ECONOMICS

ECONOMICS

JOHN SLOMAN

with the collaboration of
Mark Sutcliffe

HARVESTER WHEATSHEAF
PRENTICE HALL

New York   London   Toronto   Sydney   Tokyo   Singapore

First published 1991 by
Harvester Wheatsheaf
66 Wood Lane End, Hemel Hempstead
Hertfordshire HP2 4RG
A division of
Simon & Schuster International Group

Typeset in 10/12 pt Ehrhardt
by VAP Publishing Services

Text design by Lesley Stewart

Printed at The University Press, Cambridge

British Library Cataloguing in Publication Data

Sloman, John *1947–*
  Economics.
  1. Economics
  I. Title
  330

  ISBN 0–7450–0859–3
  ISBN 0–7450–0860–7 pbk

---

3 4 5   95 94 93 92

Contents

Preface

To the student

Economics affects all our lives. As consumers we try to make the best of our limited incomes. As workers – or future workers! – we take our place in the job market. As citizens of a country our lives are affected by the decisions of our government: decisions over taxes, decisions over spending on health and education, decisions on interest rates, decisions that affect unemployment, inflation and growth. As dwellers on the planet Earth we are affected by the economic decisions of each other: the air we breathe, the water we drink and the environment we leave to our children are all affected by the economic decisions taken by the human race.

Economics thus deals with some of the most challenging issues we face. It is this that excites me about economics, and still gives me a buzz after 20 years of teaching the subject. I hope that some of this excitement rubs off on you.

Economics is suitable for all students of economics at first-year degree level, A level or on various professional courses where a broad grounding in both principles and applications is required. It is structured to be easily understood by those of you who are new to the subject; yet it also has sufficient depth to challenge those of you who have studied the subject before, with starred sections and case studies that will provide much that is new.

It gives a self-contained introduction to the world of economics and is thus ideal for those who will not study the subject beyond introductory level. But by carefully laying a comprehensive foundation and by the inclusion of certain materials in starred sections that bridge the gap between introductory and second level economics, it provides the necessary coverage for those of you going on to specialize in economics.

The book is designed with one overriding aim: to make this exciting and highly relevant subject as clear to understand as possible. To this end the book has a number of important features:

- A direct and straightforward written style; short paragraphs to aid rapid comprehension.
- Numerous examples given: some serious, some lighthearted.
- Summaries at the end of each section (rather than each chapter).
- Definitions of all technical terms in the margin.
- A comprehensive index, including reference to all defined terms.
- Questions throughout the text (typically one or two per page) to test comprehension and stimulate thought.

- Many boxes (around 10 per chapter) providing case studies, person profiles, institutional material, news items, contemporary and historical debates and issues, anecdotes and advanced topics.
- Advanced material in starred sections/boxes, which can be omitted without affecting the flow of argument.
- Many issues are examined in their historical as well as contemporary context.

The book looks at the world from the perspective of the early 1990s. Despite huge advances in technology and despite the comfortable lives led by many people in the industrialized world, we still suffer from unemployment, poverty and inequality; our environment is polluted; our economy still goes through periodic recessions or times of rapidly rising prices; conflict and disagreement often dominate over peace and harmony.

What is more, the world order has been changing. With the collapse of the communist regimes in Eastern Europe, with the move away from the ideological simplicity of the Thatcher years, with moves towards greater economic union in Europe, with an uncertain role for the USA, and with an ever deepening crisis for many Third World countries, so there are many new economic challenges that face us.

But despite our changing environment, there are certain economic fundamentals that do not change. Despite disagreements among economists – and there are plenty – there is a wide measure of agreement on how to analyze these fundamentals.

I hope that this book will give you an enjoyable introduction to the economist's world and that it will equip you with the tools to understand and criticize the economic policies that others pursue.

Good luck and have fun.

To the instructor

Economics has the flexibility to be used on a wide variety of different courses. The depth of coverage can be varied by the inclusion or non-inclusion of starred sections, any of the boxes, the historical case studies, the policy chapters and the final three chapters.

The overall coverage of the book is fairly traditional with a roughly fifty-fifty micro/macro split. The order in which the topics arise is also fairly traditional, as a glance at the contents will show. As a result, those of you who are used to existing texts such as Begg et al., Lipsey, Hardwick et al., Beardshaw, Maunder et al., Samuelson, Dolan and Lindsey, etc, should feel quite comfortable with this book. The structure of your introductory economics courses will not have to change radically.

But despite this traditional overall structure and coverage, there are many novel features, some to do with content and others of a more purely pedagogical nature.

Style

The style of the book is direct and to the point. The paragraphs are short so as to aid rapid comprehension. Where appropriate, points are listed. The aim all the time is to provide maximum clarity. To aid digestion and provide roughage, there are numerous examples and many boxes.

The number and length of chapters

I have tried to overcome a problem that students find with conventional introductory economics textbooks. This is the problem of the number and length of chapters: too many chapters and too lengthy chapters.

This book has less chapters than most introductory economics textbooks. The reason for this is to keep the overall pattern of the book as simple as possible and not to break topics artificially. I feel that it is very important for the student to gain a clear picture of how the subject hangs together. A large number of chapters can be confusing.

But fewer chapters mean longer chapters. To overcome this problem each chapter has been divided into about three to six sections (100 in total). Each section covers a discreet 'sub topic' and should be a manageable portion of assigned work for a student. They could thus be regarded as 'mini chapters'. The sections are then further divided into sub-sections. These are typically about a page long.

This three-level approach is designed to make it possible for the student to focus on detail without losing sight of the overall structure of the subject: to be able to see each 'tree' as an individual tree whilst at the same time being able to see it in its local environment whilst also not losing sight of the whole wood!

Summaries

Summaries are given at the end of each section. This, I feel, is better than waiting to the end of the chapter, as it provides a point for reflection and checking on comprehension at reasonably frequent intervals. A chapter is usually too long (even in books where chapters are shorter than in this book) to be studied in detail in one sitting.

Definitions

All technical terms are highlighted in the text when they first appear and are defined in the margin. They are referred to in the index so that the student can simply look up a given definition as required. By defining them in the margin the student can also see the terms used in context in the text.

Boxes

Boxes are becoming a common feature of economics texts. Nevertheless the number and variety of boxes is much larger than in other texts. This is because they serve a number of important functions in this book.

- They provide a break from the main text. Many of the boxes are written in a journalistic style and demand less concentration from the student.
- Some are anecdotal; there are even some poems and jokes in boxes. Apart from being light relief, they nevertheless serve the important function of raising questions in the student's mind or putting a different perspective on an issue covered in the main text.
- They give examples which bring theory alive to the student, but which would distract too much from the flow of the argument if placed in the main narrative.
- Some are used to provide portraits of famous economists – a device used to good

effect in many American texts. This helps the student gain an insight into the historical development of the subject.

- Some are used to develop points of theory to a more advanced level. These boxes are starred. By separating this material into boxes it allows the student to cover this material (if at all) at a time appropriate to him or her – either there and then, or after having read the complete chapter, or at a later date, perhaps even at second-year level. (In my experience, second year students like to refer back to some of the more advanced parts of first year texts to help them adjust to second level economics.) Some of these starred boxes use elementary calculus. This is useful for students on straight economics degrees who are served badly by current texts. Students unfamiliar with calculus can merely skip these boxes.
- Some boxes look at how economics enters into political debate. A number of contemporary and historical controversies are examined in such boxes.
- Some boxes are used to explain relevant institutional detail: detail that would detract from the flow of the argument if placed in the main body of the text.

By placing these materials in boxes, it not only makes learning more interesting for the student, who can 'do a bit of dabbling' into the book if there is a bit of time to spare; it also gives the tutor more scope in setting work for seminars/classes.

The use of boxes also helps overcome another problem. To be comprehensive a first-year book must be long. But if it is too long it becomes daunting for the student. The additional material in the boxes makes the book comprehensive, but by taking it out of the main body of the text, the text becomes manageable.

Starred parts/sections

Certain more advanced topics are placed in optional starred parts or sections. Examples include indifference curves, isoquants, general equilibrium analysis (in both a closed economy and an international trade context), national income accounting, ISLM analysis and ISLMBP analysis (under both fixed and floating exchange rates).

Although these topics are given full treatment in these sections, (a treatment which makes the book highly suitable for students going on to study economics beyond introductory level), the material in these sections is not referred to elsewhere in the text. They may therefore be omitted without interrupting the flow of the argument. In some texts these topics are relegated to appendices. I feel it is better, however, to place these topics at the appropriate point in the chapter so that the student can see more clearly how they fit in.

An open learning approach

Questions have been incorporated into the text so as to test and reinforce the student's understanding as he/she progresses. The student is thereby encouraged to learn in a much more active way than if the questions are merely grouped at the end of the chapter, and thus easily ignored.

Some of the questions have a simple one or two word or numerical answer. Some are more philosophical or open ended. These are generally suitable for class discussion as well as a device to make the student less passive in learning and more aware of some of the broader implications of the material covered in the text.

Many of the boxes can be used as class exercises and all have questions at the end.

Suggested answers to all the questions are given in the Instructor's Manual which is available from Harvester Wheatsheaf.

Content: special features

- A range of perspectives and alternative approaches to solving economic problems, introduced right from Chapter 1.
- Many examples given of demand and supply analysis (Chapter 2).
- An examination of marginal utility theory which sets the scene for the later analysis of economic efficiency (Chapter 3).
- An extension (in boxes) of the section on indifference curve analysis to examine both the Slutsky approach and characteristics theory (Chapter 3).
- Costs and revenue put clearly into context by considering their importance right from the beginning to the determination of output (Chapter 4).
- Real-world examples of short-run factor returns (Chapter 4).
- Profit maximization considered in the general context before examining it under particular market structures (Chapter 4).
- A complete section on the theory of contestable markets (Chapter 5).
- More detail on oligopoly than in most texts (Chapter 6).
- An substantial section on game theory (Chapter 6).
- A complete chapter devoted to alternative theories of the firm – including analyses of growth and mergers, an examination of managerial utility maximization, sales revenue maximization and behavioural theories of the firm (Chapter 7).
- Marginal productivity theory put firmly into context as a means of explaining the distribution of income and not just a means of explaining factor proportions: this in my experience helps to bring it alive for students (Chapter 8).
- A consideration of the role of collective bargaining, imperfect information, non-maximizing behaviour and discrimination in the determination of wages (Chapter 8).
- A complete chapter on inequality and poverty and an examination of alternative redistributive policies, with an analysis of possible trade-offs between efficiency and equality (Chapter 9).
- Stress on the social implications of private economic decision taking (Chapter 10).
- A simple examination of Pareto optimality and the achievement of social efficiency (Chapter 10).
- A detailed examination of the case for and against government microeconomic intervention and of alternative government microeconomic policies (Chapter 10).
- A major section on cost-benefit analysis at the core of the chapter on social efficiency (Chapter 10).
- An examination of the libertarian arguments for *laissez-faire* including a box on the development of neo-Austrian thought (Chapter 10).
- A complete section on public choice theory (Chapter 10).
- An extended case study on agriculture and agricultural policy in order to illustrate potential strengths and weaknesses of the market and government intervention (Chapter 11).
- An examination of UK and European policy towards monopolies, mergers and restrictive practices (Chapter 11).
- A detailed examination of the nationalization/privatization debate (Chapter 11).
- An introductory macroeconomic chapter which looks at the range of macroeconomic problems *and* their possible causes. This unique approach prepares students for the more detailed analysis later by 'lowering them in gently', but right from the beginning stresses the relationships and trade-offs between macroeconomic objectives (Chapter 12).

- An early macro chapter devoted to the historical development of macro theory. This helps the students get a feel of the controversial nature of macroeconomics. It also puts the mainstream theories in context (Chapter 13).
- An optional (starred) section on national income accounting. In addition to examining the three ways of calculating GDP/GNP, this section raises a number of normative issues concerning the goals of macroeconomic policy (Chapter 13).
- The whole of the macro half is written in the context of an open economy. This is aided in the earlier chapters by using a JW Keynesian model rather than the simplified IS version (Chapter 14 onwards).
- A section on the Keynesian analysis of cyclical fluctuations, including a simple multiplier/accelerator model (Chapter 14).
- A chapter on fiscal policy which gives a preliminary examination of the role of Keynesian demand management policy before introducing the complications of the money market (Chapter 15).
- The incorporation of recent developments in money and banking and monetary policy (Chapter 16).
- A full examination of the effects of exchange rate changes on monetary transmission mechanisms (Chapter 16).
- Charting the rise and fall of the MTFS (Chapter 18).
- A clear division of the Keynesian–monetarist/new classical debate into issues concerned with the management of aggregate demand and issues concerned with the nature of the aggregate supply schedule (Chapters 18 and 19).
- A detailed analysis of the relationship between the money and goods markets in both a simple two market framework and in an ISLM framework. The ISLM analysis, although more detailed than in most basic texts, appears in an optional (starred) section (Chapter 18).
- A complete chapter on alternative theories of inflation and unemployment, including both adaptive and rational expectations theories and modern Keynesian theories of inflation/unemployment trade-offs (Chapter 19).
- A complete chapter on supply-side policies – both market-orientated supply-side policies and market-supplementing or market-replacing supply-side policies. This chapter includes both radical right policies (such as tax cuts and de-regulation) and interventionist policies (such as prices and incomes policies, regional policies and industrial policies) (Chapter 20).
- An international trade chapter that examines the contemporary protectionist debate (including a box on strategic trade theory) and has a complete section on preferential trading (Chapter 21).
- An examination of the economics of the single European market after 1992.
- A detailed account of the costs and benefits of alternative exchange rate regimes (Chapter 21).
- A starred section on an extension of ISLM analysis to include a BP curve. The use of this analysis to compare the effects of fiscal and monetary policies under fixed and floating exchange rates (Chapter 22).
- An examination of international macroeconomic policy harmonization, the EMS and the exchange rate mechanism, and European monetary union (Chapter 22).
- A chapter on the economics of developing countries that goes further than any other introductory text in analyzing the problems of development in both a domestic and international context. This chapter includes a complete section on the problem of Third-World debt (Chapter 23).

Instructors' Manual

An Instructors' Manual is available free only to instructors who adopt the main text for course use. It includes:

- Answers to all questions in this text.
- Suggestions on how to use the book.
- Full page diagrams that can be photocopied on to acetate for overhead projection.
- Lecture plans in large type, that again can be photocopied on to acetate.
- At least one additional case study per chapter that you can reproduce for classroom use.

Copies of the Instructor's Manual are available from Harvester Wheatsheaf.

Student Workbook (by John Sloman and Mark Sutcliffe)

A Student Workbook is designed to accompany this text. Each chapter of the workbook matches a chapter of *Economics* and consists of five sections.

1. Review questions. This section is a mixture of narrative and questions and goes through all the key material in the textbook chapter. Questions are a mixture of multiple choice, true/false, either/or, filling in blank words or phrases, matching a series of answers to a series of questions, short written answers and brief calculations. Each type of question is clearly marked with an appropriate symbol.
2. Problems, issues and applications. This section includes data response, questions on case studies (including articles from newspapers and journals) and multiple-part calculations.
3. Discussion topics and essays. This includes various thought-provoking questions that can be used for class discussion and more traditional essay questions.
4. Student projects. This includes data search exercises, games, role playing, questionnaires and debates. Guidance and sources are given to help the student.
5. Answers and comments. This includes answers to *and* comments on all section 1 questions and section 2 questions where appropriate.

Acknowledgements

Writing a book like this takes a toll not only on the author but on family and friends alike. These last two years my PC has become rather like a very demanding cuckoo, gobbling more and more of my time and attention as the book has developed. Thanks especially to Sue my wife and our sons Peter, Michael and Andrew: perhaps now I can do all the things I said I would do 'when the book is finished'.

Thanks to Chris Hunt who typed various earlier drafts and to Dennis Swann, Ken Heather and David Ulph for many valuable suggestions for improvements. Thanks too to Chris Bessant who painstakingly copy-edited the manuscript and to all the team at Harvester Wheatsheaf – to Stuart Macfarlane and Val Jones who steered the book through production and especially to Peter Johns whose total dedication to the project and whose advice, persuasion, encouragement and friendship were invaluable. We spent many hours on the phone late into the night beating the manuscript into shape.

Finally a million and one thanks to my friend and colleague Mark Sutcliffe who has contributed a great deal to the project. He has jointly or wholly written many of the boxes and has given me ideas for many more. He has obtained several of the statistics and last but not least he has kept me supplied with 'stickies' to provide sweet consolation.

Introducing Economics 1

1.1 What do economists study?

You may never have studied economics before, and yet when you open a newspaper what do you read? – a report from 'our economics correspondent'. Turn on the television news and what do you see? – an item on the state of the economy. Talk to friends and often the topic will turn to the price of this or that product, or whether you have got enough money to afford to do this or that.

The fact is that economics affects our daily lives. Continually we are being made aware of local, national and international economic problems, and continually we are faced with economic problems and decisions of our own.

So just what is economics about? What is this subject you are embarking on – with, no doubt, some trepidation?

Many people think that economics is about *money*. Well, to some extent this is true. Economics has a lot to do with money: with how much money people are paid; how much they spend; what it costs to buy various items; how much money firms earn; how much money there is in total in the economy. But despite the large number of areas in which our lives are concerned with money, economics is more than just the study of money.

It is concerned with:

- The production of goods and services: how much the economy produces; what particular combination of goods and services; how much each firm produces; what techniques of production they use; how many people they employ.
- The consumption of goods and services: how much the population as a whole spends (and how much it saves); what the pattern of consumption is in the economy; how much people buy of particular items; what particular individuals choose to buy; how people's consumption is affected by prices, advertising, fashion and other factors.

 Could production and consumption take place without money? If you think they could, give some examples.

Production

The transformation of inputs into outputs by firms in order to earn profit (or meet some other objective).

Consumption

The act of using goods and services to satisfy wants. This will normally involve purchasing the goods and services.

But we still have not quite got to the bottom of what economics is about. What is the crucial ingredient for a problem to be an *economic* one? The answer is that there is one central problem faced by all individuals and all societies. From this one problem stem all the other economic problems we shall be looking at throughout this book.

This central economic problem is the problem of *scarcity*.

BOX 1.1

What's the Latest Economics News?

- Budget news: Chancellor cuts 2p off the basic rate of income tax; government hopes that this will provide an incentive for people to work harder.
- Mortgage lending reaches record levels: house prices expected to rise rapidly.
- Recent survey reveals that business confidence is low: fall in investment predicted.
- The country continues to bask in a heatwave: record ice-cream sales reported.
- Floods hit Bangladesh: two-thirds of the country's crops ruined; massive food price rises expected.
- New report suggests that long-term contamination from Chernobyl nuclear disaster is greater than originally thought: price of lamb falls.
- Money supply growing too fast: forecasters predict that inflation will soon begin to rise.

- Further cuts in government expenditure announced: Chancellor claims that this is necessary to allow economy to continue growing and unemployment to fall. Shadow Chancellor disagrees and claims that the cuts will cause unemployment to rise.
- Record balance of trade deficit announced today: further rises in interest rates seem inevitable.
- Rumours of a take-over bid for ABC plc: ABC shares close 25p up on the day.
- Student grants raised. Student Union president says that in real terms this represents a further cut.

 What is it that makes each one of the above news items an *economics* item?

This may seem strange. 'Surely', you may say, 'we don't have a problem of scarcity. Things might have been scarce in the Second World War when there was rationing, but now, towards the end of the twentieth century, the shops are stocked full. We rarely have to queue for things, or order things a long time in advance. Most people would agree that scarcity is a problem for the poor countries of the Third World, but surely in the industrialized world, with our throw-away society and our food 'mountains', we have a problem of abundance, not of scarcity?'

But despite these objections, economists still argue that scarcity is the central economic problem, not only in Ethopia and the Sudan, but also in Britain, the USA, Japan, France, Denmark and everywhere else. For an economist, scarcity has a very specific definition . . .

 Before reading on, how would you define 'scarcity'? Must goods be at least temporarily unattainable to be scarce?

The problem of scarcity

Ask people if they would like more money, and the vast majority would answer 'Yes'. They want more money so that they can buy more goods and services; and this applies not only to poor people but also to most wealthy people too. Even people living in a large well-furnished house and with an expensive car would probably like a bigger house, a second or third car, a villa on the Mediterranean, a luxury yacht and so on. The point is that human wants are virtually unlimited.

Yet the means of fulfilling human wants are limited. At any one time the world can only produce a limited amount of goods and services. This is because the world only has a limited amount of resources. These resources, or factors of production as they are often called, are of three broad types:

- Human resources: labour
  The labour force is limited both in number and in skills.

Factors of production (or resources)

The inputs into the production of goods and services: labour, land and raw materials, and capital.

Labour

All forms of human input, both physical and mental, into current production.

- Natural resources: land and raw materials
  The world's land area is limited, as are its raw materials.
- Manufactured resources: capital
  Capital consists of all those inputs that themselves have had to be produced in the first place. The world has a limited stock of capital: a limited supply of factories, machines, transportation and other equipment. The productivity of capital is limited by the state of technology.

So here is the reason for scarcity: human wants are virtually unlimited, whereas the resources available to satisfy these wants *are* limited. We can thus define scarcity as 'the excess of human wants over what can actually be produced'.

 If we would all like more money, why does the government not print a lot more? Could it not thereby solve the problem of scarcity 'at a stroke'?

Of course, we do not all face the problem of scarcity to the same degree. A poor person unable to afford enough to eat or a decent place to live will hardly see it as a 'problem' that a rich person cannot afford a second Rolls-Royce. But economists do not claim that we all face an *equal* problem of scarcity. In fact this is one of the major issues economists study: how resources are distributed, whether between different individuals, different regions of a country or different countries of the world.

But given that people, both rich and poor, want more than they can have, this will cause them to behave in certain ways. Economics studies that behaviour. It studies people at work, producing the goods that people want. It studies people as consumers, buying the goods that they themselves want. It studies governments influencing the level and pattern of production and consumption. In short, it studies anything to do with the process of satisfying human wants.

Demand and supply

We said that economics is concerned with consumption and production. Another way of looking at this is in terms of *demand* and *supply*. It is quite likely that you already knew that economics had something to do with demand and supply. In fact, demand and supply and the relationship between them lie at the very centre of economics. But what do we mean by the terms, and what is their relationship with the problem of scarcity?

Demand is related to wants. If goods and services were free, people would simply demand whatever they wanted.

Supply is related to resources. The amount that firms can supply depends on the resources and technology available.

Given the problem of scarcity, given that human wants exceed what can actually be produced, *potential* demands will exceed *potential* supplies. Society therefore has to find some way of dealing with this problem. Somehow it has got to try to match demand and supply. This applies at the level of the economy overall: *aggregate* demand will need to be balanced against *aggregate* supply. In other words, total spending in the economy will need to balance total production. It also applies at the level of individual goods and services. The demand and supply of cabbages will need to balance, as will the demand and supply of video recorders, cars, houses and haircuts.

But if potential demand exceeds potential supply, how are *actual* demand and supply to be made equal? Either demand has to be curtailed, or supply has to be

Land (and raw materials)
Inputs into production that are provided by nature: e.g. unimproved land and mineral deposits in the ground.

Capital
All inputs into production that have themselves been produced: e.g. factories, machines and tools.

Scarcity
The excess of human wants over what can actually be produced to fulfil these wants.

increased, or a combination of the two. Economics studies this process. It studies how demand adjusts to available supplies, and how supply adjusts to consumer demands.

Dividing up the subject

Economics is traditionally divided into two main branches – *macroeconomics* and *microeconomics*, where 'macro' means big, and 'micro' means small.

Macroeconomics

The branch of economics that studies economic aggregates (grand totals): e.g. the overall level of prices, output and employment in the economy.

Macroeconomics is concerned with the economy as a whole. It is thus concerned with aggregate demand and aggregate supply. By 'aggregate demand' we mean the total amount of spending in the economy, whether by consumers, by overseas customers for our exports, by the government, or by firms when they buy capital equipment or stock up on raw materials. By 'aggregate supply' we mean the total national output of goods and services.

Aggregate demand

The total level of spending in the economy.

Microeconomics is concerned with the individual parts of the economy. It is concerned with the demand and supply of *particular* goods and services and resources: cars, butter, clothes and haircuts; electricians, secretaries, blast furnaces, computers and coal.

Aggregate supply

The total amount of output in the economy.

? Which of the following are macroeconomic issues, which are microeconomic ones and which could be either depending on the context?
(a) Inflation.
(b) Low wages in certain service industries.
(c) The rate of exchange between the pound and the D-Mark.
(d) Why the price of cabbages fluctuates more than that of cars.
(e) The rate of economic growth this year compared with last year.
(f) The decline of traditional manufacturing industries.

Microeconomics

The branch of economics that studies individual units: e.g. households, firms and industries. It studies the interrelationships between these units in determining the pattern of production and distribution of goods and services.

Macroeconomics

Because things are scarce, societies are concerned that their resources should be used *as fully as possible*, and that over time their national output should *grow*.

The achievement of growth and the full use of resources is not easy, however, as witness the periods of high unemployment and stagnation that have occurred from time to time throughout the world (for example, in the 1930s and early 1980s). Furthermore, attempts by government to stimulate growth and employment have often resulted in inflation and balance of payments crises. Even when societies do achieve growth it is often short lived. Economies have often experienced cycles, where periods of growth alternate with periods of stagnation, such periods varying from a few months to a few years.

Macroeconomics, then, studies the determination of national output and its growth over time. It also studies the problems of stagnation, unemployment, inflation, the balance of international payments and cyclical instability, and the policies adopted by governments to deal with these problems.

Macroeconomic problems are closely related to the balance between aggregate demand and aggregate supply.

If aggregate demand is *too high* relative to aggregate supply, inflation and balance of payments deficits are likely to result.

Rate of inflation

The percentage increase in the level of prices over a twelve-month period.

● Inflation refers to general rise in the level of prices throughout the economy. If aggregate demand rises substantially, firms are likely to respond by raising their prices. After all, if demand is high they can probably still sell as much as before (if not more) even at the higher prices, and thus make more profits. If firms in general put up their prices, inflation results.

BOX 1.2

Looking at Macroeconomic Data
Assessing different countries' macroeconomic performance

The objectives of rapid economic growth, low unemployment, low inflation and the avoidance of current account deficits are the major macroeconomic policy objectives of most governments round the world. To help them achieve these objectives they employ economic advisers.

But when we look at the performance of various economies, the success of government macroeconomic policies seems decidedly 'mixed'.

The table shows data for the USA, Japan, Germany and the UK from 1978 to 1989.

Macroeconomic performance of four industrialized economies (average annual figures)

	Unemployment (% of workforce)				Inflation (%)				Economic growth (%)				Balance on current account (US$bn)			
	USA	Japan	Germany	UK	USA	Japan	Germany	UK	USA	Japan	Germany	UK	USA	Japan	Germany	UK
1978–80	6.3	2.1	3.2	5.8	9.7	5.1	4.1	13.2	2.5	4.9	2.9	1.4	−5	−1	−3	2
1981–83	8.8	2.4	7.7	11.2	6.6	3.2	5.0	8.4	1.0	3.4	0.3	1.3	−16	11	2	9
1984–86	7.1	2.6	6.9	11.4	3.3	1.6	1.4	4.8	4.2	4.1	2.5	3.1	−125	57	22	2
1987–89	5.6	2.5	6.0	8.3	3.7	1.2	1.4	5.7	3.7	5.2	2.8	3.7	−131	77	50	−17

Source: *National Institute Economic Review* (NIESR).

1. Has Britain generally fared better or worse than the other three countries?
2. Was there a common pattern in the macroeconomic performance of each of the four countries over these twelve years?
3. How does the existence of inflation over the years affect the significance of the balance of payments figures?
4. In order to make a meaningful comparison of different countries' balance of payments what else would you need to know other than the simple size of their deficit or surplus?

If the government does not have much success in managing the economy it could be because:

● Economists have incorrectly analyzed the problems and hence have given the wrong advice.
● Economists disagree and hence have given conflicting advice.
● Economists have based their advice on inaccurate forecasts.
● Governments have not heeded the advice of economists.
● There is little else that governments could have done: the problems were insoluble.

● (Current account) balance of payments deficits[1] are the excess of imports over exports. If aggregate demand rises, people are likely to buy more imports. In other words, part of the extra expenditure will go on Japanese videos, German cars, French wine, etc. Also if inflation is high, home-produced goods will become uncompetitive with foreign goods. We are likely, therefore, to buy more foreign imports and foreigners are likely to buy fewer of our exports.

If aggregate demand is *too low* relative to aggregate supply, unemployment and recession may well result.

Recession is where output in the economy declines: in other words, growth becomes negative. A recession is associated with a low level of consumer spending. If people spend less, shops are likely to find themselves with unsold stocks. As a result they will buy less from the manufacturers, who in turn will cut down on production.

Current account balance of payments

Exports of goods and services minus imports of goods and services. If exports exceed imports, there is a 'current account surplus' (a positive figure). If imports exceed exports there is a 'current account deficit' (a negative figure).

Recession

A period where national output falls for a few months or more.

[1] The current account excludes investments and financial movements into and out of the country. Such movements are called the 'capital account'.

Unemployment

The number of people who are actively looking for work but are currently without a job. (Note that there is much debate as to who should officially be counted unemployed.)

- Unemployment is likely to result from cutbacks in production. If firms are producing less, they will need a smaller labour force.

Macroeconomic *policy*, therefore, tends to focus on the balance of aggregate demand and aggregate supply. It can be demand-side policy, which seeks to influence the level of spending in the economy. This in turn will affect the level of production, prices and employment. Or it can be supply-side policy. This is designed to influence the level of production directly, for example by trying to create more incentives for workers or businesspeople.

Demand-side policy

Government policy designed to alter the level of aggregate demand, and thereby the level of output, employment and prices.

Microeconomics

Microeconomics and choice

Because resources are scarce, choices have to be made. There are three main categories of choices that must be made in any society.

Supply-side policy

Government policy that attempts to alter the level of aggregate supply directly.

- *What* goods and services are going to be produced and in what quantities, given that there are not enough resources to produce all things people desire? How many cars, how much wheat, how much insurance, how many pop concerts, how many coats, etc. will be produced?
- *How* are things going to be produced, given that there is normally more than one way of producing things? What resources are going to be used and in what quantities? What techniques of production are going to be adopted? Will cars be produced by robots or by assembly line workers? Will electricity be produced from coal, oil, gas, nuclear fission, renewable resources or a mixture of these?
- *For whom* are things going to be produced? In other words, how is the nation's income going to be distributed? – after all, the higher your income, the more you can consume of the nation's output. What will be the wages of farm workers, printers, cleaners and accountants? How much will pensioners receive? How much profit will owners of private companies receive or will state-owned industries make?

All societies have to make these choices, whether they be made by individuals, by groups or by the government. These choices can be seen as *micro*economic choices since they are concerned not with the *total* amount of national output, but with the *individual* goods and services that make it up: what they are, how they are made, and who gets the incomes to buy them.

Choice and opportunity cost

Choice involves sacrifice. The more food you choose to buy, the less money you will have to spend on other goods. The more food a nation produces, the less resources will there be for producing other goods. In other words, the production or consumption of one thing involves the sacrifice of alternatives. This sacrifice of alternatives in the production (or consumption) of a good is known as its opportunity cost.

Opportunity cost

The cost of any activity measured in terms of the best alternative forgone.

If the workers on a farm can produce either 1000 tonnes of wheat or 2000 tonnes of barley, then the opportunity cost of producing 1 tonne of wheat is the 2 tonnes of barley forgone. The opportunity cost of buying a textbook is the new pair of jeans you also wanted that you have had to go without. The opportunity cost of working overtime is the leisure you have sacrificed.

Rational choices

Economists often refer to rational choices. By this is simply meant the weighing-up of the *costs* and *benefits* of any activity, whether it be firms choosing what and how much to produce, workers choosing whether to take a particular job or to work extra hours, or consumers choosing what to buy.

Imagine you are doing your shopping in a supermarket and you want to buy some meat. Do you spend a lot of money and buy best steak, or do you buy cheap mince instead? To make a rational (i.e. sensible) decision, you will need to weigh up the costs and benefits of each alternative. Best steak may give you a lot of enjoyment, but it has a high opportunity cost: because it is expensive, you will need to sacrifice quite a lot of consumption of other goods if you decide to buy it. If you buy the mince, however, although you will not enjoy it so much, you will have more money left over to buy other things: it has a lower opportunity cost.

Thus rational decision making, as far as consumers are concerned, involves choosing those items that give you the best value for money – i.e. the *greatest benefit relative to cost*.

The same principles apply to firms when deciding what to produce. For example, should a car firm open up another production line? A rational decision will again involve weighing up the benefits and costs. The benefits are the revenues the firm will earn from selling the extra cars. The costs will include the extra labour costs, raw material costs, costs of component parts, etc. It will only be profitable to open up the new production line if the revenues earned exceed the costs entailed: in other words, if it earns a profit.

In the more complex situation of deciding which model of car to produce, or how many of each model, the firm must weigh up the relative benefits and costs of each – i.e. it will want to produce the most profitable product mix.

> **?** Assume that you are looking for a job and are offered two. One is more unpleasant to do, but pays more. How would you make a rational choice between the two jobs?

Marginal costs and benefits

In economics we argue that rational choices involve weighing up marginal costs and marginal benefits. These are the costs and benefits of doing a little bit more or a little bit less of a given activity. They can be contrasted with the *total* costs and benefits of the activity.

Take a familiar example. What time will you set the alarm clock to go off tomorrow morning? Let us say that you have to leave home at 8.30. Perhaps you will set the alarm for 7.00. That will give you plenty of time to get up and get ready, but it will mean a relatively short night's sleep. Perhaps you will decide to set it for 7.30 or even 8.00. That will give you a longer night's sleep, but much more of a rush in the morning to get ready.

So how do you make a rational decision about when the alarm should go off? What you have to do is to weigh up the costs and benefits of *additional* sleep. Each extra minute in bed gives you more sleep (the marginal benefit) but gives you more of a rush when you get up (the marginal cost). The decision is therefore based on the costs and benefits of *extra* sleep, not on the *total* costs and benefits of a whole night's sleep.

This same principle applies to rational decisions made by consumers, workers and firms. For example, the car firm we were considering just now will weigh up the marginal costs and benefits of producing cars: in other words, it will compare the

---

Rational choices

Choices that involve weighing up the benefit of any activity against its opportunity cost.

Marginal costs

The additional cost of doing a little bit more (or *1 unit* more if a unit can be measured) of an activity.

Marginal benefits

The additional benefits of doing a little bit more (or *1 unit* more if a unit can be measured) of an activity.

BOX 1.3

The Opportunity Costs of Studying Economics
What are you sacrificing?

You may not have realized it, but you probably consider opportunity costs many times a day. The reason is that we are constantly making choices: what to buy, what to eat, what to wear, whether to go out, how much to study and so on. Each time we make a choice to do something, we are in effect rejecting doing some alternative. This alternative forgone is the opportunity cost of our action.

Sometimes the opportunity costs of our actions are the direct monetary costs we incur. Sometimes it is more complicated.

Take the opportunity costs of your choices as a student of economics.

Buying a textbook costing £14.95
This does involve a direct money payment. What you have to consider is the alternatives you could have bought with the £14.95. You then have to weigh up the benefit from the best alternative against the benefit of the textbook.

 What might prevent you from making the best decision?

Coming to classes
You may or may not be paying course fees. Even if you are, there is no extra (marginal) monetary cost in coming to classes once the fees have been paid. You will not get a refund by skipping classes!

So are the opportunity costs zero? No: by coming to classes you are *not* working in the library; you are *not* having an extra hour in bed; you are *not* sitting drinking coffee with friends, and so on. If you are making a rational decision to come to classes, then you will consider such possible alternatives.

 If there are several other things you could have done, is the opportunity cost the sum of all of them?

Revising for an economics exam
Again, the opportunity cost is the best alternative to which you could have put your time. This might be revising for some *other* exam. You will probably want to divide your time sensibly between your subjects. A *sensible* decision is not to revise economics on any given occasion if you will gain a greater benefit from revising for another subject. In such a case the (marginal) opportunity cost of revising economics exceeds the (marginal) benefit.

Choosing to study at university or college
What are the opportunity costs of being a student in higher education?

At first it might seem that the costs would include the following:

- Tuition fees.
- Books, stationery, etc.
- Accommodation expenses.
- Transport.
- Food, entertainment and other living expenses.

But adding these up does *not* give the *opportunity* cost. The opportunity cost is the *sacrifice* entailed by going to university or college *rather* than doing something else. Let us assume that the alternative is to take a job that has been offered. The correct list of opportunity costs of higher education would include:

- Books, stationery, etc.
- *Additional* accommodation and transport expenses over what would have been incurred by taking the job.
- Wages that would have been earned in the job *less* any student grant received.

Note that tuition fees are not included because it is assumed that these are paid by the student's local education authority.

 1. Why is the cost of food not included?
2. Make a list of the benefits of higher education.
3. Is the opportunity cost to the individual of attending higher education different from the opportunity costs to society as a whole?

costs and revenue of producing *additional* cars. If additional cars add more to the firm's revenue than to its costs, it will be profitable to produce them.

 How would this principle of weighing up marginal costs and benefits apply to a worker deciding how much overtime to work in a given week?

BOX 1.4

Scarcity and Abundance
Is lunch ever free?

The central economic problem is scarcity. But are *all* goods and services scarce? Is anything we desire truly abundant?

First, what do we mean by *abundance*? In the economic sense we mean something where supply exceeds demand at a *zero* price. In other words, even if it is free, there is no shortage. What is more, there must be no opportunity cost in supplying it. For example, if the government supplies health care free to the sick, it is still scarce in the economic sense because there is a cost to the government (and hence the taxpayer).

Two things that might seem to be abundant are air and water.

Air
In one sense air *is* abundant. There is no shortage of air to breathe for most people for most of the time.

But if we define air as clean, unpolluted air, then in some parts of the world it is scarce. In these cases, resources have to be used to make clean air available. If there is pollution in cities or near industrial plants, it will cost money to clean it up. The citizen may not pay directly – the cleaned-up air may be free to the 'consumer' – but the taxpayer or industry (and hence its customers) will have to pay.

Another example is when extractor fans have to be installed to freshen up air in buildings.

Even if you live in a non-polluted part of the country, you may well have spent money moving there to escape the pollution. Again there is an opportunity cost to obtain the clean air.

Water
Whether water is abundant depends again on where you live. It also depends on what the water is used for.

Water for growing crops in a country with plentiful rain *is* abundant. In drier countries, resources have to be spent on irrigation.

Water for drinking is not abundant. Reservoirs have to be built. The water has to be piped, purified and pumped.

? 1. There is a saying in economics, 'There is no such thing as a free lunch' (hence the sub-title for this box). What does this mean?
2. Are any other (desirable) goods or services truly abundant?

The social implications of choice

Microeconomics does not just study how choices are made. It also looks at their consequences. Under certain conditions the consequences may be an efficient allocation of the nation's resources.

There are, however, a whole series of possible problems that can arise from the choices that people make, whether they are made by individuals, by firms or by the government. These problems include such things as inefficiency, waste, inequality and pollution.

Take the case of pollution. It might be profitable for a firm to tip toxic waste into a river. But what is profitable for the firm will not necessarily be 'profitable' for society. There may be serious environmental consequences of the firm's actions.

Illustrating economic issues: the production possibility curve

Economics books and articles frequently contain diagrams. The reason is that diagrams are very useful for illustrating economic relationships. Ideas and arguments that might take a long time to explain in words can often be expressed clearly and simply in a diagram. Even when arguments are expressed fully in words, an

BOX 1.5

Green Economics
Taking account of environmental costs

People have become concerned by a number of environmental problems in recent years. These include:

- Acid rain. This is caused by sulphur and nitrogen emissions from power stations, industry and cars. It has been blamed for *Waldsterben* (forest death) in Central Europe and the contamination of many lakes and streams, with the death of fish and plant life.
- The greenhouse effect. This is caused by carbon dioxide and other gases emitted again by power stations, various industries and cars. The fear is that these gases will cause a heating of the earth's atmosphere. This will lead to climatic changes which will affect food production. It will also lead to a raising of sea levels and flooding as parts of the polar ice caps melt.
- Depletion of the ozone layer. This is caused by the use of CFC gases in aerosols, refrigerators and the manufacture of polystyrene foam. The ozone layer protects us from harmful ultra-violet radiation from the sun. A depletion of this layer could lead to increased skin cancer.
- Nuclear radiation. The fear is that accidents or sabotage at nuclear power stations could cause dangerous releases of radiation. The disposal of nuclear waste is another environmental problem.
- Land and river pollution. The tipping of toxic waste into the ground or into rivers can cause long-term environmental damage. Soils can be poisoned; rivers and seas can become polluted. It is not just industry that is to blame here. Sewage pollutes rivers and seas. Nitrogen run-off and slurry from farming are also major pollutants.

It was not until the late 1960s and early 1970s that the 'environment' became more firmly part of the political agenda in most European countries. It was largely a response not only to the spectacular growth of the Western economies, but also to the continued and extensive industrialization of the Eastern bloc countries such as Poland and the USSR.

'Green groups' sprang up round Europe. These groups realized that, if economic growth was to be sustained, then environmental damage could grow at an alarming rate.

The problems such groups have encountered in attempting to change attitudes and economic strategies have been immense. Certain governments have been reluctant to enter international environmental agreements, perceiving them to be against their national interest. The agreement to cut sulphur dioxide emissions from power stations is one example.

The costs of pollution abatement are high, especially in the short run. As long as these short-run costs are greater than the perceived costs of continuing pollution, then industry and government will continue to incur them. The consequences of this, however, could be devastating and far more costly in the long run, in both a financial and an environmental sense.

What can economists say about the causes of these environmental problems? They have three common features:

- Ignorance. It is often not for many years that the nature and causes of environmental damage are realized. Take the case of aerosols. It was not until the 1980s that scientists connected their use to ozone depletion.
- The polluters do not pay. The costs of pollution are rarely paid by the polluters. Economists call such costs *external* costs. Because polluters rarely pay to clean up their pollution or compensate those who suffer, they frequently ignore the problem.
- Present gains for future costs. The environmental costs of industrialization often build up slowly and do not become critical for many years. The benefits of industrialization, however, are more immediate. Thus governments, consumers and industry are frequently prepared to continue with various practices and leave future generations to worry about their environmental consequences. The problem is therefore a reflection of the importance that people attach to the present relative to the future.

Environmentalists recognize these problems and try through the political process and various pressure groups, such as Friends of the Earth and Greenpeace, to reduce people's ignorance and to change their attitudes.

They stress the need for clean technologies, for environmentally sound growth and for greater responsibility by industry, consumers and government alike. Policies, they argue, should prevent problems occurring and not merely be a reaction to them once they are nearing crisis point. If growth is to be sustainable into the long term, with a real increase in the quality of life, then current growth must not be at the expense of the environment.

? Should all polluting activities be banned? Could pollution ever be justified? Explain your answer.

accompanying diagram can help to make the arguments more precise and easier to grasp.

Two of the most common types of diagram used in economics are graphs and flow diagrams. In this and the next section we will look at one example of each. These examples are chosen to illustrate the distinction between microeconomic and macroeconomic issues.

We start by having a look at a production possibility curve. This diagram is a graph. Like many diagrams in economics it shows a simplified picture of reality – a picture stripped of all details that are unnecessary to illustrate the points being made. Of course, there are dangers in this. In the attempt to make a diagram simple enough to understand, we run the risk of oversimplifying. If this is the case, the diagram may be misleading.

A production possibility curve is shown in Figure 1.1. The graph is based on the data shown in Table 1.1.

Production possibility curve

A curve showing all the possible combinations of two goods that a country can produce within a specified time period with all its resources fully and efficiently employed.

Table 1.1 Maximum possible combinations of food and clothing that can be produced in a given time period

Units of food (millions)	Units of clothing (millions)
8.0	0.00
7.0	2.20
6.0	4.00
5.0	5.00
4.0	5.60
3.0	6.00
2.0	6.40
1.0	6.70
0.0	7.00

Assume that some imaginary nation devotes all its resources – land, labour and capital – to producing just two goods, food and clothing. Various possible combinations that could be produced over a given period of time (e.g. a year) are shown in the table. Thus the country, by devoting all its resources to producing food, could produce 8 million units of food but no clothing. Alternatively by producing, say, 7 million units of food it could release enough resources – land, labour and capital – to

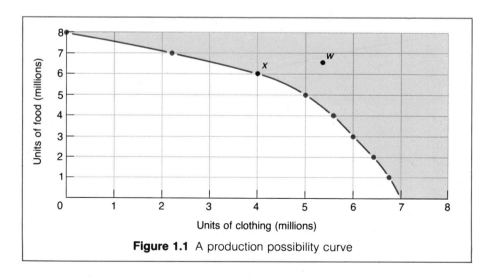

Figure 1.1 A production possibility curve

produce 2.2 million units of clothing. At the other extreme, it could produce 7 million units of clothing with no resources at all being used to produce food.

The information in the table can be transferred to a graph (Figure 1.1). We measure units of food on one axis (in this case the vertical axis) and units of clothing on the other. The curve shows all the combinations of the two goods that can be produced with all the nation's resources fully and efficiently employed. For example, production could take place at point *x*, with 6 million units of food and 4 million units of clothing being produced. Production cannot take place beyond the curve. For example, production is not possible at point *w*: the nation does not have enough resources to do this.

Note that there are two simplifying assumptions in this diagram. First it is assumed that there are just two types of good that can be produced. It is necessary to make this assumption since we only have two axes on our graph. The other assumption is that there is only one type of food and one type of clothing. This is implied by measuring their output in particular units (e.g. tonnes). If food differed in type, there would be the possibility of producing a greater tonnage of food for a given amount of clothing simply by switching production from one foodstuff to another.

These two assumptions are obviously enormous simplifications when we consider the modern complex economies of the real world. But despite this, the diagram still allows important principles to be illustrated, and illustrated simply.

Microeconomics and the production possibility curve

A production possibility curve illustrates the microeconomic issues of *choice* and *opportunity cost*.

If the country chose to produce more clothing, it would have to sacrifice the production of some food. This sacrifice of food is the opportunity cost of the extra clothing.

The fact that to produce more of one good involves producing less of the other is illustrated by the downward-sloping nature of the curve. For example, the country could move from point *x* to point *y* in Figure 1.2. In doing so it would be producing an extra 1 million units of clothing, but 1 million units less of food. Thus the opportunity cost of the 1 million extra units of clothing would be the 1 million units of food forgone.

Figure 1.2 Choice and opportunity cost

It also illustrates the phenomenon of increasing opportunity costs. By this we mean that as a country produces more of one good it has to sacrifice ever *increasing* amounts of the other. The reason for this is that different factors of production have different properties. People have different skills; land differs in different parts of the country; raw materials differ one from another; and so on. Thus as the nation concentrates more and more on the production of one good, it has to start using resources that are less and less suitable – resources that would have been better suited to producing other goods. In our example, then, the production of more and more clothing will involve a growing *marginal cost*: ever growing amounts of food have to be sacrificed for each additional unit of clothing produced.

It is because opportunity costs increase that the production possibility curve is bowed outward rather than being a straight line. Thus in Figure 1.3 as production moves from point *x* to *y* to *z*, so the amount of food sacrificed rises for each additional unit of clothing produced. The opportunity cost of the fifth million units of clothing is 1 million units of food. The opportunity cost of the sixth million units of clothing is 2 million units of food.

> **Increasing opportunity costs of production**
> When additional production of one good involves ever increasing sacrifices of another.

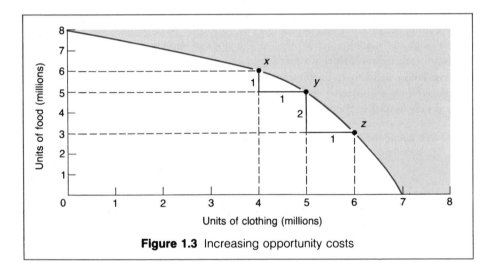

Figure 1.3 Increasing opportunity costs

> 1. What is the opportunity cost of the seventh million units of clothing?
> 2. If the country moves upward along the curve and produces more food, does this also involve increasing opportunity costs?
> 3. Under what circumstances would the production possibility curve be (a) a straight line; (b) bowed in toward the origin? Are these circumstances ever likely?

Macroeconomics and the production possibility curve

There is no guarantee that resources will be fully employed, or that they will be used in the most efficient way possible. The nation may thus be producing at a point inside the curve, for example point *v* in Figure 1.4.

What we are saying here is that the economy is producing less of both goods than it could possibly produce, either because some resources are not being used (for example, workers may be unemployed), or because it is not using the most efficient methods of production possible, or a combination of the two. By using its resources to the full, however, the nation could move out on to the curve: to point *x* or *y* for example. It could thus produce more clothing *and* more food.

Figure 1.4 Making a fuller use of resources

Here we are concerned not with the combination of goods produced (a micro-economic issue), but with whether the total amount produced is as much as it could be (a macroeconomic issue).

Over time, the production possibilities of a nation are likely to increase. Investment in new plant and machinery will increase the stock of capital; new raw materials may be discovered; technological advances are likely to take place; through education and training, labour is likely to become more productive. This growth in potential output is illustrated by an outward shift in the production possibility curve. This will then allow actual output to increase, for example from point x to point x' in Figure 1.5.

Investment

The production of goods that are not for immediate consumption.

 Will economic growth necessarily involve a *parallel outward* shift of the production possibility curve?

Illustrating economic issues: the circular flow of goods and incomes

The process of satisfying human wants involves producers and consumers. The relationship between them is two-sided and can be represented in a flow diagram.

The consumers of goods and services are labelled 'households'. Some members of households, of course, are also workers, and in some cases are the owners of other

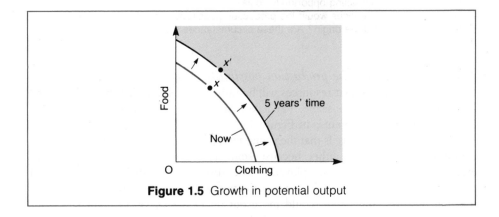

Figure 1.5 Growth in potential output

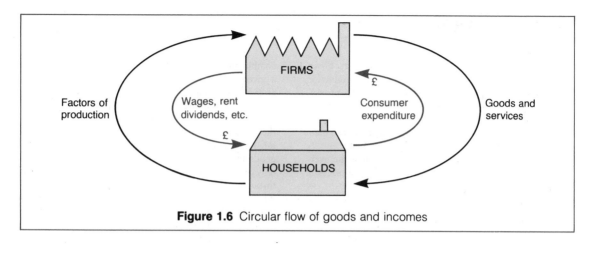

Figure 1.6 Circular flow of goods and incomes

factors of production too, such as land. The producers of goods and services are labelled 'firms' (see Figure 1.6).

Firms and households are in a twin 'demand and supply' relationship with each other.

First, on the right-hand side of the diagram, households demand goods and services, and firms supply goods and services. In the process, exchange takes place. In a money economy (as opposed to a barter economy), firms exchange goods and services for money. In other words, money flows from households to firms in the form of consumer expenditure, while goods and services flow the other way – from firms to households.

This coming together of buyers and sellers is known as a market – whether it be a street market, a shop, an auction, a mail-order system or whatever. Thus we talk about the market for apples, the market for oil, for cars, for houses, for televisions and so on.

Secondly, firms and households come together in the market for factors of production. This is illustrated on the left-hand side of the diagram. This time the demand and supply roles are reversed. Firms demand the use of factors of production owned by households – labour, land and capital. Households supply them. Thus the services of labour and other factors flow from households to firms, and in exchange firms pay households money – namely wages, rent, dividends and interest. Just as we referred to particular goods markets, so we can also refer to particular factor markets – the market for bricklayers, for secretaries, for hairdressers, for land, etc.

There is thus a circular flow of incomes. Households earn incomes from firms and firms earn incomes from households. The money circulates. There is also a circular flow of goods and services, but in the opposite direction. Households supply factor services to firms who then use them to supply goods and services to households.

This flow diagram, like the production possibility curve, can help to show the distinction between microeconomics and macroeconomics.

Microeconomics is concerned with the composition of the circular flow: *what* combinations of goods make up the goods flow; *how* the various factors of production are combined to produce these goods; *for whom* the wages, dividends, rent and interest are paid out.

Macroeconomics is concerned with the total size of the flow and what causes it to expand and contract.

Barter economy

An economy where people exchange goods and services directly with one another without any payment of money. Workers would be paid with bundles of goods.

Market

The interaction between buyers and sellers.

▲ SUMMARY

1. The central economic problem is that of scarcity. Given that there is a limited supply of factors of production (labour, land and capital), it is impossible to provide everybody with everything they want. Potential demands exceed potential supplies.
2. The subject of economics is usually divided into two main branches, macroeconomics and microeconomics.
3. Macroeconomics deals with aggregates such as the overall levels of unemployment, output, growth and prices in the economy.
4. Microeconomics deals with the activities of individual units within the economy: firms, industries, consumers, workers, etc. Because resources are scarce, people have to make choices. Society has to choose by some means or other *what* goods and services to produce, *how* to produce them and *for whom* to produce them. Microeconomics studies these choices.
5. Rational choices involve weighing up the marginal benefits of each activity against its marginal opportunity costs. If the marginal benefit exceeds the marginal cost, it is rational to choose to do more of that activity.
6. The production possibility curve shows the possible combinations of two goods that a country can produce in a given period of time. Assuming that the country is already producing on the curve, the production of more of one good will involve producing less of the other. This opportunity cost is illustrated by the slope of the curve. If the economy is producing within the curve as a result of idle resources or inefficiency it can produce more of both goods by taking up this slack. In the longer term it can only produce more of both by shifting the curve outwards through investment, technological progress, etc.
7. The circular flow of goods and incomes shows the interrelationships between firms and households in a money economy. Firms and households come together in markets. In goods markets, firms supply goods and households demand goods. In the process money flows from households to firms in return for the goods and services that the firms supply. In factor markets, firms demand factors of production and households supply them. In the process money flows from firms to households in return for the services of the factors that households supply.

1.2 Different economic systems

The classification of economic systems

All societies are faced with the problem of scarcity. They differ considerably, however, in the way they tackle the problem. One important difference between societies is in the degree of government control of the economy.

At the one extreme lies the completely planned or command economy, where all the economic decisions are taken by the government.

At the other extreme lies the completely free-market economy. In this type of economy there is no government intervention at all. All decisions are taken by individuals and firms. Households decide how much labour and other factors to supply, and what goods to consume. Firms decide what goods to produce and what factors to employ. The pattern of production and consumption that results depends on the interactions of all these individual demand and supply decisions.

In practice all economies are a mixture of the two. It is therefore the *degree* of government intervention that distinguishes different economic systems. Thus in the Soviet Union the government plays a large role (although much less than it used to), whereas in the United States the government plays a much smaller role.

It is nevertheless useful to analyze the extremes, in order to put the different mixed economies of the real world into perspective. The mixture of government and the market can be shown by the use of a *spectrum diagram* such as Figure 1.7. It shows where particular economies of the real world lie along the spectrum between the two extremes.

The diagram is useful in that it provides a simple picture of the mixture of government and the market that exists in various economies. It can also be used to show changes in the mixture over time.

Centrally planned or command economy

An economy where all economic decisions are taken by the central authorities.

Free-market economy

An economy where all economic decisions are taken by individual households and firms and with no government intervention.

Mixed economy

An economy where economic decisions are made partly by the government and partly through the market.

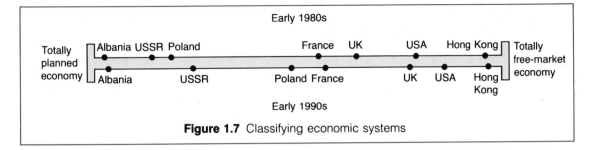

Figure 1.7 Classifying economic systems

The problem with this type of classification is that it is 'unidimensional', and thus rather simplistic. Countries also differ in the *type* of government intervention as well as the level. For example, governments intervene through planning, through nationalization, through regulation, through taxes and subsidies, through partnership schemes with private industry, and so on. Thus two countries could be in a similar position along the spectrum but have types of government intervention that were quite different. In one, the intervention could be through the public ownership of industries; in the other, it could be through rules and regulations governing the behaviour of private industries.

Notice that there has been a general movement to the right along the spectrum since 1980. In East European economies this has been a result of the abandonment of central planning and the adoption of a large measure of private enterprise, especially since the late 1980s. In Western economies it has been a result of deregulation of private industry and privatization (the selling of nationalized industries to the private sector).

> **?** Do you agree with the positions that the seven countries have been given in the spectrum diagram? Explain why or why not.

The command economy

The command economy is usually associated with a socialist or communist economic system, where land and capital are collectively owned. The state plans the allocation of resources at three important levels:

- It plans the allocation of resources between current consumption and investment for the future. By sacrificing some present consumption and diverting resources into investment, it could increase the economy's growth rate.

  The amount of resources it chooses to devote to investment will depend on its broad macroeconomic strategy: the importance it attaches to growth as opposed to current consumption.

- At a microeconomic level it plans the output of each industry and firm, the techniques that will be used, and the labour and other resources required by each industry and firm.

  In order to ensure that the required inputs are available, the state would probably conduct some form of input-output analysis. All industries are seen as users of *inputs* from other industries and as producers of *output* for consumers or other industries. For example, the steel industry uses inputs from the coal and iron-ore industries and produces output for the vehicle and construction industries. Input-output analysis shows, for each industry, the sources of all its inputs and the destination of all its output. By its use the state attempts to match up the

Input–output analysis
This involves dividing the economy into sectors where each sector is a user of inputs from and a supplier of outputs to other sectors. The technique examines how these inputs and outputs can be matched to the total resources available in the economy.

BOX 1.6

Then and Now: The Soviet Economy Under Stalin and Gorbachev
Perestroika or bust?

Early years

The Bolsheviks under the leadership of Lenin came to power in Russia with the October revolution of 1917. The Bolsheviks, however, were opposed by the White Russians and civil war ensued.

During this period of *War Communism*, the market economy was abolished. Industry and shops were nationalized; workers were told what jobs to do; there were forced requisitions of food from peasants to feed the towns; the money economy collapsed as rampant inflation made money worthless; workers were allocated goods from distribution depots.

With the ending of the civil war in 1921, the economy was in bad shape. Lenin embarked on a *New Economic Policy*. This involved a return to the use of markets. Smaller businesses were returned to private hands, and peasants were able to sell their food rather than having it requisitioned. The economy began to recover.

Lenin died in 1924 and Stalin came to power.

The Stalinist system

The Soviet economy underwent a radical transformation from 1928 onwards. The key features of the Stalinist approach were collectivization, industrialization and central planning.

Collectivization of agriculture

Peasant farms were abolished and replaced by large-scale collective farms where land was collectively owned and worked. Collectivization initially caused massive disruption and famine, with peasants slaughtering their animals rather than giving them to the collective. But despite an initial fall in output, more food was provided for the

towns, and many workers left the land to work in the new industries.

In addition to the collective farms, state farms were established. These were owned by the state and were run by managers appointed by the state. Workers were paid a wage rather than having a share in farm income.

Both collective and state farms were given quotas of output that they were supposed to deliver for which the state would pay a fixed price.

Industry and central planning

A massive drive to industrialization took place. To achieve this a vast planning apparatus was developed. At the top was *Gosplan*, the central planning agency. This prepared five-year plans and annual plans.

The five-year plans specified the general direction in which the economy was to move. The annual plans gave the details of just what was to be produced and with what resources for some 200 or so key products. Other products were planned at a lower level – by various industrial ministries or regional authorities.

The effect was that all factories were given targets that had to be achieved. It was the task of the planning authorities to ensure that the targets were realistic: that there were sufficient resources to meet the targets. The system operated without the aid of the price mechanism and the profit motive. The main incentive was the *bonus*: bonuses were paid to managers and workers if targets were achieved.

The Stalinist system remained with only minor changes until the 1980s. In the early years, very high growth rates were achieved; but this was at a cost of low efficiency. The poor flow of information from firms to the planners led to many inconsistencies in the plans. The targets

inputs and outputs of each industry so that the planned demand for each industry's product is equal to its planned supply.

- It plans the distribution of output between consumers. This will depend on the government's aims. It may distribute goods according to its judgement of people's *needs*; or it may give more to those who produce more, thereby providing an *incentive* for people to work harder.

It may distribute goods and services directly; or it may decide the distribution of money incomes and allow individuals to decide how to spend them. If it does the latter it may still seek to influence the pattern of expenditure by setting appropriate prices: low prices to encourage consumption, and high prices to discourage consumption.

BOX 1.6 (cont'd)

were often totally unrealistic, and as a result there were frequent shortages and sometimes surpluses. With incentives purely geared to meeting targets, there was little product innovation and goods were frequently of poor quality and finish.

The limits of planning

Although most resources were allocated through planning, there were nevertheless some goods that were sold in markets. Any surpluses above their quota that were produced by collective farms could be sold in collective farm markets (street markets) in the towns. In addition, the workers on collective farms were allowed to own their own small private plots of land, and they too could sell their produce in the collective farm markets.

A large 'underground economy' flourished in which goods were sold on the black market and in which people did second 'unofficial' jobs (e.g. as plumbers, electricians or garment makers).

Stalin's successors

Stalin died in 1953. His successor, Khruschev, tried some modest reforms in the late 1950s and early 1960s. But Khruschev was ousted in 1964 by Brezhnev and Kosygin. In the mid-1960s there were some further modest reforms, with a move towards bonuses being based on a firm's profitability rather than on the simple achievement of quantitative targets. But these reforms largely petered out.

Growth slowed down in the 1970s and by the time Gorbachev came to power in 1985 many people in the Soviet Union were pressing for fundamental reforms.

Gorbachev's reforms

The reforms are generally referred to by the Russian word *perestroika*, which means economic reconstruction. *Perestroika* has been concerned with creating a 'planned socialist market'. This involves a compromise between the state planning system and the Western free-market system.

Reforms have included the following:

- Making managers more involved in preparing their own plans rather than merely being given instructions.
- Insisting that firms cover their costs of production. If they cannot, the state may refuse to bale them out and they may be declared bankrupt. The aim of this is to encourage firms to be more efficient.
- Improving the incentive system by relating bonuses more closely to genuine productivity (see Box 1.8).
- Organizing workers into small teams or 'brigades' (typically of around 10–15 workers). Bonuses are then awarded to the whole brigade according to its productivity. The idea is to encourage people to work more effectively together.
- Stringent checks on quality by state officials and the rejection of substandard goods.
- Allowing co-operatives to be set up. These are generally relatively small businesses owned by the workers rather than the state.
- Allowing individuals to set up one-person businesses (e.g. taxi drivers, plumbers or hairdressers).
- Except in the case of co-operatives and one-person businesses, the state still sets prices. Nevertheless prices are now adjusted relatively frequently in order to reflect demand and supply, and the authorities are increasingly agreeing to price changes requested by firms. In many cases this has involved substantial price rises.

Nevertheless, the plan remains, and the state still operates as economic overseer, only now from a distance: regulating rather than dictating economic processes.

The future of Soviet economic growth will no doubt depend on the success of these reforms.

? If managers have more flexibility to decide their own output in a previously totally planned economy, will this make it easier or harder for the planning authorities to ensure that supply matches demand in the various sectors of the economy?

The free-market economy

Free decision making by individuals

The free-market economy is usually associated with a pure capitalist system, where land and capital are privately owned. All economic decisions are taken by households and firms, which are assumed to act in their own self-interest. These assumptions are made:

- Firms seek to maximize profits.
- Consumers seek to get the best value for money from their purchases.
- Workers seek to maximize their wages relative to the human cost of working in a particular job.

It is assumed that individuals are free to make their own economic choices. Consumers are free to decide what to buy with their incomes. Workers are free to choose where and how much to work. Firms are free to choose what to sell and what production methods to use.

The resulting supply and demand decisions of firms and households are transmitted to each other through their effect on *prices*.

The price mechanism

The price mechanism

The system in a market economy whereby changes in price in response to changes in demand and supply have the effect of making demand equal to supply.

The price mechanism works as follows. Prices respond to *shortages* and *surpluses*. Shortages cause prices to rise. Surpluses cause prices to fall.

If consumers decide they want more of a good (or if producers decide to cut back supply), demand will exceed supply. The resulting *shortage* will cause *the price of the good to rise*. This will act as an incentive to producers to supply more, since production will now be more profitable. It will discourage consumers from buying so much. *Price will continue rising until the shortage has thereby been eliminated.*

If, on the other hand, consumers decide they want less of a good (or if producers decide to produce more), supply will exceed demand. The resulting *surplus* will cause *the price of the good to fall*. This will act as a disincentive to producers, who will supply less, since production will now be less profitable. It will encourage consumers to buy more. *Price will continue falling until the surplus has thereby been eliminated.*

The same analysis can be applied to factor markets. If the demand for a particular type of labour exceeded its supply, the resulting shortage would drive up the wage rate (i.e. the price of labour), thus reducing firms' demand for that type of labour and encouraging more workers to take up that type of job. Wages would continue rising until demand equalled supply: until the shortage was eliminated.

Likewise if there were a surplus of a particular type of labour, the wage would fall until demand equalled supply.

 Can you think of any examples where prices and wages do not adjust very rapidly to a shortage or surplus? For what reasons might they not do so?

The effect of changes in demand and supply

How will the price mechanism respond to changes in consumer demand or producer supply? After all, the pattern of consumer demand changes. For example, people may decide they want more bicycles and fewer skateboards. Likewise the pattern of supply also changes. For example, changes in technology may allow the mass production of microchips at lower cost, while the production of hand-built furniture becomes relatively expensive.

In all cases of changes in demand and supply, the resulting changes in *price* act as both *signals* and *incentives*.

A change in demand. A rise in demand is signalled by a rise in price. This then acts as an incentive for supply to rise. What in effect is happening is that the high prices of these goods relative to their costs of production is signalling that consumers are willing to see resources diverted from other uses. This is just what firms do. They divert resources from goods with lower prices relative to costs (and hence lower profits) to those goods that are more profitable.

A fall in demand is signalled by a fall in price. This then acts as an incentive for supply to fall. The goods are now less profitable to produce.

A change in supply. A rise in supply is signalled by a fall in price. This then acts as an incentive for demand to rise. A fall in supply is signalled by a rise in price. This then acts as an incentive for demand to fall.

> **?** 1. Why do the prices of fresh vegetables fall when they are in season? Could an individual farmer prevent the price falling?
> 2. If you were the owner of a clothes shop, how would you set about deciding what prices to charge for each garment at the end of season sale?
> 3. The number of owners of compact disc players has grown rapidly and hence the demand for compact discs has also grown rapidly. Yet the prices of discs have fallen. Why?

The interdependence of markets

The interdependence of goods and factor markets. A rise in demand for a good will raise its price and profitability. Firms will respond by supplying more. But to do this they will need more inputs. Thus the demand for the inputs will rise, which in turn will raise the price of the inputs. The suppliers of inputs will respond to this incentive by supplying more. This can be summarized as follows:

1. Goods market

   - Demand for the good rises.
   - This creates a shortage.
   - This causes the price of the good to rise.
   - This eliminates the shortage by choking off some of the demand and encouraging firms to produce more.

2. Factor market

   - The increased supply of the good causes an increase in the demand for factors of production (i.e. inputs) used in making it.
   - This causes a shortage of those inputs.
   - This causes their prices to rise.
   - This eliminates their shortage by choking off some of the demand and encouraging the suppliers of inputs to supply more.

It is common in economics to summarize an argument like this by using symbols. It is a form of shorthand. Figure 1.8 summarizes this particular sequence of events. Goods markets thus affect factor markets.

Figure 1.8 The price mechanism: the effect of a rise in demand

Interdependence exists in the other direction too: factor markets affect goods markets. For example, the discovery of raw materials will lower their price. This will lower the costs of production of firms using these raw materials and will increase the supply of the finished goods. The resulting surplus will lower the price of the good, which will encourage consumers to buy more.

 Summarize this last paragraph using symbols like those in Figure 1.8.

The interdependence of different goods markets. A rise in the price of one good will encourage consumers to buy alternatives. This will drive up the price of alternatives. This in turn will encourage producers to supply more of the alternatives.

 Are different factor markets similarly interdependent? Give examples.

Conclusion

Even though all individuals are merely looking to their own self-interest in the free-market economy, they are in fact being encouraged to respond to the wishes of others through the incentive of the price mechanism.

Assessment of the free-market economy

The fact that a free-market economy functions automatically is one of its major advantages. There is no need for costly and complex bureaucracies to co-ordinate economic decisions. The economy can respond quickly to changing demand and supply conditions.

When markets are highly competitive, no one has great power. Competition between firms keeps prices down and acts as an incentive to firms to become more efficient. The more firms there are competing, the more responsive they will be to consumer wishes.

The more efficiently firms can combine their factors of production, the more profit they will make. The more efficiently workers work, the more secure will be their jobs and the higher their wages. The more carefully consumers decide what to buy, the greater the value for money they will receive.

Thus people pursuing their own self-interest through buying and selling in competitive markets helps to minimize the central economic problem of scarcity, by encouraging the efficient use of the nation's resources in line with consumer wishes. From this type of argument, the following conclusion is often drawn by defenders of the free market: 'The pursuit of private gain results in the social good'. This is obviously a highly significant claim and has profound moral implications.

In practice, however, markets do not achieve maximum efficiency in the allocation of scarce resources, and governments feel it necessary to intervene to rectify this and other problems of the free market. The problems of a free market are as follows:

- Competition between firms is often limited. A few giant firms may dominate an industry. In these cases they may charge high prices and make large profits. Rather than merely responding to consumer wishes, they may attempt to persuade consumers by advertising. Consumers are particularly susceptible to advertisements for products that are new to them and of which they have little knowledge.
- Lack of competition and high profits may remove the incentive for firms to be efficient.

BOX 1.7

Adam Smith (1723–1790)
and the 'invisible hand' of the market

Many economists would argue that modern economics dates from 1776. That was the year in which Adam Smith's *An Inquiry into the Nature and Causes of the Wealth of Nations* was published – one of the most important books on economics ever written.

Adam Smith was born in 1723 in Kirkcaldy, a small coastal town north of Edinburgh. His father died when Adam was just a baby, and for most of his life he lived with his mother: he never married. After graduating from Glasgow University at the age of 17, he first became a fellow of Balliol College Oxford, but then returned to Scotland and at the age of 29 became professor of moral philosophy at the University of Glasgow. At the age of 40 he resigned and spent three years touring the continent where he met many influential economists and philosophers. He then returned to Scotland, to his home town of Kirkcaldy, and set to work on *The Wealth of Nations*.

The work, in five books, is very wide ranging, but the central argument is that market economies generally serve the public interest well. Markets guide production and consumption like an *invisible hand*. Even though everyone is looking after their own private self-interest, their interaction in the market will lead to the social good.

In book I, chapter 2, he writes:

> Man has almost constant occasion for the help of his brethren and it is in vain for him to expect it from their benevolence only. He will be more likely to prevail if he can interest their self-love in his favour, and show them that it is for their own advantage to do for him what he requires of them. Whoever offers to another a bargain of any kind, proposes to do this. Give me that what I want, and you shall have this which you want, is the meaning of every such offer; and it is in this manner that we obtain from one another the far greater part of those good offices which we stand in need of. It is not from the benevolence of the butcher, the brewer, or the baker that we expect our dinner, but from their regard to their own interest. We address ourselves, not to their humanity but to their self-love, and never talk to them of our own necessities, but of their advantages.

Later in book IV, chapter 2, he continues:

> Every individual is continually exerting himself to find out the most advantageous employment of whatever

capital he can command. It is his own advantage, indeed, and not that of the society, which he has in view. But the study of his own advantage naturally, or rather necessarily, leads him to prefer that employment which is most advantageous to the society . . . he intends only his own gain, and he is in this, as in many other cases, led by an invisible hand to promote an end which was no part of his intention. Nor is it always the worse for the society that it was no part of it. By pursuing his own interest he frequently promotes that of society more effectually than when he really intends to promote it.

He argued, therefore, with one or two exceptions, that the state should not interfere in the functioning of the economy. It should adopt a *laissez-faire* or 'hands-off' policy. It should allow free enterprise for firms and free trade between countries.

This praise of the free market has led many on the political right to regard him as the father of the 'libertarian movement' – the movement that advocates the absolute minimum amount of state intervention in the economy. In fact one of the most famous of the libertarian societies is called 'the Adam Smith Institute'.

But Smith was not blind to the drawbacks of unregulated markets. In book I, chapter 7, he looks at the problem of monopoly:

> A monopoly granted either to an individual or to a trading company has the same effect as a secret in trade or manufactures. The monopolists, by keeping the market constantly under-stocked, by never fully supplying the effectual demand, sell their commodities much above the natural price, and raise their emoluments, whether they consist in wages or profit, greatly above their natural rate.

Later on he looks at the dangers of firms getting together to pursue their mutual interest:

> People of the same trade seldom meet together, even for merriment or diversion, but the conversation ends in a conspiracy against the public or in some contrivance to raise prices.

- Power and property may be unequally distributed. Those who have power and/or property (e.g. big business, unions, landlords) will gain at the expense of those without power and property.
- The practices of some firms may be socially undesirable. For example, a chemical works may pollute the environment.

- Some socially desirable goods would simply not be produced by private enterprise. What firm would build and operate a lighthouse?
- A free-market economy may lead to macroeconomic instability. There may be periods of recession with high unemployment and falling output, and other periods of rising prices.
- Finally, there is the ethical objection, that a free-market economy, by rewarding self-interested behaviour, may encourage selfishness, greed, materialism and the acquisition of power.

Assessment of the command economy

Central planning can overcome some of the problems of a free-market economy. Instead of having to rely on the decisions of millions of individuals, decisions that will not always be in the interests of society as a whole, the government could take an overall view of the economy. It could direct the nation's resources in accordance with specific national goals.

High growth rates could be achieved if the government directed large amounts of resources into investment. Unemployment could be largely avoided if the government carefully planned the allocation of labour in accordance with production requirements and labour skills. National income could be distributed more equally or in accordance with needs. The social repercussions of production and consumption (e.g. the effects on the environment) could be taken into account, provided the government was able to predict these effects.

In practice, these goals could only be achieved at considerable social and economic cost. The reasons are as follows:

- The larger and more complex the economy, the greater the task of collecting and analyzing the information essential to planning, and the more complex the plan. Complicated plans are likely to be costly to administer and involve cumbersome bureaucracy.
- If there is no system of prices, or if prices are set arbitrarily by the state, planning is likely to involve the inefficient use of resources. It is difficult to assess the relative efficiency of two alternative techniques that use different inputs, if there is no way in which the value of those inputs can be ascertained. For example, how can a rational decision be made between an oil-fired and a coal-fired furnace if the prices of oil and coal do not reflect their relative scarcity?
- It is difficult to devise appropriate incentives to encourage workers and managers to be more productive without a reduction in quality. For example, if bonuses are given according to the quantity of output produced, a factory might produce shoddy goods, since it can probably produce a larger quantity of goods by cutting quality. To avoid this problem a large number of officials may have to be employed to check quality.
- Complete state control over resource allocation would involve a considerable loss of individual liberty. Workers would have no choice where to work; consumers would have no choice what to buy.
- The government might enforce its plans even if they were unpopular.
- If production is planned, but consumers are free to spend money incomes as they wish, then the government has the problem of avoiding shortages and surpluses, should consumer wishes change.

BOX 1.8

Getting Incentives Right
When the wrong incentives caused a storm in the USSR

Any economic system will involve *incentives*. For example, under a capitalist system, firms have the incentive to make profits. This will, under certain circumstances, cause them to produce what the consumer wants and to produce as efficiently as possible.

Under the Soviet system of central planning that was developed in the 1930s and remained virtually intact until the 1980s, the main incentive for managers and workers was the *bonus*. Bonuses were awarded if *targets* were fulfilled. These targets were set by the central planning authorities and were normally expressed in quantitative units: so many tonnes, metres, cubic metres, etc. The bonuses were usually awarded monthly.

So what sort of incentive did this provide? The incentive was to meet the target, come what may. If it was clear as the month was progressing that production was slipping behind schedule, there would be a mad scramble to meet the target. Corners would be cut and quality would suffer. This process, known as *storming*, was one of the major causes of shoddy goods being produced throughout the Soviet economy.

Factory managers tended to underestimate their production potential to the authorities in order to get lower targets, which would be easier to fulfil. The authorities knew this and hence tended to increase targets. This made the problem of storming worse.

Here, then, was a case of incentives having a perverse effect: the bonus system produced shoddy goods.

Under the policy of *perestroika* (see Box 1.6), two reforms were introduced in the late 1980s to tackle the problem:

- A new government agency, 'Gospriomka', was set up. This had the task of checking quality and rejecting substandard goods. Its representatives in factories were often ex-employees of the factories and therefore knew what to look for.
- Under a system known as *Khosraschët*, factories were to be self-financing. They were required at least to break even, and to do so they would have to produce saleable goods.

Postscript
Incentives can be perverse under capitalism too. Big businesses may achieve higher profits not by being more efficient, but by driving up prices and hence 'exploiting' the consumer. This problem is examined in Chapters 6, 10 and 11.

? If you took an economics course where the sole method of assessment was two essays, would this be a good incentive to study the subject in breadth?

The mixed economy

Because of the problems of both the purely market and the purely command economies, all real-world economies are a mixture of the two systems. All 'command' economies use the market mechanism to some extent. All 'market' economies involve some degree of government intervention.

In mixed command economies, the government may, despite adopting a system of planning, allow the prices of goods and inputs to fluctuate to some extent in line with changes in demand and supply. Consumers may be free to purchase what they want. Managers may be allowed to choose what techniques to use, and where to obtain inputs. Workers may be free to choose where to work. Monetary incentives may be offered to workers and managers to increase productivity.

In mixed market economies, the government may control the following:

- Relative prices of goods and inputs, by taxing or subsidizing them or by direct price controls.
- Relative incomes, by the use of income taxes, welfare payments or direct controls over wages, profits, rents, etc.

Relative price
The price of one good compared with another (e.g. good x is twice the price of good y).

- The pattern of production and consumption, by the use of legislation (e.g. making it illegal to produce unsafe goods), by direct provision of goods and services (e.g. education and defence), by taxes and subsidies or by nationalization.
- The macroeconomic problems of unemployment, inflation, lack of growth and balance of payments deficits, by the use of taxes and government expenditure, the control of bank lending and interest rates, the direct control of prices and incomes, and the control of the foreign exchange rate.

Just how the government intervenes, and what the effects of the various forms of intervention are, will be examined in detail in later chapters.

The relative merits of alternative mixtures of government and the market depend on the weight attached to various political and economic goals: goals such as liberty, equality, efficiency in production, the fulfilling of consumer wishes, economic growth and full employment. No one type of mixed economy is likely to be superior in all respects.

▲ SUMMARY

1. The economic systems of different countries vary according to the extent to which they rely on the market or the government to allocate resources.
2. At the one extreme, in a command economy, the state makes all the economic decisions. It plans how many resources to allocate for present consumption and how many for investment for future output. It plans the output of each industry, the methods of production it will use and the amount of resources it will be allocated. It plans the distribution of output between consumers.
3. At the other extreme is the free-market economy. In this economy decisions are made by the interaction of demand and supply. Price changes act as the mechanism whereby demand and supply are balanced. If there is a shortage, price will rise until the shortage is eliminated. If there is a surplus, price will fall until that is eliminated.
4. A command economy has the advantage of being able to

address directly various national economic goals, such as rapid growth and the avoidance of unemployment and inequality. A command economy, however, is likely to be inefficient: a large bureaucracy will be needed to collect and process information; prices and the choice of production methods are likely to be arbitrary; incentives may be inappropriate; shortages and surpluses may result.
5. A free-market economy functions automatically and if there is plenty of competition between producers this can help to protect consumers' interests. In practice, however, competition may be limited; there may be great inequality; there may be adverse social and environmental consequences; there may be macroeconomic instability.
6. In practice all economies are some mixture of the market and government intervention. It is the degree and form of government intervention that distinguishes one type of economy from another.

1.3 The nature of economic reasoning

Economics is one of the social sciences. So in what sense is it a *science*? Is it like the natural sciences such as physics, chemistry, geology and astronomy. What is the significance of the word 'social' in social science? What can the economist legitimately do as an economist? What is the role of economists in helping governments devise economic policy?

In this part of the chapter we attempt to answer these questions.

Economics as a science

Economic model

A formal presentation of an economic theory.

The methodology employed by economists has a lot in common with that employed by natural scientists. Both attempt to construct theories or models which are then used for two main purposes: to *explain* and to *predict*. An astronomer, for example, constructs models of planetary movements in order to *explain* why particular planets are in the position they are and to *predict* their position at various times in the future.

Models in economics

In order to explain and predict, the economist constructs models of the economy or parts of the economy. These models are simplified representations of reality. They show the relationships between various economic phenomena. For example, a model of a market would show the relationships between demand, supply and price. A model of inflation might show the relationship between prices and the amount of money in the economy.

Although most models can be described verbally, they can normally be represented more precisely in graphical or mathematical form.

Building models

Models are constructed by making general hypotheses about the causes of economic phenomena: for example, that consumer demand will rise when consumer incomes rise. These hypotheses will often be based on observations. This process of making general statements from particular observations is known as induction.

Because reality is complex, not all possible causes can be taken into account. Thus models have to make simplifying assumptions. They ignore those possible causal factors that have only minor significance.

Induction

Constructing general theories on the basis of specific observations.

Using models

Explanation. Models explain by showing how things are caused: what are the causes of inflation; why do workers in some industries earn more than workers in other industries; why does the demand for beef rise when the price of pork rises; and so on.

Prediction. Models are sometimes used to make simple forecasts: for example, inflation will be above 20 per cent next year. Usually, however, predictions are of the 'If . . . then . . . ' variety: for example if demand for good x rises, its price will rise. This process of drawing conclusions from models is known as deduction.

When making such deductions it has to be assumed that nothing else that can influence the outcome has changed in the meantime. For example, if demand for good x rises its price will rise *assuming* the cost of producing good x has not fallen. This is known as the *ceteris paribus* assumption. *Ceteris paribus* is Latin for 'other things being equal'.

Deduction

Using a theory to draw conclusions about specific circumstances.

Ceteris paribus

Latin for 'other things being equal'. This assumption has to be made when making deductions from theories.

Assessing models

Models can be judged according to how successful they are in explaining and predicting.

If the predictions are wrong, the first thing to do is to check whether the deductions were correctly made. If they were, the model must be either adapted or abandoned. If an alternative model can be developed with better predictive ability, the original model may well be abandoned. If, however, the original model can be adapted by, say, altering its assumptions, and if its predictive powers are thereby improved, it is likely to be kept.

Sometimes an economist will want to retain a model even though it has poor predictive powers if the model helps to give some insight into the the workings of the economy. For example, a model of some idealized world in which the goals of efficiency, growth and equality were all met might be extremely useful as a yardstick against which to compare the real world and to understand its shortcomings.

BOX 1.9

Ceteris Paribus?

Because of the complexities of the real world, economic models have to make various simplifying assumptions. Sometimes, however, economists are criticized for making unrealistic assumptions, assumptions that make their models irrelevant.

The following joke illustrates the point . . .

There were three people cast away on a desert island: a chemist, an engineer and an economist. There was no food on the island and their plight seemed desperate.

Then they discovered a crate of canned food that had been washed up on the island. But their joy was soon dampened when they realized that they had no means of opening the cans. So they decided that each of them should use their expertise to find a solution.

The chemist searched around for various minerals that could be heated up to produce a compound that would burn through the lids of the cans.

The engineer hunted around for rocks and then worked out what height of tree they would have to be dropped from in order to smash open the cans.

Meanwhile the economist sat down and thought, 'Assuming we had a can opener . . .'

Economics as a social science

Despite using similar models to the natural sciences, economics lacks the ability to make precise predictions with accuracy. There are two major reasons for this.

Controlled experiments

It is impossible to conduct controlled experiments in economics.

Physicists can build models and test them using laboratory experiments under tightly controlled conditions. Economists, however, are dealing with a constantly changing environment. They are dealing with society – with the complex interactions between individuals, groups, institutions, laws, the physical environment, etc. In order to develop reasonably simple models they have to make simplifying assumptions. But while they may assume that 'other things remain constant', unlike physicists they cannot *actually* hold them constant.

Some natural scientists have this problem too. Meteorology is an example. A vast number of variables affect the course and development of weather systems. Meteorologists thus have to make a large number of simplifying assumptions. Not surprisingly, then, weather forecasting is not totally reliable and the forecasts that are made are rather imprecise. Nevertheless weather forecasting has become more accurate in recent years. Satellites have allowed better gathering of data, and computers have allowed more complex models to be developed. So too in economics: with research providing more and more information and with more complex and sophisticated models having been developed, often with the aid of computers, the predictions of economists have become more accurate.

Human behaviour

Although people may behave in broadly similar ways under similar conditions, it is impossible to predict this behaviour with any accuracy. How, for example, will firms react on a particular occasion to a rise in the rate of inflation when making their investment decisions or when making a wage offer? Such decisions will depend on unpredictable things such as the state of business confidence.

For these reasons there is plenty of scope for competing models in economics, with different models making different assumptions. Different 'schools of thought' will often take quite different views about how the economy or parts of it operate. As a result, economics can often be highly controversial, with different models leading to different policy conclusions. As we shall see later on in the book, different political parties may adhere to different schools of economic thought. Thus the political left may adhere to a model which implies that governments must intervene if unemployment is to be cured; whereas the political right may adhere to a model which implies that unemployment will be reduced if the government intervenes less and relies more on the free market.

It would be wrong to get the impression from this that economists are always disagreeing. There is a popular belief that 'if you laid all the economists of the world end to end they would still not reach a conclusion'. In practice, there is a large measure of agreement between economists about how to analyze the world and about what conclusions to draw.

Economics and policy

Economists play a major role in helping governments to devise economic policy. In order to consider this role, it is necessary to distinguish between *positive* and *normative* statements.

A positive statement is a statement of fact. It may be right or wrong, but its accuracy can be tested by appealing to the facts. 'Unemployment is rising.' 'Inflation will be over 6 per cent by next year.' 'If the government cuts taxes, imports will rise.' These are all examples of positive statements. They do not necessarily have to be true, but we can test whether they are true or false by looking at the evidence. Of course, in the case of a prediction, we will have to wait to do this.

Positive statement

A value-free statement which can be tested by an appeal to the facts.

A normative statement is a statement of value: a statement about what ought or ought not to be, about whether something is good or bad, desirable or undesirable. 'It is *right* to tax the rich more than the poor.' 'The government *ought* to reduce inflation.' 'Old-age pensions *ought* to be increased in line with inflation.' These are all examples of normative statements. They cannot be proved or disproved by a simple appeal to the facts.

Normative statement

A value judgement.

Some apparent disagreements of value may arise because people are mistaken about facts. For example, people might disagree as to whether income taxes should be cut because they disagree as to whether this would act as an incentive for people to work harder. Such a disagreement could be settled by appealing to the evidence. If, however, people agree about the facts, but still disagree about what ought to be, there is no scientific way of demonstrating who is 'right'. The choice between two such opposing views must ultimately depend on an individual's subjective judgements about what is good and bad.

Economists can only contribute in a positive way to questions of policy. That is, they can analyze the consequences of following certain policies. They can say which of two policies is more likely to achieve a given aim, but they cannot, as economists, say whether the aims of the policy are desirable. For example, economists may argue that a policy of increasing government expenditure will reduce unemployment and raise inflation, but they cannot decide whether such a policy is desirable or undesirable. Economists, then, as scientists cannot make normative judgements. They can only do so as individual people, and as such have no more moral right than any other individual.

This does not mean that economists play no role in helping governments to formulate their aims. Economists may be able to point out various unintended consequences of government policy. For example, a government for ideological reasons may choose to sell the nuclear power industry to the private sector (privatize it). Economists, by analyzing all the costs of operating the nuclear power stations, may discover that they cannot be run at a profit in the foreseeable future and may thus advise against the privatization. This is precisely what happened in Britain in 1989. The economists here were not saying that privatization is wrong on *ideological grounds*: that would be a normative judgement. What they were saying was that the pursuit of a goal irrespective of its consequences may conflict with other goals (e.g. that private industry should be able to 'stand on its own feet' without the need for government support). Thus economists, by examining the consequences of adopting various policies can help governments to formulate their policies in the first place and to amend them subsequently.

? Which of the following are positive statements, which are normative statements and which could be either depending on the context?

(a) Cutting the higher rates of income tax will redistribute incomes from the poor to the rich.
(b) It is wrong that inflation should be reduced if this means that there will be higher unemployment.
(c) It is wrong to state that putting up interest rates will reduce inflation.
(d) The government should raise interest rates in order to prevent the exchange rate falling.
(e) Current government policies should reduce unemployment.

▲ SUMMARY

1. The methodology used by economists is similar to that used by natural scientists. Economists construct models which they use to explain and predict economic phenomena. These models can be tested by appealing to facts and seeing how successfully they have been predicted or explained by the model. Unsuccessful models can be either abandoned or amended.

2. Being a social science, economics is concerned with human actions. Making accurate predictions in economics is very difficult given that economics is not a laboratory science and has to deal with a constantly changing environment.

3. Economists can help governments to devise policy by examining the consequences of alternative courses of action. In doing this it is, important to separate positive questions about what the effects of the policies are, from normative ones as to what the goals of policy should be. Economists in their role as economists have no superior right to make normative judgements on the ideological, moral or political basis of the policy. They can and do, however, play a major role in assessing whether a policy meets the political objectives of government (or opposition).

1.4 Some techniques of economic analysis

When students first come to economics many are worried about the amount of mathematics they will encounter. Will it all be equations and graphs and will there be lots of hard calculations to do and difficult theories to grasp?

As you will see if you glance through the pages of this book, there are many diagrams and tables and several equations. But this does not mean that there are many mathematical techniques that you will have to master. In fact there are relatively few techniques, but they are ones which we use many times in many different contexts. You will find that if you are new to the subject you will very quickly become familiar with these techniques. If you are not new to the subject, perhaps you could reassure your colleagues who are!

Diagrams as pictures

In many cases, we use diagrams simply to provide a picture of a relationship. Just as a photograph in a newspaper can often provide a much more vivid picture of an event than any description in words, so too a diagram in economics can often picture a relationship with a vividness and clarity that could never be achieved by description alone.

For example, we may observe that as people's incomes rise, they spend a lot more on entertainment and only a little more on food. We can picture this relationship very nicely by the use of a simple graph.

In Figure 1.9, an individual's income is measured along the horizontal axis and the expenditure on food and entertainment is measured up the vertical axis. There are just two lines on this diagram: the one showing how the expenditure on entertainment rises as income rises, the other how the expenditure on food rises as income rises. Now we could use a diagram like this to plot actual data. But we may simply be using it as a sketch – as a picture. In this case we do not necessarily need to put figures on the two axes. We are simply showing the relative *shapes* of the two curves. These shapes tell us that the person's expenditure on entertainment rises more quickly than that on food, and that above a certain level of income the expenditure on entertainment becomes greater than that on food.

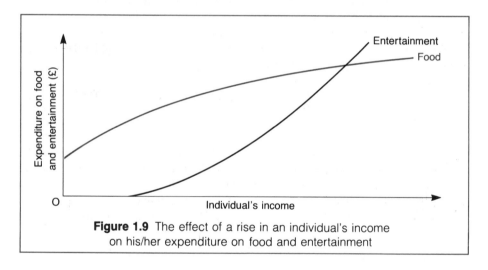

Figure 1.9 The effect of a rise in an individual's income on his/her expenditure on food and entertainment

? What else is the diagram telling us?

If you were to describe in words all the information that this sketch graph depicts, you would need several lines of prose.

Figure 1.6 (the circular flow diagram) and Figure 1.7 (the spectrum diagram) were also examples of sketches designed to give a simple, clear picture of a relationship: a picture stripped of all unnecessary detail.

Representing real-life statistics

In many cases we will want to depict real-world data. We may want to show, for example, how unemployment has changed over the years in a particular country, or how income is distributed between different groups in the population. In the first we will need to look at time-series data. In the second we will look at cross-section data.

Time series data

Table 1.2 shows the UK unemployment rate between the first quarter of 1987 and the first quarter of 1990. A table like this is a common way of representing time-series data. It has the advantage of giving the precise figures, and is thus a useful reference if we want to test any theory and see if it predicts accurately.

Time-series data

Information depicting how a variable (e.g. the price of eggs) changes over time.

Table 1.2 UK unemployment 1987 Q1–1990 Q1: time-series data

Year	1987				1988				1989				1990
	Q1	Q2	Q3	Q4	Q1	Q2	Q3	Q4	Q1	Q2	Q3	Q4	Q1
Unemployment (%)	10.9	10.6	10.1	9.5	8.9	8.5	8.0	7.6	7.0	6.6	6.3	5.9	5.7

Source: *Economic Trends* (CSO).

Notice that in this particular table the figures are given quarterly. Depending on the period of time over which we want to see the movement of a variable, it may be more appropriate to use a different interval of time. For example, if we wanted to see how unemployment had changed over the last 50 years, we might use annual figures or even average figures for longer periods of time. If, however, we wanted to see how unemployment had changed over the course of a year, we would probably use monthly figures or even weekly figures.

 The table in Box 1.2 shows time-series data for four different variables for four different countries. Would there have been any advantage in giving the figures for each separate year? Would there have been any disadvantage?

Time-series data can also be shown graphically. In fact the data from a table can be plotted directly on to a graph. Figure 1.10 plots the data from Table 1.2. Each dot on the graph corresponds to one figure from the table. The dots are then joined up to form a single line. Thus if you wanted to find the unemployment rate at any time between 1987 Q1 and 1990 Q1, you would simply find the appropriate date on the

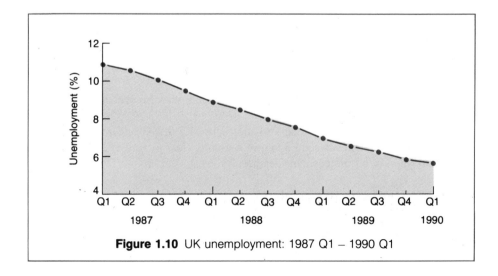

Figure 1.10 UK unemployment: 1987 Q1 – 1990 Q1

horizontal axis, read vertically upward to the line you have drawn, then read across to find the rate of unemployment.

Although a graph like this cannot give you quite such an accurate measurement of each point as a table does, it gives a much more obvious picture of how the figures have moved over time and whether the changes are getting bigger (the curve getting steeper) or smaller (the curve getting shallower). We can also read off what the likely figure would be for some point *between* two observations.

 What was the unemployment rate midway between quarters 3 and 4 of 1987?

It is also possible to combine *two* sets of time-series data on one graph to show their relative movements over time. Table 1.3 shows the figures for the UK current account on the balance of payments for the same time period. Figure 1.11 plots these data along with those from Table 1.2. This enables us to get a clear picture of how unemployment and the current account moved in relation to each other over the period in question. Note that we use a different vertical scale for the two variables. This is inevitable given that they are measured in different units.

 How would it be possible to show three different lines on the same diagram?

All developed countries publish time-series data for the major macroeconomic variables such as national income, prices, employment and unemployment, interest

Table 1.3 UK current account balance of payments 1987 Q1–1990 Q1 (quarterly figures)

Year	1987				1988				1989				1990
	Q1	Q2	Q3	Q4	Q1	Q2	Q3	Q4	Q1	Q2	Q3	Q4	Q1
Current account (£bn)	0.3	−0.7	−1.2	−2.3	−3.2	−2.9	−3.2	−5.4	−4.7	−5.5	−6.2	−4.1	−5.1

Source: *Economic Trends* (CSO).

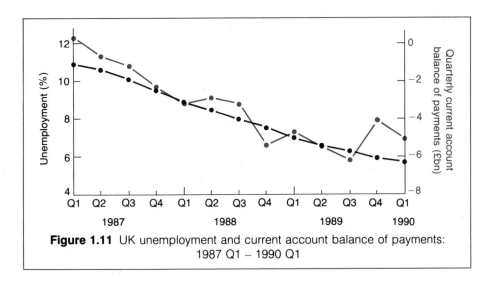

Figure 1.11 UK unemployment and current account balance of payments: 1987 Q1 – 1990 Q1

rates, and imports and exports. In the UK the figures are published by the Central Statistical Office and appear in a number of monthly and annual publications such as the *Annual Abstract of Statistics, Economic Trends* (monthly), *Economic Trends Annual Supplement, Financial Statistics* (monthly) and the *Monthly Digest of Statistics*. International economic statistics are published by, amongst others, the Organization for Economic Co-operation and Development (OECD), the International Monetary Fund (IMF), the World Bank and the European Community.

Microeconomic data on the distribution of income, the performance of particular industries, the distribution of household expenditure and so on also appear in the official government statistics. Firms, consumers' associations, charities and other organizations also publish microeconomic statistics.

Cross-section data

Cross-section data

Information showing how a variable (e.g. the consumption of eggs) differs between different groups or different individuals at a given time.

Cross-section data show different observations made at the *same point in time*. For example, they could show the quantities of food and clothing purchased at various levels of household income, or the costs to a firm or industry of producing various quantities of a product.

Table 1.4 gives an example of cross-section data. It shows the distribution of household income in the UK before the deduction of taxes and the addition of benefits. It puts households into five equal-sized groups (or 'quintiles') according to their income. Thus the poorest 20 per cent of households are in one group, the next poorest 20 per cent are in the next and so on. Looking just at the 1985 figures, they show that the poorest 20 per cent in 1985 earned just 0.3 per cent of total household incomes, whereas the richest 20 per cent earned 49.2 per cent.

Cross-section data like these are often represented in the form of a chart. Figure 1.12 shows the data as a *histogram*, and Figure 1.13 as a *pie chart*.

Table 1.4 Income before taxes and benefits

	Quintile groups of households					
	Bottom 20%	Next 20%	Middle 20%	Next 20%	Top 20%	Total
1976	0.8	9.4	18.8	26.6	44.4	100.0
1985	0.3	6.0	17.2	27.3	49.2	100.0

Source: *Social Trends* (CSO).

Figure 1.12 The distribution of UK pre-tax income (1985): the use of a histogram

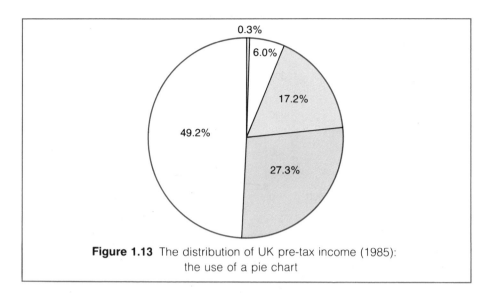

Figure 1.13 The distribution of UK pre-tax income (1985):
the use of a pie chart

It is possible to represent cross-section data at two or more different points in time, thereby presenting the figures as a time series. In Table 1.4, figures are given for just two years. With a more complete time series we could graph the movement of the shares of each of the five groups over time.

? Could histograms or pie charts be used for representing time-series data?

Getting a true picture from the statistics

'There are lies, damned lies and statistics.' This well-known saying highlights the abuse of statistics – abuse, unfortunately, that is commonplace. Have you noticed how politicians always seem to be able to produce statistics to 'prove' that they are right and that their opponents are wrong? And it's not just politicians. Newspapers frequently present statistics in the most 'newsworthy' way; companies try to show their performance in the most flattering way; pressure groups fighting for a cause (such as the protection of the environment) again present statistics in the way that best supports their case.

It is not difficult to present data in such a way as to give a grossly distorted picture of reality. Let us have a look at some of the most common examples.

Selective use of data
This is where people choose to look at only those statistics that support their case and ignore those that do not. For example, assume that unemployment has risen but inflation has fallen. The government will highlight the inflation statistics to show how successful its policies have been. The opposition parties will do the opposite: they will concentrate on the unemployment statistics to demonstrate the failure of government policy.

Graphical presentation of data
Two graphs may present exactly the same data and yet convey a quite different impression about them. Figure 1.14 shows how the amount that people buy of a

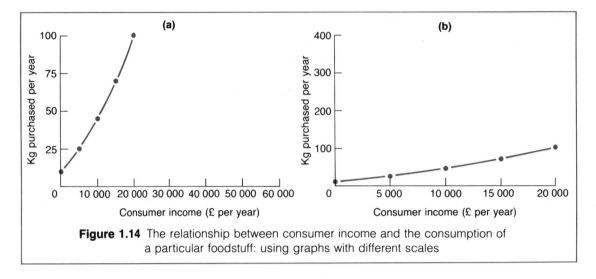

Figure 1.14 The relationship between consumer income and the consumption of a particular foodstuff: using graphs with different scales

particular foodstuff varies with their income. It is based on the information in Table 1.5.

Diagram (a) shows *exactly the same* information as diagram (b), and yet at a glance it would seem from diagram (a) that people buy a lot more as their incomes rise, whereas from diagram (b) it would seem that people only buy a little more.

Clearly the choice of *scales* for the two axes will determine the shape of the graph.

? 1. If Figure 1.11 were redrawn with the scale for unemployment running from 0 to 50 per cent, but with the original scale for the current account balance of payments, why might it seem at a glance that the government's macroeconomic policies had been less successful?
2. What are the advantages and disadvantages of presenting data graphically with the axes starting from zero?

Use of absolute or proportionate values
'People are paying more taxes now than they did when the government came to office,' claims the opposition.

'Since coming into office we have cut taxes substantially,' claims the government.

So who is right? Do we pay more or less taxes? Quite probably they are both right. If incomes have risen, we probably do pay more taxes in total. After all, the more we earn, the greater the sum of money we will be paying in income tax; and the more we spend, the more we will be paying out in VAT. Thus in *absolute* terms we probably are paying more in taxes.

On the other hand, if the government has cut the rates of tax, we may be paying a smaller *proportion* of our income. In other words, a smaller proportion of a larger total can still represent an absolute increase.

Ignoring questions of distribution
'The average person has become better off under this government,' claims a minister.

'Poverty has increased steeply under this government,' claims the opposition.

Table 1.5 Annual purchases per person of a particular foodstuff

Consumer income (£ per year)	0	5000	10 000	15 000	20 000
Foodstuff purchased per person (kg per year)	10	25	45	70	100

'More than half the population are worse off now than when the government came to office'.

Surely, this time one of the claims must be wrong? But again, both could be right. The term 'average' normally refers to the mean. The mean income is simply the total national income divided by the number in the population: i.e. income *per head*. If this is what is meant by the average, then the government may well be correct. Income per head may have risen.

If, however, a relatively few people have got a lot richer and the rest have got a little poorer, the median income will have fallen. The median income is the income of the *middle* person. For example if the population were 50 million, the median income would be the income of the twenty-five millionth richest person. This person's income may have fallen.

> **Mean (or arithmetic mean)**
> The sum of the values of each of the members of the sample divided by the total number in the sample.

> **Median**
> The value of the middle member of the sample.

Real or nominal values

'Incomes have risen by 10 per cent this last year,' claims the government.

'The standard of living has fallen,' claims the opposition.

One of the most common abuses of statistics is deliberately switching between real and nominal figures, depending on what message you want to give your audience. Nominal figures are the simple monetary values at the prices ruling at the time. For example, if you earned a wage of £100 per week last year and are earning £110 per week this year, then in nominal terms your wage has risen by 10 per cent.

But what if prices have risen by 8 per cent? Your 10 per cent increase in wages will only buy you 2 per cent more goods. Your real wages have only risen by 2 per cent. In other words, to show how much better or worse off a person or nation is, the nominal figure must be corrected for inflation. Thus:

> **Nominal values**
> Money values measured at *current* prices.

> **Real values**
> Money values corrected for inflation.

Real growth = Nominal growth − Inflation

> **?** 1. If a bank paid its depositors 12 per cent interest and inflation was 14 per cent, what would be the *real* rate of interest?
> 2. Has your real income gone up or down this last year?

The time chosen for comparison

'Between 1982 and 1990, Britain's real growth rate averaged 3.5 per cent per year,' boasts the government.

'Between 1980 and 1990, Britain could only manage a real growth rate of just over 2 per cent per year,' chides the opposition.

Again both are correct, but they have chosen either to include or to ignore the period from 1980 to 1982 when the real growth rate was negative.

Taking account of population

In 1987 Switzerland had a national income of $140 billion, whereas Brazil had a national income of $286 billion. But these figures in themselves convey nothing about living standards in the two countries. Brazil has a population over twenty times bigger than that of Switzerland. To compare living standards, therefore, the figures have to be expressed *per head* (per capita). Switzerland's per-capita national income in 1987 was $21 330, whereas Brazil's was only $2020.

Between 1980 and 1987 the annual growth rate for the Ivory Coast was 1.2 per cent and yet its population grew by 4.2 per cent. Income per head actually declined, therefore, by a massive 3 per cent. It was the same for several Third World countries in the 1980s, especially in Africa: population growth outstripped the growth in output.

International comparisons of economic performance over time must take into account population *growth*.

Index numbers

Index number

The value of a variable expressed as 100 plus or minus its percentage deviation from a base year.

Time-series data are often expressed in terms of index numbers. Consider the data in Table 1.6. It shows index numbers of manufacturing output in the UK from 1977 to 1989.

Table 1.6 UK manufacturing output: 1985 = 100

1977	1978	1979	1980	1981	1982	1983	1984	1985	1986	1987	1988	1989
105.5	106.1	106.0	96.8	91.0	91.2	93.7	97.6	100.0	100.9	106.6	114.2	119.7

Source: *Economic Trends* (CSO).

Base year (for index numbers)

The year whose index number is set at 100.

One year is selected as the base year. and this is given the value of 100. In our example this is 1985. The output for other years is then shown by their percentage variation from 100. For 1981 the index number is 91. This means that manufacturing output was 9 per cent lower in 1981 than in 1985. The index number for 1987 is 106.6. This means that manufacturing output was 6.6 per cent higher in 1987 than in 1985.

 Does this mean that the value of manufacturing output in 1987 was 6.6 per cent higher in money terms?

The use of index numbers allows us to see clearly any upward and downward movements and to make an easy comparison of one year with another. For example, Table 1.6 shows quite clearly that output fell from 1978 to 1981 and did not regain its 1978 level until 1987.

Index numbers are very useful for comparing two or more time series of data. For example, suppose we want to compare the growth of manufacturing output with that of the service industries. To do this we simply express both sets of figures as index numbers with the same base year. This is illustrated in Table 1.7.

The figures show a quite different pattern for the two sectors. The growth of the service industries was much more steady. In only one year (1980) did output fall, and that by less than 0.5 per cent.

Table 1.7 UK manufacturing and service industry output: 1985 = 100

	1977	1978	1979	1980	1981	1982	1983	1984	1985	1986	1987	1988	1989
Output of manufacturing	105.5	106.1	106.0	96.8	91.0	91.2	93.7	97.6	100.0	100.9	106.6	114.2	119.7
Output of Services	84.4	87.1	89.6	89.2	89.5	90.8	93.7	97.1	100.0	103.7	109.4	114.7	118.4

Source: *Economic Trends* (CSO).

Using index numbers to measure percentage changes

To find the annual percentage growth rate in any one year we simply look at the percentage change in the index from the previous year. To work this out we use the following formula:

$$\left(\frac{I_t - I_{t-1}}{I_{t-1}}\right) \times 100$$

where I_t is the index in the year in question and I_{t-1} is the index in the previous year.

Thus to find the growth rate in manufacturing output from 1987 to 1988 we first see how much the index has risen ($I_t - I_{t-1}$). The answer is $114.2 - 106.6 = 7.6$. But this does *not* mean that the growth rate is 7.6 per cent. According to our formula, the growth rate is equal to:

$$\frac{114.2 - 106.6}{106.6} \times 100$$

$$= 7.6/106.6 \times 100$$

$$= 7.13\%$$

 What was the growth rate in manufacturing output from 1982 to 1983?

The price index

Perhaps the best known of all price indices is the retail price index (RPI). It is an index of the prices of goods and services purchased by the average household. Movements in this index, therefore, show how the cost of living has changed. Annual percentage increases in the RPI are the commonest definition of the rate of inflation. Thus if the RPI went up from 100 to 110 over a twelve month period, we would say that the rate of inflation was 10 per cent.

> **Retail price index (RPI)**
> An index of the prices of goods bought by a typical household.

 If the RPI went up from 150 to 162 over twelve months, what would be the rate of inflation?

The use of weighted averages

The RPI is a weighted average of the prices of many items. The index of manufacturing output that we looked at above was also a weighted average, an average of the output of many individual products.

To illustrate how a weighted average works consider the case of a weighted average of the output of just three industries, A, B and C. Let us assume that in the base year (year 1) the output of A was £7 million, of B £2 million and of C £1 million, giving a total output of the three industries of £10 million. We now attach weights to the output of each industry to reflect its proportion of total output. Industry A is given a weight of 0.7 because it produces seven-tenths of total output. Industry B is given a weight of 0.2 and industry C a weight of 0.1. We then simply multiply each industry's index by its weight and then add up all these figures to give the overall industry index.

> **Weighted average**
> The average of several items where each item is ascribed a weight according to its importance. The weights must add up to 1.

The index for each industry in year 1 (the base year) is 100. This means that the weighted average index is also 100. Table 1.8 shows what happens to output in year 2. Industry A's output falls by 10 per cent, giving it an index of 90 in year 2. Industry B's output rises by 10 per cent and industry C's output rises by 30 per cent giving indices of 110 and 130, respectively. But as you can see from the table, despite the fact that two of the three industries have had a rise in output, the total industry index has *fallen* from 100 to 98. The reason is that industry A is so much larger than the other two that its decline in output outweighs their increase.

The retail prices index is a little more complicated. The reason is that it is calculated in two stages. First, products are grouped into categories such as food,

Table 1.8 Constructing a weighted average index

Industry	Weight	Year 1		Year 2	
		Index	Index times weight	Index	Index times weight
A	0.7	100	70	90	63
B	0.2	100	20	110	22
C	0.1	100	10	130	13
Total	1.0		100		98

clothing and services. A weighted average index is worked out for each group. Thus the index for food would be the weighted average of the indices for bread, potatoes, cooking oil, etc. Secondly, a weight is attached to each of the groups in order to work out an overall index.

Functional relationships

Throughout economics we will be examining how one economic variable affects another: how the purchases of cars are affected by their price; how consumer expenditure is affected by taxes, or by incomes; how the cost of producing washing machines is affected by the price of steel; how the rate of unemployment is affected by the level of government expenditure. These relationships are called functional relationships. We will need to express these relationships in a precise way. This can be done in the form of a table or a graph or an equation.

Functional relationships

The mathematical relationships showing how one variable is affected by one or more others.

Simple linear functions

These are relationships which when plotted on a graph produce a straight line. Let us take an imaginary example of the relationship between total savings in the economy (S) and the level of national income (Y). This functional relationship can be written as:

$$S = f(Y)$$

This is simply shorthand for saying that savings are a function of (i.e. depend on) the level of national income.

If we want to know just *how much* will be saved at any given level of income, we will need to spell out this functional relationship. Let us do this in each of the three ways.

As a table. Table 1.9 gives a selection of values of Y and the corresponding level of S. It is easy to read off from the table the level of savings at one of the levels of national income listed. It is clearly more difficult to work out the level of savings if national income were £23.4 billion or £47.4 billion.

Table 1.9 A savings function

National income (£bn per year	Total savings (£bn per year)
0	0
10	2
20	4
30	6
40	8
50	10

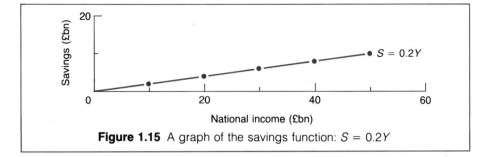

Figure 1.15 A graph of the savings function: $S = 0.2Y$

As a graph. Figure 1.15 plots the data from Table 1.9. Each of the dots corresponds to one of the points in the table. By joining the dots up into a single line we can easily read off the value for savings at some level of income other than those listed in the table. A graph also has the advantage of allowing us to see the relationship at a glance.

It is usual to plot the *independent variable* (i.e. the one that does not depend on the other) on the horizontal or *x*-axis, and the *dependent variable* on the vertical or *y*-axis. In our example, savings *depend* on national income. Thus savings are the dependent variable and national income is the independent variable.

As an equation. The data in the table can be expressed in the equation:

$$S = 0.2Y$$

This has the major advantage of being precise. We could work out *exactly* how much would be saved at any given level of national income.

This particular function starts at the origin of the graph (i.e. the bottom left-hand corner). This means that when the value of the independent variable is zero, so too is the value of the dependent variable. Frequently, however, this is not the case in functional relationships. For example, when people have a zero income, they will still have to live, and thus will draw from their past savings: they will have *negative* savings.

When a graph does not pass through the origin its equation will have the form:

$$y = a + bx$$

where this time *y* stands for the dependent variable (not 'income') and *x* for the independent variable, and *a* and *b* will have numbers assigned in an actual equation. For example, the equation might be:

$$y = 4 + 2x$$

This would give Table 1.10 and Figure 1.16.

Table 1.10 $y = 4 + 2x$

x	y
0	4
1	6
2	8
3	10
4	12
5	14
.	.
.	.

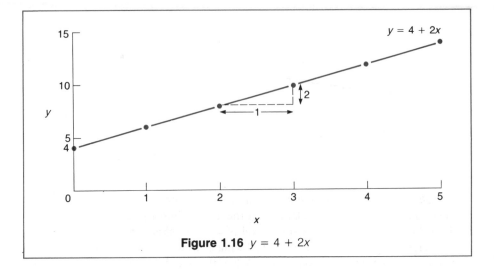

Figure 1.16 $y = 4 + 2x$

Notice two things about the relationship between the equation and the graph:

- The point where the line crosses the vertical axis (at a value of 4) is given by the constant (*a*) term. If the *a* term is negative, the line will cross the vertical axis *below* the horizontal axis.
- The slope of the line is given by the *b* term. The slope is 2/1: for every 1 unit increase in *x* there is a 2 unit increase in *y*.

? On a diagram like Figure 1.16 draw the graphs for the following equations:

$$y = -3 + 4x; y = 15 - 3x$$

Note that in the second equation of the question the *x* term is negative. This means that *y* and *x* are *inversely related*. As *x* increases, *y* decreases.

Non-linear functions

These are functions where the equation involves a squared term (or other power terms). Such functions will give a curved line when plotted on a graph. As an example, consider the following equation:

$$y = 4 + 10x - x^2$$

Table 1.11 and Figure 1.17 are based on it.

As you can see, *y* rises at a decelerating rate and eventually begins to fall. This is

Table 1.11 $y = 4 + 10x - x^2$

x	y
0	4
1	13
2	20
3	25
4	28
5	29
6	28
.	.
.	.
.	.

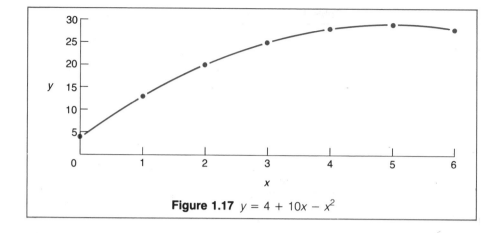

Figure 1.17 $y = 4 + 10x - x^2$

because the negative x^2 term is becoming more and more influential as x rises and eventually begins to outweigh the $10x$ term.

 What shaped graph would you get from the equations:

$y = -6 + 3x + 2x^2; y = 10 - 4x + x^2$

(If you cannot work out the answer, construct a table like Table 1.11 and then plot the figures on a graph.)

✳ Elementary differentiation

In several starred boxes we will be using some elementary calculus. The part of calculus we will be using is called differentiation. This is a technique to enable us to calculate the rate of change of a variable. The purpose of this section is not to explain why differentiation involves the procedures it does, but simply to state the rules that are necessary for our purposes. You will need to consult a maths book if you want to know how these rules are derived.

First, let us see when we would be interested in looking at the rate of change of a variable. Take the case of a firm thinking of expanding. It will want to know how much its costs will increase as its output increases. It will want to know the rate of change of costs with respect to changes in output.

Let us assume that it faces a cost function of the form:

$$C = 20 + 5Q + Q^2 \tag{1}$$

where C is the total cost of production and Q is the quantity produced. Table 1.12 and Figure 1.18 are derived from this equation.

The rate of increase in its costs with respect to increases in output is given by the *slope* of the cost curve in Figure 1.18. The steeper the slope, the more rapidly costs increase. At point a the slope of the curve is 11. This is found by drawing the tangent to the curve and measuring the slope of the tangent. At this point on the curve, what we are saying is that for each one unit increase in output there is an £11 increase in costs. (Obviously as the graph is curved, this rate of increase will vary at different outputs.)

This rate of increase in costs is known as the marginal cost. It is the same with other variables that increase with quantity: their rate of increase is known as *marginal*. For example, *marginal revenue* is the rate of increase of sales revenue with respect to output.

Differentiation

A mathematical technique to find the rate of change of one variable with respect to another.

Marginal cost

The rate of increase in costs with respect to output.

Table 1.12 $C = 20 + 5Q + Q^2$

Q	C
0	20
1	26
2	34
3	.44
4	56
5	70
6	86
7	104
.	.
.	.
.	.

We can use the technique of differentiation to derive a marginal from a total equation: in other words, to derive the slope of the total curve. Let us assume that we have an equation:

$$y = 10 + 6x - 4x^2 + 2x^3 \tag{2}$$

When we differentiate it we call the new equation dy/dx: this stands for the rate of increase in y (dy) with respect to the increase in x (dx).

The rules for differentiating a simple equation like equation (2) are very straightforward.

1. You delete the constant term (10). The reason for this is that, being constant, by definition it will not cause an increase in y as x increases, and it is the *increase* in y that we are trying to discover.
2. You delete the x from the x term which has no power attached, and just leave the number. Thus the term $6x$ becomes simply 6.
3. For any term with a power in it (a square, a cube, etc.), its value should be *multiplied* by the power term and the power term reduced by one. Thus in the term $4x^2$, the 4 would be multiplied by 2 (the power term), and the power term would be reduced from 2 to 1 (but x to the power of 1 is simply x). After differentiation, therefore, the term becomes $8x$. In the term $2x^3$, the 2 would be multiplied by 3

Figure 1.18 A total cost function: $C = 20 + 5Q + Q^2$

(the power term), and the power term would be reduced from 3 to 2. After differentiation, therefore, the term becomes $6x^2$.

Applying these three rules to the equation:

$$y = 10 + 6x - 4x^2 + 2x^3 \tag{2}$$

gives

$$dy/dx = 6 - 8x + 6x^2 \tag{3}$$

To find the rate of change of y with respect to x at any given value of x, therefore, you simply substitute that value of x into equation (3).

Thus when $x = 4$, $dy/dx = 6 - (8 \times 4) + (6 \times 16) = 70$. In other words, when $x = 4$, for every 1 unit increase in x, y will increase by 70.

Returning to our cost function in equation (1), what is the marginal cost equation? Applying the three rules to the equation:

$$C = 20 + 5Q + Q^2 \tag{1}$$

gives:

$$dC/dQ = 5 + 2Q \tag{4}$$

Thus at an output of 3, the marginal cost (dC/dQ) is $5 + (2 \times 3) = 11$, which is the slope of the tangent to point a.

? What would be the marginal cost equation if the total cost equation were:

$$C = 15 + 20Q - 5Q^2 + Q^3$$

What would be the marginal cost at an output of 8?

Finding the maximum or minimum point of a curve

The other important use we can make of calculus is to find the maximum or minimum point of a curve. This has a number of important applications. For example, a firm may want to know the minimum point on its average cost curve (a curve which shows how costs per unit of output vary as output increases). Also it is likely to want to know the output at which it will earn maximum profit. Let us examine this particular case.

Assume that the equation for total profit (Π) is:

$$\Pi = -20 + 12Q - Q^2 \tag{5}$$

This gives profit at various outputs as shown in Table 1.13. The corresponding graph is plotted in Figure 1.19.

Table 1.13 $\Pi = -20 + 12Q - Q^2$

Q	Π
0	−20
1	−9
2	0
3	7
4	12
5	15
6	16
7	15
8	12
9	7
10	0

Figure 1.19 A total profit function: $\Pi = -20 + 12Q - Q^2$

 What is the meaning of a *negative* profit?

It can be seen at a glance that profits are maximized at an output of 6 units. But we could have worked this out directly from the profit equation without having to draw up a table or graph. How is this done?

Remember that when we differentiate a curve, the equation we get (known as 'the first derivative') gives us the slope of the curve. You can see that at the point of maximum profit (the top of the curve) its slope is zero: the tangent is horizontal. So all we have to do to find the top of the curve is to differentiate its equation and set it equal to zero.

Given that:

$$\Pi = -20 + 12Q - Q^2 \tag{5}$$

then:

$$d\Pi/dQ = 12 - 2Q \tag{6}$$

Setting this equal to zero gives:

$$12 - 2Q = 0$$

$$\therefore 2Q = 12$$

$$\therefore Q = 6$$

Thus profits are maximized at an output of 6 units: the result we obtained from the table and graph.

The second derivative test

There is a problem with this technique, however. How can we tell from equation (6) that we have found the *maximum* rather than the *minimum*? The problem is that *both* the maximum *and* the minimum point of a curve have a zero slope.

The answer is to conduct a second derivative test. This involves differentiating the equation a second time. This gives the rate of change of the *slope* of the original curve. If you look at Figure 1.19, as output increases, the tangent moves from being upward sloping, to horizontal, to downward sloping. In other words, the slope is getting less and less. Its rate of change is *negative*. Thus if we differentiate the equation for the slope (i.e. the first derivative), we should get a negative figure.

Second derivative test

If on differentiating an equation a second time the answer is negative (positive), the point is a maximum (minimum).

When we differentiate a second time we get what is called the second derivative. It is written d^2y/dx^2.

Second derivative

The rate of change of the first derivative, found by differentiating the first derivative.

If we differentiate equation (6):

$$d\Pi/dQ = 12 - 2Q \qquad (6)$$

we get:

$$d^2\Pi/dQ^2 = -2 \qquad (7)$$

(Note that the rules for differentiating a second time are the same as for the first time.) Given that the second derivative in this case is negative, we have demonstrated that we have indeed found the maximum profit point (at $Q = 6$), and not the minimum.

 Given the following equation for a firm's average cost (AC) – i.e. the cost per unit of output (Q):

$$AC = 60 - 16Q + 2Q^2$$

(a) At what output is AC at a minimum?
(b) Use the second derivative test to prove that this is a minimum and not a maximum.

 # SUMMARY

1. Diagrams in economics can be used as pictures: to sketch a relationship so that its essentials can be perceived at a glance.
2. Tables, graphs and charts are also used to portray real-life data. These can be time-series data or cross-section data or both.
3. In order to get a true picture from economic data it is important to be aware of various ways that statistics can be abused: these include a selective use of data, a choice of axes on a graph to make trends seem more or less exaggerated or to make a curve more or less steep, confusing absolute and relative values, ignoring questions of distribution, confusing nominal and real values, selecting the time period to make the statistics look the most favourable or unfavourable, and ignoring the size or change in size of the population.
4. Presenting time-series data as index numbers gives a clear impression of trends and is a good way of comparing how two or more series (perhaps originally measured in different units) have changed over the same time period. A base year is chosen and the index for that year is set at 100. The percentage change in the value of a variable is given by the percentage change in the index. The formula is:

$$\left(\frac{I_t - I_{t-1}}{I_{t-1}}\right) \times 100$$

Several items can be included in one index by using a weighted value for each of the items. The weights must add up to 1, and each weight will reflect the relative importance of that particular item in the index.
5. Functional relationships can be expressed as an equation, a table or a graph. In the linear (straight-line) equation $y = a + bx$, the a term gives the vertical intercept (the point where the graph crosses the vertical axis) and the b term gives the slope. When there is a power term (e.g. $y = a + bx + cx^2$), the graph will be a curve.
* 6. Differentiation can be used to obtain the rate of change of one variable with respect to another. The rules of differentiation require that in an equation of the form:

$$y = a + bx + cx^2 + dx^3$$

the a term disappears, the bx term simply becomes b, the cx^2 term becomes $2cx$, the dx^3 becomes $3dx^2$ and so on, with each extra term being multiplied by its power term and its power term being reduced by 1.
* 7. To find the value of the x term at which the y term is at a maximum or minimum, the equation should be differentiated and set equal to zero. To check which it is – maximum or minimum – the second derivative should be calculated. If it is negative, then setting the first derivative equal to zero has yielded a maximum. If the second derivative is positive, then setting the first derivative to zero has yielded a minimum value.

2 Supply and Demand

As we saw in Chapter 1, in a free-market economy prices play a key role in transmitting information from buyers to sellers and from sellers to buyers. This chapter examines the price mechanism in more detail.

We ask what determines demand; what determines supply; just what is the relationship between demand, supply and price; how does the price mechanism transmit information; how do prices act as incentives; and how responsive are demand and supply to those incentives. We also ask what happens if the government intervenes in this mechanism.

The markets we will be examining are highly competitive markets, with many firms competing against each other. In economics we call this perfect competition. This is where consumers and producers are too numerous to have any control over prices: they are price takers.

Perfect competition
(preliminary definition)

A situation where the consumers and producers of a product are price takers. (There are other features of a perfectly competitive market; these are examined in Chapter 5.)

Price taker

A person or firm with no power to be able to influence the market price.

This is, in fact, a reasonable assumption for most markets as far as consumers are concerned. When we go into shops we have no control over prices. We have to accept the price as given. For example, when you get to the supermarket checkout you cannot start haggling with the checkout operator over the price of a can of beans or a tub of margarine.

 Give some examples where individual consumers *do* have the power to influence prices.

In the case of firms, however, the assumption that they are price takers is incorrect in many markets. In the case of manufacturing, for example, most firms set their own prices. ICI decides on the prices at which it will sell its Dulux paints to its distributors. Ford decides the prices it will charge for Escorts. This does not mean that firms can simply charge whatever they like. They will have to take account of overall consumer demand and their competitors' prices. Dulux will have to remain competitive with Crown and Berger. Escorts will have to remain competitive with Maestros and Astras. Nevertheless most firms do have some flexibility in choosing their prices.

In a perfectly competitive market, however, individual producers have *no* influence over prices. They are too small and face too much competition from other firms to be able to raise prices. Take the case of farmers selling wheat. They have to accept the price as dictated by the market. If individually they try to sell above the market price, no one will buy. They are thus price takers.

You may well ask, 'But if such highly competitive markets are the exception, why study them?'

One answer is that the analysis of perfectly competitive markets does give useful insights into real-world markets. Many markets do *approximate* to the markets we shall be describing.

Another answer concerns the normative issue of whether a free market economy is desirable. Many on the political right argue that social benefits flow from free enterprise, from the unencumbered operation of the price mechanism. These arguments are often presented in the context of a highly competitive market environment. Although economists cannot pronounce on what the goals of society ought to be, they can at least examine whether the predicted effects of a market economy are what is claimed. This involves examining what the effects of perfect competition are. It also involves examining just how far real-world markets diverge from the perfectly competitive model. Will the existence of big business, of markets dominated by multinational corporations, substantially affect the predictions about the operation of markets? For example, will British Telecom respond to an increase in demand for telephone services in the same way as Farmer Giles does to a rise in demand for cauliflowers?

Markets with powerful firms are examined in Chapters 6 and 7. For now we concentrate on price takers.

2.1 Demand

The relationship between demand and price

The headlines announce, 'Major crop failures in Brazil and East Africa: coffee prices soar.' Shortly afterwards you find that coffee prices have doubled in the shops. What do you do? Presumably you will cut back on the amount of coffee you drink. Perhaps you will reduce it from, say, six cups per day to two. Perhaps you will give up drinking coffee altogether.

This is simply an illustration of the general relationship between price and consumption: *when the price of a good rises the quantity demanded will fall*. This relationship is known as the law of demand. There are two reasons for this law:

- People will feel poorer. They will not be able to afford to buy so much of the good with their money. The purchasing power of their income (their *real income*) has fallen. This is called the income effect of a price rise.
- The good will now be dearer relative to other goods. People will thus switch to alternative or 'substitute' goods. This is called the substitution effect of a price rise.

Similarly, when the price of a good falls, the quantity demanded will rise. People can afford to buy more (the income effect), and they will switch away from consuming alternative goods (the substitution effect).

Therefore, returning to our example of the increase in the price of coffee, we will not be able to afford to buy as much as before, and we will probably drink more tea, cocoa, fruit juices or even water instead.

The amount by which the quantity demanded falls will depend on the size of the income and substitution effects.

The size of the income effect depends primarily on the proportion of income spent on the good. Thus the more coffee we buy in the first place, the more likely we will be forced to cut down on the amount we buy if the price goes up. In other words, the bigger the proportion of income spent on the good, the bigger will be the effect of a

The law of demand

The quantity of a good demanded per period of time will fall as price rises and will rise as price falls, other things being equal (*ceteris paribus*).

Income effect

The effect of a change in price on quantity demanded arising from the consumer becoming better or worse off as a result of the price change.

Substitution effect

The effect of a change in price on quantity demanded arising from the consumer switching to or from alternative (substitute) products.

price rise on people's real income, and the more they will reduce the quantity they demand.

The size of the substitution effect depends primarily on the number and closeness of substitute goods. Thus if you are quite happy to drink tea instead of coffee, a rise in the price of coffee will cause you to cut your consumption of coffee considerably, and correspondingly to increase your consumption of tea.

Quantity demanded

The amount of a good that a consumer is willing and able to buy at a given price over a given period of time.

A word of warning: be careful about the meaning of the words quantity demanded. They refer to the amount that consumers are willing and able to purchase at a given price over a given time period (e.g. a week, or a month, or a year). They do *not* refer to what people would simply *like* to consume. You might like to own a Rolls-Royce, but your demand for Rolls-Royces will almost certainly be zero.

The demand curve

Consider the hypothetical data in Table 2.1, which shows how many kilograms of potatoes per month would be purchased at various prices.

Demand schedule for an individual

A table showing the different quantities of a good that a person is willing and able to buy at various prices over a given period of time.

Columns (2) and (3) show the demand schedules for two individuals, Tracey and Darren. Column 4, by contrast, shows the total market demand schedule. This is the total demand by all consumers. To obtain the market demand schedule for potatoes, we simply add up the quantities demanded at each price by *all* consumers: i.e. Tracey, Darren and anyone else who demands potatoes. Notice that we are talking about demand *over a period of time* (not at a *point* in time). Thus we would talk about daily demand or weekly demand or annual demand or whatever.

Market demand schedule

A table showing the different total quantities of a good that consumers are willing and able to buy at various prices over a given period of time.

 Assume that there are 200 consumers in the market. Of these, 100 have schedules like Tracey's and 100 have schedules like Darren's. What would be the total market demand schedule for potatoes now?

Demand curve

A graph showing the relationship between the price of a good and the quantity of the good demanded over a given time period. Price is measured on the vertical axis; quantity demanded is measured on the horizontal axis. A demand curve can be for an individual consumer or group of consumers, or more usually for the whole market.

The demand schedule can be represented graphically as a demand curve. Figure 2.1 shows the market demand curve for potatoes corresponding to the schedule in Table 2.1. The price of potatoes is plotted on the vertical axis. The quantity demanded is plotted on the horizontal axis.

Point *E* shows that at a price of 20p per kilo, 100 000 tonnes of potatoes are demanded each month. When the price falls to 16p we move down the curve to point *D*. This shows that the quantity demanded has now risen to 200 000 tonnes per month. Similarly, if price falls to 12p we move down the curve again to point *C*: 350 000 tonnes are now demanded. The five points on the graph (*A–E*) correspond to the figures in columns (1) and (4) of Table 2.1. The graph also enables us to read off the likely quantities demanded at prices other than those in the table.

 1. How much would be demanded at a price of 6p per kilogram?
2. Assuming that demand does not change from month to month, plot the *annual* market demand for potatoes.

Table 2.1 The demand for potatoes (monthly)

	Price (pence per kg) (1)	Tracey's demand (kg) (2)	Darren's demand (kg) (3)	Total market demand (tonnes: 000s) (4)
A	4	28	16	700
B	8	15	11	500
C	12	5	9	350
D	16	1	7	200
E	20	0	6	100

Figure 2.1 Market demand curve for potatoes (monthly)

A demand curve could also be drawn for an individual consumer. Like market demand curves, individuals' demand curves generally slope downward from left to right: they have negative slope.

? 1. Draw Tracey's and Darren's demand curves for potatoes on one diagram. Note that you will use the same vertical scale as in Figure 2.1, but you will need a quite different horizontal scale.
2. At what price is their demand the same?
3. What explanations could there be for the quite different shapes of their two demand curves? (This question is explored in Section 2.4 below.)

Two points should be noted at this stage:

● In textbooks demand curves (and other curves too) are only occasionally used to plot specific data. More frequently they are used to illustrate general theoretical arguments. In such cases the axes will simply be price and quantity, with the units unspecified.
● The term 'curve' is used even when the graph is a straight line! In fact when using demand curves to illustrate arguments we frequently draw them as straight lines.

Other determinants of demand

Price is not the only factor that determines how much of a good people will buy. Demand is also affected by the following.

Tastes. The more desirable people find the good, the more they will demand. Tastes are affected by advertising, by fashion, by observing other consumers, by considerations of health and by the experiences from consuming the good on previous occasions.

The number and price of substitute goods (i.e. competitive goods). The higher the price of substitute goods, the higher will be the demand for this good as people switch from the substitutes. For example, the demand for coffee will depend on the price of tea. If tea goes up in price, the demand for coffee will rise.

The number and price of complementary goods. Complementary goods are those that are consumed together: cars and petrol, shoes and polish, chicken and stuffing,

Substitute goods

A pair of goods which are considered by consumers to be alternatives to each other. As the price of one goes up the demand for the other rises.

Complementary goods

A pair of goods consumed together. As the price of one goes up the demand for both goods will fall.

cigarettes and matches. The higher the price of complementary goods, the fewer of them will be bought and hence the less will be the demand for this good. For example, the demand for matches will depend on the price of cigarettes. If the price of cigarettes goes up, so that fewer are bought, the demand for matches will fall.

Income. As people's incomes rise, their demand for most goods will rise. Such goods are called normal goods. There are exceptions to this general rule, however. As people get richer, they spend less on inferior goods, such as cheap margarine, and switch to better quality goods.

Distribution of income. If, for example, national income were redistributed from the poor to the rich, the demand for luxury goods would rise. At the same time, as the poor got poorer they might have to turn to buying inferior goods, whose demand would thus rise too.

Expectations of future price changes. If people think that prices are going to rise in the future, they are likely to buy more now before the price does go up.

Normal good

A good whose demand rises as people's incomes rise.

Inferior good

A good whose demand falls as people's incomes rise.

 Do all these six determinants of demand affect both an individual's demand and the market demand for a product?

To illustrate these six determinants let us look at the demand for butter:

- Tastes: if it is heavily advertised, demand is likely to rise. If, on the other hand, there is a cholesterol scare, people may demand less for health reasons.
- Substitutes: if the price of margarine goes up, the demand for butter is likely to rise as people switch from one to the other.
- Complements: if the price of bread goes up, people will buy less bread and hence less butter to spread on it.
- Income: if people's income rises, they may well turn to consuming butter rather than margarine.
- Income distribution: if income is redistributed away from the poor, they may have to give up consuming butter and buy cheaper margarine instead, or simply buy less butter and be more economical with the amount they use.
- Expectations: if it is announced in the news that butter prices are expected to rise in the near future, people are likely to buy more now and stock up their freezers while current prices last.

Movements along and shifts in the demand curve

A demand curve is constructed on the assumption that 'other things remain equal' (*ceteris paribus*). In other words, it is assumed that none of the determinants of demand, other than price, changes. The effect of a change in price is then simply illustrated by a movement along the demand curve: for example, from point B to point D in Figure 2.1 when price rises from 8p to 16p per kilo.

What happens, then, when one of these other determinants does change? The answer is that we have to construct a whole new demand curve: the curve shifts. If a change in one of the other determinants causes demand to rise – say income rises – the whole curve will shift to the right. This shows that at each price more will be demanded than before. Thus in Figure 2.2 at a price of P, a quantity of Q_0 was originally demanded. But now, after the increase in demand, Q_1 is demanded. (Note that D_1 is not necessarily parallel to D_0.)

Figure 2.2 An increase in demand

If a change in a determinant other than price causes demand to fall, the whole curve will shift to the left.

To distinguish between shifts in and movements along demand curves, it is usual to distinguish between a change in *demand* and a change in the *quantity demanded*. A shift in demand is referred to as a change in demand, whereas a movement along the demand curve as a result of a change in price is referred to as a change in the quantity demanded.

> | ? |
> |---|
>
> 1. Assume that in Table 2.1 the total market demand for potatoes increases by 20 per cent at each price – due, say, to substantial increases in the prices of bread and rice. Plot the old and the new demand curves for potatoes. Is the new curve parallel to the old one?
> 2. The price of pork rises and yet it is observed that the sales of pork increase. Does this mean that the demand curve for pork is upward sloping? Explain.

Change in demand

The term used for a shift in the demand curve. It occurs when a determinant of demand *other* than price changes.

Change in the quantity demanded

The term used for a movement along the demand curve to a new point. It occurs when there is a change in price.

* Demand equations

We can represent the relationship between the market demand for a good and the determinants of demand in the form of an equation. This is called a demand function. It can be expressed either in general terms or with specific values attached to the determinants.

Demand function

An equation which shows the mathematical relationship between the quantity demanded of a good and the values of the various determinants of demand.

General form

$$Q_d = f(P_g, T, P_{s_1}, P_{s_2} \ldots P_{s_n}, P_{c_1}, P_{c_2} \ldots P_{c_m}, Y, B, P^e_{g_{t+1}}) \tag{1}$$

This is merely saying in symbols that the quantity demanded (Q_d) 'is a function of' – i.e. depends on – the price of the good itself (P_g), tastes (T), the price of substitute goods ($P_{s_1}, P_{s_2}, \ldots P_{s_n}$), the price of complementary goods ($P_{c_1}, P_{c_2} \ldots P_{c_m}$), total consumer incomes (Y), the distribution of income (B), and the expected price of the good (P_g^e) at some future time ($t + 1$). Equation (1) is thus just a form of shorthand. Expressed in this general form there are no numerical values attached to each of the determinants.

Estimated demand equations

Surveys can be conducted to show how demand depends on each one of a number of determinants, while the rest are held constant. Using statistical techniques called regression analysis a demand equation can be estimated.

Regression analysis

A statistical technique which allows a functional relationship between two or more variables to be estimated.

For example, assume that it was observed that the demand for butter (measured in 250g units) depended on its price (P_b), the price of margarine (P_m) and total annual consumer incomes (Y). The estimated weekly demand equation may then be something like:

$$Q_d = 2\,000\,000 - 50\,000P_b + 20\,000P_m + 0.01Y \qquad (2)$$

Thus if the price of butter were 50p, the price of margarine were 35p and consumer incomes were £200 million, and if P_b and P_m were measured in pence and Y was measured in pounds, then the demand for butter would be 2 200 000 units. This is calculated as follows:

$$Q_d = 2\,000\,000 - (50\,000 \times 50) + (20\,000 \times 35) + (0.01 \times 200\,000\,000)$$

$$= 2\,000\,000 - 2\,500\,000 + 700\,000 + 2\,000\,000$$

$$= 2\,200\,000$$

Simple demand functions

Demand equations are often used to relate quantity demanded to just one determinant. Thus an equation relating quantity demanded to price could be in the form:

$$Q_d = a - bP \qquad (3)$$

For example, the actual equation might be:

$$Q_d = 10\,000 - 200P \qquad (4)$$

From this can be calculated a complete demand schedule or demand curve, as Table 2.2 and Figure 2.3 show. As price (P) changes, the equation tells us how much the quantity demanded (Q_d) changes.

1. Complete the demand schedule in Table 2.2 up to a price of 50.
2. What is it about equation (4) that makes the demand curve (a) downward sloping; (b) a straight line?

This equation is based on a *ceteris paribus* assumption: it is assumed that all the other determinants of demand remain constant. If one of these other determinants changed, the equation itself would change. There would be a shift in the curve: a change in demand. If the *a* term alone changed, there would be a parallel shift in the curve. If the *b* term changed, the slope of the curve would change.

Table 2.2 Demand schedule for equation (4)

P	Q_d
5	9000
10	8000
15	7000
20	6000
.	.
.	.
.	.

---

*Box 2.1

The Demand for Butter[1]
A real-world demand function

The following is the UK's market demand curve for butter. It has been estimated (using a computer regression package) from actual data for the years 1970–83.

$$Q_d = 4.19 - 4.79P_b + 20.5P_m - 0.0198Y$$

where: Q_d is the quantity of butter sold in ounces per person per week,

P_b is the 'real' price of butter: i.e. the price of butter in pence per lb divided by the retail price index (RPI) (1975 = 100),

P_m is the 'real' price of margarine: i.e. the price of margarine in pence per lb divided by the RPI (1975 = 100),

Y is the real personal disposable income of households: i.e. household income after tax, expressed as an index (1975 = 100).

From this economists could forecast what would happen to the demand for butter if any of three variables – the price of butter, the price of margarine or income – changed.

 From this equation, calculate what would happen to the demand for butter if:
(a) The price of butter went up by 1p per lb and the RPI was 100.
(b) The price of margarine went up by 1p per lb and the RPI was 200.
(c) The index of personal disposable incomes went up by 10 points.

There is a serious problem with estimated demand functions like these: they assume that *other* determinants of demand have not changed. In the case of this demand-for-butter function, one of the other determinants *did* change. This was tastes – from 1970 to 1983 there was a massive shift in demand from butter to margarine, perhaps for health reasons, perhaps because of the advent of 'easy-to-spread' margarines, perhaps because of an improvement in the flavour of margarines. The following table shows this shift.

	Butter consumption	Margarine consumption
	(ounces per person per week)	
1970	5.90	2.82
1983	3.27	4.08

As it was assumed that the shift in taste took place steadily over time, a new demand equation was estimated for the same years:

$$Q_d = 3.73 - 4.96P_b + 12.0P_m + 0.0124Y - 0.139TIME$$

where the *TIME* term is as follows: 1970 = 1, 1971 = 2, 1973 = 3, etc.

 1. How does this affect the relationship between the demand for butter and (a) the price of margarine and (b) personal disposable income?
2. Is butter a normal good or an inferior good?

[1] Statistics for this box are from *Household Food Consumption and Expenditure* (CSO, various years); calculations by W. Thurlow.

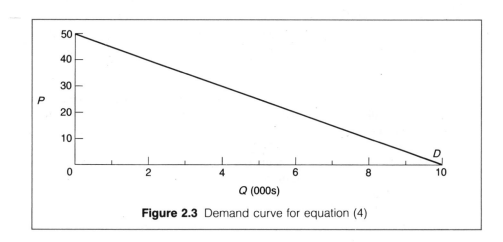

Figure 2.3 Demand curve for equation (4)

Simple equations can be used to relate demand to other determinants too. For example, an equation relating quantity demanded to income would be in the form:

$$Q_d = a + bY \tag{5}$$

1. Referring to equation (5), if the term a has a value of $-50\,000$ and the term b a value of 0.001, construct a demand schedule with respect to total income (Y). Do this for incomes between £100 million and £300 million at £50 million intervals.
2. Now use this schedule to plot a demand curve with respect to income. Comment on its shape.

Econometrics

The science of applying statistical techniques to economic data in order to identify and test economic relationships.

The branch of economics that applies statistical techniques to economic data is known as econometrics. Econometrics is beyond the scope of this book. At this stage, however, it is worth noting that, like other branches of statistics, econometrics cannot produce equations and graphs that allow totally reliable predictions to be made. The data on which the equations are based are often incomplete or unreliable, and the underlying relationships on which they are based (often ones of human behaviour) may well change over time.

▲ SUMMARY

1. When the price of a good rises, the quantity demanded per period of time will fall. This is known as the 'law of demand'. It applies both to individuals' demand and to the whole market demand.
2. The law of demand is explained by the income and substitution effects of a price change.
3. The relationship between price and quantity demanded per period of time can be shown in a table (or 'schedule') or as a graph. On the graph, price is plotted on the vertical axis and quantity demanded per period of time on the horizontal axis. The resulting demand curve is downward sloping (negatively sloped).
4. Other determinants of demand include tastes, the number and price of substitute goods, the number and price of complementary goods, income, the distribution of income and expectations of future price changes.
5. If price changes, the effect is shown by a movement along the demand curve. We call this effect 'a change in the quantity demanded'.
6. If any other determinant of demand changes, the whole curve will shift. We call this effect 'a change in demand'. A rightward shift represents an increase in demand; a leftward shift represents a decrease in demand.
*7. The relationship between the quantity demanded and the various determinants of demand (including price) can be expressed as an equation.

2.2 Supply

Supply and price

Imagine you are a farmer deciding what to do with your land. Part of your land is in a fertile valley. Part is on a hillside where the soil is poor. Perhaps, then, you will consider growing vegetables in the valley and keeping sheep on the hillside.

Your decision will depend to a large extent on the price that various vegetables will fetch in the market and likewise the price you can expect to get from sheep and wool. As far as the valley is concerned, you will plant the vegetables that give the best return. If, for example, the price of potatoes is high, you will probably use a lot of the valley for growing potatoes. If the price gets higher, you may well use the whole of the valley, being prepared maybe to run the risk of potato disease. If the price is very high indeed, you may even consider growing potatoes on the hillside, even though the yield per acre is much lower there.

In other words, the higher the price of a particular crop, the more of it you are likely to grow in preference to other crops. This illustrates the general relationship between supply and price: *when the price of a good rises the quantity supplied will also rise.* There are three reasons for this:

- As firms supply more, they are likely to find that beyond a certain level of output, costs rise more and more rapidly.

  In the case of the farm we have just considered, once potatoes have to be grown on the hillside the costs of producing them will increase. Also if the land has to be used more intensively, say by the use of more and more fertilizers, again the costs of producing extra potatoes are likely to rise quite rapidly. It is the same for manufacturers. Beyond a certain level of output, costs are likely to rise rapidly as workers have to be paid overtime and as machines approach capacity working. If higher output involves higher costs of production, producers will need to get a higher price if they are to be persuaded to produce extra output.
- The higher the price of the good, the more profitable it becomes to produce. Firms will thus be encouraged to produce more of it by switching from producing less profitable goods.
- Given time, if the price of a good remains high, new producers will be encouraged to set up in production. Total market supply thus rises.

The first two determinants affect supply in the short run. The third affects supply in the long run. We distinguish between short-run and long-run supply later in the chapter on page 82.

The supply curve

The amount that producers would like to supply at various prices can be shown in a supply schedule. Table 2.3 shows a monthly supply schedule for potatoes, both for an individual farmer (farmer X) and for all farmers together (the whole market).

The supply schedule can be represented graphically as a supply curve. A supply curve may be an individual firm's supply curve or a market curve (i.e. that of the whole industry).

Figure 2.4 shows the *market* supply curve of potatoes. As with demand curves, price is plotted on the vertical axis and quantity on the horizontal axis. Each of the points *a–e* corresponds to a figure in Table 2.3. Thus, for example, a price rise from 12p per kilogram to 16p per kilogram will cause a movement along the supply curve from point *c* to point *d*: total market supply will rise from 350 000 tonnes per month to 530 000 tonnes per month.

Supply schedule

A table showing the different quantities of a good that producers are willing and able to supply at various prices over a given time period. A supply schedule can be for an individual producer or group of producers, or for all producers (the market supply schedule).

Supply curve

A graph showing the relationship between the price of a good and the quantity of the good supplied over a given period of time.

? 1. How much would be supplied at a price of 14p per kilo?
2. Draw a supply curve for farmer X. Are the axes drawn to the same scale as in Figure 2.4?

Table 2.3 The supply of potatoes (monthly)

	Price of potatoes (pence per kg)	Farmer X's supply (tonnes)	Total market supply (tonnes: 000s)
a	4	50	100
b	8	70	200
c	12	100	350
d	16	120	530
e	20	130	700

Figure 2.4 Market supply curve of potatoes

Not all supply curves will be upward sloping (positively sloped). Sometimes they will be vertical, or horizontal or even downward sloping. This will depend largely on the time period over which firms' response to price changes is considered. This question is examined in the section on the elasticity of supply (see section 2.4 below) and in more detail in Chapters 4 and 5.

Other determinants of supply

Like demand, supply is not simply determined by price. The other determinants of supply are as follows.

The costs of production. The higher the costs of production, the less profit will be made at any price. As costs rise, firms will cut back on production, probably switching to alternative products whose costs have not risen so much.

The main reasons for a change in costs are:

- Change in input prices: costs of production will rise if wages, raw material prices, rents, interest rates or any other input prices rise.
- Change in technology: technological advances can fundamentally alter the costs of production. Consider, for example, how the microchip revolution has changed production methods and information handling in virtually every industry in the world.
- Organizational changes: various cost savings can be made in many firms by reorganizing production.
- Government policy: costs will be lowered by government subsidies and raised by various taxes.

The profitability of alternative products (substitutes in supply). If a product which is a substitute in supply becomes more profitable to supply than before, producers are likely to switch from the first good to this alternative. Supply of the first good falls. Other goods are likely to become more profitable if:

- Their prices rise.
- Their costs of production fall.

For example, if the price of carrots goes up, or the cost of producing carrots comes

Substitutes in supply

These are two goods where an increased production of one means diverting resources away from producing the other.

down, farmers may decide to produce more carrots. The supply of potatoes is therefore likely to fall.

The profitability of goods in joint supply. Sometimes when one good is produced, another good is also produced at the same time. These are said to be goods in joint supply. An example is the refining of crude oil to produce petrol. Other grade fuels will be produced as well, such as diesel and paraffin. If more petrol is produced, due to a rise in demand and hence its price, then the supply of these other fuels will rise too.

Goods in joint supply
These are two goods where the production of more of one leads to the production of more of the other.

Nature, 'random shocks' and other unpredictable events. In this category we would include the weather and diseases affecting farm output, wars affecting the supply of imported raw materials, the breakdown of machinery, industrial disputes, earthquakes, floods and fire, etc.

The aims of producers. A profit-maximizing firm will supply a different quantity from a firm that has a different aim, such as maximizing sales. For most of the time we shall assume that firms are profit maximizers. In Chapter 7, however, we consider alternative aims.

Expectations of future price changes. If price is expected to rise, producers may temporarily reduce the amount they sell. Instead they are likely to build up their stocks and only release them on to the market when the price does rise. At the same time they may plan to produce more, by installing new machines, or taking on more labour, so that they can be ready to supply more when the price has risen.

To illustrate some of these determinants let us return to the example of butter. What would cause the supply of butter to rise?

- A reduction in the costs of producing butter. This could be caused, say, by a reduction in the price of nitrogen fertilizer. This would encourage farmers to use more fertilizer, which would increase grass yields, which in turn would increase milk yields per acre. Alternatively, new technology may allow more efficient churning of butter. Or again, the government may decide to give subsidies to farmers to produce more butter.
- A reduction in the profitability of producing cream or cheese. If these products become less profitable, due say to a reduction in their price, due in turn to a reduction in consumer demand, more butter is likely to be produced instead.
- An increase in the profitability of skimmed milk. If consumers buy more skimmed milk, then an increased supply of skimmed milk is likely to lead to an increase in the supply of butter and other cream products, since they are jointly produced with skimmed milk.
- If weather conditions are favourable, grass yields and hence milk yields are likely to be high. This will increase the supply of butter and other milk products.
- If farmers expect butter prices to rise in the future, they may well build up their herds of cows in anticipation of this.

1. For what reasons might the supply of potatoes fall?
2. For what reasons might the supply of leather rise?

Movements along and shifts in the supply curve

The principle here is the same as with demand curves. The effect of a change in price is illustrated by a movement along the supply curve: for example, from point *d* to point *e* in Figure 2.4 when price rises from 16p to 20p. Quantity supplied rises from 530 000 to 700 000 tonnes.

If any other determinant of supply changes, the whole supply curve will shift. A rightward shift illustrates an increase in supply. A leftward shift illustrates a decrease in supply. Thus in Figure 2.5, if the original curve is S_0, the curve S_1 represents an increase in supply, whereas the curve S_2 represents a decrease in supply.

A movement along a supply curve is often referred to as a change in the quantity supplied, whereas a shift in the supply curve is simply referred to as a change in supply.

Change in the quantity supplied

The term used for a movement along the supply curve to a new point. It occurs when there is a change in price.

Change in supply

The term used for a shift in the supply curve. It occurs when a determinant *other* than price changes.

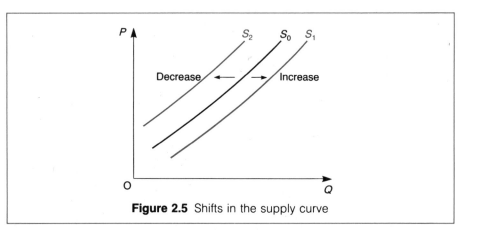

Figure 2.5 Shifts in the supply curve

This question is concerned with the supply of oil for central heating. In each case consider whether there is a movement along the supply curve (and in which direction) or a shift in it (and whether left or right).
(a) New oil fields start up in production. (b) The demand for central heating rises.
(c) The price of gas falls. (d) Oil companies anticipate an upsurge in demand for central-heating oil. (e) The demand for petrol rises. (f) New technology decreases the costs of oil refining. (g) All oil products become more expensive.

* Supply equations

A general supply function can be written in the form:

$$Q_s = f(P_g, C_g, a_1, a_2 \ldots a_n, j_1, j_2 \ldots j_m, R, A, P_{g\,t+1}^e) \tag{6}$$

In other words, quantity supplied (Q_s) depends on the price of the good (P_g), the costs of production (C_g), the profitability of alternative goods ($a_1, a_2 \ldots a_n$), the profitability of goods jointly supplied ($j_1, j_2 \ldots j_m$), nature and other random shocks (R), the aims of producers (A) and the expected price of the good (P_g^e) at some future time ($t + 1$).

Using survey data and regression analysis, equations can be estimated relating supply to some of these determinants. Note that not all determinants can be easily quantified (e.g. nature and the aims of firms), and thus may be left out of the equation.

The simplest form of supply equation relates supply to just one determinant. Thus a function relating supply to price would be of the form:

$$Q_s = c + dP \tag{7}$$

Using regression analysis, values can be estimated for *c* and *d*. Thus an actual supply equation might be something like:

$$Q_s = 500 + 1000P \qquad (8)$$

1. If *P* was originally measured in £s, what would happen to the value of the *d* term if *P* were now measured in pence?
2. Draw the schedule (table) and graph for equation (8) for prices from £1 to £10. What is it in the equation that determines the slope of the supply 'curve'?

If any determinant other than price changed, a new equation would result. For example, if costs of production fall, the equation may now be:

$$Q_s = 1000 + 1500P \qquad (9)$$

More complex supply equations would relate supply to more than one determinant. For example:

$$Q_s = 200 + 80P - 20a_1 - 15a_2 + 30j \qquad (10)$$

where *P* is the price of the good, a_1 and a_2 are the profitabilities of two alternative goods that could be supplied instead, and *j* is the profitability of a good in joint supply.

Explain why the *P* and *j* terms have a positive sign, whereas the a_1 and a_2 terms have a negative sign.

▲ SUMMARY

1. When the price of a good rises, the quantity supplied per period of time will usually also rise. This applies both to individual producers' supply and to the whole market supply.
2. There are two reasons in the short run why a higher price encourages producers to supply more: (a) they are now willing to incur the higher costs per unit associated with producing more; (b) they will switch to producing this product and away from now less profitable ones. In the long run there is a third reason: new producers will be attracted into the market.
3. The relationship between price and quantity supplied per period of time can be shown in a table (or schedule) or as a graph. As with a demand curve, price is plotted on the vertical axis and quantity per period of time on the horizontal axis. The resulting supply curve is upward

sloping (positively sloped).
4. Other determinants of supply include the costs of production, the profitability of alternative products, the profitability of goods in joint supply, random shocks and expectations of future price changes.
5. If price changes, the effect is shown by a movement along the supply curve. We call this effect 'a change in the quantity supplied'.
6. If any determinant *other* than price changes, the effect is shown by a shift in the whole supply curve. We call this effect 'a change in supply'. A rightward shift represents an increase in supply; a leftward shift represents a decrease in supply.
* 7. The relationship between the quantity supplied and the various determinants of supply can be expressed in the form of an equation.

2.3 Price and output determination

Equilibrium price and output

We can now combine our analysis of demand and supply. This will show how the actual price of a product and the actual quantity bought and sold are determined in a free and competitive market.

Let us return to the example of the market demand and market supply of potatoes, and use the data from Tables 2.1 and 2.3. These figures are given again in Table 2.4.

What will be the price and output that actually prevail? If the price started at 4p per

Table 2.4 The market demand and supply of potatoes (monthly)

Price of potatoes (pence per kg)	Total market demand (tonnes: 000s)	Total market supply (tonnes: 000s)
4	700 (*A*)	100 (*a*)
8	500 (*B*)	200 (*b*)
12	350 (*C*)	350 (*c*)
16	200 (*D*)	530 (*d*)
20	100 (*E*)	700 (*e*)

kilogram, demand would exceed supply by 600 000 tonnes (*A* − *a*). Consumers would be unable to obtain all they wanted and would thus be willing to pay a higher price. Producers, unable or unwilling to supply enough to meet the demand, will be only too happy to accept a higher price. The effect of the shortage, then, will be to drive up the price. The same would happen at a price of 8p per kilogram. There would still be a shortage; price would still rise. But as the price rises, the quantity demanded falls and the quantity supplied rises. The shortage is progressively eliminated.

 Explain the process by which the price of houses would rise if there were a shortage.

What would happen if the price started at a much higher level: say at 20p per kilogram? In this case supply would exceed demand by 600 000 tonnes (*e* − *E*). The effect of this surplus would be to drive the price down as farmers competed against each other to sell their excess supplies. The same would happen at a price of 16p per kilogram. There would still be a surplus; price would still fall.

In fact, only one price is sustainable. This is the price where demand equals supply: namely 12p per kilogram, where both demand and supply are 350 000 tonnes. When supply matches demand the market is said to clear. There is no shortage and no surplus.

This price, where demand equals supply, is called the equilibrium price. By equilibrium we mean a point of balance or a point of rest: in other words, a point towards which there is a tendency to move. In Table 2.4, if the price starts at other than 12p per kilogram, there will be a tendency for it to move towards 12p. The equilibrium price is the only price at which producers' and consumers' wishes are mutually reconciled: where the producers' plans to supply exactly match the consumers' plans to buy.

Market clearing

A market clears when supply matches demand, leaving no shortage or surplus.

Equilibrium price

The price where the quantity demanded equals the quantity supplied: the price where there is no shortage or surplus.

Demand and supply curves

The determination of equilibrium price and output can be shown using demand and supply curves. Equilibrium is where the two curves intersect.

Figure 2.6 shows the demand and supply curves of potatoes corresponding to the data in Table 2.4. Equilibrium price is P_e (12p) and equilibrium quantity is Q_e (350 000 tonnes).

At any price above 12p, there would be a surplus. Thus at 16p there is a surplus of 330 000 tonnes (*d* − *D*). More is supplied than consumers are willing and able to purchase at that price. Thus a price of 16p fails to clear the market. Price will fall to the equilibrium price of 12p. As it does so, there will be a movement along the demand curve from point *D* to point *C*, and a movement along the supply curve from point *d* to point *c*.

Equilibrium

A position of balance. A position from which there is no inherent tendency to move away.

Figure 2.6 The determination of market equilibrium (potatoes: monthly)

At any price below 12p, there would be a shortage. Thus at 8p there is a shortage of 300 000 tonnes (*B* − *b*). Price will rise to 12p. This will cause a movement along the supply curve from point *b* to point *c* and along the demand curve from point *B* to point *C*.

Point *Cc* is the equilibrium: where demand equals supply.

Movement to a new equilibrium

The equilibrium price will remain unchanged only so long as the demand and supply curves remain unchanged. If either of the curves shifts, a new equilibrium will be formed.

A change in demand

If one of the determinants of demand changes (other than price), the whole demand curve will shift. This will lead to a movement *along* the *supply* curve to the new intersection point.

For example, in Figure 2.7, if a rise in consumer incomes led to the demand curve shifting to D_2, there would be a shortage of $h − g$ at the original price P_{e_1}. This would

Figure 2.7 The effect of a shift in the demand curve

cause price to rise to the new equilibrium P_{e_2}. As it did so, there would be a movement along the supply curve from point *g* to point *i*, and along the new demand curve (D_2) from point *h* to point *i*. Equilibrium quantity would rise from Q_{e_1} to Q_{e_2}.

The effect of the shift in demand, therefore, has been a movement *along* the supply curve from the old equilibrium to the new: from point *g* to point *i*.

 What would happen to price and quantity if the demand curve shifted to the left? Draw a diagram to illustrate your answer.

A change in supply

Likewise, if one of the determinants of supply changes (other than price), the whole supply curve will shift. This will lead to a movement *along* the *demand* curve to the new intersection point.

For example, in Figure 2.8, if costs of production rose, the supply curve would shift to the left: to S_2. There would be a shortage of $g - j$ at the old price of P_{e_1}. Price would rise from P_{e_1} to P_{e_3}. Quantity would fall from Q_{e_1} to Q_{e_3}. In other words, there would be a movement along the demand curve from point *g* to point *k*, and along the new supply curve (S_2) from point *j* to point *k*.

To summarize: a shift in one curve leads to a movement along the other curve to the new intersection point.

Sometimes a number of determinants might change. This might lead to a shift in *both* curves. When this happens equilibrium simply moves from the point where the old curves intersected to the point where the new ones intersect.

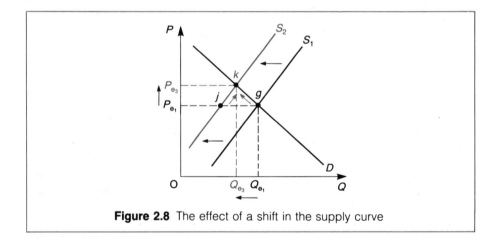

Figure 2.8 The effect of a shift in the supply curve

 1. What will happen to the equilibrium price and quantity of butter in each of the following cases? You should state whether demand or supply (or both) have shifted and in which direction.
(a) A rise in the price of margarine; (b) A rise in the demand for yoghurt; (c) A rise in the price of bread; (d) A rise in the demand for bread; (e) An expected rise in the price of butter in the near future; (f) A tax on butter production; (g) The invention of a new, but expensive, process for removing all cholesterol from butter, plus the passing of a law which states that all butter producers must use this process.
In each case assume *ceteris paribus*.

2. If both demand and supply change, and if we know in which direction they have shifted

but not by how much, why is it that we will be able to predict the direction in which *either* price *or* quantity will change, but not both? (Clue: consider the four possible combinations and sketch them if necessary: *D* left, *S* left; *D* right, *S* right; *D* left, *S* right; *D* right, *S* left.)

* Identifying the position of demand and supply curves

Both demand and supply depend on price, and yet their interaction determines price. For this reason it is difficult to identify just what is going on when price and quantity change. It is difficult to identify just what the demand and supply curves look like.

Let us say that we want to identify the demand curve for good X. We observe that when the price was 20p, 1000 units were purchased. At a later date the price has risen to 30p and 800 units are now purchased. What can we conclude from this about the demand curve? The answer is that without further information we can conclude very little. Consider Figures 2.9 and 2.10. Both are consistent with the facts.

In Figure 2.9 the demand curve has not shifted. The rise in price and the fall in sales are due entirely to a shift in the supply curve. The movement from point *a* to point *b* is thus a movement along the demand curve. If we can be certain that the demand curve has not shifted, then the evidence allows us to identify its position (or, at least, two points on it).

In Figure 2.10, however, not only has the supply curve shifted, but so also has the demand curve. Let us assume that people's tastes for the product have increased. In this case a movement from *a* to *b* does *not* trace out the demand curve. We cannot derive the demand curve(s) from the evidence of price and quantity alone.

The problem is that when the supply curve shifts, we often cannot know whether or not the demand curve has shifted, and if so by how much. How would we know, for example, just how much people's tastes have changed?

The problem works the other way round too. It is difficult to identify a supply curve when the demand curve shifts. Is the change in price and quantity entirely due to the shift in the demand curve, or has the supply curve shifted too?

The problem is known as the identification problem. It is difficult to identify just what is causing the change in price and quantity.

Identification problem

The problem of identifying the relationship between two variables (e.g. price and quantity demanded) from the evidence when it is not known whether or how the variables have been affected by *other* determinants. For example, it is difficult to identify the shape of a demand curve simply by observing price and quantity when it is not known whether changes in other determinants have *shifted* the demand curve.

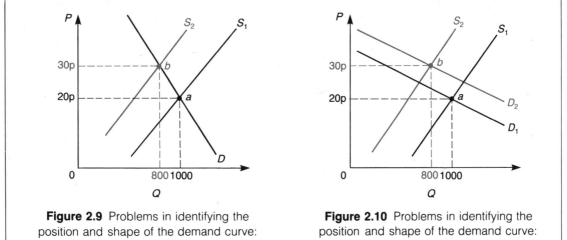

Figure 2.9 Problems in identifying the position and shape of the demand curve: shift in supply curve

Figure 2.10 Problems in identifying the position and shape of the demand curve: shift in supply *and* demand curves

Box 2.2

House Prices
A case study in shifting demand curves

Simple demand and supply analysis is a powerful tool for explaining house price movements.

Take the period of the second half of the 1980s. Britain was recovering from a recession and house prices started to soar. By 1988 house prices in some parts of the country were rising by over 30 per cent per year. Then suddenly house prices stopped rising, and in some areas even fell.

What was the cause of these movements? The analysis can be divided into two periods: the price boom and the ending of the price boom.

The house price boom up to 1988
The recovery from recession was faster in the south: people had higher incomes and these were growing faster than in the north. This is illustrated by a large rightward shift in the demand for houses in diagram (a). House prices, which were already higher in the south, thus started to rise rapidly.

(a)	(b)
Rapid growth in demand for houses in the south	Slower growth in demand for houses in the north

The recession was deeper and longer lived in the north. Recovery was slow and unemployment remained high. The demand for houses only grew slowly. This is illustrated by a small rightward shift in demand for houses in diagram (b). House prices in the north rose fairly slowly and hence the gap between south and north house prices widened.

After very high mortgage interest rates in 1985, mortgage rates gradually fell. Mortgages were easily obtainable, with banks competing with building societies to lend to house buyers. As house prices rose, so this further increased the demand, as people saw a house as a good investment. People rushed to buy before prices went any higher. Again these effects were bigger in the south, where the price rises were faster.

The breaking of the boom after 1988
By mid-1988 house prices were so high in the south that many people had huge mortgages. Then the government raised interest rates. Many people could no longer afford such large mortgages. The demand for houses in the south fell. This is illustrated in diagram (c). Demand shifted to D_3s, and prices fell to P_3s.

(c)	(d)
Breaking of the boom in the south	Slowing down of the boom in the north

Before the mortgage interest rate rise in late 1988, many people had moved out of London and the southeast. Some people working in London were prepared to commute well over 200 miles each day to avoid London house prices.

Businesses were increasingly being attracted to the north with its plentiful supply of labour, cheaper land and cheaper housing for their employees. Thus by mid 1988 the demand for houses in the north was beginning to rise faster than in the south.

This, combined with the fact that people in the north generally had smaller mortgages, meant that the mortgage rate increase had less effect in the north. Thus demand continued to rise in the north (albeit at a slower rate). This is illustrated in diagram (d), with demand rising to D_3N. As a result, the gap between south and north prices began to narrow.

? What would cause the *supply* curve for houses to shift? Which way is the supply curve likely to shift if (a) builders anticipate a boom in demand; (b) people with houses to sell think that house prices will soon rise rapidly?

▲ SUMMARY

1. If the demand for a good exceeds the supply, there will be a shortage. This will lead to a rise in the price of the good.
2. If the supply of a good exceeds the demand, there will be a surplus. This will lead to a fall in the price.
3. Price will settle at the equilibrium. The equilibrium price is the one that clears the market: the price where demand equals supply.
4. If the demand or supply curve shifts, this will lead either

to a shortage or to a surplus. Price will therefore either rise or fall until a new equilibrium is reached at the position where the supply and demand curves *now* intersect.
* 5. It is difficult to identify the position of a real-world supply (or demand) curve simply by looking at the relationship between price and quantity at different points in time. The problem is that the other curve may have shifted (by an unknown amount).

2.4 Elasticity

The responsiveness of quantity demanded to a change in price

When the price of a good rises, the quantity demanded will fall. That much is fairly obvious. But in most cases we will want to know more than this. We will want to know by just *how much* the quantity demanded will fall. In other words, we will want to know how *responsive* demand is to a rise in price.

Such information is vital to any firm considering whether to put up its prices. Take the case of two firms facing very different demand curves. These are shown in Figure 2.11. (Note that we are now dropping the assumption that firms are price takers. We are assuming that they can choose their price and face a downward-sloping demand curve. We will examine the circumstances under which firms *can* control prices in Chapters 5 and 6.)

Firm A can raise its price quite substantially – from £6 to £10 – and yet its level of sales only falls by a relatively small amount – from 100 units to 90 units. This firm will probably be quite keen to raise its price. After all, it could make significantly more profits on each unit sold (assuming no rise in costs per unit), and yet only sell slightly fewer units.

Firm B, however, will think twice about raising its price. Even a relatively modest increase in price – from £6 to £7 – will lead to a substantial fall in sales from 100 units to 40 units. What is the point of making a bit more profit on those units that it manages to sell if in the process it ends up selling a lot fewer units? In such circumstances the firm may contemplate lowering its price.

Figure 2.11 The demand for an individual firm's product

Economists too will want to know how responsive demand is to a change in price. This information is necessary to enable them to predict the effects of a shift in supply on the market price of a product.

Figure 2.12 shows the effect of a shift in supply with two quite different demand curves (D and D'). Assume that initially the supply curve is S_1, and that it intersects with both demand curves at point a, at a price of P_1 and a quantity of Q_1. Now supply shifts to S_2. What will happen to price and quantity? Economists will want to know! The answer is that it depends on the shape of the demand curve. In the case of demand curve D, there is a relatively large rise in price (to P_2) and a relatively small fall in quantity (to Q_2): equilibrium is at point b. In the case of demand curve D', however, there is only a relatively small rise in price (to P_3) but a relatively large fall in quantity (to Q_3): equilibrium is at point c. As well as the responsiveness of demand to a *rise* in price, we will often need to know how responsive it is to a fall in price too.

Figure 2.12 Market supply and demand

It is also important to know just how responsive demand is to a change in *other* determinants. How much will demand rise when incomes rise? How much will demand rise when the price of a substitute good rises? How much will demand fall when the price of a complementary good rises?

Similarly, it is important to know how responsive *supply* is to a change in price, or to some other determinant.

> **?** Draw a diagram with two supply curves, one steeply sloping and one gently sloping. Ensure that the two curves cross. Draw a demand curve through the point where they cross and mark the equilibrium price and quantity. Now assume that the demand curve shifts to the right. Show how the shape of the supply curve will determine just what happens to price and quantity.

Given the importance of knowing the responsiveness of demand and supply to a change in one of the determinants, we will need some way of measuring this responsiveness. Elasticity is the measure we use.

Elasticity

A measure of the responsiveness of a variable (e.g. quantity demanded or quantity supplied) to a change in one of its determinants (e.g. price or income).

Defining elasticity

What we will want to compare is the size of the change in quantity demanded (or supplied) of a given product with the size of the change in the determinant that caused it. Elasticity does just this. The formula for elasticity is:

$$\text{Elasticity } (\epsilon) = \frac{\text{Proportionate (or percentage) change in quantity}}{\text{Proportionate (or percentage) change in the determinant}}$$

There are four particular types of elasticity in common use: *price elasticity of demand, price elasticity of supply, income elasticity of demand* and *cross-price elasticity of demand*. Let us examine some examples of each.

Price elasticity of demand ($P\epsilon_d$)

Price elasticity of demand shows the responsiveness of quantity demanded to a change in price. It is defined as follows:

$$P\epsilon_d = \frac{\text{Proportionate (or percentage) change in quantity demanded}}{\text{Proportionate (or percentage) change in price}}$$

Price elasticity of demand
The responsiveness of quantity demanded to a change in price.

If, for example, a 20 per cent rise in the price of a product causes a 10 per cent fall in the quantity demanded, the price elasticity of demand will be:

$$-10\%/20\% = -0.5$$

Price elasticity of supply ($P\epsilon_s$)

Price elasticity of supply shows the responsiveness of quantity *supplied* to a change in price. It is defined as follows:

$$P\epsilon_s = \frac{\text{Proportionate (or percentage) change in quantity supplied}}{\text{Proportionate (or percentage) change in price}}$$

Price elasticity of supply
The responsiveness of quantity supplied to a change in price.

Thus if a 15 per cent rise in the price of a product causes a 15 per cent rise in the quantity *supplied*, the price elasticity of supply will be:

$$15\%/15\% = 1$$

? Why does price elasticity of demand have a negative value, whereas price elasticity of supply has a positive value?

In a similar vein we can measure the responsiveness of demand or supply of a product to changes in determinants *other than* price. Two useful examples both apply to demand.

Income elasticity of demand ($Y\epsilon_d$)

Income elasticity of demand measures the responsiveness of demand to a change in consumer incomes (Y). It is defined as follows:

$$Y\epsilon_d = \frac{\text{Proportionate (or percentage) change in demand}}{\text{Proportionate (or percentage) change in income}}$$

Income elasticity of demand
The responsiveness of demand to a change in consumer incomes.

For example, if a 2 per cent rise in incomes causes an 8 per cent rise in a product's demand, then its income elasticity of demand will be:

$$8\%/2\% = 4$$

Cross-price elasticity of demand ($P\epsilon_{d_{ab}}$)

Cross-price elasticity of demand measures the responsiveness of demand for one good to a change in the price of another good – either a substitute or a complement. It is defined as follows:

$$P\epsilon_{d_{ab}} = \frac{\text{Proportionate (or percentage) change in demand for good a}}{\text{Proportionate (or percentage) change in price of good b}}$$

Cross-price elasticity of demand
The responsiveness of demand for one good to a change in the price of another.

The concept is useful to a firm which wants to know how responsive the demand for its product will be to a change in the price of its rivals' products. If, for example, the demand for butter rose by 2 per cent when the price of margarine (a substitute) rose by 8 per cent, then the cross-price elasticity of demand for butter with respect to margarine would be:

$$2\%/8\% = 0.25$$

If, on the other hand, the price of bread (a complement) rose, the demand for butter would fall. If a 4 per cent rise in the price of bread led to a 3 per cent fall in demand for butter, the cross-price elasticity of demand for butter with respect to bread would be:

$$-3\%/4\% = -0.75$$

We have looked at four different types of elasticity: price elasticity of demand, price elasticity of supply, income elasticity of demand and cross-price elasticity of demand. Since there are several determinants of demand and supply, there could, in theory, be several elasticities. In practice, however, the four we have looked at are the only ones in common use.

Three things should be noted at this stage about the figure that is calculated for elasticity.

1. The use of proportionate or percentage measures

Elasticity is measured in proportionate or percentage terms for the following reasons:

- It allows comparison of changes in two qualitatively different things, which are thus measured in two different types of unit: i.e. it allows comparison of quantity changes (demand or supply) with monetary changes (price or income).
- It avoids the problem of what size units to use. For example, an increase from £2 to £4 is 2 price units. An increase from 200 pence to 400 pence is 200 price units. By measuring this change in proportionate or percentage terms the same result is obtained whichever price unit is used, thus avoiding the problems of a merely apparent difference in price change.
- It is the only sensible way of deciding *how big* a change in price or quantity is. Take a simple example. An item goes up in price by £1. Is this a big increase or a small increase? We can only answer this if we know what the original price was. If a can of beans goes up in price by £1, that is a huge price increase. If, however, the price of a house goes up by £1, that is a tiny price increase. In other words, it is the percentage or proportionate increase in price that we look at in deciding how big a price rise it is.

2. The sign (positive or negative)

If demand (or supply) increases when the determinant increases (or decreases when the determinant decreases), elasticity is a positive figure. Thus price elasticity of supply, income elasticity of demand, and cross-price elasticity of demand with respect to substitutes will all normally have a positive value.

If, however, demand (or supply) *decreases* when the determinant *increases* (or increases when the determinant decreases), elasticity will be negative: a positive figure is being divided by a negative figure (or vice versa). Thus price elasticity of demand and cross-price elasticity of demand with respect to complements will normally be negative.

3. The value (greater or less than one)

If we now ignore the sign and just concentrate on the value of the figure, this tells us whether demand (or supply) is elastic or inelastic.

Elastic (ε > 1). This is where a change in a determinant causes a proportionately larger change in demand (or supply). In this case the value of elasticity will be greater than 1, since we are dividing a larger figure by a smaller figure.

Inelastic (ε < 1). This is where a change in a determinant causes a proportionately smaller change in demand (or supply). In this case elasticity will be less than 1, since we are dividing a smaller figure by a larger figure.

Unit elastic (ε = 1). Unit elasticity is where demand (or supply) changes proportionately by the same amount as the determinant. This will give an elasticity equal to 1, since we are dividing a figure by itself.

 Go back through each of the numerical examples given above of the different types of elasticity and state whether they were elastic, inelastic or unit elastic.

Price elasticity of demand (Pε_d)

Let us now have a closer look at specific elasticities. We start with price elasticity of demand. This is one of the most useful concepts in the whole of economics. We will come across it many times throughout the book.

The demand for some goods will be highly price elastic: only a small percentage change in price will be necessary to cause a large percentage change in the quantity demanded. The demand for other goods by contrast will be highly price *in*elastic: even large percentage changes in price will have relatively little effect on the quantity demanded. But why will the price elasticity of demand vary from one good to another? What determines price elasticity of demand?

Determinants of price elasticity of demand

1. The number and closeness of substitute goods. This is the most important determinant. The more substitutes there are for a good, and the closer they are, the greater will be the price elasticity of demand. The reason is that people will be able to switch to the substitutes when the price of the good rises. The more numerous the substitutes and the closer they are, the more people will switch: in other words, the bigger will be the substitution effect of a price rise.

For example, the price elasticity of demand for a particular brand of a product will probably be fairly high. If its price goes up, people can simply switch to another brand: there is a large substitution effect. By contrast the demand for a product *in general* will normally be pretty inelastic. If the price of food in general goes up, demand for food will only fall slightly. People will buy a little less since they cannot now afford so much: this is the *income* effect of the price rise. But there is no alternative to food that can satisfy our hunger: there is therefore virtually no *substitution* effect.

 1. Rank the following in ascending order of elasticity:

Jeans	Trousers	Black Levi jeans	Outer garments
Black jeans	Clothes	Black Levi 501 jeans	

2. How might a firm set about making the demand for its brand less elastic?

2. The proportion of income spent on the good. The higher the proportion of our income that is spent on a good, the more we will be forced to cut consumption when

---

its price rises: the bigger will be the income effect and the more elastic will be the demand.

Thus salt has a very low elasticity of demand. This is because we spend such a tiny fraction of our income on salt that we would find little difficulty in paying a relatively large percentage increase in its price: the income effect of a price rise would be very small. By contrast there will be a much bigger income effect when a major item of expenditure rises in price. For example, if mortgage interest rates rise (the 'price' of loans for house purchase), people may have to cut down substantially on their demand for housing – being forced to buy somewhere much smaller and cheaper, or to live in rented accommodation.

 Will a general item of expenditure like food or clothing have a price-elastic or inelastic demand? (Consider both the determinants we have considered so far.)

3. The time period. When price rises people may take a time to adjust their consumption patterns and find alternatives. The longer the time period after a price change, then, the more elastic is the demand likely to be.

Price elasticity of demand and sales revenue

Total (sales) revenue
The amount a firm earns from its sales of a product at a particular price: *TR* = *P* × *Q*. Note that we are referring to *gross* revenue: i.e. revenue before the deduction of taxes or any other costs.

One of the most important applications of price elasticity of demand concerns its relationship with a firm's sales revenue. The total sales revenue (*TR*) of a firm is simply price times quantity:

$$TR = P \times Q$$

For example, 3000 units (*Q*) sold at £2 per unit (*P*) will earn the firm £6000 (*TR*). This is shown graphically in Figure 2.13 as the area of the shaded rectangle. But why? The area of a rectangle is simply its height multiplied by its length. *TR* is simply price (the height of the shaded rectangle) multiplied by quantity (the length of the rectangle).

Let us assume that a firm wants to increase its total revenue. What should it do? Should it raise its price or lower it? The answer depends on the price elasticity of demand.

Elastic demand

As price rises so quantity demanded falls, and vice versa. When demand is elastic, quantity changes proportionately more than price. Thus the change in quantity has a

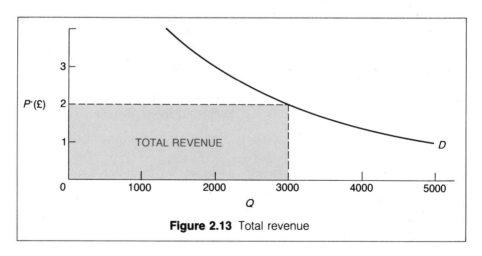

Figure 2.13 Total revenue

bigger effect on total revenue than does the change in price. This can be summarized as follows:

> *P* rises; *Q* falls proportionately more; therefore *TR* falls
> *P* falls; *Q* rises proportionately more; therefore *TR* rises

In other words, total revenue changes in the same direction as *quantity*.

This is illustrated in Figure 2.14. Demand is elastic between points *a* and *b*. A rise in price from £4 to £5 causes a proportionately larger fall in quantity demanded: from 20 to 10. Total revenue *falls* from £80 (the striped area) to £50 (the red area).

When demand is elastic, then, a rise in price will causes a fall in total revenue. If a firm wants to increase its revenue, it should *lower* its price.

Figure 2.14 Elastic demand between two points

Inelastic demand

When demand is inelastic it is the other way around. Price changes proportionately more than quantity. Thus the change in price has a bigger effect on total revenue than does the change in quantity. To summarize the effects:

> *P* rises; *Q* falls proportionately less; *TR* rises
> *P* falls; *Q* rises proportionately less; *TR* falls

In other words, total revenue changes in the same direction as *price*.

This is illustrated in Figure 2.15. Demand is inelastic between points *a* and *c*. A rise in price from £4 to £8 causes a proportionately smaller fall in quantity demanded: from 20 to 15. Total revenue *rises* from £80 (the striped area) to £120 (the red area).

If a firm wants to increase its revenue in this case, therefore, it should *raise* its price.

 Assuming that a firm faces an inelastic demand and wants to increase its total revenue, by *how much* should it raise its price? Is there any limit?

Special cases

Figure 2.16 shows three special cases: (a) a totally inelastic demand ($P\epsilon_d = 0$), (b) an infinitely elastic demand ($P\epsilon_d = \infty$) and (c) a unit elastic demand ($P\epsilon_d = -1$).

Totally inelastic demand. This is shown by a vertical straight line. No matter what happens to price, quantity demanded remains the same. It is obvious that the more

Figure 2.15 Inelastic demand between two points

the price is raised, the bigger will be the revenue. Thus in Figure 2.16 (a), P_2 will earn a bigger revenue that P_1.

 Can you think of any examples of goods which have a totally inelastic demand (a) at *all* prices; (b) over a particular price range?

Infinitely elastic demand. This is shown by a horizontal straight line. At any price above P_1 demand is zero. But at P_1 (or any price below) demand is 'infinitely' large.

This seemingly unlikely demand curve is in fact relatively common. Firms that are very small (like the small-scale grain farmer) are 'price takers'. They have to accept the price as given by supply and demand in the *whole market*. If individual farmers were to try to sell above this price, they would sell nothing at all. At this price, however, they can sell to the market all they produce. (Demand is not *literally* infinite, but as far as the farmer is concerned it is.) In this case, the more the individual farmer produces, the more revenue will be earned. In Figure 2.16 (b), more revenue is earned at Q_2 than at Q_1.

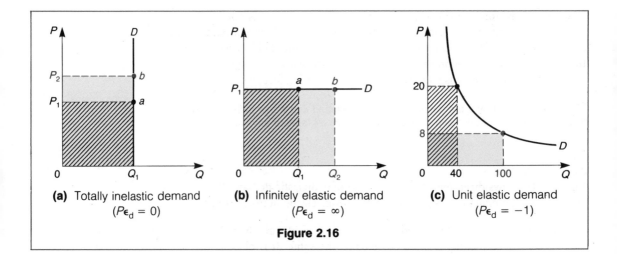

(a) Totally inelastic demand
$(P\epsilon_d = 0)$

(b) Infinitely elastic demand
$(P\epsilon_d = \infty)$

(c) Unit elastic demand
$(P\epsilon_d = -1)$

Figure 2.16

Box 2.3

Advertising and its Effect on Demand Curves
How to increase sales and price

When we are told that brand X will make us more beautiful, enrich our lives, wash our clothes whiter, give us get-up-and-go, give us a new taste sensation or make us the envy of our friends, just what are the advertisers up to? 'Trying to sell the product,' you may reply.

In fact there is a bit more to it than this. Advertisers are trying to do two things:

● Shift the product's demand curve to the right.
● Make it less price elastic.

This is illustrated in the diagram.

The effect of advertising on the demand curve

D_1 shows the original demand curve with price at P_1 and sales at Q_1. D_2 shows the curve after an advertising campaign. The rightward shift allows an increased quantity (Q_2) to be sold at the original price. If the demand is also made highly inelastic, the firm can also raise its price and still have a substantial increase in sales. Thus in the

diagram, price can be raised to P_2 and sales will be Q_3 – still substantially above Q_1. The total gain in revenue is shown by the shaded area.

How can advertising bring about this new demand curve?

Shifting the demand curve to the right
This will occur if the advertising brings the product to more people's attention and if it increases people's desire for the product.

Making the demand curve less elastic
This will occur if the advertising creates greater brand loyalty. People must be led to believe (rightly or wrongly) that competitors' brands are inferior. This will allow the firm to raise its price above that of its rivals with no significant fall in sales. There will only be a small substitution effect because consumers have been led to believe that there are no close substitutes.

 1. Think of some advertisements which deliberately seek to make demand less elastic.
2. Imagine that 'Sunshine' sunflower margarine, a well known brand, is advertised with the slogan, 'It helps you live longer' (the implication being that butter and margarines high in saturates shorten your life). What do you think would happen to the demand curve for a supermarket's *own* brand of sunflower margarine? Consider both the direction of shift and the effect on elasticity. Will the elasticity differ markedly at different prices? How will this affect the pricing policy and sales of the supermarket's own brand?'

Unit elastic demand. This is where price and quantity change in exactly the same proportion. Any rise in price will be exactly offset by a fall in quantity, leaving total revenue unchanged. In Figure 2.16 (c), the striped area is exactly equal to the red area: in both cases total revenue is £800.

You might have thought that a demand curve with unit elasticity would be a straight line at 45° to the axes. Instead it is a curve called a *rectangular hyperbola*. The reason for its shape is that the proportionate *rise* in quantity must equal the proportionate *fall* in price (and vice versa). As we move down the demand curve, in order for the *proportionate* change in both price and quantity to remain constant there must be a

Box 2.4

Any more fares?
Pricing on the buses

Imagine that a local bus company is faced with increased costs and fears that it will make a loss. What should it do?

The most likely response of the company will be to raise its fares. But this may be the wrong policy, especially if existing services are underutilized. To help it decide what to do, it commissions a survey to estimate passenger demand at three different fares: the current fare of 10p per mile, a higher fare of 12p and a lower fare of 8p. The results of the survey are shown in the first two columns of the table.

Demand turns out to be elastic. This is because of the existence of alternative means of transport. As a result of the elastic demand, total revenue can be increased by reducing the fare from the current 10p to 8p. Revenue rises from £400 000 to £480 000 per annum.

But what will happen to the company's profits? Its profit is the difference between the total revenue from passengers and its total costs of operating the service. If

buses are currently underutilized, it is likely that the extra passengers can be carried without the need for extra buses, and hence at no extra cost.

At a fare of 10p, the old profit was £40 000 (£400 000 − £360 000). After the increase in costs, a 10p fare now gives a loss of £40 000 (£400 000 − £440 000).

By raising the fare to 12p, the loss is increased to £80 000. But by lowering the fare to 8p, a profit of £40 000 can again be made.

1. Estimate the price elasticity of demand between 8p and 10p and between 10p and 12p.
2. Was the 10p fare the best fare originally?
3. The company considers lowering the fare to 6p, and estimates that demand will be 8½ million passenger miles. It will have to put on extra buses, however. How should it decide?

Fare (pence per mile) (1)	Estimated demand (passenger miles per year: millions) (2)	Total revenue (£ per year) (3)	Old total cost (£ per year) (4)	New total cost (£ per year) (5)
8	6	480 000	360 000	440 000
10	4	400 000	360 000	440 000
12	3	360 000	360 000	440 000

bigger and bigger *absolute* rise in quantity and a smaller and smaller absolute fall in price. For example, a rise in quantity from 200 to 400 is the same proportionate change as a rise from 100 to 200, but its absolute size is double. A fall in price from £5 to £2.50 is the same percentage as a fall from £10 to £5, but its absolute size is only half.

To illustrate these figures, draw the demand curve corresponding to the following table.

P	Q	TR
£2.50	400	£1000
£5	200	£1000
£10	100	£1000
£20	50	£1000
£40	25	£1000

If the curve had an elasticity of −1 *throughout* its length, what would be the quantity demanded (a) at a price of £1; (b) at a price of 10p; (c) if the good were free?

The measurement of elasticity: arc elasticity

A common mistake that students make is to think that you can talk about the elasticity of a *whole curve*. The mistake here is that in most cases the elasticity will vary along the length of the curve.

Take the case of the demand curve illustrated in Figure 2.17. Between points *a* and *b*, total revenue rises ($P_2Q_2 > P_1Q_1$): demand is thus elastic between these two points. Between points *b* and *c*, however, total revenue falls ($P_3Q_3 < P_2Q_2$). Demand here is inelastic.

Normally, then, we can only refer to the elasticity of a *portion* of the demand curve, not of the *whole* curve. There are, however, two exceptions to this rule.

The first is when the elasticity just so happens to be the same all the way along a curve, as in the three special cases illustrated in Figure 2.16. The second is where two curves are drawn on the same diagram, as in Figure 2.12. Here we can say that demand curve *D* is less elastic than demand curve *D'* at any given price. Note, however, that each of these two curves will still have different elasticities along its length.

Although we cannot normally talk about the elasticity of a whole curve, we can nevertheless talk about the elasticity between any two points on it. This is known as arc elasticity. In fact the formula for elasticity that we have used so far is the formula for arc elasticity. Let us examine it more closely. We will focus on price elasticity of demand. Remember the formula we used was:

> **Arc elasticity**
>
> The measurement of elasticity between two points on a curve.

$$\frac{\text{Proportionate } \Delta Q}{\text{Proportionate } \Delta P} \qquad \text{(where } \Delta \text{ means 'change in')}$$

The way we measure a proportionate change in quantity is to divide that change by the level of Q: i.e. $\Delta Q/Q$. Similarly, we measure a proportionate change in price by dividing that change by the level of P: i.e. $\Delta P/Q$. Price elasticity of demand can thus now be rewritten as:

$$\frac{\Delta Q}{Q} \div \frac{\Delta P}{P}$$

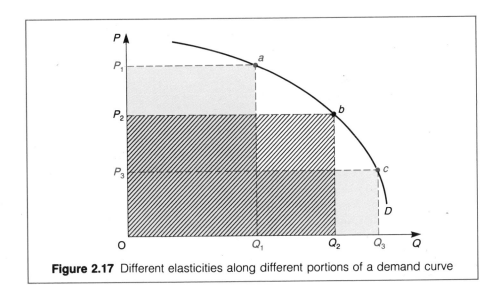

Figure 2.17 Different elasticities along different portions of a demand curve

But just what value do we give to *P* and *Q*? Consider the demand schedule given in Table 2.5 and graphed in Figure 2.18. What is the elasticity of demand between points *m* and *n*? To answer this we need to identify ΔQ and *Q*, and ΔP and *P*. Let us start with quantity.

Table 2.5

P(£)	Q(000s)
8	10
6	20
4	30
2	40

Quantity

The difference in quantity (ΔQ) between 10 (point *n*) and 20 (point *m*) is 10:

$$\Delta Q = 10$$

But what is the *proportionate* change in *Q* ($\Delta Q/Q$)? Is it 10/10, taking *Q* = 10 (point *n*) as the base from which to measure the change in *Q*? Or is it 10/20, taking *Q* = 20 (point *m*)? To avoid this problem the average of the two quantities is used: in other words, the mid-point between them:

$$Q = 15 \quad \text{i.e.} \left(\frac{10 + 20}{2}\right)$$

$$\therefore \frac{\Delta Q}{Q} = \frac{10}{15}$$

Price

The difference in price between 8 (point *n*) and 6 (point *m*) is 2:

$$\Delta P = 2$$

The *proportionate* change in *P* is found the same way as the proportionate change in *Q*.

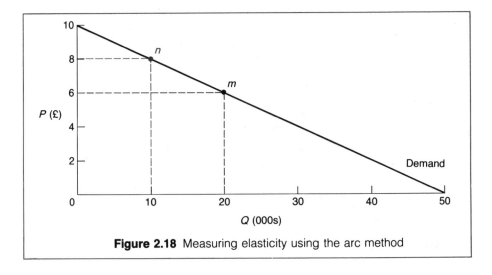

Figure 2.18 Measuring elasticity using the arc method

The base price is taken as the mid-point between the two prices:

$$P = 7 \quad \text{i.e.} \left(\frac{8 + 6}{2}\right)$$

$$\therefore \frac{\Delta P}{P} = \frac{2}{7}$$

Elasticity

Now that we have worked out figures for ΔQ, Q, ΔP and P, we can proceed to work out elasticity. Using the average (or 'mid-point') formula, price elasticity of demand is given by:

$$\frac{\Delta Q}{\text{average } Q} \div \frac{\Delta P}{\text{average } P}$$

In our example this would give the following elasticity between m and n:

$$-10/15 \div 2/7 = -7/3 = -2.33$$

Since 2.33 is greater than 1, demand is elastic between m and n.

* The measurement of elasticity: point elasticity

Rather than measuring elasticity between two points on a demand curve, we may want to measure it at a single point: for example, point r in Figure 2.19. In order to measure point elasticity we must first rearrange the terms in the formula $\Delta Q/Q \div \Delta P/P$. By doing so we can rewrite the formula for price elasticity of demand as:

$$\frac{\Delta Q}{\Delta P} \times \frac{P}{Q}$$

Since we want to measure price elasticity at a *point* on the demand curve, rather than between two points, it is necessary to know how quantity demanded would react to an *infinitesimally small* change in price. In the case of point r in Figure 2.19 we want to know how the quantity demanded would react to an infinitesimally small change from a price of 30.

An infinitesimally small change is signified by the letter 'd'. The formula for price elasticity of demand thus becomes:

$$\frac{dQ}{dP} \times \frac{P}{Q}$$

dQ/dP is the differential calculus term for the rate of change of quantity with respect to a change in price. And conversely, dP/dQ is the rate of change of price with respect to a change in quantity demanded. At any given point on the demand curve dP/dQ is given by the *slope* of the curve (its rate of change). The slope is found by drawing a tangent to the curve at that point and finding the slope of the tangent.

The tangent to the demand curve at point r is shown in Figure 2.19. Its slope is $-50/100$. dP/dQ is thus $-50/100$ and dQ/dP is the inverse of this, $-100/50 = -2$.

Returning to the formula $dQ/dP \times P/Q$, elasticity at point r equals:

$$-2 \times 30/40 = -1.5$$

Rather than having to draw the graph and measure the slope of the tangent, the technique of differentiation can be used to work out point elasticity as long as the

Average (or mid-point) formula for arc elasticity

ΔQ/average $Q \div \Delta$determinant/average value of determinant. The average in each case is the average between the two points being measured.

Formula for price elasticity of demand (arc method)

ΔQ_d/average $Q_d \div \Delta P$/average P

Point elasticity

The measurement of elasticity at a point on a curve. The formula for price elasticity of demand using the point elasticity method is $dQ/dP \times P/Q$, where dQ/dP is the inverse of the slope of the tangent to the demand curve at the point in question.

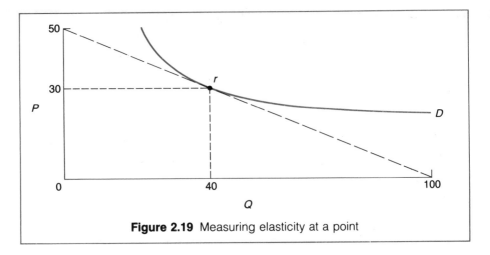

Figure 2.19 Measuring elasticity at a point

equation for the demand curve is known. An example of the use of this technique is given in Box 2.5.

Elasticity of a straight-line demand curve

A straight-line demand curve will have a different elasticity at each point on it. The only exceptions are a vertical demand curve ($P\epsilon_d = 0$), and a horizontal demand curve ($P\epsilon_d = \infty$).

The reason for this differing elasticity is demonstrated in Figure 2.20. Using the point elasticity formula:

$$dQ/dP \times P/Q$$

the slope of the demand curve (dP/dQ) is constant (i.e. $-10/50$). Thus dQ/dP is constant (i.e. $=50/-10 = -5$).

The value of P/Q, however, differs along the length of the demand curve. At point n, $P/Q = 8/10$. Thus:

$$dQ/dP \times P/Q = -5 \times 8/10 = -4$$

Figure 2.20 Different elasticities along a straight-line demand curve

*Box 2.5

Using Calculus to Calculate Price Elasticity of Demand

(A knowledge of the rules of differentiation is necessary to understand this box. No part of the text uses calculus, but a few boxes will.)

The following is an example of an equation for a demand curve:

$$Q_d = 60 - 15P + P^2$$

(where Q_d is measured in 000s of units). From this the following schedule and graph can be constructed.

P	60	−15P	+ P^2	=	Q_d(000s)
0	60	− 0	+ 0	=	60
1	60	−15	+ 1	=	46
2	60	−30	+ 4	=	34
3	60	−45	+ 9	=	24
4	60	−60	+16	=	16
5	60	−75	+25	=	10
6	60	−90	+36	=	6

Q_d (000s)

Point elasticity can be easily calculated from such a demand equation using calculus. To do this you will need to know the rules of differentiation. Remember the formula for point elasticity:

$$P\epsilon_d = dQ/dP \times P/Q$$

The term dQ/dP can be calculated by differentiating the demand equation:

Given $Q_d = 60 - 15P + P^2$

then $dQ/dP = -15 + 2P$

Thus at a price of 3, for example,

$$dQ/dP = -15 + (2 \times 3)$$

$$= -9$$

Thus price elasticity of demand at a price of 3

$$= -9 \times P/Q$$

$$= -9 \times 3/24$$

$$= -9/8 \text{ (which is elastic)}$$

 Calculate the price elasticity of demand on the above demand curve at a price of (a) 5; (b) 2; (c) 0.

At point *m*, however, $P/Q = 6/20$. Thus:

$$dQ/dP \times P/Q = -5 \times 6/20 = -1.5$$

 These questions still refer to Figure 2.20.
1. What is the price elasticity of demand at points *l* and *k*?
2. What is the price elasticity of demand at the point (a) where the demand curve crosses the vertical axis; (b) where it crosses the horizontal axis?
3. As you move down a straight-line demand curve, what happens to elasticity? Why?
4. Calculate price elasticity of demand between points *n* and *l* using the arc method. Does this give the same answer as the point method? Would it if the demand curve were actually curved?

Price elasticity of supply (Pϵ_s)

This is a measure of the responsiveness of supply to a change in price. We defined it as:

$$P\epsilon_s = \frac{\text{Proportionate (or percentage) change in quantity supplied}}{\text{Proportionate (or percentage) change in price}}$$

In Figure 2.21 curve S_2 is more elastic between any two prices than curve S_1. Thus, when price rises from P_1 to P_2 there is a larger increase in quantity supplied with S_2 (namely Q_1 to Q_3) than there is with S_1 (namely Q_1 to Q_2).

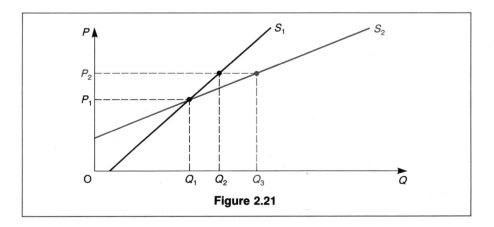

Figure 2.21

Determinants of price elasticity of supply

1. The amount that costs rise as output rises. The less the additional costs of producing additional output, the more firms will be encouraged to produce for a given price rise: the more elastic will supply be.

Supply is thus likely to be elastic if firms have plenty of spare capacity, if they can readily get extra supplies of raw materials, if they can easily switch away from producing alternative products and if they can avoid having to introduce overtime working (at higher rates of pay). If all these conditions hold, costs will be little affected by a rise in output. The less these conditions apply, the less elastic will supply be.

2. Time period (see Figure 2.22)
- Immediate time period. Firms are unlikely to be able to increase supply by much immediately. Supply is virtually fixed, or can only vary according to available stocks. Supply is highly inelastic. In the diagram S_i is drawn with $P\epsilon_s = 0$. If demand increases to D_2, supply will not be able to respond. Price will rise to P_2. Quantity will remain at Q_1. Equilibrium will move to point *b*.
- Short run. If a slightly longer time period is allowed to elapse, some inputs can be increased (e.g. raw materials) while others will remain fixed (e.g. heavy machinery). Supply can increase somewhat. This is illustrated by S_s. Equilibrium will move to point *c* with price falling again, to P_3, and quantity rising to Q_3.
- Long run. In the long run, there will be sufficient time for all inputs to be increased and for new firms to enter the industry. Supply, therefore, is likely to be highly elastic. This is illustrated by curve S_l. Long-run equilibrium will be at point *d* with price falling back even further, to P_4, and quantity rising all the way to Q_4. In some

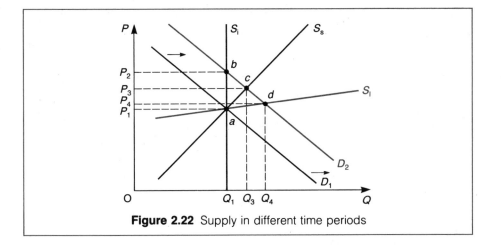

Figure 2.22 Supply in different time periods

circumstances the supply curve may even slope downward. (See the section on economies of scale in Chapter 4.)

The measurement of price elasticity of supply

A vertical supply curve has zero elasticity. It is totally unresponsive to a change in price.

A horizontal supply curve has infinite elasticity. There is no limit to the amount supplied at the price where the curve crosses the vertical axis.

Any straight-line supply curve starting at the origin will have an elasticity equal to 1 throughout its length, *irrespective of its slope*. This perhaps rather surprising result is illustrated in Figure 2.23. This shows three supply curves, each with a different slope, but each starting from the origin. On each curve two points are marked. In each case there is the *same* proportionate rise in Q as in P. For example, in curve S_1 a doubling in price from £3 to £6 leads to a doubling of output from 1 unit to 2 units.

This demonstrates nicely that it is not the *slope* of a curve that determines its elasticity, but its proportionate change.

Figure 2.23 Unit elastic supply curves

Other supply curves' elasticities will vary along their length. In such cases we have to refer to the elasticity either between two points on the curve, or at a specific point. Calculating elasticity between two points will involve the arc method. Calculating elasticity at a point will involve the point method. These two methods are just the same for supply curves as for demand curves: the formulae are the same, only the term Q now refers to quantity supplied rather than quantity demanded.

Formula for price elasticity of supply (arc method)

ΔQ_s/average $Q_s \div$ P/average P

 Given the following supply schedule:

    P: 2 4 6 8 10
    Q: 0 10 20 30 40

(a) Draw the supply curve.
(b) Using the arc method calculate price elasticity of supply (i) between *P* = 2 and *P* = 4; (ii) between *P* = 8 and *P* = 10.
(c) Using the point method, calculate price elasticity of supply at *P* = 6.
(d) Does the elasticity of the supply curve increase or decrease as *P* and *Q* increase? Why?
(e) What would be the answer to (d) if the supply curve had been a straight line but intersecting the horizontal axis to the right of the origin?

Income elasticity of demand ($Y\epsilon_d$)

As was stated above, this is a measure of the responsiveness of demand to a change in income (*Y*). It enables us to predict how much the demand curve will shift for a given change in income. We defined it as:

$$Y\epsilon_d = \frac{\text{Proportionate (or percentage) change in quantity demanded}}{\text{Proportionate (or percentage) change in income}}$$

Determinants of income elasticity of demand

1. Degree of 'necessity' of the good. In a developed country, the demand for luxury goods expands rapidly as people's incomes rise, whereas the demand for basic goods, such as bread, only rises a little. Thus items such as cars and foreign holidays have a high income elasticity of demand, whereas items such as potatoes and bus journeys have a low income elasticity of demand.

The demand for some goods actually decreases as income rises. These are inferior goods such as cheap margarine. As people earn more, so they switch to butter or better quality margarine. Inferior goods have a negative income elasticity of demand.

 Look ahead to Box 11.2 (page 420). It shows the income elasticity of demand for various foodstuffs. Explain the difference in the figures for fresh potatoes, bread and fruit juices.

2. The rate at which the desire for a good is satisfied as consumption increases. The more quickly people become satisfied, the less their demand will expand as income increases.

3. The level of income of consumers. Poor people will respond differently from rich people to a rise in their incomes. For example, for a given rise in income, poor people may buy a lot more butter, whereas rich people may buy only a little more.

Income elasticity of demand is an important concept to firms considering the future size of the market for their product. If the product has a high income elasticity of demand, sales are likely to expand rapidly as national income rises, but may also fall significantly if the economy moves into recession.

Box 2.6

Income Elasticity and the Balance of Payments

A problem for certain Third World countries

When people are poor they have to spend a large proportion of their income on basic goods such as food. As they get richer, so they can afford to buy an increasing proportion of luxury goods. This means that the income elasticity of demand for basic goods is likely to be low: their demand only rises slowly as incomes rise. The income elasticity of demand for luxury goods, on the other hand, is likely to be high.

This has important implications for international trade. If a country exports basic goods with a low income elasticity of demand, and imports luxury goods with a high income elasticity of demand, it is likely to run into long-term balance of payments problems.

As it grows richer, its demand for imports is likely to grow rapidly. As the rest of the world grows richer, however, so the demand for the country's exports is likely to grow slowly.

This has been one of the problems facing many developing countries. As exporters of commodities such as rice, sugar and tea, they have found that the demand for their exports has grown relatively slowly. As importers of manufactured products, however, their imports have grown relatively rapidly.

This affects their *terms of trade*. The terms of trade are the average price of a country's exports divided by the average price of its imports. If the demand for exports grows only slowly relative to imports, so the price of exports is likely to fall relative to imports: the terms of trade will deteriorate.

In 1985 the terms of trade for developing countries as a whole (excluding oil exporters) were only 74 per cent of their 1960 level, whereas the terms of trade for developed market economies were 86 per cent of their 1960 level.[2]

A word of caution: income elasticity of demand is only *one* factor influencing the level of a country's imports and exports, and only *one* factor determining its terms of trade.

? Would you expect the demand for Third World raw material exports to grow rapidly or slowly *over time*? Does their growth over time give a good indication as to their income elasticity of demand?

[2] See *Handbook of International Trade and Development Statistics: 1986* (United Nations Conference on Trade and Development, UNCTAD).

Cross-price elasticity of demand ($C\epsilon_{d_{ab}}$)

This is often known by it less cumbersome title of cross elasticity of demand. As explained above, it is a measure of the responsiveness of demand for one product to a change in the price of another (either a substitute or a complement). It enables us to predict how much the demand curve for the first product will shift when the price of the second product changes. We defined it as:

$$C\epsilon_{d_{ab}} = \frac{\text{Proportionate (or percentage) change in demand for good a}}{\text{Proportionate (or percentage) change in price of good b}}$$

If good b is a *substitute* for good a, a's demand will *rise* as b's price rises. For example, the demand for pork will rise as the price of beef rises. In this case, cross elasticity will be a positive figure. If b is *complementary* to a, however, a's demand will *fall* as b's price rises and thus as the quantity of b demanded falls. For example, the demand for petrol falls as the price of cars rises. In this case, cross elasticity of demand will be a negative figure.

The major determinant of cross elasticity of demand is the closeness of the substitute or complement. The closer it is, the bigger will be the effect on the first good of a change in the price of the substitute or complement, and hence the greater the cross elasticity – either positive or negative.

Firms will wish to know the cross elasticity of demand for their product when considering the effect on the demand for their product of a change in the price of a rival's product or of a complementary product. These are vital pieces of information for firms when making their production plans.

Another example of the usefulness of the concept of cross elasticity of demand is in the field of international trade and the balance of payments. A government will wish to know how a change in domestic prices will affect the demand for imports. If there is a high cross elasticity of demand for imports (because they are close substitutes for home-produced goods), and if prices at home rise due to inflation, the demand for imports will rise substantially, thus worsening the balance of payments.

 Which are likely to have the highest cross elasticity of demand: two brands of coffee, or coffee and tea?

▲ SUMMARY

1. Elasticity is a measure of the responsiveness of demand (or supply) to a change in one of the determinants.
2. It is defined as the proportionate change in quantity demanded (or supplied) divided by the proportionate change in the determinant.
3. If quantity changes proportionately more than the determinant, the figure for elasticity will be greater than 1 (ignoring the sign): it is elastic. If the quantity changes proportionately less than the determinant, the figure for elasticity will be less than 1: it is inelastic. If they change by the same proportion, the elasticity has a value of 1: it is unit elastic.
4. Price elasticity of demand measures the responsiveness of demand to a change in price. Given that demand curves are downward sloping, price elasticity of demand will have a negative value. Demand will be more elastic the greater the number and closeness of substitute goods, the higher the proportion of income spent on the good and the longer the time period that elapses after the change in price.
5. When demand is price elastic, a rise in price will lead to a reduction in total expenditure on the good and hence a reduction in the total revenue of producers.
6. Demand curves normally have different elasticities along their length. We can thus normally only refer to the specific value for elasticity between two points on the curve or at a single point.
7. Elasticity measured between two points is known as *arc*

elasticity. When applied to price elasticity of demand the formula is:

$$\frac{\Delta Q_d}{\text{average } Q_d} \div \frac{\Delta P}{\text{average } P}$$

*8. Elasticity measured at a point is known as *point elasticity*. When applied to price elasticity of demand the formula is:

$$\frac{dQ}{dP} \times \frac{P}{Q}$$

where dQ/dP is the inverse of the slope of the tangent to the demand curve at the point in question.
9. Price elasticity of supply measures the responsiveness of supply to a change in price. It has a positive value. Supply will be more elastic the less costs per unit rise as output rises and the longer the time period.
10. Income elasticity of demand measures the responsiveness of demand to a change in income. For normal goods it has a positive value. Demand will be more income elastic the more luxurious the good and the less rapidly demand is satisfied as consumption increases.
11. Cross-price elasticity of demand measures the responsiveness of demand for one good to a change in the price of another. For substitute goods the value will be positive for complements it will be negative. The cross-price elasticity will be higher the closer the two goods are as substitutes or complements.

2.5 The time dimension

The full adjustment of price, demand and supply to a situation of disequilibrium will not be instantaneous. It is necessary, therefore, to analyse the time path which supply takes in responding to changes in demand, and which demand takes in responding to changes in supply.

Short-run and long-run adjustment

As we saw in the previous section, elasticity varies with the time period under consideration. The reason is that producers and consumers take time to respond to a change in price. The longer the time period, the bigger the response, and thus the greater the elasticity of supply and demand.

This is illustrated in Figures 2.24 and 2.25. In both cases, as equilibrium moves from points *a* to *b* to *c*, there is a large short-run price change (P_1 to P_2) and a small short-run quantity change (Q_1 to Q_2), but a small long-run price change (P_1 to P_3) and a large long-run quantity change (Q_1 to Q_3).

Figure 2.24
Response of supply to an increase in demand

Figure 2.25
Response of demand to an increase in supply

Time lags in production: the cobweb

When goods take a time to produce, there will be a time lag between a change in production decisions and a change in the actual supply coming on to the market. Thus the actual supply at one time will depend on that planned at a previous time. For example, the quantity that farmers harvest now will depend on what they planted earlier.

Since supply decisions depend on price, supply at any time will depend on price at a previous time.

These time lags can lead to price fluctuations. This is illustrated in Figure 2.26: the cobweb diagram. Two important assumptions are made:

- Firms' production plans, once made, are fully carried out: they end up supplying precisely the amount they had planned to.
- There is an initial disequilibrium in the market: either demand or supply has shifted. The result is that price is now above the intersection of the new demand and supply curves.

The diagrams show just the new demand and supply curves. Note that the supply curve is the *planned* supply curve. The *actual* supply coming on to the market will be the amount planned in the previous time period.

Assume that the initial (disequilibrium) price is P_1. At P_1 producers plan to supply Q_1. Thus in the next time period Q_1 is actually supplied. But in order for Q_1 to be sold, price falls to P_2. Producers, seeing that price has fallen to P_2, now only plan to supply Q_2 for the next time period. So in the next time period Q_2 duly comes on to the market. Price now has to rise to P_3 to clear the market.

Cobweb diagram

A diagram showing the path of price and quantity adjustment over time, given a lag between the decision to supply and the goods coming to market. The path has a shape like a cobweb.

Box 2.7

Adjusting to Oil Price Shocks
Short-run and long-run demand and supply responses

Between December 1973 and June 1974, the Organiz-ation of Petroleum Exporting Countries (OPEC) put up the price of oil from $3 to $12 per barrel. It was further raised to over $30 in 1979. In the late 1980s the price fluctuated, but the trend was downward. By the late 1980s the price had fallen to around $10 per barrel: in real terms (i.e. after correcting for inflation), roughly the level prior to 1973.

The price movements can be explained using simple demand and supply analysis.

The initial rise in price

(a) An initial restriction of supply

OPEC raised the price from P_1 to P_2. To prevent a surplus at that price, OPEC members restricted their output by agreed amounts. This had the effect of shifting the supply curve to S_2, with Q_2 being produced. This reduction in output needed to be only relatively small because the short-run demand for oil was highly price inelastic: for most uses there are no substitutes in the short run.

Long-run effects on demand

The long-run demand for oil was more elastic. With high oil prices persisting, people tried to find ways of cutting back on consumption. People bought smaller cars. They converted to gas or solid-fuel central heating. Firms switched to other fuels. Less use was made of oil-fired power stations for electricity generation. Energy-saving schemes became widespread both in firms and in the home.

(b) Long-run demand response

This had the effect of shifting the short-run demand curve from D_1 to D_2. Price fell back from P_2 to P_3. This gave a long-run demand curve of D_l: the curve that joins points A and C.

The fall in demand was made bigger by a world recession in the early 1980s.

Long-run effects on supply

With oil production so much more profitable, there was an incentive for non-OPEC oil producers to produce oil. Prospecting went on all over the world and large oil fields were discovered and opened up in the North Sea, Alaska, Mexico, China and elsewhere.

In addition, OPEC members were tempted to break their 'quotas' (their allotted output) and sell more oil.

The net effect was an increase in world oil supplies. This is shown by a shift in the supply curve to S_3. Equilibrium price thus fell back to P_1 (point D).

(c) Long-run supply response

Note that the supply curves in these diagrams are all *short-run* supply curves, since each one shows supply for a particular number of oil fields.

Drawing a long-run supply curve is more difficult: it depends when in the story we start and what assumptions we make.

We could draw a long-run supply curve linking points E and F. The reasoning is as follows. After the limiting of supply to S_2, OPEC members would have supplied at point E, had the price remained at P_1. After some years with the price set at P_2 or thereabouts, more suppliers enter the market. The supply curve shifts to S_3. Had the demand curve not shifted, equilibrium would then have moved to point F: the intersection of S_3 and the original demand. A long-run supply curve thus links points E and F.

? Given the fall in demand to D_2, and the fall in price back towards original levels, what is likely to happen to the position of the (short-run) supply curve?

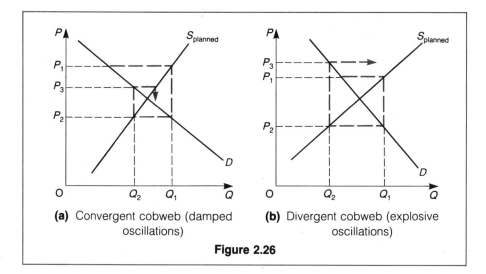

(a) Convergent cobweb (damped oscillations)　　　**(b)** Divergent cobweb (explosive oscillations)

Figure 2.26

This process continues with both price and quantity oscillating.

Whether these oscillations get smaller or larger depends on the shape of the demand and supply curves. If the supply curve is steeper than the demand curve (Figure 2.26(a)), the oscillations will be damped: they will get smaller over time. This is called a convergent cobweb. If the demand curve is steeper than the supply curve, however, the oscillations will be explosive: they will get larger over time. This is called a divergent cobweb

In practice, cobwebs will not be as clear cut as in the diagram since:

- Producers may anticipate price fluctuations and not simply rely on current prices.
- Demand and supply curves may shift in the meantime.
- There may be a lag in demand adjustment as well as in supply adjustment.
- Plans may not be fulfilled. For example, farmers may experience a better or worse harvest than anticipated.
- Producers may use stocks. They may draw on stocks when prices are high and build stocks when prices are low. Thus supply released on to the market will not fluctuate so much. This in turn will reduce price fluctuations.

Convergent cobweb

A cobweb where the path converges on the equilibrium point. The price oscillations get smaller over time.

Divergent cobweb

A cobweb where the path gets further and further away from the 'equilibrium' point. The price oscillations get larger over time.

 Go through each of these qualifications and explain how they would affect the cobweb diagram.

Nevertheless cobweb effects have been observed in various markets. Historically, 'hog' cycles and potato cycles have been identified which show clear fluctuations in pig meat and potato prices.

Speculation

In a world of shifting demand and supply curves, prices do not stay the same. Sometimes they go up; sometimes they come down. We have just seen this in the case of the cobweb theory, where prices of foodstuffs can oscillate up and down.

If prices are likely to change in the foreseeable future, this will affect the behaviour of buyers and sellers *now*. If, for example, it is now December and you are thinking of buying a new winter coat, you might decide to wait until the January sales, and in the meantime make do with your old coat. If, on the other hand, when January comes you see a new summer dress in the sales, you might well buy it now and not wait until the summer for fear that the price will have gone up by then. Thus a belief that prices will go up will cause people to buy now; a belief that prices will come down will cause them to wait.

The reverse applies to sellers. If you are thinking of selling your house and prices are falling, you will want to sell it as quickly as possible. If, on the other hand, prices are rising sharply, you will wait as long as possible so as to get the highest price. Thus a belief that prices will come down will cause people to sell now; a belief that prices will go up will cause them to wait.

Speculation

Where people make buying or selling decisions based on their anticipations of future prices.

This behaviour of looking into the future and making buying and selling decisions based on your predictions is called speculation. Speculation is often based on current trends in price behaviour. If prices are currently rising, people may then try to decide whether they are about to peak and go back down again, or whether they are likely to go on rising. Having made their prediction, they will then act on it. This speculation will thus affect demand and supply, which in turn will affect price. Speculation is commonplace in many markets: the stock exchange, the foreign exchange market and the housing market are three examples.

Self-fulfilling speculation

The actions of speculators tend to cause the very effect that they had anticipated.

Speculation tends to be self-fulfilling. In other words, the actions of speculators tend to bring about the very effect on prices that speculators had anticipated. For example, if speculators believe that the price of ICI shares is about to rise, they will buy more ICI shares. But by doing this they will ensure that the price *will* rise. The prophecy has become self-fulfilling.

Speculation can either help to reduce price fluctuations or aggravate them: it can be stabilizing or destabilizing.

Stabilizing speculation

Stabilizing speculation

Where the actions of speculators tend to reduce price fluctuations.

Speculation will tend to have a stabilizing effect on price fluctuations when suppliers and/or demanders believe that a change in price is only *temporary*.

An initial fall *in price.* In Figure 2.27 demand has shifted from D_1 to D_2; equilibrium has moved from point *a* to point *b*, and price has fallen to P_2. How do people react to this fall in price?

Given that they believe this fall in price to be only temporary, suppliers *hold back*, expecting prices to rise again: supply shifts from S_1 to S_2. After all, why supply now when, by waiting, they could get a higher price?

Buyers *increase* their purchases, to take advantage of the temporary fall in price. Demand shifts from D_2 to D_3.

The equilibrium moves to point *c*, with price rising back towards P_1.

An initial rise *in price.* In Figure 2.28 demand has shifted from D_1 to D_2. Price has risen from P_1 to P_2.

Suppliers bring their goods to market now, before price falls again. Supply shifts from S_1 to S_2. Demanders, however, hold back until price falls. Demand shifts from D_2 to D_3. The equilibrium moves to point *c*, with price falling back towards P_1.

A good example of stabilizing speculation is that which occurs in agricultural commodity markets. Take the case of wheat. When it is harvested in the autumn there will be a plentiful supply. If all this wheat were to be put on the market, the price would fall to a very low level. Later in the year, when most of the wheat would have been sold, the price would then rise to a very high level. This is all easily predictable.

So what do farmers do? The answer is that they speculate. When the wheat is harvested they know price will tend to fall, and so instead of bringing it all to market

Figure 2.27 Stabilizing speculation: initial price fall

Figure 2.28 Stabilizing speculation: initial price rise

they put a lot of it into store. The more price falls, the more they will put into store *anticipating that the price will later rise*. But this holding back of supplies prevents prices from falling. In other words, it stabilizes prices.

Later in the year, when the price begins to rise, they will gradually release grain on to the market from the stores. The more the price rises, the more they will release on to the market *anticipating that the price will fall again by the time of the next harvest*. But this releasing of supplies will again stabilize prices by preventing them from rising so much.

Rather than the farmers doing the speculation, it could be done by grain merchants. When there is a glut of wheat in the autumn, and prices are relatively low, they buy wheat on the grain market and put it into store. When there is a shortage in the spring and summer they sell wheat from their stores. In this way they stabilize prices just as the farmers did when they were the ones who operated the stores.

> **?** Would speculation help to stabilize the price fluctuations associated with the cobweb described in the previous section? How would speculation work here?

Destabilizing speculation

Speculation will tend to have a destabilizing effect on price fluctuations when suppliers and/or buyers believe that a change in price heralds similar changes to come.

An initial fall in price. In Figure 2.29 demand has shifted from D_1 to D_2 and price has fallen from P_1 to P_2. This time, believing that the fall in price heralds further falls

Destabilizing speculation
Where the actions of speculators tend to make price movements larger.

Figure 2.29 Destabilizing speculation: initial price fall

Figure 2.30 Destabilizing speculation: initial price rise

in price to come, suppliers sell now before the price does fall. Supply shifts from S_1 to S_2. And demanders wait: they wait until price does fall further. Demand shifts from D_2 to D_3.

Their actions ensure that price does fall further: to P_3.

An initial rise in price. In Figure 2.30 a price rise from P_1 to P_2 is caused by a rise in demand from D_1 to D_2. Suppliers wait until price rises further. Supply shifts from S_1 to S_2. Demanders buy now before any further rise in price. Demand shifts from D_2 to D_3.

As a result price continues to rise: to P_3.

Conclusion

In some circumstances, then, the action of speculators can help to keep price fluctuations to a minimum (stabilizing speculation). This is most likely when markets are relatively stable in the first place, with only moderate underlying shifts in demand and supply.

In other circumstances, however, speculation can make price fluctuations much worse. This is most likely in times of uncertainty, when there are significant changes in the determinants of demand and supply. Given this uncertainty, people may see price changes as signifying some trend. They then 'jump on the bandwagon' and do what the rest are doing, and further fuel the rise or fall in price.

 Redraw each of Figures 2.27–2.30, only this time assume that it was an initial shift in supply that caused price to change in the first place.

Dealing with uncertainty and risk

When price changes are likely to occur, buyers and sellers will try to anticipate them. Unfortunately, on many occasions no one can be certain just what these price changes will be. Take the case of stocks and shares. If you anticipate that the price of, say, BP shares is likely to go up substantially in the near future, you may well decide to buy some now and then sell them later after the price has risen. But you cannot be certain that they will go up in price: they may fall instead. If you buy the shares, therefore, you will be taking a gamble.

Now gambles can be of two types. The first is where you know the odds. Let us take the simplest case of a gamble on the toss of a coin. Heads you win; tails you lose. You know that the odds of winning are precisely 50 per cent. If you bet on the toss of a coin you are said to be operating under conditions of risk. *Risk is when the probability of an outcome is known.*

The second form of gamble is the more usual. This is where the odds are not known or are known only roughly. Gambling on the stock exchange is like this. You may have a good idea that a share will go up in price, but is it a 90 per cent chance, an 80 per cent chance or what? You are not certain. Gambling under this sort of condition is known as operating under uncertainty. *This is when the probability of an outcome is not known.*

You may well disapprove of gambling and want to dismiss people who engage in it as foolish or morally wrong. But 'gambling' is not just confined to horses, cards, roulette and the like. Risk and uncertainty pervade the whole of economic life, and decisions are constantly having to be made whose outcome cannot be known for certain. Even the most morally upright person will still have to decide which career to go into, whether and when to buy a house, or even something as trivial as whether or

Risk

When an outcome may or may not occur, but its probability of occurring is known.

Uncertainty

When an outcome may or may not occur and its probability of occurring is not known.

Box 2.8

The 1987 Stock Market Crash
The effects of speculation

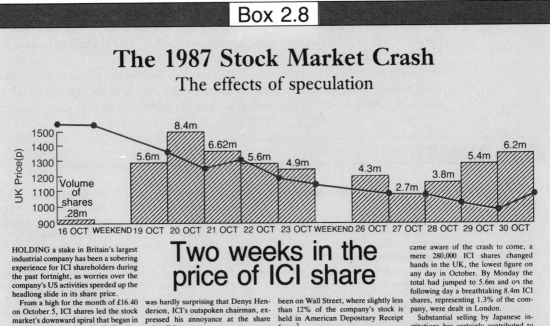

Two weeks in the price of ICI share

HOLDING a stake in Britain's largest industrial company has been a sobering experience for ICI shareholders during the past fortnight, as worries over the company's US activities speeded up the headlong slide in its share price.

From a high for the month of £16.40 on October 5, ICI shares led the stock market's downward spiral that began in earnest on "Black Monday", October 19, and hit a low of £9.89 at close of business in London on Thursday.

That trough was reached as the rest of the market began to turn upwards and the group unveiled a 38% profit leap to £1 billion for the nine months to the end of September.

With profits now firmly on course for a full-year total of around £1.3 billion it

was hardly surprising that Denys Henderson, ICI's outspoken chairman, expressed his annoyance at the share price slide.

America accounts for a quarter of the group's worldwide sales, leaving it heavily exposed to a weakening of the dollar. On top of that, there is concern that a slowing of American economic growth in 1988 will be followed by an eco-nomic downturn.

So it is perhaps surprising how small the volume of trading in ICI shares has

been on Wall Street, where slightly less than 12% of the company's stock is held in American Depositary Receipt form.[3]

During th epast month the number of ADRs traded daily has averaged 184,000, the equivalent of 736,000 shares since each ADR represents four shares. A peak was reached on Friday, October 16, the first day of the crash on Wall Street, when the equivalent of 2.4m shares were traded.

The same day, before London be-

came aware of the crash to come, a mere 280,000 ICI shares changed hands in the UK, the lowest figure on any day in October. By Monday the total had jumped to 5.6m and on the following day a breathtaking 8.4m ICI shares, representing 1.3% of the company, were dealt in London.

Substantial selling by Japanese institutions has certainly contributed to the ICI share price collapse, but followers of the company in the City do not believe that this has been matched by any great wave of selling by American or British institutions.

Friday's recovery in the price, when it closed at £10.74, up 85p on the day, suggests that ICI may outperform the market on the way up as well as down.

[3] An ADR is a bearer certificate entitling the holder to ownership of shares deposited for safekeeping with a bank in the USA.

---

not to take an umbrella when going out. Each of these decisions and thousands of others are made under conditions of uncertainty (or occasionally risk).

 Give some examples of decisions you have taken recently that were made under conditions of uncertainty. With hindsight do you think you made the right decisions?

We shall be examining how risk and uncertainty affect economic decisions on several occasions throughout the book. For example, in the next chapter we will see how it affects people's attitudes and actions as consumers and how taking out insurance can help to reduce their uncertainty. At this point, however, let us focus on firms' attitudes when supplying goods.

A simple way that suppliers can reduce risks is by holding stocks. Take the case of the wheat farmers we saw in the previous section. At the time when they are planting the wheat in the spring, they are uncertain as to what the price of wheat will be when they bring it to market. If they keep no stores of wheat, they will just have to accept whatever the market price happens to be at harvest time. If, however, they have storage facilities, they can put the wheat into store if the price is low and then wait until it goes up. Alternatively, if the price of wheat is high at harvest time, they can sell it straight away. In other words, they can wait until the price is right.

Although the keeping of stocks will substantially reduce uncertainty, it can never eliminate it. The farmer when planting the wheat cannot know just how good a harvest it will be. If it is a very good harvest, the market price is likely to remain low for a long time after the harvest, since farmers generally have full barns and are all anxious to sell the moment prices begin to rise. Also there is the problem that storage costs money. Thus the farmer must weigh up the possible benefits in terms of higher prices of waiting longer before selling against the additional storage costs involved.

▲ SUMMARY

1. A complete understanding of markets must take into account the time dimension.
2. Given that producers and consumers take a time to respond fully to price changes, we can identify different equilibria after the lapse of different lengths of time. Generally, short-run supply and demand tend to be less price elastic than long-run supply and demand. As a result any shifts in *D* or *S* curves tend to have a relatively bigger effect on price in the short run and a relatively bigger effect on quantity in the long run.
3. If there is a time lag between the decision to supply and the supply coming on to the market, price oscillations are likely to occur. High prices cause producers to plan to supply more. This extra supply when it comes on to the market depresses market price. Producers respond by

planning to produce less. When this reduced supply comes to market, market price will rise again. The path that these oscillations trace out on a demand and supply diagram is shaped like a cobweb. These cobwebs can be convergent or divergent depending on the shape of the demand and supply curves.

4. People often anticipate price changes and this will affect the amount they demand or supply. This speculation will tend to stabilize price fluctuations if people believe that the price changes are only temporary. However, speculation will tend to destabilize these fluctuations (i.e. make them more severe) if people believe that prices are likely to continue to move in the same direction as at present (at least for some time).

2.6 Government intervention in competitive markets

Forms of government intervention in the market

Futures market

A market in which contracts are made to buy or sell at some future date at a price agreed today.

The real world is one of *mixed* economies. The government intervenes in many markets, even markets which are highly competitive. This intervention can take a number of forms:

- Fixing prices, either above or below the free-market equilibrium.
- Taxing the production or sale of various goods.
- Subsidizing the production or sale of various goods.
- Taking over production. The government could nationalize various industries or run them directly from a government department (e.g. defence and health).
- Regulation. Various laws could be passed to regulate the behaviour of firms. For example, various activities, such as the dumping of toxic waste, could be made illegal; or licences or official permission might have to be obtained to produce certain goods; or a regulatory body could supervise the activities of various firms and prevent any that it felt to be against the public interest (e.g. the production of unsafe children's toys).

Supply and demand analysis is a useful tool for examining the effects of government intervention. The rest of this chapter applies the analysis to two types of intervention: price control and taxation.

The control of prices

At the equilibrium price, there will be no shortage or surplus. The equilibrium price, however, may not be the most desirable price. The government, therefore, may prefer to keep prices above or below the equilibrium price.

If the government sets a minimum price above the equilibrium (a price floor), there will be a surplus: $Q_s - Q_d$ in Figure 2.31. Price will not be allowed to fall to eliminate this surplus.

If the government sets a maximum price below the equilibrium (a price ceiling), there will be a shortage: $Q_d - Q_s$ in Figure 2.32. Price will not be allowed to rise to eliminate this shortage.

Setting a minimum (high) price

The government sets minimum prices to prevent them from falling below a certain level. It may do this for various reasons:

- To protect producers' incomes. If the industry is subject to supply fluctuations (e.g. crops, due to fluctuations in weather) and if industry demand is price inelastic, prices are likely to fluctuate severely. Minimum prices will prevent the fall in producers' incomes that would accompany periods of low prices.
- To create a surplus (e.g. of grains) – particularly in periods of glut – which can be stored in preparation for possible future shortages.
- In the case of wages (the price of labour), minimum wages legislation can be used to prevent workers' incomes from falling below a certain level.

> **?** Draw a supply and demand diagram with the price of labour (the wage rate) on the vertical axis and the quantity of labour (the number of workers) on the horizontal axis. What will happen to employment if the government raises wages from the equilibrium to some minimum wage above the equilibrium?

There are various methods that the government can use to deal with the surpluses associated with minimum prices.

- The government could buy the surplus and either store it, destroy it or sell it abroad in other markets.

Minimum price

A price floor set by the government or some other agency. The price is not allowed to fall below this level (although it is allowed to rise above it).

Maximum price

A price ceiling set by the government or some other agency. The price is not allowed to rise above this level (although it is allowed to fall below it).

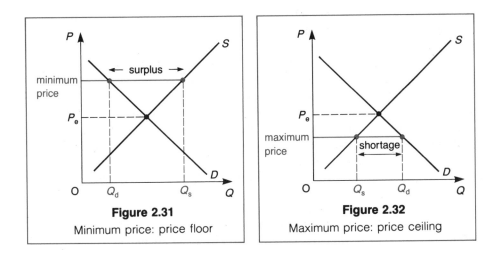

Figure 2.31
Minimum price: price floor

Figure 2.32
Maximum price: price ceiling

- Supply could be artificially lowered by restricting producers to particular quotas. In Figure 2.31, supply could therefore be reduced to Q_d.
- Demand could be raised by advertising, by finding alternative uses for the good, or by cutting down on substitute goods (e.g. by imposing taxes or quotas on substitutes, such as imports).

One of the problems with minimum prices is that firms with surpluses on their hands may try to evade the price control and cut their prices. It is possible that the minimum price was not set by the government, but by an agreement between firms in an attempt to keep their profits up. Here, too, there is the temptation for individual firms to break the agreement and undercut their rivals. This issue is examined in Chapter 6. (Note that in cases where firms can choose what prices to charge, simple supply and demand analysis needs to be replaced by a more sophisticated analysis. This is examined in Chapters 5 and 6.)

Another problem is that high prices may cushion inefficiency. Firms may feel less need to find more efficient methods of production and to cut their costs if their profits are being protected by the high price. Also the high price may discourage firms from producing alternative goods which they could produce more efficiently or which are in higher demand, but which nevertheless have a lower (free-market) price.

Setting a maximum (low) price

The government sets maximum prices to prevent them from rising above a certain level. This will normally be done for reasons of fairness. In wartime, or times of famine, the government may set maximum prices for basic goods so that poor people can afford to buy them.

The resulting shortages, however, create further problems. If the government merely sets prices and does not intervene further, the shortages will lead to:

- Allocation on a 'first come, first served' basis. This is likely to lead to queues developing, or firms adopting waiting lists. Queues have been a common feature of life in East European countries where governments have kept prices below the level necessary to equate demand and supply. In recent years, as part of their economic reforms, they have allowed prices to rise. This has had the obvious benefit of reducing or eliminating queues, but at the same time it has made life very hard for those on low incomes.
- Firms deciding which customers should be allowed to buy: for example, giving preference to regular customers.

Rationing

Where the government restricts the amount of a good that people are allowed to buy.

Black markets

Where people ignore the government's price and/or quantity controls and sell illegally at whatever price equates illegal demand and supply.

Neither of the above may be considered to be fair. Certain needy people may be forced to go without. Therefore, the government may adopt a system of rationing.

A major problem with maximum prices is likely to be the emergence of black markets, where customers, unable to buy enough in legal markets, may well be prepared to pay very high prices: prices above P_e in Figure 2.32. (See Box 2.10.)

Another problem is that the maximum prices reduce the quantity produced of an already scarce commodity. For example, artificially low prices in a famine are likely to reduce food supplies: if not immediately, then at the next harvest, because of less being sown.

To minimize these problems the government may attempt to reduce the shortage by encouraging supply: by drawing on stores, by direct government production, or by giving subsidies or tax relief to firms. Alternatively, it may attempt to reduce demand:

Box 2.9

Rationing
An alternative to the price mechanism

Given the problem of scarcity – the excess of human wants over available supplies – there has to be some mechanism for allocating scarce resources. The market is one such mechanism. Shortages are eliminated by prices rising to the level where demand equals supply.

Such a system, however, might be regarded as unfair. Those who can afford the most get the most.

The problem of a fair distribution of resources is particularly acute in wartime. Supplies are likely to be reduced and hence equilibrium prices would rise. Anticipating such price rises, consumers would hoard goods. This would magnify the shortage problem and drive prices up even further.

As a result, governments in wartime usually introduce some form of *rationing*. Rationing (originally a military term) is a system whereby each individual is allocated a *fair* share of scarce supplies. By limiting demand in this way, prices are kept down.

During the First World War (1914–18), rationing was not introduced until 1917. Sugar was rationed in 1917, and meat and lard in 1918. By 1920 all rationing had been abolished.

By contrast the Second World War (1939–45) saw rationing start as early as 1940 and continue in a somewhat limited fashion after 1945 right up until 1954. A number of different rationing systems were used.

Priority rationing entitled consumers to buy, through their holding of coupons, a fixed weekly amount of food. This system applied from 1940 to meat, bacon, sugar, fats and tea, and was extended to cheese, milk and eggs in 1941.

Other goods, however, were rationed under a *points*

system, whereby each consumer received a number of points every four weeks to spend as desired. Each food which was not under priority rationing was given a points value, calculated so as to reflect the expected demand in relation to supply. Thus luxury goods such as canned salmon had high points values, whereas cereals had low values. In June 1941 each individual was given 66 points per four-week period, which reflected 66 per cent of pre-war average consumption. Towards the end of the war this fell to only 48 points per consumer.

The points system of rationing was also applied to other goods such as footwear and clothing. A complete suit would have cost you a massive 32 points! Hence individuals, within the limits of not only their money income but also their points income, were free to allocate their expenditure as they chose.

In conjunction with the more formal process of rationing, other foods and goods were subject to what was called *controlled distribution*. Milk, for example, went to priority consumers, such as mothers and children up to five years old, who were guaranteed 7 pints a week. Seeing that supply was uncertain, once the guaranteed quota for priority consumers was distributed, the ordinary consumer got allocations as and when supplies allowed.

The rationing system in Britain was gradually phased out after the war, but it was not until 1954 that meat and bacon were finally decontrolled.

? Under which of the three systems described above would price control be necessary if high prices were to be avoided?

---

by the production of more alternative goods (e.g. homegrown vegetables in times of war) or by controlling people's incomes.

 Think of some examples where the price of a good or service is kept below the equilibrium (e.g. rent controls). In each case consider the advantages and disadvantages of the policy.

The effect of imposing taxes on goods

Another example of government intervention in markets is the imposition of taxes on goods. These indirect taxes, as they are called, include taxes such as value added tax (VAT) and excise duties on cigarettes, petrol and alcoholic drinks. These taxes can be a fixed amount per unit sold – specific tax. An example is the tax per litre of petrol.

Indirect tax

A tax on the expenditure on goods. Indirect taxes include value added tax (VAT) and duties on tobacco, alcoholic drinks and petrol. These taxes are not paid directly by the consumer, but indirectly via the sellers of the good. Indirect taxes contrast with *direct taxes* (such as income tax) which are paid directly out of people's incomes.

Box 2.10

Black Markets
A consequence of low fixed prices

When the government fixes prices a *black market* is likely to result. A black market is one where sellers ignore the government's price restrictions. But why is it in their interest to do so, given that they probably run the risk of fines or even imprisonment?

Take the case of wartime price controls. The government set maximum prices for many essential items that were in short supply. This is illustrated in the diagram.

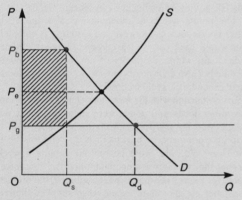

The effect of price control on black-market prices

The unacceptably high equilibrium price is P_e. The price fixed by the government is P_g. But at P_g there is a shortage of $Q_d - Q_s$. To deal with the shortage, either the government will have to accept queues, or shops only selling to 'regular' customers; or alternatively a system of rationing will have to be introduced.

But whichever system is adopted, one thing is clear: many consumers would be prepared to pay a price considerably above P_g in order to get hold of the good. The demand curve shows this: the less the supply, the higher up the demand curve will the equilibrium price be.

This is where black marketeers come in. Provided they can get supplies (maybe by some shady dealing), provided they can have access to consumers, provided consumers are willing to break the law, and provided they can escape detection, black marketeers can charge a price considerably above P_g. But what price can they charge?

Take the extreme case. Assume that the black marketeers buy up *all* the supply (Q_s) from the producers at the official price and then sell it at a price that clears the market. The black-market price will be P_b: at that price demand is equal to Q_s. The black marketeers gain the extra revenue shown by the shaded area.

In practice, of course, many people will get their supplies from official sources, and pay only P_g. On the other hand, if black marketeers are few in number and only have limited supplies, they could sell them at very high prices: above P_b even.

During the Second World War, 'spivs' (as these black marketeers were called) could often charge extortionately high prices for such items as nylon stockings and coffee.

? 1. What would be the effect on black market prices of a rise in the official price?
2. Will a system of low official prices plus a black market be more equitable or less equitable than a system of free markets?

Specific tax

An indirect tax of a fixed sum per unit sold.

Ad valorem tax

An indirect tax of a certain *percentage* of the price of the good.

Alternatively, they can be a percentage of the price or value added at each stage of production – an ad valorem tax. An example is VAT.

When a tax is imposed on a good, this will have the effect of shifting the supply curve upward by the amount of the tax (see Figure 2.33). In the case of a specific tax, it will be a parallel shift, since the amount of the tax is the same at all prices. In the case of an ad valorem tax, the curve will *swing* upward. At a zero price there would be no tax and hence no shift in the supply curve. As price rises, so the gap between the original and new supply curves will widen, since a given *percentage* tax will be a larger *absolute* amount the higher the price.

But why does the supply curve shift upward by the amount of the tax? This is illustrated in Figure 2.34. To be persuaded to produce the same quantity as before the imposition of the tax (i.e. Q_1), firms must now receive a price which allows them fully to recoup the tax they have to pay (i.e. $P_1 + $ tax).

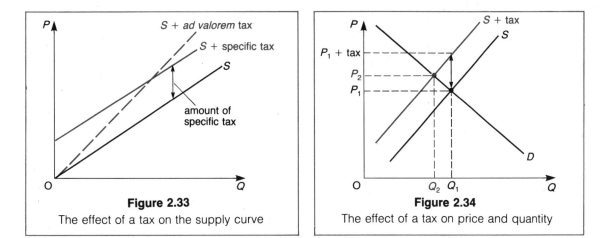

Figure 2.33

The effect of a tax on the supply curve

Figure 2.34

The effect of a tax on price and quantity

The effect of the tax is to raise price and reduce quantity. Price will not rise by the full amount of the tax, however, because the demand curve is downward sloping. In Figure 2.34, price only rises to P_2. Thus the burden or incidence of such taxes is distributed between consumers and producers. Consumers pay to the extent that price rises. Producers pay to the extent that this rise in price is not sufficient to cover the tax.

Incidence of tax

The distribution of the burden of tax between sellers and buyers.

Elasticity and the incidence of taxation

The incidence of indirect taxes depends on the elasticity of demand and supply of the commodity in question. Consider cases (1)–(4) in Figure 2.35.

In each of the diagrams (which are all drawn to the same scale), the size of the tax is the same: the supply curve shifts upward by the same amount. Price rises to P_2 in each case and quantity falls to Q_2; but as you can see, the size of this increase in price and decrease in quantity differs in each case, depending on the price elasticity of demand and supply.

The total tax revenue is given by the amount of tax per unit (the vertical difference between the two supply curves) multiplied by the new amount sold (Q_2). This is shown as the total shaded area in each case in Figure 2.35.

The rise in price from P_1 to P_2 multiplied by Q_2 (the red area) is the amount of the tax passed on to consumers and thus represents the consumers' share of the tax.

Consumers' share of a tax on a good

The proportion of the revenue from a tax on a good that arises from an increase in the price of the good.

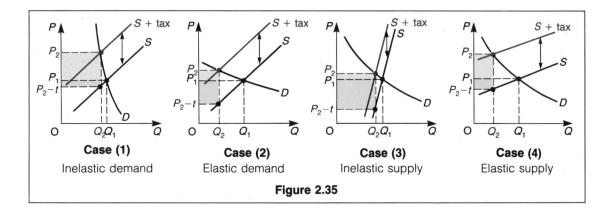

Case (1)

Inelastic demand

Case (2)

Elastic demand

Case (3)

Inelastic supply

Case (4)

Elastic supply

Figure 2.35

Producers' share of a tax on a good

The proportion of the revenue from a tax on a good that arises from a reduction in the price to the producer (after the payment of the tax).

The remainder (the grey area) is the producers' share. This is the amount by which the producers' net price $(P_2 - t)$ is below the original price (P_1) multiplied by the number of goods sold (Q_2): i.e. $(P_1 - (P_2 - t)) \times Q_2$.

From these diagrams the following conclusions can be drawn:

- Quantity will fall less, and hence tax revenue for the government will be greater, the less elastic are demand and supply (cases (1) and (3)).
- Price will rise more, and hence the consumers' share of the tax will be larger, the less elastic is demand and the more elastic is supply (cases (1) and (4)).
- Price will rise less, and hence the producers' share will be larger, the more elastic is demand and the less elastic is supply (cases (2) and (3)).

Cigarettes, petrol and alcohol have been major targets for indirect taxes. Demand for each of them is high and fairly inelastic. Thus the tax will not curb demand greatly. They are good sources, therefore, of tax revenue to the government.

> **?** Supply tends to be more elastic in the long run than in the short run. Assume that a tax is imposed on a good that was previously untaxed. How will the incidence of this tax change as time passes? How will the incidence be affected if demand too becomes more elastic over time?

▲ SUMMARY

1. There are several ways in which the government intervenes in the operation of markets. It can fix prices, tax or subsidize products, regulate production, or produce goods directly itself.
2. The government may fix minimum or maximum prices. If a minimum price is set above the equilibrium, a surplus will result. If a maximum price is set below the equilibrium price, a shortage will result.
3. Minimum prices are set as a means of protecting the incomes of suppliers or creating a surplus for storage in case of future reductions in supply. If the government is not deliberately trying to create a surplus, it must decide what to do with it.
4. Maximum prices are set as a means of keeping prices down for the consumer. The resulting shortage will cause queues, waiting lists or the restriction of sales by firms to

favoured customers. Alternatively, the government could introduce a system of rationing. If it does, then black markets are likely to arise. This is where goods are sold illegally above the maximum price.

5. If the government imposes a tax on a good, this will cause its price to rise to the consumers, but it will also cause the revenue to producers (after the tax has been paid) to fall. The distribution of the burden of the tax between producers and consumers (the 'incidence of tax') will depend on the price elasticity of demand and supply of the good. The consumers' burden will be higher and the producers' burden correspondingly lower, the less elastic the demand and the more elastic the supply of the good. The total tax revenue for the government will be higher the less elastic are both demand and supply.

Background to Demand 3

This chapter gives a more detailed explanation of the shape of the demand curve. This explanation involves considering how rational consumers behave.

Rational consumer

A person who weighs up the costs and benefits to him or her of each additional unit of a good purchased.

If we had unlimited income (and unlimited time too!), we could consume as much as we wanted. We would not have to be careful with our money. In the real world, however, given limited incomes, given the problem of scarcity, we have to make choices about what to buy. You may have to choose between that new economics textbook you feel you ought to buy and going to a rock concert, between a new pair of jeans and a meal out, between saving up for a car and having more money to spend on everyday items, and so on.

We will be assuming in this chapter that consumers behave 'rationally'. Remember from Chapter 1 how we defined rational choices. It is the weighing-up of the costs and benefits of our actions. As far as consumption is concerned, rational action involves considering the relative costs and benefits to us of the alternatives we could spend our money on. We do this in order to gain the maximum satisfaction possible from our limited incomes.

Sometimes we may act 'irrationally'. We may purchase goods impetuously with little thought to their price or quality. We may buy certain things out of habit, without any consideration of whether we really want them, or whether an alternative product or brand might be better value. In general, however, it is a reasonably accurate assumption that people behave rationally.

This does not mean that you get a calculator out every time you go shopping! When you go round the supermarket you are hardly likely to look at every item on the shelf and weigh up the satisfaction you think you would get from it against the price on the label. Nevertheless, you have probably learned over time the sort of things you like and the prices they cost. You can probably make out a 'rational' shopping list quite quickly.

With major items of expenditure such as a house, a car, a carpet or a foreign holiday, we are likely to take much more care. Take the case of a foreign holiday: you will probably spend quite a long time browsing through brochures comparing the relative merits of various holidays against their relative costs, looking for a holiday that gives good value for money. This is rational behaviour.

? 1. Do you ever purchase things irrationally? If so, what are they and why is your behaviour irrational?
2. If you buy something in the shop on the corner when you know that the same item could have been bought more cheaply two miles up the road in the supermarket, is your behaviour irrational? Explain.

Two words of warning before we go on. First, don't confuse irrationality and ignorance. We are going to assume that consumers behave rationally, but that does not mean that they have perfect information. How often have you been disappointed after buying something when you find that it is not as good as you had been led to believe by advertisements or by its packaging, or when you find later that you could have bought an alternative more cheaply? Take the case of a foreign holiday. It may not turn out to be nearly as good as the brochure led you to believe. This is a problem of ignorance. You probably nevertheless behaved rationally in the first place, *believing* (albeit wrongly) that you were getting value for money.

Secondly, the term 'rational' does not imply any moral approval. It is simply referring to behaviour that is consistent with your own particular goals, behaviour directed to getting the most out of your limited income. People may well disapprove of the things that others buy – their clothes, their records, their cigarettes, their cans of lager – but that is making a judgement about their goals: their tastes or morality. As economists we cannot make judgements about what people's goals *should* be. We can, however, look at the *implications* of people behaving rationally in pursuit of those goals. This is what we are doing when we examine rational consumer behaviour: we are looking at its implications for consumer demand.

There are two major approaches to analyzing rational consumer behaviour: the marginal utility approach and the indifference curve approach. These two approaches are described in the two sections of this chapter.

3.1 Marginal utility theory

Total and marginal utility

Total utility

The total satisfaction a consumer gets from the consumption of all the units of a good consumed within a given time period.

People buy goods and services because they get satisfaction from them. Economists call this satisfaction 'utility'.

An important distinction must be made between *total utility* and *marginal utility*.

Total utility (TU) is the total satisfaction a person gains from all those units of a commodity consumed within a given time period. Thus if Tracey drank 10 cups of tea a day, her daily total utility from tea would be the satisfaction derived from those 10 cups.

Marginal utility

The extra satisfaction gained from consuming one extra unit of a good within a given time period.

Marginal utility (MU) is the additional satisfaction gained from consuming one *extra* unit within a given period of time. Thus we might refer to the marginal utility that Tracey gains from her third cup of tea of the day or her eleventh cup.

Util

An imaginary unit of satisfaction from the consumption of a good.

A difficulty arises immediately with the utility approach to explaining demand, and that is: how do you measure utility? Utility is subjective. There is no way of knowing what another person's experiences are really like. Just how satisfying does Brian find his first cup of tea in the morning? How does his utility compare with Tracey's? We do not have utility meters that can answer these questions!

For the moment, this problem will be ignored, and it will be assumed that a person's utility can be measured in utils, where a util is one unit of satisfaction.

Principle of diminishing marginal utility

As more units of a good are consumed, additional units will provide less additional satisfaction than previous units.

Diminishing marginal utility

Up to a point, the more of a commodity you consume, the greater will be your total utility. However, as you become more satisfied, each extra unit that you consume will probably give you less additional utility than previous units. In other words, your marginal utility falls, the more you consume. This is known as the principle of diminishing marginal utility. For example, the second cup of tea in the morning gives you less additional satisfaction than the first cup. The third cup gives less satisfaction still.

At some level of consumption, your total utility will be at a maximum. No extra satisfaction can be gained by the consumption of further units within that period of time. Thus marginal utility will be zero. Your desire for tea may be fully satisfied at 12 cups per day. A thirteenth cup will yield no extra utility. It may even give you displeasure (i.e. negative marginal utility).

 Are there any goods or services where consumers do not experience diminishing marginal utility?

Total and marginal utility curves

If we could measure utility, we could construct a table showing how much total and marginal utility a person would gain at different levels of consumption of a particular commodity. This information could then be transferred to a graph. Table 3.1 and Figure 3.1 do just this. They show the imaginary utility that Darren gets from consuming packets of crisps.

Table 3.1 Darren's utility from consuming crisps (daily)

Packets of crisps consumed	TU in utils	MU in utils
0	0	–
1	7	7
2	11	4
3	13	2
4	14	1
5	14	0
6	13	−1

Referring first to the table, if Darren consumes no crisps, he obviously gets no satisfaction from crisps: his total utility is zero. If he now consumes 1 packet a day, he gets 7 utils of satisfaction. (Sorry if this sounds silly, but we will tackle this question of measurement later.) His total utility is 7, and his marginal utility is also 7. They must be equal if only 1 unit is consumed. Why?

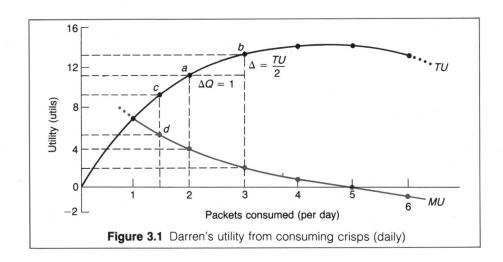

Figure 3.1 Darren's utility from consuming crisps (daily)

If he now consumes a second packet, he gains an extra 4 utils (*MU*), giving him a total utility of 11 utils (i.e. 7 + 4). His marginal utility has fallen because, having already eaten 1 packet, he has less craving for a second. A third packet gives him less extra utility still: marginal utility has fallen to 2 utils, giving a total utility of 13 utils (i.e. 11 + 2).

By the time he has eaten 5 packets, he would rather not eat any more. A sixth actually reduces his utility (from 14 utils to 13): its marginal utility is negative.

The information in Table 3.1 is plotted in Figure 3.1. Notice the following points about the two curves:

- The *MU* curve slopes downward. This is simply illustrating the principle of diminishing marginal utility.
- The *TU* curve starts at the origin. Zero consumption yields zero utility.
- It reaches a peak when marginal utility is zero. When marginal utility is zero (at 5 packets of crisps), there is no addition to total utility. Total utility must be at the maximum – the peak of the curve.
- Marginal utility can be derived from the *TU* curve. It is the slope of the line joining two adjacent quantities on the curve. For example, the marginal utility of the third packet of crisps is the slope of the line joining points *a* and *b*. The slope of such a line is given by the formula:

$$\frac{\Delta TU}{\Delta Q} \ (= MU)$$

In our example $\Delta TU = 2$ (total utility has risen from 11 to 13 utils), and $\Delta Q = 1$ (one more packet of crisps has been consumed).

- We can read off from the two curves what the *TU* and *MU* would be at points other than in the table. For example, Darren would gain a total utility of about 9¼ utils if he consumed 1½ packets of crisps (point *c*). His marginal utility would be approximately 5½ utils (point *d*). Why? Surely if his utility has gone up from 7 utils (1 packet) to 9¼ utils (1½ packets), his marginal utility is only 2¼ utils (i.e. 9¼ − 7)? No, because he has only consumed half a packet more. Remember that marginal utility is the extra utility from *one* more unit, not a half. If he gains an extra 2¼ utils from half a packet more, then this would be approximately 5½ utils for a whole packet more.
Using the formula $MU = \Delta TU / \Delta Q$:

$$MU = \frac{2¼}{½}$$

$$= 5½$$

? If Darren were to consume more and more crisps would his *total* utility ever (a) fall to zero; (b) become negative? Explain.

The ceteris paribus assumption

The table and graph we have drawn are based on the assumption that other things do not change.

In practice, other things *do* change – and frequently. The utility that Darren gets from crisps depends on what else he eats. If on Saturday he has a lot to eat, and nibbles snacks (not crisps) between meals, he will get little satisfaction from crisps. If on Monday, however, he is too busy to eat proper meals, he would probably welcome one or more packets of crisps.

*Box 3.1

Using Calculus to Derive a Marginal Utility Function

The relationship between total utility and marginal utility can be shown using calculus. If you are not familiar with the rules of calculus ignore this box!

A consumer's typical total utility function for a good might be of the form:

$$TU = 60Q - 4Q^2$$

where Q is the quantity of the good consumed.

This would give the figures shown in table (a).

Q	$60Q$	$-4Q^2$	=	TU
1	60	− 4	=	56
2	120	−16	=	104
3	180	−36	=	144
4	240	−64	=	176
.	.	.	.	.
.	.	.	.	.
.	.	.	.	.

 Complete this table to the level of consumption at which *TU* is at a maximum.

Marginal utility is the first derivative of total utility. In other words, it is the rate of *change* of total utility. Differentiating the *TU* function gives:

$$MU = \frac{dTU}{dQ} = 60 - 8Q$$

This gives the figures shown in table (b).

Q	60	$-8Q$	=	MU
1	60	− 8	=	52
2	60	−16	=	44
3	60	−24	=	36
4	60	−32	=	28
.	.	.	.	.
.	.	.	.	.

Note that the marginal utility diminishes.

 Derive a column for *MU* from the first table by taking the differences in *TU*. Why do the figures for *MU* derived in this way seem to be slightly different from the figures derived using calculus?

The *MU* function we have derived is a straight-line function. If, however, the *TU* function had contained a cubed term (Q^3), the *MU* function would be a curve.

 Derive the *MU* function from the following *TU* function:

$$TU = 200Q - 25Q^2 + Q^3$$

From this *MU* function, draw up a table (like the one above) up to the level of *Q* where *MU* becomes negative. Graph these figures.

Each time the consumption of *other* goods changed – whether substitutes or complements – a new utility schedule would have to be drawn up. The curves would shift. Remember, utility is not a property of the goods themselves. Utility is in the mind of the consumer, and consumers change their minds. Their tastes change; their circumstances change; their consumption patterns change.

The optimum level of consumption: the simplest case – one commodity

Just how much of a good should people consume if they are to make the best use of their limited income? To answer this question we must tackle the problem of how to measure utility, given that in practice we cannot measure 'utils'.

One solution to the problem is to measure utility with money. In this case utility becomes the value that people place on their consumption. Marginal utility thus becomes the amount of money a person would be prepared to pay to obtain one more unit: in other words, what that extra unit is worth to that person. If Darren is prepared to pay 25p to obtain an extra packet of crisps, then we can say that packet yields him 25p worth of utility: $MU = 25p$.

So how many packets should he consume if he is to act rationally? To answer this we need to introduce the concept of consumer surplus.

Marginal consumer surplus

Marginal consumer surplus (MCS) is the difference between what you are willing to pay for one more unit of a good and what you are actually charged. If Darren was willing to pay 25p for another packet of crisps which in fact only cost him 20p, he would be getting a marginal consumer surplus of 5p.

$$MCS = MU - P$$

Total consumer surplus

Total consumer surplus (TCS) is the sum of all the marginal consumer surpluses that you have obtained from all the units of a good you have consumed. It is the difference between the total utility from all the units and your expenditure on them. If Darren consumes four packets of crisps, and if he would have been prepared to spend £1.20 on them and only had to spend 80p, then his total consumer surplus is 40p.

$$TCS = TU - TE$$

where TE is the total expenditure on a good: i.e. $P \times Q$.

(Note that total expenditure (TE) is a similar concept to total revenue (TR). They are both defined as $P \times Q$. But in the case of total expenditure, Q is the quantity *purchased* by the consumer(s) in question, whereas in the case of total revenue, Q is the quantity *sold* by the firm(s) in question.)

Let us define rational consumer behaviour as the attempt to maximize consumer surplus. How do people set about doing this?

People will go on purchasing additional units as long as they gain additional consumer surplus: in other words, as long as the price they are prepared to pay exceeds the price they are charged ($MU > P$). But as more units are purchased, so they will experience diminishing marginal utility. They will be prepared to pay less and less for each additional unit. Their marginal utility will go on falling until $MU = P$: i.e. until no further consumer surplus can be gained. At that point, they will stop purchasing additional units. Their optimum level of consumption has been reached: consumer surplus has been maximized. Were they to continue to purchase beyond this point, MU would be less than P, and thus they would be paying more for the last units than they were worth to them.

The process of maximizing consumer surplus can be shown graphically. Let us take the case of Tina's annual purchases of petrol. Tina has her own car, but as an alternative she can use public transport or walk. To keep the analysis simple, let us assume that Tina's parents bought her the car and pay the licence duty, and that Tina does not have the option of selling the car. She does, however, have to buy the petrol. The current price is 40p per litre. Figure 3.2 shows her consumer surplus.

If she were to use just a few litres per year, she would use them for very important journeys for which no convenient alternative exists. For such trips she may be prepared to pay up to 80p per litre. For the first few litres, then, she is getting a marginal utility of around 80p per litre, and hence a marginal consumer surplus of around 40p (i.e. 80p − 40p).

By the time her annual purchase is around 250 litres, she would only be prepared to pay around 70p for additional litres. The additional journeys, although still

Consumer surplus

The excess of what a person would have been prepared to pay for a good (i.e. the utility) over what that person actually pays.

Marginal consumer surplus

The excess of utility from the consumption of one more unit of a good (MU) over the price paid: $MCS = MU - P$.

Total consumer surplus

The excess of a person's total utility from the consumption of a good (TU) over the amount that person spends on it (TE): $TCS = TU - TE$.

Rational consumer behaviour

The attempt to maximize total consumer surplus.

Figure 3.2 Tina's consumer surplus from petrol

Figure 3.3 Consumer Surplus

important, would be less vital. Perhaps these are journeys where she could have taken public transport, albeit at some inconvenience. Her marginal consumer surplus at 250 litres is 30p (i.e. 70p − 40p).

Gradually, additional litres give less and less additional utility as less and less important journeys are undertaken. The 500th litre yields 61p worth of extra utility. Marginal consumer surplus is now 21p (i.e. 61p − 40p).

By the time she gets to the 1300th litre, Tina's marginal utility has fallen to 40p. There is no additional consumer surplus to be gained. Her total consumer surplus is at a maximum. She thus buys 1300 litres, where $P = MU$.

Her total consumer surplus is the sum of all the marginal consumer surpluses: the sum of all the 1300 vertical lines between the price and the MU curve. This is represented by the total *area* between P and MU.

This analysis can be expressed in general terms. In Figure 3.3, if the price of a commodity is P_1, the consumer will consume Q_1. The person's total expenditure (*TE*) is P_1Q_1, shown by area 1. Total utility (*TU*) is the area under the marginal utility curve: i.e. areas 1 + 2. Total consumer surplus (*TU − TE*) is shown by area 2.

 If a good were free, why would total consumer surplus equal total utility? What would be the level of marginal utility?

Marginal utility and the demand curve for a good

An individual's demand curve

Individual people's demand curve for any good will be the same as their marginal utility curve for that good, measured in money.

This is demonstrated in Figure 3.4, which shows the marginal utility curve for a particular person and a particular good. If the price of the good were P_1, the person would consume Q_1: where $MU = P$. Thus point *a* would be one point on that person's demand curve. If the price fell to P_2, consumption would rise to Q_2, since this is where $MU = P_2$. Thus point *b* is a second point on the demand curve. Likewise if price fell to P_3, Q_3 would be consumed. Point *c* is a third point on the demand curve.

Thus as long as individuals seek to maximize consumer surplus and hence consume where $P = MU$, their demand curve will be along the same line as their marginal utility curve.

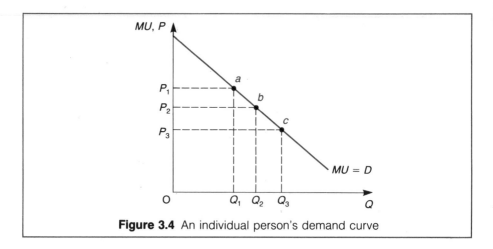

Figure 3.4 An individual person's demand curve

The market demand curve

The market demand curve will simply be the (horizontal) sum of all individuals' demand curves and hence MU curves.

The shape of the demand curve. The price elasticity of demand will reflect the rate at which MU diminishes. If there are close substitutes for a good, it is likely to have an elastic demand, and its MU will diminish slowly as consumption increases. The reason is that increased consumption of this product will be accompanied by *decreased* consumption of the alternative product(s). Since total consumption of this product *plus* the alternatives has increased only slightly (if at all), the marginal utility will fall only slowly.

For example, the demand for a given brand of petrol is likely to have a fairly high price elasticity, since other brands are substitutes. If there is a cut in the price of Texaco petrol (assuming the prices of other brands stay constant), consumption of Texaco will increase a lot. The MU of Texaco petrol will fall slowly, since people consume less of other brands. Petrol consumption *in total* may be only slightly greater, and hence the MU of petrol only slightly lower.

 Why do we get less consumer surplus from goods where our demand is relatively elastic?

Shifts in the demand curve. How do *shifts* in demand relate to marginal utility? For example, how would the marginal utility (and hence demand for) margarine be affected by a rise in the price of butter? The higher price of butter would cause less butter to be consumed. This would increase the marginal utility of margarine, since if people are using less butter, their desire for margarine is higher. The MU curve (and hence the demand curve) for margarine thus shifts to the right.

 How would marginal utility and market demand be affected by a rise in the price of a complementary good?

Weaknesses of the one-commodity version of marginal utility theory

A change in the consumption of one good will affect the marginal utility of substitute and complementary goods. It will also affect the amount of income left over to be

Box 3.2

The Marginal Utility Revolution: Jevons, Menger, Walras

Solving the diamonds–water paradox

What determines the market value of a good? We already know the answer: demand and supply. So if we find out what determines the position of the demand and supply curves, we will at the same time be finding out what determines a good's market value.

This might seem obvious. Yet for years economists puzzled over just what determines a good's value.

Some economists like Karl Marx and David Ricardo concentrated on the supply side. For them, value depended on the amount of resources used in producing a good. This could be further reduced to the amount of *labour* time embodied in the good. Thus, according to the *labour theory of value*, the more labour that was directly involved in producing the good, or indirectly in producing the capital equipment used to make the good, the more valuable would the good be.

Other economists looked at the demand side. But here they came across a paradox.

Adam Smith in the 1760s gave the example of water and diamonds. 'How is it', he asked, 'that water which is so essential to human life, and thus has such a high "value-in-use", has such a low market value (or "value-in-exchange")? And how is it that diamonds which are relatively so trivial have such a high market value?' The answer to this paradox had to wait over a hundred years until the marginal utility revolution of the 1870s. William Stanley Jevons (1835–82) in England, Carl Menger (1840–1921) in Austria, and Leon Walras (1834–1910) in Switzerland all independently claimed that the source of the market value of a good was its *marginal* utility, not its *total* utility.

This was the solution to the diamonds–water paradox. Water, being so essential, has a high total utility: a high 'value in use'. But for most of us, given that we consume so much already, it has a very low marginal utility. Do you leave the cold tap running when you clean your teeth? If you do, it shows just how trivial water is to you *at the margin*. Diamonds, on the other hand, although they have

a much lower total utility, have a much higher marginal utility. There are so few diamonds in the world, and thus people have so few of them, that they are very valuable at the margin. If, however, a new technique were to be discovered of producing diamonds cheaply from coal, their market value would fall rapidly. As people had more of them, so their marginal utility would rapidly diminish.

Marginal utility still only gives the demand side of the story. The reason why the marginal utility of water is so low is that *supply* is so plentiful. Water is very expensive in Saudi Arabia! In other words, the full explanation of value must take into account both demand *and* supply.

MU, P (£)

MU diamonds   MU water

O   Quantity of water (litres per day)
Quantity of diamonds (carats)

? The diagram illustrates a person's *MU* curves of water and diamonds. Assume that diamonds are more expensive than water. Show how the *MU* of diamonds will be greater than the *MU* of water. Show also how the *TU* of diamonds will be less than the *TU* of water. (Remember: *TU* is the area under the *MU* curve.)

spent on other goods. Thus a more satisfactory explanation of demand would involve an analysis of choices between goods, rather than looking at one good in isolation.

What is more, deriving a demand curve from a marginal utility curve measured in money assumes that money itself has a constant marginal utility. The trouble is that it does not. If people have a rise in income, they will consume more. Other things being equal, the marginal utility of the goods that they consume will diminish. Thus an extra £1 of consumption will bring less satisfaction than previously. In other words, it is likely that *the marginal utility of money diminishes as income rises*.

Unless a good occupies only a tiny fraction of people's expenditure, a fall in its price will mean that their real income has increased: i.e. they can afford to purchase more goods in general. As they do so, the marginal utility of their money will fall. We cannot, therefore, legitimately use money to measure utility in an absolute sense. We can, however, still talk about the relative utility that we get from various goods for a given increase in expenditure.

The following sections thus look at the choice between goods, and how it relates to marginal utility.

The optimum combination of goods consumed

We can use marginal utility analysis to show how a rational person decides what combination of goods to buy. As we emphasized in Chapter 1 when looking at the fundamental economic problem of scarcity, we cannot simply buy whatever we want. Given that we have limited incomes, we have to make choices. It is not just a question of choosing between two obvious substitutes (like carrots and peas or a holiday in Greece and one in Spain), but about allocating our incomes between all the goods and services we might like to consume. If you have, say, an income of £10 000 per year, what is the optimum 'bundle' of goods and services for you to spend it on?

Equi-marginal principle

Consumers will maximize total utility from their incomes by consuming that combination of goods where:

$$\frac{MU_a}{P_a} = \frac{MU_b}{P_b} = \frac{MU_c}{P_c}$$

$$= \ldots \frac{MU_n}{P_n}$$

The rule for rational consumer behaviour is known as the equi-marginal principle This states that a consumer will get the highest utility from a given level of income when the utility from the last £1 spent on each good is the same. Algebraically, this is when:

$$\frac{MU_a}{P_a} = \frac{MU_b}{P_b} = \frac{MU_c}{P_c} \ldots = \frac{MU_n}{P_n} \tag{1}$$

where a, b, c . . . n are the various goods consumed.

All we are describing here is the way in which consumers will achieve the best 'value for money' from their purchases. To explain this consider the following.

What would you do if champagne gave you twice as much satisfaction as sparkling white wine, but cost five times as much? You would buy the sparkling white wine: it would give you better value for money. What would you do if steak cost twice as much as minced beef, but gave you three times as much satisfaction? You would buy the steak. This time the more expensive item gives you better value for money.

What we are doing in each case is comparing the relative marginal utilities of the two items with their relative prices. In the case of steak and mince, when we say that steak gives three times the satisfaction of mince, we are in fact saying:

$$\frac{MU_{steak}}{MU_{mince}} = \frac{3}{1}$$

And when we say that steak costs twice as much as mince we are saying:

$$\frac{P_{steak}}{P_{mince}} = \frac{2}{1}$$

We can generalize from this to any pair of goods a and b that you buy. If:

$$\frac{MU_a}{MU_b} > \frac{P_a}{P_b}$$

you will increase your purchases of good a relative to those of good b. But as you buy more of good a, according to the principle of diminishing marginal utility, the marginal utility of good a (MU_a) will fall. Likewise as you buy less of good b, MU_b will rise. You will stop adjusting the balance of your purchases of goods a and b when the marginal utility ratios are the same as the price ratios: when

$$\frac{MU_a}{MU_b} = \frac{P_a}{P_b}$$

At this point your total utility will be maximized for any given amount of income spent on the two goods.

? Imagine that you had £10 per month to allocate between two goods a and b. Imagine that good a cost £2 per unit and good b cost £1 per unit. Imagine also that the utilities of the two goods are those set out in Table 3.2. (Note that the two goods are not substitutes for each other, so that the consumption of one does not affect the utility gained from the other.)
(a) What would be the marginal utility ratio (MU_a/MU_b) for the following combinations of the two goods: (i) 1a, 8b; (ii) 2a, 6b; (iii) 3a, 4b; (iv) 4a, 2b?
(b) Show that where the marginal utility ratio (MU_a/MU_b) equals the price ratio (P_a/P_b) total utility is maximized.
(c) If the two goods were substitutes for each other, why would it not be possible to construct a table like Table 3.2?

Table 3.2 The utility gained by a person from various quantities of two goods: A and B

Good A			Good B		
Units per month	MU (utils)	TU (utils)	Units per month	MU (utils)	TU (utils)
0	–	0.0	0	–	0.0
1	11.0	11.0	1	8.0	8.0
2	8.0	19.0	2	7.0	15.0
3	6.0	25.0	3	6.5	21.5
4	4.5	29.5	4	5.0	26.5
5	3.0	32.5	5	4.5	31.0
			6	4.0	35.0
			7	3.5	38.5
			8	3.0	41.5
			9	2.6	44.1
			10	2.3	46.4

Possible combinations of good A and good B (units per month) for a monthly expenditure of £10		Combined TU from goods A and B (utils)
Good A	Good B	
5	0	32.5
4	2	44.5
3	4	51.5
2	6	54.0
1	8	52.5
0	10	46.4

Another way of looking at the choice between two goods is to compare the ratios of their marginal utility to price (MU/P). If:

$$\frac{MU_a}{P_a} > \frac{MU_b}{P_b}$$

you would consume more a relative to b. This is because you would be getting a greater satisfaction per £1 spent on extra units of good a than you would per £1 spent on good b. In other words, good a would give you better 'value for money' than good b. You would thus buy more a and less b. But as you switched from b to a, the marginal utility of a would fall due to diminishing marginal utility, and conversely the marginal utility of b would rise, until:

$$\frac{MU_a}{P_a} = \frac{MU_b}{P_b}$$

At this point no further gain can be made by switching from one good to the other. This is the optimum combination of goods to consume.

The argument can be extended to any number of goods – a, b, c, d, e, etc. As long as the marginal utility relative to the price of any one good is greater than another, more of it will be consumed. Its marginal utility will fall until:

$$\frac{MU_a}{P_a} = \frac{MU_b}{P_b} = \frac{MU_c}{P_c} \cdots = \frac{MU_n}{P_n}$$

This is the equi-marginal principle given in equation (1) above.

The multi-commodity version of marginal utility and the demand curve

How can we derive a demand curve from the above analysis?

For a given income, and given prices of good a and all other goods, the quantity a person will demand of good a will be that which satisfies equation (1). One point on the individual's demand curve for good a is thus determined.

If the price of good a fell, such that:

$$\frac{MU_a}{P_a} > \frac{MU_{b,c,d,etc.}}{P_{b,c,d,etc.}}$$

expenditure would be switched to good a until equation (1) was once more satisfied. A second point has thus been derived.

Further changes in the price of good a would bring further changes in the quantity demanded, in order to satisfy equation (1). Further points on the individual's demand curve would thereby be derived.

If the price of *another* good changed, or if the marginal utility of any good changed (including good a), then again the quantity demanded of good a (and other goods) would change, until again equation (1) were satisfied. These changes in demand will be represented by a shift in the demand for good a.

Demand under conditions of uncertainty

So far we have assumed that when people buy goods and services they know exactly what price they will pay and how much utility they will gain. In many cases this is a reasonable assumption. When you buy a bar of chocolate you clearly do know how much you are paying for it and have a very good idea how much you will like it. But what about a video recorder, or a car, or a washing machine, or any other consumer durable? In each of these cases you are buying something that will last you a long time, and the further into the future you look, the less certain you will be of its costs and benefits to you.

Take the case of a washing machine costing you £400. If you pay cash, your

Consumer durable

A consumer good that lasts a period of time, during which the consumer can continue gaining utility from it.

Box 3.3

Taking Account of Time
Can I spare the time to enjoy myself?

Do you take a taxi or go by bus? How long do you spend soaking in the bath? Do you go to the bother of cooking a meal or will you get a take-away?

We have argued that such decisions, if they are to be rational, should involve weighing up the relative marginal utilities of these activities against their relative marginal costs.

One crucial dimension we have ignored up to now is the *time* dimension. One of the opportunity costs of doing any activity is the sacrifice of time.

A take-away meal may be more expensive than a home-cooked one, but it saves you time. Part of the cost of the home-cooked meal, therefore is the sacrifice of

time involved. The full cost is therefore not just the cost of the ingredients and the fuel used, but also the opportunity cost of the alternative activities you have sacrificed while you were cooking.

Given the high pressured lives many people lead in affluent countries, a high value is often put on time saved. Fast-food restaurants and supersonic jet travel are symptoms of this lifestyle.

Even pleasurable activities involve a time cost. The longer you spend doing pleasurable activity 'a', the less time you will have for doing pleasurable activity 'b'. The longer you laze in the bath, the less TV will you be able to watch (unless you have a TV in the bathroom!).

---

immediate outlay involves no uncertainty: it is £400. But washing machines can break down. In two years' time you could find yourself with a repair bill of £100. This cannot be predicted and yet it is a price you will have to pay, just like the original £400. In other words, when you buy the washing machine you are uncertain as to the full 'price' it will entail over its lifetime.

If the costs of the washing machine are uncertain, so too are the benefits. You might have been attracted to buy it in the first place by the manufacturer's glossy brochure, or by the look of it, or by adverts on TV, in magazines, etc. When you have used it for a while, however, you will probably discover things you had not anticipated. The spin dryer does not get your clothes as dry as you had hoped; it is noisy; it leaks; the door sticks; and so on.

Buying consumer durables thus involves uncertainty. So too does the purchase of assets, whether a physical asset such as a house or financial assets such as shares. In the case of assets the uncertainty is over their future *price*. If you buy shares in a recently privatized industry, what will happen to their price? Will they shoot up in price, thus enabling you to sell them at a large profit, or will they fall? You cannot know for certain.

So how will uncertainty affect people's behaviour? The answer is that it depends on their attitudes towards taking a gamble. To examine these attitudes let us assume that a person does at least know the *odds* of the gamble. In other words, the person is operating under conditions of *risk* rather than *uncertainty*.

? Define 'risk' and 'uncertainty'. (*See pages 92–4*).

To illustrate different attitudes towards risk, consider the case of gambling that a particular number will come up on the throw of a die. There is a one in six chance of this happening. Would you gamble? It depends on what odds you were offered and on your attitude to risk.

Odds can be of three types. They can be *favourable* odds. This is where on average you will gain. If, for example, you were offered odds of 10 to 1 on the throw of a dice, then for a £1 bet you would get nothing if you lost, but you would get £10 if your number came up. Since your number should come up on average one time in every six, on average you will gain. The longer you go on playing, the more money you are likely to win. If the odds were 6 to 1, they would be *fair* odds. On average you would break even. If, however, they were less than 6 to 1, they would be described as *unfavourable*. On average you would lose.

 Give some examples of gambling (or risk taking in general) where the odds are (a) unfavourable; (b) fair; (c) favourable.

There are three possible categories of attitude toward risk.

Risk neutral. This is where a person will take a gamble if the odds are favourable; not take a gamble if the odds are unfavourable; and be indifferent about taking a gamble if the odds are fair.

Risk loving. This is where a person is prepared to take a gamble even if the odds are unfavourable. The more risk loving a person is, the worse the odds he or she will be prepared to accept.

Risk averse. This is where a person may not be prepared to take a gamble even if the odds are favourable. The more risk averse the person is, the better would have to be the odds before he or she could be enticed to take a gamble. Few people are *totally risk averse* and thus totally unwilling to take a gamble. If I offered people a bet on the toss of a coin such that tails they pay me 10p and heads I pay them £100, few would refuse (unless on moral grounds).

Diminishing marginal utility of income and attitudes towards risk taking

Avid gamblers may be risk lovers. People who spend hours in the betting shop or at the race track may enjoy the risks, knowing that there is always the chance that they might win. On average, however, such people will lose. After all, the bookies have to take their cut and thus the odds are generally unfavourable.

Most people, however, for most of the time are risk averters. We prefer to avoid insecurity. But why? Is there a simple reason for this? Economists use marginal utility analysis to explain why.

They argue that the gain in utility to people from an extra £100 is less than the loss of utility from forgoing £100. Imagine your own position. You have probably adjusted your standard of living to your income (or are trying to!). If you unexpectedly gained £100, that would be very nice: you could buy some new clothes or have a weekend away. But if you lost £100 it could be very hard indeed. You might have very serious difficulties in making ends meet. Thus if you were offered the gamble of a 50:50 chance of winning or losing £100, you would probably decline the gamble.

 Which gamble would you be more likely to accept, a 60:40 chance of gaining or losing £10 000, or a 40:60 chance of gaining or losing £1? Explain why.

This risk-averting behaviour accords with the principle of *diminishing marginal utility*. Up to now in this chapter we have been focusing on the utility from the consumption of individual goods: Tracey and her cups of tea; Darren and his packets of crisps. In the case of each individual good, the more we consume the less satisfaction we gain from each additional unit: the marginal utility falls. But the same principle applies if we look at our *total* consumption. The higher our level of total consumption, the less additional satisfaction will be gained from each additional £1 spent. What we are saying here is that there is a diminishing marginal utility of income. The more you earn the lower will be the utility from each *extra* £1. If people on low incomes earn an extra £100, they will feel a lot better off: the marginal utility they will get from that income will be very high. If rich people earn an extra £100, however, their gain in utility will be less.

Diminishing marginal utility of income

Where each additional pound earned yields less additional utility.

 Do you think that this provides a moral argument for redistributing income from the rich to the poor? Does it *prove* that income should be so redistributed?

Why, then, does a diminishing marginal utility of income make us risk averters? The answer is illustrated in Figure 3.5, which shows the *total* utility you get from your income.

The slope of this curve gives the *marginal* utility of your income. As the marginal utility of income diminishes, so the curve gets flatter. A rise in income from £5000 to £10 000 will cause a movement along the curve from point *a* to point *b*. Total utility rises from U_1 to U_2. A similar rise in income from £10 000 to £15 000, however, will lead to a move from point *b* to point *c*, and hence a *smaller* rise in total utility from U_2 to U_3.

Now assume that your income is £10 000 and you are offered a chance of gambling £5000 of it. You are offered the fair odds of a 50:50 chance of gaining an extra £5000 (i.e. doubling it) or losing it. Effectively, then, you have an equal chance of your income rising to £15 000 or falling to £5000.

At an income of £10 000, your total utility is U_2. If your gamble pays off and as a result your income rises to £15 000, your total utility will rise to U_3. If it does not pay off, you will be left with only £5000 and a utility of U_1. Given that you have a 50:50 chance of winning, your *average* expected utility will be midway between U_1 and U_3 (i.e. $\frac{(U_1 + U_3)}{2}$) = U_4. But this is the utility that would be gained from an income of £8000. Given that you would prefer U_2 to U_4 you will choose not to take the gamble.

Thus risk aversion is part of rational utility-maximizing behaviour.

 If people are risk averse, why do they nevertheless sometimes take gambles?

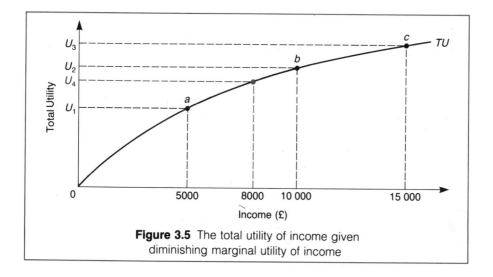

Figure 3.5 The total utility of income given diminishing marginal utility of income

On most occasions we will not know the odds of taking a gamble. In other words, we will be operating under conditions of *uncertainty*. This could make us very cautious indeed. The more pessimistic we are, the more cautious we will be.

Insurance: a way of removing risks

Insurance is the opposite of gambling. It takes the risk away. If, for example, you risk losing your job if you are injured, you can remove the risk of loss of income by taking out an appropriate insurance policy.

Given that people are risk averters, they will be prepared to pay the premiums even though they give them 'unfair odds'. The total premiums paid to insurance companies will be *more* than the amount the insurance companies pay out: that is how the companies make a profit.

But does this mean that the insurance companies are less risk averse than their customers? Why is it that the insurance companies are prepared to shoulder the risks that their customers were not? The answer is that the insurance company is able to spread its risks

Spreading risks (for an insurance company)

The more policies an insurance company issues and the more independent the risks of claims from these policies are, the more predictable will be the number of claims.

The spreading of risks

If there is a one in a hundred chance of your house burning down each year, although it is a only a small chance it would be so disastrous that you are simply not prepared to take the risk. You thus take out house insurance and are prepared to pay a premium of *more than* 1 per cent (one in a hundred).

The insurance company, however, is not just insuring you. It is insuring thousands of others at the same time. If your house burns down, there will be approximately 99 others that do not. The premiums the insurance company has collected will be more than enough to cover its payments. The more houses it insures, the smaller will be the variation in the proportion that actually burn down each year.

Law of large numbers

The larger the number of events of a particular type, the more predictable will be their average outcome.

This is an application of the law of large numbers. What is unpredictable for an individual becomes highly predictable in the mass. The more people the insurance company insures, the more predictable is the total outcome.

What is more, the insurance company will be in a position to estimate just what the risks are. It can thus work out what premiums it must charge in order to make a profit. With individuals, however, the precise risk is rarely known. Do you know your chances of living to 70? Almost certainly you do not. But a life assurance company will know precisely the chances of a person of your age, sex and occupation living to 70! It will have the statistical data to show this. In other words an insurance company will be able to covert your *uncertainty* into their *risk*.

Independent risks

Where two risky events are unconnected. The occurrence of one will not affect the likelihood of the occurrence of the other.

The spreading of risks does not just require that there should be a large number of policies. It also requires that the risks should be independent. If an insurance company insured 1000 houses *all in the same neighbourhood*, and then there were a major fire in the area, the claims would be enormous. The risks of fire were not independent. The company would, in fact, have been taking a gamble on a single event. If, however, it provides fire insurance for houses scattered all over the country, the risks *are* independent.

 1. Why are insurance companies unwilling to provide insurance against losses arising from war or 'civil insurrection'?
2. Name some other events where it would be impossible to obtain insurance.

Box 3.4

Problems for Unwary Insurance Companies
'Adverse selection' and 'moral hazard'

Adverse selection

This is where the people taking out insurance are those who have the highest risk.

For example, suppose that a company offers medical insurance. It surveys the population and works out that the average person requires £200 of treatment per year. The company thus sets the premium at £250 (the extra £50 to cover its costs and provide a profit). But it is likely that the people most likely to take out the insurance are those most likely to fall sick: those who have been ill before, those whose families have a history of illness, those in jobs that are hazardous to health, etc. These people on average may require £500 of treatment per year. The insurance company would soon make a loss.

But cannot the company then simply raise premiums to £550 or £600? It can, but the problem is that it will thereby be depriving the person of *average* health of reasonably priced insurance.

The answer is for the company to discriminate more carefully between people. You may have to fill out a questionnaire so that the company can assess your own particular risk and set an appropriate premium. There may need to be legal penalties for people caught lying!

 What details does an insurance company require to know before it will insure a person to drive a car?

Moral hazard

This is where having insurance makes you less careful and thus increases your risk to the company. For example, if your bicycle is insured against theft, you may be less concerned to go through the hassle of chaining it up each time you leave it.

Again, if insurance companies work out risks by looking at the *total* number of bicycle thefts, these figures will understate the risks to the company because they will include thefts from *uninsured* people who are likely to be more careful.

 How will the following reduce moral hazard?

(a) A no-claims bonus.

(b) The company only being prepared to insure an item for part of its value.

(c) You having to pay the first so many pounds of any claim.

(d) Offering lower premiums to those less likely to claim (e.g. lower house contents premiums for those with burglar alarms).

Another way in which insurance companies can spread their risks is by diversification. The more types of insurance a company offers (car, house, life, health, etc.), the greater is likely to be the independence of the risks.

Diversification
Where a firm expands into new types of business.

◭ SUMMARY

1. The satisfaction people get from consuming a good is called 'utility'. Total utility is the satisfaction gained from the total consumption of a particular good over a given period of time. Marginal utility is the *extra* satisfaction gained from consuming *one more* unit of the good.

2. The marginal utility tends to fall the more that people consume. This is known as the 'principle of diminishing marginal utility'.

3. Total and marginal utility can be illustrated by constructing imaginary examples using imaginary units of utility called 'utils'. These examples can be shown in the form of either a table or a graph.

4. The utility that people get from consuming a good will depend on the amount of other goods they consume. A change in the amount of other goods consumed, whether substitutes or complements, will shift the total and marginal utility curves.

5. 'Rational' consumers will attempt to maximize their consumer surplus. Consumer surplus is the excess of people's utility (measured in money terms) over their expenditure on the good. This will be maximized by purchasing at the point where the *MU* of a good is equal to its price.

6. In the simple case where the price and consumption of

other goods is held constant, a person's *MU* curve will lie along the same line as that person's demand curve.

7. The market demand curve is merely the horizontal sum of the demand curves of all the individual consumers. The elasticity of the market demand curve will depend on the rate at which marginal utility diminishes as more is consumed. This in turn depends on the number and closeness of substitute goods. If there are close substitutes, people will readily switch to this good if its price falls, and thus marginal utility will fall only slowly. The demand will be elastic.

8. Measuring the marginal utility of a good in money avoids the problem of using some imaginary unit such as utils, but it assumes that money has a constant utility. In reality, the marginal utility of money is likely to decrease as income rises.

9. A more satisfactory way of analyzing the demand for goods is to look at people's choices *between* goods. A consumer will maximize utility from a given income by consuming according to the 'equi-marginal principle'. This states that goods should be consumed in that combination which equates the *MU/P* ratio for each good.

10. When people buy consumer durables they may be uncertain of their benefits and any additional repair and maintenance costs. When they buy financial assets they may be uncertain of what will happen to their price in the future. Buying under these conditions of imperfect knowledge is therefore a form of gambling. When we take such gambles, if we know the odds we are said to be operating under conditions of *risk*. If we do not know the odds, we are said to be operating under conditions of *uncertainty*.

11. People can be divided into risk lovers, risk averters and those who are risk neutral. Because of the diminishing marginal utility of income, it is rational for people to be risk averters (unless gambling is itself pleasurable).

12. Insurance is a way of eliminating risks for policy holders. Being risk averters, people are prepared to pay premiums in order to obtain insurance. Insurance companies, on the other hand, are prepared to take on these risks because they can spread them over a large number of policies. According to the law of large numbers, what is unpredictable for a single policy holder becomes highly predictable for a large number of them provided that their risks are independent of each other.

*3.2 Indifference analysis

The limitations of the marginal utility approach to demand

Even though the multi-commodity version of marginal utility theory is useful in demonstrating the underlying logic of consumer choice, it still has a major weakness. Utility cannot be measured in any absolute sense. We cannot really say, therefore, by *how much* the marginal utility of one good exceeds another.

An alternative approach is to use *indifference analysis*. This does not involve measuring the *amount* of utility a person gains, but merely *ranking* various combinations of goods in order of preference. In other words, it assumes that consumers can decide whether they prefer one combination of goods to another. For example, if you were asked to choose between two baskets of fruit, one containing four oranges and three pears and the other containing two oranges and five pears, you could say which you prefer or whether you are indifferent between them. It does not assume that you can decide just *how much* you prefer one basket to another or just how much you like either.

The aim of indifference analysis, then, is to analyze, *without having to measure utility*, how a rational consumer chooses between two goods. As we shall see, it can be used to show the effect on this choice of (a) a change in the consumer's income and (b) a change in the price of one or both goods. It can also be used to analyze the income and substitution effects of a change in price.

Indifference analysis involves the use of *indifference curves* and *budget lines*.

Indifference curve

A line showing all those combinations of two goods between which a consumer is indifferent: i.e. those combinations that give the same level of utility.

Indifference curves

A single indifference curve

An indifference curve shows all the various combinations of two goods that give an equal amount of satisfaction or utility to a consumer.

To show how one can be constructed, consider the following example. Imagine that a supermarket is conducting a survey about the preferences of its customers for different types of fruit. One of the respondents is Clive, a student who likes a healthy diet and is a regular purchaser of fresh fruit. He is asked his preferences for various combinations of oranges and pears, and asked merely to state which he prefers or whether he is indifferent between them. Starting with the combination of 10 pears and 13 oranges, he is asked to compare this combination with others. Some combinations (such as 12 pears and 15 oranges) he prefers. Others (such as 5 pears and 6 oranges) he likes less than the original combination. Others still (such as 20 pears and 8 oranges) he says he likes the same amount as the original combination. From this is constructed a set of combinations which he likes as much as, but not more than, each other. This is shown in Table 3.3.

Table 3.3 Combinations of pears and oranges that Clive likes the same amount as 10 pears and 13 oranges

Pears	Oranges	Point in Figure 3.6
30	6	*a*
24	7	*b*
20	8	*c*
14	10	*d*
10	13	*e*
8	15	*f*
6	20	*g*

This table is known as an indifference set. It shows alternative combinations of two goods that yield the same level of satisfaction. From this we can plot an indifference curve. We measure units of one good on one axis and units of the other good on the other axis. Thus in Figure 3.6, which is based on Table 3.3, pears and oranges are measured on the two axes. The curve shows that Clive is indifferent as to whether he consumes 30 pears and 6 oranges (point *a*) or 24 pears and 7 oranges (point *b*) or any other combination of pears and oranges along the curve.

Notice that we are not saying *how much* Clive likes pears and oranges, merely that he likes all the combinations along the indifference curve the same amount. All the combinations thus yield the same (unspecified) utility.

Indifference set

A table showing the same information as an indifference curve.

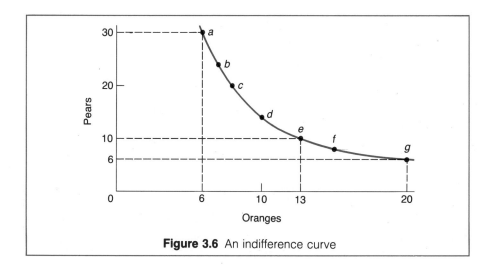

Figure 3.6 An indifference curve

The shape of the indifference curve

As you can see, the indifference curve we have drawn is not a straight line. It is bowed in towards the origin. In other words, its slope gets shallower as we move down the curve. Indifference curves are normally drawn this shape. But why?

To explain the shape of the curve, consider Figure 3.7. It shows an individual's indifference curve for two goods, X and Y.

The slope of the indifference curve is equal to $\Delta Y/\Delta X$. For example, between points *a* and *b*, $\Delta Y = -4$ and $\Delta X = 1$. Thus the slope of the curve between *a* and *b* is $-4/1 = -4$.

Another name for the slope of an indifference curve is the marginal rate of substitution (*MRS*) between X and Y. This shows the amount of Y a consumer is willing to give up (ΔY), in order to obtain one more unit of X (ΔX).

$$MRS = \frac{\Delta Y}{\Delta X}$$

(Note that we ignore the negative sign and express the *MRS* as a positive figure.) Thus in Figure 3.7, the *MRS* between points *a* and *b* is 4 and between points *c* and *d* is 1.

It can be seen that, as we move down the curve, the marginal rate of substitution diminishes as the slope of the curve gets less. Thus if we are to explain the shape of the indifference curve, we must explain why the marginal rate of substitution diminishes.

The reason for a diminishing marginal rate of substitution is related to the *principle of diminishing marginal utility* that we looked at in section 3.1. This stated that individuals will gain less and less additional satisfaction the more of a good that they consume. This principle, however, is based on the assumption that the consumption of other goods is held *constant*. In the case of an indifference curve this is not true. As we move down the curve, more X is consumed but *less* Y is consumed. Nevertheless the effect on consumer satisfaction is similar. As more X and less Y are consumed, the marginal utility of X will diminish and that of Y will increase. Consumers will thus be prepared to give up less and less Y for each additional unit of X. *MRS* diminishes.

The relationship between the marginal rate of substitution and marginal utility

In Figure 3.7, consumption at point *a* yields equal satisfaction with consumption at point *b*. Thus the utility sacrificed by giving up 4 units of Y must be equal to the utility

Marginal rate of substitution (between two goods in consumption)

The amount of one good (Y) that a consumer is prepared to give up in order to obtain one extra unit of another good (X): i.e. $\Delta Y/\Delta X$.

Diminishing marginal rate of substitution

The more a person consumes of good X and the less of good Y, the less additional Y will that person be prepared to give up in order to obtain an extra unit of X: i.e. $\Delta Y/\Delta X$ diminishes.

Figure 3.7 Deriving the marginal rate of substitution from an indifference curve

gained by consuming one more X. In other words, the marginal utility of X must be four times as great as that of Y. Therefore, $MU_X/MU_Y = 4$. But this is the same as the marginal rate of substitution:

$$MRS = \frac{MU_X}{MU_Y} = \text{slope of indifference curve (ignoring negative sign)}$$

? Although indifference curves will normally be bowed in toward the origin, on odd occasions they might not be. Which of the diagrams below correspond to which of the following?
(a) X and Y are left shoes and right shoes.
(b) X and Y are two brands of the same product, and the consumer cannot tell them apart.
(c) X is a good but Y is a 'bad' – like household refuse.

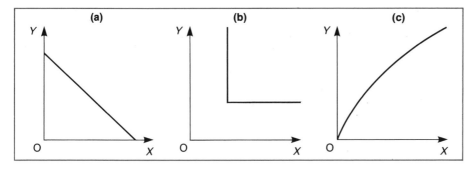

An indifference map

More than one indifference curve can be drawn. For example, referring back to Table 3.3, Clive could give another set of combinations of pears and oranges that all give him a higher (but equal) level of utility than the set shown in the table. This could then be plotted in Figure 3.6 as another indifference curve.

Although the actual amount of utility corresponding to each curve is not specified, indifference curves further out to the right would show combinations of the two goods that yield a higher utility, and curves further in to the left would show combinations yielding a lower utility.

In fact, a whole indifference map can be drawn, with each successive indifference curve showing a higher level of utility. Combinations of goods along I_2 in Figure 3.8

Indifference map

A graph showing a whole set of indifference curves. The further away a particular curve is from the origin, the higher the level of satisfaction it represents.

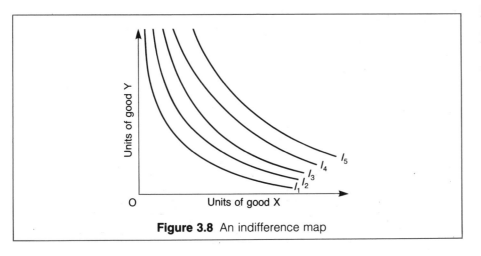

Figure 3.8 An indifference map

give a higher utility to the consumer than those along I_1. Those along I_3 give a higher utility than those along I_2, and so on. The term 'map' is appropriate here, because the indifference curves are rather like contours on a real map. Just as a contour joins all those points of a particular height, so an indifference curve shows all those combinations yielding a particular level of utility.

1. Draw another two indifference curves on Figure 3.6, one outward from and one inward from the original curve. Read off various combinations of pears and oranges along these two new curves and enter them on a table like Table 3.3.
2. By referring to Figure 3.9 and the three points *a*, *b*, and *c* on the two curves illustrated, explain why it would be logically impossible for two indifference curves to cross.

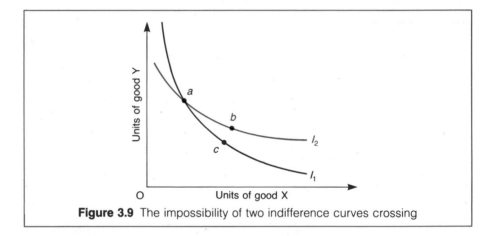

Figure 3.9 The impossibility of two indifference curves crossing

The budget line

Budget line

A graph showing all the possible combinations of two goods that can be purchased at given prices and for a given budget.

We turn now to the budget line. This is the other important element in the analysis of consumer behaviour. Whereas indifference maps illustrate people's preferences, the *actual* choices they make will depend on their *incomes*. Obviously, the more you have to spend, the more you will be able to purchase. The budget line shows what combinations of two goods you are *able* to buy, given (a) your income available to spend on them and (b) their prices.

Just as we did with an indifference curve, we can construct a budget line from a table. Table 3.4 shows various combinations of two goods X and Y that can be purchased assuming that (a) the price of X is £2 and the price of Y is £1 and (b) the consumer has a budget of £30 to be divided between the two goods.

Table 3.4 Consumption possibilities

Units of good X	Units of good Y	Point on budget line
0	30	*a*
5	20	*b*
10	10	*c*
15	0	*d*

Assumptions: budget = £30, P_X = £2, P_Y = £1.

1. How much Y could be purchased for the same budget if (a) 4 units of X and (b) 12 units of X were purchased?
2. The equation for a budget line can be given as $aX + bY = M$, where M is the total amount of money available to spend on the two goods X and Y (i.e. the budget), and a and b are the prices of the two goods. What is the equation that corresponds to Table 3.4? Confirm your answer by substituting the figures in each row of the table into your equation.

In Figure 3.10, then, if you are limited to a budget of £30 you can consume any combination of X and Y along the line (or inside it). You cannot, however, afford to buy combinations that lie outside it: i.e. in the shaded area. The shaded area is known as the *infeasible region* for the given budget.

We have said that the amount people can afford to buy will depend on (a) their budget and (b) the prices of the two goods. We can show how a change in either of these two determinants will affect the budget line.

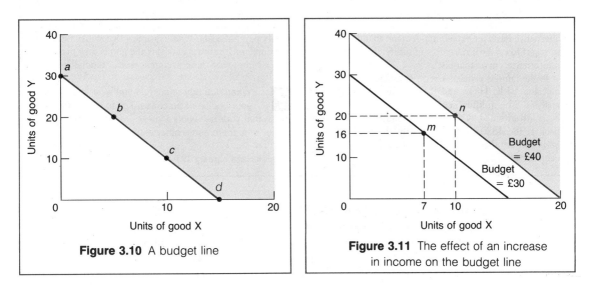

Figure 3.10 A budget line

Figure 3.11 The effect of an increase in income on the budget line

A change in income

If the consumer's income (and hence budget) increases, the budget line will shift outward, parallel to the old one. This is illustrated in Table 3.5 and Figure 3.11, which show the effect of a rise in the consumer's budget from £30 to £40. (Note that

Table 3.5 Consumption possibilities for budgets of £30 and £40

Budget of £30		Budget of £40	
Units of good X	Units of good Y	Units of good X	Units of good Y
0	30	0	40
5	20	5	30
10	10	10	20
15	0	15	10
		20	0

Assumptions: $P_X = £2$, $P_Y = £1$.

Box 3.5

Utility Under Attack
The birth of indifference curve analysis

The marginal utility theory of demand came under sustained attack in the 1930s. This attack was made by both economists and non-economists.

The weakness of the theory was its assumption that utility can be measured: the assumption that when we go shopping we weigh up the *amount* of utility that we get from our various purchases. Psychologists claimed that this is simply false. Utility cannot be measured in this absolute or *cardinal* way. Consumers do not have their own 'utility meters' inside their heads.

Faced by these criticisms, economists sought an alternative basis for explaining demand that did not have to resort to cardinal measures of utility. The answer was indifference curve analysis.

In the famous article 'A reconsideration of the theory of value',[1] J.R. Hicks and R.G.D. Allen developed the analysis. The indifference curve technique had, in fact, been first invented by the Irish economist F.Y. Edgeworth back in the 1880s. But it was with the work of Hicks in particular that the technique became popular with economists.

Indifference curve analysis does not require utility to be measured. All that is needed is that consumers should be able to order their preferences, so that for any two goods they could say whether they prefer a to b, or b to a, or are indifferent between them. Thus cardinal measures of utility were replaced by *ordinal* measures of preferences.

Indifference curve analysis had another major advantage. It could distinguish between the income and substitution effects of a price change: something that marginal utility analysis could not do. (See pp. 131–5.)

Indifference curve analysis, however, did not wholly satisfy psychologists. It still assumes that consumers are 'maximizers' by always choosing the goods they prefer. It still assumes that these preferences are 'rational'.

? When you buy goods, do you ever later regret your choice of purchases? If so, does this mean that your behaviour was not rational in the first place, or is there some other explanation?

[1] *Economica*, February 1934.

---

there is no change in the prices of X and Y, which remain at £2 and £1 respectively.)

More can now be purchased. For example, if the consumer was originally purchasing 7 units of X and 16 units of Y (point *m*), this could be increased with the new budget of £40, to 10 units of X and 20 units of Y (point *n*) or any other combination of X and Y along the new higher budget line.

A change in price
The relative prices of the two goods are given by the *slope* of the budget line. This can be demonstrated with the above example. The slope of the budget line in Figure 3.10 is 30/15 = 2. (We are ignoring the negative sign: strictly speaking, the slope should be −2.) Similarly, the slope of the new higher budget line in Figure 3.11 is 40/20 = 2. But in each case this is simply the ratio of the *price* of X (£2) to the *price* of Y (£1). Thus the slope of the budget line equals P_X/P_Y.

If the price of either good changes, the slope of the budget line will change. This is illustrated in Figure 3.12 which, like Figure 3.10, assumes a budget of £30 and an initial price of X of £2 and a price of Y of £1. The initial budget line is B_1.

Now let us assume that the price of X falls to £1 but that the price of Y remains the same (£1). The new budget line will join 30 on the Y axis with 30 on the X axis. In other words, the line pivots outward on point *a*. If the price of Y changed, the line would pivot on point *b*.

1. Assume that the budget remains at £30 and the price of X stays at £2, but that Y rises in price to £3. Draw the new budget line.
2. What will happen to the budget line if the consumer's income doubles and the prices of both X and Y double?

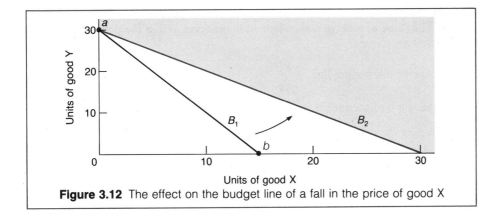

Figure 3.12 The effect on the budget line of a fall in the price of good X

Choosing the consumption point

We are now in a position to put the two elements of the analysis together: the indifference map and a budget line. This will enable us to show how much of each of the two goods the 'rational' consumer will buy from a given budget. Let us examine Figure 3.13.

The consumer would prefer to consume anywhere along indifference curve I_5 to anywhere along I_4. Similarly, points along I_4 are preferable to points along I_3. But given the budget line illustrated, it is not possible to consume anywhere along either I_5 or I_4. They are both in the infeasible region.

The consumer can, however, consume at certain points along curves I_1, I_2 and I_3. Consumption could be at point r along curve I_1. But to consume this combination of X and Y would not be 'rational'. By moving to point s a higher level of satisfaction could be gained, since point s is on the higher curve I_2. But point s is not the optimum point either. It is possible to gain a higher level of satisfaction still by consuming at point t on curve I_3. I_3 is the highest indifference curve that can be reached for this particular budget.

The optimum consumption point for the consumer, then, is where the budget line touches (is 'tangential to') the highest possible indifference curve. At any other point along the budget line the consumer would get a lower level of utility.

Figure 3.13 The optimum consumption point

If the budget line is tangential to an indifference curve, they will have the same slope. (The slope of a curve is the slope of the tangent to it at the point in question.) But as we have seen:

the slope of the budget line $= \dfrac{P_X}{P_Y}$

and the slope of the indifference curve $= MRS = \dfrac{MU_X}{MU_Y}$

Therefore, at the optimum consumption point:

$$\dfrac{P_X}{P_Y} = \dfrac{MU_X}{MU_Y}$$

i.e. $\dfrac{MU_X}{P_X} = \dfrac{MU_Y}{P_Y}$

But this is the *equi-marginal principle* that we established in the first part of this chapter: only this time, using the indifference curve approach, there has been no need to measure utility. All we have needed to do is to observe, for any two combinations of goods, whether the consumer preferred one to the other or was indifferent between them.

Just as we can use indifference analysis to show the combination of goods that maximizes utility for a given budget, so too we can show the *least-cost* combination of goods that yields a *given* level of utility. This is shown in Figure 3.14.

Let us assume that you want to obtain the level of utility indicated by the indifference curve *I*. What combination of the two goods X and Y should you consume? By drawing a series of budget lines on the diagram we can find the least costly way for you to achieve that level of satisfaction. This combination will be at the point where the indifference curve touches the *lowest* possible budget line: i.e. at point *r*. Any other combination of goods along the indifference curve will cost you more: i.e. it will be on a higher budget line.

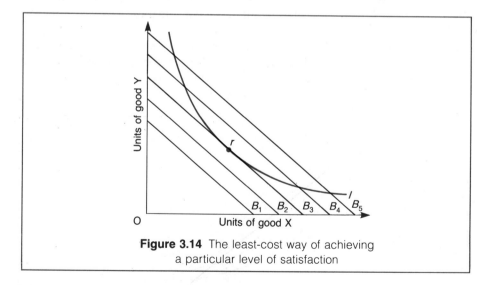

Figure 3.14 The least-cost way of achieving a particular level of satisfaction

? Refer back to Table 3.3 and plot the indifference curve like that shown in Figure 3.6. Assume that pears cost 10p each and that oranges cost 15p. Draw a series of budget lines for different levels of expenditure, making one of them tangential to the indifference curve that you have drawn. Assuming that Clive wants to gain the particular level of satisfaction from eating fruit that is shown by the indifference curve you have drawn, what is the least amount of money he must spend to achieve this? How many pears and how many oranges will he buy?

The following sections show how indifference curves and budget lines can be used to analyze the effect on consumption of changes in income and changes in price.

The effect of changes in income

An increase in income is represented by a parallel shift outward of the budget line (assuming no change in the price of X and Y). This will then lead to a new optimum consumption point on a higher indifference curve. A different consumption point will be found for each different level of income.

In Figure 3.15 a series of budget lines are drawn representing different levels of consumer income. The corresponding optimum consumption points (*r, s, t, u*) are shown. Each point is where the new higher budget line just touches the highest possible indifference curve. The line joining these points is known as the income–consumption curve.

Note that we can always draw in an indifference curve that will be tangential to a given budget line. Just because we only draw a few indifference curves on a diagram, it does not mean that there are only a few *possible* ones. We could draw as many as we liked. Again it is rather like the contours on a real map. They may be drawn at, say, 10 metre intervals. We could, however, if we liked, draw them at 1 metre or even 1 cm intervals, or at whatever height was suitable to our purpose. For example, if the maximum height of a lake were 32.45 metres above sea level, it might be useful to draw a contour at that height to show what land might be liable to flooding.

If your money income goes up and the price of goods does not change we say that your real income has risen. In other words, you can buy more than you did before. But your real income can also rise even if you do not earn any more money. This will happen if prices fall. For the same amount of money, you can buy more goods than previously. We analyze the effect of a rise in real income caused by a fall in prices in just the same way as we did when money income rose and prices stayed the same. Provided the *relative* prices of the two goods stay the same (i.e. provided they fall by the same percentage), the budget line will shift outward parallel to the old one.

Income–consumption curve

A line showing how a person's optimum level of consumption of two goods changes as income changes (assuming the prices of the goods remain constant).

Real income

Income measured in terms of how much it can buy. If your *money* income rises by 10 per cent, but prices rise by 8 per cent, you can only buy 2 per cent more goods than before. Your *real* income has risen by 2 per cent.

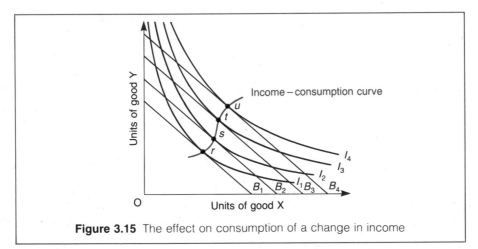

Figure 3.15 The effect on consumption of a change in income

Income elasticity of demand and the income–consumption curve

The income–consumption curve drawn in the upper half of Figure 3.16 shows how Amanda's monthly demand for two goods, bread and compact discs, rises as her income rises.

Directly after leaving school she has a low income and thus has a small monthly budget to spend. As we would expect, she buys few compact discs as they constitute a luxury she can barely afford, whereas she has to eat and bread is a major part of her diet. Initially, then, with a budget of B_1 she consumes at point a.

Later, she obtains a better paid job. Her budget line shifts to B_2 and she now consumes at point b. Her purchases of CDs have increased significantly (from Q_{cd_1} to Q_{cd_2}). They have a high income elasticity of demand. Her purchases of bread, however, have hardly increased at all (from Q_{b_1} to Q_{b_2}). Bread, being a basic good has a low income elasticity of demand.

The lower part of Figure 3.16 shows how Amanda's demand for CDs varies with her income. Each of the points a, b and c corresponds to an equivalent point in the upper part of the diagram. The line joining these points together is known as an *Engel curve*, after the German statistician Ernst Engel (1821–96) who did extensive investigations into the effects of changes in family budgets on family expenditures.

The Engel curve in Figure 3.16 illustrates a good with an income elasticity of demand greater than 1. This means that the proportionate rise in demand from Q_{cd_1} to Q_{cd_2} is greater than the proportionate rise in income from Y_1 to Y_2.

Engel curve

A line showing how much of a good people will demand at different levels of income.

Figure 3.16 Deriving an Engel curve from an income–consumption curve

The effect of a rise in income on the demand for inferior goods

If one of the two goods, X or Y, is an inferior good, such as cheap margarine or inferior cuts of meat, the effect of a rise in income will be to *reduce* the quantity purchased. Remember this is how we *defined* an inferior good in Chapter 2. This is shown in Figure 3.17.

If X is an inferior good and Y is a normal good, an outward movement of the budget line (an increase in income) will lead to *less* X being purchased. Point *b* is to the *left* of point *a*. The income–consumption curve has a negative slope.

1. The income–consumption curve in Figure 3.17 is drawn as *positively* sloped at low levels of income. Why?
2. Show the effect of a rise in income on the demand for X and Y, where this time Y is the inferior good and X is the normal good. Is the income–consumption curve positively or negatively sloped?
3. Sketch an Engel curve corresponding to Figure 3.17. What can we say about the income elasticity of demand for an inferior good?

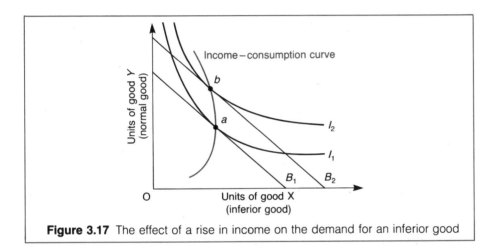

Figure 3.17 The effect of a rise in income on the demand for an inferior good

The effect of changes in price

If either X or Y changes in price, the budget line will 'pivot'. Take the case of a reduction in the price of X (but no change in the price of Y). If this happens, the budget line will swing outwards. This effect is shown in Figure 3.18.

The initial budget line B_1 corresponds to the data in Table 3.4, where the budget was £30, the price of X was £2 and the price of Y was £1. Assume now that the price of X is reduced to £1 while the price of Y remains the same as before (£1). The new budget line B_2 will therefore intersect the X axis at twice the quantity that B_1 does (i.e. 30 units of X), but will continue to intersect the Y axis at the same point. The curve has pivoted on point *a*.

The old optimum consumption point was at *j*. After the reduction in the price of good X, a new optimum consumption point is found at *k*.

Illustrate on an indifference diagram the effects of the following:

(a) A rise in the price of good X (assuming no change in the price of Y).
(b) A fall in the price of good Y (assuming no change in the price of X).

Figure 3.18 The effect of a fall in the price of good X

A series of budget lines could be drawn, all pivoting round point *a* in Figure 3.18. Each one represents a different price of good X, but with money income and the price of Y held constant. The further out the curve, the lower the price of X. At each price, there will be an optimum consumption point. The line that connects these points is known as the price–consumption curve

Price–consumption curve

A line showing how a person's optimum level of consumption of two goods changes as the price of one of the two goods changes (assuming that income and the price of the other good remain constant).

Deriving the individual's demand curve

We can use the analysis of price changes to show how in theory a person's demand curve for a product can be derived. To do this we need to modify the diagram slightly.

Let us assume that we want to derive a person's demand curve for good X. What we need to show is the effect on the consumption of X of a change in the price of X assuming the prices of all other goods are held constant. To do this we need to redefine good Y. Instead of being a *single* good, Y becomes the total of *all other* goods. But what units are we to put on the vertical axis? Each of these other goods will be in different units: litres of petrol, loaves of bread, kilograms of cheese, numbers of haircuts, etc. We cannot add them all up unless we first convert them to a common unit. The answer is to measure them as the total amount of money spent on them: i.e. what is *not* spent on good X.

With expenditure on all other goods plotted on the vertical axis and with income; tastes and the price of all other goods held constant, we can now derive the demand curve for X. This is demonstrated in Figure 3.19.

We illustrate the changes in the price of X by pivoting the budget line on the point where it intersects the Y axis. It is then possible, by drawing a price–consumption line, to show the amount of X demanded at each price. It is then a simple matter of transferring these price–quantity relationships on to a demand curve. In Figure 3.19, each of the points *a*, *b*, *c* and *d* on the demand curve in the lower part of the diagram corresponds to one of the four points on the price–consumption curve.

? As quantity demanded increases from Q_1 to Q_2 in Figure 3.19, the expenditure on all other goods *decreases*. (Point *b* is lower than point *a*.) This means, therefore, that the person's total expenditure on X has correspondingly increased. What, then, can we say about the person's price elasticity of demand for X between points *a* and *b*? What can we say about the price elasticity of demand between points *b* and *c*, and between points *c* and *d*?

Figure 3.19 Deriving the demand curve for good X from a price–consumption curve

The income and substitution effects of a price change

In Chapter 2 we argued that when the price of a good rises, consumers will purchase less of it for two reasons:

- They cannot afford to buy so much. This is the income effect
- The good is now more expensive relative to other goods. Therefore consumers substitute alternatives for it. This is the substitution effect

We can extend our arguments of Chapter 2 by demonstrating the income and substitution effects with the use of indifference analysis. Let us start with the case of a normal good and show what happens when its price changes.

A normal good

In Figure 3.20 the price of normal good X has *risen* and the budget line has pivoted *inwards* from B_1 to B_2. The consumption point has moved from point *f* to point *h*. Part of this shift in consumption is due to the substitution effect and part is due to the income effect.

The substitution effect. To separate these two effects a new budget line is drawn, parallel to B_2 but tangential to the original indifference curve I_1. This is the line B_{1a} in Figure 3.20. Being parallel to B_2, it represents the new price ratio (i.e. the higher price of X). Being tangential to I_1, however, it enables the consumer to obtain the *same utility* as before: in other words, there is no loss in *real* income to the consumer.

Income effect of a price change

That portion of the change in demand that results from the change in real income.

Substitution effect of a price change

That portion of the change in demand that results from the change in the relative price of the good.

Normal good

A good whose demand increases as income increases.

Figure 3.20 The income and substitution effects of a rise in the price of good X

By focusing on B_{1a}, then, which represents no change in real income, we have excluded the income effect. The movement from point f to point g, therefore, is due *purely* to a change in the relative prices of X and Y. The movement from Q_{x_1} to Q_{x_2}, therefore, is the *substitution* effect.

The income effect. In reality the budget line has shifted to B_2 and the consumer is forced to consume on a lower indifference curve I_2: real income has fallen. Thus the movement from Q_{x_2} to Q_{x_3} is the *income* effect.

In the case of a normal good, therefore, the income and substitution effects reinforce each other. They are both negative: they *both* involve a *reduction* in the quantity demanded as price *rises* (and vice versa).

The bigger the income and substitution effects, the higher will be the price elasticity of demand for good X.

 Illustrate on two separate indifference diagrams the income and substitution effects of the following:
(a) A decrease in the price of good X (and no change in the price of good Y).
(b) An increase in the price of good Y (and no change in the price of good X).

An inferior good

Inferior good

A good whose demand decreases as income increases.

As we saw above, when people's incomes rise they will buy less of inferior goods such as poor quality margarine and breast of lamb, since they will now be able to afford better quality goods instead. Conversely, when income falls, they will now have to reduce their living standards: their consumption of inferior goods will thus rise.

The substitution effect. If the *price* of an inferior good (good X) rises, the substitution effect will be in the same direction as for a normal good: i.e. it will be negative. People will consume less X relative to Y, since X is now more expensive relative to Y. For example, if the price of inferior quality margarine (good X) went up, people would tend to use better quality margarine or butter (good Y) instead. This is illustrated in Figure 3.21. The analysis of substitution and income effects is similar to that of Figure 3.20.

Figure 3.21 The income and substitution effects of a rise in the price of good X: X is an inferior (non-Giffen) good

Figure 3.22 The income and substitution effects of a rise in the price of good X: X is a Giffen good

The rise in price of X is signified by an inward pivot of the budget line from B_1 to B_2. As before, the substitution effect is illustrated by a movement along the original indifference curve (I_1) from point f to point g. The quantity of X demanded falls from Q_{x_1} to Q_{x_2}.

The income effect. The income effect, however, will be the opposite of that for a normal good: it will be *positive*. The reduction in real income (from the rise in price of X) will tend to *increase* the consumption of X, since with a fall in real income *more* inferior goods will now be purchased – including more X. Thus point h is to the *right* of point g: the income effect increases quantity back from Q_{x_2} to Q_{x_3}.

A Giffen good: a particular type of inferior good

If the inferior good were to account for a very large proportion of a consumer's expenditure, a change in its price would have a significant effect on the consumer's real income, resulting in a large income effect. It is conceivable, therefore, that this large abnormal income effect could outweigh the normal substitution effect. In such a case, a rise in the price of X would lead to *more* X being consumed!

This is illustrated in Figure 3.22, where point h is to the *right* of point f. In other words, the fall in consumption (Q_{x_1} to Q_{x_2}) as a result of the substitution effect is more than offset by the rise in consumption (Q_{x_2} to Q_{x_3}) as a result of the large positive income effect.

Such a good is known as a Giffen good, after Sir Robert Giffen (1837–1910), who when studying the Irish famine of the 1840s is alleged to have claimed that the consumption of potatoes by the poor rose when their price rose. Potatoes formed such a large proportion of poor people's consumption that, if their price went up, the poor could not afford to buy so much meat, other vegetables, etc. and had to buy more potatoes instead. Naturally, such cases must be very rare indeed.

Giffen good

An inferior good whose demand increases as its price increases as a result of a positive income effect larger than the normal negative substitution effect.

 Are there any Giffen goods that you consume? If not, could you conceive of any circumstances in which one or more items of your expenditure would become Giffen goods?

Box 3.6

Income and Substitution Effects: An Alternative Analysis
Slutsky's approach to defining 'real' income

The analysis of income and substitution effects that we have just been looking at is that developed by Sir John Hicks (we will be giving a 'person profile' of him in Box 18.4). Hicks defined the substitution effect as that which arises *purely* from a change in relative prices. In other words, it is the effect of a price change when *real income is held constant.*

Hicks defined a consumer's real income as constant if the level of *satisfaction* could be maintained constant: in other words, if the consumer can remain on the same indifference curve. With this definition of constant real income, the substitution effect is illustrated by sliding the budget line round the original indifference curve. In Figure 3.20, this resulted in a move from point *f* to point *g* on the original indifference curve I_1.

Hicks' definition, then, of constant real income relies on the *subjective* tastes of the consumer. It will differ from consumer to consumer depending on the shape of each one's indifference curves.

An alternative analysis was the earlier one developed by the Russian economist and mathematician Evgeny Slutsky (1880–1948). Slutsky defined constant real income as that which would allow the consumer to buy exactly the same quantity of goods after a price change as before. This definition does not involve reference to an indifference curve and hence to the subjective tastes of individual consumers.

The Slutsky analysis is shown in this diagram, which like Figure 3.20 analyzes the effect of a rise in the price of good X.

Just as in Figure 3.20, the full effect (i.e. income plus substitution effects) of the price rise is for the quantity of X consumed to fall from Q_{x_1} to Q_{x_3} (a movement from point *f* to point *h*). But this time the income and substitution effects are analyzed differently.

To keep real income constant and thus to isolate the

Slutsky's analysis of income and substitution effects

pure substitution effect, the Slutsky approach is to draw a new hypothetical budget line (B_1') through point *f*. By passing through point *f*, it shows that the consumer could (if that was what was wanted) continue to purchase the same amount of the two goods as before. But to illustrate the change in relative prices, B_1' is drawn parallel to the real new budget line B_2. With this hypothetical budget line B_1', the consumer will consume at point *g'* on indifference curve I_1'. The move from *f* to *g'* (i.e. from Q_{x_1} to Q_{x_2}) thus represents the substitution effect.

Slutsky's income effect then becomes the move from *g'* to *h* (i.e. from Q_{x_2} to Q_{x_3}).

? Show on one diagram both the Hicks and the Slutsky analysis of the income and substitution effects of a *fall* in the price of good X.

The effect of a change in price on the demand for other goods

So far we have considered the effect of the change in the price of good X on the demand for good X alone. Let us now consider the effect on the demand for good Y. There will again be an income and a substitution effect.

The income effect. *Real* income has changed: if the price of X has risen, people can afford to buy less of all goods, including good Y. The income effect is thus negative (unless Y is an inferior good).

The substitution effect. The *relative* prices of the two goods have changed: if the price of X has risen, good Y will now be relatively cheaper and thus people may buy more of it. The substitution effect is thus positive.

 Referring to Figure 3.20, show the size of the income and substitution effects on the demand for good Y of a rise in the price of good X (and hence a movement from point *f* to point *h*).

Whether more or less Y is purchased depends on which is bigger: the income effect or the substitution effect.

The income effect will be bigger the larger the proportion of income that was initially spent on good X and the more sensitive is the demand for good Y to changes in income.

The substitution effect will tend to be bigger the closer the two goods are as substitutes for each other.

The bigger the net effect on the demand for Y, the greater is the *cross-price elasticity of demand* for Y (with respect to X). If the substitution effect outweighs the income effect, the cross elasticity will be positive: a rise in the price of X leads to a rise in the demand for Y. If the income effect outweighs the substitution effect, the cross elasticity will be negative.

(Note that in a simple two-good model we cannot analyze the effect of a change in the price of one good on the demand for a *complement*. For example, we cannot show how a fall in the price of cars leads to an increase in the demand for petrol. In a two-good model, if the relative price of cars has come *down*, the relative price of petrol must have gone *up*! We would thus have to introduce a *third* good (which could be the expenditure on all other goods), to show how a fall in the price of cars (relative to the third good) leads to an increased demand for *both* cars and petrol. To introduce a third good (or more than three) we would have to move from simple graphical analysis to the use of algebra.)

The usefulness of indifference analysis

By the use of indifference analysis, it has been possible to demonstrate the logic of 'rational' consumer choice, the derivation of the individual's demand curve, and the income and substitution effects of a price change. All this has been done without having to resort to measuring utility.

Nevertheless there are limitations to the usefulness of indifference analysis:

- In practice it is virtually impossible to derive indifference curves, since it would involve a consumer having to imagine a whole series of different combinations of goods and deciding in each case whether a given combination gave more, equal or less satisfaction than other combinations.
- Consumers may not behave 'rationally', and hence may not give careful consideration to the satisfaction they believe they will gain from consuming goods. They may behave impetuously.
- Indifference curves are based on the satisfaction that consumers *believe* they will gain from a good. This belief may well be influenced by advertising. Consumers may be disappointed or pleasantly surprised, however, when they actually consume the good. In other words, consumers are not perfectly knowledgeable. Thus the 'optimum consumption' point may not in practice give consumers maximum satisfaction for their money.

Box 3.7

Consumer Theory: A Further Approach
Characteristics theory

Characteristics theory was developed in the mid-1960s by Kelvin Lancaster. He argued that people demand goods not for their own sake, but for the *characteristics* they possess.

Take cars for example. When choosing between the different makes, consumers do not just consider their relative prices, they also consider their attributes: comfort, style, horsepower, durability, reliability, fuel consumption, etc. It is these *characteristics* that give rise to utility.

Characteristics theory, then, is based on four crucial assumptions:

● All goods possess various characteristics.
● Different brands possess them in different proportions.
● The characteristics are measurable: they are 'objective'.
● The characteristics (along with price and income) determine consumer choice.

Let us assume that you are choosing between three different goods or brands of a good (e.g. a foodstuff). Each one has a different combination of two characteristics (e.g. protein and calories). Your choices can be shown graphically.

Quantity of characteristic B

The choice between brands of a product: each brand has different characteristics

The quantities of two characteristics are shown on the two axes. An indifference map can be constructed, showing the different combinations of the two characteristics that yield given levels of utility. Thus any combination of the two characteristics along indifference curve I_4 in the diagram gives a higher level of utility than those along I_3, and so on. The shape of the indifference curves (bowed in) illustrates a diminishing marginal rate of substitution between the two characteristics.

The amount of the two characteristics given by the three brands are shown by the three rays. The more that is consumed of each brand, the further up the respective ray will the consumer be. Thus at x_1, the consumer is gaining Q_{a_1} of characteristic A and Q_{b_1} of characteristic B.

Assume that, for the same money, the consumer could consume at x_1 with brand (1), x_2 with brand (2) and x_3 with brand (3). The consumer will consume brand (1): x_1 is on a higher indifference curve than x_2 or x_3.

Now assume that the price of brand (2) falls. For a given expenditure, the consumer can now move up the brand (2) ray. But not until the price has fallen enough to allow consumption at point x_4, will the consumer consider switching from brand (1). If price falls enough for consumption to be at point x_5, clearly the consumer will switch.

The characteristics approach has a number of advantages over conventional indifference curve analysis in explaining consumer behaviour.

● It helps to explain brand loyalty. When price changes, people will not necessarily gradually move from one brand to another. Rather they will stick with a brand until a critical price is reached. Then they will switch brands all at once.
● It allows the choice between *several* goods to be shown on the same diagram. Each good or brand has its own ray.
● It helps to explain the nature of substitute goods. The closer substitutes are, the more similar will be their characteristics and hence the closer will be their rays. The closer the rays, the more likely it is that there will be a shift in consumption to one good when the price of the other good changes.
● A change in the quality of a good can be shown by rotating its ray.

There are weaknesses with the approach, however:

● Some characteristics cannot be measured. Characteristics such as beauty, taste and entertainment value are subjective: they are in the minds of the consumer.
● Only two characteristics can be plotted. Most goods have several characteristics.

? 1. Make a list of the characteristics of shoes. Which are 'objective' and which are 'subjective'?

2. If two houses had identical characteristics, except that one was near a noisy airport and the other was in a quiet location, and if the market price of the first house was £80 000 and of the second was £100 000, how would that help us to put a value on the characteristic of peace and quiet?

- Certain goods are only purchased every now and again, and then only one at a time. Examples would include consumer durables such as cars, televisions and washing machines. Indifference curves are based on the assumption that marginal increases in one good can be traded off against marginal decreases in another. This will not be the case with consumer durables.

  The individual's demand curve for dish washers, for example, may look like that in Figure 3.23. Above P_1, the consumer will not purchase a dish washer: it is too expensive. Below P_1, one dish washer will be purchased. The price would have to be very low indeed to persuade the consumer to buy two.

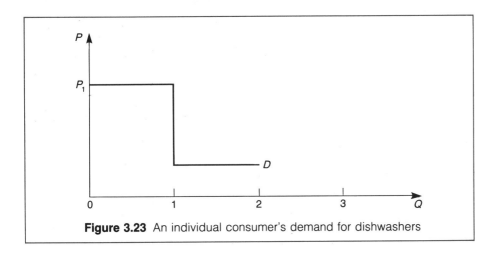

Figure 3.23 An individual consumer's demand for dishwashers

▲ SUMMARY

1. The indifference approach to analyzing consumer demand avoids having to measure utility.
2. An indifference curve shows all those combinations of two goods that give an equal amount of satisfaction to a consumer. An indifference map can be drawn with indifference curves further to the north-east representing higher (but still unspecified) levels of satisfaction.
3. Indifference curves are usually drawn convex to the origin. This is because of a diminishing marginal rate of substitution between the two goods. As more of one good is purchased, the consumer is willing to give up less and less of the other for each additional unit of the first. The marginal rate of substitution is given by the slope of the indifference curve which equals MU_X/MU_Y.
4. A budget line can be drawn on an indifference diagram. A budget line shows all those combinations of the two goods that can be purchased for a given amount of money, assuming a constant price of the two goods. The slope of the budget line depends on the relative price of the two goods. The slope is equal to P_X/P_Y.
5. The consumer will achieve the maximum level of satisfaction for a given income (budget) by consuming at the point where the budget line just touches the highest possible indifference curve. At this point of tangency the budget line and the indifference curve have the

same slope. Thus $MU_X/MU_Y = P_X/P_Y$ and therefore $MU_X/P_X = MU_Y/P_Y$, which is the 'equi-marginal principle' for maximizing utility from a given income that was established in section 3.1.
6. If the consumer's real income (and hence budget) rises, there will be a parallel outward shift of the budget line. The 'rational' consumer will move to the point of tangency of this new budget line with the highest indifference curve. The line that traces out these optimum positions for different levels of income is known as the 'income–consumption curve'.
7. From the income–consumption curve can be derived an Engel curve. This shows how the demand for a single good will vary as income varies. For a normal good, demand will rise as income rises. The Engel curve will be positively sloped. For an inferior good, demand will fall as income rises. The Engel curve will be negatively sloped.
8. If the price of one of the two goods changes, the budget line will pivot on the axis of the other good. An outward pivot represents a fall in price; an inward pivot represents an increase in price. The line that traces the tangency points of these budget lines with the appropriate indifference curves is called a 'price–consumption curve'.
9. By measuring the expenditure on all other goods on the vertical axis and by holding their price constant and

money income constant, a demand curve can be derived for the good measured on the horizontal axis. Changes in its price can be represented by pivoting the budget line. The effect on the quantity demanded can be found from the resulting price–consumption curve.

10. The effect of a change in price on quantity demanded can be divided into an income and a substitution effect. The substitution effect is the result of a change in relative prices alone. The income effect is the result of the change in real income alone. *

11. For a normal good, the income and substitution effects will both be negative and will reinforce each other. With an inferior good, the substitution effect will still be negative but the income effect will be positive and thus will to some extent offset the substitution effect. If the (positive) income effect is bigger than the (negative) substitution effect, the good is called a Giffen good. A rise in the price of a Giffen good will thus cause a *rise* in the quantity demanded.

12. Indifference analysis, although avoiding having to measure utility, nevertheless has limitations. Indifference curves are difficult to derive in practice; consumers may not behave rationally; the 'optimum' consumption point may not be optimum if the consumer lacks knowledge of the good; indifference curves will not be smooth for items where single units each account for a large proportion of income.

Background to Supply 4

The last chapter went behind the demand curve. It attempted to explain just how much of various goods people will buy if they are behaving 'rationally'. As far as consumers were concerned, rational behaviour meant weighing up the *benefits* (utility) of consuming various amounts of goods or combinations of goods against their *costs* (their price).

We now need to go behind the supply curve and find out just how the rational producer (or 'firm' as we call all producers) will behave.

In this case we shall be looking at the benefits and costs to the firm of producing various quantities of goods and using various alternative methods of production. We shall be asking:

- How much will be produced?
- What combination of inputs will be used?
- How much profit will be made?

We will examine how these decisions are affected by various costs of production and by the demand for the product.

Two important considerations govern a firm's supply, and hence the supply of the whole industry. The first is the *aims* of the firm. For example, a firm that seeks to maximize profit is likely to produce a different output from a firm that seeks to maximize sales or some other goal. The second is the degree of *competition* a firm faces. A firm competing with hundreds of others is likely to produce a different output from a firm facing little or no competition.

Profit and the aims of a firm

The traditional theory of supply, or theory of the firm, assumes that firms aim to *maximize profit*. Although the decision makers in firms may have other aims as well – e.g. pleasant working conditions – under many circumstances it is legitimate to assume that the overriding aim is the maximization of profits. The advocates of the traditional theory would argue that it enables useful and largely accurate predictions to be made about the behaviour of firms.

The traditional profit-maximizing theory of the firm is examined in this and the following two chapters.

First we examine the general principles that govern how much a firm supplies. Then, in Chapters 5 and 6, we look at how supply is affected by the amount of competition a firm faces. Different types of market are examined, right from one

Rational producer behaviour

When a firm weighs up the costs and benefits of alternative courses of action and then seeks to maximize its net benefit.

Traditional theory of the firm

The analysis of pricing and output decisions of the firm under various market conditions, assuming that the firm wishes to maximize profit.

extreme where the individual firms are so small that they are totally powerless to influence market conditions, to the other extreme where the firm is a monopoly – the only firm in the market and hence with considerable power.

In some circumstances, however, firms may not seek to maximize profits. Instead they may seek to maximize sales, or their rate of growth of sales. Alternatively, they may have no *single* aim, but rather a series of potentially conflicting aims held by different managers in different departments of the firm. Not surprisingly, a firm's behaviour will depend on just what its aims are. Chapter 7 looks at various alternative theories to profit maximization: each theory depending on the particular aims of the firm.

Alternative theories of the firm

Theories of the firm based on the assumption that firms have aims other than profit maximization.

Profit maximization

This chapter, then, provides the background to the profit maximizing theory of the firm. So just what do we mean by 'profit'?

Profit is made by firms earning more from the sale of goods than the goods cost to produce. A firm's total profit ($T\Pi$) is thus the difference between its total sales revenue (TR) and its total costs of production (TC):

$$T\Pi = TR - TC$$

(Note that we use the Greek Π (pi) for 'profit' because the letter P is normally reserved for 'price' or sometimes, as we shall see later in this chapter, for 'product'.)

In order, then, to discover how a firm can maximize its profit, we must first consider what determines costs and revenue. Sections 4.1–4.4 of this chapter examine costs. Section 4.5 examines revenue. Finally section 4.6 puts costs and revenue together to examine profit.

4.1 Background to costs: the short-run theory of production

The cost of producing any level of output will depend on the amount of inputs used and the price the firm must pay for them. Let us first focus on the quantity of inputs used.

The production function: using inputs to produce output

Entrepreneurship

The initiating and organizing of the production of new goods, or the introduction of new techniques, and the risk taking associated with it.

As explained in Chapter 1, it is usual in economics to group inputs or *factors of production* into three categories.

Labour. This includes all working people of whatever type: electricians, secretaries, doctors, foremen, unskilled workers etc.

Land. This includes not only land, but all natural resources.

Production function

The mathematical relationship between the output of a good and the inputs used to produce it. It shows how output will be affected by changes in the quantity of one or more of the inputs.

Capital. This includes all manufactured inputs: plant, tools, machinery, etc. (Note that we are referring here to physical capital, not *financial* capital. In other words we are not referring to the *money* used to finance investment.)

Some economists include a fourth category: entrepreneurship. In a capitalist economy, the owners of firms organize the other three factors, and take the risks of being in business. Entrepreneurship is this organizational activity.

The relationship between output and inputs can be shown in a production function. A production function shows the relationship between the amount of factors used and the amount of output generated per period of time (e.g. per day, per month or per year). It can be expressed in algebraic form as follows:

$$TPP = f(F_1, F_2, F_3 \ldots F_n)$$

This merely states that total output – or total physical product – (*TPP*) depends on (i.e. is a function of) the quantity of factors (F_1, F_2 etc.) that are used. Numerical examples of production functions are given in the following sections.

Firms are likely to employ many different types of workers, raw materials, tools and machines. In simple economic models, however, it is usually assumed that firms employ only one type of labour, one type of land and one type of capital. In more complex models this assumption can be relaxed.

The simplest model of all assumes just two factors of production: for example, labour and capital or labour and land. In the case of labour and capital the production function would be in the form:

$$TPP = f(K, L)$$

where K and L are the quantities of capital and labour employed.

Although in the case of most firms these two-factor production functions are a considerable abstraction from reality, useful generalizations can nevertheless be made about the relationship between production and costs.

Before we go on, let us review what we have established so far:

- Firms will want to know what output they should produce to maximize profit.
- The level of profit depends on costs and revenue.
- Costs depend on the amount of inputs used.
- The amount of inputs used depends on the amount of output produced.
- The relationship between output and inputs is shown in the production function.

Let us now examine the production function in more detail. To start with we must distinguish between short-run and long-run production functions.

Short-run and long-run changes in production

If a firm wants to increase production, it will take time to acquire a greater quantity of certain inputs. For example, a manufacturer can use more electricity by turning on switches, but it might take a long time to obtain and install more machines, and longer still to build a second or third factory.

If, then, the firm wants to increase output in a hurry, it will only be able to increase the quantity of certain inputs. It can use more raw materials, more fuel, more tools and possibly more labour (by hiring extra workers or offering overtime to its existing workforce). But it will have to make do with its existing buildings and most of its machinery.

The distinction we are making here is between fixed factors and variable factors.

A *fixed* factor is an input that cannot be increased within a given time period (e.g. buildings).

A *variable* factor is one that can.

The distinction between fixed and variable factors allows us to distinguish between the short run and the long run.

The short run is a time period during which at least one factor of production is fixed. In the short run, then, output can only be increased by using more variable factors. For example, if a shipping line wanted to carry more passengers in response to a rise in demand, it could possibly accommodate more passengers on existing

Total physical product
The total output of a product per period of time that is obtained from a given amount of inputs.

Fixed factor
An input that cannot be increased in supply within a given time period.

Variable factor
An input that *can* be increased in supply within a given time period.

Short run
The period of time over which at least one factor is fixed.

Long run
The period of time long enough for *all* factors to be varied.

sailings if there was space. It could possibly increase the number of sailings with its existing fleet, by hiring more crew and using more fuel. But in the short run it could not buy more ships: there would not be time for them to be built.

The long run is a time period long enough for all inputs to be varied. Given long enough, a firm can build a second factory and install new machines.

The actual length of the short run will differ from firm to firm. It is not a fixed period of time. Thus if it takes a farmer a year to obtain new land, buildings and equipment, the short run is any time period up to a year and the long run is any time period longer than a year. If it takes a shipping company three years to obtain an extra ship, the short run is any period up to three years and the long run is any period longer than three years.

? 1. How will the length of the short run for the shipping company depend on the state of the shipbuilding industry?
2. Up to roughly how long is the short run in the following cases?
(a) A mobile disco firm; (b) Electricity power generation; (c) A small grocery retailing business; (d) 'Superstore Hypermarkets Ltd'.
In each case specify your assumptions.

For the remainder of this section we will concentrate on *short-run* production.

Production in the short run: the law of diminishing returns

Production in the short run is subject to *diminishing returns*. You may well have heard of 'the law of diminishing returns': it is one of the most famous of all 'laws' of economics. To illustrate how this law underlies short-run production let us take the simplest possible case where there are just two factors: one fixed and one variable.

Take the case of a farm. Assume the fixed factor is land and the variable factor is labour. Since the land is fixed in supply, output per period of time can only be increased by increasing the amount of workers employed. But imagine what would happen as more and more workers crowded on to a fixed area of land. The land cannot go on yielding more and more output indefinitely. After a point the additions to output from each extra worker will begin to diminish.

Law of diminishing (marginal) returns

When one or more factors are held fixed, there will come a point beyond which the extra output from additional units of the variable factor will diminish.

We can now state the law of diminishing (marginal) returns. It says that: *when increasing amounts of a variable factor are used with a given amount of a fixed factor, there will come a point when each extra unit of the variable factor will produce less extra output than the previous unit.*

Table 4.1 Wheat production per year from a particular farm

	Quantity of variable factor: number of workers employed (*Lb*)	Total physical product: output of wheat in tonnes per year (*TPP*)
a	0	0
	1	3
	2	10
b	3	24
	4	36
	5	40
	6	42
d	7	42
	8	40

Box 4.1

Diminishing Returns in the Bread Shop
Is the baker using his loaf?

Just up the road from where I live is a bread shop. Like many others, I buy my bread there on a Saturday morning. Not surprisingly, Saturday morning is the busiest time of the week for the shop and as a result it takes on extra assistants.

During the week only one assistant serves the customers, but on a Saturday morning there are five serving. But can they serve five times as many customers? No they cannot. There are diminishing returns to labour.

The trouble is that certain factors of production in the shop are fixed:

- The shop is a fixed size. It gets very crowded on Saturday morning. Assistants sometimes have to wait while customers squeeze past each other to get to the counter. The assistants themselves get in each other's way.

- There is only one cash till. Assistants frequently have to wait while other assistants use it.
- There is only one pile of tissue paper for wrapping the bread. Again the assistants often have to wait.

The fifth and maybe even the fourth assistant end up serving very few extra customers.

? 1. How would you advise the baker as to whether he should continue employing a fifth assistant?
2. Should the baker extend his shop? (That would allow more customers to be served on a Saturday morning.)

The short-run production function: total product

Let us now see how the law of diminishing returns affects total output (*TPP*).

In the simple case of the farm with only two factors – namely, a fixed supply of land ($\overline{L}n$) and a variable supply of farm workers (Lb) – the production function would be:

$$TPP = f(\overline{L}n, Lb)$$

The production function can also be expressed in the form of a table or a graph. Table 4.1 and Figure 4.1 show a hypothetical production function for a farm producing wheat. They show how wheat output per year varies as extra workers are employed on a fixed amount of land.

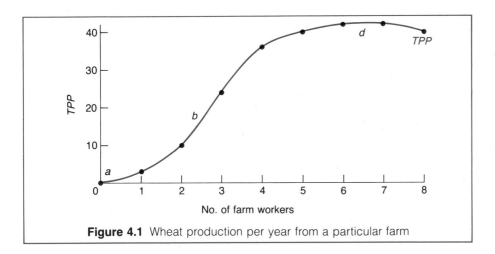

Figure 4.1 Wheat production per year from a particular farm

With nobody working on the land, output will be zero (point *a*).

As the first farm workers are taken on, wheat output initially rises more and more rapidly. The assumption behind this is that with only one or two workers efficiency is low, since the workers are spread too thinly. With more workers, however, they can work together – each, perhaps, doing some specialist job – and thus they can use the land more efficiently. In Table 4.1, output rises more and more rapidly up to the employment of the third worker (point *b*).

After point *b*, however, diminishing marginal returns set in: output rises less and less rapidly, and the *TPP* curve correspondingly becomes less steeply sloped.

When point *d* is reached, wheat output is at a maximum: the land is yielding as much as it can. Any more workers employed after that are likely to get in each other's way. Thus beyond point *d*, output is likely to fall again: eight workers produce less than seven workers.

The short-run production function: average and marginal product

In addition to total physical product, two other important concepts are illustrated by a production function: namely, average physical product (*APP*) and marginal physical product (*MPP*).

Average physical product

Total output (*TPP*) per unit of the variable factor in question: $APP = TPP/Q_v$.

Average physical product

This is output (*TPP*) per unit of the variable factor (Q_v). In the case of the farm, it is the output of wheat per worker.

$$APP = TPP/Q_v$$

Thus in Table 4.1 the average physical product of labour when four workers are employed is $36/4 = 9$ tonnes.

Marginal physical product

The extra output gained by the employment of one more unit of the variable factor: $MPP = \Delta TPP/\Delta Q_v$.

Marginal physical product

This is the *extra* output (ΔTPP) produced by employing *one more* unit of the variable factor.

Thus in Table 4.1 the marginal physical product of the fourth worker is 12 tonnes. The reason is that by employing the fourth worker, wheat output has risen from 24 tonnes to 36 tonnes: a rise of 12 tonnes.

In symbols, marginal physical product is given by:

$$MPP = \Delta TPP/\Delta Q_v$$

Thus in our example:

$$MPP = 12/1 = 12$$

The reason why we divide the increase in output (ΔTPP) by the increase in the quantity of the variable factor (ΔQ_v) is that some variable factors can only be increased in multiple units. For example, if we wanted to know the *MPP* of fertilizer and we found out how much extra wheat was produced by using an extra 20 kg bag, we would have to divide this output by 20 (ΔQ_v) to find the *MPP* of *one* more kilogram.

Let us return to the data given in Table 4.1. From these figures we can derive figures for *APP* and *MPP*. This is done in Table 4.2.

Note that the figures for *MPP* are entered in the spaces between the other figures. The reason is that *MPP* can be seen as the *difference* in output *between* one level of input and another. Thus in the table the difference in output between five and six workers is 2 tonnes.

Box 4.2

Malthus (1766–1834) and the Dismal Science of Economics

Population growth + diminishing returns = starvation

The law of diminishing returns has potentially cataclysmic implications for the future populations of the world.

If the population of the world grows rapidly, then food output may not keep pace with it. There will be diminishing returns to labour as more and more people crowd on to the limited amount of land available.

This is already a problem in some of the poorest countries of the world, especially in sub-Saharan Africa. The land is barely able to support current population levels. Only one or two bad harvests are needed to cause mass starvation. Witness the appalling famines in recent years in Ethiopia and the Sudan.

The relationship between population and food output was analyzed as long ago as 1798 by the Reverend Thomas Robert Malthus in his *Essay on the Principle of Population*. This book was a bestseller and made Robert Malthus perhaps the best known of all social scientists of his day.

Malthus argued as follows:

I say that the power of population is indefinitely greater than the power in the earth to produce subsistence for man.

Population, when unchecked, increases in a geometrical ratio. Subsistence increases only in an arithmetical ratio. A slight acquaintance with numbers will show the immensity of the first power in comparison with the second.[1]

What Malthus was saying is that world population tends to double about every 25 years or so if unchecked: 1, 2, 4, 8, 16, 32, 64, etc. But food output, because of diminishing returns, cannot keep pace with this. It is only likely to grow at an arithmetical rate: 1, 2, 3, 4, 5, 6, 7, etc. It is clear that population, if unchecked, will soon outstrip food supply.

So what is the check on population growth? According to Malthus it is starvation. As population grows, so food output per head will fall until, with more and more people starving, the death rate will rise.

Only then will population growth stabilize at the rate of growth of food output.

Have Malthus' gloomy predictions been borne out by events?

There are two factors that have mitigated the forces Malthus described:

● The rate of population growth tends to slow down as countries become more developed. Although improved health prolongs life, this tends to be more than offset by a decline in the birth rate as people choose to have smaller families.

● Technological improvements in farming have greatly increased food output per hectare. (See Box 4.4 for a relatively recent example.)

The growth in food output has thus exceeded the rate of population growth in advanced countries.

The picture is much more gloomy, however, in developing countries. There *have* been advances in agriculture. The 'green revolution', whereby new high-yielding crop varieties have been developed (especially in the cases of wheat and rice), has led to food output growth outstripping population growth in many Third World countries. India, for example, now exports grain.

Nevertheless, the Malthusian spectre is very real for some of the poorest developing countries, which are simply unable to feed their populations satisfactorily. It is these poorest countries of the world which have some of the highest rates of population growth. Kenya, for example, has a population growth of nearly 4½ per cent per annum.

? 1. Why might it be possible for there to be a zero marginal productivity of labour on many family farms in poor countries and yet just enough food for all the members of the family to survive? (Illustrate using *MPP* and *APP* curves.)

2. The figures in the following table are based on the assumption that birth rates will fall faster than death rates. Under what circumstances might these forecasts underestimate the rate of growth of world population?

World population levels and growth: actual and projected

Year	World population (billions)	Average annual rate of increase (%)		
		World	More developed regions	Less developed regions
1950	2.5			
1960	3.0	1.8	1.3	2.0
1970	3.7	2.0	1.0	2.4
1980	4.5	1.9	0.8	2.3
1990	5.2	1.7	0.6	2.0
2000	6.1	1.5	0.5	1.8
2010	7.0	1.3	0.4	1.5
2020	7.8	1.1	0.3	1.3
2030	8.6	1.0	0.3	1.1

Source: *World Population Projections* (UN, 1986).

[1] T. R. Malthus, *First Essay on Population* (Macmillan, 1926), pp. 13–14.

Box 4.3

The Relationship Between Averages and Marginals

In this chapter we have just examined the concepts of *average* and *marginal* physical product. We shall be coming across several other average and marginal concepts later on. It is useful at this stage to examine the general relationship between averages and marginals. In all cases there are three simple rules that relate them.

To illustrate these rules, consider the following example.

Imagine a room with ten people in it. Assume that the *average* age of those present is 20.

Now if a 20-year-old enters the room (the *marginal* age), this will not affect the average age. It will remain at 20. If a 56 year old now comes in, the average age will rise: not to 56, of course, but to 23. This is found by dividing the sum of everyone's ages (276) by the number of people (12). If then a child of 10 were to enter the room, this would pull the average age down.

From this example we can derive the three universal rules about averages and marginals:

- If the marginal equals the average, the average will not change.
- If the marginal is above the average, the average will rise.
- If the marginal is below the average the average will fall.

? A cricketer scores the following number of runs in five successive innings:

Innings: 1   2   3   4   5
Runs: 20   20   50   10   0

These can be seen as the marginal number of runs from each innings. Calculate the total and average number of runs after each innings. Show how the average and marginal scores illustrate the three rules above?

These figures can be represented graphically. Figure 4.2 shows *TPP* on one graph and *APP* and *MPP* on another.

The following observations can be made from the two diagrams:

- The *MPP* between two points is equal to the slope of the *TPP* curve between those two points. For example, when the number of workers increases from 1 to 2 ($\Delta Lb = 1$), *TPP* rises from 3 to 10 tonnes ($\Delta TPP = 7$). *MPP* is thus 7: the slope of the line between points *g* and *h*.
- *MPP* rises at first: the slope of the *TPP* curve gets steeper.
- *MPP* reaches a maximum at point *b*. At that point the slope of the *TPP* curve is at its steepest.

Table 4.2 Wheat production per year from a particular farm (tonnes)

	Number of workers (Lb)	TPP	APP (= TPP/Lb)	MPP (= ΔTPP/ΔLb)
a	0	0	—	
	1	3	3	3
	2	10	5	7
b	3	24	8	14
c	4	36	9	12
	5	40	8	4
	6	42	7	2
d	7	42	6	0
	8	40	5	-2

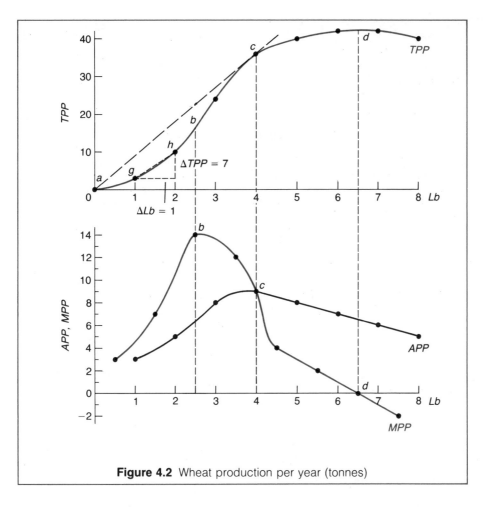

Figure 4.2 Wheat production per year (tonnes)

- After point *b*, diminishing returns set in. *MPP* falls. *TPP* becomes less steep.
- *APP* rises at first. It continues rising as long as the addition to output from the last worker (*MPP*) is greater than the average output (*APP*): the *MPP* pulls the *APP* up. (See Box 4.3.) This continues beyond point *b*. Even though *MPP* is now falling, the *APP* *goes on* rising as long as the *MPP* is still above the *APP*. Thus *APP* goes on rising to point *c*.
- Beyond point *c*, *MPP* is below *APP*. New workers add less to output than the average. This pulls the average down: *APP* falls.
- As long as *MPP* is greater than zero, *TPP* will go on rising: new workers add to total output.
- At point *d*, *TPP* is at a maximum (its slope is zero). An additional worker will add nothing to output: *MPP* is zero.
- Beyond point *d*, *TPP* falls. *MPP* is negative.

?   1. What is the significance of the slope of the line *ac* in the top part of Figure 4.2?
      2. Given that there is a fixed supply of land in the world, what implications can you draw from Figure 4.2 about the effects of an increase in world population for food output per head? (See Box 4.2.)

Box 4.4

Diminishing Returns to Nitrogen Fertilizer

Modern trends in agriculture provide a dramatic example of the law of diminishing returns.

Over the last 35 years or so, there have been large increases in yields from grasslands. This has been largely due to huge increases in the use of nitrogen fertilizer. In England and Wales this has risen over the period from around 10 kilograms per hectare to over 100. Some farmers use considerably more.

In 1976 J. Morrison and M. V. Jackson[2] reported on experiments to show the effects on grass yields of different amounts of nitrogen fertilizer.

The experiments were conducted over a four-year period on a number of different sites up and down the country. The findings from three of the sites are shown in the table.

A similar pattern emerges from all the sites. Total output of grass (*TPP*) rises at a roughly constant rate (in other words, *MPP* is roughly constant) with up to about 300 kg/ha of fertilizer. These rises are substantial. Just look at the Gleadthorpe figures! Above 300 kg/ha, however, diminishing returns set in. Additional applications of fertilizer yield less and less extra output: *MPP* falls.

Maximum yield is obtained at around the 600 kg/ha of nitrogen level.

Above that, *MPP* is negative. Why?

If the soil has a high *natural* level of nitrogen, the effects of adding nitrogen fertilizer will be more limited. Diminishing returns will set in before the 300 kg/ha level. Consider the graph. It shows the effects of fertilizer

Average (dry matter) grass yields: tonnes per hectare (total physical product: *TPP*)

| Site | Nitrogen fertilizer applied: kg/ha/year | | | | | | Mean rainfall |
	0	150	300	450	600	750	May–August (mm)
Cambridge	1.3	3.4	5.6	6.1	6.1	5.9	175
Gleadthorpe, Nottingham	0.7	4.8	9.0	10.7	11.1	10.9	252
South–west Wales (4 sites)	3.2	7.3	11.1	13.2	14.1	13.6	311

on two more sites: Bangor in North Wales and Wenvoe in South Wales.

At Wenvoe there is very little natural nitrogen in the soil. At Bangor, however, the soil supplies about 150 kg/ha of nitrogen. In other respects the sites are similar.

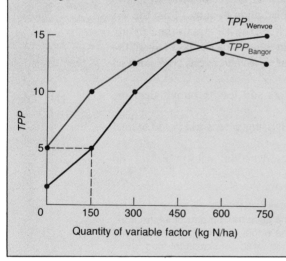

? 1. Draw the *TPP* and *MPP* curves for the three sites in the table.

2. Rainfall and the amount of nitrogen naturally occurring in the soil will cause differences in the positions of the *TPP* curves between sites. One will cause vertical differences in the curves and one will cause horizontal differences. Explain which one causes which effect (and why).

3. Apart from figures on yields, what else will a farmer need to know before deciding whether to use 600 kg/ha of nitrogen fertilizer?

[2] This box is based on J. Morrison and M. V. Jackson, 'The response of grass to fertilizer nitrogen', *Span*, vol. 19 (1976), no. 1.

*Box 4.5

The Relationship Between TPP, MPP and APP

Using calculus again

The total physical product of a variable factor (e.g. fertilizer) can be expressed as an equation. For example:

$$TPP = 100 + 32Q_f + 10Q_f^2 - Q_f^3 \qquad (1)$$

where *TPP* is the output of grain in tonnes per hectare, and Q_f is the quantity of fertilizer applied in kilograms per hectare.

From this we can derive the *APP* function. *APP* is simply TPP/Q_f: i.e. output per kilogram of fertilizer. Thus:

$$APP = \frac{100 + 32 + 10Q_f - Q_f^2}{Q_f} \qquad (2)$$

We can also derive the *MPP* function. *MPP* is the rate of increase in *TPP* as additional fertilizer is applied. It is thus the first derivative of *TPP*: $dTPP/dQ_f$. Thus:

$$MPP = 32 + 20Q_f - 3Q_f^2 \qquad (3)$$

From these three equations the following table can be derived.

Q_f	TPP	APP	MPP
1	141	141	49
2	196	98	60
3	259	86	65
4	324	81	64
5	385	77	57
6	436	72	44
7	471	67	25
8	484	60	0
9	469	52	-31

 Check out some figures by substituting values of Q_f into each of the three equations.

Maximum output (484 tonnes) is achieved with 8 kg of fertilizer per hectare. At that level, *MPP* is zero: no additional output can be gained.

This maximum level of *TPP* can be discovered from the equations by using a simple technique. If *MPP* is zero at this level, then simply find the value of Q_f where:

$$MPP = 32 + 20Q_f - 3Q_f^2 = 0 \qquad (4)$$

Solving this equation[3] gives $Q_f = 8$.

[3] If you know the second derivative test, you could verify that $Q_f = 8$ gives the *maximum TPP* rather than the *minimum*. (Both the maximum *and* the minimum point of a curve have a slope equal to zero.)

◭ SUMMARY

1. A production function shows the relationship between the amount of inputs used and the amount of output produced from them (per period of time).
2. In the short run it is assumed that one or more factors (inputs) are fixed in supply. The actual length of the short run will vary from industry to industry.
3. Production in the short run is subject to diminishing returns. As greater quantitities of the variable factor(s)

are used, so each additional unit of the variable factor will add less to output than previous units: marginal physical product will diminish and total physical product will rise less and less rapidly. As long as marginal physical product is above average physical product, average physical product will rise. Once *MPP* has fallen below *APP*, however, *APP* will fall.

4.2 Background to costs: the long-run theory of production

In the long run *all* factors of production are variable. There is time for the firm to build a new factory (maybe in a different part of the country), to install new machines, to use different techniques of production, and in general to combine its inputs in whatever proportion and in whatever quantities it chooses.

In the long run, then, there are a number of decisions that a firm will have to make: decisions about the scale of its operations, the location of its operations and the techniques of production it will use. These decisions will affect the costs of production. It is important, therefore, to get them right.

The scale of production

If a firm were to double all of its inputs – something it could do in the long run – would it double its output? Or will output more than double or less than double? We can distinguish three possible situations:

Constant returns to scale. This is where a given percentage increase in inputs will lead to the *same* percentage increase in output.

Increasing returns to scale. This is where a given percentage increase in inputs will lead to a *larger* percentage increase in output.

Decreasing returns to scale. This is where a given percentage increase in inputs will lead to a *smaller* percentage increase in output.

Notice the terminology here. The words 'to scale' mean that *all* inputs increase by the same proportion. Decreasing returns to *scale* are therefore quite different from diminishing *marginal* returns (where only the *variable* factor increases). The differences between marginal returns to a variable factor and returns to scale are illustrated in Table 4.3.

In the short run, input 1 is assumed to be fixed in supply (at 3 units). Output can only be increased by using more of the variable factor (input 2). In the long run, however, both input 1 and input 2 are variable.

 Referring still to Table 4.3, are there diminishing or increasing marginal returns, and are there decreasing or increasing returns to scale?

Economies of scale

Economies of scale

When increasing the scale of production leads to a lower cost per unit of output.

The concept of increasing returns to scale is closely linked to that of economies of scale. A firm experiences economies of scale if costs per unit of output fall as the scale of production increases. Clearly, if a firm is getting increasing returns to scale from its

Table 4.3 Short-run and long-run increases in output

Short run			Long run		
Input 1	Input 2	Output	Input 1	Input 2	Output
3	1	25	1	1	15
3	2	45	2	2	35
3	3	60	3	3	60
3	4	70	4	4	90
3	5	75	5	5	125

factors of production, then as it produces more it will be using smaller and smaller amounts of factors per unit of output. Other things being equal this means that it will be producing at a lower unit cost.

There are a number of reasons why firms are likely to experience economies of scale. Some are due to increasing returns to scale; some are not.

Specialization and division of labour. In large-scale plants workers can do more simple, repetitive jobs. With this specialization and division of labour less training is needed; workers can become highly efficient in their particular job, especially with long production runs; there is less time lost in workers switching from one operation to another; and supervision is easier. Workers and managers can be employed who have specific skills in specific areas.

Indivisibilities. Some inputs are of a minimum size: they are indivisible. The most obvious example is machinery. Take the case of a combine harvester. A small scale farmer could not make full use of one. They only become economical to use, therefore, on farms above a certain size. The problem of indivisibilities is made worse when different machines, each of which is part of the production process, are of a different size. For example, if there are two types of machine, one producing 6 units a day, and the other packaging 4 units a day, a minimum of 12 units would have to be produced, involving two production machines and three packaging machines, if all machines are to be fully utilized.

The 'container principle'. Any capital equipment that contains things (e.g. blast furnaces, oil tankers, pipes, vats, etc.) will tend to cost less per unit of output the larger its size. The reason has to do with the relationship between a container's volume and its surface area. A container's cost will depend largely on the materials used to build it and hence roughly on its *surface area*. Its output will depend largely on its *volume*. Large containers have a bigger volume relative to surface area than do small containers. For example, a container with a bottom, top and four sides, with each side measuring 1 metre, has a volume of 1 cubic metre and a surface area of 6 square metres (six surfaces of 1 square metre each). If each side were now to be doubled in length to 2 metres, the volume would be 8 cubic metres and the surface area 24 square metres (six surfaces of 4 square metres each). Thus an eightfold increase in capacity has been gained at only a fourfold increase in the container's surface area, and hence an approximate fourfold increase in cost.

Greater efficiency of large machines. Large machines may be more efficient in the sense that more output can be gained for a given amount of inputs. For example, only one worker may be required to operate a machine whether it be large or small. Also, a large machine may make more efficient use of raw materials.

By-products. With production on a large scale, there may be sufficient waste products to enable them to make some by-product.

Multi-stage production. A large factory may be able to take a product through several stages in its manufacture. This saves time and cost in moving the semi-finished product from one firm or factory to another. For example, a large cardboard-manufacturing firm may be able to convert trees or waste paper into cardboard and then into cardboard boxes in a continuous sequence.

All the above are examples of plant economies of scale. They are due to an individual factory or workplace or machine being large. There are other economies of scale that are associated with the *firm* being large – perhaps with many factories.

Specialization and division of labour

Where production is broken down into a number of simpler, more specialized tasks, thus allowing workers to acquire a high degree of efficiency.

Indivisibilities

The impossibility of dividing a factor into smaller units.

Plant economies of scale

Economies of scale that arise because of the large size of the factory.

Rationalization

The reorganizing of production (often after a merger) so as to cut out waste and duplication and generally to reduce costs.

Organizational economies. With a large firm, individual plants can specialize in particular functions. There can also be centralized administration of the firms. Often, after a merger between two firms, savings can be made by rationalizing their activities in this way.

Spreading overheads. There are some expenditures that are only economic when the *firm* is large, for example research and development: only a large firm can afford to set up a research laboratory. This is another example of indivisibilities, only this time at the level of the firm rather than the plant. The greater the firm's output, the more these overhead costs are spread.

Overheads

Fixed costs: costs that do not vary with the level of output.

Financial economies. Large firms may be able to obtain finance at lower interest rates than small firms. They may be able to obtain certain inputs cheaper by buying in bulk.

 1. Which of the economies of scale we have considered are due to increasing returns to scale and which are due to other factors?
2. What economies of scale is a large department store likely to experience?

Diseconomies of scale

Diseconomies of scale

Where costs per unit of output increase as the scale of production increases.

When firms get beyond a certain size, costs per unit of output may start to increase. There are several reasons for such diseconomies of scale:

● Management problems of co-ordination may increase as the firm becomes larger and more complex, and as lines of communication get longer. There may be a lack of personal involvement by management.
● Workers may feel 'alienated' if their jobs are boring and repetitive, and if they feel an insignificantly small part of a large organization. Poor motivation may lead to shoddy work.
● Industrial relations may deteriorate as a result of these factors and also as a result of the more complex interrelationships between different categories of worker.
● Production-line processes and the complex interdependencies of mass production can lead to great disruption if there are hold-ups in any one part of the firm.

Whether firms experience economies or diseconomies of scale will depend on the conditions applying in each individual firm.

 Why are firms likely to experience economies of scale up to a certain size and then diseconomies of scale after some point beyond that?

Location

In the long run, a firm can move to a different location. The location will affect the cost of production since locations differ in terms of the availability and cost of raw materials, suitable land and power supply, the qualifications, skills and experience of the labour force, wage rates, transport and communications networks, the cost of local services, and banking and financial facilities. In short, locations differ in terms of the availability, suitability and cost of the factors of production.

Transport costs will be an important influence on a firm's location. Ideally, a firm will wish to be as near as possible to both its raw materials and the market for its finished product. When market and raw materials are in different locations, the firm will minimize its transport costs by locating somewhere between the two. In general, if the raw materials are more expensive to transport than the finished product, the firm should be located as near as possible to the raw materials. This will normally apply to firms whose raw materials are heavier or more bulky than the finished product. Thus heavy industry, which uses large quantities of coal and various ores, tends to be

Box 4.6

The Division of Labour in the Pin-Making Industry

Adam Smith began his famous book *The Wealth of Nations* (1776) by discussing the division of labour. He argued that it was the most important single ingredient in explaining economic development.

Chapter 1 begins:

> The greatest improvement in the productive powers of labour, and the greater part of the skill, dexterity, and judgement with which it is anywhere directed, or applied, seems to have been the effects of the division of labour.
>
> The effects of the division of labour, in the general business of society, will be more easily understood by considering in what manner it operates in some particular manufactures . . .
>
> To take an example, therefore, from a very trifling manufacture, but one in which the division of labour has been very often taken notice of, the trade of the pin-maker; a workman not educated to this business (which the division of labour has rendered a distinct trade), not acquainted with the use of the machinery employed in it (to the invention of which the same division of labour has probably given occasion), could scarce, perhaps, with his utmost industry, make one pin in a day, and certainly could not make twenty. But in the way in which this business is now carried on, not only the whole work is a peculiar trade, but it is divided into a number of branches, of which the greater part are likewise peculiar trades. One man draws out the wire, another straights it, a third cuts it, a fourth points it, a fifth grinds it at the top for receiving the head; to make the head requires three distinct operations; to put it on is a peculiar business, to whiten the pins is another; it is even a trade by itself to put them into the paper; and the important business of making a pin is, in this manner, divided into about eighteen distinct operations, which, in some manufactories, are all performed by distinct hands, though in others the same man will sometimes perform two or three of them. I have seen a small manufactory of this kind where ten men only were employed, and where some of them consequently performed two or three distinct operations. But though they were very poor, and therefore but indifferently accommodated with the necessary machinery,

they could, when they exerted them-selves, make among them about twelve pounds of pins in a day. There are in a pound upwards of four thousand pins of a middling size. Those ten persons, therefore, could make among them upwards of forty-eight thousand pins, in a day. Each person, therefore, making a tenth part of forty-eight thousand pins, might be considered as making four thousand eight hundred pins in a day. But if they had all wrought separately and independently, and without any of them having been educated to this peculiar business, they could certainly not each of them have made twenty, perhaps not one pin in a day; that is, certainly, not the two hundred and fortieth, perhaps not the four thousand eight hundredth part of what they are at present capable of performing, in consequence of a proper division and combination of their different operations.

> In every other art and manufacture, the effects of the division of labour are similar to what they are in this very trifling one; though, in many of them, the labour can neither be so much subdivided, nor reduced to so great a simplicity of operation. The division of labour, however, so far as it can be introduced, occasions, in every art, a proportionable increase of the productive powers of labour. The separation of different trades and employments from one another seems to have taken place in consequence of this advantage. This separation, too, is generally carried farthest in those countries which enjoy the highest degree of industry and improvement . . .
>
> This great increase of the quantity of work which, in consequence of the division of labour, the same number of people are capable of performing, is owing to three different circumstances; first, to the increase of dexterity in every particular workman; secondly, to the saving of the time which is commonly lost in passing from one species of work to another; and lastly, to the invention of a great number of machines which facilitate and abridge labour, and enable one man to do the work of many.

? Were there likely to have been any *diseconomies* of scale in the pin factory.

concentrated near the coal fields or near the ports. If, on the other hand, the finished product is more expensive to transport (e.g. bread and beer), the firm will probably be located as near as possible to its market.

When raw materials or markets are in many different locations, transport costs will be minimized at the 'centre of gravity'. This location will be nearer to those raw materials and markets whose transport costs are greater per mile.

? How is the opening-up of trade and investment between Eastern and Western Europe likely to affect the location of industries within Europe that have (a) substantial economies of scale; (b) little or no economies of scale?

The size of the whole industry

External economies of scale

Where a firm's costs per unit of output decrease as the size of the whole *industry* grows.

Industry's infrastructure

The network of supply agents, communications, skills, training facilities, distribution channels, specialized financial services, etc. that supports a particular industry.

External diseconomies of scale

Where a firm's costs per unit of output increase as the size of the whole *industry* increases.

As an *industry* grows in size, this can lead to external economies of scale for its member firms. This is where a firm, whatever its own individual size, benefits from the *whole industry* being large. For example, the firm may benefit from having access to specialist raw material or component suppliers, labour with specific skills, firms which specialize in marketing the finished product, and banks and other financial institutions with experience of the industry's requirements. What we are referring to here is the industry's infrastructure: the facilities, support services, skills and experience that can be shared by its members.

 1. Name some industries where external economies of scale are gained. What are the specific external economies in each case?
2. Would you expect external economies to be associated with the concentration of an industry in a particular region?

The member firms of a particular industry might experience external diseconomies of scale. For example, as an industry grows larger this may create a growing shortage of specific raw materials or skilled labour. This will push up their prices, and hence the firms' costs.

The optimum combination of factors: the marginal product approach

In the long run, all factors can be varied. The firm can thus choose what techniques of production to use: what design of factory to build, what types of machine to buy, how to organize the factory, whether to use highly automated processes or more labour-intensive techniques. It must be very careful in making these decisions. Once it has built its factory and installed the machinery these then become fixed factors of production, maybe for many years: the subsequent 'short-run' time period may in practice last a very long time!

For any given scale, how should the firm decide what technique to use? How should it decide the optimum 'mix' of factors of production?

The profit-maximizing firm will obviously want to use the least costly combination of factors to produce any given output. It will therefore substitute factors, one for another, if by so doing it can reduce the cost of a given output. What then is the optimum combination of factors?

The simple two-factor case

Take first the simplest case where a firm uses just two factors: labour (L) and capital (K). The least-cost combination of the two will be where:

$$\frac{MPP_L}{P_L} = \frac{MPP_K}{P_K}$$

in other words, where the extra product (MPP) from the last pound spent on each factor is equal. But why should this be so? The easiest way to answer this is to consider what would happen if they were not equal.

If they were not equal, it would be possible to reduce cost per unit of output, by using a different combination of labour and capital. For example, if:

$$\frac{MPP_L}{P_L} > \frac{MPP_K}{P_K}$$

more labour should be used relative to capital, since the firm is getting a greater physical return for its money from extra workers than from extra capital. As more labour is used per unit of capital, however, diminishing returns to labour set in. Thus MPP_L will fall. Likewise, as less capital is used per unit of labour, the MPP_K will rise. This will continue until:

$$\frac{MPP_L}{P_L} = \frac{MPP_K}{P_K}$$

At this point the firm will stop substituting labour for capital.

Since no further gain can be made by substituting one factor for another, this combination of factors or 'choice of techniques' can be said to be the most efficient. It is the least-cost way of combining factors for any given output. Efficiency in this sense of using the optimum factor proportions is known as technical or productive efficiency

Technical or productive efficiency
The least-cost combination of factors for a given output.

The multi-factor case

Where a firm uses many different factors, the least-cost combination of factors will be where:

$$\frac{MPP_a}{P_a} = \frac{MPP_b}{P_b} = \frac{MPP_c}{P_c} \cdots = \frac{MPP_n}{P_n}$$

where a . . . n are different factors.

The reasons are the same as in the two-factor case. If any inequality exists between the MPP/P ratios, a firm will be able to reduce its costs by using more of those factors with a high MPP/P ratio and less of those with a low MPP/P ratio until they all become equal.

A major problem for a firm in choosing the least-cost technique is in predicting future factor price changes.

If the price of a factor were to change, the MPP/P ratios would cease to be equal. The firm, to minimize costs, would then like to alter its factor combinations until the MPP/P ratios once more became equal. The trouble is that, once it has committed itself to a particular technique, it may be several years before it can switch to an alternative one. Thus if a firm invests in labour-intensive methods of production and is then faced with an unexpected wage rise, it may regret not having chosen a more capital-intensive technique.

 If factor X costs twice as much as factor Y ($P_X/P_Y = 2$), what can be said about the relationship between the *MPP*s of the two factors if the optimum combination of factors is used?

*The optimum combination of factors: the isoquant/isocost approach

A firm's choice of optimum technique can be shown graphically. This graphical analysis takes the simplest case of just two variable factors – for example, labour and capital. The amount of labour used is measured on one axis and the amount of capital used is measured on the other.

The graph involves the construction of *isoquants* and *isocosts*.

Isoquants

Imagine that a firm wants to produce a certain level of output: say 5000 units. Let us assume that it estimates all the possible combinations of labour and capital that could produce that level of output. Some of these estimates are shown in Table 4.4.

Technique *a* is a capital-intensive technique, using 40 units of capital and only 5 workers. As we move towards technique *e*, labour is substituted for capital. The techniques become more labour intensive.

These alternative techniques for producing a given level of output can be plotted on a graph. The points are joined to form an isoquant. Figure 4.3 shows the 5000 unit isoquant corresponding to Table 4.4.

Isoquant

A line showing all the alternative combinations of two factors that can produce a given level of output.

Table 4.4 Various capital and labour combinations to produce 5000 units of output

	a	b	c	d	e
Units of capital (K)	40	20	10	6	4
Number of workers (L)	5	12	20	30	50

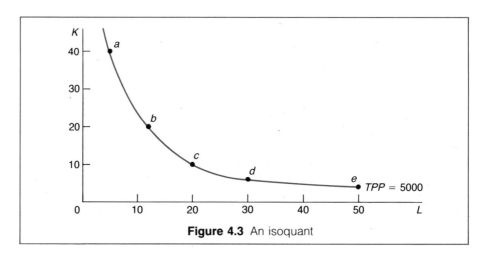

Figure 4.3 An isoquant

The isoquant shows the whole *range* of alternative ways of producing a given output. Thus Figure 4.3 shows not only points *a* to *e* from the table, but all the intermediate points too.

Like an indifference curve, an isoquant is rather like a contour on a map. And like contours and indifference curves, a whole series of isoquants can be drawn, each one representing a different level of output (*TPP*). The higher the output, the further out to the right will the isoquant be. Thus in Figure 4.4, isoquant I_5 represents a higher level of output than I_4, and I_4 a higher output than I_3, and so on.

1. Could isoquants ever cross?
2. Could they ever slope upward to the right? Explain your answers.

Marginal rate of factor substitution

The rate at which one factor can be substituted by another while holding the level of output constant:
$MRS = \Delta F_1/\Delta F_2 = MPP_{F_2}/MPP_{F_1}$.

The shape of the isoquant. Why is the isoquant 'bowed-in' toward the origin? This illustrates a diminishing marginal rate of factor substitution (*MRS*). This, as we shall see in a minute, is due to the law of diminishing returns.

The *MRS*[4] is the amount of one factor (e.g. *K*) that can be replaced by a 1 unit

---

[4] Note that we use the same letters *MRS* to refer to the marginal rate of *factor* substitution as we did in the last chapter to refer to the marginal rate of substitution *in consumption*. Sometimes we use the same words too – just 'marginal rate of substitution' rather than the longer title. In this case we must rely on the context in order to tell which is being referred to.

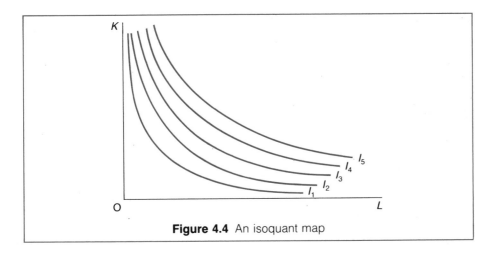

Figure 4.4 An isoquant map

increase in the other factor (e.g. *L*), if output is to be held constant. So if 2 units of capital ($\Delta K = 2$) could be replaced by 1 unit of labour ($\Delta L = 1$) the *MRS* would be 2. Thus:

$$MRS = \frac{\Delta K}{\Delta L} = \frac{2}{1} = 2$$

The *MRS* between two points on the isoquant will equal the slope of the line joining those two points. Thus in Figure 4.5, the *MRS* between points *g* and *h* is 2 ($\Delta K/\Delta L = 2/1$). But this is merely the slope of the line joining points *g* and *h* (ignoring the negative sign).

When the isoquant is bowed in toward the origin, the slope of the isoquant will diminish as one moves down the curve, and so too, therefore, will the *MRS* diminish. Referring again to Figure 4.5, between points *g* and *h* the *MRS* = 2. Lower down the curve between points *j* and *k*, it has fallen to 1.

? Calculate the *MRS* moving *up* the curve in Figure 4.3 between each of the points: *e–d, d–c, c–b,* and *b–a*. Does the *MRS* diminish moving in this direction?

Figure 4.5 Diminishing marginal rate of factor substitution

The relationship between MRS *and* MPP. As one moves down the isoquant, total output, by definition, will remain the same. Thus the loss in output due to less capital being used (i.e. $MPP_K \times \Delta K$) must be exactly offset by the gain in output due to more labour being used (i.e. $MPP_L \times \Delta L$). Thus:

$$MPP_L \times \Delta L = MPP_K \times \Delta K$$

This equation can be rearranged as follows:

$$\frac{MPP_L}{MPP_K} = \frac{\Delta K}{\Delta L} \quad (= MRS)$$

Thus the *MRS* is equal to the inverse of the marginal productivity ratios of the two factors.

Diminishing MRS *and the law of diminishing returns.* The principle of diminishing *MRS* is related to the law of diminishing returns. As one moves down the isoquant, increasing amounts of labour are being used relative to capital. Thus, given diminishing returns, we would expect the *MPP* of labour to fall relative to the *MPP* of capital. But since $MRS = MPP_L/MPP_K$, if MPP_L/MPP_K diminishes, so must *MRS*.

The less substitutable factors are for each other, the faster *MRS* will diminish, and therefore the more bowed in will be the isoquant.

Isoquants and returns to scale. We can use isoquants to illustrate constant, increasing and decreasing returns to scale.

In each of the three diagrams of Figure 4.6 we show the effect of equal percentage increases in the inputs of the two factors (K, L). As we increase both by the same proportion, we move up a straight line through the origin (or 'ray'). The ray illustrated in the three diagrams (R) is drawn with a slope of 45°, but it could be drawn with any slope.

What happens as we increase capital and labour from 1 unit of each to 2 units to 3 units, and thus move from point *a* to *b* to *c*? In diagram (a) the isoquants are equally spaced. Output increases from 200 to 400 to 600 units. There are *constant returns* to scale. In diagram (b) the isoquants get progressively closer. As we move from *a* to *b* to *c* this time output increases from 200 to 400 to 700 units. There are *increasing returns* to scale. Finally in diagram (c) the isoquants get progressively further apart. Output increases from 200 to 400 to 500 units. There are *decreasing returns* to scale.

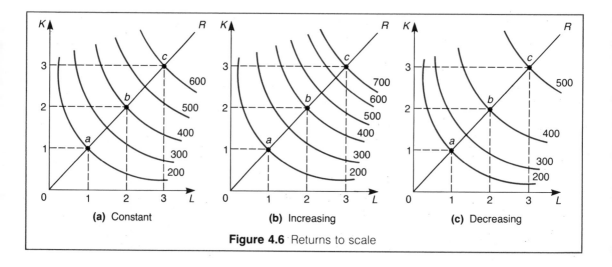

Figure 4.6 Returns to scale

? Draw an isoquant map that illustrates increasing returns to scale up to a certain level of output, and then decreasing returns beyond that.

Isoquants and marginal returns. We can also illustrate what happens to output when one factor is held constant.

In Figure 4.7, it is assumed that capital is fixed in supply at a level of $\overline{K}$. Output can only be increased by increasing the amount of the variable factor (L). This will involve moving along the horizontal line. If there are constant returns *to scale* and hence the isoquants are equally spaced, ever *increasing* amounts of labour will be required to produce equal amounts of extra output: $(L_6 - L_5) > (L_5 - L_4) > (L_4 - L_3)$, etc. This demonstrates the law of diminishing marginal returns.

The diagram also illustrates how a diminishing marginal rate of substitution is dependent on the law of diminishing returns. It is the fact that the isoquants are bowed in toward the origin (giving a diminishing *MRS*) that makes the gap between L_1, L_2, L_3, etc. grow larger and larger (diminishing marginal returns). If the isoquants were downward-sloping *straight lines* and hence the *MRS* did *not* diminish, the gaps between L_1, L_2, L_3, etc. would *not* grow larger. There would be no diminishing returns.

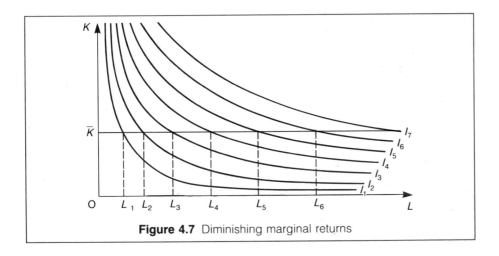

Figure 4.7 Diminishing marginal returns

? Would it be possible to have constant *marginal* returns if there were increasing returns to *scale*?

Isocosts

We have seen how factors combine to produce different levels of output, but how do we choose the level of output? This will involve taking costs into account.

Assume that factor prices are fixed. A table can be constructed showing the various combinations of factors that a firm can use for a particular sum of money.

For example, assuming that P_K is £20 000 per unit and P_L is £10 000 per worker, Table 4.5 shows various combinations of capital and labour that would cost the firm £300 000.

Table 4.5 Combinations of capital and labour costing the firm £300 000

Units of capital (at £20 000 per unit)	0	5	10	15
No. of workers (at a wage of £10 000)	30	20	10	0

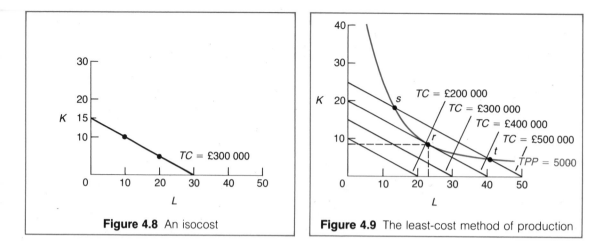

Figure 4.8 An isocost

Figure 4.9 The least-cost method of production

Isocost

A line showing all the combinations of two factors that cost the same to employ.

These figures are plotted in Figure 4.8. The line joining the points is called an isocost. It shows all the combinations of labour and capital that cost £300 000.

As with isoquants, a series of isocosts can be drawn. Each one represents a particular cost to the firm. The higher the cost, the further out to the right will the isocost be.

 1. What will happen to an isocost if the prices of both factors rise by the same percentage?
2. What will happen to the isocost of Figure 4.8 if the wage rate rises to £15 000?

The slope of the isocost will always be equal to:

$$\frac{P_L}{P_K}$$

This can be shown in the above example. The slope is $15/30 = \frac{1}{2}$. But this is P_L/P_K (i.e. £10 000/£20 000).

Isoquants and isocosts can now be put on the same diagram. The diagram can be used to answer either of two questions: (a) What is the least-cost way of producing a particular level of output? (b) What is the highest output that can be achieved for a given cost of production?

These two questions are examined in turn.

The least-cost combination of factors to produce a given level of output

First the isoquant is drawn for the level of output in question: for example, the 5000 unit isoquant of Figure 4.3. This is reproduced in Figure 4.9.

Then a series of isocosts are drawn representing different levels of total cost. The higher the level of total cost, the further out will be the isocosts.

The least-cost combination of labour and capital is shown at point *r*, where $TC = £400 000$. This is where the isoquant just touches the lowest possible isocost. Any other point on the isoquant (e.g. *s* or *t*) would be on a higher isocost.

 Draw the isoquant corresponding to the data in Table 4.6. Assuming that capital costs are £20 per day and the wage rate is £10 per day, what is the least-cost method of producing 100 units? What will the daily total cost be? (Draw in a series of isocosts.)

Table 4.6 Alternative combinations of labour and capital required to produce 100 units of output per day of good x

K	16	20	$26\frac{2}{3}$	40	60	80	100
L	200	160	120	80	$53\frac{1}{3}$	40	32

Comparison with the marginal productivity approach. We showed earlier that the least-cost combination of labour and capital was where:

$$\frac{MPP_L}{P_L} = \frac{MPP_K}{P_K}$$

In this section it has just been shown that the least-cost combination is where the isoquant is tangential to an isocost (i.e. point *r* in Figure 4.9). Thus their slope is the same. The slope of the isoquant equals *MRS*, which equals MPP_L/MPP_K; and the slope of the isocost equals P_L/P_K.

$$\therefore \frac{MPP_L}{MPP_K} = \frac{P_L}{P_K}$$

$$\therefore \frac{MPP_L}{P_L} = \frac{MPP_K}{P_K}$$

Thus, as one would expect, the two approaches yield the same result.

Highest output for a given cost of production

An isocost can be drawn for the particular level of total cost outlay in question. Then a series of isoquants can be drawn, representing different levels of output (*TPP*). The higher the level of output, the further out will lie the corresponding isoquant. The point at which the isocost touches the highest isoquant will give the factor combination yielding the highest output for that level of cost. This will be at point *h* in Figure 4.10.

Again this will be where the slopes of the isocost and isoquant are the same: where $P_L/P_K = MRS$.

If the prices of factors change, new isocosts will have to be drawn. Thus in Figure 4.10, if wages go up, less labour can be used for a given sum of money. The

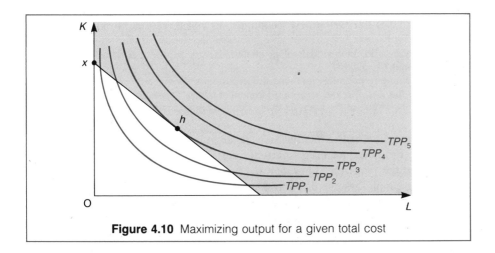

Figure 4.10 Maximizing output for a given total cost

isocost will swing inward round point *x*. The isocost will get steeper. Less labour will now be used relative to capital.

 Referring to the question on Table 4.6, assume that the wage rate rises to £20 per day. Draw a new set of isocosts. What will be the least-cost method of producing 100 units now? How much labour and capital will be used?

*Postscript: Decision making in different time periods

We have distinguished between the short run and the long run. Let us introduce two more time periods to complete the picture. The complete list then reads as follows.

Very short run (immediate run). All factors are fixed. Output is fixed. The supply curve is vertical. On a day-to-day basis a firm may not be able to vary output at all. For example, a flower seller, once the day's flowers have been purchased from the wholesaler, cannot alter the amount of flowers available for sale on that day. In the very short run, all that may remain for a producer to do is to sell an already produced good.

 Why are Christmas trees and fresh foods often sold cheaply on Christmas Eve? (See Box 4.7 below.)

Short run. At least one factor is fixed in supply. More can be produced, but the firm will come up against the law of diminishing returns as it tries to do so.

Long run. All factors are variable. The firm may experience constant, increasing or decreasing returns to scale. But although all factors can be increased or decreased, they are of a fixed *quality*.

Very long run. All factors are variable, *and* their quality and hence productivity can change. Labour productivity can increase as a result of education, training, experience and social factors. The productivity of capital can increase as a result of new inventions (new discoveries) and innovation (putting inventions into practice).

Improvements in factor quality will increase the output they produce: *TPP*, *APP* and *MPP* will rise. These curves will shift vertically upward.

New isoquants will also have to be drawn. An increase in productivity will shift the isoquants inward towards the origin: less capital and labour will be required to produce any given level of output.

Just how long the 'very long run' is will vary from firm to firm. It will depend on how long it takes to develop new techniques, new skills or new work practices.

1. Will an advance in technology shift the isoquants inward *parallel* to the old ones? Explain.
2. Could the long run and the very long run ever be the *same* length of time?
3. What will the long-run and very-long-run market supply curves for a product look like? How will the shape of the long-run curve depend on returns to scale?

It is important to realize that decisions *for* all four time periods can be made *at* the same time. Firms do not make short-run decisions *in* the short run and long-run decisions *in* the long run. They can make both short-run and long-run decisions today. For example, assume that a firm experiences an increase in consumer demand and anticipates that it will continue into the foreseeable future. It thus wants to increase output. Consequently it makes the following four decisions *today*.

- *(Very short run)* It accepts that for a few days it will not be able to increase output. It informs its customers that they will have to wait. It may temporarily raise prices to choke off some of the demand.
- *(Short run)* It negotiates with labour to introduce overtime working as soon as possible, to tide it over the next few weeks. It orders extra raw materials from its suppliers. It launches a recruitment drive for new labour so as to avoid paying overtime longer than is necessary.
- *(Long run)* It starts proceedings to build a new factory. The first step may be to discuss requirements with a firm of consultants.
- *(Very long run)* It institutes a programme of research and development and/or training in an attempt to increase productivity.

Although we distinguish these four time periods, it is the middle two we are primarily concerned with. The reason for this is that there is very little the firm can do in the *very* short run. And in the *very* long run, although the firm will obviously want to increase the productivity of its inputs, it will not be in the position to make precise calculations of how to do it. It will not know precisely what inventions will be made, or just what will be the results of its own research and development.

▲ SUMMARY

1. In the long run a firm is able to vary the quantity it uses of all factors of production. There are no fixed factors.
2. If it increases all factors by the same proportion, it may experience constant, increasing or decreasing returns to scale.
3. Economies of scale occur when costs per unit of output fall as the scale of production increases. This can be due to a number of factors, some of which are directly due to increasing (physical) returns to scale. These include the benefits of specialization and division of labour, the use of larger and more efficient machines, and the ability to have a more integrated system of production. Other economies of scale arise from the financial and administrative benefits of large-scale organizations.
4. Long-run costs are also influenced by a firm's location. The firm will have to balance the need to be as near as possible both to the supply of its raw materials and to its market. The optimum balance will depend on the relative costs of transporting the inputs and the finished product.
5. To minimize costs per unit of output a firm should choose that combination of factors which gives an equal marginal product for each factor relative to its price: i.e. $MPP_a/P_a = MPP_b/P_b = MPP_c/P_c$, etc. (where a, b and c are different factors). If the *MPP/P* ratio for one factor is greater than for another, more of the first should be used relative to the second.
* 6. An isoquant shows the various combinations of two factors to produce a given output. A whole map of such isoquants can be drawn with each isoquant representing a

different level of output. The slope of the isoquant ($\Delta K/\Delta L$) gives the marginal rate of factor substitution (MPP_L/MPP_K). The bowed-in shape of isoquants illustrates a diminishing marginal rate of factor substitution, which in turn arises because of diminishing marginal returns. If isoquants get progressively closer, this illustrates increasing returns to scale. If they get progressively further apart, this represents decreasing returns to scale.
* 7. An isocost shows the various combinations of two factors that cost a given amount to employ. It will be a straight line. Its slope is equal to the price ratio of the two factors (P_L/P_K).
* 8. The tangency point of an isocost with an isoquant represents the optimum factor combination. It is the point where MPP_L/MPP_K (the slope of the isoquant) = P_L/P_K (the slope of the isocost). By drawing a single isoquant touching the lowest possible isocost we can show the least-cost combination of factors for producing a given output. By drawing a single isocost touching the highest possible isoquant we can show the highest output obtainable for a given cost of production.
* 9. Four distinct time periods can be distinguished. In addition to the short- and long-run periods, we can also distinguish the very-short- and very-long-run periods. The very short run is when all factors are fixed. The very long run is where not only the quantity of factors but also their quality is variable (as a result of changing technology, etc.).

4.3 Costs in the short run

Having looked at the background to costs in both the short and long run, we now turn to examine the costs themselves. Again we divide our analysis into the short run and the long run. We will be examining how costs change as a firm changes the amount it produces. Obviously, if it is to decide how much to produce, it will need to know just what the level of costs will be at each level of output.

But first we must be clear on just what we mean by the word 'costs'. The term is used differently by economists and accountants.

Measuring costs of production

Opportunity cost

Cost measured in terms of the next best alternative forgone.

When measuring costs economists always use the concept of opportunity cost Remember from Chapter 1 how we defined opportunity cost. It is the cost of any activity measured in terms of the *sacrifice* made in doing it: in other words, the cost measured in terms of the opportunities forgone.

How do we apply this principle of opportunity cost to a firm? First we must discover what factors of production it has used. Then we must measure the sacrifice involved in using them. To do this it is necessary to put factors into two categories.

Factors not owned by the firm: explicit costs

The opportunity cost of those factors not already owned by the firm is simply the price the firm has to pay for them. Thus if the firm uses £100 worth of electricity, the opportunity cost is £100. The firm has sacrificed £100 which could have been spent on something else.

Explicit costs

The payments to outside suppliers of inputs.

These costs are called explicit costs, because they involve direct payment of money by firms.

Factors already owned by the firm: implicit costs

Implicit costs

Costs which do not involve a direct payment of money to a third party, but which nevertheless involve a sacrifice of some alternative.

When the firm already owns factors (e.g. machinery) it does not as a rule have to pay out money to use them. Their opportunity costs are thus implicit costs. They are equal to what the factors could earn for the firm in some alternative use, either within the firm or hired out to some other firm.

Here are some examples of implicit costs:

- A firm owns some buildings. The opportunity cost of using them is the rent it could have received by letting them out to another firm.
- A firm draws £100 000 from the bank out of its savings in order to invest in new plant and equipment. The opportunity cost of this investment is not just the £100 000 (an explicit cost), but also the interest it thereby forgoes (an implicit cost).
- The owner of the firm could have earned £15 000 per annum by working for someone else. This £15 000 then is the opportunity cost of the owner's time.

Historic costs

The original amount the firm paid for factors it now owns.

If there is no alternative use for a factor of production, as in the case of a machine designed to produce a specific product, and if it has no scrap value, the opportunity cost of using it is *zero*. In such a case, if the output from the machine is worth more than the cost of all the *other* inputs involved, the firm might as well use the machine rather than let it stand idle.

Replacement costs

What the firm would have to pay to replace factors it currently owns.

What the firm paid for the machine – its historic cost – is irrelevant. Not using the machine will not bring that money back. It has been spent. These are sometimes referred to as 'sunk costs'.

Likewise the replacement cost is irrelevant. That should only be taken into account when the firm is considering replacing the machine.

Box 4.7

The Fallacy of Using Historic Costs
Or there's no point crying over spilt milk

'What's done is done.'

'Write it off to experience.'

'You might as well make the best of a bad job.'

These familiar sayings are all everyday examples of a simple fact of life: once something has happened, you cannot change the past. You have to take things as they are *now*.

If you fall over and break your leg, there is little point in saying, 'If only I hadn't done that I could have gone on that skiing holiday; I could have taken part in that race; I could have done so many other things (sigh).' Wishing things were different won't change history. You have to manage as well as you can *with* your broken leg.

It is the same for a firm. Once it has purchased some inputs, it is no good then wishing it hadn't. It has to accept that it has now got them, and make the best decisions about what to do with them.

Take a simple example. The local greengrocer in early December decides to buy 100 Christmas trees for £3 each. At the time of purchase this represents an oppor-

tunity cost of £3 each, since the £3 could have been spent on something else. The greengrocer estimates that there is enough local demand to sell all 100 trees at £5 each, thereby making a reasonable profit (even after allowing for handling costs).

But the estimate turns out to be wrong. On 23 December there are still 50 trees unsold. What should be done? At this stage the £3 that was paid for the trees is irrelevant. It is a historic cost. It cannot be recouped: the trees cannot be sold back to the wholesaler!

In fact the opportunity cost is now zero. It might even be negative if the greengrocer has to pay to dispose of any unsold trees. It might, therefore, be worth selling the trees at £3, £2 or even £1. Last thing on Christmas Eve it might even be worth giving away any unsold trees.

? Why is the correct price to charge (for the unsold trees) the one at which the price elasticity of demand equals -1? (Assume no disposal costs.)

Costs and inputs

A firm's costs of production will depend on the factors of production it uses. The more factors it uses, the greater will its costs be. More precisely, this relationship depends on two elements:

- The productivity of the factors. The greater their physical productivity, the smaller will be the quantity of them that is needed to produce a given level of output, and hence the lower will be the cost of that output. In other words, there is a direct link between *TPP*, *APP* and *MPP* and the costs of production.
- The price of the factors. The higher their price, the higher will be the costs of production.

In the short run, some factors are fixed in supply. Their total costs, therefore, are fixed, in the sense that they do not vary with output. Rent on land is a fixed cost. It is the same whether the firm produces a lot or a little.

The cost of variable factors, however, does vary with output. The cost of raw materials is a variable cost. The more that is produced, the more raw materials are used and therefore the higher is their total cost.

? The following are some costs incurred by a shoe manufacturer. Decide whether each one is a fixed cost or a variable cost or has some element of both.
(a) The cost of leather; (b) The fee paid to an advertising agency; (c) Wear and tear on machinery; (d) Uniform business rates on the factory; (e) Electricity for heating and lighting; (f) Electricity for running the machines; (g) Basic minimum wages agreed with the union; (h) Overtime pay; (i) Depreciation of machines as a result purely of their age (irrespective of their condition).

Fixed costs

Total costs that do not vary with the amount of output produced.

Variable costs

Total costs that do vary with the amount of output produced.

Total cost

Total cost

The sum of total fixed costs and total variable costs: $TC = TFC + TVC$.

The total cost (TC) of production is the sum of the *total variable costs* (TVC) and the *total fixed costs* (TFC) of production:

$$TC = TVC + TFC$$

Consider Table 4.7 and Figure 4.11. They show the total costs for an imaginary firm of producing different levels of output (Q). Let us examine each of the three cost curves in turn.

Table 4.7 Total costs for firm X

Output (Q)	TFC (£)	TVC (£)	TC (£)
0	12	0	12
1	12	10	22
2	12	16	28
3	12	21	33
4	12	28	40
5	12	40	52
6	12	60	72
7	12	91	103
.	.	.	.
.	.	.	.
.	.	.	.

Total fixed cost (TFC)
In our example, total fixed cost is assumed to be £12. Since this does not vary with output, it is shown by a horizontal straight line.

Total variable cost (TVC)
With a zero output, no variable factors will be used. Thus $TVC = 0$. The TVC curve, therefore, starts from the origin.

The shape of the TVC curve follows from the law of diminishing returns. Initially, *before* diminishing returns set in, TVC rises less and less rapidly as more variable factors are added. For example, in the case of a factory with a fixed supply of machinery, initially as more workers are taken on the workers can do increasingly

Figure 4.11 Total costs for firm X

specialist tasks and make a fuller use of the capital equipment. This corresponds to the portion of the *TPP* curve that rises more rapidly (up to point *b* in Figure 4.1).

As output is increased beyond point *m*, diminishing returns set in. Given that extra workers (the extra variable factors) are producing less and less extra output, the extra units of output they do produce will be costing more and more in terms of wage costs. Thus *TVC* rises more and more rapidly. The *TVC* curve gets steeper. This corresponds to the portion of the *TPP* curve that rises less rapidly (between points *b* and *d* in Figure 4.1).

Total cost (TC)

Since $TC = TVC + TFC$, the *TC* curve is simply the *TVC* curve shifted vertically upwards by £12.

Average and marginal cost

Average cost (*AC*) is cost per unit of production:

$$AC = TC/Q$$

Thus if it cost a firm £2000 to produce 100 units of a product, the average cost would be £20 for each unit (£2000/100).

Like total cost, average cost can be divided into the two components, fixed and variable. In other words, average cost equals average fixed cost (*AFC = TFC/Q*) plus average variable cost (*AVC = TVC/Q*):

$$AC = AFC + AVC$$

Marginal cost (*MC*) is the *extra* cost of producing *one more unit*: that is, the rise in total cost per one unit rise in output:

$$MC = \frac{\Delta TC}{\Delta Q}$$

To explain this formula, consider the following two examples.

Example 1

A firm is currently producing 100 units of output at a cost of £2000. It now increases its output to 101 units and its total cost rises to £2030. It has thus incurred an extra cost of £30 to produce this 101st unit. Thus the marginal cost of the 101st unit is £30.

Putting these figures into the formula gives:

$$MC = \frac{\Delta TC}{\Delta Q} = \frac{(£2030 - £2000)}{101 - 100} = \frac{£30}{1}$$

But why do we have to divide the rise in cost by 1? In cases like this, where output can be increased one unit at a time, it is obviously not necessary to divide the rise in cost by the rise in output. Marginal cost is simply the rise in costs of producing that extra unit. There are cases, however, where output can only be increased in batches ...

Example 2

Assume that a firm is currently producing 1 000 000 boxes of matches a month. It now increases output by 1000 boxes, (another batch): $\Delta Q = 1000$. As a result its total costs rise by £30: $\Delta TC = £30$. What is the cost of producing one more box of matches? It is:

$$\frac{\Delta TC}{\Delta Q} = \frac{£30}{1000} = 3p$$

Average (total) cost

Total cost (fixed plus variable) per unit of output: $AC = TC/Q = AFC + AVC$.

Average fixed cost

Total fixed cost per unit of output: $AFC = TFC/Q$.

Average variable cost

Total variable cost per unit of output: $AVC = TVC/Q$.

Marginal cost

The cost of producing one more unit of output: $MC = \Delta TC/\Delta Q$.

Box 4.8

Putting on a Duplicate
Marginal costs of an extra coach

Recently I had to travel to London by coach and decided to book my seat early in case the coach was full. 'There is no need to do that,' I was told, 'because we will always put on an extra coach if there is not enough room on the first.'

Is this an example of 'irrational' behaviour on the part of the coach company? What is the cost of providing me with a seat on that second coach? Will the company make a loss on my custom?

Let us assume that the cost of putting on a second coach to London holding 50 passengers is £500. *When deciding whether to put on the coach*, what is the marginal cost that the firm must take into account? The answer is that it depends on how many people travel on it. Remember that the formula for marginal cost is $\Delta TC/\Delta Q$. If I have the coach to myself ($\Delta Q = 1$), the marginal cost will be £500. In other words, the coach company is having to pay an extra £500 to let me have a seat. Clearly it will be making a loss by putting on that extra coach.

If, however, 50 people use the second coach, the marginal cost of providing the extra seats is only £10 per seat: $\Delta TC/\Delta Q = £500/50 = £10$. Presumably, with a full

coach, the company will make a profit.

Once it has had to put on a second coach and has thus incurred the extra £500 cost, the marginal cost of extra passengers on that coach will be zero. In other words, the marginal cost of the first passenger is £500; thereafter there are no extra costs to be incurred (except maybe for a little extra fuel to cope with the extra weight) until a third coach is put on.

If, then, the question is *whether* to put on a second coach, and if all the company is thinking about is its short-term profits, the marginal cost it will look at is the marginal cost per passenger on it: i.e. $\Delta TC/\Delta Q$. If, however, it has already put on that second coach and it has vacant seats, the marginal cost of taking one more passenger (say, a person arriving at the coach station at the last minute and wanting to buy a ticket on the coach) will be virtually zero.

 Why may it still make economic sense for the company to put on a coach for just one or two passengers, rather than turning them away?

(Note that all marginal costs are variable, since, by definition, there can be no extra fixed costs as output rises.)

Given the *TFC*, *TVC* and *TC* for each output, it is possible to derive the *AFC*, *AVC*, *AC* and *MC* for each output using the above definitions.

For example, using the data of Table 4.6 in the previous section, Table 4.8 can be constructed.

Fill in the missing figures in Table 4.8. (Note that the figures for *MC* come in the *spaces* between each level of output.)

Table 4.8

Output (Q) (Units)	TFC (£)	AFC (TFC/Q) (£)	TVC (£)	AVC (TVC/Q) (£)	TC (TFC + TVC) (£)	AC (TC/Q) (£)	MC (ΔTC/ΔQ) (£)
0	12	–	0	–	12	–	
1	12	12	10	10	22	22	10
2	?	6	16	?	28	?	?
3	?	?	21	7	?	?	?
4	?	3	?	?	40	?	7
5	?	2.4	?	?	52	10.4	12
6	?	?	?	10	?	12	?
7	?	1.7	91	13	103	?	31

What will be the shapes of the *MC*, *AFC*, *AVC* and *AC* curves? These follow from the nature of the *MPP* and *APP* curves that we looked at in section 4.1 above. You may recall (hopefully) that the typical shapes of the *APP* and *MPP* curves are like those illustrated in Figure 4.12.

Marginal cost (MC)

The shape of the *MC* curve follows directly from the law of diminishing returns. Initially, in Figure 4.13, as more of the variable factor is used, extra units of output cost less than previous units. *MC* falls. This corresponds to the rising portion of the *MPP* curve in Figure 4.12 and the portion of the *TVC* curve in Figure 4.11 to the left of point *m*.

Beyond a certain level of output, diminishing returns set in. This is shown as point *x* in Figure 4.13 and corresponds to point *b* in Figure 4.12 (and point *m* in Figure 4.11). Thereafter *MC* rises as *MPP* falls. Additional units of output cost more and more to produce, since they require ever increasing amounts of the variable factor.

Average fixed cost (AFC)

This falls continuously as output rises, since *total* fixed costs are being spread over a greater and greater output.

Average variable cost (AVC)

The shape of the *AVC* curve depends on the shape of the *APP* curve. As the average product of workers rises (up to point *c* in Figure 4.12), the average labour cost per unit of output (the *AVC*) falls: up to point *y* in figure 4.13. Thereafter, as *APP* falls, *AVC* must rise.

Average (total) cost (AC)

This is simply the vertical sum of the *AFC* and *AVC* curves. Note that as *AFC* gets less, the gap between *AVC* and *AC* narrows.

The relationship between average cost and marginal cost

This is simply another illustration of the relationship that applies between *all* averages and marginals. (See Box 4.3.)

Figure 4.12 Average and marginal physical product

Figure 4.13 Average and marginal costs

Box 4.9

Deriving Cost Curves from Total Physical Product Information

In section 4.1 we argued that a firm's costs depend on the output of its factors. If we want to know precisely what a firm's cost curves will be, we need to know two pieces of information: (a) how its output varies with the amount of each factor it uses; (b) the price of those factors.

Let us take a simple production function and see how cost curves may be derived from it. Assume that a firm uses just two factors: capital and labour.

Assume that capital is *fixed* in supply at 5 units (column (1)) and costs £60 per unit per week. Thus total fixed costs are £300 (column (4)).

Labour is the variable factor (column (2)). The effects on output (*TPP*) of employing different amounts of labour are shown in column (3).

It is assumed that workers are paid a wage rate of £100 per week.

Total (weekly) variable costs, then, are simply the number of workers employed multiplied by this wage rate: column (5) = column (2) × £100.

Total costs are the sum of total fixed and total variable costs: TC = column (4) + column (5).

Inputs		Output	Total costs			Average costs			Marginal cost
Capital (units)	Labour (number)	Total physical product (*TPP*) (units)	Fixed (*TFC*) (£)	Variable (*TVC*) (£)	(Total) (*TC*) (£)	Fixed (*AFC*) (£)	Variable (*AVC*) (£)	(Total) (*AC*) (£)	(*MC*) (£)
			(1) × £60	(2) × £100	(4) + (5)	(4) ÷ (3)	(5) ÷ (3)	(6) ÷ (3)	Δ(6) ÷ Δ(3)
(1)	(2)	(3)	(4)	(5)	(6)	(7)	(8)	(9)	(10)
5	1	100	300	100	400	3.00	1.00	4.00	
5	2	250	300	200	500	1.20	0.80	2.00	0.67
5	3	400	300	300	600	0.75	0.75	1.50	0.67
5	4	500	300	400	700	0.60	0.80	1.40	1.00
5	5	560	300	500	800	0.54	0.89	1.43	1.67

To find the three average costs (*AFC*, *AVC* and *AC*) we have to divide the appropriate total cost column by output (column(3)). Thus *AFC = TFC/TPP* = column (4) ÷ column (3). Similarly, *AVC = TVC/TPP* = column (5) ÷ column (3). Finally, *AC = TC/TPP* = column (6) ÷ column (3). Alternatively, *AC* can be found by adding *AFC* and *AVC*: i.e. column (7) + column (8). (Check that this gives the same result.)

Marginal cost can be found by using the formula *MC = ΔTC/ΔTPP*. In other words, it is the extra cost of producing *one more* unit. Thus when the firm employs a fifth worker, for example, its costs have gone up (Δ*TC*) by £100 (i.e. the cost of the fifth worker). Its output has

increased (Δ*TPP*) by 60 units (from 500 to 560.) Thus if it is costing the firm an extra £100 to produce an extra 60 units, it is costing it £100/60 = £1.67 to produce *one* more unit.

1. Draw a graph showing the *AFC*, *AVC*, *AC* and *MC* curves corresponding to the figures in the above table.

2. Calculate a new set of figures for each of the columns (4)–(10) if (a) the price of capital rose from £60 to £100; (b) the wage rate rose from £100 to £150. Why in the case of (a) is the marginal cost not affected?

As long as new units of output cost less than the average, their production must pull the average cost down. That is, if *MC* is less than *AC*, *AC* must be falling. Likewise, if new units cost more than the average, their production must drive the average up. That is, if *MC* is greater than *AC*, *AC* must be rising. Therefore, the *MC* crosses the *AC* at its minimum point (point *z* in Figure 4.13).

Since all marginal costs are variable, the same relationship holds between *MC* and *AVC*.

Why is the minimum point of the *AVC* curve at a lower level of output than the minimum point of the *AC* curve?

▲ SUMMARY

1. When measuring costs of production we should be careful to use the concept of opportunity cost. In the case of factors not owned by the firm, the opportunity cost is simply the explicit cost of purchasing or hiring them. It is the price paid for them. In the case of factors already owned by the firm, it is the implicit cost of what the factor could have earned for the firm in its next best alternative use.

2. In the short run, some factors are fixed in supply. Their total costs are thus fixed with respect to output. In the case of variable factors, their total cost will increase as more output is produced and hence as more of the variable factor is used.

3. Total cost can be divided into total fixed and total variable costs. Total variable cost will tend to increase less rapidly at first as more is produced, but then when diminishing returns set in they will increase more and more rapidly.

4. Marginal cost is the cost of producing one more unit of output. It will probably fall at first (corresponding to the part of the *TVC* curve where the slope is getting shallower), but will start to rise as soon as diminishing returns set in.

5. Average cost, like total cost, can be divided into fixed and variable costs. Average fixed cost will decline as more output is produced. The reason is that the total fixed cost is being spread over a greater and greater number of units of output. Average variable cost will tend to decline at first, but once the marginal cost has risen above it, it must then rise.

4.4 Costs in the long run

When it comes to making long-run production decisions the firm has much more flexibility. It does not have to operate with plant and equipment of a fixed size. It can expand the whole scale of its operations. All its inputs are variable, and thus the law of diminishing returns does not apply. The firm may experience constant returns to scale, or it may experience economies of scale or diseconomies of scale.

Since there are no fixed factors in the long run, there are no long-run fixed costs. For example, the firm may rent more land in order to expand its operations. Its rent bill therefore goes up as it expands its output.

All costs, then, in the long run are variable costs.

Long-run average costs

Long-run average cost (*LRAC*) curves can take various shapes.

If the firm experiences economies of scale, its *LRAC* curve will fall as the scale of production increases (diagram (a) in Figure 4.14). This, after all, is how we define

Long-run average cost curve

A curve that shows how average cost varies with output on the assumption that *all* factors are variable. (It is assumed that the least-cost method of production will be chosen for each output.)

(a) Economies of scale   (b) Diseconomies of scale   (c) Constant costs

Figure 4.14 Alternative long-run average cost curves

economies of scale: namely, a reduction in average costs as the scale of production increases. If diseconomies of scale predominate, the *LRAC* curve will rise (diagram (b)). Alternatively, if the firm experiences neither economies nor diseconomies of scale, the *LRAC* curve will be horizontal (diagram (c)).

 What would the firm's long-run total cost curve look like in each of these three cases?

It is often assumed that as a firm expands, it will initially experience economies of scale and thus face a downward-sloping *LRAC* curve. After a point, however, all such economies will have been achieved and thus the curve will flatten out. Then (possibly after a period of constant *LRAC*) the firm will get so large that it will start experiencing diseconomies of scale and thus a rising *LRAC*. At this stage, production and financial economies will begin to be offset by the managerial problems of running a giant organization.

The effect of this is to give a ⌣ -shaped or saucer-shaped curve, as in Figure 4.15.

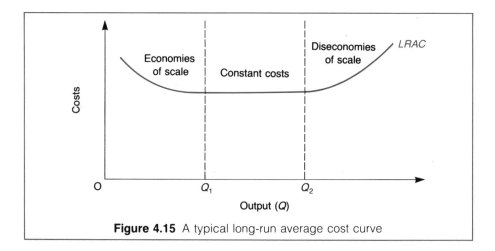

Figure 4.15 A typical long-run average cost curve

Assumptions behind the long-run average cost curve
There are three key assumptions that we make when constructing long-run average cost curves.

Factor prices are given. At each output a firm will be faced with a given set of factor prices. It may be the case, however, that factor prices will be different at *different* levels of output. For example, one of the economies of scale that many large firms enjoy is the ability to obtain bulk discount on raw materials and other supplies.

If factor prices change, both short- and long-run cost curves will shift. Thus an increase in wages would shift the curves upwards.

The state of technology and factor quality are given. These are assumed only to change in the *very* long run. If a firm gains economies of scale, it is because it is being able to exploit *existing* technologies and make better use of the existing availability of factors of production.

Firms choose the least-cost combination of factors for each output. The assumption here is that firms operate efficiently: that they choose the cheapest possible way of producing any level of output. In other words, at every point along the *LRAC* curve the firm will adhere to the cost-minimizing formula:

$$\frac{MPP_a}{P_a} = \frac{MPP_b}{P_b} = \frac{MPP_c}{P_c} \cdots = \frac{MPP_n}{P_n}$$

where a ... n are the various factors the firm uses.

If the firm did not choose the optimum factor combination, it would be producing at a point above the *LRAC* curve.

Long-run marginal costs

The relationship between long-run average and long-run marginal cost curves is just like that between any other averages and marginals (see Box 4.3). Diagrams (a) to (c) in Figure 4.16 show this relationship in the three cases we looked at in Figure 4.14.

If there are economies of scale (diagram (a)), additional units of output will add less to costs than the average. The *LRMC* curve must be below the *LRAC* curve and thus pulling the average down as output increases. If there are diseconomies of scale (diagram (b)), additional units of output will cost more than the average. The *LRMC* curve must be above the *LRAC* curve, pulling it up. If there are no economies or diseconomies of scale, so that the *LRAC* curve is horizontal, any additional units of output will cost the same as the average and thus leave the average unaffected (diagram (c)).

Long-run marginal cost

The extra cost of producing one more unit of output assuming that all factors are variable. (It is assumed that the least-cost method of production will be chosen for this extra output.)

1. Explain the shape of the *LRMC* curve in diagram (d).
2. What would the *LRMC* curve look like if the *LRAC* curve were 'flat bottomed' as in Figure 4.15?

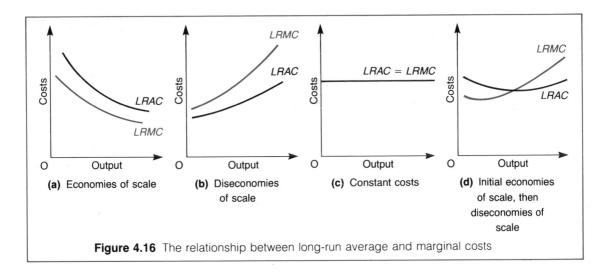

Figure 4.16 The relationship between long-run average and marginal costs

The relationship between long-run and short-run average cost curves

Take the case of a firm which has just one factory and faces a short-run average cost curve illustrated by $SRAC_1$ in Figure 4.17.

In the long run, it can build more factories. If it thereby experiences economies of scale (due, say, to savings on administration), each successive factory will allow it to

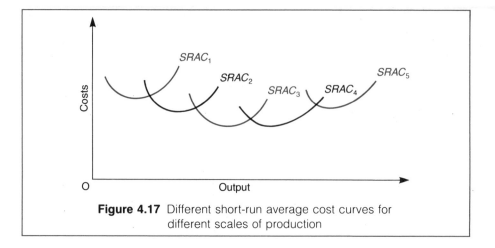

Figure 4.17 Different short-run average cost curves for different scales of production

produce with a new lower *SRAC* curve. Thus with two factories it will face $SRAC_2$; with three factories $SRAC_3$, and so on. Each *SRAC* curve corresponds to a particular amount of the factor that is fixed in the short run: in this case, the factory.

From this succession of short-run average cost curves we can construct a long-run average cost curve. This is shown in Figures 4.18 and 4.19.

If a firm could only build factories of a particular size, the *LRAC* curve would be 'wavy' as in Figure 4.18. Up to output Q_1, it would be cheaper to use just one factory, but for an output between Q_1 and Q_2 it would be cheaper to use two factories. Likewise between Q_2 and Q_3 it would be cheaper to use three factories.

It is usual, however, to show the *LRAC* curve as a smooth line tangential to the *SRAC* curves (as in Figure 4.19). This is known as the envelope curve. The assumption here is that the short-run fixed factor(s) can be varied by *any* amount in the long run. For example, factories of any size can be built or existing ones can be expanded. The result is that there will be an unlimited number of *SRAC* curves.

Envelope curve

A long-run average cost curve drawn as the tangency points of a series of short-run average cost curves.

> **?** Will the envelope curve be tangential to the *bottom* of each of the short-run average cost curves? Explain why it should or should not be.

Figure 4.18 Constructing long-run average cost curves from short-run average cost curves: factories of fixed size

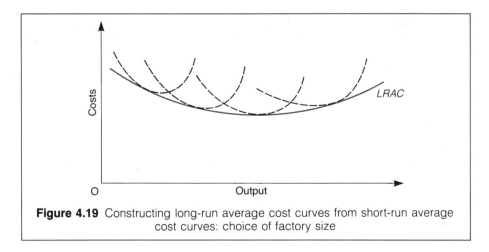

Figure 4.19 Constructing long-run average cost curves from short-run average cost curves: choice of factory size

Long-run cost curves in practice

Firms do experience economies of scale. Some experience continuously falling *LRAC* curves, as in Figure 4.14(a). Others experience economies of scale up to a certain output and thereafter constant returns to scale.

Evidence is inconclusive on the question of diseconomies of scale.

There is little evidence to suggest the existence of *technical* diseconomies, but the possibility of diseconomies due to managerial and industrial relations problems cannot be ruled out.

Some evidence on economies of scale in the UK is considered in Box 4.10.

* Derivation of long-run costs from an isoquant map

Cost curves are drawn on the assumption that, for any output, the least-cost combination of factors is used: that is, that production will take place at the tangency point of the isoquant and an isocost: where $MPP_K/P_K = MPP_L/P_L$. By drawing a series of isoquants and isocosts, long-run costs can be derived for each output.

In Figure 4.20, isoquants are drawn for some hypothetical firm at 100 unit

Figure 4.20 Deriving an *LRAC* curve from an isoquant map

Box 4.10

Minimum Efficient Plant Size (MEPS)
The extent of economies of scale in practice

One of the most important studies of economies of scale in the UK was made in the late 1960s by C. F. Pratten.[5] Pratten found strong evidence that most firms experienced economies of scale.

For some firms long-run average costs fell continuously as output increased. For others it fell up to a certain level of output and then remained constant, (a ⌣-shaped *LRAC* curve).

Pratten found little evidence, however, to suggest that firms experienced *dis*economies of scale. This may be due to the fact that he was concentrating on the production costs of operating different-sized *plants*. Diseconomies of scale are usually associated with the managerial inefficiencies of large-scale *organizations*.

If firms are to gain the full economies of scale, they must have plants of a certain minimum size. Pratten used a measure called *minimum efficient plant size (MEPS)* to identify this size. He defined *MEPS* as the minimum size above which a subsequent doubling in size would reduce average cost by less than 5 per cent. In other words, *MEPS* is the size beyond which no significant additional economies of scale can be achieved: it is at virtually the bottom of the *LRAC* curve.

The *MEPS* can be compared with total industry demand. Pratten observed that in some industries economies of scale were exhausted with plants that were still small relative to total UK market demand: in other words, *MEPS* is a small percentage of the total UK market. In other industries, however, even if a plant were large enough to supply the whole market, it would still not be large enough to experience the full potential economies of scale: the *MEPS* is greater than 100 per cent of the market.

In 1978 a government green paper was published on monopolies and mergers policy.[6] Contained within it was a review of the evidence on *MEPS* as a percentage of the UK market for a number of different industries. The evidence was drawn from several different sources. Some examples of the findings are given in the table.

In the next few chapters we will be looking at the effects of competition (or lack of it) on a firm's prices. If the *MEPS* is a large percentage of the market, and if the firms are to be large enough to gain the full economies of

Product	MEPS as % of UK sales
Shoes	0.2–0.5
Bricks	0.4–0.9
Bread	0.5–1.0
Oil refining	4–9
Bicycles	8
Paint	7
Potato crisps	10
Detergent powder	20
Cigarettes	21
Sulphuric acid	26
Electric cookers	30
Motor cars	29–57
Diesel engines (industrial)	56
Tractors	76
TV tubes	around 100
Aircraft	at least 100
Electronic calculators	over 100
Turbo generators	120–200

Note: Where a range of figures is given this is due to there being more than one source and/or different assumptions.

Source: *A Review of Monopolies and Mergers Policy* (Dept of Prices and Consumer Protection, 1978), Cmnd 7198.

scale, there will not be room for many firms in the market. Hence competition will be limited.

If the *MEPS* exceeds 50 per cent there is only room for one firm large enough to gain full economies of scale. In this case the industry is said to be a *natural monopoly*.

? 1. How will the existence of imports and an export market affect the relationship between *MEPS* and competition?
2. Will the liberalization of trade within Europe make any difference to the *MEPS* for British producers in the cases of (a) bricks; (b) TV tubes; (c) motor cars; (d) bread?

[5] *Economies of Scale in Manufacturing Industry* (Cambridge University Press, 1971).
[6] *A Review of Monopolies and Mergers Policy* (Dept of Prices and Consumer Protection, 1978), Cmnd 7198.

intervals. Up to 400 units of output, the isoquants are getting closer together. Thereafter, the gap between the isoquants widens again.

Expansion path

The line on an isoquant map that traces the minimum

The line from *a* to *g* is known as the expansion path. It traces the tangency points of the isoquants and isocosts, and thus shows the minimum-cost combinations of labour and capital to produce each output: the (long-run) total cost being given by the isocost.

Up to point *d*, less and less *extra* capital (*K*) and labour (*L*) are required to produce each extra 100 units of output. Thus long-run marginal cost is falling. Above point *d*, more and more extra *K* and *L* are required and thus *LRMC* rises.

Thus the *isoquant* map of Figure 4.20 gives an *LRMC* curve that is ⌣-shaped. The *LRAC* curve will therefore also be ⌣-shaped (only shallower) with the *LRMC* coming up through the bottom of the *LRAC*.

cost combinations of two factors as output increases.
It is drawn on the assumption that both factors can be varied. It is thus a long-run path.

 What would the isoquant map look like if there were (a) continuously increasing returns to scale; (b) continuously decreasing returns to scale?

Using an isoquant map to compare the behaviour of short- and long-run costs

Consider the isoquant map shown in Figure 4.21. It shows a firm currently producing at point *a*. It is producing 200 units of output per time period (shown by the isoquant passing through point *a*) and is using K_1 units of capital and L_1 units of labour. The cost of this much capital and labour is assumed to be £40 000 (shown by the isocost passing through point *a*). Let us assume that the plant which the firm is using is designed to produce 200 units of output at the least possible cost. Therefore point *a* is on the long-run expansion path. Both short-run and long-run average costs are £40 000/200 = £200.

Now let us see what will happen to the firm's costs if it chooses to expand output to 300 units in (a) the short run and (b) the long run.

Short run. In the short-run capital is fixed in supply at K_1. If the firm wants to increase output to 300 units, it must therefore take on L_3 labour. It will be producing at point b_S on the 300 unit isoquant. Its total costs will rise to £66 000 (the isocost passing through point b_S). The short-run average cost will rise to £66 000/300 = £220.

Long run. In the long run, if the firm still wants to produce 300 units of output, the firm can increase the amount of capital as well as the amount of labour. It can thus move up the expansion path in Figure 4.21 to point b_L, using K_2 capital and L_2 labour. This time the total cost will only be £60 000. The long-run average cost thus remains at the original £200 (£60 000/300).

 Referring again to Figure 4.21 and assuming that the firm is currently producing at point a using K_1 capital and L_1 labour, what will be the short-run and long-run costs of reducing production to 100 units?

Figure 4.21 Deriving short-run costs from an isoquant map

SUMMARY

---

1. In the long run all factors are variable. There are thus no long-run fixed costs.
2. When constructing long-run cost curves it is assumed that factor prices are given, that the state of technology is given and that firms will choose the least-cost combination of factors for each given output.
3. The *LRAC* curve can be downward sloping, upward sloping or horizontal, depending in turn on whether there are economies of scale, diseconomies of scale or neither. Typically, *LRAC* curves are drawn as ⌣-shaped but with a flat bottom, or as ⌣ -shaped. As output expands, initially there are economies of scale. When these are exhausted the curve will become flat. When the firm becomes very large it may begin to experience diseconomies of scale. If this happens, the *LRAC* curve will begin to slope upward again.

4. The long-run marginal cost curve will be below the *LRAC* curve when *LRAC* is falling, above it when *LRAC* is rising and equal to it when *LRAC* is neither rising nor falling.
5. An envelope curve can be drawn which shows the relationship between short-run and long-run average cost curves. The *LRAC* curve envelops the short-run *AC* curves: it is tangential to them.
* 6. Costs can be derived from an isoquant map. Long-run total costs are found from the expansion path, which shows the least-cost combination of factors to produce any given output. It traces out the tangency points of the isocosts and isoquants. Short-run total costs are found by holding one of the two factors constant and reading off the intersections of isocosts and isoquants *at that quantity* of the fixed factor.

4.5 Revenue

Throughout this chapter we are building up a theory of profit maximization. We are attempting to find the output and price at which a firm will maximize its profits, and how much profit will be made at that level. Remember that we defined a firm's total profit as its total revenue minus its total costs of production:

$$T\Pi = TR - TC$$

We have been looking at costs in some detail. We must now turn to the revenue side of the equation. As with costs, we distinguish between three revenue concepts: total revenue (TR), average revenue (AR) and marginal revenue (MR).

Total, average and marginal revenue

Total revenue (TR)

Total revenue

A firm's total earnings from a specified level of sales within a specified period: $TR = P \times Q$.

Total revenue is the firm's total earnings per period of time from the sale of a particular amount of output (Q).

For example, if a firm sells 1000 units (Q) per month at a price of £5 each (P), then its monthly total revenue will be £5000: in other words, £5 × 1000 ($P \times Q$). Thus:

$$TR = P \times Q$$

Average revenue (AR)

Average revenue

Total revenue per unit of output. When all output is sold at the same price, average revenue will be the same as price: $AR = TR/Q = P$.

Average revenue is the amount the firm earns per unit sold. Thus:

$$AR = TR/Q$$

So if the firm earns £5000 (TR) from selling 1000 units (Q), it will earn £5 per unit. But this is simply the price! Thus:

$$AR = P$$

(The only exception to this is when the firm is selling its products at different prices to different consumers. In this case *AR* is simply the (weighted) average price.)

Marginal revenue (MR)

Marginal revenue is the extra total revenue gained by selling one more unit (per time period). So if a firm sells an extra 20 units this month compared with what it expected to sell, and in the process earns an extra £100, then it is getting an extra £5 for each extra unit sold: $MR = £5$. Thus:

$$MR = \Delta TR/\Delta Q$$

We now need to see how each of these three revenue concepts (*TR*, *AR* and *MR*) varies with output. We can show this graphically in the same way as we did with costs.

The relationships will depend on the market conditions under which a firm operates. A firm which is too small to be able to affect market price will have different-shaped looking revenue curves from a firm which is able to choose the price it charges. Let us examine each of these two situations in turn.

Marginal revenue	
The extra revenue gained by selling one more unit per time period: $MR = \Delta TR/\Delta Q$.	

Revenue curves when price is not affected by the firm's output

Average revenue

If a firm is very small relative to the whole market, it is likely to be a price taker. That is, it has to accept the price given by the intersection of demand and supply in the whole market. But, being so small, it can sell as much as it is capable of producing at that price. This is illustrated in Figure 4.22.

The left-hand part of the diagram shows market demand and supply. Equilibrium price is £5. The right-hand part of the diagram looks at the demand for an individual firm which is tiny relative to the whole market. (Look at the difference in the scale of the horizontal axes in the two parts of the diagram.)

Being so small, any change in its output will be too insignificant to affect the market price. It thus faces a horizontal demand 'curve' at this price. It can sell 200 units, 600 units, 1200 units or whatever without affecting this £5 price.

Average revenue is thus constant at £5. The firm's average revenue curve must therefore lie along exactly the same line as its demand curve.

Price taker

A firm that is too small to be able to influence the market price.

Figure 4.22 Deriving a firm's *AR* and *MR*: price-taking firm

Marginal revenue

In the case of a horizontal demand curve, the marginal revenue curve will be the same as the average revenue curve, since selling one more unit at a constant price (*AR*) merely adds that amount to total revenue. If an extra unit is sold at a constant price of £5, an extra £5 is earned.

Total revenue

Table 4.9 shows the effect on total revenue of different levels of sales with a constant price of £5 per unit.

As price is constant, total revenue will rise at a constant rate as more is sold. The *TR* 'curve' will therefore be a straight line through the origin, as in Figure 4.23.

 What would happen to the *TR* curve if the market price rose to £10? Try drawing it.

Table 4.9 Deriving total revenue

Quantity (units)	Price ≡ AR = MR (£)	TR (£)
0	5	0
200	5	1000
400	5	2000
600	5	3000
800	5	4000
1000	5	5000
1200	5	6000
.	.	.
.	.	.
.	.	.

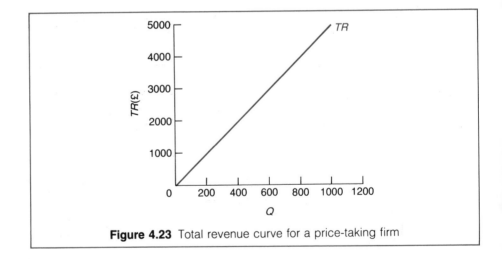

Figure 4.23 Total revenue curve for a price-taking firm

Revenue curves when price varies with output

The three curves (*TR*, *AR* and *MR*) will look quite different when price does vary with the firm's output.

If a firm has a relatively large share of the market, it will face a downward-sloping demand curve. This means that if it is to sell more, it must lower the price. It could also choose to raise its price. If it does so, however, it will have to accept a fall in sales.

Average revenue

Remember that average revenue equals price. If, therefore, price has to be lowered to sell more output, average revenue will fall as output increases.

Table 4.10 gives an example of a firm facing a downward-sloping demand curve. The demand curve (which shows how much is sold at each price) is given by the first two columns.

Note that as in the case of a price-taking firm, the demand curve and the *AR* curve lie along exactly the same line. The reason for this is simple: $AR = P$, and thus the curve relating price to quantity (the demand curve) must be the same as that relating average revenue to quantity (the *AR* curve).

Table 4.10 Revenues for a firm facing a downward-sloping demand curve

Q (units)	P = AR (£)	TR (£)	MR (£)
1	8	8	
2	7	14	6
3	6	18	4
4	5	20	2
5	4	20	0
6	3	18	-2
7	2	14	-4
.	.	.	.
.	.	.	.
.	.	.	.

Marginal revenue

When a firm faces a downward sloping demand curve, marginal revenue will be less than average revenue, and may even be negative. But why?

If a firm is to sell more per time period, it must lower its price (assuming it does not advertise). This will mean lowering the price not just for the extra units it hopes to sell, but also for those units it would have sold had it not lowered the price.

Thus the marginal revenue is the price at which it sells the last unit, *minus* the loss in revenue it has incurred by reducing the price on those units it could otherwise have sold at the higher price. This can be illustrated with Table 4.10.

Assume that the price is currently £7. Two units are thus sold. The firm now wishes to sell an extra unit. It lowers the price to £6. It thus gains £6 from the sale of the third unit, but loses £2 by having to reduce the price by £1 on the two units it could otherwise have sold at £7. Its net gain is therefore £6 − £2 = £4. This is the marginal revenue: it is the extra revenue gained by the firm from selling one more unit.

There is a simple relationship between marginal revenue and *price elasticity of demand*. Remember from Chapter 2 (p. 73) that if demand is price elastic, a *decrease* in price will lead to a proportionately larger increase in the quantity demanded and hence an *increase* in revenue. Marginal revenue will thus be positive. If, however, demand is inelastic, a decrease in price will lead to a proportionately smaller increase in sales. In this case the price reduction will more than offset the increase in sales and as a result revenue will fall. Marginal revenue will be negative.

If, then, marginal revenue is a positive figure (i.e. if sales per time period are 4 units or less in Figure 4.24), the demand curve will be elastic at that point, since a rise in quantity sold (as a result of a reduction in price) would lead to a rise in total revenue. If, on the other hand, marginal revenue is negative (i.e. at a level of sales of 5 or more

Figure 4.24 *AR* and *MR* curves for a firm facing a downward-sloping demand curve

Figure 4.25 Total revenue for a firm facing a downward-sloping demand curve

units in Figure 4.24), the demand curve is inelastic at that point, since a rise in quantity sold would lead to a *fall* in total revenue.

Thus the demand (*AR*) curve of Figure 4.24 is elastic to the left of point *r* and inelastic to the right.

Total revenue

Total revenue equals price times quantity. This is illustrated in Table 4.10. The *TR* column from Table 4.10 is plotted in Figure 4.25.

Unlike in the case of a price-taking firm, the *TR* curve is not a straight line. It is a curve that rises at first and then falls. But why? As long as marginal revenue is positive (and hence demand is price elastic), a rise in output will raise total revenue. However, once marginal revenue becomes negative (and hence demand is inelastic), total revenue will fall. The peak of the *TR* curve will be where $MR = 0$. At this point the price elasticity of demand will be equal to -1.

Shifts in revenue curves

We saw in Chapter 2 that a change in *price* will cause a movement along a demand curve. It is similar with revenue curves, except that here the causal connection is in the other direction. Here we ask what happens to revenue when there is a change in the firm's *output*. Again the effect is shown by a movement along the curves. The assumption here is that the price charged will be that which will ensure that the output is sold. Thus the causal sequence is: price determines the output that can be sold (a movement along the demand curve); this then determines the level of revenue earned (a movement along the three revenue curves).

The effect of a change in any *other* determinant of demand, such as tastes, income or the price of other goods, will shift the demand curve. By affecting the price at which each level of output can be sold, there will be a shift in all three revenue curves. An increase in revenue is shown by a vertical shift upward; a decrease by a shift downward.

? Copy Figures 4.24 and 4.25 (which are based on Table 4.10). Now assume that incomes have risen and that, as a result, two more units per time period can be sold at each price. Draw a new table and plot the resulting new *AR*, *MR* and *TR* curves on your diagrams. Are the new curves parallel to the old ones? Explain.

▲ SUMMARY

1. Just as we could identify total, average and marginal costs, so too we can identify total, average and marginal revenue.
2. Total revenue (*TR*) is the total amount a firm earns from its sales in a given time period. It is simply price times quantity: $TR = P \times Q$.
3. Average revenue (*AR*) is total revenue per unit: $AR = TR/Q$. In other words, $AR = P$.
4. Marginal revenue is the extra revenue earned from the sale of one more unit per time period.
5. The *AR* curve will be the same as the demand curve for the firm's product. In the case of a price taker, the demand curve and hence the *AR* curve will be a horizontal straight line and will also be the same as the *MR* curve.

The *TR* curve is an upward-sloping straight line from the origin.
6. A firm that faces a downward-sloping demand curve must obviously also face the same downward sloping *AR* curve. The *MR* curve will also slope downwards, but will be below the *AR* curve and steeper than it. The *TR* curve will be an arch shape starting from the origin.
7. When demand is price elastic, marginal revenue will be positive and the *TR* curve will be upward sloping. When demand is price inelastic, marginal revenue will be negative and the *TR* curve will be downward sloping.
8. A change in output is represented by a movement along the revenue curves. A change in any other determinant of revenue will shift the curves up or down.

4.6 Profit maximization

We are now in a position to put costs and revenue together to find the output at which profit is maximized, and also to find out how much that profit will be.

There are two ways of doing this. The first and simpler method is to use total cost and total revenue curves. The second method is to use marginal and average cost and marginal and average revenue curves. Although this method is a little more complicated (but only a little!), it is more useful when we come to compare profit maximizing under different market conditions.

We will look at each method in turn. In both cases we will concentrate on the short run: namely, that period in which one or more factors are fixed in supply. In both cases we take the instance of a firm facing a downward-sloping demand curve.

Short-run profit maximization: using total curves

Table 4.11 shows the total revenue figures from Table 4.10. It also shows figures for total cost. These figures have been chosen so as to produce a *TC* curve of a typical shape.

Total profit (*TΠ*) is found by subtracting *TC* from *TR*. Check this out by examining the table. Where *TΠ* is negative, the firm is making a loss. Total profit is maximized at

Table 4.11

Q (units)	TR (£)	TC (£)	TΠ (£)
0	0	6	−6
1	8	10	−2
2	14	12	2
3	18	14	4
4	20	18	2
5	20	24	−4
6	18	33	−15
7	14	49	−35
.	.	.	.
.	.	.	.

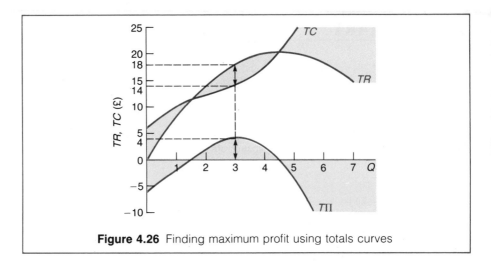

Figure 4.26 Finding maximum profit using totals curves

an output of 3 units: namely, where there is the greatest gap between total revenue and total costs. At this output, total profit is £4 (£18 − £14).

The *TR*, *TC* and *TII* curves are plotted in Figure 4.26. The size of the maximum profit is shown by the arrows.

 What can we say about the slope of the *TR* and *TC* curves at the maximum profit point? What does this tell us about marginal revenue and marginal cost?

Short-run profit maximization: using average and marginal curves

Table 4.12 is based on the figures in Table 4.11.

 1. Fill in the missing figures (without referring to Table 4.10).
2. Why are the figures for *MR* and *MC* entered in the spaces between the lines in Table 4.12?

Finding the maximum profit a firm can make is a two-stage process. The first stage is to find the profit-maximizing output. To do this we use the *MC* and *MR* curves. The second stage is to find out just how much profit is at this output. To do this we use the *AR* and *AC* curves.

Table 4.12

Q (units)	P = AR (£)	TR (£)	MR (£)	TC (£)	AC (£)	MC (£)	TII (£)	AII (£)
0	9	0		6	−		−6	−
			8			4		
1	8	8		10	10		?	−2
			?			2		
2	7	14		12	?		2	1
			4			2		
3	6	?		14	$4\frac{2}{3}$		4	$1\frac{1}{3}$
			2			?		
4	5	20		18	$4\frac{1}{2}$		?	?
			0			6		
5	4	?		24	$4\frac{4}{5}$		−4	$-\frac{4}{5}$
			−2			?		
6	3	18		33	?		?	?
			?			16		
7	2	14		49	7		−35	−5
·	·	·	·	·	·	·	·	·
·	·	·	·	·	·	·	·	·
·	·	·	·	·	·	·	·	·

Stage 1: Using marginal curves to arrive at the profit-maximizing output

There is a very simple profit-maximizing rule: if profits are to be maximized, *MR must equal MC*. From the table it can be seen that $MR = MC$ at an output of 3. This is shown as point *e* in Figure 4.27.

But why are profits maximized when $MR = MC$? The simplest way of answering this is to see what the position would be if *MR* did not equal *MC*.

Referring to Figure 4.27, at a level of output below 3, *MR* exceeds *MC*. This means that by producing more units there will be a bigger addition to revenue (*MR*) than to cost (*MC*). Total profit will *increase. As long as MR exceeds MC, profit can be increased by increasing production.*

At a level of output above 3, *MC* exceeds *MR*. All levels of output above 3 thus add more to cost than to revenue and hence *reduce* profit. *As long as MC exceeds MR, profit can be increased by cutting back on production.*

Profits are thus maximized where $MC = MR$: at an output of 3. This can be confirmed by reference to the *T*Π column in Table 4.12.

Students worry sometimes about the argument that profits are maximized when $MR = MC$. Surely, they say, if the last unit is making no profit, how can profit be at a *maximum*? The answer is very simple. If you cannot *add* anything more to a total, the total must be at the maximum. Take the simple analogy of going up a hill. When you cannot go any higher, you must be at the top.

Profit-maximizing rule

Profit is maximized where marginal revenue equals marginal cost.

Stage 2: Using average curves to measure the size of the profit

Once the profit-maximizing output has been discovered, we now use the average curves to measure the *amount* of profit at the maximum. Both marginal and average curves corresponding to the data in Table 4.12 are plotted in Figure 4.28.

First, average profit (*A*Π) is found. This is simply $AR - AC$. At the profit-maximizing output of 3, this gives a figure for *A*Π of $£6 - £4\frac{2}{3} = £1\frac{1}{3}$. Then total profit is obtained by multiplying average profit by output:

$$T\Pi = A\Pi \times Q$$

This is shown as the shaded area. It equals $£1\frac{1}{3} \times 3 = £4$. This can again be confirmed by reference to the *T*Π column in Table 4.12.

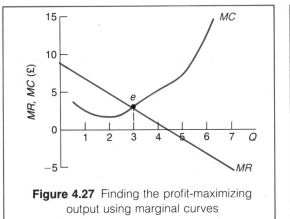

Figure 4.27 Finding the profit-maximizing output using marginal curves

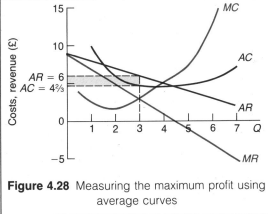

Figure 4.28 Measuring the maximum profit using average curves

From the information for a firm given in the table below, construct a table like Table 4.12.

Q	0	1	2	3	4	5	6	7
P	12	11	10	9	8	7	6	5
TC	2	6	9	12	16	21	28	38

Use your table to draw diagrams like Figures 4.26 and 4.28. Use these two diagrams to show the profit-maximizing output and the level of maximum profit. Confirm your findings by reference to the table you have constructed.

Some qualifications

Long-run profit maximization

Assuming that the *AR* and *MR* curves are the same in the long run as in the short run, long-run profits will be maximized at the output where *MR* equals the *long-run MC*. The reasoning is the same as with the short-run case.

The meaning of 'profit'

One element of cost is the opportunity cost to the owners of the firm of being in business. This is the minimum return the owners must make on their capital in order to prevent them from eventually deciding to close down and perhaps move into some alternative business. It is a *cost* because, just as with wages, rent, etc., it has to be covered if the firm is to continue producing. This opportunity cost to the owners is sometimes known as normal profit, and is included in the cost curves.

Normal profit is the profit that the owners could have earned in the next best alternative business. If they can earn more than normal profit, they will prefer to stay in this business. If they earn less than normal profit, then after a time they will consider leaving and using their capital for some other purpose.

Normal profit

The opportunity cost of being in business: the profit that could have been earned in the next best alternative business. It is counted as a cost of production.

 What determines the size of this 'normal profit'? Will it vary with the general state of the economy?

Given that normal profits are included in costs, any profit that is shown diagrammatically (e.g. the shaded area in Figure 4.28) must therefore be over and above normal profit. It is known by several alternative names: supernormal profit, pure profit, economic profit, abnormal profit, producer's surplus or sometimes simply profit. They all mean the same thing: the excess of profit over normal profit.

Supernormal profit
(also known as **pure profit**, **economic profit**, **abnormal profit**, **producer's surplus** or simply **profit**)

The excess of total profit above normal profit.

Loss minimizing

It may be that there is no output at which the firm can make a profit. Such a situation is illustrated in Figure 4.29: the *AC* curve is above the *AR* curve at all levels of output.

In this case, the output where *MR = MC* will be the loss minimizing output. The amount of loss at the point where *MR = MC* is shown by the shaded area in Figure 4.29.

When MC = MR at two different outputs

Figure 4.30 illustrates a case where *MR = MC* at two different points. Which is the one that maximizes profit? The answer is Q_2. At Q_1, a move in either direction would *increase* profit (or reduce loss). For example, as output is increased above Q_1, *MR* becomes greater than *MC* and thus output should increase further: *away* from Q_1 and toward Q_2.

*Box 4.11

Using Calculus to Find the Maximum Profit Output

Imagine that a firm's total revenue and total cost functions were:

$$TR = 48Q - Q^2$$

$$TC = 12 + 16Q + 3Q^2$$

From these two equations the following table can be derived.

Q	TR	TC	TⅡ (= TR − TC)
0	0	12	−12
1	47	31	16
2	92	56	36
3	135	87	48
4	176	124	52
5	215	167	48
6	252	216	36
7	287	271	16
.	.	.	.
.	.	.	.

1. How much is total fixed cost?
2. Continue the table for $Q = 8$ and $Q = 9$.
3. Plot *TR*, *TC* and *T*Ⅱ on a diagram like Figure 4.26.

It can clearly be seen from the table that profit is maximized at an output of 4, where $T\Pi = 52$.

This profit-maximizing output and the level of profit can be calculated without drawing up a table. The calculation involves calculus. There are two methods that can be used.

Finding where MR = MC

Marginal revenue can be found by differentiating the total revenue function.

$$MR = dTR/dQ$$

The reason is that marginal revenue is the rate of change of total revenue. Differentiating a function gives its rate of change.

Similarly, marginal cost can be found by differentiating the total cost function:

$$MC = dTC/dQ$$

Differentiating *TR* and *TC* gives:

$$dTR/dQ = 48 - 2Q = MR$$

$$dTC/dQ = 16 + 6Q = MC$$

Profit is maximized where $MR = MC$: in other words, where:

$$48 - 2Q = 16 + 6Q$$

Solving this for *Q* gives:

$$32 = 8Q$$

$$\therefore Q = 4$$

The equation for total profit ($T\Pi$) is:

$$
\begin{aligned}
T\Pi &= TR - TC \\
&= 48Q - Q^2 - (12 + 16Q + 3Q^2) \\
&= -12 + 32Q - 4Q^2
\end{aligned}
$$

Substituting $Q = 4$ into this equation gives:

$$T\Pi = -12 + (32 \times 4) - (4 \times 4^2)$$

$$\therefore T\Pi = 52$$

These figures can be confirmed from the table.

Maximizing the total profit equation

To maximize an equation we want to find the point where the slope of the curve derived from it is zero. In other words, we want to find the top of the *T*Ⅱ curve.

The slope of a curve gives its rate of change and is found by differentiating the curve's equation. Thus to find maximum *T*Ⅱ we differentiate it (to find the slope) and set it equal to zero (to find the top).

$$T\Pi = -12 + 32Q - 4Q^2 \text{ (see above)}$$

$$\therefore dT\Pi/dQ = 32 - 8Q$$

Setting this equal to zero gives:

$$32 - 8Q = 0$$

$$\therefore 8Q = 32$$

$$\therefore Q = 4$$

This is the same result as was found by the first method. Again $Q = 4$ can be substituted into the *T*Ⅱ equation to give:

$$T\Pi = 52$$

Given the following equations:

$$TR = 72Q - 2Q^2; \ TC = 10 + 12Q + 4Q^2$$

calculate the maximum profit output and the amount of profit at that output using both methods.

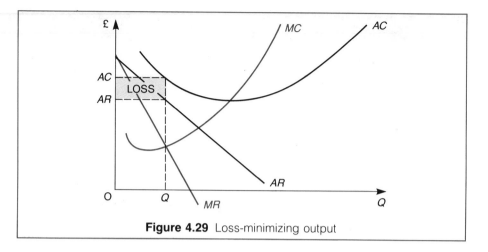

Figure 4.29 Loss-minimizing output

The rule for profit maximization then can be redefined as: the firm should produce where $MR = MC$ *provided that* above that output MC exceeds MR and below that output MR exceeds MC.

Whether or not to produce at all

The short run. Fixed costs have to be paid even if the firm is producing nothing at all. Rent has to be paid, business rates have to be paid, etc. Providing, therefore, that the firm is more than covering its *variable* costs, it can go some way to paying off these fixed costs and therefore will continue to produce.

It will shut down if it cannot cover its variable costs: that is, if the AVC curve is above, or the AR curve below, that illustrated in Figure 4.31. This situation is known as the short-run shut-down point

The long run. All costs are variable in the long run. If, therefore, the firm cannot cover its long-run average costs (which include normal profit), it will close down. The long-run shut-down point will be where the AR curve is tangential to the $LRAC$ curve.

Short-run shut-down point

Where the AR curve is tangential to the AVC curve. The firm can only just cover its variable costs. Any fall in revenue below this level will cause a profit-maximizing firm to shut down immediately.

Long-run shut-down point

Where the AR curve is tangential to the $LRAC$ curve. The firm can just make normal profits. Any fall in revenue below this level will cause a profit-maximizing firm to shut down once all costs have become variable.

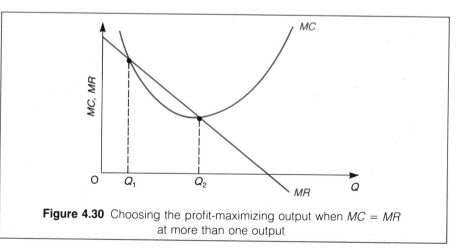

Figure 4.30 Choosing the profit-maximizing output when $MC = MR$ at more than one output

Figure 4.31 The short-run shut-down point

▲ SUMMARY

1. Total profit equals total revenue minus total cost. By definition, then, a firm's profits will be maximized at the point where there is the greatest gap between total revenue and total cost.
2. Another way of finding the maximum profit point is to find the output where marginal revenue equals marginal cost. Having found this output, the level of maximum profit can be found by finding the average profit ($AR - AC$) and then multiplying it by the level of output.
3. Normal profit is the minimum profit that must be made to persuade a firm to stay in business in the long run. It is counted as part of the firm's cost. Supernormal profit is any profit over and above normal profit.
4. For a firm that cannot make a profit at any level of output, the point where $MR = MC$ represents the loss-minimizing output.
5. In the short run a firm will close down if it cannot cover its variable costs. In the long run it will close down if it cannot make normal profits.

5 Profit Maximizing Under Perfect Competition and Monopoly

5.1 Alternative market structures

As we saw in Chapter 4, a firm's profits are maximized where its marginal cost equals its marginal revenue: $MC = MR$. But we will want to know more than this.

- What determines the *amount* of profit that a firm will make? Will profits be large, or just enough for the firm to survive, or so low that it will be forced out of business?
- Will the firm produce a high level of output or a low level?
- Will it be producing efficiently?
- Will the price charged to the consumer be high or low?
- More generally, will the consumer benefit from the decisions a firm makes? This is, of course, a *normative* question (see Chapter 1). Nevertheless, economists can still identify and analyze the effects on consumers of these decisions.

The answers to all these questions depend on the amount of *competition* that a firm faces. A firm in a highly competitive environment will behave quite differently from a firm facing little or no competition.

It is traditional to divide industries into categories according to the degree of competition that exists between the firms within the industry. There are four such categories.

At one extreme is perfect competition where there are very many firms competing. Each firm is so small relative to the whole industry that it has no power to influence price. It is a price taker. At the other extreme is monopoly, where there is just one firm in the industry, and hence no competition from within the industry. In the middle come monopolistic competition, where there are quite a lot of firms competing and where there is freedom for new firms to enter the industry, and oligopoly, where there are only a few firms and where entry of new firms is restricted.

To distinguish more precisely between these four categories, the following must be considered:

- The freedom with which firms can enter the industry. Is entry free or restricted? If it is restricted, just how great are the barriers to the entry of new firms?
- The nature of the product. Do all firms produce an identical product, or do firms produce their own particular brand or model or variety?
- The degree of control that the firm has over price. Is the firm a price taker or does it have the freedom to choose its price, and if it does, how will changing its price affect its profits? What we are talking about here is the nature of the demand curve

---

Perfect competition

A market structure where there are many firms; where there is freedom of entry into the industry; where all firms produce an identical product; and where all firms are price takers.

Monopoly

A market structure where there is only one firm in the industry.

Monopolistic competition

A market structure where, like perfect competition, there are many firms and freedom of entry into the industry, but where each firm produces a differentiated product and thus has some control over its price.

Oligopoly

A market structure where there are few enough firms to enable barriers to be erected against the entry of new firms.

it faces. How elastic is it? If it puts up its price, will it lose (a) all its sales (a horizontal demand curve), or (b) a large proportion of its sales (a relatively elastic demand curve), or (c) just a small proportion of its sales (a relatively inelastic demand curve)?

Table 5.1 shows the differences between the four categories.

Table 5.1 Features of the four market structures

Type of market	Number of firms	Freedom of entry	Nature of product	Examples	Implication for demand curve for firm
Perfect competition	Very many	Unrestricted	Homogeneous (undifferentiated)	Cabbages, carrots (these approximate to perfect competition)	Horizontal. The firm is a price taker
Monopolistic competition	Many/several	Unrestricted	Differentiated	Plumbers, restaurants	Downward sloping, but relatively elastic. The firm has some contol over price
Oligopoly	Few	Restricted	1. Undifferentiated or 2. Differentiated	1. Cement 2. Cars, electrical applicances	Downward sloping, relatively inelastic but depends on reactions of rivals to a price change
Monopoly	One	Restricted or completely blocked	Unique	British Gas, local bus service (in many towns)	Downward sloping, more inelastic than oligopoly. Firm has considerable control over price

1. Give one more example in each category.
2. Would you expect plumbers and restaurateurs to have the same degree of control over price?

The market structure under which a firm operates will determine its behaviour. Firms under perfect competition will behave quite differently from firms which are monopolists, who will behave differently again from firms under oligopoly or monopolistic competition.

This behaviour (or 'conduct') will in turn affect the firm's performance: its prices, profits, efficiency, etc. In many cases it will also affect other firms' performance: *their* prices, profits, efficiency, etc. The collective conduct of all the firms in the industry will affect the whole industry's performance.

Economists thus see a causal chain running from market structure to the performance of that industry.

Structure → Conduct → Performance

First we shall look at the two extreme market structures: perfect competition and monopoly. Then we shall turn to look at the two intermediate cases of monopolistic competition and oligopoly (Chapter 6).

The two intermediate cases are sometimes referred to collectively as imperfect competition. The vast majority of firms in the real world operate under imperfect competition. It is still worth studying the two extreme cases, however, because they provide a framework within which to understand the real world. Some industries tend more to the competitive extreme, and thus their performance corresponds to some extent to perfect competition. Other industries tend more to the other extreme: for

Imperfect competition

The collective name for monopolistic competition and oligopoly.

Box 5.1

Concentration Ratios
Measuring market structure

We can determine what type of market we are observing by the number of firms. However, this does not tell us anything about how *concentrated* the market might be. There may be *many* firms (suggesting a situation of perfect competition or monopolistic competition), but the largest two firms may have 90 per cent of the market's sales. This market power makes these two firms more like oligopolists.

Thus even though a large number of producers may make the market *seem* highly competitive, this could be deceiving.

The simplest measure of industrial concentration involves adding together the market share of the largest so many firms: e.g. the largest three or the largest five. This would give what is known as the '3-firm' or '5-firm concentration ratio'. Consider the total UK production of beer in 1985 and 1989, as shown in Table (a).

(a) Concentration in the UK brewing industry

	Percentage share of UK output	
	1985	1989
Bass	20	22
Allied	13	14
Whitbread	11	13
Scottish & Newcastle	9	11
Watney-Truman	9	13
Courage	9	10
Others	29	17

Source: *The Economic Review*, January 1989.

 Work out the 3-firm, 5-firm and 6-firm concentration ratios for each of the two years.

The beer industry this century has seen large numbers of mergers and takeovers. As Table (b) shows, the number of brewing firms has fallen dramatically. But despite this, output has remained roughly constant at about 40 million barrels per annum right from 1900 to the present day.

(b) Increasing concentration in the brewing industry

Number of brewing companies in the UK	
1900	1466
1910	1284
1920	941
1930	559
1940	428
1950	362
1960	247
1970	96
1980	81
1988	64

Source: *Brewers Society Statistical Handbook.*

Although the UK brewing industry has become more and more concentrated – the largest two firms in 1989 having over 36 per cent of the market – international comparisons show that concentration is far greater in some other countries. For example, in Australia the largest two firms produce 90 per cent of the nation's output; in Austria 60 per cent; in Belgium 55 per cent.

Regional brewers (approximately 20 companies UK wide) and local brewers (approximately 40) do exist, but they provide little competition to the 'big six', who through economies of scale and retailing and marketing strategies dominate the UK beer market.

1. In 1988 there were 64 brewers in the UK. How would you classify this industry?
2. Is it useful to judge the industry by the number or concentration of domestic producers when beer can be imported?

example, when there is one dominant firm and a few much smaller firms. In such cases their performance corresponds more to monopoly.

Chapters 5 and 6 assume that firms, under whatever market structure, are attempting to maximize profits. Chapter 7 questions this assumption. It looks at alternative theories of the firm: theories based on assumptions *other* than profit maximizing.

5.2 Perfect competition

The theory of perfect competition illustrates an extreme form of capitalism. In it firms are entirely subject to market forces. They have no power whatsoever to affect the price of the product. The price they face is that determined by the interaction of demand and supply in the whole *market*.

Assumptions

The model of perfect competition is built on four assumptions:

- There is *a very large number of firms* in the industry. As a result, the individual firm produces an insignificantly small portion of total industry output. Any change in its output, therefore, will not noticeably affect industry supply, and therefore will not affect price. The firm is thus a price taker. It faces a *horizontal demand 'curve'*.
- There is complete *freedom of entry* of new firms into the industry. Existing firms are unable to stop new firms setting up in business. Setting up a business takes time, however. Freedom of entry, therefore, applies in the long run. An extension of this assumption is that there is complete factor mobility in the long run. If profits are higher than elsewhere, capital will be freely attracted into that industry. Likewise if wages are higher than for equivalent work elsewhere, workers will freely move into that industry and will meet no barriers.
- All firms produce an *identical product*. (The product is 'homogeneous'.) There is therefore no branding or advertising.
- Producers and consumers have *perfect knowledge* of the market. That is, producers are fully aware of prices, costs and market opportunities. Consumers are fully aware of the price, quality and availability of the product.

These assumptions are very strict. Few, if any, industries in the real world meet these conditions. Certain agricultural markets perhaps are closest to perfect competition. The market for fresh vegetables is an example.

Nevertheless, despite the lack of real-world cases, the model of perfect competition plays a very important role in economic analysis and policy. Its major relevance is as an 'ideal type'. Many on the political right argue that perfect competition brings a number of important advantages. The model can thus be used as a standard against which to judge the shortcomings of real-world industries. It can help governments to formulate policies towards industry.

> **?** 1. It is sometimes claimed that the market for various stocks and shares is perfectly competitive, or nearly so. Take the case of the market for shares in a large company like ICI. Go through each of the four assumptions above and see if they apply in this case. (Don't be misled by the first assumption. The 'firm' in this case is not ICI itself.)
>
> 2. Is the market for gold perfectly competitive?

The short run and the long run

Before we can examine what price, output and profits will be, we must first distinguish between the short run and the long run as they apply to perfect competition.

In the short run the number of firms is fixed. Depending on its costs and revenue, a

The short run under perfect competition

The period during which there is too little time for new firms to enter the industry.

Box 5.2

Is Perfect Best?

Be careful of the word 'perfect'.

'Perfect' competition refers to competition that is total. Perhaps 'total' competition would be a better term. There is a total absence of power, a total absence of entry barriers, a total absence of product differentiation between producers, and total information for producers and consumers on the market. It is thus useful for understanding the effects of power, barriers, product differentiation and lack of information.

Perfect does not mean 'best', however.

Just because it is at the extreme end of the competition spectrum, it does not follow that perfect competition is desirable. You could have a perfect bomb – i.e. one that kills everyone in the world. You could have a perfect killer virus – i.e. one that is totally immune to drugs, and against which humans have no natural protection at all. Such things, though perfect, are hardly desirable!

To say that perfect competition is desirable and that it is a goal towards which government policy should be directed are normative statements. Economists, in their role as economists, cannot make such statements.

This does not mean, of course, that economists cannot identify the effects of perfect competition, but whether these effects are *desirable* or not is an ethical question.

The danger is that by using perfect competition as a yardstick, and by using the word 'perfect' rather than 'total', economists may be surreptitiously persuading their audience that perfect competition is a goal we *ought* to be striving to achieve.

1. Can economists list advantages and disadvantages of an economic policy?
2. Have economists the right to advise governments?

---

firm might be making large profits, small profits, no profits or a loss; and in the short run it may continue to do so.

The long run under perfect competition

The period of time which is long enough for new firms to enter the industry.

In the long run, however, the level of profits will affect entry and exit from the industry. If profits are high, new firms will be attracted into the industry, whereas if losses are being made, firms will leave.

This leads us to the distinction we made in Chapter 4: that between *normal* and *supernormal* profits. Let us examine them in the context of perfect competition.

Normal profit

This is the level of profit that is just enough to persuade firms to stay in the industry in the long run, but not high enough to attract new firms. If less than normal profits are made, firms will leave the industry in the long run.

Although we shall be talking about the *level* of normal profit (since that makes our analysis of pricing and output decisions simpler to understand), in practice it is usually the *rate* of profit that will determine whether a firm stays in the industry or leaves. The rate of profit (r) is the level of profit ($T\Pi$) as *a proportion of the level of capital (K) employed:* $r = T\Pi/K$. As you would expect, larger firms will require to make a larger *total* profit to persuade them to stay in an industry. Total normal profit is thus larger for them than for a small firm. The *rate* of normal profit, however, will probably be similar.

Rate of profit

Total profit ($T\Pi$) as a proportion of the capital employed (K): $r = T\Pi/K$.

1. Why do economists treat normal profit as a cost of production?
2. What determines (a) the level and (b) the rate of normal profit for a particular firm?

Supernormal profit

This is any profit above normal profit. If supernormal profits are made, new firms will be attracted into the industry in the long run.

Thus whether the industry expands or contracts in the long run will depend on the rate of profit. Naturally, since the time taken for a firm to set up in business will vary from industry to industry, the length of time before the long run is reached will also vary from industry to industry.

The short-run equilibrium of the firm

The determination of price, output and profit in the short run under perfect competition can best be shown in a diagram.

Figure 5.1 shows a short-run equilibrium for both industry and a firm under perfect competition. Both parts of the diagram have the same scale for the vertical axis. The horizontal axes have totally different scales, however. For example, if the horizontal axis for the firm were measured in, say, thousands of units, the horizontal axis for the whole industry might be measured in millions or tens of millions of units, depending on the number of firms in the industry.

Let us examine the determination of price, output and profit in turn.

Price

The price is determined in the industry by the intersection of demand and supply. The firm faces a horizontal demand (or average revenue) 'curve' at this price. It can sell all it can produce at the market price (P_e), but nothing at a price above P_e.

Output

The firm will maximize profit where marginal cost equals marginal revenue ($MR = MC$), at an output of Q_e. Note that, since the price is not affected by the firm's output, marginal revenue will equal price. The reason is that the firm is not having to reduce its price in order to sell more. An extra unit produced will therefore earn its full price for the firm. Thus the firm's MR 'curve' and demand 'curve' are the same horizontal straight line.

Profit

If the average cost (AC) curve (which includes normal profit) dips below the average revenue (AR) 'curve', the firm will earn supernormal profit. Supernormal profit per unit at Q_e is the vertical difference between AR and AC at Q_e. Total supernormal profit is the shaded rectangle in Figure 5.1.

Figure 5.1 Short-run equilibrium of industry and firm under perfect competition

What happens if the firm cannot make a profit at *any* level of output? This situation would occur if the *AC* curve were above the *AR* curve at all points. This is illustrated in Figure 5.2, where the market price is P_1. In this case, the point where $MC = MR$ represents the *loss-minimizing* point (where loss is defined as anything less than normal profit). This amount of the loss is represented by the shaded rectangle.

As we saw in Chapter 4, whether the firm is prepared to continue making a loss in the short run or whether it will close down immediately depends on whether it can cover its *variable* costs.

Provided price is above average variable cost (*AVC*), the firm will still continue producing in the short run. It will only shut down in the short run if the market price falls below P_2 in Figure 5.2.

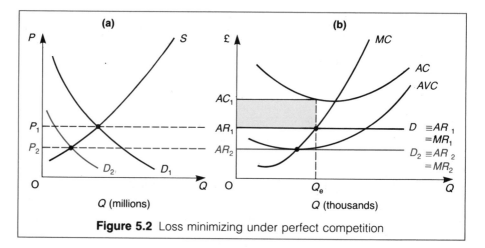

Figure 5.2 Loss minimizing under perfect competition

The short-run supply curve

The *firm's* short-run supply curve will be its (short-run) marginal cost curve.

A supply curve shows how much will be supplied at each price: it relates quantity to price. The marginal cost curve relates quantity to marginal cost. But under perfect competition, given that $P = MR$, and $MR = MC$, P must equal MC. Thus the supply curve and the *MC* curve will follow the same line.

For example, in Figure 5.3, if price were P_1, profits would be maximized at Q_1 where $P_1 = MC$. Thus point *a* is one point on the supply curve. At a price of P_2, Q_2 would be produced, thus point *b* is another point on the supply curve, and so on.

Thus, under perfect competition, the firm's supply curve is entirely dependent on costs of production. This demonstrates why the firm's supply curve is upward sloping. Given that marginal costs rise as output rises (due to diminishing marginal returns), a higher price will be necessary to induce the firm to increase its output.

Note that the firm will not produce at a price below *AVC*. Thus the supply curve is only that portion of the *MC* curve above point *e*.

What will be the short-run supply curve of the whole *industry*? This is simply the sum of the short-run supply curves (and hence *MC* curves) of all the firms in the industry. Graphically this will be a *horizontal* sum, since it is *quantities* that are being added.

? Will the industry supply be zero below a price of P_5 in Figure 5.3?

(a) Industry   **(b)** Firm

Figure 5.3 Deriving the short-run supply curve

The long-run equilibrium of the firm

In the long run, if typical firms are making supernormal profits, new firms will be attracted into the industry. Likewise, if existing firms can make supernormal profits by increasing the scale of their operations, they will do so, since all factors of production are variable in the long run.

The effect of the entry of new firms and/or the expansion of existing firms is to increase industry supply. This is illustrated in Figure 5.4.

The industry supply curve shifts to the right. This in turn leads to a fall in price. Supply will go on increasing and price falling until firms are making only normal profits. This will be when price has fallen to the point where the demand 'curve' for the firm just touches the bottom of its long-run average cost curve. Q_L is thus the long-run equilibrium output of the firm, with P_L the long-run equilibrium price.

 Illustrate on a diagram similar to Figure 5.4 what would happen in the long run if price were initially below P_L.

(a) Industry   **(b)** Firm

Figure 5.4 Long-run equilibrium under perfect competition

Figure 5.5 Long-run equilibrium of the firm under perfect competition

Since the *LRAC* curve is tangential to all possible short-run *AC* curves, (see section 4.4), the full long-run equilibrium will be as shown in Figure 5.5 where:

$$LRAC = AC = MC = MR = AR$$

The long-run industry supply curve

If industry demand increased, what would happen to industry price and output in the long run? The long-run supply curve gives the answer.

Each of the diagrams in Figure 5.6 shows an increase in demand. The demand curve shifts from D_1 to D_2. Equilibrium in the short run moves from point *a* to point *b*, where D_2 and S_1 intersect. After the initial rise in price, the resulting supernormal profit attracts new firms into the industry. The short-run supply curve shifts to S_2 and equilibrium moves to point *c*. Thus the long-run effect of the increase in demand has been to move the equilibrium from point *a* to point *c*. This means, therefore, that the *long-run* supply curve will pass through points *a* and *c*. This is illustrated in each of the three diagrams.

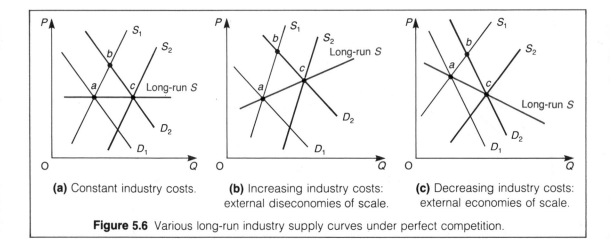

(a) Constant industry costs.

(b) Increasing industry costs: external diseconomies of scale.

(c) Decreasing industry costs: external economies of scale.

Figure 5.6 Various long-run industry supply curves under perfect competition.

Box 5.3

When Is a Profit Not a Profit?
A confusion of terminologies

We have used the terms *normal* and *supernormal* profit. Unfortunately not all economists and all textbooks use these terms. Economists can't seem to agree on what titles to use. The table shows some alternative titles.

Normal profit	Supernormal profit
Normal profit	Supernormal profit
Zero profit	Abnormal profit
The opportunity cost of	Economic profit
the owners' capital	Pure profit
	Profit

Looking at the left-hand column first, normal profit is the bare minimum return that owners must receive on their capital (after taking risks into account) in order to persuade them to stay in business. It can be seen as the opportunity cost of capital: namely, what could be earned on that capital by using it elsewhere. If it is counted as a 'cost', then in one sense it is not profit at all. If the owners are not getting anything extra over what they could get elsewhere, then in a sense normal profit is zero profit.

Turning now to the right-hand column, all five terms mean the same!

The last term needs some explanation, however. If we argue that normal profit is not really profit at all, that it is zero profit, then 'profit' must be anything earned above the opportunity cost of capital (i.e. supernormal profits).

The important thing to learn from this is to be very careful in the use of words. Be clear what is meant by a term when it is used. If the term 'profit' is used, does the user just mean supernormal profit or does it include normal profits as well?

Does it matter which terms you use? Not really, as long as everyone (including you) is clear about what you mean.

If price falls back to its original level (i.e. points *a* and *c* are at the *same* price) the *long-run* supply curve will be horizontal (see diagram (a)). This would occur if there were no change in firms' average cost curves. Price would simply return to the bottom of firms' *LRAC* curve.

If, however, the entry of new firms creates a shortage of factors of production, this will bid up factor prices. Firms' *LRAC* curve will shift vertically upwards, and so the long-run equilibrium price will be higher. The long-run supply curve of the industry, therefore, will slope upwards, as in diagram (b). This is the case of *increasing industry costs* or *external diseconomies of scale*: i.e. diseconomies external to the firm (see section 4.2).

If the expansion of the industry lowers firms' *LRAC* curve, due, say, to the building-up of an industrial infrastructure (distribution channels, specialist suppliers, banks, communications, etc.), the long-run supply curve will slope downwards, as in diagram (c). This is the case of *decreasing industry costs* or *external economies of scale*.

The incompatibility of perfect competition and substantial economies of scale

Why is perfect competition so rare in the real world – if it even exists at all? One important reason for this has to do with economies of scale.

In many industries, firms may have to be quite large if they are to experience the full potential economies of scale. But perfect competition requires there to be *many* firms. Firms must therefore be small under perfect competition: too small in most cases for economies of scale.

Once a firm expands sufficiently to achieve economies of scale, it will usually gain market power. It will be able to undercut the prices of smaller firms, which will thus be driven out of business. Perfect competition is destroyed.

1. What other reasons can you think of why perfect competition is so rare?
2. Why does the market for fresh vegetables approximate to perfect competition, whereas that for aircraft does not?

Perfect competition and the public interest

There are a number of features of perfect competition which could be argued to be advantageous to society:

- Price equals marginal cost. As we shall see in Chapter 10, this has important implications for the allocation of resources between alternative products. Given that price equals marginal utility (see Chapter 3), marginal utility will equal marginal cost. This is argued to be an *optimal* position.

  To demonstrate why, consider the cases where they are not equal. At levels of output *below* the equilibrium, price is greater than marginal cost. This means that consumers put a higher value on additional consumption than it costs to produce additional output. It could be argued, therefore, that *more* ought to be produced. If, on the other hand, *output* is above equilibrium, price will be below marginal cost. Here it could be argued that *less* should be produced because consumers put a lower value on this additional output than it costs to produce. Clearly, if more should be produced when output is below equilibrium, and less should be produced when output is above equilibrium, the equilibrium represents an optimum level of output. As we shall see later, it is only under perfect competition that price will equal marginal cost.

- If a firm becomes less efficient than other firms, it will make less than normal profits and be driven out of business. If it is more efficient, it will earn supernormal profits (until other firms copy its more efficient methods). Thus the competition between firms will act as a spur to efficiency.

- Similarly, the desire for supernormal profit, and the desire to avoid loss, will encourage the development of new technology.

- There is no point in advertising under perfect competition, since all firms produce a homogeneous product: (unless, of course, the firm believes that by advertising it can differentiate its product from its rivals' and thereby establish some market power; but then, by definition, the firm would cease to be perfectly competitive).

  This and the previous two factors will lead to low *AC* curves, and hence to an economical use of the nation's scarce resources.

- Long-run equilibrium is at the bottom of the firm's long-run *AC* curve. That is, for any *given* technology, the firm, in the long run, will produce at the least-cost output.

- The consumer gains from low prices, since not only are costs kept low, but also there are no long-run supernormal profits to add to cost.

- If consumer tastes change, the resulting price change will lead firms to respond (purely out of self-interest). An increased consumer demand will call forth extra supply with only a short-run increase in profit.

Consumer sovereignty

A situation where firms respond to changes in consumer demand without being in a position in the long run to charge a price above average cost.

Because of these last two points, perfect competition is said to lead to consumer sovereignty. Consumers, through the market, determine what and how much is to be produced. Firms have no power to manipulate the market. They cannot control price. The only thing they can do to increase profit in the long term is to become more efficient, and that benefits the consumer too.

Even under perfect competition, however, the free market has various limitations. For example, there is no guarantee that the goods produced will be distributed to the members of society in the fairest proportions. There may be considerable inequality of income. What is more, a redistribution of income would lead to a different pattern of consumption and hence production. Thus there is no guarantee that perfect competition will lead to the optimum combination of goods produced.

Another limitation is that the production of certain goods may lead to various undesirable side-effects, such as pollution. Perfect competition cannot safeguard against this either.

What is more, perfect competition may be less desirable than other market structures such as monopoly:

- Even though firms under perfect competition may seem to have an incentive to develop new technology (in order to gain supernormal profits, albeit temporarily), they may not be able to afford the necessary research and development due to a lack of current supernormal profit. Also they may be afraid that if they did develop new more efficient methods of production, their rivals would merely copy them, in which case the investment would have been a waste of money.
- Perfectly competitive industries produce undifferentiated products. This lack of variety might be seen as a disadvantage to the consumer. Under monopolistic competition and oligopoly there is often intense competition over the quality and design of the product. This can lead to pressure on firms to improve their products. This pressure will not exist under perfect competition.

The whole question of the efficiency or otherwise of perfect markets and the various failings of real-world markets is examined in more detail in Chapter 10.

At this stage, however, it is important to emphasize that the whole question of advantages and disadvantages is a normative one, and as such it is a question to which the economist cannot give a definitive answer. After all, people have very different views as to what constitutes 'good' or 'bad'.

 # SUMMARY

1. The assumptions of perfect competition are: a very large number of firms, complete freedom of entry, a homogeneous product and perfect knowledge of the good and its market by both producers and consumers.
2. In the short run there is not time for new firms to enter the market, and thus supernormal profits can persist. In the long run, however, any supernormal profits will be competed away by the entry of new firms.
3. The short-run equilibrium for the firm will be where the price, as determined by demand and supply in the market, is equal to marginal cost. At this output the firm will be maximizing profit. The firm's short-run supply curve is the same as its marginal cost curve (that portion of it above the *AVC* curve).
4. The long-run equilibrium will be where the market price is just equal to firms' long-run average cost. The long-run industry supply curve will thus depend on what happens to firms' *LRAC* curves as industry output expands. If their *LRAC* curves shift upward (due to external diseconomies of scale), the long-run industry supply

curve will slope upwards. If their *LRAC* curves shift downward (due to external economies of scale), the long-run industry supply curve will slope downwards.
5. There are no substantial economies of scale to be gained in a perfectly competitive industry. If there were, the industry would cease to be perfectly competitive as the large, low-cost firms drove the small high-cost ones out of business.
6. Under perfect competition, production will be at the point where $P = MC$. This can be argued to be optimal. Perfect competition can act as a spur to efficiency and bring benefits to the consumer in terms of low costs and low prices.
7. On the other hand, perfectly competitive firms may be unwilling to invest in research and development or may have insufficient funds to do so. They may also produce a lack of variety of goods. Finally, perfect competition does not necessarily lead to a fair distribution of income or guarantee an absence of harmful side-effects of production.

5.3 Monopoly

What is a monopoly?

This may seem a strange question because the answer seems obvious. A monopoly exists when there is only one firm in the industry.

But whether an industry can be classed as a monopoly is not always clear. It depends how narrowly the industry is defined. For example, Courtaulds has a monopoly on certain types of fabric, but it does not have a monopoly on fabrics in general. The consumer can buy alternative fabrics to those supplied by Courtaulds. British Rail may have a monopoly over rail services between London and Glasgow, but it does not have a monopoly over public transport between these two cities. People can travel by coach or air. They could also use private transport.

To some extent, the boundaries of an industry are arbitrary. What is more important for a firm is the amount of monopoly *power* it has, and that depends on the closeness of substitutes produced by rival industries. The electricity boards have a monopoly supply of electricity. They also have virtually no rivals in supplying power for lighting and running many domestic appliances. In the case of central heating, however, they have serious rivals in the form of coal, oil and gas.

The monopolist's demand curve

Since there is, by definition, only one firm in the industry, the firm's demand curve is also the industry demand curve.

Compared with other market structures, demand under monopoly will be relatively inelastic at each price. The monopolist can raise its price and consumers have no alternative firm to turn to within the industry. They either pay the higher price, or go without the good altogether.

The actual elasticity will depend on whether reasonably close substitutes are available in other industries. The demand for a rail service will be much more elastic if there is also a bus service to the same destination.

Barriers to entry

In order for a firm to maintain its monopoly position there must be barriers to the entry of new firms. Barriers also exist under oligopoly, but in the case of monopoly they must be high enough to block the entry of new firms. Barriers can be of various forms.

Economies of scale. If the monopolist's costs go on falling significantly up to the output that satisfies the whole market, the industry may not be able to support more than one producer. In Figure 5.7, D_1 represents the industry demand curve, and hence the demand curve for the firm under monopoly. The monopolist can gain supernormal profit at any output between points *a* and *b*. If there were two firms, however, each charging the same price and supplying half the industry output, they would both face

Natural monopoly

A situation where long-run average costs would be lower if an industry were under monopoly than if it were shared between two or more competitors.

the demand curve D_2. There is no price that would allow them to cover costs.

This case is known as natural monopoly. It is particularly likely if the market is small. For example, two bus companies might find it unprofitable to serve the same routes, each running with perhaps only half-full buses, whereas one company with a monopoly of the routes could make a profit.

Even if a market could support more than one firm, a new entrant is unlikely to be able to start up on a very large scale. Thus the monopolist who is already experiencing

Box 5.4

When Is a Monopoly Not a Monopoly?

As an illustration of the difficulty in identifying monopolies,
try and decide which of the following are monopolies:

British Telecom
British Gas
The Royal Mail
The London
    Underground
Guinness
Tipp-Ex

Your local milkman
Your local evening newspaper
The village post office
Interflora
Ice-creams in the cinema
Food on British Rail trains
The board game 'Monopoly'

As you will quickly realize in each case, it depends how
you define the industry.

economies of scale can charge a price below the cost of the new entrant and drive it
out of business. If, however, the new entrant is a firm already established in another
industry, it may be able to survive this competition.

Product differentiation and brand loyalty. If a firm produces a clearly differentiated
product, where the consumer associates the product with the brand, it will be very
difficult for a new firm to break into that market. This barrier can occur even though
the market is potentially big enough for two firms each gaining all the available
economies of scale. In other words, the problem for the new firm is not in being able
to produce at low enough costs, but in being able to produce a product sufficiently
attractive to consumers who are loyal to the familiar brand.

Lower costs for an established firm. An established monopoly is likely to have
developed specialized production and marketing skills. It is more likely to be aware of
the most efficient techniques and the most reliable and/or cheapest suppliers. It is
likely to have access to cheaper finance. Thus new firms would find it hard to
compete and could not win a price war.

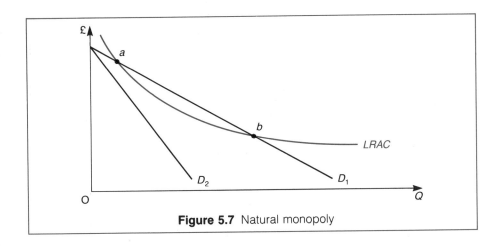

Figure 5.7 Natural monopoly

Ownership of, or control over, key factors of production. If a firm governs the supply of vital inputs (say, by owning the sole supplier of some component part), it can deny access to these inputs to potential rivals.

Ownership of, or control over, wholesale or retail outlets. Similarly, if a firm controls the outlets through which the product must be sold, it can prevent potential rivals from gaining access to consumers.

Legal protection. The firm's monopoly position may be protected by patents on essential processes, by copyright, by various forms of licensing (allowing, say, only one firm to operate in a particular area) and by tariffs (i.e. customs duties) and other trade restrictions to keep out foreign competitors.

Mergers and take-overs. The monopolist can put in a take-over bid for any new entrant. The sheer threat of take-overs may discourage new entrants.

Aggressive tactics. An established monopolist can probably sustain losses for longer than a new entrant. Thus it can start a price war, mount massive advertising campaigns, offer an attractive after-sales service, introduce new brands to compete with new entrants, and so on.

Intimidation. The monopolist may resort to various forms of harassment, legal or illegal, to drive a new entrant out of business.

Equilibrium price and output

Unlike the firm under perfect competition, the monopoly firm is a 'price maker'. It can choose what price to charge. Nevertheless, it is still constrained by its demand curve. A rise in price will lower the quantity demanded.

As with firms in other market structures, a monopolist will maximize profit where $MR = MC$. In Figure 5.8 profit is maximized at Q_m. The supernormal profit obtained is shown by the shaded area.

Since there are barriers to the entry of new firms, these supernormal profits will not be competed away in the long run. The only difference, therefore, between short-run and long-run equilibrium is that in the long run the firm will produce where $MR = long-run MC$.

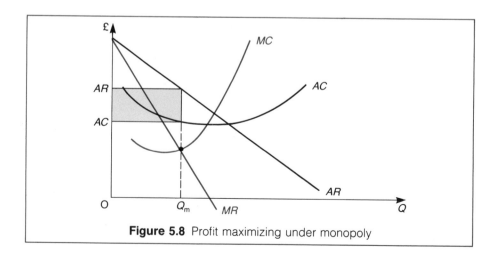

Figure 5.8 Profit maximizing under monopoly

Try this brain teaser. A monopoly would be expected to face an inelastic demand. After all, there are no direct substitutes. And yet, if it produces where *MR* = *MC*, *MR* must be positive and demand must therefore be *elastic*. Therefore the monopolist must face an elastic demand! Can you solve this conundrum?

Limit pricing

If the barriers to the entry of new firms are not total, and if the monopolist is making very large supernormal profits, there may be a danger in the long run of potential rivals breaking into the industry. In such cases the monopolist may keep its price down and thereby deliberately limit the size of its profits so as not to attract new entrants.

In Figure 5.9, two *AC* curves are drawn: one for the monopolist and one for a potential entrant. The monopolist, being established, has a lower *AC* curve. The new entrant, if it is to compete successfully with the monopolist, must charge the same price or a lower one. Thus provided the monopolist does not raise price above P_L, the other firm, unable to make supernormal profit, will not be attracted into the industry.

P_L may well be below the monopolist's short-run profit-maximizing price, but the monopolist may prefer to limit its price to P_L in order to protect its long-run profits from damage by competition.

Fear of government intervention to curb the monopolist's practices (e.g. the government referring the firm to the Monopolies and Mergers Commission: see section 11.2) may have a similar restraining effect on the price that the monopolist charges.

Figure 5.9 Limit pricing

1. On a diagram like Figure 5.9, by drawing in *MR* and *MC* curves, demonstrate that P_L could be below the short-run profit-maximizing price.
2. What does this analysis assume about the price elasticity of demand for the new entrant (a) above P_L; (b) below P_L?

Monopoly and the public interest

Disadvantages of monopoly
There are several reasons why monopolies may be against the public interest. As we shall see in section 11.2, these have given rise to legislation to regulate monopoly power and/or behaviour.

Higher price and lower output than under perfect competition (short run). Figure 5.10 compares the profit-maximizing position for an industry under monopoly with that under perfect competition. The monopolist will produce Q_1 at a price of P_1. This is where $MC = MR$.

If the same industry were under perfect competition, however, it would produce at Q_2 and P_2 – a higher output and a lower price. But why? Remember that the *firm* under perfect competition faces a perfectly elastic demand (*AR*) curve, which also equals *MR*. Thus $P = MR$ (see Figure 5.1). The firm under perfect competition is thus equating price and marginal cost: the *MC* curve is the supply curve (see section 5.2). When *all* firms under perfect competition do this, price and quantity in the *industry* will be given by P_2 and Q_2 in Figure 5.10. That is, price and quantity will be where industry supply (*MC*) equals industry demand.

(This analysis is based on the assumption that the industry has the same *AC* and *MC* curves whether under perfect competition or run as a monopoly. An example would be the case of potato farmers who initially operate under perfect competition. Then they set up a marketing agency through which they all sell their potatoes. The agency therefore acts as a monopoly supplier to the market. Since it is the same farmers before and after, production costs are unlikely to have changed much. But as we shall see below, even if an industry has *lower AC* and *MC* curves under monopoly than under perfect competition, it is still likely to charge a higher price and produce a lower output.)

When we were looking at the advantages of perfect competition, we said that where $P = MC$ could be argued to be the *optimum* level of production. Clearly, if a monopolist is producing below this level (at only Q_1 in Figure 5.10 – where $P > MC$), the monopolist can be argued to be producing at *less* than optimal output. Consumers would be prepared to pay more for additional units than they cost to produce.

Higher price and lower output than under perfect competition (long run). Under perfect competition, freedom of entry eliminates supernormal profit and forces firms to produce at the bottom of their *LRAC* curve. The effect, therefore, is to keep long-run prices down. Under monopoly, however, barriers to entry allow profits to remain supernormal in the long run. The monopolist is not forced to operate at the bottom of the *AC* curve. Thus, other things being equal, long-run prices will tend to be higher, and hence output lower, under monopoly.

Figure 5.10 Equilibrium of the industry under perfect competition and monopoly: with same *MC* curve

Possibility of higher cost curves due to lack of competition. The sheer survival of a firm in the long run under perfect competition requires that it uses the most efficient known technique, and develops new techniques wherever possible. The monopolist, however, sheltered by barriers to entry, can still make large profits even if it is not using the most efficient technique. It has less incentive, therefore, to be efficient.

On the other hand, if it can lower its costs by using and developing more efficient techniques, it can gain extra supernormal profits which will not be competed away.

Unequal distribution of income. The high profits of monopolists may be considered as unfair, especially by competitive firms, or anyone on low incomes for that matter. The scale of this problem obviously depends on the size of the monopoly and the degree of its power. The monopoly profits of the village store may seem of little consequence when compared to the profits of a giant national or international company.

 If the shares in a monopoly (such as British Gas) were very widely distributed among the population, would the shareholders necessarily want the firm to use its monopoly power to make larger profits?

In addition to these problems, monopolies may lack the incentive to introduce new product varieties, and large monopolies may be able to exert political pressure and thereby get favourable treatment from governments.

Advantages of monopoly

Despite these arguments, monopolies can have some advantages.

Economies of scale. The monopoly may be able to achieve substantial economies of scale due to larger plant, centralized administration and the avoidance of unnecessary duplication (e.g. a monopoly gas company would eliminate the need for several sets of rival gas pipes under each street). If this results in an *MC* curve substantially below that of the same industry under perfect competition, the monopoly will produce a *higher* output at a *lower* price. In Figure 5.11 the monopoly produces Q_1 at a price of P_1, whereas the perfectly competitive industry produces Q_2 at the higher price P_2.

Note that this result only follows if the monopoly *MC* curve is below point *x* in Figure 5.11. Note also that an industry cannot exist under perfect competition if substantial

Figure 5.11 Equilibrium of the industry under perfect competition and monopoly: with different *MC* curves

Box 5.5

X Inefficiency
The cost of a quiet life

The major criticism of monopoly has traditionally been that of the monopoly's power in selling the good. Facing a relatively inelastic demand, the monopoly can charge a high price. A higher price than under competitive conditions means a lower output (see Figure 5.10). The criticism here is that monopoly leads to *allocative inefficiency*. Fewer resources are being allocated to the monopoly industry and less is being produced than if it were under perfect competition. Under monopoly, price is above MC. This is seen as allocatively inefficient because at the margin consumers are willing to pay more than it is costing to produce ($P > MC$); and yet the monopolist is deliberately holding back, so as to keep its profits up. Allocative inefficiency is examined in detail in section 10.1.

Monopolies may also be inefficient for another reason: they may have higher costs. But why?

A major reason for this is that monopolies may be X inefficient.[1] Without competitive pressure on profit margins, cost controls may become lax. The result may be overstaffing and spending on prestige buildings and equipment, as well as less effort to keep technologically up to date, scrap old plant, research new products, or develop new domestic and export markets.

Thus the more comfortable the situation, the less may be the effort which is expended to improve it.

The effect of X inefficiency is to make the AC and MC curves higher than they would otherwise be.

A good example of an improvement in X inefficiency occurred in the 1950s and 1960s. A wave of anti-monopoly legislation over this twenty-year period (see section 11.2) saw many firms with previously comfortable profit margins faced by new competition. As profits were eroded, a cost-cutting drive was launched by many companies. Much out-of-date plant was closed down and replaced with new technologically advanced machinery. Overstaffed factories saw their employment cut and there was a decline in managerial perks. In most cases the firms in question became both more competitive and more efficient.

? 1. How does the existence of X inefficiency contribute to arguments concerning monopoly policy?
2. How might you measure X inefficiency?
3. Another type of inefficiency is *technical or productive inefficiency*. What do you think this is? (Clue: it has to do with the proportions in which factors are used.)

[1] This term was coined by Harvey Leibenstein, 'Allocative efficiency or X efficiency', *American Economic Review*, June 1966.

economies of scale can be gained. It is thus somewhat hypothetical to compare a monopoly with an alternative situation that could not exist. What is more, were the monopolist to follow the $P = MC$ rule observed by perfectly competitive firms, it would charge an even lower price (P_3) and produce an even higher output (Q_3).

Possibility of lower cost curves due to more research and development and more investment. Although the monopolist's sheer survival does not depend on its finding ever more efficient methods of production, it can use part of its supernormal profits for research and development and investment. It thus has a greater ability to become efficient than has the small firm with limited funds.

Innovation and new products. The promise of supernormal profits, protected perhaps by patents, may encourage the development of new (monopoly) industries producing new products.

▲ SUMMARY

1. A monopoly is where there is only one firm in an industry. In practice it is difficult to determine where a monopoly exists because it depends on how narrowly an industry is defined.
2. Barriers to the entry of new firms will normally be necessary to protect a monopoly from competition. Such barriers include economies of scale (making the firm a natural monopoly or at least giving it a cost advantage over new (small) competitors), control over supplies of inputs or over outlets, patents or copyright, and tactics to eliminate competition (such as take-overs or aggressive advertising).
3. Profits for the monopolist (as for other firms) will be maximized where $MC = MR$. In the case of monopoly, this will probably be at a higher price relative to marginal cost than for other firms, due to the less elastic nature of its demand at any given price.
4. If entry barriers are not total, the monopolist may limit its

price to the level of its potential rivals' average cost. That way there would be insufficient potential profits to encourage them to enter.
5. Monopolies may be against the public interest to the extent that they charge a higher price relative to cost than do competitive firms; to the extent that they may cause a less desirable distribution of income; to the extent that a lack of competition removes the incentive to be efficient and innovative; and to the extent that they may exert undesirable political pressures on governments.
6. On the other hand, any economies of scale will in part be passed on to consumers in lower prices, and the monopolist's high profits may be used for research and development and investment, which in turn may lead to better products at possibly lower prices.
7. The relative importance of the advantages and disadvantages of monopoly will vary from industry to industry.

5.4 Potential competition or potential monopoly? The theory of contestable markets

Potential competition

In recent years economists have developed the theory of contestable markets. This theory argues that what is crucial in determining price and output is not whether an industry is *actually* a monopoly or competitive, but whether there is the real *threat* of competition.

If a monopoly is protected by high barriers to entry – say that it owns all the raw materials – then it will be able to make supernormal profits with no fear of competition.

If, however, another firm *could* take over from it with little difficulty, it will behave much more like a competitive firm. The threat of competition has a similar effect to actual competition.

As an example, consider a catering company that is given permission by a factory to run its canteen. The catering company has a monopoly over the supply of food to the workers in that factory. If, however, it starts charging high prices or providing a poor service, the factory could offer the running of the canteen to an alternative catering company. This threat may force the original catering company to charge 'reasonable' prices and offer a good service.

Perfectly contestable markets

A market is perfectly contestable when the costs of entry and exit by potential rivals are zero, and when such entry can be made very rapidly. In such cases, the moment the possibility of earning supernormal profits occurs, new firms will enter, thus

Perfectly contestable market

A market where there is free and costless entry and exit.

driving profits down to a normal level. The sheer threat of this happening, so the theory goes, will ensure that the firm already in the market will (a) keep its prices down, so that it just makes normal profits, and (b) produce as efficiently as possible, taking advantage of any economies of scale and any new technology. If the existing firm did not do this, entry would take place, and potential competition would become actual competition.

Contestable markets and natural monopolies

So why in such cases are the markets not *actually* perfectly competitive? Why do they remain monopolies?

The most likely reason has to do with economies of scale and the size of the market. To operate on a minimum efficient scale, the firm may have to be so large relative to the market that there is only room for one such firm in the industry. If a new firm does come into the market, then one or other of the two firms will not survive the competition. The market is simply not big enough for both of them.

If, however, there are no entry or exit costs, new firms will be perfectly willing to enter even though there is only room for one firm, provided they believe that they are more efficient than the existing firm. The existing firm, knowing this, will be forced to produce as efficiently as possible and with only normal profit.

The importance of costless exit

Setting up in a new business usually involves large expenditures on plant and machinery. Once this money has been spent, it becomes fixed costs. If these fixed costs are no higher than those of the existing firm, then the new firm could win the battle. But, of course, there is always the risk that it might lose.

But does losing the battle really matter? Cannot the firm simply move to another market?

It does matter if there are substantial costs of exit. This will be the case if the capital equipment cannot be transferred to other uses. In this case these fixed costs are known as sunk costs. The losing firm is left with capital equipment that it cannot use. The firm may therefore be put off entering in the first place. The market is not perfectly contestable, and the established firm can make supernormal profit.

Sunk costs
Costs that cannot be recouped (e.g. by transferring assets to other uses).

If, however, the capital equipment can be transferred, the exit costs will be zero (or at least very low), and new firms will be more willing to take the risks of entry. For example, a rival coach company may open up a service on a route previously operated by only one company, and where there is still only room for one operator. If the new firm loses the resulting battle, it can still use the coaches it has purchased. It simply uses them for a different route. The cost of the coaches is not a sunk cost.

Costless exit, therefore, encourages firms to enter an industry, knowing that, if unsuccessful, they can always transfer their capital elsewhere.

The lower the exit costs, the more contestable the market. This implies that firms already established in other similar markets may provide more effective competition against monopolists, since they can simply transfer capital from one market to another. For example, studies of airlines in the USA show that entry to a particular route may be much easier for an established airline, which can simply transfer planes from one route to another.

Costless exit can also allow effective potential competition for oligopolies. As we shall see in Chapter 6, if an oligopolistic market is contestable, this will reduce the level of supernormal profits that can be made, just as it does with a monopoly.

> In which of the following industries are exit costs likely to be low: (a) steel production; (b) market gardening; (c) nuclear power generation; (d) specialist financial advisory services; (e) production of fashion dolls; (f) production of a new drug; (g) contract catering; (h) mobile discos; (j) car ferry operators? Are these exit costs dependent on how narrowly the industry is defined?

Hit-and-run competition

When entry and exit costs are low, and entry can be made speedily, firms may engage in hit-and-run tactics. They may enter a market for a short period when high profits can be made and then quickly withdraw again.

For example, a small goods delivery company may set up a rival parcels service to the national postal service at Christmas time over certain major routes if the national service has high (monopoly) postal charges. The fear of such competition may prevent the national service from charging high prices in the first place. Similarly, a local builder serving a small village may suddenly find itself facing competition after a storm from 'cowboy' operators offering to mend roofs cheaply for cash. The fear of this may again dissuade the local builder from raising its prices, even if several roofs have been damaged.

Hit-and-run competition

When a firm enters an industry to take advantage of temporarily high profits and then leaves again as soon as the high profits have been exhausted.

> Give some other examples of hit-and-run competition.

Assessment of the theory

The theory of contestable markets is an improvement on simple monopoly theory, which merely focuses on the existing structure of the industry and makes no allowance for potential competition.

The theory of limit pricing goes some way toward considering potential competition, but focuses on one particular barrier to entry: namely, the higher average cost of the new entrant.

The theory of contestable markets takes this further and considers the size of the barriers to entry and the costs of exit. The bigger these are, the less contestable is the market, and therefore the greater is the monopoly power of the existing firm. Various attempts have been made to measure monopoly power in this way.

Perfectly contestable markets may exist only rarely. But like perfect competition they provide an *ideal type* against which to judge the real world. It is increasingly argued that they provide a more useful ideal type than perfect competition, since the extent of divergence from this ideal provides a better means of predicting firms' price and output behaviour than does the simple portion of the market currently supplied by the existing firm.

One criticism of the theory, however, is that it does not take sufficient account of the possible reactions of the established firm. There may be no cost barriers to entry or exit (i.e. a perfectly contestable market), but the established firm may let it be known that any firm that dares to enter will face all out war! This may act as a deterrent to entry. In the meantime, the established firm may charge high prices and make supernormal profits.

Contestable markets and the public interest

If a monopoly operates in a perfectly contestable market, it might bring the 'best of both worlds'. Not only will it be able to achieve low costs through economies of scale, but also the potential competition will keep profits and hence prices down.

Box 5.6

Deregulated Airlines in the USA
A case of contestable markets?[2]

The airline industry in the United States has been deregulated (i.e. free from government control) for over ten years, and the impact of this policy on air travel has been dramatic.

Prior to deregulation, air routes were allocated by the government with the result that many airlines operated as monopolies or shared the route with just one other airline. Now there exists a policy of 'open skies'. The consequences have been highly significant, with lower fares and, over many routes, a greater choice of airlines. Moreover, this has taken place despite a rapid rise in operating costs: in 1989 costs rose by 9 per cent exceeding the growth in combined airline revenues of 7 per cent.

Even where routes continue to be operated by just one or two airlines, fares have still fallen if the route is contestable: if the entry and exit costs remain low.

But deregulation has not made all routes more contestable. In some cases the reverse has happened. In a situation of rising costs and falling revenues, there are likely to be take-overs of the vulnerable airlines. Some eight airlines now account for 90 per cent of American domestic air travel, compared with fifteen in 1984. With this move towards greater monopolization, some airlines have managed to make their routes *less* contestable.

In recent times a system has developed of air routes radiating out from key or 'hub' airports. With waves of flights scheduled to arrive and depart within a short space of time, passengers can make easy connections at these hub airports.

The problem is that several of these hub airports have become dominated by single airlines, which through economies of scale and the ownership or control of various airport facilities, such as landing gates or check-in areas, can effectively keep out potential entrants. The problem is worse in airports which are congested and where room for a new entrant could only be made if existing airlines cut back their flights: something they will obviously resist. In those hub airports where a single airline operates more than 75 per cent of departures, fares were nearly 20 per cent higher than the national average.

So how could routes from these hub airports be made more contestable?

Part of the answer may be to deregulate even further. For example, the practice could be ended whereby new take-off or landing slots at certain airports are auctioned among airlines already operating out of that airport.

Part of the answer, however, may be to introduce *new* regulations to prevent airlines which already have more than a certain percentage of slots from obtaining new ones.

? 1. Make a list of those factors that determine the contestability of a particular air route.
2. Are there any advantages to the traveller of the government allocating routes?

[2] This box is based on material from *The Economist*, 10 March 1990.

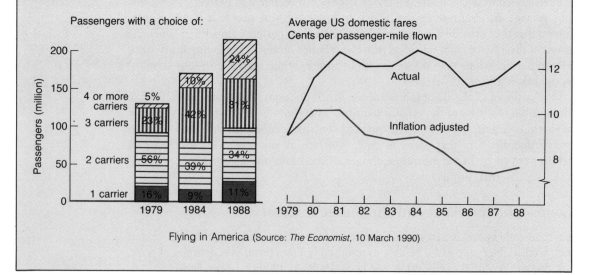

Flying in America (Source: *The Economist*, 10 March 1990)

For this reason the theory has been seized on by politicians on the political right to justify a policy of *laissez-faire* (non-intervention). They argue that the theory vindicates the free market. There are two points in reply to this:

- Markets may not be *perfectly* contestable. If entry and exit are not costless, a monopoly can still make supernormal profits in the long run.
- There are other possible failings of the market besides monopoly power (e.g. inequality, pollution). These failings are examined in Chapters 9 and 10.

Nevertheless the theory of contestable markets has highlighted the importance of entry barriers in determining monopoly behaviour. The size of the barriers has therefore become the focus of attention of many politicians and academics when considering anti-monopoly policy.

 Think of three examples of monopolies (local or national) and consider how contestable their markets are.

▲ SUMMARY

1. Potential competition may be as important as actual competition in determining a firm's price and output strategy.
2. The threat of this competition is greater the lower are the entry and exit costs to and from the industry. If the entry and exit costs are zero, the market is said to be *perfectly* contestable. Under such circumstances an existing monopolist will be forced to keep its profits down to the normal level if it is to resist entry of new firms. Exit costs will be lower, the lower are the sunk costs of the firm.
3. Hit-and-run competition can be an important feature of highly contestable markets.
4. The theory of contestable markets provides a more realistic analysis of firms' behaviour than theories based simply on the *existing* number of firms in the industry.

⑥ Profit Maximization Under Imperfect Competition

Very few markets in practice can be classified as perfectly competitive or as a pure monopoly. The vast majority of firms do compete with other firms, often quite aggressively, and yet they are not price takers: they do have some degree of market power. Most markets, therefore, lie between the two extremes of monopoly and perfect competition, in the realm of 'imperfect competition'.

There are two types of imperfect competition: namely, monopolistic competition and oligopoly. Under monopolistic competition there will normally be quite a large number of relatively small firms, whereas under oligopoly there will normally only be a few – say, between two and twenty.

> **?** Think of ten different products or services and estimate roughly how many firms there are in the market. (You will need to decide whether 'the market' is a local one, a national one or an international one.) In what ways do the firms compete in each of the cases you have identified?

6.1 Monopolistic competition

We will start by looking at monopolistic competition. This is nearer to the competitive end of the spectrum. It can best be understood as a situation where there are a lot of firms competing but where each firm does nevertheless have some degree of market power (hence the term 'monopolistic' competition): each firm has some discretion as to what price to charge for its products.

Assumptions of monopolistic competition

- There is *quite a large number of firms*. As a result each firm has an insignificantly small share of the market, and therefore its actions are unlikely to affect its rivals to any great extent. What this means is that each firm in making its decisions does not have to worry how its rivals will react. It assumes that what its rivals choose to do will *not* be influenced by what it does.

Independence (of firms in a market)
Where the decisions of one firm in a market will not have any significant effect on the demand curves of its rivals.

  This is known as the assumption of independence. (As we shall see later, this is not the case under oligopoly. There we assume that firms believe that their decisions *do* affect their rivals, and that their rivals' decisions will affect them. Under oligopoly we assume that firms are *inter*dependent.)

- There is *freedom of entry* of new firms into the industry. If any firm wants to set up in business in this market, it is free to do so.

In these two respects, therefore, monopolistic competition is like perfect competition.

- Unlike perfect competition, however, each firm produces a product or provides a service in some way different from its rivals. As a result it can raise its price without losing all its customers. Thus its demand curve is downward sloping, albeit relatively elastic given the large number of competitors to whom customers can turn. This is known as the assumption of product differentiation.

Petrol stations, chemist shops, hairdressers and builders are all examples of monopolistic competition.

 Give some other examples of monopolistic competition. (Try looking through the *Yellow Pages* if you are stuck.)

A typical feature of monopolistic competition is that, although there are many firms in the industry, there is only one firm in a particular location. This applies particularly in retailing. There may be many greengrocers in a town, but only one in a particular street. In a sense, therefore, it has a local monopoly. People may be prepared to pay higher prices there for their vegetables to avoid having to go elsewhere.

It is similar with the general food store. Once a week people may go to the supermarket where prices are cheaper, but if they run out of one or two items during the week they will go to the shop on the corner, even though it is dearer.

Product differentiation

Where one firm's product is sufficiently different from its rivals' to allow it to raise the price of the product without customers all switching to the rivals' products. A situation where a firm faces a downward-sloping demand curve.

Equilibrium of the firm

Short run

As with other market structures, profits are maximized at the output where $MC = MR$. The diagram will be the same as for the monopolist, except that the AR and MR curves will be more elastic. This is illustrated in Figure 6.1(a). As with perfect competition, it is possible for the monopolistically competitive firm to make supernormal profit in the short run. This is shown as the shaded area.

Just how much profit the firm will make in the short run depends on the strength of demand: the position and elasticity of the demand curve. The further to the right the

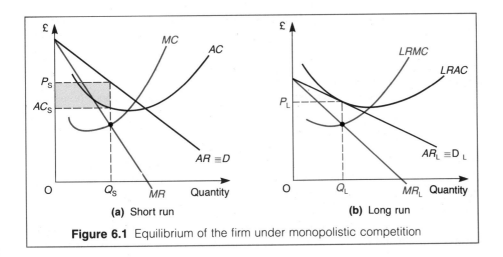

Figure 6.1 Equilibrium of the firm under monopolistic competition

---

Box 6.1

A Case Study in Monopolistic Competition
The motor vehicle repair and servicing industry[1]

The typical British small garage is stereotyped as untidy, messy, cluttered with hoists and equipment, with a few overall-clad figures working to the clatter of tools and blaring radio.

This picture is quite different from that of the early years of the automobile. In those days, work on the car was the domain of the chauffeur or blacksmith, or the manufacturer if repairs were beyond both.

This was to change following the Second World War. As the volume of cars grew, the motor repair sector began to expand, giving employment to the many mechanically trained ex-servicemen.

The market grew so quickly that there was little chance of erecting entry barriers. For example, although there were moves to introduce specific (City and Guilds) qualifications for mechanics and thereby impose a degree of restricted entry on the industry, this was never fully established. The result is to be seen today.

The motor vehicle repair industry has developed into a good example of a monopolistically competitive industry.

Some 20 000 workshops maintain and repair vehicles; three-quarters of these employ fewer than ten staff and have an average turnover of little more than £100 000.

The vehicle repair and servicing industry is diverse, being made up of general repairers, specialist repairers (i.e. bodywork, electrics), dealers and petrol stations. With so many garages the industry has remained a highly competitive one. However, specialism and locality enable the various garages to maintain a fairly constant degree of control over their price.

1. What are the specific features of the motor vehicle repair industry that have restricted the growth of large-scale operations?
2. What other industries can you think of that exhibit similar characteristics?

[1] This box is based on A. Bollard, *Small Beginnings* (Intermediate Technology Publications, 1983).

---

demand curve is relative to the average cost curve, and the less elastic the demand curve is, the greater will be the firm's short-run profit. Thus a firm facing little competition and whose product is considerably differentiated from its rivals may be able to earn considerable short-run profits.

Take the case of a petrol station near a new housing estate. If it is the only one in the neighbourhood, it will have considerable market power. It may face a relatively high and inelastic demand. Motorists may have to travel a long way to get to the next filling station. *Some* motorists may be prepared to do just that if the price of its petrol were high. Others, however, may find it inconvenient to go to another station, or may have to use extra petrol to do so (thus cancelling out any cost advantage). In the short run, therefore, it may be able to charge a high price and make large supernormal profits.

1. Why may a food shop charge higher prices than supermarkets for 'essential items' and yet very similar prices for delicatessen items?
2. Which of these two items is a petrol station more likely to sell at a discount: (a) oil; (b) sweets? Why?

Long run

If typical firms are earning supernormal profit, new firms will enter the industry in the long run. In the case of the petrol station we were looking at just now, new ones are likely to open in the neighbourhood: not necessarily in the same place, but maybe at the other end of the estate.

As new firms enter, they will take some of the customers away from the existing firms. The demand for the existing firms will therefore fall. Their demand (*AR*) curve

Box 6.2

Joan Robinson (1903–83)
Person profile

At the same time that Edward Chamberlin was developing the theory of monopolistic competition in America, Joan Robinson was developing an alternative theory of imperfect competition in England. There were some differences in their approaches but they both analyzed the effects of product differentiation and advertising and thereby extended traditional theory, which had been based almost solely on the two models of perfect competition and monopoly.

Joan Robinson's career, however, was very different from Chamberlin's. He is famous for just one theory; she is famous for the sheer variety and unorthodoxy of her contributions.

She was very much associated with Cambridge. She was a student at Girton College, Cambridge, graduating in 1925. Soon after, she married fellow economist Austin Robinson. After living in India for a time, they returned to Cambridge University where she taught until her retirement in 1971.

During the 1930s she was one of a small group of economists who worked alongside John Maynard Keynes (see Box 13.7 below), in developing the new macroeconomic theories of employment and money: theories that we shall be looking at in detail from Chapter 13 onwards.

Joan Robinson's contributions to economics were both radical and extensive. She was frequently scathing of traditional economics and of the concerns of economists. For example, she argued that capitalism's failure to eliminate poverty or to aid the development of the Third World were issues which economists should address with urgency.

In 1973, along with John Eatwell, a fellow Cambridge economist, she wrote *An Introduction to Modern Economics*, a book that the authors hoped would revolutionize the teaching of economics. It discarded much of what they considered to be irrelevant in traditional theory (including her early work on imperfect competition!). The book was poorly received, however. Perhaps users of economics textbooks prefer the traditional and familiar!

John Eatwell said of Joan Robinson:

> Her books and articles are often outstanding examples of English prose, and the ideas are novel and exciting, but they do not fit within the framework used by most economists to define their subject.[2]

This non-orthodox approach became very much Joan Robinson's trademark. Such unorthodoxy, however, did not prevent her from being acknowledged as one of the world's most important economic theorists.

[2] J. Eatwell, 'Joan Robinson: Portrait', *Challenge*, vol. 20, no. 1.

will shift to the left, and will continue doing so as long as supernormal profits remain and thus new firms continue entering.

Long-run equilibrium will be reached when only normal profits remain: when there is no further incentive for new firms to enter. This is illustrated in Figure 6.1(b). The firm's demand curve settles at D_L, where it is tangential to the firm's *LRAC* curve. Output will be Q_L: where $AR_L = LRAC$. (At any other output, *LRAC* is greater than *AR* and thus less than normal profit would be made.)

?
1. Why does the *LRMC* curve cross the MR_L curve directly below the tangency point of the *LRAC* and AR_L curves?
2. Assuming that supernormal profits can be made in the short run, will there be any difference in the long-run and short-run elasticity of demand? Explain.

Limitations of the model

There are various problems in applying the model of monopolistic competition to the real world:

- Information may be imperfect. Firms will not enter an industry if they are unaware of the supernormal profits currently being made, or if they underestimate the demand for the particular product they are considering selling.

- Given that the firms in the industry produce different products, it is difficult if not impossible to derive a demand curve for the industry as a whole. Thus the analysis has to be confined to the level of the firm.
- Firms are likely to differ from each other not only in the product they produce or the service they offer, but also in their size and in their cost structure. What is more, entry may not be *completely* unrestricted. Two petrol stations could not set up in exactly the same place – on a busy crossroads, say. Thus although the typical or 'representative' firm may only earn normal profit in the long run, other firms may be able to earn long-run supernormal profit. They may have some cost advantage or produce a product that is impossible to duplicate perfectly.
- Existing firms may make supernormal profits, but if a new firm entered this might reduce everyone's profits below the normal level. Thus a new firm will not enter and supernormal profits will persist into the long run. An example would be a small town with two chemist shops. They may both make more than enough profit to persuade them to stay in business. But if a third set up (say mid-way between the other two) there would not be enough total sales to allow them all to earn even normal profit. This is a problem of *indivisibilities*. Given the overheads of a chemist shop, it is not possible to set up one small enough to take away just enough customers to leave the other two with normal profits.
- One of the biggest problems with the simple model outlined in the previous section is that it concentrates on price and output decisions. In practice, the profit-maximizing firm under monopolistic competition will also need to decide the exact variety of product to produce and how much to spend on advertising it. This will lead the firm to take part in non-price competition.

Non-price competition

Non-price competition

Competition in terms of product promotion (advertising, packaging, etc.) or product development.

Non-price competition involves two major elements: product development and advertising.

The major aims of product development are to produce a product that will sell well (i.e. one in high or potentially high demand) and that is different from rivals' products (i.e. has an inelastic demand due to lack of close substitutes). In the case of shops or other firms providing a service, 'product development' will take the form of attempting to provide a service which is better than, or at least different from, that of rivals: personal service, late opening, certain lines stocked, etc.

 Are there any shops in your area that stay open later than others? If so, are their prices similar? Why, do you think, do they charge the prices they do?

The major aim of advertising is to sell the product. This can be achieved not only by informing the consumer of the product's existence and availability, but also by deliberately trying to persuade consumers to purchase the good. Like product development, successful advertising will not only increase demand but also make the firm's demand curve less elastic since it stresses the specific qualities of this firm's product over its rivals'. (See Box 2.3.)

Product development and advertising not only increase a firm's demand and hence revenue, they also involve increased costs. So how much should a firm advertise, say to maximize profits?

For any given price and product the optimal amount of advertising is where the revenue from *additional* advertising (MR_A) is equal to its cost (MC_A). As long as $MR_A > MC_A$, additional advertising will add to profit. But extra amounts spent on

Box 6.3

A Case Study in Non-Price Competition
The corner shop and the hypermarket

The general store corner shop run by Mr Brown has recently seen its trade dwindle. This family business, passed from generation to generation, is on the verge of closure. The thorn in Mr Brown's side is a new hypermarket rapidly planned and constructed on a site no more than 2 miles away.

Mr Brown is unable to undercut the hypermarket's prices because he is prevented from making bulk purchases due to his limited storage space. Thus he must consider how he might compete on non-price terms.

Lower prices are not the only advantage the hypermarket has over Mr Brown. It is able to offer a wider range of goods, not only groceries but consumer durables, clothing and hardware. It has superior display and hygiene, easier parking, self-service and longer opening hours as well as credit card facilities. What is Mr Brown

to do? What non-price means of competition are open to the small trader?

Mr Brown does surprisingly have a number of options, chief amongst which is his ability to offer a more personal service, including such things as delivery. Alternatively, he might turn to a local advertising campaign, stressing the shop's convenience and place within the community: i.e. he might try and create a degree of shop loyalty.

Temporary credit and longer hours are further strategies Mr Brown could adopt, fighting the hypermarket on its own terms.

Mr Brown's successes in using these methods will determine his future. One thing is certain: he and others like him will have to be flexible if they are to meet the challenges posed by superstores.

---

advertising are likely to lead to smaller and smaller increases in sales. Thus MR_A falls, until $MR_A = MC_A$. At that point no further profit can be made. It is at a maximum.

 Why will additional advertising lead to smaller and smaller increases in sales?

Two problems arise with this analysis:

- The effect of product development and advertising on demand will be difficult for a firm to forecast.
- Product development and advertising are likely to have different effects at different prices. Profit maximization, therefore, will involve the more complex choice of the optimum combination of price, type of product, and level and variety of advertising.

Monopolistic competition and the public interest

Comparison with perfect competition

It is often argued that monopolistic competition leads to a less efficient allocation of resources than perfect competition.

Figure 6.2 compares the long-run equilibrium positions for two firms. One firm is under perfect competition and thus faces a horizontal demand curve. It will produce an output of Q_1 at a price of P_1. The other is under monopolistic competition and thus faces a downward-sloping demand curve. It will produce the lower output of Q_2 at the higher price of P_2. A crucial assumption here is that a firm would have the *same* long-run average cost (*LRAC*) curve in both cases. Given this assumption, monopolistic competition has the following disadvantages:

- Less will be sold and at a higher price.
- Firms will not be producing at the least-cost point.

Figure 6.2 Long-run equilibrium of the firm under perfect and monopolistic competition

Excess capacity (under monopolistic competition)

In the long-run firms under monopolistic competition will produce at an output below their minimum-cost point.

By producing more, firms would move to a lower point on their *LRAC* curve. Thus firms under monopolistic competition are said to have excess capacity. In Figure 6.2 this excess capacity is shown as $Q_1 - Q_2$. In other words, monopolistic competition is typified by quite a large number of firms (e.g. petrol stations), all operating at less than optimum output, and thus being forced to charge a price above that which they could charge if they had a bigger turnover. How often have you been to a petrol station and had to queue for the pumps?

? Does this imply that if, say, half of the petrol stations were closed down, the consumer would benefit? (Clue: what would happen to the demand curves of the remaining stations?)

On the other hand, it is often argued that these wastes of monopolistic competition may be insignificant. In the first place, although the firm's demand curve is downward sloping, it is still likely to be highly elastic due to the large number of substitutes. In the second place, although the firm under monopolistic competition will not be operating quite at the bottom of its *LRAC* curve, the nature of the industry may allow some economies of scale to be gained. The *LRAC* curve would thus be lower than in the case of the larger number of smaller firms that would be necessary if the industry were to be perfectly competitive. The size of the economies of scale, if any, will obviously vary from industry to industry.

Furthermore, the consumer may benefit from monopolistic competition by having a greater variety of products to choose from. Each firm may satisfy some particular requirement of particular consumers.

? Which would you rather have: five restaurants to choose from, each with very different menus and each having spare tables so that you could always guarantee getting one; or just two restaurants to choose from, charging a bit less but with less choice and where you have to book a table quite a long time in advance?

If monopolistic competition brings the disadvantage of excess capacity but the advantage of diversity, is the consumer necessarily worse off under monopolistic competition than under perfect competition? The answer is no. For a start it is rather a bogus question. There is no possibility that industries offering a highly differentiated product could ever be under perfect competition. It is not *logically* possible for a firm *both* to have a horizontal demand curve *and* to provide for some specific demand (like a shop within a few minutes' walk).

Secondly, even if we identify the cost to consumers from having to pay a price above minimum average cost, this has to be traded off against the gain to consumers from the extra diversity. Only if the cost exceeded the benefit would monopolistic competition be seen as wasteful.

Comparison with monopoly

The arguments here are very similar to those when comparing perfect competition and monopoly.

On the one hand, freedom of entry for new firms and hence the lack of long-run supernormal profits under monopolistic competition are likely to help keep prices down for the consumer and encourage cost saving. On the other hand, monopolies are likely to achieve greater economies of scale and have more funds for investment and research and development.

▲ SUMMARY

1. Monopolistic competition occurs where there is free entry to the industry and quite a large number of firms operating independently of each other, but where each firm has some market power by producing differentiated products or services.
2. In the short run, firms can make supernormal profits. In the long run, however, freedom of entry will drive profits down to the normal level. The long-run equilibrium of the firm is where the (downward-sloping) demand curve is tangential to the long-run average cost curve.
3. The long-run equilibrium is one of excess capacity. Given that the demand curve is downward sloping, its tangency point with the *LRAC* curve will not be at the bottom of the *LRAC* curve. Increased production would thus be possible at *lower* average cost.
4. In practice, supernormal profits may persist into the long

run: firms have imperfect information; entry may not be completely unrestricted; there may be a problem of indivisibilities; firms may use non-price competition to maintain an advantage over their rivals.
5. Non-price competition may take the form of product development or product promotion (advertising, etc.).
6. Monopolistically competitive firms, because of excess capacity, may have higher costs than perfectly competitive firms, but consumers may gain from a greater diversity of products.
7. Monopolistically competitive firms may have fewer economies of scale than monopolies and conduct less research and development, but the competition may keep prices lower than under monopoly. Whether there will be more or less choice for the consumer is debatable.

6.2 Oligopoly

Oligopoly occurs when just a few firms between them share a large proportion of the industry.

There are, however, significant differences in the structure of industries under oligopoly and similarly significant differences in the behaviour of firms. The firms may produce a virtually identical product (e.g. metals, chemicals, sugar, petrol). Most oligopolists, however, produce differentiated products (e.g. cars, soap powder, cigarettes, electrical appliances). Much of the competition between such oligopolists is in terms of the marketing of their particular brand. Marketing practices may differ considerably from one industry to another.

The two key features of oligopoly

Despite the differences between oligopolies, there are two crucial features that distinguish oligopoly from other market structures.

Barriers to entry

Unlike firms under monopolistic competition, there are various barriers to the entry of new firms. These are similar to those under monopoly (see page 202). The size of the barriers, however, will vary from industry to industry. In some cases entry is relatively easy, whereas in others it is virtually impossible.

Interdependence of the firms

Because there are only a few firms under oligopoly, each firm will have to take account of the others. This means that they are mutually dependent: they are interdependent. Each firm is affected by its rivals' actions. If a firm changes the price or specification of its product, for example, or the amount of its advertising, the sales of its rivals will be affected. The rivals may then respond by changing their price, specification or advertising. No firm can therefore afford to ignore the actions and reactions of other firms in the industry.

It is impossible, therefore, to predict the effect on a firm's sales of, say, a change in its price without first making some assumption about the reactions of other firms. Different assumptions will yield different predictions. For this reason there is no single generally accepted theory of oligopoly. Firms may react differently and unpredictably.

> **Interdependence (under oligopoly)**
> One of the two key features of oligopoly. Each firm will be affected by its rivals' decisions. Likewise its decisions will affect its rivals. Firms recognize this interdependence. This recognition will affect their decisions.

Competition and collusion

Oligopolists are pulled in two different directions:

- The interdependence of firms may make them wish to *collude* with each other. If they could club together and act as if they were a monopoly, they could jointly maximize industry profits.
- On the other hand, they will be tempted to *compete* with their rivals to gain a bigger share of industry profits for themselves.

These two policies are incompatible. The more fiercely firms compete to gain a bigger share of industry profits, the smaller these industry profits will become! For example, price competition will drive down the average industry price, while competition through advertising will raise industry costs. Either way, industry profits are likely to be reduced.

Sometimes firms will collude. Sometimes they will not. The following sections examine first collusive oligopoly (both open and tacit), and then non-collusive oligopoly

> **Collusive oligopoly**
> Where oligopolists agree (formally or informally) to limit competition between themselves. They may set output quotas, fix prices, limit product promotion or development, or agree not to 'poach' each other's markets.

The equilibrium of the industry under collusive oligopoly

When firms under oligopoly engage in collusion, they may agree on prices, market share, advertising expenditure, etc. Such collusion will reduce the uncertainty they face. It will reduce the fear of engaging in competitive price cutting or retaliatory advertising, both of which could reduce total industry profits.

A formal collusive agreement is called a cartel. The cartel will maximize profits if it acts like a monopoly: if the members behave as if they were a single firm. This is illustrated in Figure 6.3.

The total market demand curve is shown with the corresponding market *MR* curve. The cartel's *MC* curve is the horizontal sum of the *MC* curves of its members.

> **Non-collusive oligopoly**
> Where oligopolists have no agreement between themselves, formal, informal or tacit.

> **Cartel**
> A formal collusive agreement.

 Why is the cartel's *MC* curve the *horizontal* sum of the firms' *MC* curves and not the *vertical* sum?

Box 6.4

Oligopoly or Monopolistic Competition?
Big firms and little firms: the case of bakeries

Despite barriers to entry of other *large-scale* firms, many oligopolies face competition at the margin from many small firms. The reason for this is that the small firms often produce a specialist product or serve a local market. These small firms are in a position somewhat like monopolistic competition: they produce a differentiated product and face little if any entry barriers themselves.

A good example of this is bakers. Two giant producers (RHM and Allied) produce bread for a nationwide market. But then there are thousands of small bakeries, often where the bread is baked in the shop. Their bread is usually more expensive than the mass-produced bread of the two giants, but they often sell a greater variety of loaves, cakes, etc., and many people prefer to buy their bread freshly baked.

In the 1950s and 1960s the giant bakers gradually captured a larger and larger share of the market. This was due to technical developments that allowed economies of scale: developments such as mechanical handling of bread, processes that allowed rapid large-scale proving of

dough, and bulk road tankers for flour. Also, with the development of supermarkets where people tended to shop for the week, there was a growth in large-volume retail outlets where there was a demand for wrapped bread with a long sell-by date. These presented real barriers to the small baker.

But then in the 1970s the rise in oil prices and hence the rise in transport costs gave a substantial cost advantage to locally produced bread. What is more, some of the technical developments of the 1960s were adapted to small-scale baking. Finally there was a shift in consumer tastes away from mass-produced bread and towards the more individual styles of bread produced by the small baker.

The effect was a growth in the number of small bakers, who now found that entry barriers were very small.

? Are the large oligopolistic bakers and the small bakers catering for the same market?

Profits are maximized at Q_1 where $MC = MR$. The cartel must therefore set a price of P_1 (at which Q_1 will be demanded).

Having agreed on the cartel price, the members may then compete against each other using *non-price competition*, to gain as big a share of resulting sales (Q_1) as they can.

? What effect will advertising have on the cartel's *MC* and *AR* curves? How will this affect the profit-maximizing output? Is there any problem here for the cartel in fixing the price?

Figure 6.3 Profit-maximizing cartel

Quota (set by a cartel)

The output that a given member of a cartel is allowed to produce (production quota) or sell (sales quota).

Alternatively, the cartel members may somehow agree to divide the market between them. Each member would be given a quota. The sum of all the quotas must add up to Q_1. If the quotas exceeded Q_1, either there would be output unsold if price remained fixed at P_1, or the price would fall.

But if quotas are to be set by the cartel, how will it decide the level of each individual member's quota? One way is to set quotas at the level that will minimize overall industry costs. To do this, each firm should be instructed to produce a level of output such that all firms' marginal costs are *the same*. If they were *not* the same, if firm A's marginal costs were greater than firm B's, total costs would be reduced by switching some of industry production from A to B. In fact, by constructing an industry MC curve which is the horizontal sum of the members' MC curves, we are assuming that, at any given *industry* marginal cost, each member's marginal cost will be that same level.

The trouble with this cost-minimizing solution to carving up the market between the members is that members may have very different costs, in which case the members with lower costs will be given a high quota, whereas the members with high costs may be given a very low quota or no quota at all. Clearly it would not be in the interests of the high-cost producers to agree to such quotas!

Another method would be for the cartel to divide the market between the members according to their current market share. This is the solution most likely to be accepted as 'fair'.

 If this 'fair' solution were adopted, what effect would it have on the industry MC curve in Figure 6.3?

Collusion and the law

Cartels were prohibited in Britain under the 1956 Restrictive Trade Practices Act, unless the firms involved could prove to the Restrictive Practices Court that their agreement was in the public interest. Anti-oligopoly and anti-monopoly legislation is examined in detail in section 11.2.

Where open collusion is illegal, firms may simply break the law, or get round it. There have been various examples of firms breaking the law. For example, construction firms have colluded from time to time when tendering for local authority contracts. They get together beforehand and all agree to put in high-priced estimates for the job. The 'cartel' chooses one firm to get the contract, and that firm therefore puts in a slightly lower (but still high) estimate. On the next occasion the cartel will choose another firm to get the job, and so on, thus dividing the contracts 'fairly' between the 'members'. Such illegal practices are very difficult to prove, provided the firms are careful not to make their agreement too obvious.

Alternatively, firms may stay within the law, but still *tacitly* collude by watching each other's prices and keeping theirs similar. Firms may tacitly 'agree' to avoid price wars or aggressive advertising campaigns.

Tacit collusion: price leadership

Tacit collusion

Where oligopolists take care not to engage in price cutting, excessive advertising or other

One form of tacit collusion is where firms set the same price as an established leader. The leader may be the largest firm: the firm which dominates the industry. This is known as dominant firm price leadership. Alternatively, the price leader may simply be the one that has emerged over time as the most reliable one to follow: the one that is the best barometer of market conditions. This is known as barometric firm price leadership. Let us examine each of these two types of price leadership in turn.

Dominant firm price leadership

How does the leader set the price? The leader will maximize profits where its marginal revenue is equal to its marginal cost.

In Figure 6.4(a), the total market demand curve is shown. The supply curve of all followers is also shown. These firms, like perfectly competitive firms, accept the price as given, only in this case it is the price set by the leader, and thus their joint supply curve is simply the sum of their *MC* curves – the same as under perfect competition.

The leader's demand curve can be seen as that portion of market demand unfilled by the other firms. In other words, it is market demand minus other firms' supply. At P_1 the whole of market demand is satisfied by the other firms, and so the demand for the leader is zero (point *a*). At P_2 the other firms' supply is zero, and so the leader faces the full market demand (point *b*). The leader's demand curve thus connects points *a* and *b*.

The leader's profit will be maximized where its marginal cost equals its marginal revenue. This is shown in Figure 6.4(b). The diagram is the same as Figure 6.4(a) but with the addition of *MC* and *MR* curves for the leader. The leader's marginal cost equals its marginal revenue at an output of Q_L, (giving a point *l* on its demand curve). The leader thus sets a price of P_L, which the other firms then duly follow. They supply Q_F (i.e. at point *f* on their supply curve). Total market demand at P_L is Q_T (i.e. point *t* on the market demand curve), which must add up to the output of both leader and followers (i.e. $Q_L + Q_F$).

> ❓ Draw a pair of diagrams like those in Figure 6.4. Illustrate what would happen if there were a rise in market demand and no rise in the costs of either the leader or the followers. Would there be an equal percentage increase in the output of both leader and followers?

In practice, however, it is very difficult for the leader to apply this theory. The leader's demand and *MR* curves depend on the followers' supply curve – something the leader will find virtually impossible to estimate with any degree of accuracy. The leader will thus have to make a rough estimate of what its profit maximizing price and output will be, and simply choose that. That is the best it can do!

A simpler model is where the leader assumes that it will maintain a constant *market share* (say 50 per cent). It makes this assumption because it also assumes that all other

forms of competition. There may be unwritten 'rules' of collusive behaviour such as price leadership.

Dominant firm price leadership

Where firms (the followers) choose the same price as that set by a dominant firm in the industry (the leader).

Barometric firm price leadership

Where the price leader is the one whose prices are believed to reflect market conditions in the most satisfactory way.

(a) Division of the market between leader and followers

(b) Determination of price and output

Figure 6.4 Dominant firm price leadership

firms will follow its price up and down. This is llustrated in Figure 6.5. It knows its current position on its demand curve (say, point *a*). It then estimates how responsive its demand will be to industry-wide price changes and thus constructs its demand and *MR* curves on that basis. It then chooses to produce Q_L at a price of P_L: at point *l* on its demand curve (where *MC* = *MR*). Other firms then follow that price. Total market demand will be Q_T, with followers supplying that portion of the market not supplied by the leader, namely $Q_T - Q_L$.

There is one problem with this model. That is the assumption that the followers will want to maintain a constant market share. It is possible that if the leader raises its price, the followers may want to supply more, given that the new price (= *MR* for a price-taking follower) may well be above their marginal cost. On the other hand, the followers may decide merely to maintain their market share for fear of invoking retaliation from the leader, in the form of price cuts or an aggressive advertising campaign.

Figure 6.5 A price leader aiming to maximize profits for a given market share

Barometric firm price leadership

A similar exercise can be conducted by a barometric firm. Although the firm is not dominating the industry, its price will be followed by the others.

It merely tries to estimate its demand and *MR* curves – assuming, again, a constant market share – and then produces where *MR* = *MC* and sets price accordingly.

In practice, which firm is taken as the barometer will frequently change. Whether we are talking about oil companies, car producers or banks, any firm may take the initiative in raising prices. If the other firms are merely waiting for someone to take the lead – say, because costs have risen – they will all quickly follow suit. For example, if one of the bigger building societies raises its mortgage rates by 1 per cent, then this is likely to stimulate the others to follow suit.

Tacit collusion: rules of thumb

Average cost pricing

Where a firm sets its price by adding a certain percentage for (average) profit on top of average cost.

An alternative to having an established leader is for there to be an established set of simple 'rules of thumb' that everyone follows.

One such example is average cost pricing. Here producers, instead of equating *MC* and *MR*, simply add a certain percentage for profit on top of average costs. Thus, if average costs rise by 10 per cent, prices will automatically be raised by 10 per cent.

Box 6.5

The Wholesale Market for Petrol

The wholesale market for petrol within the UK exhibits various oligopolistic features. These include the following:

- The market share of the top five firms – Esso, Shell, BP, Texaco and Conoco (Jet) – stood at 81.9 per cent in 1970, although by 1980 this had declined by almost 10 per cent to 72.3 per cent. This still represented a very high level of industrial concentration.
- Petrol's price elasticity of demand is low, i.e. it has few substitutes. With so few firms in the industry this will discourage individual companies from price cutting (to increase market share) for fear of starting a price war and causing a large loss in revenue.
- There has generally been a low level of product differentiation, especially since the star grading of petrol was introduced in 1968. In 1989, however, a 'new product', namely super unleaded petrol, entered the market and at first this was only sold by three of the companies: Esso, Shell and BP.

- With relatively little product differentiation and hence little brand loyalty, barriers to entry consist mainly in the ownership of retail outlets. By 1979, 72.7 per cent of retail sales were through wholesaler-owned outlets.
- Similar cost structures among the major companies have provided favourable conditions for collusion.
- Competition within the industry has been mainly in non-price terms, i.e. in the use of promotional gifts and advertising. However, there have been occasional periods when the apparent price collusion broke down, mainly when the world price of oil or the exchange rate was rapidly changing.

? What other entry barriers might there be into this market?

This is a particularly useful rule of thumb in times of inflation, when all firms will be experiencing similar cost increases.

Another rule of thumb is to have certain price benchmarks. Thus clothes may sell for £9.95, £14.95, £19.95, (but not £12.31 or £16.42). If costs rise, then firms simply raise their price to the next benchmark, knowing that other firms will do the same.

Rules of thumb can also be applied to advertising – e.g. you do not criticize other firms' products, only praise your own – or to the design of the product – e.g. lighting manufacturers tacitly agreeing not to bring out an everlasting light bulb.

Price benchmark
A price which is typically used. Firms, when raising a price will usually raise it from one benchmark to another.

Factors favouring collusion

Collusion between firms, whether formal or tacit, is more likely when firms can clearly identify with each other or some leader and when they trust each other not to break agreements. It will be easier for firms to collude if the following conditions apply:

- There are only very few firms and hence they are well known to each other.
- They are not secretive with each other about costs and production methods.
- They have similar production methods and average costs, and will thus be likely to want to change prices at the same time and by the same percentage.
- They produce similar products and can thus more easily reach agreements on price.
- There is a dominant firm.
- There are significant barriers to entry and thus there is little fear of disruption by new firms.
- The market is stable. If industry demand or production costs fluctuate wildly, it will be difficult to make agreements, partly due to difficulties in predicting and partly because agreements may frequently have to be amended. There is a particular

---

Box 6.6

OPEC: The Rise and Fall of a Cartel
The history of the world's most famous cartel

OPEC is probably the best known of all cartels. It was set up in 1960 by the five major oil-exporting countries: Saudi Arabia, Iran, Iraq, Kuwait and Venezuela. Its stated objectives were as follows:

- The co-ordination and unification of the petroleum policies of member countries.
- The organization of means to ensure the stabilization of prices, eliminating harmful and unnecessary fluctuations.

The years leading up to 1960 had seen the oil-producing countries increasingly in conflict with the international oil companies, which extracted oil under 'concessionary agreement'. Under this scheme, oil com-panies were given the right to extract oil in return for royalties. This meant that the oil-producing countries had little say over output and price levels.

Iran was the first to seek greater control over its country's oil production by forming a nationalized oil company as long ago as 1951. Other countries took time to follow suit, however, and it was not until 1973 that control of oil production was effectively transferred from the oil companies to the oil countries, with OPEC making the decisions on how much oil to produce and thereby determining its oil revenue. By this time OPEC consisted of thirteen members.

The table shows the relative importance of the cartel members in regard to output, as well as the significance of non-OPEC countries – the competitive fringe.

Estimated production of oil (barrels per day: 000s)

	1972	1973	1974	1975	1976	1977	1978	1979	1980	1981	1982	1983	1984	1985	1986	1987	1988
OPEC																	
Indonesia	1 027	1 300	1 457	1 300	1 500	1 690	1 650	1 600	1 570	1 607	1 341	1 292	1 332	1 376	1 443	1 312	1 318[1]
Iran	4 900	6 000	6 128	5 600	5 875	5 650	5 250	2 900	1 280	1 375	1 896	2 606	2 166	2 183	1 871	2 314	2 263
Iraq	1 500	1 882	1 829	2 400	2 070	2 150	2 500	3 370	2 600	892	914	905	1 218	1 427	1 680	2 138	2 665
Kuwait	2 750	2 890	2 600	1 950	1 820	1 700	1 900	2 210	1 400	916	675	912	925	1 061	1 412	1 284	1 500
Qatar	450	556	546	410	485	350	480	480	470	414	360	270	404	306	332	287	338
Saudi Arabia	5 255	7 418	8 400	7 000	8 570	8 950	7 800	9 250	9 620	9 642	6 484	4 872	4 345	3 176	5 043	4 230	5 113
UAE	1 130	1 509	1 987	1 800	1 945	2 030	1 740	1 825	1 740	1 512	1 247	1 119	1 142	1 211	1 378	1 397	1 486
Algeria	1 064	1 035	889	935	950	990	1 260	1 240	1 000	750	750	687	608	631	600	654	663
Gabon	125	145	182	200	220	225	170	192	145	147	130	150	150	151	159	158	175
Libya	2 230	2 117	1 700	1 400	1 900	2 050	2 050	2 050	1 780	1 063	1 127	1 020	1 090	1 024	1 034	1 072	1 024
Nigeria	1 800	2 000	7 300	1 850	2 020	2 150	1 800	2 370	2 100	1 369	1 324	1 232	1 414	1 502	1 474	1 256	1 404
Equador	59	197	232	165	185	180	200	220	230	204	215	236	254	280	287	175	305[1]
Venezuela	3 200	3 370	3 025	2 400	2 290	2 280	2 150	2 330	2 150	2 093	1 826	1 791	1 724	1 681	1 791	1 819	1 912
Total OPEC	25 487	30 419	31 275	27 410	29 830	30 395	29 044	30 037	26 085	21 984	18 269	17 092	16 972	16 009	18 504	18 096	20 166
Other																	
non-communist	15 202	15 482	15 107	14 691	15 021	15 983	17 139	18 411	19 009	19 292	20 083	21 222	22 148	22 040	21 859	22 341	21 648[1]
incl. Mexico	440	478	514	710	850	990	1 270	1 490	1 960	2 390	2 734	2 702	2 743	2 609	2 428	2 592	2 582
USA	9 500	9 225	8 945	8 370	8 105	8 240	8 660	8 650	8 650	8 588	8 655	8 669	8 750	8 803	8 539	8 349	8 151
Norway	34	38	30	170	300	270	350	390	530	508	488	600	688	794	870	1 054	1 216
UK	2	2	2	40	230	775	1 100	1 570	1 600	1 790	2 050	2 260	2 452	2 454	2 428	2 355	2 220
Total non-communist world	40 789	45 901	46 382	42 101	44 851	46 378	46 183	48 448	45 094	41 276	38 352	38 314	39 120	39 049	40 363	40 437	41 814

1 Estimates.

Source: *Oil and Gas Journal.*

---

problem in a declining market where firms may be tempted to undercut each other's prices in order to maintain their sales.
- There are no government measures to curb collusion.

 In which of the following industries is collusion likely to occur: bricks, beer, margarine, cement, crisps, washing powder, blank audio or video cassettes, carpets?

Non-collusive oligopoly: the breakdown of collusion

In some oligopolies, there may only be a few (if any) factors favouring collusion. In such cases the likelihood of price competition is greater.

Box 6.6 (cont'd)

OPEC's pricing policy over the 1970s consisted of setting a market price for Saudi Arabian crude (the market leader), and leaving other OPEC members to set their prices in line with this: a form of dominant 'firm' price leadership.

As long as demand remained buoyant, and was price inelastic, this policy allowed large price increases with consequent large revenue increases. In 1973/74, after the Arab–Israeli war, OPEC raised the price of oil from around $3 per barrel to over $12. The price was kept at roughly this level until 1979. And yet, as the table shows, the sales of oil did not fall significantly after 1973 (except for a 10 per cent fall in the recession of 1975).

? Illustrate what was happening here on a demand and supply diagram. Remember that demand was highly inelastic and was increasing over time.

After 1979, however, following a further increase in the price of oil from around $15 to $40 per barrel, demand did fall. This was largely due to the recession of the early 1980s (although, as we shall see later on when we look at macroeconomics, this recession was in turn largely caused by governments' responses to the oil price increases).

? Was this decline in demand a shift in the demand curve or a movement along the demand curve?

Faced by declining demand, OPEC after 1982 agreed to limit output and allocate production quotas in an attempt to keep the price up. A production ceiling of 16 million barrels per day was agreed in 1984.

The cartel was beginning to break down, however, due to the following:

- The world recession and the resulting fall in demand for oil.
- Growing output from non OPEC members (see the table).
- 'Cheating' by some OPEC members who exceeded their quota limits.

With a glut of oil, OPEC could no longer maintain the price. The 'spot' price of oil (the day-to-day price at which oil was trading on the open market) was falling, as the graph shows.

Movements in the spot price of oil. Real crude oil price (Arab light $ per barrel, deflated by US GNP deflator, 1982 = 100). Source: *Financial Times*, 14 June 1990.

Attempts at monitoring and greater regulations between OPEC members proved to be unsuccessful.

Today OPEC exists largely in name only. The collapse of the oil price in 1985/86 signalled the failure of the cartel to co-ordinate and stabilize the petroleum production industry.

? 1. It is generally in the sellers' interest to combine in order to raise the price of their product. What conditions facilitate the formation of a cartel?
2. Which of these conditions are to be found in the oil market?
3. Was there anything OPEC could have done to prevent its virtual collapse?
4. How did the Iraqi invasion of Kuwait in 1990 and the resulting Gulf crisis influence (a) the price of oil and (b) the power of OPEC?

Even if there is collusion, there will always be the temptation for individual oligopolists to 'cheat', by cutting prices or by selling more than their allotted quota. Let us take the case of a relatively small member of a cartel. As a small firm it is a price taker. Its position is illustrated in Figure 6.6(b).

Let us assume that before the cartel is set up the industry price is P_1. As a price taker the firm maximizes its profits by producing at q_1 where $MC = P_1 = MR_1$. Its profits are shown by the grey shaded area.

Now assume that a cartel is set up and that a price is chosen to maximize industry profits. This will be P_2 where industry MC = industry MR in Figure 6.6(a). Total industry output must be reduced to Q_2. Let us assume that our particular firm is

Figure 6.6 The incentive for a firm to produce more than its quota

allocated a quota of q_2. At that output its profits will increase to the pink shaded area. As long as price remains fixed at P_2, however, the firm could increase its profit even further (at the expense of the other members) by selling more than its quota, since at q_2, price is greater than MC. It will maximize its profits at q_3, where $MC = MR_2$.

The danger, of course, is that this would invite retaliation from the other members of the cartel, with a resulting price war. Price would then fall and the cartel could well break up in disarray.

When considering whether to break a collusive agreement, even if only a tacit one, a firm will ask: (1) 'How much can we get away with without inviting retaliation?' and (2) 'If a price war does result, will we be the winners? Will we succeed in driving some or all of our rivals out of business and yet survive ourselves, and thereby gain greater market power?'

The position of rival firms, therefore, is rather like that of the generals of opposing armies or the players in a game. It is a question of choosing the appropriate *strategy*: the strategy that will best succeed in outwitting your opponents.

The strategy a firm adopts will, of course, be concerned not just with price but also with advertising and product development.

Non-collusive oligopoly: game theory

The behaviour of a firm under non-collusive oligopoly will depend on how it thinks its rivals will react to its policies.

Game theory (or the theory of games)
The study of alternative strategies that oligopolists may choose to adopt, depending on their assumptions about their rivals' behaviour.

Economists have developed game theory which examines the best strategy a firm can adopt for each assumption about its rivals' behaviour.

Simple dominant strategy games

The simplest case is where there are just two firms with identical costs, products and demand. They are both considering which of two alternative prices to charge. Table 6.1 shows typical profits they could each make.

Let us assume that at present both firms (X and Y) are charging a price of £2 and

Box 6.7

The Captains of Industry
Oligopoly and warfare

The behaviour of oligopolists has often been likened to that of leaders of hostile or potentially hostile nations, or to that of generals of opposing armies. For example, a cut-throat price war could be likened to a full-scale war between countries, while the meeting of competitive firms to find some way of agreeing on prices or advertising levels could be likened to a peace conference.

See if you can think of some examples of business practice that correspond to each of the following:

1. Nuclear deterrence.
2. The forming of an alliance during a war.
3. The decision not to use gas during the Second World War.
4. A siege.
5. Spying.
6. Border skirmishes.
7. The development of new weapons.
8. A summit conference.
9. Trench warfare.
10. A 'cold war'.
11. The annexation of one country by another.

? Why has it been so difficult to achieve peace in the Lebanon? Are there any lessons here for oligopolistic competition or collusion?

that they are each making a profit of £10 million, giving a total industry profit of £20 million. This is shown in the top left-hand box (A).

Now assume they are both (independently) considering reducing their price to £1.80. In making this decision they will need to take into account what their rival might do, and how this will affect them. Let us consider X's position. In our simple example there are just two things that its rival, firm Y, might do. Either Y could cut its price to £1.80, or it could leave its price at £2. What should X do?

One alternative is to go for the cautious approach and think of the worst thing that its rival could do. If X kept its price at £2, the worst thing for X would be if its rival Y cut its price. This is shown by box C: X's profit falls to £5 million. If, however, X cut its price to £1.80, the worst outcome would again be for Y to cut its price, but this time X's profit only falls to £8 million. In this case, then, if X is cautious, it will *cut its price to £1.80*. Note that Y will argue along similar lines, and if it is cautious it too will cut its price to £1.80. This policy of adopting the safer strategy is known as maximin. Following a maximin strategy, the firm will opt for the alternative that will *maxi*mize its *mini*mum possible profit.

Maximin
The strategy of choosing the policy whose worst possible outcome is the least bad.

Table 6.1 Profits for firms A and B at different prices

		X's price	
		£2	£1.80
Y's price	£2	**A** £10m each	**B** £5m for Y £12m for X
	£1.80	**C** £12m for Y £5m for X	**D** £8m each

Box 6.8

The Prisoners' Dilemma

Game theory is not just relevant to economics. A famous non-economic example is the prisoners' dilemma.

Nigel and Amanda have been arrested for a joint crime of serious fraud. Each is interviewed separately and given the following alternatives:

- First, if they say nothing, the court has enough evidence to sentence both to a year's imprisonment.
- Secondly, if either Nigel or Amanda *alone* confesses, he or she is likely to get only a three-month sentence but the partner could get up to ten years.
- Thirdly, if both confess, they are likely to get three years each.

What should Nigel and Amanda do?

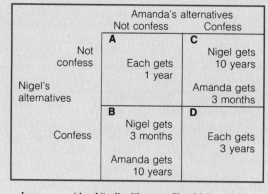

Let us consider Nigel's dilemma. Should he confess in order to get the short sentence (the maximax strategy)?

This is better than the year he would get for not confessing. There is, however, an even better reason for confessing. Suppose Nigel doesn't confess but, unknown to him, Amanda does confess. Then Nigel ends up with the long sentence. Better than this is to confess and to get no more than three years: this is the safest (maximin) strategy.

Amanda is in the same dilemma. The result is simple: when both prisoners act selfishly by confessing, they both end up in position D with long prison terms. Only when they collude will they end up in position A with short prison terms, the best combined solution.

Of course the police know this and will do their best to prevent any collusion. They will keep Nigel and Amanda in separate cells and try to persuade each of them that the other is bound to confess.

Thus the choice of strategy depends on:

- Nigel's and Amanda's risk attitudes: i.e. are they 'risk lovers' or 'risk averse'?
- Nigel's and Amanda's estimates of how likely the other is to own up.

? 1. How would Nigel's choice of strategy be affected if he had instead been involved in a joint crime with Jeremy, Pauline, Diana and Dave, and they had all been caught?
2. Can you think of any other non-economic examples of the prisoners' dilemma?

Maximax

The strategy of choosing the policy which has the best possible outcome.

Dominant strategy game

Where the *same* policy is suggested by different strategies.

Prisoners' dilemma

Where two or more firms (or people), by attempting independently to choose the best

An alternative strategy is to go for the optimistic approach and assume that your rivals react in the way most favourable to you. Here the firm will go for the strategy that yields the highest possible profit. In X's case this will again be to cut price, only this time on the optimistic assumption that firm Y will leave its price unchanged. If firm X is correct in its assumption, it will move to box B and achieve the maximum possible profit of £12 million. This strategy of going for the maximum possible profit is known as maximax. Note that again the same argument applies to Y. Its maximax strategy will be to cut price and hopefully end up in box C.

Given that in this 'game' *both* approaches, maximin and maximax, lead to the *same* strategy (namely cutting price), this is known as a dominant strategy game.

But, given that both X and Y will be tempted to lower prices, they will both end up earning a lower profit (£8 million profit each in box D) than if they had charged the higher price (£10 million profit each in box A). Thus collusion, rather than a price war, would have benefited both, and yet both would be tempted to cheat and cut prices. This is known as the prisoners' dilemma. An example is given in Box 6.8.

More complex games with no dominant strategy

More complex 'games' can be devised with more than two firms, many alternative prices, differentiated products and various forms of non-price competition (e.g. advertising). Table 6.2 illustrates a more complex game.

strategy for whatever the other(s) are likely to do, end up in a worse position than if they had co-operated in the first place.

Table 6.2 Profit possibilities for firm X (£m)

		a	b	c	d	e	f	
Strategies	1	100	60	−20	10	30	80	(Maximax − a)
for	2	40	50	20	30	25	60	(Maximin − c)
firm X	3	90	15	30	25	20	50	(Best compromise)

Other firms' responses

It shows the profits that will result from three alternative strategies that firm X can pursue (e.g. price cut, advertising campaign, new model) and six possible responses from rivals (e.g. all rivals cutting price, some cutting price, all increasing advertising). It is assumed that firm X can calculate the effects on its profits of these various reactions.

Which strategy will X choose? It may go for the safe strategy – *maximin*. Here it will choose strategy 2. The worst outcome from strategy 2 (response c) will still give a profit of £20 million, whereas the worst outcome from strategy 3 (response b) is a profit of only £15 million, and the worst outcome from strategy 1 (response c) is a loss of £20 million.

Alternatively, firm X may go for a high-risk strategy: the one with highest maximum profit – *maximax*. Here it would choose strategy 1. This has a potential maximum profit of £100 million (response a), whereas the best outcome from strategy 3 is only £90 million (response a), and for strategy 2 only £60 million (response f).

Alternatively, it may go for a compromise strategy. Here it could choose strategy 3. The best outcome from strategy 3 (response a) is only slightly lower than strategy 1 (response a) – £90 million compared with £100 million. The worst outcome (response b) is only slightly lower than strategy 2 (response c) – £15 million compared with £20 million.

Alternatively, it may go for a strategy which gives the *best most likely outcome*, or the *best average outcome*.

Compromise strategy
A strategy whose worst outcome is better than under the maximax strategy and whose best outcome is better than under the maximin strategy.

? Assume that firm X is considering four possible strategies: 1, 2, 3 and 4 (for example, one strategy could be a 10 per cent price cut, another could be to spend £1 million on an advertising campaign, another could be to launch a modified product, and so on). Assume that firm X estimates that there are five possible responses (a, b, c, d and e) that its rivals might make to its actions. It estimates the effects on its profits in the case of each of these five responses to each of its four strategies. Its estimates are given in Table 6.3.

(a) Which of the strategies (1, 2, 3 or 4) should it adopt if it is hoping to make the maximum possible profit (maximax)?

Table 6.3 Profit possibilities for firm X (£m)

		a	b	c	d	e
Alternative	1	30	20	80	−10	100
strategies	2	−5	105	40	100	30
for firm X	3	90	0	50	45	60
	4	30	15	10	20	25

Rivals' responses

(b) Which of the strategies should it adopt if it is very cautious and decides to assume that the worst will happen (maximin)?

(c) Which of the strategies might be the best compromise between these two extreme positions? Explain.

The advantage of the game-theory approach is that the firm does not need to know which response its rivals will make. It does, however, need to be able to measure the effect of each possible response. This will be virtually impossible to do when there are many firms competing and many different responses that could be made. The approach is only useful, therefore, in relatively simple cases, and even here the estimates of profit from each outcome may amount to no more than a rough guess.

It is thus difficult for an economist to predict with any accuracy what price, output and level of advertising the firm will choose. This problem is compounded by the difficulty in predicting the type of strategy – safe, high risk, compromise – that the firm will adopt.

In some cases, firms may compete hard for a time (in price or non-price terms) and then realize that maybe no one is winning. Firms may then jointly raise prices and reduce advertising. Later, after a period of tacit collusion, competition may break out again. This may be sparked off by the entry of a new firm, by the development of a new product design, by a change in market demand, or simply by one or more firms no longer being able to resist the temptation to 'cheat'.

Non-collusive oligopoly: the kinked demand curve

In 1939 a theory of non-collusive oligopoly was developed simultaneously on both sides of the Atlantic: in America by Paul Sweezy and in Britain by R. L. Hall and C. J. Hitch. This kinked demand theory has since become perhaps the most famous of all theories of oligopoly. The model seeks to explain how it is that, even when there is no collusion at all between oligopolists, prices can nevertheless remain stable.

The theory is based on two asymmetrical assumptions:

- If an oligopolist cuts its price, its rivals will feel forced to follow suit and cut theirs, to prevent losing customers to the first firm.
- If an oligopolist raises its price, however, its rivals will *not* follow suit since, by keeping their prices the same, they will thereby gain customers from the first firm.

> **Kinked demand theory**
>
> The theory that oligopolists face a demand curve that is kinked at the current price: demand being significantly more elastic above the current price than below. The effect of this is to create a situation of price stability.

On these assumptions, each oligopolist will face a demand curve that is *kinked* at the current price and output (see Figure 6.7). A rise in price will lead to a large fall in sales as customers switch to the now lower priced rivals. The firm will thus be reluctant to raise its price. Demand is relatively elastic above the kink. On the other hand, a fall in price will bring only a modest increase in sales, since rivals lower their prices too and therefore customers do not switch. The firm will thus also be reluctant to lower its price. Demand is relatively inelastic below the kink. Thus oligopolists will be reluctant to change prices at all.

This price stability can be shown formally by drawing in the firm's marginal revenue curve, as in Figure 6.8.

To see how this is done, imagine dividing the diagram into two parts either side of Q_1. At quantities less than Q_1 (the left-hand part of the diagram), the *MR* curve will correspond to the shallow part of the *AR* curve. At quantities greater than Q_1 (the right-hand part), the *MR* curve will correspond to the steep part of the *AR* curve. To see how this part of the *MR* curve is constructed, imagine extending the steep part of

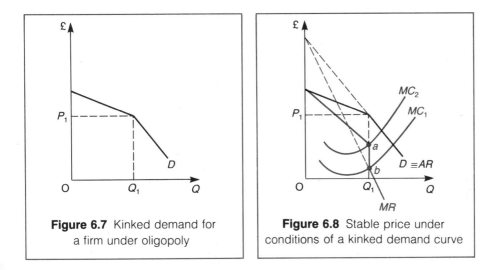

Figure 6.7 Kinked demand for a firm under oligopoly

Figure 6.8 Stable price under conditions of a kinked demand curve

the *AR* curve back to the vertical axis. This and the corresponding *MR* curve are shown by the dotted lines in Figure 6.8.

As you can see, there will be a gap between points *a* and *b*. In other words, there is a vertical section of the *MR* curve between these two points.

Profits are maximized where $MC = MR$. Thus, if the *MC* curve lies anywhere between MC_1 and MC_2, (i.e. between points *a* and *b*), the profit-maximizing price and output will be P_1 and Q_1. Thus prices will remain stable *even with a considerable change in costs*.

Despite its simple demonstration of the real-world phenomenon of price stability, the model does have two major limitations:

- Price stability may be due to *other* factors. Firms may not want to change prices too frequently as it will involve modifying price lists, working out new revenue predictions and revaluing stocks of finished goods, and it may upset customers. Price stability, therefore, is not proof of the accuracy of the model.
- Although the model can help to explain price stability, it does not explain how prices are set in the first place. To do this, some other model would be required. This is a serious limitation in times of inflation, when oligopolists, like other firms, will raise prices in response to higher costs and higher demand. What the model does predict, however, is that the price will be raised only after marginal cost has risen above MC_2 in Figure 6.8, and that once it has been raised, a new kink will form at that price. Price will then remain fixed at that level until higher costs once more force a further price rise.

Oligopoly and the public interest

If oligopolists act collusively and jointly maximize industry profits, they will in effect be acting together as a monopoly. In such cases the disadvantages to society experienced under monopoly will also be experienced under oligopoly. (See section 5.3.)

Furthermore, in two respects, oligopoly may be more disadvantageous than monopoly:

- Depending on the size of the individual oligopolists, there may be less scope for economies of scale to mitigate the effects of market power.

- Oligopolists are likely to engage in much more extensive advertising than a monopolist. (See pages 236–7.)

These problems will be less, however, if oligopolists do not collude, if there is some degree of price competition and if barriers to entry are weak.

Also the power of oligopolists in certain markets may to some extent be offset if they sell their product to other powerful firms. Thus oligopolistic producers of baked beans sell a large proportion of their output to giant supermarket chains who can use their market power to keep down the price at which they purchase the beans. This phenomenon is known as countervailing power

Countervailing power

Where the power of a monopolistic/ oligopolistic seller is offset by powerful buyers who can prevent the price from being pushed up.

 Which of the following are examples of effective countervailing power?

(a) Power stations buying coal from British Coal.
(b) A large factory hiring a photocopier from Rank Xerox.
(c) Marks and Spencer buying clothes from a garment manufacturer.
(d) A small village store (but the only one for miles around) buying food from a wholesaler.

In some respects, oligopoly may have *advantages* to society over other market structures:

- Oligopolists, like monopolists, can use part of their supernormal profit for research and development. Unlike monopolists, however, oligopolists will have a considerable *incentive* to do so. If the product design is improved, this may allow the firm to capture a larger share of the market, and it may be some time before rivals can respond with a similarly improved product. If, in addition, costs are lowered by technological improvement, the resulting higher profits will enable the firm to withstand better a price war should one break out.
- Non-price competition through product differentiation may result in greater choice for the consumer.

It is difficult to draw any general conclusions since oligopolies differ so much in their performance.

Advertising and the public interest

There is no point in advertising under perfect competition since there is no product differentiation. There is no point in farmer Jones advertising his/her potatoes if they are no different from farmer Brown's. Under monopoly too there is little point in advertising since, by definition, there are no rivals to compete with.

 Why do monopolies like British Gas and British Rail advertise?

However, under imperfect competition (both monopolistic competition and especially oligopoly), advertising is often a major means of competing.

Supporters of advertising claim that it is an important freedom for firms. Moreover, they claim that it brings specific benefits for consumers:

- Advertising provides information to consumers on what products are available.
- Advertising may be necessary in order to introduce new products. Without it, firms would find it difficult to break into markets in which there were established brands. In other words, it is a means of breaking down barriers to entry.
- It can aid product development by helping the firm emphasize the special features of its product.

- It may encourage price competition, if prices feature significantly in the advertisement.
- By increasing sales, it may allow the firm to gain economies of scale, which in turn will help to keep prices down.

Critics of advertising, however, claim that advertising imposes serious costs on the consumer and on society in general:

- Advertising is designed to persuade people to buy the product. Consumers do not have perfect information and may thus be misled into purchasing goods which may be inferior in quality to those goods which are not advertised.
- Scarcity is defined as the excess of human wants over the means of fulfilling them. Advertising is used to *create* wants. It could thus be argued to increase scarcity.
- It increases materialism.
- Advertising costs money: it uses resources. These resources could be put to alternative uses in producing more goods.
- If there are no economies of scale, the costs of advertising will tend to raise the price paid by the consumer. Even if the firm has potential economies of scale, it may be prevented from expanding its sales by retaliatory advertising from its rivals.
- Advertising can create a barrier to the entry of new firms by promoting brand loyalty to existing firms' products. New firms may not be able to afford the large amount of advertising necessary to create a new brand image, whereas existing firms can spread the cost of their advertising over their already large number of sales. In other words, there are economies of scale in advertising which act as a barrier to entry.

  This barrier is strengthened if existing firms sell many brands each (e.g. in the washing powder industry many brands are produced by just two firms). This makes it even harder for new firms successfully to introduce a new brand, since the consumer already has so many to choose from.

  The fewer the competitors, the less elastic will be the demand for each individual firm, and the higher, therefore, will be the profit-maximizing price.
- People are constantly subjected to advertisements, on television, in magazines, on bill-boards, etc., and often find them annoying, tasteless or unsightly. Thus advertising imposes costs on society in general. These costs are external to the firm: that is, they do not cost the firm money, and hence are normally ignored by the firm.

> **Beneath this slab**
> **John Brown is stowed.**
> **He watched the ads**
> **but not the road.**
>
> Ogden Nash

? 1. Could annoyance to the public ever rebound as a direct cost to the firm?
2. Choose two products which are extensively advertised. Make out a case for and a case against these particular advertisements.

The effect of advertising on competition, costs and prices is an empirical issue. The evidence, however, is inconclusive. Most of the other questions raised in the above discussion are normative and thus cannot be settled by a simple appeal to facts.

Oligopoly and contestable markets

The new theory of contestable markets has been applied to oligopoly as well as to monopoly, and similar conclusions are drawn.

The lower the entry and exit costs for new firms, the more difficult it will be for oligopolists to collude and make supernormal profits. If oligopolists do form a cartel (whether legal or illegal), this will be difficult to maintain if it very soon faces competition from new entrants. What a cartel has to do in such a situation is to erect entry barriers, thereby making the 'contest' more difficult. For example, the cartel could form a common research laboratory, denied to outsiders. It might attempt to control the distribution of the finished product by buying up wholesale or retail outlets. Or it might simply let it be known to potential entrants that they will face all-out price, advertising and product competition from all the members if they should dare to set up in competition.

The conclusions of the theory, as far as the public interest is concerned, are straightforward. The industry is likely to behave competitively if entry and exit costs are low, with all the benefits and costs of such competition – even if the new firms do not actually enter. If entry and/or exit costs are high, however, the degree of competition will simply depend on the relations between existing members of the industry.

 Which of the following markets do you think are contestable?
(a) Credit cards; (b) Brewing; (c) Petrol retailing; (d) Insurance services;
(e) Compact discs.

▲ SUMMARY

1. An oligopoly is where there are just a few firms in the industry with barriers to the entry of new firms. Firms recognize their mutual dependence.
2. Oligopolists will want to maximize their joint profits. This will tend to make them collude to keep prices high. On the other hand, they will want the biggest share of industry profits for themselves. This will tend to make them compete.
3. Whether they compete or collude depends on the conditions in the industry. They are more likely to collude if there are few of them; if they are open with each other; if they have similar products and cost structures; if there is a dominant firm; if there are significant entry barriers; if the market is stable; and if there is no government legislation to prevent collusion.
4. Collusion can be open or tacit.
5. A formal collusive agreement is called a 'cartel'. A cartel aims to act as a monopoly. It can set price and leave the members to compete for market share, or it can assign quotas. There is always a temptation for cartel members to 'cheat' by undercutting the cartel price if they think they can get away with it and not trigger a price war.
6. Tacit collusion can take the form of price leadership. This is where firms follow the price set by either a dominant firm in the industry or a firm seen as a reliable 'barometer' of market conditions. Alternatively, tacit collusion can simply involve following various rules of thumb such as average cost pricing and benchmark pricing.
7. Non-collusive oligopolists will have to work out a price strategy. This will depend on their attitudes towards risk and on the assumptions they make about the behaviour of their rivals. Game theory examines various strategies that firms can adopt when the outcome of each is not certain. They can adopt a low risk 'maximin' strategy of choosing the policy that has the least-bad worst outcome, or a high-risk 'maximax' strategy of choosing the policy with the best possible outcome, or some compromise.
8. Because firms are likely to face a kinked demand curve, they are likely to keep their prices stable unless there is a large shift in costs or demand.
9. Whether oligopoly behaviour is in the public interest depends on the particular oligopoly and how competitive it is; whether there is any countervailing power; whether the firms engage in extensive advertising and of what type; whether product differentiation results in a wide range of choice for the consumer; how much of the profits are ploughed back into research and development; and how contestable the market is. Since these conditions vary substantially from oligopoly to oligopoly, it is impossible to state just how well or how badly oligopoly in general serves the public interest.

6.3 Price discrimination

Up to now we have assumed that a firm will sell its output at a single price. Sometimes, however, firms may practise price discrimination. This is where a firm sells the same product to different consumers at different prices. There are three major varieties of price discrimination:

- First-degree price discrimination is where the firm charges each consumer the maximum price he or she is prepared to pay for each unit. For example, stallholders in a bazaar will attempt to do this when bartering with their customers.
- Second-degree price discrimination is where the firm charges customers different prices according to how much they purchase. It may charge a high price for the first so many units, a lower price for the next so many units, a lower price again for the next, and so on. For example, electricity companies in some countries charge a high price for the first so many kilowatts. This is the amount of electricity that would typically be used for lighting and running appliances: in other words, the uses for which there is no substitute fuel. Additional kilowatts are charged at a much lower rate. This is electricity that is typically used for heating and cooking, where there are alternative fuels.
- Third-degree price discrimination is where consumers are grouped into two or more independent markets and a separate price is charged in each market. Examples include different priced seats on buses for adults and children, and different prices charged for the same product in different countries. Third-degree price discrimination is much more common than first- or second-degree discrimination.

Conditions necessary for price discrimination to operate

As we shall see, a firm will be able to increase its profits if it can engage in price discrimination. But under what circumstances will it be able to charge discriminatory prices? There are three conditions that must be met:

- The firm must be able to set its price. Thus price discrimination will be impossible under perfect competition, where firms are price takers.
- The markets must be separate. Consumers in the low priced-market must not be able to resell the product in the high-priced market. For example, children must not be able to resell a half-priced child's cinema ticket for use by an adult.
- Demand elasticity must differ in each market. The firm will charge the higher price in the market where demand is less elastic, and thus less sensitive to a price rise.

Advantages to the firm

Price discrimination will allow the firm to earn a higher revenue from any given level of sales. Let us examine the case of third-degree price discrimination.

Figure 6.9 represents a firm's demand curve. If it is to sell 200 units without price discrimination it must charge a price of P_1. The total revenue it earns is shown by the grey area. If, however, it can practise third-degree price discrimination by selling 150 of those 200 units at the higher price of P_2, it will gain the red area in addition to the grey area in Figure 6.9.

Price discrimination

Where a firm sells the same product at different prices.

First-degree price discrimination

Where a firm charges each consumer for each unit the maximum price which that consumer is willing to pay for that unit.

Second-degree price discrimination

Where a firm charges a consumer so much for the first so many units purchased, a different price for the next so many units purchased, and so on.

Third-degree price discrimination

Where a firm divides consumers into different groups and charges a different price to consumers in different groups, but the same price to all the consumers within a group.

 Explain why, if the firm can practise *first*-degree price discrimination by selling every unit at the maximum price each consumer is prepared to pay, its revenue from selling 200 units will be the grey area plus the red area in Figure 6.10.

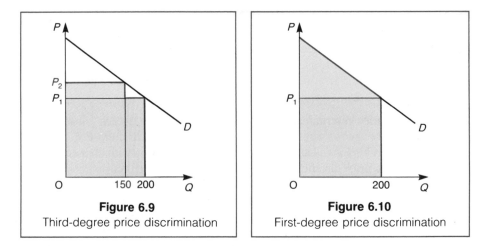

Figure 6.9
Third-degree price discrimination

Figure 6.10
First-degree price discrimination

Another advantage to the firm of price discrimination is that it may be able to use it to drive competitors out of business. If a firm has a monopoly in one market (e.g. the home market), it may be able to charge a high price due to relatively inelastic demand, and thus make high profits. If it is under oligopoly in another market (e.g. the export market), it may use the high profits in the first market to subsidize a very low price in the oligopolistic market, thus forcing its competitors out of business.

Profit-maximizing prices and output

Assuming that the firm wishes to maximize profits, what discriminatory prices should it charge and how much should it produce? Let us first consider the case of first-degree price discrimination.

First-degree price discrimination

Since an increase in sales does not involve lowering the price for any unit save the *extra* one sold, the extra revenue gained from the last unit (MR) will be its price. Thus profit is maximized at Q_1 in Figure 6.11, where $MC = MR$ ($= P$ of the *last* unit).

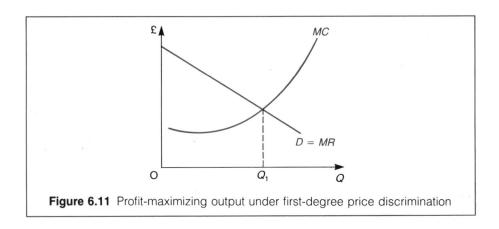

Figure 6.11 Profit-maximizing output under first-degree price discrimination

Box 6.9

What's the Train Fare to London?
Price discrimination on the trains

Ask the question, 'What's the fare to London?' at ticket enquiries, and you may receive any of the following replies:

- Do you want 1st or standard class?
- Do you want single or return?
- How old are you?
- Do you have a railcard (family, young person's, student, senior citizens)?
- Do you want a day return, a 'saver' or a period return?
- Will you be travelling back on a Friday?
- Will you be travelling out before 10 a.m.?
- Will you be leaving London between 4 p.m. and 6 p.m.?

- Do you want to reserve a seat?
- Do you want to take advantage of our special low-priced winter Saturday fare?

 1. Look at each of the above questions. In each case decide whether price discrimination is being practised. If it is, is it sensible for British Rail to do so? Is it discriminating between people with different price elasticities of demand?

2. Are these various forms of price discrimination in the traveller's interest?

Third-degree price discrimination

Assume that a firm sells an identical product in two separate markets X and Y with demand and *MR* curves as shown in Figure 6.12.

Diagram (c) shows the *MC* and *MR* curves for the firm as a whole. This *MR* curve is found by adding the amounts sold in the two markets at each level of *MR* (in other words, the horizontal addition of the two *MR* curves). Thus, for example, with output of 1000 units in market X and 2000 in market Y, making 3000 in total, revenue would increase by £5 if one extra unit were sold, whether in market X or Y.

Total profit is maximized where *MC* = *MR*: i.e. at an output of 3000 units in total. This output must then be divided between the two markets so that *MC* is equal to *MR* in each market: i.e. *MC* = *MR* = £5 in each market. *MR* must be the same in both markets, otherwise revenue could be increased by switching output to the market with the higher *MR*.

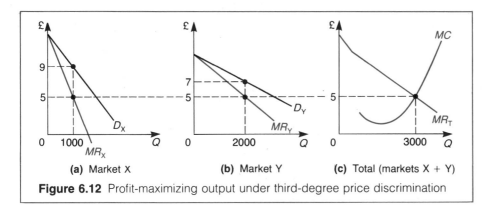

Figure 6.12 Profit-maximizing output under third-degree price discrimination

The profit-maximizing price in each market will be given by the relevant demand curve. Thus, in market X, 1000 units will be sold at £9 each, and in market Y, 2000 units will be sold at £7 each. Note that the higher price is charged in the market with the less elastic demand curve.

> **?** How would profit-maximizing output and price be determined under third-degree price discrimination if there were three separate markets? Draw a diagram to illustrate your answer.

Price discrimination and the public interest

No clear-cut decision can be made over the social desirability of price discrimination. Some people will benefit from it; others will lose. This can be illustrated by considering the effects of price discrimination on the following aspects of the market.

Distribution

Those paying the higher price will probably feel that price discrimination is unfair to them. On the other hand, those charged the lower price may thereby be able to obtain a good or service they could not otherwise afford: for example, concessionary bus fares for old-age pensioners. Price discrimination is likely to increase output and make the good or service available to more people.

Competition

As explained above, a firm may use price discrimination to drive competitors out of business. On the other hand, it might use the profits from its high-priced market to break into another market and withstand a possible price war. Competition is thereby increased.

Profits

Price discrimination raises a firm's profits. This could be seen as an undesirable redistribution of income in society, especially if the average price of the product is raised. On the other hand, the higher profits may be reinvested and lead to lower costs in the future. What is more, price discrimination may allow goods or services to be produced that otherwise would not.

In Figure 6.13 there is no *one* price at which revenue will cover costs. If Q_1 is sold entirely at P_1, the firm will make a loss shown by the striped area. If, however, part of the output is sold at P_2, extra revenue will be gained (the red area) which might be sufficient to eliminate the loss and transform it into a profit.

Figure 6.13 How price discrimination could enable a loss-making firm to make a profit

▲ SUMMARY

1. Price discrimination is where a firm sells the same product at different prices. It can be first-degree, second-degree or third-degree price discrimination.
2. Price discrimination allows the firm to earn a higher revenue from a given level of sales.
3. Under first-degree price discrimination, the profit-maximizing output is where $MC = P$. Under third-degree price discrimination, profit-maximizing output is

where the firm's MC is equal to the overall MR (found by adding horizontally the MR curves in each of the separate markets). This is then divided between the markets by selling that amount in each market where $MC = MR$, at a price given by the demand curve in each market.

4. Some people will gain from price discrimination; others will lose.

7 Alternative Theories of the Firm

7.1 Problems with traditional theory

The traditional profit-maximizing theories of the firm have been criticized for being unrealistic. The criticisms are mainly of two sorts: (a) that firms wish to maximize profits but for some reason or other are unable to do so; or (b) that firms have aims other than profit maximization. Let us examine each in turn.

Difficulties in maximizing profit

One criticism of traditional theory sometimes put forward is that firms do not use *MR* and *MC* concepts. This may be true, but firms could still arrive at maximum profit by trial and error adjustments of price, or by finding the output where *TR* and *TC* are furthest apart. Provided they end up maximizing profits, they will be equating *MC* and *MR*, even if they do not know it! In this case, traditional models will still be useful in predicting price and output.

The main difficulty in trying to maximize profits is a lack of information.

Firms may well use accountants' cost concepts not based on opportunity cost. If it were thereby impossible to measure true profit, a firm would not be able to maximize profit except by chance.

> **?** What cost concepts are there other than those based on opportunity cost? Would the use of these concepts be likely to lead to an output greater or less than the profit-maximizing one?

More importantly, firms are unlikely to know precisely (or even approximately) their demand curves and hence their *MR* curves. Even though (presumably) they will know how much they are selling at the moment, this only gives them one point on their demand curve and no point at all on their *MR* curve. In order to make even an informed guess of marginal revenue they must have some idea of how responsive demand will be to a change in price. But how are they to estimate this price elasticity? Market research may help. But even this is frequently very unreliable. Such information takes time to acquire and act on, by which time market conditions may have changed, thus making the information out of date. The firm will therefore have to decide whether the possibly small benefit from market research is worth its cost.

The biggest problem in estimating the firm's demand curve is in estimating the actions and reactions of *other* firms and their effects. Collusion between oligopolists or price leadership would help, but there will still be a considerable area of uncertainty, especially if the firm faces competition from abroad. Even other *industries'* products may be substitutes or complements to some degree, and thus changes in their price or quality will affect the firm's demand curve.

Game theory may help a firm decide its price and output strategy: it may choose to sacrifice the chance of getting the absolute maximum profit (the high-risk, maximax option), and instead go for the safe strategy of getting probably at least reasonable profits (maximin). But even this assumes that it knows the consequences for its profits of each of the possible reactions of its rivals. In reality, it will not even have this information to any degree of certainty, because it simply will not be able to predict just how consumers will respond to each of its rivals' alternative reactions.

Finally there is the problem of deciding the *time period* over which the firm should be seeking to maximize profits. Firms operate in a changing environment. Demand curves shift; supply curves shift. Some of these shifts occur as a result of factors outside the firm's control, such as changes in competitors' prices and products, or changes in technology. Some, however, change as a direct result of a firm's policies, such as an advertising campaign, the development of a new improved product, or the installation of new equipment. The firm is not, therefore, faced with static cost and revenue curves from which it can read off its profit-maximizing price and output. Instead it is faced with a changing (and often highly unpredictable) set of curves. If it chooses a price and output that maximizes profits *this* year, it may as a result jeopardize profits in the future.

Let us take a simple example. The firm may be trying to decide whether to invest in new expensive equipment. If it does, its costs will rise in the short run and thus short-run profits will fall. On the other hand, if the quality of the product thereby increases, demand is likely to increase over the longer run. Also variable costs are likely to decrease if the new equipment is more efficient in its use of fuel or raw materials, or requires less labour per unit of output to operate it. In other words, long-run profit is likely to increase, but probably by a highly uncertain amount.

Given these extreme problems in deciding profit maximizing price and output, firms may fall back on simple rules of thumb for pricing.

Alternative aims

An even more fundamental attack on the traditional theory of the firm is that firms do not even *aim* to maximize profits (even if they could).

The traditional theory of the firm assumes that it is the *owners* of the firm who make price and output decisions. It is reasonable to assume that owners *will* want to maximize profits: this much most of the critics of the traditional theory accept. The question is, however, whether the owners do in fact make the decisions.

In public limited companies the shareholders are the owners and presumably will want the firm to maximize profits so as to increase their dividends and the value of their shares. Shareholders elect directors. Directors in turn employ professional managers who are often given considerable discretion in making decisions. There is therefore a *separation between the ownership and control* of a firm.

Public limited company

A company owned by its shareholders. The shares may be bought and sold publicly – on the Stock Exchange.

But what are the objectives of managers? Will *they* want to maximize profits, or will they have some other aim?

Managers may be assumed to want to *maximize their own utility*. This may well involve pursuits that conflict with profit maximization. They may, for example, pursue higher salaries, greater power or prestige, better working conditions, greater sales, etc. Different managers in the same firm may well pursue different aims.

Box 7.1

Managerial Utility Maximization
Williamson's alternative alternative

The belief that managerial discretion has an important influence on the resource allocation process within the business firm has a long and recurrent history among economists.

O. E. Williamson[1]

Williamson makes reference to a galaxy of famous names in support of his proposition. These include Adam Smith, Alfred Marshall and John Maynard Keynes, all of whom, according to Williamson, questioned the dominant theory of the firm – namely, profit maximization.

The theory of profit maximization came under increasing attack during the 1950s and 1960s, when a whole range of new and alternative theories were developed. The common element of these theories was the replacement of profit maximizing by a profit constraint.

Provided that satisfactory levels of profit were achieved, managers were seen to be free to pursue a whole range of discretionary policies: that is, they were free to maximize their own utility.

Williamson identified a number of factors that would determine a manager's utility. These included the following:

● Salary.
● Security.
● Dominance – including status, power and prestige.
● Professional excellence.

Of these variables only salary was directly measurable. The rest would have to be measured indirectly through other variables that reflected them. For this purpose Williamson developed the concept of 'expense preference'. This was a means of illustrating the satisfaction that managers gained from spending money – in particular on *staff*, on *perks* (such as company cars and a plush office) and on *discretionary investment*. He suggested that such spending reflected the manager's power, status, prestige, security and professional excellence.

Increased *spending on staff* was suggested by Williamson to be equivalent to promotion. Power, status and prestige would all be enhanced as the staff under the manager's control grew in number. The number of staff was a symbol of the manager's professional importance.

Emoluments (perks) in the form of expense accounts, company cars, etc., reflect the manager's position within the firm. The higher the level of perks, the more secure and dominant the manager is likely to be.

Discretionary investment by managers is possible when earnings above the minimum profit constraint are achieved. This allows managers to expand staff and perks and undertake any other projects that the manager wishes to pursue. How the money is invested is at the manager's discretion.

Having identified these factors that influence a manager's utility, Williamson developed several models in which managers maximize their utility function. He used these models to predict managerial behaviour under various conditions and argued that they performed better than traditional profit-maximizing theory. To support these claims he conducted a number of case studies. These showed, for example, that staff and perks were cut during recessions and expanded during booms, and that new managers were frequently able to cut staff without influencing the productivity of firms.

Although Williamson's work has produced and stimulated a whole range of investigations into the behaviour of managers, the evidence gathered remains inconclusive. Many economists suggest that the nature of the market in which the firm operates will determine which of the theories is the most relevant: profit maximization, managerial utility or some other.

[1] *The Economics of Discretionary Behaviour* (Prentice-Hall, 1964), p. 3.

Managers will still have to ensure that *sufficient* profits are made to keep shareholders happy, but that may be very different from *maximizing* profits.

Profit satisficing

Where decision makers in a firm aim for a target level of profit rather than the absolute maximum level.

Alternative theories of the firm to those of profit maximization, therefore, tend to assume that large firms are profit satisficers. That is, managers strive hard for a minimum target level of profit, but are less interested in profits above this level.

Such theories fall into two categories: first, those theories that assume that firms attempt to maximize some other aim, provided that sufficient profits are achieved (these are examined in section 7.2); and secondly, those theories that assume that

Box 7.2

What Do You Maximize?
Or managers are only human too

You are a student studying economics. So what do you maximize?

Do you attempt to maximize the examination marks you will get? If so, you will probably have to spend most of each week studying. Obviously you will have to have breaks for food and sleep, and you will need some recreation, but you will probably still spend a lot more time studying than you do now!

What is more likely is that you will, in some rather vaguely defined way, try to maximize your happiness. Getting a good mark in your exams is just one element contributing to your happiness, and you will have to weigh it against the opportunity cost of studying – namely, time not spent out with friends, watching television, pursuing your hobby, etc.

To argue that managers seek to maximize profits to the exclusion of everything else is rather like arguing that you seek to maximize your exam marks. Managers' happiness (or utility) will depend on their salaries, the pleasantness of their job, their power, their respect, the friendship or their colleagues, etc.

Achieving profits may be an important aim (after all it does contribute to a manager's utility), but the effort required to make extra profits involves an opportunity cost to the manager. For example, the manager may have to work longer hours! Managers are only human too.

? 1. When are increased profits in the manager's personal interest?
2. Do you carefully allocate your time between study and leisure? If not, why not?

firms pursue a number of potentially conflicting aims, of which sufficient profit is merely one (these are examined in section 7.3).

 Make a list of six possible aims that a manager of a high street department store might have. Identify some conflicts that might arise between these aims.

Survival: the ultimate aim?

Aiming for profits, sales, salaries, power, etc. will be useless if the firm does not survive! Trying to *maximize* any of the various objectives may be risky. For example, if a firm tries to maximize its market share by aggressive advertising or price cutting, it might invoke a strong response from its rivals. The resulting war may drive it out of business. Some of the managers may easily move to other jobs and may actually gain from the experience, but the majority are likely to lose. Concern with survival, therefore, may make firms cautious.

Not all firms, however, make survival the top priority. Some are adventurous and are prepared to take risks. Adventurous firms are most likely to be those dominated by a powerful and ambitious individual – an individual prepared to take gambles.

The more dispersed the decision-making power is in the firm, however, and the more worried managers are about their own survival, the more cautious are their policies likely to be: preferring collusion to competition, preferring to stick with products that have proved to be popular, and preferring to expand slowly and steadily.

If a firm is too cautious, however, it may not after all survive. It may find that it loses markets to more aggressive competitors. Ultimately, therefore, if a firm is concerned to survive, it must be careful to balance caution against keeping up with competitors, ensuring that the customer is sufficiently satisfied and that costs are kept sufficiently low by efficient management and the introduction of new technology.

▲ SUMMARY

1. There are two major types of criticism of the traditional profit-maximizing theory: (a) firms may not have the information to maximize profits; (b) they may not even want to maximize profits.
2. Lack of information on demand and costs and on the actions and reactions of rivals, and a lack of use of opportunity cost concepts, may mean that firms adopt simple 'rules of thumb' for pricing.
3. In large companies there is likely to be a divorce between ownership and control. The shareholders (the owners) may want maximum profits, but it is the managers who make the decisions and managers are likely to aim to maximize their own utility rather than that of the shareholders. This leads to profit 'satisficing'. This is where managers aim to achieve sufficient profits to keep shareholders happy, but this is a secondary aim to one or more alternative aims.
4. Some alternative theories assume that there is a single alternative aim that firms seek to maximize. Others assume that managers have a series of (possibly conflicting) aims.

7.2 Alternative maximizing theories

Long-run profit maximization

The traditional theory of the firm is based on the assumption of *short-run* profit maximization. Many actions of firms may be seen to conflict with this aim and yet could be consistent with the aim of long-run profit maximization. For example, policies to increase the size of the firm or the firm's share of the market may involve heavy advertising or low prices to the detriment of short-run profits. But if this results in the firm becoming larger, with a larger share of the market, the resulting economic power may enable the firm to make larger profits in the long run.

At first sight, a theory of long-run profit maximization would seem to be a realistic alternative to the traditional short-run profit-maximization theory. In practice, however, the theory is not a very useful predictor of firms' behaviour and is very difficult to test.

One question is whether long-run profit maximization is merely the result of managers pursuing other aims, or whether it is the prime aim itself.

What is more, 'long-run maximization' could be an excuse for virtually any policy. When challenged as to why the firms had, say, undertaken expensive research or high-cost investment, or had engaged in a damaging price war, the managers could reply, 'Ah, yes, but in the long run it will pay off.' This is very difficult to refute (until it is too late!).

If long-run profit maximization *is* the prime aim, the means of achieving it are extremely complex. The firm will need a plan of action for prices, output, investment, etc., stretching from now into the future. But today's prices affect tomorrow's demand. Therefore, future demand curves cannot be taken as given. Today's investment decisions will affect tomorrow's costs. Therefore, future cost curves cannot be taken as given. Quite apart from this, the actions of competitors, suppliers, unions and so on are difficult to predict. Thus the picture of firms making precise calculations of long-run profit-maximizing prices and outputs is a false one.

A precise theory of long-run profit maximization is therefore not useful in explaining how firms actually behave. Either the theory would be too simplistic to be realistic, because there could be no simple formula for predicting price and output and the level of investment, or it would have to be so complex that it would be quite unworkable.

It may be useful, however, simply to observe that firms, when making current price, output and investment decisions, try to judge the approximate effect on new entrants,

---

Long-run profit maximization

An alternative theory which assumes that managers aim to shift cost and revenue curves so as to maximize profits over some longer time period.

Box 7.3

When Is a Theory Not a Theory?

Have you heard the joke about the man sitting in a railway carriage who was throwing pieces of paper out of the window? A fellow traveller was curious and asked him why he kept doing this.

'It keeps the elephants down' was the reply.

'But,' said the other man, 'there are no elephants around here.'

'I know,' said the first man. 'Effective, isn't it?'

Let's reformulate this joke.

Once upon a time there was this boss of a company who kept doing strange things. First he would spend a massive amount of money on advertising, and then stop. Then he would pay a huge wage increase 'to keep his workforce happy'. Then he would close the factory for

two months to give everyone a break. Then he would move the business, lock, stock and barrel, to a new location.

One day he was talking to an accountant friend, who asked, 'Why do you keep doing these strange things?'

'I have to do them to make the business profitable' was the reply.

'But your business *is* profitable,' said the accountant.

'I know. It just goes to show how effective my policies are.'

 1. Why might it be difficult to refute a theory of long-run profit maximization?

2. If a theory cannot *in principle* be refuted, is it a useful theory?

---

consumer demand, future costs, etc., and try to avoid decisions that would appear to conflict with long-run profits. Often this will simply involve avoiding making decisions (e.g. cutting price) that may stimulate an unfavourable result from rivals (e.g. rivals cutting their price).

Sales revenue maximization (short run)

Perhaps the most famous of all alternative theories of the firm is that developed by William Baumol in the late 1950s. This is the theory of sales revenue maximization. Unlike the theory of long-run profit maximization, it is easy to identify the price and output that meet this aim – at least in the short run.

So why should managers want to maximize their firm's sales revenue? The answer is that the success of managers, and in particular sales managers, may be judged according to the level of the firm's sales. Sales figures are an obvious barometer of the firm's health. Managers' salaries, power and prestige may depend directly on sales revenue. The firm's sales representatives may be paid commission on their sales. Thus sales revenue maximization may be a more dominant aim in the firm than profit maximization, particularly if it has a dominant sales department.

Sales revenue will be maximized at the top of the *TR* curve at output Q_1 in Figure 7.1. Profits, by contrast, would be maximized at Q_2. Thus, for given total revenue and total cost curves, sales revenue maximization will tend to lead to a higher output and a lower price than profit maximization.

Sales revenue maximization

An alternative theory which assumes that managers aim to maximize the firm's short-run total revenue.

 Draw a diagram with *MC* and *MR* curves. Mark the output (a) at which profits are maximized; (b) at which sales revenue is maximized.

The firm will still have to make sufficient profits, however, to keep the shareholders happy. Thus firms can be seen to be operating with a profit constraint. They are *profit satisficers*.

Figure 7.1 Sales revenue maximizing output

Figure 7.2 Sales revenue maximizing
with a profit constraint

The effect of this profit constraint is illustrated in Figure 7.2. The diagram shows a total profit ($T\Pi$) curve. (This is found by simply taking the difference between TR and TC at each output.) Assume that the minimum acceptable profit is Π (whatever the output). Any output greater than Q_3 will give a profit less than Π. Thus the sales revenue maximizer who is also a profit satisficer will produce Q_3 not Q_1. Note, however, that this output is still greater than the profit-maximizing output Q_2.

If the firm could maximize sales revenue and still make more than the minimum acceptable profit, it would probably spend this surplus profit on advertising to increase revenue further. This would have the effect of shifting the TR curve upward and also the TC curve (since advertising costs money).

Sales revenue maximization will tend to involve more advertising than profit maximization. Ideally the profit-maximizing firm will advertise up to the point where the marginal revenue of advertising equals the marginal cost of advertising (assuming diminishing returns to advertising). The firm aiming to maximize sales revenue will go beyond this, since further advertising, although costing more than it earns the firm, will still add to total revenue. The firm will continue advertising until surplus profits above the minimum have been used up.

 1. Since advertising increases a firm's costs, will prices necessarily be lower with sales revenue maximization than with profit maximization?
2. We have seen that a firm aiming to maximize sales revenue will tend to produce more than a profit-maximizing firm. This conclusion certainly applies under monopoly and oligopoly. Will it also apply under (a) perfect competition and (b) monopolistic competition, where in both cases there is freedom of entry?

Growth maximization

Rather than aiming to maximize *short-run* sales revenue, managers may take a longer-term perspective and aim for growth maximization in the size of the firm. They may directly gain utility from being part of a rapidly growing 'dynamic' organization; promotion prospects are greater in an expanding organization since new posts tend to be created; large firms may pay higher salaries; managers may obtain greater power in a large firm.

Growth is probably best measured in terms of a growth in sales revenue, since sales revenue (or 'turnover') is the simplest way of measuring the size of a business. An

Growth maximization
An alternative theory which assumes that managers seek to maximize the growth in sales revenue (or the capital value of the firm) over time.

alternative would be to measure the capital value of a firm, but this will depend on the ups and downs of the stock market and is thus a rather unreliable method.

If a firm is to maximize growth, it needs to be clear about the time period over which it is setting itself this objective. For example, maximum growth over the next two or three years might be obtained by running factories to absolute maximum capacity, cramming in as many machines and workers as possible, and backing this up with massive advertising campaigns and price cuts. Such policies, however, may not be sustainable in the longer run. The firm may simply not be able to finance them. A longer-term perspective (say 5–10 years) may therefore require the firm to 'pace' itself, and perhaps to direct resources away from current production and sales into the development of new products that have a potentially high and growing long-term demand.

How is a firm to grow? Growth may be achieved either by internal expansion or by merger.

Growth by internal expansion

Internal growth requires an increase in sales, which in turn requires an increase in the firm's productive capacity.

In order to increase its *sales*, the firm is likely to engage in extensive product promotion and it is also likely to try to launch new products. In order to increase *productive capacity* the firm will require new investment. Both product promotion and investment will require finance.

In the short run, the firm can finance growth by borrowing or by retaining profits or by a new issue of shares. The proportions of UK company investment financed from these sources is shown in Table 7.1.

As you can see, the bulk of investment in the UK is financed by internal funds (i.e. from ploughed-back profit). Nevertheless, in recent years there has been a growing proportion of company investment financed by bank borrowing. Also, until the stock market crash of October 1987, a growing proportion of investment was being financed by the issue of new shares and debentures (fixed-interest loan stock).

What limits the amount of finance a firm can acquire, and hence the rate at which the firm can grow? If the firm *borrows* too much, the interest payments it incurs are likely to make it difficult to maintain the level of dividends to shareholders. Similarly,

Table 7.1 Sources of capital funds of UK industrial and commercial companies

Year	Total from all sources (£ million)	Internal funds[1] (%)	Borrowing from banks, etc. (%)	Shares and debentures (%)	Overseas sources (%)
1970	6 336	60.7	22.4	3.2	13.7
1975	13 736	73.5	7.1	8.8	10.6
1980	28 913	66.1	22.3	4.9	6.7
1982	27 356	62.1	26.9	4.7	6.3
1984	36 980	83.5	20.7	3.7	−7.9
1986	48 715	58.5	21.6	12.5	7.4
1987	71 387	52.2	20.8	19.4	7.6
1988	84 430	45.1	41.2	7.1	6.6
1989	90 251	35.1	47.3	6.2	11.4

[1] Includes grants and tax relief.

Source: *Financial Statistics* (CSO).

if the firm *retains* too much *profit*, there will be less to pay out in dividends. Also if it attempts to raise capital by a *new issue of shares*, the distributed profits will have to be divided between a larger number of shares. Whichever way it finances investment, therefore, the more it invests, the more the dividends on shares in the short run will probably fall. This could lead shareholders to sell their shares, unless they are confident that *long-run* profits and hence dividends will rise again, thus causing the share price to remain high in the long run. If shareholders do *not* have this confidence, they may well sell their shares. This will cause share prices to fall. If they fall too far, the firm runs the risk of being taken over and of certain managers losing their jobs.

Take-over constraint

The effect that the fear of being taken over has on a firm's willingness to undertake projects that reduce distributed profits.

This take-over constraint, therefore, requires that the growth-maximizing firm must distribute sufficient profits to avoid being taken over.

In the long run, a rapidly growing firm may find its profits increasing, especially if it can achieve economies of scale and a bigger share of the market. These profits can then be used to finance further growth. The firm will still not have unlimited finance, however, and therefore will still be faced by the take-over constraint if it attempts to grow too rapidly.

Growth by merger

A merger may be the result of the mutual agreement of two firms to come together. Alternatively, one firm may put in a take-over bid for another. This involves the first firm offering to buy the shares of the second for cash, to swap them for shares in the acquiring company, or to issue fixed-interest securities (debentures). The shareholders of the second firm then vote on whether to accept the offer. (Technically this is an 'acquisition' or 'take-over' rather than a merger, but the term 'merger' is generally used to include both mutual agreements and acquisitions.)

There are three types of merger:

Horizontal merger

Where two firms in the same industry at the same stage in the production process merge.

Vertical merger

Where two firms in the same industry at different stages in the production process merge.

Conglomerate merger

Where two firms in different industries merge.

- A horizontal merger is where firms in the same industry and at the same stage of production merge: e.g. two car manufacturers.
- A vertical merger is where firms in the same industry but at different stages in the production of a good merge: e.g. a car manufacturer with a car component parts producer.
- A conglomerate merger is where firms in different industries merge: e.g. when British Aerospace acquired Austin Rover.

Merger activity

Merger activity tends to go in waves: several years of low merger activity are followed by periods of feverish activity, where both the number and value of mergers can increase several hundred per cent. Merger activity in the UK since 1970 is shown in Table 7.2. It illustrates the two major booms that have occurred since the Second World War.

Table 7.2 Acquisitions and mergers by UK industrial and commercial companies

Year	1970	1971	1972	1973	1974	1975	1976	1977	1978	1979	1980	1981	1982	1983	1984	1985	1986	1987	1988	1989	1990
Number of companies acquired	793	884	1210	1205	504	315	353	481	567	534	469	452	463	447	568	474	842	1527	1499	1330	600*
Expenditure (£m)	1122	911	2532	1304	508	291	448	824	1140	1656	1475	1144	2206	2344	5475	7090	15 363	16 486	22 740	27 052	6200*

* approximate

Source: *Financial Statistics* (CSO).

Box 7.4

Sir Clive Sinclair
A case study in growth by internal expansion

Clive Sinclair is an inventor in a modern guise, being principally involved in electronics and micro-computers. His success at inventing was reflected in his firm's £100 million turnover a year in the mid-1980s. However, Sinclair's rise to prominence was an uncertain one.

In 1962 he founded Sinclair Radionics, which sold radio and amplifier kits by mail order. Five years later the company had progressed to selling complete hi-fis and produced a turnover of £100 000 per annum. The hi-fi and electronics market in general was a rapidly developing area of business and ideal for massive levels of expansion, given the right type of product innovation.

Sinclair's success was to lie in product innovation, as well as in launching an extensive and wholly new kind of advertising campaign – the half-page spread.

By 1973 Sinclair was the leader in pocket calculators within the UK market. From here he moved into digital watches and pocket televisions. Each invention was financially demanding, almost causing Sinclair's bankruptcy in 1976. He was saved by the development of the ZX80 personal computer, which was aimed at the cheap bottom end of the personal computer market. Five million computers, sold in over 70 countries, highlight Sinclair's success at that time. His development of the Spectrum and QL computers represented his challenge

to a developing and continually growing market for sophistication and quality. But it was at this stage that things began to go wrong. In an increasingly competitive market the QL computer sold badly.

Then Sinclair suffered a major setback. Never short of inventive ideas, he introduced the C5 electronic car/tricycle. This was hailed by the media as a revolution in transport: cheap to run, cheap to purchase, non-polluting and compact. But it was a disaster for Sinclair. It was seen by the public as slow, dangerously vulnerable and silly. Sales were no more than a few hundred and production ceased after only a few months. It was damaging to Sinclair's reputation, and he was seen to have lost his 'golden touch'.

Sinclair's entrepreneurial story illustrates graphically the potentially huge gains that can be made from finding an 'untapped' market and producing the right product for it at the right time. But it also illustrates the risks of such a policy, especially for a company that relies heavily on one or two path-breaking products.

?
1. The ZX80 was sold at a very low price. Was this an appropriate policy in a rapidly expanding market?
2. Could the failure of the C5 have been predicted?

The first of these booms had begun in the mid-1960s. In 1968, for example, there were 946 mergers with an amount paid of £11 145 million. Then during the mid-1970s and early 1980s there were relatively few mergers. This period of low merger activity continued until 1983, when first the value of mergers and then the number began to increase dramatically. By the late 1980s mergers were occurring at four times the rate of a decade earlier. This latest boom has been different in a number of ways from the boom of the late 1960s and early 1970s, and from previous (more minor) booms:

- There have been some exceptionally large mergers. For example, in the third quarter of 1989 (a record quarter with more than twice the value of acquisitions of any previous quarter), of 212 mergers, the value of the largest three accounted for 58 per cent of the total. Hanson paid £3.2 billion for Consolidated Gold Fields (26 per cent of the total value of mergers in that quarter); GEC Siemens paid around £2 billion for Plessey (16 per cent) as did Isosceles for Gateway (16 per cent).
- There was a marked shift in the method of financing acquisitions after the Stock Exchange crash of October 1987. This is illustrated in Table 7.3.

From the start of the merger boom, there had been a move away from cash finance towards finance through the issue of shares. With a fall in the value of shares in 1987, however, and with an accompanying fall in new share issues (see

Table 7.3 The finance of mergers in the UK

	1973	1975	1977	1979	1981	1983	1985	1987				1988				1989				1990		
								Q1	Q2	Q3	Q4	Q1	Q2	Q3	Q4	Q1	Q2	Q3	Q4	Q1	Q2	Q3
% of expenditure																						
Cash	53	59	62	56	68	44	40	19	34	35	52	73	51	81	61	14	76	84	86	76	84	57
Issues of shares	36	32	37	31	30	54	52	66	65	63	45	23	35	16	22	17	22	12	9	21	14	27
Issues of debentures	11	9	1	13	3	2	7	15	1	1	4	5	13	3	18	9	1	4	5	2	2	15

Source: *Aquisitions and Mergers*, Business Bulletin no. 10 (CSO, 1990).

Table 7.1), there was a dramatic fall in the percentage of expenditure on acquisitions financed from share issue. This fell from 65 per cent in the third quarter of 1987 to 11 per cent in the third quarter of 1989.

- There has been an increase in the proportion of conglomerate mergers. In the 1960s less than 10 per cent of expenditure on mergers was on conglomerate ones. By the 1980s this had risen to around 30 per cent.

Mergers have become commonplace. It is not just large firms that take over small ones. Firms of any size are involved in take-overs, and in many cases it is large firms that are taken over by smaller ones (see Box 7.5).

Motives for merger

But why do firms want to take over others? Is it purely that they want to grow: are mergers simply evidence of the hypothesis that firms are growth maximizers? Or are there other motives that influence the predatory drive?

Economists have identified a number of possible motives.

Merger for growth. If the aims of the decision makers within the firm are to maximize growth, mergers are an obvious means. They provide a much quicker means to growth than does internal expansion. Not only does the firm acquire new capacity, it also acquires additional consumer demand. There is a danger for growth-maximizing firms, however, and this is from being taken over themselves. If they are currently growing rapidly and yet have a relatively low profit and a low stock market value, they will be attractive to other predator firms.

Merger for economies of scale. Once the merger has taken place, the constituent parts can be reorganized through a process of 'rationalization'. The result can be a reduction in costs. For example, only one head office will now be needed.

Evidence for such motivation is sparse, however. The problem is in separating the desire to reduce costs from the desire to achieve other objectives. Reduced costs are a way of increasing profits and thereby of increasing the rate of growth. It is probably unlikely that managers will want to reduce costs for their own sake.

In fact the evidence on costs suggests that most mergers result in little if any cost savings: either potential economies of scale are not exploited due to a lack of rationalization, or diseconomies result from the disruptions of reorganization or a lack of control over the acquired part of the organization by the parent company. In many cases, managers seem to know little about the businesses their companies have bought. New managers installed by the parent company are often seen as unsympathetic, and morale may go down.

Merger for monopoly power. Here the motive is simple: essentially it is to reduce competition and thereby gain greater market power and larger profits. With less competition, the firm will face a less elastic demand and will be able to charge a

Box 7.5

Sir Terence Conran's Storehouse
A case study in growth by merger

Terence Conran, often seen as one of the 'hot shot' designers of the 1960s, has failed to shake off his 'trendy' image, despite his massive success in retailing with Habitat, Mothercare and BHS. This 'trendiness', even with over £500 million worth of business per year, has seen a reluctance on the part of the banking sector and the City to supply sufficient capital for Conran's expansion, especially into the United States market.

Terence Conran was by trade a designer and he originally supplied designer furniture to the business world. In 1963, however, he established his first Habitat and thereby expanded into the consumer retail market.

Expansion, however, was slow. After nine years Habitat comprised only fifteen stores. Nevertheless, by 1969 Conran had taken over Lupton Morton, a mail-order firm, and merged with Rymans, a large stationery and office supplier. These early mergers, however, brought serious problems. The aims of the constituent firms were too diverse. There were no economies of scale to be gained, only disruptions.

The take-over of Mothercare in January 1982 for £120 million was Conran's first major coup. Mothercare was three times the size of Habitat, with profits in the region of £20.6 million compared to Habitat's £6.6 million, and with 429 stores to Habitat's 52. It would therefore not appear to be the type of firm Habitat should be taking over; rather the reverse.

During the 1970s however, Mothercare had 'lost its way' in the market. Even though it still held 35 per cent of market sales, it had lost many of its traditional middle-class customers. Conran believed that new designs and initiatives could increase Mothercare's market considerably, bringing back the middle-class customers. Habitat financed this venture by going public.

Subsequent moves saw Conran take over Heals, a Habitat competitor, which Conran envisaged as developing into a 'mature person's Habitat'. Moves into fashion have seen Conran acquire 48 per cent of Richard Shops and establish a new chain of teenage clothes shops called Now. His merger with Octopus shows Conran's diversification into publishing.

Perhaps the most obvious to the high street customer, however, was the take-over of British Home Stores for £500 million. Conran immediately set about changing its image. From a 'poor person's Marks and Spencer', he has attempted to transform it into a chain bringing quality and design to a mass market.

In the late 1980s and early 1990s, however, the home furnishing market experienced a massive downturn in business. Habitat profits fell by more than 90 per cent in 1988/89, and a loss of around £11 million in the following year led to a move to close twelve of its stores – some two-fifths of its trading space.

Conran's expansion into the retailing market in recent years has been rapid – some suggest too rapid. Escalating costs, falling demand and changing consumer tastes all conspired to suggest that 'big is not necessarily beautiful or successful'.

? 1. What are the advantages and disadvantages to the firm of growth by merger?
2. What are the advantages and disadvantages to the consumer?

---

higher percentage above marginal cost. This obviously fits well with the traditional theory of the firm. Empirical evidence, however, is inconclusive and in certain cases contradictory. One influential study[4] suggested that mergers within the USA illustrate managers' desire to avoid rigorous competition, whereas another[5] found no evidence to suggest that mergers are greater in those markets where a significant increase in market power would result.

 Which of the three types of merger (horizontal, vertical and conglomerate) are most likely to lead to (a) reductions in average costs; (b) increased market power?

[4] S. Nelson, *Merger Movements in American Industry 1895–1956*, National Bureau of Economic Research, General Series 66 (Princeton University Press, 1959).
[5] M. Gort, 'An economic disturbance theory of mergers', *Quarterly Journal of Economics*, vol. 83 (1969).

Box 7.6

Merger Activity: A European Perspective[2]

Merger activity within Europe throughout the 1960s, 1970s and 1980s has been predominantly horizontal in nature rather than vertical or conglomerate. This has led to a steady increase in industrial concentration within a wide range of manufacturing and service-sector industries in a number of European countries, especially in the UK, Germany, Holland and Sweden. Such merger activity has been found from investigations to have led to few gains in efficiency and only minimal improvements in competitiveness.

Diagram (a) shows that the number of mergers and acquisitions involving the 1000 largest EC firms steadily increased during the 1980s.

(a) Numbers of mergers and acquisitions of majority stakes involving the 1000 largest European firms

(a) Main motives for inter-EC mergers and acquisitions in 1985/86 and 1986/87 (cases for which precise information about mergers is available)

	1985/86 (%)	1986/87 (%)
Rationalization, restructuring	35.0	29.7
Expansion	18.1	22.1
Complementarity	14.4	12.4
Strengthening of market position	11.3	11.5
Diversification	12.5	5.7
R&D	2.5	5.3
Specialization	1.9	1.3
Other	4.4	11.9
	100.0	100.0

One point to note is that the vast majority of merger activity within Europe still remains within national boundaries. In 1986/87, 69.6 per cent of mergers involved companies from within the same country. Nevertheless, mergers involving cross-border activity have been growing over the last few years, exceeding merger activity involving non-European companies. In 1986/87 there were 75 EC-based mergers as compared with 52 the previous year. An important factor explaining the increase in inter-EC mergers is the establishment of a single European market after 1992 (see section 21.4). Firms have been taking the opportunity to establish a European network and restructure their operations as well as to expand productive capacity.

Merger for increased market valuation. Here merger is seen to benefit shareholders of *both* firms by leading to a potential increase in the stock market valuation of the merged firm. If both sets of shareholders believe that they will make a capital gain, then they are more likely to give the go-ahead to the merger.

Evidence for this motive is inconclusive. One survey of 2500 mergers in the UK and the USA between 1955 and 1985[6] showed that, although shares in the companies that were the target of a take-over bid were pushed up by the bid, the shareholders of the bidding companies initially gained (or lost) very little. After two years, however, although the shares of cash-bidding companies had appreciated as fast as they did before the merger, those which acquired other companies through issuing shares ('equity bidders') found that their shares did 18 per cent worse in the USA and 9 per cent worse in the UK. Other studies have confirmed a relatively poor share performance of companies after merger. One possible reason for this is the

[6] J. Franks, R. Harris and C. Mayer in A. Auerbach (ed.), *Corporate Takeovers: Causes and consequences* (University of Chicago Press, 1989).

Box 7.6 (cont'd)

(b) Mergers by nationality of acquirer

A notable feature of European merger activity is the size of the firms involved. In 1986/87, 57 per cent of merger activity involved firms with sales of over ECU 1 billion (£0.65 billion). The implication of this is that markets are and will become increasingly concentrated. This may well lead the EC to adopt a more strict long-term policy of control over monopoly practices.

Differences between member states' merger activity is highly significant, and is a reflection as much of economic, institutional and legal differences as of opportunity and business practice. A study by Booz, Allen and Hamilton[3] found a number of trends.

For UK companies, mergers with European firms have tended to be much less important than mergers within the US market. However, in recent years the decline in British–European mergers, down to only 20 per cent of the total in 1987 (see table (b)), has been reversed in line with generally improved opportunities within Europe and the prospect of the 1992 single market.

For German companies, inter-EC mergers have been much more significant, accounting for 66 per cent of total German mergers in 1987. But here too this was lower than previously. In 1984, 86 per cent of German mergers had involved European firms.

Whereas total British and German merger activity increased substantially during the 1980s, in France merger activity was at a low level until 1987. After that it grew substantially, but the proportion of French inter-EC mergers declined somewhat to around 50 per cent of total French mergers.

Although common themes such as a general increase in merger activity can be identified within a European perspective, significant variations remain between EC members in attitudes and direction. However, a degree of convergence, primarily stimulated by the single market after 1992, has become more apparent over the last few years. In the light of this, one factor that will inevitably represent a key concern of competition policy is the potential domination of European markets by single firms once trading barriers have been removed.

(b) Share of acquisitions and mergers involving other EC firms in total

	1982	1983	1984	1985	1986	1987
UK	37	34	39	31	27	20
France	95	60	63	47	77	50
Germany (Fed. Rep.)	n.a.	83	86	77	72	66

[2] This box and the tables and figures are based on *European Economy*, vol. 40 (May 1989).
[3] The study is referred to in *European Economy*, *op. cit.*

---

increases in costs referred to above. This suggests that mergers may be more appealing to the shareholders of target companies than to those of bidding companies.

Merger to reduce uncertainty. There are two major sources of uncertainty for firms. The first is the behaviour of rivals. Mergers, by reducing the number of rivals, can correspondingly reduce uncertainty. At the same time they can reduce the costs of competition (e.g. by reducing advertising).

The second source of uncertainty is the domestic and international economic environment. Looking at evidence from the UK merger boom in 1967/68, Newbould[7] found that there were strong connections between an uncertain economic environment and levels of merger activity. The introduction of corporation tax in 1965, devaluation of sterling in 1967, increasing pressure by the government to remove restrictive practices, attempts to join the EEC, and changes in technology, all contributed, according to Newbould, to the 1967/68 merger spree.

[7] G. Newbould, *Management and Merger Activity* (Guthstead, 1970).

Merger due to opportunity. Sometimes mergers may occur in response to opportunities that may suddenly and unexpectedly arise. Many firms are on the lookout for new markets, new products, new expertise and new ideas. Many firms simply want to show that they are a 'dynamic organization' and not stuck in a rut. At the same time, managers may be unwilling to plan a strategy of take-overs in advance, in case this gives signals to the market (and encourages other bidders or pushes up the share prices of the target firms). All this suggests that the actual mergers that take place will be very difficult to predict.

Other motives. Other motives that have been suggested for mergers include the following:

- Getting bigger so as to become less likely to be taken over oneself.
- Defending another firm from an unwanted predator (the 'White Knight' strategy).
- Asset stripping. This is where a firm buys another and then breaks it up, selling off the profitable bits and probably closing down the remainder.
- Empire building. This is where owners or managers like the power or prestige of owning or controlling several (preferably well-known) companies.
- Broadening the geographical base of the company by merging with a firm in a different part of the country or the world.

None of these theories is generally accepted and several of them overlap. Most are in need of greater empirical investigation and support.

 1. Which of the above theories overlap and in what way?
2. Why, do you think, is it difficult to find adequate empirical support for any of them?

Mergers and the relationship between growth and profit

In order for a firm to be successful in a take-over bid, it must be sufficiently profitable to finance the take-over. Thus the faster it tries to grow and the more take-overs it attempts, the higher must be its profitability.

In addition to being an obvious means to the growth of the firm, mergers may be a means of increasing profits, since mergers can lead to both lower average costs through economies of scale and higher average revenue through increased market power over prices. These profits in turn may be seen as a means of financing further growth.

It can therefore be seen that, whichever way it is financed, growth is closely linked to profits. High profits can help a firm grow. Rapid growth can lead to a rapid growth in profits.

These are not inevitable links, however. For example, long-run profits may not increase if a firm, as part of its growth policy, invests in risky projects or projects with a low rate of return. Expansion alone is no guarantee of profits. Also, high profits will not necessarily lead to growth if a large proportion is distributed to shareholders and only a small proportion is reinvested. High profits may help growth, but they do not guarantee it.

Equilibrium for a growth-maximizing firm

What will a growth-maximizing firm's price and output be? Unfortunately there is no simple formula for predicting this.

In the short run, the firm may choose the profit-maximizing price and output – so as to provide the greatest funds for investment. On the other hand, it may be prepared to sacrifice some short-term profits in order to mount an advertising campaign. It all depends on the strategy it considers most suitable to achieve growth.

In the long run, prediction is more difficult still. The policies that a firm adopts will depend crucially on the assessments of market opportunities made by managers. But this involves judgement, not fine calculation. Different managers will judge a situation differently.

One prediction can be made. Growth-maximizing firms are likely to diversify into different products, especially as they approach the limits to expansion in existing markets.

Alternative maximizing theories and the public interest

It is difficult to draw firm conclusions about the public interest.

In the case of sales revenue maximization, a higher output will be produced than under profit maximization, but the consumer will not necessarily benefit from lower prices, since more will be spent on advertising – costs that will be passed on to the consumer.

In the case of growth and long-run profit maximization, there are many possible policies that a firm could pursue. To the extent that a concern for the long run encourages firms to look to improved products, new products and new techniques, the consumer may benefit from such a concern. To the extent, however, that growth encourages a greater level of industrial concentration through merger, the consumer may lose from the resulting greater level of monopoly power.

As with the traditional theory of the firm, the degree of competition a firm faces is a crucial factor in determining just how responsive it will be to the wishes of the consumer.

? How will competition between growth maximizing firms benefit the consumer?

▲ SUMMARY

1. Rather than seeking to maximize short-run profits, a firm may take a longer-term perspective. It is very difficult, however, to predict the behaviour of a long-run profit-maximizing firm, since (a) different managers are likely to make different judgements about how to achieve maximum profits and (b) demand and cost curves may shift unpredictably both in response to the firm's own policies and as a result of external factors.

2. Managers may gain utility from maximizing sales revenue. They will still have to ensure that a satisfactory level of profit is achieved, however. The output of a firm which seeks to maximize sales revenue will be higher than that for a profit-maximizing firm. Its level of advertising will also tend to be higher. Whether price will be higher or lower depends on the relative effects on demand and cost of the additional advertising.

3. Many managers aim for maximum growth of their organization, believing that this will help their salaries, power, prestige, etc.

4. Growth may be by internal expansion. This can be financed by ploughing back profits, by share issue or by borrowing. Whichever method a firm uses, it will require sufficient profits if it is to avoid becoming vulnerable to a take-over.

5. Growth may be by merger. Mergers can be horizontal, vertical or conglomerate. Merger activity tends to occur in waves. A major increase in merger activity began in the mid-1980s. Various motives have been suggested for mergers, including growth, economies of scale, market power, increased share values, reduction in uncertainty, and simply taking advantage of opportunities as they occur.

6. As with long-run profit-maximizing theories, it is difficult to predict the price and output strategies of a growth maximizing firm. Much depends on the judgements of particular managers about growth opportunities.

7. Alternative aims will benefit the consumer to the extent that they encourage firms to develop new products and to find more efficient methods of production. They may be against the consumer's interest to the extent that they lead firms to engage in extensive advertising or to merge with a resulting increased concentration of market power.

7.3 Multiple aims

Satisficing and the setting of targets

Firms may have more than one aim. For example, they may try to achieve increased sales revenue *and* increased profit. The problem with this is that if two aims conflict, it will not be possible to maximize both of them. For example, sales revenue will probably be maximized at a different price and output from that at which profits are maximized. Where firms have two or more aims, a compromise may be for targets to be set for individual aims which are low enough to achieve simultaneously and yet which are sufficient to satisfy the interested parties.

Such target setting is also likely when the maximum value of a particular aim is unknown. If, for example, the maximum achievable profit is unknown, the firm may well set a target for profit which it feels is both satisfactory and achievable.

Behavioural theories of the firm: the setting of targets

Behavioural theories of the firm

Theories that attempt to predict the actions of firms by studying the behaviour of various groups of people within the firm and their interactions under conditions of potentially conflicting interests.

A major advance in alternative theories of the firm has been the development of behavioural theories.[8] Rather than setting up a model to show how various objectives could in theory be achieved, behavioural theories of the firm are based on observations of how firms *actually* behave.

Large firms are often complex institutions with several departments (sales, production, design, purchasing, personnel, finance, etc.). Each department is likely to have its own specific set of aims and objectives which may possibly come into conflict with those of other departments. These aims in turn will be constrained by the interests of shareholders, workers, customers and creditors, who will need to be kept sufficiently happy.

Behavioural theories do not lay down rules of how to *achieve* these aims, but rather examine what these aims are, the motivations underlying them, the conflicts that can arise between aims, and how these conflicts get resolved.

It is assumed that targets will be set for production, sales, profit, stock holding, etc. If, in practice, target levels are not achieved, a 'search' procedure will be started to find what went wrong and how to rectify it. If the problem cannot be rectified, managers will probably adjust the target downwards. If, on the other hand, targets are easily achieved, managers may adjust them upwards. Thus the targets to which managers aspire depend to a large extent on the success in achieving *previous* targets. Targets are also influenced by expectations of demand and costs, by the achievements of competitors and by expectations of competitors' future behaviour.

If targets conflict, the conflict will be settled by a bargaining process between managers. The outcome of the bargaining, however, will depend on the power and ability of the individual managers concerned. Thus a similar set of conflicting targets may be resolved differently in different firms.

Behavioural theories of the firm: organizational slack

Since changing targets often involves search procedures and bargaining processes and is therefore time consuming, and since many managers prefer to avoid conflict, targets tend to be changed fairly infrequently. Business conditions, however, often change rapidly. To avoid the need to change targets, therefore, managers will tend to

---

[8] See in particular R. M. Cyert and J. G. March, *A Behavioural Theory of the Firm* (Prentice-Hall, 1963).

Box 7.7

Types of Theory: Descriptive and Prescriptive

The behavioural theory does not state how a firm *ought* to behave in order to achieve certain objectives. Rather, it examines just how firms *do* behave. It *describes* their behaviour and looks at the consequences for, say, profit. It is thus a descriptive theory.

The traditional theory of the firm *may* be used in this way. Advocates of the theory may claim that firms do maximize short-run profits, and do equate MR and MC.

Others, however, would claim that the traditional theory is 'prescriptive'. It says what firms must do *if* they are to maximize profits. 'If you wish to maximize profits then you must equate MR and MC', or 'If you are a risk-averse oligopolist, and prefer to go for a safe strategy, then you should adopt the maximin alternative.'

?
1. Are the theories of sales revenue maximization prescriptive or descriptive?
2. If prescriptive theories tell firms what they ought to do, are they normative? Is there a problem here?

---

be fairly conservative in their aspirations. This leads to the phenomenon known as organizational slack.

When the firm does better than planned, it will allow slack to develop. This slack can then be taken up if the firm does worse than planned. For example, if the firm produces more than it planned, it will build stocks of finished goods and draw on them if subsequently production falls. It would not, in the meantime, increase its sales or production target. If it did, and production then fell below target, the production department might not be able to supply the sales department with its full requirement.

Thus keeping targets fairly low and allowing slack to develop allows all targets to be met with minimum conflict.

Organizational slack
Where managers allow spare capacity to exist thereby enabling them to respond more easily to changed circumstances.

Multiple goals: some predictions of behaviour

Conservatism
Some firms may be wary of unnecessary change. Change is risky. They may prefer to stick with tried and tested practices. 'If it works, stick with it.' This could apply to pricing policies, marketing techniques, product design and range, internal organization of the firm, etc.

If something does not work, managers will probably change it, but again they may be conservative and only try a cautious change: perhaps imitating successful competitors.

This safe, satisficing approach makes prediction of any given firm's behaviour relatively easy. You simply examine its past behaviour. Making generalizations about all such cautious firms, however, is more difficult. Different firms are likely to have established different rules of behaviour depending on their own particular experiences of their market.

Comparison with other firms
Managers may judge their success by comparing their firm's performance with that of rival firms. For example, growing market share may be seen as a more important

Box 7.8

J. K. Galbraith (1908–)
A lofty view of economics

No review of alternative theories of the firm can be complete without an examination of the contribution of John Kenneth Galbraith, who for decades has attacked the traditional theory of the firm for its unrealistic assumptions. But that is not all he has been famous for.

Tall in stature (6′8″) and deed, Galbraith has been a prolific writer, producing academic works not only in economics, but also in sociology and politics. Not many economists can lay claim to writing best-sellers, yet Galbraith has written four.[10] He has also been a frequent contributor to newspapers, radio and television. With his dead-pan voice and razor-sharp wit he has delighted audiences with acid attacks on big business and free-market capitalism, with its 'private affluence and public squalor'. As a lifelong liberal and an active supporter of Democrat causes, he has been vehemently opposed to the philosophy of the New Right and to leaders such as Ronald Reagan, George Bush and Margaret Thatcher.

As a highly original thinker and maverick he has frequently challenged mainstream economics. This unorthodox approach was apparent in the early years of his career. On appointment as deputy head of the Office of Price Administration during the Second World War, he was a strong advocate of wartime price controls and rationing, and also argued that widespread price fixing should be seriously considered in peacetime too. After all, he maintained, it was no more than large firms already practised as normal business behaviour! His forced resignation in 1943 stemmed largely from the unpopularity of his views.

The great part of Galbraith's career has centred on Harvard, where from 1949 to his retirement in 1975 he was Professor of Economics, although for a period under the Kennedy administration he was US ambassador to India. His active participation in politics as speech writer and adviser to a long line of Democrat politicians, including John F. Kennedy, has ensured that his views have been heard in the highest political circles. In many cases Galbraith has used his political experiences to enhance and develop his theories and to explain the place of power in economic theory – power of the state, power of big business and power of pressure groups.

In *The New Industrial State* (1967) and *Economics and the Public Purpose* (1973), he argued that power structures in big business make the traditional assumptions of profit maximization irrelevant. And yet, economists continue to assume that firms are profit maximizers:

> The corporate reality is ignored. Discussion begins with the observation: 'Profit maximization, of course, assumed'.[11]

The basis of power in big business is what Galbraith calls the 'technostructure'. This is the experts – the scientists, engineers and economists(!) – and the professional managers:

> As the firm grows larger, the technostructure becomes the effective governing power for reasons that are not mysterious. Unless you have the knowledge that allows you to participate in making decisions and do participate, you can't be influential.[12]

According to Galbraith, the technostructure has its own goals, such as job satisfaction, growth and status, and it will try to shape decisions to achieve these objectives. What has happened is that the capitalists (the owners) have lost power as a result of the increasing complexity of the modern business world. They are no longer in a position to insist on policies of profit maximization. As Galbraith remarks:

> [The modern large corporation] loses its legitimacy as an entrepreneurial and capitalist institution. It becomes instead an instrument of its own organization . . .
>
> Having independent power and being the creation of its own organization, the modern corporation, not surprisingly, serves the purposes of its own management. These purposes are frequently different from those of the public, or substantial parts of it, and the latter are less than pleased. Specifically, the corporate bureaucracy, like all organizations, seeks its own expansion.[13]

Like many of Galbraith's theories, his analysis of the structure of big business challenges the very foundations of traditional economics. But one person's heresy can be another's orthodoxy. Galbraith's theories have much in common with the other alternative theories of the firm we have considered in this chapter. It is just that Galbraith has a way of reaching out to a mass audience with his views: something that no other economist has managed to do, with the possible exceptions of his arch academic 'enemies', Milton Friedman (see Box 13.9) and Friedrich von Hayek (see Box 10.9).

[10] *American Capitalism: The concept of countervailing power* (Houghton Mifflin, 1952); *The Affluent Society* (Houghton Mifflin, 1958; Penguin, 1962); *The New Industrial State* (Houghton Mifflin, 1967; Penguin, 1969); *Economics and the Public Purpose* (Houghton Mifflin, 1973; Penguin, 1975).

[11] *Economics and the Public Purpose* (Penguin, 1975), p. 106.

[12] *Almost Everyone's Guide to Economics* (André Deutsch, 1979), p. 55.

[13] *Annals of an Abiding Liberal* (André Deutsch, 1980), pp. 75, 77.

indicator of 'success' than simple growth in sales. Similarly, they may compare their profits, their product design, their technology or their industrial relations with those of rivals. To many managers it is *relative* performance that matters, rather than absolute performance.

What predictions can be made if this is how managers behave? The answer is that it depends on the nature of competition in the industry. The more profitable, innovative and efficient are the competitors, the more profitable, innovative and efficient will managers try to make their particular firm.

The further ahead of their rivals that firms try to stay, the more likely it is that there will be a 'snowballing' effect: each firm trying to outdo the other.

 Will this type of behaviour tend to lead to profit maximization?

Satisficing and the public interest

Firms with multiple goals will be satisficers. The greater the number of goals of the different managers, the greater is the chance of conflict, and the more likely it is that organizational slack will develop. Satisficing firms are therefore likely to be less responsive to changes in consumer demand and changes in costs than profit-maximizing firms. They may thus be less efficient.

On the other hand, such firms may be less eager to exploit their economic power by charging high prices, or to use aggressive advertising, or to pay low wages.

The extent to which satisficing firms do act in the public interest will, as in the case of other types of firm, depend to a large extent on the amount and type of competition they face, and their attitudes towards this competition. Firms that compare their performance with that of their rivals are more likely to be responsive to consumer wishes than firms that prefer to stick to well-established practices. On the other hand, they may be more concerned to 'manipulate' consumer tastes than the more traditional firm.

 Are satisficing firms more likely to suffer from X inefficiency (see Box 5.5) than firms which seek to maximize profit or sales revenue?

▲ SUMMARY

1. In large firms, decisions are taken by or influenced by a number of different people, including various managers, shareholders, workers, customers, suppliers and creditors. If these different people have different aims, a conflict between them is likely to arise. A firm cannot maximize more than one of these conflicting aims. The alternative is to seek to achieve a satisfactory target level of a number of aims.

2. Behavioural theories of the firm examine how managers and other interest groups actually behave, rather than merely identifying various equilibrium positions for output, price, investment, etc.

3. If targets were easily achieved last year, they are likely to be made more ambitious next year. If they were not achieved, a search procedure will be conducted to identify how to rectify the problem. This may mean adjusting

targets downwards, in which case there will be some form of bargaining process between managers.

4. Life is made easier for managers if conflict can be avoided. This will be possible if slack is allowed to develop in various parts of the firm. If targets are not being met, the slack can then be taken up without requiring adjustments in other targets.

5. Satisficing firms may be less innovative, less aggressive and less willing to initiate change. If they do change, it is more likely to be in response to changes made by their competitors. Managers may judge their performance by comparing it with that of rivals.

6. Satisficing firms may be less aggressive in exploiting a position of market power. On the other hand they may suffer from greater X inefficiency.

⑧ The Theory of Distribution of Income

8.1 The market for factors of production

Why do pop stars, footballers and stockbrokers earn such large incomes? Why, on the other hand, do cleaners, hospital porters and workers in clothing factories earn very low incomes? These are the types of question that the theory of distribution seeks to answer. It attempts to explain why some people are rich and others poor.

It does this by examining the incomes earned by the various *factors of production*. In the case of labour, this income takes the form of wages and salaries. In the case of land it is the rent earned by landlords. In the case of capital it is the profits or interest earned by the owners of capital. Notice in the last two cases that we are not talking about the price at which a factor is sold (i.e. the price of land or the price of capital equipment). Rather we are talking about the incomes earned from the use of these factors.

Size distribution of income

Measurement of the distribution of income according to the levels of income received by individuals (irrespective of source).

The question of distribution can be examined at three levels. First of all there is the question of how equally incomes are distributed among the population. This is known as the size distribution of income. For example, we might want to know how much richer the top 10 per cent of income earners are than the bottom 10 per cent.

Then there is the question of distribution between the general factor categories: labour, land and capital. This is known at the functional distribution of income. For example, there is the question of the relative shares of wages and profits in national income.

Functional distribution of income

Measurement of the distribution of income according to the source of income (e.g. from employment, from profit, from rent, etc.).

Finally, at the narrowest level, there is the question of distribution within the factor categories. For example, there is the question of what determines wages in a particular occupation. Why are some jobs well paid while others are badly paid? Why are rents higher in some areas than in others?

In a free-market economy the distribution of income may be highly unequal. This raises the normative question of whether this inequality is desirable. Although economists cannot answer this question directly, they can examine the causes of the inequality. They can also examine various government policies to redistribute incomes, and the various consequences of these policies for other questions such as economic efficiency and economic growth.

This chapter examines the theory of income distribution. In doing so it concentrates on the narrower question of what determines the rewards to particular factors of production. Chapter 9, on the other hand, looks at income distribution in practice. It looks at inequality and poverty in the UK and at government policies to tackle the problem. It thus concentrates mainly on the size distribution of income.

Distribution of income in perfect markets

It is useful to make a similar distinction to that made in the theory of the firm: the distinction between perfect and imperfect markets. Although in practice few factor markets are totally perfect, many do at least approximate to it. Also, when we come to study imperfect markets it is useful to have a yardstick against which to judge the effects of such imperfections. Perfect markets provide that yardstick. (A word of caution: as Box 5.2 pointed out, 'perfect' does not necessarily mean 'desirable'.)

Assumptions

The assumption of perfect factor markets are similar to those of perfect goods markets:

- *Everyone is a price taker.* No one has any economic power to affect factor prices. In the labour market, both employers and workers have to accept the market wage. Similarly, landlords and tenants have to accept the rent of land as given by the market. Likewise those who supply and those who demand capital have to accept the market rate of return on that capital.
- There is *freedom of entry.* There are no restrictions on the movement of labour or capital, or on changes in the use of land. For example, workers are free to move to jobs and areas of the country where wages are higher. There are no barriers erected by, say, unions, professional associations or the government. Of course it takes time for workers to change jobs and perhaps to retrain. Similarly, the use of land cannot be changed overnight. This assumption therefore applies only in the long run.
- There is *perfect knowledge.* Workers are fully aware of what jobs are available at what wages and with what conditions of employment. Likewise employers know what labour is available and how productive that labour is. Similarly, those who supply and demand other factors are fully aware of their price and quality.
- *Factors are homogeneous.* It is usually assumed that in perfect markets factors of a particular type are identical. For example, it would be assumed that all bricklayers are equally skilled and motivated.

> **?** Which of the above four assumptions do you think would be correct in each of the following cases?
> (a) Shorthand typists. (e) A hectare of prime agricultural land.
> (b) Shepherds. (f) A herd of Friesian cows.
> (c) Unskilled workers. (g) A warehouse.
> (d) Economics teachers. (h) Oxyacetylene welding equipment.

The workings of the market

In a perfect market, factor earnings are determined by demand and supply. In this way factor markets are very similar to goods markets, but the roles of supplier and demander are reversed. In goods markets, firms supply goods and households demand goods. In factor markets, firms demand factors while households supply them. These demand and supply relationships can be illustrated in the circular flow of income shown in Figure 8.1.

Starting at the bottom of the diagram and moving anti-clockwise, households demand goods and services. The price of each good and service is determined by the interaction of this demand and firms' supply. In the process, money flows from households to firms.

To produce these goods firms need to employ factors of production. The demand

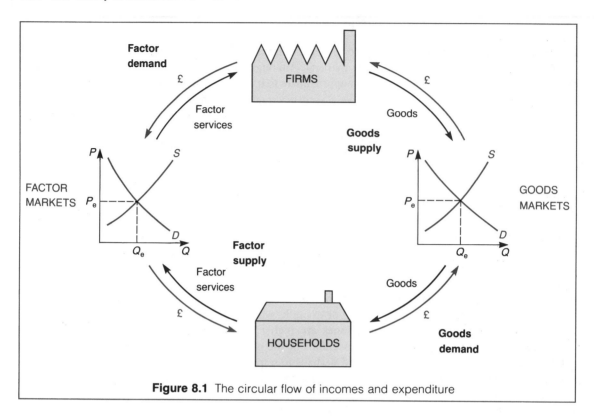

Figure 8.1 The circular flow of incomes and expenditure

Derived demand

The demand for a factor of production depends on the demand for the good which uses it.

for goods thus creates a demand for factors. The demand for factors is thus said to be a derived demand. For example, the demand for bricklayers is derived from the demand for new houses. The demand for factors then interacts with their supply by households. This determines the price paid to the factor owners for the use of those factors.

Generally it would be expected that the supply and demand curves for factors of production slope the same way as for goods and services. Take the case of labour. The higher the wages paid for a certain type of job, the more workers will want to do that job. This gives an upward-sloping supply curve of labour. On the other hand, the higher the wages that employers have to pay, the less labour they will want to employ. Either they will simply produce less output, or they will substitute other factors, like machinery, for labour. Thus the demand curve for labour slopes downwards.

These upward-sloping supply curves and downward-sloping demand curves are for the *whole market*. They determine the market price of each factor. Individual firms and households under perfect competition then have to accept these prices as given (the first assumption we made above). As individuals they have no power to influence them: they are *price takers*. Figure 8.2 illustrates the case of labour.

Diagram (b) shows how the equilibrium hourly wage is determined by the intersection of the demand and supply of labour hours.

Diagram (a) shows how an individual employer has to accept this wage. The supply of labour to that employer is infinitely elastic. In other words, at the market wage W_m, there is no limit to the number of workers available to that employer (but no workers at all will be available below it: they will all be working elsewhere). At the market wage W_m, the employer will employ Q_1 hours of labour.

Diagram (c) shows how an individual worker also has to accept this wage. The

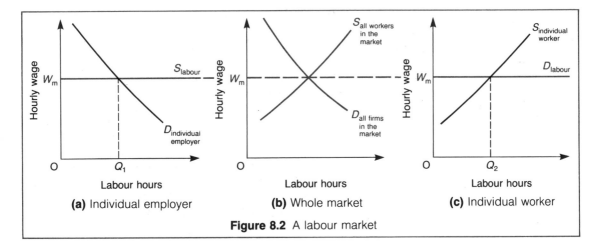

Figure 8.2 A labour market

(a) Individual employer (b) Whole market (c) Individual worker

demand curve for that worker is also infinitely elastic. In other words, there is as much work as the worker cares to do at this wage (but none at all above it).

The determination of income distribution

So what determines income distribution in perfect markets? There are two determinants.

The prices paid to factor owners. The position of the market demand and supply curves will determine the equilibrium price paid to the factor owners for the use of the factor. The price will be high when there is a high demand for the factor relative to supply. So if, for example, the demand for computer programmers grows faster than their supply, their wages will rise.

To explain the causes of inequality in factor earnings, then, it is necessary to examine what determines the position of the demand and supply curves. This is done in subsequent sections of this chapter.

The ownership of factors of production. There are two aspects to this:

- The *quantity* of factors that people own. Some people own lots of land and capital. Some people own only a little. Others own none: all they have to sell is their own labour. The more factors people own, the more they will earn. Thus however 'perfect' the market, and however equal wages are, inequality will persist if there is an unequal distribution of property.
- The *quality* of factors that people own. Different factors of production have different productivities. The higher the productivity of a factor, the more it will earn for its owner. Thus fertile land or city centre property will earn high rents. Efficient modern capital equipment will earn more than old inefficient equipment. Likewise workers differ in strength, intelligence, education and training.

Is there a tendency toward equality under perfect competition?

At first sight the answer to this question might seem to be yes. If wages are higher in one industry than in another, workers will be encouraged to move from the low-paid to the high-paid industry. The resulting surplus of labour in the high-paid industry would reduce wages there, while the shortage of labour in the low-paid industry would raise its wages. The differential would be reduced. Similarly, if capital is attracted to industries with a high return, this will depress the return because the increased output will depress industry prices. Likewise if farmers transfer the use of their land to produce more profitable crops, the extra output will reduce the crop's price and hence the return on the land.

But even under perfect competition inequality will persist. One reason is that the costs of supplying factors may differ. In the case of labour, it is far nicer to do a clean and pleasant job than a dirty, unpleasant or dangerous job. Other things being equal, nasty jobs would have to pay more than nice jobs in order to attract labour. Similarly, owners of capital would expect a higher return on risky projects than on totally safe projects.

 Why, do you think, are some of the lowest-paid jobs the most unpleasant? (The next paragraph might provide part of the answer. When you have read it, consider whether it contains the whole answer.)

The other reason is the unequal ownership of factors, both in terms of quantity and quality. In the long run, all nurses may be paid the same and all brain surgeons may be paid the same, but nurses will not be paid the same as brain surgeons. Two landowners may earn the same rent per acre for the same sort of land, but one farmer may own 10 hectares, whereas the other may own 1000 hectares, and of course many people own no land at all.

Distribution of income in imperfect markets

In real-world factor markets it is usual for one or more of the assumptions of perfect competition to break down.

Various groups have economic power. Large employers, trade unions, large landlords and large owners of capital all may have significant economic power. In general, the greater a group's power and the more it is exercised, the greater will be that group's share of national income.

Markets may be imperfect in other respects:

- There may be *restrictions on the movement of factors* into various firms or industries. For example, trade unions may try to restrict the employment of non-union labour. The government may impose ceilings on rents. Oligopolists may collude to try to prevent new capital entering their industry.
- Firms and households may have *imperfect knowledge*. Workers will not apply for better paid jobs if they do not know such jobs exist. Capitalists will not always make the best investments: they can only really guess at how successful an investment will be.
- People *do not always try to maximize their own economic interest*. Firms may not be profit maximizers. They may not be ruthless employers whose only concern for their workforce is as an 'input' into production. Likewise workers may be motivated by questions of loyalty or commitment rather than by pure selfishness. At the other extreme, employers may treat their workforce badly, even if productivity suffers as a result. They may discriminate between workers on other than economic grounds (e.g. by sex or race). Likewise workers may behave in a belligerent and unco-operative way, even if it means that they lose bonuses or sacrifice their chance of promotion.

To the extent that these imperfections affect the rewards that people earn, so they will affect the distribution of income.

 If a firm is a profit 'satisficer' rather than a profit maximizer, how will this affect the wages that it pays?

Box 8.1

Labour as a Factor of Production
Is this any way to treat a worker?

The theory that wages depend on demand and supply is often referred to as the 'neo-classical' theory of wages. Treated as pure theory it is value free and does not involve moral judgements. It does not say, for example, whether the resulting distribution of income is fair or just.

In practice, however, the neo-classical theory is often used in such a way as to imply moral judgements. It is a theory that tends to be associated with the political right and centre: those who are generally in favour of markets and the capitalist system. Many on the political left are critical of its implied morality. They make the following points:

● By treating labour as a 'factor of production', it demeans labour. Labour is *not* the same as a piece of land or a machine.
● It somehow legitimizes the capitalist system, where some people own land and capital whereas others only have their own labour. It seems to imply that people have a right to the incomes from their property even if that property is highly unequally distributed among the population.
● It implies that labour has no rights to the goods that it produces. These goods are entirely the property of the employer, even though it is the workers who made them.

Karl Marx (1818–83) was highly critical of these values and the way that the capitalist system led to extremes of wealth and poverty. He argued that labour was the only true source of value. After all it is labour that makes machines, labour that tills the land and makes it yield, labour that mines coal and other natural resources. Property, he argued, is therefore a form of theft. When capitalists extract profits from their enterprises, he continued, they are stealing part of the value produced by labour.

Neo-classical economists defend their position against the Marxist 'labour theory of value' by arguing the following:

● They are merely describing the world. If people want to draw pro-capitalist conclusions from their theory, then that is up to them.
● If the labour theory of value is used in any practical way to evaluate costs and output, it will lead to a misallocation of resources. Labour is not the only scarce resource. Land, for example, is also scarce and needs to be included in calculations of costs, otherwise it will be used wastefully.

?   1. Could demand and supply analysis of factor markets be used to criticize a free-market allocation of factor incomes?
2. Assume that it is agreed by everyone that it is morally wrong to treat labour as a mere 'factor of production', with no rights over the goods produced. Does this make the neo-classical theory wrong?

▲ SUMMARY

1. The distribution of income can be examined at a number of levels. We can look at the size distribution of income, the functional distribution of income, and the incomes earned by particular factors of production in particular uses.
2. In perfect markets, factor rewards will be determined by the interaction of the market demand and supply of the factor. Income distribution will depend on the prices of the factors and how their ownership is distributed.
3. Although in perfect markets there will be a tendency for the price of a given type of factor to be equalized by market forces, inequality will persist because of differences in the costs of supplying factors, differences in the quality of factors and inequality in the ownership of factors.
4. In imperfect markets, factor prices (and hence the distribution of income) will be affected by economic power, restrictions on factor movements, imperfect knowledge of market opportunities and non-maximizing behaviour.

8.2 Wage determination under perfect competition

Wages under perfect competition will be determined by the interaction of the demand and supply of labour. To explain the distribution of wage incomes, it is thus necessary to examine the determinants of the supply of and demand for labour.

The supply of labour

We can look at the supply of labour at three levels. The supply of hours by an individual worker, the supply of workers to an individual employer and the total market supply of a given category of labour. Let us examine each in turn.

The supply of hours by an individual worker
Work involves two major costs (or 'disutilities') to the worker:

- When people work they sacrifice leisure.
- The work itself may be unpleasant.

Marginal disutility of work

The extra sacrifice/ hardship to a worker of working an extra unit of time in any given time period (e.g. an extra hour per day).

Each extra hour worked will involve additional disutility. This marginal disutility of work (*MDU*) will tend to *increase* as people work more hours. There are two reasons for this. First, the less the leisure they have left, the greater is the disutility they experience in sacrificing a further hour of leisure. Secondly, the unpleasantness they experience in doing the job will tend to increase due to boredom or tiredness.

This increasing marginal disutility (see Figure 8.3 (a)) will tend to give an upward-sloping supply curve of hours by an individual worker (see Figure 8.3 (b)). The reason is that, in order to persuade people to work more hours, a higher hourly wage must be paid to compensate for the higher marginal disutility incurred. This helps to explain why overtime rates are higher than standard rates.

(a) The marginal disutility of hours worked

(b) The supply of hours worked

Figure 8.3

Under certain circumstances, however, the supply of hours curve might bend backwards (see Figure 8.4). The reason is that when wage rates go up there will be two opposing forces operating on the individual's labour supply.

On the one hand, with higher wages people will tend to work more hours since leisure would now involve a greater sacrifice of income and hence consumption. They

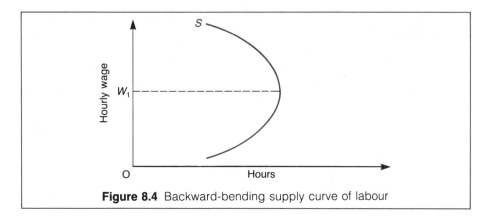

Figure 8.4 Backward-bending supply curve of labour

substitute income for leisure. This is called the substitution effect of the increase in wage rates.

On the other hand, people may feel that with higher wage rates they can afford to work less and have more leisure. This is called the income effect.

The relative magnitude of these two effects determines the slope of the individual's supply curve. It is normally assumed that the substitution effect outweighs the income effect, especially at lower wages. A rise in wages acts as an incentive: it encourages a person to work more hours. It is possible, however, that the income effect might outweigh the substitution effect. Particularly at very high wage rates people say, 'There's not so much point now in doing overtime. I can afford to spend more time at home.'

If the wage rate becomes high enough for the income effect to dominate, the supply curve will begin to slope backwards. This occurs above a wage rate of W_1 in Figure 8.4.

These considerations are particularly important for a government considering tax cuts. The Conservative government of the 1980s argued that cuts in income taxes are like giving people a pay rise, and thus provide an incentive for people to work harder. This analysis is only correct, however, if the substitution effect dominates. If the income effect dominates, people will work *less* after the tax cut. These questions are examined in Chapter 9.

The supply of labour to an individual employer

Under perfect competition the supply of labour to a particular firm will be perfectly elastic, as in Figure 8.2(a). The firm is a 'wage taker' and thus has no power to influence wages. Take the case of a small firm that wishes to employ a temporary typist and thus goes to a secretarial agency. It has to pay the 'going rate', and presumably will be able to employ as many typists as it likes (within reason) at that wage rate.

The market supply of a given type of labour

This will typically be upward sloping. The higher the wages offered in a particular type of job, the more people will want to do that job.

The *position* of the market supply curve of labour will depend on the number of people willing and able to do the job at each given wage rate. This depends on three things:

- The number of qualified people.
- The non-wage benefits of the job, such as the pleasantness of the working

Substitution effect of a rise in wages

Workers will tend to substitute income for leisure as leisure now has a higher opportunity cost. This effect leads to *more* hours being worked as wages rise.

Income effect of a rise in wages

Workers get a higher income for a given number of hours worked and may thus feel they need to work *fewer* hours as wages rise.

*Box 8.2

Using Indifference Curve Analysis to Derive the Individual's Supply Curve of Labour

Indifference curve analysis (see section 3.2) can be used to derive the individual's supply curve of labour. The analysis can show why the supply curve may be backward bending.

(a) The alternatives of income and leisure open to an individual

Assume that an individual can choose the number of hours to work and has 12 hours a day to divide between work and leisure (the remaining 12 being for sleep, shopping, travelling, etc.). In diagram (a) with an hourly wage rate of £5 the individual can move along budget line B_1, which shows all the possible combinations of daily income and leisure hours. For example, at point x the individual has an income of £40 by working 8 hours and taking 4 hours off as leisure.

At an hourly wage of £10 the budget line becomes B_2.

An indifference map can be drawn on this diagram. Each indifference curve shows all those combinations of income and leisure that give the individual a particular level of utility.

Diagram (b) shows three such indifference curves. The curves are bowed in toward the origin, showing that increasingly higher incomes are necessary to compensate for each hour of leisure sacrificed. Curve I_3 shows a higher level of utility than I_2, and I_2 a higher level than I_1.

At a wage rate of £5 per hour, the individual can move

(b) The choice of hours worked at different wage rates

along a budget line of B_1. Point x shows the highest level of utility that can be achieved. The individual thus supplies 8 hours of labour (and takes 4 off in leisure).

At the higher wage rate of £10 per hour, the individual is now on budget line B_2 and maximizes utility at point y by working 9 hours. Thus the higher wage has encouraged the individual to work one more hour. So far, then, the individual's supply curve would be upward sloping: a higher wage rate leading to more labour hours supplied.

At the higher wage rate still of £12.50 per hour, the individual is on budget line B_3, and now maximizes utility at point z. But this means that only 8 hours are now worked. The supply curve has begun to bend backwards. In other words, the individual is now in a position to be able to afford to take more time off in leisure. The income effect has begun to offset the substitution effect.

? 1. Using the analysis developed in Chapter 3, try to show the size of the income and substitution effects when moving from point x to point y and from point y to point z.
2. Illustrate on an indifference diagram the effect on the hours a person works of (a) a cut in the rate of income tax; (b) an increase in child benefit (assuming the person has children).

environment, job satisfaction, status, power, job security, holidays, perks and other fringe benefits.
- The wages and non-wage benefits in alternative jobs.

A change in wages will cause a movement along the supply curve. A change in any of these other three determinants will shift the whole curve.

Which way will the supply curve shift if the wage rates in alternative jobs rise?

Elasticity of supply

We concentrate here on the *market* supply curve of labour for a particular type of job.

The determinants of elasticity of supply

How responsive will the supply of labour be to a change in wages? If market wages go up, will a lot more labour become available or only a little? This responsiveness (elasticity) depends on (a) the difficulties and costs of changing jobs and (b) the time period.

Another way of looking at the elasticity of supply of labour is in terms of the 'mobility of labour': the willingness and ability of labour to move to another job. The greater the difficulties and costs of changing jobs, and the shorter the time period involved, the more immobile will labour be, and hence the less elastic will be the supply curve of labour.

Immobility is of two types: geographical and occupational.

Geographical immobility. Sometimes people have difficulty in moving to another part of the country, or are unwilling to do so. The possible reasons for this geographical immobility include the following:

- The financial costs of moving home.
- The inconvenience of moving.
- Social and family ties.
- Poor availability of housing or other facilities (e.g. schooling) in the new area.
- The higher cost of living in the new area, including perhaps higher commuting costs.
- Ignorance of available jobs elsewhere in the country.
- Fear of the unknown.

Geographical immobility

The lack of ability or willingness of people to move to jobs in other parts of the country.

Occupational immobility. Even if there are alternative jobs vacant in the same town, people may be unable or unwilling to change jobs. This occupational immobility can be due to the following:

- Lack of qualifications or ability to do alternative jobs.
- Less desirable working conditions or fringe benefits in the alternative jobs.
- Ignorance of available jobs.
- Fear of the unknown.

Occupational immobility

The lack of ability or willingness of people to move to other jobs irrespective of location.

The mobility of labour is thus higher when there are alternative jobs in the same location, when alternative jobs require similar skills and when people have good information about these jobs. It is also much higher in the long run, when people have the time to acquire new skills and when the education system has time to adapt to the changing demands of industry.

1. Assume that there is a growing demand for computer programmers. As a result more people train to become programmers. Does this represent a rightward shift in the supply curve of programmers, or merely the supply curve becoming more elastic in the long run, or both? Explain.
2. Which is likely to be more elastic, the supply of coal miners or the supply of shop assistants? Explain.

Box 8.3

It's a Long Way to Commute

A novel way to overcome the problem of geographical immobility has been adopted by many construction firms in London.

There is a shortage of bricklayers, carpenters, plumbers, etc., in London, with jobs available on many construction sites but not enough workers to fill them. In the north of England, however, there are construction workers available but not enough jobs. So why don't the workers move south? The main reason for this geographical immobility is the cost of living in London, especially the cost of accommodation – rents and house prices.

The answer the construction firms have come up with is to 'bus' the workers to the jobs. On Sunday night or Monday morning, coaches or mini-buses bring the workers south. During the week they are accommodated in caravans or huts on the construction site. Then on Friday evening they are taken back north again.

> **?** 1. What effect will this policy have on the relative wages of construction workers in the north and south?
> 2. If construction firms were not prepared to lay on this transport, what would happen?

Economic rent and transfer earnings

The earnings of a factor of production can be split into two elements. The relative size of these two elements depends on the elasticity of supply of that factor.

Transfer earnings are what a factor must earn to prevent it from moving to an alternative use. In the case of labour it is what people must be paid to persuade them to stay in their present job.

Economic rent is anything over and above transfer earnings.

For example, take the case of Mary Jones. She is the manager of a high street store and earns £20 000 per year. She could earn £15 000 in another job and would indeed transfer to that other job if her salary were cut below £15 000. Thus her transfer earnings are £15 000. The remaining £5000 is her economic rent. Economic rent equals total earnings minus transfer earnings.

Now take the case of a market supply curve – say the market for nurses. This is illustrated in Figure 8.5. Starting at point *a* and moving towards point *b*, as the wage rate is raised so more nurses are attracted to the profession. At each higher wage the *new* nurses attracted are getting just enough to persuade them to transfer into the profession: the wage for them is entirely transfer earnings. But nurses *already* in the profession will get economic rent; after all, they are now getting more than the minimum necessary to keep them in the profession.

Workers' economic rent is thus the difference between the actual wage rate and the point on the supply curve at which they entered the market.

Thus at the market wage W_m (in Figure 8.5) the total economic rent of all those employed is shown by area 1 – the area above the supply curve. Area 2 shows transfer earnings.

The less elastic the supply curve, the greater will be the proportion that is economic rent. Why? The bigger the wage increase necessary to attract extra workers, the more economic rent existing workers will gain.

> **Transfer earnings**
> What a factor must earn to prevent it from moving to another use/occupation. Total transfer earnings are the area under the supply curve to the left of current factor employment.

> **Economic rent**
> The excess that a factor is paid over its transfer earnings. Total economic rent is the area between the supply curve and the factor price.

 Draw a perfectly elastic supply curve. Will workers receive any economic rent? Explain the reason for your answer.

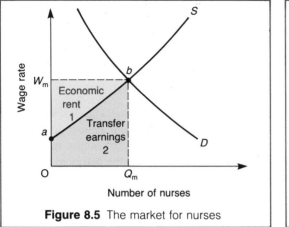

Figure 8.5 The market for nurses

Figure 8.6 The market for Dame Edna Everidge

Now take the extreme position of a totally inelastic supply curve. The simplest example is that of a person with a unique talent, like a famous show business megastar, such as Dame Edna Everidge (see Figure 8.6). The quantity of Dame Ednas is fixed. There is only one: she is unique. As a result her income is determined entirely by demand, and is entirely economic rent. The more popular she is, the higher the demand for her performances and the higher the income she can command. Thus megastars can earn very high incomes.

Conversely, once a star's popularity wanes, his or her income can plummet, as many show business failures can confirm.

Identifying transfer earnings and economic rent. The precise division of a worker's income between transfer earnings and economic rent will depend on the context.

Only a small cut in wages will be necessary before workers are encouraged to move to the same job in another firm in the same town (assuming there are such jobs). In this context the elasticity of labour supply is high. Thus economic rents are low and transfer earnings are high.

The same workers, however, would need a much larger cut in wages to persuade them to move to another town and into a totally new job. Transfer earnings thus tend to be much lower between different occupations. Supply is less elastic and consequently economic rents are correspondingly higher.

> **?** If a firm faces a shortage of workers with very specific skills, it may decide to undertake the necessary training itself. If, on the other hand, it faces a shortage of unskilled workers, it may well offer a small wage increase in order to obtain the extra labour. In the first case it is responding to an increase in demand for labour by attempting to shift the supply curve. In the second case it is merely allowing a movement along the supply curve. Use a demand and supply diagram to illustrate each case. Given that elasticity of supply is different in each case, do you think that these are the best policies for the firm to follow? What would happen to wages and economic rent if it used the second policy in the first case?

Quasi-rent. In the long run, people's economic rent may be competed away as newly trained workers enter the market. In other words, labour supply curves may be inelastic in the short run, but much more elastic in the long run.

Economic rent that applies only in the short run as a result of skill shortages is known as quasi-rent.

Quasi-rent
Temporary economic rent arising from short-run supply inelasticity.

The demand for labour: the marginal productivity theory

The traditional 'neo-classical' theory of the firm assumes that firms aim to maximize profits. The same assumption is made in the neo-classical theory of labour demand. This theory is generally known as the marginal productivity theory

The profit-maximizing approach

How many workers will a profit-maximizing firm want to employ? The firm will answer this question by weighing up the costs of employing extra labour against the benefits. It will use exactly the same principles as in deciding how much output to produce.

In the goods market, the firm will maximize profits where the marginal cost of an extra unit of *goods* produced equals the marginal revenue from selling it: $MC=MR$.

In the labour market, the firm will maximize profits where the marginal cost of employing an extra *worker* equals the marginal revenue that the worker's output earns for the firm: MC of labour = MR of labour. The reasoning is simple. If an extra worker adds more to a firm's revenue than to its costs, the firm's profits will increase. It will be worth employing that worker. But as more workers are employed, diminishing returns to labour will set in. Each extra worker will produce less than the previous one, and thus earn less revenue for the firm. Eventually the marginal revenue from extra workers will fall to the level of their marginal cost. At that point the firm will stop employing extra workers. There are no additional profits to be gained. Profits are at a maximum.

Measuring the marginal cost and revenue of labour

Marginal cost of labour (MC_L). This is the extra cost of employing one more worker. Under perfect competition the firm is too small to affect the market wage. It faces a horizontal supply curve (see Figure 8.2(a)). Thus the additional cost of employing one more person will simply be the wage: $MC_L = W$.

Marginal revenue of labour (MRP_L). The marginal revenue the firm gains from employing one more worker is called the marginal revenue product of labour. The MRP_L is found by multiplying two elements – the *marginal physical product* of labour (MPP_L) and the marginal revenue gained by selling one more unit of output (MR):

$$MRP_L = MPP_L \times MR$$

The MPP_L is the extra output produced by the last worker. Thus if the last worker produces 100 tonnes of output per week (MPP_L), and if the firm earns an extra £2 for each additional tonne sold (MR), then the worker's MRP is £200. This extra worker is adding £200 to the firm's revenue.

A related concept is the value of the marginal product of labour (VMP_L). This is the MPP_L multiplied by the *price* of the good (rather than its MR):

$$VMP_L = MPP_L \times P$$

As we saw in Chapter 5, under perfect competition $P = MR$, since the firm is a price taker in the goods market. Thus $MRP_L = VMP_L$ under perfect competition. The distinction between MRP_L and VMP_L becomes significant, however, when we consider firms operating in imperfect markets (see section 8.3).

The profit-maximizing level of employment for a firm

The MPP_L curve is illustrated in Figure 8.7. As more workers are employed there will come a point when diminishing returns set in (point *x*). The MPP_L curve thus slopes

Figure 8.7 Marginal physical product of labour curve

Figure 8.8 The profit-maximizing level of employment

down after this point. The MRP_L curve will be a similar shape to the MPP_L curve, since it is merely being multiplied by a constant figure, MR. (Under perfect competition $MR = P$ and does not vary with output.) The MRP_L curve is illustrated in Figure 8.8, along with the MC_L 'curve'.

? Why is the MC_L curve horizontal?

Profits will be maximized at an employment level of Q_e, where MC_L (i.e. W) = MRP_L. Why? At levels of employment below Q_e, MRP_L exceeds MC_L. The firm will increase profits by employing more labour. At levels of employment above Q_e, MC_L exceeds MRP_L. In this case the firm will increase profits by reducing employment.

Derivation of the firm's demand curve for labour
No matter what the wage rate, the quantity of labour demanded will be found from the intersection of W and MRP_L (see Figure 8.9).

Thus the MRP_L curve will show the quantity of labour employed at each wage rate. But this is just what the demand curve for labour shows. Thus the MRP_L curve is the demand curve for labour.

There are three determinants of the demand for labour:

- The wage. This determines the position *on* the demand curve. (Strictly speaking, we should refer here to the wage determining the 'quantity demanded' rather than the 'demand'.)
- The productivity of labour (MPP_L). This determines the position *of* the demand curve.
- The demand for the good. The higher the market demand for the good, the higher will be its market price, and hence the higher will be the MR, and thus the MRP_L. This too determines the position of the demand curve. It illustrates just how the demand for labour (and other factors) is *derived* from the demand for the good.

A change in the wage will be represented by a movement *along* the demand curve for labour. A change in the productivity of labour or the demand for the good will *shift* the curve.

Figure 8.9 Deriving the firm's demand curve for labour

Figure 8.10 Using the firm's demand curves for labour to derive the industry demand curve for labour

Derivation of the industry demand curve for labour

This will not simply be the sum of the demand curves of the individual firms. The firm's demand curve is based on a constant *P* and *MR*, no matter how many workers the firm employs (this is one of the assumptions of perfect competition). In Figure 8.10, when the wage falls from W_1 to W_2 the firm will employ more labour by moving from point *a* to point *b* along its demand curve MRP_1.

The trouble with this analysis is that when the wage rate falls it will affect *all* employers. They will all want to employ more labour. But when they do, the total industry output will increase, and hence *P* (and *MR*) will be pushed down. This will shift the firm's *MRP* curve to the left and lead to a lower level of employment at point *c*. Therefore, when we allow for the effect of lower wages on the market price of the good, the firm's demand curve for labour will be the dotted line passing through points *a* and *c*.

Thus the *industry* demand curve for labour is the (horizontal) sum of the *dotted* lines for each firm, and is therefore less elastic than the firm's *MRP* curve.

> **?** What will determine the elasticity of this curve?

The elasticity of demand for labour

The elasticity of demand for labour (with respect to changes in wages) will be greater:

- The greater the price elasticity of demand for the good. A fall in *W* will lead to higher employment and more output. This will drive *P* down. If the demand for the good is elastic, this fall in *P* will lead to a lot more being sold and hence to a lot more people being employed.
- The easier it is to substitute labour for other factors and vice versa. If labour can be readily substituted for other factors, then a reduction in *W* will lead to a large increase in labour used to replace these other factors.
- The greater the elasticity of supply of complementary factors. If wages fall, a lot more labour will be demanded if plenty of complementary factors can be obtained at little increase in their price.

- The greater the elasticity of supply of substitute factors. If wages fall and more labour is used, fewer substitute factors will be demanded and their price will fall. If their supply is elastic, a lot fewer will be supplied and therefore a lot more labour will be used instead.
- The greater the wage cost as a proportion of total costs. If wages are a large proportion of total costs and wages fall, total costs will fall significantly; therefore production will increase significantly, and so too will the demand for labour.
- The longer the time period. Given sufficient time, firms can respond to a fall in wages by reorganizing their production processes to make use of the now relatively cheap labour.

? For each of the following jobs, check through the above list of determinants (excluding the last), and try to decide whether demand would be relatively elastic or inelastic: Firemen; Bus conductors; Typists; Carpenters; Bus drivers; Punch and Judy operators; Farm workers; Car workers

Wages and profits under perfect competition

The wage rate (W) will be determined by the interaction of demand and supply in the labour market. This will be equal to the value of the output that the last person produces (VMP_L or MRP_L).

Profits to the individual firm will arise from the fact that the MRP_L (VMP_L) curve slopes downward (diminishing returns). Thus the last worker adds less to the revenue of firms than previous workers already employed.

If *all* workers in the firm receive a wage equal to the MRP of the *last* worker, everyone but the last worker will receive a wage less than their MRP. This excess of MRP_L over W of previous workers provides a surplus to the firm (see Figure 8.11). In a simple two-factor model (labour and capital), this surplus will be the same as profits.

Perfect competition between firms will ensure that profits are kept down to *normal* profits. If the surplus over wages is such that *supernormal* profits are made, new firms will enter the industry. The price of the good (and hence VMP_L and MRP_L) will fall, and the wage will be bid up, until only normal profits remain.

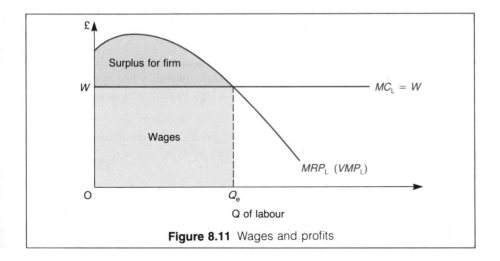

Figure 8.11 Wages and profits

Equality and inequality under perfect competition

The mythical world of perfect wage equality

Under certain very strict assumptions a perfectly competitive market will lead to perfect equality of wages. All workers will earn exactly the same. These strict assumptions are as follows:

- All workers have identical abilities.
- There is perfect mobility of labour.
- All jobs are equally attractive.
- All workers and employers have perfect knowledge.
- Wages are determined entirely by demand and supply.

Given these assumptions, if consumer demand rose in any industry, the demand for labour would rise. As a result, wages would begin to rise. Immediately workers would flood into this industry, attracted by the higher wages. Very quickly, then, the wage would be competed back down to the level in the rest of the economy. Likewise if wages began to fall in any industry, workers would leave, thereby eliminating any labour surplus and preventing the fall in wages.

Under these conditions, therefore, not only would the labour supply curve to a *firm* be infinitely elastic, but so too would the labour supply curve to each *industry* at the universal wage.

Of course, in the real world these conditions do not hold. Huge inequalities of wages exist. A stockbroker in the City can earn fifty times as much a shop assistant. But even if markets *were* perfect, inequality would be expected to persist.

Causes of inequality under perfect competition

In the short run, inequality will exist under perfect competition because of the time it takes for changes in demand and supply conditions to bring new long-run equilibria. Thus expanding industries will tend to pay higher wages than contracting industries.

But even after enough time has elapsed for all adjustments to be made to changes in demand and supply, long-run wage differentials will still exist for the following reasons:

- Workers do not have identical abilities. Some people are strong while others are weak. Some people are intelligent, while others are not. Some people are dextrous while others are clumsy. Education and training can only go a certain way to eliminating these differences in ability.
- Workers are not perfectly mobile, even in the long run. People have different preferences about where they want to live and the jobs they like to do.
- Jobs differ enormously in terms of the skills they require and in terms of their pleasantness or unpleasantness.

What is more, since demand and supply conditions are constantly changing, long-run general equilibrium throughout the economy may never be reached.

Conclusions: Who are the poor? Who are the rich?

The poor will be those whose labour is in low demand or high supply. Low demand will be due to low demand for the good or low labour productivity. High supply will be due to low mobility out of contracting industries or to a surplus of people with the same skills or qualifications. Thus workers will be poor, for example, who possess few skills, are unfit, are working in contracting industries, do not want to move from the area and will not or cannot retrain.

The rich will be those whose labour is in high demand or low supply. Thus workers who possess skills or talents which are in short supply, especially those skills which take a long time for others to acquire, and those who are working in expanding industries will tend to earn high wages.

Although the movement of labour from low-paid to high-paid jobs will tend to reduce wage differentials, considerable inequality will persist even under perfect competition. It is a fallacy, therefore, to believe that simply by 'freeing up' markets and encouraging workers to 'stand on their own feet' or 'get on their bikes' poverty and inequality will be eliminated.

What is more, in the real world there exist many market imperfections. These tend to make inequality greater. These imperfections are examined in the next section.

Finally, income inequality under capitalism will also be due to unequal distribution of the ownership of land and capital. Even under perfect competition, considerable inequality will therefore exist if wealth is concentrated in the hands of the few.

▲ SUMMARY

1. Wages in a perfect market will be determined by supply and demand.
2. The supply curve of hours by an individual worker will reflect the increasing marginal disutility of work. Its shape will depend on the relative sizes of the substitution and income effects of a wage change. The substitution effect will be positive. A higher wage will encourage people to work more by substituting wages for leisure. The income effect, however, will be negative. A higher wage will make people feel that they can afford to work less. If the income effect is bigger than the substitution effect, the supply of hours curve will bend backwards.
3. The supply of labour to a particular employer under perfect competition will be infinitely elastic.
4. The market supply will typically be upward sloping. Its elasticity will depend on labour mobility. Immobility is of two types: geographical and occupational.
5. The elasticity of supply will determine what proportion of wages consists of transfer earnings and what proportion consists of economic rent. Transfer earnings are the wages that must be paid to prevent a worker transferring

to another job. Economic rent is any wages above transfer earnings.
6. The demand for labour will depend on a worker's marginal revenue product. This is the extra revenue that a firm will gain from the output of an extra worker. The profit-maximizing firm will continue taking on extra workers until MRP_L is equal to MC_L (= W under perfect competition).
7. The elasticity of demand for labour will depend on the elasticity of demand for the good, the ease of substituting labour for other factors and vice versa, the elasticity of supply of substitute and complementary factors, wages as a proportion of total costs, and the time period involved.
8. Although market forces will tend to lead to the elimination of differentials as workers move from low-paid to high-paid jobs, nevertheless inequality can persist even under perfect competition. People have different abilities and skills; people are not perfectly mobile; and jobs differ in their labour requirements.
9. Inequality is also caused by market imperfections and by unequal ownership of land and capital.

8.3 Wage determination in imperfect markets

In the real world, firms and/or workers are likely to have the power to influence wages. This is one of the major types of market imperfection.

Firms may have market power in selling goods: in other words, they may be operating under conditions of monopoly, oligopoly or monopolistic competition.

Firms may also have market power in employing labour. When a firm is the only employer of a certain type of labour, this situation is called a monopsony. British Rail is a monopsony employer of train drivers. When a factory is the only employer of

Monopsony
A market with a single buyer or employer.

certain types of labour in that district, it therefore has local monopsony power. When there are just a few employers, this is called oligopsony

Oligopsony

A market with just a few buyers or employers.

Workers may have market power as members of unions. When a single union bargains on behalf of a certain type of labour, it is acting as a monopolist. When there is more than one union, they are oligopolists.

Bilateral monopoly

Where a monopsony buyer faces a monopoly seller.

When a monopsonist employer faces a monopolist union, the situation is called bilateral monopoly

Firms with market power in selling goods (monopoly, etc.)

This section assumes that there is still perfect competition in the labour market, but that there is power in the goods market. This type of situation is not uncommon. Often large firms have considerable market power in selling their output and yet compete for certain categories of labour (e.g. electricians, secretaries) with many other firms.

According to the theory we developed above, an employer will maximize profits by employing labour up to the point where $W = MRP_L$. Where firms operate under *perfect competition* in the goods market, MR will equal P: they are price takers and thus one more unit sold earns the full market price. Thus, as we saw, MRP_L (i.e. $MPP_L \times MR$) = VMP_L (i.e. $MPP_L \times P$). Therefore if $W = MRP_L$, W also equals VMP_L. In other words, workers will be paid a wage equal to the value of the last worker's output (VMP_L).

Where firms have market *power* in the goods market, however, MR will be *less* than P. Thus MRP_L will be less than VMP_L. But this will mean that workers will now be paid a wage less than the value of the last worker's output: ($W < VMP_L$). This has been referred to as one form of 'monopoly exploitation' of labour.

In Figure 8.12 instead of employing Q_2 labour (where $W = VMP_L$) the monopolist will employ Q_1 labour (where $W = MRP_L$). Note that at Q_1, $W < VMP_L$.

Other things being equal, a monopolist will produce less than a competitive industry. There will thus be a lower demand for labour. If a lot of firms employing a particular type of labour have market power in their respective goods markets, the general level of demand for this type of labour will be lower and thus wages will tend to be lower. The ratio of profits to wages in such industries is likely to be higher than under perfect competition, since there is not the competition from new entrants to

Figure 8.12 Firms with power in the goods market but perfect competition in the labour market

drive profits down and wages up. This has also been referred to as a form of exploitation of labour.

Nevertheless, economies of scale in such industries may lead to greater output and possibly greater employment (unless the economies of scale involve using less of this type of labour) and hence higher wages. Also the higher profits may lead to higher investment, faster growth and hence higher wages in the long run.

Firms with market power in employing labour (monopsony, etc.)

When only one or a few firms employ a particular type of labour, they have power to influence wages. Thus monopsonists or oligopsonists are 'wage makers' not 'wage takers'. A large employer in a small town, for example, may have considerable power to resist wage increases or even to force wages down.

Such firms face an upward-sloping supply curve of labour. This is illustrated in Figure 8.13. If the firm wants to take on more labour, it will have to pay higher wages to attract workers away from other industries. But conversely, by employing less labour it can get away with paying lower wages.

The supply curve shows the wage that must be paid to attract a given quantity of labour. The wage it pays is the *average cost* to the firm of employing labour (AC_L). The supply curve is also therefore the AC_L curve.

The *marginal cost* of employing one more worker (MC_L) will be above the wage (AC_L). The reason is that wages have to be raised to attract extra workers. The MC_L will thus be the new higher wage paid to the new employee *plus* the small rise in the total wages bill for existing employees: after all, they will be paid the higher wage too.

The profit-maximizing employment of labour would be at Q_1, where $MC_L = MRP_L$. The wage paid would thus be W_1.

If this had been a perfectly competitive labour market, employment would have been at the higher level Q_2, and the wage at the higher level W_2, where $W = MRP_L$. What in effect the monopsonist is doing, therefore, is forcing the wage rate down by restricting the number of workers employed. This will allow the monopsonist to make larger profits, while at the same time workers are getting less than even the *last* worker's *MRP*. Critics of the capitalist system have referred to this as another form of exploitation.

Figure 8.13 Monopsony

1. Table 8.1 shows data for a monopsonist employer. Fill in the missing figures for columns (3) and (4). How many workers should the firm employ if it wishes to maximize profits?

Table 8.1

Number of workers (1)	Wage rate (£) (2)	Total cost of labour (£) (3)	Marginal cost of labour (£) (4)	Marginal revenue product (£) (5)
1	100	100		230
			110	
2	105	210		240
			120	
3	110	330		240
			130	
4	115	460		230
			140	
5	120	600		210
			150	
6	125	755		190
			160	
7	130	910		170
			170	
8	135	1080		150
			180	
9	140	1260		130
			190	
10	145	1450		

2. Will a monopsony typically be a monopoly? Try to think of some examples of monopsonists that are not monopolists, and monopolists that are not monopsonists.

Labour with market power (union monopoly or oligopoly)

The extent to which unions will succeed in pushing up wages depends on their power and militancy. It also depends on the power of firms to resist and on their ability to pay higher wages. In particular, the scope for unions to gain a better deal for their members depends on the sort of market in which the employers are producing.

If the employers are producing under perfect or monopolistic competition, unions can only raise wages at the expense of employment. Firms are only earning normal profit. Thus if unions force up wages, the marginal firms will go bankrupt and leave the industry. Fewer workers will be employed. The fall in output will lead to higher prices. This will enable the remaining firms to pay higher wages.

Figure 8.14 illustrates these effects. If unions force wages up from W_1 to W_2, employment will fall from Q_1 to Q_2. There will be a surplus of people ($Q_3 - Q_2$) wishing to work in this industry for whom no jobs are available.

The union is in a doubly weak position. Not only will jobs be lost as a result of

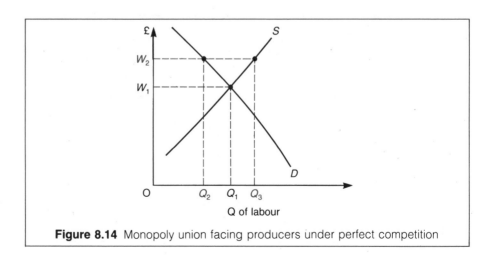

Figure 8.14 Monopoly union facing producers under perfect competition

Box 8.4

Life at the Mill
Monopsony in Victorian times

A dramatic illustration of the effects of extreme monopsony power is that of the textile mill in Victorian England. When a mill was the only employer in a small town, or when factory owners colluded as oligopsonists, and when there was no union to counterbalance the power of the employer, things could be very bad for the worker. Very low pay would be combined with often appalling working conditions.

Friedrich Engels described the life of the textile factory worker as follows:

> The factory worker is condemned to allow his physical and mental powers to become atrophied. From the age of eight he enters an occupation which bores him all day long. And there is no respite from this boredom. The machine works ceaselessly. Its wheels, belts and spindles hum and rattle ceaselessly in his ears, and if he thinks of taking even a moment's rest, the overlooker is always there to punish him with a fine. It is nothing less than torture of the severest kind to which the workers are subjected by being condemned to a life-sentence in the factory, in the service of a machine which never stops. It is not only the body of the worker which is stunted, but also his mind. It would indeed be difficult to find a better way of making a man slow-witted than to turn him into a factory worker.[1]

What were these fines that the overlooker could impose on the worker? Engels quotes an example of some typical factory rules:

> 1st. The door of the lodge will be closed ten minutes after the engine starts every morning, and no weaver will afterwards be admitted till breakfast-time. Any weaver who may be absent during that time shall forfeit three-pence per loom.
> 2nd. Weavers absent at any other time when the engine is working, will be charged three-pence per hour each loom for such absence; and weavers leaving the room when the engine is working without the consent of the overlooker, shall forfeit three-pence.

> 3rd. Weavers not being provided with nippers or shears, shall forfeit one penny for every day they are so unprovided.
> 9th. All shuttles, temples, brushes, oil-cans, wheels, windows, etc., if broken, shall be paid for by the weaver.
> 10th. One week's notice will be required previous to any weaver leaving the mill, or the work in hand will be forfeited. The master may discharge any hand without notice, for bad work or mis-conduct.
> 11th. If any hand in the mill be seen talking to another, whistling, or singing [he or she] will be fined sixpence.[2]

I have before me another set of factory rules, which state that a worker who is three minutes late loses a quarter of an hour's pay, while anyone who is 20 minutes late loses a quarter of a day's pay. An operative who does not arrive at the factory until after breakfast is fined 1s. on Mondays and 6d. on other days. These regulations were in force at the Phoenix Mill, Jersey Street, Manchester. It will be argued that such rules are necessary to ensure the smooth co-ordination of the various processes carried on in a big, well-run factory. It will be said that stern discipline of this kind is just as necessary in the factory as in the army. That may be true enough, but how can one defend the state of society which can only survive by the exercise of such shameful tyranny?[3]

? 1. Why did competition between employers not force up wages and improve working conditions?
2. Were the workers making a 'rational economic decision' when they chose to work in such factories?

[1] F. Engels, *The Condition of the Working Class in England*, translated by W. O. Henderson and W. H. Chaloner (Basil Blackwell, 1971), pp. 199–200.
[2] These rules appeared in J. Leach, *Stubborn Facts from the Factories*, p. 13, quoted in Engels *op. cit.*, pp. 200–1.
[3] Engels, *op. cit.*, pp. 201–2.

---

forcing up the wage, but there is also a danger that these unemployed people could undercut the union wage, unless the union can prevent firms employing non-unionized labour.

Wages can only be increased without a reduction in the level of employment if, as part of the bargain, the productivity of labour is increased. This is called a productivity deal.

? Which of the following unions find themselves in a weak bargaining position for the above reasons?
(a) The National Union of Seamen.
(b) The shopworkers' union (USDAW).
(c) The National Union of Mineworkers.
(d) The farmworkers' union (part of the Transport and General Workers' Union).

Productivity deal
Where, in return for a wage increase, a union agrees to changes in working practices that will increase output per worker.

In a competitive market, then, the union is faced with the choice between wages and jobs. Its actions will thus depend on its objectives.

If it wants to *maximize employment*, it will have to content itself with a wage of W_1 in Figure 8.14, unless productivity deals can be negotiated. At W_1, Q_1 workers will be employed. Above W_1 fewer than Q_1 workers will be *demanded*. Below W_1 fewer than Q_1 workers will be *supplied*.

If, on the other hand, it wants to *maximize the total amount of wages* paid by employers, it will continue pushing up the wage rate as long as the demand for labour is inelastic. As long as it is inelastic the increase in wage rates will be proportionately larger than the fall in employment, thereby causing total wage payments to rise. As wages are raised, however, firms will increasingly be forced to cut back on labour. The elasticity of demand is likely to increase as wages rise. When the elasticity has risen to unity, total incomes of workers will be at a maximum.

Unions may press for a higher wage still, even though it will mean that the firm pays out less in total wages. This is likely if unions are merely concerned to *maximize the incomes of remaining members* after natural wastage. Natural wastage is when people leave their job not because they have been made redundant, but because they have retired or moved to another job.

An example will show how the remaining workers will benefit by pushing wages above the level that maximizes the firm's wage bill. In Table 8.2 a wage of £200 maximizes the total wages paid. The union may still prefer a wage of £250, however, even though the wage bill falls to £17 500, if the reduction of 30 in the workforce can be made by natural wastage.

Natural wastage

Where a firm wishing to reduce its workforce does so by not replacing those who leave or retire.

Table 8.2

Wage rate (weekly)	Number of workers employed	Total wages paid (per week)
£150	120	£18 000
£200	100	£20 000
£250	70	£17 500

Firms and labour with market power (bilateral monopoly)

What happens when a union monopoly faces a monopsony employer? What will the wage be? What will the level of employment be? Unfortunately economic theory cannot give a precise answer to these questions. There is no 'equilibrium' level as such. Ultimately the level of wages and employment will depend on the relative bargaining strengths and skills of unions and management.

Nevertheless, economic theory can make some contribution to predicting the outcome of negotiations. It can identify the limits within which wages will be set. The lower limit will be that which a monopsonist would pay in the absence of a union. The upper limit will be where a firm would be driven into bankruptcy. Also economic theory can examine the consequences of various wage rates for employment.

Strange as it may seem, unions may well be in a stronger position to make substantial gains for their members when they are facing a powerful employer. There is often considerable scope for them to increase wages *without* this leading to a reduction in employment, or even for them to increase both wages *and* employment. Figure 8.15 shows how this can be so.

Assume first that there is no union. The monopsonist will maximize profits by employing Q_1 workers at a wage of W_1. (Q_1 is where $MRP_L = MC_L$.)

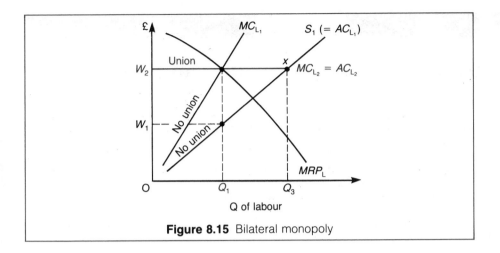

Figure 8.15 Bilateral monopoly

What happens when a union is introduced into this situation? Wages will now be set by negotiation between unions and management. Once the wage has been agreed, any reduction in the labour force will not affect that wage. In other words, the employer can no longer drive the wage rate down by employing fewer workers. If it tried to pay less than the agreed wage, it could well be faced by a strike, and thus have a zero supply of labour!

Similarly, if the employer decided to take on *more* workers, it would not have to *increase* the wage, as long as the negotiated wage were above the free-market wage: as long as the wage rate were above that given by the supply curve S_1.

The effect of this is to give a new supply curve that is horizontal up to the point where it meets the original supply curve. For example, let us assume that the union succeeds in negotiating a wage rate of W_2 in Figure 8.15. The supply curve will be horizontal at this level to the left of point x. To the right of this point it will follow the original supply curve S_1, since to acquire more than Q_3 workers the employer would have to raise the wage above W_2.

If the supply curve is horizontal to the left of point x at a level of W_2, so too will be the MC_L curve. The reason is simply that the extra cost to the employer of taking on an extra worker (up to Q_3) is merely the wage rate: no rise has to be given to existing employees. If MC_L is equal to the wage, the profit-maximizing level of employment ($MC_L = MRP_L$) will now be where $W = MRP_L$. At a negotiated wage rate of W_2, the firm will therefore choose to employ Q_1 workers.

What this means is that the union can push the wage right up from W_1 to W_2 and the firm will still *want* to employ Q_1. In other words, a wage rise can be obtained *without* a reduction in employment.

 If the negotiated wage rate were somewhere between W_1 and W_2, what would happen to employment?

The union could go further still. By threatening industrial action, it may be able to gain wages above W_2 and still insist that Q_1 workers are employed (i.e. no redundancies). The firm may be prepared to see profits drop right down to normal level rather than face a strike and risk losses. The absolute upper limit to wages will be that at which the firm is forced to close down.

Box 8.5

The Origins of the Labour Movement

Perhaps rather surprisingly, the origins of the labour movement do *not* lie within a general political movement or amongst unskilled workers, despite the fact that such workers would probably have had the most to gain from the market power that unions provided.

Instead, the early unions, or 'artisan societies' as they were known, were conservative in their views and had a membership based on skilled handicraft workers – the 'aristocracy of labour'. Their principal interest, like many professional associations today, was to support the level of their members' incomes by regulating the flow of labour. The printers, for example, immediately prior to industrialization had policies whereby not only were foreigners excluded from the trade, but new workers were expected to undertake a seven-year apprenticeship with tight restrictions on the number of apprentices allowed.

Unionism amongst *unskilled* workers developed during the 1880s. Industrialization had caused the nature of many jobs to change. Technical innovation had brought about a high degree of deskilling, and there was a massive shift of labour from agriculture to industry, expanding the potential union base. Coupled with this there was the capitalist system itself, which in its early years was openly exploitative, with low wages, long hours and poor working conditions.

Thus the unions that developed as a result of these forces were different in character and nature. Their memberships were large by comparison to previous unions; they were less conservative and were often politically linked to socialism; and last but not least, these unions were prepared to use strike tactics to gain their demands, tactics which (as a result of the modified Combination Laws of 1799) were viewed as a 'criminal conspiracy'.

Hostility from both the legal system and the capitalist entrepreneur was a key factor in the slow development of union membership. Only 11 per cent or 1 576 000 of adult males in manual occupations were in an effective union in 1892. It was not until after the First World War that there was a substantial growth in the labour movement. By 1920, 8 348 300 workers (45 per cent of the total labour force) were union members.[4]

There are two points of interest concerning this historical development of the union movement. First, as union membership grew, unions' tactics became more violent and aggressive. Secondly, during these early years, unions generally had more success in improving working conditions than in influencing money wages.

1. What professional associations can you identify that have adopted strategies similar to those of the early skilled-worker unions?
2. What factors following 1919 might account for the growth in union membership?

[4] K. Hawkins, *Trade Unions* (Hutchinson University Library, 1981), p. 78.

Collective bargaining

Sometimes when unions and management negotiate, *both* sides can gain from the resulting agreement. For example, the introduction of new technology may allow higher wages, improved working conditions and higher profits. Usually, however, one side's gain is the other's loss. Higher wages mean lower profits. Either way, both sides will want to gain the maximum for themselves.

The outcome of the negotiations will depend on the relative bargaining strengths of both sides. In bargaining there are various threats or promises that either side can make. To be effective, of course, it must be believed by the other side that the threat or promise will be carried out.

Union threats

Strikes. These are the union's ultimate weapon. Their effectiveness will depend on whether they can bring production to a halt. This in turn depends on the following:

- The number of workers involved.
- How crucial those workers are to the production process.

- The length of time the strike continues.
- The ability of the firm to by-pass the strike by drawing on stocks, using non-unionized labour, using other techniques of production that avoid having to use the workers on strike, and using other factories not involved in the dispute.

Picketing. Picketing is where union members gather at the entrance to a firm and attempt to dissuade workers from entering – not only the members of the union on strike, but also the members of other unions not directly involved and whose support would be helpful in the dispute. Workers are often unwilling to cross picket lines, even if they are not directly involved in the dispute themselves.

Unions may also attempt to engage in secondary picketing. This is where the union pickets a firm not directly involved in the dispute. Thus coal miners might picket a power station to try to prevent the shipment of coal into it. Secondary picketing was made illegal in the UK by the 1980 Employment Act.

Working to rule. This is where union members are instructed to stick to the letter of their job descriptions and to refuse to take on any extra duties. The effect is to slow down production. It is obviously less effective than a strike in the short run, but at the same time it is much less costly to union members, who still continue to be paid. A union can thus continue with this type of action for much longer, and, despite the fact it can also survive longer, the firm may eventually be forced to give in.

Non-co-operation. This is simply where the union refuses to co-operate in ways to increase the efficiency of the firm, such as through the introduction of new machines, new work practices, new factory organization and so on. Even though the firm may well be able to impose these changes on the workforce, it would probably get better results if it had the goodwill of the union.

Union promises

In return for higher wages and better working conditions, the union may offer one or more of the following.

No strikes. This could be a formal no-strike agreement, or an informal promise not to strike or take other industrial action provided the firm honours its side of the bargain.

Increased productivity. The union could agree to a reorganization of the workforce and to the introduction of new machines and/or new methods of production; or it could simply promise that its members would work more efficiently.

Reductions in the workforce. The union could co-operate in reducing the size of the workforce. Unless the firm were facing a financial crisis, the union would normally only be prepared to co-operate in this if it were through natural wastage, or if those made redundant were given generous redundancy payments.

Long-term deals. In return for a substantial pay increase, the union may be prepared not to submit another claim for at least two years.

Employers' threats

Plant closure. The ultimate threat of an employer is to close down a plant with the loss of jobs to the workers. This threat might be taken seriously by the unions if the firm can simply move its business to another plant which does not employ union members. The major newspapers in England moved out of Fleet Street during the 1980s to escape what they claimed were costly union restrictive practices.

Picketing

Where people on strike gather at the entrance to the firm and attempt to dissuade workers or delivery vehicles from entering.

Secondary picketing

Where workers picket a firm not directly involved in the dispute.

Lock-outs. This is where union members are temporarily laid off until they are prepared to agree to the firm's conditions.

Redundancies. Employers frequently use this threat to try to resist wage increases. In terms of Figure 8.15, they attempt to argue that they cannot afford to employ so many workers: they claim that they are forced to move back up along their demand curve. This might involve reducing output, or substituting machinery for labour, or a bit of both.

Using non-union labour. The firm may threaten to bring in non-union labour unless the union agrees to its terms.

Employers' promises

In return for lower wage increases, the firm may offer various other 'perks' such as productivity bonuses, profit-sharing schemes, better working conditions, more chances for overtime, better holidays, security of employment, or a closed shop

Closed shop

Where a firm agrees to employ only union members.

Strikes, lock-outs and other forms of action impose costs in the short run. Unions lose pay. Firms lose revenue. If either side therefore carries out its threats, there is likely to be a net loss while the action continues. It is usually in both sides' interests, therefore, to settle without resort to industrial action. Nevertheless if each side is to gain the maximum from the negotiations, it must persuade the other side that it will carry out its threats if pushed.

The approach described so far has essentially been one of confrontation. The alternative is for both sides to concentrate on increasing the total net income of the firm (after other costs, excluding wages, have been met). This could be done by co-operating on ways to increase efficiency or the quality of the product. This approach is more likely when unions and management have built up an atmosphere of trust over time, and where each side believes that the other will only demand a fair share of the net income for themselves.

? The relationship between unions and management has a lot in common with that between rival oligopolists. Recall the various strategies that an oligopolist can adopt and then see what parallels there are in union and management strategies.

The outcome of negotiations

Given these various 'carrots' and 'sticks' that both sides can wield, what will be the outcome of the bargain? This will depend on a number of factors.

Power

The greater the power of either side to pursue its objectives, the more likely it is to succeed. A *union*'s power depends on the following:

- The finances of the union. The greater its reserves, the longer it can hold out in a strike and the more seriously will an employer have to take a strike threat.
- The size and influence of the union. A union that is large and bargains with many different firms may be able to use its influence elsewhere to gain support for its wage claim. It might be able to persuade firms elsewhere to put pressure on the firm in dispute to settle. It might also be in a better position to gain support from the general public.
- The percentage of the labour force in the union. If the union has a closed-shop agreement, it will not have to fear non-unionized labour or labour from other unions undermining its position.

- Support from other unions. For example, railway unions could refuse to transport coal in support of a miners' strike.
- National/local/industrial employment levels. The easier it is for union members to get jobs elsewhere, the less worried they will be by threats of redundancy.

A *firm*'s power depends on the following:

- Its financial strength. The more reserves it has, the longer it can withstand a strike or other industrial action.
- The attitudes of its creditors. If banks are willing to lend to it and if suppliers are prepared to wait for payment, then it will be able to hold out longer.
- The size of the whole company relative to the part in dispute. A large multinational corporation, for example, may be able to use profits in one part of the organization to subsidize the part that is making a loss because of the union action.
- Solidarity with other firms in dispute. If the dispute extends beyond just one firm, then each firm's bargaining position will be stronger if the other firms adopt a tough line.
- Its ability to substitute machines or non-union labour for the workers in dispute.

Attitudes
It is not just power that is important, but also the determination of either side to win.

As far as the union is concerned, the more solid the support from members and their families, and the more the members are prepared to undergo hardships while the dispute lasts, the more likely they are to succeed. Similarly, the tougher the management and the more determined it is not to give in, the more likely management is to succeed.

Of course, if both sides are determined, the dispute can last a very long time. The protracted miners' dispute (over pit closures) in 1985–6 and the ambulance workers' dispute (over pay and a long-term pay formula) in 1989–90 were two examples in Britain of great determination on both sides not to give in.

Scope for movement by the employer
When firms are operating in a competitive goods market their scope for giving wage increases is limited. In the extreme case where a firm operates under perfect competition and where the wage demand is confined to that one firm only, it will have virtually no scope at all to meet the demand. It is only making normal profits. Any rise in its wage bill would force it to close down (in the long run), unless, of course, there was an accompanying increase in productivity.

If, however, the firm's rivals are *also* facing similar wage demands, there is more scope for granting them. What is crucial here is the industry-wide demand curve for labour. It will show how much employment will fall for any given rise in wages (see Figure 8.14). The less the elasticity of this demand curve, the less employment will fall as wages rise. This elasticity will depend on the elasticity of demand for the good: the less elastic it is, the less elastic will be the demand for labour and thus the stronger will be the union's position. Unions are thus better off bargaining in these circumstances when there are no close substitutes for the industry's product.

When the firm has market power in the goods market, its demand curve for the good and hence for labour will be relatively inelastic. It therefore has much more scope to pass on wage increases to the consumer in higher prices.

Bargaining skills
The more skilful the negotiators are on one side, the more likely they are to gain at the expense of the other.

Information

A lot of bargaining involves bluff and counter-bluff. A firm may well attempt to persuade the union that it cannot afford to meet its wage demands without substantial cuts in the labour force, whereas in reality it could do so. In these circumstances the union's bargaining position would be strengthened if it had clear information on the firm's finances and its market potential.

Likewise union negotiators may attempt to persuade management that the members are willing to strike, whereas in reality they may be very reluctant. The firm's position will be strengthened if it knows the true feelings of the workforce.

The role of government

There are a number of ways in which the government can influence the outcome of collective bargaining.

As provider of social security. If workers can draw social security benefits, then they can sustain a strike for longer. If the government withdraws such benefits, the position of unions will be correspondingly weakened.

As macroeconomic policy maker. In its fight against inflation the government can use various weapons to prevent general wage and price increases. One of these is prices and incomes policy. This involves setting limits to the level of wage or price increases that it will permit. Such policy therefore imposes a constraint on collective bargaining. Prices and incomes policy is examined in Chapter 20.

Prices and incomes policy
Where the government seeks to restrain wage and/or price increases.

As employer. The government may take a tough line in resisting wage demands by government employees, hoping thereby to set an example to employers in the private sector.

As purchaser of supplies from private companies. The government could refuse to purchase supplies from firms which give in to wage demands that the government feels are 'excessive'.

As arbitrator. Past governments have attempted to mediate in pay disputes which they felt were damaging to the economy. 'Beer and sandwiches at No. 10 Downing Street' for the two sides in a dispute were not uncommon in the Labour government of the 1960s. More formally, the government can set up arbitration or conciliation machinery. For example, the Advisory Conciliation and Arbitration Service (ACAS) conciliates in over a thousand disputes each year, trying to help both sides in the dispute to come to an agreement. It also provides, on request by both sides, an arbitration service, where its findings will be binding on both sides.

As legislator. The government can pass laws that restrict the behaviour of employers or unions. It can pass laws that set minimum wages, or prevent discrimination against workers on various grounds (such as sex or race). Similarly, it can pass laws that curtail the power of unions. In Britain the Conservative government of the 1980s used the law quite extensively to reduce union power. The following Acts were passed:

- 1980 Employment Act. This Act required unions to put closed-shop agreements to a secret ballot to those employees affected. It also made secondary action unlawful against a firm not directly involved in a dispute. If unions do take secondary action, the firm affected can seek damages from the union in the civil courts. If the union disobeys a court ruling, it will be in contempt and could be fined or have its assets sequestrated (confiscated).
- 1982 Employment Act. This tightened up the 1980 Act, by making political strikes and strikes against other unions illegal. The effect of the 1980 and 1982 Acts was

| Box 8.6 |

Sailing Close to the Wind
The case of secondary action by the National Union of Seamen

In the spring of 1988 the National Union of Seamen was in dispute with P & O.

P & O and Sealink were the two main cross-Channel ferry operators, and both were getting worried about the effects that the opening of the Channel Tunnel would have on their business. P & O, which had a more aggressive style of management, wished to cut back on the number of workers per ship. The NUS did not agree to its proposals and negotiations broke down. The NUS took strike action against P & O. In response to this, P & O recruited non-union labour to staff its ferries.

The NUS picketed Dover and other Channel ports, trying to persuade the non-union workers and the few NUS workers still at work on the P & O ferries to change their minds. This much was legal.

To try and make the industrial action against P & O more effective, strikes and picketing spread to other ferries round the country. This was secondary action.

The most dramatic example of such secondary action was against Sealink. Although the NUS was not in dispute with Sealink, the members were called out on strike (without the statutory secret ballot) and Sealink ferries were picketed. In this way it was hoped that much more chaos would be brought to the Channel ports, and that P & O would be forced back to the negotiating table. But this secondary action was illegal.

Sealink tried to avoid legal conflict by offering to provide extra jobs for some of the NUS members made redundant by P & O. This was felt to be inadequate by NUS members, and the secondary action continued.

The NUS was brought to court. It was fined and ordered to stop the secondary action. It refused and was thus in contempt of court. As a result of this, the court ordered that the NUS's £2.8 million assets should be sequestrated, and additional fines were imposed.

Mr Justice Davies, in giving his judgment said, 'The law and the authority of the court must be upheld. There has been unlawful action on a wide scale and, of course, no lawful ballot.'

It was ironic that at this time P & O ships were sailing, whereas Sealink were strikebound.

Eventually the NUS action collapsed and P & O and Sealink resumed a full normal service, with P & O operating with its new lower staffing levels.

to confine lawful action to that against workers' own direct employers, even to their own particular place of work.

- 1984 Trade Union Act. This Act made (secret) ballots mandatory of the membership for (a) the operation of a political fund (where the union contributes to a political party), (b) the election of senior union officials and (c) strikes and other official industrial action.

The determinants of the outcome of negotiations between unions and management are thus many and complex. It is therefore difficult to predict in advance what the agreed wage rate (and other conditions) will be. Certainly there is no simple economic model that can specify the 'equilibrium' wage.

Other labour market imperfections

The possession of power by unions and/or firms is not the only way in which real-world labour markets diverge from the perfectly competitive model:

- Workers or employers may have imperfect information about wages and job opportunities elsewhere, about the availability of labour and so on.
- Wages may respond very slowly to changes in demand and supply, causing disequilibrium in labour markets to persist.

- Firms may not be profit maximizers. Likewise workers may not seek to maximize their 'worker surplus' – the excess of benefits from working (i.e. wages) over the disutility of working (displeasure in doing the job and lost leisure).

Some of the forms and effects of these imperfections are examined in the next three sections.

Imperfect information

In the real world, workers are unaware of many jobs that are available. They may well be willing to move jobs, but end up staying where they are due to ignorance. The effect of this ignorance is to decrease the elasticity of supply of labour. For firms wishing to take on extra labour, the less the elasticity of supply, the higher the wages they will have to pay to attract a given number of extra workers.

Firms too suffer from imperfect information. They may be ignorant of what quality and quantity of labour is available. In other words, they may not know the position and shape of the labour supply curve. This makes it difficult for them to decide what wage rate to offer when recruiting labour.

Search theory

This examines people's behaviour under conditions of ignorance where it takes time to search for information.

Economists have developed search theory to explain how workers and firms will deal with this problem of ignorance. Workers will spend time searching for better jobs. This could be after quitting their previous job, or while currently in a job (e.g. by searching through the job advertisements in the local/national newspapers). Likewise employers will spend time searching for suitable labour. Maybe they will advertise and then spend time interviewing a number of applicants.

In both cases search is costly, both in time and effort and in money. If workers give up a job to look for a better one, they lose pay. Even if they do not give up their job, they still have to sacrifice leisure time in searching and perhaps spend money travelling to interviews. Thus rational workers/employers will weigh up the benefits of search (namely a better job/quality of labour) against the costs of search.

They might decide at the outset that the costs outweigh the benefits. Workers in a good job might say, 'What's the point?' Firms might say, 'We'll make do with the labour we've got.'

If they do decide to search, how long should they carry on? If they perceive that the benefits of continuing searching exceed the benefits, then they will carry on. If the costs are perceived to exceed the benefits, however, they will settle for what they can get.

The problem here is that the benefits of searching cannot be calculated in advance. It was because people were ignorant that they were searching in the first place. All they can do, then, is to use their 'judgement' about when to stop – a judgement based on the evidence they have accumulated so far and coloured by either optimism or pessimism.

What will be the effect of searching on the wage level? This is illustrated in Figure 8.16. This diagram has two curves. The first is the 'wage offered' curve. This shows that, as the period of search increases, the average worker will get better wage offers. This curve will gradually flatten out as the worker's search becomes complete. The top of the curve represents the maximum wage that this type of worker can receive. The second curve shows the wage rate that the worker would accept. As time progresses, and the costs of search increase, so the typical worker would settle at a lower and lower wage. This curve bottoms out as it approaches the minimum that the worker would accept under any circumstances.

? What determines this minimum?

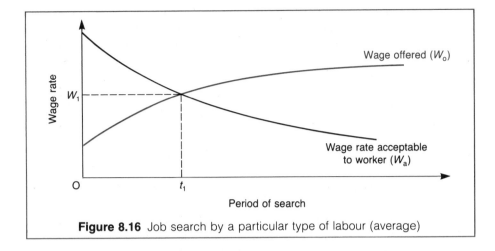

Figure 8.16 Job search by a particular type of labour (average)

As long as the wage offered is below the level acceptable, the worker will continue searching. The worker will stop searching at t_1, and settle for a wage of W_1.

This wage will be higher:

- The more optimistic workers are about finding a high-paid job. This will shift the W_a line up. It will thus also increase the average search time.
- The less the costs of search to workers. Better job information by firms or by the government, and better social security payments for those who have quit their job to search, are examples of things which reduce the costs of searching. This too will shift the W_a line up.

  In both these cases, workers will be prepared to search longer and thus firms will be forced to pay a higher wage to get the required labour.

- The more pessimistic firms are about the difficulties in finding suitable labour. This will shift the W_o line up.
- The higher the costs of search to firms. This too will shift the W_o line up.

> **?** 1. When you finish studying and start looking for a job (assuming you have not already got one), what factors will you take into account when deciding whether to accept a job offer or to continue looking? How will the level of unemployment affect your decision?
> 2. In what ways could the government reduce the problem of imperfect information?

Persistent disequilibrium

Apart from unions pushing wages above the equilibrium, there are other reasons why an imbalance of demand and supply may persist in a given labour market.

Wages set for a period of time. Typically when wage rates are set through a process of collective bargaining the agreement will last for a period of time – usually a year. But during the year the demand and supply curves of labour could shift, causing a disequilibrium that cannot be corrected until the next wage round.

Custom and practice. A firm may have agreed to a formula for setting various wage rates in its organization. A higher grade of job may always get, say, 20 per cent more than a lower grade, even though changes in demand and supply may have made this differential no longer appropriate.

A given wage rate covering several types of labour. An employer may pay all its workers the same rate, even though there is a shortage of one type of labour and a surplus of another. For example, many schools cannot recruit maths teachers because they can only pay them the same rate as other teachers, despite the fact that maths teachers are in short supply.

National or industry-based wage agreements. When wages are set nationally or centrally within a large organization they will not reflect the local supply and demand conditions. For example, it is difficult to recruit nurses in parts of the south where the cost of living is higher, when they are only being paid the same as nurses elsewhere in the country.

Longer-term considerations. Firms are concerned to gain the goodwill and loyalty of their workforce. Without it long-term profits will fall. To gain this goodwill, wages must be seen as fair. Wages that are frequently raised or lowered according to demand and supply, with some workers gaining and others losing, will hardly be seen as 'fair' wages by the workers. Firms may find it in their long-term interests, therefore, to let disequilibrium wages persist for quite a long time.

Another example is where pay is related to age or length of service. Often younger workers, once they have gained some experience, are more efficient than older workers. Yet it is in the firm's interests to pay more to older workers in order to encourage workers to stay with the company. It gives them more of a 'career structure'.

All these considerations mean that the labour market is not like the market for cattle or antiques. It is not like an auction, with wages fluctuating according to demand and supply. Wages tend to be relatively 'sticky'.

Non-maximizing behaviour

Not all employers are ruthless profit maximizers. The owners of some small businesses may treat their employees more as family members than as 'factors of production'. They may pay them better wages and give them better conditions of work than they would if they were purely concerned to make money. Large companies too may not squeeze the maximum profit from their workers. Where there is a separation between the ownership and control of a company, profits may take a second place to other goals that interest managers (see Chapter 7). Managers may prefer an 'easy life'. Paying good wages and keeping a contented workforce may give them that easy life. Of course it could be argued that in some cases keeping a contented workforce is a way of improving productivity, and thus is really only a way of increasing long-run profits.

Not all workers are 'rational economic maximizers' either, carefully weighing up the costs and benefits of each job. Workers may give little thought to such issues, and may simply stay put in a job through 'sheer inertia'. This has the effect of reducing the elasticity of supply of labour, and can therefore increase inequality. If workers are not prepared to leave low-paid jobs, the pay will remain low, and in relative terms will become lower.

Economic discrimination

Where workers of identical *ability* are paid different wages or are otherwise discriminated against because of race, age, sex, etc.

Discrimination

This can be another major factor in determining wages. Discrimination can take many forms: it can be by race, sex, age, class, dress, etc.; it can occur in many different aspects of society. This section is concerned with economic discrimination

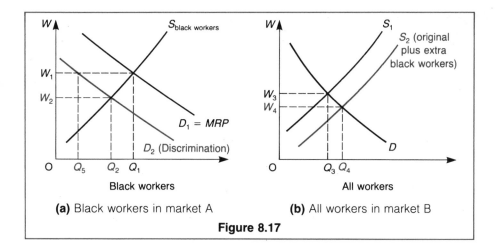

(a) Black workers in market A **(b)** All workers in market B

Figure 8.17

This is defined as a situation where otherwise identical workers receive different pay for doing the same job, or are given different chances of employment or promotion.

Take the case of racial discrimination by employers. Figure 8.17 illustrates the wages and employment of black workers in two labour markets. In market A there is discrimination against black workers, in market B there is not.

The diagram for market A shows the demand and supply curves for black workers. If there was no discrimination, the demand curve would be D_1 and the wage W_1. (Note that the demand curve slopes downwards. This is due to the falling marginal productivity of black workers. But this is only partially due to *diminishing returns* because extra black workers may largely simply displace white workers. The main explanation is that as extra black workers are employed the better qualified and hence more productive ones will be employed first.) If the firm now discriminates, the demand for black workers will shift to D_2. Employment will fall to Q_2 and wages will fall to W_2, below the *MRP* of black workers.

But the effects of discrimination are not just confined to those industries where discrimination takes place. Most of the workers displaced from market A ($Q_1 - Q_2$) will seek employment elsewhere. This will increase the supply of workers coming on to other labour markets, especially those that do *not* discriminate. Market B in Figure 8.17 illustrates one such market. It shows the demand and supply of all workers, black and white. The extra black workers coming on to this market will shift the supply curve to S_2. Employment will rise from Q_3 to Q_4, but the wage rate will fall from W_3 to W_4. Discrimination in one market, therefore, will tend to push wages down in other markets.

If the government now insists on equal pay for equal work, then employers who discriminate will respond by further cutting back on black workers. In market A, if employers are now forced to pay a wage of W_1, their demand for black workers will fall to Q_5. This in turn will mean that even more black workers move to market B, with the result that wages there will fall below W_4.

The answer to *this* problem would seem to be for the government to pass laws that insist not only that black workers be paid the same as white for doing the same job, but also that they be treated equally when applying for jobs. The problem here is that an employer who wants to continue discrimination can always claim that the black applicants were less well qualified than the white applicant who got the job. Such laws are, therefore, difficult to enforce.

Box 8.7

Equal Pay for Equal Work!

(a) Average gross hourly earnings, excluding the effects of overtime, for full-time UK employees, aged 18 and over, 1970–89 (pence per hour)

	1970	1974	1975	1976	1977	1978	1979	1980	1981	1982	1983	1984	1985	1986	1987	1988	1989
Men	67·4	104·8	136·6	162·9	177·4	200·3	226·9	280·7	322·5	354·8	387·6	417·3	445·3	481·8	526·2	573·0	629·0
Women	42·5	70·6	98·3	122·4	133·9	148·0	165·7	206·4	241·2	262·1	287·5	306·3	329·9	358·2	386·2	429·0	478·0
Differential	24·9	34·2	38·0	39·5	43·5	52·3	61·2	74·3	81·3	92·7	100·1	110·5	115·4	123·6	140·0	144·0	151·0
Women's earnings as a % of men's	63·1	67·4	72·1	75·1	75·5	73·9	73·0	73·5	74·8	73·9	74·2	73·5	74·0	74·3	73·3	75·0	76·0

Source: *New Earnings Surveys* (HMSO).

One of the key characteristics shown in table (a) is that female gross hourly earnings relative to male gross hourly earnings increased substantially during the early 1970s, reaching a high of 75.5 per cent in 1977. However, since then differential earnings have remained at a relatively constant level, below 75 per cent.

The inequality between male and female earnings can in part be explained by the fact that men and women are occupationally segregated. Seeing that women predominate in poorly paid occupations, the difference in earnings is somewhat to be expected. But if you consider table (b), you can see that quite substantial earnings differentials persist *within* particular occupations.

1. If we were to look at weekly rather than hourly pay and included the effects of overtime, what do you think would happen to the pay differentials in table (a)?
2. In table (b), which of the occupations have a largely female workforce?

So why has this inequality persisted? There are a number of possible reasons:

● The marginal productivity of labour in typically female occupations may be lower than in typically male occupations. This may in part be due to simple questions of physical strength. Very often, however, it is due to the fact that women tend to work in more labour-intensive occupations. If there is less capital equipment per female worker than there is per male worker, then it would be expected that the marginal product of a woman would be less than that of a man.

● Women may on average undertake less training than men. If, therefore, the resulting level of skills obtained by women is less than those obtained by men, women will have a lower marginal productivity.

There are various reasons for differences in training and qualifications. The educational system may favour boys rather than girls. Even if this is not deliberate policy, the attitudes of parents, teachers and pupils may be such as to give more encouragement to boys to think of qualifications for a future career. Employers are also more willing to invest money in training men, fearing that women may leave after a short time to have children.

● Women tend to be less geographically mobile than men. If social norms are such that the man's job is seen as somehow more 'important' than the woman's,

The type of discrimination considered so far can be seen as 'irrational' if the firm wants to maximize profits. After all, to produce a given amount of output it would be paying out more in wages to employ white workers than black workers. In a competitive market environment such firms may be forced to end discrimination simply to survive the competition from non-discriminating rivals. If, however, the firm has market power, it will probably be making sufficient profits to allow it to continue discriminating. The main pressure here to end discrimination is likely to come from shareholders, unions, customers or race relations organizations.

Not all cases of discrimination result in lower profits, however. A firm may agree not to employ black workers because of pressure from white workers. If it ignores this pressure, it might face industrial relations problems and a resulting loss of profits. Discrimination in this case could be part of profit-maximizing behaviour.

Box 8.7 (cont'd)

(b) Average gross hourly earnings, excluding the effects of overtime, for selected occupations, full-time UK employees on adult rates, 1986

Occupation	Men	Women	Women's earnings as a % of men's
	(pence per hour)		
Police officers (below sergeant)	617.2	566.8	91.8
Registered and enrolled nurses, midwives	421.7	381.1	90.3
Bar staff	266.7	238.1	89.3
Records and library clerks	357.1	317.4	88.9
Supervisors of clerks	533.9	452.6	84.7
Storekeepers	327.3	275.1	84.0
Chefs/cooks	322.2	270.4	83.9
General clerks	389.7	323.5	83.0
Cash handling clerks	426.7	349.2	81.8
Laboratory technicians (scientific/medical)	473.0	380.8	80.5
Packers, bottlers, canners and fillers	337.8	271.1	80.2
Shipping and travel clerks	424.2	336.2	79.2
Sales staff, shop assistants, shelf fillers	305.4	240.5	78.7
Repetitive assemblers (metal and electrical)	367.2	280.2	76.3
Finance insurance, etc. clerks	508.2	380.9	74.9
Inspectors and testers (metal and electrical)	426.3	315.7	74.0
Footwear workers	358.8	262.7	73.2
Sales supervisors	488.3	317.4	65.0
All occupations	486.6	360.7	74.1

Source: *New Earnings Survey* (HMSO).

then a couple will often move if necessary for the man to get promotion. The woman, however, will have to settle for whatever job she can get in the same locality as her partner.

● A smaller proportion of women workers are members of unions than men. Even when they are members of unions, these are often in jobs where unions are weak (e.g. clothing industry workers, shop assistants and secretaries).

● Part-time workers (mainly women) have less bargaining power, less influence and less chance of obtaining promotion.

● Custom and practice. Despite equal pay legislation many jobs done wholly or mainly by women continue to be low paid, irrespective of questions of productivity.

● Prejudice. Some employers may prefer to give senior posts to men on grounds purely of sexual prejudice. This is very difficult to legislate against when the employer can simply claim that the 'better' person was given the job.

? 1. If employers were forced to give genuinely equal pay for equal work, how would this affect the employment of women and men? What would determine the magnitude of these effects?

2. What measures could a government introduce to increase the number of women getting higher-paid jobs?

There are other types of discrimination which are not strictly *economic* discrimination. The education system might discriminate against black children, with the result that they end up with poor qualifications. Under these circumstances employers, preferring to employ the best qualified applicants, are likely to choose white people. This is particularly so in the more highly paid jobs that require a higher level of educational attainment. Tackling this problem at source means tackling weaknesses in the education system or problems of inner-city deprivation. Nevertheless there may still be a benefit to be gained from passing laws that tackle more than just pure economic discrimination. For example, firms could be required to employ a minimum quota of black people. This at least would help to guard against any prejudices of employers against the ability of black workers.

Box 8.8

How Useful is the Marginal Productivity Theory?

Reality or the fantasy world of economists?

The marginal productivity theory of income distribution has come in for a lot of criticisms. Are they justified?

To start with, you cannot criticize something unless you know precisely what it is you are criticizing. Marginal productivity theory has been criticized for assuming perfect competition. It doesn't!

Marginal productivity theory merely states that to maximize profits an employer will employ workers up to the point where the worker's marginal cost equals the extra revenue added by that worker: $MC_L = MRP_L$. This applies equally under perfect competition, monopoly and monopsony.

What it does say is that, *if* there is perfect competition, then the worker's *wage* will equal MRP_L. It certainly does not say that there will always be perfect competition, or that $W = MRP_L$ in other market structures.

A second criticism is that employers simply do not behave in this 'marginal way', weighing up each additional worker's costs and revenues for the firm. There are three possible reasons for this.

Ignorance of the theory of profit maximization

The employer may use some rule of thumb, but nevertheless is attempting to maximize profits.

This is only a criticism of the theory if the theory is supposed to describe how employers actually behave. It does not. It merely states that, if firms are attempting to maximize profits, they will in fact be equating MC_L and MRP_L, whether they realize it or not!

A worker's marginal productivity cannot be calculated

When workers are part of a team, it is not usually possible to separate out the contribution to output of each individual. What is the marginal productivity of a cleaner, a porter, a secretary, a security guard, or even a member of a production line? Similarly, it may not be possible to separate the contribution of workers from that of their tools. A lathe operator is useless without a lathe, as is a lathe without a lathe operator.

This is a more fundamental criticism. Nevertheless it is possible to amend the theory to take this into account.

First of all, an employer can look at the composition of the team, or the partnership of worker and tools, and decide whether any reorganizations or alternative production methods will increase the firm's profitability. In doing this, the changes in costs resulting from the reorganization must be weighed against changes in output and hence revenue. Secondly, the employer can decide whether to expand or contract the overall size of the team, or the number of workers plus machines. Here the whole team or the worker plus machine is the 'factor of production' whose marginal productivity must be weighed against its costs.

Firms are not always profit maximizers

This is only a criticism if the theory states that firms are. As long as the theory is merely used to describe what would happen *if* firms maximized profits, there is no problem.

This criticism, then, is really one of how the theory is used. And even if it is used to predict what will actually happen in the real world, it is still relatively accurate in the large number of cases where firms' behaviour only slightly diverges from profit maximizing. It is clearly wrong in other cases.

A final criticism is the moral one. If economists focus their attention exclusively on how to maximize profits, it might be concluded that they are putting their seal of approval on this sort of behaviour. Of course, economists will respond by saying that they are doing no such thing: they are confining themselves to positive economics. Nevertheless the criticism has some force. What an economist chooses to study is in part a normative decision.

 Do any of the following contradict marginal productivity theory?
(a) Wage scales related to length of service (incremental scales).
(b) *Nationally* negotiated wage rates.
(c) Discrimination.
(d) Firms taking the lead from other firms in determining this year's pay increase.

Conclusions: who are the poor and who are the rich?

To the list we made at the end of section 8.2 we can now add the following factors which will tend to make people poor:

- Lack of economic power, not belonging to a union or belonging to a union with only weak bargaining power.
- Working for firms which operate in a highly competitive goods market.
- Ignorance of better job opportunities.
- Lack of will to search for a better job.
- Discrimination against them by employers or fellow workers.

Thus many people of Asian origin, especially women, working in the garment industry in back-street 'sweatshops' in London and other cities earn pitifully low wages.

Conversely, belonging to a powerful union, working for a profitable employer who nevertheless is not a ruthless profit maximizer, being aware of new job opportunities and having the 'get up and go' to apply for better jobs, and being white, male and middle class are all factors that help to contribute to people earning high wages.

▲ SUMMARY

1. If firms have market power in the goods market, they will tend to produce a lower output and hence employ fewer workers. They will maximize profits at the level of employment where the marginal revenue product of labour ($MRP_L = MPP_L \times MR$) is equal to the wage rate.
2. If a firm is a monopsony employer, it will employ workers to the point where $MRP_L = MC_L$. Since the wage is below MC_L, the monopsonist, other things being equal, will employ fewer workers at a lower wage than would be employed in a perfectly competitive labour market.
3. If a union has monopoly power, its power to raise wages will be limited if the employer operates under perfect or monopolistic competition in the goods market. A rise in wages will force the employer to cut back on employment.
4. In a situation of bilateral monopoly (where a monopoly union faces a monopsony employer) the union may have considerable scope to raise wages above the monopsony level, without the employer wishing to reduce the level of employment. There is no unique equilibrium wage. The wage will depend on the outcome of a process of collective bargaining between union and management.
5. Each side can make various threats or promises. A union can threaten strikes or other forms of industrial action such as working to rule. On the other hand, it can offer such things as no strikes, increased productivity, or reductions in the workforce. Management can threaten redundancies, lockouts, plant closures, or taking on non-union labour. Alternatively, it can offer better working conditions, shorter hours, longer holidays, profit-sharing schemes, job security, etc.
6. The outcome of the bargaining will depend on the relative power of both sides, their attitudes, the scope for movement on the part of the employer, the information each side has about the other, and their bargaining skills. The outcome also depends on the legal framework within which the negotiations take place.
7. Power is not the only factor that makes actual wage determination different from the perfectly competitive model. Firms and workers may have imperfect knowledge of the labour market. Each side will probably have to go through a search procedure. The equilibrium wage will depend on how long and how hard each side is prepared to search.
8. Labour markets do not adjust instantly to changes in demand or supply: disequilibrium can persist. The reasons are that wages are only changed at intervals (typically annually); wages may be set by custom and practice; a given wage rate may cover several types of labour; agreements may be national or industry wide.
9. Firms may not be profit maximizers and as such may be prepared to continue employing workers beyond the profit-maximizing level and paying above the profit-maximizing wage.
10. Firms may exercise discrimination (by race, sex, age, etc.) in their employment policy. By discriminating against a particular group, an employer with market power can drive down the wages of the members of that group. Unless firms are forced not to discriminate, equal pay legislation may well lead to a reduction in the employment of members of groups that are discriminated against.

8.4 Land and capital

The non-human factors of production

In this final section of the chapter we consider the market for *other* factors of production. These non-human factors can be divided into two broad groups:

- *Land*: this includes all those productive resources supplied by nature: in other words, not only land itself, but also all natural resources.
- *Capital*: this includes all manufactured products that are used to produce goods and services. Thus capital includes such diverse items as a blast furnace, a bus, a cinema projector, a typewriter, a factory building and a screwdriver.

One problem with this classification is that some non-human factors are partly land and partly capital. For example, raw materials when they are delivered to factories have been extracted, processed and transported. They cannot be classified, therefore, as pure land. Even land itself contains elements of capital if it has in any way been improved from its natural state – say by levelling or drainage.

Despite this, the distinction can still be useful. It helps to focus on the different sorts of properties different factors can have.

(Note that when we are talking about capital as a factor of production we are talking about *physical* assets such as machines, not the *paper* assets that people hold, such as money, stocks and shares. These paper assets are merely *claims* on physical assets. If these paper assets were real wealth-producing resources, all we would need to do is to print more of them and, hey presto, we could all be better off!)

Factor prices versus the price of factor services

A feature of most non-human factors of production is that they last a period of time. A machine may last 10 years; a coal mine may last 50 years before it is exhausted; farmland will last for ever if properly looked after. There are some exceptions, however. For example, raw materials can usually only be used once.

Given that most of these factors do last, this leads to an important distinction. This is the distinction between the income the owner will get from *selling* the factor and that which the owner will get from *using* it or *hiring* it out:

- The income from selling the factor is the factor's *price*. It is a once-and-for-all payment. Thus a factory might sell for £1 million, a machine for £20 000, or a hectare of land for £20 000.
- The income gained from using a factor is its *return*, and the income gained from hiring a factor out is its *rental*. This is income gained not by selling the factor, but by using its services. This income therefore represents the value or price of the factor's *services*. It is expressed as an income per period of time. Thus a machine might give a return (i.e. earn for the firm) £1000 per year. A hectare of land might earn £1000 rent per year for a landlord.

Obviously the price of a factor will be linked to the value of its services. The price that a hectare of land will fetch if sold will depend on the return or rent that can be earned on that land. If it is highly productive farmland, it will sell for a higher price than a piece of scrubby moorland.

? When we were looking at wages, were we talking about the price of labour or the price of labour services? Is this distinction between the price of a factor and the price of factor services a useful one in the case of labour? Was it in Roman times?

Box 8.9

Stocks and Flows

The discussion of the rewards to capital and land leads to a very important distinction: that between stocks and flows.

A *stock* is a quantity of something held. A landowner may own 200 hectares. A farmer may have a barn with 500 tonnes of grain. You may have £1000 in a savings account. A factory may contain 100 machines. These are all stocks: they are all quantities held at a given point in time.

A *flow* is an increase or decrease in quantity over a specified time period. The landowner may buy another 10 hectares during the course of the year. The farmer may use 10 tonnes of grain from the barn each week as animal feed. You may save £10 per month. The factory may invest in another 20 machines next year.

Wages, rent and interest are all rewards to *flows*. Wages are the amount paid not to purchase a person (as a slave!), but for the services of that person's labour for a week. Rent is the amount paid per period of time to use the services of land, not to buy it outright. Likewise interest is the reward paid to people per year for the use of their money.

If an asset is sold, its value is the value of the *stock*. It is a simple payment at a single point in time. If a person buys a house for £100 000, the vendor is not paid in instalments. It is a single payment at a single point in time for the transfer of a whole asset. Thus the price of land and the price of capital are stock concepts.

An important example of stocks and flows arises with capital and investment. If a firm has 100 machines, that is a stock of capital. It may choose to build up its stock by investing. Investment is a flow concept. The firm may choose to invest in 10 new machines each year. This may not add 10 to the stock of machines, however, as some may be wearing out (a negative flow).

? Which of the following are stocks and which are flows?
(a) Unemployment.
(b) Redundancies.
(c) Profits.
(d) A firm's stock market valuation.
(e) The value of property after a period of inflation.

The profit-maximizing employment of land and capital

On the demand side, the same rules apply for land and capital as for labour, if a firm wishes to maximize profits. Namely, it should demand factors up to the point where the marginal cost of the factor equals its marginal revenue product: $MC_f = MRP_f$. This same rule applies whether the firm is buying the factor outright, or merely renting it.

Figure 8.18 illustrates the two cases of perfect competition and monopsony. In both diagrams the MRP curve slopes downwards. This is just another illustration of the law of diminishing returns, but this time applied to land or capital. For example, if a farmer increases the amount of land farmed while *holding other factors constant*, diminishing returns to land will occur. If the same number of farm workers and the same amount of agricultural machinery and fertilizers are used but on a larger area, then returns per hectare will fall. Diminishing returns will equally apply whether the farmer is buying the extra land or renting it.

In diagram (a) the firm is a price taker. The factor price is given at P_{f_1}. Profits are maximized at Q_{f_1} where $MRP_f = P_f$ (since $P_f = MC_f$).

In diagram (b) the firm has monopsony power. The factor price will vary, therefore, with the amount that the firm uses. The firm will again use factors to the point where $MRP_f = MC_f$. In this case it will mean using Q_{f_2} at a price of P_{f_2}.

What is the difference between buying a factor and renting it? Although the $MRP_f = MC_f$ rule remains the same, there are differences. As far as buying the factors is concerned, the MC_f is the extra outlay for the firm in *purchasing* one more unit of the

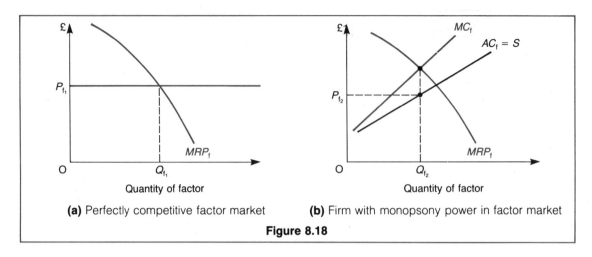

(a) Perfectly competitive factor market   **(b)** Firm with monopsony power in factor market

Figure 8.18

factor; and the MRP_f is all the revenue produced by that factor over its *whole life* (but measured in terms of what this is worth when purchased: see page 309). In the case of renting, MC_f is the extra outlay for the firm in rent *per year*, while MRP_f is the extra revenue earned from it *per year*. (These calculations could alternatively be of weekly or monthly rent and revenue.)

The remaining sections look first at the determination of the rental value of capital, and then at the determination of the price of capital. Then the rent and price of land are examined.

The demand for and supply of capital services

What we are talking about in this section is the hiring of capital equipment for a period of time.

Demand for capital services

The analysis is virtually identical to that of the demand for labour. As with labour we can distinguish between an individual firm's demand and the whole market demand.

Individual firm's demand. Take the case of a small painting and decorating firm that requires some scaffolding in order to complete a job. It could possibly use ladders, but the job would take longer to complete. It goes along to a company that hires out scaffolding and is quoted a daily rate.

If it hires the scaffolding for one day, it can perhaps shorten the job by, say, two or three days. If it hires it for a second day, it can perhaps save another one or two days. Hiring it additional days may save extra still. But diminishing returns are occurring: the longer the scaffolding is up, the less intensively it will be used, and the less additional time it will save. Perhaps for some of the time it will be used when ladders could have been used equally easily.

The time saved allows the firm to take on extra work. Thus each extra day the scaffolding is hired gives the firm extra revenue. This is the scaffolding's marginal revenue product of capital (MRP_K). Diminishing returns mean that it has the normal downward sloping shape.

This MRP_K curve is illustrated in Figure 8.19. The firm is assumed to be under perfect competition and thus has no power to influence the daily rental charge (R_K). It will maximize profits by hiring the scaffolding for 10 days. The MRP_K curve is the

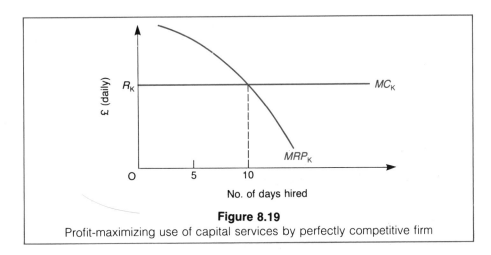

Figure 8.19

Profit-maximizing use of capital services by perfectly competitive firm

demand curve for capital, in the same way that the MRP_L curve was the demand curve for labour.

If the firm has monopsony power, the diagram will look like Figure 8.18(b). Most firms that hire capital rather than buying it outright will, however, be small firms, and thus closer to perfect competition.

Market demand. The market demand for capital services is derived in exactly the same way as the market demand for labour (see Figure 8.10 on page 278). It is the horizontal sum of the MRP_K curves of the individual firms, corrected for the fact that increased use of capital will increase output, drive down the price of the good and hence reduce MRP. This means that the market demand curve for capital is steeper than the horizontal sum of the demand curves (MRP_K) of all the firms in the market.

 Under what circumstances would the market demand for renting a type of capital equipment be (a) elastic; (b) inelastic? (Clue: turn back to section 8.2 and see what determines the elasticity of demand for labour.)

Supply of capital services

It is necessary to distinguish (a) the supply *to* a single firm, (b) the supply *by* a single firm and (c) the market supply.

Supply to a single firm. The small firm renting capital equipment is probably a price taker. If so, it faces a horizontal supply curve at the going rental rate, R_K in Figure 8.19. If, however, it has monopsony power, it will face an upward-sloping supply curve as in Figure 8.18(b).

Supply by a single firm. Again, the firm is likely to be a price taker. It has to accept the going rental rate established in the market. If it tries to charge more, then customers are likely to turn to rival suppliers. This means that individual suppliers under such conditions will face an infinitely elastic *demand* curve.

But what will the individual supplier's *supply* curve look like? The theory has a lot in common with perfect competition in the goods market: the supply curve is the firm's *MC* curve, only here the *MC* is the extra cost of supplying one more unit of capital equipment for rent over a given time period. But just what will this *MC* be?

The problem with working out the marginal cost of renting out capital equipment is that the piece of equipment probably cost a lot to buy in the first place, but lasts a long time. How then are these large costs to be apportioned to each new rental? If scaffolding is hired out for a week, say, what extra costs are incurred? What proportion, if any, of the large costs of buying scaffolding should be included in the calculations? The answer is that it depends on the time period under consideration. Are we talking about the *short* run, where the firm already has its stock of equipment to hire out, or the *long* run, where the firm is considering purchasing additional equipment?

In the *short run*, we do not include the cost of the original purchase or the replacement cost of the equipment when calculating marginal cost. As Chapter 4 explained, as economists we are concerned with *opportunity* costs. In the case of our scaffolding firm, this is simply the additional expenditures incurred by hiring *existing* scaffolding out. There are no new purchases involved. So what are these additional costs? There are two:

- Depreciation. Scaffolding has second-hand value. The hire company could always sell its equipment second hand. Each time the scaffolding is hired out, however, it deteriorates, and thus its second-hand value falls. This loss in value is called 'depreciation', and is an opportunity cost. It must therefore be included in calculating MC.
- Maintenance and handling. When equipment is hired out it can get damaged and thus incur repair costs. The equipment might need servicing. Also hiring out equipment involves labour time (e.g. in the office) and possibly transport costs. All these variable costs, being opportunity costs, must also be included in the calculation of MC.

The MC of depreciation and maintenance and handling are likely to be relatively constant. In other words, for each extra day a piece of equipment is hired out the company will incur the same additional costs. The effect of this is to give a supply curve like the one illustrated in Figure 8.20.

Q_{max} shows the total supply of equipment available for renting over a given time period. R_1 is the marginal cost per period of hiring it out. Thus up to Q_{max} the supply curve is infinitely elastic, whereas at Q_{max} it becomes totally inelastic since there is no more equipment to hire out. Provided the firm can get a rental above R_1, it will be worth hiring out all its equipment. If, however, the market rent is below R_1, it will be worth the firm selling off its equipment second hand.

> ❓ Assume now that the firm has monopoly power in hiring out equipment, and thus faces a downward-sloping demand curve. Draw in two such demand curves on a diagram like Figure 8.20, one crossing the MC curve in the horizontal section, and one in the vertical section. How much will the firm supply in each case and at what price? (You will need to draw in MR curves too.) Is the MC curve still the supply curve?

In the *long run*, the hire company will consider purchasing additional equipment. What is the marginal cost of this? In this case there are three elements:

- The opportunity cost of purchasing the equipment. This is the interest that the firm sacrifices by not saving the money in a bank or investing it elsewhere.
- Depreciation. This is the loss in value of the equipment over its life: the difference between its purchase price and its scrap value.
- Maintenance and handling costs. These are the total ongoing costs over the life of the equipment.

These three elements then have to be expressed as a rate per year (or month, or

Figure 8.20 Short-run supply of capital by a hire company

week, or day). This is necessary if this *MC* is to be compared with the rent charged to the customer (*MR*), since this is expressed as a rate per period.

How is this done? An illustration will make it easier to understand.

Assumptions:

- A piece of capital equipment costs £10 000 to purchase.
- The current rate of interest that the firm could earn by investing elsewhere is 10 per cent per year: (i.e. £1000).
- The equipment lasts 20 years and has no scrap value at the end. It depreciates at a steady rate of £500 per year.
- Maintenance and handling costs are also £500 each year.

In this example the annual cost that the hire firm will incur if it buys the equipment is £1000 + £500 + £500 = £2000. This then is the marginal cost of the equipment per year. If, therefore, the equipment earns more than £2000 per year in rental for the firm, it will be profitable to buy the equipment.

It is normal to express this *MC* as a rate: as a percentage of the purchase price. In this case the *MC* is 20 per cent per year. If the equipment earns a rental of more than 20 per cent of the purchase price, then it is profitable to purchase.

What will the firm's long-run supply curve look like? If the firm is a price taker in purchasing capital equipment, the supply curve will be horizontal, at least up to a fairly high level of output. But it will be vertically higher than the short-run curve: say going through R_2 in Figure 8.20. The reason is that the *MC* now includes the opportunity cost of purchasing new equipment. There will also be no vertical section, since the firm can increase the supply of capital for hire by simply purchasing more. Beyond a certain level of output the curve may begin to slope upward, due to diseconomies of scale and hence rising handling costs.

Market supply. The market supply curve of capital services is the sum of the quantities supplied by all the individual firms. Either it can be the total supply of a particular type of capital (e.g. scaffolding), or more narrowly it can be the supply of a particular type of capital to a certain industry (e.g. the catering industry, or the coal industry).

In the case of the total supply of a particular type of capital, the *short-run* supply curve will be virtually totally inelastic. The reason is that capital is *heterogeneous*. This means that one piece of capital equipment is not the same as another. If there is a shortage of scaffolding, you cannot use a cement mixer instead: people would fall off!

If supply is totally inelastic, what determines the rental value of capital equipment in the short run?

In the case of supply to a particular industry, supply will not be totally inelastic because capital equipment to a limited extent can be transferred from one industry to another: but *only* to a limited extent. Supply is still pretty inelastic.

In the *long run*, the supply curve will be more elastic because extra capital equipment can be produced. It will not be horizontal, however, but upward sloping. The reason for this is that, if the supply of capital services is to increase, the hire firms will require a bigger stock of capital. This means that they will have to purchase a bigger amount each year to replace worn-out or obsolete stock. But this will push up the purchase price and therefore increase the *MC* of supplying capital services. Thus to make it worth supplying extra capital services a higher rental charge must be obtained. This makes the supply curve upward sloping.

Determination of the price of capital services

The analysis parallels that of the determination of the equilibrium wage in a given labour market.

Figure 8.21 draws together the analysis of the last section, and shows how the equilibrium rental rate is determined for the services of a particular type of capital equipment. The interaction of demand and supply in diagram (b) gives an equilibrium rate of R_e. This is then the rate given to the user of capital services in diagram (a) who demands Q_1. It is also the rate given to the supplier of capital services in diagram (c), who supplies Q_2.

 What will happen to the demand for capital services and the equilibrium rental if the price of some other factor, say labour, changes? Assume that wage rates fall. Trace through the effects on a three-section diagram like that of Figure 8.21. (Clue: a fall in wages will have two significant effects: it will reduce costs and hence the price of the product, so that more will be sold; and it will make labour cheaper relative to capital. How will these two things affect the demand for capital?)

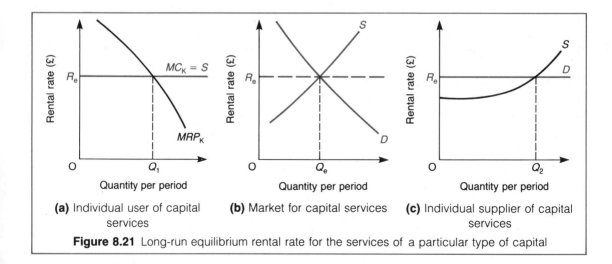

(a) Individual user of capital services   **(b)** Market for capital services   **(c)** Individual supplier of capital services

Figure 8.21 Long-run equilibrium rental rate for the services of a particular type of capital

* The demand for and supply of capital for purchase

The alternative to hiring capital is to buy it outright. This section examines the demand and supply of capital for purchase. The next section puts demand and supply together and examines what determines the price of capital.

The demand for capital: investment

How many computers will an engineering firm want to buy? Should a steelworks install another blast furnace? Should a removal firm buy another furniture lorry? Should it buy another warehouse? These are all investment decisions. Investment is the purchasing of additional capital.

The demand for capital, or 'investment demand', by a profit-maximizing firm is based on exactly the same principles as the demand for labour or the demand for capital services. The firm must weigh up the marginal revenue product of that investment (i.e. the money it will earn for the firm) against its marginal cost.

The problem is that the benefits of the investment do not occur all at once, but over a number of years. This is because capital is durable. It goes on producing goods, and hence yielding revenue for the firm, for a considerable period of time. Calculating these benefits therefore involves taking account of their timing.

There are two ways of approaching the problem. The first involves calculating the monetary benefits and comparing them with the monetary costs. This is called the present value approach. The second involves calculating the benefits as a percentage *rate of return* on the investment and comparing it with the rate of interest that the firm would have to pay to borrow the money in order to make the investment. In both cases the firm is comparing the marginal benefits with the marginal costs of the investment.

Present value approach. To work out the benefit of an investment (its *MRP*), the firm will need to estimate all the future earnings it will bring and then convert them to a *present value*. Let us take a simple example.

Assume that a firm is considering buying a machine. It will produce £1000 per year (net of operating costs) for four years and then wear out and sell for £1000 as scrap. What is the benefit of this machine to the firm? At first sight the answer would seem to be £5000. This, after all, is the total income earned from the machine. Unfortunately it is not as simple as this. The reason is that money earned in the future is less beneficial to the firm than having the same amount of money today: if the firm has the money today, it can earn interest on it by putting it in the bank or reinvesting it in some other project. (Note that this has nothing to do with inflation. In the case we are considering, we are assuming constant prices.)

To illustrate this assume that you have £100 today and can earn 10 per cent interest by putting it in a bank. In one year's time that £100 will have grown to £110, in two years' time to £121, in three years' time to £133.10 and so on. This process is known as compounding.

From this it follows that if someone offered to give you £121 in two years' time that would be no better than giving you £100 today, since, with interest, £100 would grow to £121 in two years. What we say, then, is that, with a 10 per cent interest rate, £121 in two years' time has a *present value* of £100.

The procedure of reducing future values back to a present value is known as discounting. When we do discounting, the rate which we use is not called the rate of *interest* but rather the rate of discount: in this case 10 per cent. The formula for discounting is as follows:

$$PV = \Sigma \frac{X_t}{(1 + r)^t}$$

Investment
The purchase by the firm of equipment or materials that will add to its stock of capital.

Present value approach to appraising investment
This involves estimating the value *now* of a flow of future benefits (or costs).

Compounding
The process of adding interest each year to an initial capital sum.

Discounting
The process of reducing the value of future flows to give them a present valuation.

Rate of discount
The rate that is used to reduce future values to present values.

where PV is the present value

X_t is the earnings from the investment in year t

r is the rate of discount (expressed as a fraction: i.e. $10\% = 0.1$)

Σ is the sum of each of the years' discounted earnings.

So what is the present value of the investment in the machine that produced £1000 for four years and then is sold as scrap for £1000 at the end of the four years? According to the formula it is:

Year 1	Year 2	Year 3	Year 4

$$= \frac{£1000}{1 \cdot 1} + \frac{£1000}{(1 \cdot 1)^2} + \frac{£1000}{(1 \cdot 1)^3} + \frac{£2000}{(1 \cdot 1)^4}$$

$$= £909 + £826 + £751 + £1366$$

$$= £3852$$

Thus the present value of the investment (i.e. its *MRP*) is £3852, *not* £5000 as might seem at first sight. In other words, if the firm had £3852 today and deposited it in a bank at a 10 per cent interest rate, the firm would earn exactly the same as it would by investing in the machine.

So is the investment worthwhile? It is now simply a question of comparing the £3852 benefit with the cost of buying the machine. If the machine costs less than £3852, it will be worth buying. If it costs more, the firm would be better off by keeping its money in the bank and earning the 10 per cent rate of interest.

The difference between the present value of the benefits (PV_b) of the investment and its cost (C) is known as the net present value (*NPV*):

$$NPV = PV_b - C$$

If the *NPV* is positive, the investment is worthwhile.

Net present value of an investment

The discounted benefits of an investment minus the cost of the investment.

> **?** What is the present value of a machine that lasts three years, earns £100 in year 1, £200 in year 2 and £200 in year 3, and then has a scrap value of £100? Assume that the rate of discount is 5 per cent. If the machine costs £500, is the investment worthwhile? Would it be worthwhile if the rate of discount were 10 per cent?

Rate of return approach. The alternative approach when estimating whether an investment is worthwhile is to calculate the investment's *rate of return*. This rate of return is known as the firm's marginal efficiency of capital (*MEC*) or internal rate of return (*IRR*).

The way this is calculated is to use the formula that we used for calculating present value:

Marginal efficiency of capital or internal rate of return

The rate of return of an investment: the discount rate that makes the net present value of an investment equal to zero.

$$PV = \Sigma \frac{X_t}{(1 + r)^t}$$

and then to calculate what value of r would make the *PV* equal to the cost of investment: in other words, to calculate the rate of discount that would make the investment just break even. Say this worked out at 20 per cent. What we would be saying is that the investment would just cover its costs if the current rate of interest (rate of discount) were 20 per cent. In other words, this investment is equivalent to receiving 20 per cent interest: it has a 20 per cent rate of return.

So should the investment go ahead? Yes, if the actual rate of interest (i) is less than 20 per cent. The firm is better off investing its money in this project than keeping its money in the bank. If $MEC > i$ the investment should go ahead.

This is just one more application of the general rule that if $MRP_f > MC_f$ then more

Figure 8.22 The profit-maximizing stock of capital

of the factor should be used: only in this case *MRP* is expressed as a rate of return (*MEC*), and *MC* is expressed as a rate of interest (*i*).

The profit-maximizing position is illustrated in Figure 8.22. As the firm invests more, and thus builds up its stock of capital, so *MEC* will fall due to diminishing returns. As long as *MEC* is greater than *i*, the firm should invest more. It should stop when the stock of capital has reached Q_1. Thereafter it should cut investment to a level just sufficient to replace worn-out machines, and thus keep the capital stock at Q_1.

The risks of investment. One of the problems with investment is that the future is uncertain. The return on an investment will depend on the value of the goods it produces. But this will depend on the goods market. For example, the return to investment in the car industry will depend on the demand for and price of cars. But future markets cannot be predicted with accuracy: they depend on consumer tastes, the actions of rivals and the whole state of the economy. Investment is thus risky.

How is this risk accounted for when calculating the benefits of an investment? The answer is to use a higher rate of discount. The higher the risk, the bigger the premium that must be added to the rate.

The supply of capital

It is necessary to distinguish the supply of *physical* capital from the supply of *finance* to be used by firms for the purchase of capital.

Supply of physical capital. The principles here are just the same as those in the goods market. It does not matter whether a firm is supplying lorries (capital) or cars (a consumer good): it will still produce up to the point where *MC* = *MR* if it wishes to maximize profits.

Supply of finance. When firms borrow to invest, this creates a demand for finance (or 'loanable funds'). The supply of loanable funds comes from the deposits that individuals and firms make in financial institutions. These deposits are savings, and represent the resources released when people refrain from consumption. In other words, the less people consume, the more loanable funds there will be available to finance investment.

Amongst other things, savings depend on the rate of interest that depositors receive. The higher the rate of interest, the more people will be encouraged to save. This would be illustrated by an upward-sloping supply curve of loanable funds.

Savings also depend on the level of people's incomes, their expectations of future price changes, and their general level of 'thriftiness' (their willingness to forgo present consumption in order to be able to have more in the future). A change in any of these other determinants will shift the supply curve.

* Determination of the price of capital equipment

In a competitive market, the price and quantity sold of a particular type of capital equipment (e.g. a computer) will be determined by the interaction of demand and supply. The demand will depend on the present value of investment in that capital good. The demand curve slopes downward due to diminishing returns (diminishing present value) to that investment.

The supply will depend on the profit maximizing behaviour of suppliers. The higher the price, the more existing firms will be prepared to produce and the more firms will enter the market.

If the rate of interest goes up, the present value of investment will fall. This is because a higher discount rate will now be used to work out the present value. This means that the demand curve for capital goods will shift to the left. As a result the equilibrium price and quantity of capital goods will fall.

> **?** What will happen to the equilibrium price and quantity of capital equipment in each of the following cases? (In each case you should consider which way the demand or supply curve shifts.)
> (a) A rise in the price of raw materials used to make the capital equipment.
> (b) A rise in the demand for the good that the capital equipment is used to make.
> (c) Technical progress that increases the efficiency of the capital equipment.
> (d) A rise in the supply of savings in the economy.
>
> If you can't work out the answer to (d), read on!

* Determination of the rate of interest

But what determines the rate of interest, the rate that is used for working out the present value of investment? Again the answer lies in demand and supply: only on this occasion it is the demand and supply of loanable funds.

The long-run position is illustrated in Figure 8.23. The supply curve is the total supply of savings, which in the long run can be used to build up the capital stock. The demand curve includes the demand by households for credit and also the demand by firms to finance their investment.

Why is this demand curve downward sloping? There are two reasons. First, households will borrow more at lower rates of interest. It effectively makes goods cheaper for them to buy. Secondly, it reflects the falling rate of return on investment as investment increases. This is simply due to diminishing returns to investment. As rates of interest fall, it will now become profitable for firms to invest in these projects that have a lower rate of return (provided their rate of return is now above the rate of interest): the demand for loanable funds then rises.

Equilibrium will be achieved where demand equals supply at an interest rate of i_e and a quantity of loanable funds $£_e$.

How will this market adjust to a change in demand or supply?

Assume that there is a rise in demand for capital equipment, due, say, to an improvement in technology which increases the productivity of capital. There is thus an increase in demand for loanable funds. The demand curve shifts to the right in Figure 8.23. The equilibrium rate of interest will rise and this will encourage more

Figure 8.23 The market for loanable funds

savings. The end result is that more money will be spent on capital equipment.

This does not necessarily mean that there will be much more capital equipment installed, however, especially in the short run. The reason is that the total supply of capital equipment in the economy for purchase is relatively inelastic in the short run. The capital goods industries cannot suddenly supply many more machines (although some of the extra demand can be met by imports). The increased demand will thus push up the price of capital equipment. Much of the extra expenditure on investment, then, is simply being spent on paying higher *prices* for capital equipment. What is more, these higher prices will reduce the rate of return on capital, which in turn will curtail the demand for investment.

In the long run, the supply of capital equipment is more elastic. An increase in demand for investment will thus have a bigger effect on the amount of equipment installed.

Capital and profit

What does the analysis so far tell us about the amount of profit firms will earn? After all, profit is the reward that the owners of firms get from having and using capital. This is what makes them 'capitalists'.

Remember from Chapter 5 the distinction between normal and supernormal profit. In a perfectly competitive world all supernormal profits will be competed away in the long run.

Another way of putting this is that a perfectly competitive firm in the long run will only earn a normal rate of return on capital. What this means is that the return on capital (after taking risk into account) will be just the same as if the owners of capital had simply deposited their money in a bank instead. If firm's capital yields a higher rate of return than this normal level (i.e. supernormal returns), other firms will be attracted to invest in similar capital. The resulting increased level of capital will increase the supply of goods. This in turn will lower the price of the goods and hence lower the rate of return on capital. This process will continue until the return on capital has fallen back to the normal level.

> **Normal rate of return**
> The rate of return (after taking risks into account) that could be earned elsewhere.

 Can a perfectly competitive firm earn a supernormal rate of return on capital if it *continuously* innovates?

If, however, capital owners have monopoly/oligopoly power and can thus restrict the entry of new firms or the copying of innovations – for example, by having a patent on a particular process – they can continue to get a supernormal return on their capital. They do not have the same competitive pressure to make further innovations.

If an investment entails *risks*, it will have to bring the possibility of returns higher than the market rate of interest, otherwise no one will be willing to take the risk. If the investor is lucky and the investment pays off, then a rate of profit considerably higher than the rate of interest can be earned. This will not be competed away by other firms if they too face similar risks: the reason is that *on average* such investments only yield an approximately normal rate of return.

An example of a risky investment is prospecting for oil. An oil company may be lucky and have a major strike, but it may simply drill dry well after dry well. If it does get a major strike and hence earn a large return on its investment, these profits will not be competed away by competitors prospecting in other fields, because they too still run the risk of drilling dry holes.

Rent: the reward to landowners

We turn now to land. The income it earns for landowners is the *rent* charged to the users of the land. This rent, like the rewards to other factors, is determined by demand and supply.

What makes land different from other factors of production is that it has an inelastic supply. In one sense this is obvious. The total supply of land in any area is fixed. It is in the very nature of land that it cannot be moved from one place to another! For example, the amount of land in Britain is fixed. In this sense, therefore, the supply of land is totally inelastic: the supply curve is vertical.

In another sense supply is not *totally* inelastic. This is where we are talking about the supply of a certain *quality* of land in a given area. Land can be improved. It can be cleared, levelled, drained, fertilized, etc. Thus the supply of a certain type of land can be increased by expending human effort on improving it. The question here, though, is whether *land* has thereby increased, or whether the improvements constitute *capital* invested in land, and if so whether the higher rents that such land can earn really amount to a return on the capital invested in it.

To keep the analysis simple let us assume that land *is* fixed. What then determines rent? Let us take the case of an area of 10 000 hectares surrounding the village of Oakleigh. This is shown as a vertical supply 'curve' in Figure 8.24. The demand

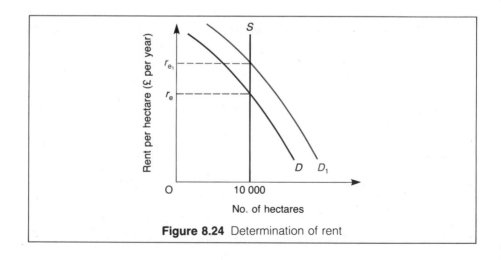

Figure 8.24 Determination of rent

Box 8.10

Is Rent the Same as Economic Rent?

Remember the distinction we made near the beginning of the chapter between *economic rent* and *transfer earnings*. It should now be clear why it was called economic 'rent'. Economic rent was that proportion of a factor's earnings that depended on demand. But in the case of land, *all* its earnings depend on demand and hence are entirely economic rent. There are no transfer earnings on land. It cannot be transferred to another part of the country where rents are higher!

As far as other factors of production are concerned, then, their economic rent is that portion of their earnings that is like rent on land – determined by demand.

 So far we have been considering rent on land. But what about rent on accommodation: is this all *economic* rent?

---

curve for that land will be like the demand curve for other factors of production. It is the *MRP* curve and slopes down due to diminishing returns to land.

The equilibrium rent is r_e, where demand and supply intersect.

The important thing to notice is that the level of this rent depends entirely on *demand*. For example, suppose that a new housing development takes place in Oakleigh, due perhaps to a growth in employment in a nearby town. The demand curve will shift to D_1 and the equilibrium rent will rise to r_{e_1}. But no more land will be forthcoming as a result: it remains fixed at 10 000 acres. Landowners will earn more rent, but they themselves have done nothing: the higher rent is a pure windfall gain.

So why are rents higher in some parts of the country than others? Why are rents in the centre of London many times higher per hectare than they are in the north of Scotland? The answer is that demand is very much higher in London.

Demand for land depends on its marginal revenue product. Thus it is differences in the *MRP* of land that explain the differences in rent from one area to another. There are two reasons for differences in *MRP*. Remember that $MRP = MPP$ (marginal physical product of the factor) $\times MR$ (marginal revenue of the good produced by that factor).

Differences in MPP

Land differs in productivity. Fertile land will produce a higher output than deserts or moorland. Similarly, land near centres of population will be of much more use to industry than land in the middle of nowhere.

 What other factors will determine the *MPP* of land for industry?

Differences in MR

The higher the demand for a particular good, the higher its price and marginal revenue, and hence the higher the demand and rent for the land on which that good is produced. Thus if the demand for housing rises relative to the demand for food, then the rent on land suitable for house building will rise relative to the rent on agricultural land. Likewise if the demand for dairy products goes up relative to that for wheat, the rent on land suitable for dairy production will go up relative to that on land suitable for wheat.

To summarize: rents will be high on land which is physically productive (high *MPP*) and produces goods in high demand (high *MR*).

Box 8.11

Rent Control
Cheap housing for all?

The purpose of rent control is to protect the consumer from high rent, as well as to provide cheap housing for the very poor.

In practice, however, many economists argue that such rent controls only succeed in making a larger part of the population worse off. How is this so?

Assume that legislation is passed which limits the rent that landlords can charge and this means that rents must be reduced in many cases. The supply of rented property will hardly fall in the short run, as landlords cannot quickly transfer their accommodation to other uses. In the diagram this is shown by the inelastic supply curve S.

The effect of rent control

With a rent ceiling of R_1 there is a relatively small shortage of rented property with Q_1 supplied and Q_2 demanded. As a result Q_1 households will get accommodation at the lower rent, while others, $Q_2 - Q_1$ will fail to find housing at all.

In the long run, landlords will respond to the lower rent by putting their accommodation to other uses. The supply curve will become flatter and the supply of rented property will fall. The supply curve is now S'.

In the long run, then, at the rent ceiling R_1, the quantity of rental accommodation supplied falls to Q_3. Shortages now increase as less rental housing is available, and more people become homeless – more, perhaps, than in an unregulated market.

Rent controls may have further adverse effects. First, on equity grounds it is somewhat arbitrary as to who gets and who does not get housing at the lower rent. Secondly, in the long run, those landlords who still keep their property available for rent may respond to the low rents by cutting maintenance costs and letting their property fall into a poor state of repair.

Thus in practice it could be argued that rent control may be more detrimental than beneficial to those to whom it should have been of greatest value.

Those in favour of rent controls counter these arguments by claiming that the demand and supply curves of rented accommodation are very inelastic.

Take the case of the demand curve. People have got to live somewhere. If rent control is abolished, people will just have to pay the higher rent or become homeless; and given that people will only sacrifice their home as a last resort, demand remains inelastic and rents could rise to a very high level.

1. How could housing supplied by the public sector be made to rectify some of the problems we have identified above? (What would it do to the supply curve?)
2. Using supply and demand curves, show the likely effect of rent control on (a) the supply of private flats; (b) the demand for rent collectors.
3. If the government gives poor people rent allowances (i.e. grants), how will this affect the level of rents in an uncontrolled market?
4. The case for and against rent controls depends to a large extent on the long-run elasticity of supply. Do you think it will be relatively elastic or inelastic? Give reasons.

We defined the factor of production 'land' to include raw materials. Does the analysis of rent that we have just been looking at apply to raw materials?

The price of land

Not all land is rented. Much of it is bought and sold outright. What determines its price? The price will depend on what the purchaser is prepared to pay, and this will depend on the land's rental value.

Let us say that a piece of land can earn £1000 per year. What would a person be prepared to pay for it? There is a simple formula for working this out. It is:

$$\frac{R}{i}$$

where R is the rent per year and i is the market rate of interest.

Let us assume that the market rate of interest is 10 per cent (i.e. 0.1). Then according to the formula, a purchaser would be prepared to pay:

$$\frac{£1000}{0.1} = £10\,000$$

Why should this be so? If a person has £10 000 to invest, they can deposit it in the bank. With an interest rate of 10 per cent this will earn that person £1000 per year. An alternative is to buy land. Assuming our piece of land is guaranteed to earn a rent of £1000 per year (with no risk attached), then provided it costs less than £10 000 to buy, it is a better investment than putting money in the bank. The competition between people to buy this land will drive its price up until it reaches £10 000.

1. What price would the same piece of land sell for if it still earned £1000 rent per year, but if the rate of interest were now 5 per cent?
2. What does this tell us about the relationship between the price of an asset (like land) and the rate of interest?

Conclusions: who are the rich and who are the poor?

We have been building up an answer to this question as this chapter has progressed. The final part of the answer concerns the ownership of land and capital. Many people own no land or capital at all. These people will therefore earn no profit, rent or interest.

For those who are fortunate enough to own productive assets their income from them will depend on (a) the quantity they own and (b) their rental value.

The quantity of assets owned
This will depend on the following.

- Inheritance. Some people have rich parents who leave them substantial amounts of land and capital.
- Past income and savings. If people have high incomes and save a large proportion of them, this helps them to build up a stock of assets.
- Skill in investment (entrepreneurial skill). The more skilful people are in investing and in organizing production the more rapidly will their stock of assets grow.
- Luck. When people open up a business there are usually substantial risks. The business might fail. But people may be lucky. Demand may grow and the business may flourish.

The rental value
This is the income earned per unit of land and capital. It will depend on the following.

- The level of demand for the factor. This depends on the factor's *MRP*, which in turn depends on its physical productivity (*MPP*) and the demand for the good it produces and hence the good's *MR*.
- The elasticity of demand for the good. The greater the monopoly power that capital owners have in the goods market, the less elastic will be the demand for the product and the greater will be the supernormal returns they can earn on their capital.

- The elasticity of supply of the factor. The less elastic its supply, the more factor owners can gain from a high demand. The high demand will simply push up the level of economic rent that the factor will earn.
- The total factor supply by other factor owners. The further to the left the total factor supply curve, the higher the level of economic rent that each unit of the factor can earn for any given level of demand.

Thus if you are lucky enough to have rich parents who leave you a lot of money when you are relatively young; if you are a skilful investor and save and reinvest a large proportion of your earnings; if you have luck in owning assets that few other people own, and which cannot be reproduced, and which produce goods in high demand: then you may end up very rich.

If you have no assets, you will have no property income at all. If at the same time you are on a low wage or are unemployed, then you may be very poor indeed.

In Chapter 9 we examine the problem of poverty and inequality. We look at the extent of the problem, at its causes, and at the various alternative policies a government can adopt to tackle the problem.

 ## SUMMARY

1. It is necessary to distinguish between buying the *services* of land (by renting) or capital (by hiring) from buying them outright.
2. The profit-maximizing employment of land and capital services will be where the factor's *MRP* is equal to its price (under perfect competition) or its *MC* (where firms have monopsony power).
3. The demand for capital services will be equal to MRP_K. Due to diminishing returns, this will decline as more capital is used.
4. The supply of capital services to a firm will be horizontal or upward sloping depending on whether the firm is perfectly competitive or has monopsony power. The supply of capital services by a firm in the short run is likely to be infinitely elastic up to its maximum use, and then totally inelastic. In the long run, the supplying firm can purchase additional capital equipment for hiring out. Its decision to do so will depend on its marginal cost. This will normally be expressed as a rate per year, which will take into account the opportunity cost of borrowing money to make the purchase, the annual depreciation of the equipment, and maintenance and handling costs.
5. The market supply of capital services is likely to be highly inelastic in the short run, given that capital equipment tends to have very specific uses and cannot normally be transferred from one use to another. In the long run it will be more elastic.
6. The price of capital services will be determined by the interaction of demand and supply.
*7. The demand for capital for purchase will depend on the return it earns for the firm. To calculate this return, all

future earnings from the investment have to be reduced to a present value by discounting at a market rate of interest (discount). If the present value exceeds the cost of the investment, the investment is worthwhile. Alternatively, a rate of return from the investment can be calculated and then this can be compared with the return that the firm could have earned by investing elsewhere.
*8. The supply of *physical* capital will be governed by the same principles as the supply of goods. A firm will maximize profits by supplying them up to the point where *MC* = *MR*. The supply of *finance* for investment depends on the supply of loanable funds, which in turn depends on the rate of interest, on the general level of thriftiness and on expectations about future price levels and incomes.
*9. The rate of interest will be determined by the demand and supply of loanable funds. When deciding whether to make an investment a firm will use this rate for discounting purposes. If, however, an investment involves risks, the firm will require a higher rate of return on the investment than current market interest rates.
10. Rent on land, like the price of other factor services, will be determined by the interaction of demand and supply. Its supply is totally inelastic (or nearly so). Its demand curve will be downward sloping and will equal the *MRP* of land.
11. The price of land will depend on its potential rental value (its marginal benefit) and the repayment costs of borrowing to pay for the land (its marginal cost). Equilibrium will be where the two are equal.

Inequality, Poverty and Policies to Redistribute Incomes

9.1 Inequality and poverty

Inequality is one of the most contentious issues in the world of economics and politics.

The political right argues that a certain amount of inequality and poverty is the inevitable price paid for an efficient, growing economy. People need the incentives of high incomes to encourage them to work, train, invest and take risks. This may mean that some people are poor, and most on the right argue in favour of government measures to alleviate poverty. Nevertheless they worry that any significant redistribution from rich to poor may seriously reduce growth and efficiency by undermining incentives. People on the right also argue from a moral standpoint that the freedom to own property and to pass it on to children, and the freedom to keep the bulk of the income from that property, are fundamental rights.

The left, not surprisingly, disagrees. A fundamental tenet of socialism is that the distribution of income should be based on need, rather than on private property ownership and the workings of the market. A truly socialist society would be a much more equal society. Most socialists nevertheless do accept that there will have to be some incentives for an economy to function, and that therefore there will have to be some minimum level of inequality.

Whether the current distribution of income is desirable or not is a normative question. Economists therefore cannot settle the debate between left and right over how much the government should redistribute incomes from rich to poor. Nevertheless economists do have a major role to play in the analysis of inequality. They can do the following:

- Identify the extent of inequality and analyze how it has changed over time.
- Explain why a particular level of income distribution occurs and what causes inequality to grow or to lessen.
- Examine the relationship between equality and other economic objectives such as efficiency.
- Identify various government policies to deal with problems of inequality and poverty.
- Examine the effects of these policies, both on inequality itself and on other questions such as efficiency, inflation and unemployment.

This chapter first looks at different ways of measuring inequality. It then shows how these different approaches can be used to examine the extent of inequality and poverty in the UK. The causes of inequality are examined next, and section 9.1

concludes by describing the various attitudes that governments take towards the question of inequality.

Section 9.2 examines various policies. In particular it focuses on taxes and benefits as means of redistributing income from the rich to the poor. The advantages and disadvantages of specific types of tax and benefit are examined. In particular, the relationship between income redistribution and economic efficiency is analyzed: for example, will high taxes on the rich discourage them from working and investing?

Types of inequality

There are a number of different ways of looking at the distribution of income and wealth. Each way highlights a different aspect of inequality.

Size distribution of income

This simply looks at how evenly incomes are distributed. It says nothing about how those incomes were earned, or the sort of people who receive them. The size distribution can be expressed between *households*, or between *individual earners*, or between *all individuals*. It can be expressed either *before* or *after* the deduction of taxes and the receipt of benefits.

Functional distribution of income

This is the distribution of income according to the *source* of that income.

At the broadest level it is the distribution between the major *factor categories*: labour, land and capital. This aspect of income distribution has figured prominently in the debate between left and right over the last 200 years, socialists claiming that rent and profit constitute an exploitation of labour, and conservatives claiming that rent and profit are the just rewards to the owners of property.

At a narrower level it is the distribution between groups *within* the broad factor categories: for example, the average wages of manual compared with non-manual workers, or the rate of return on capital in large businesses (however defined) compared with small businesses.

At the narrowest level it is the distribution between *individual types of factors of production*. In the case of labour it is the occupational distribution of income. This shows the differences in earnings between doctors, librarians, electricians, typists, bricklayers and so on. In the case of land it is the difference in rent per acre of different types of land. This is the type of distribution we examined in Chapter 8.

Distribution of income by recipient

This can be by *class of person*: women, men, single people, married people, people within a particular age group and so on. Alternatively, it can be by *geographical area*. Typically this is expressed in terms of differences in incomes between officially defined regions such as the North, the West Midlands, the South West and so on.

Distribution of wealth

Income is a *flow*. It measures the receipt of money per period of time (e.g. £10 000 per year). Wealth, by contrast, is a stock (see Box 8.9). It measures the value of a person's assets at a particular point in time. The distribution of wealth can be measured as a size distribution (how evenly it is distributed among the population); as a functional distribution (the proportion of wealth held in various forms, such as dwellings, land, company shares, building society deposits, etc.); or according to the holders of wealth, classified by age, sex, geographical area, etc.

Box 9.1

How Can We Define Poverty?

In attempting to solve a social problem such as poverty, it is normal for the policy-making body to adopt the following four-stage approach:

- The problem is defined.
- The problem is measured.
- The problem's causes are identified.
- Alternative policies are considered to cure the problem.

The importance of defining the problem of poverty correctly is that it determines the subsequent stages: the number of poor, possible causes of poverty and ways of tackling the problem.

There are two ways of looking at poverty.

Absolute poverty (or subsistence poverty)

As its name suggests, this definition involves identifying a poverty line measured in terms of those basic items considered essential to life: items such as adequate clothing, food and shelter.

By defining poverty in absolute terms, it is assumed that all individuals have similar minimum requirements, and that those whose means fall below the required minimum are poor.

Attempts have been made to include minimum social/cultural needs in such definitions: for example, adequate leisure and recreation, education and security.

? Compile your own list of basic necessities. Are these the same for all people?

Relative poverty

Relative poverty, by contrast, is a far more flexible concept.

The definition is based on judgements, made by each particular society, as to what is considered a reasonable and acceptable standard of living, according to the conventions of the day. Hence an individual who is unable to attain this reasonable and acceptable standard is considered poor. For example, if fridges, TVs and videos are considered part of 'civilized existence', then without them you are considered poor!

The flexibility of this definition lies in the fact that the standard of living considered to be acceptable by society will differ not only over time, but also from one society to another. Thus poverty measured in this way reflects changes within society.

? 1. If poverty is defined in absolute terms, will the list of necessities still vary from society to society?
2. If we use a relative definition of poverty, what difficulties will we encounter in comparing poverty over time?

Analysis of incomes below a certain level: the analysis of poverty

A major problem here is in defining just what is meant by poverty. The dividing line between who is poor and who is not is necessarily arbitrary. Someone who is classed as poor in the UK may seem comparatively rich to an Ethiopian. Where the line is drawn is important, however, to the extent that it determines who receives state benefits and who does not.

The extent and nature of poverty can be analyzed in a number of ways:

- The number of people or the proportion of the population falling into the category.
- The size distribution of income between poor people.
- The occupational distribution of poverty.
- The geographical distribution of poverty.
- The distribution of poverty according to age, sex, ethnic origin, marital status, educational attainment, etc.

It is not possible in this chapter to look at all aspects of inequality in the UK. Nevertheless some of the more important facts are considered, along with questions of their measurement and interpretation.

The size distribution of income in the UK

Table 9.1 shows the size distribution of income in the UK. It covers income from all sources. In these figures, households are grouped into five equal-sized groups or quintiles, from the poorest 20 per cent of households up to the richest 20 per cent.

Quantiles

Divisions of the population into equal-sized groups.

Quintiles

Divisions of the population into five equal-sized groups (an example of a quantile).

Table 9.1 Size distribution of UK income (by quintile group of households)

	Quintile groups of households					
	Bottom 20%	Next 20%	Middle 20%	Next 20%	Top 20%	Total
Income before taxes and benefits						
1976	0.8	9.4	18.8	26.6	44.4	100.0
1986	0.3	5.7	16.4	26.9	50.7	100.0
Income after taxes and benefits						
1976	7.0	12.6	18.2	24.1	38.1	100.0
1986	5.9	11.0	16.9	24.1	42.2	100.0

Source: *Social Trends* (CSO, 1989).

The following points can be drawn from these statistics:

- In 1986 the richest 20 per cent of households earned over 50 per cent of national income, and even after the deduction of taxes this was still over 42 per cent.
- The poorest 20 per cent, by contrast, earned a mere 0.3 per cent of national income, and even after the receipt of benefits this had only risen to 5.9 per cent.
- Inequality grew between 1976 and 1986. The pre-tax-and-benefits share of national income of the bottom 40 per cent of households fell from 10.2 per cent to 6.0 per cent; while the share of the top 20 per cent grew from 44.4 per cent to 50.7 per cent.

Deciles

Divisions of the population into ten equal-sized groups (another example of a quantile).

Figure 9.1 shows the distribution of income in 1984/85 before and after tax. This time there are ten equal-sized groups or deciles. Benefits are included in both the before-tax and the after-tax data. The chart dramatically depicts the level of inequality at the top end of the range. The top 10 per cent in 1984/85 earned 29.5 per cent of pre-tax income, nearly double that of the next 10 per cent, who earned 16.8 per cent.

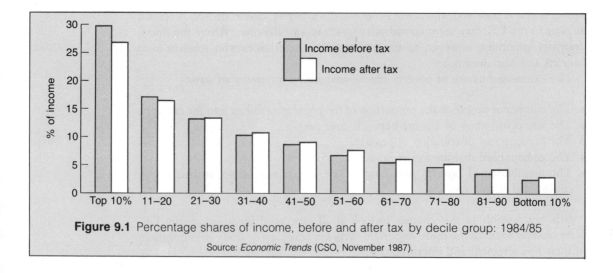

Figure 9.1 Percentage shares of income, before and after tax by decile group: 1984/85

Source: *Economic Trends* (CSO, November 1987).

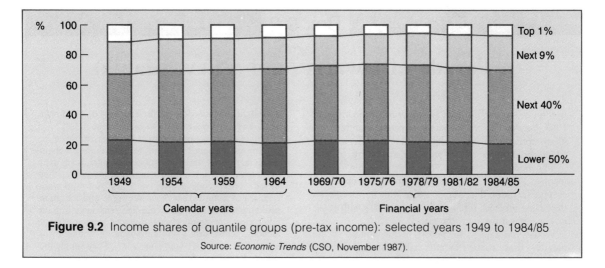

Figure 9.2 Income shares of quantile groups (pre-tax income): selected years 1949 to 1984/85
Source: *Economic Trends* (CSO, November 1987).

Figure 9.2 shows how the size distribution of pre-tax incomes has changed over the years. From 1949 to 1978/79 the share of the top income earners steadily declined. The share of the top 1 per cent was 11.2 per cent in 1949. It had fallen to 5.3 per cent by 1978/79, but then rose again to reach 6.4 per cent in 1984/85. The share of the bottom 50 per cent in 1978/79 has only changed slightly since 1949. It remained around the 23–24 per cent level until the 1980s, when it fell slightly, reaching 22.2 per cent in 1984/85. The general pattern that is apparent from this chart is a gradual distribution from high-income earners to middle-income earners from 1949 to 1978/79 and then a reversal of this trend from 1978/79 to 1984/85.

Ways of measuring the size distribution of income

Apart from tables and charts, two of the most widely used methods for measuring inequality are the *Lorenz curve* and the *Gini coefficient*.

Lorenz curve

Figure 9.3 shows the Lorenz curve for the UK based on 1984/85 pre-tax incomes.

The horizontal axis measures percentages of the population from the poorest to the richest. Thus the 40 per cent point represents the poorest 40 per cent of the population. The vertical axis measures the percentage of national income they receive.

The curve starts at the origin: zero people earn zero incomes. If income were distributed totally equally, the Lorenz curve would be a straight 45° line. The 'poorest' 20 per cent of the population would earn 20 per cent of national income. The 'poorest' 60 per cent would earn 60 per cent, and so on. The curve ends up at the top right-hand corner, with 100 per cent of the population earning 100 per cent of national income.

In practice the Lorenz curve will 'hang below' the 45° line. Point *x*, for example, shows that the poorest 50 per cent of UK households earned only 22.2 per cent of national income. The further the curve drops below the 45° line, the greater will be the level of inequality.

The Lorenz curve is quite useful for showing the change in income distribution over time. From 1949 to 1978/79 the curve moved inwards towards the 45° line,

Lorenz curve

A curve showing the proportion of national income earned by any given percentage of the population (measured from the poorest upwards).

Box 9.2

A Parade of Dwarfs (and a Few Giants)

In this extract from his book *Income Distribution* written in 1963, Jan Pen describes a parade of people marching by. They represent the whole population of the UK, and the whole parade takes exactly one hour to pass by.

The height of each person represents his or her income. People of average height are the people with average incomes. The parade starts with the people on the lowest incomes (the dwarfs) and finishes with those on the highest incomes (the giants).

Would you expect the people in the middle of the parade – those passing by after half an hour – to be of average height? Read on and see . . .

In the first few seconds a remarkable thing already happens. If we have superhuman powers of observation (and why shouldn't we confer them upon ourselves?) we see a number of people of negative height passing. On closer inspection they prove to be businessmen who have suffered losses and whose capital is reduced. They are not necessarily short people. In fact, right in the front we spot a few very tall men, with their feet on the ground and their heads deep in the earth. The first one may be as tall as ten yards – he must be rich to indulge in that kind of thing. It's an unhealthy way of carrying on, and most of them don't keep it up long.

After this tragi-comic opening we see tiny gnomes pass by, the size of a matchstick, a cigarette. We think we see among them housewives who have worked a short time for some money and so have not got anything like an annual income, schoolboys with a paper round and once again a few entrepreneurs who didn't make it.

Suddenly we see an increase by leaps and bounds. The people passing by are still very small ones – about three feet – but they are noticeably taller than their predecessors. They form a heterogeneous group; they include some young people, especially girls who work regularly in factories, but above all people who are not in paid employment; very many old-age pensioners without other means of support, some divorced women without alimony, people with a physical handicap. Among them are owners of shops doing poor trade. They supply the smooth transitions. And we see artists – they may include geniuses, but the public does not understand their work and the market does not reward their capacities.

After them – the parade has been going on for about ten minutes – come the ordinary workers about whom there is nothing out of the ordinary except that they are in the lowest-paid jobs. Dustmen, Underground ticket collectors, some miners. The unskilled clerks march in front of the unskilled manual workers. Precisely among these lower-paid categories each group applies the principle of ladies first – particularly in Britain equal pay is far from being a reality. We now also see large numbers of coloured persons. These groups take their time to pass; we have ample opportunity to observe them at our leisure. It takes almost fifteen minutes before the passing marchers reach a height of substantially more than four feet. For you and me this is a disturbing sight; fifteen minutes is a long time to keep seeing small people pass

---

suggesting a lessening of inequality. Since then it has moved downwards away from the 45° line, suggesting a deepening of inequality.

The problem with simply comparing Lorenz curves by eye is that it is imprecise. This problem is overcome by using Gini coefficients.

Gini coefficient

Gini coefficient

The area between the Lorenz curve and the 45° line divided by the total area under the 45° line.

The Gini coefficient is a precise way of measuring the position of the Lorenz curve. It is the ratio of the area between the Lorenz curve and the 45° line to the whole area below the 45° line. In Figure 9.3 this is the ratio of the shaded area A to the whole area $(A + B)$.

If income is totally equally distributed so that the Lorenz curve follows the 45° line, area A disappears and the Gini coefficient is zero. As inequality increases, so does area A. The Gini coefficient rises. In the extreme case of total inequality, where one person earns the whole of national income, area B would disappear and the Gini coefficient would be 1. Thus the Gini coefficient will be between 0 and 1. The higher it is, the greater is the inequality. In 1949 the Gini coefficient in the UK was 0.41. It gradually fell over the years until by the late 1970s it was 0.37. It then rose again and by the mid-1980s was once more at a level of 0.41.

Gini coefficients have the advantage of being relatively simple to understand and

Box 9.2 (cont'd)

by who barely reach to our midriff. More than a third of them are women, dwarf-like human beings. In embarrassment we avert our gaze and look in the direction of the approaching parade to catch sight at long last of normal people.

But a new surprise awaits us here. *We keep on seeing dwarfs*. Of course they gradually become a little taller, but it's a slow process. They include masses of workers, just ordinary people with not inconsiderable technical knowledge, but shorties. After we have waited another ten minutes small people approach who reach to our collar-bones. We see skilled industrial workers, people with considerable training. Office workers, respectable persons so to speak. We know that the parade will last an hour, and perhaps we expected that after half-an-hour we would be able to look the marchers straight in the eye, but that is not so. We are still looking down on the tops of their heads, and even in the distance we do not yet see any obvious improvement. The height is growing with tantalizing slowness, and forty-five minutes have gone by before we see people of our own size arriving. To be somewhat more exact: about twelve minutes before the end the average income recipients pass by.

After the average income recipients have passed, the scene changes rather quickly. The marchers' height grows; six minutes later we see the arrival of the top ten per cent. The first to arrive are around six feet six inches, but to our surprise we see that they are still people with modest jobs.

In the last few minutes giants suddenly loom up. A lawyer, not exceptionally successful; eighteen feet tall. A colonel, also of much the same height. Engineers who work for nationalized industries. The first doctors come into sight, seven to eight yards, the first accountants.

There is still one minute to go, and now we see towering fellows. University professors, nine yards, senior officers of large concerns, ten yards, a Permanent Secretary thirteen yards tall, and an even taller High Court judge; a few accountants, eye surgeons and surgeons of twenty yards or more.

During the last seconds the scene is dominated by colossal figures: people like tower flats. Most of them prove to be businessmen, managers of large firms and holders of many directorships and also film stars and a few members of the Royal Family.

The rear of the parade is brought up by a few participants who are measured in miles. Indeed they are figures whose height we cannot even estimate: their heads disappear into the clouds and probably they themselves do not even know how tall they are.

Suddenly the parade is gone – the income recipients disappear from sight and leave the spectators behind them with mixed feelings.[1]

1. Draw a sketch graph of the parade. On the vertical axis put the height of the passers-by (their income). On the horizontal axis measure the time from 0 to 60 minutes (the cumulative number of people from poorest to richest). What shape is the graph? Why is it not a straight line?

2. Why is the person in the middle of the parade (the *median* person) not of average (*mean*) height? How is the answer to this question related to the answer to question 1?

[1] Jan Pen, *Income Distribution* (Penguin, 1971).

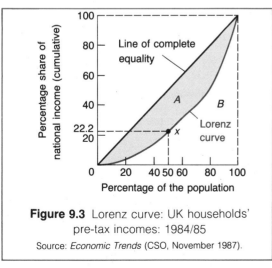

Figure 9.3 Lorenz curve: UK households' pre-tax incomes: 1984/85

Source: *Economic Trends* (CSO, November 1987).

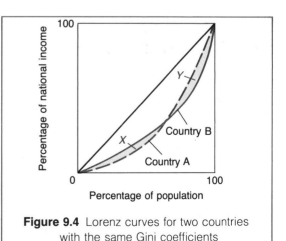

Figure 9.4 Lorenz curves for two countries with the same Gini coefficients

use. They provide a clear way of comparing income distribution either in the same country at different times, or between different countries. They suffer two main drawbacks, however.

First, a single measure cannot take into account all the features of inequality. Take the case of the two countries illustrated in Figure 9.4. If area *X* is equal to area *Y*, they will have the same Gini coefficient, and yet the pattern of their income distribution is quite different.

> **?** In which country in Figure 9.4 would you expect to find the highest number of poor people? Describe how income is distributed in the two cases.

Secondly, there is the problem of what statistics are used in the calculation. Are they pre-tax or post-tax; do they include benefits; do they include non-monetary incomes (such as food grown for own consumption: a major item in many Third World countries); are they based on individuals, households or tax units? Unfortunately, different countries use different types of statistics. International comparisons of inequality are thus fraught with difficulties.

Ratios of the shares in national income of two quantile groups

This is a very simple method of measuring income distribution. A ratio quite commonly used is that of the share of national income of the *bottom 40 per cent* of the population to that of the *top 20 per cent*. Thus if the bottom 40 per cent earned 15 per cent of national income and the top 20 per cent earned 50 per cent of national income, the ratio would be 15/50 = 0.3. The lower the ratio, therefore, the greater the inequality. Table 9.2 gives some examples of this ratio from different countries.

Table 9.2 Ratio of income shares of bottom 40% to top 20% of households (after taxes and benefits)

Country	Year	Ratio	Country	Year	Ratio
Brazil	1972	0.10	UK	1986	0.40
Peru	1972	0.11	USA	1980	0.43
Kenya	1976	0.15	Denmark	1981	0.45
Philippines	1985	0.27	Yugoslavia	1978	0.48
India	1975/6	0.33	Norway	1982	0.49
Hong Kong	1980	0.34	West Germany	1978	0.52
South Korea	1976	0.37	Hungary	1982	0.57
Bangladesh	1981/2	0.38	Japan	1979	0.58
France	1975	0.40	Netherlands	1981	0.62

Source: *World Development Report* (World Bank, 1989).

> **?** 1. Why, do you think, are the ratios for developing countries lower than those for developed countries?
> 2. Make a list of reasons why the figures in this table may not give an accurate account of relative levels of inequality between countries.
> 3. What would the ratio be if national income were absolutely equally distributed?

The functional distribution of income in the UK

Distribution of income by source

Table 9.3 shows the sources of household incomes in 1975 and 1986. Wages and salaries constitute by far the largest element. However, their share fell from 74.8 per cent to 64.3 per cent of national income between 1975 and 1986. Conversely, the share coming from social security benefits and pensions rose from 11.9 per cent to

Table 9.3 Sources of UK household income as a percentage of total household income

	Wages and salaries	Income from self-employment	Income from investments	Pensions and annuities	Social security benefits	Imputed rent	Other	Total
1975	74.8	5.5	3.5	2.3	9.6	3.4	0.9	100.0
1986	64.3	7.7	4.2	4.3	13.0	5.4	1.1	100.0

Source: *Annual Abstract of Statistics* (CSO, 1989).

17.3 per cent reflecting the higher levels of unemployment in the mid-1980s and the growing proportion of the population past retirement age.

In contrast to wages and salaries, investment income (dividends, interest and rent) accounted for a very small percentage of household income – a mere 4.2 per cent.

If you own property and rent it out, the income you earn will count as investment income. This rent is what people pay you for the benefits of living in the property. If, however, you live in your own house, you still get benefits from it (i.e. of living in it) and yet there is no rent actually paid. To account for these benefits to owner occupiers, therefore, an element for imputed rent is included in the statistics for household income. It is not a money income, except in the sense that it is a saving of rent from not having to live in rented accommodation.

The overall shares illustrated in Table 9.3 hide the fact that the sources of income differ quite markedly between different income groups. These differences are shown in Table 9.4.

Column (1) shows that higher income groups get a larger proportion of their income from wages and salaries than do lower income groups. This can be largely explained by examining column (5). As would be expected, the poor tend to get a larger proportion of their incomes in social security benefits than do people further up the income scale.

It is interesting to note that the second poorest 20 per cent of households have a larger proportion of their income from pensions and imputed rent than any other group. As far as pensioners are concerned, they are clustered in this group because they tend to be fairly poor (pensions being less than wages), but not as poor as the unemployed or families on low incomes with a large number of dependants. As far as imputed rent is concerned, the poorest group tend not to be home owners and thus have little imputed rent allocated to them.

Imputed rent

The benefits that owner occupiers gain from living in their own property, measured as the rent they would have to pay for living in equivalent rented accommodation.

 Why do higher income groups have proportionately less imputed rent?

Table 9.4 Sources of UK household income as a percentage of total household income by quintile groups: 1987

Gross household weekly incomes (quintiles)	Wages and salaries (1)	Income from self-employment (2)	Income from investments (3)	Pensions and annuities (4)	Social security benefits (5)	Imputed rent (6)	Other (7)	Total (8)
Lowest 20%	4.4	1.7	3.0	4.8	78.2	5.8	2.1	100.0
Next 20%	26.4	5.4	5.6	10.0	43.0	7.3	2.3	100.0
Middle 20%	61.1	6.9	4.8	6.9	13.0	5.8	1.5	100.0
Next 20%	73.6	6.7	3.6	3.8	5.9	5.2	1.3	100.0
Highest 20%	72.2	11.1	5.6	3.1	2.5	4.2	1.3	100.0
All households	63.5	8.4	4.9	4.6	12.1	5.1	1.5	100.0

Source: *Family Expenditure Survey 1987* (HMSO, 1989).

One perhaps surprising feature to note is that the proportion of income coming from profits, rent and interest (column (3)) varies little between the income groups. In fact only for those people in the top 1 or 2 per cent is it significantly higher. The conclusion from this, plus the fact that investment incomes account for only 4.9 per cent of household incomes in total, is that incomes from capital and land are only of relatively minor significance in explaining income inequality.

The major cause of differences in incomes between individuals in employment is the differences in wages and salaries between different occupations.

Distribution of wages and salaries by occupation

Differences in full-time wages and salaries are illustrated in Table 9.5. This table shows the average gross weekly earnings of full-time adult male workers in selected occupations in 1987. As can be seen there are considerable differences in earnings between different occupations. The causes of differences in wages from one occupation to another were examined in Chapter 8.

Table 9.5 Average gross weekly earnings of UK full-time adult male employees (selected occupations: 1987)

Occupation	Average Gross weekly earnings (£)	Occupation	Average gross weekly earnings (£)
Finance, insurance, tax specialists	475	Telephone fitters	224
Medical practitioners	462	Welders	197
Personnel managers	363	Bus and coach drivers	175
Journalists	343	Nurses	173
Scientists and mathematicians	300	Painters and decorators	160
Mechanical engineers	299	Footwear workers	156
Accountants	294	Refuse collectors	154
Policemen below sergeant	265	Records and library clerks	152
Technical sales representatives	253	Bakers, confectioners	149
Secondary school teachers	248	Barmen	132
Face-trained coal workers	226	General farm workers	123

Source: *New Earnings Survey* (HMSO, 1987).

? If fringe benefits (such as long holidays, company cars, free clothing/uniforms, travel allowances and health insurance) were included, do you think the level of inequality would increase or decrease? Explain why.

About 15 per cent of the earnings in Table 9.5 come from overtime (on average about 5.5 hours per week). The amount of overtime worked differs markedly, however, between occupations. Thus it is not just the basic hourly wage rate (or annual salary) that explains differences in earnings from one occupation to another, but also the number of hours worked and the overtime rate.

Table 9.6 Weekly income for different types of UK household: 1987

	One adult (not retired)	One adult, two or more children	One man, one woman (not retired)	Two adults, four or more children
Gross normal weekly household income (£)	181.75	118.35	322.81	258.91

Source: *Family Expenditure Survey 1987* (HMSO).

Other determinants of income inequality

Differences in household composition

Other things being equal, the more dependants there are in a household, the lower the income will be *per member* of that household. Table 9.6 gives an extreme example of this. It shows the average household income in Britain in 1987 of four different categories of household.

Households with two adults and four or more children had a lower average *gross* income than households with only one man and one woman. This means that they had a very much lower income *per member* of the household.

There is a twin problem for many large households. Not only may there be relatively more children and old-aged dependants, but also the total household income will be reduced if one of the adults stays at home to look after the family, or only works part time.

Differences by sex

Box 8.7 looked at some of the aspects of income inequality between the sexes. Table 9.7 gives examples of average gross weekly earnings of full-time adult female workers in 1987. The average for all occupations was £145. This compares with £219 for men. There are three important factors to note:

- Women are paid less than men in the same occupations. You will see this if you compare some of the occupations in Table 9.7 with the same ones in Table 9.5.
- Women tend to be employed in lower-paid occupations than men.
- Women do much less overtime than men (on average about 1.5 hours per week, compared with 5.5 for men).

Table 9.7 Average gross weekly earnings of full-time adult female employees (selected occupations: 1987)

Occupation	Average gross weekly earnings (£)	Occupation	Average gross weekly earnings (£)
Policewomen (below sergeant)	238	Telephonist	133
Professional (management)	237	Records and library clerks	127
Secondary teachers	215	Cleaners	105
Secretaries/shorthand typists	154	Shop assistants	98
Nurses	150	Barmaids	94
Inspectors and testers	136	Kitchen hands	93

Source: *New Earnings Survey* (HMSO, 1987).

List the reasons for each of the three factors above. (Re-read section 8.3 and Box 8.7 if you need help.)

Differences in the geographical distribution of income

Table 9.8 shows the gross weekly household incomes in different types of geographical area in the UK in 1985. These incomes reflect the following factors:

- Differences in the types of occupation between areas. This in turn reflects differences in the types of industry in different areas.
- Differences in the relative demand and supply of workers with particular qualifications. Areas with higher unemployment will tend to pay lower average wages. Areas with skill shortages will tend to pay higher average wages.

Table 9.8   Gross weekly median household incomes (£): 1985

Greater London	Metropolitan districts	Non-metropolitan districts	
		High population density	Low population density
208	160	176	194

- Differences in the costs of living between areas. The higher the cost of living, the higher the wage that must be paid to attract sufficient labour and the higher the wages that will be demanded by trade unions.
- Differences in household composition between areas. Areas where there are relatively large numbers of owner-occupied houses and two-or-more-earner households will have higher average household incomes.

Geographical differences in income are also apparent on a regional basis. For example, average incomes are lower in the North than in the South East and East Anglia. Regional inequality is explored in section 20.4.

The distribution of wealth

Wealth is difficult to measure. Being a *stock* of assets (such as a house, land, furniture, personal possessions and investments), it only has an easily measurable value when it is sold. What is more, individuals are not required to keep any record of their assets. Only when people die and their assets are assessed for inheritance tax does a record become available. Official statistics are thus based on Inland Revenue data of the assets of those who have died that year. These statistics are suspect for two reaons. First, the people who have died are unlikely to be a representative sample of the population. Secondly, many items may not be included, especially household and personal items, and items passed automatically to the surviving spouse.

Tables 9.9 and 9.10 give official statistics on the UK composition and distribution of wealth. As can be seen from Table 9.10, inequality of wealth is far greater than inequality of income. The wealthiest 1 per cent of the adult population owned 18 per cent of the marketable wealth in 1987, and the wealthiest 10 per cent owned 50 per cent. These figures do not include pension rights, which are much more equally distributed. Even when they are included, however, the wealthiest 1 per cent and 10 per cent still owned 10 per cent and 34 per cent respectively of the nation's wealth.

The four major causes of inequality in the distribution of wealth are as follows:

- *Inheritance*: this allows inequality to be perpetuated from one generation to another.
- *Income inequality*: people with higher incomes can save more.
- *Different propensities to save*: people who save a larger proportion of their income will build up a bigger stock of wealth.
- *Entrepreneurial and investment talent/luck*: some people are successful in investing their wealth and making it grow rapidly.

Even though wealth was still highly concentrated in 1985, there had been a significant reduction in inequality of wealth over time. From 1971 to 1981 the Gini coefficient of wealth fell a full ten percentage points from 0.80 to 0.70. A major reason for this was the increased taxation of inherited wealth. Another reason in the early 1970s was a substantial fall in the real value of shares when share prices failed to keep pace with inflation. Since 1981, however, this reduction in inequality has been halted.

Table 9.9 Composition of UK wealth: 1986

Type of wealth	% of total
Dwellings (net of mortgage debt)	33.4
Other fixed assets	6.5
Non-marketable tenancy rights	7.9
Consumer durables	8.2
Building society shares	7.8
National savings, bank deposits	7.6
Stocks and shares	10.5
Other financial assets	18.1
	100.0

Source: *Social Trends* (CSO, 1990).

Table 9.10 Size distribution of UK wealth

	Proportion of marketable wealth (%)		
	1971	1981	1987
Wealthiest 1%	31	21	18
Wealthiest 5%	52	40	36
Wealthiest 10%	65	54	50
Wealthiest 25%	86	77	74
Wealthiest 50%	97	94	93
Gini coefficient	0.80	0.70	0.67

Sources: *Inland Revenue Statistics* (HMSO, 1987); *Social Trends* (CSO, 1990).

Causes of inequality

We turn now to identify the major causes of inequality. The problem has many dimensions and there are many factors that determine the pattern and depth of inequality. It is thus wrong to try to look for a single cause, or even the major one. What follows then is a list of the possible determinants of inequality:

- Inequality of wealth. People with wealth are able to obtain an income other than from their own labour. The greater the inequality of wealth, the greater is the inequality of income likely to be.
- Differences in ability. People differ in strength, intelligence, dexterity, etc. Some of these differences are innate and some are acquired through the process of 'socialization' – education, home environment, peer group, etc.
- Differences in attitude. Some people are adventurous, willing to take risks, willing to move for better jobs, keen to push themselves forward. Others are much more cautious.
- Differences in qualifications. These are reflections of a number of things: ability, attitudes toward study, access to educational establishments, the quality of tuition, attitudes and income of parents, etc.
- Differences in hours worked. Some people do a full-time job plus overtime, or a second job; others only work part time.
- Differences in job utility/disutility. Other things being equal, unpleasant, arduous or dangerous jobs will need to pay higher wages.
- Differences in power. Monopoly power in the supply of factors or goods, and monopsony power in the demand for factors, is unequally distributed in the economy.
- Differences in the demand for goods. Factors employed in expanding industries will tend to have a higher marginal revenue product because their output has a higher market value.
- Differences in household composition. The greater the number of dependants relative to income earners, the poorer the household will be (other things being equal).
- Discrimination, whether by race, sex, age, social background, etc.
- Degree of government support. The greater the support for the poor, the less will be the level of inequality in the economy.
- Unemployment. As explained in the previous section, this has become one of the major causes of poverty and hence inequality in recent years.

 Which of the above causes are reflected in differences in the marginal revenue product of factors?

Box 9.3

Poverty in the Past

Consider from the following passage whether it is reasonable or even possible to compare poverty today with poverty in the 1800s.

Every great city has one or more slums, where the working class is crowded together. True, poverty often dwells in hidden alleys close to the palaces of the rich; but, in general, a separate territory has been assigned to it, where, removed from the sight of the happier classes, it may struggle along as it can. These slums are pretty equally arranged in all the great towns of England, the worst houses in the worst quarters of the towns; usually one- or two-storied cottages in long rows, perhaps with cellars used as dwellings, almost always irregularly built. These houses of three or four rooms and a kitchen form, throughout England, some parts of London excepted, the general dwellings of the working class. The streets were generally unpaved, rough, dirty, filled with vegetable and animal refuse, without sewers or gutters, but supplied with foul, stagnant pools instead. Moreover, ventilation is impeded by the bad, confused method of building of the whole quarter, and since many human beings live crowded into a small space, the atmosphere that prevails in these working-men's quarters may readily be imagined. Further, the streets serve as drying grounds in fine weather; lines are stretched across from house to house, and hung with wet clothing.

The houses are occupied from cellar to garret, filthy within and without, and their appearance is such that no human being could possibly wish to live in them. But all this is nothing in comparison with the dwellings in the narrow courts and alleys between the streets, entered by covered passages between the houses, in which the filth and tottering ruin surpass all description. Scarcely a whole window-pane can be found, the walls are crumbling, doorposts and window-frames loose and broken, doors of old boards nailed together, or altogether wanting in this thieves' quarter, where no doors are needed, there being nothing to steal. Heaps of garbage and ashes lie in all directions, and the foul liquids emptied before the doors gather in stinking pools. Here the poorest of the poor, the worst-paid workers with thieves and the victims of prostitution indiscriminately huddled together, the majority Irish, or of Irish extraction, and those who have yet sunk in the whirlpool of moral ruin which surrounds them, sinking daily deeper, losing daily more and more of their power to resist the demoralizing influence of want, filth, and evil surroundings.[2]

? 1. If we were to measure poverty today and in the 1800s in *absolute terms* (see Box 9.1), in which would there be the greater number of poor?

2. If we measure poverty in *relative terms*, must a society inevitably have a problem of poverty, however rich it is?

[2] F. Engels, *The Condition of the English Working Class* (Progress Publishers, 1973), pp. 166–7.

Government attitudes towards inequality

The political right sees little problem with inequality as such. In fact, inequality has an important economic function. Factor price differences are an essential part of a dynamic market economy. They are the price signals that encourage resources to move to sectors of the economy where demand is growing, and away from sectors where demand is declining. If the government interferes with this process by taxing high incomes and subsidizing low incomes, working people will not have the same incentive to gain better qualifications, to seek promotion, to do overtime, or to move for better jobs. Similarly, owners of capital will not have the same incentive to invest.

If inequality is to be reduced, claims the political right, it is better done by encouraging greater factor mobility. If factor supply curves are more elastic (greater mobility), then any shifts in demand will cause smaller changes in factor prices and thus less inequality. But how is greater mobility to be encouraged? The answer, they say, is to create a culture of self-help: where people are not too reliant on state support; where they will 'get on their bikes' and look for higher incomes. At the same time they argue that the monopoly power of unions to interfere in labour markets should be curtailed. The net effect of these two things, they claim, is to create a more competitive labour market which will help to reduce inequality as well as promoting economic growth and efficiency.

State support, say those on the right, should be confined to the relief of 'genuine' poverty. Benefits should be simply a minimum safety net for those who cannot work (e.g. the sick or disabled), or on a temporary basis for those who, through no fault of their own, have lost their jobs. Even at this basic level, however, the right argues that state support can be a serious disincentive to effort.

Although many on the political left accept that there is some possibility of a trade-off between equality and efficiency, they see it as a far less serious problem. Questions of efficiency and growth, claims the left, are best dealt with by encouraging investment. This, they argue, is best achieved by creating an environment of industrial democracy where workers participate in investment decisions. This common purpose is in turn best achieved in a more equal and less individualistically competitive society. The left also sees a major role for government in providing support for investment: for example, through government-sponsored research, by investment grants, by encouraging firms to get together and plan a co-ordinated strategy, or by maintaining low interest rates which make borrowing cheaper for investment.

These policies on growth and efficiency, claims the left, will leave the government freer to pursue a much more active policy on redistribution.

▲ SUMMARY

1. Inequality can be examined by looking at the size distribution of income, the functional distribution of income (whether by broad factor categories, narrow factor categories, occupation or other individual factor reward), the distribution of income by recipient (whether by class of person or geographical area), the distribution of wealth, or the extent and nature of poverty.

2. An analysis of the size distribution of income in the UK shows that inequality has grown.

3. The size distribution of income can be illustrated by means of a Lorenz curve. The greater the inequality, the more bowed the curve will be towards the bottom right-hand corner.

4. Size distribution can also be measured by a Gini coefficient. This will give a figure between 0 (total equality) and 1 (total inequality). It can also be measured as the ratio of the share of national income of a given lower income quantile to that of a higher income quantile.

5. Wages and salaries constitute by far the largest source of income, and thus inequality can be explained mainly in terms of differences in wages and salaries. Nevertheless state benefits are an important moderating influence on

inequality and constitute the largest source of income for the poorest 20 per cent of households. Investment earnings are only a minor determinant of income except for the richest 1 or 2 per cent.

6. Apart from differences in wages and salaries between occupations, other determinants of income inequality include differences in household composition, sex and where people live.

7. The distribution of wealth is less equal than the distribution of income. The trend towards greater equality of wealth stopped in the early 1980s.

8. Attitudes towards government redistribution of income vary among political parties. The political right stresses the danger that redistributive policies may destroy incentives. The best approach to inequality, according to the right, is to 'free up' markets so as to encourage greater mobility. The left, by contrast, sees fewer dangers in reducing incentives and stresses the moral and social importance of redistribution from rich to poor. The left argues that growth and employment are best encouraged by direct state support for investment.

9.2 Taxes, benefits and the redistribution of income

In this section we will look at policies to redistribute incomes more equally. This is one of the major roles of government intervention in the economy. There are two other major roles, however, that we will be examining in later chapters and which it is important at least to identify at this stage.

The role of government intervention in the economy

Policies to redistribute incomes

There are four main types of redistributive policy.

Taxation. By taxing the rich proportionately more than the poor, the post-tax distribution of income will be more equal than the pre-tax distribution.

Subsidies. These are of two broad types. First, *cash benefits* can be seen as subsidies to people's incomes. They include such things as family credit, child benefit and old-age pensions. Secondly, *benefits in kind* provide subsidized goods and services, which may be provided free (e.g. education and health care) or at a reduced price (e.g. concessionary bus fares for the elderly). Subsidies will lessen inequality if they account for a larger proportion of a poor person's income than a rich person's.

Legislation. Examples include minimum wage legislation and anti-discrimination legislation.

Structural. This encompasses a wide range of policies where the government tries to alter those institutions and attitudes of society which increase or at least perpetuate inequalities. Examples of such policies include attacking privileges, instituting universal comprehensive education, encouraging worker share ownership, encouraging industries to move to areas of high unemployment and encouraging the provision of crèche facilities at work.

We shall just focus on two of these policies: taxes and benefits.

Provision of goods and services not provided efficiently (or at all) by the market

Markets in the real world are imperfect and thus do not lead to an optimum allocation of resources for any *given* distribution of income. Sometimes the government will choose to provide certain goods and services directly, such as education, health, defence, roads and the administration of justice. These, as we shall see in Chapter 10, are unlikely to be provided adequately by the market. Alternatively, the government can subsidize their provision by the private sector.

Either way, government expenditure has to be financed. Although some finance can be obtained from government borrowing, from the goods and services sold by nationalized industries, from selling publicly owned assets (privatization), from various charges, such as prescriptions, and even from printing more money, the bulk of government expenditure has to be financed from taxes.

Taxes also have an allocative function themselves. They can be used to correct market signals. For example, taxes can be imposed on activities causing harmful side-effects, such as pollution or smoking and drinking, thereby reducing them to an 'optimum' level. The use of taxes and benefits to correct market distortions is examined in section 10.3.

Fiscal policy

Finally, government expenditure and taxation have a macroeconomic role in stabilizing the economy. The Chancellor of the Exchequer can adjust government expenditure and taxation in order to affect the level of unemployment, the rate of inflation, the rate of growth of the economy, the balance of payments, or the exchange rate of the pound into other currencies. Adjusting taxes and/or government expenditure for these purposes is known as 'fiscal policy'. It is examined extensively in later chapters.

Box 9.4

Adam Smith and the Maxims of Taxation

There are four maxims with regard to taxes in general,

1. equality,

   The subjects of every state ought to contribute towards the support of the government, as nearly as possible, in proportion to their respective abilities; that is, in proportion to the revenue which they respectively enjoy under the protection of the state.

2. certainty,

   The tax which each individual is bound to pay ought to be certain, and not arbitrary. The time of payment, the manner of payment, the quantity to be paid, ought all to be clear and plain to the contributor, and to every other person.

3. convenience of payment,

   Every tax ought to be levied at the time, or in the manner, in which it is most likely to be convenient for the contributor to pay it.

4. and economy of collection,

   Every tax ought to be so contrived as both to take out and to keep out of the pockets of the people as little as

possible, over and above what it brings into the public treasury of the state.

which have recommended themselves to all nations.

The evident justice and utility of the foregoing maxims have recommended them more or less to the attention of all nations. All nations have endeavoured, to the best of their judgement, to render their taxes as equal as they could contrive; as certain, as convenient to the contributor, both in the time and the mode of payment, and in proportion to the revenue which they brought to the prince, as little burdensome to the people.[3]

 Consider Box 9.5 on the poll tax, and assess the tax's merits on the above criteria.

[3] A. Smith, *The Wealth of Nations* (Routledge, 1890), pp. 651–3.

Before we turn to look at the use of taxation and government expenditure to redistribute incomes, we must first look at what taxes are available to a government and what are the requirements of a good tax system.

The requirements of a good tax system

Whatever the purpose of taxation, when it comes to devising and administering particular taxes there are various principles that many people argue should be observed. In 1776 Adam Smith argued that there were four such principles, or 'maxims' as he called them (see Box 9.4). The following is a more complete list of the requirements of a good tax system.

Horizontal equity. According to horizonal equity, people in the *same circumstances* should be taxed equally. In other words, taxes should be levied impartially. For example, people earning the same level of income and with the same personal circumstances (e.g. number and type of dependants, size of mortgage, etc.) should pay the same level of income tax.

 Is it horizontally equitable for smokers and drinkers to pay more tax than non-smokers and non-drinkers?

Vertical equity. According to vertical equity, taxes should be 'fairly' apportioned between rich and poor. What constitutes fairness here is highly controversial. No one likes paying taxes and thus a rich person's concept of a fair tax is unlikely to be the same as a poor person's. This whole question of using taxes as a means of redistributing incomes will be examined in detail below.

Equitable between recipients of benefits. Under the benefit principle it is argued that those who receive the most benefits from government expenditure ought to pay the

Horizontal equity
The equal treatment of people in the same situation.

Vertical equity
The redistribution from the better off to the worse off. In the case of taxes this means the rich paying proportionately more taxes than the poor.

Benefit principle of taxation
The principle that people ought to pay taxes in proportion to the amount that they use government services.

most in taxes. For example, it can be argued that roads should be paid for from fuel tax. That way those who use the roads the most will pay the most towards their construction and maintenance.

 1. Does the benefit principle conflict with either vertical or horizontal equity?
2. Would this be a good principle to apply in the case of health care?

In most cases the benefits principle would be difficult to put into practice. There are two reasons why. First, a specific tax would have to be devised for each particular good and service provided by the state. Secondly, in the case of many goods and services provided by the state it would be difficult to identify the amount of benefit received by each individual. Just how much benefit (in money terms) do you derive from street lighting, from the police, from the navy, from clean air, etc?

Cheap to collect. Taxes cost money to collect. These costs should be kept to a minimum relative to the revenue they yield.

Difficult to evade. If it is desirable to have a given tax, people should not be able to escape paying it. A distinction here is made between tax evasion and tax avoidance:

Tax evasion

The illegal non-payment of taxes (e.g. by not declaring income earned).

Tax avoidance

The rearrangement of one's affairs so as to reduce one's tax liability.

- Tax evasion is illegal. This is where, for example, people do not declare income to the Inland Revenue.
- Tax avoidance is legal, albeit from the government's point of view undesirable. This is where people try to find ways of managing their affairs so as to reduce their tax liability. They may employ an accountant to help them.

Non-distortionary. Taxes alter market signals: taxes on goods and services alter market prices; taxes on income alter wages. They should not do this in an undesirable direction.

If prices are not distorted in the first place, it is best to use taxes that have the same percentage effect on prices of all goods and services. That way *relative* prices remain the same. For example, VAT in the UK is levied on virtually all goods and services at a single rate of 15 per cent. If goods were taxed at different rates, this would create distortions, switching consumption and production from goods with high taxes to goods with low taxes.

If, however, the government feels that market prices *are* distorted in the first place, taxes can be used to alter price signals in the desired direction.

 How can the market distortions argument be used to justify putting excise duties on specific goods such as petrol, alcohol and tobacco? Is this the only reason why excise duties are put on these particular products?

Convenient to the taxpayer. Taxes should be *certain* and *clearly understood* by taxpayers so that they can calculate their tax liabilities. The method of payment should be *straightforward.*

Convenient to the government. Governments use tax changes as an instrument for managing the economy. Tax rates should thus be *simple to adjust.* Also the government will need to be able to *calculate* as accurately as possible the effects of tax changes, both on the total tax yield and on the distribution of the burden between taxpayers.

Minimal discincentive effects. Taxes may discourage people from working longer or harder, from saving, from investing or from taking initiative. For example, a high rate of income tax may discourage people from seeking promotion or from doing overtime. 'What is the point,' they may say, 'if a large proportion of my extra income is taken away in taxes?' It is desirable that these disincentives should be kept to a minimum.

Of course, not all these requirements can be met at the same time. There is no perfect tax. The government thus has to seek a compromise when there is a conflict between any of the requirements. One of the most serious conflicts is between vertical equity and the need to keep disincentives to a minimum. The more steeply the rich are taxed, it is argued, the more serious are the disincentive effects on them likely to be. This particular conflict is examined below.

Types of tax in the UK

We will now look at the main taxes currently operating in the UK. They can be divided into two broad categories. *Direct taxes* are payable either on *income* or *wealth* or, in the form of a *poll tax. Indirect taxes* are paid via a middle person.

Direct taxes

The main direct taxes on income are personal income tax, corporation tax, capital gains tax and national insurance contributions.

Personal income tax. This is the tax that individuals pay on their income. All types of income are included – wages, salaries, interest, dividends and rent. For most people, income taxes on their wages or salaries are deducted by their employer through the pay-as-you-earn scheme (PAYE).

The system of personal income tax in the UK works as follows:

- Everyone can earn a certain amount tax free. This is known as their personal allowance. In 1990/91 this was £3005. An additional tax-free allowance is granted to married couples (£1720 in 1990/91). Single parents, old people and people with special needs also get additional tax-free allowances.
- Beyond this tax-free level of income, people then pay the basic rate of income tax on each extra pound earned. In 1990/91 the basic rate was 25 per cent.
- There is an upper limit to the taxable income on which the basic rate is paid. Beyond this, each extra pound earned is charged at a higher rate of income tax. Since 1988 there has been a single higher rate of 40 per cent. In 1990/91 this was paid on any taxable income (i.e. income above the tax-free allowance level) above £20 700.

It is necessary to distinguish the marginal rate of income tax from the average rate This is illustrated in Table 9.11 and Figure 9.5, which use 1990/91 rates.

The *marginal* rate is the rate a person would pay on an extra pound earned. In 1990/91 this was zero, 25 per cent or 40 per cent depending on a person's total income.

The *average* rate is a person's total income tax as a fraction of total income. This will always be less than the marginal rate since part of a person's income will be tax free; and for higher tax rate payers, part will be taxed at the basic rate.

Corporation tax. This is a tax on the profits of limited companies. In 1990/91 the rate was 25 per cent for companies with profits below £200 000, rising to 35 per cent for those with profits over £1 million. Profits can be offset against capital expenditure and interest payments when working out liability to corporation tax. This effectively means that profits that are reinvested are not taxed.

Capital gains tax. This is a tax payable when a person sells assets, such as property or shares. It is payable on the gain in value of these assets since a set date in the past or since they were purchased if this was after the set date. It is only payable if a person's capital gains exceed a certain amount in any year. In 1990/91 this amount was £5000.

Tax allowance
An amount of income that can be earned tax free. Tax allowances vary according to a person's circumstances.

Basic rate of tax
The main marginal rate of tax, applying to most people's incomes.

Higher rate tax(es)
The marginal rate(s) of tax on incomes above the basic rate limit.

Marginal rate of income tax
The tax rate. The rate paid on each *additional* pound earned: $\Delta T/\Delta Y$.

Average rate of income tax
Taxes (T) as a proportion of a person's total (gross) income (Y): T/Y.

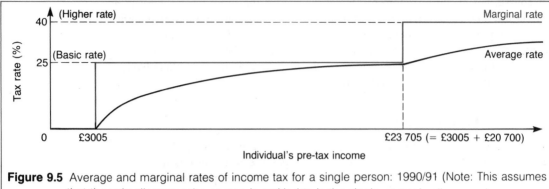

Figure 9.5 Average and marginal rates of income tax for a single person: 1990/91 (Note: This assumes that the only allowance the person is entitled to is the single person's allowance.)

Table 9.11 UK marginal and average income tax rates: 1990/91

	Single persons/married women[1] (annual figures)		
Income (£) (1)	Marginal tax rate (%) (2)	Total paid in income tax (£) (3)	Average tax rate (%) (3) ÷ (1) (4)
3 000	0	0	0.0
4 000	25	249	6.2
5 000	25	499	10.0
6 000	25	749	12.5
7 000	25	999	14.3
8 000	25	1 249	15.6
9 000	25	1 499	16.7
10 000	25	1 749	17.5
12 000	25	2 249	18.7
14 000	25	2 749	19.6
16 000	25	3 249	20.3
18 000	25	3 749	20.8
20 000	25	4 249	21.2
25 000	40	5 693	22.8
30 000	40	7 693	25.6
40 000	40	11 693	29.2
50 000	40	15 693	31.4
60 000	40	19 693	32.8
70 000	40	23 693	33.8

[1] Or married men if the wife receives the married couple's allowance.

Source: *Financial Times*, (21 March 1990).

The rate of tax was the same as income tax (25 per cent or 40 per cent depending on a person's total taxable income). The sale of owner-occupied houses is excluded from the tax.

National insurance contributions (NICs). These are payments made by individuals and their employers to the Department of Social Security. They are used to finance pensions and social security. Although they do not officially count as taxes, to all intents and purposes they are so. Individuals' contributions are a percentage of their income.

The marginal rates in 1990/91 are shown in Table 9.12. For most people – that is, those with an income between £3005 and £18 200 – the combined marginal rate of income tax and NIC was 34 per cent, (i.e. 25 per cent + 9 per cent). Above this the rate fell to 25 per cent (the marginal NIC rate was zero), rising again to 40 per cent when people reached the higher rate of income tax.

Table 9.12 Marginal national insurance rates for individuals: 1990/91

Income per annum (£)	Marginal national insurance rate
0– 2 392	2%
2 392–18 200	9%
18 200–	0%

Wealth taxes are paid on either the general assets or specific assets held or acquired by individuals. The two main forms of wealth tax in the UK have been *inheritance tax* and *local authority rates*.

Inheritance tax. This is a tax paid when assets are transferred from one person to another, either on death or during the donor's lifetime if the donor dies within seven years of the gift. In 1990/91, transfers below £128 000 were exempt. Amounts above this were taxed at a rate of 40 per cent on the excess.

Local authority rates. Before 1990 in England and Wales and 1989 in Scotland, 'rates' on individuals and businesses were the tax used to finance part of local authority expenditure (the remaining part being financed by the government through general taxation). Rates were a property tax based on the value of houses, other buildings, businesses and land. The rates on a person's house would be the same no matter how many wage earners lived in it.

Today rates are only levied on businesses. The *uniform business rate* is levied at a single rate throughout the country, but varies with the size and value of the business. Businesses are given a 'rateable value' by the Inland Revenue and then all businesses are charged at the same percentage of their rateable value. The moneys from the business rates go to a central pool and then all local authorities draw from this pool according to the size of their population. The money they draw does *not* depend on the amount of business rates paid in their area.

The *community charge* which replaced the *domestic* rates is not a property tax: it is not a tax on wealth but is a poll tax. A poll tax is a tax per head of the population irrespective of people's income or wealth.

The community charge is a fixed sum per head of the adult population paid to the person's local authority. The amount of the community charge does nevertheless vary from local authority to local authority depending on the size of their expenditure relative to their population. It is the only element of local authority revenue (the other two being business rates and central government grants) that the local authority can vary. Unlike a *pure* poll tax, the community charge is levied at a reduced rate for those on very low incomes (including students!).

The community charge is the only example of a poll tax in the UK. It is thus generally referred to as 'the' poll tax.

Poll tax

A lump-sum tax per head of the population. Since it is a fixed *amount*, it has a marginal rate of zero with respect to both income and wealth.

Box 9.5

The Poll Tax
Accountability versus equity?

The new system of local government finance will usher in a new era – a new attitude in local government. The relationship between councils and their electors will change to one where every council has to concentrate on local rather than national issues, on providing value for money in the services they provide and on serving their customers as their first priority. That will be a great improvement for many authorities controlled by Opposition parties – high time, too, I believe that in time the community charge will come to be seen as a watershed in terms of the strengthening of local democracy.

Nicholas Ridley MP,
Secretary of State for the Environment

The community charge is repressive, inefficient and unfair. The arguments in its favour were always thin and they have grown shabby and worn with repetition. Claims about increased accountability are wildly exaggerated and the statistics deployed in aid are, at best, questionable.

Sir Barney Hayhoe MP

What is the community charge or 'poll tax'? It represents a flat-rate charge on all adults with an income above the income-support benefit level.

It is part of the means of financing local authority expenditure.

The other means are grants from central government and business rates. These latter two cannot be varied by local authorities. If, therefore, a local authority wants to increase its expenditure, it has to increase the size of the poll tax in its area.

To summarize: the poll tax varies from one local authority to another, but is a flat-rate charge on virtually all adults *within* each authority.

The main case against it (as stated in the second quotation above) is that the tax is not calculated on the individual's ability to pay: a clear breach of the generally accepted principle of direct taxation, that taxes on individuals ought to be in relation to their means. Other arguments against include the following:

● It is an expensive tax to collect.
● It is difficult to prevent evasion by people who do not have a permanent address.
● It is not horizontally equitable between people living in different local authorities. The tax varies enormously from one authority to another.

The government's reply is that the poll tax is not so much a tax as a charge for local services: services which we all receive. Hence we should all contribute. The local authorities' provision of these services will in consequence be more accountable to the public, enhancing notions of local democracy. If local people have to pay in full for any additional local authority expenditure, they will think twice before voting for a party that advocates increased expenditure. This pressure will make local authorities more efficient in the use of their revenues.

Finally, being a flat charge, there is no disincentive effect: people are not discouraged from earning extra money.

? 1. Do you believe that the poll tax is a fairer or less fair system than the old system of rates based on the value of property? Why?
2. The Liberal Democrats advocate the use of a local *income* tax. This, they claim, is vertically equitable since it is levied according to people's ability to pay. What are the advantages and disadvantages of such a tax?

Indirect taxes
There are three types of indirect tax in the UK. All three are taxes on expenditure, and are paid to HM Customs and Excise.

Value added tax. This is the main indirect tax throughout the EC. It was introduced in the UK in 1973 on joining the EC.

VAT is paid on the value that firms add to goods and services at each stage of their production and distribution. For example, if a firm purchases supplies costing £10 000 and with them produces goods which it sells for £15 000 (before VAT), it is liable to pay VAT on the £15 000 minus £10 000: in other words, on the £5000 value it has added. Suppliers must provide invoices to show that the VAT has already been paid on all the inputs.

Table 9.13 Calculating VAT: an example

	Value added (1)	VAT (2)	Value added plus VAT (3)	Price sold to next stage (4)
Firm A sells raw materials to firm B for £11 000	£10 000	£1 000	£11 000	£11 000
Firm B processes them and sells them to a manufacturer, firm C, for £19 800	£8 000	£800	£8 800	£19 800
Firm C sells the manufactured goods to a wholesaler, firm D, for £27 500	£7 000	£700	£7 700	£27 500
Firm D sells them to a retailer, firm E, for £33 000	£5 000	£500	£5 500	£33 000
Firm E sells them to consumers for £44 000	£10 000 **£40 000**	£1 000 + **£4 000** =	£11 000 **£44,000**	£44 000

The example in Table 9.13 can be used to show how the tax eventually gets passed on to the consumer. For simplicity's sake, assume that the rate of VAT is 10 per cent and that each firm uses only one supplier.

The value added at each stage plus VAT adds up to the total amount paid by the consumer: £44 000 in this case. The total VAT paid, therefore, amounts to a tax on the consumer. In the example, the £4000 VAT is 10 per cent of the (pre-tax) consumer price of £40 000. VAT in Britain in the early 1990s is levied at 17½ per cent on most goods and services. Some goods, however, are zero rated. These include food, domestic fuel, books and children's clothes.

Small firms and financial institutions are exempt from paying VAT. Unless they sell direct to the consumers, the VAT will be paid by the next firm up the production chain.

Excise duties. These are taxes on particular goods and services. They include alcoholic drinks, tobacco products, petrol and diesel, new cars and gambling. They are a single-stage tax levied on the manufacturer. They are paid in addition to VAT.

VAT is an ad valorem tax. This means that the tax is levied at a *percentage* of the value of the good. The higher the value of the good, the higher the tax paid. Excise duties, by contrast, are a specific tax. This means that they are levied at a *fixed amount*, irrespective of the value of the good. Thus the duty on a litre of petrol is the same for a cut-price filling station as for a full-price one.

Customs duties. Economists normally refer to these as tariffs. They are duties on goods imported from outside the EC and levies imposed on agricultural imports (see section 11.1).

Table 9.14 shows the amount and the percentage raised from each of the various taxes in the three financial years 1977/78, 1987/88 and 1990/91.

? To what extent do (a) income tax, (b) VAT, (c) the old local authority domestic rates and (d) the poll tax meet the various requirements for a good tax system on pages 335–7 above? (Some of the answers to this question are given below.)

Ad valorem tax

A tax on a good levied as a percentage of its value. It can be a single-stage tax or a multi-stage tax (such as VAT).

Specific tax

A tax on a good levied at a fixed amount per unit of the good, irrespective of the price of that unit.

Tariff

A tax on imported goods.

Taxes as a means of redistributing income

If taxes are to be used as a means of achieving greater equality, the rich must be taxed proportionately more than the poor. The degree of redistribution will depend on the

Table 9.14 UK taxes, national insurance, rates, community charge and licences

	1977/78		1987/88		1990/91	
	Amount (£bn)	Percentage of total taxes	Amount (£bn)	Percentage of total taxes	Amount (£bn)	Percentage of total taxes
Inland Revenue						
Income tax	17.5	33.9	41.4	26.1	55.0	26.8
Corporation tax	3.3	6.4	15.6	9.8	20.7	10.1
Capital gains tax	0.3	0.6	1.4	0.9	2.1	1.0
Petroleum revenue tax	0	0	2.3	1.4	1.1	0.5
Inheritance tax	0.4	0.8	1.1	0.7	1.2	0.6
Stamp duties	0.4	0.8	2.4	1.5	1.9	0.9
(Total Inland Revenue)	21.9	42.5%	64.2	40.5%	81.9	39.9%
Customs and Excise						
VAT	4.2	8.1	24.1	15.2	32.1	15.6
Petrol, derv, etc.	2.5	4.8	7.8	4.9	9.7	4.7
Cigarettes and other tobacco	2.1	4.1	4.8	3.0	5.4	2.6
Alcoholic beverages	2.1	4.1	4.4	2.8	4.9	2.4
Betting and gaming	0.3	0.6	0.8	0.5	1.0	0.5
Car tax	0.3	0.6	1.1	0.7	1.5	0.7
Customs duties (EC)	0.6	1.2	1.5	0.9	1.9	0.9
Agricultural levies (EC)	0.2	0.4	0.2	0.1	0.1	0.0
(Total Customs and Excise)	12.3	23.8%	44.7	28.2%	56.7	27.6%
Other						
National insurance contribs	9.7	18.8	28.7	18.1	35.9	17.5
Local authority rates/community charge	5.1	9.9	16.9	10.6	23.4	11.4
Vehicle excise duties	1.1	2.1	2.7	1.7	3.0	1.5
Broadcasting receivg licences	0.3	0.6	1.0	0.6	4.4	2.1
Other	1.2	2.3	0.5	0.3		
(Total other)	17.4	33.7%	49.8	31.3%	66.7	32.5%
Total	**51.6**	**100.0%**	**158.7**	**100.0%**	**205.3**	**100.0%**

Source: *Financial Statement and Budget Reports 1978/79, 1988/89, 1990/91* (HMSO, various dates).

degree of 'progressiveness' of the tax. In this context, taxes may be classified as *proportional*, *progressive* or *regressive*:

Progressive tax

A tax whose average rate with respect to income rises as income rises.

Regressive tax

A tax whose average rate with respect to income falls as income rises.

Proportional tax

A tax whose average rate with respect to income stays the same as income rises.

- Progressive tax: As people's income (Y) rises, the percentage of their income paid in the tax (T) rises. In other words, the *average* rate of tax (T/Y) rises.
- Regressive tax: As people's income rises, the percentage of their income paid in the tax falls: T/Y falls.
- Proportional tax: As people's income rises, the percentage of their income paid in the tax stays the same: T/Y is constant.

In other words, progressiveness is defined in terms of what happens to the average rate of tax as incomes rise. (Note that it is not defined in terms of the *marginal* rate of tax.)

? 1. If a person earning £5000 per year pays £500 in a given tax and a person earning £10 000 per year pays £800, is the tax progressive or regressive?
2. A proportional tax will leave the distribution of income unaffected. Why should this be so, given that a rich person will pay a larger absolute amount than a poor person?

An extreme form of regressive tax is a lump-sum tax. This is levied at a fixed *amount* (not rate) irrespective of income.

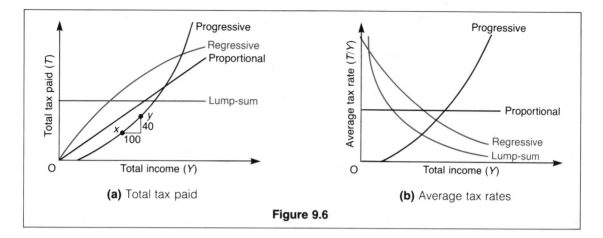

(a) Total tax paid   **(b)** Average tax rates

Figure 9.6

Figure 9.6 illustrates these different categories of tax. Diagram (a) shows the total amount of tax a person pays. With a progressive tax the curve gets progressively steeper, showing that the average rate of tax (T/Y) rises. The marginal rate of tax $(\Delta T/\Delta Y)$ is given by the slope. Thus between points x and y the marginal tax rate is 40 per cent.

Diagram (b) shows the average rates. With a proportional tax a person pays the same amount of tax on each pound earned. With a progressive tax a larger proportion is paid by a rich person than by a poor person, and vice versa with a regressive tax.

> **?** 1. What is the *marginal* rate of a lump-sum tax?
> 2. Draw a diagram similar to Figure 9.5 showing UK income tax for a single person, only this time plot *total* tax paid on the vertical axis. Is the line a curve? Explain.

The more steeply upward sloping the average tax curve, the more progressive is the tax, and the more equal will be the post-tax incomes of the population.

UK taxes and the redistribution of income

How progressive or regressive are UK taxes, and how has this changed over time?

Direct taxes

Income tax. Income tax in the UK is progressive. In other words, the average rate of tax rises with income. There are two reasons for this:

• Tax allowances account for a larger proportion of a poor person's income than a rich person's.
• Above a certain level of income a higher marginal rate of tax is paid.

Average and marginal rates of income tax in 1990/91 were shown in Figure 9.5.

Although income tax is still mildly progressive, it is much less so now than it used to be. This is due to various changes in income tax rates that were made by the Conservative government during the 1980s. One change was a series of reductions in the basic rate: from 33 per cent in 1979 to 25 per cent in 1988. This resulted in income taxes accounting for a smaller fraction of total taxation, and since income taxes are more progressive than most other taxes, this in turn led to a reduction in the redistribution of income.

Table 9.15 Marginal income tax rates in the UK

1978/79		1979/80		1987/88		1988/89	
Taxable income[1] (£)	Marginal tax rate (%)	Taxable income[1] (£)	Marginal tax rate (%)	Taxable income[1] (£)	Marginal tax rate (%)	Taxable income[1] (£)	Marginal tax rate (%)
1–750	25	1–750	25	1–17 900	27[2]	1–19 300	25[2]
751–7000	34[2]	751–10 000	30[2]	17 901–20 400	40	over 19 300	40
7001–8000	40	10 001–12 000	40	20 401–25 400	45		
8001–9000	45	12 001–15 000	45	25 401–33 300	50		
9001–10 000	50	15 001–20 000	50	33 301–41 200	55		
10 001–11 500	55	20 001–25 000	55	over 41 200	60		
11 501–13 000	60	over 25 000	60				
13 001–15 000	65						
15 001–17 500	75						
17 501–23 000	80						
over 23 000	83						

[1] After taking allowances into account.
[2] Basic rate.

The most dramatic change was introduced in the 1988 budget. Before that time there were several higher rates of taxation above the 40 per cent rate. In 1988 these were all abolished. Table 9.15 shows the rates before and after these changes.

National insurance contributions. NIC rates were shown in Table 9.12. They are mildly progressive up to the upper limit of income (£18 200 in 1990/91). Thereafter they are regressive.

The old system of local authority rates and the community charge. A larger proportion of rich people are home owners. Richer people tend to live in bigger houses. For these two reasons rich people tended to pay more rates than poor people. Whether they were actually progressive or not, however, depended on how much more they paid: did they pay a larger proportion of their income? This varied with (a) the particular local authority in question and (b) the number of occupants in any given house.

The community charge or poll tax is a lump-sum tax, save for those on very low incomes. Except for these very poor people, therefore, it is a highly regressive tax.

 Look through the list of other direct taxes (see pages 337–9). In each case decide whether the tax is progressive, regressive or proportional.

Indirect taxes

These tend to be regressive. The reason is that the rich tend to spend a smaller proportion of their income than the poor: the poor cannot afford to save; the rich can.

The regressive nature of indirect taxes is lessened by two features:

- Some basic goods and services which are consumed proportionately much more by the poor are zero rated for VAT. These include food, children's clothes and domestic fuel.
- Excise duties (levied on top of VAT) only apply to certain items. Some of these, such as petrol, are consumed proportionately more by the rich. Others, however, such as cigarettes, are consumed proportionately more by the poor.

Indirect taxes used to be less regressive than they are today for the following reasons:

- Before 1973, when VAT was introduced, there was a tax called 'purchase tax' on various goods. This was levied at higher rates on luxury goods.

Table 9.16 Distribution of the tax burden in the UK

Quintile groups of households (ranked by original income)	1978			1986		
	Income tax and NICs as % of gross income[1]	Indirect taxes as % of gross income[1]		Income tax and NICs as % of gross income[1]	Indirect taxes as % of gross income[1]	
	(1)	(2)	(1)+(2)	(1)	(2)	(1)+(2)
Poorest 20%	0.6	20.6	21.6	0	25.1	25.1
Next 20%	11.1	20.7	31.8	6.0	27.9	33.9
Middle 20%	17.9	18.7	36.6	16.1	24.6	40.7
Next 20%	20.1	17.2	37.3	19.3	20.6	39.9
Richest 20%	23.2	14.8	38.0	22.2	16.7	38.9
All households	18.5	17.1	35.6	17.5	20.5	38.0

[1] Gross income = original income plus cash benefits.

Source: *Social Trends* (CSO, 1980; 1990).

- There used to be more than one rate of VAT (other than zero). There was a basic rate and a luxury rate.
- VAT was raised from 8 per cent to 15 per cent in 1979 as part of a general shift from direct to indirect taxes.

The relative progressiveness of income tax and NICs on the one hand and indirect taxes on the other is shown in Table 9.16 for the years 1978 and 1986. These data are based on the *Family Expenditure Survey*.

1. Had taxes become more or less progressive between 1978 and 1986?
2. How do you think the 1988 budget changes will have affected these figures?

Problems with using taxes to redistribute incomes

Assuming that it is desirable to redistribute incomes from rich to poor, how successfully can taxes accomplish this, and at what economic cost?

Problems in achieving redistribution
How to help the very poor. Taxation takes away income. It can thus reduce the incomes of the rich. But no taxes, however progressive, can *increase* the incomes of the poor. This will require subsidies.

But what about tax cuts? Cannot bigger tax cuts be given to the poor? This is only possible if the poor are already paying taxes in the first place. Take the two cases of income tax and taxes on goods and services.

If the government were to cut income tax, then anyone currently paying it would benefit. A cut in tax *rates* will give proportionately more to the rich, since they have a larger proportion of taxable income relative to total income. An increase in personal *allowances*, on the other hand, will give the same *absolute* amount to everyone above the new tax threshold. This will therefore represent a smaller proportionate gain to the rich. In either case, however, there will be no gain at all to those people below the tax threshold. They paid no income tax in the first place. These poorest of all people therefore gain nothing at all from income tax cuts.

Since taxes on goods and services are generally regressive, any cut in their rate will benefit the poor proportionately more than the rich. A more dramatic effect would be obtained by cutting the rate most on those goods consumed relatively more by the poor.

The government may not wish to cut the overall level of taxation, given its expenditure commitments. In this case it can switch the burden of taxes from regressive to progressive taxes: it can cut certain indirect taxes and raise certain direct taxes. That way at least some benefit is gained by the very poor.

Tax evasion and tax avoidance. The higher the rates of tax, the more likely are people to try to escape paying some of their taxes.

People who are subject to higher rates of income tax will be more tempted not to declare all their income. This tax *evasion* will be much easier for people not paying all their taxes through the PAYE scheme. This will include the self-employed, or people doing casual work on top of their normal job ('moonlighting' as it is called). Furthermore, richer people can often reduce their tax liability – tax *avoidance* – by a careful use of various allowances (such as mortgage tax relief) and tax loopholes such as being allowed to offset 'business expenses' against income.

Part of the government's justification for abolishing income tax rates above 40 per cent in 1988 was that many people escaped paying these higher taxes.

 Why may a steeply progressive income tax which is designed to achieve greater *vertical* equity lead to a reduction in *horizontal* equity?

Undesired incidence of tax. High rates of income tax on high wage earners may simply encourage employers to pay higher wages. Indeed, high salaries for top business executives have often been justified as being necessary to compensate for high taxes. At the other end of the scale, tax cuts for low-paid workers may simply allow employers to cut wages. In other words, part of the incidence of income taxes will be borne by the employer and only part by the employee. Thus attempting to make taxes more 'progressive' will fail if employers simply adjust wages to compensate.

What will determine the incidence of income tax? The answer is the elasticity of supply and demand for labour. The effect of different elasticities of supply of labour is illustrated in Figures 9.7 and 9.8.

In both diagrams the initial supply and demand curves for labour (before the imposition of the tax) intersect at point (1), giving Q_1 labour employed at a wage of W_1. Now an income tax is imposed. Graphically this has the effect of shifting the labour supply curve vertically upwards by the amount of the tax, giving the new labour supply curve, S + tax. In other words, workers are only prepared to work the same amount as before if they get a wage rise equal to their tax increase. But, of course, employers will

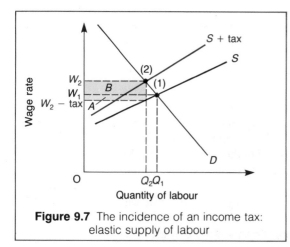

Figure 9.7 The incidence of an income tax: elastic supply of labour

Figure 9.8 The incidence of an income tax: inelastic supply of labour

demand less labour at higher wages. The new equilibrium is thus reached at point (2) with Q_2 labour employed at a (gross) wage of W_2. Workers, after their taxes have been paid, only take home $W_2 -$ tax.

The incidence of the tax, therefore, is as follows: .

- The total tax revenue for the government is shown by the total shaded area.
- Workers' income is cut to $W_2 -$ tax. Their share of the tax is thus $W_1 - (W_2 -$ tax$)$. They pay area A.
- Employers have to pay workers a rise of $W_2 - W_1$. This is their share of the tax. They pay area B.

In Figure 9.7 supply is relatively elastic. In this case the main burden of the tax falls on employers: a significantly higher wage has to be paid in order to continue attracting enough workers. Area B is bigger than area A.

In Figure 9.8, by contrast, supply is relatively inelastic. Here it is workers who pay the bulk of the tax. Area A is bigger than area B.

1. Do poor people gain more from a cut in income tax with an elastic or an inelastic supply of labour? Is the supply of unskilled workers likely to be elastic or inelastic?
2. Draw two diagrams like Figures 9.7 and 9.8, but this time keep the two sets of supply curves the same in each and vary the slope of the demand curve. How does the elasticity of demand affect the incidence of the income tax?

Of course income taxes are not just imposed on workers in one industry alone. People, therefore, cannot move to another industry to avoid paying taxes. This fact will cause a relatively inelastic supply response to any rise in income tax, since the only alternative to paying the income tax is not to work so much. The less elastic this response, the more will the burden of the tax fall on the taxpayer and the more effectively can income taxes be used to redistribute incomes.

The economic costs of redistribution

Administrative costs. It is sometimes argued that using taxes to redistribute incomes is costly because income taxes are more expensive to administer than indirect taxes. Income taxes are levied on individuals whereas indirect taxes are levied on firms. There are fewer firms than individuals. Therefore, other things being equal, there ought to be lower collection and other administrative costs associated with indirect taxes.

This argument, however, has a number of weaknesses:

- With the PAYE system of income tax, the tax is collected from firms not individuals. It is true that individuals have to fill in income tax returns and these have to be checked by the Inland Revenue, but with computerization the PAYE system has been made much more streamlined.
- Excise duties are relatively cheap to collect since they are single-stage taxes applying to only relatively few firms. VAT, however, is much more expensive as so many more firms are involved.
- Unless income tax were abolished – and virtually no one advocates that – the costs of collecting it exist anyway. Raising the *rates* of income tax will impose very few *additional* costs. A swing from indirect to direct taxes as a means of redistributing income should therefore have very little effect on costs.

Nevertheless, if income tax is to be made horizontally as well as vertically equitable, there may need to be a complex system of personal allowances – and this *will* raise administrative costs.

Costs of resource reallocation. The argument is that the imposition of taxes on goods creates market distortions, and that the loss to those paying the tax is greater than the gain to the community from the tax revenues.

Take first the case of an indirect tax applied to one good only. Assume that there is universal perfect competition. Raising the price of this good relative to other goods will introduce a market distortion. Consumption will shift away from this good towards other goods which people preferred less at the original prices. What is more, the loss to consumers and producers (other things being equal) will be greater than the gain to the community from the tax revenue. This is illustrated in Figure 9.9.

With no tax, price will be at P_1 and output at Q_1, where demand equals supply. By imposing a tax on the good, the supply curve shifts upward to S + tax. Price rises to P_2 and output falls to Q_2. Producers are left with P_2 − tax after they have paid the tax. There is thus a loss to both consumers and producers, but a gain to the government (and hence the community at large) from the tax revenue. The net cost of the tax arises from these losses being bigger than the gain. What are the losses and gains?

Consumers, by having to pay a higher price, lose consumer surplus (see section 3.1). Originally their consumer surplus was areas $A + B + C$ in Figure 9.9. With the price now at P_2, the consumer surplus falls to area C alone. The loss to consumers is thus areas $A + B$.

Producers, by receiving a lower price after tax and selling fewer units, lose profits. Profits can be shown by the area between the MC curve and the price line. The reason is that total profits are simply the sum of all the marginal profits ($P (= MR) − MC$) on each of the units sold. Thus before the tax is imposed, firms receive total profits of areas $D + E + F$. After the tax is imposed they receive a profit of area F alone. The loss in profits to producers is therefore areas $D + E$.

The total loss to consumers and producers is areas $A + B + D + E$. The gain to the government in tax revenue is areas $B + E$: the tax rate times the number of units sold (Q_2). There is thus a net loss to the community of areas $A + D$. This is shown as the red area in the diagram.

This analysis assumes that the loss by consumers and producers can be compared with the gain by the government. If, however, the money raised from the tax is redistributed to the poor, their gain in welfare is likely to exceed the loss in welfare from the higher tax. The reason is that a pound sacrificed by the average consumer is probably of less value to him or her than a pound gained by a poor person. In other words, as people get richer, so the utility of each extra pound gets less.

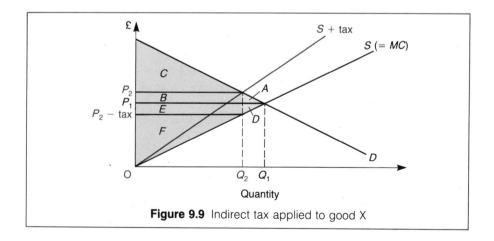

Figure 9.9 Indirect tax applied to good X

What is more, if the tax is applied at a uniform rate to *all* goods, there is no distortion resulting from reallocation between goods. This is one of the major justifications for having a single rate of VAT.

Of course, in the real world, markets are highly imperfect and there is no reason why taxes will necessarily make these imperfections worse. In fact it might be desirable on efficiency grounds to tax certain goods and services, such as cigarettes, alcohol, petrol and gambling, at higher rates than other goods and services. We will examine these arguments in the next chapter.

Disincentives A problem with income taxes is that, if they lead to less employment, then, other things being equal, less will be produced. Redistribution will be achieved at the expense of total output and consumption.

The problem is one of disincentives. High tax rates may discourage people from working. But do they? It depends on the elasticity of supply of labour.

Critics of high marginal rates of income tax claim that labour supply is relatively elastic. Putting up income tax rates, they say, will act as a disincentive. What is the point of seeking promotion; what is the point of doing overtime; what is the point of obtaining better qualifications; what is the point of working harder – and so on, if a large proportion of any rise in income is simply taken in taxes? In short, critics argue that high income tax rates will significantly reduce national income.

Those in favour of high income taxes, on the other hand, argue that the supply curve of labour is highly inelastic and may even be downward sloping. A rise in taxes, they argue, will cut people's income. They will not be able to afford to cut down on the amount they work. They may even have to work harder or longer to try to maintain their living standards.

Who is correct? The arguments are examined in the next section.

Taxation and incentives

One of the major justifications given by the Conservative governments after 1979 for cutting both the basic and higher rates of income tax was that it increased the incentive to work.

This whole question of incentives is highly charged politically. If the Conservatives are correct, then there is a trade-off between output and equity. High and progressive income taxes can lead to a more equal distribution of income, but a smaller national output. Alternatively, by cutting taxes there will be a bigger national output, but less equally divided. If many socialists are correct, we can have both a more equal society and a bigger national output: there is no trade-off.

To analyze these arguments we need to return to the distinction between the income and substitution effects of changes in income on the supply of labour. Section 8.2 looked at these effects in the general context of changes in wages. But how can the analysis be applied to taxation?

Income and substitution effects of higher income taxes
The key to understanding these effects is the role of leisure. People want leisure. They also want various goods and services. The problem is that in order to obtain goods and services they have to sacrifice leisure by working, and in order to obtain leisure they have to sacrifice goods and services by not working. Thus the opportunity cost of leisure is the goods and services sacrificed (and vice versa).

Raising taxes does two things.

It reduces incomes. With higher taxes people cannot afford to have the same amount of both leisure and goods and services as before. They thus sacrifice some of each. They cut their consumption somewhat, but they also cut their leisure by working more. The more they work, the less they will have to cut their consumption. This is the income effect. Higher taxes encourage people to work more.

Income effect of a tax rise

Tax increases reduce people's incomes and thus encourage people to work more.

Substitution effect of a tax rise

Tax increases reduce the opportunity cost of leisure and thus encourage people to work less.

It reduces the opportunity cost of leisure. With higher taxes an hour's work buys less consumption than before, but it still involves the sacrifice of an hour's leisure. Conversely, an extra hour taken in leisure now involves a smaller sacrifice in consumption. Thus people may well substitute leisure for the consumption of goods and services. This is the substitution effect. Higher taxes encourage people to work less.

Which is greater, the income effect or the substitution effect? The relative size of the income and substitution effects is likely to differ for different types of people and different types of tax change.

Different types of people

The *income* effect is likely to dominate for those people with a substantial proportion of long-term commitments: for example, people with families and with mortgages and other debts.

The income effect is also likely to be relatively large for people on higher incomes. This may seem strange at first sight. It might be thought that poor people would have a higher income effect. After all, with their low level of consumption, they may find it difficult to make further cutbacks. The reason why the income effect is larger for high income earners is that an increase in tax rates represents a substantial cut in income for them and only a small cut for poor people. This is illustrated in Table 9.17.

The table shows the effect on the incomes of two people of a rise in the tax rate from 25 per cent to 30 per cent. In both cases it assumes that the personal allowances are £4000. For the person on £5000 close to the tax threshold, net income falls by only £50. For the person on £50 000 net income falls by £2300.

 Who is likely to work harder as a result of a cut in income tax rates, a rich person or a poor person? Why? Would your answer be different if personal allowances were zero?

The *substitution* effect is likely to dominate for those with few commitments: those whose families have left home, the single, and second income earners in families where that second income is not relied on for 'essential' consumption.

 How will tax cuts affect the willingness of married women to return to employment after having brought up a family?

Although high income earners may work more when there is a tax *rise*, they may still be discouraged by a steeply progressive tax *structure*. If they have to pay very high marginal rates of tax, it may simply not be worth their while seeking promotion or working harder or longer. At some level of the marginal tax rate this is inevitable. At a

Table 9.17 Effects of increasing the rate of income tax on the amount people pay

Tax rate	Person on £5000 (taxable income £1000)	Person on £50 000 (taxable income £46 000)
25%	£250	£11 500
30%	£300	£13 800

Box 9.6

The Laffer Curve
Having your cake and eating it

Professor Art Laffer was one of President Reagan's advisers during his first administration (1981–4). He was a strong advocate of tax cuts, arguing that substantial increases in output would result.

He went further than this. He argued that tax cuts would actually *increase* the amount of tax revenue the government earned.

Tax revenue = Average tax rate × Income

If tax cuts cause income to rise (due to incentives) proportionately more than the tax rate has fallen, then tax revenues will increase. These effects are illustrated by the now famous 'Laffer curve'.

If the average tax rate were zero, no revenue would be raised. As the tax rate is raised above zero, tax revenues will increase. The curve will be upward sloping. Eventually, however, the curve will peak (at tax rate t_1). Thereafter tax rates become so high that the resulting fall in output more than offsets the rise in tax rate. When the tax rate reaches 100 per cent, the revenue will once more fall to zero, since no one will bother to work.

The curve may not be symmetrical. It may peak at a 40 per cent, 50 per cent, 60 per cent or even 90 per cent rate. Nevertheless, Laffer and others on the political right have argued that current tax rates are above t_1.

This, of course, is an empirical issue and most evidence suggests that current tax rates are well below t_1.

?
1. What is the elasticity of supply of output with respect to changes in tax rates at a tax rate of t_1? What is it below t_1? What is it above t_1?
2. If the substitution effect of a tax cut outweighs the income effect, does this necessarily mean that the economy is to the right of point t_1?

marginal rate of 100 per cent no one would work harder (unless they wanted to for the fun of it!). Would the effect be any different if the rate were 98 per cent or 95 per cent?

Different types of tax change

If the government wishes to raise income taxes in order to redistribute incomes, there are three main ways it can do it: raising the higher rates of tax; raising the basic rate; and reducing tax allowances.

Raising the higher rates of tax. This may seem the most effective way of redistributing incomes: after all, it is only the rich who will suffer. There are, however, serious problems:

- The income effect will be relatively small, since it is only that part of incomes subject to the higher rates that will be affected.
- The substitution effect is likely to be quite large. Given the diminishing marginal utility of income as people get richer (an extra pound is worth less to a rich person than to a poor person), the rich may be prepared to sacrifice a relatively large amount of consumption to avoid sacrificing leisure.

- It may discourage risk taking by business people, if a large proportion of their profits are to be taken in taxes. This may have a serious effect on future output and growth.
- The rich may be more mobile internationally, their talents being in high demand overseas and they being more willing to emigrate. There may therefore be a 'brain drain'.

These problems may only become serious when rates are raised to very high levels. There may be little problem, for example, in raising the higher rate of tax from 40 per cent to 45 per cent. The substitution effect would become very serious, however, if it were raised, say, to 98 per cent. At what tax level the substitution effect does become serious is an empirical question. In other words, we would have to examine the evidence.

Raising the basic rate of tax. Here, as explained above, the income effect is likely to be relatively large for those with higher incomes. They will suddenly be faced with a substantial loss in income, for which they may feel the need to compensate by working harder – especially if they have substantial commitments like a large mortgage.

For those just above the tax threshold, there will be very little extra to pay on *existing* income since most of it is tax free anyway. Thus there will be hardly any income effect. The substitution effect is therefore likely to outweigh the income effect. Each *extra* pound earned will be taxed at the new higher rate. There will therefore be a net disincentive here.

For those below the tax threshold, there will probably be no effect from a rise in the basic rate. Their marginal rate remains at zero. It might nevertheless deter them from undertaking training in order to get a better wage.

What about those people who are not employed? If they are not looking for work anyway, a rise in tax rates will make no difference. If they are looking for work, a rise in tax rates may make them feel that it is no longer worthwhile and that they would be better off on social security. Those who remain looking might take a job *more* readily: there is no longer so much point in searching for a well-paid job if a higher proportion of wages is going to be taken in taxes. They may as well settle for a lower-paid job.

Reducing tax allowances. A lot here depends on *which* allowances are lowered. Take first the simple case of the basic personal allowance. For all those above the old tax threshold there is no *substitution* effect here at all. The rate of tax has not changed. There is an *income* effect, however. The effect is like a lump-sum tax. Suddenly everyone's take-home pay is cut by a fixed sum. This will therefore have a positive incentive effect. People will need to work harder to make up some of the shortfall. This is particularly the case for people only just above the threshold. They have a high marginal utility of income. This type of tax change, however, is highly regressive. If everyone pays the same *amount* of extra tax, this represents a bigger percentage for poorer people than for richer people.

For those now brought into tax for the first time (i.e. those just below the old threshold but above the new lower one), there *will* be a substitution effect. These people may thus be discouraged from working so hard.

For those below even the new tax threshold there will be no effect, except that it may discourage them from seeking better qualifications.

If specific allowances are cut, the effects may be different. For example, a cut in the allowance for married women may have a substantial disincentive effect if, as a result, many women choose to leave the labour force.

The conclusion from the theoretical arguments is that tax changes will have very different effects depending on (a) whom they affect and (b) the nature of the change.

> **?**   1. Go through each of the above types of tax change and consider the effects of a tax *cut*.
> 2. What tax changes (whether up or down) will have a positive incentive effect and also redistribute incomes more equally?

One final point should be stressed. For many people there is no choice in the amount they work. The job they do dictates the number of hours worked. People on a '9 to 5' job cannot suddenly decide to leave at 4 o'clock or stay until 7.30 because of changes in taxes. They still have to finish at 5 o'clock like everyone else.

Evidence
All the available evidence suggests that the effects of tax changes on output are relatively small. Labour supply curves seem highly inelastic to tax changes.

Whether the tax cuts of the late 1980s will have a bigger incentive effect remains to be seen. This may be so if the government has brought about a substantial change in attitudes through its advocacy of the virtues of incentives, individual initiatives and an enterprise culture.

Cash benefits

Cash benefits fall into two broad categories: *means-tested benefits* and *universal benefits*.

Means-tested benefits
Means-tested benefits are available only to those whose income (and savings in some instances) falls below a certain level. In order to obtain such benefits, therefore, people must apply for them and declare their personal circumstances to the authorities: usually the Department of Social Security. The benefits could be given as grants or merely as loans. They could be provided as general income support or for the meeting of specific needs, such as rents, fuel bills and household items. Under a new system introduced in the UK in 1988 there are four main categories of means-tested benefit.

> **Means-tested benefits**
> Benefits whose amount depends on the recipient's income or assets.

Income support. This is available to all adults who work less than a specified number of hours per week. It is particularly designed to help the unemployed. The government sets 'target incomes' which vary according to a person's circumstances – marital status, number of children, disability, etc.

The amount of income support received is based on the difference between people's target income and their actual income. For example, if a person's circumstances gave them a target income of £75 per week and they actually earned only £30, then income support will be based on £75 − £30 = £45. They will not be entitled to the full £45, however, otherwise there would be no incentive to earn more. Savings over a certain level disqualify a person from receiving income support.

Family credit. This is a tax-free benefit to anyone on low income who is supporting a child, but who works too many hours to be entitled to income support. If the family's income is below a certain level, they are entitled to the full benefit, whose amount depends on the number of children. As the family's income rises above this level, so the family credit is correspondingly reduced.

*Box 9.7

Tax Cuts and Incentives
An application of indifference curve analysis[4]

Will tax cuts provide an incentive for people to work harder? This question can be analyzed using indifference curves (see section 3.2). The analysis is similar to that developed in Box 8.2.

It is assumed that individuals have a choice of how many hours a day to work, but that the effort required per hour is constant.

The position with no income taxes
First let us assume that there are no income taxes in the country.

? Why are the curves bowed in towards the origin? (Clue: the answer has something to do with diminishing marginal utility.)

The optimum combination of income and leisure is at Y^* and L^* where the individual is on the highest possible indifference curve: point a.

The position with taxes
Now let us introduce a system of income taxes. This is illustrated in diagram (b).

(a) Optimum combination of income and leisure: no taxes

(b) Optimum combination of income and leisure: income tax in force

Diagram (a) shows a budget line and a set of indifference curves for an individual. The budget line shows the various combinations of leisure and income open to an individual at a given wage rate. By taking no leisure (L_0) a maximum income can be earned (Y_{max}). At the other extreme, the individual can chose to do no work (Y_0) and take all the time in leisure (L_{max}).

? Why is the budget line straight? What would it look like if overtime were paid at higher rates per hour? What will the budget line look like for a person with higher qualifications?

The indifference curves show all the combinations of income and leisure that give the person equal satisfaction. The further out the curve, the higher the level of satisfaction.

Assume that the tax has the following features:

- Up to an income of Y_1 no tax is paid: Y_1 is the individual's personal allowance.
- From Y_1 to Y_2 the basic rate of tax is paid. The budget line thus gets flatter, since less extra income is earned for each extra hour of leisure sacrificed.
- Above Y_2 the higher rate of tax is paid. The budget line becomes flatter still.

The particular individual illustrated in the diagram will now choose to earn a take-home pay of Y^{**} and have L^{**} hours of leisure: point b. Note that this is more leisure than in the no-tax situation (point a). In this diagram, then, the tax has acted as a disincentive. The substitution effect has outweighed the income effect.

Box 9.7 (cont'd)

? Redraw diagram (b), but in such a way that the income effect outweighs the substitution effect.

A cut in the basic tax rate

We are now in a position to analyze the effects of tax cuts. Assume first a cut in the basic rate. This is shown in diagram (c).

(c) Cut in the basic rate of tax

The tax cut makes the budget line steeper above point *q* (the tax threshold).

For people on the tax threshold – like person X – the cut in the basic rate makes no difference. Person X was originally taking L_x hours of leisure (point *q*) and will continue to do so.

For people above the tax threshold – like person W – the tax cut will enable them to move to a higher indifference curve. Person W will move from point *r* to point *s*. The way this diagram is drawn, point *s* is to the left of point *r*. This means that person W will work harder: the substitution effect is greater than the income effect.

? Try drawing two or three diagrams like diagram (c), with the tangency point at different points along the budget line to the left of *q*. You will find that the further to the left you move, the *less* likely is the substitution effect to outweigh the income effect: i.e. the *more* likely are people to work less when given a tax cut.

A rise in the tax threshold

Now assume that personal allowances rise, but that the tax rate stays the same. This is shown in diagram (d).

The point at which people start paying taxes rises from point *t* to point *u*. The *slope* of the budget line remains the same, however, since the tax *rate* has not changed.

(d) Increase in the tax threshold

For people paying taxes, the increase in allowances represents a lump-sum increase in income: there will thus be an income effect. But since tax *rates* have not changed, there is no substitution effect. People therefore work less. The person in the diagram moves from point *m* to point *n*, taking L_2 rather than L_1 hours in leisure.

? What about those people actually on the old tax threshold (i.e. those whose indifference curve/budget line tangency point is at *t*)? Will they work more or less? (Try drawing it.)

A cut in the higher rate of tax

It is likely that the income effect of this will be quite small except for those on very high incomes.

? Why should this be so?

The substitution effect is therefore likely to outweigh the income effect, thus causing people to work more.

? 1. All the above analysis assumes that taxes will not affect people's *gross* wage rates. If part of the incidence of taxes is borne by the employer, after-tax wages will be affected less. There will therefore be a smaller shift in the budget line. How will this affect the argument for tax cuts?
2. Think of ten different jobs. In how many of them do workers have the choice of how many hours to work? How will this affect the argument for tax cuts?
3. In what ways, other than working longer hours, may a person work 'harder'?

[4] This box is based on D. Ulph, 'Tax Cuts: will they work?', *Economic Review*, March 1987.

Social Fund. This provides money for specific needs. It is primarily for people on income support. Some people are entitled to grants from the fund. These are people who would otherwise probably have to live in an institution: a hospital, an old people's home, a hostel, etc. The majority of payments from the fund, however, are in the form of loans. These are either 'budgeting loans', to enable people to buy specific items such as essential household furniture and equipment, or 'crisis loans' for such things as temporary board and lodging or loss of money. The loans are interest free, but they will not be given unless they can be repaid. Repayments are made weekly by deductions from people's income support.

Housing benefit. This is a grant paid to help meet the cost of rents or rates. This benefit was substantially reduced in the 1988 measures.

Means-tested benefits are thus of two types: *general support* (income support and family credit) and *payments for specific purposes* (grants and loans from the social fund and housing benefit).

The 1988 measures changed the pattern of support. Previously, much more money had been available as grants for specific purposes, such as buying a cooker. Today many people are referred to private charities if they require money for specific items. On the other hand, support for families (through the introduction of family credit) was increased in the 1988 measures, with more than double the previous number being eligible for benefits.

Universal benefits (by category of person)

Universal benefits

Benefits paid to everyone in a certain category irrespective of their income or assets.

Universal benefits are those that everyone is entitled to, irrespective of their income, if they fall into a certain category. Examples include child benefit, state pensions, and unemployment, sickness and invalidity benefits.

With the exception of child benefit these are examples of 'social insurance'. People who are working pay national insurance contributions, based on their earnings. When they retire, become unemployed or fall sick they are entitled to benefits. Unemployment and sickness benefits are only paid for a certain number of weeks. After that, the unemployed have to rely on income support, and the sick on invalidity benefit.

Child benefit is a flat payment to parents (usually the mother) for each child. Single parents receive an additional payment.

Benefits in kind

Benefits in kind

Goods or services which the state provides directly to the recipient at no charge or at a subsidized price. Alternatively, the state can subsidize the private sector to provide them.

Individuals receive other forms of benefit from the state, not as direct monetary payments, but in the form of the provision of free or subsidized goods or services. These are known as benefits in kind The major categories of benefit in kind are given in Table 9.18. This table shows how they are distributed between different income groups.

The two largest items are health care and education. They are very differently distributed, however. This difference can largely be explained on age grounds. Old people have lower than average incomes and are thus concentrated in the lower quintiles. Old people use a large proportion of health services, but virtually no education services. Thus higher income groups consume more education, whereas lower income groups consume more health services – a fact also explained by various poverty-related illnesses.

Benefits in kind are consumed roughly equally by the different income groups (in fact slightly more by higher income groups). Nevertheless they do have some

Table 9.18 Distribution of benefits in the UK: 1985 (average per family to nearest £10)

Benefit	Bottom 20%	Next 20%	Middle 20%	Next 20%	Top 20%	All households
Education	370	450	650	850	850	630
National Health Service	910	870	730	710	720	790
Bus and rail subsidies	50	60	50	50	100	60
Housing subsidy	130	80	50	30	20	60
Free school meals and other welfare foods	50	40	30	20	20	30
Total benefits in kind	1510	1500	1510	1660	1710	1570
Cash benefits	3370	2720	1250	870	680	1780
Total benefits	4880	4220	2760	2530	2390	3350

Source: *Social Trends* (CSO, 1990).

equalizing effect, since they represent a much larger proportion of poor people's income than rich people's. However, they still have a far smaller redistributive effect than cash benefits, as Table 9.18 shows.

Benefits and the redistribution of income

It might seem that means-tested benefits are a much more efficient system for redistributing income from the rich to the poor: the money is directed to those most in need. With universal benefits, by contrast, many people may receive them who have little need for them. Do families with very high incomes need child benefit? Would it not be better for the government to redirect the money to those who are genuinely in need?

There are, however, serious problems in attempting to redistribute incomes by the use of means-tested benefits:

• Not everyone entitled to means-tested benefits actually receives them. This may be due to a number of factors:

Ignorance of the benefits available. This in turn may be due to the complexities of the system.
Difficulties in applying for the benefits. People may give up rather than having to face difficult forms or long queues or harassed benefit office staff.
Reluctance to reveal personal circumstances.
The perception that the benefits are 'charity' and therefore demeaning.

Thus some of the poorest families may receive no support.
• Even when people do apply and receive benefits, the need first to discover their personal circumstances may make the application procedure lengthy and unpleasant.
• The level of income above which people become ineligible for benefits may be set too low. Of course, this is partly an argument for raising the level. Even so, there will always be some people just above the level who will still find difficulties. By receiving various universal benefits, however, such as child benefit, or benefits in kind such as health and education, these people's difficulties could be alleviated.
• Means tests based purely on *income* (or even universal benefits based on broad

categories) ignore the very special needs of many poor people. A person earning £50 a week and living in a small, well-appointed flat with a low rent will have less need of assistance than another person who also earns £50 per week but lives in a cold, draughty and damp house with large bills to meet. If means tests are to be fair, *all* of a person's circumstances need to be taken into account.

In the 1988 measures the government moved away from payments for specific needs and tried to simplify the system by treating people in broad categories (according to marital status, number of children, etc.). This inevitably meant that some people with particular needs received inadequate benefit.

The government did attempt to give more support to some of the poorest of the population, especially through family credit. But it was not willing to contemplate a substantial increase in the *overall* level of benefits. The effect, therefore, was that some very poor families were helped not at the expense of the rich, but at the expense of the moderately poor and the 'able-bodied' single poor.

There were serious problems too in adopting a system of loans. The obvious point here is that loans only tide people over. They do not redistribute incomes.

 Is this strictly true if the loans are interest free?

Then there is the problem of repayment. If income support is designed to cover only the bare essential weekly expenditures, how can people afford to pay back loans out of their income support? Finally, there is the limited amount of money available in the Social Fund. Once social security offices have run out of money, no further loans or grants can be made.

The tax/benefit system and the problem of disincentives: the poverty trap

When means-tested benefits are combined with a progressive income tax system there can be a serious problem of disincentives. As poor people earn more money, so not only will they start paying income taxes and national insurance, but also they will begin losing means-tested benefits. Theoretically, it is possible to have a marginal tax-plus-lost-benefit rate in excess of 100 per cent. In other words, for every extra £1 earned, taxes and lost benefits add up to more than £1. This obviously acts as a serious disincentive. What is the point of getting a job or trying to earn more money, if you end up earning no more or actually losing money?

Poverty trap

Where poor people are discouraged from working or getting a better job because any extra income they earn will be largely taken away in taxes and lost benefits.

This situation is known as the poverty trap. People are trapped on low incomes with no realistic means of bettering their position.

Before 1988, in some cases the marginal rate *did* in fact exceed 100 per cent. Today this is no longer the case, since benefits are now based on after-tax not pre-tax incomes. Nevertheless, benefits taper off very steeply as people earn more, giving an effective marginal rate of tax-plus-lost-benefit of between 70 and 90 per cent for many people.

The problem of the poverty trap would be overcome by switching to a system of universal benefits unrelated to income. For example, *everyone* could receive a flat payment from the state fixed at a sufficiently high level to cover their basic needs. There would still be *some* disincentive, but this would be confined to an income effect: people would not have the same need to work if the state provided a basic income. But there would no longer be the disincentive to work caused by a resulting *loss* of benefits (a substitution effect).

Box 9.8

Negative Income Tax and Redistribution
A unified system of tax and social security

The complexities of welfare provision have led many economists to look for a more simplified and effective means to cure poverty and redistribute income, whilst avoiding the poverty trap. One such solution is the negative income tax system, which works as follows.

First, a minimum income level must be set. This will generally be on or about the poverty line. Let us assume for the sake of argument that this level is £2000. Under the negative income tax system, everyone is entitled to this fixed level of benefit. If you earn nothing, then you just get this £2000.

Secondly, as a person earns income, so right from the first pound, income tax is paid. Assume that the tax rate is 25 per cent.

These taxes are then offset against the fixed benefit. If taxes exceed the benefit, a person pays the difference to the Inland Revenue. If taxes are less than the benefit, the person receives the difference from the Inland Revenue – a negative tax. The table shows how it works. With earnings up to £8000, people receive a net benefit (a negative income tax). Over £8000, people pay a positive net tax.

A negative income tax system

Earnings (£) (1)	Tax on earnings @ 25% (£) (2)	Benefit (£) (3)	Tax minus benefit (£): (2) − (3) (4)	Net income (£): (1) − (4) (5)
0	0	2 000	−2 000[1]	2 000
4 000	1 000	2 000	−1 000[1]	5 000
8 000	2 000	2 000	0	8 000
12 000	3 000	2 000	1 000	11 000
16 000	4 000	2 000	2 000	14 000

[1] Negative income tax.

The level of fixed benefit can be made to vary with people's circumstances. Thus if a single person's benefit were £2000, a married couple's with four children could be, say, £5000.

The advantages claimed for the system are as follows:

● It eliminates the poverty trap. There are no levels of earnings where benefits suddenly disappear.
● It is simple to administer. A single agency – the Inland Revenue – is involved.
● It would have a high take-up rate.

There are, however, various problems associated with the system:

● If the Inland Revenue is responsible for paying a negative income tax, it will be paid in arrears. This could be a major problem for the poor. An alternative is for everyone to receive the full fixed benefit – say, through the Post Office – and then simply to pay taxes on *every* pound earned. The effect is just the same.
● There may still need to be special payments for

specific needs: for example, for the sick and for those with housing problems.
● The main problem is the cost. If the marginal tax rate is to be kept low (say, at a standard rate of 25 per cent), and if the basic benefit for the poor is to be sufficiently high (say, £5000), then anyone earning less than *£20 000* will receive a negative income tax payment! This would put a tremendous cost burden on indirect taxes: a burden paid disproportionately by the poor!
● Alternatively, the marginal tax rate could be increased. But then the problem of disincentives is likely to arise.

Thus the conflict between equity and efficiency is not resolved.

? Draw up a similar table to the one above, only this time assume that the basic benefit is £6000. Assume that the marginal tax rate is 20 per cent up to £10 000 and 40 per cent from £10 000 to £20 000. To what extent would this particular system help to tackle the problems of (a) equity; (b) cost of provision; (c) incentives?

The big drawback with universal benefits, however, is their cost. If they were given to everyone and were large enough to help the poor, their cost would be enormous. Thus although the benefits themselves would not create much disincentive effect, the necessary taxation to fund them probably would.

There is no ideal solution to this conundrum. On the one hand, the more narrowly benefits are targeted on the poor, the greater is the problem of the poverty trap. On the other hand, the more widely they are spread, the greater is the cost of providing any given level of support to individuals. A compromise proposal is that of a negative income tax This is examined in Box 9.8.

Negative income tax

A combined system of tax and benefits. As people earn more they gradually lose their benefits until beyond a certain level they begin paying taxes.

Conclusions

Redistribution is not costless. Whether it takes place through taxes or benefits or both, it is possible that there will be a problem of disincentives. Nevertheless the size of the disincentive problem varies enormously from one tax to another and from one benefit to another, and in some cases there may even be an *in*centive effect: for example, when the income effect of a tax outweighs the substitution effect. It is therefore important to estimate the particular effects of each type of proposal not only on income distribution itself, but also on economic efficiency.

Ultimately the questions of how much income should be redistributed and whether the costs are worth bearing are normative questions, and ones therefore that an economist cannot answer. They are moral and political questions. It would be nice if the 'utility' gained by the poor and lost by the rich could be quantified so that any net gain from redistribution could be weighed up against lost output. But such 'interpersonal comparisons of utility' are not possible. For example, the benefit that a person receives from a cooker or an electric fire cannot be measured in 'utils' or any other 'psychic unit'. What people are prepared to pay for the items is no guide either, since a poor person obviously cannot afford to pay nearly as much as a rich person, and yet will probably get the same if not more personal benefit from them.

Yet decisions have to be made!

? How would you go about deciding whether person A or person B gets more personal benefit from each of the following: (a) an electric fire; (b) a clothing allowance of £x; (c) draught-proofing materials; (d) child benefit.
Do your answers help you in deciding how best to allocate benefits?

▲ SUMMARY

1. Government intervention in the economy has a number of purposes including redistribution, the correction of market distortions and macroeconomic stabilization.

2. The government can redistribute incomes through taxation, benefits, legislation or structural policies.

3. There are various requirements of a good tax system, including horizontal and vertical equity, payment according to the amount of benefit received, being cheap to collect, difficult to evade, non-distortionary and convenient to the taxpayer and the government, and having the minimum disincentive effects.

4. Taxes can be divided into those paid directly to the authorities (direct taxes) and those paid via a middle person (indirect taxes). Direct taxes in the UK are of three types: (a) Taxes on income: these include personal income tax, corporation tax (on company profit) and capital gains tax. National insurance contributions are also assessed on a person's income. (b) Taxes on wealth: these include inheritance tax and business rates. (c) Poll taxes: the community charge. Indirect taxes include VAT, excise duties and customs duties.

5. Taxes can be categorized as progressive, regressive or

proportional. Progressive taxes have the effect of reducing inequality. The more steeply progressive they are, the bigger is the reduction in inequality.

6. Income taxes in the UK are progressive, but less steeply so than they used to be. National insurance contributions are mildly progressive at lower levels of income and then steeply regressive (with a zero marginal rate) above a certain level of income. The community charge is highly regressive, with all but very poor people having to pay the same absolute amount within any given local district. VAT in the UK is regressive, but the regressiveness is moderated by zero rates on certain basic items. Excise duties vary in their progressiveness/regressiveness depending on how much the goods on which they are imposed are consumed by the rich or the poor.

7. There are various limitations to using taxes to redistribute incomes. First, they cannot on their own increase the incomes of the poor. (Cutting taxes, however, *can* help the poor if the cuts are carefully targeted.) Secondly, high taxes on the rich may encourage evasion or avoidance. Thirdly, higher income taxes on the rich will probably lead to them receiving higher (gross) wages as well as reduced take-home pay. The balance of the two effects will depend on the elasticities of demand and supply of labour in each labour market.

8. Using taxes to redistribute incomes involves costs: these include administrative costs, costs of resource reallocation and disincentive effects.

9. Raising taxes has two effects on the amount people wish to work. On the one hand, people will be encouraged to work more in order to maintain their incomes. This is the income effect. On the other hand, they will be encouraged to substitute leisure for income, since an hour's leisure now costs less in forgone income. This is the substitution effect. The relative size of the income and substitution effects will depend on the nature of the tax change. The substitution effect is more likely to outweigh the income effect for those with few commitments, for people just above the tax threshold of the newly raised tax and in cases where the highest rates of tax are increased.

10. Benefits can be cash benefits or benefits in kind. Means-tested cash benefits in the UK include income support, family credit, grants and loans from the Social Fund, and housing benefit. Universal benefits include child benefit, state pensions, unemployment benefits, and sickness and invalidity benefits. Benefits in kind include health care, education and free school meals.

11. Means-tested benefits can be specifically targeted to those in need and are thus more 'cost-effective'. However, there can be serious problems with such benefits, including: limited take-up, time-consuming procedures for claimants, some relatively needy people falling just outside the qualifying limit and inadequate account taken of *all* relevant circumstances affecting a person's needs.

12. The poverty trap occurs when the combination of increased taxes and reduced benefits removes the incentive for poor people to earn more. The more steeply progressive this combined system is at low incomes, the bigger is the disincentive effect.

10 Markets, Efficiency and the Public Interest

In Chapter 9 we examined the problem of inequality and the various redistributive policies that a government could pursue. In this chapter we turn to examine another major area of concern. This is the question of the *efficiency* of markets in allocating resources. The arguments we shall be looking at provide the basis for many of the microeconomic policies adopted by government.

In section 10.1 we show how a *perfect* market economy could under certain conditions lead to 'social efficiency'. In section 10.2 we examine the *real* world and show how markets in practice fail to meet social goals. This second section presents the major arguments in favour of government intervention in a market economy. In section 10.3 we turn to discuss the alternative ways in which a government can intervene to correct these various market failings. If the government is to replace the market and provide goods and services directly it will need some way of establishing their costs and benefits. Section 10.4 looks at 'cost–benefit analysis'. This is a means of establishing the desirability of a public project such as a new motorway or a new hospital. Then in section 10.5 we look at the case for restricting government intervention. We examine the advantages of real-world markets and the drawbacks of government intervention. Finally, in section 10.6 we look at recent attempts to apply economic analysis to the political process itself.

The optimum amount of government intervention depends on two things: first, the *positive* question of the relative successes of government and the market in achieving various social goals; and secondly, the *normative* question of the relative desirability of various, possibly conflicting, social goals – goals such as efficiency and equity.

10.1 Efficiency under perfect competition

Perfect competition has been used by many economists and policy makers as an ideal against which to compare the benefits and shortcomings of real-world markets.

As was shown in Chapter 5, perfect competition has various advantages for society. Under perfect competition, firms' supernormal profits are competed away in the long run by the entry of new competitors. As a result firms are forced to produce at the bottom of their average cost curves. What is more, the fear of being driven out of business by the entry of new firms forces existing firms to try to find lower cost methods of production, thus shifting their AC curves downward.

Perhaps the most wide-reaching claim for perfect competition is that under certain conditions it will lead to a *socially efficient* use of a nation's resources.

Box 10.1

Vilfredo Pareto (1848–1923)
Person profile

Pareto came to economics late in his life: his first writing on the subject did not appear until 1896 when he was 48 years old. He had, however, replaced Leon Walras in the Chair of Economics at the University of Lausanne in 1892 and his economic career had started somewhat earlier. Like many notable economists of the past, Pareto had been trained in a discipline away from economics. He was a successful engineer and mathematician, and later became an iron works manager.

Pareto was Italian by nationality, although he was born in Paris. He was, much to his disappointment, to spend a large part of his life away from Italy. He did, however, involve himself deeply in Italian political, economic and social life, and this was to have a profound influence on his work in a number of ways. His contact with Italian socialism, and late in his life fascism, was to lead to a general disillusionment with political regimes irrespective of their aims.

Pareto's economic and political philosophy was subtly to change his life. In his early writings he expounded a strong belief in economic liberalism, being an advocate of free trade and competition. Such beliefs, however, diminished in later years.

His two outstanding works – the *Cours d' Economie Politique* (1896) and *Manuale d' Economia Politica* (1907) – represent a mixture of economics and sociology (another discipline in which Pareto was to make valuable contributions).

One feature that stands out in these texts is Pareto's

belief that, in order for economics to be scientific (i.e. concerned with model building, explanation and prediction), it must be ethically neutral. Values and biases must be kept to a minimum. In this respect Pareto was one of the first advocates of *positive* economics. What is rather surprising given this standpoint is that Pareto is most well known for his work on welfare economics – one of the potentially most value-laden areas of study.

Pareto is often seen as the founder of modern welfare economics. The Pareto criterion, which states that 'in order for a maximum welfare position to be reached then the "ophelimity"[1] of some should not increase to the detriment of others', was intended to represent a neutral standard of welfare, but nevertheless a standard against which the effects of economic changes can be judged to be an improvement or not. This at Pareto's time of writing was a path-breaking piece of work. Although the original Pareto criterion has since been refined and modified,[2] it still represents a crucial historical step in the development of modern welfare economics.

Pareto's contribution to economics has been a lasting one. It is interesting to speculate, however, just how much greater his contribution would have been had he not turned solely to the study of sociology from about 1912.

[1] Pareto uses this term as an alternative to utility.
[2] See, for example, the Hicks–Kaldor criterion in section 10.4 (page 404).

Social efficiency: 'Pareto optimality'

If it were possible to make changes in the economy – changes in the combination of goods produced or consumed, or changes in the combination of inputs used – and if such changes benefited some people without anyone else being made worse off, this would be said by economists to be an improvement in social efficiency, or a Pareto improvement, after Vilfredo Pareto, the Italian social scientist (see Box 10.1).

 Do you agree that, if some people gain and if no one loses, then this will be an 'improvement' in the well-being of society?

When all Pareto improvements have been made – in other words, when any additional changes in the economy would benefit some people only by making others worse off – the economy is said to be socially efficient, or Pareto optimal.

Pareto optimality, however, is a weak test of social welfare, since it ignores the question of the best or fairest distribution of income. It may be a *necessary* condition for an ideal allocation of resources that all Pareto improvements are made: that all

An improvement in social efficiency

A Pareto improvement.

Pareto improvement

Where changes in production or consumption can make at least one person better off without making anyone worse off.

Social efficiency

A situation of Pareto optimality.

Pareto optimality

Where all possible Pareto improvements have been made: where, therefore, it is impossible to make anyone better off without making someone else worse off.

waste is eliminated. It is not *sufficient*, however. If, for example, the government redistributed income from the rich to the poor, there would be no Pareto improvement since the rich would lose. Both an equal and a highly unequal distribution of income could be Pareto optimal, and yet it could be argued that a more equal distribution is socially more desirable.

The argument we shall be examining is that under certain conditions a perfect market will lead to Pareto optimality and hence social efficiency. But a word of caution. Just because social *efficiency* is achieved in a particular market environment, it does not necessarily make that environment *ideal*. There may be *other* problems such as those we looked at in Chapter 9: the problems of inequality and poverty. But for the moment we will ignore these other problems.

So why may a perfect market lead to social efficiency? The following sections explain.

The simple analysis of social efficiency: marginal benefit and marginal cost

Remember how we defined 'rational' choices. A rational person will choose to do an activity if the gain from so doing exceeds any sacrifice involved. In other words, whether as a producer, a consumer or a worker, a person will gain by expanding any activity whose marginal benefit (*MB*) exceeds its marginal cost (*MC*) and by contracting any activity whose marginal cost exceeds its marginal benefit. Remember that when economists use the term 'cost' they are referring to 'opportunity cost': in other words, the *sacrifice* of alternatives. Thus when we say that the marginal benefit of an activity is greater than its marginal cost, we mean that the additional benefit gained exceeds any sacrifice in terms of alternatives forgone.

Rational economic behaviour

Doing more of those activities whose marginal benefit exceeds their marginal cost and doing less of those activities whose marginal cost exceeds their marginal benefit.

Thus the economist's rule for rational economic behaviour is that a person should expand or contract the level of any activity until its marginal benefit is equal to its marginal cost. At that point the person will be acting efficiently in his or her own private interest. Only when $MB = MC$ can no further gain be made. This is known as a situation of private efficiency

By analogy, *social* efficiency will be maximized where, for any activity, the marginal benefit to *society* (*MSB*) is equal to the marginal (opportunity) cost to *society* (*MSC*). Where $MSB = MSC$, Pareto optimality is achieved. But why? If *MSB* is greater than *MSC*, there will be a Pareto improvement if there is an increase in the activity. For example, if the benefits to consumers from additional production of a good exceed the cost to producers, the consumers could fully meet the cost of production in the price they pay, and so no producer loses, and yet there would still be a net gain to consumers. Thus society has gained. Likewise if *MSC* is greater than *MSB*, society will gain from a decrease in production.

Private efficiency

Where a person's marginal benefit from a given activity equals the marginal cost.

Externalities

Costs or benefits of production or consumption experienced by society but not by the producers or consumers themselves. Sometimes referred to as 'spillover' or 'third-party' costs or benefits.

It is argued by economists that under certain circumstances the achievement of *private* efficiency will result in *social* efficiency also. Two major conditions have to be fulfilled, however:

● There must be *perfect competition* throughout the economy. This is examined in the following sections.
● There must be *no* externalities. Externalities are additional costs or benefits to society, *over and above* those experienced by the individual producer or consumer. Pollution is an example. It is a cost that society experiences from production, but it is not a cost that the individual producer has to pay. In the *absence* of externalities, the only costs or benefits to society are the ones that the individual producer or consumer experiences: i.e. marginal social benefit (*MSB*) is the same as marginal

private benefit (*MB*), and marginal social cost (*MSC*) is the same as marginal private cost (*MC*).

To understand just how social efficiency is achieved we must look at how people maximize their interests through the market. We will look first at the demand side and then at the supply side, and then finally put the two sides together.

Achieving social efficiency through the market

Consumption: MU = P

The marginal benefit to a consumer from the consumption of any good is its marginal utility. The marginal cost is the price the consumer has to pay.

As demonstrated in Chapter 3, the 'rational' consumer will maximize consumer surplus where *MU* = *P*: in other words, where the marginal benefit from consumption is equal to the marginal cost of consumption. Do you remember the case of Tina and her purchases of petrol? (See page 106.) She goes on making additional journeys and hence buying extra petrol as long as she feels that the journeys are worth the money she has to spend: in other words, as long as the marginal benefit she gets from buying extra petrol (its marginal utility to her) exceeds its marginal cost (its price). She will stop buying extra petrol when its marginal utility has fallen (the law of diminishing marginal utility) to equal its price. At that point her consumer surplus is maximized: she has an 'efficient' level of consumption.

 Assume that the price of the good falls. How will an 'efficient' level of consumption be restored?

Production: P = MC

The marginal benefit to a producer from the production of any good is its marginal revenue (which under perfect competition will be the same as the price of the good). As demonstrated in Chapter 5, the 'rational' firm will maximize its profit where its marginal revenue (i.e. the price under conditions of perfect competition) is equal to its marginal cost of production. This is the same thing as saying that it will produce where the marginal benefit from production is equal to the marginal cost from production.

Social efficiency in the market: MSB = MSC

Provided the two conditions of (a) perfect competition and (b) the absence of externalities are fulfilled, Pareto optimality will be achieved. Let us take each condition in turn.

Perfect competition. Since *MU* = *P* (for each consumer) and *P* = *MC* (for each producer), then, since the market price (*P*) for any good is the same for *all* producers and consumers:

MU = *MC* (for all producers and all consumers)

No externalities. In the absence of externalities, *MSB* = *MU* (i.e. the benefits of consumption within society are confined to the direct consumers) and *MSC* = *MC* (i.e. the costs of production to society are simply the costs paid by the producers). Thus:

$$MSB = MU = P = MC = MSC$$

i.e. *MSB* = *MSC*

Inefficiency would arise if (a) competition were not perfect and hence if marginal revenue were *not* equal to price and as a result marginal cost were not equal to price or (b) there were externalities and hence either marginal social benefit were different from marginal utility (i.e. marginal *private* benefit) or marginal social cost were different from marginal (private) cost.

1. If monopoly power existed in an industry, would production be above or below the socially efficient level (assuming no externalities)? Which would be greater, *MSB* or *P*?

2. Assuming perfect competition and no externalities, social efficiency will also be achieved in factor markets. Demonstrate that this will be where:

$$MSB_f = MRP_f = P_f = MDU_f = MSC_f$$

(where f is any factor – see section 8.2).

3. Why will marginal social benefit *not* equal marginal social costs in the labour market if there exists (a) union monopoly power and/or (b) firms with monopsony power?

Interdependence, efficiency and the 'invisible hand': the simple analysis of general equilibrium

If there is perfect competition and an absence of externalities throughout the economy, then the whole economy, when in equilibrium, will be socially efficient. A state of general Pareto optimality will exist.

No economy, however, is static. Conditions of demand and supply are constantly changing. Fashions change, technology changes and so on. Thus old patterns of consumption and production will cease to be Pareto optimal. Nevertheless, provided there is perfect competition and no externalities, forces will come into play to restore Pareto optimality.

In this perfect market economy, Pareto optimality is restored not by government action, but rather by the individual actions of producers, consumers and factor owners all seeking their own self-interest. It is as if an 'invisible hand' were working to guide the economy towards social efficiency. (See Box 1.7.)

The economic system will respond to any change in demand or supply by a whole series of subsequent changes in various interdependent markets. Social efficiency will thereby be restored. The whole process can be illustrated with a circular flow of income diagram (see Figure 10.1).

Assume, for example, that tastes change such that the marginal utility of a particular good rises. This is illustrated on the right-hand side of the diagram by a shift in the *MU* curve (i.e. the demand curve) from MU_1 to MU_2 (i.e. D_1 to D_2). This will lead to the following sequence of events, which you can follow round the diagram in an anti-clockwise direction.

Consumer demand
The rise in marginal utility (i.e. the rise in marginal social benefit) leads to increased consumption. The resulting shortage will drive up the market price.

Producer supply
The rise in the market price will mean that price is now above the marginal (social) cost of production. It will thus be profitable for firms to increase their production. This in turn will lead to an increase in marginal cost (a movement up along the marginal cost curve) due to diminishing returns. There is a movement up along the supply curve. Price will continue to rise until equilibrium is reached at P_2Q_2, where $MSB_{g2} = MSC_g$.

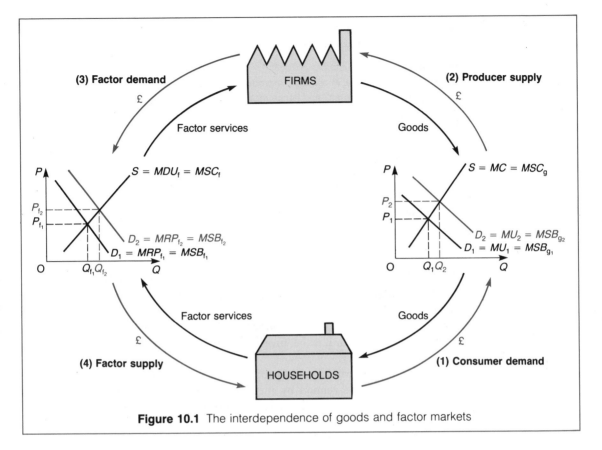

Figure 10.1 The interdependence of goods and factor markets

Factor demand

The rise in the price of the good will lead to an increase in the marginal revenue product of factors that are employed in producing the good. The reason for this is that the marginal *revenue* product of a factor is its marginal *physical* product multiplied by the *price* of the good (see section 8.2). But since the price of the good has now gone up, the output of factors will be worth correspondingly more. The following takes just one factor (f) as an example.

A rise in the value of the factor's output (due to the higher price of the good) will make its marginal revenue product higher than its marginal cost to the firm. This will increase the demand for the factor. This in turn will drive up the price of the factor.

Factor supply

The rise in the price of the factor will raise the marginal benefit of supplying it (and hence the marginal social benefit). This will mean that the marginal benefit now exceeds the marginal cost (the marginal disutility) of supplying the factor. There is thus a movement up along the factor supply curve as more units of the factor are supplied. The price of the factor will continue to rise until equilibrium is reached at $P_{f2}Q_{f2}$, where $MSB_{f2} = MSC_f$.

These effects in the four quadrants of Figure 10.1 are summarized in Figure 10.2.

The process of adjustment does not end here. If supernormal profits are made, new firms will enter. If factor rewards are supernormal, new factors will be attracted from other industries. This in turn will affect prices and hence quantities in *other* industries in both goods and factor markets.

---

(1) Consumer demand

$MU\uparrow$ (i.e. $MSB\uparrow$) $\rightarrow D\uparrow$ (i.e. D_1 to D_2) $\rightarrow MU > P \rightarrow$ consumption $\uparrow \rightarrow D > S \rightarrow P\uparrow$

(2) Producer supply

$P\uparrow \rightarrow P > MC$ (i.e. $P > MSC$) $\rightarrow$ production $\uparrow \rightarrow MC\uparrow$ (i.e. $MSC\uparrow$)
(movement up along MC and hence MSC curve)

(3) Factor demand

$MRP_f\uparrow$ (i.e. $MSB_f\uparrow$) $\rightarrow MRP_f > P_f \rightarrow$ employment of factor $\uparrow \rightarrow P_f\uparrow$

(4) Factor supply

$P_f\uparrow \rightarrow P_f > MDU$ (i.e. $P_f > MSC_f$) $\rightarrow$ supply of factor $\uparrow \rightarrow MDU\uparrow$
(movement up along MDU and hence MSC_f curve)

Figure 10.2 The effects of an initial increase in consumers' marginal utility for a good

---

In other words, a single change in tastes will create a ripple effect throughout the economy, through a whole series of interdependent markets. Eventually, long-run equilibrium will be restored with $MSB = MSC$ in all markets. The economy has returned to a position of Pareto optimality. And all this has taken place with no government intervention. It is the 'invisible hand' of the market that has achieved this state of social efficiency.

These arguments form a central part of the neo-classical case for *laissez-faire*: the philosophy of non-intervention by the government. Under ideal conditions, it is argued, the free pursuit of individual self-interest will lead to the social good.

? Trace through the effects in both factor and goods markets of the following:

(a) An increase in the productivity of a particular type of labour.
(b) An increase in the supply of a particular factor.
Show in each case how social efficiency will initially be destroyed and then how market adjustments will restore social efficiency.

The following pages examine social efficiency in more detail. You may omit these and skip straight to section 10.2 (page 373) if you want to.

* The intermediate analysis of social efficiency: marginal benefit and marginal cost ratios

In practice, consumers do not consider just one good in isolation. They make choices between goods. Likewise firms make choices as to which goods to produce and which factors to employ. A more satisfactory analysis of social efficiency, therefore, considers the choices that firms and households make.

Whether as a producer, consumer or worker, a person will gain by expanding activity X relative to activity Y if:

$$\frac{MB_X}{MB_Y} > \frac{MC_X}{MC_Y}$$

The reason is straightforward. Activity X is giving a greater benefit relative to its cost than is activity Y. Only when:

$$\frac{MB_X}{MB_Y} = \frac{MC_X}{MC_Y}$$

can no further gain be made by switching from the one activity to the other. At this point, people will be acting efficiently in their own private interest.

By analogy, *social* efficiency will be maximized when:

$$\frac{MSB_X}{MSB_Y} = \frac{MSC_X}{MSC_Y}$$

This is the requirement for Pareto optimality. If, however:

$$\frac{MSB_X}{MSB_Y} > \frac{MSC_X}{MSC_Y}$$

there would be a Pareto improvement if there were an increase in activity X relative to activity Y. For example, if the marginal benefit to consumers from good X relative to good Y was greater than the marginal cost to producers from good X relative to good Y, then if more X was produced relative to Y, the additional gain to consumers would be greater than the additional cost to producers. Thus consumers could fully compensate the producers (in the price they pay for X) and still have a net gain.

As with the simple analysis of social efficiency, it can be shown that, provided there is perfect competition and no externalities, the achievement of private efficiency will result in social efficiency also. This will be demonstrated in the following sections.

* Efficiency in the goods market (intermediate analysis)

Private efficiency under perfect competition

Consumption. The optimum combination of two goods X and Y consumed for any consumer will be where:

$$\frac{MU_X}{MU_Y} \text{ (i.e. } MRS) = \frac{P_X}{P_Y}$$

(Note: section 3.2 explained that the *marginal rate of substitution in consumption (MRS)* is the amount of good Y a consumer would be willing to sacrifice for an increase in consumption of good X (i.e. $\Delta Y/\Delta X$). It is given by the slope of the indifference curve. $MRS = MU_X/MU_Y$ since, if X gave twice the marginal utility of Y, the consumer would be prepared to give up two of Y to obtain one of X (i.e. $MRS = 2/1$). See pages 120–1.)

 If MU_X/MU_Y were greater than P_X/P_Y, how would consumers behave? What would bring consumption back to equilibrium where $MU_X/MU_Y = P_X/P_Y$?

Production. The optimum combination of two goods X and Y produced for any producer will be where:

$$\frac{MC_X}{MC_Y} \text{ (i.e. } MRT) = \frac{P_X}{P_Y}$$

(Note: the *marginal rate of transformation in production (MRT)*, is the amount of good Y that the producer will have to give up producing for an increase in production of good X (i.e. $\Delta Y/\Delta X$) if total costs of production are to remain unchanged. $MRT = MC_X/MC_Y$ since, if the marginal cost of good X were twice that of Y, the firm's costs would remain constant if it gave up producing two of Y in order to produce one extra X (i.e. $MRT = 2/1$).)

 If MC_X/MC_Y were greater than P_X/P_Y how would firms behave? What would bring production back into equilibrium where $MC_X/MC_Y = P_X/P_Y$?

Social efficiency under perfect competition

In each of the following three cases, it will be assumed that there are no externalities and that therefore $MU = MSB$ and thus $MU_X/MU_Y = MSB_X/MSB_Y$, and that $MC = MSC$ and thus $MC_X/MC_Y = MSC_X/MSC_Y$.

Social efficiency between consumers. If MU_X/MU_Y for person a is greater than MU_X/MU_Y for person b, *both* people would gain if person a gave person b some of good Y in exchange for some of good X. There would be a Pareto improvement. The Pareto optimal distribution of consumption will therefore be where:

$$\frac{MU_X}{MU_Y} \text{ person a} = \frac{MU_X}{MU_Y} \text{ person b} \ldots = \frac{MU_X}{MU_Y} \text{ person n}$$

i.e. $MRS_a = MRS_b \ldots = MRS_n$

But this will be achieved *automatically* under perfect competition, since each consumer will consume that combination of goods where $MU_X/MU_Y = P_X/P_Y$ and all consumers face the *same* (market) prices and hence the *same* P_X/P_Y.

Social efficiency between producers. If MC_X/MC_Y for producer g is greater than MC_X/MC_Y for producer h, then if producer g produced relatively more Y and producer h produced relatively more X, the same output could be produced at a lower total cost (i.e. with less resources). There would be a Pareto improvement. The Pareto optimum distribution of production between firms will therefore be where:

$$\frac{MC_X}{MC_Y} \text{ producer g} = \frac{MC_X}{MC_Y} \text{ producer h} \ldots = \frac{MC_X}{MC_Y} \text{ producer n}$$

i.e. $MRT_g = MRT_h \ldots = MRT_n$

But this too will be achieved *automatically* under perfect competition, since each producer will maximize profits where $MC_X/MC_Y = P_X/P_Y$ and all producers face the *same* (market) prices and hence the *same* P_X/P_Y.

Social efficiency in exchange. If MU_X/MU_Y (i.e. *MRS*) for all consumers is greater than MC_X/MC_Y (i.e. *MRT*) for all producers, then there would be a Pareto improvement if resources were reallocated to produce relatively more X and less Y.

This can be demonstrated as follows.

Assume the *MRS* (i.e. $\Delta Y/\Delta X$) = 3/1 and the *MRT* (i.e. $\Delta Y/\Delta X$) = 2/1. Thus $MRS > MRT$. Consumers will be prepared to give up 3 units of Y to obtain 1 unit of X, and yet producers only have to sacrifice producing 2 units of Y to produce 1 unit of X. Thus for each extra unit of X that is produced and consumed, consumers gain the equivalent of 3 units of Y for the loss to producers of only 2 units of Y. Thus consumers can pay producers in full for the X they produce and there will still be a net gain to consumers. Some people have gained; no one has lost. There has therefore been a Pareto improvement.

The Pareto optimum allocation of resources will be where:

Social *MRS* (*SMRS*) = Social *MRT* (*SMRT*)

Assuming no externalities, this will be achieved automatically under perfect competition since (a) with no externalities, social and private marginal rates of substitution will be the same, and similarly social and private marginal rates of transformation will be the same and (b) P_X/P_Y is the same for all producers and consumers. In other words:

Figure 10.3 The achievement of social efficiency under perfect competition

$$SMRS = MRS_{\text{all consumers}} = \frac{MU_X}{MU_Y}_{\text{all consumers}} = \frac{P_X}{P_Y}$$

$$\text{and } SMRT = MRT_{\text{all producers}} = \frac{MC_X}{MC_Y}_{\text{all producers}} = \frac{P_X}{P_Y}$$

i.e. $SMRS = SMRT$

Thus the pursuit of *private* gain, it is argued, has led to the achieving of *social* efficiency. This is a momentous conclusion. It is clearly very attractive to people to think that, simply by looking after their own interests, *social* efficiency will thereby be achieved!

This is illustrated graphically in Figure 10.3. A production possibility curve shows the various combinations of two goods X and Y that can be produced (see page 11). Its slope is given by $\Delta Y / \Delta X$ and shows how much Y must be given up to produce 1 more of X. Its slope, therefore, is the marginal rate of transformation (*MRT*).

Social indifference curves can be drawn showing the various combinations of X and Y that give particular levels of satisfaction to consumers as a whole. Their slope is given by $\Delta Y / \Delta X$ and shows how much Y consumers are prepared to give up to obtain 1 more unit of X. Their slope, therefore, is the marginal rate of substitution in consumption (*MRS*).

The Pareto optimum combination of goods will be at point S, where the production possibility curve is tangential to the highest possible indifference curve. At any other point on the production possibility curve, a lower level of consumer satisfaction is achieved. The slope of the tangent at S is equal to both *MRT* and *MRS*, and hence also to P_X/P_Y.

 If production were at a point on the production possibility curve below point S, describe the process whereby market forces would return the economy to point S.

** Efficiency in the factor market (intermediate analysis)

A similar analysis to the above can be applied to factor markets. It is possible to show that perfect competition and the absence of externalities will lead to efficiency in the use of factors between firms, efficiency in the supply of factors between factor suppliers, and efficiency in the exchange or hire of factors.

The following will serve as an illustration. It examines the use of factors between firms.

Private efficiency in the use of factors under perfect competition

The optimum combination of any two factors (e.g. labour (L) and capital (K)) used by any firm will be where:

$$\frac{MP_L}{MP_K} = \frac{P_L}{P_K}$$

where MP_L/MP_K is the MRS_p – the marginal rate of factor substitution in production. This was demonstrated in section 4.2. MP_L/MP_K is the slope of the isoquant. P_L/P_K is the slope of the isocost. The optimum combination of labour and capital is where the isocost is tangential to the isoquant: i.e. where they have the same slope.

Social efficiency between firms in the use of factors

If MP_L/MP_K for firm g is greater than MP_L/MP_K for firm h, then if firm g were to use relatively more labour and firm h relatively more capital, more could be produced for the same total input. There would be a Pareto improvement.

The Pareto optimum distribution of factors between firms will therefore be where:

$$\frac{MP_L}{MP_K} \text{ firm g} = \frac{MP_L}{MP_K} \text{ firm h} \ldots = \frac{MP_L}{MP_K} \text{ firm n}$$

But this will be achieved automatically under perfect competition since each producer will be producing where $MP_L/MP_K = P_L/P_K$ and each producer will face the same factor prices and hence P_L/P_K.

Provided there are no externalities, and assuming $P_L/P_K = MSC_L/MSC_K$, then:

$$\frac{MSB_L}{MSB_K} = \frac{MSC_L}{MSC_K}$$

*The intermediate analysis of general equilibrium

General equilibrium

Where all the millions of markets throughout the economy are in a simultaneous state of equilibrium.

General equilibrium is where equilibrium exists in all markets. Under perfect competition and in the absence of externalities, general equilibrium will give Pareto optimality.

If any change in the conditions of demand or supply occurs, general equilibrium will be temporarily destroyed. Pareto optimality will no longer exist. But this disequilibrium will automatically create a whole series of interdependent reactions in various markets.

Assume, for example, that tastes change such that MU_X rises and MU_Y falls. This will lead to the following sequence of events in the goods market:

$MU_X/MU_Y > P_X/P_Y \rightarrow$ consumers buy more X relative to Y $\rightarrow MU_X/MU_Y \downarrow$ (due to diminishing marginal utility) and $P_X/P_Y \uparrow$ (due to a relative shortage of X and a surplus of Y).

$P_X/P_Y \uparrow \rightarrow P_X/P_Y > MC_X/MC_Y \rightarrow$ firms produce more X relative to Y $\rightarrow$ $MC_X/MC_Y \uparrow$ (due to diminishing returns).

The process of price and quantity adjustment continues until once more:

$$\frac{MU_X}{MU_Y} = \frac{P_X}{P_Y} = \frac{MC_X}{MC_Y}$$

Similar adjustments will take place in the factor market. The price of those factors used in producing good X will be bid up and those used in producing Y will be bid down. This will encourage factors to move from industry Y and into industry X. If X is a labour-intensive industry and Y a capital-intensive industry, an increase in X production relative to Y production will bid up the price of labour relative to capital: $(P_L/P_K)\uparrow$. This in turn may lead to an increased supply of labour and a reduced supply of capital.

To the extent that X and Y are substitutes or complements for other goods, a change in their price will create disequilibrium and subsequent adjustments in other goods markets.

To the extent that industry X and Y are competing for factors with other industries, any change in factor prices will create disequilibrium in other industries, which in turn will affect their costs and supply and their demand for other factors of production.

And so the whole process of adjustment continues until general equilibrium and Pareto optimality are restored.

▲ SUMMARY

1. Social efficiency (Pareto optimality) will be achieved when it is not possible to make anyone better off without making someone else worse off. This will be achieved if people behave 'rationally' under perfect competition providing there are no externalities.

2. Rational behaviour involves doing more of any activity whose marginal benefit (*MB*) exceeds its marginal cost (*MC*) and less of any activity whose marginal cost exceeds its marginal benefit. The optimum level of consumption or production for the individual consumer or firm will be where $MB = MC$. This is called a situation of 'private efficiency'.

3. In a perfectly competitive goods market, the consumer will achieve private efficiency where $MU = P$; and the producer where $P = MC$. Thus $MU = MC$. In the absence of externalities, private benefits and costs will equal social benefits and costs. Thus $MU = MSB$ and $MC = MSC$. Thus $MSB = MSC$: a situation of social efficiency (Pareto optimality).

4. In perfectly competitive factor markets, the employer will achieve private efficiency where $MRP_f = P_f$; and the factor supplier where $P_f = MDU_f$. Thus $MRP_f = MDU_f$. In the absence of externalities, $MRP_f = MSB_f$ and $MDU_f = MSC_f$. Thus $MSB_f = MSC_f$: a situation of social efficiency in the factor market.

5. Given perfect competition and an absence of externalities, if the equality of marginal benefit and marginal cost is destroyed in any market (by shifts in demand or supply), price adjustments will take place until general equilibrium is restored where $MSB = MSC$ in all markets: a situation of general Pareto optimality.

*6. The rational producer or consumer will choose the combination of any two pairs of goods where their marginal benefit ratio is equal to their marginal cost ratio. Consumers will achieve private efficiency where:

$$\frac{MU_X}{MU_Y}(MRS) = \frac{P_X}{P_Y}$$

Producers will achieve private efficiency where:

$$\frac{P_X}{P_Y} = \frac{MC_X}{MC_Y}(MRT)$$

Thus:

$$\frac{MU_X}{MU_Y} = \frac{MC_X}{MC_Y}$$

In the absence of externalities this will give a situation of social efficiency where:

$$\frac{MSB_X}{MSB_Y} = \frac{MSC_X}{MSC_Y}$$

*7. Similarly, in factor markets, social efficiency will be achieved if there is perfect competition and an absence of externalities. This will be where the *MSB* ratio for any two factors is equal to their *MSC* ratio.

*8. Again assuming perfect competition and an absence of externalities, general equilibrium will be achieved where there is a socially efficient level of production, consumption and exchange in all markets: where the *MSB* ratio for any pair of goods or factors is equal to the *MSC* ratio.

10.2 The case for government intervention

In the real world, markets will fail to achieve social efficiency. Part of the problem is the lack of perfect competition, part is the existence of externalities, and part is the fact that markets may take a long time to adjust to any disequilibrium given the often considerable short-run immobility of factors. What is more, social efficiency (i.e. Pareto optimality) is not the *only* economic goal of society. Markets may also fail to the extent that they fail to achieve objectives such as greater equality, faster growth, full employment, stable prices and the provision of public goods and services such as roads, the police and sewerage systems.

The various possible failures of the market are examined below. They provide the major part of the case for government intervention in the economy.

Externalities

The market will not lead to social efficiency if the actions of producers or consumers affect people other than themselves: in other words, when there are *externalities* (side-effects). Whenever other people are affected beneficially, there are said to be external benefits. Whenever other people are affected adversely, there are said to be external costs.

Thus the full costs to society (the social costs) of the production of any good are the private costs faced by firms plus any side-effects of production. Likewise the full benefits to society (the social benefits) from the consumption of any good are the private benefits enjoyed by consumers plus any side-effects.

There are four major types of externality.

External benefits

Benefits from production (or consumption) experienced by people *other* than the producer (or consumer).

External costs

Costs of production (or consumption) borne by people *other* than the producer (or consumer).

Social cost

Private cost plus externalities in production.

Social benefit

Private benefit plus externalities in consumption.

External costs of production (MSC > MC)

When a chemical firm dumps waste in a river or pollutes the air, the community bears costs additional to those borne by the firm. The marginal *social* cost (*MSC*) of chemical production exceeds the marginal private cost (*MC*). Diagrammatically, the *MSC* curve is above the *MC* curve.

In Figure 10.4 the socially optimum output for the firm would be Q_2, where $P = MSC$. The firm, however, produces Q_1 which is more than the optimum. Thus external costs lead to overproduction from society's point of view.

The problem of external costs arises in a capitalist society because no one has legal ownership of the air or rivers and can prevent or charge for their use as a dump for waste. Control must, therefore, be left to the government or local authorities.

Other examples include extensive farming that destroys hedgerows and wildlife, acid rain caused by smoke from coal-fired power stations, and nuclear waste from nuclear power stations.

External benefits of production (MSC < MC)

Imagine a bus company that spends money training its bus drivers.Each year some drivers leave to work for coach and haulage companies. These companies' costs are reduced as they do not have to train such drivers. Society has benefited from their training even though the bus company has not. The marginal *social* cost of the bus service, therefore, is less than the marginal *private* cost.

In a diagram like Figure 10.4, the *MSC* curve would be *below* the *MC* curve. The level of output (i.e. number of passenger miles) provided by the bus company would be where $P = MC$, a *lower* level than the social optimum where $P = MSC$.

Another example of external benefits in production is that of research and development. If other firms have access to the results of the research, then clearly the benefits extend beyond the firm which finances it. Given that the firm only receives the private benefits, it will conduct a less than optimal amount of research.

Figure 10.4 External costs in production

Figure 10.5 External costs in consumption

External costs of consumption (MSB < MB)

When people use their cars, other people suffer from their exhaust, the added congestion, the noise, etc. These 'negative externalities' make the marginal social benefit of using cars less than the marginal private benefit (i.e. marginal utility).

Figure 10.5 shows the marginal utility and price to a consumer of using a car. The optimal distance travelled for this motorist will be Q_1 miles: i.e. where $MU = P$ (where price is the cost of petrol, oil, wear and tear, etc. per mile). The *social* optimum, however, would be less than this, namely Q_2, where $MSB = P$.

Other examples are noisy radios in public places, cigarettes and their smoke, and litter.

> **?** Is it likely that the *MSB* curve will be parallel to the *MU* curve? Explain your reasoning.

External benefits of consumption (MSB > MB)

When people travel by train rather than by car, other people benefit by there being less congestion and exhaust and fewer accidents on the roads. Thus the marginal social benefit of rail travel is *greater* than the marginal private benefit (i.e. marginal utility). There are external benefits from rail travel.

Other examples are deodorants, vaccinations and attractive clothing.

> **?** On a diagram like Figure 10.5 demonstrate that there will be a less than optimum output where there are external benefits in consumption.

In general, whenever there are external benefits, there will be too little produced or consumed. Whenever there are external costs, there will be too much produced or consumed. The market will not equate *MSB* and *MSC*.

The above arguments have been developed in the context of perfect competition, with prices given to the producer or consumer by the market. Externalities also occur in all other types of market.

> **?** 1. Give other examples of each of the four types of externality.
> 2. Redraw Figures 10.4 and 10.5, only this time assume that the producer (in the first diagram) or the consumer (in the second) has economic power and is thus *not* a price taker. How does the existence of power affect the relationship between the private and the social optimum positions?

Box 10.2

Can the Market Provide Adequate Protection for the Environment?

In recent years people have become acutely aware of the damage being done to the environment by pollution. But if the tipping of chemicals and sewerage into the rivers and seas and the spewing of toxic gases into the atmosphere cause so much damage, why does it continue? If we all suffer from these activities, both consumers and producers alike, then why will a pure market system not deal with the problem? After all, a market should respond to people's interests.

The reason is that the costs of pollution are largely *external* costs. They are borne by society at large and only very slightly (if at all) by the polluter. If, for example, 10 000 people suffer from the smoke from a factory (including the factory owner) then that owner will only bear approximately 1/10 000 of the suffering. That personal cost may be quite insignificant when the owner is deciding whether the factory is profitable. And if the owner lives far away, the personal cost of the pollution will be zero.

Thus the *social* costs of polluting activities exceed the *private* costs. If people behave selfishly and only take into account the effect their actions have on themselves, there will be an *overproduction* of polluting activities.

Thus it is argued that governments must intervene to prevent or regulate pollution, or alternatively to tax the polluting activities or subsidize measures to reduce the pollution.

But if people are purely selfish, why do they buy 'green' products? Why do they buy, for example, 'ozone-friendly' aerosols? After all, the amount of damage done to the ozone layer from their own personal use of 'non-friendly' aerosols would be absolutely minute. The answer is that many people have a social conscience. They *do* sometimes take into account the effect their actions have on other people. They are not totally selfish. They like to do their own little bit, however small, towards protecting the environment.

Nevertheless to rely on people's consciences may be a very unsatisfactory method of controlling pollution. In a market environment where people are all the time being encouraged to consume more and more goods and where materialism is the religion of the age, there would have to be a massive shift towards 'green thinking' if the market were to be a sufficient answer to the problem of pollution. Certain types of environmental problem may get high priority in the media, like acid rain, the greenhouse effect, damage to the ozone layer and brain damage to children from leaded petrol. Nevertheless the sheer range of polluting activities makes reliance on people's awareness of the problems and their social consciences far too arbitrary.

? The following table gives the costs and benefits of an imaginary firm operating under perfect competition whose activities create a certain amount of pollution. (It is assumed that the costs of this pollution to society can be accurately measured.)

(a) What is the profit-maximizing level of output for this firm?

(b) What is the socially efficient level of output?

(c) Why might the marginal pollution costs increase in the way illustrated in this example?

Output (units)	Price per unit (MSB) (£)	Marginal (private) costs to the firm (MC) (£)	Marginal external (pollution) costs (MEC) (£)	Marginal social costs (MSC = MC + MEC) (£)
1	100	30	20	50
2	100	30	22	52
3	100	35	25	60
4	100	45	30	72
5	100	60	40	100
6	100	78	55	133
7	100	100	77	177
8	100	130	110	240

Market power

Lack of Pareto optimality

Whenever markets are imperfect, whether as pure monopoly or monopsony or as some form of imperfect competition, the market will fail to equate *MSB* and *MSC*. Pareto optimality will not be achieved.

For example, a monopoly faces a downward-sloping demand curve, and therefore marginal revenue is below average revenue ($= P$). Profits will be maximized where marginal revenue equals marginal cost. Thus, since price is above marginal revenue, price must also be above marginal cost. If there are no externalities and thus $P = MSB$ and $MC = MSC$, the firm will produce *less* than the Pareto optimal output, since if P is greater than MC, then MSB must be greater than MSC. Pareto optimum would be at the higher output where $P = MC$ and thus $MSB = MSC$.

This is illustrated in Figure 10.6, which shows revenue and cost curves for a monopolist. It assumes no externalities. The socially efficient (Pareto optimal) output is Q_2, where $MSB = MSC$. The monopolist, however, produces the lower output Q_1, where $MR = MC$.

Similarly, a firm with monopsony power in a factor market equates the marginal revenue product of a factor (MRP_f) with its marginal cost (MC_f). But under monopsony the factor's marginal cost will exceed its price (P_f) (see page 304). If there are no externalities and thus $MRP_f = MSB_f$ and $P_f = MSC_f$, then the firm will employ factors at a point where $MSB > MSC$ (since $MRP > P$). Thus it is employing less than the Pareto optimum amount of factors.

Figure 10.6 The monopolist producing less than the Pareto optimum

Deadweight loss under monopoly

Another way of analyzing the welfare loss that occurs under monopoly is to use the concepts of *consumers'* and *producers' surplus*. We examined consumers' surplus in Chapter 3 (page 106): it is the excess of consumers' total utility from consuming a good over their total expenditure on it. Producers' surplus is just another name for profit, but we measure it by a different method from the one we used in Chapters 4–6. The two concepts are illustrated in Figure 10.7, which is similar to Figure 10.6. The diagram shows an industry which is initially under perfect competition and then becomes a monopoly (but faces the same revenue and cost curves).

Under *perfect competition* the industry will produce an output of Q_{pc} at a price of P_{pc}, where $MC(= S) = P(= AR)$: i.e. at point a. Consumers' total utility is given by the area under the demand (MU) curve (the sum of all the areas 1 to 7). Consumers' total expenditure is $P_{pc} \times Q_{pc}$ (areas $4 + 5 + 6 + 7$). Consumers' surplus is the difference between total utility and total expenditure: in other words, the area between the price and the demand curve (areas $1 + 2 + 3$).

Producers' surplus (profit) is the difference between total revenue and total cost. Total revenue is $P_{pc} \times Q_{pc}$ (areas $4 + 5 + 6 + 7$). Total cost is the area under the MC

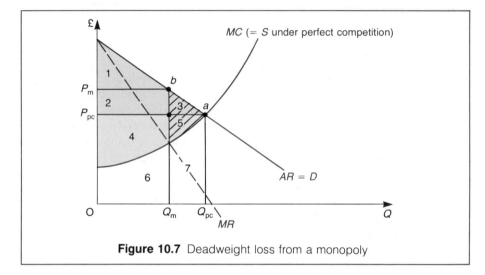

Figure 10.7 Deadweight loss from a monopoly

curve (areas 6 + 7). Producers' surplus is thus the area between the price and the *MC* curve (areas 4 + 5). Total consumers' plus producers' surplus is therefore the area between the demand and *MC* curves. This is shown by the total shaded area (areas 1 + 2 + 3 + 4 + 5).

What happens when the industry is under *monopoly*? The firm will produce where $MC = MR$, at an output of Q_m and a price of P_m (at point *b* on the demand curve). Total revenue is $P_m \times Q_m$ (areas 2 + 4 + 6). Total cost is the area under the *MC* curve (area 6). Thus the producer's surplus is areas 2 + 4. This is clearly a *larger* surplus than under perfect competition (since area 2 is larger than area 5). The consumers' surplus, however, will fall dramatically. With consumption at Q_m, total utility is given by areas 1 + 2 + 4 + 6, whereas consumer expenditure is given by areas 2 + 4 + 6. Consumers' surplus, then, is simply area 1. (Note that area 2 has been transformed from consumers' surplus to the producer's surplus.)

Total surplus under monopoly is therefore areas 1 + 2 + 4: a smaller surplus than under perfect competition. 'Monopolization' of the industry has resulted in a loss of total surplus of areas 3 + 5. The producer's gain has been more than offset by the consumers' loss. This loss of surplus is known as the deadweight welfare loss of monopoly.

Deadweight welfare loss

The loss of consumers' plus producers' surplus in imperfect markets (when compared with perfect competition).

Conclusions

The firm with market power uses fewer factors and produces less output than the Pareto optimum. It also causes deadweight welfare loss. To the extent, however, that the firm seeks aims *other* than profit maximization and thus may produce more than the profit-maximizing output, so these criticisms must be relaxed.

As was shown in Chapter 5, there are possible social advantages from powerful firms: advantages such as economies of scale and more research and development. These advantages may outweigh the lack of Pareto optimality. It can be argued that an ideal situation would be where firms are large enough to gain economies of scale and yet are somehow persuaded or compelled to produce where $P = MC$ (assuming no externalities).

With oligopoly and monopolistic competition further wastes may occur because of possibly substantial resources involved in non-price competition. Advertising is the major example. It is difficult to predict just how much oligopolists will diverge from the Pareto optimum, since their pricing and output depends on their interpretation of the activities of their rivals.

 Why will Pareto optimality not be achieved in markets where there are substantial economies of scale in production?

Ignorance and uncertainty

Perfect competition assumes that consumers, firms and factor suppliers have perfect knowledge of costs and benefits. In the real world there is often a great deal of ignorance and uncertainty. Thus people are unable to equate marginal benefit with marginal cost.

Consumers purchase many goods only once or a few times in a lifetime. Cars, washing machines, televisions and other consumer durables fall into this category. Consumers may not be aware of the quality of such goods until they have purchased them, by which time it is too late. Advertising may contribute to people's ignorance by misleading them as to the benefits of a good.

Firms are often ignorant of market opportunities, prices, costs, the productivity of factors (especially white-collar workers), the activity of rivals, etc.

Many economic decisions are based on expected future conditions. Since the future can never be known for certain, many decisions are taken that in retrospect will be seen to have been wrong.

In some cases it may be possible to obtain the information through the market. There may be an agency who will sell you the information or a newspaper or magazine that contains the information. In this case you will have to decide whether the cost to you of buying the information is worth the benefit it will provide you. A problem here is that you may not have sufficient information to judge how reliable the information is that you are buying!

 1. Assume that you wanted the following information. In which cases could you
  (i) buy perfect information, (ii) buy imperfect information, (iii) be able to obtain information without paying for it, (iv) not be able to obtain information?
(a) Which washing machine is the most reliable?
(b) Which of two jobs that are vacant is the most satisfying?
(c) Which builder will repair my roof most cheaply?
(d) Which builder will make the best job of repairing my roof?
(e) Which builder is best value for money?
(f) How big a mortgage would it be wise for me to take out?
(g) What course of higher education should I follow?
(h) What brand of washing powder washes whiter?
In which cases are there non-monetary costs to you of finding out the information? How can you know whether the information you acquire is accurate or not?
2. Make a list of pieces of information that a firm might want to know, and consider whether it could buy the information and how reliable that information might be.

Public goods

There is a category of goods that the free market, whether perfect or imperfect, will underproduce or may not produce at all. They are called public goods. Examples include lighthouses, pavements, flood-control dams, public drainage, public services such as the police and even government itself.

Public goods have two important characteristics:

- They have large external benefits relative to private benefits. This makes them socially desirable, but privately unprofitable. No one person alone would pay to

Public goods

Goods which when consumed by one person can still be consumed by other people (who would get a 'free ride' if the goods were paid for by the first person).

have a pavement built along his or her street. The private benefit would be too small relative to the cost. And yet the social benefit to all the other people using the pavement may far outweigh the cost.

Free-rider problem

When it is not possible to exclude other people from consuming a good that someone has bought.

- Once public goods are provided, it is not possible to exclude people from using them. This feature of *non-excludability* is known as the free-rider problem. It would be impossible for a private company to build pavements and then charge people each time they walk on them. Toll booths would be totally impractical.

Thus public goods can only be provided by the government or by the government subsidizing private firms. (Note that not all goods produced by the public sector are public goods.)

 1. Give some other examples of public goods. Does the provider of these goods (the government or local authority) charge for their use? If so, is the method of charging based on the amount of the good that people use? Is it a good method of charging? Could you suggest a better method?
2. Name some goods or services provided by the government or local authorities that are not public goods.

Immobility of factors and time lags in response

The long-run equilibrium under perfect competition with no externalities can be said to be socially optimal. $MSB = MSC$; there is maximum consumers' plus producers' surplus; all firms are producing at the bottom of their $LRAC$ curves; no firm is making supernormal profits.

Even under perfect competition, however, factors may be very slow to respond to changes in demand or supply conditions. Labour, for example, may be highly immobile both occupationally and geographically. This can lead to large price changes and hence to large supernormal profits and high wages for those in the sectors of rising demand or falling costs. The long run may be a very long time coming!

In the meantime, there will be further changes in the conditions of demand and supply. Thus the economy is in a constant state of disequilibrium and the long run never comes. The social optimum is never achieved. It is a bit like chasing rainbows. As you move towards the rainbow's end, so the rainbow moves. Likewise as firms and consumers respond to market signals and move towards equilibrium, so the equilibrium position moves.

Whenever monopoly/monopsony power exists, the problem is made worse as firms or unions put up barriers to the entry of new firms or factors.

Protecting people's interests

Dependants

People do not always make their own economic decisions. They are often dependent on decisions made by others. Parents make decisions on behalf of their children; spouses on each other's behalf; younger adults on behalf of old people; managers on behalf of shareholders; etc.

A free market will respond to these decisions, however good or bad they may be, and whether or not they are in the interests of the dependant. Thus the government may feel it necessary to protect dependants.

 Give examples of how the government intervenes to protect the interests of dependants from bad economic decisions taken on their behalf.

Box 10.3

The Police as a Public Service
Could policing be provided privately?

A good example of a public good or service is that of the police. Take the case of police officers on the beat. They are providing a general service to the community by deterring and detecting crime.

If individuals had to employ privately their own police officers, this would create considerable external benefits relative to private benefits. One police officer can provide protection to *many* individuals. But for most people it would be out of the question to employ their own police officer: the private cost would hugely exceed the private benefit. Also, once such privately employed police were on duty catching and deterring criminals, it would not be possible to exclude those people from benefiting who were not employing their own police officers. There would be a 'free-rider' problem.

It obviously makes sense, therefore, that policing should be provided as a public service.

But do all aspects of policing come into this category? The answer is no. When there is a *specific* task of guarding specific property, policing could be provided by the market. This is in fact done by security firms. Security guards are employed by banks, shops, factories, etc. to prevent theft or criminal damage to specific property. In these cases the private benefits are perceived to exceed the private costs.

Should such security services be provided privately or are they better provided by the police? Since the *private* benefits in such cases are large, there is a strong argument for charging the recipient. But why should not the police charge firms for specific guard duties? The problem here is that, if private security firms were not allowed to operate, the police would have a monopoly and could charge very high prices unless the prices were regulated by the government. Also the quality of the service might be poorer than that provided by private security companies which were competing against each other for business.

On the other hand, the police are likely to have greater expertise to bring to the job. Also there are economies of scale to be gained: for example, the police may have knowledge of criminal activities in other parts of the area which may pose a threat to the particular property in question. Finally, there is the problem that private security guards may not show the same level of courtesy as the police in dealing with the public (or criminals for that matter).

? 1. The police charge football clubs for policing inside football grounds. Do you think this is a good idea?
2. Some roads could be regarded as a public good, but some could be provided by the market. Which types of road could be provided by the market? Why? Would it be a good idea?

Poor economic decision making by individuals on their own behalf

The government may feel that people need protecting from poor economic decisions that they make on their *own* behalf. It may feel that in a free market people will consume too many harmful things. Thus if the government wants to discourage smoking and drinking, it can put taxes on tobacco and alcohol. In more extreme cases it could make various activities illegal: activities such as prostitution, certain types of gambling, and the sale and consumption of drugs.

On the other hand, the government may feel that people consume too little of things that are good for them: things such as education, drugs on prescription and sports facilities. When the government feels that it knows better than individuals about what items are good for them, such goods are known as merit goods. The government could either provide them free or subsidize their production.

? How do merit goods differ from public goods?

Merit goods

Goods which the government feels that people will underconsume and which therefore ought to be subsidized or provided free.

Box 10.4

Should the Provision of Health Care Be Left to the Market?
A case of multiple market failures

When you go shopping you may well pay a visit to the chemist and buy a bottle of paracetamol, some sticking plasters or a tube of ointment. These health-care products are being sold through the market system in much the same way as other everyday goods and services such as food, household items and petrol.

But many health-care services and products are not allocated through the market in this way. In the UK, the National Health Service provides free hospital treatment, a free general practitioner service and free prescriptions for certain categories of people (such as pensioners and children). Their marginal cost to the patient is thus zero. Of course, these services use resources and they thus have to be paid for out of taxes. In this sense they are not free. (Have you heard the famous saying, 'There's no such thing as a free lunch'?)

But why are these services not sold directly to the patient, thereby saving the taxpayer money? Why is it considered that certain types of health care should be provided free, whereas food should not? After all, they could both be considered as basic necessities of life.

The advocates of free health-care provision argue that there are a number of fundamental objections to relying on a market system of allocation of health care, many of which do not apply in the case of food, clothing, etc. So what are the reasons why a free market would fail to provide the optimum amount of health care?

People may not be able to afford treatment

This is a problem connected with the distribution of income. Because income is unequally distributed, some people will be able to afford better treatment than others, and the poorest people may not be able to afford

treatment at all. On grounds of equity, therefore, it is argued that health care should be provided free – at least for poor people.

The concept of equity that is usually applied to health care is that of treatment according to medical need rather than according to the ability to pay.

? Does this argument also apply to food and other basic goods?

Difficulty for people in predicting their future medical needs

If you were suddenly taken ill and required a major operation, or maybe even several, it could be very expensive indeed for you if you had to pay. On the other hand, you may go through life requiring very little if any medical treatment. In other words, there is great uncertainty about your future medical needs. As a result it would be very difficult to plan your finances and budget for possible future medical expenses if you had to pay for treatment. Medical insurance is a possible solution to this problem, but there is still a problem of equity. Would the chronically sick or very old be able to obtain cover, and if so, would the premiums be very high? Would the poor be able to afford the premiums? Also would insurance cover be comprehensive?

Externalities

Health care generates a number of benefits *external* to the patient. If you are cured of an infectious disease, for example, it is not just you who benefit, but also others since you will not infect them. Also your family and friends benefit from seeing you well; and if you have a job you will be able to get back to work, thus reducing the

Other objectives

As we saw in the Chapter 9, one of the major criticisms of the free market is the problem of *inequality*. The Pareto criterion gives no guidance, however, as to the most desirable distribution of income. A redistribution of income will benefit some and make others worse off. Thus Pareto optimality can be achieved for *any* distribution of income. Pareto optimality merely represents the efficient allocation of resources for any *given* distribution of income.

Social efficiency is one possible social goal. Greater equality is another, as is economic growth. Other possible social goals also can be identified: goals such as

Box 10.4 (cont'd)

disruption there. These external benefits of health care could be quite large.

If the sick have to pay the cost of their treatment, they may decide not to be treated – especially if they are poor. They may not take into account the effect that their illness has on other people. The market, by equating *private* benefits and costs, would produce too little health care.

Patient ignorance

Markets only function well to serve consumer wishes if the consumer has the information to make informed decisions. If you are to buy the right things, you must know what you want and whether the goods you buy meet these wants. In practice, consumers do have pretty good knowledge about the things they buy. For example, when you go to the supermarket you will already have tried most of the items that you buy, and will therefore know how much you like them. Even with new products, provided they are the sort you buy more than once, you can learn from any mistakes.

In the case of health care, 'consumers' (i.e. patients) may have very poor knowledge. If you have a pain in your chest, it may be simple muscular strain, or it may be a symptom of heart disease. You rely on the doctor (the *supplier* of the treatment) to give you the information: to diagnose your condition. Two problems could arise here if there were a market system of allocating health care.

The first is that unscrupulous doctors might advise more expensive treatment than is necessary, or that drug companies might try to persuade you to buy a more expensive branded product rather than an identical cheaper version.

The second is that patients suffering from the early stages of a serious disease might not consult their doctor until the symptoms become acute, by which time it might be too late to treat the disease, or very expensive to do so. With a free health service, however, there is likely to be an earlier diagnosis of serious conditions. On the other hand some patients may consult their doctors over trivial complaints.

Oligopoly

If doctors and hospitals operated in the free market as profit maximizers, it is unlikely that competition would drive down their prices. Instead it is possible that they would collude to fix standard prices for treatment, so as to protect their incomes.

Even if doctors did compete openly, it is unlikely that consumers would have the information to enable them to 'shop around' for the best value. Doctor A may charge less than doctor B, but is the quality of service the same? Simple bedside manner – the thing that may most influence a patient's choice – may be a poor indicator of the doctor's skill and judgment.

To argue that the market system will fail to provide an optimal allocation of health-care resources does not in itself prove that *free provision* is the best alternative. In the USA there is much more reliance on *private medical insurance*. Only the very poor get free treatment. Alternatively, the government may simply *subsidize* the provision of health care, so as to make it cheaper rather than free. This is the case with prescriptions and dental treatment in the UK, where many people have to pay part of the cost of treatment. Also the government can *regulate* the behaviour of the providers of health care, so as to prevent exploitation of the patient. Thus only people with certain qualifications are allowed to operate as doctors, nurses, pharmacists, etc.

? 1. Does the presence of external benefits from health care suggest that health care should be provided free?
2. If health care is provided free, the demand is likely to be high. How is this high demand dealt with? Is this a good way of dealing with it?
3. Go through each of the market failings identified in this box. In each case consider what alternative policies are open to a government to tackle them. What are the advantages and disadvantages of these alternatives?

moral behaviour (however defined), enlightenment, social consciousness, co-operation, the development of more refined tastes, fulfilment, freedom from exploitation, and freedom to own, purchase and inherit property. The unfettered free market may not be very successful in achieving social efficiency. It may be even less successful in achieving many other social goals.

Finally, the free market is unlikely to achieve simultaneously the *macroeconomic objectives* of rapid economic growth, full employment, stable prices and a balance of international payments. These problems and the methods of government intervention are examined in later chapters.

Conclusions

It is not within the scope of economics to make judgements as to the relative importance of social goals. Economics can only consider means to achieving stated goals. First, therefore, the goals have to be clearly stated by the policy makers. Secondly, they have to be quantifiable so that different policies can be compared as to their relative effectiveness in achieving the particular goal. Certain goals, such as growth in national income, changes in the distribution of income and greater efficiency, are relatively easy to quantify. Others, such as enlightenment, are virtually impossible to quantify. For this reason, economics tends to concentrate on the means to achieving a relatively narrow range of goals. The danger is that, by economists concentrating on a limited number of goals, they may well influence the policy makers – the government, local authorities, various pressure groups, etc. – into doing the same, and thus into neglecting other perhaps important social goals.

Different objectives are likely to conflict. For example, economic growth may conflict with greater equality. In the case of such 'trade-offs', all the economist can do is to demonstrate the effects of a given policy, and leave the policy makers to decide whether the benefits in terms of one goal outweigh the costs in terms of another goal.

Where there are two or more alternative policies, economists can go further than this. They may be asked to consider the relative effectiveness of the various policies or even themselves to suggest alternative policies. In such cases it may be possible to say that policy A is preferable to policy B because its benefits are greater or its costs lower in terms of all stated goals. On the other hand, if policy A better achieves one goal and policy B better achieves another, once more all the economist can do is to point this out and leave the policy makers to decide.

If people's interests conflict, the economist cannot say who is the more deserving. That is a normative issue.

> **?** Summarize the economic policies of the major political parties. (If it is near an election, you could refer to their manifestos.) How far can an economist go in assessing these policies?

◭ SUMMARY

1. Real-world markets will fail to achieve Pareto optimality. What is more, there are objectives other than social efficiency, and real-world markets may fail to achieve these too.
2. Externalities are spill-over costs or benefits. Whenever there are external costs, the market will (other things being equal) lead to a level of production and consumption *above* the socially efficient level. Whenever there are external benefits, the market will (other things being equal) lead to a level of production and consumption *below* the socially efficient level.
3. Monopoly power will (other things being equal) lead to a level of output below the socially efficient level. It will lead to a deadweight welfare loss: a loss of consumers' plus producers' surplus.
4. Ignorance and uncertainty may prevent people from consuming or producing at the levels they would otherwise choose. Information may sometimes be provided (at

a price) by the market, but it may be imperfect; in some cases it may not be available at all.
5. Public goods will be underprovided by the market. The problem is that they have large external benefits relative to private benefits, and without government intervention it would not be possible to prevent people having a 'free ride' and thereby escaping contributing to their cost of production.
6. Markets may respond sluggishly to changes in demand and supply. The time lags in adjustment can lead to a permanent state of disequilibrium and to problems of instability.
7. In a free market there may be inadequate provision for dependants and an inadequate output of merit goods; there are likely to be macroeconomic problems (which we shall look at in later chapters); there are likely to be problems of inequality and poverty (which we looked at in Chapter 9); finally, there may be a whole series of social,

moral, attitudinal and aesthetic problems arising from a market system.

8. Being normative questions, the economist cannot make ultimate pronouncements on the rights and wrongs of the market. The economist can, however, point out the consequences of the market and of various government policies, and also the trade-offs that exist between different objectives.

10.3 Forms of government intervention

Faced with all the problems of the free market, what is a government to do?

There are several policy instruments that the government can use. At one extreme it can totally replace the market by providing goods and services itself. At the other extreme it can merely seek to persuade producers, consumers or workers to act differently. Between the two extremes the government has a number of weapons that it can use to change the way markets operate: weapons such as taxes, subsidies, laws and regulatory bodies. The following sections examine the different forms of government intervention.

Before looking at different forms of government intervention and their relative merits, it is first necessary to look at a general problem concerned with all forms of intervention. This is known as the problem of the second best.

In an ideal free market, where there are no market failures of any sort (the 'first-best' world), there would be no need for government intervention at all. If in this world there did then arise just one failure, in theory its correction would be simple. Say a monopoly arose, or some externality (e.g. pollution) was produced by a particular firm, with the result that the marginal social cost was no longer equal to the marginal social benefit. In theory the government should simply intervene to restore production to the point where $MSC = MSB$. This is known as the first-best solution.

Of course the real world is not like this. It is riddled with imperfections. What this means is that, if one imperfection is 'corrected' (i.e. by making $MSB = MSC$), it might aggravate problems elsewhere. For example, if an airport like Gatwick banned night-time flights so as not to disturb the sleep of local residents, the airlines might simply use Heathrow instead. This simply passes the buck. It now imposes an additional cost on those people living near Heathrow.

 Give some examples of how correcting problems in one part of the economy will create problems elsewhere.

As the first-best solution of a perfectly efficient, distortion-free world is obviously not possible, the second-best solution needs to be adopted. Essentially this involves seeking the best compromises. This will mean attempting to minimize the *overall* distortionary effects of the policy measure. There are some second-best *rules* that can be applied in certain cases. We will examine these in the following sections as we look at specific policy measures.

Taxes and Subsidies

A policy instrument particularly favoured by many economists is that of taxes and subsidies. They can be used for two main purposes: (a) to promote greater social efficiency by altering the composition of production and consumption; and (b) to

---

Problem of the second best

The difficulty of working out the best way of correcting a specific market distortion if distortions in other parts of the market continue to exist.

First-best solution

The solution of correcting a specific market distortion by ensuring that the whole economy operates under conditions of social efficiency (Pareto optimality).

Second-best solution

The solution to a specific market distortion that recognizes distortions elsewhere and seeks to minimize the overall distortionary effects to the economy of tackling this specific distortion.

redistribute incomes. We examined their use for the second purpose in the last chapter. Here we examine their use to achieve greater social efficiency.

When there are imperfections in the market (such as externalities, monopoly power, imperfect knowledge and irrational behaviour), Pareto optimality will not be achieved. Marginal social benefit (*MSB*) will not equal marginal social cost (*MSC*). A different level of output would be more desirable.

Taxes and subsidies can be used to correct these imperfections. Essentially the approach is to tax those goods or activities where the market produces too much, and subsidize those where the market produces too little.

Taxes to correct externalities

Assume, for example, that a chemical works emits smoke from a chimney and thus pollutes the atmosphere. This creates external costs for the people who breathe in the smoke. The marginal social cost of producing the chemicals thus exceeds the marginal private cost to the firm:

$$MSC > MC$$

This is illustrated in Figures 10.8 and 10.9. Figure 10.8 looks at the case of the first-best world. Figure 10.9 looks at the real world.

The first-best world. In Figure 10.8 the firm is producing in an otherwise perfect world. It produces Q_1 where $P = MC$ (its profit-maximizing output), but in doing so takes no account of the external pollution costs it imposes on society. If the government imposes a tax on production equal to the marginal pollution cost, it will effectively internalize the externality. The firm will now maximize profits at Q_2, which is the socially optimum output where $MSB = MSC$.

In the first-best world, then, the optimum tax is equal to the marginal external cost.

By analogy, if a firm produced an external benefit, then in the first-best world it ought to be given a subsidy equal to that marginal external benefit. It should be noted that a tax or subsidy ought to be directed as closely as possible to the source of the externality. For example, if a firm trains labour, and that creates a benefit to society, then ideally it ought to be given a subsidy for each person trained, rather than a general output subsidy. After all, an output subsidy is not only encouraging the firm to train more people (the desired effect), but it is also encouraging it to use more capital and raw materials (an undesired side-effect). This is a general maxim of welfare economics: *a distortion should be corrected at source if side-effect problems are to be avoided.*

Figure 10.8 Using taxes to correct a distortion: the first-best world

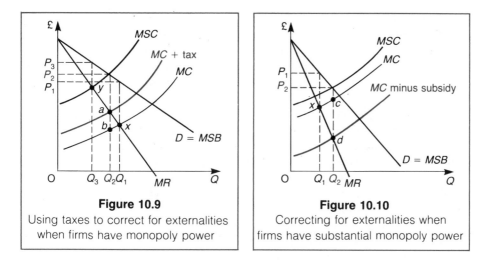

Figure 10.9

Using taxes to correct for externalities
when firms have monopoly power

Figure 10.10

Correcting for externalities when
firms have substantial monopoly power

Second-best tax and subsidy policies. In reality, the government must tackle imperfections
in a world that has many other imperfections besides. An example is given in Figure 10.9.
Here a firm both produces an external cost ($MSC > MC$), and *also* has monopoly
power. It will maximize profits at Q_1 where $MC = MR$ (point x).

What is the socially efficient level of output in this case, and how can a tax (or
subsidy) be used to achieve it?

MSB equals MSC at output Q_2. To persuade the monopolist to produce at this
level, a tax of $a - b$ must be imposed (since at point a $MR = MC + $ tax). This tax is *less*
than the full amount of the externality because of the problem of monopoly power.
Were the monopolist to be charged a tax *equal* to the externality (so that its $MC + $ tax
curve was equal to the MSC curve), it would maximize profits at point y, at a price of P_3
and an output of Q_3. This would not be socially efficient since MSB would now be
above MSC.

There is a possible problem with the tax solution to an externality in the case of a
monopolist. If the monopoly power were large enough and external costs were small
or non-existent, a tax would no longer be suitable. Instead a *subsidy* would seem to be
the answer. This is illustrated in Figure 10.10.

The monopolist initially produces at Q_1, where $MR = MC$ (point x). MSB equals MSC
at output Q_2. But this is *higher* than Q_1.

To persuade the monopolist to produce at Q_2 a subsidy must be paid. The amount
of the subsidy will be $c - d$, (since at point d, $MR = MC$ minus the subsidy).

But should a monopolist be subsidized?! Two points arise here:

- Subsidizing the monopoly gives it even bigger supernormal profits. This could be
  seen as *unfair* even if the resulting level of output it produced was now the desirable
  level. In other words, the *benefit* of allocative efficiency is being achieved at the *cost*
  of greater inequality. An answer to this problem would be to impose a lump-sum
  tax on the monopolist (see below).
- In the second-best world, it is not necessarily desirable for firms to charge a price
  equal to MSC anyway! If other firms in general were charging a price, say, 20 per cent
  above MSC, then this firm ought also to do so. If it charged a price *equal* to MSC, it
  would be charging a price lower relative to MSC than other firms. This would *itself*
  be a distortion: causing a reallocation of consumption to it and away from other firms.

This is an important conclusion of the theory of the second best. Where the rest of the economy has distorted prices, it is *not* necessarily desirable to charge a price equal to marginal social cost in any one given market. It is better for the firm (other things being equal) to have the same percentage difference between price and *MSC* as the average of other firms. This minimizes the firm's *relative* distortion.

Taxes to correct for monopoly

So far we have considered the use of taxes to correct for externalities. Taxes can also be used to regulate the behaviour of monopolies and oligopolies.

If the problem of monopoly that the government wishes to tackle is that of excessive profits, it can impose a lump-sum tax on the monopolist: that is, a tax of a fixed absolute amount irrespective of what the monopolist produces, or the price it charges. This is illustrated in Figure 10.11.

Being of a fixed amount, a lump-sum tax is a fixed cost to the firm. It does not affect the firm's marginal cost. It shifts the AC curve upwards.

Since the marginal cost and marginal revenue curves are unaffected by the tax, profits continue to be maximized at an output of Q_1 and a price of P_1. But profits are reduced from areas $1 + 2$ to area 1 alone. Area 2 now represents the amount of tax paid to the government. If the lump-sum tax were large enough to make the $AC +$ lump-sum tax curve cross the demand curve at point *a*, *all* the supernormal profits would be taken as tax.

If, however, the government also wants to increase the monopolist's output to the socially efficient level of Q_2, and wants it to charge a price of P_2, it could do this with a careful combination of a per-unit subsidy (which will shift both the AC and the MC curves downwards) and a lump-sum tax. The required level of subsidy will be that which shifts the MC curve downwards to the point where it intersects MR at output Q_2. Then a lump-sum tax would be imposed that would be big enough to shift the AC curve back up again so that it crosses the demand curve at point *b*.

 What could we say about the necessary subsidy if the *MR* curve crossed the horizontal axis to the left of point *b*?

Figure 10.11 Using a lump-sum tax to reduce monopoly profits

Advantages of taxes and subsidies

Many economists favour the tax/subsidy solution to market imperfections (especially the problem of externalities) because it still allows the market to operate. It forces

Box 10.5

A Way of Reducing Pollution from Car Exhausts

The use of lower taxes on unleaded petrol

The following is an extract from Nigel Lawson's Budget speech in March 1988:

> In my Budget speech last year, I sought to promote the use of lead-free petrol, with all the environmental benefits it brings, by introducing a duty differential in its favour. As a result, the number of garages selling lead-free petrol has more than trebled. But consumption remains disappointingly low.
>
> Accordingly, I propose to double the duty differential in its favour by exempting it altogether from the duty increase I have just announced for leaded petrol.
>
> This means that despite the higher production costs, the pump price of unleaded petrol should in future be below that of ordinary 2-star petrol. I very much hope the petrol companies will now reinforce this concession by vigorously promoting the use of lead-free petrol.

The effect of these measures was to make unleaded petrol about 6p cheaper than 4-star (leaded) petrol.

About 10 per cent of cars in the UK at that time could switch to unleaded petrol without any adjustments to their engines. A further 50 per cent or so could do so after minor adjustments costing around £20.

To reinforce these measures, the Chancellor also increased the tax on 2-star petrol to bring it up to the price of 4-star. This had the rapid effect of removing 2-star petrol from the market as it no longer had any advantage for the motorist. This gave garages an incentive to sell unleaded petrol as it released pumps which had previously sold 2-star petrol.

?
1. What alternative measures could the government have adopted to encourage or force people to switch to unleaded petrol?
2. Compare the relative advantages and disadvantages of Mr Lawson's measures with the alternative measures you have identified.
3. How would you set about determining whether 6p was the 'correct' differential between unleaded and leaded petrol?

---

firms to take on board the full social costs and benefits of their actions. It also has the flexibility of being adjustable according to the magnitude of the problem. For example, the bigger the external costs of a firm's actions, the bigger the tax can be.

What is more, by taxing firms for polluting, say, they are encouraged to find cleaner ways of producing. The tax thus acts as an incentive over the longer run to reduce pollution: the more a firm can reduce its pollution, the more taxes it can save.

Likewise, by subsidizing *good* practices, firms are given the incentive to adopt more good practices.

It might be argued that taxes are a bad way of dealing with pollution, because they still allow the pollution to continue. Advocates of the tax solution, however, argue that just because a firm pollutes, it does not mean that it should be shut down. The benefits to society of having the product may considerably outweigh the costs of its production, *including* the costs of the pollution.

The most suitable situation for imposing a pollution tax is when there is a clearly measurable emission, like a particular chemical waste. The government can then impose a tax per litre or per tonne of that waste. The firm would be required to install a meter and an inspector could then read the meter and the firm be sent the appropriate tax bill.

Disadvantages of taxes and subsidies

Infeasible to use different tax and subsidy rates. Each firm produces different levels and types of externality and operates under different degrees of imperfect competition. It would be administratively very difficult and expensive, if not impossible, to charge every offending firm its own particular tax rate (or grant every relevant firm its own particular rate of subsidy).

Even in the case of pollution where it is possible to measure a firm's emissions, there would still have to be a different tax rate for each pollutant and even for each environment depending on its ability to absorb the pollutant.

As for using combinations of lump-sum taxes and per-unit subsidies to correct monopoly distortions to price, output and profit, again this solution would probably be totally impractical. Given that cost and revenue curves differ substantially from one firm to another, separate tax and subsidy rates would be needed for each firm. An army of tax inspectors would be necessary to administer the system!

Lack of knowledge. Even if a government did decide to charge a tax equal to each offending firm's marginal external costs, it would still have the problem of measuring those costs. The damage from pollution is often extremely difficult to assess. It is also difficult to apportion blame. For example, the damage to lakes and forests from acid rain has been a major concern since the beginning of the 1980s. But just how serious is that damage? What is its current monetary cost? How long lasting is the damage? What will be the position in twenty years? Just what and who are to blame? These are questions that cannot be answered precisely. It is thus impossible to fix the 'correct' pollution tax on, say, a particular coal-fired power station.

> **?** 1. Why is it easier to use taxes and subsidies to tackle the problem of car exhaust pollution than to tackle the problem of peak-time traffic congestion in cities?
> 2. If the precise environmental costs of aerosol propellants were known, would the tax solution be a suitable remedy for the problem?

Changes in property rights

One cause of market failure is the limited nature of property rights. If someone dumps a load of rubble in your garden, the law should protect you. It is *your* garden, *your* property, and you can thus insist that it is removed. If, however, someone dumps a load of rubble in his or her *own* garden, but which is next door to yours, what can you do? You can still see it from your window. It is still an eyesore. But you have no property rights over the next-door garden.

It is similar with the air you breathe. It is not your property. You cannot insist that it is clear air. Likewise the skies over your head. Noisy aircraft may disturb you, but it is not *your* airspace! You cannot insist that the aircraft fly elsewhere.

One solution, then, to the problem of market failure (again especially in the case of externalities) is to extend property rights.

Property rights define who owns property, to what uses it can be put, the rights other people have over it and how it may be transferred. By extending these rights, individuals may be able to prevent other people from imposing costs on them.

The ultimate form of this type of policy would be to extend property rights so completely that everyone would have the right to prevent people imposing any costs on them whatsoever, or to charge them for the privilege. For example, if I were disturbed by noisy lorries outside my home, I would have the right to prohibit them from coming down my street, or to charge them. The charge would be negotiated between me and the lorry firm.

The trouble is that in many instances this type of solution is totally impractical. It is impractical when *many* people are *slightly* inconvenienced, especially if there are many culprits imposing the costs. The case of the lorries is an example. How could I negotiate with every lorry firm? What if I wanted to ban the lorries from the street but my next-door neighbour wanted to charge them 10p per journey? Who gets their way? Likewise it would be totally impractical for me to negotiate with various airlines about diverting their aircraft because of my loss of sleep!

Where the extension of private property rights becomes a more practical solution is where the culprits are few in number, are easily identifiable and impose clearly defined costs. Thus a noise abatement Act could be passed which allowed me to prevent my neighbours from playing noisy radios, having noisy parties or otherwise disturbing the peace in my home. The onus would be on me to report them. Or if I chose, I could agree not to report them if they paid me adequate compensation.

But even in cases where only a few people are involved, there may still be the problem of litigation. I may have to incur the time and expense of taking people to court. Justice may not be free, and thus there is again the conflict with equity. The rich can afford 'better' justice. They can employ top lawyers. Thus even if I have a right to sue a large company for dumping toxic waste near me, I may not have the legal muscle to win.

Finally there is the broader question of *equity*. The extension of private property rights may favour the rich at the expense of the poor. Ramblers may get great pleasure from strolling across a great country estate, along public rights of way. This may annoy the owner. If the owner's property rights were now extended to exclude the ramblers, would this be a social gain?

Of course equity considerations can also be dealt with by altering property rights, but in a different way. *Public* property, like parks, open spaces, libraries and historic buildings, could be extended. Also the property of the rich could be redistributed to the poor. Here it is less a question of the rights that ownership confers, and more a question of altering the ownership itself.

> **?** 1. To what extent could property rights (either public or private) be successfully extended and invoked to curb the problem of industrial pollution (a) of the atmosphere; (b) of rivers; (c) by the dumping of toxic waste; (d) by the erection of ugly buildings; (e) by the creation of high levels of noise?
> 2. What protection do private property rights in the real world give to sufferers of noise (a) from neighbours; (b) from traffic; (c) from transistor radios at the seaside?

Laws prohibiting or regulating undesirable structures or behaviour

Laws are frequently used to correct market imperfections. This section examines three of the most common cases.

Laws prohibiting or regulating behaviour that imposes external costs

Laws can be applied both to individuals and to firms. In the case of individuals it is illegal to drive when drunk. Drunk driving imposes costs on others in the form of accidents and death. Another example is the banning of smoking in public places.

In the case of firms, various polluting activities can be banned or restricted. Another example is the legal imposition of various safety standards in the place of work. Another is the prohibition of building houses or factories in green-belt areas.

Advantages of legal restrictions

- They are simple and clear to understand and are often relatively easy to administer. Inspectors or the police can conduct spot checks to see that the law is being obeyed.

Of course, if the law is to be effective, the penalties for breaking the law must be sufficiently harsh, and the inspections must be sufficiently frequent and rigorous.

● When the danger is very great, it might be much safer to ban various practices altogether rather than to rely on taxes or on individuals attempting to assert their property rights through the civil courts. For example, the anti-nuclear power lobby argues that the dangers of long-term exposure to low-level radiation and the risks of accident and sabotage are serious problems that are too easily dismissed by the authorities. Imposing 'radiation' taxes on such power stations would seem quite inappropriate. Similarly, if the dangers to the ozone layer (and the resulting risks of skin cancer) from the use of certain aerosol cans are as serious as some scientists suggest, the offending propellant ought to be banned, not merely taxed. In other words, if the potential risks are grave, would not banning be a safer solution?

● When a decision needs to be taken quickly it might be possible to invoke emergency action. For example, in a city like Athens or Los Angeles it would be simpler to ban or restrict the use of private cars during a chemical smog emergency than to tax their use.

Disadvantages of legal restrictions. The main problem is that legal restrictions tend to be a rather blunt weapon. If, for example, a firm were required to reduce the effluent of a toxic chemical to 20 tonnes per week, there would be no incentive for the firm to reduce it further. With a tax on the effluent, however, the more the firm reduced the effluent, the less tax it would pay. Thus with a system of taxes there is a *continuing* incentive to cut pollution.

The other problem is that in practice inspections may be few and/or penalties may be small. In such cases the pollution would simply continue.

Laws to prevent or regulate monopolies and oligopolies

The law can be used to affect either the structure of an industry or the behaviour of the firms within it.

Laws affecting structure. Various mergers or take-overs could be made illegal. The criterion would probably have to be the level of market concentration that results. Thus the merger could be illegal if the merged firm controlled over a certain percentage of the market or it resulted in assets over a certain level. The merger could be illegal if as a result the 'x firm concentration ratio' exceeded a certain level (see Box 5.1). For example, the law could set a limit of 60 per cent of the market to be controlled by the five largest firms. The merger could be illegal if the *degree* of concentration in the industry rose by a certain amount. This is the current position of anti-merger legislation in the USA. The law could require that firms which had more than a certain percentage share of the market, or were more than a certain size, be split up into smaller firms.

Laws affecting behaviour. Firms could be prohibited from engaging in various types of oligopolistic collusion. Individual firms could be prohibited from various monopolistic practices. For example, manufacturers could be prevented from fixing the prices that retailers must charge, or from refusing to supply certain retailers.

The various ways the law has been used to regulate monopolies and oligopolies in the UK are examined in section 11.2.

 How suitable are legal restrictions in the following cases?

(a) Ensuring adequate vehicle safety (e.g. that tyres have sufficient tread or that the vehicle is roadworthy).
(b) Reducing traffic congestion.
(c) Preventing the abuse of monopoly power.
(d) Ensuring that mergers are in the public interest.
(e) Ensuring that firms charge a price equal to marginal cost.

Laws to prevent firms from exploiting people's ignorance

Given that consumers have imperfect information, firms could sometimes take advantage of this by making false claims for their products or by producing poor quality or unsafe goods. This is particularly a problem where consumers are unlikely to want to purchase the same item from that firm on another occasion: in such cases the firm has no worry about people finding out how poor the product is after they have purchased it. Shoddy toys at Christmas, estate agents who make exaggerated claims about properties, and 'cowboy' builders offering to do cheap repairs are examples where consumers may be 'taken for a ride'.

Consumer protection laws can make it illegal for firms to sell shoddy or unsafe goods, or to make false or misleading claims about their products. The problem is that the firms most likely to exploit the consumer are often the ones that are most elusive when it comes to prosecuting them. Also it may be very difficult to frame the legislation tightly enough to prevent firms from getting around it.

Regulatory bodies

Rather than using the blunt weapon of general legislation to ban or restrict various activities, a more 'subtle' approach can be adopted. This involves the use of various regulatory bodies. What would these bodies do?

First, they would seek out, or some agent would seek out for them, any potential cases for investigation: e.g. potential cases of pollution, or the abuse of monopoly power.

Secondly, they would conduct an investigation to decide whether these activities should be permitted, reduced, modified or banned. They would obviously have to make their decisions according to various laid-down criteria. Such criteria could be embodied in the legislation establishing the regulatory body.

Thirdly, they would take action themselves to enforce their decisions – again, power to do this would have to be embodied in legislation – or they would report to some higher authority (the government or some other official body) which would decide whether to take action on the recommendation. An example of such a body is the Monopolies and Mergers Commission (MMC), which investigates various monopolies, oligopolies and mergers to establish whether or not they are operating in the public interest. The work of the MMC is examined in section 11.2.

The advantage of this approach is that a case-by-case method can be used. All the various circumstances surrounding a particular case can be taken into account, with the result that the most appropriate solution can be adopted.

The problems with this approach are (a) that investigations may be expensive and time consuming, (b) that only a few cases may be examined and (c) that the offending firms may make various promises of good behaviour which, owing to a lack of follow-up by the regulatory body, may not in fact be carried out.

 What other forms of intervention are likely to be necessary to back up the work of regulatory bodies?

Price controls

Price controls could be used to prevent a monopoly or oligopoly from charging excessive prices. Thus in the late 1970s the Labour government's Price Commission, which had to give permission for many types of price increase, used its power to deny price increases which were not warranted by an increase in costs.

Price controls are also used with the objective of redistributing incomes. Prices can be fixed either above or below equilibrium.

High minimum prices (above market equilibrium). These are used to support the incomes of certain suppliers. For example, under the Common Agricultural Policy of the European Community, high prices for food are set so as to increase farmers' incomes above the free-market level (see Chapter 11). Another example is minimum wage legislation. This involves setting minimum wages for workers either throughout the economy or in certain jobs.

Low maximum prices (below market equilibrium). These are used to redistribute incomes to the consumers of certain goods and services. For example, the government may impose rent controls on private rented accommodation, so that poor people can afford housing. Another example is the use of price ceilings on food during a war or other emergency.

As was argued in section 2.6, the problem with price controls is that they cause shortages (in the case of low prices) or surpluses (high prices).

Provision of information

When ignorance is a reason for market failure, the direct provision of information by the government may help to correct that failure, especially when the information is not sold by some private-sector agency. Some examples would be the following:

- The provision of job centres. These provide information on jobs to those looking for work, and put firms in touch with possibly suitable labour. They thus help the labour market to work better and increase the elasticity of supply of labour.
- The provision of consumer information, for example on the effects of smoking, or the dangers of inflammable furniture.
- The provision of government statistics on prices, costs, employment, sales trends, etc. This enables firms to plan with greater certainty.

The provision of information may also put pressure on firms to reduce external costs. For example, if the government advertises the effect of dumping toxic chemicals, offending firms may decide to stop doing it, because of either conscience or the fear of a hostile public reaction and a resulting loss of sales.

> **?** Information may not be provided by the private sector if it can be used by those who do not pay: if it is a public good (service). Do all the examples above come into the category of public goods? Give some other examples of information which is a public good. (Clue: do not confuse a public good with something merely provided by the government, which *could* also be provided by the private sector.)

The direct provision of goods and services

In the case of public goods and services, such as streets, pavements, seaside illumination and national defence, the market may completely fail to provide. In this case the government must take over the role of provision. Central government, local government or some other public agency could provide these goods and services directly. Alternatively, they could pay private firms to do so. The public would pay through taxes and rates.

But just what quantity of the public good should be provided? How can the level of public demand or public 'need' be identified? Should any charge at all be made to consumers for each unit consumed?

With a pure public good, once it is provided the marginal cost of supplying one more consumer is zero. Take the case of a lighthouse. Once it is constructed and in operation, there is no extra cost of providing the service to additional passing ships. Even it were *possible* to charge ships each time they make use of it, it would not be socially desirable. Assuming no external costs, MSC is zero. Thus $MSB = MSC$ at a price of zero. Zero is thus the socially efficient price.

But what about the construction of a new public good, like a new road or a new lighthouse? How can a rational decision be made by the government as to whether it should go ahead? This time the marginal cost is not zero: extra roads and lighthouses cost money to build. The solution is to identify all the costs and benefits to society from the project, and to weigh them up. This is where cost–benefit analysis comes in – the subject of section 10.4.

The government could also provide goods and services directly which are *not* public goods. Examples include health and education. There are four reasons why such things are provided free or at well below cost.

Social justice. Society may feel that these things should not be provided according to ability to pay. Rather they should be provided as of right: an equal right based on need. Obviously this is a highly normative issue, and it is an issue that people feel strongly about, an issue that frequently determines which political party they vote for.

Large positive externalities. People other than the consumer may benefit substantially. If a person decides to get treatment for an infectious disease, other people benefit by not being infected. A free health service thus helps to combat the spread of disease. This argument is particularly important if the externalities are thought to be substantial but difficult to measure. Is it worth risking sacrificing these benefits by charging for the service?

Dependants. If education were not free, and if the quality of education depended on the amount spent, and if parents could choose how much or little to buy, then the quality of children's education would depend not just on their parents' income, but also on how much they cared. A government may choose to provide such things free in order to protect children from 'bad' parents. A similar argument is used for providing free prescriptions and dental treatment for all children.

Ignorance. Consumers may not realize how much they will benefit. If they had to pay, they might choose (unwisely) to go without. Providing health care free may persuade people to consult their doctors for what they perceive to be a minor complaint, which is then diagnosed to be the first symptom of something serious.

Public ownership

This is different from direct provision, in that the goods and services produced by publicly owned (nationalized) industries are sold in the market. There are many arguments concerned with the costs and benefits of public ownership and these are examined in detail in section 11.3.

▲ SUMMARY

1. If there were a distortion in just one part of the economy, the 'first-best' solution would be possible. This would be to bring production to the point where $MSC = MSB$. In the real world, where there are many distortions, the first-best solution will not be possible. The second-best solution will be to seek the best compromise that minimizes the *relative* distortions between the industry in question and other parts of the economy.

2. Taxes and subsidies are one means of correcting market distortions. In the first-best world, externalities can be corrected by imposing tax rates equal to the size of marginal external costs, and granting rates of subsidy equal to marginal external benefits. In the second-best world, taxes and subsidies can be used to correct externalities that create *relative* distortions between this industry and others, or externalities that exist along with other distortions within this industry.

3. Taxes and subsidies can also be used to affect monopoly price, output and profit. Subsidies can be used to persuade a monopolist to increase output to the competitive level. Lump-sum taxes can be used to reduce monopoly profits without affecting price or output.

4. Taxes and subsidies have the advantages of 'internalizing' externalities and of providing incentives to reduce external costs. On the other hand, they may be impractical to use when different rates are required for each case, or when it is impossible to know the full effects of the activities that the taxes or subsidies are being used to correct.

5. An extension of property rights may allow individuals to prevent others from imposing costs on them. This is not practical, however, when many people are affected to a small degree, or where several people are affected but differ in their attitudes towards what they want doing about the 'problem'.

6. Laws can be used to regulate activities that impose external costs, to regulate monopolies and oligopolies, and to provide consumer protection. Legal controls are often simpler and easier to operate than taxes, and are safer when the danger is potentially great. Nevertheless, legal controls tend to be rather a blunt weapon, although discretion can sometimes be allowed in the administration of the law.

7. Regulatory bodies can be set up to monitor and control activities against the public interest (e.g. anti-competitive behaviour of oligopolists). They can conduct investigations of specific cases and can be very thorough. The investigations, however, may be expensive and time consuming, and may not be acted on by the authorities.

8. The government may provide information in cases where the private sector fails to provide an adequate level. It may also provide goods and services directly. These could be either public goods or other goods where the government feels that provision by the market is inadequate. The government could also influence production in publicly owned industries.

*10.4 Cost-benefit analysis

Cost–benefit analysis

The identification, measurement and weighing-up of the costs and benefits of a project in order to decide whether or not it should go ahead.

If the market produces the wrong amount of various goods and services, how is the government to determine the right amount? This is obviously a highly normative question because it depends on social goals. Nevertheless economists have developed a technique known as cost benefit analysis (CBA). It is used to help governments decide whether to go ahead with various projects such as a new motorway, a bypass, an underground line, a hospital, a health-care programme, a dam, and so on. The analysis seeks to establish whether the benefits to society from the project outweigh the costs, in which case the project should go ahead; or whether the costs outweigh the benefits, in which case it should not.

CBAs are usually commissioned either by a government department or by a local authority. Unlike the techniques of project evaluation used by private firms, which only take into account *private monetary* costs and benefits, CBA takes into account *externalities* and private *non-monetary* costs and benefits as well. Thus the cost–benefit study on the siting of a third London airport attempted to assess the external costs of noise to local residents as well as the direct costs and benefits to the travellers.

The procedure

The procedure at first sight seems fairly straightforward.

- All costs and benefits are identified. This includes all private monetary and non-monetary costs and benefits and all externalities.
- A monetary value is assigned to each cost and benefit. This is essential if costs and benefits are to be added up: a common unit of measurement must be used. As might be expected, assigning monetary values to externalities like noise, pollution, the quality of life, etc. is fraught with difficulties!
- Account is taken of the likelihood of a cost or benefit occurring. The simplest way of doing this is to multiply the monetary value of a cost or benefit by the probability of its occurrence. So if there were a 60 per cent chance of a cost of £100 occurring, it would be valued at £60.
- Account is taken of the timing of the costs and benefits. £100 of benefits received today would be regarded as more desirable than having to wait, say, ten years to receive the £100. Likewise it is a greater sacrifice to pay £100 today than being able to wait ten years to pay it. Thus future costs and benefits must be reduced in value to take this into account. *Discounting techniques* (similar to those we examined in section 8.4) are used for this purpose.
- Some account may also be taken of the distribution of the costs and benefits. Is it considered fair that, although some people will gain from the project, others will lose? Will the losers be compensated in any way?
- A recommendation is then made by weighing up the costs and benefits. In simplest terms, if the benefits exceed the costs, it will be recommended that the project goes ahead.

Each of these stages involves a number of difficulties. These are examined in the following sections.

Identifying the costs and benefits

Identifying costs and benefits is relatively easy, although there are some problems in predicting what types of external effect are likely to occur.

Costs

Direct (private) monetary costs. These are easy to identify. They simply include all the construction costs and the operating and maintenance costs.

External costs. These fall into two categories:

- *Monetary costs*, such as the loss of profits to competitors. Thus in the case of a CBA of a tunnel under a river, external monetary costs would include the loss of profits to ferry operators.
- *Non-monetary costs*, such as pollution, spoiling the landscape, noise and various other forms of inconvenience to local residents. In some projects like a tunnel, these costs will be largely confined to the construction phase. With other projects, however, like a new airport, there may be considerable externalities resulting from its operation (e.g. noise). These non-monetary externalities are usually the most difficult costs to identify.

Benefits

Direct (private) monetary benefits. These are also easy to identify. They consist of the revenues received from the users of the project. The direct monetary benefits of a toll bridge, for example, are the tolls paid.

Private non-monetary benefits. These are the benefits to consumers over and above

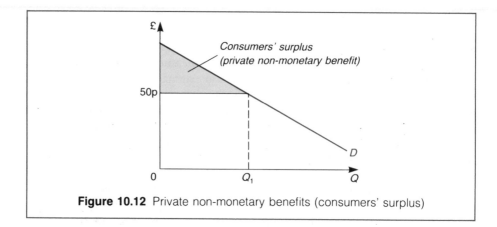

Figure 10.12 Private non-monetary benefits (consumers' surplus)

what they actually pay: in other words, the consumers' surplus. For example, if a bridge had a toll of 50p, and yet a person was prepared to pay £2 if necessary to avoid the long trip round the estuary, then the person's consumer's surplus is £1.50. Total consumers' surplus is thus the area between the demand curve (which shows what people are willing to pay) and the price charged. This is illustrated in Figure 10.12.

External benefits. These are the benefits to the non-users of the project. For example, the Victoria underground line CBA identified external benefits to road users in central London. The roads would become less congested as people used the new underground line. Usually these benefits are non-monetary benefits, but sometimes they may result in direct financial gain (e.g. higher profits to companies from reduced transport costs on less crowded roads).

Measuring the costs and benefits

Identifying costs and benefits may be relatively easy: measuring them is another matter. Difficulties in measurement depend on the type of cost and benefit. There are four types.

Direct private monetary costs and benefits

These would seem to be the simplest to measure. Normally the simple financial costs and revenues are used. In the case of a new underground line, for example, such costs would include excavation, construction and capital costs (such as new rolling stock) and the operating costs (such as labour, electricity, and maintenance). Revenues would be the fares paid by travellers. There are two problems, nevertheless:

● What *will* these financial costs and revenues be? It is all very well using current prices, but prices rise over time, and at different and unpredictable rates. Also it is difficult to forecast demand and hence revenues. There is thus a large element of *uncertainty*.
● The prices will often be distorted by the existence of monopoly power. Should this be taken into account? Should, for example, fuel costs be estimated at prices that *would* be charged under perfect competition? In an otherwise perfect world (the first-best situation), the answer would be yes. But in the real world these price distortions exist throughout the economy. If a rational choice is to be made about whether to build a new underground line, say, then generally speaking, actual market prices should be used. After all, these are the prices that have to be paid by

car drivers and taxi and bus users (the alternatives to using the underground). Thus the second-best solution is to use actual market prices *unless* there is a price distortion that applies *only* to the specific project.

 What price should be used when there is such a distortion?

Non-monetary private benefits: consumers' surplus

Consumers' surplus is a private benefit – it accrues to the users of the project – but is not part of the money earned from the project. There are two ways of estimating it.

The first way is to estimate the demand curve and then estimate the shaded area in Figure 10.12. Estimating demand is very difficult, since it depends on the price and availability of substitutes. The demand for the Channel Tunnel will depend on the price, frequency and convenience of ferry crossings. It will also depend on the overall level of activity in the economy and perhaps the world generally. Thus estimates of air traffic (an essential piece of information when deciding whether to build a new airport) have often been proved wrong as the world economy has grown more rapidly or less rapidly than previously forecast.

Another problem is that the consumers' surplus gained from this project (e.g. the Channel Tunnel) may replace the albeit smaller consumers' surplus from a competing service (e.g. cross-Channel ferries). In this case the non-monetary private benefit is merely the *additional* consumer surplus of those who switch, but still the *full* consumer surplus of those who would not otherwise have crossed the Channel. This makes calculation less straightforward.

An alternative approach is to focus on specific non-monetary benefits to consumers. This approach is more useful when the service is to be provided free and thus no estimate of a demand curve can be made. For example, if a new motorway or bridge or airport saves travellers' time, then an estimate can be made of the value of that time saved. Assume that a new motorway saves 20 000 hours of travelling time per week. (This, of course, will first have to be estimated, and again a prediction will have to be made of the number of people using the motorway.) How is this 20 000 hours to be evaluated? In the case of businesspeople and lorry drivers, the average hourly wage rate will be used to estimate the value of each hour saved. In the case of leisure time there is less agreement on how to value an hour saved. Usually it is simply assumed to be some fraction of the average hourly wage. This method is somewhat arbitrary, however, and a better approach, though probably impractical, would be to attempt to measure how the travellers themselves evaluate their time.

Another way of measuring time saved would be to see how much money people would be prepared to spend to save travelling time. For example, how much extra would people be prepared to pay for a taxi which saved, say, ten minutes over the bus journey? This method, however, has to take account of the fact that taxis may be more desirable for other reasons too, such as comfort.

 How would you attempt to value time that you yourself save (a) getting to work; (b) going on holiday; (c) going out in the evening?

Similar calculations would need to be made for fuel saved by the traveller. This calculation is relatively easy to make. A much more difficult type of private benefit to estimate, however, would be the pleasure of travelling along that road (due, say, to the scenery). Note that, although some of these benefits do involve *money* savings to the consumer, they do not earn *revenue* for the project. It is in this sense that they are non-monetary benefits.

Monetary externalities

These would normally be counted at face value. Thus the external monetary costs of a new underground would include the loss of profits to taxi and bus companies. The external monetary benefits of a new motorway would include the profits to be made by the owners of the motorway service stations.

Non-monetary externalities

These are likely to be the hardest to measure. The general principle employed is to try and find out how much people would be prepared to pay to obtain the benefits or avoid the costs, if they were able to do so. There are two approaches here.

Ask people (questionnaires). Take the case of noise from an airport or motorway. People could be asked how much they would need to be compensated. There are two problems with this:

- Ignorance. People will not know just how much they will suffer *until* the airport or motorway is built.
- Dishonesty. People will tend to exaggerate the compensation they would need. After all, if compensation is actually going to be paid, people will want to get as much as possible. But even if it is not, the more people exaggerate the costs to them, the more likely it is they can get the project stopped.

These problems can be lessened if people are questioned who have already experienced a similar project elsewhere. They have less to gain from being dishonest.

Make inferences from people's behaviour. Take the case of noise again. In similar projects elsewhere, how have people actually reacted? How much have they spent on double glazing or other noise insulation? How much financial loss have they been prepared to suffer to move somewhere quieter? What needs to be measured, however, is not just the financial cost, but also the loss of consumer surplus. The Roskill Commission in 1968 examined the siting of the third London airport. It attempted to evaluate noise costs, and looked at the difference in value of house prices round Gatwick compared with elsewhere. A problem with this approach is in finding cases elsewhere that are directly comparable. Were the four potential sites for the third London airport directly comparable with Gatwick?

Another example of externalities would be a reduction in accidents from a safer road. How is this to be measured? Obviously there are the monetary benefits from reduced medical expenditures. But how would you value a life saved? This question is examined in Box 10.6.

 How would you evaluate (a) the external effects of building a reservoir in an area of outstanding natural beauty; (b) the external effects of acid rain pollution from a power station?

Risk and uncertainty

Sensitivity analysis

Where a range of possible values of uncertain costs and benefits are given to see whether the project's desirability is sensitive to these different values.

Taking account of *risk* is relatively straightforward. The value of a cost or benefit is simply multiplied by the probability of its occurrence.

The problem is that *risk* is less frequent than *uncertainty*. As was explained in Chapter 3, in the case of risk at least the probability of various outcomes is known. In the case of uncertainty all that is known is that an outcome *might* occur. The likelihood of its occurring, however, is uncertain.

How then can uncertainty be taken into account? The best approach is to use sensitivity analysis. Let us consider two cases.

Box 10.6

What Price a Human Life?
A difficult question for cost–benefit analysis

Many projects involve saving lives, whether they be new hospitals or new transport systems. This is obviously a major benefit, but how is a life to be evaluated?

Some people argue, 'You can't put a price on a human life: life is priceless.' But just what are they saying here? Are they saying that life has an *infinite* value? If so, this project must be carried out *whatever* the costs, and even if other benefits from it were zero! Clearly, when evaluating lives saved from the project a value less than infinity must be given.

Other people might argue that human life cannot be treated like other costs and benefits and put into mathematical calculations. But what are these people saying? That the question of lives saved should be excluded from the cost–benefit study? If so, the implication is that life has a *zero* value! Again this is clearly not the case.

So if a value somewhere between zero and infinity should be used, what should it be?

Some economists have suggested that a life be valued in terms of a person's future earning potential. But this implies that the only value of a person is as a factor of production! Would the life of a disabled person, for example, who is unable to work and draws state benefit be given a *negative* value? Again this is clearly not the solution.

Can any inferences be drawn from people's behaviour?

How much are people prepared to spend on safety: on making their car roadworthy, on buying crash helmets, etc? This approach too has serious drawbacks. People are wishful thinkers. They obviously do not want to be killed, but simply believe that accidents happen to other people, not to them.

Then again, there are the problems of estimating the effects on other people: on family and friends. Can the amount that people are willing to spend on life assurance be a guide here? Again people are wishful thinkers. Also it is not the family and friends who buy the assurance; it is the victim, who may not take the effect on others fully into account.

As a result of these problems, an arbitrary value is usually put on a human life. This, it is argued, is at least better than ignoring the question altogether.

 1. Can you think of any other ways of getting a more 'rational' evaluation of human life? Would the person's age make any difference?
2. If you had to decide whether more money from a hospital's budget were to be spent on hip replacements (which do not save lives, but do dramatically improve the quality of the patient's life), or on heart transplants (which do save lives, but which are expensive), how would you set about making a rational decision?

Individual uncertain outcomes

A range of possible values can be given to an uncertain item in the CBA: for example, damage from pollution. Table 10.1 illustrates two possible cases.

The lowest estimate for pollution damage is £10 million; the highest is £50 million. In case A, given a very high margin of benefits over *other* costs, the project's

Table 10.1 The effect of different estimates of the costs of pollution on the viability of a project

	Total costs other than pollution (£m)	Total pollution costs (£m)	Total benefits (£m)	Net benefits (Total benefits − costs) (£m)
Case A				
	100	10	200	90
	100	20	200	80
	100	50	200	50
Case B				
	140	10	160	10
	140	20	160	0
	140	50	160	−30

desirability is *not* sensitive to different values for pollution damage. Even with the highest value (£50 million), the project still yields a net benefit.

In case B, however, the project's desirability is sensitive to pollution damage. If the damage exceeds £20 million, the project becomes undesirable. In this case the government will have to decide whether it is prepared to take the gamble.

A number of uncertain outcomes

When there are several uncertain outcomes the typical approach is to do three cost–benefit calculations: the most optimistic (where all the best possible outcomes are estimated), the most pessimistic (where all the worst possible outcomes are estimated), and the most likely (where all the middle-of-the-range outcomes are estimated). This approach can give a good guide to just how 'borderline' the project is.

Discounting future costs and benefits

As we saw in section 8.4, discounting is a procedure for giving a present value to costs and benefits that will not occur until some time in the future.

Discounting in cost-benefit analysis

The procedure is as follows:

- Work out the costs and benefits for each year of the life of the project.
- Subtract the costs from the benefits for each year, to give a net benefit for each year.
- Discount each year's net benefit to give it a present value.
- Add up all of these present values. This gives a *net present value* (*NPV*).
- If the *NPV* is greater than zero, the benefits exceed the costs: the project is worthwhile.

Choosing the discount rate

Apart from the problems of measuring the costs and benefits, there is the problem of choosing the rate of interest/discount.

If it were a private-sector project, the firm would probably choose the market rate of interest as its rate of discount. This is the rate it would have to pay to borrow money to finance the project.

Social rate of discount

A rate of discount that reflects *society's* preferences for present benefits over future ones.

In the case of CBA, however, it is argued that the government ought to use a social rate of discount. This rate should reflect society's preference for present benefits over future benefits. But just what is this rate? If a high rate is chosen, then future net benefits will be discounted more, and projects with a long life will appear less attractive than projects yielding a quick return. Since the government has a responsibility to future generations and not just to the present one, it is argued that a relatively low discount rate should be chosen.

> **?** Imagine that a public project yields a return of 13 per cent (after taking into account all social costs and benefits), whereas a 15 per cent private return could typically be earned in the private sector. How would you justify diverting resources from the private sector to this project?

Inevitably the choice of discount rate is arbitrary. As a result the analysis will normally be done using two or three alternative discount rates to see whether the outcome is sensitive to the choice of discount rate. If it is, then again the project will be seen as borderline.

Box 10.7

Calculating Net Present Value
The use of discounting techniques in CBA

The formula for calculating the net present value (*NPV*) of a project is as follows:

$$NPV = (B - C)_0 + \frac{(B - C)_1}{(1 + d)} + \frac{(B - C)_2}{(1 + d)^2} + \frac{(B - C)_3}{(1 + d)^3} \cdots + \frac{(B - C)_n}{(1 + d)^n}$$

where: $B_{1, 2, 3}$, etc. are the benefits in years 1, 2, 3, etc., $C_{1, 2, 3}$, etc. are the costs in years 1, 2, 3 etc., n is the life of the project in years, and d is the rate of discount expressed as a fraction (i.e. 10% = 0.1).
Now assume that the following:

- A project has an initial construction cost of £30 000 (in year 0).
- It has a life of 4 years.
- It yields a net benefit of £10 000 each year in years 1–4.
- The rate of discount is 10 per cent.

Given these assumptions, the *NPV* can be worked out as follows:

$$NPV = -£30\ 000 + \frac{£10\ 000}{1.1} + \frac{£10\ 000}{1.21} + \frac{£10\ 000}{1.331} + \frac{£10\ 000}{1.4641}$$

$$= -£30\ 000 + £9090.91 + £8264.46 + £7513.15 + £6830.13$$

$$= -£30\ 000 + £31\ 698.65$$

$$= £1698.65$$

This is a positive figure. The project would thus be judged as desirable.
If, however, the rate of discount were 15 per cent, the figures would be:

$$NPV = -£30\ 000 + £28\ 549.78$$

$$= -£1450.22$$

This is negative. Thus at a 15 per cent discount rate the project would be judged as undesirable. This particular project's desirability, therefore, is relatively sensitive to a change in the discount rate.

 Assume that a project has an initial construction cost of £10 000, takes a year to come into operation and then has a life of three years. Assume that it yields £5000 per year in each of these three years. Is the *NPV* positive at (a) a 10 per cent discount rate; (b) a 15 per cent discount rate?

CBA and the distribution of costs and benefits

Virtually all projects involve gainers and losers. For example, the majority may gain from the construction of a new motorway, but not those whose homes lie alongside it. So how is the distribution of costs and benefits to be taken into account?

The strict Pareto criterion
According to the strict Pareto criterion, a project is only unequivocally desirable if there are some gains and *no one* is made worse off. According to this, then, a project would only be accepted if the gainers *fully* compensated the losers, with the gainers still being better off after doing so.

In practice this never happens. Often compensation is simply not paid. Even when it is, the recipients rarely feel as well off as before, and there will still be many who do

Box 10.8

Catastrophic Risk
Thinking the unthinkable

Some projects involve the remote chance that a total catastrophe might occur. A tunnel might collapse; a bridge might fall down; or, perhaps worst of all, a nuclear power station might explode. This last possibility was dramatically brought home to people with the Chernobyl disaster in the USSR in 1986.

How are such disasters to be evaluated in a cost–benefit study? This is the subject of catastrophic risk.

First of all, a mathematical conundrum. What do you get when you multiply a number by zero? The answer is zero. What do you get when you multiply a number by infinity? The answer is infinity. What, then, do you get when you multiply infinity by zero? The answer is . . .? In fact there is no sensible answer to this question other than, 'It can't be done', or 'Something between zero and infinity'.

A similar problem is raised in the measurement of catastrophic risk. Remember that the simplest way of measuring a risky outcome is to multiply its value (its cost or benefit) by the probability of its occurring. For example, if there is a 20 per cent chance of a benefit of £100 occurring, then the simplest way of valuing it is at £20. But what happens if you use a similar approach to measuring the cost of a nuclear disaster?

The power companies argue that the chance of such a disaster occurring is so remote that its probability can be regarded as zero. Many environmentalists argue that the costs to life, health and the environment generally, if such a disaster did occur, are so horrendous that the costs are virtually infinite.

So here is the conundrum. If both sides are right, then we have to multiply a cost that is virtually infinite by a probability that is virtually zero.

Of course, the costs are not *actually* infinite. But they are exceedingly large, and there may be long-term consequences (e.g. slowly developing cancers) which nobody can estimate. Likewise the probability may not actually be zero. There may be a very remote possibility of a disaster occurring, due, say, to human error or sabotage. But if you multiply a very very large number by a very very small fraction, the result is still highly suspect.

? Assume that a disaster is estimated to cost society £1 000bn (£1 000 000 000 000). The chances of the disaster occurring are said to be minute, however. Estimates vary from a probability of one in a million to one in a billion. What estimate of this cost would you include in a cost–benefit analysis?

Are there any solutions to the problem of measuring catastrophic risk? Pessimists would argue that uncertainty of the risks ought to make us cautious. They might quote Murphy's law: 'If anything can go wrong, it eventually will.'

Advocates of the project will argue that life is full of dangers. We could be run over or even struck by lightning (both of which may have a higher probability than the disaster). But we don't stay locked indoors. Thus rather than being 'negative' we ought to focus on ways of increasing safety and eliminating the possibilities of a disaster.

But what all this says is that there is no real solution to the conundrum. Apart from the mathematical puzzle, there remain two serious problems:

- The costs and the probability of the disaster occurring are impossible to measure with any accuracy.
- People's attitudes to risk vary. Some people are prepared to take great risks for relatively modest benefits. These people are 'risk lovers'. Others are very cautious. These people are 'risk averse'.

There are also other questions raised by the possibility of disaster:

- What discount rate would be used for measuring the long-term effects of, say, radiation?
- Which is worse, a thousand small disasters, or one disaster a thousand times bigger? (How is this relevant to the issue?)
- Should the effects on the rest of the world be included in a cost–benefit study, or just the effects on the UK?

? Why are many Third World countries apparently prepared to accept riskier projects than are industrialized countries?

not get compensation. Also the compensation is usually paid not by the project users, but by the general taxpayer (who will thus be *worse* off).

The Hicks–Kaldor criterion

To get round this problem J. R. Hicks and N. Kaldor suggested an alternative criterion. This states that a project is desirable if it leads to a *potential* Pareto improvement: in other words, if the gainers could *in principle* fully compensate the losers and still have a net gain, even though in practice they do not pay any compensation at all.

This criterion is what lies behind conventional CBA. If the benefits of a project are greater than the costs, then in principle the losers could be fully compensated with some net benefits left over.

But what is the justification for using this test? The losers, after all, will still lose. Its advocates argue that questions of *efficiency* should be kept separate from questions of *equity*. Projects, they argue, should be judged on efficiency grounds. They are efficient if their benefits exceed their costs. Questions of fairness in distribution, on the other hand, should be dealt with through the general system of taxation and welfare.

This is a 'useful' argument because it lets the proponents of the project off the hook. Nevertheless the problem still remains that some people will lose. People do not like living near a new motorway, airport or power station. These people cannot expect to receive special welfare benefits from general taxation.

Thus other economists have argued that a more specific account should be taken of distributional effects when *measuring* costs and benefits.

Taking specific account of distributional consequences
The way this could be done would be to give a higher weighting to the costs of individual (as opposed to corporate) losers. The justification is simple. Most people would argue that the pain of losing £1000 is greater than the pleasure of gaining £1000. Just how much higher this weighting should be, however, is a matter of judgement, not of precise calculation.

Another way distribution can be taken into account is to give a higher weighting to the costs incurred by poor people than to those incurred by rich people. For example, assume that a new airport is built. As a result house prices nearby fall by 10 per cent. A rich person's house falls in value from £200 000 to £180 000 – a loss of £20 000. A poor person's house falls from £50 000 to £45 000 – a loss of £5000. Is the loss to the rich person four times as painful as that to the poor person? Probably not. It is argued, therefore, that the poorer people are, the higher the weighting that should be given to each £1 lost. Just what this weighting should be, however, is controversial.

▲ SUMMARY

1. Cost–benefit analysis (CBA) can help a government decide whether or not to go ahead with a particular public project, or which of alternative projects to choose. CBA involves a number of stages.

2. All costs and benefits must be identified. These include the direct costs of constructing and operating the project, the direct monetary benefits to the operators and the consumer surplus of the users. They also include external costs and benefits to non-users.

3. Direct monetary costs and benefits are relatively easy to measure. Nevertheless there is still the uncertainty of how much these will be in the *future*. Also there is the problem that prices are distorted, although the theory of the second best would suggest that this is only a problem if the distortions are *different* for this project.

4. Non-monetary private benefit (consumer surplus) is difficult to estimate because of the difficulty of estimating

the shape and position of the demand curve. The alternative approach is to focus on specific non-monetary benefits such as journey time saved and then to evaluate how much people would be prepared to pay for them if they could.

5. Monetary externalities would normally be counted at face value. Non-monetary externalities are much more difficult to estimate. The approach is to try to estimate the value that consumers would put on them in a market environment. Questionnaire techniques could be used, or inferences could be drawn from people's actual behaviour elsewhere.

6. Figures would then have to be adjusted for risk and uncertainty.

7. Discounting techniques would then have to be used to reduce future benefits and costs to a present value.

8. The study may also take distributional questions into

account. The Hicks–Kaldor criterion suggests a compensation test for deciding whether a project is desirable. But given that in practice full compensation would be unlikely, the distributional questions may need to be taken into account more specifically. The weighting that the government chooses to attach to the costs to the losers is essentially a value judgement, which may be determined by its views on the weightings that should be attached to the incomes of different income groups, or may be determined by simple political expedience.

9. Having adjusted the costs and benefits for risk and uncertainty, timing and distributional effects, a recommendation to go ahead with the project will probably be given if its net present value (*NPV*) is positive: in other words, if the discounted social benefits exceed the discounted social costs.

10.5 The case for *laissez-faire*

Government intervention in the market can itself lead to problems. The case for non-intervention (*laissez-faire*) or very limited intervention is not that the market is the *perfect* means of achieving given social goals, but rather that the problems created by intervention are greater than the problems overcome by that intervention. The proponents of *laissez-faire*, therefore, concentrate on (a) criticizing government intervention and (b) demonstrating that the problems of the free market are relatively minor.

Drawbacks of government intervention

Shortages and surpluses
If the government intervenes by fixing prices at levels other than the equilibrium, this will create either shortages or surpluses.

If the price is fixed *below* the equilibrium, there will be a shortage. For example, if the rent of council houses is fixed below the equilibrium in order to provide cheap housing for poor people, demand will exceed supply. In the case of shortages resulting from fixing prices below the equilibrium, either the government will have to adopt a system of waiting lists, or rationing, or giving certain people preferential treatment, or alternatively it will have to allow allocation to be on a first-come, first-served basis or allow queues to develop. Black markets are also likely to develop. People unable to obtain the good or service at the fixed price may be prepared to pay considerably more. Their marginal utility may be well above the price. This could lead to very high profits for black marketeers. (see page 98.)

If the price is fixed *above* the equilibrium price, there will be a surplus. For example, if the price of food is fixed above the equilibrium in order to support farmers' incomes, supply will exceed demand. Government will have to purchase such surpluses and then perhaps store them, throw them away or sell them cheaply in another market, or ration suppliers by allowing them to produce only a certain quota, or allow suppliers to sell to whom they can. Such surpluses are obviously wasteful. High prices may protect inefficient producers. (The problem of food surpluses in the European Community is examined in section 11.1.)

? What are the possible arguments in favour of fixing prices (a) below and (b) above the equilibrium? Are there any means of achieving the same social goals without fixing prices?

Poor information
The government may not know the full costs and benefits of its policies. It may genuinely wish to pursue the interests of consumers or any other group, and yet may

be unaware of people's wishes or misinterpret their behaviour. It may be poorly informed of the consequences of its policies, particularly if there is a considerable range of possible outcomes and if the factors influencing such outcomes are themselves uncertain.

Bureaucracy and inefficiency

Government intervention involves administrative costs. The more wide reaching and detailed the intervention, the greater the number of people and material resources that will be involved. These resources may be used wastefully. Civil servants and local authority officials may not be as accountable as employees of private industry. Government decision-making processes may be highly inflexible and bureaucratic, and may involve considerable duplication and red tape.

Lack of market incentives

If government intervention removes market forces or cushions their effect (by the use of subsidies, welfare provisions, guaranteed prices or wages, etc.), it may remove certain useful incentives. Subsidies may allow inefficient firms to survive. Welfare payments may discourage effort. The market may be imperfect, but it does tend to encourage efficiency by allowing the efficient to receive greater rewards. It also encourages factor mobility into those sectors of the economy offering higher rewards.

Shifts in government policy

The economic efficiency of industry may suffer if government intervention changes too frequently. It makes it difficult for firms to plan if they cannot predict tax rates, subsidies, price and wage controls, etc. Government policy is likely to change with a change in government, but even existing governments may change policies as they succumb to various political pressures or as a general election approaches.

Voters' ignorance

The economic issues before the electorate are often highly complex. The average voter is unlikely to appreciate the costs and benefits of the programmes of alternative political parties. Voters may be highly susceptible to political propaganda and deceit. Thus a government's programme may not really represent the 'will of the people'.

Unrepresentative government

Once elected, those in power may pursue their *own* interests rather than those of the people. Governments may not follow through the programmes on which they were elected. Also, the government may have a majority of seats, but have been elected by only a minority of the population.

Lack of freedom for the individual

One of the major arguments put forward by those advocating *laissez-faire* is that government intervention involves a loss of freedom for individuals to make economic choices. The argument is not just that the pursuit of individual gain is seen to lead to the social good, but that it is desirable in itself that individuals should be as free as possible to pursue their own interests with the minimum of government interference: that minimum being largely confined to the maintenance of laws consistent with the protection of life, liberty and property.

 Go through the above arguments and give a reply to the criticisms made of government intervention.

Box 10.9

Mises, Hayek and the Mont Pelerin Society
The birth of post-war libertarianism

After the Second World War, governments in the Western world were anxious to avoid a return to the high levels of unemployment and poverty experienced in the 1930s. The free market was seen to have failed. Governments, it was therefore argued, should take on the responsibility for correcting or counteracting these failings. This would involve various measures such as planning, nationalization, the restriction of monopoly power, controls on prices, the macroeconomic management of the economy and the provision of a welfare state.

But this new spirit of intervention deeply troubled a group of economists and other social scientists who saw it leading to an erosion of freedom. In 1947 this group met in an hotel in the Swiss Alps. There they formed the Mont Pelerin society: a society pledged to warn against the dangers of socialism and to advocate the freedom for individuals to make their own economic choices.

Two of the most influential figures in the society were the Austrians Ludwig von Mises (1881–1973) and Friedrich von Hayek (1899–). They were the intellectual descendants of the nineteenth-century 'Austrian school'. Carl Menger, the originator of the school, had (along with Jevons and Walras (see Box 3.2)) emphasized the importance of individuals' marginal utility as the basis of demand. The Austrian school of economists was famous for its stress on individual choice as the basis for rational economic calculation and also for its advocacy of the free market.

Mises and Hayek (the 'Neo-Austrians' as they became known) developed these ideas, both before and after the Second World War. Although both were born in Austria and both taught at the University of Vienna, both left for professorships in the English-speaking world. In 1932 Hayek became a professor at the London School of Economics and then in 1950 at the University of Chicago. Mises emigrated to the USA in 1940 to take up a chair in Economics at New York University.

Mises and Hayek provided both a critique of socialism and an advocacy of the free market. There were two main strands to their arguments.

The impossibility of rational calculation under socialism
In his famous book *Socialism* (1922) Mises argued that centrally planned socialism was logically incapable of achieving a rational allocation of resources. Given that scarcity is the fundamental economic problem, all societies, whether capitalist or socialist, will have to make choices. But rational choices must involve weighing up the costs and benefits of alternatives. Mises argued that this cannot be done in a centrally planned economy. The reason is that costs and benefits can only be measured in terms of money prices, prices which reflect demand and supply. But such prices can only be established in a market economy.

In a centrally planned economy, prices will be set by the state and no state will have sufficient information of demand and supply to set rational prices. Prices under centrally planned socialism will thus inevitably be arbitrary. Also with no market for land or capital these factors may not be given a price at all. The use of land and capital, therefore, may be highly wasteful.

Many democratic socialists criticized Mises' arguments that rational prices *logically* cannot be established under socialism. In a centrally planned economy the state can in theory, if it chooses, set prices so as to balance supply and demand. It can, if it chooses, set an interest rate for capital and a rent for land, even if capital and land are owned by the state. And certainly in a mixed-market socialist economy, prices will merely reflect the forces of demand and supply that have been modified by the state in accordance with its various social goals.

Hayek modified Mises' arguments somewhat. He conceded that some imperfect form of pricing system could be established under socialism, even under centrally planned socialism. Hayek's point was that such a system

Advantages of the free market

Although markets in the real world are not perfect, even imperfect markets can be argued to have positive advantages over government provision or even government regulation.

Automatic adjustments
Government intervention requires administration. A free-market economy, on the other hand, leads to the automatic, albeit imperfect, adjustment of demand to supply

Box 10.9 (cont'd)

would inevitably be inferior to capitalism. The problem was one of imperfect information under socialism.

Calculation of costs and benefits requires knowledge. But that knowledge is dispersed amongst the millions of consumers and producers throughout the economy. Each consumer possesses unique information about his or her own tastes; each manager or worker possesses unique information about his or her own job. No government could hope to have this knowledge. Planning will inevitably, therefore, be based on highly imperfect information.

The market, by contrast, is a way of co-ordinating this dispersed information: it co-ordinates all the individual decisions of suppliers and demanders, decisions based on individuals' own information. And it does it all without the need for an army of bureaucrats.

> The economic problem of society is thus not merely a problem of how to allocate 'given' resources – if 'given' is taken to mean given to a single mind which deliberately solves the problem set by these 'data'. It is rather a problem of how to secure the best use of resources known to any of the members of society, for ends whose relative importance only these individuals know. Or, to put it briefly, it is a problem of the utilization of knowledge not given to anyone in its totality.[4]

Lack of dynamic incentives under socialism

A planned socialist economy will, according to Mises and Hayek, lack the incentives for people to take risks. Even a 'market socialist' society, where prices are set so as to equate demand and supply, will still lack the crucial motivating force of the possibility of large personal economic gains. Under capitalism, by contrast, a firm which becomes more efficient or launches a new or improved product can gain huge profits. The prospect of such profits is a powerful motivator.

> The motive force of the whole process which gives rise to market prices for the factors of production is the cease-less search on the part of capitalists and the entrepreneurs to maximize their profits by serving the consumers' wishes. Without the striving of entrepreneurs (including the shareholders) for profit, of the landlords for rent, of the capitalists for interest and the labourers for wages, the successful functioning of the whole mechanism is not to be thought of. It is only the prospect of profit which

directs production into those channels in which the demands of the consumer are best satisfied at least cost. If the prospect of profit disappears the mechanism of the market loses its mainspring, for it is only this prospect which sets it in motion and maintains it in operation. The market is thus the focal point of the capitalist order of society; it is the essence of capitalism. Only under capitalism, therefore, is it possible; it cannot be 'artificially' imitated under socialism.[5]

In addition to these economic criticisms of socialism, Mises and Hayek saw government intervention as leading down the road towards totalitarianism. The more governments intervened to correct the 'failings' of the market, the more this tended to erode people's liberties. But the more people saw the government intervening to help one group of people, the more help they would demand from the government for themselves. Thus inexorably the role of the state would grow and grow, and with it the size of the state bureaucracy.

In the early years after the war, the Mont Pelerin society had little influence on government policy. Government intervention and the welfare state were politically popular.

In the late 1970s, however, the society, along with other similar libertarian groups, gained increasing influence as a new breed of politicians emerged who were wedded to the free market and were looking for an intellectual backing for their beliefs.

Libertarian thinkers such as Hayek and Milton Friedman (see Box 13.9) have had a profound effect on many right-wing politicians, and have considerably influenced the economic programmes of the Thatcher, Reagan and Bush administrations. Hayek, although in his eighties, was still giving advice on putting free-market policies into action, and had become very much the 'elder statesman' of the libertarian movement.

? Do the arguments of Mises and Hayek necessarily infer that a *free* market is the most desirable alternative to centrally planned socialism?

[4] F. von Hayek, 'The price system as a mechanism for using knowledge', *American Economic Review*, September 1945, p. 519.
[5] L. von Mises, *Socialism: An economic and sociological analysis* (Jonathan Cape, 1936), p. 138.

changes and supply to demand changes. If, therefore, the costs of correcting imperfections in a market outweigh the costs of those imperfections themselves, then a case has been made out for *laissez-faire*.

The advocates of *laissez-faire* argue that the costs of such imperfections are relatively small. Even under oligopoly, it is claimed, the competition between firms will be enough to encourage firms to produce goods that are desirable to consumers and at not excessively high prices, and will encourage more efficient production methods. Cases of pure monopoly with total barriers to entry are extremely rare. On the other hand, they argue that the costs of intervention are relatively high.

Dynamic advantages of capitalism

The chances of making high monopoly/oligopoly profits will encourage capitalists to invest in new products and new techniques. The benefits to growth from such innovations may considerably outweigh any problem of resource misallocation. Given time, the high profits will be so attractive to potential competitors that they will find some way of breaking into the industry even with substantial barriers to entry. If the government tries to correct the misallocation of resources under monopoly/oligopoly either by regulating monopoly power or by nationalization, any resulting benefits could be outweighed by a loss in innovation and growth.

 Are there any features of free-market capitalism which would *discourage* innovation?

A high degree of competition even under monopoly/oligopoly

Even though an industry at first sight may seem to be highly monopolistic, competitive forces may still work for the following reasons.

Fear of competition. Firms may fear that the possibility of high profits will encourage firms to attempt to break into an industry. Existing firms will therefore need to remain relatively efficient and not charge excessively high prices if they are to avoid such competition. These arguments have been developed into the theory of contestable markets which we examined in section 5.4.

Even if a small firm cannot overcome the barriers to entry of a monopolistic industry, a large powerful firm from another industry may well have the power to do so. Thus the possible diversification of firms from other industries is an important source of potential competition.

Competition from closely related industries. There are relatively close substitutes for many products. If, for example, a firm had a monopoly over the supply of tinned cans to food producers, food could always be packed in glass or plastic containers instead, if the price of tinned cans was too high.

Foreign competition. Even if a firm is the only producer in the country of a certain product, it may still face stiff competition from foreign producers, especially if the government does not intervene by imposing customs duties on imports.

Countervailing powers. Large powerful producers often sell to large powerful buyers. Powerful producers of raw materials may sell to powerful manufacturers. Powerful manufacturers may sell to powerful department stores or supermarket chains. Thus there are often countervailing powers. The power of detergent manufacturers to drive up the price of washing powder is countered by the power of supermarket chains to drive down the price at which they purchase it. Thus power is to some extent neutralized.

Should there be more or less intervention in the market?

No firm conclusions can be drawn in the debate between those who favour more and those who favour less government intervention, for the following reasons:

- Many normative issues are involved which cannot be settled by economic analysis. For example, it could be argued that freedom to set up in business and freedom from government regulation are desirable *for their own sake*. As a fundamental ethical point of view this can be disputed, but not disproved.
- In principle, the issue of whether a government ought to intervene in any situation

could be settled by weighing up the costs and benefits of that intervention. Such costs and benefits, however, even if they could be identified, are extremely difficult, if not impossible, to measure, especially when the costs are borne by different people from those who receive the benefits and when externalities are involved.

- Often the effect of more or less intervention simply cannot be predicted: there are too many uncertainties.

Nevertheless, economists can make a considerable contribution to analyzing problems of the market and the effects of government intervention. Chapter 11 illustrates this by examining specific problem areas.

▲ SUMMARY

1. Government intervention in the market may lead to shortages or surpluses; it may be based on poor information; it may be costly in terms of administration; it may stifle incentives; it may be disruptive if government policies change too frequently; it may not represent the majority of voters' interests if the government is elected by a minority, or if voters did not fully understand the issues at election time, or if the policies were not in the government's manifesto; it may remove certain liberties.

2. By contrast, a free market leads to automatic adjustments to changes in economic conditions; the prospect of monopoly/oligopoly profits may stimulate risk taking and hence research and development and innovation, and this advantage may outweigh any problems of resource misallocation; there may still be a high degree of actual or potential competition under monopoly and oligopoly.

3. It is impossible to draw firm conclusions about the 'optimum' level of government intervention. This is partly due to the normative nature of the question, partly due to the difficulties of measuring costs and benefits of intervention/non-intervention, and partly due to the difficulties of predicting the effects of government policies, especially over the longer term.

10.6 Public choice theory: the economics of politics?

Economists have attempted to extend their analysis of markets to the field of political decision making. The result is public choice theory, sometimes called 'the economics of politics'. It involves using the tools of economic analysis to analyze various political phenomena such as voter behaviour, party politics and the actions of the government.

Public choice theory adopts a number of simple assumptions (some would argue simplistic ones) similar to those made in neo-classical market economics:

- Voters are seen as customers and politicians as businesspeople. Politicians produce decisions and outcomes which are 'sold' to the voters.
- The 'money' for which these political decisions are sold is votes. If people want, say, a new ring-road built, they will vote for the politician or party who will support it. The more actively and successfully the politician or party supports it, the more votes they are likely to get.
- Voters and politicians (and state bureaucrats too) are assumed to be rational utility maximizers, aiming for their own personal gain. Everyone weighs up his or her own personal marginal costs and benefits when deciding between alternatives: voters when deciding how to vote; politicians when deciding what policies to pursue.
- In the simplest public choice models it is assumed that politicians' utility is achieved through winning votes. They are thus vote maximizers. (In other models it is recognized that there may be other factors affecting politicians' utility. For

Public choice theory

The application of economic methods of analysis to the study of political decision taking.

example, in some cases their utility may be maximized by preferment within the party: appealing to the party leader may be more important than appealing to the electorate.)

As J. Buchanan, one of the founders of public choice theory, argues:

> We make choices as voters. We make choices as members of political parties. We make choices as bureaucrats if we hold government jobs. Economic analysis of these choices is just as appropriate as the economic analysis of the choices made in the market place to buy bread and fish.[6]

An analogy with perfect competition?

Will a free democratic system of one person one vote lead to an 'optimum' set of public decisions? To the extent that politicians and parties are competing for the public's votes and that the voters have perfect information and a genuine free choice of a complete range of alternative politicians and policies, then there may seem to be parallels with a perfect market.

But even if these conditions are fulfilled, there are some important differences.

Perhaps the most important is that political decisions are rarely made on behalf of *individual* voters; they are made for voters *collectively*. If you vote for a party that supports tougher sentences for criminals or mass screening for heart disease or a process of disarmament, then you are voting for something that affects the whole community.

Contrast this with your own personal economic decisions. If you buy a cabbage or a pair of jeans, the benefits are confined to you. Some people can buy many cabbages, some can buy few, others can buy none, according to their tastes. People do not have to agree whether *everyone* should have more or fewer cabbages. With political decisions it is rare that everyone will agree, and yet in most cases the same decision will necessarily apply to everyone. Without unanimity, then, the minority will lose from majority decision making. These decisions, therefore, will not be *Pareto improvements* unless the majority compensates the minority – and this it never does.

With a multi-party system, the outcome may be desirable to even fewer people. Particularly with a 'first-past-the-post' system, as in the UK, a government is likely to be elected with only a minority supporting it.

Another problem is that in general elections people vote for a party with its complete manifesto. In most countries they do not have separate votes on each separate issue. The problem here is that you may like some of a party's policies and not others. When voting, therefore, you have to choose between one complete package and another. Your choice is thus probably for the best compromise.

Political responses to voters' wishes

How will the desire to gain votes affect political decisions?

Moves towards the centre
Politicians may well be pulled toward the centre ground of politics.

Take the case of a simple two-party system. It is likely that the opinions of the electorate will be 'normally' distributed along a left-right spectrum. This normal distribution is illustrated in Figure 10.13. It shows that the number of voters favouring a particular position increases towards the centre and decreases towards the extremes.

---

[6] J. Buchanan, 'Economics, democracy and the constitution', *The World of Economics*, (IEA video).

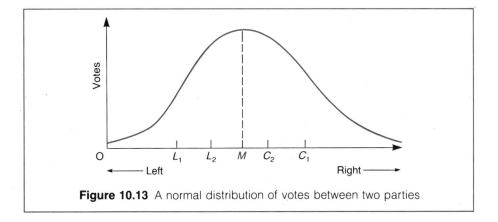

Figure 10.13 A normal distribution of votes between two parties

Assume that the positions of the two parties, Labour and Conservative, are initially at L_1 and C_1 respectively. They both want to win the next election. What do they do? The answer given by public choice theory is that they will both go for the centre ground. Take the case of Labour. If it shifts its position to the right, it can hope to gain a majority of that large block of votes between L_1 and C_1; but it will probably lose very few of the votes to the left of L_1, since its policies are still more appealing to this group than the Conservatives'. It thus moves, say, to position L_2. Similarly, the Conservatives move to position C_2. The effect is to make the two parties' policies very similar and to squeeze out any other parties in the centre.

There are two major criticisms of this analysis, however. The first is that it views politicians in too cynical a light. Politicians may *not* be motivated entirely by achieving power at all costs. They may be wedded to a particular cause, however unpopular, believing that it is genuinely the best policy for the country. The second is that politicians may not passively accept voters' opinions. Instead, by propaganda and argument, they may attempt to *shift* political opinion. This is what the Conservative government did after 1979. They attempted to shift public opinion in favour of the free market. In other words, instead of moving C_1 to the modal position M, they attempted to shift M towards C_1.

The effects of lobbying

Assume that you feel strongly about a particular issue: for example, about whether or not abortion should be permitted. With only one vote you will have little chance of swaying politicians to your point of view. The best course of political action will be to form a 'pressure group' of like-minded people. They can then lobby politicians and threaten to withhold their votes (and to persuade others to do likewise) if the politicians do not support them.

This is analogous to consumer groups using their monopsony/oligopsony power to put pressure on suppliers.

The use of such power may not be to the interests of the country, however. The American car industry, for example, managed to persuade the US government to restrict imports of Japanese cars. In 1984 it was estimated that they had substantially benefited from this policy, adding $300 million to their profits. However, the cost to the consumer of this measure in terms of higher car prices was estimated to be over $2000 million. Politicians were clearly swayed by lobbying from the car industry on this matter.

Political 'horse-trading'

This is when one politician or party is prepared to do deals with other politicians or parties in order to get their way. This is particularly likely in coalition politics. Assume that the coalition has two parties, the Greens and the Blues. The Greens may agree to cut grants to local authorities (a demand of the Blues) in return for the Blues agreeing to increase expenditure on reducing pollution (a demand of the Greens). For both parties, the cost of the agreement (agreeing to the other's demand) is less than the gain, namely achieving a more important demand to them.

This is analogous to trade, whether through simple barter or through the market. *Both* parties gain because their marginal benefit exceeds their marginal cost. When it comes to election time, the gain will be even greater if a coalition enables two minority parties to form a government.

Public choice theory and the optimum constitution

Public choice theory has been used to analyze the advantages and disadvantages of different types of voting system. Let us focus on the *costs* of different decisions.

There are two major categories of cost: (a) the time it takes to reach a decision and (b) the suffering of people for whom it was the wrong decision. These two sets of costs will vary according to the number of people who must support the decision.

At the one extreme there is the sort of decision that must be supported by *everyone*. There must be unanimous support: in other words, everyone has a veto. In this type of system it may be very difficult to get any decisions made at all, especially when large numbers of people are involved. Thus the first type of cost will be very high (if not infinite). On the other hand, the second type of cost will be very low (if not zero) since everyone supports the decision.

At the other extreme there is the system where just one person decides – an elected president with sole power, or a dictator. Here decision making can be very quick. Thus the first type of cost will be very low. On the other hand, the decision could be very unpopular, especially if the president is not standing again for office or if the dictator does not fear a military coup.

Between these two extremes there are all sorts of voting systems which require different levels of support for a decision to be made. In the middle there are decisions which require a simple majority: over 50 per cent of the vote. Towards the unanimity extreme there are decisions which may require 60 per cent, 70 per cent, 75 per cent or more of the vote. This is the case in many countries or organizations when changes to the rules or constitution are involved. In other cases, less than 50 per cent support is required. This is the case in the UK in the first-past-the-post system of electing Members of Parliament. The candidate with the most votes wins, however few those votes happen to be. On a low turnout, and with several candidates standing, this could mean a person elected with, say, only 25 per cent of the electorate's support.

Public choice theorists have attempted to identify and measure these costs of different systems in order to establish the most efficient way of achieving the public interest. (Of course, it is necessary to analyze the benefits of each system as well as the costs.)

Imperfections in the political system

Just as market economists analyze the failings of the market to achieve an optimal allocation of resources, so too do public choice theorists analyze the failings of a political system. Failings of a democratic system include the following.

Imperfect information. This prevents both voters and politicians alike from making informed decisions. Voters do not know exactly what politicians will do once they are elected. Politicians do not know exactly how popular their policies will be. Sometimes a system of 'rational ignorance' will develop. This is where the costs of acquiring information to make rational political decisions are greater than the benefits the information would provide.

Unequal distribution of power. The unequal distribution of power and resources means that certain groups or individuals can lobby politicians more effectively.

'Short-termism'. Politicians like many businesspeople tend to operate within a short time horizon. The need to be re-elected in four or five years may restrict long-term planning. Politicians may feel obliged to look for less risky or less costly programmes, even though the more costly programmes would in the end benefit the public more.

> **?** 1. Are there any other failings of a democratic system? If so, what are they?
> 2. Assume that there are two types of cost associated with decision making:
> (a) the time and effort involved in trying to secure support from people and in ironing out any problems they foresee; (b) the adverse effects on certain people of the decision itself. The relative size of these costs will depend on the nature of the decision and the system under which it is made. Which of the following decisions would be best made by
> (i) an individual, (ii) unanimous decision, (iii) a simple majority of those involved (50% +),
> (iv) a 'super majority' (e.g. 70% or 75% +) of those involved, or (v) a certain minimum number of those involved (e.g. 30%)?
> (a) Whether a group of friends should go on holiday together.
> (b) Whether taxes should be raised.
> (c) What colour coat you should buy.
> (d) Whether a certain person or people should be excluded from attending a club meeting.
> (e) Which of three parties should form a government.
> (f) Whether capital punishment should be reinstated.
> (g) Whether a new member country should be admitted to the European Community.
> In each case you should specify *who* is involved in the decision taking and whether you feel other people also ought to be involved.

▲ SUMMARY

1. Public choice theory borrows a lot of assumptions and concepts from neo-classical economics to study political decision making.
2. Politicians (the producers) are assumed to respond to the wishes of the general public (the consumers) expressed through the ballot box, pressure groups and other political avenues. In a simple analogy with markets, politicians are seen to be competing for votes.
3. There are, however, significant differences between political decisions and economic decisions made by consumers and firms. Political decisions are made on behalf of voters collectively and will often affect certain people adversely. There can rarely be a Pareto improvement with political decisions.
4. Political choice theorists examine various political phenomena such as the tendency of parties to converge on the centre ground, the effects of pressure groups on the

behaviour of parties and individual politicians, and the 'horse trading' that takes place especially in coalitions.
5. Public choice theorists also examine the efficiency of decision making under different political systems. Systems that require a high level of consent may lead to popular decisions, but may be quite unsuitable in situations where decisions have to be made quickly. They may also lead to very few decisions and hence little change (a situation that may be very unpopular). By contrast, systems that require little consent may lead to unpopular decisions being made, but at least decisions can probably be made quickly.
6. Just as imperfections in markets can be identified, so too can imperfections in political systems. These include imperfect information, unequal distribution of power and an overemphasis on the short term.

11 Applied Microeconomics

Just how far should things be left to the market in practice? Just how much should a government intervene? These are clearly normative questions, and the answers to them will depend on a person's politics.

Conservative politicians tend to favour the absolute minimum degree of intervention, to ensure the 'efficient' working of the market. Socialist politicians, on the other hand, prefer a much greater degree of intervention, to ensure not only that the inefficiencies of the market are corrected, but also that questions of 'fairness' and 'equality' are taken into account.

This chapter examines three topics which illustrate well the possible strengths and weaknesses of both the market and government intervention. Ultimately, you the reader must be left to judge where the correct balance lies, according to your political and ethical beliefs.

11.1 Agriculture and agricultural policy
The paradox of agriculture

The first topic is agricultural policy. Agriculture is an interesting area to start with because it poses somewhat of a conundrum. A *free* market in agricultural products would be about as close as one could get to perfect competition in the real world:

- There are thousands of farmers, each insignificantly small relative to the total market. Each farmer thus faces a virtually *horizontal demand curve*.
- Products are *homogeneous* and are not sold by brand. There may be different varieties of products – for example, in the case of potatoes, there are King Edwards, Whites, Reds, Wilja, etc. – but you do not go into the greengrocer and ask for Farmer Brown's!
- There is *freedom of entry*. People can freely buy land and set up in business as farmers.

Yet despite these features, there is more government intervention in agriculture throughout the world than in virtually any other industry!

Why intervene?

What reasons, then, are given for government intervention in agriculture? The following are the most commonly cited problems of the free market.

Agricultural prices are subject to considerable fluctuations

- Fluctuating prices cause fluctuating farm incomes. There is thus a direct problem here that in some years farm incomes may be very low.
- In other years, of course, the consumer will suffer by having to pay very high prices.
- Fluctuating prices make the prediction of future prices very difficult. This in turn makes rational economic decision making very difficult. How is a farmer to choose which of two or more crops to plant if their prices cannot be predicted?
- This uncertainty may discourage farmers from making long-term investment plans. A farmer may be reluctant to invest in, say, a new milking parlour, if in a couple of years it might be more profitable to switch to sheep rearing or arable farming. A lack of investment by farmers will reduce the growth of efficiency in agriculture.

Farm incomes rise less quickly over time than other incomes

Over the years, farming is likely to take a smaller and smaller share of national income. Without intervention, therefore, both the profits of farmers and the wages of farm workers are likely to fall relative to incomes in other parts of the economy, unless there is a substantial movement of the population out of agriculture.

The lack of economic power of farmers

It might be desirable to have lots of competition throughout the economy, but it could be seen as unfair if farmers are competitive while other sectors are not. A particular complaint of farmers here is that they have to buy their inputs (tractors, fertilizers, etc.) from oligopolists or monopolists who charge high prices. Then they often have to sell their produce to oligopsonist or monopsonist food processors, packers and distributors, who keep the price low to farmers. Farmers thus feel squeezed from both directions.

 To what extent can this be seen as a problem of the second best?

Traditional rural ways of life may be destroyed

The pressure on farm incomes may cause unemployment and bankruptcies; smaller farms may be taken over by larger ones; and generally, as the rural population declines, village life may be threatened – with the break-up of communities and the closure of schools, shops and other amenities.

Competition from abroad

- Farming may well be threatened by cheap food imports from abroad. Farmers may be driven out of business.
- If a country becomes too reliant on food imports, there may be severe problems in times of war, or at any other time when supplies may be cut off.

Against all these arguments must be set the argument that intervention involves economic costs. These may be costs to the taxpayer in providing financial support to farmers, or costs to the consumer in higher prices of foodstuffs, or costs to the economy as a whole in keeping resources locked into agriculture that could have been more efficiently used elsewhere.

Causes of short-term fluctuations: supply problems

There are two aspects of supply that help explain price fluctuations of agricultural products.

Fluctuations in the harvest. A field is not like a machine. It cannot produce a precisely predictable amount of output according to the inputs fed in. The harvest is affected by a number of unpredictable factors such as the weather, pests and diseases. The outputs of various foodstuffs for the years 1982–6 are shown in Table 11.1. Fluctuating harvests mean that farmers' incomes will fluctuate.

Time lags in supply: the cobweb theory. Crops and animals take time to grow. There is thus a time lag between farmers planning to produce a certain level of output and that output eventually coming to the market. These time lags can cause prices to fluctuate. These fluctuations are explained by the 'cobweb theory' which we examined in section 2.5.

Table 11.1 UK yields of selected crops: 1982–86

	Potatoes		Wheat		Sugar beet	
	Yield per hectare (tonnes)	% change	Yield per hectare (tonnes)	% change	Yield per hectare (tonnes)	% change
1982	37.3	–	6.2	–	49.8	–
1983	31.0	−16.9	6.4	+3.2	38.1	−23.1
1984	39.2	+26.4	7.7	+20.3	46.0	+20.1
1985	36.7	−6.4	6.3	−18.2	38.3	−16.6
1986	37.6	+2.5	7.0	+11.1	40.3	+5.2

Source: *Agricultural Statistics 1986* (MAFF, 1987).

Causes of short-term fluctuations: demand problems (low price elasticity)

The price elasticity of demand for food is low. The reason for this has to do with substitutes. Food, being a basic necessity of life, has no substitute. If, therefore, the price of food in general goes up, people cannot switch to an alternative: they either have to pay the higher price or consume less food. They might consume a bit less, but not much! The price elasticity for food in general, therefore, is very low.

It is not quite so low for individual foodstuffs, because if the price of one goes up, people can always switch to an alternative. If beef goes up in price, people can buy pork or lamb instead. Nevertheless, certain foodstuffs still have a low price elasticity, especially if:

● They are considered to be basic foods rather than luxuries.
● There are no close substitutes.
● They account for a relatively small portion of consumers' income.

With an inelastic demand curve, any fluctuation in supply will cause a large fluctuation in price. This is illustrated in Figure 11.1.

Causes of declining farm incomes: demand problems (low income elasticity)

There is a limit to the amount that people wish to eat. As people get richer, therefore, they tend not to consume much more food. They might buy better cuts of meat, or more convenience foods, but they will spend very little extra on basic foodstuffs. Their income elasticity of demand for basic foods, therefore, is very low.

 Why don't farmers benefit from a high income elasticity of demand for convenience foods?

Box 11.1

Price Elasticities of Demand for Various Foodstuffs

The statistics in the table were compiled by the Ministry of Agriculture. They show the average price elasticities of demand for various foodstuffs for the years 1980–5 (or 1978–85 in some cases).

Food	Price elasticity of demand	Food	Price elasticity of demand
Milk	−0.45	Fruit juices	−0.89
Cheese	−0.32	Fresh fruit	−0.39
Carcase meat	−1.30	Apples	−0.18
Beef	−1.49	Pears	−0.94
Lamb	−1.67	Oranges	−1.20
Pork	−2.08	Fresh potatoes	−0.12
Fish	−0.46	Fresh green vegetables	−0.43
Sugar and preserves	−0.70	Other fresh vegetables	−0.10
Bread	−0.50	Frozen vegetables	−1.07
Beverages	−0.28		

Source: *Household Food Consumption and Expenditure 1985* (CSO).

?

1. Arrange the products in ascending order of elasticity. Is the order as you would expect? Does it depend on the number and closeness of substitutes? Do staple foods have a different elasticity from non-staple foods?

2. Why do fresh vegetable prices fluctuate more than frozen vegetable prices? (Clue: the answer has partly to do with the elasticities presented in the table, but also partly to do with market structures.)

This very low income elasticity of demand has a crucial effect on farm incomes. It means that a rise in national income of 1 per cent leads to a rise in food consumption of considerably less than 1 per cent. As a result, total farm incomes will grow much more slowly than the incomes of other sectors. Unless people leave the land, farmers' incomes will grow less rapidly than those of other entrepreneurs, and farm workers' wages will grow less rapidly than those of other workers.

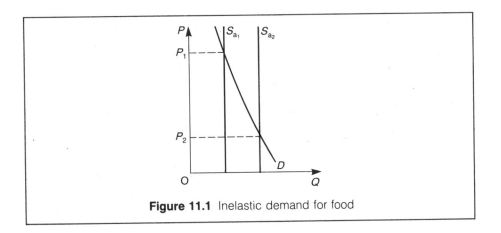

Figure 11.1 Inelastic demand for food

Box 11.2

Income Elasticities of Demand for Various Foodstuffs

The statistics in the table show the income elasticity of demand for various foodstuffs.

Remember, the income elasticity of demand is:

% change in quantity demanded
―――――――――――――――――
% change in income

This means that if the figure is less than 1 (an income-inelastic demand), then a rise in income will give a smaller percentage rise in the demand for that foodstuff. The lower the figure, the greater will be the long-term problems for farmers, since the more slowly will their sales rise.

The figures have been corrected to take into account changes in food prices, and thus show:

% change in consumer *expenditure*
――――――――――――――――――
% change in income

The demand for butter (with respect to income)

? 1. What does it mean when there is a negative income elasticity? What implications are there for farmers producing these foods?
2. The diagram shows a demand curve for butter with respect to *income*. The curve is inelastic. (Note that butter has an income elasticity of 0.18.)

(a) What would be the effect on this demand curve if there were growing health worries over the consumption of butter?
(b) Why might this make the calculation of income elasticity of demand difficult?
3. What would be the shape of the demand curve for margarine with respect to income?

Foodstuff	Income elasticity of demand	Foodstuff	Income elasticity of demand
Milk	−0.05	Sugar and preserves	−0.16
Cheese	0.38	Cakes and pastries	0.32
Eggs	−0.03	Fresh potatoes	−0.23
Carcase meat	0.22	Fresh green vegetables	0.42
Beef	0.26	Processed vegetables	0.04
Lamb	0.19	Fresh fruit	0.71
Pork	0.14	Fruit juices	1.09
Bread	−0.06	Tea	−0.32
Butter	0.18	Coffee	0.38
Margarine	−0.17		
		All foods	0.16

Source: *Household Food Consumption and Expenditure 1985* (CSO).

Causes of declining farm incomes: increases in supply

What can farmers do to increase their profits, given that demand is sluggish? The obvious solution would seem to be to reduce costs. That way, farmers can make more profit without having to sell more. As a result, farmers over the years have striven hard to improve efficiency, and have been keen to invest in new technology and improved farming methods.

The trouble is, though, that with a given supply of land, reduced costs mean

Figure 11.2 Decline in food prices over time

increased yields and hence increased supply. This, given the price-inelastic demand for food, will lower the price of food, thus largely offsetting any reduction in costs. And given the income-inelastic demand for food, the long-term rise in demand will be less than the long-term rise in supply.

These effects are illustrated in Figure 11.2, which shows a basic foodstuff like potatoes or other vegetables. Rising productivity leads to an increase in supply from S_1 to S_2. But given that demand is price inelastic and only shifts slightly to the right over time, from D_1 to D_2, price falls from P_1 to P_2.

Even if some farmers manage to get costs to fall faster than prices for certain crops, and thus earn supernormal profits, the highly competitive nature of farming will mean that other farmers will soon switch to these crops and copy their methods. This will further drive down prices and eliminate the supernormal profits.

Government intervention

There are five main types of government intervention that can be used to ease the problems examined above.

Buffer stocks. The government can buy food and place it in store when harvests are good, and then release the food back on to the market when harvests are bad. Buffer stocks are suitable only for *stabilizing* prices or farm incomes, not for providing long-term support to farmers.

Subsidies (or tax relief). The government can pay subsidies or grant tax relief to farmers to compensate for low market prices. Subsidies and tax relief can be used to increase farm incomes as well as to stabilize them.

High fixed prices. The government can fix a minimum price for food – normally above the market equilibrium – and buy up any surpluses that result. It will then have either to store the surpluses indefinitely, or find some way of disposing of them, for example by selling them abroad or giving them away as emergency food aid to famine-stricken countries. Guaranteed prices, like subsidies, can be used to increase farm incomes as well as to stabilize them.

Reducing supply. The government can introduce schemes to reduce the amount of food that farmers are allowed to produce or to sell. The government can also restrict food imports.

Structural policies. The government can provide retraining or financial help for people to leave agriculture. It can provide grants or other incentives for farmers to

Box 11.3

The Fallacy of Composition
Or when good is bad

Ask farmers whether they would like a good crop of potatoes this year, or whether they would rather their fields be ravaged by pests and disease, and the answer is obvious. After all, who would wish disaster upon themselves!

And yet, what applies to an individual farmer does not apply to farmers as a whole. Disaster for all may turn out not to be disaster at all.

Why should this be? The answer has to do with price elasticity. The demand for food is highly price inelastic. A fall in supply, due to a poor harvest, will therefore cause a proportionately larger rise in price. Farmers' incomes will therefore *rise*, not fall.

Look at diagram (a). Farmer Giles is a price taker. If he alone has a bad harvest, price will not change. He simply sells less (Q_2) and thus earns less. His revenue falls by the amount of the shaded area. But if all farmers have a bad harvest the picture is quite different, as shown in diagram (b). Supply falls from Q_1 to Q_2, and consequently price rises from P_1 to P_2. Revenue thus rises from areas (1 + 2) to areas (1 + 3).

And so what applies to a single farmer in isolation (a fall in revenue) does not apply to farmers in general. This is known as the fallacy of composition: *what applies in one case will not necessarily apply when repeated in all cases.*

What sort of harvest, then, would suit Farmer Giles best? The best possible situation would be for him to have a good harvest and everyone else to have a bad one. That way, price is high and yet he also sells a lot. The worst possible situation would be for him to have a bad harvest and everyone else to have a good one.

But if everyone is to have the same harvest, a generally bad one will be preferable for farmers to a generally good one.

(a) Farmer Giles   **(b)** All farmers

? 1. Can you think of any other (non-farming) examples of the fallacy of composition?
2. Would the above arguments apply in the case of foodstuffs that can be imported as well as being produced at home?

diversify into forestry, tourism, rural industry or different types of food, such as organically grown crops, or other foods with a high income elasticity of demand.

Buffer stocks

Buffer stocks to stabilize prices
If the government merely wants to stabilize prices, it can simply fix a price which balances demand and supply over the long term. Assume that this is P_g in Figure 11.3. At this price demand is Q_d.

If there is a good harvest (S_{a_1}), the government buys up the surplus, $Q_{s_1} - Q_d$, and puts it into store. If there is a bad harvest (S_{a_2}), it releases $Q_d - Q_{s_2}$ from the store on to the market.

Buffer stocks to stabilize farm incomes
If buffer stocks are used to maintain fixed prices (as in Figure 11.3), farmers' *incomes* will still fluctuate, only this time (in contrast to a free market) the bigger the harvest, the *bigger* will farmers' incomes be. Therefore the more the harvest fluctuates, the

Figure 11.3
Buffer stocks to stabilize prices

Figure 11.4
Buffer stocks to stabilize incomes

more their incomes will fluctuate. An alternative, then, is to *vary* the government price in such a way as to keep farmers' incomes stable.

In Figure 11.4 the average annual supply over the years is Q_1. Demand is price inelastic and is shown by the demand curve D. If output were in fact S_{a_1}, in any year, the equilibrium price would be P_1 and the income earned by farmers would be P_1 times Q_1.

Assume now that the government wants to stabilize farm incomes at this level. The curve Y shows all the combinations of P and Q that would achieve this. Note that this is the same as a demand curve with a price elasticity of demand equal to -1 passing through point a. As Chapter 2 explained, a demand curve of unit elasticity gives the same total revenue at any point along it: a given percentage rise in price leads to the same percentage fall in the quantity demanded.

If there is a good harvest (S_{a_2}), output will rise to Q_2. Price must only fall to P_2' (not P_2) if income is to stay constant. But at P_2' only Q_2' is demanded. Thus $Q_2 - Q_2'$ (i.e. $b - c$) must be purchased by the government and put into store.

If there is a bad harvest (S_{a_3}), output will fall to Q_3. Price must only rise to P_3' (not P_3) if income is to stay constant. But at P_3', Q_3' is demanded. Thus $Q_3' - Q_3$ (i.e. $d - e$) must be released from the store on to the market.

Conclusions

Buffer stocks can only be used with food that can be stored: i.e. non-perishable foods like grain, wine or milk powder; or food that can be put into frozen storage: e.g. butter and meat.

To prevent stores from mounting over time, the government price will have to be the one that balances demand and supply over the years. Surpluses in good years will have to match shortages in bad years. In this case, then, buffer stocks only stabilize prices or incomes, they do not increase farm incomes over the long term.

Subsidies

Governments may feel that the market price is too low for farmers. One method of supporting farmers' incomes, therefore, is to pay them a subsidy (per unit produced) which they will receive in addition to the market price. This, of course, will encourage farmers to produce more, which in turn will depress the market price.

Figure 11.5 illustrates the case of a foodstuff where the country is self-sufficient. Without a subsidy the market price would be P_e, where supply equals demand.

Box 11.4

Seven Years of Plenty and Seven Years of Famine
Buffer stocks in biblical Egypt

The idea of buffer stocks is not a new one. According to Genesis chapter 41, a buffer stock scheme was employed in the land of Egypt by Joseph.

King Pharaoh had had two dreams. In one, seven fat cows were devoured by seven thin cows. In the other, seven fat ears of corn were devoured by seven thin ears. The only person who could interpret these dreams was Joseph who was in prison. He was thus summoned to Pharaoh and interpreted the dreams as follows:

29. Behold, there come seven years of great plenty throughout all the land of Egypt:
30. And there shall arise after than seven years of famine; and all the plenty shall be forgotten in the land of Egypt; and the famine shall consume the land . . .
35. And let them gather all the food of those good years that come, and lay up corn under the hand of Pharaoh, and let them keep food in the cities.
36. And that food shall be in store to the land against the seven years of famine, which shall be in the land of Egypt; that the land perish not through the famine . . .
46. And Joseph was thirty years old when he stood before Pharaoh, King of Egypt. And Joseph went out from the presence of Pharaoh, and went throughout all the land of Egypt.
47. And in the seven plenteous years the earth brought forth by handfuls.

48. And he gathered up all the food of the seven years, which were in the land of Egypt, and laid up the food in the cities: the food of the field, which was round about every city, laid he up in the same.
49. And Joseph gathered corn as the sand of the sea, very much, until he left numbering; for it was without number . . .
53. And the seven years of plenteousness, that was in the land of Egypt, were ended.
54. And the seven years of dearth began to come, according as Joseph had said: and the dearth was in all the lands; but in all the land of Egypt there was bread . . .
56. And the famine was over all the face of the earth: and Joseph opened all the storehouses, and sold unto the Egyptians; and the famine waxed sore in the land of Egypt.
57. And all countries came into Egypt to Joseph for to buy corn; because that the famine was so sore in all lands.

? Would you expect the demand for corn from the storehouses to be price elastic or inelastic? What implications does your answer have for the price Joseph could have charged if he had wanted to maximize revenue for Pharaoh?

Assume now that the government wishes farmers to receive a price of P_g. If farmers do receive this price, they will plan to increase production to Q_1, which will push the market price down to P_m. The size of the subsidy that the government must pay, therefore, will be $P_g - P_m$. The total amount of taxpayers' money spent will be the

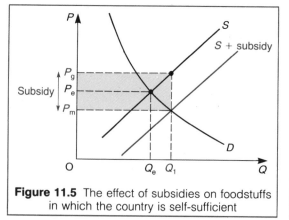

Figure 11.5 The effect of subsidies on foodstuffs in which the country is self-sufficient

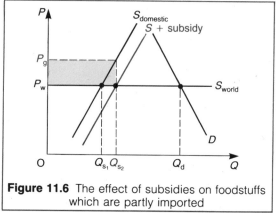

Figure 11.6 The effect of subsidies on foodstuffs which are partly imported

shaded area. The effect of the subsidy is to shift the effective supply curve downward by the amount of the subsidy, to S + subsidy.

When some of the food is imported, and when therefore the equilibrium price is the world price, the effect is slightly different. In Figure 11.6 the world price is P_w. Without a subsidy, domestic supply is Q_{s_1}. Domestic demand is Q_d. Imports are therefore the difference: $Q_d - Q_{s_1}$.

Assume now that the government wants farmers to receive a price of P_g. At that price domestic supply increases to Q_{s_2}, but the price paid by the consumer does not fall. It remains at P_w. The subsidy paid per unit is $P_g - P_w$. The cost to the taxpayer is again shown by the shaded area.

> **?** 1. The total amount paid in subsidies is greater in Figure 11.5 than in Figure 11.6. Will it always be the case that, for a given after-subsidy price to the farmer (P_g), a greater amount will be paid out in subsidies if the country is self-sufficient in the foodstuff than if it has to import part of the total amount consumed? (Assume that the demand curve is the same in both cases.)
> 2. We have been discussing a subsidy *per unit of output*. What would be the effect of a lump-sum subsidy: i.e. a total subsidy paid irrespective of output?

The old UK deficiency payments system

If the aim of subsidies is to guarantee prices to farmers, there is a problem. Actual supply fluctuates and thus diverges from planned supply. If there is a fixed subsidy, therefore, the price the farmer receives will fluctuate along with the market price.

The alternative, then, is to have variable subsidies. This system was used in the UK after the Second World War and continued until entry to the EEC in 1973. The system was one of deficiency payments. The government, in consultation with the National Farmers' Union set guaranteed minimum prices to farmers for a number of products such as wheat, barley, oats, potatoes, eggs, wool and livestock. If the market price for any product fell below the guaranteed price, the difference was paid as a subsidy or 'deficiency payment'. The size of deficiency payment varied, therefore, with the market price, which in turn varied with fluctuations in supply.

An advantage of the system was that the deficiency payment was based on the *average* market price. There was therefore an incentive for farmers to improve quality and get a better than average price without thereby sacrificing any subsidy.

Farmers gained from high stable prices, which both supported their incomes and helped them plan their future investments with more certainty. Consumers gained from low prices. The costs of the deficiency payments were borne by the taxpayer.

> **?** 1. Refer back to Figure 11.5 and use the diagram to illustrate each of the points made in this last paragraph.
> 2. Referring to Figure 11.6, will the consumer gain from deficiency payments in the case of foodstuffs where the country remains a net importer?

High fixed prices: the system in the European Community

The Common Agricultural Policy of the EC is a system of high fixed prices which are not only received by the producer but also paid by the consumer. The EC sets a target price for each major foodstuff. This has a different effect depending on whether the EC is self-sufficient in the foodstuff or a net importer.

Foodstuffs where the EC is a net importer

The target price will usually be above the world price. A tax or 'levy' is thus imposed on imports to bring them up to the required price. Given that the world price will

Deficiency payments
Variable subsidies where the amount paid per unit is that which is necessary to make up the deficiency between the market price and the previously agreed guaranteed price.

Target price (of a foodstuff in the EC)
The price the Community wants producers to receive (and consumers to pay). The Community will intervene through import levies (taxes) or buying up surpluses in order to ensure that price does not fall below the target level.

Box 11.5

Who Gains and Who Loses from Subsidies?

'There is no such thing as a free lunch.' We are frequently reminded by politicians that subsidized food – or anything for that matter – has to be paid for by someone. That someone is the taxpayer.

Whenever some people gain but others lose, we are faced with a question of redistribution.

So what is the redistribution arising from food subsidies? Let us take the case of foods where the UK is self-sufficient. The gainers in this case are both farmers and consumers. In Figure 11.5 the farmer gains from an increase in price received, from P_e to P_g. The consumer gains from a reduction in price paid, from P_e to P_m.

But is the redistribution from taxpayers to consumers a redistribution from rich to poor, or poor to rich, or no redistribution at all?

Poor people spend a large proportion of their income

on food, but pay a small proportion in tax. Rich people, on the other hand, spend a smaller proportion of their income on food than the poor, but pay a larger proportion in tax.

Subsidies that lower food prices, therefore, have the effect of redistributing incomes from the rich to the poor. They therefore tend to be favoured more by the political left.

? 1. If the demand for food is very price inelastic, will there be a bigger or smaller redistribution from rich to poor? (Imagine swinging the demand curve in Figure 11.5 so that it becomes steeper.)

2. Is there any redistribution from rich to poor in Figure 11.6?

Variable import levy

A tax on imports to bring the price of imported food up to the target price. The size of the tax will vary as the world price varies.

Threshold price

The price at which an imported foodstuff enters the EC: the world price plus the variable import levy. The threshold price is set at the target price minus transport costs from the port.

fluctuate, this tax has to be variable. The system is thus known as one of variable import levies. To work out the size of the necessary levy a threshold price is set. This is the port equivalent of the target price. Given that food has to be transported from the port to the market and this costs money, the price at the port (the threshold price) does not have to be quite as high as the target price. The threshold price is thus the target price minus transport costs from the port. Provided, then, that the levy is equal to the difference between the world price and the threshold price, this will bring the EC price of imports up to the target price.

The effects of this system are illustrated in Figure 11.7. To keep the analysis simple, let us assume that transport costs are zero and that therefore the target and threshold prices are the same. If trade took place freely at the world price P_w, Q_{d_1}, would be demanded and Q_{s_1} supplied within the EC. The difference $(Q_{d_1} - Q_{s_1})$ would be imported.

If a target price P_t is now set and a levy imposed on imports to raise their price to P_t, domestic prices will also rise to this level. Demand will fall to Q_{d_2}. Supply by EC countries will rise to Q_{s_2}. Imports will fall to $Q_{d_2} - Q_{s_2}$.

Figure 11.7 The EC system of high prices where some food is imported

The amount paid in import levies is shown by the shaded area. These moneys are paid into the Community budget.

Foodstuffs where the EC is self-sufficient

In this case an intervention price is set. This will be a few percentage points below the target price. If the market price falls below the intervention price, the Intervention Boards of the EC will buy up any surpluses at the intervention price. In the case of foodstuffs that can be stored, such as wheat, the surpluses will be put into intervention stores.

Intervention price

The price at which the EC is prepared to buy a foodstuff if the market price is below it.

The effects of this system are illustrated in Figure 11.8. Assume that the EC demand is D_{EC}. Assume also that the world price is P_w. This will be the equilibrium price, since any surplus at P_w (i.e. $b - a$) will be exported at that price. Thus before intervention, EC demand is Q_{d_1} and EC supply is Q_{s_1}.

Now assume that the EC sets an intervention price of P_i. Given that this is above the equilibrium (world) price, there will be a surplus of $d - e$ (i.e. $Q_{s_2} - Q_{d_2}$). This will be bought by the appropriate Intervention Board. The cost to the EC of buying this surplus is shown by the total shaded area ($edQ_{s_2}Q_{d_2}$). Unless the food is thrown away or otherwise disposed of, there will obviously then be the additional costs of storing this food: costs which could be very high over time, especially if the food has to be frozen.

An alternative to storing the food is for the Boards to sell the surpluses on the world market. In this case the net cost to the Intervention Boards would only be area *edcf*.

[?] What will be the amount paid out in Figure 11.8 if instead of the Intervention Boards buying the surpluses, export subsidies were given to farmers so as to guarantee them a price (after subsidy) of P_i?

When surpluses are bought by the EC or export subsidies are given, the money comes from the European Agricultural Guarantee and Guidance Fund (known as FEOGA – the initials of its French name). Originally it was thought that the money earned from port levies would be sufficient to finance these payments. Over the years, however, as the EC has become increasingly self-sufficient in food, and as food surpluses have grown, so member countries have had to make increasingly large additional budget contributions to enable FEOGA to purchase these surpluses.

Figure 11.8
The EC system of high prices in foodstuffs where the EC is self-sufficient

Justification for the Common Agricultural Policy

The EC was established in 1957 with the signing of the Treaty of Rome. Article 39 of that treaty set out various objectives of agricultural policy including the following:

- Assured supplies of food.
- A fair standard of living for those working in agriculture.
- A growth in agricultural productivity.
- Stable prices.
- Reasonable prices for consumers.

The CAP has had some success in meeting some of these objectives, but in each case the extent of the 'success' is open to question. Let us examine each in turn.

Assured supplies of food. Memories of a war-ravaged Europe were still fresh in people's minds when the Treaty of Rome was signed. The goal of a guaranteed supply of food was thus seen as very important. The growing self-sufficiency of the EC in most foodstuffs could therefore be argued to be an important success. It could be a major strategic advantage should the EC ever be involved in a war, or if world food prices rose substantially.

These arguments are questionable, however. World food prices are much lower than EC prices, and there is no prospect in the foreseeable future of difficulties in obtaining food imports at reasonable prices. Also making provisions against a future war is difficult when the nature of any such war is uncertain. Nuclear war or invasion would make previous self-sufficiency irrelevant.

Fair standard of living for farmers and farm workers. A system of high prices, other things being equal, will give farmers larger incomes. Some farmers have benefited greatly from the CAP, but despite the high prices, average incomes in agriculture have continued to lag behind those of other sections of the economy. In the UK, agricultural income per head of the rural population fell by 28 per cent relative to national income per head between 1976 and 1986.

To what extent things would have been even worse for farmers and farm workers without the CAP is difficult to gauge. Prices would have been lower, but whether farm costs would have been higher or lower depends on what would have happened to agricultural productivity and to the prices of farm inputs. Feedstuffs and seeds would have been cheaper, and also probably the price of land. But has the CAP increased or decreased agricultural productivity?

Agricultural productivity. The argument is that higher prices lead to higher profits and therefore more money for farmers to invest in land improvement, agricultural machinery, etc. On the other hand, higher profits may allow farmers to survive without having to become more efficient. The continuance of many small-scale inefficient farms using outdated techniques, especially in continental Europe, has been blamed directly on the CAP. The evidence shows that agricultural yields have improved dramatically over the years, especially in certain crops. Table 11.2 gives some examples of the growth in yields in the UK since it joined the EC.

A large proportion of this rise in productivity has been due to technological improvements and a greater use of chemicals. It is difficult, however, to judge the extent to which this greater use has been the direct result of higher food prices rather than the simple availability of new techniques, or competition from other farmers.

Stable prices. By fixing prices which do not fluctuate with demand and supply, stable prices are guaranteed – at least for a year. But these stable prices are high prices, so

Table 11.2 UK yields of selected crops

	1974–78 (average)	1983–87 (average)
	(tonnes per hectare)	
Wheat	4.7	6.7
Barley	4.0	5.1
Oilseed rape	2.2	3.1
Potatoes	28.8	36.5

Source: *Agricultural Statistics* (MAFF).

they do not benefit the consumer. They go some way to helping the farmer in making production plans, but only if the prices are not abruptly changed by the EC, and if there are no other shifts in policy that favour one product or another.

But as was demonstrated in Figure 11.3, even if prices are stable, farm incomes will still fluctuate with supply. The better the harvest, the higher will farm incomes be.

Reasonable prices for consumers. In the short run a policy of high prices is inconsistent with reasonable prices for consumers (if 'reasonable' is defined as 'low' or at any rate 'not high'). In the long run, however, it can be argued that, if prices above the market equilibrium encourage investment and productivity increases, then after a number of years they will end up lower than they would have been without the policy.

> **?** The EC is more than self-sufficient in a number of commodities. Does this mean that the objectives of the CAP have been achieved? What has been the cost of achieving this success? What do you think would have happened in the absence of the CAP?

Criticisms of the CAP

If the arguments in favour of the CAP are questionable, the arguments against are substantial.

Agricultural surpluses (not sold on to world markets)

Apart from the moral question of whether it is right to grow food that is not consumed, especially given the extent of famines and malnourishment in the Third World and the problem of poverty within the EC, there are substantial direct costs of food surpluses. These costs are borne by consumers and taxpayers. They can be divided into static costs (the costs of the CAP with any given demand and supply curves) and dynamic costs (the costs arising from shifts in the curves over time as a result of the CAP).

Static costs. The cost to consumers and taxpayers is greater than the gain to farmers. So what is the net cost? This is illustrated in Figure 11.9, which considers the case of a single foodstuff. P_e is the free-market equilibrium price, and P_i is the intervention price. To keep the analysis simple, let us assume that P_e is the world price too.

- The cost to consumers of the higher price is the loss of consumer surplus: area afP_eP_i.
- The gain to farmers is the increase in profits: area bfP_eP_i.
- There is a net gain, therefore, to farmers over consumers of area abf.
- But there is an additional cost to taxpayers of purchasing the surplus. This is area $abcd$.
- There is therefore an overall net loss of area $afbcd$.

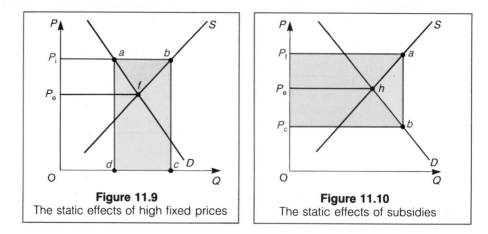

Figure 11.9
The static effects of high fixed prices

Figure 11.10
The static effects of subsidies

? Assume that the world price were above point *f* (but still below P_i). Draw a diagram to illustrate the static costs in this case.

The static costs of high prices are greater than those of *subsidies*. The costs of subsidies are shown in Figure 11.10. P_f is the price to farmers. P_c is the price to consumers. The per-unit subsidy is $P_f - P_c$.

- The gain to farmers is the increase in profits: area $P_f ah P_e$.
- The gain to consumers is the increase in consumer surplus: area $P_e hb P_c$.
- The total gain to farmers and consumers, therefore, is the area $P_f ahb P_c$.
- The cost to taxpayers is the area $P_f ab P_c$.
- There is therefore an overall net loss of the triangle *abh*. Other things being equal, this is a considerably smaller net loss than with the EC system.

? What assumptions are we making here when we say 'other things being equal'?

Dynamic costs. To the extent that higher prices encourage more investment in farming and therefore greater increases in long-run supply, so surpluses and their attendant costs will increase over time.

- First, there will be the growing cost of purchasing each new year's surplus.
- Secondly, there will be the growing cost of storing previous years' surpluses.

These costs are costs to the taxpayer, and therefore will be offset to a small extent by an additional net gain to farmers over consumers.

The costs of surpluses to EC taxpayers are shown in Table 11.3. The table shows the expenditure by FEOGA on intervention to guarantee high prices, and also on various other forms of market support (e.g. export subsidies). Over half of the expenditure goes on storage and disposal. The figures are given in European Currency Units (ECUs). The ECU is an EC unit of account – a way of valuing EC goods. It is worth approximately 70p, but varies with the exchange rate of the pound.

As the table shows, FEOGA's 'Guarantee expenditure' has accounted for some two-thirds of the total Community budget. FEOGA also provides 'Guidance' support for farm modernization and help for rural communities. This, however, has accounted for less than 5 per cent of FEOGA expenditure.

Until recently, agricultural support accounted for a growing proportion of the gross domestic product (GDP) of the EC countries. (GDP is a measure of a country's national output: its measurement is explained in section 13.6.)

Table 11.3 The cost of price and other market support for agriculture in the EC

Year	Total EC budget (ECU m)	Gross FEOGA Guarantee expenditure		
		Total (ECU m)	% of total EC budget	% of total EC GDP
1977	8 924	6 830	76.5	0.48
1978	11 367	8 673	76.3	0.55
1979	14 373	10 441	72.6	0.59
1980	16 301	11 315	69.4	0.56
1981	17 785	10 980	61.7	0.51
1982	20 429	12 406	60.7	0.52
1983	24 357	15 812	64.9	0.60
1984	27 528	18 346	66.6	0.66
1985	28 101	19 744	70.3	0.66
1986	35 174	22 137	63.0	0.63
1987	35 783	22 968	64.2	0.63
1988	43 820	28 795	65.7	0.75
1989	45 030	28 323	62.9	0.68

Source: *The Agricultural Situation in the Community* (Commission of the EC).

Irrational relative prices

Although food prices are kept high generally, some are kept much higher above free-market prices than others. The effect is to cause a misallocation of resources within agriculture. For example, the yellow fields of rape that dominate much of the British landscape have been the direct result of the high levels of support given to oilseed production.

Table 11.4 shows the proportion of total agricultural output (by value) accounted for by various foodstuffs and the proportions of total Guarantee expenditure they receive.

Table 11.4 Unequal support given to different foodstuffs in the EC: 1987

	Percentage of total EC output (by value)	Percentage of FEOGA Guarantee expenditure
Milk	17.8	22.4
Cereals	10.2	18.2
Sugar	2.2	8.8
Tobacco	0.5	3.5
Oilseeds	2.2	11.6
Fruit and vegetables	14.8	4.2
Pigmeat	8.6	0.7
Poultrymeat and eggs	6.8	0.7

Source: A. Burrell, B. Hill and J. Medland, *Agrifacts: A handbook of UK and EEC agriculture and food statistics* (Harvester Wheatsheaf, 1990).

Removes disciplines of markets

Under a system of subsidies, all farm products are sold on the market. Thus the price that farmers are able to receive will depend on the quality of their produce.

Under the EC system, where prices are guaranteed, food sold into intervention may be of inferior quality. Inspectors thus have to be employed to ensure that a minimum standard of quality of the surplus food is maintained. This further adds to the costs of the surpluses.

Increases inequalities in agriculture

The bigger the farm, the bigger its output, and therefore the bigger the benefit the farmer receives from high prices. Similarly, richer agricultural regions of the EC receive more support than poorer ones. The effect of the CAP, therefore, is to increase inequalities in agriculture. These effects might be seen as beneficial if the aim of the CAP were simply to increase productivity: higher incomes would be the rewards for higher output. But then why give any support at all to the small inefficient farmer? If, however, in the light of food surpluses, the main aim of continuing to give support is to redistribute incomes from rich to poor, the policy is clearly a failure.

Increases inequalities generally

Poor people spend a larger proportion of their income on food than the rich, but pay a lower proportion of their income in taxes than the rich. A system of high prices for food therefore directly penalizes the poor and reduces the burden on taxpayers. It thus increases inequality.

A system of subsidies, on the other hand, leads to lower prices for the consumer, the cost being borne entirely by the taxpayer. It therefore leads to greater equality.

Inequitable between member countries of the EC

There are two reasons why the CAP is inequitable between the member countries. The first is that lower levels of support are given to foodstuffs produced in the poorer Mediterranean EC countries.

The second is that the countries which import the most food from outside the EC – countries like the UK – pay the most in import levies into FEOGA. The countries with the greatest food surpluses draw most from FEOGA. The UK also loses in having the smallest proportion of the working population in agriculture: 2.4 per cent, compared with 5.2 per cent in West Germany, 7.1 per cent in France, 10.5 per cent in Italy, 15.4 per cent in Ireland and 27 per cent in Greece.

The UK pays £20–£30 per head of the population more into the Community budget each year than it receives. This is exceeded only by West Germany. At the other extreme Denmark receives £40–£50 per head more than it pays, and Ireland around £150 more than it pays.

Externalities

By encouraging increased output, the CAP has encouraged the destruction of hedgerows, and the increased use of chemical fertilizers and pesticides. Many of these chemicals have caused pollution. For example, nitrates are now the biggest single cause of river pollution in the UK, especially in the east.

Member countries not 'playing the game'

The CAP is supposed to be a *common* agricultural policy. In practice individual countries have frequently sought to flout its regulations.

In the face of mounting surpluses, countries have sought to protect their own farmers against competition from other member countries. They have used illegal methods (or methods that 'get round' European law) to subsidize their own farmers or to reduce imports from other EC countries.

Effects on the rest of the world

The CAP has had a very damaging effect on agriculture in non EC countries in two ways.

Import levies. Levies on imported food substantially reduce the amount of food that other countries are able to export to the EC. For example, Australia, a low-cost producer of butter, and once a major exporter to the UK, now finds it impossible to export any butter at all to the EC.

'Dumping' surpluses on world markets. Export subsidies allow EC surpluses to be sold at very low prices on world markets. This has a doubly damaging effect on Third World agriculture: (a) Third World exporters of foodstuffs find it very difficult to compete with subsidized EC exports; (b) farmers in the Third World who are producing for their domestic market find that they cannot compete with cheap imports of food.

Third World agriculture thus declines. Farmers' incomes are too low to invest in the land. Many migrate to the overcrowded cities and become slum dwellers in shanty towns, with little or no paid employment (see Chapter 23). The neglect of agriculture can then lead to famines if there is poor rainfall in any year. Calls are then made for European (and North American) food surpluses to be used for emergency aid: the same food surpluses that contributed to the problem in the first place!

Reforming the CAP

A number of proposals for reform have been discussed by the EC. Most focus on the growing problem of food surpluses. Some tentative steps have been taken to implement some of the proposals, but so far the effects have been limited.

Price reductions
The most obvious solution is a reduction in the levels of intervention prices. In theory this should reduce supply, increase demand and thereby reduce or even eliminate surpluses.

There have been some attempts to reduce the rate of increase in intervention prices. Also in 1988 a system of budget stabilizers was introduced. These involve automatic price cuts if *total* FEOGA expenditure exceeds a stated level. To act as a real disincentive to farmers who overproduce, however, it would have to apply to each farm individually. For example, the farmer could be given a lower price for each foodstuff once a certain quota was exceeded. Clearly this would be more expensive to administer.

An alternative is to impose a tax on output, thereby reducing the (after-tax) price to the farmer. Such a scheme was introduced in 1986 when a tax (or co-responsibility levy as it is called) of 3 per cent was imposed on cereal production. This was later extended with supplementary levies being imposed on output that exceeded quotas.

The problem with any substantial price cuts, however, is that many small farmers would be driven out of business: something that the CAP was designed to prevent. Large farms with substantial economies of scale would survive, but the traditional character of the countryside would be further eroded. Politically, it would probably not be possible for large numbers of small farmers to be made bankrupt.

As a result of the difficulties in instituting price reductions, various proposals have been put forward to restrict supply.

Production quotas
This system would restrict farmers' permitted output. Quotas have already been introduced for sugar and milk. It is more difficult, however, to have a quota system for grains and vegetables where yields fluctuate with the harvest, and where it would thus

Budget stabilizers
A system introduced into the EC in 1988 of limiting total expenditure on agricultural support. Intervention prices are cut when an agreed budget limit is reached.

Co-responsibility levy
A tax on food production in the EC so as to reduce the level of agricultural support.

be difficult to monitor the system. And if quotas are only applied to a limited range of products, this will merely encourage farmers to switch to other products which may also be in surplus.

Dairy farmers have been bitterly opposed to quotas (introduced in 1984). They naturally see them as a barrier against expansion, efficiency and increased profit. They claim that quotas freeze current production patterns and prevent efficient farmers from entering the market. There is now a trade in quotas, however, as farmers buy and sell their right to produce milk. As a result milk quotas have become a valuable asset.

Acreage controls

Another way of reducing cereal production has been to reduce the area cultivated. Subsidies are paid to farmers to leave their land fallow. Under this set-aside scheme, as it is called, farmers are paid not to produce!

A problem with set-aside is that farmers tend to set aside their least productive land, thereby making little difference to total output. Another problem is that farmers tend to put in extra effort on the remaining land, again hoping to maintain total output. If they are successful, supply will not be reduced and the problem of surpluses will remain. To increase yields they would probably use more chemicals with the attendant problems of pollution.

> **Set-aside**
> A system in the EC of paying farmers not to use a certain proportion of their land.

Diversification

Farmers could be paid subsidies or given tax concession to encourage them to diversify into food products that are not in surplus, or into forestry, rural industry or tourism. FEOGA Guidance payments can be used for this purpose.

Low-intensity farming

Another option would be to encourage the use of less fertilizers and other chemicals. This would reduce yields per hectare. To some extent this is happening anyway with the shift in consumer preferences towards organic foods. Nevertheless measures could be taken to encourage this trend with the use of subsidies on organically grown food and taxes on various chemicals.

Replacing high prices with subsidies

A more radical possibility, and one that has so far received little support within the Community, would be to introduce a system like the old UK deficiency payments scheme. This would allow surpluses to be eliminated. It might even be possible to pay a larger per-unit subsidy to smaller farmers. But given the current scale of the overproduction, the price inelasticity of demand for food and the extent to which EC prices are above world prices, the necessary size of the subsidies would be very large. This would put a consequently large additional burden on Community taxpayers. This would be politically difficult given complaints that the current cost of intervention is already excessive.

Income support ('lump-sum' subsidies)

Given the size of the surpluses, there is no simple solution. The one most favoured by academic economists, however, is that of a straight grant to farmers, not related to output. Grants will protect farmers' incomes, but unlike both high prices and subsidies, grants will not (in theory) encourage them to increase output, since extra output only earns them the market price.

 Demonstrate graphically that the use of a lump-sum subsidy will not affect output. (Clue: see Figure 10.11 for the effects of a lump-sum tax.)

In practice, grants would be resisted by politicians, who would see them as 'handouts' for doing nothing at all. Also if they are paid grants, farmers may simply reinvest them in their farms, thereby increasing long-term output.

The approach to agricultural support is gradually changing in the EC. Although the European Commission has planned for a slight growth of Guarantee expenditure in real terms in the early 1990s, it is nevertheless planned to grow much less rapidly than other parts of EC expenditure. In particular there is a shift in emphasis towards viewing agriculture as part of the whole rural environment. This involves increasing the relative size of the Guidance expenditure of FEOGA, and using it for helping to set up alternative rural industries and 'environmentally friendly' farm activities. This expenditure is being co-ordinated with the European Regional Development Fund and the European Social Fund, the aim being to take account of local economic, social and environmental issues when giving support. In other words there is a shift towards *discretionary* payments and away from automatic (compulsory) market support.

On the international front there has been growing pressure on the EC to reduce the level of agricultural support. In 1990, as part of the 'Uruguay' round of trade negotiations (see Section 21.2 and Box 21.8) the USA demanded that the EC made a 75 per cent cut in the level of support. The EC considered making a 30 per cent cut – far too little for the US negotiators.

 SUMMARY

1. Despite the fact that a free market in agricultural produce would be highly competitive, there is large-scale government intervention in agriculture throughout the world. The aims of intervention include preventing or reducing price fluctuations, encouraging greater national self-sufficiency, increasing farm incomes, encouraging farm investment, and protecting traditional rural ways of life and the rural environment generally.

2. Price fluctuations are the result of fluctuating supply combined with a price-inelastic demand. The supply fluctuations are due to fluctuations in the harvest and time lags in supply (the cobweb effect).

3. The demand for food is generally income inelastic and thus grows only slowly over time. Supply, on the other hand, has generally grown rapidly as a result of new technology and improved farm methods. This puts downward pressure on prices – a problem made worse for farmers by the price inelasticity of demand for food.

4. Government intervention can be in the form of buffer stocks, subsidies, price support, quotas and other ways of reducing supply, and structural policies.

5. If buffer stocks are used to stabilize prices, farm incomes will fluctuate *positively* with the harvest. If they are used to stabilize farm incomes, intervention must be such as to allow price to rise (fall) by the same percentage as farm output falls (rises).

6. Subsidies will increase farm incomes but will lower consumer prices to the world price level (or to the point where the market clears). Under the old UK deficiency payments system, subsidies were paid to farmers to make

up the deficiency between the expected (post-subsidy) market price and the price the government wished farmers to receive.

7. In the EC prices are kept high to both farmer and consumer. In the case of partly imported foodstuffs, this is achieved by imposing variable import levies. In cases where the EC is self-sufficient, surpluses are purchased at an intervention price.

8. The Common Agricultural Policy of the EC has been justified as providing assured supplies of food, a fair standard of living for farmers, incentives to increase productivity, stable prices, and, in the *long* term, possibly lower prices for consumers.

9. The CAP has been criticized, however, on a number of counts: it leads to food surpluses, the static costs of which are greater than those of subsidies; price support has been unequal as between foodstuffs, with a resulting misallocation of resources; it reduces the incentive to produce high-quality food; it has aggravated inequalities within agriculture; it has been inequitable between member countries; it has encouraged environmental damage; import levies and the surpluses 'dumped' on world markets have had a damaging effect on the agricultural sector of non-EC countries.

10. Reforms have included production quotas, acreage controls (set-aside), taxing output (co-responsibility levies), capping the level of FEOGA expenditure on price support (budget stabilizers) and increased expenditure on rural diversification and restructuring.

11.2 Policies towards monopolies and oligopolies

Competition, monopoly and the public interest

Most markets in the real world are imperfect, with firms having varying degrees of market power. But will this power be against the public interest? This is the question that has been addressed by successive governments in framing legislation to deal with monopolies and oligopolies.

It might be thought that market power is always 'a bad thing', certainly as far as the consumer is concerned. After all, it enables firms to make supernormal profit, thereby 'exploiting' the consumer. The greater the firm's power, the higher will prices be relative to the costs of production. Also a lack of competition removes the incentive to become more efficient.

The point is that businesspeople are primarily looking after their own interests, and will only be concerned with the consumer's interest to the extent that competition forces them to be. Reduce competition, so the argument goes, and the consumer will suffer.

But market power is not necessarily a bad thing. Firms may not fully exploit their position of power – perhaps for fear that very high profits would eventually lead to other firms overcoming entry barriers, or perhaps because they are not aggressive profit maximizers. Even if they do make large supernormal profits, they may still charge a lower price than more competitive sectors of the industry because of their economies of scale. Finally, they may use their profits for research and development and for capital investment. The consumer might then benefit from improved products at lower prices.

The general approach of UK policy in dealing with market power is therefore to look at firms on a case by case basis. It is not presumed that the mere *possession* of power is against the public interest, but rather that certain uses of that power may be. UK legislation has therefore sought to regulate firms' behaviour rather than to impose an outright ban on monopolistic market structures.

? Try to formulate a definition of 'the public interest'.

The targets of UK policy

Competition policy in the UK has targeted three main aspects of market power.

The existing power of monopolies and oligopolies: monopoly policy

This type of policy aims to prevent firms abusing their market power. Although it is referred to as 'monopoly' policy, it also applies to many larger oligopolists. The approach has been to weigh up the gains and losses to the public of individual firms' behaviour.

To illustrate this consider Figure 11.11, which compares a monopoly with the same industry under perfect competition. Assuming that the monopoly wishes to maximize profits, it will produce an output Q_1 where marginal cost (MC) equals marginal revenue (MR). Its supernormal profits are shown by the shaded rectangle. Being large, this particular monopoly is able to produce with a lower MC curve than if the industry were perfectly competitive.

On the plus side, if the MC curve is a lot lower, the industry will operate with a lower price and higher output than it would under perfect competition. The

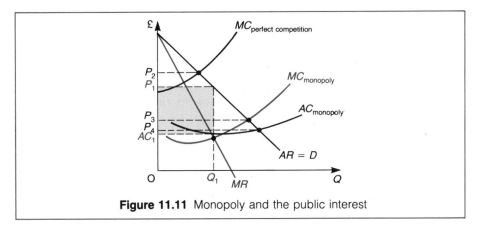

Figure 11.11 Monopoly and the public interest

monopoly price is P_1, whereas the perfectly competitive price is P_2. Also, the supernormal profits may be ploughed back into research and development: part of the reason, perhaps, why it has achieved a lower MC curve.

On the negative side, the MC curve may not be low enough to give a lower price and higher output. Even if it were, the monopoly could still have produced at an even lower price and higher output. At P_3 it would be equating MC and P, and thus producing at the Pareto optimal level. At P_4, a lower price still, it would still be making normal profits.

Thus the government has to work out, if it insisted on a reduction in price, whether research and development and investment would thereby suffer, and whether the consumer would, therefore, lose in the long run.

The growth of power through mergers and acquisitions: merger policy

The aim of merger policy is to monitor mergers and prevent those that are considered to be against the public interest. Again the approach has been one of weighing up the gains and losses to the public. On the basis of the findings, the government must then decide whether a prospective merger should be prevented or allowed to proceed.

On the plus side, the merged firms may be able to *rationalize*. Horizontal mergers particularly may allow economies of scale to be gained. Production may be able to be concentrated on fewer sites, with a more intensive utilization of capital and labour. Also a more efficient use may be made of transport fleets, with distribution in greater bulk. Savings may be made in warehousing costs too.

There may also be some scope for rationalization with vertical mergers. Various stages in the production process may be able to be concentrated on one site, with consequent savings in transport and handling costs.

Then there are cost savings that apply to all types of merger: horizontal, vertical and conglomerate. One of the two head offices may be closed down. The greater financial power may allow the merged firm to drive down the prices charged by its suppliers. The combined profits may allow larger-scale investment and R & D.

Finally, if two relatively small firms merge, their increased market power may allow them to compete more effectively against large firms.

On the negative side, mergers lead to a greater concentration of economic power, which could be used against the consumer's interests. This is particularly true of horizontal mergers, which will result in fewer firms for the consumer to choose from. But even conglomerate mergers can lead to certain anti-competitive activities. In particular, a conglomerate can use large profits gained in one market where it already has monopoly power to cross-subsidize prices in a competitive market, thereby driving out competitors and establishing itself as a monopoly or oligopolist in that market too.

What is more, rationalization may lead to redundancies. While this may be a potential Pareto gain, it is unlikely that the redundant will be fully compensated by the gainers.

In deciding how tough to be with mergers, the government must consider how this will affect firms' behaviour. It is not just actual mergers once they have taken place that will determine firms' price, output, investment, etc. It is also the *prospect* of mergers: either of an agreed merger, or of taking over another firm or of being taken over.

If the government has a liberal policy towards mergers, the competition for ownership and control of other companies may force firms to be more efficient. If the managers of a firm are afraid that it will be taken over, they will need to ensure that the firm is economically strong. Strength is not just a question of making profits at present: it is a question of being seen by shareholders as better able to make profits than an alternative ownership or control. This competition for corporate control may lead to lower costs and thereby benefit the consumer. It may, however, make firms even more keen to exploit any monopoly power they have, either in their battle for other firms, or in the battle to persuade shareholders not to vote for being taken over.

The government's policy towards this market for corporate control has been to try to ensure that mergers and the possibility of mergers encourage competition rather than reducing it.

Oligopolistic collusion: restrictive practice policy

The approach towards restrictive practices has been different. Governments have assumed that the losses to the public will usually outweigh the gains. After all, the firms are combining to exploit their joint power to make bigger profits. They could combine to try to keep out new entrants. They could agree to keep prices high and/or restrict output. They could divide up the market between them, agreeing not to 'poach' on each other's territory. For example, two or more supermarket chains could agree to open only one supermarket in each district.

The aim of government policy, therefore, has generally been to prevent collusion unless firms can prove that they are acting in the public interest – that the resulting higher profits are going to be used for investment or product development.

Banning formal cartels is easy. Preventing tacit collusion is another matter. It may be very difficult to prove that firms are making informal agreements behind closed doors.

UK legislation 1948–68: laying the foundation

1948: Monopolies and Restrictive Practices Act

This Act set up the Monopolies and Restrictive Practices Commission to investigate firms with monopoly power and submit reports to the government. Firms could be investigated if either individually or collectively they controlled one-third or more of the UK market and the Commission would consider whether the firm or firms referred to it were operating in the public interest. The 'public interest' was rather vaguely defined in the Act, but included objectives such as efficiency, a full use of resources, meeting the requirements of consumers in terms of price, quantity and quality, developing and taking advantage of new technology, and developing and expanding markets.

There were a number of shortcomings of the Commission. Not least because it was slow in dealing with individual cases and the ambiguity generated by the vague definition of the 'public interest'. Nevertheless its reports provided important conclusions.

Monopoly power itself was not necessarily a problem: it depended on how it was exercised. Restrictive practices, however, were generally against the public interest, and were found to be very widespread at the time, with firms quite blatantly agreeing to fix prices and punishing any member who broke the agreement (e.g. by 'persuading' suppliers to boycott it). The conclusions were used in justification for the next piece of legislation.

1956: Restrictive Trade Practices Act

This Act sought to ban all formal restrictive practices that could not be proved to be in the public interest. It set up a Registrar of Restrictive Trading Agreements and a Restrictive Practices Court to administer the legislation. The procedure for dealing with restrictive practices was as follows:

- All firms that had an agreement over prices, quantity, product specifications, the markets to be supplied, or any other aspect that limited competition, had to register that agreement with the Registrar.
- The firms would then be required to appear before the Restrictive Practices Court to justify the agreement (unless they were prepared to end it voluntarily).
- The onus was on firms to prove that their agreement was in the public interest. If they could not do so, the Court would terminate the agreement. In other words, firms were assumed guilty unless they could prove themselves innocent.
- To prove that the public interest was being served, the firms would have to show that their agreement passed at least one of seven 'gateways'. The gateways were that the agreement would:

  1. Protect the public against injury.
  2. Provide specific benefits to the public.
  3. Help prevent other restrictive practices.
  4. Help secure fairer terms from the firms' suppliers or purchasers.
  5. Help protect jobs.
  6. Promote exports.
  7. Support another agreement acceptable to the Court.

- There was a final hurdle for the firms. The Act specified a 'tail-piece'. This was a catch-all clause that allowed the Court to terminate the agreement if it felt on balance that the public interest was not served, even if it satisfied one or more gateways.

One of the earlier cases where the Court allowed an agreement to continue was that of the Permanent Magnets Association (PMA), a group of industrial magnet producers. The PMA had an agreement to fix minimum prices. It also had a common research laboratory and a technical committee to advise members. The PMA argued, under gateway 2, that the public gained from this common research facility, which in the long run led to better and cheaper magnets. The Court accepted these arguments and felt that the agreement also passed the tail-piece, since profits were not excessive, there were no significant entry barriers, and customers did not complain of unreasonable prices.

Such cases were unusual, however. Of the 50 or so cases that have come before the Restrictive Practices Court, only around a quarter have been permitted to continue.

On the surface, the 1956 Act seemed to have a powerful effect. Within a few years, several hundred agreements were registered. (Today around 4500 have been registered). The vast majority were voluntarily terminated, the firms realizing that they had little or no hope of winning their case before the Court.

Prohibiting open collusion, however, may simply drive it underground. Firms may continue to collude behind closed doors, or may simply avoid aggressive competition.

An additional Act, the *1968 Restrictive Practices Act* went a small way toward preventing tacit collusion by making *information agreements* registrable as a restrictive practice. An information agreement is when firms agree to keep each other informed about plans for price changes, product design, distribution policy, etc. All this did, however, was to prevent *formal* information agreements. It could not stop business-people talking to each other!

The 1968 Act also added an eighth gateway: that an agreement does not restrict competition.

1964: Resale Prices Act

Resale (or retail) price maintenance

Where the manufacturer of a product (legally) insists that the product should be sold at a specified retail price.

One form of monopolistic/oligopolistic practice is that of resale price maintenance (RPM). This is where a manufacturer or distributor can legally insist that retailers charge a set price for its products. It is a way of keeping prices high to the consumer and thereby discouraging firms from forcing down the price they pay to the manufacturer. It was particularly criticized for curtailing the development of large multiple retailers, which with their economies of scale could otherwise have charged lower prices to the consumer. Manufacturers feared the countervailing power of these retailers.

The 1956 Act had only covered *collective* RPM by two or more manufacturers. The 1964 Act also covered RPM by *individual* manufacturers or distributors. Any firm wishing to continue with RPM had to register it with the Registrar of Restrictive Practices. The firm would then have to appear before the Restrictive Practices Court and justify it under one or more of several gateways, and show that its benefit to the public outweighed its costs.

As with oligopolistic collusion, the Court was very tough. RPM was allowed to continue only in the case of books and certain medicines. (In both cases it was argued that abandoning RPM would make it unprofitable to supply such a wide range.)

1965: Monopolies and Mergers Act

One way in which colluding firms could get around the 1956 Act was to merge. This, plus the fact that the 1960s had seen a rapid growth in mergers and hence in industrial concentration, led to the passing of the 1965 Act. This created a Mergers Panel which monitored proposed mergers.

Any merger leading to the new company having more that one-third of the market (or assets of more than £5 million) could be referred to the Monopolies Commission by the Mergers Panel and held up while the investigation took place. As with monopolies, the Monopolies Commission would prepare a report on whether the merger was in the public interest. The Board of Trade (today the Secretary of State for Trade and Industry) would then decide whether to allow the merger to go ahead, and if so whether it would insist on any condition being met.

Some significant mergers were prevented: for example, that between Barclays, Lloyds and Martins banks (although the merger between Barclays and Martins was allowed to go ahead). Nevertheless only a very small proportion (less than 4 per cent) of mergers have been referred to the Monopolies Commission, and only one-third of these have been found to be against the public interest, although several were abandoned before the Commission reported.

UK legislation: the current position

The current state of legislation concerning monopolies, mergers and restrictive practices is set out in four Acts of 1973, 1976 (2) and 1980. These build on the foundations laid down in the previous Acts.

1973: Fair Trading Act

An Office of Fair Trading was created. Its Director-General (DG) took over the responsibility for referring cases to the Restrictive Practices Court. The DG is also responsible for advising the Secretary of State for Trade and Industry on the administration of monopoly and merger policy, and for monitoring cases where firms may be acting uncompetitively or against the interests of consumers. Specific details of the Act included the following:

- The scope of the 1956 Act was extended to cover restrictive practices between firms supplying commercial services (e.g. travel agents, banks, insurance companies). It was not extended, however, to cover professional services (e.g. architects, solicitors, doctors).
- The minimum market share criterion for both monopoly and merger investigations by the renamed Monopolies and Mergers Commission (MMC) was reduced from one-third to one-quarter of the UK market. Mergers could also be investigated if the companies' joint assets exceeded £15 million (raised to £30 million in 1984.)
- Nationalized industries also could now be investigated by the MMC; so too could firms controlling more than one-quarter of a local market; so too could restrictive labour practices.
- Two or more firms which jointly had more than one-quarter of the market could now be investigated by the MMC, if it was felt that they might be jointly restricting competition, even though they had no formal agreements and could not, therefore, be referred to the Restrictive Practices Court. It was hoped that this would help to control tacit collusion.
- A Consumer Protection Advisory Committee (CPAC) was established. If the DG or Secretary of State suspected that any firm's practices were adversely affecting the consumer, he could refer the case to the CPAC for investigation. The CPAC's recommendations could then be enforced by the Secretary of State.

The Act also gave a much clearer remit to the MMC. Rather than considering whether firms were operating in the 'public interest' – a vaguely defined term – firms were now to be judged in terms of their competitiveness. Is there effective competition in the industry? Do the firms promote the interests of the consumers – in terms of price, quality, variety and service? Is there sufficient competition to promote lower costs and technical progress?

1976: Restrictive Trade Practices Act

This tightened up the 1956 and 1968 Restrictive Trade Practices Acts and also the 1973 Fair Trading Act. It brought together the provisions of these Acts and extended the range of services that could be referred to the Restrictive Practices Court. Under the Act the Director General of Fair Trading can apply for an injunction to prevent the continuance of an unlawful restrictive practice. Also any consumer adversely affected can bring proceedings for damages.

1976: Resale Prices Act

This too tightened up the previous legislation by specifying more clearly what constitutes the fixing of minimum prices by manufacturers or distributors. Any complaints of such price fixing can be taken to the Office of Fair Trading (OFT), which will investigate the complaint. If necessary the DG will take proceedings against the perpetrators.

1980: Competition Act
This Act extended the 1973 Act. The aim was to promote greater competition.

- Various types of anti-competitive practice were specified in the Act. These included price discrimination, predatory pricing (selling below cost to drive competitors from the market), and vertical price squeezing (where a vertically integrated firm, which controls the supply of an input, charges competitors a high price for that input so that they cannot compete with it in selling the finished good).

   They also included policies to restrict supply: for example, tie-in sales (where a firm controlling the supply of a first product insists that its customers also buy a second product from it rather than its rivals), selective distribution (where a firm is only prepared to supply certain selected retail outlets) and rental-only contracts (where a firm is only prepared to rent equipment, e.g. a photocopier, rather than to sell it).

- The Office of Fair Trading could investigate and report on any such alleged cases of anti-competitive practice (but only where the firms controlled over one-quarter of the UK market). It would first try to get firms to comply voluntarily with its recommendations. Failing this, it would refer them to the MMC.

- The Act extended the grounds on which nationalized industries can be referred to the MMC. The aim was to improve the efficiency of these industries, and increase their accountability to consumers.

Assessment of UK policy

Policy towards restrictive practices has contrasted markedly with policy towards monopolies and mergers.

Restrictive practice policy
On the surface, restrictive practice legislation has been tough. Formal open collusion has virtually been eliminated. If this is the objective of the policy, then it has been successful. If, however, the aim is to reduce tacit as well as open collusion, the success is much less certain. If there is no *formal* agreement between firms, their actions fall outside the scope of the Restrictive Practices Court.

Nevertheless, if firms' joint actions result in any of the anti-competitive practices specified in the 1980 Act, they can be investigated by the Office of Fair Trading, and if necessary be referred to the MMC.

The question is, will their collusion be discovered? It can only be investigated once it is known about. If firms are careful, they may well be able to keep their price fixing, or other collusive actions, secret. Some cases have come to light, however. For example, one of the most widespread practices is that of collusive tendering. This is where two or more firms put in a tender for a contract at secretly agreed (high) prices. A well-known case is that of firms supplying ready-mixed concrete agreeing on prices they would tender to local authorities. But provided the firms do not tender at exactly the same price, it is very difficult to spot when such collusion is taking place. The cases that have been discovered may well be simply the tip of an iceberg.

What is more, the *dis*incentive for such collusion is very small. The worst that is likely to happen is an OFT investigation and a court injunction to prevent *further* price fixing. Only then would heavy fines be imposed if the firms continued, for then they would be in contempt of court.

Box 11.6

Cycling Restrictions
The supply of Raleigh bicycles by T. I. Raleigh Industies Ltd (1981)

The market share of Raleigh bicycles in 1979 was 46 per cent. Although still high, this represented a fall of 20 per cent in market share since 1968 (primarily due to a surge in cheaper imports).

It was not, however, Raleigh's near-monopoly position on the domestic market which led to it being referred to the Monopolies and Mergers Commission; rather it was its refusal to supply certain retailers such as Argos, Asda, Comet, Tesco and Woolworth. Between September 1979 and September 1980, from 189 requests to Raleigh for supply, 96 were refused and only 93 were accepted. Raleigh protested that its refusals to supply were based on sound arguments:

● These discount stores had no interest in the long-run development of the bicycle market.
● Such retailers would be detrimental to brand image.
● It is advantageous to limit the number of retailers in any one area, so as to maintain supplier loyalty and long-term market commitments.

The Director-General decided that Raleigh's claims were unfounded and declared that the company's actions constituted an anti-competitive practice. Once the case was passed on to the Monopolies Commission it was further declared that Raleigh's policy also succeeded in maintaining a generally higher price for its bicycles than would otherwise have been the case.

The Raleigh policy in restricting supply was therefore seen to be working against the public interest, and Raleigh was ordered to supply the discount stores.

1. Do you think there was any merit in Raleigh's arguments?
2. Did the discount stores have any real cause for complaint? After all, could they not sell other makes and undercut Raleigh's prices?

Monopoly policy

The policy towards firms with monopoly power has been much more cautious. Unlike cases before the Restrictive Practices Court where firms are presumed to be operating against the public interest unless they can prove otherwise, cases of monopoly power are treated on their own merits. It is not presumed that the mere possession of power is detrimental. The OFT and the MMC are concerned with how that power is *used*.

In the early years the public interest was vaguely defined. As a result the judgments of the MMC depended very much on the personal views of its members. The 1973 and 1980 Acts tightened up the criteria, but even now there is considerable scope for disagreement within the MMC as to whether a firm's practices are detrimental or not. There is also the problem that the MMC's recommendations are not binding. The Secretary of State can reject the MMC's findings, and has done so on a number of occasions.

Nevertheless, the Office of Fair Trading has collected a vast amount of information on the behaviour of firms. On many occasions, firms have agreed to modify their behaviour to make it more competitive. The trouble is that there has often been too little follow up to ensure that firms have stuck to the agreement – both the letter and the spirit.

In the 1980s the attentions of the OFT and the MMC shifted substantially towards the nationalized industries. Critics claimed that too little attention was now paid to the practices of private sector monopolies.

In assessing monopoly policy it is not enough to ask what has been done. It is necessary to know what *needs* to be done. Many on the political right argue that there is little need for intervention at all. Many large firms, which on the surface may seem very powerful, do face substantial competition, often from abroad. This, they argue, will usually be enough to prevent the abuse of apparent market power. Then there is the argument about contestability. If entry and exit costs are relatively low, monopolistic and oligopolistic firms will have to take account of potential competition. Even if firms do use their power to gain substantial profits, the consumer, they claim, will still benefit in the long run from improved products at a lower cost and eventually a lower price.

Generally, however, it is agreed that the more effective the competition, the more the consumer will benefit. At least this question of competition is now the prime concern of the OFT. But is the OFT pursuing the issue rigorously enough?

Critics of the UK legislation argue that certain anti-competitive *practices* ought to be made illegal and not just subject to investigation by the OFT and the MMC. This is more the sort of approach adopted by the EC (see below).

Merger policy

It is easier to stop a powerful firm being formed by merger than to break it up, or even control it, once it has been formed. The bulk of the work of the MMC in recent years, therefore, has been in investigating proposed mergers.

As with monopolies, there is no presumption that mergers are against the public interest: in fact the onus of proof has been on the MMC to demonstrate this. There are potential costs of greater market power in terms of higher prices and less choice, but also potential benefits from economies of scale, greater research and development, greater investment and greater power to compete internationally.

In the 1960s, the government actually encouraged many mergers, and even set up a body, the Industrial Reorganization Corporation, to help finance mergers that were thought to be desirable.

Over 3000 mergers have taken place since 1965, and yet only just over 100 have been referred to the MMC. Of those cases that were referred, there were several where the MMC felt that the public interest would have been seriously damaged. Most of these were stopped, either voluntarily or by the Secretary of State.

Does this mean that all of the remaining mergers were in the public interest, or does it mean that the policy has not been tough enough? In several cases the OFT accepted assurances from the firms involved and agreed not to refer them to the MMC. But in many more cases the merger simply went ahead.

Studies have shown, however, that mergers have generally *not* been in the public interest. Significant benefits from cost reduction and research have not occurred, and yet mergers have contributed to a growing degree of market concentration in the UK. The conclusion, then, would seem to be that merger policy has not been tough enough. Several commentators have argued that the burden of proof ought to be changed so that the companies would have to demonstrate the benefits to the public of the merger if it were to be allowed to proceed.[1]

The other major criticism of the policy is that it has been too arbitrary. The references to the MMC, the MMC recommendations and the decisions of the Secretary of State have frequently, it is alleged, been decided according to political criteria. Although such allegations are difficult to prove, there does seem to have been a degree of inconsistency in the various decisions.

[1] See, for example, M. Fleming and D. Swann, 'Competition policy: the pace quickens and 1992 approaches', *Royal Bank of Scotland Review*, June 1989.

Box 11.7

Freedom of the Air
The proposed merger between British Airways plc and the British Caledonian Group plc (1987)

In 1986, British Airways (BA) accounted for 60 per cent of the total carrying capacity of all UK airlines. British Caledonian (BCAL) held a further 15 per cent. The proposed merger would mean the new firm was some eleven times larger than any of its UK competitors. In the light of this situation how did BA and BCAL support their merger proposal?

They argued as follows:

● The civil aviation industry had undergone substantial changes in recent years with greater levels of competition and a general liberalization of international regulations, especially concerning routes.
● Such had been the extent of this change that, in order to survive, one of two conditions had to be met. Either the airline had to be large so as to gain economies of scale, which would allow it to cut costs and hence compete; or alternatively it would have to supply a specialized service. BCAL met neither condition.
● BA believed that the merger would, without affecting market competitiveness, strengthen its own service. This would enable it to compete not only in a future deregulated UK market, but also with other foreign airline companies.

BA claimed that there would be two substantial benefits to the consumer:

● Lower prices, as operating costs were reduced.
● As a result of an enlarged aircraft fleet, greater flexibility in flight scheduling which would be better suited to passenger requirements.

The case against the merger, presented by a wide range of organizations including other airlines, unions and airport authorities, consisted of the following arguments:

● The BA/BCAL merger would leave certain domestic routes with very little or no competition.
● The powerful market position of the merged airline would provide a large number of opportunities for anti-competitive behaviour.
● The merged airline would be in a strong position to restrict the supply of a wide range of facilities to competing airlines, such as maintenance, repairs and training.

From these various criticisms of the proposed merger it was suggested that a powerful monopoly would be established. However, the Monopolies and Mergers Commission ruled in favour of the merger. They suggested that the benefits, cost savings, international competitiveness, etc., plus various concessions BA were willing to undertake, such as opening up certain routes, would mean that the merger would not be expected to operate against the public interest.

 Which of the two sides to the argument do you find the more convincing? Why?

The merger went ahead in late 1987. As a result BA's profits were seriously eroded, undermined by the debt inherited from BCAL. Some attempts were made at rationalization. But cost cutting and route restrictions led to many BCAL staff, especially pilots, having to occupy inferior positions (such as co-pilot jobs).

EC legislation

EC legislation is contained in Articles 85 and 86 of the Treaty of Rome, and, since 1990, in new regulations governing mergers.

Article 85 is concerned with restrictive practices and Article 86 with monopolies and mergers. The Articles are largely confined to firms trading between EC members and thus do not cover monopolies or oligopolies operating solely within a member country. The policy is implemented by the European Commission. If any firm appears to be breaking the provisions of either of the Articles, the Commission can refer it to the European Court of Justice.

Article 85 covers *agreements* between firms, *joint decisions*, and concerted *practices* which prevent, restrict or distort competition. It is so worded as to include all types of oligopolistic collusion. On the surface, Article 85 appears to be similar to UK restrictive practice legislation: the presumption in both cases is that collusion is against the public interest; both allow for exemptions in specific cases.

But in other respects they are quite different. The UK legislation is designed to prevent oligopolistic *structures*. The presumption here is that all such agreements are undesirable, irrespective of the behaviour of the parties to the agreement. The problem with the UK approach is that it does not prevent tacit collusion no matter how anti-competitive this may be. Article 85, by contrast, focuses on collusive *behaviour*. No matter what form collusion takes, if the European Commission finds that firms are committing anti-competitive *practices* they will be banned from doing so and possibly fined, although firms do have the right of appeal to the European Court of Justice. Practices considered anti-competitive include firms jointly fixing prices, limiting output, charging discriminatory prices and sharing out markets between them.

The other major difference between UK restrictive practice legislation and Article 85 is that there is little power of enforcement in the UK. If firms do not register agreements and are subsequently found to be operating a restrictive practice, they will merely be told to stop it. Only if they continue will they be fined, and even then the fines are not very heavy. By contrast, the European Commission has much greater powers to ban collusive behaviour.

Article 86 relates to the abuse of monopoly power and has also been extended to cover mergers. As with Article 85, it is the *behaviour* of firms that is the target of the legislation: for example, charging unfair prices or restricting output to the disadvantage of consumers. As with Article 85, such practices can be banned. In contrast to the UK legislation, a firm does not have to have some specified minimum market share before Article 86 can be invoked. This is sensible given the difficulties of identifying the boundaries of a market, either in terms of geography or in terms of type of product.

The 1990 merger control measures tightened up the legislation in Article 86. Any proposed merger with a combined *worldwide* turnover exceeding ECU 5 billion (approximately £3.5 billion) and where the aggregate EC turnover of at least two of the companies exceeds ECU 250 million must be notified to the European Commission within one week of the announcement of a merger (or its completion, whichever is the earlier). At this point the merger will be automatically suspended for three weeks, although this can be waived by the Commission under certain circumstances. Within one month of the notification the Commission, on the basis of preliminary investigations, must decide whether to conduct a formal investigation or to let the merger proceed. (Even if the Commission does not object to the merger, a member state can still intervene to prevent it, if the merger threatens competition in a distinct market within that country.)

If the Commission does institute a formal investigation, it must establish whether the merger violates Article 86 by impeding effective competition within the EC. At the end of the investigation, which must be completed within four months, the Commission can decide to block the merger, permit it, or permit it subject to various conditions to safeguard competition.

Although it would appear that the EC legislation is tougher than that in the UK, it is more limited in scope (being confined to trade between member countries) and few cases have been examined, albeit with the 1990 measures it is hoped to examine some 50 mergers per year. Nevertheless it is seen by many to be the model for future UK anti-monopoly/oligopoly legislation.

Proposals for reform

Towards the end of the 1980s, after the publication of two Department of Trade and Industry reports,[2] the government began a review of restrictive practice and merger policy.

The recommendations on restrictive practices were the most sweeping. The old approach, followed since 1956, should be abandoned in favour of the approach contained in Article 85. In other words, the control of collusion should focus not on the *form* of the agreement, but on the *effects* of the collusion. This means that agreements would no longer be registrable, but that certain *activities* (such as price fixing, collusive tendering and sharing out the market) would be banned. The OFT or some other body would be given increased powers to investigate firms' behaviour and to impose penalties, which would be tougher than before. There would still, as with Article 85, be the possibility of exemptions, but only if certain criteria could all be satisfied. It is proposed, however, to make these criteria simpler and fewer than the gateways in the 1956 and 1968 Acts.

The proposals for mergers were relatively minor and were merely concerned with making merger investigations quicker and more efficient. The government did not feel that it was necessary to make the legislation tougher. Instead it believed that the disciplines contained in the market for corporate control (i.e. the fear of being taken over) are generally a better means than government regulation of ensuring that firms operate in the public interest.

  1. Does this imply that the 'public' interest is the same as the 'shareholders'' interests?
2. What imperfections are there in the market for corporate control?

There have been no proposals for changing the approach to monopolies (and other dominant firms). The government believed that in most cases there was still adequate competition, either existing or potential (in contestable markets).

▲ SUMMARY

1. The UK approach to monopolies, mergers and restrictive practices has recognized that market power can bring both costs and benefits to the consumer. The policy on restrictive practices has been tougher than that on monopolies and mergers.

2. Monopolies and other dominant firms (with more than one-quarter of the market) can be referred to the Monopolies and Mergers Commission by the Secretary of State for Trade and Industry. The MMC prepares a report and the government decides on what action, if any, to take. The same procedure applies to mergers. Mergers can be held up while the investigation takes place. The criterion for judging whether a monopoly or merger is in the public interest has become largely that of whether or not it damages competition.

3. Restrictive practices must be registered with the Office of Fair Trading. If firms want to continue their agreement, it will be referred to the Restrictive Practices Court. The

onus is on firms to prove that their agreement is in the public interest. To do so they must 'pass through' (satisfy) at least one of eight gateways and demonstrate to the satisfaction of the Court that the public interest on balance is served by the agreement.

4. European Community legislation applies to firms trading between EC countries. Article 85 applies to restrictive practices. Article 86 applies to monopolies and dominant firms, but can also be used against mergers. These Articles focus on specific practices that are against the public interest. They can be banned unless exemption can be claimed.

5. Government proposals put forward at the end of the 1980s recommended adopting an approach to restrictive practices like that of Article 85. Instead of focusing on the agreements themselves, the approach would be to ban certain activities. The government, however, proposed no major changes to monopoly and merger legislation.

---

[2] *Review of Restrictive Trade Practices Policy*, Cm 331 (HMSO, 1988);
Mergers Policy: A DTI paper on the policy and procedures of merger control (HMSO, 1988).

11.3 Nationalization versus privatization

One solution to market failure, advocated by the political left, is nationalization. If industries are not being run in the public interest by the private sector, then bring them into public ownership. This way, so the argument goes, the market failures can be corrected. Problems of monopoly power, externalities, inequality, etc. can be dealt with directly if these industries are run with the public interest at heart rather than private gain.

Clause 4 of the Labour Party constitution advocates 'the common ownership of the means of production, distribution and exchange'. Although this has been official Labour Party policy for over 70 years, there has been considerable debate within the party over its interpretation. Just how much of industry should be under public ownership is not agreed.

The political right is against nationalization. The failures of the market (which are often relatively small) are best dealt with by encouraging more competition, and by generally improving the market. Public ownership, they argue, far from serving the public interest, actually creates more problems than it solves. Nationalized industries, they claim, are bureaucratic, inefficient, unresponsive to consumer wishes and often a burden on the taxpayer.

The Thatcher government thus engaged in an extensive programme of 'privatization', especially after its second election victory in 1983. Many of the nationalized industries have been returned to the private sector, with shares in many of these industries being offered for sale to the public.

The nationalized industries

Nationalized industries

State-owned industries that produce goods or services that are sold in the market.

Public corporations

State-owned organizations set up by statute and technically free to manage their own affairs within broad ministerial or parliamentary guidelines. They include nationalized industries and other organizations such as the BBC.

Nationalized industries are public corporations owned by the state, and which produce goods or services that are sold in the market. They include industries such as coal, railways and the Post Office.

Officially they are separate from the government. Although their boards of directors are appointed by the appropriate government minister, the boards are theoretically independent from government control. In practice, however, there has frequently been considerable government interference in their running.

Not all public corporations are classed as nationalized industries. For example, the BBC and the Bank of England are not, as they are not primarily concerned with producing goods or services directly for sale.

Nationalized firms are generally monopolies (e.g. railways and coal): these are therefore truly nationalized *industries*. Other firms may be publicly owned (or partly so) but still compete with other private-sector firms. Thus Rolls-Royce and British Airways before they were privatized were nationalized *firms*, but not nationalized *industries*. Even where a whole industry is nationalized it may still compete with the private sector or with other nationalized industries. Thus British Coal has to compete with oil, gas and electricity in many markets.

The bulk of nationalization took place during the Labour government of 1945–51. The industries nationalized during this period were coal, railways, gas and steel. Table 11.5 shows the dates when the various nationalizations took place.

 The National Health Service and state education are not counted as nationalized industries. Do you think that they should be?

Table 11.5 The major nationalized industries

Industry	First nationalized	Subsequent reorganizations
Electricity	1926	1926 Central Electricity Board 1948 Area Electricity Boards added 1958 Reorganized into Electricity Council, Central Electricity Generating Board (CEGB) and Area Electricity Boards 1990–1 Privatized
Coal	1947	1947 National Coal Board (now called British Coal)
Gas	1949	1949 Gas Council and Area Boards 1973 Re-established as British Gas Corporation (later called British Gas) 1986 Privatized
Water	1972	1973 Regional Water Authorities (10) took over from local government 1989 Privatized as 10 separate companies
Oil	1976	1976 British National Oil Corporation (BNOC) (part of industry only) 1982 Privatized as Britoil
Posts and telecommunications	1961	Previously a government department 1981 Split into the Post Office and British Telecom (BT) 1984 BT privatized
Railways, etc.	1948	1948 British Transport Commission 1963 Split into British Railways, London Transport (and also British Transport Docks Board, British Waterways Board, Transport Holding Company)
Buses	1969	1969 National Bus Company 1986 Privatized
Road haulage	1947	1953 Privatized Re-nationalized as National Freight Corporation 1982 Privatized (management and worker buyout)
Car manufacturing	1976	1976 British Leyland 1984 Jaguar privatized 1988 Rover Group privatized
Shipbuilding	1977	1977 British Shipbuilders 1985–6 Privatized
Aero engines	1971	1971 Rolls-Royce 1987 Privatized
Airways	1940	1940 British Overseas Airways Corporation (non-European) 1946 British European Airways (European) 1974 BOAC and BEA combined to form British Airways 1987 Privatized
Airports	1966	1966 British Airports Authority 1987 Privatized
Aerospace	1977	1977 British Aerospace (part of industry only) 1981 Privatized
Steel	1951	1951 Iron and Steel Corporation 1953 Privatized 1967 Re-nationalized as British Steel Corporation 1988 Privatized
Shipbuilding	1977	1977 British Shipbuilders 1985–6 Privatized

Forms of privatization

Privatization can take different forms:

- The introduction of private contractors to supply goods and services to parts of the public sector: e.g. private arms factories selling to the Ministry of Defence; private agencies supplying cleaners to hospitals or schools; and so on.

- The introduction into the public sector of firms selling directly to the public: e.g. private caterers on trains or in public-sector canteens.
- Selling various public-sector assets: e.g. the sale of council houses.
- Selling part or all of the public sector's shareholdings in otherwise private companies: e.g. the sale of BP shares.
- Selling a state-owned corporation by the sale of shares to the public (e.g. British Gas) or by selling it to another firm (e.g. the Rover Group to British Aerospace) or by selling it to the managers or workers in the firm (e.g. the National Freight Corporation).

Although all five forms of privatization have been pursued since 1979, we will concentrate on the last of these forms – the de-nationalizing of nationalized industries/firms.

History of privatization

Table 11.6 illustrates which industries have been privatized and when.

When it came to power in 1979, the Conservative government gave a low priority to privatization, with the one exception of council house sales. The firms that were privatized in the first few years were not the giant state monopolies. Rather they were companies that were already competing in the market, and where a change in ownership would make a relatively small difference to their operation. Some of the firms had only been partly owned by the government anyway – firms such as ICL, Ferranti and British Sugar.

After a few years, however, the government began to see the political advantages in privatization:

- It was proving increasingly popular with the electorate, as more and more people became first-time share owners. There was often a substantial capital gain to be made as the share prices quickly rose after flotation.
- The revenues earned for the government were a convenient way of financing tax cuts.
- It was seen as the 'flagship' in the whole policy of 'rolling back the frontiers of the state'. It was a means of helping the government re-establish the 'enterprise culture' and promote the advantages of capitalism.

The second and third terms of office of the government (1983–87 and 1987–   ) thus saw a much more ambitious programme of privatization. The major state monopolies such as telecommunications, gas, water, steel and electricity were now to be sold. These companies are giants compared with earlier privatizations, as Table 11.6 shows. With the possible exception of the Post Office, the government seemed to be keen to sell the remainder of the nationalized industries too, including British Rail and British Coal, provided they could first be made sufficiently profitable to attract purchasers.

The debate for and against privatization has been heated. Strong feelings are aroused on both sides, and ever since the first privatizations of the early 1980s the issue has rarely been out of the public's attention.

In the late 1940s the debate was equally heated, but then it was not about privatization; it was about nationalization. The newly elected Labour government saw nationalization as the best way of rebuilding the economy after the war in a way that was consistent with its vision of 'the common ownership of the means of production, distribution and exchange'.

We turn now to look at the arguments on both sides. We start by examining the arguments for public ownership.

Table 11.6 UK privatization: 1979–

Year	Company	Business	Proceeds (£m)
1979	British Petroleum (1st part)[1]	Oil	276
	ICL[1]	Computers	37
1980	Fairey	Construction	22
	Ferranti[1][2]	Hi-tech industrial	55
	Motorway service stations (Dept of Transport)[2]	Motorway services	28
1981	British Aerospace (1st part)	Aerospace	43
	British Petroleum (2nd part)	Oil	200
	British Sugar Corporation[1]	Sugar refining	44
	Cable and Wireless (1st part)	Telecommunications systems	182
1982	Amersham International	Radio-chemicals	64
	National Freight Corporation[3]	Road haulage	7
	Britoil (1st part)	Oil	627
1983	Associated British Ports (1st part)[1][2]	Seaports	−34
	International Aeradio[2]	Aviation communications	60
	British Rail Hotels[2]	Hotels	51
	British Petroleum (3rd part)[1]	Oil	543
	Cable and Wireless (2nd part)	Telecommunications systems	263
1984	British Gas (onshore)[2]	Oil	82
	Associated British Ports (2nd part)[1][2]	Seaports	48
	Enterprise Oil	Oil	380
	Sealink[2]	Ferries	66
	Jaguar	Cars	297
	British Telecom (govt. retains 49.8% of shares)	Telecommunications	3916
	Inmos[2]	Computer systems	95
1985	British Aerospace (2nd part)	Aerospace	350
	British Shipbuilders (1st part)[2][3]	Various shipyards	220
	Britoil (2nd part)	Oil	449
	Cable and Wireless (3rd part)	Telecommunications systems	900
1986	British Shipbuilders (2nd part)[3]	Various shipyards	67
	Royal Ordance (1st part)[2]	Weapons manufacture	11
	National Bus Company	Bus and coach carriers	260
	BA Helicopters[2]	Helicopter carriers	135
	British Gas	Gas	5600
1987	Unipart[3]	Car parts	30
	Leyland Bus[3]	Bus manufacture	4
	British Airways	Airline	900
	Royal Ordance (2nd part)[2]	Weapons manufacture	190
	British Rail Doncaster Wagon Works[3]	Rolling stock manufacture	7
	Rolls-Royce	Aero engines	1100
	British Airports Authority (BAA)	Airports	600
	British Petroleum (4th part)[1]	Oil	7200
1988	British Steel	Steel	2400
	Rover Group (sold to British Aerospace)[2]	Car manufacture	−435
1989	Water companies (10)	Water supply and sewage treatment	5240
1990	Electricity distributors (12)	Area supply of electricity	5200
1991	National Power, PowerGen	Electricity generation	

[1] In these cases the companies were only partly government owned in the first place.
[2] These were private sales to other companies.
[3] These were management and/or worker buyouts.

Sources: *The Economist*, 23 February 1985; *Financial Times*, 16 September 1987; *Observer*, 25 October 1987; *Financial Statistics* (CSO); various other newspaper articles.

Arguments for public ownership: ideological

There are two main types of argument in favour of public ownership. The first is *ideological*.

Many on the political left argue that it is morally desirable to have the means of production in public ownership. Such a system, they argue, is socially preferable to one based on private ownership. Private ownership not only is highly unequal, but also involves the division of society into classes: a class of workers who only have their own labour to earn them money and who receive a wage below their marginal productivity; and a class of capitalists whose income is largely derived not from their own toil, but from the capital they are lucky enough to own – capital that is often inherited. Such a social division is seen as unjust. Nationalization is one means of rectifying that injustice.

The political right, not surprisingly, challenges these arguments. Their counter-argument is that it is morally desirable for people to be free to own property and to pass it on to their children.

There is no way an economist can make a fundamental moral judgement as to the desirability of capitalism and socialism. All we can do is to note that these ideological questions often play a major role in the nationalization/privatization debate.

Those in the political centre take a more pragmatic view. They would rather judge individual nationalized industries on their own merits, in each case attempting to assess whether the benefits outweigh the costs or vice versa.

Arguments for public ownership: market failure

The other type of argument for public ownership is based on *market failure*. If the market fails to achieve various objectives, such as efficiency, growth and equality, then nationalization may be a suitable means of correcting these failures.

In each case, however, there are likely to be means *other* than nationalization for correcting the market failures: means such as taxes and subsidies, regulation, or the direct encouragement of competition. Even if nationalization is superior to the free market, it does not follow that nationalization is necessarily the *best* form of intervention.

Given this reservation, what are the arguments based on market failure?

Natural monopoly
Some industries have such great economies of scale that there is only room for one firm in the industry.

The cost of providing a national electricity grid or a national gas pipe network is a relatively high proportion of the total cost of providing electricity or gas. The more intensively these grids are used, however, the lower their cost will become per unit of fuel supplied. Similarly with railways: the relatively high costs of providing track and signalling, etc. will become smaller per passenger, the more passengers use the railway.

In the short run, these costs are fixed costs. Average fixed costs must necessarily decline as more is produced: overheads are being spread over a greater output.

In the long run, when new lines can be built (electricity, gas, railway), these costs become variable costs. It is still likely, however, that they will decline per unit of output, the higher the output becomes. A pylon carrying ten lines does not cost five times as much as a pylon carrying two. A double-track railway does not cost twice as much to build and service as a single-track railway, and it can carry more than twice as many passengers. What this means is that long-run average costs fall as more is produced. This is illustrated in Figure 11.12.

Assume initially that the firm just seeks to cover long-run average costs ($P = LRAC$), and that, therefore, if it is in the private sector it does not exploit its monopoly power to earn supernormal profits. Q_1 will be sold at a price P_1 and at a cost of $LRAC_1$.

Now assume that the industry is shared between two equal-sized producers.

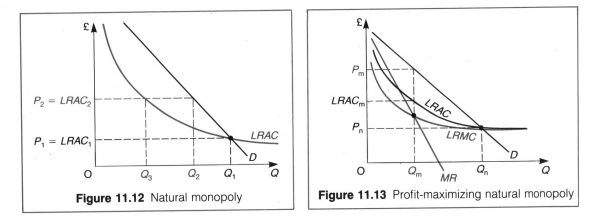

Figure 11.12 Natural monopoly

Figure 11.13 Profit-maximizing natural monopoly

Neither would be able to achieve the full economies of scale. There would be much duplication of resources. There might even be two sets of pipes or cables under each street and two sets of railway lines between each pair of towns!

The average cost of each supplier would be considerably higher than that of a single supplier. In Figure 11.12, continuing with the assumption that a price is charged that just covers *LRAC*, the market price will have to rise to P_2, with total consumption of Q_2. This is divided equally between the two suppliers, who each supply Q_3 at a cost of $LRAC_2$ (= P_2).

It is potentially more efficient, therefore, to have a single monopoly supplier whenever there is a natural monopoly. It avoids wasteful duplication.

The problem is that the monopoly producer in a free market could use its power to drive up prices. The long-run profit-maximizing position is illustrated in Figure 11.13. The monopolist produces Q_m at a price of P_m and at a cost of $LRAC_m$. There is a misallocation of resources.

Nationalization can provide an answer to the problem. The industry can be run as a monopoly and thus achieve the full economies of scale. And yet it can choose a price where it just covers costs (including normal profits), and thus makes no more profit than a highly competitive industry. In Figure 11.13, it would produce Q_n at a price of P_n.

It may, however, be possible to achieve the same result without nationalization. A private monopoly supplier could be ordered by the government or some regulatory agency to charge a price that just earns normal profits (or 'reasonable' profits, however defined). The USA has preferred this approach to that of nationalization. Many of the 'utilities' (electricity, gas, water) are privately owned but state regulated.

High capital costs and barriers to entry
A related problem is that of industries with high capital costs. Once established, a monopoly will have an effective barrier to the entry of competitors if it is very capital intensive. Potential entrants may be unable to raise sufficient capital to break into the market. Even if they can, they may be unwilling to take the risks of making such a vast capital investment, only to find that they cannot capture sufficient market share from the established firm. The market is not contestable, since the entry and exit costs are too high. Such industries are therefore likely to remain monopolies.

High capital costs and a lack of investment
Certain industries may require investment on such a large scale that they would find it difficult to raise the necessary capital from financial markets. This was one of the

main arguments used to support the re-nationalization of the steel industry in 1967 (it had been privatized in 1953).

The problem is made worse if large amounts of money are required for research and development, or if the investment is risky.

Planning and the co-ordination of industry

Road use and road construction affect the demand for railways and vice versa. Decisions in the coal, electricity, gas and oil industries (and to a large extent in the steel industry) all affect each other. Rational decision making, it is argued, requires co-ordination of these decisions. Each industry cannot make sensible decisions without knowing what the others are doing.

Nationalization of these industries should make their decisions easier to co-ordinate in the public interest. It could help the sensible planning of the nation's infrastructure. If these industries were under private enterprise, however, either there would be little co-ordination, or alternatively co-ordination might degenerate into oligopolistic collusion, with the consumer losing out.

Externalities

Various industries may create substantial external benefits and yet may be privately unprofitable. A railway or an underground line, for example, may considerably ease congestion on the roads, thus benefiting road as well as rail users. If nationalized, these industries could be run at a loss and subsidized by the taxpayer – perhaps by an extra tax on petrol.

Other industries may cause substantial external costs. Nuclear power stations may produce nuclear waste that is costly to dispose of safely and/or provides hazards for future generations. Coal-fired power stations may pollute the atmosphere and cause acid rain. If the industry were privately owned, these questions of pollution and safety might be ignored or underplayed. Even with government regulation the firms might attempt to get round the regulations.

If these various industries were nationalized, their statutory objectives could, it is argued, include taking account of these externalities.

'Lame ducks'

Another argument where externalities are relevant is the 'lame duck' argument. If a major firm is about to go bankrupt, then nationalization may be a means of rescuing it. Jobs will be saved, not only in the firm itself, but also in other firms servicing it and in the local community. Thus the nationalization provides benefits outside the firm itself.

What is more, nationalization of these firms may allow substantial investment to take place, which will eventually return them to solvency. At that stage they could then be privatized, if the government of the day so chose. Examples of the nationalization of ailing firms/industries are Rolls-Royce in 1971, BL in 1976 and British Shipbuilders in 1977.

Fair provision of services

It costs the Post Office much more to deliver a letter to a remote rural area than to a city. If it were run as a profit-maximizing firm, many rural deliveries would be withdrawn or charged at much higher prices. For reasons of equity it is argued that these should continue to be 'cross-subsidized' by the more profitable parts of the service. Similarly, it can be argued that rural bus services or railway lines should be kept operating at cross-subsidized prices. It is also argued that certain needy people should be charged lower prices (e.g. pensioners).

All this is easier to achieve, it is argued, under nationalization.

Industrial relations

The early advocates of nationalization in the 1930s and 1940s hoped that it would improve industrial relations. The old class antagonisms between workers and owners would be broken down. In theory this is possible, provided there is genuine industrial democracy in the nationalized industries, with workers participating in decision making, or at least being fully informed and consulted.

In practice the divide between workers and management in the nationalized industries has often been as deep as in the private sector. The bitter dispute between the management of British Coal and the NUM in 1985–6 over pit closures illustrates the possible extent of such divisions.

Management of the economy

Governments may wish to have certain key industries under nationalization in order to make it easier for them to manage the economy.

- During the 1970s, the government on a number of occasions attempted to restrain wages in the nationalized industries as a way of controlling inflation. Similarly, they attempted to keep nationalized industry price increases small.
- In the 1980s, the Thatcher government deliberately raised prices in the nationalized industries above the rate of inflation as a way of increasing their profitability and earning more money for the Treasury. This helped the government to finance tax cuts.
- Nationalized industry investment could be directed to regions of high unemployment.

Strategic

If certain industries such as aerospace and nuclear power were nationalized, it might be easier for the government to ensure that they were operated in the defence interests of the country.

> **?** This is a long list of arguments in favour of nationalization. Yet the critics of nationalization would claim that not one of these arguments is conclusive. All of the ten problem areas could be dealt with by other means. Try going through each of the arguments and think of other ways of dealing with the problems. Do you think that nationalization is the best way of tackling each one? If so, why? If not, why not?

* Short-run pricing and output decisions under public ownership

Assuming that these industries are run 'in the public interest', how much should they produce, and at what price?

The answer to this question depends on what problems need to be taken into account. Take three cases. In the first, the nationalized industry has monopoly power (perhaps it is a natural monopoly), but there are no other problems. In the second case there are also externalities to be considered, and in the third, questions of fairness too.

The nationalized industry has monopoly power

The 'first-best' situation: $P = MC$. Assume that all other firms in the economy are operating under perfect competition, and thus producing where $P = MC$. This is the imaginary 'first-best' situation. If this were so, the nationalized industry should follow the same pricing rule: $P = MC$. In Figure 11.14 this gives a price of P_n and an output of Q_n. But why should the nationalized industry do this?

Figure 11.14 Marginal cost pricing

If price (given by the demand curve) measures the marginal social benefit, and if the marginal social cost is given by the MC curve, then net social gain from this industry is the area between these two curves. In Figure 11.14 this area is maximized with production at point a, giving an area abc. Pareto optimality is achieved.

If the industry had instead been run as a profit-maximizing monopoly, it would have produced only Q_m at a price P_m: where $MC = MR$. The social gain from production would have been only $bcde$: a *deadweight welfare loss* of the shaded area aed.

The theory of the 'second best': $P = MC + X$. Now let us drop the assumption that the rest of the economy operates under perfect competition. The first-best situation now no longer holds. If other industries on average are charging a price, say, 10 per cent above MC, then what should the nationalized industry do? The theory of the second best suggests that perhaps it too should charge a price 10 per cent above MC. At least that way it will not cause a diversion of consumption away from relatively low-cost industries (at the margin) to a relatively high-cost one. For example, if oil is charged at 10 per cent above MC, then perhaps coal should be too. That way price differences between the two fuels will reflect differences in their costs of supply.

The second-best rule is therefore to set $P = MC + X$, where X in this case is 10 per cent.

The nationalized industry produces externalities

If the nationalized industry produces external benefits (e.g. railways reducing traffic congestion on the roads), then marginal social cost is less than marginal private cost: $MSC < MC$. If it produces external costs (e.g. power stations producing acid rain), then marginal social cost is greater than marginal private cost: $MSC > MC$.

In such cases the rule for Pareto optimality can be simply amended. In the first-best situation, the nationalized industry should produce where $P = MSC$ (not MC). The second-best solution is to produce where $P = MSC + X$ (where X is the average of other industries' price above their MSC).

The difficulty of following these rules in practice is to identify and measure the externalities: not an easy task! Some intelligent 'guesstimates' may have to be made. (See section 10.4.)

The nationalized industry involves questions of fairness

If the government wishes to charge a price below MC because it wishes to help certain groups (e.g. pensioners, children, rural dwellers, those below certain incomes), then what price should it charge?

There is no simple answer to this question, because it depends on how much help the government wishes to give. In practice the industry will probably adopt one or other of two simple rules. Either the same price will be charged as elsewhere, despite higher costs (this applies in the case of rural postal services); or a simple formula will be used (e.g. half price for pensioners and children). These are often the only practical solutions given the impossibility of identifying the specific needs of individual consumers.

Two further questions arise:

- Should the lower price be subsidized by the *government* from general taxation, or by *other users* of the service (i.e. by a cross-subsidy)? Justice would suggest that if these customers require support it should come from the community as a whole – the taxpayer – and not just other users of the service: after all, what have they got to do with the people who require help?

  In the case of railways, a subsidy is paid by the government to support various loss-making lines. In the case of postal services, profitable parts of the service cross-subsidize the unprofitable parts.

- If people require help, should they not be given *general* tax relief or benefits, rather than specifically subsidized services?

? Try thinking through the arguments here yourself.

*Long-run pricing, output and investment decisions under public ownership

In the short run certain factors of production are fixed in supply. For example, electricity output can be increased by using *existing* power stations more fully, but the *number* of power stations is fixed. There will thus be a limit to the amount of electricity that can be generated in the short run. As that limit is approached, the marginal cost of electricity is likely to rise rapidly. For example, oil-fired power stations, which are more costly to operate, will have to be brought on line.

In the long run all factors are variable. New power stations can be built. The *long*-run marginal costs, therefore, will probably not rise as more is produced. In fact they may even fall due to economies of scale.

Long-run marginal costs, however, unlike short-run marginal costs, will include the extra capital costs of increasing output. The long-run marginal cost of electricity will thus be all the extra costs of producing one more unit: namely, the extra operating costs (fuel, labour, etc.) *plus* the extra capital costs (power stations, pylons, etc.).

How are these marginal capital costs, say of a power station, to be calculated? The simplest way is to assume that a loan was taken out to build the power station. Assume that the power station produces 100 million kilowatts of electricity per year and that the interest payments on the loan are £1 million per year. The marginal capital cost of 1 kilowatt is therefore 1p (i.e. £1 million/100 million).

The rule for long-run pricing and output decisions is simple. The industry should produce where price equals *long-run* marginal social cost (*LMSC*). This is illustrated in Figure 11.15.

In the short run, optimum price and output are P_S and Q_S: where P = (short-run) *MSC*. This might mean that production is at quite a high cost: existing capital equipment is being stretched and diminishing returns have become serious.

In the long run, then, it will be desirable to increase capacity if $LMSC < MSC$. Optimum long-run price and output are thus at P_L and Q_L: where $P = LMSC$.

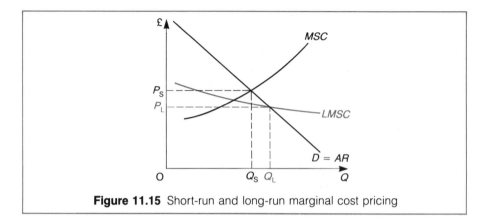

Figure 11.15 Short-run and long-run marginal cost pricing

This is the rule for the first-best situation. In the second-best situation, the industry should produce where $P = LMSC + X$ (where X is the average of other industries' price above their $LMSC$).

*Problems with marginal cost pricing

There are a number of difficulties in using marginal cost pricing.

Decreasing LMSC

If the long-run marginal social cost is falling, it will be below the long-run *average* social cost. An example would be where a new power station generates cheaper electricity than the average. If price is set equal to $LMSC$, it will be below $LASC$. The industry will thus make a loss. This is illustrated in Figure 11.16. The loss is shown by the shaded area. If this loss is not covered, the nationalized industry will not be able to afford to replace old capital. (Note: it is assumed in this case that there are no externalities.)

Who, then, will pay for the loss? Presumably the taxpayer. In the first-best world this would lead to a misallocation of resources. A subsidy would be being provided to the nationalized industry, thereby giving it an unfair advantage over other (competing) industries. In practice, however, in the second-best world, there is not so much of a problem. The rule '$P = LMSC + X$' will prevent a loss being made, provided X is sufficient to close the gap between $LMSC$ and $LASC$.

Figure 11.16 Loss when $LMSC < LASC$

*Box 11.8

Peak Load Pricing

Peak load pricing is where people using a service at a busy or 'peak' time pay more, whereas off-peak consumers are charged at a lower rate. Examples would be higher rush hour tolls on bridges, higher-priced rush-hour trains, lower-priced off-peak electricity and lower-priced off-peak telephone call charges. In each of these cases marginal cost is much lower at off-peak times when there is spare capacity, and much higher at peak times. The higher peak costs could be due to a number of factors:

● Diminishing returns, and hence higher *short*-run *MC*.
● Higher-priced inputs being used: for example, high-priced fuels (e.g. oil) for generating extra electricity at peak times.
● The whole of the capital costs of the extra capacity required for the peak user being attributable to the peak user. After all, this capital would not be required if demand was always at the off-peak level.
● Externalities. Rush-hour traffic causes congestion and thus imposes external costs on other travellers. The

more the traffic, the higher the marginal *social* cost. By charging people a higher price at peak times, those people who are less concerned about when they consume the product will switch to a lower-priced off-peak time. Telephone calls home will be made in the evening; people will switch to night-storage heating.

? 1. British Telecom is now a private company. Does it charge a lower off-peak rate in order to achieve an optimal allocation of the nation's resources? Would it make any difference to peak load pricing whether the supplier was a profit-maximizing private monopolist or a nationalized industry using a marginal cost pricing rule?
2. Can you think of any reasons why it would not be a good idea to charge (a) much higher rush-hour bridge tolls; (b) higher underground fares in the rush hour; (c) higher postage rates at Christmas?

Difficulty in estimating LMSC

To calculate *LMSC* it must be known *in advance* how much it will cost to make a new investment. Estimates of such costs, however, are often hopelessly optimistic. For example, estimates of the cost of building and operating nuclear power stations have been far lower than the costs eventually turned out to be. The reasons are as follows:

● Construction may take longer than planned.
● There may be unforeseen expenditures.
● The cost of labour and construction materials may rise more than had been anticipated.

When there are several alternative ways of producing a product, the problem is made worse. Which methods of production do you assume will be used? Each one may involve a different marginal cost.

A final problem is that *LMSC* includes externalities; but externalities are very difficult to quantify.

Difficulty in estimating demand

Using a $P = LMSC$ rule involves producing where *LMSC* intersects with the demand curve. Demand, however, can fluctuate and is often very difficult to forecast. For example, just how much electricity will the UK need in ten years' time? An answer to this question is crucial when deciding whether to build a new power station. The answer, though, is uncertain. It depends not only on the total demand for fuel, which in turn will depend on the rate of growth of the economy, a very difficult thing to predict, but also on the relative prices of oil, coal and gas, also very difficult to predict.

Prices may be market determined

Where the nationalized industry faces competition from other industries (e.g. coal from oil, railways from buses, the Royal Mail from private parcel carriers), prices may be largely outside the industry's control. It may be forced to set a price that matches its competitors'.

Marginal cost varies at different times and in different parts of the industry

The marginal cost of an extra passenger on a half-empty train is virtually zero. At peak times, however, trains are full and thus extra trains would have to be put on to accommodate extra passengers. The marginal cost would thus be quite high.

Charging a single price for all people at all times and in all places will not, therefore, be allocatively efficient. The alternative is for price to vary with marginal cost. In theory, an efficient allocation of resources would be achieved if everyone paid a price equal to the marginal cost that they individually imposed. In practice, of course, this is quite impossible. You cannot have everyone paying a different price.

Nevertheless, a movement in this direction can be made by having more than one price. An example of this is peak load pricing: this is examined in Box 11.8.

Peak load pricing

Where a higher price is charged on a good or service at times of higher demand in order to reflect the higher marginal cost of production.

Assessing the performance of nationalized industries

One of the major arguments for privatization is the relatively poor performance of the nationalized industries. Assessing this performance, however, is fraught with difficulties.

A good example is when *profit* is used as a yardstick. Nationalized industries are often criticized for having had a poor profit record. But using profits as a means of assessment has very little validity for the following reasons:

● Many industries or firms were nationalized *because* they were having difficulty making profits. To say, therefore, that such industries have not been profitable under nationalization is hardly a fair criticism.
● Loss-making parts of the nationalized industries are sometimes kept operating for *social* reasons. This will reduce the profitability of the industry as a whole.
● If a first-best marginal cost pricing rule, or a break-even rule, is followed, the industry would be expected to make lower profits than other industries.
● The government may deliberately keep nationalized industry prices low to restrain inflation. This will reduce profits.
● Even if the nationalized industry does make large profits, is this good or bad? Is it due to a high level of efficiency, or to its charging monopoly prices?

An alternative is to try to assess nationalized industry *costs*. Are they higher or lower than costs in other industries? The problem here is to compare like with like. What is the nationalized industry to be compared with?

● If the whole industry is nationalized, it would have to be compared with another *industry*. But the conditions in another industry may be quite different. What meaningful comparison can be made of the costs of extracting a tonne of coal and those of obtaining a barrel of oil? Most of the differences between these two industries have nothing to do with whether they are publicly or privately owned.
● An alternative is to compare it with the same industry abroad. For example, cost per passenger mile of British Rail could be compared with that of French Railways (SNCF). But this too poses serious problems. Conditions may be quite different between the two countries. SNCF has a higher proportion of freight traffic and a smaller proportion of commuter passengers than BR. The level and spread of subsidies differs between the two countries. SNCF has a much higher rate of

investment per mile in track and rolling stock than BR. How, then, is any meaningful comparison to be made?

- Another possibility is to compare the costs of those parts of the nationalized sector that do compete with the private sector: for example, British Airways (before it was privatized) with British Caledonian, British Midland, Laker Airways, etc.; or Royal Mail parcels with private parcel carriers; or electricity and gas showrooms with private-sector retailers; or Austin Rover with private sector car companies; and so on. Again, however, the problem is whether ownership is the *only* thing that causes differences in efficiency. The Royal Mail has to carry parcels to any part of the country. Private carriers may confine themselves to certain high-density routes, and are thus able to carry full loads and operate with a lower cost per tonne/mile.

Even if it could be demonstrated that *competitive* parts of the nationalized industries would be less efficient than identical parts operating in the private sector, it does not prove that natural *monopolies* are less efficient under public than private ownership.

Even if meaningful comparisons of costs could be made, low costs are not the only objective of a nationalized industry. High-cost pits may be kept open to protect miners' jobs. High-cost railway lines and bus routes may be kept open to provide a service to local communities. If any judgement is to be made about performance, the objectives must be clearly stated first.

Of course, just because it is difficult to *prove* that nationalized industries operate less in the public interest than private-sector firms, they may still do so! The belief that private ownership better serves the public is one of the central arguments for privatization.

 Can you think of any test which would allow a fair assessment of the performance of nationalized industries?

The arguments for privatization

The arguments in favour of privatization are to a large extent the same as the arguments *against* nationalization.

Market forces

The first argument is that privatization will expose these industries to market forces, from which will flow the benefits of greater efficiency, greater growth and greater responsiveness to the wishes of the consumer. There are three parts to this argument.

Greater competition in the goods market. Under certain circumstances, a privatized industry may be more competitive than a nationalized one.

If it was previously a monopoly under nationalization and is now split into competing parts (e.g. separate power stations competing to sell electricity to different area electricity boards, or separate coal mines competing against each other), then supernormal profits may be competed down. This competition in the goods market will then force the competing firms to keep their costs as low as possible in order to stay in business. It may also reduce the power of unions to increase wages unrelated to productivity, or to continue with inefficient working practices. Of course this argument depends on there being little or no oligopolistic collusion. If the privatized companies colluded with each other, the consumer might not benefit at all.

Alternatively, when nationalized the company may have already been competing with the other companies (e.g. British Airways with other airlines). Nevertheless it may still have been *cushioned* by government subsidies or by various barriers to the

Deregulation

Where the government removes official barriers to competition (e.g. licences and minimum quality standards).

entry of competition (e.g. when BA or the National Bus Company were granted sole licences to operate a particular route). If privatization also involves deregulation, such that the newly privatized firm is forced to compete on *equal* terms with other firms, then again the consumer might gain from increased competition.

Greater competition for finance. After privatization a company no longer has direct access to government finance. To finance investment it must now go to the market: it must issue shares or borrow from banks or other financial institutions. In doing so, it will be competing for funds with other companies, and thus must be seen as capable of using these funds profitably.

Accountability to shareholders. Shareholders want a good return on their shares and will thus put pressure on the privatized company to perform well. If the company does not make sufficient profits, shareholders will sell their shares. The share price will fall, and the company will be in danger of being taken over. The market for corporate control thus provides incentives for private firms to be efficient.

Ultimately there is also the threat of bankruptcy. A nationalized industry can always rely on the government to bale it out. A privatized company, so the argument goes, cannot.

Reduced government interference

In nationalized industries, managers may frequently be required to adjust their targets for political reasons. At one time they may have to keep prices low as part of the government drive against inflation. At another they may have to raise their prices substantially in order to raise extra revenue for the government and help finance tax cuts. At another they may find their investment programmes cut as part of a government economy drive.

Privatization frees the company from these constraints and allows it to make more rational economic decisions and plan future investments with greater certainty.

Even if interference were desirable, it has not always been very effective. Governments have found that their ability to impose strict control on the nationalized industries has been limited.

Reducing the public-sector borrowing requirement (PSBR)

The PSBR is the amount of money the public sector has to borrow each year to make up the shortfall between public-sector expenditure and public-sector receipts (taxes, rates, nationalized industries' sales). Reducing the PSBR was a major aim of the Thatcher government, since it was seen as the way of bringing down the rate of inflation and allowing reductions in the rate of taxation. (These arguments are examined in later chapters.)

The privatization issue of shares directly earns money for the government and thus reduces the amount it needs to borrow. Effectively, then, the government can use the proceeds of privatization to finance tax cuts. Cuts in taxation are not only popular politically, but also seen as a means of increasing incentives to work and invest, and thus a means of stimulating increased output in the economy.

Increased share ownership and popular capitalism

This is largely a political/ideological argument. The Conservative Party believes that 'true' public ownership is not state ownership. Although in theory the nationalized industries are owned by everyone in the UK, people do not feel a sense of ownership or participation. Instead the industry is run by 'bureaucrats'. This is not so after privatization. Shares are now owned by members of the public who thus feel a much greater sense of involvement. In this sense, then, the Conservatives argue that privatization is really a return of industries to the public. It is a form of 'popular capitalism'.

By 1988 there were some 9.5 million direct shareholders in the UK, nearly five times the number a decade earlier.[3] A large proportion of these new shareholders, however, hold only a very small number of shares in one or two of the privatized companies. Over half hold shares in only one company, and only around 100 000 hold shares in more than three companies.

The arguments against privatization

The arguments against privatization are in part a rebuttal of the arguments for, and in part a restatement of the arguments for nationalization.

Natural monopolies

The market forces argument for privatization largely breaks down if a public monopoly is simply replaced by a private monopoly. British Telecom faces virtually no competition: Mercury, its only competitor, is tiny by comparison. British Gas, although facing competition from other fuels, is still the only supplier of piped gas. Once equipment has been installed to burn gas, such as a cooker or more significantly a gas-only burning furnace in industry, there is no competitor to whom the customer can turn. At least, say the critics of privatization, when nationalized the company was not out to maximize profits and thereby exploit the consumer.

But will not competition for finance and pressure from shareholders force the privatized company to be more efficient? The problem here is that the monopoly has less need to rely on efficiency to make profits. It can make large profits for its shareholders simply by raising prices. In such cases the interests of shareholders will be in conflict with the interests of customers.

Likewise monopoly profits can be used to finance investment. A monopoly has less need to rely on the capital market and is thus not put in competition with other firms for finance. Even if it were, it could simply use its promise of monopoly profits to attract new shareholders or bank loans.

But what about the ultimate sanction of bankruptcy? Surely this will ensure that a privatized industry behaves efficiently? Critics also dismiss this argument. In the case of highly profitable industries such as telecommunications and gas, there *is* no fear of bankruptcy. Profits can always be ensured by raising prices.

In the case of industries like coal, railways and steel, there may be no overall fear of bankruptcy under nationalization, but unprofitable pits, railway lines and steelworks have been closed with a consequent loss of jobs. In other words, if the government chooses to be tough with the nationalized industries it can be, and has been. If these industries were privatized, there is no reason why they would necessarily operate under a harsher regime. If a government were unhappy about closures, it might always step in and provide a rescue package or even re-nationalize. After all, Rolls-Royce and British Leyland were rescued by the government.

Insufficient regulations

An answer to the problem of monopoly power is for the government to regulate the behaviour of privatized companies. There are three ways this can be done. Critics say that, even using all three, regulations will still be insufficient to prevent the abuse of monopoly power.

---

[3] There are many more than this if people's indirect shareholdings via pension funds and insurance companies are counted.

Regulations built into the Act of privatization. The privatized industry may have constraints imposed on its pricing policy. Thus British Telecom must keep its average price rises 4 per cent below the rate of inflation. (If inflation is less than 4 per cent there must be a corresponding price reduction.) In the case of gas, BG can raise its prices to domestic consumers by the full amount of any increases in the cost of gas and 2 per cent below the rate of inflation for any rises in non-gas costs. Similar types of price regulation are in force in other cases, such as the water companies.

Also the government may retain a 'golden share'. This effectively permits the government to veto any policy which might threaten the public interest. For example, it could block a take-over bid by a foreign company.

Critics argue that these safeguards are too weak. Thus BT could perhaps still make large profits and charge unnecessarily high prices even with the inflation minus 4 per cent rule, given the rapid progress in technology and thus the opportunities for cost savings.

Establishment of regulatory agencies. OFTEL (Office of Telecommunications) and OFGAS (Office of Gas Supply) were established when these industries were privatized. Their aim is to monitor the industries' behaviour and if necessary to regulate their policies. Critics argue that these agencies are not powerful enough.

Use of existing legislation. The privatized industries could be investigated by the Office of Fair Trading and if necessary referred to the Monopolies and Mergers Commission. If they engaged in any restrictive agreements, they could be referred to the Restrictive Practices Court. The problem here is likely to be one of abuse of monopoly power rather than oligopolistic collusion. But it is this part of UK legislation that is weakest. The MMC has not been very effective in regulating monopoly behaviour in the past.

The public interest

Will not the questions of externalities and social justice be ignored after privatization? The advocates of privatization argue that externalities are a relatively minor problem, and anyway can be dealt with by appropriate taxes, subsidies and regulations even if the industry is privatized. Likewise questions of fairness and social justice can be dealt with by subsidies or regulations. A loss-making bus service can be subsidized so that it can be run profitably by a private bus company. Regulations can insist that 999 calls can be made free from call boxes.

Critics argue that only the most glaring examples of externalities and injustice can be taken into account, given that the whole ethos of a private company is different from a nationalized one: private profit is the goal rather than public service. Externalities, they argue, are extremely widespread and need to be taken into account by the industry itself and not just by an occasionally intervening government.

In assessing these arguments, a lot depends on the toughness of government legislation and the attitudes and powers of regulatory agencies after privatization. For example, in the case of water and the environment, it depends on how tough the government's anti-pollution legislation is and on the vigour of the National Rivers Authority in insisting that environmental standards are maintained or improved.

The PSBR

The privatization issue of shares will directly reduce the PSBR, but there are problems here:

- The nation's *capital* assets are being sold to finance *current* expenditure. This is what ex-prime minister Harold Macmillan called 'selling off the family silver'.

Box 11.9

The Price of Privatization

A principal criticism of the government's privatization drive is the low share valuation put on the nationalized industries being sold. The table shows a substantial divergence between the price at which the shares were issued to the public, and the price at which they were traded on the Stock Exchange. Even after the stock market crash of October 1987, only BAA and British Airways fell below their issue price.

? What arguments might the government offer for undervaluing the nationalized industries' share prices?

Share prices of privatization issues

	Date of sale	Issue price	First-day close	Price on 1/9/87	Low price Nov./Dec. 1987
British Telecom	12/84	50p	93p	104p[1]	80p[1]
British Gas	12/86	50p	63p	91p[1]	62p[1]
British Airways	2/87	65p	109p	102p[1]	61p[1]
Rolls-Royce	5/87	85p	147p	113p	104p
BAA	7/87	100p	146p	133p	83p
Water (10 companies)	12/89	100p	140p[2]	–	–
Electricity distributors (12 companies)	12/90	100p	151p[3]	–	–

[1] Issue price in these cases was a part-paid price only; subsequent market prices have been reduced to take this into account.
[2] Average of the 10 water companies.
[3] Average of the 12 companies.

Source: *Financial Times*, various dates.

- The profits of nationalized industries also help to reduce the PSBR. Once sold, there will be no further profits accruing to the state from these industries. In other words, there is a short-term gain from the sale of shares, but a long-term loss from reduced profits. Of course, if these industries were made *much* more profitable by privatization, the extra corporation tax they would pay would go some way towards offsetting this.
- Why does the government want to reduce its borrowing? A major reason is that, if less has to be lent to the government, there will be more finance available to be lent to the private sector, and this should stimulate investment and growth. Reducing the PSBR by privatization, however, does not do this, since the money released is simply being used to buy the privatization shares and is *not* being diverted to the rest of industry.
- There is a conflict between reducing the PSBR and avoiding monopoly exploitation. This is one of the biggest problems with privatization. In order to earn the maximum revenue for the government from the privatization issue, the industry must have the greatest possible potential for earning profit. This will be so if the industry is sold as a monopoly. But this directly conflicts with the aims of efficiency and the interests of the consumer, which are best served by splitting the industry up and selling it as competing parts.

Problems in the valuation of shares

It is very difficult for the government to predict the market price of shares in advance of their sale. If the price of the privatization issue is set too high, the shares may be unattractive to shareholders. The government thus has to employ the service of underwriters. These are financial institutions which will guarantee to buy up any

Box 11.10

Selling Power to the People
Electricity privatization

Electricity is one of the country's most important industries. Its privatization is expected to raise between £15 billion and £20 billion in revenue – more than all previous privatizations put together. But it is not simply the sheer size of the electricity industry that makes its privatization interesting. It also raises a number of interesting questions about the best form in which to sell an apparent natural monopoly.

Under nationalization the industry was organized as a monopoly with the Central Electricity Generating Board (CEGB) supplying 99 per cent of all electricity. It operated the power satations and supplied the electricity via the national grid to the consumer. However, the CEGB did not sell electricity directly to the consumer;

rather it sold it to twelve regional boards, which in their turn charged the user.

The main argument put forward in favour of privatizing electricity is that of competition. Competition, it is claimed, will lead to enhanced efficiency and lower prices to the consumer. But how was greater competition to be achieved? Could the industry be reorganized, or would a public monopoly simply be turned into a private monopoly?

Three methods of privatizing the industry were initially proposed. The first was to leave the industry as it was, simply transferring the public monopoly into the private sector. It was suggested by the CEGB that this was the simplest and best way to ensure the existing level of service and retain the full economies of scale. Predictably, this view was seen by most observers to be quite at odds with the desire for greater competition.

The second privatization strategy involved leaving the CEGB intact. The national grid, however, would be run by a separate company which would search for the cheapest electricity, whether produced domestically or abroad, predominantly in France. Once again the principle criticism is that the CEGB would face a level of competition that was too small to make any difference to its pricing policy.

A third proposal involved going one step further than solely removing the grid from CEGB control. Here the

unsold shares. Thus when the sale of BP shares came just after the stock market collapse in October 1987, the underwriters had to buy up the vast bulk of these shares. This underwriting is not free! The government has to pay the underwriters large amounts in commission (whether or not they have to take up any shares).

If the price is set too low, the government will sacrifice revenues. Box 11.9 shows how difficult it was to get various issue prices just right.

Critics argue that the government will deliberately set the price too low. The windfall gain that this gives to the purchasers of the shares will encourage them to buy future issues, and will also encourage people to become shareholders for the first time. This spread of 'popular capitalism' is thus achieved at a sacrifice of revenues for the government.

Ideological objections

Critics argue that people are being sold shares in industries they already own, whereas those who do not buy them are being dispossessed. Privatization, they claim, far from making ownership more widespread, actually further concentrates ownership. After privatization, many shareholders sell their shares for a quick profit, and the industries end up with relatively few shareholders.

One radical alternative to privatization would be to issue everyone with an (equal)

Box 11.10 (cont'd)

CEGB itself would be split into five companies, each in competition. The national grid would buy from the cheapest source. The resulting structure was seen as the most desirable if competition was the principal aim of the sale. But even so there would be the possibility of oligopolistic collusion between the generating companies. There were other difficulties too with this proposal. It was suggested that the system would be highly complex in both an administrative and a technical sense. As a result some economists argued that the industry could become very inefficient in this form.

The government announced its decision on the form of the privatization on 25 February 1988. It was somewhat of a compromise between these last two proposals. It involved splitting the CEGB into two unequally sized companies. The larger company (National Power) would have 70 per cent of the generating capacity and would include nuclear power stations. Since it was estimated that the nuclear stations would not be profitable given their large capital and decommissioning costs, it was necessary to make National Power large enough to cover the costs of nuclear power. The other company (Powergen) would have the remaining 30 per cent of capacity and would not include nuclear stations. In conjunction with this split, the creation of new private-sector stations was to be actively encouraged. Also electricity could be imported from France.

The grid would be under separate ownership. It would be a non-profit-making organization owned by the twelve regional boards.

As for the regional boards, their position was somewhat enhanced. They would be able to generate electricity, control the grid, buy electricity from anywhere and, most importantly, set their own price.

To prevent the potential abuse of this structure a new post of Director-General of Electricity Supply would be set up to supervise the privatized industry. The Director-General would have a degree of control over prices. Such regulation would be of crucial importance if the electricity industry was to operate in the consumers' interests and not just the shareholders'.

In November 1989, however, it was announced that the nuclear power stations would be withdrawn from the privatization. They would remain as a separate nationalized sector, where they could be subsidized as necessary. This would still leave National Power as a much larger company than Powergen, although the main reason for their unequal size had been removed.

?

1. Will there be any effective competition between the regional boards in supplying electricity to (a) households; (b) firms not considering moving their location; (c) firms considering moving?
2. Would it be in the regional boards' interest to practise price discrimination between different industrial users of electricity?
3. Given that nuclear power generation remains nationalized, is there any justification for splitting the remaining power generation into just two private companies: one very large and one moderately large?

share certificate in the nationalized industries. Once a year they could go along to the Post Office and draw their dividend. The bigger the profit, the bigger the dividend. This, it is claimed, would make the nationalized industries more accountable and give people a greater sense of ownership and involvement.

Conclusions

Since the debate is so bound up with ideology, it is difficult to draw any clear conclusions. The issue is highly normative. Nevertheless the following generalizations can be made:

- Ownership is only a minor determinant of an industry's efficiency. What is much more important is the degree of competition that the firm(s) face. Both private- and public-sector monopolies can be inefficient. Both can be made much more efficient if they face effective competition. The issue, then, is much more one of liberalization and deregulation than one of simple ownership.
- The functioning of both private- and public-sector industries depends on the attitudes of the government. Industries in both sectors can be given an 'easy ride' by government if it is prepared to provide subsidies or if it chooses not to regulate

their behaviour. Alternatively, the government can be tough with both sectors. Nationalized industries in the 1980s were forced to become much more efficient because of the appointment of tough managers, the imposition of cash limits on their expenditure and minimum government support. Likewise privatized industries can be forced to be more efficient if price regulation is tough and rigorously enforced.

● Externalities and questions of the public interest generally can be taken into account in both sectors. Again it depends on government attitudes. Probably it is easier to impose a 'public minded' regime in nationalized industries, but privatized firms too can be forced to behave in the public interest if the government is rigorous enough in its intervention.

Despite these 'middle of the road' conclusions, privatization has caught the political imagination all around the world. Countries as diverse as France, Japan, Italy, Malaysia, Turkey, Brazil, Mexico, Canada and Spain (and many others too) have embarked on programmes of privatization. None, however, is so advanced and so thorough as that in the UK.

▲ SUMMARY

1. In the period after the Second World War, the Labour government carried through a large programme of nationalization. The arguments used to justify bringing industries into public ownership were partly ideological and partly economic, based on market failures under private enterprise.

2. The market failure arguments for nationalization include the problems of monopoly power (due to industries being natural monopolies or there being high entry costs), lack of investment, lack of planning and co-ordination of key infrastructural industries, large external costs and benefits, and a lack of provision of non-profitable but socially desirable services. In addition 'lame duck', strategic and industrial relations arguments have been used to justify nationalization.

3. From around 1983 the Conservative government embarked on a large programme of privatization. Again the justification was partly ideological and partly to do with the perceived economic failures of the nationalized industries and their better prospects under private ownership.

4. The economic arguments for privatization include: greater competition, not only in the goods market but in the market for finance and for corporate control; reduced government interference, which was particularly damaging if the industries were being used for political purposes or as a means of controlling the macroeconomy; and making these industries more accountable to the public via share ownership.

5. The economic arguments against privatization are largely the market failure arguments that were used to justify nationalization. In reply the advocates of privatization argue that these problems can be overcome through appropriate regulation. The question here is whether that regulation can be comprehensive enough and tough enough.

6. Privatization raises money for the government and thus in the short term the government can use these revenues to finance tax cuts. There is, however, a potential conflict between this objective and that of making the industry as competitive as possible. The more competition is introduced, the less profitable it is likely to be, and thus the less revenue is likely to be raised from the share flotation. There is also the problem of deciding the share issue price.

* 7. Whether under public or regulated private ownership, the question arises of the socially optimum price and output for these industries. In the first-best world it would be socially efficient to set price equal to marginal social cost. In the real world this is not the case given that prices elsewhere are not equal to marginal social costs. Ideally, prices should still *reflect* marginal social costs, but there are difficulties in identifying and measuring social costs.

8. Assessing the performance of nationalized and privatized industries is difficult given the political constraints under which they have operated. It is possible for both or neither to be run in 'the public interest' (however defined): it depends crucially on the government's attitude towards them, the degree of competition they face and the regulatory framework within which they operate.

Macroeconomic Issues 12

12.1 The scope of macroeconomics

The distinction between microeconomics and macroeconomics

We turn now to *macroeconomics*. This will be the subject for the second half of the book.

As we have already seen, *microeconomics* focuses on *individual* markets. It studies the demand for and supply of oranges, videos, petrol and haircuts; of bricklayers, doctors, office accommodation and blast furnaces. It examines the choices people make *between* goods, and what determines their relative prices and the relative quantities produced.

In macroeconomics we take a much loftier view. We examine the economy as a whole. We still examine demand and supply, but now it is the *total* level of spending in the economy and the *total* level of production. In other words, we examine *aggregate demand* and *aggregate supply*.

We still examine output, but now it is *national* output. What determines the size of national output? What causes it to grow? Why do growth rates fluctuate? These are typical macroeconomic questions to do with output.

We still examine employment, but now it is *national* employment. Here we will want answers to the question: what causes unemployment?

We still examine the determination of prices, but now it is the *general* level of prices. In particular we will want to know what causes prices to rise: what causes *inflation*.

In macroeconomics we will not just focus on a country in isolation. We will need to examine its economic relationships with the rest of the world. We will ask: what determines the level of its imports and exports? What determines the rate of exchange of its currency into other nations' currencies? How do these relationships with other countries affect the domestic economy?

These are all big issues: the sort of issues we constantly read about in the papers and hear about on radio and television; the sort of issues that the electorate is concerned about when deciding which way to vote in elections. In particular we will be focusing on four issues. These are the issues that seem of most concern to the electorate and hence to governments anxious to retain office.

Although we will be focusing largely on the UK economy in examining these key issues, our analysis will be equally applicable to other countries. We will also consider from time to time the comparative economic performance of other countries.

The major macroeconomic issues

Economic growth

A growing economy means that there will be more goods and services for people to consume.

Rate of economic growth

The percentage increase in output over a twelve-month period.

The UK has generally had a poor economic growth record compared with its major industrial competitors – countries such as Japan, West Germany and France. We will need to examine why this is so. We will need to discover what the causes of long-term growth are, and whether governments have pursued policies conducive to long-term growth.

There is a short-term problem too. Growth fluctuates. In some years output may grow at 3 per cent or more. In other years, however, the economy may slide into recession: growth may be very low or even negative. By negative growth we mean a fall in output.

Governments, therefore, would not only like to achieve high long-run rates of growth, but they would also like to achieve stable growth and avoid recessions.

Unemployment

For many years after the Second World War, people believed that the problem of unemployment had been largely solved. Throughout the 1950s and 1960s unemployment never rose above 600 000.

This contrasted dramatically with the inter-war period, where mass unemployment was a problem from 1921 right through to the outbreak of war in 1939. In 1932, at the depths of the 'Great Depression', unemployment reached 3 million (23 per cent of the working population).

In the 1970s, confidence in the ability of governments to prevent unemployment was gradually eroded again as unemployment began to rise. By 1976 it had reached 1 million. Then in the early 1980s the situation deteriorated rapidly. Unemployment soared. By the mid-1980s it was well over 3 million. Then, as the economy recovered from recession from the mid-1980s onwards, it began to fall again, only to rise once more with the recession in the early 1990s.

So, what causes unemployment? Why was it high in the 1930s and 1980s and so low in the 1950s and 1960s? Can the government do anything about unemployment, and if so, what? These are questions we shall need to explore.

Inflation

Rate of inflation

The percentage increase in prices over a twelve-month period.

By 'inflation' we mean a general rise in prices throughout the economy.

During the 1950s and 1960s the annual rate of inflation fluctuated up and down, but averaged around only 4 per cent. In the 1970s, however, inflation rose dramatically. By 1975 it had reached 26 per cent. It then fell back to 8 per cent in 1978.

When the Thatcher government was elected in 1979 inflation was beginning to rise. The government soon declared inflation to be 'Public enemy number one': it had to be got down if the nation's economic health was to be restored. At first, however, inflation rose, reaching 21 per cent in 1980. Then it began to fall again, and by the mid-1980s it was back down around the 4 per cent level. By the end of the 1980s, however, it was rising again and peaked at nearly 11 per cent in 1990.

Just how serious a problem is inflation? What are its causes? What is the relationship between inflation and the other macroeconomic objectives? What can the government do to control inflation? Are there any undesirable side-effects of policies to control inflation? These are all questions we will be examining.

The balance of payments and the exchange rate

The final issue has to do with the country's foreign trade and its economic relationships with other countries.

The UK's balance of payments account records all transactions between the UK and the rest of the world. These transactions enter as either debit items or credit items. The debit items include all payments *to* other countries: these include the UK's purchases of imports, the investments it makes abroad and the interest and dividends paid to foreigners who have invested in the UK. The credit items include all the UK's receipts *from* other countries: these include the sales of exports, investments made by foreigners in the UK and earnings of interest and dividends from abroad.

The sale of exports and any other receipts earn foreign currency. The purchase of imports or any other payments abroad use up foreign currency. If we start to spend more foreign currency than we earn, one of two things must happen. Both are likely to be a problem.

The balance of payments will go into deficit. In other words, there will be a shortfall of foreign currencies. The government will therefore have to borrow money from abroad, or draw on its foreign currency reserves to make up the shortfall. This is a problem because, if it goes on too long, overseas debts will mount, along with the interest that must be paid; and/or reserves will begin to run low.

The exchange rate will fall. The exchange rate is the rate at which one currency exchanges for another. For example, the exchange rate of the pound into the dollar might be £1 = \$1.60.

If the government does nothing to correct the balance of payments deficit, then the exchange rate must fall. (We will show just why this is so in section 12.5.) A falling exchange rate is a problem because it pushes up the price of imports and may fuel inflation. Also if the exchange rate fluctuates, this can cause great uncertainty for traders and can damage international trade and economic growth.

How serious have these problems been for the UK? What are their underlying causes? How do the balance of payments and the exchange rate relate to the other macroeconomic issues? What are the best policies for governments to adopt? These are the questions we must look at here.

Balance of payments account

A record of the country's transactions with the rest of the world. It shows the country's payments to or deposits in other countries (debits) and its receipts or deposits from other countries (credits). It also shows the balance between these debits and credits under various headings.

Exchange rate

The rate at which one national currency exchanges for another. The rate is expressed as the amount of one currency that is necessary to purchase *one unit* of another currency (e.g. DM2.80 = £1).

Government macroeconomic policy

From the above four issues we can identify four macroeconomic policy objectives that governments typically pursue:

● High and stable economic growth.
● Low unemployment.
● Low inflation.
● The avoidance of balance of payments deficits and excessive exchange rate fluctuations.

Unfortunately, these policy objectives may conflict. For example, a policy designed to accelerate the rate of economic growth may result in a higher rate of inflation and a balance of payments deficit. We will be examining these policy conflicts in the following chapters.

The actual policies a government pursues will depend on two major factors.

Its order of priorities

If its economic goals conflict, then the government must choose which is the most important. For example, if it makes the fight against inflation its major short-term objective, it may be prepared to accept, at least for the time being, a lower rate of growth and a higher level of unemployment. On the other hand, if it is anxious to reduce unemployment significantly in time for the next general election, it might be prepared to allow the rate of inflation to rise and the exchange rate to fall.

Which macroeconomic theories it believes to be the most accurate

There is not just one set of macroeconomic theories. If there were, it would make *your* life simpler – there would be less to learn! On the other hand, macroeconomics would be less controversial and hence less exciting.

One broad distinction between macroeconomic theories is between those that imply that the four policy objectives are generally best achieved through the free market, and those that imply that the market will probably fail to achieve some or all of them. Obviously a government that believes in the first set of theories is likely to pursue policies designed to 'free up' markets: policies that involve the minimum of government interference. In contrast, a government that believes in the second set of theories is likely to intervene much more actively in trying to steer the economy.

Macroeconomic theories are thus frequently associated with political parties: the non-interventionist, market-orientated theories are adopted by the political right; the interventionist theories are adopted by the political left.

It would be wrong to suggest that there are just two schools of macroeconomic thought. Just as there are many shades of political opinion about the success or otherwise of the market economy, so too there are many shades of economic opinion about how the market works or fails to work to achieve the macroeconomic goals. For the rest of this chapter we will look at the range of *possible* causes of macroeconomic problems. Later we will see which schools of thought stress which causes, and what policy implications follow.

▲ SUMMARY

1. Macroeconomics, like microeconomics, looks at issues such as output, employment and prices; but it looks at them in the context of the whole economy.
2. The four main macroeconomic goals that are generally of most concern to governments are economic growth, reducing unemployment, reducing inflation, and avoiding balance of payments and exchange rate problems.
3. Unfortunately these goals are likely to conflict. Which policies a government adopts, therefore, will depend on its order of priorities. It will also depend on which school of economic thought the government adheres to.

12.2 Economic growth

The distinction between actual and potential growth

Before examining the causes of economic growth, it is essential to distinguish between *actual* and *potential* economic growth. People frequently confuse the two.

Actual growth is the percentage annual increase in national output: the growth in what is actually produced. (See section 13.6 for alternative ways of measuring national output and income.) When statistics on growth rates are published, it is actual growth they are referring to.

Actual growth

The percentage annual increase in national output actually produced.

Potential growth is the speed at which the economy *could* grow, if it were to use all its resources: if it had no workers, machines, factories or land left idle. Two of the major factors contributing to potential economic growth are:

Potential growth

The percentage annual increase in the capacity of the economy to produce.

- An increase in resources – natural resources, labour or capital.
- An increase in the efficiency with which these resources are used, through advances in technology, improved labour skills or improved organization.

Whether *actual* output increases will depend on whether this increase in potential is exploited.

Growth and the production possibility curve

The distinction between actual and potential growth in output can be illustrated on a production possibility diagram. If you remember, a production possibility curve shows all the possible combinations of two goods that can be produced at any one time (see pages 9–14). For purposes of illustration we could lump all goods and services together into two categories: for example, agricultural goods (good X) and manufactured goods and services (good Y).

The production possibility curve itself shows potential *output*. Potential *growth*, then, is illustrated by a shift outward of the curve (e.g. curve I to curve II in Figure 12.1). Actual growth is represented by a movement outward of the production point (e.g. point *a* to *b* to *c* to *d*).

In the short run, actual growth can arise from a fuller use of resources (e.g. a movement from point *a* to point *b*). This would involve taking up slack in the economy: using machinery more fully and reducing unemployment. For actual growth to be sustained over a number of years, however, there would also have to be an increase in potential output. In other words, to get beyond point *b* in Figure 12.1, the production possibility curve itself would have to shift outward beyond curve I.

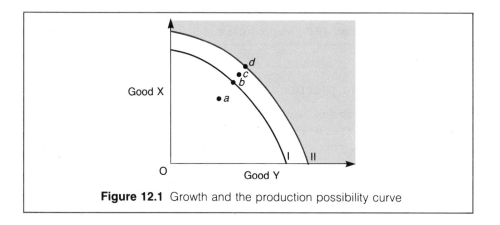

Figure 12.1 Growth and the production possibility curve

Economic growth and the trade cycle

Although growth in potential output will vary to some extent over the years – depending on the rate of advance of technology, the level of investment and the discovery of new raw materials – it will nevertheless tend to be much more steady than the growth in actual output.

Actual growth will tend to fluctuate. In some years, countries will experience high rates of economic growth: the country experiences a boom. In other years, economic growth will be low or even negative: the country experiences a recession. This cycle of booms and recessions is known as the trade cycle or business cycle.

There are four 'phases' of the trade cycle. They are illustrated in Figure 12.2.

Trade cycle or business cycle

The periodic fluctuations of national output round its long-term trend.

- The upturn. In this phase a stagnant economy begins to recover, and growth in actual output resumes.
- The boom. During this phase there is rapid economic growth. A fuller use is made of resources, and the gap between actual and potential output narrows.
- The peaking out. During this phase, growth slows down or even ceases.
- The slowdown, recession or slump. During this phase there is little or no growth or even a decline in output. Increasing slack develops in the economy.

A word of caution: do not confuse a high *level* of output with a high *growth* in output. The level of actual output is highest in phase 3. Growth in actual output is highest in phase 2.

 Figure 12.2 shows a decline in actual output in recessions. Redraw the diagram, only this time show a mere slowing down of growth in phase 4.

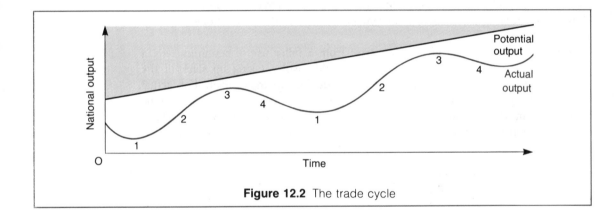

Figure 12.2 The trade cycle

The trade cycle in practice

The trade cycle illustrated in Figure 12.2 is a 'stylized' cycle. It is nice and smooth and regular. Drawing it this way allows us to make a clear distinction between each of the four phases. In practice, however, trade cycles are highly irregular. They are irregular in two ways.

The length of the phases. Some booms are short lived, lasting only a few months or so. Others are much longer, lasting perhaps three or four years. Likewise some recessions are short while others are long.

The magnitude of the phases. In some booms there is a very high rate of economic growth, perhaps 5 per cent per annum or more, while in others growth is much gentler. Some recessions are severe, with an actual decline in output. Others are merely 'pauses', with growth simply slowing down.

Nevertheless, despite the irregularity of the fluctuations, cycles are still clearly discernable. Figure 12.3 shows the fluctuations in UK *gross domestic product* (GDP)

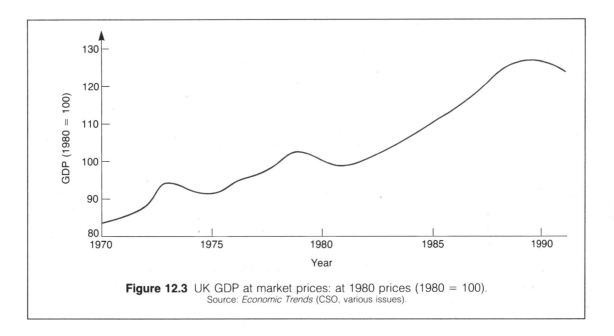

Box 12.1

International Fluctuations

Countries throughout the world experience trade cycles. The diagram illustrates the cyclical fluctuations of the seven main industrial economies from 1978 to 1989.

As you can see, all seven economies suffered a recession in the early 1980s, with four of the countries experiencing negative growth for a year (or two in the case of the UK). In the second half of the 1980s all the countries experienced relatively rapid economic growth.

But despite this broad similarity in their experience, there were nevertheless significant differences in the magnitude and timing of their individual cycles. For example, the UK plunged into recession in 1980, whereas it was not until 1982 that most of the other countries experienced their lowest level of growth. France, by contrast, experienced only a modest slowdown in the rate of growth (and even a slight increase in 1982); on the other hand, it experienced a smaller increase in growth between 1983 and 1985.

Another point to note is that some countries have had persistently higher rates of growth than others. For example, Japan experienced relatively high rates of economic growth in the 1980s, whereas Germany experienced relatively low rates.

? Identify the peaks and troughs in economic growth for each of the seven countries. Is the length of time between them the same for each country?

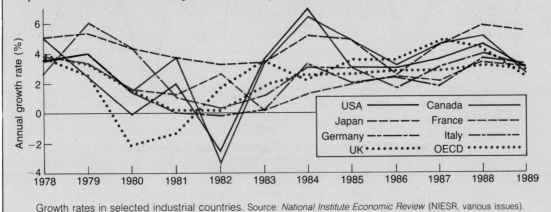

Growth rates in selected industrial countries. Source: *National Institute Economic Review* (NIESR, various issues).

Figure 12.3 UK GDP at market prices: at 1980 prices (1980 = 100).
Source: *Economic Trends* (CSO, various issues).

since 1970. GDP is simply a measure we use for national output. We will explain this measure and others in detail in section 13.6.

These fluctuations show up much more dramatically if we plot *growth* on the vertical axis rather than the *level* of output. This is done in Figure 12.4. This time we plot the figures right back to 1950.

1. At what phases of the trade cycle are points *w*, *x* and *y* in Figure 12.4?
2. Why do cyclical swings seem much greater when we plot growth on the vertical axis rather than the level of output?
3. How long was the average duration of the cycle from peak to peak between 1950 and 1990?

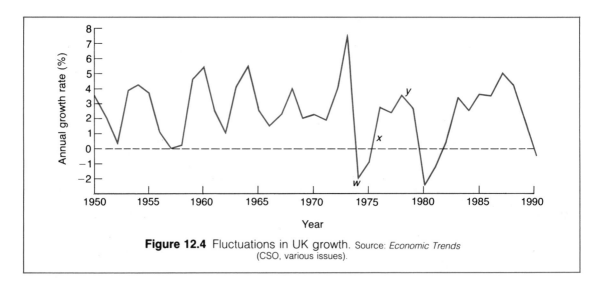

Figure 12.4 Fluctuations in UK growth. Source: *Economic Trends* (CSO, various issues).

Causes of actual growth

The major determinants of variations in the rate of actual growth in the *short run* are variations in the growth of aggregate demand.

Aggregate demand

Total spending on goods and services made in the economy. It consists of four elements, consumer spending (*C*), investment (*I*), government spending (*G*) and the expenditure on exports (*X*), less any expenditure on foreign goods and services (*M*): $AD = C + I + G + X - M$.

The UK's aggregate demand (*AD*) is the total spending on goods and services made in the UK. This spending consists of four elements: consumer spending (*C*), investment expenditure by firms (*I*), government spending (*G*), and the expenditure by foreigners on UK goods and services (i.e. their purchases of UK exports and their new investments in the UK) (*X*). From these four must be subtracted any expenditure that goes on imports (*M*), since this is expenditure that 'leaks' abroad, and is not therefore spent on UK goods and services. Thus:

$$AD = C + I + G + X - M$$

Another way of saying the same thing is merely to count that element of consumption, investment, government expenditure and foreign expenditure that is spent on goods and services produced in the UK. Thus:

$$AD = C_d + I_d + G_d + X_d$$

where 'd' stands for the part of each one that is spent on *domestically* produced goods and services.

Would you expect *X* to equal X_d? Explain.

A rapid rise in aggregate demand will create shortages. This will tend to stimulate firms to increase output, thus reducing slack in the economy. Likewise, a reduction in aggregate demand will leave firms with increased stocks of unsold goods. They will therefore tend to reduce output.

Aggregate demand and actual output, therefore, fluctuate together in the short run. A boom is associated with a rapid rise in aggregate demand: the faster the rise in aggregate demand, the higher the short-run actual rate of growth. A recession, by contrast, is associated with a slowing down or reduction in aggregate demand.

A rapid rise in aggregate demand, however, is not enough to ensure a continuing high level of growth over a *number* of years. Without an expansion of potential output too, rises in actual output must eventually come to an end. Once spare capacity has been used up, once there is full employment of labour and other resources, the rate of growth of actual output will be restricted to the rate of growth of potential output. This is illustrated in Figure 12.2. As long as actual output is below potential output, the actual output curve can slope upward more steeply than the potential output curve. But once the gap between the two curves has been closed, the actual output curve can only slope as steeply as the potential output curve: the two curves cannot cross – actual output cannot be above potential output.

In the long run, therefore, there are two determinants of actual growth:

- The growth in aggregate demand. This determines whether potential output will be realized.
- The growth in potential output.

Causes of potential growth

We turn now to the *supply* side of the question. Here we are not concerned with the amount of *spending*, but rather with what determines the capacity of the economy to *produce*. There are two main determinants of this potential output: (a) the amount of resources available and (b) the efficiency with which these resources can be used. If supply potential is to grow, then either (a) or (b) or both must grow.

Increases in the quantity of resources: capital, labour, land and raw materials

1. Capital. The nation's output depends on its stock of capital (K). An increase in this stock will increase output. If we ignore the problem of machines wearing out or becoming obsolete and needing replacing, then the stock of capital will increase by the amount of investment: $\Delta K = I$.

But by how much will this investment raise output? This depends on the productivity of this new capital: on the *marginal efficiency of capital* (see page 310). Let us define the nation's marginal efficiency of capital (*MEC*) as the annual extra income (ΔY) yielded by an increase in the capital stock, relative to the cost of that extra capital (ΔK).

$$MEC = \frac{\Delta Y}{\Delta K} = \frac{\Delta Y}{I}$$

Thus if £100 million of extra capital yields an annual income of £25 million, the marginal efficiency of capital would be £25 million/£100 million = ¼.

The rate of growth will depend on the fraction (*i*) of national income devoted to new investment (i.e. investment over and above what is necessary to replace worn-out equipment). The higher this rate of new investment, the higher will be the potential growth rate.

The relationship between the investment rate and the potential growth rate (g_p) is given by the simple formula:

$$g_p = i \times MEC$$

Thus if 20 per cent of national income went in new investment (i), and if each £1 of new investment yielded 25p of extra income per year ($MEC = \frac{1}{4}$), then the growth rate would be 5 per cent. A simple example will demonstrate this. If national income is £100 billion, then £20 billion will be invested ($i = 20$ per cent). This will lead to extra annual output of £5 billion ($MEC = \frac{1}{4}$). Thus national income grows to £105 billion: a growth of 5 per cent.

Over the long term, if investment is to increase, then *savings* must increase in order to finance that investment. Put another way, people must be prepared to forgo a certain amount of consumption in order to allow resources to be diverted into producing more capital goods: factories, machines, etc.

2. Labour. If there is an increase in the working population, there will be an increase in potential output. The size of this increase in output will depend on the marginal productivity of labour.

There is a problem here, of course. If there is a rise in the overall population, there will be an increase in the number of 'mouths to feed'. Output per head may not rise at all. Whether output per head does rise depends on two factors:

- The working population as a proportion of total population. If this proportion were to rise, then there would be a rise in output per head. In practice, many developed countries are faced with a growing proportion of their population above retirement age, and thus a potential fall in output per head.
- The relationship between the average and marginal product of labour. If the *marginal* product of new workers joining the labour force were above the *average* for the nation, then output per worker would rise. This is an example of the general rule that if the marginal value of something is above the average, the average will rise.

 What in practice will determine the size of the marginal product of labour relative to the average product?

3. Land and raw materials. Land is virtually fixed in quantity. Land reclamation schemes and the opening-up of marginal land can only add tiny amounts to national output.

Whether new raw materials can be discovered is largely a matter of the luck of nature. A country might strike it lucky and discover vast new deposits of coal, oil or some other mineral. North Sea oil was one such bonanza. Such discoveries, however, are usually 'one-off' benefits. They simply provide short-term growth, while the rate of their exploitation is building up. Once their rate of extraction is at a maximum, growth will cease. Output will simply remain at the new higher level, until eventually the raw materials will begin to run out. This will cause output to fall.

The problem of diminishing returns. If a single factor of production increases in supply whilst others remain fixed, diminishing returns will set in. Remember the problem that Thomas Malthus referred to: the problem of a growing population with a fixed supply of land (see Box 4.2). As more and more workers crowd on to a fixed amount of land, so the marginal product of workers will fall.

At first the marginal product of labour may be above the average product, as illustrated in Figure 12.5. Beyond Q_{L1}, however, the output per worker (the average product) will fall.

Figure 12.5 The average and marginal product of labour

The same argument applies to capital. If the quantity of capital increases with no increase in other factors of production, then diminishing returns to capital will set in. The rate of return on capital will fall.

Unless *all* factors of production increase, therefore, the rate of growth is likely to slow down. This was the worry of the classical economists of the nineteenth century who were pessimistic about the future prospects for growth, (see Box 12.2).

The solution to the problem of diminishing returns is an increase in the *productivity* of resources.

Increases in the productivity of resources

Most economists of the twentieth century have not shared the pessimism of the classical economists. Although they do not deny the law of diminishing returns, they argue that the marginal productivity of factors can be increased in various ways.

Technological improvements can increase the marginal productivity of capital. Much of the investment in new machines is not just in extra machines, but in superior machines producing a higher rate of return. Consider the microchip revolution of recent years. Modern computers can do the work of many people and have replaced many machines which are cumbersome and expensive to build. Improved methods of transport have reduced the costs of moving goods and materials. Improved communications (such as fax machines and satellites) have reduced the costs of transmitting information. The high-tech world of today would seem a wonderland to a person of 100 years ago.

As a result of technical progress, the marginal efficiency of capital has tended to increase, not decrease, over time. Similarly, as a result of new skills, improved education and training, and better health, the marginal productivity of labour has also tended to increase over time.

> **?** For what reasons might the productivity of land increase over time?

The effects of rising factor productivity are shown in Figure 12.6. Even though, at any *given* time, diminishing returns will apply (and therefore a factor's marginal physical productivity curve will slope downward), over time the marginal physical productivity curve will shift outward. If the quantity of the factor rises from Q_0 to Q_1, then with no increase in productivity the marginal productivity will fall. There is a movement from point *a* to point *b*.

*Box 12.2

The Classical Theory of Growth
Dismal economics

The classical economists of the nineteenth century were very pessimistic about the prospects for economic growth. They saw the rate of growth petering out as diminishing returns to both labour and capital led to low wages and a falling rate of profit. The only gainers would be landlords, who, given the fixed supply of land, would receive higher and higher rents as the demand for scarce land rose.

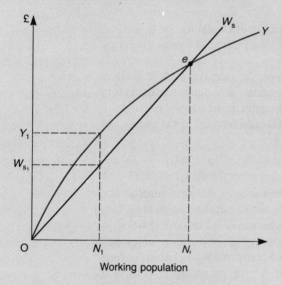

Equilibrium in the classical model

The classical position can be shown graphically. The size of the working population is plotted on the horizontal axis. If it is assumed that there is a basic minimum 'subsistence' wage that workers must earn in order to survive, then the line W_s traces out the total subsistence wage bill. It is a straight line because a doubling in the number of workers would lead to a doubling of the subsistence wage bill.

The line Y shows the total level of income that will be generated as more workers are employed, after subtracting rents to landlords. In other words, it is total wages plus profits. It gets less and less steep due to diminishing returns to labour and capital given the fixed supply of land.

As long as Y is above W_s (say, at a population of N_1), firms can make a profit. They will try to expand and will thus take on more labour.

Initially this will bid up the wage and will thus erode the level of profits. But the higher wages will encourage the population to expand. This increased supply of labour will compete wages back down to the subsistence level and will thus allow *some* recovery in profits. But profits will not be as high as they were before because, with an increase in workers, the gap between Y and W_s will have narrowed.

Firms will continue to expand and the population will continue to grow until point e is reached. At that point, even with wages at bare subsistence level, no profit can be made. Growth will cease. The economy will be in a long-run stationary state.

This process was described by David Ricardo, perhaps the most famous of all the classical economists. In *The Principles of Political Economy and Taxation* (1817), he wrote:

> The natural tendency of profits is to fall; for, in the progress of society and wealth, the additional quantity of food required is obtained by the sacrifice of more and more labour . . .
> . . . [A]s soon as wages should equal . . . the whole receipts of the farmer, there must be an end of accumulation; for no capital can then yield any profit whatever, and no additional labour can be demanded, and consequently population will have reached its highest point. Long indeed before this period, the very low rate of profits will have arrested all accumulation, and almost the whole produce of the country, after paying the labourers, will be the property of the owners of the land and the receivers of tithes and taxes.[1]

Ricardo did recognize that improvements in technology could put off the day when growth would cease. (It would have the effect of shifting the Y line upward.)

> This tendency, this gravitation as it were of profits, is happily checked at repeated intervals by the improvements in machinery, connected with the production of necessaries, as well as by discoveries in the science of agriculture which enable us to relinquish a portion of labour before required.[2]

Nevertheless, classical economists still held the pessimistic view that in the long run growth would cease. Economies would settle at a stationary state with just basic subsistence wages.

No wonder economics became dubbed 'The dismal science'.

[1] P. Sraffa (ed.), *The Works and Correspondence of David Ricardo*, (Cambridge University Press, 1951), p. 120.
[2] *Ibid.*

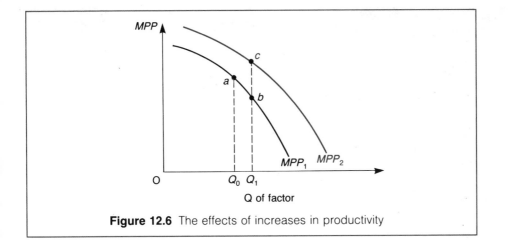

Figure 12.6 The effects of increases in productivity

If, however, the curve shifts outward to MPP_2, marginal productivity will rise. There is a movement to point c instead.

Show diagrammatically how there could be an increase in the productivity of a factor and yet a fall in its actual marginal product.

The main determinant of long-term growth is the rate of advance of technology. Invention, however, is not enough. There must also be the institutions and attitudes that encourage *innovation*. In other words. the inventions must be exploited. One reason often cited for the UK's poor growth performance compared with other countries is its lack of innovation, despite a relatively good record of inventions.

Policies to achieve growth

Can governments increase a country's growth rate? Most economists and politicians argue that they can, but just what policies should be adopted is a highly controversial issue. Policies differ in two ways.

First, they may focus on the demand side or the supply side of the economy. In other words, they may attempt to create sufficient *aggregate demand* to ensure that firms wish to invest and that potential output is realized. Or alternatively they may seek to increase *aggregate supply* by concentrating on measures to increase potential output: measures to encourage research and development, innovation and training.

Secondly, they may be market-orientated or interventionist policies. Many economists and politicians, especially those on the political right, believe that the best environment for encouraging economic growth is one where private enterprise is allowed to flourish: where entrepreneurs are able to reap substantial rewards from investment in new techniques and new products. Such economists, therefore, advocate policies designed to free up the market. Others, however, argue that a free market will be subject to considerable cyclical fluctuations. The resulting uncertainty will discourage investment. These economists, therefore, tend to advocate active intervention by the government to reduce these fluctuations. Some go further and argue for economic planning and/or control of industry by the state. Only that way, they argue, can the high levels of investment necessary for high long-term rates of growth be sustained.

Throughout this second half of the book we will be looking at these various

Box 12.3

The Costs of Economic Growth
Is more necessarily better?

For many Third World countries economic growth is a necessity if they are to remove mass poverty. When the majority of their population is underfed, poorly housed, with inadequate health care and little access to education, few would quarrel with the need for an increase in productive potential. The main query is whether the benefits of economic growth will flow to the mass of the population, or whether they will be confined to the few who are already relatively well off.

For developed countries the case for economic growth is less clear cut. True, there can be major advantages and certainly the majority of the population wants higher real incomes. Nevertheless there are important disadvantages too. These disadvantages have caused some people to call for a policy of *zero economic growth*.

So, what are the benefits and costs of economic growth?

The benefits of growth

Increased levels of consumption
Provided economic growth outstrips population growth, it will lead to higher real income per head. This can lead to higher levels of consumption of goods and services. If human welfare is related to the level of consumption, then growth provides an obvious gain to society.

It can help avoid other macroeconomic problems
People have aspirations of rising living standards. Without a growth in productive potential, people's demands for rising incomes are likely to lead to higher inflation, balance of payments crises (as more imports are purchased), industrial disputes, etc. Growth in productive potential helps to meet these aspirations and avoid macroeconomic crises.

It can make it easier to redistribute incomes to the poor
If incomes rise, the government can redistribute incomes from the rich to the poor *without the rich losing*. For example, as people's incomes rise, they automatically pay more taxes. These extra revenues for the government can be spent on programmes to alleviate poverty.

Without a continuing rise in national income the scope for helping the poor is much more limited.

Society may feel that it can afford to care more for the environment.
As people grow richer, they may become less preoccupied with their own private consumption and more concerned to live in a clean environment. The regulation of pollution tends to be tougher in developed countries than in the Third World.

The costs of growth

In practice, more consumption may not make people happier; economies may be no less crisis riven; income may not be redistributed more equally; the environment may not be better protected. More than this, some people argue that growth may worsen these problems and create additional problems besides.

The current opportunity cost of growth
To achieve faster growth, firms will probably need to invest more. This will require financing. The finance can come from higher savings or higher taxes. Either way, there must be a cut in consumption. In the short run, therefore, higher growth leads to *less* consumption, not more.

In the diagram, assume that consumption is currently at a level of C_1. Its growth over time is shown by the line out from C_1. Now assume that the government pursues a policy of higher growth. Consumption has to *fall* to finance the extra investment. Consumption falls to, say, C_2. The growth in consumption is now shown by the line out from C_2. Not until time t_1 is reached (which may be several years into the future) does consumption overtake the levels it would have reached with the previous lower growth rate.

government policies. We will look at demand-side and supply-side policies. We will also look at market-orientated and interventionist policies.

Postscript: the role of investment

Investment plays a twin role in economic growth. It is a component of aggregate demand and thus helps determine the level of actual output. It is also probably the major determinant of potential output, since investment both increases the capital stock and also leads to the development of new technology.

There is a problem here, however: if investment rises, the resulting rise in

Box 12.3 (cont'd)

High and low growth paths

Growth may simply generate extra demands

'The more people have, the more they want.' If this is so, more consumption may not increase people's utility at all. (Diagrammatically, indifference curves may move outward as fast as, or even faster than, consumers' budget lines: see section 3.2). It is often observed that rich people tend to be miserable!

As people's incomes grow, they may become more materialistic and less fulfilled as human beings.

Social effects

Many people claim that an excessive pursuit of material growth by a country can lead to a more greedy, more selfish and less caring society. As society becomes more industrialized, violence, crime, loneliness, stress-related diseases, suicides, divorce and other social problems are likely to rise.

Environmental costs

A richer society may be more concerned for the environment, but it is also likely to do more damage to it. The higher the level of consumption, the higher is likely to be the level of pollution and waste. What is more, many of the environmental costs are likely to be underestimated due to a lack of scientific knowledge. Acid rain and the depletion of the ozone layer have been two examples.

Non-renewable resources

If growth involves using a greater amount of resources, rather than using the same amount of resources more efficiently, certain non-renewable resources will begin to run out. Unless viable alternatives can be found for various minerals and fossil fuels, present growth may lead to shortages for future generations.

Effects on the distribution of income

While some people may gain from a higher standard of living, others are likely to lose. If the means to higher growth are greater incentives (such as cuts in higher rates of income tax), then the rich might get richer, with little or no benefits 'trickling down' to the poor.

Growth involves changes in production: both in terms of the goods produced and in terms of the techniques used and the skills required. The more rapid the rate of growth, the more rapid the rate of change. People may find that their skills are no longer relevant. Their jobs may be replaced by machines. People may thus find themselves unemployed, or forced to take low-paid, unskilled work.

Conclusion

So should countries pursue growth? The answer depends on (a) just what costs and benefits are involved, (b) what weighting people attach to them, and (c) how opposing views are to be reconciled.

A problem is that the question of the desirability of economic growth is a normative one. It involves a judgement about what a 'desirable' society should look like.

A simpler point, however, is that the electorate seems to want economic growth. As long as that is so, governments will tend to pursue policies to achieve growth. That is why we need to study the causes of growth and the policies that governments can pursue.

One thing the government can do is to view the problem as one of *constrained optimization*. It sets constraints: levels of environmental protection, minimum wages, maximum rates of depletion of non-renewable resources, etc. It then seeks policies that will maximize growth, whilst keeping within these constraints.

? 1. Is a constrained optimization approach a practical solution to the possible costs of economic growth?
2. Are worries about the consequences of economic growth a 'luxury' that only rich countries can afford?

aggregate demand may not match the resulting rise in aggregate supply.

If the rise in aggregate supply is greater than the rise in aggregate demand, potential growth will be greater than actual growth. Increased slack will develop in the economy, with a resulting rise in unemployment (of both labour and other resources). If, however, the rise in aggregate demand is greater than the rise in aggregate supply, slack will be taken up and unemployment will fall. Eventually, as firms approach full capacity, the economy will 'overheat'. Shortages will develop as supply cannot keep up with demand. Prices will rise.

Some economists argue that it will only be by chance that the supply effects and the demand effects of investment will match. This whole debate is examined in Chapter 14.

▲ SUMMARY

1. Actual growth must be distinguished from potential growth. The actual growth rate is the percentage annual increase in the output that is actually produced, whereas potential growth is the percentage annual increase in the capacity of the economy to produce (whether or not it is actually produced).
2. Actual growth is represented by a movement outward of the production *point* on a production possibility diagram, whereas potential growth is represented by an outward shift of the whole curve.
3. Actual growth will fluctuate with the course of the trade cycle. The cycle can be broken down into four phases: the upturn, the boom, the peaking-out, and the slowdown or recession. In practice the length and magnitude of these phases will vary: the cycle is thus irregular.
4. Actual growth is determined by potential growth and by the level of aggregate demand. If actual output is below potential output, actual growth can temporarily exceed potential growth, if aggregate demand is rising sufficiently. In the long-term, however, actual output can only grow as fast as potential output will permit.
5. Potential growth is determined by the rate of increase in the *quantity* of resources: capital, labour, land and raw materials; and by the *productivity* of resources. Increases in the *quantity* of resources will affect output according to their marginal productivity. Marginal productivity will decline (diminishing returns) if only *some* factors are increased. Increases in the *productivity* of factors, however, will shift factors' *MPP* curves outward. The productivity of capital can be increased by technological improvements and the more efficient use of the capital stock; the productivity of labour can be increased by better education, training, motivation and organization.
6. Whether governments can best achieve rapid growth through market-oriented or interventionist policies is highly controversial.
7. Investment plays a key role in determining growth, since it affects both actual and potential growth: it affects both aggregate demand and aggregate supply. Whether investment leads to more or less slack developing in the economy depends on which of these effects is the larger.

12.3 Unemployment

The data for the official unemployment figures for the UK since 1970 are plotted in Figure 12.7. As this clearly shows, the problem of unemployment rapidly worsened in the late 1970s and early 1980s.

This picture was repeated throughout the industrialized world. In Europe, in North America, in Australasia, and in many developing countries too, the problem of unemployment rapidly worsened in the early 1980s as the world plunged into the

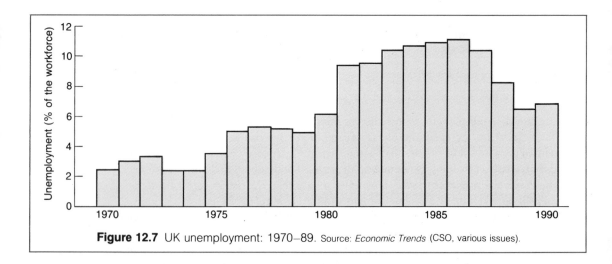

Figure 12.7 UK unemployment: 1970–89. Source: *Economic Trends* (CSO, various issues).

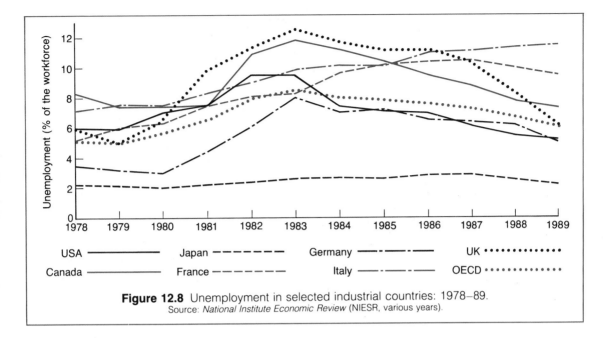

Figure 12.8 Unemployment in selected industrial countries: 1978–89.
Source: *National Institute Economic Review* (NIESR, various years).

greatest recession since the Great Depression of the 1930s. Figure 12.8 shows percentage unemployment rates for selected countries.

In this section we will survey the problem of unemployment. We will first of all ask just what is meant by 'unemployment'. (The answer is not quite as obvious as it might at first seem.) Then we will ask what are the costs of unemployment: not just to the unemployed themselves, but to the whole economy. Then we will turn to the causes of unemployment. At this preliminary stage all we will do is to look at the range of *possible* causes. As the book progresses, however, we will see that different schools of thought put the major blame for unemployment on one or other specific cause. Finally, we will survey the possible policies that can be adopted to tackle unemployment.

The meaning of 'unemployment'

Unemployment can be expressed either as a number (e.g. 2.5 million) or as a percentage (e.g. 8 per cent). But just who should be included in the statistics? Should it be everyone without a job? The answer is clearly no, since we would not want to include children and pensioners. We would probably also want to exclude those who were not looking for work, such as parents choosing to stay at home to look after children.

The most usual definition that economists use for the number unemployed is: *those who want a job, but who are not currently employed*. If the figure is to be expressed as a percentage, then it is as a percentage of the total labour force. The labour force is defined as: *those in employment plus those unemployed*. Thus if 21 million were employed and 3 million were unemployed, the unemployment rate would be:

$$\frac{3}{21 + 3} \times 100 = 12.5\%$$

The government uses a much narrower definition. In official statistics, the number unemployed is defined as: *those in receipt of unemployment benefit and who are available to do any suitable work.* The government statistics thus exclude those who are unemployed but not in receipt of benefits: people such as school leavers under 18 and men over 60.

It is difficult to get politicians to agree on who should be counted as unemployed. Naturally, a government wants the unemployment figures to be as low as possible. Equally naturally, opposition parties want the statistics to include everyone who could possibly be considered as unemployed. This lack of objectivity on the part of politicians makes it very difficult to get a clear, unbiased picture of the problem.

Nevertheless it is possible to identify ways in which official statistics may underestimate or overestimate the extent of unemployment.

Reasons why the statistics may underestimate unemployment

In the UK only those in receipt of unemployment-related benefits are counted in the statistics. As a result the following are ignored.

People returning to the workforce. The main category of people here is parents who up to now have been at home raising children, but who are now looking for employment. These people are ineligible for benefits as they have not recently worked.

School leavers. Those who cannot find jobs are found places on government youth training schemes (YTS). Whether such schemes should be seen as causing a genuine reduction in unemployment is a matter of debate.

Men between 60 and 65 who are seeking employment. Men are not entitled to state pensions until they are 65. Unemployed men over 60, however, do not count in the statistics, since they can receive benefits without having to register as being available for employment.

The temporarily unemployed. People temporarily out of work are not entitled to benefits. Whether they should be regarded as 'genuinely' unemployed is debatable. A lot depends on (a) how long is 'temporary' and (b) just why people are temporarily out of work. If people voluntarily quit their job and then spend two or three weeks looking for a better one, this is far less serious a problem for them than if they were made redundant and after two or three weeks settled for a much lower-paid job.

People seeking part-time work. Such people are not entitled to benefits and therefore do not count as unemployed, even though they cannot find employment.

Underemployment. Some people may want to work full time and yet are only able to find part-time work. They are thus 'underemployed'. They do not show up in the statistics – not even as a fraction of an unemployed person. Underemployment is a particular problem in Third World countries (this is examined in Chapter 23).

Disguised unemployment. Some industries are reluctant to shed labour even when they are clearly overstaffed. If four people are employed to do the work of three, then it can be said that there is 'disguised' unemployment of one person. Other examples of disguised unemployment are where skilled people are forced to take low-paid jobs that do not utilize their skills. This was a major problem in the USSR and other countries which were centrally planned and where people had guaranteed jobs.

 At which point in the trade cycle is the level of disguised unemployment likely to be the highest? Explain.

Reasons why the statistics may overestimate unemployment

Some people who are in receipt of benefits, and who are thus officially available for work, may have no intention of doing a job. Examples of such people are those who have taken early retirement and who are in receipt of an occupational pension; those who have given up employment in order to raise a family; those who would rather live on unemployment benefit than take a job.

Other people may already have a job but pretend that they are unemployed so as to be able to claim benefits. The Department of Employment has tightened up its checks on claimants in recent years in order to prevent fraudulent claims.

Other people may turn down several offers of employment in the hope of getting a better offer.

Some people do more than one job. Others do substantial amounts of overtime. It could be argued that this means that the unemployment figures overstate the lack of jobs in the economy.

There are always some jobs vacant even when unemployment is high (e.g. due to a lack of workers with specific skills). It could be argued that this too means that the unemployment figures overstate the lack of jobs.

It can thus be argued that some people are *voluntarily* unemployed. This, some claim, is not nearly such a serious problem as *in*voluntary unemployment. The distinction between voluntary and involuntary unemployment is examined below.

 How would you distinguish between voluntary and involuntary unemployment? How would you classify people who are made redundant and turn down the only job they can find, where that job pays a much lower wage?

The duration of unemployment

A few of the unemployed may never have had a job and may never will. For the rest, however, unemployment only lasts a period of time. For some it may be just a few days while they are between jobs. For others it may be a few months. For others – the long-term unemployed – it could be several years.

Table 12.1 shows the composition of unemployment by duration.

What determines the average duration of unemployment? There are two important factors here.

Table 12.1 UK unemployment by duration

	Up to 26 weeks	Over 26 weeks and up to 52 weeks	Over 52 weeks	Total
Oct 1979 (thousands)	771.6	194.2	337.0	1302.8
(per cent)	59.2	14.9	25.9	100.0
Oct 1981 (thousands)	1514.5	689.5	784.6	2988.6
(per cent)	50.7	23.1	26.2	100.0
Oct 1986 (thousands)	1341.1	555.0	1341.0	3237.2
(per cent)	41.5	17.0	41.5	100.0
Oct 1988 (thousands)	873.0	360.4	885.5	2118.9
(per cent)	41.2	17.0	41.8	100.0
Oct 1990 (thousands)	873.4	289.5	507.7	1670.6
(per cent)	52.3	17.3	30.4	100.0

Source: *Employment Gazette* (Dept of Employment).

The number unemployed (the size of the stock of unemployment). Unemployment is a 'stock' concept. It measures a *quantity* (i.e. the number unemployed) at a particular *point in time.* Another example of a stock concept is a firm's stock of finished goods in the warehouse. The higher the stock of unemployment, the longer will tend to be the duration of unemployment. There will be more people competing for vacant jobs. Likewise, the bigger a firm's stock of finished goods, the longer they will tend to stay in the warehouse.

The rate of inflow and outflow from the stock of unemployment. The people making up the unemployment total are constantly changing. Each week some people are made redundant or quit their jobs. They represent an inflow to the stock of unemployment. Other people find jobs and thus represent an outflow from the stock of unemployment. The various inflows and outflows are shown in Figure 12.9.

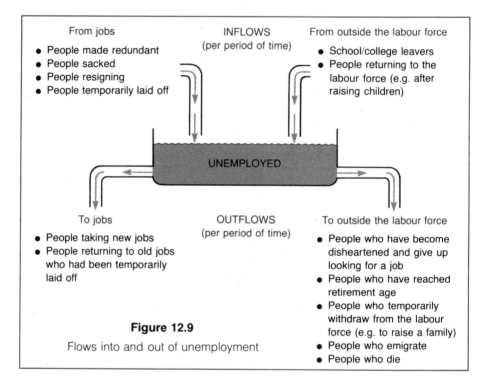

Figure 12.9

Flows into and out of unemployment

Unemployment is often referred to as 'the pool of unemployment'. This is quite a good analogy. If the water flowing into a pool exceeds the water flowing out, the level of water in the pool will rise. Similarly, if the inflow of people into unemployment exceeds the outflow, the level of unemployment will rise.

The duration of unemployment will depend on the *rate* of inflow and outflow. The rate is expressed as the number of people per period of time. Table 12.2 shows the inflows and outflows in selected years.

Note the magnitude of the flows. In each of the years, the outflows (and inflows) exceed the total number unemployed. The bigger the flows are, the less will be the

Table 12.2 UK unemployment flows (millions)

	1980	1982	1984	1986	1988
Inflow	3.85	4.53	4.50	4.49	3.81
Outflow	3.21	4.24	4.40	4.88	4.43
Total level of unemployment	1.66	2.92	3.16	3.29	2.37

Source: *Employment Gazette* (Department of Employment).

average duration of unemployment. This is because people move into and out of the pool more quickly, and hence their average stay will be shorter.

> **?** 1. If the number unemployed exceeded the total annual outflow, what could we conclude about the average duration of unemployment?
> 2. Make a list of the various inflows to and outflows from employment from and to (a) unemployment; (b) outside the workforce.

The costs of unemployment

The most obvious cost of unemployment is to the *unemployed themselves*. There is the direct financial cost of the loss in their earnings, measured as the difference between their previous wage and their unemployment benefit. Then there are the personal costs of being unemployed. The longer people are unemployed, the more dispirited they may become. Their self-esteem is likely to fall, and they are more likely to succumb to stress-related illness.

Then there are the costs to the *family and friends* of the unemployed. Personal relations can become strained, and there may be an increase in domestic violence and the number of families splitting up.

Then there are the *broader costs to the economy*. Unemployment represents a loss of output. In other words, actual output is below potential output. Apart from the lack of income to the unemployed themselves, this under-utilization of resources leads to lower incomes for other people too:

- The government loses tax revenues, since the unemployed pay no income tax and national insurance, and, given that the unemployed spend less, they pay less VAT and excise duties. The government also incurs administrative costs associated with the running of benefit offices. It may also have to spend extra on health care, the social services and the police.
- Firms lose the profits that could have been made, had there been full employment.
- Other workers lose any additional wages they could have earned from higher national output.

Finally, there is some evidence that higher unemployment leads to increased *crime and vandalism*. This obviously imposes a cost on the sufferers.

The costs of unemployment are to some extent offset by benefits. If workers voluntarily quit their jobs to look for a better one, then they must reckon that the benefits of a better job more than compensate for their temporary loss of income. From the nation's point of view, a workforce that is prepared to quit jobs and spend a short time unemployed will be a more adaptable, more mobile workforce – one that is responsive to changing economic circumstances. Such a workforce will lead to greater allocative efficiency in the short run and more rapid economic growth over the longer run.

Long-term involuntary unemployment is quite another matter. The costs clearly outweigh any benefits, both for the individuals involved and for the economy as a whole. A demotivated, deskilled pool of long-term unemployed is a serious economic and social problem.

Unemployment and the labour market

We now turn to the causes of unemployment. These causes fall into two broad categories: *equilibrium* unemployment and *disequilibrium* unemployment. To make

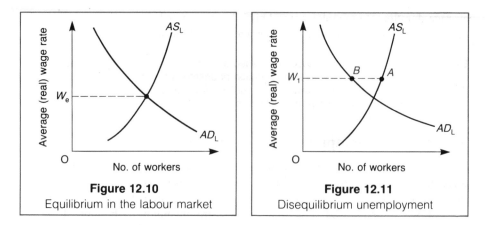

Figure 12.10
Equilibrium in the labour market

Figure 12.11
Disequilibrium unemployment

clear the distinction between the two, it is necessary to look at the working of the labour market.

Figure 12.10 shows the aggregate demand for labour and aggregate supply of labour: that is, the total demand and supply of labour in the whole economy. The *real* wage is plotted on the vertical axis. This is the wage expressed in terms of its purchasing power: in other words, after taking inflation into account.

The aggregate supply of labour curve (AS_L) shows the number of workers *willing to accept jobs* at each wage rate. This curve is relatively inelastic, since the size of the workforce at any one time cannot change significantly. Nevertheless it is not totally inelastic because (a) a higher wage will encourage some people to enter the labour market (e.g. parents raising children), and (b) the unemployed will be more willing to accept job offers rather than continuing to search for a better-paid job.

The aggregate demand for labour curve (AD_L) slopes downward. The higher the wage, the more firms will attempt to economize on labour. They will be encouraged to substitute other factors of production for labour.

The labour market is in equilibrium at a wage of W_e – where the demand for labour equals the supply.

If the wage were above W_e, the market would be in a state of disequilibrium. This is illustrated in Figure 12.11. At a wage rate of W_1, there is an excess supply of labour of $A - B$. This is called disequilibrium unemployment.

For disequilibrium unemployment to occur, two conditions must hold:

● The aggregate supply of labour must exceed the aggregate demand.
● There must be a 'stickiness' in wages. In other words, the wage rate must not immediately fall to W_e.

Even when the labour market *is* in equilibrium, however, not everyone looking for work will be employed. Some people will hold out, hoping to find a better job. This is illustrated in Figure 12.12.

The curve N shows the total number in the labour force. The horizontal difference between it and the aggregate supply of labour curve (AS_L) gives equilibrium unemployment. This is shown by the distance $D - E$. Equilibrium unemployment can be defined as the excess of people looking for work over those actually willing to accept jobs.

Note that the AS_L curve gets closer to the N curve at higher wages. The reason for this is that the unemployed will be more willing to accept jobs, the higher the wages they are offered. Figure 12.13 shows both equilibrium *and* disequilibrium unemploy-

Aggregate demand for labour curve

A curve showing the total demand for labour in the economy at different levels of real wages.

Aggregate supply of labour curve

A curve showing the total number of people willing and able to work at different real wage levels.

Disequilibrium unemployment

Unemployment resulting from real wages in the economy being above the equilibrium level.

Equilibrium ('natural') unemployment

The difference between those who would like employment at the current wage and those willing and able to take a job.

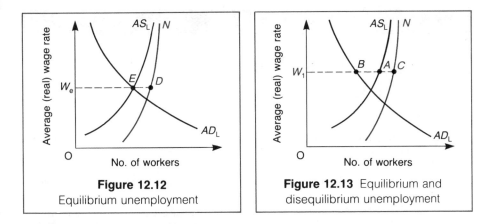

Figure 12.12
Equilibrium unemployment

Figure 12.13 Equilibrium and
disequilibrium unemployment

ment. At a wage of W_1, disequilibrium unemployment is $A - B$; equilibrium unemployment is $C - A$; thus total unemployment is $C - B$.

But what are the causes of disequilibrium unemployment? What are the causes of equilibrium unemployment? We will examine each in turn.

Disequilibrium unemployment

What causes the actual average wage rate to be above the market equilibrium wage rate? There are three possible reasons:

● The wage rate is pushed up above the equilibrium.
● There is a fall in the aggregate demand for labour with no corresponding fall in wages.
● There is an increase in the aggregate supply of labour with no corresponding fall in wages. Each of these three causes gives rise to a distinct type of disequilibrium unemployment.

Real-wage (classical) unemployment

Real-wage or classical unemployment is where trade unions use their monopoly power to drive wages above the market-clearing level. It could also be caused by governments introducing minimum wage legislation, or operating a 'prices and incomes policy' where one of the provisions is for workers automatically to get wage increases above the rate of inflation. (See section 20.3.)

In Figure 12.14, if the average wage rate is pushed up from W_e to W_1, the supply of labour will rise to Q_1 as higher wages encourage more people to join the labour force and to accept job offers. The demand for labour will fall to Q_2 as firms, faced by higher labour costs, cut back on production and attempt to substitute other factors of production for labour. (For example, firms may replace workers by robots on assembly lines.)

Disequilibrium unemployment will thus be $Q_1 - Q_2$ (i.e. the amount $A - B$).

The final effect on unemployment, however, may not be quite so bad. The extra wages paid to those who are still employed could lead to extra *consumer* expenditure. This addition to aggregate demand would in turn lead to firms demanding more labour, as they attempted to increase output to meet the extra demand. If the effect of this is to shift the demand for labour to AD_{L2}, real-wage unemployment will fall to $A - B'$.

The 'classical' economists in the 1920s and 1930s blamed the mass unemployment of that period on real wages being too high (hence the alternative name 'classical

Classical unemployment

Disequilibrium unemployment caused by real wages being driven up above the market clearing level.

Box 12.4

The Conservative Party's Analysis of Unemployment

In his speech to the Conservative Party conference in 1985, the then Chancellor of the Exchequer, Nigel Lawson, made the following statement about unemployment:

> You won't reduce unemployment by increasing what government spends, or what government borrows, nor by printing more money. That approach has already been tested to destruction during the 1970s and unemployment went on rising . . .
>
> The main cause of high unemployment in Britain today, and it's much the same in the rest of Europe, is the

determination of monopolistic trades unions to insist on levels of pay that price men out of work altogether.

On 13 December 1990, the Prime Minister, John Major commenting on a dramatic rise in unemployment, said:

> Everyone regrets the rise in unemployment that we have seen, but I have been warning for some months that if wage rises stay high, that will have a necessary effect on jobs.

---

unemployment'). Excessive real wages have also been blamed by Conservative governments for the high unemployment of recent years (see Box 12.4).

The solution to real-wage unemployment is a reduction in real wages. This seemingly obvious solution, however, has a number of drawbacks:

● If the government reduces minimum wages, it will be the poorest workers who will suffer. It will not affect the wages or employment of those already on above minimum wages.

● It may be very difficult to reduce the power of unions to push up wages.

● Even if the government succeeds in reducing the average real wage, there will then be a problem of reduced consumer expenditure and a reduced demand for labour.

 How would you show this last problem in a diagram like Figure 12.14?

Demand-deficient (cyclical) unemployment

Demand-deficient (cyclical) unemployment

Disequilibrium unemployment caused by a fall in aggregate demand with no corresponding fall in the real wage rate.

Demand-deficient (cyclical) unemployment is associated with economic recessions. As the economy moves into recession, consumer demand falls. Firms find that they are unable to sell their current level of output. For a time they may be prepared to build up stocks of unsold goods, but sooner or later they will start to cut back on production and cut back on the amount of labour they employ. The deeper the recession becomes and the longer it lasts, the higher will demand-deficient unemployment become.

As the economy recovers and begins to grow again, so demand-deficient unemployment will start to fall again. Because demand-deficient unemployment fluctuates with the trade cycle, it is sometimes referred to as 'cyclical unemployment'.

Demand-deficient unemployment is illustrated in Figure 12.15. Assume initially that the economy is at the peak of the trade cycle. The aggregate demand for and supply of labour are equal at the current wage of W_1. There is no disequilibrium unemployment. Now assume that the economy moves into recession. Consumer demand falls and as a result firms demand less labour. The demand for labour shifts to AD_{L2}. If there is a resistance to wage cuts, such that the wage remains fixed at W_1, there will now be disequilibrium unemployment of $Q_1 - Q_2$.

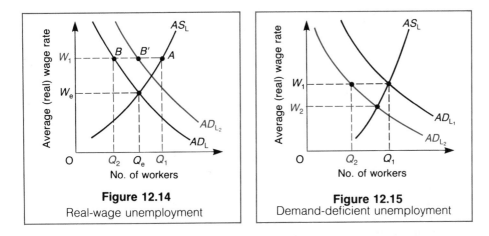

Figure 12.14
Real-wage unemployment

Figure 12.15
Demand-deficient unemployment

Even if wages were to fall to W_2, demand-deficient unemployment could still persist. The reason is that this general cut in wages throughout the economy would reduce workers' incomes and hence reduce their *consumption of goods*. As the aggregate demand for goods fell, there would be a further reduction in demand for labour: the aggregate demand for labour curve would shift to the left of AD_{L2}. By the time the wage had fallen to W_2, W_2 would no longer be the equilibrium wage. There would still be demand-deficient unemployment.

 If this analysis is correct, namely that a reduction in wages will reduce the aggregate demand for goods, what assumption must we make about the relative proportions of wages and *profits* that are spent (given that a reduction in wages will lead to a corresponding increase in profits)?

Demand-deficient unemployment can also exist in the longer term if the economy is constantly run at below full capacity and labour markets continue not to be in equilibrium. Even at the peak of the trade cycle, actual output may be considerably below potential output.

In an attempt to reduce demand-deficient unemployment, governments have sought to ensure that aggregate demand is high enough. Policies that raise aggregate demand may, however, worsen inflation and balance of payments deficits. (We will look at these effects later.)

Growth in the labour supply

If labour supply rises with no corresponding increase in the demand for labour, the equilibrium wage rate will fall. If the wage rate is 'sticky' downward, disequilibrium unemployment will occur.

 On a diagram similar to that of Figure 12.15, illustrate how a growth in labour supply can cause disequilibrium unemployment.

This tends not to be such a serious cause of unemployment as demand-deficiency, since the supply of labour changes relatively slowly. Nevertheless there is a problem of providing jobs for school leavers each year with the sudden influx of new workers on to the labour market.

There is also the potential problem over the longer term if social trends lead more women with children to seek employment. In practice, however, with the rapid growth of part-time employment, and the lower level of average wages paid to women, this has not caused a major problem of excess labour supply.

Equilibrium ('natural') unemployment

Even when there is no general disequilibrium in the economy at the current wage levels – even when there are as many job vacancies as people unemployed – there will still be some unemployment. For various reasons, not all vacancies will be filled. The problem is one of mismatching. There may be excess demand for labour (vacancies) in some markets and excess supply (unemployment) in others. There may be vacancies for computer technicians and unemployment in the steel industry, but unemployed steel workers cannot immediately become computer technicians. There may even be vacancies *and* unemployment in the same market, but the unemployed may be unable, unwilling or unsuitable to take up the vacancies, or simply unaware of their existence.

Although there may be overall *macro*economic equilibrium, with the *aggregate* demand for labour equal to the *aggregate* supply, and thus no disequilibrium unemployment, at a *micro*economic level supply and demand may not match. This is when equilibrium unemployment will occur.

There are various types of equilibrium unemployment.

Frictional (search) unemployment

> **Frictional (search) unemployment**
>
> Unemployment that occurs as a result of imperfect information in the labour market. It often takes time for workers to find jobs (even though there *are* vacancies) and in the meantime they are unemployed.

Frictional (search) unemployment occurs when people leave their jobs, either voluntarily or because they are sacked or made redundant, and are unemployed for a period of time while they are looking for a new job. They may not get the first job they apply for, despite a vacancy existing. The employer may continue searching, hoping to find a better-qualified person. Likewise unemployed people may choose not to take the first job they *are* offered. Instead they may continue searching, hoping that a better one will turn up.

The problem is that information is imperfect. Employers are not fully informed about what labour is available; workers are not fully informed about what jobs are available and what they entail. Both employers and workers, therefore, have to search: employers searching for the right labour and workers searching for the right jobs.

Searching for a job takes time. The longer people search for a job, the better the wage offers they are likely to be made. This is illustrated in Figure 12.16 by the curve W_o. It shows the highest wage offer that the typical worker will have received since being unemployed.

When they first start looking for a job, people may have high expectations of getting a good wage. The longer they are unemployed, however, the more anxious they are

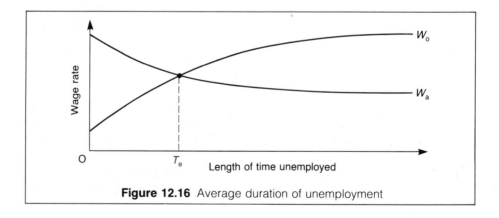

Figure 12.16 Average duration of unemployment

likely to be to get a job, and therefore the lower will be the wage they will be prepared to accept. The curve W_a shows the wage that is acceptable to the typical worker.

? Why are W_o and W_a curves rather than straight lines?

The average duration of unemployment will be T_e. That is, workers will remain unemployed until they find a job at an acceptable wage.

One obvious remedy for frictional unemployment is for there to be better job information. This could be provided by government job centres, by private employment agencies, or by local and national newspapers. This would have the effect of making the curve W_o reach its peak earlier, and thus of shifting the intersection of W_o and W_a to the left.

Another much more controversial remedy is for the government to reduce the level of unemployment benefit. This will make the unemployed more desperate to get a job and thus prepared to accept a lower wage. It will therefore have the effect of shifting the W_a curve downwards and again of shifting the intersection of W_o and W_a to the left.

Structural unemployment

Structural unemployment is where the structure of the economy changes. Employment in some industries may expand while in others it contracts. There are two main reasons for this.

A change in the pattern of demand. Some industries experience declining demand. This may be due to a change in consumer tastes. Certain goods may go out of fashion. Or it may be due to competition from other industries. For example, consumer demand may shift away from coal and to other fuels. This will lead to structural unemployment in mining areas.

A change in the methods of production (technological unemployment). New techniques of production often allow the same level of output to be produced with fewer workers. This is known as 'labour-saving technical progress'. Unless output expands sufficiently to absorb the surplus labour, people will be made redundant. This creates technological unemployment.

Structural unemployment often occurs in particular regions of the country. When it does, it is referred to as regional unemployment. Regional unemployment is due to the concentration of particular industries in particular areas. For example, the decline in the South Wales coal-mining industry led to high unemployment in the Welsh valleys. The level of structural unemployment will depend on three factors.

The degree of regional concentration of industry. The more diversified is a region's economy, the less it will be affected by the decline of one particular industry.

The speed of change of demand and supply in the economy. The more rapid the rate of technological change or the shift in consumer tastes, the more rapid will be the rate of redundancies.

The immobility of labour. The less able or willing workers are to move to a new job, the higher will be the level of structural unemployment. Remember from Chapter 8 the distinction we made between geographical and occupational immobility. Geographical immobility is a particular problem with regional unemployment. Occupational

Structural unemployment

Unemployment that arises from changes in the pattern of demand or supply in the economy. People made redundant in one part of the economy cannot immediately take up jobs in other parts (even though there are vacancies).

Technological unemployment

Structural unemployment that occurs as a result of the introduction of labour-saving technology.

Regional unemployment

Structural unemployment occurring in specific regions of the country.

Box 12.5

Technology and Employment
Does technological progress create or destroy jobs?[3]

Does technological progress destroy jobs? The obvious answer may seem to be Yes. After all, new technology often involves machines taking over jobs that were previously done by people.

There is another view, however. This argues that a failure to introduce new technology and ultimately to remain competitive will offer an even worse long-term employment problem. Markets, and hence employment, will be lost to more efficient competitors.

The relative merits of each of these views is difficult to assess, since they depend greatly upon the type of technology, its organization in the workplace and the market within which it is located. The diagram isolates four stages in the effects of new technology on jobs.

Four effects of new technology on employment.
Source: A. Rajan and G. Cooke, 'The impact of IT on employment', *National Westminster Bank Quarterly Review*, August 1986.

Stage (1) Design and installation
Here labour requirements grow as first designers and then construction workers are employed. As construction/installation is completed, employment from this source will then disappear.

Stage (2) Implementation
Here labour requirements decline, especially if the technology is concerned with improving existing processes rather than creating new products.

Stage (3) Servicing
Maintenance and repair may have positive employment effects. This may gradually decrease over time as 'teething troubles' are eliminated, or it may increase as the stock of initially new machines begins to grow older.

Stage (4) Market expansion
This represents the long-term impact of technology on employment levels as the improved and/or cheaper products lead to more sales.

The *optimistic* view holds that, historically, technology has generated more jobs than it has destroyed. The Institute for Employment Research at Warwick University suggested in the early 1980s that, although approximately 340 000 jobs would have been displaced by new technology in the six years up to 1990, this would have been more than compensated by the creation of 420 000 new jobs, both directly in the industries experiencing technical innovation, and also indirectly in related non-innovating industries.

The *pessimists*, however, are less certain about the potential employment benefits of new technology.

At the end of the 1980s, Rolls-Royce in Derby had 3 workers producing what 30 did twenty years previously. Plessey reduced their Liverpool workforce by 825 in two years as they expanded their production of digital telephone exchanges. In Japan, the number of workers in TV production was cut by 50 per cent during the 1970s. Output, however, grew by 25 per cent.

White-collar work is seen as equally under threat by technological innovation. One branch of the Halifax Building Society, in moving from electronic typewriters to sixteen IBM word processors, managed to treble its workload without taking on any extra staff. Littlewoods mail order introduced a new computer system and during 1985 cut 600 jobs.

Long-term employment estimates can be equally pessimistic. In West Germany, estimates made in the early 1980s predicted that by 1990 office employment would have fallen by 40 per cent, or over 2 million jobs.

The question of technology and employment is one that poses a serious dilemma. A failure to innovate reduces a country's competitive position and hence its employment potential in the longer term. Yet technological innovation can represent a serious source of job loss in the immediate future.

? In what areas of the economy are jobs growing most rapidly? Is this due to a lack of technological innovation in these areas?

[3] This box is based on material in C. Rowe, *People and Chips: The human implications of information technology* (Paradigm, 1986).

immobility is a particular problem with technological unemployment where old skills are no longer required.

? For what reasons are people (a) geographically and (b) occupationally immobile?

There are two broad approaches to tackling structural unemployment: *market orientated* and *interventionist*.

A market-orientated approach involves encouraging people to 'get on their bikes' and look for jobs, if necessary in other parts of the country. It involves encouraging people to adopt a more willing attitude towards retraining, and if necessary to accept some reduction in wages.

An interventionist approach involves direct government action to match jobs to the unemployed. Two examples are providing grants to firms to set up in areas of high unemployment (regional policy), and government-funded training schemes.

Policies to tackle structural unemployment are examined in detail in sections 20.4 and 20.5.

Seasonal unemployment

Seasonal unemployment occurs when the demand for certain types of labour fluctuates with the seasons of the year. This problem is particularly severe in holiday areas such as Cornwall, where unemployment can reach very high levels in the winter months. Policies for tackling seasonal unemployment are similar to those for structural unemployment.

Seasonal unemployment
Unemployment associated with industries or regions where the demand for labour is lower at certain times of the year.

▲ SUMMARY

1. Who should be counted as 'unemployed' is a matter for some disagreement. If everyone without a job who would like one is included, the figure will be much higher than if it only includes those who are actively looking for work and are in receipt of benefit.

2. The 'stock' of unemployment will grow if the inflow of people into unemployment exceeds the outflow (to jobs or out of the labour market altogether). The more rapid these flows, the shorter the average duration of unemployment.

3. The costs of unemployment include the financial and other personal costs to the unemployed person, the costs to relatives and friends, and the costs to society at large in terms of lost tax revenues, lost profits and lost wages to other workers, and in terms of social disruption.

4. Unemployment can be divided into disequilibrium and equilibrium unemployment.

5. Disequilibrium unemployment occurs when real wages are above the level that will equate the aggregate demand and supply of labour. It can be caused by unions or government pushing up wages (classical or real-wage unemployment), by a fall in aggregate demand but a downward 'stickiness' in real wages (demand-deficient unemployment), or by an increase in the supply of labour with again a downward stickiness in wages.

6. Equilibrium unemployment occurs when there are people unable or unwilling to fill job vacancies. This may be due to poor information in the labour market and hence a time lag before people find suitable jobs (frictional unemployment), to a changing pattern of demand or supply in the economy and hence a mismatching of labour with jobs (structural unemployment – specific types being technological and regional unemployment), or to seasonal fluctuations in the demand for labour.

12.4 Inflation

The rate of inflation measures the annual percentage increase in prices. The most usual measure is that of *retail* prices. The government publishes an index of retail prices each month, and the rate of inflation is the percentage increase in that index over the previous twelve months.

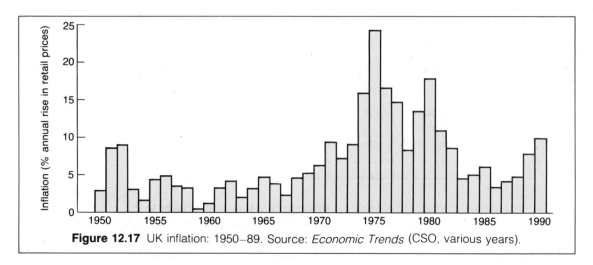

Figure 12.17 UK inflation: 1950–89. Source: *Economic Trends* (CSO, various years).

Figure 12.17 shows the rates of UK inflation from 1950 to 1990. As you can see, inflation was particularly severe between 1973 and 1981.

Figure 12.18 shows the rates of inflation for various countries from 1977 to 1989. There are marked differences between the countries, with Japan having very low rates of inflation and Italy having comparatively high rates. UK inflation was slightly worse than the OECD[4] average.

It is also possible to give the rates of inflation for other prices. For example, indices are published for commodity prices, for food prices, for house prices, for import prices, for prices after taking taxes into account (the 'tax and price index') and so on. Their respective rates of inflation are simply their annual percentage increases. Likewise it is possible to give the rate of inflation of wages ('wage inflation').

A word on terminology: if prices rise, we refer to that as 'inflation'. If prices fall, however, this is normally referred to as 'negative inflation' rather than 'deflation'. The

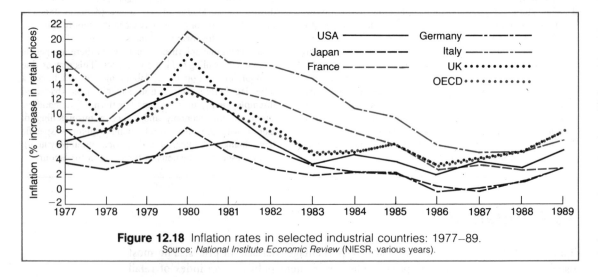

Figure 12.18 Inflation rates in selected industrial countries: 1977–89.
Source: *National Institute Economic Review* (NIESR, various years).

[4] OECD: Organization for Economic Co-operation and Development. Its membership consists of the developed countries of the world.

word 'deflation' is normally used to refer to a government policy of reducing aggregate demand – a policy designed to reduce excessive spending in the economy.

Finally, before we proceed, a word of caution: be careful not to confuse a rise or fall in *inflation* with a rise or fall in *prices*. A rise in inflation means a *faster* increase in prices. A fall in inflation means a *slower* increase in prices (but still an increase as long as inflation is positive).

The costs of inflation

A lack of growth is obviously a problem if people want higher living standards. Unemployment is obviously a problem, both for the unemployed themselves and also for society, which suffers a loss in output and has to support the unemployed. But why is inflation a problem? If prices go up by 10 per cent does it really matter? Provided your wages kept up with prices, you would have no cut in your living standards.

Apart from the problem of having to adjust our concept of what a 'fair' price is for each item when we go shopping, are there any other problems of inflation? In other words, is inflation anything more than a minor inconvenience?

Inflation is regarded as a problem for the following reasons.

Redistribution. Inflation redistributes income away from those on fixed incomes and those in a weak bargaining position, and to those who can use their economic power to gain large pay, rent or profit increases. It redistributes wealth to those with assets (e.g. property) which rise in value particularly rapidly during periods of inflation, and away from those with savings which pay rates of interest below the rate of inflation and hence whose value is eroded by inflation. Pensioners may be particularly badly hit by rapid inflation.

1. Do you personally gain or lose from inflation? Why?
2. Make a list of those who are most likely to gain and those who are most likely to lose from inflation.

Uncertainty. Inflation tends to cause uncertainty among the business community, especially when the rate of inflation fluctuates. (Generally, the higher the rate of inflation, the more it fluctuates.) If it is difficult for firms to predict their costs and revenues, they may be discouraged from investing. This will reduce the rate of economic growth. On the other hand, as will be explained below, policies to reduce the rate of inflation may themselves reduce the rate of economic growth, especially in the short run. This may then provide the government with a policy dilemma.

Why does uncertainty reduce investment?

Balance of payments. Inflation is likely to worsen the balance of payments. If UK inflation is higher than in other countries, it will make UK exports less competitive in world markets. At the same time, imports will become relatively cheaper than home-produced goods. Thus exports will fall and imports will rise. As a result the balance of payments will deteriorate and/or the exchange rate will fall. Both of these effects can cause problems. This is examined in more detail in section 12.5.

Resources. Extra resources are likely to be used to cope with the effects of inflation. Price lists will have to be issued more frequently; and accountants and other financial experts may have to be employed by companies to help them cope with the uncertainties caused by inflation.

Box 12.6

Hyperinflation in Germany: 1923
When prices went crazy

In recent years in the UK we have come to expect relatively stable prices. If the rate of inflation were to rise to anywhere near the levels reached in the mid-1970s (24 per cent) or the early 1980s (18 per cent), it would be looked upon as a clear sign of economic failure.

But such rates are mild compared with those experienced by many other countries in the past, or in some cases the present. In 1990 the rate of inflation in Yugoslavia exceeded 300 per cent and in Brazil it was over 1000 per cent. But even these cases of hyperinflation are mild compared with those experienced by several countries in the early 1920s!

In Austria and Hungary prices were several thousand times their pre-war level. In Poland they were over 2 million times higher, and in the USSR several billion times higher. But even these staggering rates of inflation seem insignificant beside those of Germany.

Following the chaos of the First World War, the German government resorted to printing money, not only to meet its domestic spending requirements in rebuilding a war-ravaged economy, but also to finance the crippling war reparations imposed on it by the allies in the Treaty of Versailles.

In 1919 the currency in circulation increased by a massive 80 per cent and prices increased by 91 per cent. At the end of 1919, however, a new socialist government attempted to slow this inflationary spiral. New taxes were imposed and government revenues increased. But public debt continued to grow, and by mid-1921 the government once more resorted to the printing presses to finance its expenditure.

Inflation now really began to take off, and by autumn 1923 the annual rate of inflation had reached a mind-boggling 7 000 000 000 000 per cent!

The table charts the rise in money supply and inflation over this period. (Note that the figures for inflation are *quarterly*.)

As price increases accelerated, people became reluctant to accept money: before they knew it, the money would be worthless. People thus rushed to spend their money as

		Currency[1]	Prices[1]	Unemployment[2]	Real wages[3]
1919	I	12.5	11.8		
	II	14.7	12.4	3.7	26.7
	III	–0.1	60.1		
	IV	18.6	62.9		
1920	I	18.8	112.8		
	II	14.6	–19.1	3.8	–34.6
	III	11.0	8.3		
	IV	7.8	–3.9		
1921	I	–1.5	–7.1		
	II	5.6	2.1	2.8	18.1
	III	11.8	51.3		
	IV	29.5	68.7		
1922	I	14.3	55.8		
	II	28.6	29.4	1.5	–53.6
	III	84.0	308.3		
	IV	289.5	413.9		
1923	I	331.1	231.1		
	II	213.8	297.0	10.2	49.3
	III	1622.9	1234.4		
	IV	17580.7	52678.8		

[1] Percentage change from previous quarter.
[2] Percentage of the labour force.
[3] Percentage annual rate of change.

Source: A. Sommariva and G. Tullio, *German Macroeconomic History 1880–1979* (Macmillan, 1987).

quickly as possible. But this in turn further drove up prices.

For many Germans the effect was devastating. People's life savings were wiped out. Others whose wages were not quickly adjusted found their real incomes plummeting. Many were thrown out of work as businesses, especially those with *money* assets, went bankrupt. Poverty and destitution were widespread.

By the end of 1923 the German currency was literally worthless. In 1924, therefore, it was replaced by a new currency – one whose supply was kept tightly controlled by the government.

The costs of inflation may be relatively mild if inflation is kept to single figures. They can be very serious, however, if inflation gets out of hand. If inflation develops into 'hyperinflation', with prices rising perhaps by several hundred per cent or even thousands per cent per year, the whole basis of the market economy will be undermined. Firms constantly raise prices in an attempt to cover their rocketing costs. Workers demand huge pay increases in an attempt to stay ahead of the rocketing cost of living. Thus prices and wages chase each other in an ever-rising inflationary spiral. People will no longer want to save money. Instead they will spend it as quickly as possible before its value falls any further. People may even resort to barter in an attempt to avoid using money altogether.

Box 12.6 looks at perhaps the most severe case of hyperinflation ever: that of Germany in the early 1920s.

Aggregate demand and supply and the level of prices

The level of prices in the economy is determined by the interaction of aggregate demand and aggregate supply. The analysis is similar to that of demand and supply in individual markets, although as we shall see in later chapters there are some crucial differences. Figure 12.19 shows an aggregate demand and an aggregate supply curve. Let us examine each in turn.

Aggregate demand curve

Remember what we said about aggregate demand earlier in the chapter.

It is the total level of spending in the economy: that is, by consumers, by the government, by firms on investment, and by foreigners. This total level of spending will depend on people's money incomes and the prices people have to pay. For any *given* level of money incomes, the higher the level of prices, the less people will be able to buy. In other words, if there is a given amount of money income in the economy and prices go up, less will be purchased: aggregate demand will be lower. Thus the aggregate demand curve has a negative slope, as in Figure 12.19. (This analysis ignores any changes in interest rates. We will drop this assumption in later chapters.)

Aggregate supply curve

The aggregate supply curve slopes upwards. In other words, the higher the level of prices, the more will be produced. The reason for this is that higher output will involve higher marginal costs. If firms face rising marginal costs, they will need to receive higher prices to encourage them to produce more. Put another way, if the price level rises, it will now be profitable to produce additional units, even though they cost more to produce. But why should marginal costs rise? There are two main reasons.

Diminishing returns. With some factors of production fixed in supply, firms will experience a diminishing marginal physical product from their variable factors.

Figure 12.19 Aggregate demand and aggregate supply

Growing shortages of certain variable factors. As firms produce more, even factors that can be varied may increasingly become in short supply. Skilled labour may be harder to find; certain raw materials may be harder to obtain; monopoly suppliers of component parts may raise their price to take advantage of the higher level of demand.

Thus rising costs explain the upward-sloping aggregate supply curve. The more steeply costs rise, the less elastic will the curve be. (Note that we are making important simplifying assumptions here too. The main one is that firms are assuming that their cost curves do not *shift*: that they face no rise in the price of raw materials, labour, etc. Again we will need to drop this assumption in subsequent chapters.)

Equilibrium

The equilibrium price level will be where aggregate demand equals aggregate supply. To demonstrate this, consider what would happen if aggregate demand exceeded aggregate supply, for example at P_2 in Figure 12.19. The resulting shortages throughout the economy would drive up prices. This would encourage firms to produce more: there would be a movement up *along* the *AS* curve. At the same time, for a given level of money income, people would not purchase so much: there would be a movement back up *along* the *AD* curve. The shortage would be eliminated when price had risen to P_e.

This explains how inflation occurs. An excess of aggregate demand over aggregate supply drives up prices. This excess can be caused by a rightward shift in *AD*, or a leftward shift in *AS*, or a combination of the two.

When inflation results from a rightward shift in aggregate demand it is known as demand-pull inflation (or 'demand-side' inflation). When it originates from a leftward shift in aggregate supply it is known as cost-push inflation (or 'supply-side' inflation). Let us examine each in turn.

Demand-pull inflation

Inflation caused by persistent rises in aggregate demand.

Cost-push inflation

Inflation caused by persistent rises in costs of production (independently from demand).

Monetarists

Those who attribute inflation solely to rises in money supply.

Demand-pull inflation

This is caused by rises in aggregate demand. These rises in aggregate demand may be due to rises in consumer demand, in the level of government expenditure, in investment by firms, or in foreigners' demand for UK exports, or any combination of these four.

Just what causes rises in aggregate demand is a matter of considerable debate amongst economists. Some economists attribute rises in demand entirely (or virtually so) to an increase in money supply. If there is more money in the economy there will be more spending. These economists, called monetarists, therefore see the cure for inflation to lie in the government controlling the supply of money in the economy.

Other economists see a much more tenuous link between money and spending. They argue that there can be an autonomous rise in spending with no increase in money supply. For example, consumer spending could rise substantially if the government cut the rate of income tax by 2 or 3 per cent, or if there was an upsurge in business confidence and hence investment.

Thus a distinction is frequently made between *monetary* and *non-monetary* explanations of demand-pull inflation.

So just what will happen if aggregate demand rises? Firms will respond to a rise in demand partly by raising prices and partly by increasing output. Just how much they raise prices depends on how much their costs rise as a result of increasing output. In other words, it will depend on the shape of the *AS* curve.

The effect is illustrated in Figure 12.20. The rise in aggregate demand is

Figure 12.20 Demand-pull inflation

illustrated by a rightward shift in the aggregate demand curve, from AD_1 to AD_2. Prices rise from P_1 to P_2, and output rises from Q_1 to Q_2. The steeper the aggregate supply curve, the more prices will rise and the less output will increase.

The aggregate supply curve will tend to become steeper as the economy approaches the peak of the trade cycle. In other words, the closer actual output gets to potential output, and the less slack there is in the economy, the more will firms respond to a rise in demand by raising their prices.

What we have illustrated so far is a *single* increase in demand (or a 'demand shock'). This could be due, for example, to an increased level of government expenditure. The effect is to give a *single* rise in the price level. Although this causes inflation in the short run, once the effect has taken place inflation will fall back to zero. For inflation to persist there must be *continuing* rightward shifts in the *AD* curve, and thus continuing rises in the price level. If *inflation* is to rise, these rightward shifts must get *faster*.

Demand-pull inflation is typically associated with a booming economy. Many economists therefore argue that it is the counterpart of demand-deficient unemployment. When the economy is in recession, demand-deficient unemployment will be high, but demand-pull inflation will be low. When, on the other hand, the economy is near the peak of the trade cycle, demand-pull inflation will be high, but demand-deficient unemployment will be low.

Cost-push inflation

Cost-push inflation is associated with a leftward (upward) shift in the aggregate supply curve. It occurs when costs of production rise *independently* of aggregate demand.

If firms face a rise in costs, they will respond partly by raising prices and passing the costs on to the consumer, and partly by cutting back on production. This is illustrated in Figure 12.21. The leftward shift in the aggregate supply curve from AS_1 to AS_2 causes the price level to rise to P_3 and the level of output to *fall* to Q_3.

Just how much firms raise prices and cut back on production depends on the shape of the aggregate demand curve. The less elastic the *AD* curve, the less will sales fall as a result of any price rise, and hence the more will firms be able to pass on the rise in their costs to consumers as higher prices.

Box 12.7

Cost-Push Illusion
When rising costs are *not* cost-push inflation

It is easy to get confused between demand-pull and cost-push inflation.

Frequently, inflationary pressures *seem* to come from the cost side. Shopkeepers blame their price rises on the rise in their costs – the wholesale prices they have to pay. The wholesalers blame their price rises on a rise in *their* costs – the prices they are charged by the various manufacturers. The manufacturers in turn blame rising raw material costs, rising wage rates, rising rents and so on. Everyone blames their price rises on the rise in their costs.

But why have these costs risen?

It could well be due to a rise in aggregate *demand*! Wages may go up because of falling unemployment and a shortage of labour. Firms *have* to pay higher wages in order to recruit or maintain enough labour. Rents may rise because of the upsurge in demand. So too with raw materials: higher demand may pull up their prices too.

What we have then is a 'cost-push illusion'. Costs rise, it is true, but they rise because of an increase in *demand*.

So when does genuine cost-push inflation occur? This occurs when costs of production rise *independently* of demand. This will normally involve an increased use of monopoly power: unions becoming more powerful or militant; firms using their monopoly/oligopoly power to push up prices; commodity producers such as the OPEC countries forming cartels to push up their prices; the government using its power to raise indirect taxes (such as VAT).

? If trade unions take increased industrial action and if they gain higher wage increases, will any increased inflation that results necessarily be cost-push inflation?

Note that the effect on output and employment will be the opposite of demand-pull inflation. With demand-pull inflation, output and hence employment will tend to rise. With cost-push inflation, however, output and employment will tend to fall.

As with demand-pull inflation, we must distinguish between *single* shifts in the aggregate supply curve (known as 'supply shocks') and *continuing* shifts. If there is a single leftward shift in aggregate supply, there will be a single rise in the price level. For example, if the government raises the excise duty on oil, there will be a single rise in oil prices and hence in industry's fuel costs. This will cause *temporary* inflation while the price rise is passed on through the economy. Once this has occurred, prices will stabilize at the new level and the rate of inflation will fall back to zero again. If cost-push inflation is to continue over a number of years, therefore, the aggregate supply curve must *continually* shift to the left. If cost-push inflation is to *rise*, these shifts must get *faster*.

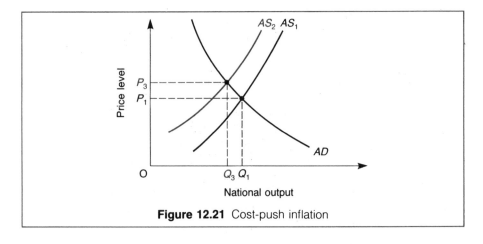

Figure 12.21 Cost-push inflation

The rise in costs may originate from a number of different sources. As a result we can distinguish various types of cost-push inflation.

- Wage-push inflation. This is where trade unions push up wages independently of the demand for labour.
- Profit-push inflation. This is where firms use their monopoly power to make bigger profits by pushing up prices independently of consumer demand.
- Import-price-push inflation. This is where import prices rise independently of the level of aggregate demand. An example is when OPEC quadrupled the price of oil in 1973/74.

In all these cases, inflation occurs because one or more groups are exercising economic power. The problem is likely to get worse, therefore, if there is an increasing concentration of economic power over time (for example, if firms or unions get bigger and bigger, and more monopolistic) or if groups become more militant.

These causes are likely to interact. Firms and unions may compete with each other for a larger share of national income. This can lead to wages and prices chasing each other upwards.

Additional causes of cost push inflation include the following.

- Tax-push inflation. This is where increased taxation adds to the cost of living. For example, when VAT was raised from 8 per cent to 15 per cent in 1979, prices rose as a result.
- The exhaustion of natural resources. If major natural resources become depleted, the *AS* curve will shift to the left. Examples include the gradual running-down of North Sea oil, pollution of the seas and hence a decline in incomes for nations with large fishing industries, and, perhaps the most devastating of all, the problem of 'desertification' in sub-Saharan Africa. Temporary inflationary problems could also arise due to short-run supply problems, such as a bad harvest.

The interaction of demand-pull and cost-push inflation

Demand-pull and cost-push inflation can occur together, since wage and price rises can be caused both by increases in aggregate demand and by independent causes pushing up costs. Even when an inflationary process *starts* as either demand-pull or cost-push, it is often difficult to separate the two. An initial cost-push inflation may encourage the government to expand aggregate demand to offset rises in unemployment. Alternatively, an initial demand-pull inflation may strengthen the power of certain groups which then use this power to drive up costs.

The interaction of the two causes is illustrated in Figure 12.22. Assume that powerful groups are constantly pushing up the costs of production. The *AS* curve is constantly shifting to the left. At the same time assume that the government, in order to prevent a rise in unemployment, is constantly boosting the level of aggregate demand (say, by cutting taxes). The *AD* curve is constantly shifting to the right. The net effect on output and employment may be very small, but prices may rise substantially.

If these shifts get more and more rapid, a wage–price spiral will result. Unions demand higher and higher wages to cover higher and higher costs of living. Firms put up their prices to higher and higher levels to cover the higher and higher costs of production. The government, in an attempt to avoid a recession, accommodates these price and wage rises by printing more and more money. Wage and price rises accelerate as these shifts get faster and faster. Inflation goes on rising.

Wage–price spiral

Wages and prices chasing each other as aggregate demand continually shifts to the right and aggregate supply continually shifts to the left.

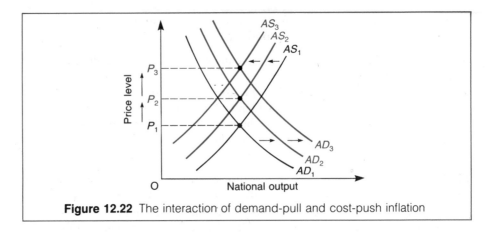

Figure 12.22 The interaction of demand-pull and cost-push inflation

Structural (demand-shift) inflation

When the *pattern* of demand (or supply) changes in the economy, certain industries will experience increased demand and others decreased demand. If prices and wages are inflexible downwards in the contracting industries, and prices and wages rise in the expanding industries, the overall price and wage level will rise. The problem will be made worse, the less elastic is supply to these shifts.

Thus a more rapid structural change in the economy can lead to both increased structural unemployment and increased structural inflation. An example of this problem is the so-called north–south divide. The north has experienced high structural unemployment as old industries have declined, while the south has experienced excess demand. This excess demand in the south has, amongst other things, led to rapid house price inflation, and rapid increases in incomes for various groups of workers and firms. With many prices and wages being set *nationally*, the inflation in the south then 'spills over' into the north.

Expectations and inflation

Workers and firms take account of the *expected* rate of inflation when making decisions.

Imagine that a union and an employer are negotiating a wage increase.

Let us assume that both sides expect a rate of inflation of 10 per cent. The union will be happy to receive a wage rise somewhat above 10 per cent. That way the members would be getting a *real* rise in incomes. The employers will be happy to pay a wage rise somewhat below 10 per cent. After all, they can put their price up by 10 per cent, knowing that their rivals will do approximately the same. The actual wage rise that the two sides agree on will thus be somewhere around 10 per cent.

Now let us assume that the expected rate of inflation is 20 per cent. Both sides will now negotiate around this benchmark, with the outcome being somewhere round about 20 per cent.

Thus the higher the expected rate of inflation, the higher will be the level of pay settlements and price rises, and hence the higher will be the resulting actual rate of inflation.

The importance of expectations in explaining the actual rate of inflation has been increasingly recognized by economists in recent years. As a result economists have been concerned to discover just what determines people's expectations. As you might expect, there is considerable disagreement, and in fact it is one of the most controversial areas of economics.

Policies to tackle inflation

We will be examining a number of different anti-inflationary policies in later chapters. These policies can be directed towards the control of either aggregate demand or aggregate supply, and hence are referred to as demand-side and supply-side policies respectively.

Demand-side policies

The two types of demand-side policies are *fiscal policy* and *monetary policy*.

Fiscal policy. Fiscal policy involves altering government expenditure and/or taxation. Aggregate demand can be reduced by cutting government expenditure (one of the four elements in aggregate demand) or by raising taxes and hence reducing consumer expenditure. These are both examples of deflationary fiscal policy.

(Fiscal policy could also be used to *boost* aggregate demand if there were a problem of demand-deficient unemployment. In this case the government would raise government expenditure and/or cut taxes. This is called reflationary fiscal policy.)

Monetary policy. Monetary policy involves altering the supply of money in the economy or manipulating the rate of interest. The government can reduce aggregate demand (a *deflationary* monetary policy) by reducing the money supply, thereby making less money available for spending, or by putting up interest rates and thus making borrowing more expensive. If people borrow less, they will spend less.

Supply-side policies

The aim here is to reduce the rate of increase in costs. This will help reduce leftward shifts in the aggregate supply curve. This can be done either by restraining monopoly influences on prices and incomes (e.g. by various forms of wage and price control, policies to restrict the activities of trade unions, or policies to restrict mergers and take-overs), or by designing policies to increase productivity (e.g. giving various tax incentives, encouraging various types of research and development, giving grants to firms to invest in up-to-date equipment or in the training of labour).

We will examine all these various policies as the book progresses. As we shall see, just as economists cannot agree on the causes of inflation, so too they cannot agree on the most appropriate cures.

Demand-side policies
Policies designed to affect aggregate demand: fiscal policy and monetary policy.

Supply-side policies
Policies designed to affect aggregate supply. Policies to affect costs or productivity.

Fiscal policy
Policy to affect aggregate demand by altering the balance between government expenditure and taxation.

Deflationary policy
Fiscal or monetary policy designed to reduce the rate of growth of aggregate demand.

Reflationary policy
Fiscal or monetary policy designed to increase the rate of growth of aggregate demand.

Monetary policy
Policy to affect aggregate demand by altering the supply or cost of money (rate of interest).

▲ SUMMARY

1. Inflation redistributes incomes from the economically weak to the economically powerful; it causes uncertainty in the business community and as a result reduces investment; it tends to lead to balance of payments problems and/or a fall in the exchange rate; it leads to resources being used to offset its effects. The costs of inflation can be very great indeed in the case of hyperinflation.

2. Equilibrium in the economy occurs when aggregate demand equals aggregate supply. Inflation can occur if there is a rightward shift in the aggregate demand curve or an upward (leftward) shift in the aggregate supply curve.

3. Demand-pull inflation occurs as a result of increases in aggregate demand. This can be due to monetary or non-monetary causes.

4. Cost-push inflation occurs when there are increases in the costs of production independent of rises in aggregate demand. Cost-push inflation can be of a number of different varieties: wage-push, profit-push, import-price-push, tax-push or that stemming from reductions in potential output.

5. Cost-push and demand-pull inflation can interact to form spiralling inflation.

6. Inflation can also be caused by shifts in the pattern of demand in the economy, with prices rising in sectors of increasing demand but being reluctant to fall in sectors of declining demand.

7. Expectations play a crucial role in determining the level of inflation. The higher people expect inflation to be, the higher it will be.

8. Policies to tackle inflation can be either demand-side policies (fiscal or monetary) or supply-side policies (to reduce costs or increase productivity).

12.5 The balance of payments and exchange rates

The balance of payments and the rate of exchange influence each other. The two issues must therefore be examined together.

We will first explain what is meant by the 'balance of payments'. In doing so we will see just how the various monetary transactions between the UK and the rest of the world are recorded.

Then we will examine how rates of exchange are determined, and how they are related to the balance of payments. Then we will see what causes exchange rate fluctuations, and what will happen if the government intervenes in the foreign exchange market to prevent these fluctuations.

The balance of payments account

The UK's balance of payments account records all the monetary transactions between UK residents and the rest of the world.

UK *receipts* of money from abroad are regarded as *credits*. These will be from the export of goods and services, foreign investment in the UK, deposits of money in the UK by non-residents and various loans made to the UK.

Outflows of money are regarded as *debits*. These will be from the purchase of imports, UK investment abroad, the deposit of money abroad by UK residents,

Table 12.3 UK balance of payments (£millions)

	1981		1985		1989	
CURRENT ACCOUNT						
Visible trade						
Exports (credits)	+50 668		+77 991		+92 526	
Imports (debits)	−47 416		−81 119		−115 638	
Visible balance		+3 252		−3 128		−23 112
Invisibles						
Credits	+57 322		+80 583		+108 530	
Debits	−53 933		−74 290		−106 268	
Invisible balance		+3 390		+6 293		+2 261
Current account balance		+6 642		+3 165		−20 850
CAPITAL ACCOUNT						
(Transactions in UK external assets and liabilities)						
Long-term capital account (investments)						
Overseas investment in UK (credits)	+3 255		+11 334		+27 914	
UK investment overseas (debits)	−10 473		−28 093		−56 943	
Long-term capital balance		−7 218		−16 759		−29 029
Short-term capital flows						
Overseas deposits in UK and borrowing from overseas residents (credits)	+40 143		+32 874		+61 713	
Deposits overseas by UK residents and lending to overseas residents (debits)	−42 739		−23 286		−33 785	
Short-term capital balance		−2 596		+9 588		+27 928
Reserves (drawing on +, adding to −)		+2 577		−1 758		+5 439
Net transactions in external assets and liabilities (capital balance)		−7 237		−8 929		+4 341
TOTAL CURRENT + CAPITAL ACCOUNTS		−595		−5 592		−16 509
(balancing item)		+595		+5 592		+16 509
		0		0		0

Source: *Economic Trends* and *Economic Trends Annual Supplement* (CSO).

various loans to non-residents made by UK banks and the paying back of loans made to UK residents by foreign banks.

There are two main parts of the balance of payments account: the *current account* and the *capital account*. Each part is then subdivided. Table 12.3 gives a summary of the UK balance of payments for 1981, 1985 and 1989, and shows these divisions and subdivisions.

The current account

The current account records the imports and exports of goods and services. It is normally divided into two parts.

The visible trade account. This records imports and exports of physical goods. Exports result in an inflow of money and are therefore a credit item. Imports result in an outflow of money and are therefore a debit item. The balance of these is called the visible balance or the balance of trade. A *trade surplus* is when exports exceed imports. A *trade deficit* is when imports exceed exports.

The invisible account. This records receipts from the provision of UK services to overseas residents, and the expenditure on foreign services by UK residents. These services include such things as banking, insurance, transport and tourism. The invisible account also includes the payment to and receipt from overseas of interest and dividends. The inflows of money are credit items (sometimes referred to as 'invisible exports'). The outflows of money are debit items (sometimes referred to as 'invisible imports'). The balance of all the invisible items is called the invisible balance. If the invisible credits exceed the invisible debits, there is an *invisible surplus*. If invisible debits exceed invisible credits, there is an *invisible deficit*.

> **?** Which of the following invisibles are credits and which are debits?
> (a) The expenditure by British tourists on foreign holidays.
> (b) The payment of dividends by foreign companies to UK investors.
> (c) Foreigners taking out British insurance policies.

The current account balance is the balance of both visibles and invisibles. A *current account surplus* is where credits exceed debits. A *current account deficit* is where debits exceed credits. The record of Britain's balance of payments on current account since 1970 is shown in Figure 12.23.

Current account of the balance of payments

The record of a country's imports and exports of goods and services.

Visible balance or balance of trade

Exports of goods minus imports of goods.

Invisible balance

Exports of services minus imports of services.

Balance of payments on current account

Exports of goods and services minus imports of goods and services: i.e. the visible balance plus the invisible balance.

Figure 12.23 UK balance of payments on current account: 1970–89

The capital account

Capital account of the balance of payments (or transactions in external assets and liabilities)

The record of all capital movements into and out of the country.

The official title for the capital account part of the balance of payments is the *transactions in external assets and liabilities*. It records investments and other financial flows. There are three main sections in this part of the balance of payments.

The long-term capital account. This records long-term capital investments. Investment by foreigners in the UK (e.g. a new Japanese car factory) represents an inflow of money when the investment is made, and is thus a credit item. (Any subsequent profit from this investment that flows abroad will be an invisible debit.) UK investment abroad represents an outflow of money when the investment is made. It is thus a debit item. Over the last few years, UK overseas investment has greatly exceeded foreign investment in the UK. This part of the balance of payments has thus been in substantial deficit.

? Is it a 'bad thing' to have a deficit on the long-term capital account?

The combined balance of the current and long-term capital account is referred to as the basic balance.

Basic balance

The current account plus the long-term capital account balance.

Short-term capital flows. These consist of various types of short-term monetary movement between the UK and the rest of the world. Foreign deposits in UK banks and loans to the UK from abroad are credit items since they represent an inflow of money. Deposits by UK residents in overseas banks and loans by UK banks to overseas residents are debit items. They represent an outflow of money.

Short-term monetary flows are common between international financial centres to take advantage of differences in countries' interest rates and changes in exchange rates.

? Why may inflows of short-term deposits create a problem?

The reserves. The UK, like all other countries, holds reserves of gold and foreign currencies. From time to time the Bank of England (acting as the government's agent) will sell some of these reserves to purchase sterling on the foreign exchange market. It does this normally as a means of supporting the rate of exchange (see below). The drawing on reserves represents a *credit* item in the balance of payments accounts: the reserves are an *inflow* to the balance of payments (albeit an outflow from the reserves account). The reserves can thus be used to support a deficit elsewhere in the balance of payments. Conversely, if there is a surplus elsewhere in the balance of payments, the Bank of England can use it to build up the reserves. Building up the reserves counts as a debit item in the balance of payments, since it represents an outflow from it (to the reserves).

When all the components of the balance of payments account are taken together, the balance of payments should exactly balance: credits should equal debits. As we shall see below, if they were not equal, the rate of exchange would have to adjust until they were, or the government would have to intervene to make them equal.

Balancing item

A statisical adjustment to ensure that the two sides of the balance of payments account balance. It is necessary because of errors in compiling the statistics.

When the statistics are compiled, however, a number of errors are likely to occur. As a result there will not be a balance. To 'correct' for this a balancing item is included in the accounts. This ensures that there will be an exact balance. The main reason for the errors is that the statistics are obtained from a number of sources, and there are often delays before items are recorded and sometimes omissions too.

Box 12.8

World Trade Imbalance: Japan and the USA
Mirror images in the balance of payments

The old saying that one person's gain is another person's loss is certainly true when we consider the trade imbalance between the USA and her trading partners, most notably Japan.

In recent years the United States has run a huge current account deficit. This has been funded by a massive inflow of capital, causing a correspondingly huge capital account surplus. The major proportion of this capital is supplied by Japan, which has a huge current account surplus and uses this surplus to invest and lend abroad.

As the chart shows, the imbalance between these two countries has widened considerably since 1982.

To rephrase the old saying, one person's surplus is another person's deficit!

? What are the costs and benefits of this imbalance to the two countries?

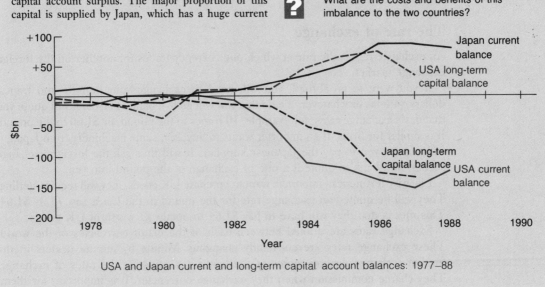

USA and Japan current and long-term capital account balances: 1977–88

Assessing the balance of payments figures

It is often regarded as being desirable to have a *basic balance* or *basic surplus*. In other words, it is seen as *undesirable* for the combined current and long-term capital accounts to be in deficit. If they were in deficit, this would have to be covered by borrowing from abroad or attracting deposits from abroad. This might necessitate paying high rates of interest. It also leads to the danger that foreigners might at some time in the future suddenly withdraw their money from the UK and cause a 'run on the pound'. An alternative would be to draw on reserves. But this too causes problems. If the reserves are run down too rapidly, it may cause a crisis of confidence, and again a run on the pound. Also, of course, reserves are limited and hence there is a limit to which they can be used to pay for a balance of payments deficit.

It is also often regarded as undesirable for a country to have a *current account* deficit, even if it is matched by a long-term capital account surplus (and hence there is a basic balance). Although this will bring the short-term benefit of a greater level of consumption through imports, and hence a temporarily higher living standard, the excess of imports over exports is being financed by foreign investment in the UK. This represents a greater claim on UK assets by foreigners. For example, the current account deficits of Western oil importing countries after the oil price increases of the 1970s were partly offset by the purchase of large quantities of assets in the West by OPEC countries. On the other hand, investment by foreigners may lead to increased production and hence possibly increased incomes for UK residents.

 With reference to the above, provide an assessment of the UK balance of payments in each of the three years illustrated in Table 12.3.

What causes deficits to occur on the various parts of the balance of payments? The answer has to do with the demand for and supply of sterling on the foreign exchange market. Thus before we can answer the question, we must examine this market and in particular the role of the rate of exchange.

The rate of exchange

An exchange rate is the rate at which one currency trades for another on the foreign exchange market.

If you want to go abroad, you will need to exchange your pounds into francs, dollars, pesetas or whatever. To do this you will go to a bank. The bank will quote you that day's exchange rates: for example, 10 francs to the pound, or $1.60 to the pound. It is similar for firms. If an importer wants to buy, say, some machinery from Japan, it will require yen to pay the Japanese supplier. It will thus ask the foreign exchange section of a bank to quote it a rate of exchange of the pound into yen.

Likewise if American importers want to purchase UK goods, they will require sterling. They will be quoted an exchange rate for the pound in the USA: say, £1 = $1.64. This means that they will have to pay $1.64 to obtain £1 worth of UK goods.

Exchange rates are quoted between each of the major currencies of the world. These exchange rates are constantly changing. Minute by minute dealers in the foreign exchange dealing rooms of the banks are adjusting the rates of exchange. They charge commission when they exchange currencies. It is important for them, therefore, to ensure that they are not left with a large amount of any currency unsold. What they need to do is to balance the supply and demand of each currency: to balance the amount they purchase to the amount they sell. To do this they will need to adjust the price of each currency, namely the exchange rate, in line with changes in supply and demand.

Not only are there day-to-day fluctuations in exchange rates, but also there are long-term changes in them. Table 12.4 shows the average exchange rate between the pound and various currencies for each of the years 1980–9.

One of the problems in assessing what is happening to a particular currency is that its rate of exchange may rise against some currencies (weak currencies) and fall against others (strong currencies). In order to gain an overall picture of its fluctuations, therefore, it is best to look at a weighted average exchange rate against all other currencies. This is known as the exchange rate index. The weight given to each currency in the index depends on the proportion of transactions done with that country. The last column in Table 12.4 shows the sterling exchange rate index based on 1985 = 100. Box 12.9 looks at the different weightings attached to each of the currencies in the index.

Note that all the exchange rates must be consistent with each other. For example, if in 1980 £1 exchanged for $2.33 or 526 yen, then $2.33 would have to exchange for

Exchange rate index
A weighted average exchange rate expressed as an index, where the value of the index is 100 in a given base year. The weights of the different currencies in the index add up to 1.

Box 12.9

The Sterling Index
What goes into the basket?

The UK's *effective* exchange rate measures the value of the pound against a group or 'basket' of other currencies. Each currency's exchange rate with the pound enters with a weight somewhere between 0 and 1. The size of each currency's weight depends on the relative importance of that country as a competitor to the UK. The more important it is, the bigger its weight. All the weights must add up to 1.

The effective exchange rate is expressed as an index with the base year equal to 100. The effective increase or decrease in the value of the pound can thus be expressed in terms of the percentage increase or decrease in this index.

A new official sterling index was introduced in January 1989. The previous index was based on 1975 = 100. The new index is based on 1985 = 100. The new index uses new weights for the various currencies (sixteen in all). These new weights were chosen to reflect the changes in importance of UK trade with the various countries. The table shows the old and new weights.

The weights of foreign currencies in the sterling exchange rate index

	Old	New		Old	New
USA	0.2463	0.2044	Sweden	0.0373	0.0379
Germany	0.1408	0.2001	Ireland	0.0405	0.0242
France	0.1039	0.1175	Spain	0.0186	0.0202
Japan	0.1367	0.0883	Canada	0.0151	0.0190
Italy	0.0718	0.0766	Denmark	0.0109	0.0145
Switzerland	0.0300	0.0548	Finland	0.0085	0.0145
Belgium	0.0404	0.0525	Norway	0.0211	0.0131
Netherlands	0.0480	0.0500	Austria	0.0100	0.0124
			(Australia)	0.0199	–

? What are the new and old total weights of the EC countries? Comment.

Table 12.4 Sterling exchange rates 1980–89

	US dollar	French franc	Japanese yen	German mark	Italian lira	Sterling exchange rate index (average 1985 = 100)
1980	2.33	9.83	526	4.23	1992	117.7
1981	2.03	10.94	445	4.56	2287	119.0
1982	1.75	11.48	435	4.24	2364	113.7
1983	1.52	11.55	360	3.87	2302	105.3
1984	1.34	11.63	317	3.79	2339	100.6
1985	1.30	11.55	307	3.78	2463	100.0
1986	1.47	10.16	247	3.18	2186	91.5
1987	1.64	9.84	237	2.94	2123	90.1
1988	1.78	10.60	228	3.12	2315	95.5
1989	1.64	10.45	226	3.08	2247	92.6

Source: *Economic Trends* (CSO).

526 yen directly, otherwise people could make money by moving around in a circle between three currencies.

? How did the pound 'fare' compared with the dollar, the lira and the yen from 1980 to 1989? What conclusions can be drawn about the relative movements of these three currencies?

The determination of the rate of exchange in a free market

In a free foreign exchange market the rate of exchange is determined by demand and supply: the demand for and supply of currencies. Thus the sterling exchange rate is determined by the demand and supply of pounds. This is illustrated in Figure 12.24.

For simplicity, assume that there are just two countries: the UK and the USA. When UK importers wish to buy goods from the USA, or when UK residents wish to invest in the USA, they will *supply* pounds on the foreign exchange market in order to obtain dollars. The higher the exchange rate, the more dollars they will obtain for their pounds. This will effectively make American goods cheaper to buy, and investment more profitable. Thus the *higher* the exchange rate, the *more* pounds will be supplied. The supply curve of pounds will therefore typically slope upwards.

When US residents wish to purchase UK goods or to invest in the UK, they will require pounds. They *demand* pounds by selling dollars in the foreign exchange markets. The lower the $ price of the pound (the exchange rate), the cheaper it will be for them to obtain UK goods and assets, and hence the more pounds they are likely to demand. The demand curve for pounds, therefore, will typically slope downwards.

The equilibrium exchange rate will be where the demand for pounds equals the supply. In Figure 12.24 this will be at an exchange rate of £1 = $1.60. But what is the mechanism that equates demand and supply?

If the current exchange rate were above the equilibrium, the supply of pounds being offered to the banks would exceed the demand. For example, in Figure 12.24 if the exchange rate were $1.80, there would be an excess supply of pounds of *a − b*. The banks, wishing to make money by *exchanging* currency, would have to lower the exchange rate in order to encourage a greater demand for pounds and in order to reduce the excessive supply. They would continue lowering the rate until demand equalled supply.

Similarly, if the rate were below the equilibrium, say at $1.40, there would be a shortage of pounds. The banks would find themselves with too few pounds to meet all the demand. At the same time they would have an excess supply of dollars. The banks would thus raise the exchange rate until demand equalled supply.

In practice the process of reaching equilibrium is extremely rapid. The foreign exchange dealers in the banks are continually adjusting the rate as new customers make new demands for currencies. What is more, the banks have to watch closely what each other is doing. Banks are constantly in competition with each other and thus have to keep their rates in line. The dealers receive minute by minute updates on their computer screens of the rates being offered round the world.

Figure 12.24 Determination of the rate of exchange

Box 12.10

Dealing in Foreign Exchange
A daily juggling act

Imagine that a large car importer in the UK wants to import 5000 cars from Germany costing DM75 million. What does it do?

It will probably contact a number of banks' foreign exchange dealing rooms in London and ask them for exchange rate quotes. It thus puts all the banks in competition with each other. Each bank will want to get the business and thereby obtain the commission on the deal. To do this they must offer a higher rate than the other banks, since the higher the DM/£ exchange rate, the more D-Marks the firm will get for its money. (For an importer a rate of, say, DM3.10 to £1 is better than a rate of, say, DM3.08.)

Now it is highly unlikely that any of the banks will have a spare 75 million D-Marks. But a bank cannot say to the importer 'Sorry, you will have to wait before we can agree to sell them to you.' Instead the bank will offer a deal and then, if the firm agrees, the bank will have to set about obtaining the DM75 million. To do this it must offer Germans who are *supplying* D-Marks to obtain pounds a

sufficiently *low* DM/£ exchange rate. (The lower the DM/£ exchange rate, the fewer D-Marks the Germans will have to pay to obtain pounds.)

The banks' dealers thus find themselves in the delicate position of wanting to offer a *high* enough exchange rate to the car importer in order to gain its business, but a *low* enough exchange rate in order to obtain the required amount of D-Marks. The dealers are thus constantly having to adjust the rates of exchange in order to balance the demand and supply of each currency.

In general, the more of any foreign currency that dealers are asked to supply (by being offered sterling), the lower will be the exchange rate they will offer. In other words, a higher supply of sterling pushes down the foreign currency price of sterling.

? Assume that an American firm wants to import Rolls-Royces from the UK. Describe how foreign exchange dealers will respond.

Exchange rates and the balance of payments: no government intervention

In a free foreign exchange market the balance of payments will *automatically* balance. But why?

The credit side of the balance of payments constitutes the demand for sterling. For example, when foreigners buy UK exports they will demand sterling in order to pay for them. The debit side constitutes the supply of sterling. For example, when UK residents buy foreign goods, the importers of these goods will require foreign currency to pay for them. They will thus supply pounds. A floating exchange rate will ensure that the demand for pounds is equal to the supply. It will thus also ensure that the credits on the balance of payments are equal to the debits: that the balance of payments balances.

This does not mean that each part of the balance of payments account will separately balance, but simply that any current account deficit must be matched by a capital account surplus and vice versa.

For example, suppose initially that each part of the balance of payments *did* separately balance. Then let us assume that aggregate demand expanded rapidly (the economy was experiencing a boom). Consumers would buy more goods and services, including more imports. The current account would begin to move into deficit. The supply of sterling would shift to the right. The exchange rate would fall.

As the exchange rate fell, so there would be a movement along the demand curve for sterling: amongst other things, the lower exchange rate would attract long-term foreign investment into the UK. The capital account would thus move into surplus and would exactly offset any deficit on the current account.

Floating exchange rates

If the government does not intervene in the foreign exchange market, the exchange rate will fluctuate up and down according to demand and supply. This is known as a system of floating exchange rates.

Floating exchange rate

When the government does not intervene in the foreign exchange markets, but simply allows the exchange rate to be freely determined by demand and supply.

If the demand or supply curves of sterling shift, the exchange rate will alter. This is illustrated in Figure 12.25. This time let us look at the Deutschmark/sterling exchange rate.

Assume, for example, that the supply curve shifts to the right and the demand curve to the left. The rate of exchange will simply fall from the old equilibrium of £1 = DM3.00 to the new equilibrium of £1 = DM2.75. (Dealers mark the rate down in order to balance their books.)

But why should the demand and supply curves shift in this way? The following are the major reasons.

Changes in UK prices relative to foreign prices. If, for example, the UK inflation rate is higher than abroad, UK exports will become less competitive. The demand for sterling will fall. At the same time, imports will become relatively cheaper for UK consumers. The supply of sterling will rise.

Changes in relative incomes. If UK incomes rise, the demand for imports, and hence the supply of sterling, will rise. If foreign incomes fall, the demand for UK exports, and hence the demand for sterling, will fall.

Changes in relative interest rates. If UK interest rates fall relative to those abroad, UK residents are more likely to deposit their money abroad, since they will earn a higher return there. The supply of sterling rises. At the same time overseas residents are less likely to put their money in the UK. The demand for sterling falls.

Changes in relative investment prospects. If investment prospects become brighter abroad than in the UK, perhaps because of better incentives abroad, or because of worries about an impending recession in the UK, again the demand for sterling will fall and the supply of sterling will rise.

Figure 12.25 Floating exchange rates: movement to a new equilibrium

Speculators believe that the rate of exchange will change. By speculators we do not just mean people who make a living by financial dealing. We also include importers and exporters who want to choose the most favourable time to buy or sell currency. If they think that the exchange rate is about to fall, they will sell pounds *now* before the rate does fall. The supply of sterling will thus rise. At the same time people requiring pounds will *wait* until the rate has fallen before they purchase them. Thus the demand for pounds will fall.

Longer-term changes in international trading patterns. Over time the pattern of imports and exports is likely to change as (a) consumer tastes change, (b) the nature and quality of goods change and (c) the costs of production change. If as a result British goods become less competitive than, say, Japanese goods, the demand for sterling will fall and the supply will rise. These shifts, of course, are gradual, taking place over many years.

In each of the above cases the exchange rate will fall. We call this a depreciation of the pound. If the exchange rate rises, we call this an appreciation.

 Go through each of the above reasons for shifts in the demand for and supply of sterling and consider what would cause an *appreciation* of the pound.

Depreciation

A fall in the free-market exchange rate of the domestic currency with foreign currencies.

Appreciation

A rise in the free-market exchange rate of the domestic currency with foreign currencies.

Government intervention in the foreign exchange market

The government may be unwilling to let the pound float freely. Frequent shifts on the demand and supply curves would cause frequent changes on the exchange rate. This, in turn, might cause uncertainty for businesses, which might curtail their trade and investment.

The government may thus intervene in the foreign exchange market. But what can it do? The answer to this will depend on its objectives. It may simply want to reduce the day-to-day fluctuations in the exchange rate, or it may want to prevent longer-term, more fundamental shifts in the rate.

Reducing short-term fluctuations

Assume in Figure 12.25 that the government believes that an exchange rate of DM3.00 to the pound is approximately the long-term equilibrium rate. It thus decides to intervene to prevent excessive fluctuations from that level. Assume now that the demand and supply curves shift to D_2 and S_2 respectively, albeit temporarily. There are three possible things that the government can do to prevent the rate falling to DM2.75.

Using reserves. The Bank of England can sell gold and foreign currencies from the reserves to buy pounds. This will shift the demand for sterling to the right.

Borrowing from abroad. The government can negotiate a foreign currency loan from other countries or from an international agency such as the International Monetary Fund. It can then use these moneys to buy pounds on the foreign exchange market, thus again shifting the demand for sterling to the right.

Raising interest rates. If the government raises interest rates, it will encourage people to deposit money in the UK and encourage UK residents to keep their money in the country. The demand for sterling will increase and the supply of sterling will decrease.

Maintaining a fixed rate of exchange over the longer term

Governments may choose to maintain a fixed rate over a number of months or even years. Indeed from 1945 to 1972 the whole world operated under such a system. Countries used to 'peg' (i.e. fix) their currencies against the US dollar. This meant, therefore, that every currency was fixed with respect to every other currency.

But how can a government maintain an exchange rate that is persistently above the equilibrium? How can it resist the downward pressure on the exchange rate? After all, it cannot *order* dealers to keep the rate up: the dealers will run out of foreign currency. Also it cannot go on and on using its reserves to support the rate: the reserves will begin to run out. Also it will probably not want to go on borrowing from abroad and building up large international debts.

So what can it do? It must attempt to shift the demand and supply curves back again so that they once more intersect at the fixed exchange rate. The following are possible methods it can use.

Deflation. This is where the government deliberately curtails aggregate demand by either fiscal policy or monetary policy or both.

Deflationary fiscal policy will involve raising taxes and/or reducing government expenditure. Deflationary monetary policy will involve reducing the supply of money and raising interest rates. Note that in this case we are not just talking about the temporary raising of interest rates to prevent a short-term outflow of money from the country, but the use of higher interest rates to reduce borrowing and hence dampen aggregate demand.

A reduction in aggregate demand will work in two ways:

- It will reduce the level of consumer spending. This will directly cut imports since there will be reduced spending on Japanese videos, German cars, Spanish holidays and so on. It will also indirectly cut imports when UK firms, themselves facing a reduction in demand, cut back on their purchases of raw materials and equipment, part of which comes from abroad. The supply of sterling coming on to the foreign exchange market thus decreases.
- It will reduce the rate of inflation. This will make UK goods more competitive abroad, thus increasing the demand for sterling. It will also cut back on imports as UK consumers switch to the now more competitive home-produced goods. The supply of sterling falls.

Supply-side policies. This is where the government attempts to increase the long-term competitiveness of UK goods by encouraging reductions in the costs of production and/or improvements in the quality of UK goods. For example, the government may give grants or tax incentives to encourage firms to engage in research and development. Or it may attempt to improve the quantity and quality of education and training.

Controls on imports and or foreign exchange dealing. This is where the government restricts the outflow of money, either by restricting people's access to foreign exchange, or by the use of tariffs and quotas. Tariffs are another word for customs duties. As taxes on imports, they raise their price and hence reduce their consumption. Quotas are quantitative restrictions on various imports.

1. What problems might arise if the government were to adopt this third method of maintaining a fixed exchange rate?
2. What policy measures could a government adopt to maintain a fixed rate of exchange in a situation where the rate would otherwise *rise*?

Conclusions

Both fixed exchange rates and freely floating exchange rates create problems. To avoid these problems, various compromises have been tried between the two extremes of totally fixed and totally free exchange rates. These alternative exchange rate regimes and their advantages and disadvantages are examined in Chapter 22.

▲ SUMMARY

1. The balance of payments account records all payments to and receipts from foreign countries. The current account records payments for visible and invisible imports and exports. The capital account records all capital movements, both short term and long term; it also includes dealings in the country's foreign exchange reserves.

2. The whole account must balance, but surpluses or deficits can be recorded on any specific part of the account. Thus the current account could be in deficit, but it would have to be matched by an equal and opposite capital account surplus.

3. It is generally regarded as undesirable to have persistent current account deficits, since these lead to increased foreign ownership of domestic assets.

4. The rate of exchange is the rate at which one currency exchanges for another. Rates of exchange are determined by demand and supply in the foreign exchange market. Demand for the domestic currency consists of all the credit items in the balance of payments account. Supply consists of all the debit items.

5. The exchange rate will depreciate (fall) if the demand for the domestic currency falls or the supply increases. These shifts can be caused by increases in domestic prices or incomes relative to foreign ones, reductions in domestic interest rates relative to foreign ones, worsening investment prospects at home compared with abroad, or the belief by speculators that the exchange rate will fall. The opposite in each case would cause an appreciation (rise).

6. The government can attempt to prevent the rate of exchange from falling by central bank purchases of the domestic currency in the foreign exchange market, either by selling foreign currency reserves or by using foreign loans. Alternatively, the government can raise interest rates. The reverse actions can be taken if it wants to prevent the rate from rising.

7. In the longer term it can prevent the rate from falling by pursuing deflationary policies, protectionist policies, or supply-side policies ·to increase the competitiveness of the country's exports.

12.6 The relationship between the four objectives

Aggregate demand and the short-term relationship between the four objectives

In the short term (up to about two years), the four objectives of faster growth in output, lower unemployment, lower inflation and the avoidance of balance of payments deficits (either current account or basic) are all related. They all depend on aggregate demand, and all vary with the course of the trade cycle. This is illustrated in Figure 12.26.

In the expansionary phase of the trade cycle (phase 2), aggregate demand grows rapidly. The gap between actual and potential output will narrow. There will be relatively rapid growth in output and (demand-deficient) unemployment will fall. Thus two of the problems are getting better. On the other hand, the other two problems will be getting worse. The growing shortages lead to higher (demand-pull) inflation and current account balance of payments deficits as the extra demand 'sucks in' more imports and as higher prices make UK goods less competitive internationally. As a result the equilibrium exchange rate is likely to fall, which will raise the price of imports, thus further stoking up inflation. This will probably increase inflationary expectations.

Box 12.11

The Political Trade Cycle (Part I)
Getting things looking right on the night

Any government standing for re-election would like the economy to look as healthy as possible. It can then claim to the electorate that its economic policies have been a success.

Governments are able to engineer booms and recessions by the use of demand-side policies (fiscal and monetary). For example, by cutting taxes and/or increasing government expenditure, and by cutting interest rates, they can generate a period of economic expansion.

But how is this of any use politically, if the improvement in two of the objectives is at the cost of a deterioration in the other two? That would not help the government's election prospects.

The answer is that there is one point in the trade cycle where *all four* objectives are likely to be looking good. This 'window of opportunity' for the government is in the middle of phase 2 – the period of rapid expansion. At this point, growth is at its highest and unemployment is *falling* most rapidly. In fact falling unemployment is probably more popular with the electorate than simply a *low level* of unemployment. Three million unemployed but falling will win more votes than one million and rising!

But what about the other two objectives? Surely, in the middle of phase 2, inflation and the balance of payments will be deteriorating? The answer is that they will probably not yet have become a serious problem. Inflation takes a time to build up. It will probably only really start to rise rapidly as the peak of the trade cycle is approached

and shortages and bottlenecks occur. As far as the balance of payments is concerned, this tends only to become a serious *political issue* when the current account deficit gets really severe, or if the pound starts to plummet on the foreign exchange market. In the middle of phase 2, it is unlikely that this stage will yet have been reached.

By careful economic management, then, the government can get the four objectives to look good at the time of the election. Of course, economic management is not perfect and policies may take longer (or shorter) to work than the government had anticipated. Things are made easier for governments in countries like the UK, however, where the government can choose when to call an election. It is less easy in countries like the USA where elections are at fixed times.

Once a government has won an election it can then deflate the economy in order to remove inflationary pressures and improve the balance of payments. A recession is likely to follow. This will probably be highly unpopular with the electorate. But no matter: the government, having created sufficient slack in the economy, can then reflate the economy again in time for the next general election!

It is thus possible to observe a *political* trade cycle. Recessions follow elections. Rapid growth precedes elections.

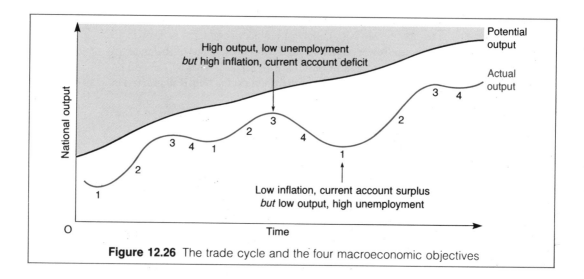

Figure 12.26 The trade cycle and the four macroeconomic objectives

At the peak of the cycle (phase 3), unemployment is probably at its lowest and output at its highest (for the time being). But growth has already ceased or at least slowed down. Inflation and balance of payments problems are probably acute.

As the economy moves into phase 4, the recession, the reverse will happen to that of phase 2. Falling aggregate demand will make growth negative and demand-deficient unemployment higher, but inflation is likely to slow down and the balance of payments will improve. These two improvements may take some time to occur, however.

Governments are thus faced with a dilemma. If they reflate the economy, they will make two of the objectives better (growth and unemployment) but the other two worse (inflation and balance of payments). If they deflate the economy, it is the other way round: inflation and the balance of payments will improve, but unemployment will rise and growth or even output will fall.

Is there any point in the trade cycle where all four objectives are looking reasonable? If so, that would be the time when it would be wise for a government to call a general election! (See Box 12.11.)

The Phillips curve

The analysis of the last section suggests that in the short run governments are faced with a simple trade-off between the objectives. One such trade-off, namely that between inflation and unemployment, was illustrated by the famous Phillips curve.

A. W. Phillips in 1958 showed the statistical relationship between wage inflation and unemployment in the UK from 1861 to 1957. With wage inflation ($\dot{W}$) on the vertical axis and the unemployment rate (U) on the horizontal axis, a scatter of points was obtained. Each point represented the observation for a particular year. The curve that best fitted the scatter has become known as the 'Phillips curve'. It is illustrated in Figure 12.27 and shows an inverse relationship between inflation and unemployment.[5]

Given that wage increases over the period were approximately 2 per cent above price increases (made possible because of increases in labour productivity), a similar-shaped, but lower curve could be plotted showing the relationship between *price* inflation and unemployment.

The curve has often been used to illustrate the effects of changes in aggregate demand. When aggregate demand rose (relative to potential output), inflation rose

Phillips curve

A curve showing the relationship between (price) inflation and unemployment. The original Phillips curve plotted *wage* inflation against unemployment for the years 1861–1957.

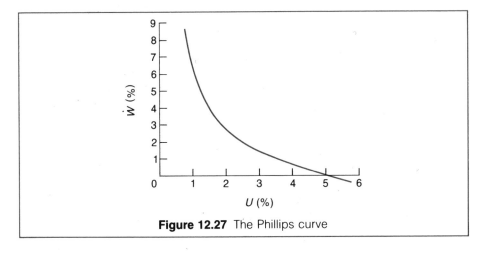

Figure 12.27 The Phillips curve

[5] Phillips' estimated equation was $\dot{W} = -0.9 + 9.638U^{-1.394}$

and unemployment fell: there was an upward movement along the curve. When aggregate demand fell, there was a downward movement along the curve.

There was also a second reason given for the inverse relationship. If wages rose, the unemployed may have believed that the higher wages they were offered represented a *real* wage increase. That is, they did not realize that the higher wages would be 'eaten up' by price increases: they suffered from *money illusion*. They would thus accept jobs more readily. The average duration of unemployment therefore fell. This is a reduction in *frictional* unemployment and is illustrated by an upward shift in the W_0 curve in Figure 12.16.

The Phillips curve was bowed in to the origin. The usual explanation for this is that, as aggregate demand expanded, at first there would be plenty of surplus labour, which could meet the extra demand without the need to raise wages very much. But as labour became increasingly scarce, firms would find they had to offer increasingly higher wages to obtain the labour they required, and the position of trade unions would be increasingly strengthened.

The *position* of the Phillips curve depended on *non*-demand factors causing inflation and unemployment: frictional and structural unemployment; and cost-push, structural and expectations-generated inflation. If any of these non-demand factors changed so as to raise inflation or unemployment, the curve would shift outward to the right. The relative stability of the curve over the 100 years or so observed by Phillips suggested that these non-demand factors had changed little.

The Phillips curve seemed to present governments with a simple policy choice. They could trade off inflation against unemployment. Lower unemployment could be bought at the cost of higher inflation, and vice versa. Unfortunately, the experience of the 1970s and 1980s has suggested that no such simple relationship exists beyond the short run.

The problem of 'stagflation'

From about 1966 the Phillips curve relationship seemed to break down. The UK, and many other countries in the Western world too, began to experience growing unemployment *and* higher rates of inflation as well.

Figure 12.28 shows price inflation and unemployment in the UK from 1955 to 1989. From 1955 to 1966 a curve similar to the Phillips curve can be fitted through the data (diagram (a)). From 1967 to 1989, however, no simple picture emerges.

Money illusion

When people believe that a money wage or price increase represents a *real* increase: in other words, they ignore or underestimate inflation.

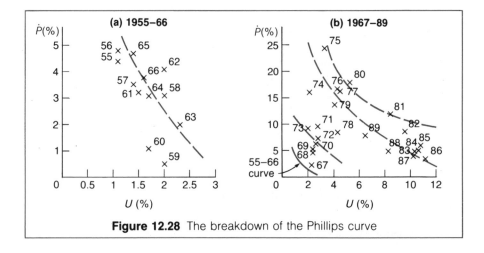

Figure 12.28 The breakdown of the Phillips curve

Certainly the original Phillips curve can no longer fit the data; but whether the curve has been shifting to the right (the dotted lines), or whether the relationship has broken down completely, or whether there is some quite different relationship between inflation and unemployment, is not clear. There is much controversy amongst economists on this issue. The controversy will be examined in later chapters and particularly in Chapter 19.

Not only were inflation and unemployment generally worse in the 1970s and 1980s than in the 1950s and 1960s, but also growth had slowed down – at least it had until the mid-1980s. The combination of stagnation (high unemployment and low growth) and high inflation has been called stagflation. These problems were compounded for non-oil-producing countries by large current account balance of payments deficits following the large oil price rises of 1973/74 and 1978/79.

Table 12.5 illustrates the problem of stagflation in the UK. In the late 1970s the UK economy was faring worse in terms of all four objectives than it was in the early 1960s. By the early 1980s, with the economy in deepest recession, unemployment had reached levels that would not have been believed a decade earlier, and yet inflation was still high compared with the 1950s and 1960s.

Stagflation

A combination of stagnation (and hence high unemployment) with high inflation.

Table 12.5 UK macroeconomic indicators: 1959–1988

	Inflation[1]	Unemployment[2]	Growth[3]	Current account balance[4]
1959–63	2.3	1.9	3.5	+149
1964–68	4.1	1.9	3.2	−947
1969–73	8.7	3.0	3.4	+1 516
1974–78	22.1	4.3	1.2	−4 415
1979–83	14.0	8.1	0.8	+17 969
1984–88	4.7	10.2	3.6	−11 773

[1] Average annual percentage increase in retail prices.
[2] Average percentage unemployed (excluding school leavers).
[3] Average annual growth rate in real GDP at market prices.
[4] Total current account deficit(−) or surplus(+) per 5 year period (£m).

Source: *Economic Trends Annual Supplement* (CSO).

By the mid-1980s inflation had fallen back again and growth had, but unemployment, although now falling, was still at very much higher levels than in the 1950s, 1960s *and* 1970s; and despite North Sea oil, which had given a current account surplus in the early 1980s, the current account was now moving deeply into deficit.

By 1990 the economy was moving back into recession with unemployment rising again, and yet the current account was still in massive deficit, and inflation, although now falling, was over 10 per cent – much higher than in the boom years of the 1950s and 1960s.

Conclusions

Today the relationship between the four objectives seems far less simple than it did back in the 1950s.

In the short run, they still do seem to fluctuate with the trade cycle. This does not necessarily make short-run prediction easy, however, since the course of the trade cycle is irregular. Both booms and slumps can be long lived or short lived, lasting anything from a few months to a few years. What is more, even if accurate forecasts could be made, short-term management of the economy is still very difficult. We will be examining these difficulties as the book progresses.

In the long run, the relationship between the objectives is at the heart of the debate between the various schools of macroeconomic thought. These schools of thought are described in Chapter 13.

▲ SUMMARY

---

1. In the short run, the four macroeconomic objectives are related to aggregate demand and the trade cycle. In the boom phase, growth is high and unemployment is falling, but inflation is rising and the current account of the balance of payments is moving into deficit. In the recession, the reverse is the case.

2. The Phillips curve showed the trade-off between two of the problems: inflation and unemployment. There seemed to be a simple inverse relationship between the two.

3. After 1966 the relationship broke down as inflation *and* unemployment rose.

4. Although economists recognize that the relationships between the four objectives are more complex than was thought back in the 1950s, there is considerable disagreement as to precisely what these relationships are.

Macroeconomic Ideas 13

13.1 Macroeconomic controversies

Macroeconomics and politics

Macroeconomics is highly controversial. There is no universal agreement amongst economists as to how the economy functions at a macroeconomic level. Instead there are various schools of thought.

These schools of thought see very different roles for the government in managing the economy. Some economists argue that the economy is more likely to achieve the various macroeconomic objectives if the capitalist market economy is allowed to function pretty well freely, without hindrance from the government. Other economists argue that the government must intervene if macroeconomic objectives are to be met. There is further division among those who argue in favour of government intervention over the appropriate amount and type of intervention.

These divisions amongst economists tend to parallel political divisions. Politicians have tended to embrace schools of economic thought whose vision of the economy and the role of government is the same as their own. There is a big danger here, however. When economics is made to serve the political purposes of politicians, objectivity can fly out the window. Economic analysis can become economic dogma. Evidence which is uncomfortable to a politician's point of view may be rejected, ignored or twisted. Evidence which supports the point of view may be given undue weight or accepted uncritically.

Later in the chapter we will examine the development of macroeconomic ideas over the last 60 years or so. We will identify various schools of macroeconomic thought, along with the political factions that have embraced them.

First, however, we need to identify those areas where debate takes place. Most of the debate centres on the working of the market mechanism: just how well or how badly it will achieve the various macroeconomic objectives. There are three major areas of disagreement: (a) how flexible are wages and prices, (b) how flexible is aggregate supply and (c) what is the role of expectations? We examine each in turn.

Issue 1: The flexibility of prices and wages

Generally, the political right tends to ally with those economists who argue that prices and wages are relatively flexible. Markets tend to clear, they say, and clear fairly quickly.

Disequilibrium unemployment is likely to be fairly small, according to their view, and normally only a temporary, short-run phenomenon. Any long-term unemployment, therefore, will be equilibrium (or 'natural') unemployment. To cure this, they argue, encouragement must be given to the free play of market forces: to a rapid response of both firms and labour to changes in market demand and supply, to a more rapid dissemination of information on job vacancies, and generally to greater labour mobility, both geographical and occupational.

There are some on the political right, however, who argue that in the short run wages may not be perfectly flexible. This occurs when unions attempt to keep wages above the equilibrium. (See Box 12.4.) In this case, disequilibrium unemployment may continue for a while. The solution here, they argue, is to curb the power of unions so that wage flexibility can be restored and disequilibrium unemployment cured.

The political centre and left tend to ally with economists who reject the assumption of highly flexible wages and prices. Generally, as one moves leftwards along the political spectrum, a greater degree of inflexibility of wages and prices is assumed. If there is a deficiency of demand for labour in the economy, during a recession say, there will be a resistance from unions to cuts in real wages and certainly to cuts in money wages. Any cuts that do occur will be insufficient to eliminate the disequilibrium, and will anyway only serve further to reduce aggregate demand so that workers have less money to spend. The demand curve in Figure 12.15 (see page 493) would shift to the left.

The prices of goods may also be inflexible in response to changes in demand. As industry has become more concentrated and more monopolistic over the years, firms, it is argued, have become less likely to respond to a general fall in demand by cutting prices. Instead, they are likely to build up stocks if they think the recession is temporary, or cut production and hence employment if they think the recession will persist. It is also argued that firms typically use cost-plus methods of pricing. If wages are inflexible downwards, and if they form a major element of costs, prices will also be inflexible downwards.

Thus according to those who criticize the right, markets cannot be relied upon automatically to correct disequilibria and hence cure disequilibrium unemployment.

 Why are *real* wages likely to be more flexible downwards than *money* wages?

Issue 2: The flexibility of aggregate supply

The question here is, how responsive is national output (i.e. aggregate supply), and hence also employment, to a change in aggregate demand?

The right tends to argue that aggregate supply does not respond, except perhaps in the short run, to changes in aggregate demand. Aggregate supply is determined *independently* of demand. It depends on the quantity and productivity of factors of production, *not* on the level of aggregate demand. An expansion of aggregate demand will merely lead to (demand-pull) inflation. It cannot lead to a long-term growth in output and employment. Likewise a contraction in aggregate demand will not lead to a long-term fall in output and a rise in unemployment. It will merely lead to a fall in prices.

Supply-side economics

An approach which focuses directly on aggregate supply and how to shift the aggregate supply curve outwards.

If the government, therefore, wants to expand aggregate supply and get more rapid economic growth, it is no good, they argue, concentrating on demand. Instead, governments should concentrate directly on supply by encouraging enterprise and competition, and generally by encouraging markets to operate more freely. For this reason, this approach is often labelled supply-side economics.

Other economists and other politicians disagree – from the left of the Conservative Party ('the Wets') leftwards. They argue that rises in aggregate demand *will* cause aggregate supply to rise, and if the rise in aggregate demand is sufficient, unemployment will fall. This rise in output and employment can persist into the long run if governments maintain a high and expanding level of aggregate demand. Buoyant and expanding markets for their products will encourage firms to produce up to capacity, to employ more people and to invest for the future, thus increasing capacity further.

However, these conditions will not be achieved, they argue, if the government pursues a non-interventionist, *laissez-faire* policy. The government instead must seek to control aggregate demand, to ensure that it continues to grow, and at a steady, non-fluctuating rate.

There is disagreement among those who criticize the right, however, over the extent to which expansion of demand will be inflationary. Some argue that the effects on inflation can be minimal. If a rise in aggregate demand causes a real growth in output, and productivity, workers can have real wage rises without it being inflationary. Others argue that inflation could be quite high with such policies, and could get worse over time as people come to expect ever bigger rises in their standard of living and/or ever bigger rises in prices (see issue 3 below). In such cases, additional policies to curb rising prices – such as prices and incomes policies – may be desirable.

All these arguments centre on the nature of the aggregate supply curve (*AS*). Three different *AS* curves are shown in Figure 13.1. The *AD* curves are drawn as downward sloping, showing that the higher the level of prices, the less will people be able to purchase for a given level of money incomes. In each of the three cases, it is assumed that the government now raises aggregate demand, by, say, increasing the amount of money in the economy. Aggregate demand shifts from AD_1 to AD_2. The effect on prices and output will depend on the shape of the *AS* curve.

The political right argues that there will be little or no effect on output. Instead, the rise in aggregate demand will simply lead to a rise in prices. They therefore envisage an *AS* curve like that in diagram (a).

Their critics, however, argue that a rise in aggregate demand will lead to a rise in output. In the extreme case, prices will not rise at all. In this case the *AS* curve is like that in diagram (b). Output will rise to Y_2 with the price level remaining at P.

Others argue that both prices and output will rise. In this case, the short-term curve will be like that in diagram (c). If there is plenty of slack in the economy – idle machines, unemployed labour, etc. – output will rise a lot and prices only a little. But as slack is taken up, the *AS* curve becomes steeper. Firms, finding it increasingly

Figure 13.1 Different aggregate supply curves

difficult to raise output in the short run, simply respond to a rise in demand by raising prices. In the longer term, if increased demand leads to more investment and increased capacity (potential output), the short-run *AS* curve will shift to the right. A long-term *AS* curve, in this view, therefore, would be more elastic than the short-term one.

 Would it be possible for a short-run *AS* curve to be horizontal (as in diagram (b)) at *all* levels of output?

Issue 3: The role of expectations in the working of the market

How quickly and how fully will individuals and firms anticipate changes in prices and changes in output? How are their expectations formed, and how accurate are they? What effect do these expectations have? This is the third major controversial topic.

The political right tends to ally with those economists who argue that people's expectations adjust rapidly and fully to changing economic circumstances. They emphasize the role of expectations of *price* changes.

If aggregate demand expands, they argue, people will expect higher prices. Workers will realize that the apparently higher wages they are offered are an illusion. The higher wages are 'eaten up' by higher prices. Thus workers are not encouraged to work longer hours, and unemployed workers are not encouraged to take on employment more readily. Likewise firms realize that any increased demand for their products is an illusion. Very soon all firms will raise their prices in response to the demand increase, and given that firms' costs are rising due to higher wages and the higher prices of raw materials, machinery, etc., their price rises will fully choke off the extra demand. There will be no increase in sales, and hence no increase in output and employment.

Thus, they argue, increased aggregate demand merely fuels inflation and can do no more than give a very temporary boost to output and employment. If anything, the higher inflation could damage business confidence and thus worsen long-term output and employment growth by discouraging investment.

Those who criticize the right argue that the formation of expectations is more complex than this, and that whether people expect an increase in demand to be fully matched by inflation depends on the current state of the economy and how any increase in demand is introduced.

If there is a lot of slack in the economy – if unemployment is very high and there are many idle resources – and if an increase in demand is in the form, say, of direct government spending on production – on roads, hospitals, sewers and other infrastructure – then output and employment may quickly rise. Here the effect of expectations may be beneficial. Rather than expecting inflation from the increased demand, firms may expect faster growth and an expansion of markets. As a result they may choose to invest, and this in turn will produce further growth in output and employment.

Views on expectations, therefore, parallel views on aggregate supply. The right argues that a boost to demand will not produce extra output and employment: aggregate supply is inelastic (as in Figure 13.1 (a)) and therefore the higher demand will merely fuel expectations of inflation. Their critics argue that a boost to demand will increase aggregate supply and employment. Firms will expect this and therefore produce more.

 If firms believe the aggregate supply curve to be moderately elastic, what effect will this belief have on the outcome of an increase in aggregate demand?

Policy implications

Generally, then, the economists supported by the political right tend to favour a policy of *laissez-faire*. At most, governments should intervene to remove hindrances to the free and efficient operation of markets: for example, by legislation to reduce the power of trade unions. This way, they argue, disequilibrium unemployment will be removed and the greatest opportunity will be given for long-term growth in output and the reduction in equilibrium unemployment. Any intervention by government to boost demand will merely be inflationary and will thus damage long-term growth and employment.

Economists supported by the political centre and left argue that disequilibrium unemployment may persist for many years and may be very great. The answer is to boost demand, thereby increasing aggregate supply and employment.

These different schools of economic thought will be examined in the following sections. But first, to help understand the debate it is necessary to develop a simple model of the economy. This is the circular flow of income model.

▲ SUMMARY

1. There is considerable debate amongst economists and politicians over how the market mechanism works at a macroeconomic level. Those on the right argue that markets work relatively well and adjust quickly to changes in demand and supply. Their critics argue that there are various rigidities and that disequilibrium may persist.

2. The right argues (a) that prices and wages are relatively flexible, (b) that aggregate supply is determined independently of aggregate demand and (c) that people's price and wage expectations adjust rapidly to shifts in aggregate demand so as to wipe out any output effect.

3. The centre and left to varying degrees argue (a) that prices and wages are inflexible downwards, (b) that output depends on the level of aggregate demand and that aggregate supply is relatively elastic when there is slack in the economy and (c) that people's expectations of prices and wages depend on their expectations of output and employment, and anyway may be relatively slow to adjust to shifts in aggregate demand.

13.2 The circular flow of income

Figure 13.2 depicts the flows of money round the domestic economy. It is an extension of the model we looked at in previous chapters. In the diagram, the economy is divided into two major groups: *firms* and *households*. Each group has two roles. Firms are producers of goods and services; they are also the employers of labour and other factors of production. Households (which is the word we use for individuals) are the consumers of goods and services; they are also the suppliers of labour and various other factors of production. In the diagram there is an inner flow and various outer flows of incomes between these two groups.

Before we look at the various parts of the diagram, a word of warning. Do not confuse *money* and *income*. Money is a stock concept. At any given time there is a certain quantity of money in the economy (e.g. £1 billion). But that does not tell us the level of national *income*. Income is a flow concept (as is expenditure). It is measured as so much *per period of time*. The relationship between money and income depends on how rapidly the money *circulates*: its 'velocity of circulation'. (We will examine this concept in detail later on.) If there is £1 billion of money in the economy and each £1 on average is paid out as income five times per year, then annual national income will be £5 billion.

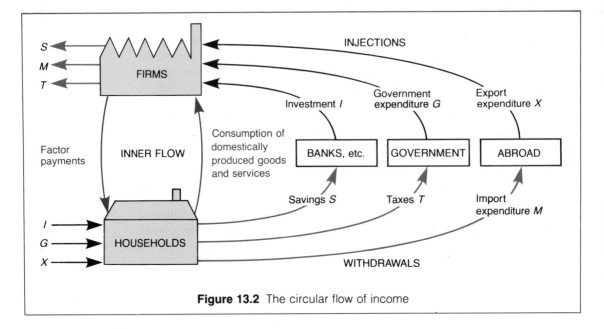

Figure 13.2 The circular flow of income

The inner flow, withdrawals and injections

The inner flow

Firms pay money to households in the form of wages and salaries, dividends on shares, interest and rent. These payments are in return for the services of the factors of production – labour, capital and land – that are supplied by households. Thus on the left-hand side of the diagram, money flows directly from firms to households as 'factor payments'.

The consumption of domestically produced goods and services (C_d)

The direct flow of money payments from households to firms.

Households, in turn, pay money to UK firms when they consume domestically produced goods and services (C_d). This is shown on the right-hand side of the inner flow. There is thus a circular flow of payments from firms to households to firms and so on.

If households spend *all* their incomes on buying domestic goods and services, and if firms pay out *all* this income they receive as factor payments to domestic households, and if the velocity of circulation does not change, the flow will continue at the same level indefinitely. The money just goes round and round at the same speed and incomes remain unchanged.

 Would this argument still hold if prices rose?

In the real world, of course, it is not as simple as this. Not all income gets passed on round the inner flow; some is *withdrawn*. At the same time, incomes are injected into the flow from outside. Let us examine these withdrawals and injections.

Withdrawals (W)

Only part of the incomes received by households will be spent on the goods and services of domestic firms. The remainder will be withdrawn from the inner flow. Likewise only part of the incomes generated by firms will be paid to UK households.

The remainder of this will also be withdrawn. There are three forms of withdrawals (or 'leakages' as they are sometimes called).

Savings (S). This is income that households choose not to spend but to put aside for the future. Savings will normally be deposited in financial institutions such as banks, building societies, the Post Office, pension funds, etc. This is shown in the bottom right of the diagram. Money flows from households to 'banks, etc.'.

It is not just households that save. Firms also save. This is from profits that they choose not to pay out as dividends to shareholders. Like households they will probably deposit these savings in some financial institution. This saving by firms is shown in the top left of the diagram. Imagine that this flow goes to the 'banks, etc.' box. (This is not shown otherwise the diagram would become a tangle of spaghetti!)

Taxes (T). Taxes withdraw income from the inner flow in much the same way as savings, only in this case people have no choice. In the model, 'taxes' include all taxes and national insurance contributions paid to central and local government. Some taxes, such as (PAYE) income tax and employees' national insurance contributions, are paid out of household incomes. Others, such as VAT and excise duties, are paid out of consumer expenditure. Others, such as corporation tax, are paid out of firms' incomes.

Import expenditure (M). Not all consumption is of home-produced goods. Households spend some of their incomes on imported goods and services. Likewise firms do not just use domestic resources. They spend money on imported raw materials, machinery, etc. This expenditure on imports, whether by households or firms, constitutes the third withdrawal from the inner flow.

This category also includes other income flowing abroad, such as the purchases by households of shares in foreign companies and deposits by UK residents in banks abroad. In other words, it includes debit items on the balance of payments account.

Total withdrawals are simply the sum of savings, taxes and imports:

$$W = S + T + M$$

Injections (J)

Only part of the money flowing into firms comes from consumer expenditure. The remainder comes from other sources outside the inner flow. Likewise only part of the incomes received by households will come from domestic firms. In both cases these inflows of money are known as 'injections'. There are three forms of injections.

Investment (I). This is the money that firms spend which they draw from various financial institutions – either past savings or loans. They may invest in plant and equipment or may simply spend the money on building up stocks of inputs and semi-finished or finished goods. When households borrow money from financial institutions, for example from a building society to buy a house, this too constitutes an injection into the inner flow.

Government expenditure (G). This can be in the form of direct government expenditure on goods and services (such as roads and hospitals), of government grants to firms, of wages to government employees or of transfer payments to households, such as pensions and child benefit.

Export expenditure (X). Money flows into the circular flow from abroad when foreigners buy UK exports. This category also includes investment by foreigners in the UK and receipts of money from abroad by UK households (e.g. the dividends earned on foreign shares). These are credit items in the balance of payments.

Withdrawals (W) (or leakages)

Incomes of households or firms that are not passed on round the inner flow. Withdrawals equal savings (S) plus taxes (T) plus import: expenditure (M)
$W = S + T + M$.

Injections (J)

Incomes received by firms that do not come from domestic households, plus incomes received by households that do not come from domestic firms. In other words, inflows of income from outside the inner flow. Injections equal investment (I) plus government expenditure (G) plus export expenditure (X):
$J = I + G + X$.

Transfer payments

Moneys transferred from one person or group to another (e.g. from the government to individuals) without production taking place.

Total injections are thus the sum of investment, government expenditure and exports:

$$J = I + G + X$$

The relationship between the withdrawals and injections

There are indirect links between savings and investment, taxation and government expenditure, and imports and exports via financial institutions, the government (central and local) and foreign countries respectively. If more money is saved, there will be more available for banks and other financial institutions to lend out. If tax receipts are higher, the government may be more keen to increase its expenditure. Finally, if imports increase, foreigners' incomes will increase, which will enable them to purchase more of our exports.

These links, however, do not guarantee that $S = I$ or $G = T$ or $M = X$. For a period of time, financial institutions can lend out (I) more than they receive from depositors (S) or vice versa; governments can spend (G) more than they receive in taxes (T) or vice versa; and the UK can run a basic balance of payments deficit ($M > X$) or surplus ($X > M$).

A major point here is that the decisions to save and invest are made by different people, and thus they plan to save and invest different amounts. Likewise the demand for imports may not equal the demand for exports. As far as the government is concerned, it may choose not to make $T = G$. It may choose not to spend all its tax revenues: to run a 'budget surplus' ($T > G$). Or it may choose to spend more than it receives in taxes – to run a budget deficit ($G > T$) – by borrowing or printing money to make up the difference.

Thus planned injections (J) may not equal planned withdrawals (W).

If they are not equal, what will happen next? This is at the centre of the debate between the various schools of economic thought. The question will be examined in the following sections.

? Are the following net injections, net withdrawals or neither? If there is uncertainty, explain your assumptions.
(a) Firms are forced to take a cut in profits in order to give a pay rise.
(b) Firms spend money on research.
(c) The government increases personal tax allowances.
(d) The government raises taxes in order to fund a programme of public works.
(e) The general public invests more money in building societies.
(f) UK investors earn higher dividends on overseas investments.
(g) UK investors earn higher dividends on domestic investments.
(h) The government purchases USA military aircraft.
(i) People draw on their savings to finance holidays abroad.
(j) People draw on their savings to finance holidays in the UK.
(k) The government runs a budget deficit and finances it by borrowing from the public.
(l) The government runs a budget deficit and finances it by printing more money.

Measuring national income

The final part of this chapter examines in detail how national income is measured in practice. But it is important to make a few preliminary points here.

The circular flow of income model we have been looking at is *not* a means of *measuring* national income. All it does is to picture in a stylized way the flows of money round the economy, and to identify the sources of injections and withdrawals.

'National income' measures incomes earned from *production*, not simply the amount of money changing hands. If we are to measure this, we must be much more precise. Take the case of government injections to households. If the government decides to increase social security benefits or child benefit, this will directly increase household incomes and thus boost aggregate demand. It will *not*, however, represent an increase in *national income*. No more has been produced. The benefits are merely *transfer payments* from taxpayers to householders.

Take another case. If householders earn dividends from shares in foreign companies, this is an injection (*X*) from abroad into the household sector, but it does not represent an increase in *domestic* production. Although there is no problem in classifying this as an injection, there is a problem in deciding whether it should be counted as national income: it *is* money the country earns, but not from any goods or services it has produced! As section 13.6 shows, we get round this problem by having two measures of national income, one which includes these foreign earnings and one which does not.

It is not necessary to get into these details to understand the debates as to how the economy functions at a macro level. The simple analysis of an inner flow plus various injections and withdrawals is all we need at this point.

▲ SUMMARY

1. The circular flow of income model depicts the flows of money round the economy. The inner flow shows the direct flows between firms and households. Money flows from firms to households in the form of factor payments, and back again as consumer expenditure on domestically produced goods and services.
2. Not all incomes get passed on directly round the inner flow. Some is withdrawn in the form of savings, some is paid in taxes, and some goes abroad as expenditure on imports, etc.
3. Likewise not all incomes received come from within the

inner flow. Some is injected in the form of investment expenditure, some as government expenditure and some as payments from abroad.
4. Planned injections and withdrawals are unlikely to be the same. What happens when they are not is a major area of debate among macroeconomists.
5. If we wish to measure national income, there are a number of qualifications we need to make to the simple analysis of the circular flow. These qualifications are examined in section 13.6.

13.3 Classical macroeconomics

The classical economists of the early nineteenth century held a pessimistic view of the long-term prospects for economic growth (see Boxes 4.2, 12.2 and 13.1). Population growth combined with the law of diminishing returns would undermine any benefits from improved technology or the discovery of new sources of raw materials. What is more, there was little the government could do to improve these prospects. In fact governments, they argued, by interfering with competition and the functioning of the market would be likely to make things worse. They therefore advocated a policy of *laissez-faire* and free trade.

The classical school continued into the twentieth century. By then, its predictions about economic growth had become less pessimistic. After all, the Victorian years had been ones of rapid industrialization and growth, with a massive expansion of Britain's overseas trade. This growing optimism had, if anything, strengthened the advocacy of *laissez-faire*. In the early years of this century, then, most economists, most politicians and virtually all bankers and businesspeople were relatively confident in the power of the free market to provide growing output and low unemployment.

The main role for the government was to provide 'sound finance' (i.e. not to print too much money), so as to maintain stable prices.

The classical analysis of output and employment

The classical theory predicted that, in the long run, equilibrium in the economy would be at virtually full employment. In the long run, any unemployment would be merely *frictional* unemployment: namely, people in the process of changing jobs.

There were two important elements in the classical theory.

The free market economy works to equate demand and supply in all markets

This element of classical theory assumes flexible prices: of goods and services, of labour (i.e. wages) and of money (i.e. the rate of interest).

The classical economists argued that flexible prices would ensure that savings equalled investment ($S = I$) and that imports equalled exports ($M = X$). From this it follows that, if the government were to 'balance its budget' and make taxation equal to government expenditure ($T = G$), then total withdrawals would equal total injections ($W = \mathcal{J}$).

$$\left.\begin{array}{c} S = I \\ M = X \\ T = G \end{array}\right\} \rightarrow W = \mathcal{J}^1$$

But why should flexible prices ensure that $S = I$ and $M = X$? The reasoning of the classical economists was as follows.

$S = I$. This would be brought about by flexible rates of interest (r) in the market for 'loanable funds'. When firms want to invest in new plant and equipment they will require finance. Investment demand, therefore, represents a demand for loanable funds from financial institutions. The higher the rate of interest (*r*), the more expensive will borrowing be, and hence the less will be the demand for investment. The investment schedule will therefore be downward sloping.

Savings represent a supply of loanable funds. The savings schedule will be upward sloping. The higher the rate of interest, the more people will save: that is, the more they will deposit in financial institutions.

In Figure 13.3 equilibrium will be at r_e, where $S = I$. If the rate of interest were above r_e, say at r_1, financial institutions would have surplus funds. They would have to lower the rate of interest to attract sufficient borrowers. If the rate of interest were

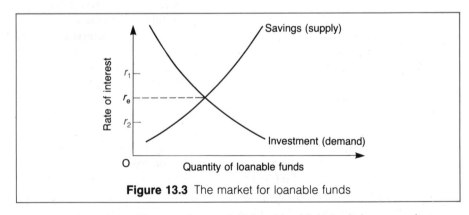

Figure 13.3 The market for loanable funds

---

[1] The classical economists did not use the terms 'withdrawals' and 'injections': these are modern terms. Nevertheless, their analysis implied an automatic equation of W and $\mathcal{J}$ if markets cleared and the government balanced its budget.

below r_e, say at r_2, financial institutions would be short of funds. They would raise the rate of interest.

> **?** Assume that rates of interest are initially above the equilibrium and that one particular financial institution chooses *not* to reduce its rate of interest. What will happen? What will be the elasticity of supply of loanable funds to an individual institution?

$M = X$. This would be brought about by flexible UK prices and wages. Before 1914, and from 1925 to 1931, the UK was on the gold standard. This was a *fixed* exchange rate system in which each participating country's currency was valued at a certain fixed amount of gold.

If a country had a balance of payments deficit ($M > X$), this had to be paid in gold from its reserves. A country was then supposed to respond to this outflow of gold by reducing the amount of money in the economy and hence reducing total expenditure. This would create surpluses in the goods and labour markets, which would, in turn, lead to a fall in prices and wages. This fall in the prices of UK goods would increase the sale of exports and reduce the consumption of the now relatively expensive imports. This whole process would continue until the balance of payments deficit was eliminated: until $M = X$.

> **Gold standard**
>
> The system whereby countries' exchange rates were fixed in terms of a certain amount of gold and whereby balance of payments deficits were paid in gold.

> **?** What would have happened if countries in deficit had not responded to an outflow of gold by reducing total expenditure?

(Note that, under a system of freely floating exchange rates, it is the flexibility in exchange rates, rather than the prices of goods and factors, that will ensure $M = X$.)

Provided the government balanced its budget ($T = G$), therefore, flexibility in the various markets would ensure that withdrawals equal injections.

Say's law

J. B. Say was a French economist of the early nineteenth century (see Box 13.1). The law named after him states that: *supply creates its own demand.*

What this means is that the production of goods and services will generate expenditures sufficient to ensure that they are sold. There will be no deficiency of demand and no need to lay off workers. There will be full employment. The justification for the law is as follows.

When firms produce goods, they pay out money either directly to other firms, or as factor payments to households. The income that households receive is then partly paid back to firms in the form of consumption expenditure (C_d): the inner flow of the circular flow of income.

But any withdrawals by firms or households are also fully paid back to firms in the form of injections, since $S = I$, $M = X$ and $T = G$. Thus all the incomes generated by firms' supply will be transformed into demand for their products, either directly in the form of consumption, or indirectly via withdrawals and then injections. There will thus be no deficiency of demand.

Of course, it is possible that, although aggregate demand might equal aggregate supply, consumers may shift their demand away from some industries in favour of others. Unemployment may then temporarily occur. But then wages would fall in the declining industries and rise in the expanding industries. Equilibrium would be restored. Unemployment would be eliminated.

The restoration of equilibrium, and thus the correction of this temporary

Box 13.1

Thomas Malthus, David Ricardo and Jean-Baptiste Say
How gloomy was classical economics?

Thomas Robert Malthus (1766–1834) and David Ricardo (1772–1823) were probably the two most famous economists of the early nineteenth century. They were in fact close friends and spent much of their time in discussion, in correspondence and also in social gatherings – both men loving to entertain.

The two men came from quite different backgrounds and pursued very different careers.

Malthus, the gifted son of a gifted and eccentric father, with whom he would debate for hours, gained a degree in mathematics from Cambridge, took holy orders and became a rector (but left two curates to run the parish while he continued his academic research), and in 1804 became England's first professor of political economy.

While Malthus pursued an academic career, Ricardo was making a fortune in the world of finance. He was the third of seventeen children born to Jewish parents who had migrated to London from Holland. His father was a wealthy merchant banker, and at the age of 14 David went to work for him. But then when he was 21, against the wishes of his parents, he married a Quaker. Disinherited by his father, he set up in business on his own as a stockbroker. He was so successful that in 1814, when he was still only 42, he retired from the world of business to concentrate on writing and politics. Representing an Irish constituency in Parliament, he strongly advocated liberal reforms.

Malthus and Ricardo agreed on one thing: there was a gloomy long-term prospect for the human race.

As we saw back in Chapter 4, Malthus argued that population growth would outstrip the growth in food supplies. The future of the planet, therefore, was to be one of mass starvation, rather than one of growing abundance.

Ricardo's theory of long-term growth (outlined in Box 12.2) was more sophisticated than that of Malthus, but it too predicted a gloomy future, with the rate of profit eventually falling to a level where firms would no longer find it worth investing. Growth would ultimately grind to a halt.

But while Malthus and Ricardo agreed about the fate of the world in the distant future, that was about all they did agree on!

Malthus was also pessimistic about the more immediate future. Malthus saw the capitalist system as inheritantly unstable. He looked around him at a world in recession following the Napoleonic wars. Yet this recession with its high level of unemployment was not due to a lack of productive capacity. Quite the opposite: the warehouses were full; there was a general 'glut'. The problem according to Malthus was one of underconsumption, of a lack of 'effectual demand'. If consumers would not buy, firms would not produce.

Ricardo was totally dismissive of Malthus's ideas.

---

unemployment, will be quicker (a) the more flexible are wages and (b) the more willing and able are workers to move to industries and towns where jobs are available (labour mobility). In other words, the better markets work, the sooner will full employment be restored.

Classical analysis of prices and inflation

Quantity theory of money

The price level (*P*) is directly related to the quantity of money in the economy (*M*$_s$).

The classical economists based their analysis of inflation on the quantity theory of money. In its simplest form it states that the general level of prices (*P*) in the economy depends on the supply of money (*M*$_s$):

$$P = f(M_s)$$

The higher the quantity of money, the higher the level of prices. Under this theory inflation is simply caused by a rise in money supply. The quantity theory of money is one of the oldest explanations of price changes, as Box 13.2 illustrates.

Box 13.1 (cont'd)

Ignoring the evidence around him, Ricardo denied the possibility of a general glut. He denied the possibility of mass unemployment. If wages were too high to clear the labour market, they would simply fall until the disequilibrium was eliminated. In reply to Malthus he wrote:

> You say 'we know from repeated experience that the money price of labour never falls till many workmen have been for some time out of work.' I know no such thing, and if wages were previously high, I can see no reason whatever why they should not fall before many labourers are thrown out of work.[2]

Ricardo's more optimistic view about short-term growth and employment, even though it flew in the face of the evidence, carried public opinion with it. Ricardo was held in great respect, if not awe. A persuasive public speaker, a highly successful businessman, a writer of very difficult to understand economics: his ideas must be correct!

Jean-Baptiste Say (1776–1832) was a French economist and industrialist who was greatly influenced by both Adam Smith and David Ricardo. He was largely responsible for introducing to the continent Smith's ideas on the workings of markets and the 'invisible hand', and for a time fell out of favour with Napoleon for advocating a policy of extreme *laissez-faire*.

Say, who was a good friend of Malthus and Ricardo and visited England many times, was more optimistic than either of them. Himself a capitalist – he owned a cotton mill – he believed that free-market capitalism would provide both short-term and long-term prosperity. In the debate between Malthus and Ricardo, he sided with Ricardo, and claimed that a problem of general overproduction and unemployment is impossible. In what became known as Say's law of markets, or more simply Say's law, he argued:

> [A] product is no sooner created, than it, from that instant, affords a market for other products to the full extent of its own value. When the producer has put the finishing hand to his product, he is most anxious to sell it immediately, lest its value should vanish in his hands. Nor is he less anxious to dispose of the money he may get for it; for the value of money is also perishable. But the only way of getting rid of money is in the purchase of some product or other. Thus the mere circumstance of the creation of one product immediately opens a vent for other products.[3]

Thus, according to Say, the production of goods would generate sufficient incomes to ensure that these goods were sold. Prolonged unemployment would be impossible.

This optimism about the free market, despite the criticisms of Karl Marx and others, was to dominate the thinking of mainstream economists right up to the 1930s. Even the *long-run* gloomy prognostications of Ricardo and Malthus were eventually dismissed, as the prospect of sustained technological progress seemed to allow economic growth to go on indefinitely. The attention of economists thus became increasingly focused on microeconomic considerations: on questions of efficiency and distribution.

It was not until the 1920s and 1930s, with the UK and then the rest of the world plunged into recession, with all the horrors of mass unemployment and poverty, that Say's law was seriously questioned and the possibility of deficient aggregate demand was once more entertained – this time by Keynes.

[2] P. Sraffa (ed.), *The Works and Correspondence of David Ricardo* (Cambridge University Press, 1951), p. 24.
[3] J. B. Say, *Treatise on Political Economy* (1803), p. 167.

A useful version of the quantity theory for helping understand the classical approach is that developed in Cambridge in the early 1900s. In this version, the *demand* for money (M_d) depends on national *income* (Y). The higher the level of national income, the more money balances people will require to hold in order to finance their transactions. When we refer to 'money balances' we are not talking about people's savings, but rather the amount of money they *currently* feel the need to hold. Obviously, the higher people's incomes are, the bigger the total money balances they will choose to hold. The Cambridge version of the quantity theory is expressed by the following equation:

$$M_d = kY$$

where k is the proportion of national income that people desire to hold in money balances. National income (Y) is the *value* of the nation's output: i.e. the physical level of national output (Q) times the average price (P) of that output. Thus:

$$M_d = kPQ$$

Box 13.2

The Quantity Theory of Money
A sixteenth century version

Plenty of money maketh generally things dear and scarcity of money maketh likewise things generally good cheap. Whereas things particularly are also dear or good cheap according to plenty or scarcity of the things themselves, or the use of them.[4]

Malynes

[4] Quoted in E. Victor Morgan, *A History of Money* (Penguin, 1969), pp. 184–5.

Assuming flexible interest rates, and therefore that the money market will clear, the demand for money will equal the supply of money.

$$M_d = M_s$$

thus:

$$M_s = kPQ$$

and:

$$P = M_s/kQ$$

The classical economists argued that k was constant. The value of k depends on the banking and other institutional arrangements for holding money. They also argued that Q was independent of money supply. Say's law would ensure that actual output (Q) was kept at the full employment level. With k and Q as constants, therefore, the quantity theory must hold:

$$P = f(M_s)$$

Increases in money supply simply lead to inflation.

? Assuming that Q rises each year as a result of increases in productivity, can money supply rise without causing inflation? Would this destroy the validity of the quantity theory?

The Great Depression and the return to the gold standard

The classical economists had predicted that there would be virtual full employment. Any unemployment would simply be the frictional unemployment of people being 'between jobs'. Before the First World War their predictions were not far from the truth. Unemployment did fluctuate somewhat with the trade cycle, but averaged around only $4\frac{1}{2}$ per cent of the workforce.

Between the wars, however, Britain experienced a prolonged recession of unparalleled severity. Throughout this 'Great Depression' unemployment was very much higher than before the war, reaching over 22 per cent in the winter of 1932–3 with 3 million people unemployed. Even in the best years between the wars, the unemployment rate was still higher than in the worst years before 1914. The depression eliminated inflation, however. In every year from 1921 to 1934 prices either were constant or fell (see Figure 13.4).

At first Britain was virtually alone in suffering depression. While output slumped and unemployment soared, most of the rest of the industrialized world was

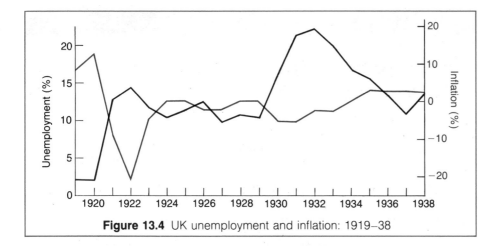

Figure 13.4 UK unemployment and inflation: 1919–38

experiencing a boom. But in 1929, after a decade of rapid growth and a huge rise in share values, the US stock exchange crashed. The Wall Street crash sent the US economy plunging into deep recession, with the rest of the world following suit. As the world economy slumped, so too did international trade. With a collapse of its exports, Britain dived even deeper into depression.

The Great Depression was closely associated with Britain's return to the gold standard, a system that it had left in 1914 at the outbreak of the war. From 1918 to 1925 Britain adopted a flexible exchange rate system, a system felt necessary because of the disruption to foreign trade following the war and the monetary chaos in Europe. In 1925, however, Britain returned to the gold standard.

Britain's prosperity before the First World War was crucially dependent on its international trade and its position as provider of international financial services. This was the view of classical economists and bankers in the 1920s. Free trade must be encouraged, they argued, and the best way of doing this was to return to the gold standard.

The classical position was that the gold standard had worked well before the war. Britain's trade had grown and the role of sterling had been that of an 'international currency'. Because the government had guaranteed that a pound sterling could be exchanged for a fixed amount of gold, foreigners had been willing to accept pounds, both in exchange for their exports and as a reserve currency.

The experience of international inflation in the years straight after the war made many countries anxious to return to the certainties of the gold standard, a system that forced countries to keep inflation under control.

The government and the Treasury felt it was important to return at the old rate to create confidence in the strength of sterling and to protect the value of sterling reserves held by various countries round the world. In 1925 Winston Churchill, who was Chancellor of the Exchequer at the time, made the fateful announcement: Britain was returning to the gold standard and at the pre-war rate of $4.86.

There was a serious problem, however, in returning to the gold standard at the old pre-war rate. Britain had developed a large balance of payments deficit. Export markets had been lost during the war and industries had been diverted away from exporting to producing for the war effort. Imports were high, as post-war reconstruction took place. Also high inflation immediately after the war had reduced the competitiveness of Britain's exports and made imports relatively cheaper.

To return to the gold standard at the old rate would therefore require harshly

Box 13.3

Release from the Gold Cage
Keynes' cinema news broadcast in 1931

John Maynard Keynes, the most prominent critic of the classical view, welcomed the collapse of the gold standard. Broadcasting to the nation in 1931, he said:

> There is no danger of the exchange rate falling too far. There is no danger of a serious rise in the cost of living. The worst I should expect would be a return to the prices of some two years ago.[5] But meanwhile British trade will

have received an enormous stimulus, much more than most of us have yet realized. It is a wonderful thing for our businessmen and our manufacturers and our unemployed to taste hope again. But they must not allow anyone to put them back in the gold cage where they have been pining their hearts out all these years.

[5] Prices had been falling the last two years.

deflationary policies. In fact such policies had already been adopted from the beginning of the 1920s in preparation for the return, and had already been largely responsible for the depression that had begun four years earlier.

Nevertheless, according to the Treasury view, based on classical economics, deflationary policies were necessary. The resulting fall in wages and prices would restore Britain's competitiveness and thus correct the balance of payments deficit. Once Britain had actually returned to the gold standard, such policies seemed to be essential.

There followed a period of great pain. The balance of payments remained in severe deficit. At such a high exchange rate, prices and wages could not be forced downwards rapidly enough to restore the competitiveness of exports or to stem the flood of imports. The result was that gold poured out of the country. So how was this haemorrhage to be stopped? The classical answer was to dampen domestic demand even further, put even more downward pressure on prices and wages, and as a result make British goods more competitive again.

But the cure was worse than the disease. The high interest rate policy succeeded in deepening the already severe depression.

What is more, other countries made Britain's problem worse. The rules of the gold standard required not only that deficit countries should deflate, but also that surplus countries should *reflate*. The idea was that, as these countries earned gold from their balance of payments surpluses, they should increase their money supply and reduce their interest rates, thereby expanding aggregate demand and raising prices. The result would be higher imports and lower exports, thus eliminating their balance of payments surplus. In the process, the deficit countries would be helped. *Their* exports would rise and their imports fall.

The problem was that the surplus countries did not reflate. They were quite happy simply to build up their stock of gold. This put the whole burden of correction on Britain and other deficit countries. As a result they had to deflate that much harder. Eventually, with the collapse of world trade following the Wall Street crash of 1929, and a resulting further decline in Britain's exports, the country could no longer support the exchange rate: there was simply not enough gold left in the Bank of England. Britain left the gold standard in 1931. The pound was allowed to depreciate.

The classical response to the Great Depression

The deflationary policies, designed to lower prices and make UK goods more competitive, seemed to be directly responsible for increasing unemployment. Many critics argued that the government ought deliberately to *expand* aggregate demand.

What was the reply of the Treasury and other classical economists? First, they rejected the analysis that unemployment was caused by a lack of demand; secondly, they rejected policies of reflation (policies such as increased government expenditure).

The classical Treasury view on unemployment

Would not deflation of demand lead to unemployment? According to the Treasury view, unemployment would only occur if labour markets *failed to clear*.

In Figure 13.5, if the aggregate demand for labour falls from AD_{L_1} to AD_{L_2}, then real wages (i.e. wage costs (W) as a proportion of the price (P) the employer receives for the good) must fall from W_1 to W_2 if equilibrium is to be restored in the labour market.

The mass unemployment of the 1920s and 1930s was therefore caused, according to the classical view, by a failure of labour markets to clear: a failure of real wage costs to fall sufficiently. Trade unions were resisting real wage cuts.

?   What type of unemployment was this (if the analysis was correct)?

The following policy conclusions were thus drawn by the Treasury:

- People should be encouraged to take wage cuts. This would help to reduce prices and restore export demand, thus correcting the balance of payments. Also it would help to reduce unemployment (assuming that money wages fell faster than prices and hence that *real* wages fell).
- People should be encouraged to save. This would, via flexible interest rates, lead to more investment and hence growth of output and demand for labour. 'Real' jobs would be created.

The classical Treasury view on public works

During the 1920s and 1930s some politicians and economists argued that unemployment could be reduced by the government pursuing a programme of public works:

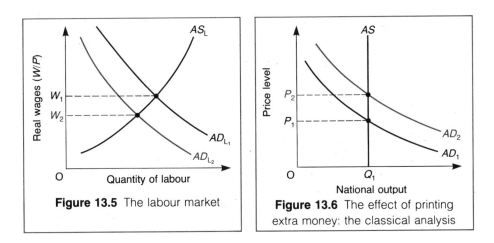

Figure 13.5 The labour market

Figure 13.6 The effect of printing extra money: the classical analysis

Box 13.4

Balance the Budget at All Cost
Fiscal policy in the early 1930s

The budget must be balanced. All government expenditure should be financed from taxation. This was orthodox opinion in the 1920s.

But as unemployment increased during the Great Depression, spending on unemployment benefits (the most rapidly growing item of government expenditure) threatened the balanced budget principle. Other spending had to be cut to restore balance. The result was more unemployment, and hence the payment of more unemployment benefits.

Treasury officials and classical economists called for cuts in unemployment benefits. The May Committee, set up to investigate the budgetary problem, recommended a 20 per cent reduction. Even the Labour government, elected on a mandate to tackle the unemployment problem, proposed a 10 per cent reduction in 1931. This contributed to its subsequent collapse.

The extent to which people tolerated the cuts in government social expenditure – the direct result of the balanced budget philosophy – was surprising. As Philip Snowdon, Labour's Chancellor of the Exchequer, was to remark in 1931:

This morning my post was like my post everyday for a

week past. Old aged pensioners had returned their pension books. War pensioners had offered to forgo their pensions for the year. Postal orders large and small pour in. Factory girls come to me with collections taken in workshops. Children, even, have sent from their savings boxes shillings and half-crowns to help the nation in its need.[6]

And yet, as Keynes argued, it was not savings that were necessary to cure the unemployment, but spending (see Box 13.7). Government deficits were *desirable*. Attempts to balance the budget merely deflate the economy further and deepen the problem of unemployment. As he was to write in the *New Statesman* in 1931:

At the present time all governments have large deficits. For government borrowing of one kind or another is nature's remedy, so to speak, for preventing business losses from being, in so severe a slump as the present one, so great as to bring production altogether to a standstill.[7]

[6] Open University D284 TV programme 1.
[7] R. Middleton, *Towards the Managed Economy: Keynes, the Treasury and the fiscal policy debate of the 1930s* (Methuen, 1985), p. 112.

Year	Receipts (total) (£m)	Expenditure (total) (£m)	Expenditure on unemployment benefits (£m)	Balance
1929/30	815.0	829.5	59.7	−14.5
1930/31	857.8	881.0	103.5	−23.2
1931/32	851.5	851.1	125.1	+ 0.4
1932/33	827.0	859.3	–	−32.3

Source: League of Nations.

the building of roads, hospitals, houses, etc. The Treasury view, however, was that this would not work and could have costly side-effects.

There are three ways in which a programme of public works could be funded. *None* of these three ways would, according to the classical Treasury view, solve the unemployment problem.

From extra taxation. This, it was argued, would merely have the effect of reducing the money consumers would spend on private industry.

$$G \uparrow, T \uparrow \rightarrow C_d \downarrow$$

Extra public-sector demand would be offset by a fall in private-sector demand.

From extra government borrowing. To persuade people to lend to the government, it must offer higher interest rates. The private sector will then in turn have to offer higher interest rates to compete for funds. As interest rates go up, private borrowing goes down. Thus public investment crowds out private investment (see Box 13.5).

Crowding out

Where increased public expenditure diverts money or resources away from the private sector.

Box 13.5

The Crowding-Out Effect (Part I)
When public expenditure replaces private

Critics of the use of government expenditure to stimulate output and employment often refer to the problem of *crowding out*. In its starkest form the argument goes like this.

There is no point in the government embarking on a programme of public works to bring the economy out of recession. If it attempts to spend more, it can only do so by reducing private expenditure. The effect on total spending will be zero.

There are two main types of crowding out that could occur – *resource crowding out* and *financial crowding out*.

Resource crowding out

This is when the government uses resources such as labour and raw materials that would otherwise be used by the private sector. This would clearly be possible if the economy were operating near full capacity. Workers cannot be in two places at once. If they work for the government, they cannot at the same time work for a private company.

The argument is far less convincing, however, if there is slack in the economy. If the government merely mobilizes otherwise *idle* resources, there need be no reduction in private-sector output. Quite the opposite: if there is a growth in public-sector output and employment, this will stimulate a demand for goods produced by the private sector too. If these private-sector firms have spare capacity, they will respond by producing more themselves. This is the argument put forward by Keynesians: extra aggregate demand will stimulate extra production.

Financial crowding out

This occurs when extra government spending diverts *funds* from private-sector firms and thus deprives them of the finance necessary for investment. The mechanism is as follows.

If the government spends more (without raising taxes or printing more money), it will have to borrow more. In order to attract people to buy government securities or put their money in National Savings, the government will have to offer higher rates of interest. Private companies in turn will then have to offer higher rates of interest themselves in order to attract funds. Alternatively, if they borrow from banks, and banks have less funds, the banks will charge them higher interest rates. Higher interest rates will discourage firms from borrowing and hence discourage investment.

In short, if the government spends more money, there will be less money for the private sector to spend.

The weakness with this argument is that it assumes that the supply of money is fixed. If the government spends more but *increases* the amount of money in the economy, it need not deprive the private sector of finance. Interest rates will not be bid up.

But would that not be inflationary? No, say Keynesians, not if there are idle resources and hence the extra money can be spent on extra output. Only if *resource* crowding out takes place would it be inflationary.

The debate about crowding out will be examined in more detail in later chapters and boxes.

> **?** Could resource crowding out take place at less than full employment?

There may, however, be *some* increase in the supply of loanable funds as higher interest rates encourage more saving. But then there will be less private consumption and lower receipts by firms from sales.

Thus either way, government expenditure merely replaces private expenditure.

$$G \uparrow \rightarrow I \downarrow, C_d \downarrow$$

By printing extra money. Printing extra money could, in theory, allow the extra government expenditure to be financed without reducing money available to the private sector. But according to the quantity theory of money, extra money would simply lead to inflation. The assumption here is that the aggregate supply 'curve' is vertical. In Figure 13.6, a rise in aggregate demand from AD_1 to AD_2 (as a result of the extra money supply) would simply lead to a rise in the price level from P_1 to P_2. National output (and hence employment) would not increase. It would remain constant at Q_1.

There was a great fear of a return of inflation. The deflationary policies of the 1920s had eliminated the inflation of the 1910s, and the reductions in wages and prices had gone some way to restoring the UK's competitiveness. Any reflation would erode that competitiveness and jeopardize the return to the gold standard. Also there was the lesson of Germany and some East European countries of the early 1920s where severe 'hyperinflation' had virtually destroyed their economies (see Box 12.6).

Treasury orthodoxy insisted, therefore, that government should attempt to balance its budget, even if this meant cutting welfare benefits to the rising numbers of unemployed (see Box 13.4).

The governments of the 1920s and early 1930s followed these classical recommendations. They attempted to balance their budgets and rejected policies of reflation. Yet mass unemployment persisted.

▲ SUMMARY

1. The classical analysis of output and employment is based on the assumption that markets clear. More specifically, it assumes that the there are flexible wages, flexible prices and flexible rates of interest. The result will be that demand and supply are equated in the labour market, in the goods market and in the market for loanable funds.

2. Given that markets will clear, Say's law will operate. This law states that supply creates its own demand. In other words, the production of goods and services will generate incomes for households, which in turn will generate consumption expenditure, ensuring that the goods are sold. If any incomes are not directly spent on domestic goods, flexible prices will help to ensure that any money withdrawn is reinjected. Flexible interest rates will ensure that investment equals savings, and flexible prices and wages will ensure that exports equal imports. Provided the government balances its budget, withdrawals will equal injections and Say's law will hold.

3. The classical economists based their analysis of prices on the quantity theory of money. This states that the level of prices is directly related to the quantity of money in the economy. The Cambridge equation expresses this relation-

ship formally in terms of the demand for money (M_d):

$$M_d = kPQ$$

where P is the price level and Q is the quantity of money. Assuming that the demand for money equals the supply of money (M_s) and that k and Q are independent of money supply. then it follows that:

$$P = f(M_s)$$

Increases in the money supply simply lead to inflation.

4. In 1925 Britain returned to the gold standard system of fixed exchange rates at the pre-war rate. But given the massive balance of payments deficit at this rate, it had to pursue tough deflationary policies. The result was mass unemployment.

5. The classical economists saw the remedy to the problem to lie in downward flexibility of wages and prices. According to the classical theory this would allow Say's law to operate and full employment to be restored. They rejected public works as the solution, arguing that it would lead to crowding out if financed by borrowing, and to inflation if financed by printing money.

Keynes Tower : Uni of Essex : Tribute to the great man.

13.4 The Keynesian revolution

Keynes' rejection of classical macroeconomics

The main critic of classical macroeconomics was John Maynard Keynes. In his major work, *The General Theory of Employment, Interest and Money* (1936), he rejected the classical assumption that markets would clear. Disequilibrium could persist and mass unemployment could continue. There are two crucial markets in which disequilibrium could persist.

The labour market

Workers would resist wage cuts. Wages were thus 'sticky' downwards. In a recession, when the demand for labour is low, wages might not fall far or fast enough to clear the labour market.

In Figure 13.7 the recession has caused the aggregate demand for labour to shift to

Figure 13.7 The problem of demand deficiency in the labour market

AD_{L_2}. If the real wage rate were to remain at W_1, the supply and demand for labour would no longer be in equilibrium. There would exist disequilibrium (demand-deficient) unemployment. But even if wage cuts could be introduced, as advocated by classical economists, Keynes rejected that as the solution to demand deficiency. Workers are also consumers. A cut in workers' wages would mean less consumer spending. Firms would respond to this by reducing their demand for labour. Thus a lowering of wages below W_1 would lead to a leftward shift in the AD_L curve, and this would more than offset the reduction in wages. Wages would not fall fast enough to clear the market. Disequilibrium would worsen. The recession would deepen.

Employers might well find that labour was cheaper to employ, but if demand for their product was falling, they would hardly be likely to take on more labour.

The market for loanable funds

Keynes also rejected the classical solution of increased savings as a means of stimulating investment and growth. Again the problem was one of market disequilibrium.

A rise in savings will cause a disequilibrium in the market for loanable funds. The rate of interest will fall from r_1 to r_2 in Figure 13.8. But a rise in savings means a fall in consumption. As a result, firms will sell less and will thus be discouraged from investing. The investment demand curve will shift to the left. The rate of interest will have to fall *below* r_2 to clear the market.

The demand for investment, according to Keynes, depends very much on business confidence in the future. A slide into recession could shatter such confidence. The resulting fall in investment would deepen the recession.

Figure 13.8 Disequilibrium in the market for loanable funds

Box 13.6

Will Wage Cuts Cure Unemployment?
Keynes' dismissal of the classical remedy

In *The General Theory of Employment, Interest and Money*, Keynes rejects the classical argument that unemployment is due to excessive wages. In chapter 2 he argues:

[T]he contention that the unemployment which characterises a depression is due to a refusal by labour to accept a reduction of money wages is not clearly supported by the facts. It is not very plausible to assert that unemployment in the United States in 1932 was due either to labour obstinately refusing to accept a reduction of money wages or to its obstinately demanding a real wage beyond what the productivity of the economic machine was capable of furnishing. Wide variations are experienced in the volume of employment without any apparent change either in the minimum real demands of labour or in its productivity. Labour is not more truculent in the depression than in the boom – far from it. Nor is its physical productivity less. These facts from experience are a *prima facie* ground for questioning the classical analysis . . .

. . . A classical economist may sympathise with labour in refusing to accept a cut in its money-wage, and he will admit that it may not be wise to make it to meet conditions which are temporary; but scientific integrity forces him to declare that this refusal is, nevertheless, at the bottom of the trouble.[8]

[8] J. M. Keynes, *The General Theory of Employment Interest and Money* (Macmillan, 1967), p. 9.

The problem of disequilibrium in the market for loanable funds was made worse, according to Keynes, by two other factors. Firstly, neither savings nor investment is very responsive to changes in interest rates, and thus very large changes in interest rates would be necessary if ever equilibrium were to be restored after any shift in the savings or investment curves.

Secondly, interest rates respond not only to savings and investment decisions, but also to speculation in other parts of the money market. According to Keynes, there is considerable speculation in money markets. The resulting interest rates may not equate savings and investment at full employment.

Keynes also rejected the simple quantity theory of money. Increases in money supply will not necessarily lead merely to rises in prices. There are two reasons for this. Firstly, not all extra money will be spent. Some of it may simply stay in people's bank accounts. Thus in the equation $M_s = kPQ$, k may vary. Secondly and more importantly, increases in money supply may lead to increases in *real output*. If there is a lot of slack in the economy, with high unemployment, idle machines and idle resources, an increased spending of money may lead to substantial increases in output (Q) and leave prices (P) little affected.

? Demonstrate this argument on an aggregate demand and supply diagram.

If the government were to cut money supply in an attempt to reduce prices, the major effect might be to reduce output and employment instead.

All these arguments meant a rejection of Say's law. Far from supply creating demand and thus ensuring full employment, Keynes argued that it was *demand that created supply*. If aggregate demand rose, firms would respond to the extra demand by producing more and employing more people. But a fall in demand would lead to less output and rising unemployment.

Keynes' central point was that an unregulated market economy *could not ensure sufficient demand*. Governments should therefore abandon *laissez-faire*. Instead they should intervene to *control* aggregate demand.

Keynes' analysis of employment and inflation

Keynes' analysis of unemployment can be explained most simply in terms of the circular flow of income diagram. Figure 13.9 shows a simplified version of the circular flow with injections entering at just one point, and likewise withdrawals leaving at just one point. This simplification does not affect the argument. Keynes himself did not use this exact model, but it clearly explains the essence of his argument.

If injections (J) do not equal withdrawals (W), a state of disequilibrium exists. What will bring them back into equilibrium, however, is not a change in prices (of labour or of loanable funds), but rather a change in national income and employment.

Start with a state of equilibrium, where injections equal withdrawals. If there is now a rise in injections – say, firms decide to invest more – aggregate demand ($C_d + J$) will be higher. Firms will respond to this increased demand by using more labour and other resources and thus paying out more incomes (Y) to households. Household consumption will rise and so firms will sell more.

Firms will respond by producing more, and thus using more labour and other resources. Household incomes will rise again. Consumption and hence production will rise again, and so on. There will thus be a multiplied rise in incomes and employment. This is known as the multiplier effect.

The process, however, does not go on for ever. Each time household incomes rise, households save more, pay more taxes and buy more imports. In other words, withdrawals rise. When withdrawals have risen to match the increase in injections, equilibrium will be restored and national income and employment will stop rising. The process can be summarized as follows:

$$J > W \rightarrow Y\uparrow \ \rightarrow W\uparrow \ \text{until } J = W$$

Similarly, an initial fall in injections (or rise in withdrawals) will lead to a multiplied fall in national income and employment:

$$J < W \rightarrow Y\downarrow \ \rightarrow W\downarrow \ \text{until } J = W$$

Thus equilibrium in the circular flow of income can be at *any* level of output and employment.

If aggregate demand is too low, there will be a recession and high unemployment.

> **Multiplier effect**
>
> An initial increase in aggregate demand of £xm leads to an eventual rise in national income that is greater than £xm.

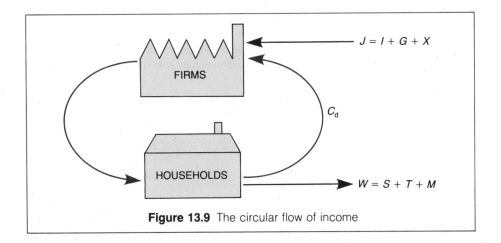

Figure 13.9 The circular flow of income

Figure 13.10 The effects of increases in aggregate demand on national output

In Figure 13.10 it is assumed that there is some potential level of national income and output (Y_p) at which there would be full employment of resources. This represents a limit to output. If aggregate demand were initially at AD_1, equilibrium would be at Y_1, considerably below the full employment potential.

In this case, argued Keynes, governments should intervene to boost aggregate demand. There are two policy weapons they can use.

Fiscal policy
Remember how we defined this in Chapter 12. It is where the government alters the balance between government expenditure (G) and taxation (T), and thereby alters the balance between injections and withdrawals. In this way it controls aggregate demand. Faced with a recession, it should raise G and/or lower T. In other words, the government should run a budget deficit rather than a balanced budget. There will then be a multiplier effect:

$$G\uparrow \text{ or } T\downarrow \ \rightarrow J > W \rightarrow Y\uparrow \ \rightarrow W\uparrow \text{ until } J = W$$

If the eventual rise in aggregate demand were to, say, AD_2 in Figure 13.10, output would rise to Y_2.

Monetary policy
This is where the government alters the supply of money in the economy or manipulates interest rates. If it were to raise money supply, there would be more available in the economy for spending, interest rates would fall and aggregate demand would rise. Keynes argued that this was a less reliable policy than fiscal policy, since some of the extra money could be used for speculating in paper assets rather than spending on real goods and services. The details of how money supply is controlled and the effects it has on the economy are examined in later chapters.

It is most effective if both policies are used simultaneously. For example, if the government were to undertake a programme of public works (fiscal policy) and finance it through increases in money supply (monetary policy), there would be no crowding out. There would be a significant rise in output and employment.

 What would be the classical economists' criticisms of this argument?

If aggregate demand rises too much, however, inflation becomes a problem. (This was the case during the Second World War, with the high expenditure on the war effort.) As Y_p is approached, with more and more firms reaching full capacity and with fewer and fewer idle resources, so additional increases in aggregate demand lead more and more to higher prices rather than higher output. This can be seen in Figure 13.10 as aggregate demand rises from AD_2 to AD_3 to AD_4.

 Might the *AS* curve shift to the right in the meantime? If it did, how would this influence the effects of the rises in aggregate demand?

Governments faced with the resulting demand-pull inflation should, according to Keynes, use *contractionary* fiscal and monetary policies to reduce demand. Contractionary fiscal policy would involve reducing government expenditure and/or raising taxes. Contractionary monetary policy would involve reducing the rate of growth of money supply. Keynes argued that here too fiscal policy was the more reliable, but again that the best solution was to combine both policies.

The Keynesian policies of the 1950s and 1960s

During the 1920s and 1930s, governments of all parties adopted the classical Treasury view of balanced budgets. After the Second World War and up to the mid-1970s, governments adopted the Keynesian approach of deliberately managing aggregate demand. In both periods, therefore, there was a high degree of agreement between the parties as to the way the economy worked and therefore the appropriate macroeconomic policies.

As demand fluctuated with the trade cycle, so government was seen as having the role of smoothing out such fluctuations. Governments pursued Keynesian demand management policies in an attempt to stabilize the economy and avoid excess or deficient demand.

When the economy began to grow too fast, with rising inflation and balance of payments deficits, the government adopted *deflationary* fiscal and monetary policies. When inflation and the balance of payments were sufficiently improved, but probably with recession looming, threatening rising unemployment and little or no growth, governments adopted *expansionary* fiscal and monetary policies. This succession of deflationary and reflationary policies to counteract the effect of the trade cycle became known as stop–go policies.

Figure 13.11 illustrates the inflation and unemployment rates experienced during the 1950s and 1960s. During this period the average rate of inflation was 3.77 per cent and the average rate of unemployment was a mere 1.72 per cent.

Stop–go policies
Alternate deflationary and reflationary policies to tackle the currently most pressing of the four problems which fluctuate with the trade cycle.

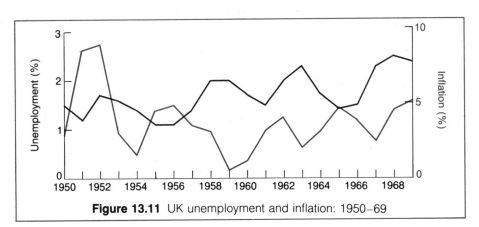

Figure 13.11 UK unemployment and inflation: 1950–69

Box 13.7

John Maynard Keynes (1883–1946)
Person profile

Modern macroeconomics had its birth in 1936. That was when Keynes' *General Theory of Employment Interest and Money* was published. Probably no other economist and no other book has ever had such a profound influence on the subject and on the policies pursued by governments. Indeed, throughout the 1950s and 1960s, governments in the UK and the USA, and many other countries too, considered themselves to be 'Keynesian'.

John Maynard Keynes came from an intellectual family. His father, John Neville Keynes, himself an economist and logician, spent his whole career at Cambridge first as a fellow and then as university registrar. His mother was a justice of the peace and at one time mayor of Cambridge.

Maynard (as he was called) won a scholarship to Eton. After a brilliant school career he progressed to King's College, Cambridge, to study classics and mathematics. There he made a profound impression on his tutors, who included the two great economists Alfred Marshall and Arthur Pigou. Marshall wanted him to become a full-time economist, but Keynes' interests were much broader. He loved debating and was elected secretary of the Cambridge Union and president of its famous debating society; he loved writing on all kinds of public issues; he loved climbing mountains; he loved socializing and mixing with famous literary and artistic figures – in fact he became one of the members of the 'Bloomsbury group', which included such famous literary people as Virginia Woolf, E. M. Forster and Bertrand Russell.

After leaving Cambridge, Keynes became a civil servant and worked in the Indian Office – a job he thoroughly disliked. But two years later, in 1908, he returned to King's College as a fellow, and in 1911 was made editor of the *Economic Journal*, Britain's foremost economics publication. He was to retain the editorship for 33 years.

With the outbreak of war in 1914, he left Cambridge temporarily and joined the Treasury. He gained rapid promotion, and was one of the major advisers to the government at the Versailles peace conference at the end of the war. Disgusted at the terms of the peace treaty, which was more concerned with making Germany pay than paving the way for the reconstruction of Europe, he resigned from the Treasury and wrote a damning critique of the treaty. *The Economic Consequences of the Peace* became a bestseller and rocketed him to international fame.

He returned to Cambridge. But he did not just teach and write. He began to speculate in international commodity and exchange markets. At first he had little success and just avoided going broke, but soon he was making huge amounts of money. He eventually built a fortune worth several million pounds at today's prices. Like Ricardo, he was not just a *theoretical* economist!

He made money for other people too. He acted as economic adviser to several companies, and then later became bursar of King's College. Through speculation he made the college very rich. A well-known story recounts how one day Keynes was walking across the

From the mid-1960s onwards there was increasing criticism of short-term demand management policies. Criticisms included the following:

- The policies were not very successful in stabilizing the economy. Fluctuations still existed. Some economists even claimed that demand management policies made fluctuations worse. The main reason given was the time it took for policies to be adopted and to work. If time lags are long enough, a deflationary policy may only begin to work when the economy has already turned down into recession. Likewise a reflationary policy may only begin to work when the economy is already booming, thus further fuelling inflation.

- The UK's long-term growth at around 2.8 per cent per annum was appreciably lower than that of other industrialized countries. Some of the blame for this was attributed to an over-concentration on short-term policies of stabilization, and a neglect of underlying structural problems in the economy.

- Persistent balance of payments problems meant that governments often had to

Box 13.7 (cont'd)

quad with a friend, when he looked up at the famous King's College chapel and muttered to himself, 'Too small. Far too small.' 'Too small for what?' enquired his friend. 'If I have to take delivery of all the corn I have just bought for the college,' replied Keynes, 'it will never all go in there!'

He also continued his association with the artistic world, including the ballet. He married Lydia Lopokova, a popular Russian ballerina. On marrying Keynes she gave up her career in the ballet, but later became a Shakespearean actress and on one occasion was leading lady in a new Cambridge theatre with which Keynes was closely associated – another of his ventures.

Throughout the 1920s he wrote many pamphlets and articles critical of the *laissez-faire*, balanced budget policies of successive governments. Full employment, maintained Keynes, was not a natural state of affairs. To achieve full employment, the government would have to intervene actively in the economy to ensure a sufficient level of aggregate demand. This might well mean running a budget deficit: in other words, the government spending more than it receives in taxes.

His views gradually became more and more influential, but for years were steadfastly resisted by the Treasury and the Bank of England, which were steeped in balanced budget orthodoxy.

Then in 1936 the *General Theory* was published. Although this is a difficult and rather dry work, it took the economic world by storm. It caused a revolution – the Keynesian revolution. Gone was the economist's cosy view of the world where unemployment was a mere temporary aberration. In its place was adopted a new orthodox view, that an economy could slide into a slump – *and stay there*. This, however, was not the long-term pessimistic picture painted by Malthus and Ricardo. A slump was essentially a short-term problem, a problem that a government could cure. Keynes was not particularly interested in the long-run future of the world. 'Take care of the short run and the long run will look after itself' might have been Keynes' maxim. Keynes himself put it more succinctly: 'In the long run we are all dead.'

By the outbreak of the Second World War, Keynes and the Treasury were reconciled. He was recruited as an adviser to the government on its wartime finances. But his health was ailing. He had suffered a heart attack in 1937, and never fully recovered. Despite his ill health, however, he made a major contribution to the management of the wartime economy and was made a baron in 1942.

He made several trips to the USA, with Lydia at his side as nurse, to negotiate wartime financial assistance. He was also concerned to map out with the Americans a new post-war economic order. This culminated in 1944 in an international conference at Bretton Woods, New Hampshire, at which Lord Keynes was the chief British negotiator. The system devised at that conference (albeit not entirely to Keynes' liking) was to last 27 years and was to provide the framework for the international post-war recovery.

Keynes died in 1946, an untimely end for someone who undoubtedly would have had much to contribute toward the shaping of the post-war world.

It might have been expected that the economic revolution which overthrew classical theory would have come from the left. But Keynes, stern critic of *laissez-faire* and advocate of government intervention though he was, was no socialist. His was a centrist revolution: not one that advocated the overthrow of capitalism, but one that advocated measures to support it – not by leaving it alone, but by intervening to make up for its shortcomings.

pursue deflationary policies even when the economy was running below capacity and unemployment was rising.

- The simple Phillips curve relationship between inflation and unemployment was breaking down. If reflationary policies were the cure for unemployment and deflationary policies were the cure for inflation, what policies should be pursued when both inflation *and* unemployment were rising?

- The most fundamental criticism of all came from monetarists. They rejected Keynesianism as a whole, with its concentration on demand. They returned to the earlier classical analysis, with its concentration on supply, and extended it to take account of the increasingly important role of price expectations in explaining 'stagflation'.

From the mid-1970s onwards the Keynesian/monetarist split between economists was reflected in the political parties. The Conservative leadership embraced monetarism, whereas the other political parties continued to embrace variants of Keynesianism.

Box 13.8

'You've Never Had It So Good'
Prosperity in the late 1950s

By the late 1950s people had come to expect rising living standards and the absence of economic depressions. True, the economy still fluctuated, and for short periods there would be only low rates of economic growth, but generally there was optimism that the government could ensure growing prosperity over the longer term.

Harold Macmillan was Prime Minister from 1957 to 1963, and his attitude epitomized this optimism (or complacency!). In a famous speech at Bedford in July 1957 he said:

> Indeed let us be frank about it: most of our people have never had it so good. Go round the country, go to the industrial towns, go to the farms and you will see a state of prosperity such as we have never had in my lifetime – nor indeed ever in the history of this country.

A few days later in the Commons he expanded on this claim:

> I confess that I find it rather a strange experience to sit here day after day and listen to the arguments and problems presented by high prices and over-full employment. When I first stood for the House of Commons in 1923, soon after the post-war boom broke, and for the next twelve or fifteen years, including four general elections, one problem and one problem only held the political field. It was the problem of deflation, violently

and rapidly falling prices, and massive unemployment. We debated it, as many of the older members here remember, week by week and day by day. We put forward all kinds of rival views as to how it should be solved . . .

> Today, it has somehow solved itself, but this new trouble has come which seems to dog our footsteps. Having solved one problem we have now the one we are discussing, that of rising prices. Every honourable Member knows, and every man and woman in the country knows, that for the mass of the people – I would say for the great mass of the people – there has never been such a good time or such a high standard of living as at the present day. I repeat what I said at Bedford, that they have 'never had it so good' . . .

> I can only repeat that I have been grateful to see the change. I believe that all of us in the House, certainly the older members, feel grateful that there has been this great change. When I am told by some people, some rather academic writers, that inflation can be cured or arrested only by returning to substantial or even massive unemployment, I reject that utterly.

Not everyone in the country was this 'grateful'. Although the UK's economic performance was vastly better than in the inter-war period, the rate of growth was nevertheless poor compared with countries like France and West Germany.

 SUMMARY

1. Keynes rejected the classical assumption that markets would clear. Disequilibrium could persist in the labour market. A fall in aggregate demand would not simply lead to a fall in wages and prices and a restoration of the full employment equilibrium. Instead there would be demand-deficient unemployment: as demand fell there would be less demand for labour.

2. Disequilibrium could also persist in the market for loanable funds. As aggregate demand fell, and with it business confidence, so the demand for loanable funds for investment would shrink. Reductions in interest rates would be insufficient to clear the market for loanable funds.

3. Keynes also rejected the simple quantity theory. If there is slack in the economy, an expansion of the money supply can lead to an increase in *output* rather than an increase in prices.

4. Keynes argued that there would be a multiplier effect from changes in injections or withdrawals. A rise in investment, for example, would cause a multiplied rise in

national income, as additional expenditures flowed round and round the circular flow stimulating more and more production and thus generating more and more real incomes.

5. If the economy is operating below full employment, the government can use fiscal and/or monetary policies to boost aggregate demand and thereby take up the slack in the economy. Excessive aggregate demand, however, causes inflation. Here deflationary fiscal and monetary policies can be used to remove this excess demand.

6. Keynesianism became the orthodoxy of the 1950s and 1960s. Governments used fiscal (and to a lesser extent monetary) policies to manage the level of aggregate demand.

7. After the mid-1960s, however, there was growing criticism of Keynesian demand management. The economy still fluctuated and the various macroeconomic problems seemed to be getting worse. Monetarists argued that Keynesian analysis was fundamentally flawed, and instead returned to the classical analysis.

13.5 Modern developments

The monetarist counter-revolution

The most powerful criticisms of the Keynesian conventional wisdom came from monetarists, whose chief advocate was Milton Friedman, Professor of Economics at Chicago University. Monetarists returned to the old classical theory as the basis for their analysis, and extended it to take account of the growing problem of 'stagflation'.

At the heart of monetarism is the quantity theory of money. Friedman examined the historical relationship between money supply and prices, and concluded that inflation was 'always and everywhere a monetary phenomenon'. If money supply over the long run rises faster than the potential output of the economy, inflation will be the inevitable result.

Monetarists argue that over the long run, in the equation $M_s = kPQ$, both k and Q are 'exogenous variables'. In other words, k and Q are independently determined and are not, therefore, affected by changes in M_s. Any change in money supply (M_s), therefore, will only affect prices (P).

$$M_s \uparrow, \bar{k}, \bar{Q} \rightarrow P \uparrow$$

Whether or not monetarists are correct in arguing that k and Q are exogenous will be examined in later chapters.

Monetarists draw two important conclusions from their analysis.

First, the rising inflation from 1967 onwards was entirely due to the growth in money supply increasingly outstripping the growth in output. Part of the problem was seen to be that increases in money supply raise aggregate demand, which in turn raises output and employment in the short run – perhaps after six months to a year. But soon people's expectations will adjust. Workers and firms expect higher wages and prices. Their actions then ensure that wages and prices *are* higher. Thus after 1–2 years the extra demand is fully taken up in inflation, and so output and employment fall back again. Thus governments are tempted to raise money supply and aggregate demand again in a further attempt to get unemployment down. The effect of this over a number of years is for inflation simply to get higher and higher.

Secondly, reducing the rate of growth of money supply will reduce inflation without leading to long-run increases in unemployment. It will lead to temporary increases in unemployment, they argue, as the demand for goods and labour fall. But once price and wage inflation have adjusted down to this new level of demand, disequilibrium unemployment will be eliminated. This process will be hindered and high unemployment is likely to persist if workers persist in demanding excessive wage increases, or if firms and workers continue to expect high inflation rates.

Monetarists argue that inflation is damaging to the economy because it creates uncertainty for businesspeople and therefore reduces investment, and also because it is damaging to UK competitiveness in international trade. They see it as essential, therefore, for governments to keep a tight control over money supply and advocate the setting of money supply targets. Modest and well-publicized targets should help to reduce the *expected* rate of inflation. The UK government from the late 1970s to the mid-1980s set targets for the growth of money supply, and such targets were central to the Thatcher government's 'medium-term financial strategy'.

Apart from controlling the money supply, governments, according to monetarists, should intervene in the economy as little as possible, save to remove hindrances to the efficient functioning of the market (like various restrictive practices of unions). This way, they argue, aggregate supply will be encouraged to grow as firms and workers respond to market incentives. Monetarist 'supply-side policy', therefore, is essentially one of encouraging free enterprise.

Monetarist reappraisal of the Phillips curve

The monetarist position on inflation and unemployment can best be summarized by referring to their version of the long-run Phillips curve.

Unemployment

Unemployment may be temporarily reduced by raising aggregate demand, or increased by lowering aggregate demand, but in the long run it will tend to a 'natural' level (U_n). This is the equilibrium level of unemployment and is independent of aggregate demand. Disequilibrium unemployment will not exist in the long run. Equilibrium unemployment (U_n) consists of frictional, structural and technological unemployment. It can be reduced by increasing the mobility of labour by improved retraining, for example, or by reducing social security benefits. This should encourage a quicker matching of workers to jobs.

Inflation

Inflation is entirely dependent on aggregate demand, which in turn is entirely dependent on money supply. Inflation is thus of the demand-pull variety. Higher demand in the long run simply leads to more inflation. In the short run, higher demand will reduce unemployment below the natural level, but in the long run, once expectations have adjusted, unemployment rises back to the natural level. Thus the long-run Phillips curve is vertical (see Figure 13.12). A change in demand will lead in the long run to a move up or down this 'curve'. A shift in the 'curve' will be caused by a change in the level of equilibrium unemployment (U_n), *not* by a change in demand.

 What effects, according to monetarists, would successful supply-side policies have on the Phillips curve?

Stagflation

Over time the vertical Phillips curve has moved to the right both in the UK and throughout the developed world. Natural (equilibrium) unemployment had increased, in the UK from around 1½ per cent of the labour force in the 1960s to

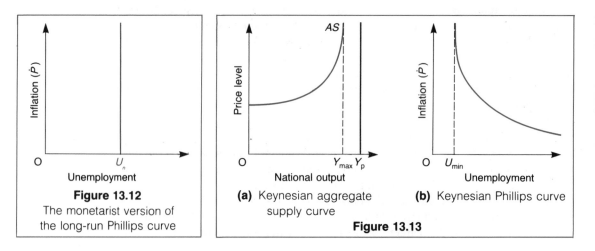

Figure 13.12
The monetarist version of the long-run Phillips curve

(a) Keynesian aggregate supply curve

(b) Keynesian Phillips curve

Figure 13.13

around 6–8 per cent in the 1980s. This was due to increased frictional and structural problems caused by the growth of union power and generous unemployment benefits which reduce the incentive to get a job.

Governments up to the late 1970s responded to rising unemployment by boosting aggregate demand (the balance of payments permitting). This, however, only led to more inflation fuelled by rising expectations of inflation.

When governments eventually did curb the growth in aggregate demand, as did the Thatcher government after 1979, it took a time for expectations to adjust downwards. In the meantime, there was a further temporary rise in unemployment (due to wage rises being slow to adjust downward) over and above that corresponding to the rightward shift of the long-run Phillips curve.

Modern-day Keynesians

Keynesians agreed with monetarists on one point. If demand is expanded too fast and for too long, inflation will result – and there will be a certain amount of unemployment of labour (and other resources too) that cannot be eliminated simply by expanding aggregate demand.

In Figure 13.13(a) there is a maximum level of output (Y_{max}) that can be achieved at any one time simply by expanding aggregate demand. This is below the potential output (Y_p) that could be achieved if all resources were used to the full.

Likewise in Figure 13.13(b) there is a minimum level of unemployment (U_{min}) that can be achieved by expanding aggregate demand. The Phillips curve becomes vertical at this point. Keynesians and monetarists alike argue that reductions in unemployment below U_{min} can only be brought about by improved factor mobility or other structural policies. In other words, supply-side policies will be needed.

In other respects, Keynesians differ markedly from monetarists.

Keynesian analysis of stagflation

Keynesians blame stagflation on a wider set of causes than do monetarists.

Inflation. Inflation may in the past have been caused by excess demand feeding into higher and higher expectations of inflation. But from the mid-1970s onwards there ceased to be a problem of general excess demand. Instead, excess demand was confined to certain sectors. The inflationary pressures here, however, were not offset by the deflationary pressures in sectors with excess supply because of the 'stickiness' downward of wages and prices. Demand-shift inflation was the result.

Inflation has also been caused by increased cost-push pressures: the increasing concentration of economic power in large multinational companies and large trade unions, and the large oil price increases of 1973/74 and 1978/79.

Finally, workers came to expect real wage increases each year which could simply not be met from real increases in national income. The problem here for the long term was not so much the expectations of price increases, but rather the expectations of increases in real living standards.

Unemployment. Keynesians blame a deficiency of aggregate demand for the massive rise in unemployment in the 1980s. Aggregate supply is highly elastic downwards in response to a reduction in aggregate demand. Firms respond to falling demand by producing less and employing fewer people. This may be further aggravated by firms running down stocks to try to reduce costs and maintain profits.

Expectations are relevant here. But it is not so much the expectation of lower inflation that reduces inflation (as monetarists claim); rather it is the expectation of

Box 13.9

Milton Friedman (1912–)
Person profile

Ask the average person to name a monetarist and the answer you get will almost certainly be 'Milton Friedman'. He is one of the few economists widely known outside the profession. He is also a public figure who is strongly associated with the political right, being a staunch advocate of the free market.

His fame (or infamy to his opponents) spread dramatically in the early 1980s when he made a series of TV documentaries called *Free to Choose*. Here was no mere economist. Here was an evangelist. The free market that he advocated was not just a means to achieving economic growth, efficiency and full employment. Far more, it was the guarantor of human liberty; it was the best environment in which humans could develop their talents and their creative energies; it was a system which encouraged individuals to be responsible.

To economists he is much more than a TV personality. He is associated with a number of major developments in monetary theory, the theory of expectations and economic methodology.

Milton Friedman was born in New York in 1912. After teaching for many years at Columbia University, he became Professor of Economics at Chicago University in 1948 – a post he retained until his retirement in 1979. He was one of the leading lights of the 'Chigago school' of monetarist economics.

In his *Studies in the Quantity Theory of Money* (1956), Friedman developed his thesis that 'inflation is always and everywhere a monetary phenomenon'. This was a return to the classical belief in the quantity theory of money: that the level of prices depends on the quantity of money in the economy. The policy implications were simple. If the government wishes to control inflation, it must restrain the growth in the money supply.

These monetarist arguments were given added weight with the publication of a monumental work, *A Monetary History of the United States 1867–1960* (1963), which he wrote jointly with Anna Schwartz. The message was that 'money matters', and that explanations for fluctuations in prices, output and employment were to be found in monetary fluctuations, for which *governments* must bear responsibility.

The other major contribution he made to the development of economic theory was his re-examination of the Phillips curve. By incorporating expectations into his analysis of inflation he was able to demonstrate that the Phillips curve would be *vertical* in the long run.

The policy implications of this were profound. If he was correct, governments could not trade off lower unemployment against higher inflation. This seemed to run directly counter to orthodox Keynesian analysis, which had argued that a policy of expanding aggregate demand would reduce unemployment (albeit at a cost of somewhat higher inflation). What Friedman was saying was that a policy of expanding aggregate demand would, in the long run, lead merely to inflation. Unemployment would be unaffected. It would remain at its 'natural' level.

So how could this 'natural' level be reduced? Do we simply have to put up with it? No, says Friedman – and this is where we come back full circle to Friedman the apostle of the free market – the answer lies in incentives. The labour market must be freed up. Wages must be flexible and workers must be mobile. In other words, workers must respond to market signals. Excessive government welfare schemes and monolithic trade unions only stifle this process.

And so we return to Friedman, darling of the right and bogeyman of the left – skilled debater, media personality and popularizer of *laissez-faire* economics.

lower sales that reduces production, investment and employment. The problem is not merely a short-term difficulty that markets will soon correct. Unless the government adopts a deliberate policy of reflation, the problem will continue. Mass unemployment and recession are likely to persist.

Structural problems, such as the long-term decline of certain industries, or the continuing shift away from labour-intensive processes in manufacturing, are also to blame for high unemployment. Again, these are not temporary problems that markets will put right. They are problems that require large-scale government intervention: for example, in the form of regional development policy.

 How will these various factors that worsen the problem of stagflation affect the Phillips curve?

Keynesian criticisms of monetarism

Keynesians criticize monetarists for putting too much reliance on markets. The problems of inflation, unemployment and industrial decline are much too deep seated and complex to be rectified by a simple reliance on controlling the money supply and then leaving private enterprise and labour to respond to unregulated market forces.

Free markets are often highly imperfect and will not lead to an optimum allocation of resources. What is more, markets frequently reflect short-term speculative movements of demand and supply, and do not give a clear indication of long-term costs and benefits. In particular, the stock market, the money market and the foreign exchange market can respond quite violently to short-term pressures. Such fluctuations can be very damaging to investment. For example, violent swings in exchange rates, as experienced in the early 1980s, can dissuade firms from making long-term invest-ment decisions to develop export markets. A sudden rise in exchange rates may make it impossible to compete abroad, even though at a lower exchange rate an exporter could have made a large profit.

The fluctuations inherent in free markets cause uncertainty about future demand, supply and prices. This uncertainty reduces investment and hence reduces growth. Government, therefore, should intervene much more to stimulate growth and investment. Keynesians frequently refer to the cases of Japan, France and Germany where there is a much closer collaboration between government and industry than there is in the UK.

Keynesian policy proposals

A sustained increase in demand

A substantial increase in demand may be necessary initially if unemployment levels are very high. The best way of doing this is for the government to increase its expenditure on public works such as roads and housing, since these projects have a relatively low import content and therefore increased expenditure does not lead to balance of payments problems. Thereafter the government should maintain a high and stable demand, by appropriate demand management policies. This should keep unemployment down and set the environment for long-term investment and growth.

A prices and incomes policy

To prevent the higher demand leading to higher inflation, the government may have to adopt some form of prices and incomes policy. Previously such policies had been introduced in booming conditions to control already high levels of inflation, and they had therefore had little long-term success. The policies created frustrations for workers and firms, and they eventually broke down, only to be followed by a wage and price explosion. Many Keynesians argue, however, that a prices and incomes policy introduced in a recession and accompanied by expanding demand and output and hence rises in living standards would be much more acceptable to trade unions. (The support for prices and incomes policies by Keynesians has waned somewhat in recent years.)

Control of exchange rates and interest rates

To reduce uncertainties, the government should intervene in foreign exchange and money markets to prevent excessive short-term fluctuations in exchange rates and interest rates. More stable rates will encourage investment and growth.

Protection (import controls)

One of the problems of expanding aggregate demand is the effect it has on imports and hence the balance of payments. To *some* extent a higher level of imports will be acceptable given that the exchange rate is likely to depreciate. Keynesians argue that a steady depreciation of a country's currency is probably desirable to increase the competitiveness of its exports. But to prevent excessive rises in imports some control over imports may be necessary. For example, the government could impose tariffs (customs duties) on imports, or restrict people's access to foreign exchange.

International reflation

Balance of payments constraints would be further eased if there was an internationally co-ordinated reflation. Each country's exports would then rise roughly in line with imports. A significant reflation by other countries may eliminate the need for import controls.

Greater co-operation between government and industry

To promote long-term growth and to avoid the uncertainties of the market, the government should work much more closely with industry. The government should help to co-ordinate the plans of interdependent sectors of industry, and should channel finance to the more promising industries.

Some Keynesians argue that the government should go further and engage in full-scale national planning. This would not be the 'command planning' that used to exist in Eastern Europe, but rather 'indicative planning', whereby the government, along with representatives of industry and probably trade unions, works out a strategy for industrial regeneration and growth. The effect, it is argued, will be for the government to provide an infrastructure (transport, communications, energy, etc.) that better meets the needs of private industry, and for private industry to increase the level of investment, confident in the growth of its markets.

Structural policies

To reduce structural unemployment the government should pursue regional policies to encourage firms to move to areas of high unemployment, and retraining policies to encourage greater occupational mobility of labour.

Extremists and moderates

Not all monetarists agree with each other. Not all Keynesians agree with each other. There are moderate and extreme monetarists and moderate and extreme Keynesians.

Extreme monetarists (new classical/rational expectations school)

New classical school

A body of economists who believe that markets are highly competitive and clear very rapidly; any expansion of demand will feed through virtually instantaneously into higher prices, giving a vertical *short*-run as well as a vertical long-run Phillips curve.

The new classical school maintains that markets clear very quickly and expectations adjust virtually instantaneously to new situations. These expectations are based on firms' and workers' rational assessment of what is happening in the economy and in their particular sector of it. They may be wrong, but they are as likely to overpredict as to underpredict the rate of inflation and hence their equilibrium price. On average they will guess it about right.

Expanding money supply will virtually instantaneously lead to higher expectations of inflation. Therefore it can only cause inflation; it cannot reduce unemployment. The short-run Phillips curve is vertical, as well as the long-run. Likewise tight monetary policy will reduce inflation. It does not increase unemployment. Rising unemployment is entirely due to a rise in the natural level of unemployment.

This school favours *laissez-faire* policies and is part of what is often called the 'radical right'.

Moderate monetarists

Moderate monetarists maintain that markets adjust fairly quickly – perhaps within one or two years.

A rise in money supply and hence aggregate demand will lead to a temporary reduction in unemployment, but as expectations of inflation (and hence of wage increases) adjust upwards, so eventually the level of unemployment will rise again. Thus the short-run Phillips curve is downward sloping, but the long-run curve is vertical.

If the economy is faced with high inflation, a sudden tight monetary policy may temporarily lead to a recession. Thus sudden extreme policies should be avoided. Instead there should be a gradual reduction in the growth of the money supply.

Any temporary demand-deficient unemployment will be reduced if workers can be encouraged to take reductions in real wages. Ultimately, though, any policies to make long-term reductions in unemployment must be aimed at the supply side of the economy: reducing natural unemployment by increasing labour mobility.

Extreme Keynesians

Extreme Keynesians argue that there is no automatic mechanism to eliminate demand-deficient unemployment even in the long run.

Not only are wages sticky downwards, but also any reductions in wages that do take place will further reduce consumer demand. Money circulating will automatically fall as banks lend out less and less in response to falling demand. Firms are unlikely to borrow for investment since they have no confidence in their market. Expectations are likely to remain pessimistic.

Under these circumstances, government must intervene to expand demand. By raising government expenditure and cutting taxes, the nation must spend its way out of recession. Extensive import controls must be used if necessary.

After the economy has pulled out of recession, it is still important for the government to maintain a high level of demand. Not only will this maintain low unemployment and keep actual national income close to potential national income, but also it will provide the most favourable environment for research and development, innovations and investment generally. Thus *potential* national income will grow more rapidly.

Moderate Keynesians

Moderate Keynesians argue that economies will probably eventually pull out of recession even if governments do not boost demand. There will be a natural upturn in the trade cycle. Wage increases will slow down and the average real wage (W/P) will probably eventually fall. At the same time, the surplus funds in the banking sector will encourage banks to find borrowers, and this will help to arrest the fall in aggregate demand. Finally, after a period of recession when investment has been low and stocks have been run down, there will be some resumption of investment to replace worn-out machinery and some resumption of purchasing of stocks.

Nevertheless a recession can be deep and long lived, and the recovery slow and faltering. Thus moderate Keynesians, like extreme Keynesians, argue for active intervention by government to boost demand.

Once the economy is back to near full employment, the government must continue to control aggregate demand to prevent fluctuations in output and employment. Keynesians generally advocate the use of anti-cyclical demand management policy.

Moderate Keynesians recognize a wider range of important causes of macro-economic problems than do extreme Keynesians. As a result moderate Keynesians normally recommend a package of policies selected from those outlined in the previous section and possibly including targets for the growth of money supply and certain supply-side policies to reduce the natural level of unemployment, such as retraining schemes and better and more efficient job centres.

The radical left

Some economists make a far more fundamental attack on the market economy. Most Keynesians, although they see a *free* market leading to serious problems, nevertheless argue that government intervention can rectify these problems. Those on the radical left disagree. They see the market economy as so flawed that mere intervention will not solve its problems. Instead the market economy needs to be *replaced* by some alternative system such as state planning and/or worker control of industry. Marxist economists see the problems of capitalism to be so severe that ultimately there will be a revolution and it will be overthrown.

The fact that there are so many different views as to how the macroeconomy functions makes it impossible to do justice to them all in an introductory book. Nevertheless it is hoped that you will get some insight into the major schools of thought and why they advocate the policies they do. If nothing else, you will probably begin to see why economists never seem to be able to agree: why, as Bernard Shaw once said, 'If you laid all the economists of the world end to end, they would still never reach a conclusion.'

 Two economists disagree over the best way of tackling the problem of unemployment. For what reasons might they disagree? Are these reasons positive or normative?

▲ SUMMARY

1. Monetarists argue that there is a close correlation between the growth of the money supply and the level of inflation. Increases in money supply cause increases in aggregate demand, which in turn cause inflation. Along with the classical economists, they argue that output and employment are determined independently of money supply (at least in the long run). This means that a deflationary policy to cure inflation will *not* in the long run cause a fall in output or a rise in unemployment.

2. Monetarists thus argue that the long-run Phillips curve is vertical. Its position along the horizontal axis will depend on the level of equilibrium or 'natural' unemployment.

3. According to monetarists, stagflation has been caused by a combination of (a) rightward shifts in the vertical Phillips 'curve' due to increased frictional and structural problems in the economy, and (b) governments attempting to reduce unemployment by continuously expanding the money supply.

4. Modern-day Keynesians reject the notion of a totally vertical Phillips curve, but do accept that demand-side policies alone cannot cure unemployment completely. Keynesians blame the combination of high inflation and high unemployment on a number of factors, each of which has the effect of shifting the Phillips curve to the right. These factors include cost-push and demand-shift pressures on inflation, and government attempts to cure inflation by continually pursuing deflationary policies.

5. Keynesians argue that markets do not clear rapidly and that in the meantime expectations of output and employment changes can have major effects on investment plans.

6. Whereas monetarists generally favour policies of freeing up markets (within the framework of strict government control over money supply), Keynesians favour a much more interventionist approach by the government. From time to time they advocate such policies as controls over prices and incomes, import controls and controls over the exchange rate and interest rates. At the same time they advocate greater co-operation, planning and consultation both domestically and internationally so as to achieve co-ordinated and sustained economic growth.

7. There are many shades of opinion amongst the different groups of economists, from extreme new classical economists who advocate almost complete *laissez-faire* to the extreme left where economists advocate the virtual abandonment of markets. In between comes a whole spectrum of opinions and theories about the relative effectiveness of markets and the government in achieving the various macroeconomic goals.

*13.6 Measuring national income and output

Comparing national incomes

- How does UK national income compare with that of other countries? Does the UK, for example, have a higher or lower national income than Germany or France or Spain or Portugal or . . .?
- How much has the economy grown over the last five years?
- Are we really better off than we were ten years ago?
- Which country in the world has the highest living standard?
- How fast is the economy growing at the moment?
- Did the economy grow faster in the 1980s or the 1970s?

These are typical questions that economists will be asked on the subject of national output and its growth. They are questions that are at the forefront of political debate: after all, economic growth is a major objective of governments. When a government stands for re-election, voters will consider how much their living standards have improved over the government's term of office. Voters will also consider whether the opposition parties would be likely to do better. Voters will also look at other countries and ask how their growth performance compares with ours.

To assess how fast the economy has grown we must have a means of *measuring* the value of the nation's output. The measure we use is called gross domestic product (GDP).

This section shows how GDP is calculated. It looks at some alternative ways of measuring national output, and at various complications that arise in the measurement process. It also looks at difficulties in interpreting GDP statistics. Does GDP give a good indication of human welfare? Can the figures be meaningfully used to compare one country's standard of living with another? Can the figures be used to show how living standards have changed over the years: in other words, can the figures be used to show the real growth in living standards?

Gross domestic product (GDP)

The value of output produced within the country over a twelve-month period.

The three ways of calculating GDP

There are three different ways in which GDP can be calculated. To understand why three different methods are used and why they should all add up to the same figure, let us recall the circular flow of income diagram that we examined in section 13.2. In it, you will remember, we divided the economy into two major groups of people: households and firms. Incomes flow from firms to households when firms employ factors of production to produce goods and services. The money flows back again to firms when households consume goods and services. To keep the analysis simple let us assume for the moment that there are no injections and withdrawals. This simplified circular flow of income is illustrated in Figure 13.14

The first method of measuring GDP is to add up the value of all the goods and services produced in the country, industry by industry. In other words, we focus on firms and add up all their production. Thus method number one is known as the *product method*.

The production of goods and services generates incomes for households in the form of wages and salaries, profits, rent and interest. The second method of measuring GDP, therefore, is to add up all these incomes. This is known as the *income method*.

The third method is to focus on the expenditures necessary to purchase the nation's production. In our simplified model of the circular flow of income, where

Box 13.10

Il Sorpasso?
Who are better off: the British or the Italians?

In 1987 the Italian press proudly claimed that Italy's economy had overtaken the UK's. They called it 'il sorpasso'.

For the Italian government this was very important. It was a major achievement to put before the Italian electorate. But more than this it gave Italy a claim to be represented in the *Group of Five* most important economies of the world. The Group of Five consists of the USA, Japan, Germany, France and the UK, and meets at regular intervals to discuss world economic events (such as exchange rate and interest rate policies). Italy is excluded and only participates (along with Canada) in the *Group of Seven*, which often simply rubber stamps decisions already taken by the Group of Five.

Not surprisingly, many British politicians and economists rejected the claim. So what are the facts? Had Italy overtaken the UK? The table gives the relevant figures.

The Italians claimed that the difference was even bigger than these figures suggested. The reason is Italy's large 'underground' economy, a thriving sector of undeclared, and therefore untaxed and unrecorded activities. If this were included, it could boost the Italian GDP figures by as much as 15 per cent. The UK underground economy is thought to be quite a bit smaller.

There is a big problem with comparing GDP figures of different countries. They are measured in the local currency and thus have to be converted into a common currency (e.g. dollars) at the current exchange rate. But the exchange rate may be a poor indicator of the purchasing power of the currency at home. For example, £1 may exchange for, say, 2000 lire. But will £1 in the UK buy the same amount of goods as L2000 in Italy? The answer is almost certainly no. Estimates by the European Commission suggested that a person on average income in the UK could purchase 15 per cent more goods than a person on average income in Italy. The point is that prices are lower in the UK, and thus people's money goes further.

The same applies when comparing the UK with many other seemingly much richer countries, such as Germany and Japan. They may have a much higher average money income, but their prices are quite a bit higher too. Thus according to the same European Commission estimates, the average Briton is only about 10 per cent worse off than the average German.

? The Italians claimed that they were better off than the British because they had more cars per head (359 per 1000 people compared with 312 in the UK), more doctors per head (3.6 per 1000 compared with only 0.5 in the UK), more washing machines, more dishwashers and so on. The British, however, had more televisions and more telephones per head. Are these sort of statistics good indicators of countries' relative standards of living?

Italian and UK GDP at market prices: 1987

	Italy	UK
Gross domestic product	L982 594bn	£408.55bn
Exchange rate (1987 average)	L1000 = $0.77	£1 = $1.64
GDP in dollars	$756.60bn	$670.02bn
Population	57.33m	56.89m
Dollar GDP per capita	$13 197	$11 777

Sources: *International Financial Statistics* (IMF, various issues);
National Institute Economic Review (NIESR, various issues).

there are no injections or withdrawals, whatever is produced is sold. The value of what is sold must therefore be the value of what is produced. The *expenditure method* measures this value of sales.

Because of the way the calculations are made, the three methods of calculating GDP *must* yield the same result. In other words:

National product ≡ National income ≡ National expenditure

In our simplified circular flow of income this is obvious. In the real world, however,

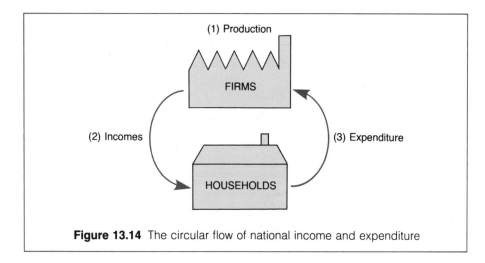

Figure 13.14 The circular flow of national income and expenditure

where there are injections and withdrawals, we must be careful to avoid making mistakes. We must take into account the role of government, foreign trade and investment. We must also be careful not to engage in 'double counting'. This is where we count the same items twice (an easy thing to do if you are not careful) and thus put too big a figure on GDP.

We will look at each of the three methods in turn, and examine the various factors that have to be taken into account to ensure that the figures are accurate.

The product method of measuring GDP

This approach simply involves adding up the value of everything produced in the country during the year in question: the output of cars, beef, timber, fridges, lollipops, shirts, plastic dolls, etc.; and all the myriad of services such as football matches, pop concerts, haircuts, bus rides and insurance services. The list is obviously enormous and it is clearly a major statistical exercise to gather information from firms all over the country. In the national accounts these figures are grouped together into broad categories such as manufacturing, construction and distribution. The figures for the UK economy for 1987 are shown in Figure 13.15.

The problem of double counting

When we add up the output of various firms we must be careful to avoid *double counting*. For example, if a manufacturer sells a television to a retailer for £200 and the retailer sells it to the consumer for £300, how much has this television contributed to GDP? The answer is *not* £500. We do not add the £200 received by the manufacturer to the £300 received by the retailer: that would be double counting.

There are two ways of estimating the true value of the output and avoiding double counting. The first is just to count the *final* value of the output. Thus in the case of the television set we would just count the £300 when the set is sold to the consumer. This is the approach we adopt in the *expenditure* method of calculating GDP (see page 567). The alternative is just to include the *extra* value that each firm adds to an item: this is known as *value added*.

The measurement of value added

In our complex modern economy, virtually every single item goes through several stages of production and distribution with several firms involved. Take an item as

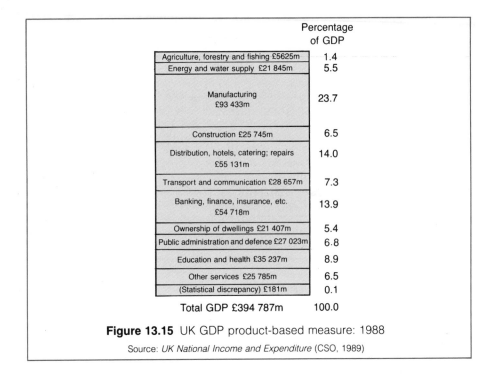

	Percentage of GDP
Agriculture, forestry and fishing £5625m	1.4
Energy and water supply £21 845m	5.5
Manufacturing £93 433m	23.7
Construction £25 745m	6.5
Distribution, hotels, catering; repairs £55 131m	14.0
Transport and communication £28 657m	7.3
Banking, finance, insurance, etc. £54 718m	13.9
Ownership of dwellings £21 407m	5.4
Public administration and defence £27 023m	6.8
Education and health £35 237m	8.9
Other services £25 785m	6.5
(Statistical discrepancy) £181m	0.1
Total GDP £394 787m	100.0

Figure 13.15 UK GDP product-based measure: 1988

Source: *UK National Income and Expenditure* (CSO, 1989)

simple as a pad of writing paper. A forestry company will grow trees from which the paper is made. The logs are sold to a timber merchant, which then sells the timber to the paper manufacturer. Another firm may then cut the paper and form it into pads. The pads will then be sold to wholesalers, which in turn will sell them to retailers. At each stage, transport companies may be involved in the distribution process. Each firm, all the way up the line from producing the basic raw materials to selling the finished good, adds value to the product. We then count up all this value added to arrive at the final value of the product.

To illustrate this process let us examine the case of an imaginary product that passes through three stages.

Stage 1. Firm A produces the necessary raw materials and sells them for £1000 to firm B.

Stage 2. Firm B manufactures them into finished products and sells them to a retailer, firm C, for £1800.

Stage 3. Finally, firm C sells them to households for £2500.

How much has been contributed to GDP? We could simply look at the final sales value: £2500. But we will get the same answer by counting up the *values added* at each stage. Firm A does not make any purchases from other firms. Its value added is thus the full value of its sales of raw materials to the manufacturer: i.e. £1000. Firm B buys these materials for £1000 and sells the finished products to firm C for £1800. It thus adds £800 of value to the products. Finally, firm C sells the products to consumers for £2500 and thus adds £700 of value. Total value added is therefore £1000 + £800 + £700 = £2500.

Some qualifications

Stocks. We must be careful only to include the values added in the *particular year in question*. A problem here is that some goods start being produced *before* the year begins. Thus when we come to work out GDP we must ignore the values that had previously been added to stocks of raw materials and goods, and only include the additional values added in *this* year.

Similarly, other goods are only sold to the consumer *after* the end of the year. Nevertheless we must still count the values that have been added during *this* year to these stocks of partially finished goods.

A final problem concerned with stocks is that they may increase in value simply due to increased prices. This is known as stock appreciation. Since there has been no real increase in output, stock appreciation must be deducted from value added.

Stock appreciation

The increase in monetary value of stocks due to increased prices. Since this does not represent increased output, it is not included in GDP.

Government services. The output of private industry is sold on the market and can thus be easily valued. This is not the case with most of the services provided by government departments. When a government official gives you advice on your taxes, what contribution does that service make to GDP? Given that the advice is not sold to you, we have to value it in terms of what it costs to provide. For example, ten minutes of advice may cost £5 in staff time and overheads to provide. That ten minutes has thus added £5 to GDP.

Ownership of dwellings. When a landlord rents out a flat, this service is valued as the rent that the tenant pays. But how do we value the benefit for owner occupiers of living in their own property? They do not pay rent and yet they are 'consuming' a similar 'service'. The answer is that a rental value for owner occupation is 'imputed'. In other words, a figure corresponding to a rent is included in the GDP statistics.

The income method of measuring GDP

The second approach is to focus on the incomes generated from the production of goods and services. A moment's reflection will show that this must be the same as the sum of all values added. Value added is simply the difference between a firm's revenue from sales and the costs of its purchases from other firms. This difference is made up of wages and salaries, rent, interest and profit. In other words, it consists of the incomes earned by those involved in the production process.

Value added = Wages and salaries + Rent + Interest + Profit
= Factor incomes

Since GDP is the sum of all values added, it must also be the sum of all incomes generated: the sum of all wages and salaries, rent, interest and profit.

> **?** If a retailer buys a product from a wholesaler for £80 and sells it to a consumer for £100, then the £20 of value that has been added will go partly in wages, partly in rent and partly in profits. Thus £20 of income has been generated at the retail stage. But the good actually contributes a total of £100 to GDP. Where, then, is the remaining £80 worth of income recorded?

Figure 13.16 shows how these incomes are grouped together in the official statistics. By far the largest category is income from employment: in other words, wages and salaries. The next largest category is that of profit and interest, which is broken down into (a) the gross trading profits of companies, (b) the income from self-employment and (c) the gross trading surplus of public corporations and general government enterprises. Next comes income from rent, which includes an element of imputed rent for owner-occupied dwellings. The final category, 'other', includes an adjustment for statistical errors and also an imputed profit on capital in non-market

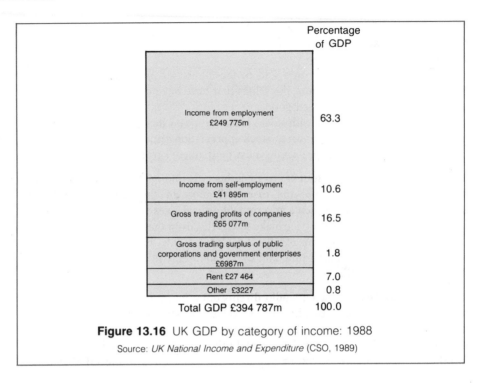

Figure 13.16 UK GDP by category of income: 1988

Source: *UK National Income and Expenditure* (CSO, 1989)

parts of the economy (such as education, health and public administration) where there are no actual profits.

As you will see, the total in Figure 13.16 is the same as that in Figure 13.15, even though the components are quite different. Gross domestic product is the same as 'gross domestic income', or put in the more usual way, GDP is the same whether calculated by the product or the income method. But this is not surprising since, as we have seen, the values added that comprise the product approach are simply the factor incomes contributed by each sector of the economy.

Some qualifications

Transfer payments. GDP only includes those incomes that arise from the production of goods and services. We would not, for example, include a gift that one person makes to another. If an aunt gives you £50, this transfer of income has not increased GDP! It is the same with all *transfer payments*. Any income that is merely transferred from one person to another is not included in GDP. By far the largest category of transfer payments is government benefits such as pensions, social security, child benefit and family credit. Since these are not payments for the production of goods and services, they are excluded from GDP.

Conversely, part of people's gross income is paid in taxes. Since it is this *gross* (pre-tax) income that arises from the production of goods and services, we count wages, profits, interest and rent *before* the deduction of taxes.

Stock appreciation. As in the case of the product approach, any gain in profits from stock appreciation must be deducted. The reason why profits arising from stock appreciation are not included is that they do not arise from a real increase in output.

Indirect taxes and subsidies on goods and services. When a firm receives revenues from its sales, it will have to pay part of these as VAT, and in the case of petrol and oil, alcoholic drinks, tobacco and gambling part will also go as excise duties. The part of its revenues it pays in these indirect taxes will *not* be available for wages, profits, rent or interest. It must not, therefore, be included in the GDP calculations.

In the case of subsidies on goods and services the reverse is true. When the government pays a subsidy to a firm, it forms part of the firm's revenues and hence part of the incomes earned by factors. Subsidies must therefore be *added* to the revenues gained from consumers when calculating GDP.

If we do *not* make these adjustments for taxes and subsidies, and just look at the prices consumers pay – i.e. at the gross incomes of firms before they pay the taxes or obtain the subsidies – the figure we get is called GDP at market prices. The figure, however, that represents the true income to factors of production (i.e. after the *deduction* of indirect taxes from and the *addition* of subsidies to the market value of sales) is called GDP at factor cost. Thus:

GDP at factor cost = GDP at market prices − Indirect taxes + Subsidies

The figures shown in Figures 13.15 and 13.16 are GDP at *factor cost*.

 GDP at factor cost represents the payments made to factors of production. To get this figure we have to deduct indirect taxes from firms' sales revenues. Why do we not also deduct income taxes?

The expenditure method of measuring GDP

The final approach is to add up all expenditure on final output. This will include the following items.

Consumer expenditure on domestically produced goods and services (C_d*)*
This includes all consumer spending on final goods and services produced within the country.

Government expenditure on final domestically produced goods and services (G_d*)*
We do *not* include government expenditure on pensions, social security, child benefit, etc. These transfer payments are not part of government spending on *final* output. We do, however, include non-marketed items such as the services provided by government departments. Since these services are not sold they are valued at cost.

Investment expenditure within the country (I_d*)*
This is divided into three categories.

Fixed capital. This includes expenditure on buildings, machinery and other equipment. Although these investment goods are not sold to households, they are still *finished* items and thus count as *final* goods.

Stocks and work in progress. This consists of firms' expenditure on increased stocks of raw materials, semi-finished goods and finished goods that have not yet been sold to the final consumer. This expenditure is counted as 'investment' since it is items produced for future consumption. Note that we only include *additions* to stocks that have been made during the year. We would be double counting if we included stocks produced in previous years. If there has been a net decline in stocks during the year, stock investment will be negative.

Housing. Expenditure on *new* housing is counted as investment, whether the houses are bought for commercial purposes or by owner occupiers. The reason why we count

GDP at market prices
The value of output in terms of the price paid by consumers. These prices will reflect any indirect taxes and subsidies on the goods and services.

GDP at factor cost
The value of output in terms of the resources used to produce it. It is thus GDP at market prices *less* indirect taxes and *plus* subsidies on goods and services.

the expenditure on new housing as investment rather than consumption is that houses yield benefits over many years to their owners.

 Should the sale of houses that are not new be included in the GDP statistics?

Expenditure on exports (X_d)

Although this expenditure comes from abroad, it is nevertheless expenditure on goods and services produced within the domestic economy. Note that we must exclude any component of exports that have *not* been made within the country. Thus if raw materials are imported and then manufactured into goods for export, we must exclude the cost of these imported raw materials from the value of the exports.

You will see that in each of the categories of expenditure we exclude any expenditure that is not on domestically produced goods. In other words, we must exclude all *imports* (M) from the calculations, whether these are imports of consumer goods, of capital equipment, of intermediate goods, of raw materials or of services. If we were to include that component of consumption, government expenditure, investment and exports that was imported, we would then have to subtract imports again in order to get back to domestic expenditure alone. Thus we can define GDP by expenditure in two ways. Either:

$$GDP = C_d + G_d + I_d + X_d$$

where C_d, G_d, I_d and X_d exclude any imported component, or:

$$GDP = C + G + I + X - M$$

where C, I, G and X include any imported component.

The official statistics use the second of these methods. It is easier to deduct imports as one lump sum than to deduct the imported element from each item of expenditure separately.

From total domestic expenditure to GDP at factor cost

In the official statistics, expenditure is measured at a number of different stages before a figure for GDP at factor cost is reached. The stages are as follows.

Total domestic expenditure at market prices (TDE)

The total annual expenditure on final goods and services by *domestic residents*. It includes expenditure on both domestic goods and services *and* imports (at prices that *include* indirect taxes and subsidies).

Total domestic expenditure (TDE) (at market prices). This is the starting point for calculating GDP. Total domestic expenditure at market prices consists of the total expenditure on final goods and services by the residents of the country, whether these goods and services were produced at home or abroad. It thus includes consumer expenditure, government expenditure on final goods and services, and investment. (Note that it excludes exports and includes imports.)

$$TDE = C + G + I$$

Total final expenditure (TFE) (at market prices). The next step is to add in exports. This gives total final expenditure at market prices which is the total expenditure that takes place within the country, whether by domestic residents or by people abroad. (Note that it includes *both* imports *and* exports.)

Total final expenditure at market prices (TFE)

Total expenditure within the country: i.e. *TDE* plus exports.

$$\begin{aligned} TFE &= TDE + X \\ &= C + G + I + X \end{aligned}$$

Gross domestic product at market prices. The next step is to subtract imports. This gives us gross domestic product at market prices, which is total expenditure on *domestically produced goods.* In other words, we ignore that component of consumption, government expenditure and investment that goes on imports.

$$GDP \text{ at market prices} = TFE - M$$
$$= C + G + I + X - M$$
$$= C_d + G_d + I_d + X_d$$

Gross domestic product at factor cost. So far we have been using market prices: prices that have been increased by indirect taxes and reduced by any subsidies. If we are to have a true measure of the expenditure on actual *output*, we must correct for these taxes and subsidies. The final step to get to GDP at factor cost is thus to subtract indirect taxes and add subsidies. This gives us the formula we used above when looking at the income method of calculating GDP:

GDP at factor cost = *GDP* at market prices − Indirect taxes + Subsidies

Table 13.1 shows each of these stages in the calculation of the 1988 GDP at factor cost.

Table 13.1 UK GDP at market prices by category of expenditure: 1988

	£million
Consumers' expenditure	293 569
Government final consumption	91 847
Gross domestic fixed capital formation (including new housing)	88 751
Value of physical increase in stocks and work in progress	4 371
Total domestic expenditure	**478 538**
Plus Exports of goods and services	108 533
Total final expenditure	**587 071**
Less Imports of goods and services	−125 194
GDP at market prices	**461 877**
Statistical discrepancy	2 056
Less Taxes on expenditure	−75 029
Plus Subsidies	5 883
GDP at factor cost	**394 787**

Source: *UK National Income and Expenditure* (CSO, 1989).

Gross national product

Some of the output produced in the country (and thus included in GDP) is produced by *foreign* companies. When these companies make a profit the dividends will flow out of the country to the foreign owners. These 'property' incomes will therefore be lost to the country. On the other hand, some of the incomes earned by UK residents will come from overseas investments. Although these property incomes are earned abroad, they will still form part of the incomes of UK residents.

Gross *domestic* product does not take into account these property incomes flowing into and out of the country. It is only concerned with incomes generated *within* the country, irrespective of ownership. If we are to take net property incomes into account, therefore, we need a new measure. This is gross national product (GNP). It is defined as follows:

GNP at factor cost = *GDP* at factor cost + Net property income from abroad

Thus GDP focuses on the value of domestic production, whereas GNP focuses on the value of incomes earned by domestic residents.

> **?** 1. If a country persistently runs a long-term capital account deficit on the balance of payments, would you expect GNP to be bigger or smaller than GDP? (Clue: if there is a long-term capital account deficit, what is the balance between the country's investment abroad and foreign investment within the country?)
> 2. Define GNP at market prices.

Net national product ('national income')

Depreciation

The decline in value of capital equipment due to age or wear and tear.

Net investment

Total investment minus depreciation.

Net national product (NNP) or national income

GNP minus depreciation.

One problem with the measures we have used so far is that they ignore the fact that each year some of the country's capital equipment will wear out or become obsolete: in other words, they ignore capital depreciation. If we subtract an allowance for depreciation (or 'capital consumption' as it is called in the official statistics), what we are left with is net investment:

Net investment = Gross investment − Depreciation

GNP is calculated using gross investment figures (as is GDP). This is why it is called 'gross' national product. If we deduct depreciation from these figures, we get *net* national product (NNP), or national income as it is sometimes called:

NNP at factor cost (national income) = *GNP* at factor cost − Depreciation

Table 13.2 shows the 1988 GDP, GNP and NNP figures for the UK.

Table 13.2 UK GDP, GNP and NNP at factor cost: 1988

	£million
Gross domestic product	**394 787**
Plus Net property income from abroad	5 619
Gross national product	**400 406**
Less Capital consumption (depreciation)	−54 769
Net national product (national income)	**345 637**

Source: *UK National Income and Expenditure* (CSO, 1989).

Although NNP gives a truer picture of the nation's income than GNP, economists tend to prefer to use gross figures. The reason is that depreciation is hard to estimate with accuracy. The figures are largely based on estimates for tax purposes: estimates of investment expenditure that can be offset against company income. These figures are thus governed by tax regulations and do not give an accurate picture of the genuine depreciation in the country's capital stock. But since the level of depreciation only changes relatively slowly over time, the rate of growth in gross figures will tend to be very similar to the rate of growth of net figures.

> **?** If the government altered tax regulations so that a firm is allowed to offset a higher proportion of the value of its capital against income, how would this affect the figure for depreciation?

Personal disposable income

The income available for households to spend: i.e. personal incomes after deducting taxes on incomes and adding benefits.

Personal disposable income

Finally, we come to a measure that is useful for analyzing consumer behaviour. If we are to examine how consumption responds to changes in households' disposable income, the measure we require is called personal disposable income.

Let us start with GNP at factor cost. This measures the incomes generated by production. To get from this to personal disposable income we must first subtract company incomes that are *not* paid to households: namely, company taxes and undistributed profits. This gives us the incomes received by households from firms. To get from this to what is available for households to spend we must subtract the money that households have to pay in income taxes and national insurance contributions, but add all benefits to households, such as pensions and family credit: in other words, we must *include* transfer payments.

Personal disposable income = *GNP* at factor cost − Company taxes
− Depreciation − Undistributed profits
− Personal taxes + Benefits

Taking account of inflation

If we are to make a sensible comparison of one year's national income with another, we must take into account any inflation that has taken place. For example, if this year national income is 10 per cent higher than last year, but at the same time prices are also 10 per cent higher, then the average person will be no better off at all. There has been no *real* increase in income.

An important distinction here is between nominal national income and real national income. *Nominal* national income, sometimes called 'money national income', measures national income in the prices ruling at the time and thus takes no account of inflation. *Real* national income, however, measures national income in the prices that ruled in some particular year – the *base year*. Thus we could measure each year's national income in, say, 1980 prices. This would enable us to see how much *real* income had changed from one year to another. In other words, it would eliminate increases in money national income that were merely due to an increase in prices.

The official statistics give both nominal and real figures for all the measures: GDP, GNP, NNP, etc. Box 13.11 shows in more detail how real national income figures are calculated.

Nominal national income

National income measured at current prices.

Real national income

National income after allowing for inflation: i.e. national income measured in constant prices: i.e. in terms of the prices ruling in some base year.

Taking account of population: the use of per-capita measures

The figures we have been looking at up to now are *total* figures for the country. Although such figures are useful in comparing the size of one economy with another, they are no good for comparing living standards. For example, if we want to know how well off the average American is in comparison to the average Swiss, it is no good comparing the *total* GDP of the two countries. Clearly, since the population of the USA is many times larger than that of Switzerland, you would expect the USA's GDP to be many times higher than Switzerland's.

If we want to look at a country's living standards, therefore, we must look at national income *per head of the population*. In other words, we must divide national income by the size of the population. The total GDP for the USA in 1987 was $4488.6 billion, whereas for Switzerland it was only $157.4 billion (at an exchange rate of $1 = SF1.49). The US GDP was over 28 times bigger than the Swiss. American GDP *per capita*, however, was $18 301 compared with $24 223 for Switzerland. To the extent that GDP figures give an indication of living standards (but see below) the Swiss would seem to have a higher living standard than the Americans.

There are other per-capita measures that are sometimes useful. For example, measuring GDP per head of the *employed* population allows us to compare how much

Box 13.11

The GDP Deflator
Taking account of inflation

In 1987 the UK's GDP was £352 billion. In 1979 it was £172 billion. Does this mean that the average Briton in 1987 was over twice as well off as in 1979? It's obvious that the answer is no. Prices rise over time and thus a pound in 1987 would not be worth as much as a pound in 1979.

To get a true picture of how a country's output has changed we must correct the figures for inflation. The *uncorrected* figures are known as the *nominal* figures. Thus in 1987 the UK's nominal GDP was £352 billion. The *corrected* figures are known as *real* GDP.

But how do we convert nominal GDP into real GDP? The answer is to measure each year's GDP at the prices that ruled in one particular year: the *base year*. Thus if 1985 were chosen as the base year, each year's GDP would be measured in 1985 prices. So if we wanted to measure the 1990 statistics in 1985 prices, we would need to know how much prices had risen between the two years. If prices had increased by 50 per cent then *nominal* GDP in 1990 would be 50 per cent higher than the *real* 1990 GDP measured in 1985 prices. To get the figures for real GDP, then, we must reduce the nominal figures by an appropriate amount.

The calculations are done by expressing average prices each year as an index, with the index for the base year being set at 100. If average prices are 20 per cent higher this year than in the base year, the index this year will be 120.

The price of each item which is entering into the average must be given a weight which reflects its proportion of GDP. Thus if the value of cars produced is twice that of bread, then car prices will have twice the weighting of bread prices. The weights of all items entering into the index must add up to 1.

The formula for calculating real GDP is as follows:

$$\text{Real } GDP_{\text{year a}} = \text{Nominal } GDP_{\text{year a}} \times \frac{\text{Index}_{\text{base year}}}{\text{Index}_{\text{year a}}}$$

Let's look at an example. Assume that Ruritania's nominal GDP was $150 billion in 1985 and $300 billion in 1990. Let us also assume that prices have risen by 50 per cent over the period. Thus if the index was 100 in

1985 it would be 150 in 1990. What is *real* GDP in 1990 measured in 1985 prices? Applying the formula we get:

Real 1990 GDP = $300 billion × 100/150 = $200

The figures are given in the table.

Ruritania's nominal and real GDP

Year	Nominal GDP	Price index	Real GDP
1985	$150bn	100	$150bn
1990	$300bn	150	$200bn

Which prices should we use in calculating the index? The most usual index of prices is the *retail price index* (RPI). This shows the average prices of goods and services bought by consumers: in other words, prices *in the shops*. The RPI is the index used in calculating the rate of inflation. If the current rate of inflation is 6 per cent, this means that the RPI has risen by 6 per cent over the last twelve months.

When calculating real GDP, however, we must use a slightly different index. This is called the *GDP deflator*. It is an index of the average prices of *all* the components of GDP. Thus it includes not just consumer goods prices, but also the prices of investment goods, goods and services consumed by the government, and exports; it excludes the price of imported goods.

? The following table shows UK (nominal) GDP at factor cost for the years 1979, 1981, 1985 and 1987. It also shows the GDP deflator with 1985 = 100. Work out the real GDP for each year based on 1985 prices. How much did *real* GDP grow between 1979 and 1981, and between 1981 and 1987?

	1979	1981	1985	1987
Nominal GDP at factor cost (£bn at current prices)	172.4	217.8	304.7	352.2
GDP deflator (1985 = 100)	61.0	79.7	100.0	107.7

the average worker produces. A country may have a relatively high GDP per head of population but also have a large proportion of people at work. Its output per worker will therefore not be so high.

 By what would we need to divide GDP in order to get a measure of labour productivity per hour?

Do national income statistics give a good indication of a country's standard of living?

If we take into account both inflation and the size of the population, and use figures for *real* per-capita GNP, will this give us a good indication of a country's standard of living compared with other countries, or compared with some point in the past? The figures *do* give quite a good indication of the level of production of goods and the incomes generated from it (provided we are clear about the distinction between factor cost and market prices, between GDP and GNP, and between GNP and NNP and just what each one is attempting to measure). But even here there are some omissions and distortions that are likely to occur.

When we come to ask the more general question of whether the figures give a good indication of the welfare or happiness of the country's citizens, then there are serious problems in relying exclusively on national income statistics.

Problems of measuring national output
The main problem here is that the output of some goods and services goes unrecorded and thus the GNP figures will understate the nation's output. There are two reasons why these items are not recorded.

Non-marketed items. If you employ a decorator to paint your living room, this will be recorded in the GNP statistics. If, however, you paint the room yourself, it will not. Similarly, if a farmer grows cabbages and sells them, this output will form part of GNP. If, however, you grow cabbages on your allotment, it will not. The exclusion of these 'do-it-yourself' activities means that the GNP statistics understate the true level of production in the economy. If over time there is an increase in the amount of do-it-yourself activities that people *perform* the figures will also understate the *rate of growth* of national output. On the other hand, if in more and more families both partners go out to work and employ people to do the housework, this will overstate the rate of growth in output. The housework which was previously unrecorded now enters into the GNP statistics.

The 'underground' economy. The underground economy consists of illegal and hence undeclared transactions. These could be transactions where the goods and services are themselves illegal, such as drugs and prostitution. Alternatively, they could be transactions that are only illegal in that they are not declared for tax purposes. For example, a garage may be prepared to repair your car slightly more cheaply if you pay cash. That way the garage can avoid paying VAT. Another example is that of 'moonlighting'. This is where people do extra work outside their normal job and do not declare the income for income tax purposes. For example, an electrician employed by a building contractor during the day may rewire people's houses in the evenings, again for cash. Unemployed people may do casual jobs which again they do not declare, this time for fear of losing unemployment or social security benefit.

Problems of using national income statistics to measure welfare
GNP is essentially an indicator of a nation's *production*. But production may be a poor indicator of the well-being of society for the following reasons.

Production does not equal consumption. Production is hardly desirable for its own sake. It is only desirable to the extent that it enables us to *consume* more. If GNP rises as a result of a rise in *investment*, this will not lead to an increase in *current* living standards. It will, of course, help to raise *future* consumption.

The same applies if GNP rises as a result of an increase in exports. There has been

Box 13.12

How Big Is the Underground Economy?
The factors that determine its size

Estimates for the size of the underground economy vary enormously from country to country, from a few per cent of GNP in countries like Japan and Germany to 15 per cent or more in countries such as Sweden and Italy (see Box 13.10). Clearly it is impossible to get precise estimates because, by their very nature, the details are largely hidden from the authorities. Nevertheless economists have tried to identify the factors that determine the size of the underground economy.

The first determinant is the level of taxes and regulations. The greater their level, the greater the incentive for people to evade the system and 'go underground'.

The second is the determination of the authorities to catch up with evaders, and the severity of the punishments for those found out.

A third is the size of the service sector relative to the manufacturing sector. It is harder for the authorities to detect the illicit activities of motor mechanics, gardeners and window cleaners than the output of cars, bricks and soap.

Another determinant is the proportion of the population that is self-employed. It is much easier for the self-employed to evade taxes than it is for people receiving a wage where taxes are deducted at source.

Some indication of the size of the underground economy is given by the demand for cash in the economy. Since most underground transactions are conducted in cash, if the demand for cash increases relative to the use of cheques or credit cards, it is an indication that underground activities are on the increase. For example, in some parts of the USA which have witnessed a large rise in drug use the banks have reported an increased demand for cash.

 1. Is the size of the underground economy likely to increase or decrease as the level of unemployment rises?
2. If the amount of cash used in the economy falls, does this mean that the size of the underground economy must have fallen?

---

an increase in *production*, but unless there is a resulting increase in imports it will be foreign consumers that benefit, not domestic consumers.

The human costs of production. If production increases, this may be due to technological advance. If, however, it increases as a result of people having to work harder or longer hours, its net benefit will be less. Leisure is a desirable good, and so too are pleasant working conditions, but these items are not included in the GNP figures. If, therefore, as part of an increase in 'efficiency' people are expected to work harder or longer, the growth in GNP will overstate the growth in human well-being. If, however, the length of the typical working day or week decreases over time, the growth in GNP will understate the growth in well-being.

GNP ignores externalities. The rapid growth in industrial society is recorded in GNP statistics. What the statistics do not record are the environmental side-effects: the polluted air and rivers, the ozone depletion, the problem of global warming. If these external costs were taken into account, the *net* benefits of industrial production might be much less.

 Name some external *benefits* that are not included in GNP statistics.

The production of certain 'bads' leads to an increase in GNP. As we have seen, external costs are not deducted from GNP. In some cases the production of undesirable things can actually count as an *increase* in GNP. If you have to travel a long distance to work, this will be a personal *cost* to you. The costs include both the monetary cost of the transport and also the lost leisure time, the frustration and the inconvenience. Yet

Box 13.13

A Measure of Economic Welfare
MEW: an alternative to GNP?

GNP is not a complete measure of economic welfare; nor is it meant to be. So is there any alternative that takes other factors into account and gives a more complete picture of the level of human well-being?

In 1972 two economists, William Nordhaus and the subsequent Nobel prize winner James Tobin, introduced what they called a *measure of economic welfare* (MEW). This started with GNP and NNP. To this was added an allowance for leisure, for various non-marketed goods and services such as housework and underground activities, for the services of various public amenities such as parks and roads, and for private durable goods such as furniture and jewellery.

On the other hand, various items were subtracted. These included 'regrettables' such as expenditure on defence and commuting to work, and various 'bads' or 'disamenities' such as pollution. Also various intermediate items such as the benefits of education were subtracted. The logic for excluding these was that the benefits show up later in increased labour productivity and earnings, and to include them now would be to double count. Finally, amounts have to be deducted for the extra capital and extra current output required to meet any growth in population: after all, the objective is per-capita welfare and not merely some gross figure.

The table shows how Nordhaus and Tobin reworked the US GNP for 1965 to produce a value for MEW.

MEW has been growing at a slower pace than GNP. The reason for this is that, although leisure has been increasing, it has increased less quickly than the output of goods and services, whereas the output of 'bads' and

US GNP and MEW: 1965

Item	$bn
GNP	617.8
Capital consumption	−54.7
NNP	563.1
Regrettables and intermediates	
Government	−63.2
Private	−30.9
Items not included in GNP	
Leisure	626.9
Non-market activity	295.4
Disamenities	−34.6
Services of public and private capital	78.9
Additional capital consumption	−92.7
Growth requirement	−101.8
Sustainable MEW	**1241.1**

Source: W. Nordhaus and J. Tobin, 'Is growth obsolete?' in *Economic Growth* (National Bureau of Economic Research, Columbia University Press, 1972).

'regrettables' has increased more rapidly than the output of goods and services.

The big problem with using MEW is in obtaining reliable estimates of all the additional items it includes. As a result it has not been adopted by governmental statistical agencies around the world.

? If defence should be excluded as a 'regrettable', should we also exclude expenditure on health, heating and double glazing?

---

the provision of these transport services count as part of GNP. The further people have to travel to work, the bigger this will make GNP!

Total GNP figures ignore the distribution of income. As we saw in Chapter 10, if some people gain and others lose, we cannot say that there has been an unambiguous increase in welfare even if there has been an overall increase in incomes. In practice an increase in GNP will often be accompanied by a redistribution of income. Many people may gain, but almost certainly others will lose. A typical feature of many rapidly growing countries is that some people grow very rich while others are left behind. The result is a growing inequality. If this is seen as undesirable, then clearly total GNP statistics are an inadequate measure of welfare.

A related point here is that a given percentage growth in a rich person's income will add much more to GNP than the same percentage growth in a poor person's income. For example, a 10 per cent growth in income for a person earning £100 000 per year will add £10 000 to GNP, whereas a 10 per cent growth in income for a person earning £10 000 will add only £1000 to GNP. Yet can it be said that the rich person has gained ten times more happiness than the poor person? What we are saying here is that the marginal utility of an extra £1 is greater for a poor person who has very little than it is for a rich person who already has a great deal.

A way of dealing with this problem is to put a greater weighting on the growth in incomes of poor people than rich people.

Conclusions

If a country's citizens put a high priority on a clean environment, a relaxed way of life, greater self-sufficiency, a less materialistic outlook, more giving rather than selling, and greater equality, then such a country will probably have a lower GNP than a similarly endowed country where the pursuit of wealth is given high priority. Clearly, though, we cannot conclude that the first country will have a lower level of well-being.

It would be easy to argue from this that GNP statistics ought to be rejected as a means of judging the economic performance of countries. This would be to go much too far. GNP statistics are not meant to be a measure of economic welfare. They are a measure of *output*, and should be seen in that context. If politicians choose to misuse them and make out that they give an accurate portrait of economic success, then it is up to economists to point out their weaknesses.

▲ SUMMARY

1. National income is usually expressed in terms of gross domestic product. This is simply the value of domestic production over the course of the year. It can be measured by the product, expenditure or income methods.
2. The product method measures the values added in all parts of the economy. Care must be taken in the evaluation of stocks, government services and the ownership of dwellings.
3. The income method measures all the incomes generated from domestic production: wages and salaries, rent, interest and profit. Transfer payments are not included, nor is stock appreciation.
4. The expenditure method adds up all the categories of expenditure: consumer expenditure, government expenditure and investment. If imports are included as well, this gives total domestic expenditure. If in addition exports are included, this gives total final expenditure. If imports are then deducted from total final expenditure, this gives GDP. Thus $GDP = C + G + I + X - M$.
5. GDP at *market prices* measures what consumers pay for output (including taxes and subsidies on what they buy). GDP at *factor cost* measures what factors receive. GDP at factor cost is thus GDP at market prices minus indirect taxes plus subsidies on goods and services.
6. Gross *national* product (GNP) takes account of incomes earned on assets held overseas and payments made to foreigners who hold assets in the country. Thus $GNP = GDP$ plus net property income from abroad.
7. Net national product takes account of depreciation of capital.
8. Personal disposable income is a measure of household income after the deduction of income taxes and the addition of benefits.
9. *Real* national income takes account of inflation by being expressed in the prices of some base year.
10. In order to compare living standards of different countries, national income has to be expressed per capita. Even if it is there are still problems in using national income statistics for comparative purposes. Certain items will not be included: items such as non-marketed products, services in the family and activities in the underground economy. Moreover, the statistics include certain 'bads' and ignore externalities, and they also ignore questions of the distribution of income.

The Simple Keynesian Analysis of National Income, Employment and Inflation

14.1 Background to the theory

Throughout the 1950s and 1960s and into the 1970s, Keynesian analysis was generally accepted by economists and politicians alike. It was only after the breakdown of the Phillips curve and the emergence of stagflation that a sustained attack was mounted by the critics of Keynesianism. Even given this attack, many economists still hold that the Keynesian arguments are essentially true.

Keynesians argue that aggregate demand determines the level of economic activity in the economy. In other words, the nation's production and employment depend on the amount of spending. Too little spending will lead to unemployment. More spending will stimulate firms to produce more and employ more people. Too much spending, however, will cause inflation.

This chapter examines this relationship between aggregate demand and national income, production, employment and inflation.

One important simplifying assumption is made throughout the chapter: *the rate of interest is fixed*. This allows us for the time being to ignore what is happening to the amount of money in the economy. Our assumption of fixed interest rates effectively means that the supply of money will passively rise or fall as aggregate demand rises or falls. In other words, if there is an increase in spending and hence an increase in demand for money from the banking system, there will be a corresponding increase in the amount of money made available and hence no need for interest rates to rise. In subsequent chapters we will drop this assumption and take specific notice of the role of money in the economy.

The relationship between aggregate demand and national income

In the simple Keynesian theory, the consumption of domestically produced goods (C_d) and the three withdrawals (W) – savings (S), taxes (T) and spending on imports (M) – all depend on the level of national income (Y) (see Figure 14.1). In fact, in the model, national income must always equal consumption of domestic goods plus withdrawals: there is nothing else people can do with their incomes!

$$Y \equiv C_d + W$$

Total spending in the economy on the goods and services of domestic firms is what we have already defined as aggregate demand (AD). It is also referred to as national

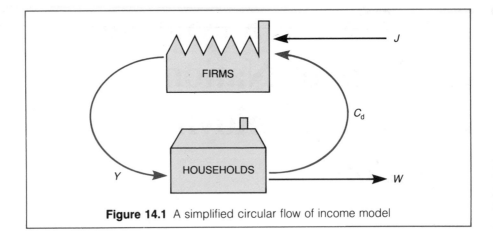

Figure 14.1 A simplified circular flow of income model

expenditure on domestic product (*E*). It consists of C_d plus the three injections (J) – investment in the domestic economy (*I*), government expenditure in the domestic economy (*G*) and overseas spending on UK exports (*X*).

$$AD \equiv E \equiv C_d + J$$

In equilibrium, withdrawals equal injections. (We demonstrated this in Chapter 13.) Since national income (*Y*) is simply withdrawals plus C_d, and national expenditure on domestic product (*E*) is simply injections plus C_d, it follows that in equilibrium national income must equal national expenditure on domestic product (aggregate demand). To summarize:

$$W = J$$
$$\therefore C_d + W = C_d + J$$
$$\therefore Y = E \, (= AD)$$

The level of national income is *determined* by aggregate demand. If aggregate demand exceeds current national income, firms will respond to the extra demand by producing more and hence employing more factors of production (assuming there are unemployed resources available). National income will thus rise.

How long will national income go on rising? Until a new equilibrium is reached where withdrawals equal injections and national income equals expenditure.

The process of reaching a new equilibrium is as follows. Whenever national expenditure ($C_d + J$) exceeds national income ($C_d + W$), injections will exceed withdrawals. National income will rise. But as national income rises, so too will savings, imports and the amount paid in taxes: in other words, withdrawals will rise. Withdrawals will go on rising until they equal injections: until a new equilibrium has been reached.

$$J > W \rightarrow Y\uparrow \; \rightarrow W\uparrow \text{ until } W = J$$

The question is, *how much* will income rise when aggregate demand (expenditure) rises. What will the new equilibrium level of national income be? Any government seeking to control national income by managing the level of aggregate demand will want to know the answer to this question.

To answer this question we must examine the relationship between national income and the component parts of the circular flow of income: consumption, withdrawals and injections. This relationship is shown in the Keynesian '45° line diagram'.

Introducing the Keynesian 45° line diagram

In this model it is assumed that the levels of consumption and withdrawals are determined by the level of national income. Since national income is part of the model, we say that consumption and withdrawals are endogenous. This means that they vary with one of the other components of the model (i.e. income). Injections, however, are assumed to be exogenous. This means that they are determined independently of what is going on in the model. In other words, we assume that injections do *not* depend on the level of national income.

We will justify these assumptions and examine just how each of the component parts fits into the model in the following sections. But first we must look at how the diagram is constructed, and at the significance of the 45° line.

We plot real national income (i.e. national income matched by output) on the horizontal axis, and the various component parts of the circular flow (C_d, W and J) on the vertical axis. The 45° line out from the origin plots $C_d + W$ against Y. It is a 45° line because by definition $Y = C_d + W$. For example, if Y were £100 billion, then $C_d + W$ must also be £100 billion (see Figure 14.2).

We turn now to look at each of the components of the circular flow and see how they fit into the 45° line diagram.

> **Endogenous variable**
> A variable whose value is determined by the model of which it is part.

> **Exogenous variable**
> A variable whose value is determined independently of the model of which it is part.

Figure 14.2 The 45° line

Consumption

We will need to distinguish total consumption (C) from that part of consumption that goes purely on the output of domestically produced goods (C_d). C_d excludes expenditure taxes (e.g. VAT) and expenditure on imports. We start by looking at *total* consumption.

The relationship between consumption and national income: the consumption function

As national income increases, so does consumption. The reason is simple: if people earn more, they can afford to spend more. The relationship between consumption and income is expressed by the consumption function:

$$C = f(Y)$$

It can be shown graphically on the 45° line diagram (see Figure 14.3). As in the previous diagram, national income is plotted on the horizontal axis. Consumption is

> **Consumption function**
> The relationship between consumption and national income. It can be expressed algebraically or graphically.

plotted on the vertical axis. The consumption function slopes upwards. This illustrates that, as national income rises, so does consumption. To keep the analysis simple the consumption function is drawn as a straight line. It is based on the data of Table 14.1.

Table 14.1

National income (£bn)	Consumption (£bn)
0	10
10	18
20	26
30	34
40	42
50	50
60	58
70	66
80	74
90	82
100	90
110	98

The following points should be noted about the consumption function:

● At very low levels of national income, it will lie above the 45° line. This is because when people are very poor they may be forced to spend more than they earn merely to survive. They will do this by borrowing or drawing on savings. For a nation to be on this portion of its consumption function would mean that it was accumulating international debts: a problem that many Third World countries have faced since the early 1970s.
● At a certain point the consumption function will cross the 45° line. In Figure 14.3 this is at an income of £50 billion. At this point consumption equals income. The nation spends exactly what it earns.
● Above this point consumption is less than income. This means that some of people's incomes will go towards savings and the payment of income taxes. The higher the level of income, the larger the proportion that will go in savings and taxes, and the smaller the proportion that will be consumed.
● It follows from these three observations that the slope of the consumption function

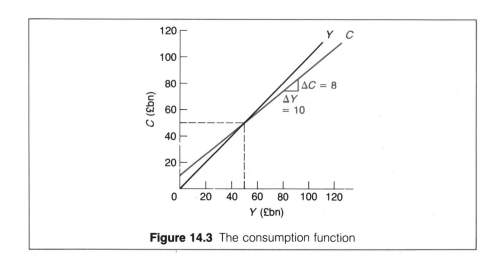

Figure 14.3 The consumption function

is less than that of the 45° line. The slope of the consumption function is given by the 'marginal propensity to consume'.

The marginal propensity to consume (mpc)

Sorry about this term. Like several terms in economics it lacks a certain elegance!

The marginal propensity to consume is the proportion of any increase in national income that goes on consumption. In Table 14.1 for each £10 billion rise in national income there is an £8 billion rise in consumption. Thus the marginal propensity to consume is £8 billion/£10 billion = 8/10 or 4/5 or 0.8. The formula is:

$$mpc = \Delta C/\Delta Y$$

> **Marginal propensity to consume**
> The proportion of a rise in national income that goes on consumption:
> $mpc = \Delta C/\Delta Y$.

Turning to Figure 14.3, it can be seen that the *mpc* is given by the slope of the consumption function. Being a straight line, the consumption function has a *constant* slope, and hence the *mpc* is also constant. No matter whether income is high or low, for every £1 that income rises (measured horizontally), consumption rises by 80p (measured vertically).

> **?** It is possible that as people get richer they will spend a smaller and smaller fraction of each rise in income (and save a larger fraction). Why might this be so? What effect will it have on the shape of the consumption function?

The average propensity to consume (apc)

One other important concept (though not as important as the *mpc*) is the average propensity to consume. This is the proportion of *total* national income that is consumed. The formula is:

$$apc = C/Y$$

> **Average propensity to consume**
> The proportion of total national income that goes on consumption:
> $apc = C/Y$.

Thus again referring to Table 14.1, at a national income of £100 billion, £90 billion goes on consumption. The *apc* is 90/100 = 0.9.

> **?** 1. Referring to Table 14.1, what is the *apc* at a national income of (a) £50 billion; (b) £20 billion?
> 2. What happens to the *apc* as national income rises?
> 3. Would the *apc* ever equal the *mpc* in Table 14.1 if it were continued to a high enough income?

The average propensity to consume can be derived graphically. This is shown in Figure 14.4, which reproduces the consumption function of Figure 14.3.

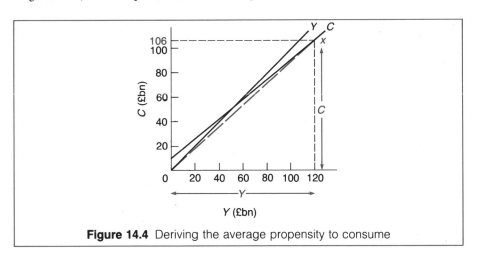

Figure 14.4 Deriving the average propensity to consume

Box 14.1

Keynes' Views on the Consumption Function

The absolute income hypothesis

Keynes argued that consumption depends on the level of current *disposable* income (i.e. income after the payment of taxes).[1] As disposable income rises, so will consumption, but it will account for a decreasing *proportion* of income. Savings, by contrast, will account for an increasing proportion of income.

But, apart from short-period *changes* in the level of income, it is also obvious that a higher absolute level of income will tend, as a rule, to widen the gap between income and consumption. For the satisfaction of the

immediate primary need of a man and his family is usually a stronger motive than the motives towards accumulation, which only acquire effective sway when a margin of comfort has been attained. These reasons will lead, as a rule, to a greater *proportion* of income being saved as real income increases.[2]

But just what does this imply about the shape of the consumption function?

Typically, consumption functions are drawn in one of four ways. These are illustrated in the four diagrams.

(a)　　　　　(b)　　　　　(c)　　　　　(d)

Different consumption functions

What is the *apc* at point *x*? It is the slope of the line from the origin to that point. The slope of the line is given by the vertical distance (106) divided by the horizontal distance (120): in other words, *C* divided by *Y*. But this was how we defined the *apc*. Note that the slope of this line is greater than the slope of the consumption function. This means that the *apc* is greater than the *mpc*.

 Is this what you would expect? Is your own *apc* greater than your *mpc*?

The other determinants of consumption

Of course, people's incomes are not the only determinants of the amount they consume. There are several other determinants.

Assets held. The more wealth people have, whether as savings, as shares or as property, the more they are likely to spend out of current income. This is particularly true if people have a sudden change in their wealth. If you inherit a fortune, you are quite likely to go on a spending spree, even though your current income has not changed. There is a problem here with the definition of 'income'. If the *acquisition* of assets is counted as *income*, then it is not a separate determinant: only the *level* of wealth can be regarded as separate from income.

Box 14.1 (cont'd)

Consumption function C_1 has the form:

$$C = bY_d$$

When income is zero, consumption is zero too. As income rises, so does consumption, but at a constant rate: the *mpc* is constant. Consumption also always accounts for a constant *proportion* of income: the *apc* is constant too. This is *not* consistent with Keynes' assumptions. The quote from Keynes above implies a decreasing *apc* as income rises.

Consumption function C_2 has the form:

$$C = bY_d - cY_d^2$$

This does give a decreasing *apc*. It also gives a decreasing *mpc*. You can see this easily by inspecting the curve. Its slope gets flatter (a decreasing *mpc*). Also consumption accounts for a declining proportion of income (a decreasing *apc*).

But this diagram is not consistent with another assumption of Keynes:

[A] decline in income due to a decline in the level of employment, if it goes far, may even cause consumption to exceed income . . .[3]

Consumption function C_3 has the form:

$$C = a + bY_d$$

and consumption function C_4 the form:

$$C = a + bY_d - cY_d^2$$

In both cases, provided the term *a* is a positive figure,

consumption will exceed income at very low levels of income: the consumption function will cross the 45° line.

> **?** Using these two equations, what will be the level of consumption when national income is zero?

Keynes' argument that people's consumption depends on the level of their current income, irrespective of what their previous incomes were or what their future incomes are expected to be, and irrespective of what other people's incomes are, has led economists to call this the '*absolute income* theory of consumption'. Alternative theories of the consumption function are examined in Box 14.3.

> **?** What will happen to the shape of the consumption function in diagram (d) in each of the following cases?
> (a) When the value of term *a* increases.
> (b) When the value of term *b* decreases.
> (c) When the value of term *c* decreases.

[1] The theory we are developing in this chapter relates consumption to *gross* income (*Y*). If we relate consumption to *disposable* income (Y_d), as we are doing in this box, we must remember that the consumption function we get is not the one we will be using later on in the chapter.
[2] J. M. Keynes, *The General Theory of Employment, Interest and Money* (Macmillan, 1967), p. 97.
[3] *Ibid.*, p. 98.

Taxation. The higher the level of taxes, the less will people have left to spend out of their gross income: consumption depends on disposable income. If taxes are raised, *how much* will consumption fall? This depends on the marginal propensity to consume. The bigger the *mpc*, the more will consumption fall.

The availability and cost of credit. The easier it is to get credit and the lower the rate of interest that has to be paid, the more people are likely to borrow at any given level of income.

There is a problem here with the definition of 'consumption'. If borrowing is regarded as an *injection* of expenditure (since it is not from current income), then it cannot also count as consumption. It is equivalent to investment, since it comes from the banking sector. The same problem applies to drawing on past savings when considering the level of assets as a determinant of consumption.

Expectations of future prices and incomes. If people expect rapid price rises in the future, they will tend to buy durable goods such as furniture and cars *now* before prices do rise. The cost of the interest they have to pay if they have to borrow the money, or the interest they lose if they have to draw on savings, will be more than offset by purchasing the good at the current lower price.

If people expect a rise in their incomes in the future, they are likely to spend more

Disposable income

Household income after the deduction of taxes and the addition of benefits.

now. If, on the other hand, they are uncertain about their future income prospects, they are likely to be cautious in their spending. This is often the case when people fear losing their job and becoming unemployed.

The distribution of income. The poor have a higher *mpc* and *apc* than the rich. A redistribution of national income from the poor to the rich will therefore tend to reduce the total level of consumption in the economy.

Tastes and attitudes. If people have a 'buy now, pay later' mentality, they are likely to have a higher level of consumption than if they are anxious to avoid getting into debt. Similarly, if people have a craving for more and more consumer goods, they will spend more than if their tastes are more frugal. The more 'consumerist' and materialistic a nation becomes, therefore, the higher will its consumption be for any given level of income.

The age of durables. If people's car, carpets, clothes, etc. are getting old, they will tend to have a high level of 'replacement' consumption. This is particularly likely after a period of recession during which people had cut back on their consumption of durables. Conversely, as the economy reaches the peak of the boom, people will probably spend less on durables as they have already bought a new car, a new video and that three-piece suite they had wanted.

Movements along and shifts in the consumption function

The effect on consumption of a change in national income is shown by a movement *along* the consumption function. A change in any of the other determinants is shown by a *shift* in the consumption function.

? What effect will the following have on (1) the *apc* and (2) the *mpc*?
(a) A rise in the rate of income tax; (b) The economy begins to recover from recession; (c) People anticipate that the rate of inflation is about to rise; (d) The government redistributes income from the rich to the poor.
In each case sketch what would happen to the consumption function.

Long-run and short-run consumption functions

The long-run consumption function is likely to be steeper than the short-run one. This is illustrated in Figure 14.5.

In the short run, people may be slow to respond to a rise in income. Perhaps this is

Figure 14.5 Long-run and short-run consumption functions

*Box 14.2

Using Calculus to Derive the MPC

The consumption function can be expressed as an equation. For example, the consumption function of Table 14.1 and Figure 14.3 is given by the equation:

$$C = 10 + 0.8Y \qquad (1)$$

 Try using this equation to derive the figures in Table 14.1.

From this equation we can derive an equation for *apc* and *mpc*.

The apc

Remember how we defined *apc*:

$$apc = C/Y \qquad (2)$$

Substituting (1) into (2) gives:

$$apc = \frac{10 + 0.8Y}{Y} \qquad (3)$$

$$= 0.8 + 10/Y \qquad (4)$$

 Check out a few of the figures from Table 14.1 first by dividing consumption by income and then by substituting the figures into equation (4). The answer should be the same!

The mpc

The *mpc* is found by differentiating the consumption function. Remember from previous calculus boxes what it is we are doing when we differentiate an equation. We are finding its rate of change. Thus by differentiating the consumption function we are finding the rate of change of consumption with respect to income. But this is what we mean by the *mpc*.

The difference between using differentiation and the formula $\Delta C/\Delta Y$ is that with the former we are looking at the *mpc* at a single point on the consumption function. With the $\Delta C/\Delta Y$ formula we were looking at the *mpc* between two points.

Differentiating equation (1) gives:

$$mpc = dC/dY = 0.8 \qquad (5)$$

Note that, since the consumption function is a straight line in this case, the *mpc* (which measures the slope of the consumption function) is constant.

Finding the apc and mpc of a non-linear consumption function

What would we do to find the *apc* and *mpc* of a curved consumption function? The procedures are the same.

Assume that the consumption function is given by the following equation:

$$C = 20 + 0.9Y - 0.001Y^2 \qquad (6)$$

 First of all try constructing a table like Table 14.1 and then graph the consumption function that it gives. What is it about equation (6) that gives the graph its particular shape?

The apc
The *apc* is given by C/Y:

$$apc = \frac{20 + 0.9Y - 0.001Y^2}{Y}$$

$$= 0.9 + 20/Y - 0.001Y$$

The mpc
The *mpc* is given by dC/dY:

$$mpc = 0.9 - 0.002Y$$

 1. What are the values of *apc* and *mpc* at incomes of (a) 20; (b) 100?
2. What happens to the value of *mpc* as national income increases? Is this what you would expect by examining the shape of the consumption function?

because they are cautious about whether their higher income will last (unless, of course, they have just been promoted to a better-paid and *secure* job). Perhaps they are slow to change their consumption habits. Perhaps it takes them time to move house and start purchasing new items of furniture, etc. In the short run, then, people may have a relatively low *mpc*.

In the long run, however, people have time to adjust their consumption patterns. Assuming that national income rises over time, the long-run consumption function

Box 14.3

The Relationship Between Income and Consumption

Three alternative theories of the consumption function

The absolute income hypothesis

This is the title of the Keynesian theory of consumption that we have been looking at so far. It assumes that people's consumption depends on their *current* disposable income. It assumes a declining *apc*.

This theory fits quite well with the evidence on *short-run* consumption behaviour. Unfortunately, it fits much less well with *long-run* consumption behaviour. The evidence suggests that, over the long term, the *apc* is roughly constant as income rises, and that the *apc* is approximately equal to the *mpc*. This gives a long-run consumption function that is a straight line out from the origin, as illustrated in the diagram.

How can we explain short-run consumption that tails off as income rises, but long-run consumption that rises proportionately with income? There are two alternative theories of consumption which provide such an explanation.

The long-run consumption function

The relative income hypothesis

This theory was put forward by J. S. Duesenberry in 1947.[4] It assumes that people's consumption behaviour is influenced by others. If other people in your street have

videos or CDs or a second car, then you will probably buy these items too, even if you are poorer.

In other words, if your income is relatively low compared

---

will be intersected by a series of short-run ones. Each year's short-run function will be above the previous year's.

 Which is likely to show the greater variation from one person to another at any given level of income: the short-run *mpc* or the long-run *mpc*?

Consumption of domestically produced goods (C_d)

Part of consumption goes on imports; part goes on VAT and excise duties. These two parts constitute withdrawals from the circular flow of income and thus do not contribute to aggregate demand. We shall need to concentrate on the part of consumption that *does*: namely, the consumption of domestic product (C_d). The C_d function will lie below the C function, as in Figure 14.6. The gap between them constitutes imports of consumer goods and indirect taxes.

Withdrawals

All three withdrawals – savings, taxes and import expenditure – depend on the level of national income. They are thus all *endogenously* determined within the model. Let us examine each in turn.

Box 14.3 (cont'd)

with your neighbours, you will probably spend a large proportion of it in your attempt 'to keep up with the Joneses'. Your *apc* will be high. If, on the other hand, your income is *high* relative to others, you will not need to spend such a large proportion of your income. Your *apc* will be lower.

This explains the discrepancy between the short-run and long-run consumption functions. In the short run, if people have a rise in their incomes, they will feel *relatively* better off compared with others. They will therefore only increase their consumption by a modest amount.

In the long run, if national income increases, people will not feel better off *relative* to others. As average incomes increase, people generally consume more as they see others consuming more.

The permanent income hypothesis

This was put forward by Milton Friedman in 1957.[5] Friedman divided a person's income into two types: permanent and transitory.

Permanent income is the average (discounted) income a person expects to receive over his or her lifetime. To estimate this, people look at their current wages and what they are likely to be earning in the future. It is on this that people base their normal planned spending. Thus the house, furniture, car, etc. that you buy, and the amount you allow each week for food and household items, all depend on your permanent income.

The permanent income hypothesis has been extended by various economists who have looked at the typical

patterns of income that people earn over their life span. (These are known as 'life cycle theories'.)

Transitory income is defined as temporary, unexpected income. People do not base their consumption plans on this. If people have an unexpected rise in income, they are likely to save most, if not all of it.

How can this distinction be used to explain the difference between short- and long-run consumption functions?

In the short run, a rise in national income may well lead to *unexpected* rises in individuals' incomes. For example, a boom in the trade cycle can lead to unexpected overtime for many workers. Since this is transitory income, it is largely saved. Consumption only rises slightly and the *apc* falls.

In the long run, if higher incomes persist, people are likely to adjust their expectations of their permanent income upwards. They will thus adjust their standard of living upwards. Their *apc* will not fall.

? Is it a reasonable assumption that consumption does not depend on transitory income? If it did, what would this do to the shape of the short-run consumption function?

[4] J. S. Duesenberry, *Income, Saving and the Theory of Consumer Behaviour* (Harvard University Press, 1947).
[5] M. Friedman, *A Theory of the Consumption Function* (Princeton University Press, 1957).

Savings

The savings function. As with consumption, the major determinant of savings is income. In fact savings and consumption are closely linked. If taxes are constant, the more people spend on consumption, the less they will save, and vice versa. This relationship gives us a clue about the shape of the *savings function*, which is illustrated

Figure 14.6 The consumption of domestic product

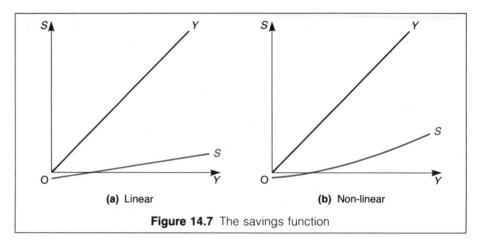

Figure 14.7 The savings function

in Figure 14.7. In diagram (a) the savings function is linear; in (b) it is curved. As income increases and a decreasing fraction of it goes on consumption, so an increasing fraction of it will be saved. The rich can afford to save a larger proportion of their income than the poor.

Average propensity to save

The proportion of national income saved: $aps = S/Y$.

Average and marginal propensities to save. Just as we did with consumption, we can distinguish between the average and marginal propensities to save. The average propensity to save (*aps*) is the proportion of total income saved:

$$aps = S/Y$$

The marginal propensity to save (*mps*) is the proportion of an *increase* in income that is saved:

$$mps = \Delta S/\Delta Y$$

Marginal propensity to save

The proportion of an increase in national income saved: $mps = \Delta S/\Delta Y$.

The *mps* is given by the slope of the savings function. The *aps* is given by the slope of the line from the origin to the relevant point on the savings function.

The determinants of savings. Apart from national income there are a number of other determinants of savings. To a large extent these are the same as the determinants of consumption, since most things that encourage people to spend more will thereby encourage them to save less.

> **?** Go through each of the determinants of consumption that were listed in the previous section and consider how they will affect savings. Are there any determinants of consumption in that list which will *not* cause savings to rise if consumption is caused to fall?

It might be easy to get the impression that savings are merely what is left over after consumption has taken place. In fact for many people the decision to save is a very positive one. They might be saving up for something they are eager to buy but cannot afford at the moment: for example, the deposit on a house. They might be saving for a summer holiday. They might be saving for a time in the future when their income will be lower: for example, when they retire. They may make the positive decision to save a regular amount each week or month.

But despite all this, savings and consumption are still closely linked, and what determines the one will usually determine the other.

Box 14.4

Consumption and Savings in the UK

Consumer spending follows a regular cyclical pattern each year, reaching its peak in the fourth quarter as Christmas approaches. The graph shows the levels of disposable national income and total consumer expenditure (i.e. consumption before indirect taxes and imports have been deducted) from 1983 Q2 to 1988 Q3. The annual cyclical pattern can clearly be seen, with consumption actually falling in quarter 1 of each year, despite a rise in disposable income.

UK disposable income, consumption and savings

The area between consumer expenditure and disposable income represents that fraction of income that is saved.

?
1. From the diagram, what can we say about the short-run and long-run consumption functions in the UK?
2. What are the implications for the economy of consumer expenditure exceeding total disposable income?

The long-term trend of a decline in the *aps*, which can be clearly seen in the diagram, has worried the government in recent years. In an attempt to reverse the trend, the then Chancellor of the Exchequer, John Major, in his 1990/91 Budget announced a new scheme to encourage savings. This was the Tax Exempt Special Savings Accounts (TESSA) that people could hold in banks or building societies whose interest would be tax free.

Taxes

Marginal and average propensities to pay taxes. The *mpt* and *apt* are defined in the same way as the other marginal and average propensities. The average tax propensity (*apt*) is the proportion of national income paid in taxes:

$$apt = T/Y$$

The marginal tax propensity (*mpt*) is the proportion of an *increase* in national income paid in taxes:

$$mpt = \Delta T/\Delta Y$$

The *mpt* depends on tax rates. In a simple world where there was only one type of tax, which was charged at a constant rate – for example, an income tax of 22 per cent – the *mpt* would be given directly by the tax rate. In this example, for each extra pound

Average tax propensity

The proportion of national income paid in taxes:
$apt = T/Y$.

Marginal tax propensity

The proportion of an increase in national income paid in tax:
$mpt = \Delta T/\Delta Y$.

earned, 22p would be paid in income tax. The $mpt = \Delta T/\Delta Y = 22/100 = 0.22$. In practice, of course, there are many types of tax charged at many different rates, and thus working out the *mpt* is more complicated.

Various tax functions. Generally, as income increases so does the amount paid in taxes. The pattern, however, varies enormously from one type of tax to another. The four diagrams of Figure 14.8 illustrate the possible different types of tax function.

Diagram (a) shows the tax function for a *lump-sum* tax. This is one that does *not* vary with income. Algebraically, the function is of the form:

$$T = \bar{T}$$

An example of a lump-sum tax is the community charge (the poll tax). The amount paid does not depend on a person's income. With the exception of the very poor, everyone in a given local authority pays the same. The *mpt* for such a tax is zero. The *apt* declines as income increases.

Diagram (b) shows a *proportional* tax. It is a constant fraction of income: the *apt* is constant. The way it is drawn in the diagram, the *mpt* is constant too. Algebraically, it is of the form:

$$T = bY$$

The term b gives the *apt* and *mpt*. For example, if the tax rate were 10 per cent the term b would equal 0.1.

Diagram (c) shows a *progressive* tax. The proportion paid in this type of tax increases as income increases. Both the *mpt* and the *apt* increase as income increases. A progressive tax function is of the form:

$$T = bY + cY^2 \tag{1}$$

or

$$T = a + bY + cY^2 \tag{2}$$

With equation (1) the tax function goes through the origin. With equation (2) the function intercepts the horizontal axis if the term a is negative. This would be the case if people were exempt from the tax if they earned below a certain level of income.

> **?** With a progressive tax, which is higher: the *mpt* or the *apt*?

Diagram (d) shows a *regressive* tax. This accounts for a smaller proportion of income as income rises: the *apt* and the *mpt* fall. A regressive tax function is of the form:

$$T = bY - cY^2$$

or

$$T = a + bY - cY^2$$

There are more complicated tax functions than these, where marginal rates are constant over a large range of income but then suddenly rise. The most obvious example is income tax.

The aggregate tax function. This shows the relationship between total tax payments and national income. Figure 14.9 shows a typical aggregate tax function. It is progressive: in other words, lump sum, regressive and proportional taxes are outweighed by progressive taxes. In practice the aggregate tax function became much *less* progressive during the 1980s.

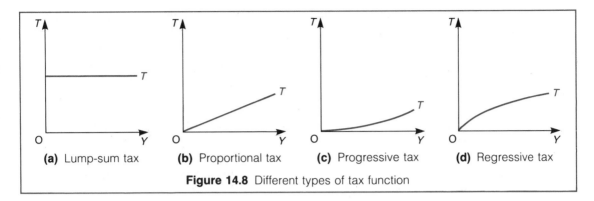

Figure 14.8 Different types of tax function

> **?** What would cause (a) a momement along the tax function; (b) a parallel downward shift in the tax function; (c) a steepening of the tax function and an increase in its curvature?

Expenditure taxes and the definition of 'consumption of domestic product'. When we talk about the marginal propensity to consume we must be careful to avoid ambiguity. When we spend £10 in a shop, part of that goes to the government in VAT and possibly excise duties. The net amount earned by firms is thus less than £10.

When we refer to 'consumption of domestic product' we only count that part of consumer expenditure which is actually received by UK firms as payment for the goods and services they have produced.

Imports

The marginal and average propensities to import. The average propensity to import (*apm*) is the proportion of national income that goes on imports and capital outflows from the country:

$$apm = M/Y$$

Average propensity to import

The proportion of total national income that goes abroad: $apm = M/Y$.

The marginal propensity to import (*mpm*) is the proportion of a *rise* in national income that goes on imports and capital outflows:

$$mpm = \Delta M/\Delta Y$$

Notice that we only count that part of the expenditure on imports that actually goes abroad. If you buy a Japanese personal stereo costing £40, that does not constitute £40 worth of imports. Part of the £40 will go to the government as VAT; part will be kept by the shop to cover its wages, overheads and profits; part will go to the wholesaler and part to the UK importer.

Marginal propensity to import

The proportion of an increase in national income that goes abroad: $mpm = \Delta M/\Delta Y$.

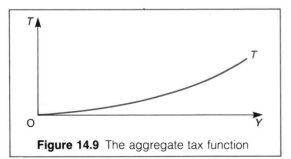

Figure 14.9 The aggregate tax function

Figure 14.10 Import functions

The import function. The higher the level of national income, the higher will be the level of imports. The import function, like all the others we have considered, is thus upward sloping. Two possible import functions are illustrated in Figure 14.10.

Curve (a) would be the function for a country which imported predominantly basic goods. Such goods have a relatively low income elasticity of demand.[6] The rate of increase in the consumption of such goods tails off rapidly as incomes increase. The *mpm* for such a country would thus also rapidly decrease. The import function thus gets less and less steep as imports account for a smaller and smaller proportion of any increase in income.

Curve (b) would be the function for a country whose imports were mainly of luxury goods. In this case, imports account for an increasing proportion of any rise in national income.

> **?** If a country imports a whole range of goods whose average income elasticity of demand is the same as for home-produced goods, what will the import function look like?

The determinants of the level of imports. Apart from national income, there are a number of other determinants of the level of imports:

- *Relative prices.* If UK goods go up in price relative to the price of imports, the level of imports will rise. The rate of exchange is a major influence here. The higher the rate of exchange, the cheaper will imports be and hence the more will be spent on them.
- *Tastes.* If consumer tastes shift towards foreign goods and services, imports will rise. For example, it might become more popular to go abroad for your holidays.
- *Relative quality.* If the quality of foreign goods and services increases relative to that of UK goods and services, imports will rise.
- *Interest rates.* If foreign interest rates rise relative to domestic rates, more money will flow abroad. M will rise.
- *Speculation.* If people believe that the exchange rate is about to depreciate, there will be an outflow of capital. M will rise.
- *The determinants of consumption.* Since imports of goods and services are part of *total* consumption (as opposed to C_d), the various determinants of consumption that we looked at in the last section will also be determinants of imports. If any of these determinants change, the whole import function will shift.

The total withdrawals function

Remember that withdrawals consist of the three elements: savings, taxes and imports. The withdrawals function, therefore, is simply the vertical sum of the savings, tax and import functions. A withdrawals function along with the corresponding consumption of domestic goods function is shown in Figure 14.11.

Note the relationship between the C_d and W curves. The steeper the slope of the one, the flatter the slope of the other. The reason for this is that C_d and W add up to total income:

$$Y = C_d + W$$

Since the 45° line measures $C_d + W$, the distance between the C_d function and the

---

[6] Note the definition of the two similar yet quite distinct concepts of income elasticity of demand ($Y\epsilon_d$) and the marginal propensity to import. The definitions are:

$Y\epsilon_d = \Delta M_a/M_a \div \Delta Y/Y$ (where M_a refers to the demand for a particular imported good 'a')
$mpm = \Delta M/\Delta Y$ (where M refers to total imports).

Figure 14.11 The W and C_d functions

45° line must equal withdrawals. Thus at point x, where national income is £100 billion and C_d is £70 billion, W must be £30 billion – the gap between C_d and the 45° line. The position of one of the two curves automatically determines the position of the other. If either of the curves shifts, the other one must shift by an equal and opposite amount.

Average and marginal propensities to withdraw

The formulae for the average propensity to withdraw (*apw*) and the marginal propensity to withdraw (*mpw*) are as we would expect:

$$apw = W/Y$$

$$mpw = \Delta W/\Delta Y$$

The *mpw* is the slope of the withdrawals function. The *apw* is the slope of the line from the origin to the withdrawals function.

Note that, since $W = S + T + M$, the *apw* must equal the *aps + apt + apm*. For example, if 1/10 of national income is saved, 2/10 paid in taxes, and 2/10 spent on imports, then 5/10 must be withdrawn. Similarly, *mpw = mps + mpt + mpm*.

Note also that, since $C_d + W = Y$, the *apc_d* + *apw* must add up to 1. If your income is £20 000 and you spend £13 000 on UK goods, the remaining £7000 must go in withdrawals. Your *apc_d* is 13/20 and your *apw* is 7/20. But 13/20 + 7/20 = 1. Likewise, *mpc_d* + *mpw* = 1. If you spend, say, 3/5 of any rise in income on UK goods, the remaining 2/5 must go in withdrawals.

 If the slope of the C_d function is 3/4, what is the slope of the W function?

Average propensity to withdraw

The proportion of national income that is withdrawn from the circular flow of income: *apw = W/Y*, where *apw = aps + apt + apm*.

Marginal propensity to withdraw

The proportion of an increase in national income that is withdrawn from the circular flow: *mpw = ΔW/ΔY*, where *mpw = mps + mpt + mpm*.

Injections

In simple Keynesian theory, injections are assumed not to depend on the level of national income: they are *exogenously* determined. This means that the injections function will be a horizontal straight line. Injections will be at a given level irrespective of the level of national income.

This is illustrated in Figure 14.12. The injections function is the vertical addition of the investment, government expenditure and export functions, each of which is a horizontal straight line.

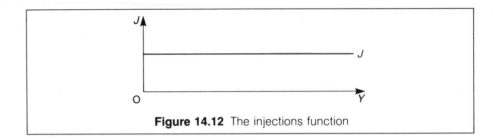

Figure 14.12 The injections function

The assumption that injections are independent of national income makes the theory simpler. (It is possible to drop this assumption, however, without destroying the theory.) But is the assumption sufficiently realistic? Let us examine each of the injections in turn.

Investment
There are four major determinants of investment.

The rate of interest. The higher the rate of interest, the more expensive will it be for firms to finance investment, and hence the less profitable will the investment be. The relationship between interest and investment at a microeconomic level was examined in section 8.4. Just how responsive total investment in the economy is to changes in interest rates is a highly controversial issue. It is one we will be examining in later chapters. (Keynesians argue that the relationship between interest rates and investment is a highly unstable one.)

Increased consumer demand. Investment is to provide extra capacity. This will only be necessary, therefore, if consumer demand increases. The bigger the increase in consumer demand, the more the investment that will be needed.

You might think that, since consumer demand depends on the level of national income, investment must also, and that therefore our assumption that investment is independent of national income is wrong. But we are not saying that investment depends on the *level* of consumer demand; rather it depends on *how much it has risen*. If income and consumer demand are high but *constant*, there will be no point in firms expanding their capacity: no point in investing.

The relationship between investment and increased consumer demand is examined by the 'accelerator theory'. We will look at this theory in section 14.4.

The cost and efficiency of capital equipment. If the cost of capital equipment goes down or machines become more efficient, the return on investment will increase. Firms will invest more. Technological progress is an important determinant here.

Expectations. Since investment is made in order to produce output for the future, investment must depend on firms' expectations about future market conditions.

So if these are the main determinants of investment, does it mean that investment is totally independent of the level of national income? Not quite. Part of firms' investment is to replace worn out or outdated equipment. This 'replacement investment' *will* depend on the level of national income. The higher the current level of national income, the greater will be the stock of capital and therefore the more will need replacing each year.

Finally, it is possible that, if the level of national income is high and firms' profits are high, they will be able to *afford* more investment. This is likely to be a more

Box 14.5

The Shaping of Expectations
CBI surveys of business expectations and intentions

The following three articles from *The Times* and *Financial Times* reported on the state of business expectations in early 1988, 1989 and 1990 respectively.

After the stock market crash of autumn 1987 and fears of an economic recession, and given at the same time a high exchange rate with fears that this would damage exports, the government was pursuing a reflationary monetary policy of low interest rates. As a result the economy grew rapidly and business optimism was high:

> The Confederation of British Industry (CBI) yesterday reported strong growth in output, healthy orders and a record proportion of companies planning to increase investment over the next 12 months.
>
> There was little indication in the CBI's latest Quarterly Survey of Industrial Trends of any effects on exporters following the pound's recent rise. But Mr David Wigglesworth, the chairman of the CBI's Economic Situation Committee, said that the pound's rise, together with its recent volatility, would have adverse effect on industry in the long term.
>
> The April survey, carried out between March 25 and April 13, showed some evidence of pressures on industrial capacity and of higher inflation, but CBI officials denied that these signalled an emerging overheating problem in the economy.
>
> The proportion of companies working below full capacity, 32 per cent, was the lowest since January 1958, and there was an increase to 26 per cent from 21 per cent at the time of the previous quarterly survey in January, in the percentage of companies reporting capacity as a constraint on output.
>
> This figure, on the face of it worrying, is balanced by the investment optimism shown in the survey, with 48 per cent of companies planning to increase plant and machinery investment during the next 12 months and only 16 per cent expecting to invest less. The balance, of 32 per cent, compared with 20 per cent in January.
>
> The main surprise of the survey was the buoyancy of output and orders both at home and abroad in spite of the strength of the pound and recent indications from official figures of a slowdown in the economy.[7]

The booming economy led to a record current account balance of payments deficit and rising inflation. In response the government began to pursue a deflationary monetary policy of high interest rates towards the end of 1988. By early 1989 business optimism was falling, as the second article, which reported on smaller firms' intentions, shows:

> Business optimism among smaller firms has been in sharp decline this year, according to a Confederation of British Industry study published today. Confidence fell more than at any time since October 1982.

Smaller businesses – those employing up to 200 people – expect the growth in both domestic and export demand to slow down; costs to rise; and the effect of higher interest rates to start working through.

> A continuation of this trend would threaten recently strong growth rates of both investments by and employment in smaller firms, the study says. Since smaller firms have become increasingly important in the UK manufacturing sector in recent years this could put in jeopardy the notion of a 'soft landing' for the economy, it warns.[8]

Despite the deflationary policy of high interest rates, consumer expenditure remained high throughout 1989 and inflation continued to rise. As a result the government felt it necessary to continue with its policy of high interest rates in order to slow down the growth in demand. By early 1990 the CBI was forecasting a *fall* in investment.

> The Confederation of British Industry today warns that 1990 will be a disappointing year for companies that depend on the home market but a good one for exporters.
>
> The CBI's post-Budget forecasts show that the British economy is expected to grow by only 1.1% this year, compared with 2.4% last year and 4.5% in 1988.
>
> However, if interest rates fall, output growth is forecast to pick up slightly to 1.55% in 1991.
>
> ... [The CBI] forecasts that total fixed investment will fall 1.3% in 1990, with manufacturing investment declining by 0.9% this year. It previously forecast that investment would be flat.[9]

Extracts from the April 1990 CBI forecast

	1989	1990	1991
	(% change on previous year)		
GDP (output)	2.4	1.1	1.5
Fixed investment	5.5	−1.3	1.5

1. What factors in the three reports were influencing business expectations?
2. How will the existence of such reports affect firms' expectations and actions?
3. Why if the growth in output is expected to slow down (but still be *positive*), is investment expected to *fall* (i.e. be *negative*)? (We will examine this question in section 14.4 when we look at the accelerator theory.)

[7] *The Times*, 27 April 1988.
[8] *Financial Times*, 9 May 1989.
[9] *Financial Times* 2 May 1990.

important determinant of investment in a country like the UK, where the bulk of investment is financed from ploughed-back profit, than in a country like Germany which relies much more on long-term bank loans to finance investment.

Despite these two links between investment and the level of income, it is not a gross distortion of reality to assume that they are independent.

Government expenditure

Government expenditure depends on present and past government policy.

To some extent, especially over the longer term, government expenditure *will* depend on national income. The higher the level of national income, the higher is the amount of tax revenue that the government receives, and hence the more it can afford to spend. This can be clearly seen around the world where the governments of richer nations spend much more than those of the Third World.

Nevertheless governments can run a budget deficit or surplus. There is thus no inevitable link between tax revenues and government spending. What is more, the government can always raise or lower taxes if it wants to. Certainly then, in the short run at least, government expenditure can be regarded as independent of national income.

 Are there any types of government expenditure that automatically *decrease* as national income rises, despite the fact that tax revenues will also be rising?

Exports

The amount that foreigners spend on UK exports depends largely on *their* national incomes. Nevertheless there are two indirect links between UK incomes and exports:

- Via foreign countries' circular flows of income. If UK incomes rise, more will be spent on imports. But UK imports are other countries' exports and thus an injection into their circular flows. This will cause a rise in their incomes and lead them to buy more imports, part of which will be UK exports.
- Via the exchange rate. A rise in UK incomes will lead to a rise in imports. Other things being equal, this will lead to a depreciation in the exchange rate. This will make it cheaper for foreigners to buy UK exports. Export sales will rise.

However, it is useful in simple Keynesian models to assume that exports are determined independently of domestic national income.

The determinants of exports are similar to the determinants of imports: relative prices, tastes, relative quality, interest rates and speculation.

 Referring to this list of determinants, what would cause an *increase* in exports?

One final point should be noted about the injections function. It is assumed to be constant with respect to income – it is drawn as a horizontal straight line. This does not mean, however, that it will be constant *over time*. Quite the opposite. Injections can be highly volatile. Investment can suddenly rise or virtually collapse as the confidence of businesspeople changes. Exports can change dramatically too with shifts in the exchange rate or with speculation. The injections line, then, is constantly shifting up and down.

Where do we go from here?

We have now covered the preliminary material for the Keynesian model. We have laid the pieces of the jigsaw puzzle on the table. We are now ready to fit the pieces together.

Remember, we want to know not just what determines the level of national income, but precisely what that level will be. We want to know just *how much* income will change if the level of injections or withdrawals changes.

▲ SUMMARY

1. In the simple Keynesian model, equilibrium national income is where withdrawals equal injections, and where national income equals the total expenditure on domestic products: where $W = J$ and where $Y = E$.
2. The relationships between national income and the various components of the circular flow of income can be shown on a 45° line diagram. In the diagram, C, C_d, W and J are endogenous variables. Each one rises as income rises. The relationships can also be expressed in terms of average and marginal propensities. The average propensity of each variable is given by V/Y (where V is the variable in question). The marginal propensity is given by $\Delta V/\Delta Y$.
3. Apart from being determined by national income, consumption is determined by wealth, taxation, the availability and cost of credit, expectations about future prices and incomes, the distribution of income, tastes and attitudes, and the average age of durables. Consumption of domestic product (C_d) is total consumption minus imports and minus indirect taxes and plus subsidies on goods and services.
4. Like consumption, withdrawals (S, T and M) vary with national income. Savings are also determined by the various factors that determine consumption: if these factors cause consumption to rise, then except in the case

of a cut in income taxes they will cause savings to fall and vice versa. Tax revenues, apart from being dependent on incomes, will depend on the rates of tax the government sets and how progressive or regressive they are. Imports (which includes all leakages abroad) will depend on the relative prices and quality of domestic and foreign goods, total consumption, tastes, interest rates and speculation.
5. In the simple Keynesian model, injections are assumed to be exogenous variables. They are therefore drawn as a horizontal straight line in the 45° line diagram. In practice there will be *some* relationship between injections and national income. Replacement investment depends to some extent on the level of output; government expenditure depends to some extent on the level of tax revenues; and exports depend on exchange rates and foreign incomes, both of which will depend on the level of imports. Nevertheless in the short run it is reasonable to assume that injections are independent of national income.
6. The determinants of investment include the rate of interest, the size of increases in consumer demand, the cost and efficiency of capital equipment, and expectations about prices, consumer demand, interest rates and other costs. The list of determinants of exports is similar to the list of determinants of imports.

14.2 The determination of national income

Equilibrium national income

We can now put the various functions together on one diagram. This is done in Figure 14.13. Note that there is a new line on the diagram that we have not looked at so far. This is the aggregate demand (or national expenditure) function. We defined aggregate demand as $C_d + J$. Graphically, then, the *AD* function is simply the C_d function shifted upward by the amount of J. Equilibrium national income can be found in either of two ways.

$W = J$

Withdrawals equal injections at point *x* in the diagram. Equilibrium national income is thus Y_e. If national income were below this level, say at Y_1, injections would exceed withdrawals (by an amount $a - b$). This additional net expenditure injected into the economy would encourage firms to produce more. This in turn would cause national income to rise. But as people's incomes rose, so they would save more, pay more taxes and buy more imports. In other words, withdrawals would rise. There would be a movement up along the W function. This process would continue until $W = J$ at point *x*.

If, on the other hand, national income were at Y_2, withdrawals would exceed

Figure 14.13 Equilibrium national income

injections (by an amount $c - d$). This deficiency of demand would cause production and hence national income to fall. As it did so, there would be a movement down along the W function until again point x was reached.

$Y = E$

If $W = \mathcal{J}$, then $C_d + W = C_d + \mathcal{J}$. In other words, another way of describing equilibrium is where national income ($Y \equiv C_d + W$) equals national expenditure ($E \equiv C_d + \mathcal{J}$). This is shown at point z in Figure 14.13. This is where the expenditure function ($C_d + \mathcal{J}$) crosses the 45° line ($C_d + W$).

> **?** Why is point z vertically above point x?

If national expenditure exceeded national income, say at Y_1, there would be excess demand in the economy (of $e - f$). In other words, people would be buying more than was currently being produced. Firms would thus find their stocks dwindling and would therefore increase their level of production. In doing so they would employ more factors of production. National income would thus rise. As it did so, consumption and hence national expenditure would rise. There would be a movement up along the expenditure function. But because not all the extra income would be consumed (i.e. some would be withdrawn), expenditure would rise less quickly than income: (the E line is flatter than the Y line). As income rises towards Y_e, the gap between Y and E gets smaller. Once point z is reached, $Y = E$. There is then no further tendency for income to rise.

If national income exceeded national expenditure, at say Y_2, there would be insufficient demand for the goods and services currently being produced. Firms would find their stocks of unsold goods building up. They would thus respond by producing less and employing fewer factors of production. National income would thus fall and go on falling until Y_e was reached.

> **?** Why do $a - b = e - f$, and $c - d = g - h$?

The multiplier: the withdrawals and injections approach

When injections rise this will cause national income to rise. But by how much?

In fact, national income will rise by *more* than the level of injections: Y rises by a *multiple* of the rise in J.

$$\Delta Y > \Delta J$$

The number of times that the increase in income (ΔY) is greater than the increase in injections (ΔJ) is known as the multiplier (k). (We use the letter 'k' as the symbol for the multiplier because that was the letter Keynes chose to use.)

$$k = \Delta Y/\Delta J$$

Thus if a £10 billion rise in injections caused a £30 billion rise in national income, the multiplier would be 3.

What causes the multiplier effect? Why will national income rise by more than the rise in injections that caused it? The answer is that, when extra spending is injected into the economy, it will then stimulate further spending, which in turn will stimulate yet more spending and so on. For example, if firms decide to invest more, this will lead to more people being employed and hence more incomes being paid to households. Households will then spend part of this increased income on UK goods (the remainder will be withdrawn). This increased consumption will encourage firms to produce more goods to meet the demand. Firms will thus employ more people and other factors of production. This leads to even more incomes being paid out to households. Consumption will thus increase yet again. And so the process continues. Think of it this way: if extra money is injected into the economy, it will circulate round and round the economy, stimulating the production of extra goods and services and thus generating extra incomes in the process.

Note that in this simple Keynesian theory we are assuming that prices are constant and hence that any increase in income is a *real* increase in income matched by extra production. So when we talk about extra money being injected into the economy causing extra spending, it is the extra *output* that this spending generates that we are concerned with. If the multiplier were 3, for example, this would mean that an injection of £1 of expenditure into the economy would lead to an increase in *output* of £3.

But even if there were limitless resources, an increase in injections would not cause national income to go on rising for ever: the multiplier is not infinite. Each time money circulates round the flow, some of it will be withdrawn. Each time people receive extra income they will save some of it, pay some of it in taxes and spend some of it on imports. Eventually, as income goes on rising, all the extra injections will have leaked away into the three withdrawals. At that point the multiplier process will have ceased; a new equilibrium will have been reached.

What determines the size of the multiplier? This can be shown graphically using either withdrawals and injections or income and expenditure. The income/expenditure approach will be examined shortly. For now we will use the withdrawals/injections approach. This is illustrated in Figure 14.14.

Assume that injections rise from J_1 to J_2. Equilibrium will move from point a to point b. Income will thus rise from Y_{e_1} to Y_{e_2}. The multiplier is therefore:

$$\frac{Y_{e_2} - Y_{e_1}}{J_2 - J_1} \quad \left(\text{i.e. } \frac{\Delta Y}{\Delta J}\right)$$

(Injections) multiplier

The number of times by which a rise in income exceeds the rise in injections that caused it: $k = \Delta Y/\Delta J$.

Figure 14.14 The multiplier: a shift in injections

It can be seen that the size of the multiplier depends on the *slope of the W function*. Remember that the slope of the *W* function is given by the marginal propensity to withdraw ($\Delta W/\Delta Y$). The flatter the line (and hence the lower the *mpw*), the bigger will be the rise in national income: the bigger will be the multiplier.

? Try this simple test of the above argument. Draw a series of *W* lines of different slopes all crossing the *J* line at the same point. Now draw a second *J* line above the first. Mark the original equilibrium and all the new ones corresponding to each of the *W* lines. It should be quite obvious that the flatter the *W* line is, the more *Y* will have increased.

The point here is that the less is withdrawn each time money circulates, the more will be recirculated and hence the bigger will be the rise in national income. The size of the multiplier thus varies inversely with the size of the *mpw*. The bigger the *mpw*, the smaller the multiplier; the smaller the *mpw*, the bigger the multiplier. In fact the multiplier formula simply gives the multiplier as the inverse of the *mpw*:

(Injections) multiplier formula

The formula for the multiplier is $k = 1/mpw$ or $1/(1 - mpc_d)$.

$$k = 1/mpw$$

or alternatively, since $mpw + mpc_d = 1$ and thus $mpw = 1 - mpc_d$:

$$k = 1/(1 - mpc_d)$$

Thus if the *mpw* were $\frac{1}{4}$ (and hence the mpc_d were $\frac{3}{4}$), the multiplier would be 4. So if J increased by £10 billion, *Y* would increase by £40 billion.

But why is the multiplier given by the formula $1/mpw$? This can be illustrated by referring to Figure 14.14. The *mpw* is the slope of the *W* line. In the diagram this is given by the amount $(b - c)/(c - a)$. The multiplier is defined as $\Delta Y/\Delta J$. In the diagram this is the amount $(c - a)/(b - c)$. But this is merely the inverse of the *mpw*. Thus the multiplier equals $1/mpw$.[10]

A shift in withdrawals

A multiplied rise in income can also be caused by a fall in withdrawals. This is illustrated in Figure 14.15.

The withdrawals function shifts from W_1 to W_2. This means that, at the old equilibrium of Y_{e_1}, injections now exceed withdrawals by an amount $a - b$. This will cause national income to rise until a new equilibrium is reached at Y_{e_2} where $J = W_2$.

---

[10] In some elementary textbooks, the formula for the multiplier is given as $1/mps$. The reason for this is that it is assumed (for simplicity!) that there is only one withdrawal, namely savings, and only one injection, namely investment. In other words it is assumed that there is no foreign trade and no government. The problem with this approach is that this totally unrealistic assumption has to be dropped later, and so, having just learnt one version of the multiplier, this then has to be unlearnt and replaced by the full version. This can be very confusing.

Figure 14.15 The multiplier: a shift in withdrawals

Thus a downward shift of the withdrawals function of $a - b$ (ΔW) causes a rise in national income of $c - a$ (ΔY). The multiplier in this case is given by $\Delta Y/\Delta W$: in other words, $(c - a)/(a - b)$.

? Why is the 'withdrawals multiplier' strictly speaking a negative figure?

The multiplier: a numerical illustration

The multiplier effect does not work instantaneously. When there is an initial increase in injections, it takes time before this brings about the full multiplied rise in national income: it takes time for money to go round and round the circular flow of income.

Consider the following example. Let us assume for simplicity that the *mpw* is $\frac{1}{2}$. This will give an mpc_d of $\frac{1}{2}$ also. Let us also assume that there is an increase in injections into the economy of £160 million. Table 14.2 shows what will happen.

Table 14.2 The multiplier 'round'

Period	ΔJ (£m)	ΔY (£m)	ΔC_d (£m)	ΔW (£m)
1	160	160	80	80
2	–	80	40	40
3	–	40	20	20
4	–	20	10	10
5	–	10	5	5
6	–	5	.	.
.		.	.	.
.		.	.	.
.		.	.	.
$1 \rightarrow \infty$		320	160	160

The initial injection of £160 million will generate an immediate increase in national income of £160 million. When this income is received by households, half will be withdrawn (*mpw* $= \frac{1}{2}$) and half will be spent on the goods and services of UK firms. This increase in consumption thus generates additional incomes for firms of £80 million over and above the initial £160 million. When this additional £80 million of incomes is received by households (period 2), again half will be withdrawn and half will go on consumption of domestic product. This increases national income by a further £40 million (period 3). And so each time we go around the circular flow of income, national income increases, but by only half as much as the previous time (*mpc_d* $= \frac{1}{2}$).

If we add up the additional income generated in each period (assuming the process

---

Box 14.6

Deriving the Multiplier Formula
An algebraic proof

The formula for the multiplier can be derived using simple algebra. First of all remember how we defined the multiplier:

$$k \equiv \Delta Y / \Delta \mathcal{J} \qquad (1)$$

and the marginal propensity to withdraw:

$$mpw \equiv \Delta W / \Delta Y \qquad (2)$$

If we now take the inverse of equation (2) we get:

$$1/mpw \equiv \Delta Y / \Delta W \qquad (3)$$

But in equilibrium we know that $W = \mathcal{J}$. Hence any change in injections must be matched by a change in withdrawals and vice versa, to ensure that withdrawals and injections remain equal. Thus:

$$\Delta W = \Delta \mathcal{J} \qquad (4)$$

Substituting equation (4) in equation (3) gives:

$$1/mpw = \Delta Y / \Delta \mathcal{J} \ (= k)$$

i.e. the multiplier equals $1/mpw$.

---

goes on indefinitely), the total will be £320 million: twice the initial injection. The multiplier is 2.

The bigger the mpc_d (and hence the smaller the mpw), the more will expenditure rise each time national income rises, and hence the bigger will be the multiplier.

> **?**
> 1. Construct a table similar to Table 14.1, only this time assume that the mpc_d is $\frac{3}{4}$. Show that national income will increase by £640 million.
> 2. Assume that the multiplier has a value of 3. Now assume that the government decides to increase aggregate demand in an attempt to reduce unemployment.
>
> It raises government expenditure by £100 million with no increase in taxes. Firms, anticipating a rise in their sales, increase investment by £200 million, of which £50 million consists of purchases of foreign machinery. How much will national income rise? (Assume *ceteris paribus*.)

The multiplier: the income and expenditure approach

The multiplier can also be demonstrated using the income/expenditure approach. Assume in Figure 14.16 that the expenditure function shifts to E_2. This could be due either to a rise in one or more of the three injections, or to a rise in the consumption of domestic goods (and hence a fall in withdrawals). Equilibrium national income will rise from Y_{e_1} to Y_{e_2}. What is the size of the multiplier? The initial rise in expenditure was $b - a$. The resulting rise in income is $c - a$. The multiplier is thus $(c - a)/(b - a)$.

> **?**
> 1. What determines the slope of the E function?
> 2. How does the slope of the E function affect the size of the multiplier? (Try drawing diagrams with E functions of different slopes and see what happens when they shift.)

*The multiplier: some qualifications

There are some possible errors that can easily be made in calculating the value of the multiplier. These often arise from a confusion over the meaning of terms.

Box 14.7

The Paradox of Thrift
When prudence is folly

The classical economists argued that savings were a national virtue. More savings would lead via lower interest rates to more investment and faster growth. Keynes was at pains to show the opposite. Savings, far from being a national virtue, could be a national vice.

Remember the fallacy of composition (see Box 11.2). Just because something is good for an individual, it does not follow that it is good for society as a whole. This fallacy applies to savings. If individuals save more, they will increase their consumption possibilities in the future. If society saves more, however, this may *reduce* its future income and consumption.

This can be demonstrated quite simply by reference to Figure 14.15. If people generally choose to save more, the withdrawals function will shift upwards. As people save more, they will spend less. Firms will thus produce less. There will thus be a multiplied *fall* in income. The phenomenon of higher savings leading to *lower* national income is known as 'the paradox of thrift'.

But this is not all. Far from the extra savings encouraging more investment, the lower consumption will *discourage* firms from investing. If investment falls, the *J* line will shift downwards. There will then be a further multiplied fall in national income. (This response of investment to changes in consumer demand is examined in section 14.4 under the 'accelerator theory'.)

The paradox of thrift had in fact been recognized before Keynes, and Keynes himself referred to various complaints about 'underconsumption' that had been made back in the sixteenth and seventeenth centuries:

> In 1598 Laffemas . . . denounced the objectors to the use of French silks on the grounds that all purchasers of French luxury goods created a livelihood for the poor, whereas the miser caused them to die in distress. In 1662 Petty justified 'entertainments, magnificent shews, triumphal arches, etc.', on the ground that their costs flowed back into the pockets of brewers, bakers, tailors, shoemakers and so forth. Fortrey justified 'excess of apparel'. Von Schrtter (1686) deprecated sumptuary regulations and declared that he would wish that display in clothing and the like were even greater. Barbon (1690) wrote that 'Prodigality is a vice that is prejudicial to Man, but not to trade . . . Covetousness is a vice, prejudicial both to Man and Trade.' In 1695 Cary argued that if everybody spent more, all would obtain larger incomes 'and might then live more plentifully'.[11]

But despite these early recognitions of the danger of underconsumption, the belief that savings would increase the prosperity of the nation was central to classical economic thought.

? Is an increase in savings ever desirable?

[11] J. M. Keynes, *The General Theory of Employment, Interest and Money* (Macmillan, 1967), pp. 358–9.

Figure 14.16 A shift in the expenditure function

The marginal propensity to consume domestic product

Remember the formula for the multiplier:

$$k = 1/(1 - mpc_d)$$

It is important to realize just what is meant by the mpc_d. It is the proportion of a rise in households' gross (i.e. pre-tax) income that actually accrues to UK firms. It thus excludes that part of consumption that is spent on imports and that part which is paid to the government in VAT and other indirect taxes.

Let us call the proportion of a rise in *disposable* income that people spend the *mpc* (without the subscript 'd'). How do we derive the mpc_d from this? We use the following formula:

$$mpc_d = mpc \ (1 - t_E)(1 - t_Y) - mpm$$

where t_Y is the marginal rate of income tax, and t_E is the marginal rate of expenditure tax.

To illustrate this formula consider the following effects of an increase in national income of £100 million. It is assumed that $T_Y = 20$ per cent, $T_E = 10$ per cent and $mpc = 7/8$. It is also assumed that the $mps = 1/10$ and the $mpm = 13/100$.

Table 14.3

(£m)	ΔY	$-$	ΔT_Y	$=$	ΔY_{dis}		
	100		20		80		
(£m)	ΔY_{dis}	$-$	ΔS	$=$	ΔC		
	80		10		70		
(£m)	ΔC	$-$	ΔT_E	$-$	ΔM	$=$	ΔC_d
	70		7		13		50

Gross income rises by £100 million. Of this, £20 million is taken in income tax ($t_Y = 20$ per cent). This leaves a rise in disposable income of £80 million. Of this, £10 million is saved ($mps = 1/10$) and £70 million is spent. Of this, £7 million goes in expenditure taxes ($t_E = 10$ per cent) and £13 million leaks abroad ($mpm = 13/100$). This leaves £50 million that goes on the consumption of domestic product ($mpc_d = 50/100 = \frac{1}{2}$). Substituting these figures in the above formula gives:

$$mpc_d = mpc(1 - t_E)(1 - t_Y) - mpm$$
$$= 7/8(1 - 1/10)(1 - 2/10) - 13/100$$
$$= 7/8 \ . \ 9/10 \ . \ 8/10 - 13/100$$
$$= 63/100 - 13/100 = 50/100 = \frac{1}{2}$$

Note that the mpc_d, *mps*, *mpm* and *mpt* are all based on the rise in *gross* income not disposable income. They are 50/100, 10/100, 13/100 and 27/100 respectively.

? Assume that the rate of income tax is 15 per cent, the rate of expenditure tax is 12½ per cent, the *mps* is 1/20, the *mpm* is 1/8 and the *mpc* (from disposable income) is 16/17. What is the mpc_d? Construct a table like Table 14.3 assuming again that national income rises by £100 million.

The effects of changes in injections and withdrawals on other injections and withdrawals

In order to work out the size of a multiplied rise or fall in income it is necessary to know first the size of the initial *total* change in injections and/or withdrawals. The trouble is that a change in one injection or withdrawal can affect other ones. For example, a rise in exports of £10 million may encourage firms to increase investment by £5 million. In this case the total rise in injections is thus £15 million, and it is on this that the multiplier effect is based.

 Give some other examples of changes in one injection or withdrawal that can affect others.

The relationship between the 45° line diagram and the aggregate demand and supply diagram

We have used two diagrams to show the determination of equilibrium national income: the aggregate demand and supply diagram and the 45° line diagram. The first shows aggregate demand dependent on the price level. The second shows aggregate demand (E) dependent on the level of national income. Figure 14.17 shows the multiplier effect simultaneously on the two diagrams. Initially equilibrium is at Y_{e_1} where aggregate demand equals aggregate supply and where the expenditure function crosses the 45° line.

Now assume that there is an autonomous increase in expenditure. Perhaps business confidence rises and firms decide to invest more, or perhaps there is an improvement on the current account of the balance of payments. In diagram (b) the E line shifts to E_2. There is a multiplied rise in income to Y_{e_2}. In diagram (a) the aggregate supply curve is drawn as a horizontal straight line between Y_{e_1} and Y_{e_2}. This means that an increase in aggregate demand from AD_1 to AD_2 will raise income to Y_{e_2} with no increase in prices.

But what if the economy is approaching full employment? Surely we cannot expect the multiplier process to work in the same way as when there is plenty of slack in the economy? In this case the aggregate supply curve will be upward sloping. This means that an increase in aggregate demand will raise prices and not just output. How do we analyze this with the 45° line diagram? This is the subject of section 14.3.

Figure 14.17 Showing the multiplier effect on the 45° line and *AD/AS* diagrams

▲ SUMMARY

1. Equilibrium national income can be shown in the 45° line diagram at the point where $W = J$ and $Y = E$.
2. If there is an increase in injections (or a reduction in withdrawals), there will be a multiplied rise in national income. The multiplier is defined as $\Delta Y/\Delta J$.
3. The size of the multiplier depends on the marginal propensity to withdraw (mpw). The smaller the mpw, the less will be withdrawn each time incomes are generated round the circular flow, and thus the more will go round again as *additional* demand for domestic product. The multiplier formula is $k = 1/mpw$ or $1/(1 - mpc_d)$.

* 4. When working out the size of the multiplier you must be careful to identify clearly the mpc_d (which is based on *gross* income and only includes expenditure that actually accrues to domestic firms) and not to confuse it with the mpc (which is based on *disposable* income and which includes consumption of imports and the payment of indirect taxes). It is also necessary to identify the *full* changes in injections and withdrawals on which any multiplier effect is based.
5. The multiplier effect can also be illustrated on an aggregate demand and supply diagram.

14.3 The simple Keynesian analysis of unemployment and inflation

'Full employment' national income

In the simple Keynesian theory it is assumed that there will be a maximum level of national output, and hence real income, that can be obtained at any one time. If the equilibrium level of income is at this level, there will be no deficiency of aggregate demand and hence no disequilibrium unemployment. This level of income is referred to as the full employment level of national income. (In practice there would still be some unemployment at this level because of the existence of equilibrium unemployment – structural, frictional and seasonal.)

Post-war governments of the 1950s, 1960s and early 1970s aimed to achieve this full employment income (Y_f), if inflation and the balance of payments permitted. To do this they attempted to manipulate the level of aggregate demand.

Full employment level of national income

The level of national income at which there is no deficiency of demand.

The deflationary gap

If the equilibrium level of income (Y_e) is below the full employment level (Y_f), there will be excess capacity in the economy and hence demand-deficient unemployment.

If under these circumstances the economy were *initially* at the full employment level of income, the sum of C_d, I, G and X would be less than that of C_d, S, T and M. This shortfall in expenditure is shown by the shaded area in Figure 14.18. This lack of demand would cause a multiplied fall in national income and a rise in unemployment until equilibrium income (Y_e) was reached.

This shortfall in expenditure at full employment is known as the deflationary gap. If the government wants to achieve full employment, it must endeavour to close the gap so that equilibrium income coincides with the full employment income.

Deflationary gap

The excess of national income over expenditure (and withdrawals over injections) at the full employment level of national income.

? What would happen to the income and expenditure blocks in Figure 14.18 as income fell? Why would the height of the two blocks eventually become equal? What could the government do to close the deflationary gap (the shaded area) in Figure 14.18?

The deflationary gap can also be illustrated on the 45° line diagram. This is done in Figure 14.19. The gap is $a - b$: namely, the amount that the E line is below the 45° line

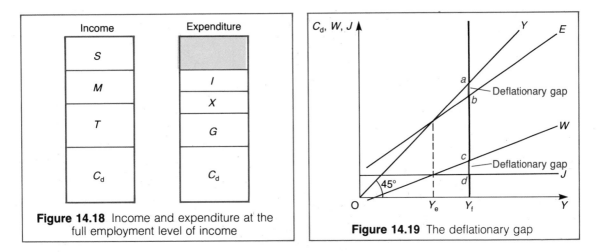

Figure 14.18 Income and expenditure at the full employment level of income

Figure 14.19 The deflationary gap

at the full employment level of income (Y_f). It is also $c - d$: the amount that withdrawals exceed injections at the full employment level of income.

? Why does $a - b$ equal $c - d$?

Note that the size of the deflationary gap is *less* than the amount by which Y_e falls short of Y_f. This is another illustration of the multiplier. If injections are raised by $c - d$, income will rise by $Y_f - Y_e$. The multiplier is thus given by:

$$\frac{Y_f - Y_e}{c - d}$$

The inflationary gap

If at the full employment level of income national expenditure exceeds national income, there will be a problem of *excess* demand. Y_e will be above Y_f. The problem is that Y_f represents a real ceiling to output. In the short run, national income *cannot* expand beyond this point. Y_e cannot be reached. The result will therefore be demand-pull inflation.[12]

This situation involves an inflationary gap. This is the amount by which expenditure exceeds income or injections exceed withdrawals at the full employment level of national income. This is illustrated by the gaps $e - f$ and $g - h$ in Figure 14.20.

To eliminate this inflation, the inflationary gap must be closed by either raising withdrawals or lowering injections or some combination of the two until Y_e equals Y_f. This can be done by a deliberate government policy of deflation. This could be either a deflationary *fiscal* policy of lowering government expenditure or raising taxes, or a deflationary *monetary* policy of reducing the amount of money in the economy and/or deliberately raising interest rates.

Even if the government does not actively pursue a deflationary policy, the inflationary gap may still be closed. If the rich are better able to defend themselves

Inflationary gap

The excess of national expenditure over income (and injections over withdrawals) at the full employment level of national income.

---

[12] Note that the horizontal axis in the 45° line diagram represents *real* national income. If incomes were to rise by, say, 10 per cent but prices also rose by 10 per cent, real income would not have risen at all. People could not buy any more than before. In such a case there will have been no rightward movement along the horizontal axis.

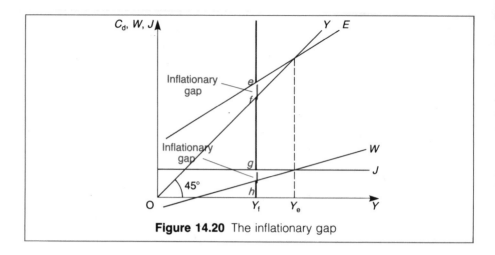

Figure 14.20 The inflationary gap

against inflation than the poor, there will be a redistribution from the poor to the rich. But the rich tend to have a higher marginal propensity to save than the poor. Thus savings will rise and consumption will fall. This will shift the *W* line up and the *E* line down, thus narrowing the inflationary gaps.

Inflation will also tend to worsen the balance of payments. Higher money incomes at home will lead to more imports being purchased. Higher UK prices will lead to fewer exports being sold and more imports being bought in preference to the now dearer home-produced goods. The effect of this will be to shift the *W* line up and the *J* and *E* lines down, thus helping to close the inflationary gap.

Finally, as money incomes go up, people will tend to find themselves paying higher rates of tax (unless the government increases tax bands and allowances in line with inflation). This will shift the *W* line up.

> **?** The present level of a country's exports is £12 billion; investment is £2 billion; government expenditure is £4 billion; *total* consumer spending (not C_d) is £36 billion; imports are £12 billion; and expenditure taxes are £2 billion. The economy is currently in equilibrium. It is estimated that an income of £50 billion is necessary to generate full employment. The *mps* is 0.1, the *mpt* is 0.05 and the *mpm* is 0.1.
> (a) Is there an inflationary or deflationary gap in this situation?
> (b) What is the size of the gap? (Don't confuse this with the difference between Y_e and Y_f.)
> (c) What would be the appropriate government policies to close this gap?

Unemployment and inflation at the same time

The simple analysis of the preceding pages implies that the aggregate supply curve looks like AS_1 in Figure 14.21. Up to Y_f, output and employment can rise with no rise in prices at all. The deflationary gap is being closed. At Y_f no further rises in output are possible. Any further rise in aggregate demand is entirely reflected in higher prices. An inflationary gap opens.

In other words, this implies that either inflation *or* unemployment can occur, but not both simultaneously.

Keynesians make two important qualifications to this analysis to explain the occurrence of both unemployment *and* inflation at the same time.

First, there are *other* types of inflation and unemployment not caused by an excess or deficiency of aggregate demand: for example, cost-push and expectations-generated inflation; frictional and structural unemployment.

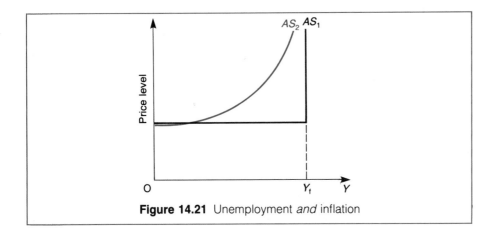

Figure 14.21 Unemployment *and* inflation

Thus, even if a government could manipulate national income so as to get Y_e and Y_f to coincide, this would not eliminate all inflation and unemployment – only demand-pull inflation and demand-deficient unemployment. Keynesians argue, therefore, that governments should use a whole package of policies, each tailored to the specific type of problem. But certainly one of the most important of these policies will be the management of aggregate demand.

Secondly, not all firms operate with the same degree of slack. This may be due to different policies of firms over how much spare capacity to maintain and how many stocks to carry. It may be due to shifts in consumer demand away from some firms and towards others.

The implication of this is that a rise in aggregate demand can lead to *both* a reduction in unemployment *and* a rise in prices: some firms responding to the rise in demand by taking up slack and hence increasing output; other firms, having little or no slack, responding by raising prices; others doing both. Similarly, labour markets have different degrees of slack and therefore the rise in demand will lead to various mixes of higher wages and lower unemployment.

Thus the *AS* curve will look like AS_2 in Figure 14.21.

> ? How does the above argument about firms' responses to a rise in demand relate to the shape of their marginal cost curves?

It was these types of argument that were used to justify a belief in a downward-sloping Phillips curve by the majority of economists and politicians in the 1960s and into the 1970s. A modified version of these arguments is still used today by Keynesian economists. This is examined in more detail in Chapter 19.

The problem is that if there is a trade-off between unemployment and inflation, demand management policies used to make one of the objectives better will only succeed in making the other one worse. It then becomes a matter of political judgement as to which of the objectives is the right one to direct demand management policies towards. Is *inflation* public enemy number one, or is it *unemployment*?

The relationship between the AD/AS diagram and the 45° line diagram

Now that we have introduced the argument that inflation can begin to occur *before* the full employment level of income is reached, how does this affect the relationship

Figure 14.22 Allowing for inflation in the 45° line and *AD/AS* diagrams

between our two models: the *AD/AS* model and the 45° line model? This is examined in Figure 14.22. Initial equilibrium is at Y_{e_1} in both parts of the diagram, where $AD_1 = AS$ and where E_1 crosses the 45° line.

Now let us assume that there is a rise in aggregate demand. The *E* line shifts initially to E_2 in diagram (b). If this rise in demand were to lead to a full multiplied rise in real income, equilibrium income would rise to Y_{e_2}. But we are now assuming that inflation can occur *before* the full employment level of income is reached. In other words, we are assuming that the *AS* curve is upward sloping (not horizontal as it was in Figure 14.17).

In diagram (a) the rise in aggregate demand has shifted the *AD* curve from AD_1 to AD_2. Part of this increase in demand is reflected in higher prices – the price level rises to P_2 – and only *part* is reflected in higher output. Equilibrium real income therefore only rises to Y_{e_3} and not Y_{e_2}.

In diagram (b) the effect of the higher prices is to reduce the real value of expenditure (*E*). In other words, a given amount of money buys fewer goods. If there is no compensating increase in money supply by the government (which would shift the *AD* curve further to the right in diagram (a)), the *E* line must fall to the point where it intersects the 45° line at a real income of Y_{e_3}: the *E* line must fall to E_3.

What is the mechanism that drives down the expenditure function from E_2 to E_3? There are three main causes:

- The shortage of money drives up interest rates. This will reduce investment and encourage savings.
- Higher prices will reduce the real value of people's savings. They may therefore save more to compensate for this.
- Higher prices of UK goods will reduce exports and increase imports.

 If money supply *did* increase sufficiently for the *E* line to remain at E_2, what would be the position of the new *AD* curve?

▲ SUMMARY

1. If equilibrium national income (Y_e) is below the full employment level of national income (Y_f), there will be a deflationary gap. This gap is equal to $Y - E$ or $W - \mathcal{J}$ at Y_f. This gap can be closed by reflationary fiscal or monetary policy, which will then cause a multiplied rise in national income (up to a level of Y_f) and will eliminate demand-deficient unemployment.

2. If equilibrium national income exceeds the full employment level of income, the inability of output to expand to meet this excess demand will lead to demand-pull inflation. This excess demand gives an inflationary gap, which is equal to $E - Y$ or $\mathcal{J} - W$ at Y_f. This gap can be closed by deflationary policies.

3. This simple analysis tends to imply that the AS curve will be horizontal up to Y_f and then vertical. If allowance is made for other types of inflation and unemployment, the AS curve will be upward sloping but getting steeper as full employment is approached and as bottlenecks increasingly occur.

4. An initial rise in aggregate demand (and an upward shift in the E curve) will be eroded to the extent that inflation reduces the real value of this demand: the E curve will shift back downward again somewhat, unless there is a further boost to demand.

14.4 The Keynesian analysis of the trade cycle

Keynesians blame fluctuations in output and employment on fluctuations in aggregate demand. Theirs is therefore a 'demand-side' explanation of the trade cycle.

In the upturn (phase 1), aggregate demand starts to rise. It rises rapidly in the expansionary phase (phase 2). It then slows down and may start to fall in the peaking-out phase (phase 3). It then falls or remains relatively stagnant in the recession (phase 4) (see Figure 14.23).

Keynesians seek to explain why aggregate demand fluctuates, and then to devise appropriate stabilization policies to iron out these fluctuations. In Chapter 15 we examine the major policy weapon that Keynesians advocate for stabilizing aggregate demand: namely, fiscal policy. For the remainder of this chapter we examine the possible causes of fluctuations. In fact, as we shall see, there are several possible causes, all or only some of which could be operating in any one particular cycle. Given the multiplicity of causes, it is extremely difficult to combine them all into a single comprehensive theory of the trade cycle, especially since some of the causes operate earlier in each phase than do others, and since some operate with time lags – lags which can be highly variable. Nevertheless Keynesian theorists and forecasters have

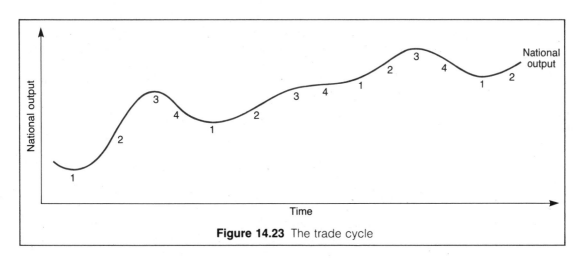

Figure 14.23 The trade cycle

built often highly complex models of the trade cycle, which take into account many different variables.

A demand-side theory of the trade cycle must explain the following:

- Why does aggregate demand *continue* to rise (or fall) once it has started to rise (or fall)?
- Why does a boom break or a recession end? In other words, why does aggregate demand stop moving in one direction and start moving in the other?
- What determines the length of each phase? Why do some recessions last several years, whereas others last only a few weeks?
- What determines the magnitude of each phase? Why are some recessions really severe with a considerable fall in output, whereas others are merely 'pauses' before rapid growth resumes?.

A comprehensive theory will seek to answer all these questions. All we can attempt to do at this level, however, is to *identify* the range of possible causes and to show how they can contribute to the instability of aggregate demand.

Instability of investment: the accelerator

One of the major factors contributing to the ups and downs of the trade cycle is the instability of investment.

When an economy begins to recover from a slump, investment can rise very rapidly. In percentage terms the rise in investment may be several times that of the rise in income. When the growth of the economy slows down, however, investment can fall dramatically, and during a recession investment can all but disappear. Since investment is an injection into the circular flow of income, these changes in investment will cause multiplied changes in income and thus heighten a boom or deepen a recession.

The theory that explains these fluctuations in investment is called the accelerator theory. This theory relates investment to *changes* in national income. Note that this is still consistent with the simple Keynesian assumption that investment does not depend on the *level* of income. What the accelerator theory argues is that it is not whether national income is high or low that determines how much firms will choose to invest, but rather whether income is rising or falling.

When there is no change in income and hence no change in consumption, the only investment needed is a relatively small amount of replacement investment for machines that are wearing out or have become obsolete. When income and consumption increase, however, firms will probably wish to expand output to meet the new higher demand. There will thus have to be *new* investment in order to increase production capacity. This is called induced investment (I_i). Once this has taken place, investment will fall back to mere replacement investment (I_r) unless there is a further rise in income and consumption.

Thus induced investment depends on *changes* in income (ΔY):

$$I_i = \alpha \Delta Y$$

where α is the amount by which induced investment depends on changes in national income. α is known as the accelerator coefficient. Thus if a £1 million *rise* in national income caused the *level* of induced investment to be £2 million, the accelerator coefficient would be 2.

The size of α will depend on the economy's marginal capital/output ratio ($\Delta K/\Delta Y$). This is the cost of extra capital required to produce a £1 increase in

---

Accelerator theory

The *level* of investment depends on the *rate of change* of national income, and as result tends to be subject to substantial fluctuations.

Induced investment

Investment firms make to enable them to meet extra consumer demand.

Accelerator coefficient

The level of induced investment as a proportion of a rise in national income: $\alpha = I_i/\Delta Y$.

Marginal capital/ output ratio

The amount of extra capital (in money terms) required to produce a £1 increase in national output. Since $I_i = \Delta K$, the marginal capital/ output ratio $\Delta K/\Delta Y$ equals the accelerator coefficient (α).

national output. Thus if an increase in the country's capital stock of £2 million (i.e. an investment of £2 million) is required to produce £1 million extra national output, the marginal capital output ratio would be 2. It is easy to see that (other things being equal) the accelerator coefficient and the marginal capital/output ratio will be the same.

? How is it that the amount of money a firm will have to spend on investment will exceed the value of the output that the investment will yield? Surely that would make the investment unprofitable? (Clue: the increase in output refers to output over a specific time period, usually a year.)

Why is the relationship between investment and changes in national income called the 'accelerator'? The reason is that a relatively modest rise in national income can cause a much larger percentage rise in investment. There are two reasons for this:

- When national income is constant, only a relatively small amount of replacement investment is needed. When income rises, and induced investment now occurs, the percentage rise in investment can as a result be quite large.
- α is likely to be greater than 1. A machine may last many years and have a value considerably in excess of one year's output. A rise in consumer demand, therefore, may lead to a much bigger rise in the capital stock (ΔK).

The following example (see Table 14.4) illustrates some important features of the accelerator. It looks at the investment decisions made by a firm in response to changes in the demand for its product. This firm is taken as a representative firm, so that what it chooses to do will be typical of what firms generally throughout the economy will choose to do. The example is based on various assumptions:

- The firm's machines last exactly 10 years and then need replacing.
- At the start of the example, the firm has 10 machines in place, one 10 years old, one 9 years old, one 8 years old, one 7, one 6 and so on. Thus one machine needs replacing each year.
- Machines produce exactly 100 units of output per year. This figure cannot be varied.
- The firm always adjusts its output and its stock of machinery to match consumer demand.

These assumptions are obviously very restrictive, but they enable us to illustrate the accelerator phenomenon quite clearly. The example shows what happens to the firm's investment when there is first a substantial rise in consumer demand, then a levelling off and then a slight fall. The example covers a six-year period. In year 2 consumer demand shoots up from 1000 units to 2000 units. In year 3 it goes up by a further 1000 units to 3000 units. In year 4 the rise begins to slow down: demand goes up by

Table 14.4 The accelerator effect

	Year						
	0	1	2	3	4	5	6
Quantity demanded by consumers (sales)	1000	1000	2000	3000	3500	3500	3400
Number of machines required	10	10	20	30	35	35	34
Induced investment (I_i) (extra machines)		0	10	10	5	0	0
Replacement investment (I_r)		1	1	1	1	1	0
Total investment ($I_i + I_r$)		1	11	11	6	1	0

500 units to 3500 units. In year 5 there is no further rise in demand at all: demand is constant at 3500 units. In year 6 there is a slight fall in demand to 3400 units.

This example illustrates the following features of the accelerator.

Investment will rise when the growth of national income (and hence consumer demand) is rising: $\Delta Y_{t+1} > \Delta Y_t$. Years 1 to 2 illustrate this. The rise in consumer demand is zero in year 1 and 1000 units in year 2. Investment rises from 1 to 11 machines. The growth in investment may be considerably greater than the growth in consumer demand, giving a large accelerator effect. Between years 1 and 2, consumer demand doubles but investment goes up by a massive *eleven* times!

Investment will be constant even when national income is growing, if the increase in income this year is the same as last year: $\Delta Y_{t+1} = \Delta Y_t$. Years 2 to 3 illustrate this. Consumer demand continues to rise by 1000 units, but investment is constant at 11 machines.

Investment will fall even if national income is still growing, if the rate of growth is slowing down: $\Delta Y_{t+1} < \Delta Y_t$. Years 3 to 4 illustrate this. Consumer demand rises now by 500 units (rather than the 1000 units last year). Investment falls from 11 to 6 machines.

If national income is constant, investment will be confined to replacement investment only. Years 4 to 5 illustrate this. Investment falls to the one machine requiring replacement.

If national income falls, even if only slightly, investment can be wiped out altogether. Years 5 to 6 illustrate this. Even though demand has only fallen by 1/35, investment will fall to zero. Not even the machine that is wearing out will be replaced.

In practice the accelerator will not be as dramatic as this, and certainly the effect will be extremely difficult to predict precisely. The reasons for this are as follows:

- Many firms may have spare capacity and/or carry stocks. This will enable them to meet extra demand without having to invest.
- The willingness of firms to invest will depend on their confidence in *future* demand. Just because demand has currently risen, firms are not going to rush out and spend large amounts of money on machines that will last many years if it is quite likely that next year demand will fall back again.
- Firms may make their investment plans a long time in advance and may be unable to change them quickly.
- Even if firms do decide to invest more, the producer goods industries may not have the capacity to meet a sudden surge in demand for machines.
- Machines do not as a rule suddenly wear out. A firm could thus delay replacing machines and keep the old ones for a bit longer if it was uncertain about its future level of demand.

But despite the fact that all these points tend to reduce the magnitude of the accelerator and to make it very difficult to predict, nevertheless the effect still exists. Firms still take note of changes in consumer demand when deciding how much to invest.

Box 14.8 looks at investment and national income from 1978 to 1989. It shows how fluctuations in investment were far more severe than fluctuations in national income. This evidence does tend to suggest (but not conclusively) that there was a substantial accelerator effect operating during the period.

Box 14.8

Was There an Accelerator Effect in the 1980s?

Investment is highly volatile. It is subject to far more violent swings than national income. If we look at the period from 1978–1989, the maximum annual rise in GDP was 5.6 per cent and the maximum fall was 2.8 per cent. By contrast, the maximum annual rise in investment was 17.6 per cent and the maximum fall was 11.7 per cent.

If we focus on *manufacturing* investment, the swings were even greater. The maximum annual rise in manufacturing investment in plant and machinery was 20 per cent and the maximum fall was 28 per cent, and in new buildings and works the maximum annual rise was a massive 64 per cent and the maximum fall was 38 per cent.

These figures are consistent with the accelerator theory which argues that the *level* of investment depends on the *rate of change* of national income. A relatively small percentage change in national income can give a much bigger percentage change in investment. The graph shows this pattern over the 11 years from 1978 to 1989.

As you can see, the ups and downs in GDP and investment do not completely match. This is because there are additional factors that determine investment other than simple changes in national income.

Interest rates

Real interest rates rose dramatically after 1979 but then fell again after 1983.

Exchange rates

The exchange rate rose sharply from 1978 to 1981 and then fell sharply until early 1985, after which it rose initially and then remained relatively stable at the end of the period.

A high exchange rate makes UK goods more expensive abroad and thus more difficult to sell. This discourages UK exporting firms from investing.

Business expectations

Investment does not just depend on current or recent changes in demand, it also depends on business expectations of future demand. (Box 14.5 examined the role of these business expectations.) Although business expectations are naturally to some extent dependent on the current rate of growth of GDP, they are also influenced by many other domestic and international economic and political events.

1. Are there any time lags that you can identify in the graph? Why might there be time lags?
2. Why does investment in construction and producer goods industries tend to fluctuate more than investment in retailing and the service industries?

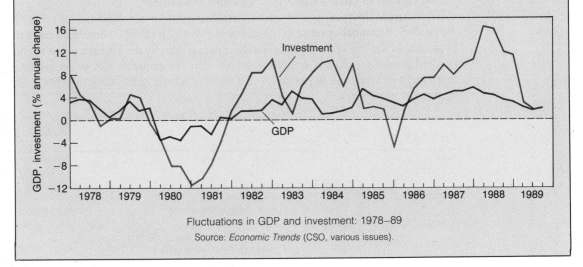

Fluctuations in GDP and investment: 1978–89

Source: *Economic Trends* (CSO, various issues).

The multiplier/accelerator interaction

If there is an initial change in injections or withdrawals, then theoretically this will set off a chain reaction between the multiplier and accelerator. For example, if there is a rise in government expenditure, this will lead to a multiplied rise in national income. But this *rise* in national income will set off an accelerator effect: firms will respond to the rise in income and the resulting rise in consumer demand by investing more. But this rise in investment constitutes a further rise in injections and thus will lead to a second multiplied rise in income. If this rise in income is larger than the first, there will then be a second rise in investment (the accelerator), which in turn will cause a third rise in income (the multiplier). And so the process continues indefinitely. Each time investment changes it will cause a change in national income. Each time national income changes it will cause a change in investment.

But does this lead to an exploding rise in national income? Will a single injection cause national income to go on rising for ever? The answer is no. There are two reasons for this. The first is the obvious one that national income, in real terms, cannot go on rising faster than the growth in potential output. It will bump up against the ceiling of full employment, whether of labour or of other resources. Firms cannot go on investing if there are not the machines available to buy, or the space to install them, or the workers to operate them.

But there is a second reason why the multiplier/accelerator interaction will not lead to an ever growing national income. If investment is to go on rising, it is not enough that national income should merely go on *rising*: instead, national income must *rise faster and faster*. Once the growth in national income slows down, investment will begin to fall, and then the whole process will be reversed. A fall in investment will lead to a fall in national income, which will lead to a massive fall in investment. But then, perhaps after several years of little or no investment, firms will find that their stock of capital has fallen so much, or that their machines have become so out of date, that they will have to start making replacement investment. This can then trigger off an upswing in the economy, and once more the multiplier and accelerator will interact to create an economic boom.

You can see from this that the interaction of the multiplier and accelerator alone will be enough to cause cyclical upswings and downswings.

To illustrate the process a bit more formally, consider the sequence of events in Table 14.5. An initial upsurge in injections in period t leads to a cumulative increase in income as the multiplier and accelerator interact. But by the time the economy has reached period $t + 2$, it is no longer certain that the economy will go on growing. Investment will only rise in period $t + 2$ if national income grew more in period $t + 1$ than it did in period t.

Table 14.5 The multiplier/accelerator interaction

Period t	$J\uparrow \rightarrow Y\uparrow$	(Multiplier)
Period $t + 1$	$Y\uparrow \rightarrow I$	(Accelerator)
	$I\uparrow \rightarrow Y\uparrow$	(Multiplier)
Period $t + 2$	If $\uparrow Y_{t+1} > \uparrow Y_t$ then $I\uparrow$	
	If $\uparrow Y_{t+1} = \uparrow Y_t$ then I stays the same	(Accelerator)
	If $\uparrow Y_{t+1} < \uparrow Y_t$ then $I\downarrow$	
	This in turn will have a multiplied upward effect, no effect, or a multiplied downward effect respectively on national income.	
Period $t + 3$	This will then lead to a further accelerator effect and so on . . .	

Note that the full multiplier effect will not have taken place each time before there is an accelerator effect. Only one 'round' of the multiplier effect will be necessary to trigger a change in investment. By a 'round' we mean one complete time round the circular flow of income, or one 'period'.

Fluctuations in stocks

Firms hold stocks of finished goods. These stocks tend to fluctuate with the course of the trade cycle, and these fluctuations in stocks themselves contribute to fluctuations in output.

Imagine an economy that is recovering from a recession. At first firms may be cautious about increasing production. Doing so may involve taking on more labour or entering into a contract with suppliers for more inputs or even making additional investment. Firms may not want to make these commitments if the recovery could soon peter out. As a result firms respond to the extra demand by initially running down their stocks rather than increasing output. This will mean that initially the recovery from recession will be slow.

After a time, however, if the recovery does continue, firms will start to gain more confidence. As a result they will increase their production. Also they will find that their stocks have got rather low and will need building up. This gives a further boost to production, and for a time the growth in output will exceed the growth in demand. This extra growth in output will then, via the multiplier, lead to a further increase in demand.

Once stocks have been built up again, the growth in output will slow down to match the growth in demand. This slowing down in output will, via the accelerator and multiplier, contribute to the ending of the expansionary phase of the trade cycle.

As the economy slows down, retailers will find themselves with unsold goods on their shelves. They will thus order less from the wholesalers, who in turn will find that their stocks begin to build up. The wholesalers will thus order less from the manufacturers, who, unless they cut back production immediately, will find their stocks building up too. Initially, then, as the recession sets in, production will fall only slowly. The increase in stocks cushions the effect of falling demand on output and employment.

If the recession continues, however, and hopes for a quick recovery wane, firms will be unwilling to go on building up stocks: they will soon run into cash flow problems if they do. But as firms attempt to reduce their stocks back to the desired level, production will fall below the level of sales, despite the fact that sales themselves are lower. This could therefore lead to a dramatic fall in output, which, via the multiplier, will lead to an even bigger fall in sales. The problem is made even worse if firms, in an attempt to cut their costs and arrest their falling profits, cut back production even further and run their stocks down to an even lower level than normal.

Eventually, once stocks have been run down to the minimum, production will have to rise again to match the level of sales. This will contribute to a recovery and the whole cycle will start again.

Analyzing the phases of the trade cycle

Having identified some of the major factors contributing to fluctuations in aggregate demand, we are now in a position to paint a more complete Keynesian picture of the trade cycle. We shall look at each phase in turn and identify the range of possible reasons why aggregate demand is moving in that particular direction.

Box 14.9

Heavenly Cycles
Looking for spots on the sun

Many different theories of the trade cycle have been put forward over the years. Unlike Keynesian theories, some of them have focused on the supply side, and some of these have looked to natural phenomena as the cause of supply fluctuations.

One of the most bizarre of these theories was that put forward by Jevons in the late nineteenth century. He blamed trade cycles on sunspots!

The sun goes through cycles of activity. When the sun is at its most active there is a high occurrence of sunspots. Jevons noted that these sunspot cycles had an average duration of 10.45 years and that trade cycles between 1721 and 1878 had an average duration of 10.46 years!

Of course this could have been a sheer fluke. Certainly mere statistical correlation does not prove causality: just because two things occur at the same time it does not prove that one *causes* the other. Nevertheless Jevons believed that the correlation between the two cycles was too close to be accidental.

So what was the causal mechanism? Sunspots, argued Jevons, affect the weather; weather affects the harvest; harvests affect economic prosperity. In a predominantly agricultural country, bumper harvests can cause boom conditions, whereas poor harvests can cause declining incomes. Even if price elasticities of demand for food are low, so that good harvests depress farm incomes, this will be more than compensated for by rising real incomes of food consumers (i.e. everyone else).

There turned out to be a serious flaw in Jevons' theory, however: on recalculation, the sunspot cycles were found to be 11 years long, not 10.45. So much for that theory!

? Invent a theory. Find two seemingly unrelated things that tend to go together. (They need not be economic.) Then construct a hypothesis to show how they might be related. Is your theory a good theory? Could your theory be disproved other than by an appeal to contradictory *evidence*?

Notice that it is the *demand* side of the economy we are focusing on. This is why we call the analysis 'Keynesian'.

In an advanced analysis the possible causes of fluctuations in demand could be combined into a mathematical model. Economic forecasters use such models in predicting the future course of the economy. At this level, however, we must confine ourselves merely to *identifying* the possible causes. We will take each phase of the trade cycle in turn.

Phase 1: The upturn

During the recession fewer machines were needed and thus many worn-out machines were not even replaced. Investment was very low. Gradually, as the stock of machines is reduced, replacement investment re-emerges. This can be more dramatic if a lot of machines were purchased within a short time during the previous expansionary phase and now need replacing. This is an 'echo' effect of the previous expansion. $I \uparrow \rightarrow AD \uparrow$

Consumer durables (cars, televisions, washing machines, etc.) that were bought in the previous period of expansion will now be wearing out and will start needing to be replaced. This is another echo effect. $C_d \uparrow \rightarrow AD \uparrow$

Firms during the recession initially found that their stocks of finished goods increased as sales fell. They therefore cut back on production while drawing on these surplus stocks. Once stocks are back down to the desirable level again, production will increase. $AD \uparrow$

As the rate of inflation falls during the recession, and there may be a time lag before this occurs, so exports should rise as they become relatively less expensive for foreigners to buy. At the same time imports should fall as home-produced substitutes become relatively cheaper. Consumers of both exports and imports may take a time to respond to the changing relative prices. The effects on aggregate demand may therefore only become significant after the recession has continued for some time. $X\uparrow, M\downarrow \rightarrow AD\uparrow$

After the recession has continued for some time, people may begin to believe that a recovery will soon be on the way. After all, there is the experience of previous trade cycles: recessions have never lasted for ever. This anticipation of recovery may encourage firms to start investing again and consumers to start buying more durables. $I\uparrow, C_d\uparrow \rightarrow AD\uparrow$

Consumption and investment are low during the recession. Borrowing from banks is therefore likely to be low. Banks will thus have surplus funds and interest rates (r) will be low. This stimulates borrowing, especially if people begin to anticipate that recovery is just around the corner. $r\downarrow \rightarrow C_d\uparrow, I\uparrow \rightarrow AD\uparrow$

As the balance of payments improves during the recession and the rate of inflation falls, the government may turn its attention to tackling the growing unemployment and falling or stagnant output. It will use reflationary fiscal and/or monetary policy. In other words, it will use some combination of lower taxes, higher government expenditure and lower interest rates. $T\downarrow, G\uparrow, r\downarrow \rightarrow AD\uparrow$

Firms and consumers may anticipate such government policy and spend more even before the measures are announced. $I\uparrow, C_d\uparrow \rightarrow AD\uparrow$

Random events may stimulate demand: for example, the settling of a major international dispute, a fall in the world oil price, the election of a new US president, or the discovery of large new oil fields in the country. These 'random shocks', as they are called, can occur at any point in the trade cycle, and if large enough can have a significant effect on its course.

Phase 2: The expansion

Most of the factors that caused the recovery are likely to go on stimulating the economy for some time.

Initial increases in aggregate demand will cause a *multiplied* rise in income and hence demand.

Rises in income will lead, via the *accelerator*, to increases in investment. This accelerator effect will be large at first, given that there had been little or no rise in consumer demand during the recession.

The multiplier and accelerator will interact.

Firms, finding that stocks are beginning to run low, will increase production not only to meet extra sales but also to rebuild stocks.

People begin to anticipate rising prices. Thus both firms and consumers stock up now while prices are still relatively low.

Firms anticipate further rises in demand and hence invest now in both capital and stock.

Phase 3: The peaking out

Many firms reach capacity and hence cannot increase output further even if they would like to.

The consumer spending boom levels out. People have now purchased all the consumer durables they can currently afford. $C_d\downarrow \rightarrow AD\downarrow$

According to the accelerator theory, a levelling-out of consumption will lead to a fall in investment. $I\downarrow \rightarrow AD\downarrow$

Firms anticipate the impending recession and invest less. $I\downarrow \rightarrow AD\downarrow$

The growing demand for bank loans during the period of expansion has driven up interest rates. This will help to curtail further growth in consumption and investment. $r\uparrow \rightarrow C_d\downarrow, I\downarrow \rightarrow AD\downarrow$

Inflation has been rising during the latter part of the expansionary phase. The government is likely to take counter-inflationary measures. This will involve some combination of lower government expenditure, higher taxes or higher interest rates. $G\downarrow, T\uparrow \rightarrow AD\downarrow; r\uparrow \rightarrow C_d\downarrow, I\downarrow \rightarrow AD\downarrow$

Higher inflation makes exports less competitive abroad. Exports thus fall. $X\downarrow \rightarrow AD\downarrow$

Higher inflation makes imports relatively cheaper than home-produced goods. Imports thus rise. $M\uparrow \rightarrow AD\downarrow$

Various random shocks may bring a boom to an abrupt end: e.g. a war, a sudden oil price rise or a stock market crash.

Phase 4: The recession

Many of the factors that led to a downturn in aggregate demand in the previous phase are still operative. Some work with a time lag and their effect is still building up.

Business prospects are poor. Confidence is low. Investment remains very low. The effects on the capital goods industries may thus be very severe.

If aggregate demand actually falls (as opposed to merely being stagnant), there will be a resulting multiplied fall in income.

The government may be unwilling to stimulate the economy as long as the inflation rate remains high and/or the balance of payments current account remains in deficit. These problems may take some time to be brought under control.

Firms, finding their stocks of unsold goods rising, cut back on production. They may even attempt to reduce stocks to the bare minimum in order to save costs. In such cases the cuts in production may be very large indeed.

Conclusions

Let us return to the first two of the four questions we posed back at the beginning of this section.

Why do booms and recessions last for several months or even years?
Explanations for this include the following.

Time lags. It takes time for changes in injections and withdrawals to be fully reflected in changes in national income, output and employment. The multiplier process takes time: it takes time for money to go round and round the circular flow of income. Consumers, firms and government may not all respond immediately to new situations. Their responses are spread out over a period of time.

'Bandwagon' effects. Once the economy starts expanding, expectations become buoyant. People think ahead and adjust their expenditure behaviour: they consume and invest more *now*. Likewise in a recession a mood of pessimism may set in. The effect is cumulative. The multiplier and accelerator interact: they feed on each other.

Why do booms and recessions come to an end? What determines the turning points?
Explanations for this include the following.

Ceilings and floors. Actual output can only go on growing more rapidly than potential output as long as there is slack in the economy. As full employment is approached and as more and more firms reach full capacity, so a ceiling to output will be reached. Firms simply cannot produce more, even though they would like to.

There is a basic minimum level of consumption that people will maintain. During a recession people may not buy much in the way of luxury and durable goods, but they will still continue to buy food and other basic goods. There is thus a floor to consumption.

The industries supplying these basic goods will need to maintain their level of replacement investment. Also there will always be some minimum investment demand as firms, in order to survive competition, feel the need to install the latest equipment as it becomes available. There is thus a floor to investment too.

Echo effects. Durable consumer goods and capital equipment may last several years, but eventually they will need replacing. The replacement of goods and capital purchased in a previous boom may help to bring a recession to an end.

The accelerator. For investment to continue rising, consumer demand must rise at a *faster and faster* rate. If this does not happen, investment will fall back and the boom will break.

Random shocks. National or international political, social or natural events can affect the mood and attitudes of firms, governments and consumers, and thus affect aggregate demand.

Changes in government policy. In a boom, a government may become most worried by inflation and balance of payments deficits and thus pursue deflationary policies. In a recession, it may become most worried by unemployment and lack of growth and thus pursue reflationary policies. These government policies, if successful, will bring about a turning point in the cycle.

Keynesians argue that governments should attempt to reduce cyclical fluctuations by the use of active stabilization policies. A more stable economy will provide a better climate for long-term investment. It will help to reduce uncertainty about the future. Higher long-term investment will increase the growth in *potential* output and thus allow a faster growth in actual output to be maintained.

The policy most favoured by Keynesians for stabilizing the economy is *fiscal policy*. This is the subject of Chapter 15.

 SUMMARY

1. Keynesians explain cyclical fluctuations in the economy by examining the causes of fluctuations in the level of *demand*.
2. A major part of the Keynesian explanation of the trade cycle is the instability of investment. The accelerator theory explains this instability. It relates the level of investment to *changes* in national income and consumer demand. An initial increase in consumer demand can result in a very large percentage increase in investment; but as soon as the rise in consumer demand begins to level off investment will fall; and even a slight fall in consumer demand can reduce investment to virtually zero.
3. The accelerator effect will be dampened by the carrying of stocks, the cautiousness of firms, forward planning by firms and the inability of producer goods industries to supply the capital equipment.
4. The interaction of the multiplier and accelerator will cause cycles.
5. Keynesians identify other causes of cyclical fluctuations, such as cycles in the holding of stocks, time lags, 'bandwagon' effects, ceilings and floors to output, echo effects, swings in government policy and random shocks.

15 Fiscal policy

15.1 The nature of fiscal policy

For most of the 1950s and 1960s fiscal policy was seen as the major way of controlling the economy. There were two reasons for this. The first was that economists and politicians were generally of the Keynesian view that it was aggregate *demand* that determined the level of output, employment, inflation and the balance of payments. Given the belief that a free-market economy could not be relied upon to achieve the right amount of aggregate demand, it would be necessary for it to be managed by the government. The second reason for favouring fiscal policy was the belief that the alternative way of controlling demand, namely monetary policy, was ineffective.

Fiscal policy was seen to have two main roles. The first was to remove any severe deflationary or inflationary gaps. In other words, expansionary fiscal policy could be used to prevent a recurrence of the mass unemployment that was experienced between the wars, and deflationary fiscal policy could be used to prevent rampant inflation. This first role was to prevent the occurrence of *fundamental* disequilibrium in the economy. Keynesian economists today still argue that fiscal policy has this role.

The second role was to smooth out the fluctuations in the economy associated with the trade cycle. This would involve reducing government expenditure or raising taxes during phase 2 of the cycle. This would dampen down the expansion and prevent 'overheating' of the economy with its attendant rising inflation and deteriorating balance of payments. Conversely, during phase 4, as the problems of unemployment and declining output get worse, the government should cut taxes or raise government expenditure in order to boost the economy. If these stabilization policies are successful, they will amount merely to fine tuning. Problems of excess or deficient demand will never be allowed to get severe. Any movement of aggregate demand away from a steady growth path would be immediately 'nipped in the bud'. Virtually no economist argued then or now that perfect fine tuning is possible. There will always be some fluctuations in aggregate demand. Nevertheless many Keynesians argue that the careful use of fiscal policy can make the economy much *more* stable than it would otherwise be.

Fine tuning

The use of demand management policy (fiscal or monetary) to smooth out cyclical fluctuations in the economy.

Government finances: some terminology

Budget deficits and surpluses

An expansionary fiscal policy will involve raising government expenditure and/or lowering taxes. This will have the effect of either increasing the budget deficit or

Box 15.1

A Little Bit Less of This and a Little Bit More of That
Fine tuning in 1959 and 1960

The following extracts are from the Budget television broadcasts in 1959 and 1960 by the Conservative Chancellor, Derick Heathcoat Amory.

In the first, Heathcoat Amory explained that inflation was sufficiently under control and that there was enough slack in the economy to allow a modest reflation. The interviewer asked him, 'We understood about a year ago that having more unemployed was part of the price we had to pay for stabilizing the cost of living. Now if we are going to have less unemployment in the next year does that mean that the cost of living is likely to go up?'

Heathcoat Amory replied:

No I don't think so. It's all a question of balance, and up to a year or so ago we'd been suffering ever since the war from inflation and excess demand, and that was pushing up prices and also involving us in balance of payments difficulties. So we had to damp down demand a bit until we could see that we'd got rid of inflation. Now we've got rid of inflation we can go steadily ahead again with

production without running the risk, I think, of pushing up prices.

A year later the economy was growing more rapidly and showing signs of overheating. In his Budget television interview he this time justified a deflationary Budget:

If you remember last year we had a situation where then things were a bit slack. There was spare manpower and spare factory capacity and things wanted just brisking up a bit and stimulating, and so we had a sort of reflationary Budget and then I was able to do all sorts of pleasant things like reduce taxation. But now things are a little bit the other way around and we've had a prosperous year of expansion, and I'm very glad of it. Now we've just got to watch our step. We don't want to hold back things and stop expansion, far less reverse it, but the time's come when it is right just to steady the pace a bit.

? Did Heathcoat Amory's 1960 Budget broadcast suggest that he had been wrong in 1959 to reflate the economy?

---

reducing the budget surplus. A budget deficit in any one year is where central government's expenditure exceeds its revenue from taxation. A budget surplus is where tax revenues exceed central government expenditure.

The government ran a budget deficit through most of the 1950s and 1960s. For a short period at the end of the 1960s the government had a surplus. After 1971, however, the budget was once more back in deficit and stayed so until 1987. Substantial budget surpluses were then experienced until 1991.

Financing a deficit

If the government spends more than it receives in taxes, how is it to finance this deficit? The answer is that it will have to borrow the money. It can do this either by borrowing from the Bank of England or by selling government securities. There are two types of government security: Treasury bills and government bonds. Treasury bills are short-term loans to the government (three months). Bonds are long-term loans (several years). At the end of the loan period, the government redeems the securities at their face value. To persuade people to buy these securities the government has to pay interest or, what amounts to the same thing, sell them below their redemption value.

Details of the two types of security and how their rates of interest are determined are given in Chapters 16 and 17, but for now we will simply observe that, if the government wants to sell more of these securities, it will have to sell them at a lower price or offer a higher rate of interest.

Budget deficit
The excess of central government's spending over its tax receipts.

Budget surplus
The excess of central government's tax receipts over its spending.

The national debt

The budget deficit refers to the debt that the government incurs in one year. If the government runs persistent deficits over many years, these debts will accumulate. The accumulated debt is known as the national debt. Note that the national debt is *not* the same thing as the country's overseas debt. Only a relatively small fraction of the national debt is owed overseas. The bulk of it is owed to UK citizens. In other words, the government finances its budget deficits largely by borrowing at home and not from abroad.

The PSBR and PSDR

So far we have looked at merely the *central* government deficit or surplus. To get a more complete view of the overall 'stance' of fiscal policy – just how expansionary or contractionary it is – we would need to look at the deficit or surplus of the entire public sector: namely, central government, local government and public corporations. If the public sector spends more than it earns (through taxes and the revenues of the nationalized industries, etc.), the amount of this deficit is known as the public-sector borrowing requirement (PSBR). It is defined as: the total expenditure of central government, local government, nationalized industries and other public sector expenditure minus the tax revenues of central and local government, the sales revenues of the nationalized industries and licence fees of public corporations (such as the BBC): i.e. public sector expenditure minus public sector receipts.

The reason for the name 'public-sector borrowing requirement' is simple. If the public sector runs a deficit in the current year of, say, £1 billion, then it will have to borrow £1 billion this year in order to finance it.

If the public sector runs a surplus, it will be able to repay some of the public-sector debts that have accumulated from previous years. In 1987, when for the first time since 1971 the UK ran a public-sector surplus, this was given the name public-sector debt repayment (PSDR) by the then Chancellor, Nigel Lawson. Table 15.1 shows the PSBR/PSDR from 1965 to 1989.

National debt

The accumulated budget deficits (less surpluses) over the years: the total amount of government borrowing.

Public-sector borrowing requirement (PSBR)

The (annual) deficit of the public sector (central government, local government and public corporations), and thus the amount that the public sector must borrow.

Public-sector debt repayment (PSDR)

The (annual) surplus of the public sector, and thus the amount of debt that can be repaid.

Table 15.1 UK public-sector deficits/surpluses: 1965–89

Year	1965	1966	1967	1968	1969	1970	1971	1972	1973	1974
PSBR (£m)	1170	949	1844	1252			1320	1950	4093	6452
PSDR (£m)					534	51				
GDP (£bn)	31.6	33.5	35.2	38.0	40.2	44.3	50.0	56.6	65.5	75.3

Year	1975	1976	1977	1978	1979	1980	1981	1982	1983	1984
PSBR (£m)	10 161	9000	5466	8195	12 551	11 786	10 507	4880	11 605	10 281
GDP (£bn)	95.2	112.0	128.9	148.8	172.4	200.0	217.8	237.3	259.8	279.1

Year	1985	1986	1987	1988	1989
PSBR (£m)	7476	2418			
PSDR (£m)			1432	11 611	9147
GDP (£bn)	304.7	322.2	352.2	391.6	426.0

Source: *Annual Abstract of Statistics* (CSO, 1990).

The public-sector debt

Just as the national debt was the total outstanding debt of central government, so the public-sector debt is the total outstanding debt of the entire public sector. Table 15.2 shows the level of public-sector debt since 1977. As can be seen from the figures, although the total debt increased over the period (due to persistent annual deficits)

Table 15.2 UK national and public-sector debt

Year	National debt (£m)	Public-sector debt (£m)	Public-sector debt as a percentage of GDP	Public-sector debt held overseas as a percentage of GDP
1977	52 748	88 287	62.9	9.8
1982	103 884	147 640	54.4	6.2
1987	168 129	205 050	53.2	6.9

Source: *Annual Abstract of Statistics* (CSO).

the size of the debt as a proportion of national income fell. Note the relatively small proportion of UK public-sector debt owed abroad.

Public-sector deficits and surpluses and the government's 'fiscal stance'

The government's fiscal stance refers to whether it is pursuing an expansionary or contractionary fiscal policy. Does the fact that there was a public-sector deficit right from 1971 to 1986 mean that the government's fiscal stance was reflationary throughout this period? Would the mere existence of a *surplus* mean that the stance was deflationary? The answer is no.

Fiscal stance
How deflationary or reflationary the Budget is.

What we need to discover is whether the current *size* of the public-sector deficit or surplus is causing aggregate demand to expand or contract (and by how much). This will depend on two things:

● The previous level of the deficit (or surplus). If the deficit this year is lower than last year, then (*ceteris paribus*) aggregate demand will be lower this year than last. It is thus whether the deficit (or surplus) is rising or falling that is important rather than its simple level.
● Changes in other components of aggregate demand. Government expenditure is only one of the three injections into the circular flow of income. Taxation is only one of the three withdrawals. If one of the *other* injections or withdrawals changes, then this will affect the required size of the public-sector deficit or surplus to achieve any given level of national income. For example, if business optimism was low and as a result investment had fallen by £2 million, then even if the level of government expenditure was increased, with a consequent increase in the public-sector deficit, the increase in government expenditure would have to be more than £2 million if there was to be an increase in national income. If it only rose by, say, £1 million, there would be a fall in national income.

The mere existence of a deficit or surplus therefore tells us very little about whether the economy will expand or contract.

Another problem is that the size of the deficit or surplus is not entirely due to deliberate government policy. It may not give a very good guide, therefore, to government intentions. The size of the deficit or surplus will depend on the state of the economy. If the economy is booming with people earning high incomes, the amount paid in taxes will be high. In a booming economy the level of unemployment will be low. Thus the amount paid out in unemployment benefits will also be low. The combined effect of increased taxes and reduced government expenditure is to give a public-sector surplus (or a reduced deficit). By contrast, if the economy was depressed, tax revenues would be low and government expenditure on benefits would be high. The public-sector deficit would thus be high.

This relationship between the budget deficit or surplus and the state of the

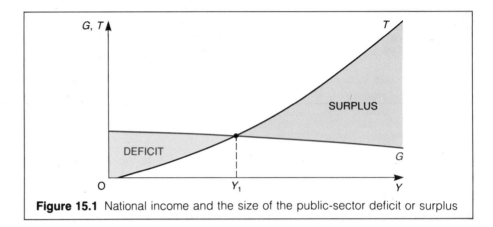

Figure 15.1 National income and the size of the public-sector deficit or surplus

economy is illustrated in Figure 15.1. The tax function is upward sloping. Its slope is given by the marginal propensity to pay taxes (*mpt*), which in turn depends on tax rates. The government expenditure function is drawn as downward sloping, showing that at higher levels of income and employment less is paid out in benefits. As can be clearly seen, there is only one level of income (Y_1) where there is a public-sector financial balance. Below this level of income there will be a public-sector deficit. Above this level there will be a surplus. The further income is from Y_1, the bigger will be the deficit or surplus.

To conclude, the size of the deficit or surplus is a poor guide to the stance of fiscal policy. A large deficit *may* be due to a deliberate policy of reflation, but it may be due simply to the fact that the economy is depressed.

Automatic fiscal stabilizers

We saw from Figure 15.1 that the size of the public-sector surplus or deficit will automatically vary according to the level of national income. The effect of this will be to reduce the level of fluctuations in national income without the government having to take any deliberate action.

Taxes whose revenues rise as national income rises and government expenditures that fall as national income rises are called automatic stabilizers. They have the effect of reducing the size of the multiplier. They therefore reduce both upward movements and downward movements of national income. Thus, in theory, the trade cycle should be dampened by such built-in stabilizers. The more taxes rise (i.e. the bigger the *mpt*) and the more government expenditure falls, the bigger will be the stabilizing effect.

To illustrate how they work let us concentrate on taxes. Figure 15.2 looks at two

Automatic fiscal stabilizers

Tax revenues that rise and government expenditure that falls as national income rises. The more they change with income, the bigger the stabilizing effect on income.

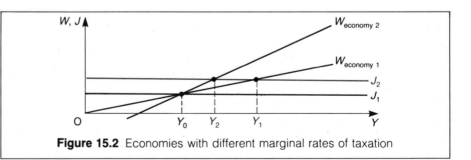

Figure 15.2 Economies with different marginal rates of taxation

economies. Economy 1 has a low marginal rate of taxation (a low *mpt*). As a result its withdrawals function is relatively gently sloping. Economy 2 has a much higher marginal rate of tax. Its withdrawals function is relatively steep. As we shall see, taxes act as a bigger automatic stabilizer in economy 2 than in economy 1.

Assume that the two economies both have the same initial level of injections J_1 and that the withdrawals functions of the two economies both intersect J_1 at an equilibrium national income of Y_0. Now assume that there is an autonomous rise in injections – perhaps the level of business confidence has risen with a corresponding rise in investment. The effect in economy 1 is for national income to rise to Y_1. The relatively shallow *W* line (i.e. a low *mpw*) gives a large multiplier effect. In economy 2, however, national income only rises to Y_2. The relatively steep *W* line (i.e. a high *mpw*), caused by a high *mpt*, gives a smaller multiplier effect.

To summarize: the higher the *mpt*, the higher the *mpw* and hence the smaller the multiplier, and hence the bigger the stabilizing effect of the taxes.

1. The withdrawals functions in Figure 15.2 were based on the assumption that the rate of tax, although higher in economy 2, was nevertheless constant in each case. Redraw the diagram, only this time assume that the rate of tax in economy 2 is progressive: i.e. that it increases as income increases. How will this affect the stabilizing properties of the tax?
2. Will a highly progressive tax system have as strong an effect on reducing slumps as it does on reducing booms? (Draw a diagram showing the effect of an equal-sized fall and rise in injections.)

Virtually all taxes (except the community charge) fall into the category of automatic stabilizers. The only government expenditures to fall into this category, however, are unemployment and social security benefits and possibly various subsidies that are paid to ailing industries or to support agricultural incomes. These automatic changes in government expenditure also reduce the multiplier. Being transfer payments, as opposed to direct government expenditures on goods and services, these benefits only reduce the multiplier indirectly via reductions in people's incomes. The formula for the multiplier would now be:

$$\frac{1}{mpw + (mpc_d' \times mrg)}$$

where *mrg* is the marginal reduction in government expenditure (the reduction in government expenditure divided by the rise in national income) and mpc_d' is the proportion of it that would have been spent. Thus if a rise in national income of £100 million led to benefits being cut by £10 million (*mrg* = 0.1) and as a result consumption being cut by £8 million (mpc_d' = 0.8), then the term ($mpc_d' \times mrg$) would be 0.8 × 0.1 = 0.08.

The bigger the cut in benefit as income rises, and hence the bigger the value of *mrg*, the bigger will the term $mpw + (mpc_d' \times mrg)$ be, and hence the smaller the multiplier, and hence the bigger the stabilizing effect.

Will the mpc_d' (the proportion of a change in benefits being spent on domestic consumption) be the same as the overall mpc_d? Explain.

The stabilizing effect of benefits is shown in Figure 15.3. Again two economies are shown. In economy 1 there are no income-related benefits. The *J* 'curve' is horizontal. In economy 2 there are such benefits. They have the effect of making the *J* curve downward sloping.

Assume initially that in both economies equilibrium is at the same level of income,

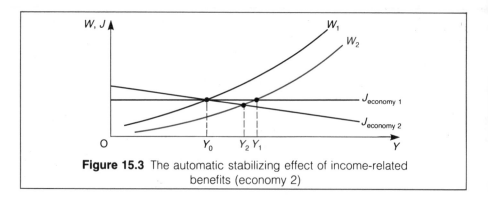

Figure 15.3 The automatic stabilizing effect of income-related benefits (economy 2)

with both J curves intersecting with W_1 at Y_0. Now assume that the W curve shifts downwards, causing a multiplied rise in national income. In the case of economy 1, where there are no income-related benefits (and hence no automatic stabilizer on the government expenditure side), national income rises to Y_1. In the case of economy 2, the income-related benefits have the effect of dampening the rise in national income. Income only rises to Y_2.

Discretionary fiscal policy

Automatic stabilizers cannot prevent fluctuations. They merely reduce their magnitude. If there is a fundamental disequilibrium in the economy or substantial fluctuations in other injections and withdrawals, the government may choose to *alter* the level of government expenditure or the rates of taxation. This is known as discretionary fiscal policy. It involves *shifting* the J and W lines.

Discretionary fiscal policy

Deliberate changes in tax rates or the level of government expenditure in order to influence the level of aggregate demand.

Changes in government expenditure for the next financial year (April to March) are announced by the Chancellor of the Exchequer in October. This is known as the Chancellor's 'autumn statement'. Changes in taxation for the coming financial year are announced in the Budget. This is held in early spring just before the start of the financial year.

In the past, governments sometimes felt it necessary to have more than one Budget a year in order to be able to respond more quickly to changing economic circumstances. These additional Budgets were known as 'mini Budgets'. Nowadays, however, Budgets are only held once a year. 'Fine tuning' aggregate demand on a week-by-week or month by month basis is left to monetary policy – to changes in interest rates (see Chapter 17).

Discretionary changes in taxation or government expenditure, as well as being used to alter the level of aggregate demand, are also used for other purposes, including the following:

- Altering aggregate supply. The tax system may be altered so as to provide more incentives (e.g. by cutting the top rates of income tax). This, it is argued, will encourage more investment, more initiative and more risk taking. Government expenditure may be directed into building up the infrastructure of the economy (e.g. new roads) or into providing grants for research and development or the training of labour.
- Altering the distribution of income. As Chapter 9 explained, government transfer payments and taxation are major weapons in redistributing incomes from the rich to the poor.

- Altering the degree of state ownership and intervention. For ideological reasons governments may want a larger or smaller amount of state ownership and intervention in industry.

When we refer to 'fiscal policy', however, we are normally referring to the use of government expenditure and taxation specifically to control aggregate demand. Of course, changes in G or T can be made for more than one purpose. For example, if an expansionary fiscal policy were required, taxes could be reduced so as to boost aggregate demand, but at the same time bigger tax cuts could be given to the poor than to the rich so as to redistribute incomes more equally.

Let us now compare the relative effects of changing government expenditure and changing taxes. Will a £1 million increase in government expenditure have the same effect as a £1 million cut in taxes? Will the multiplier be the same in each case?

Discretionary fiscal policy: changing G

If government expenditure on goods and services (roads, health care, education, etc.) is raised, this will create a full multiplied rise in national income. The reason is that all the money gets spent and thus all of it goes to boosting aggregate demand.

Diagrammatically, it has the effect of shifting the J line upward by the full amount of the increase in government expenditure. In Figure 15.4 this is shown as a shift in the J line from J_1 to J_2. This gives a full multiplied rise in income from Y_{e_1} to Y_{e_2}. The size of the multiplier (as you should know by now!) is given by $1/mpw$.

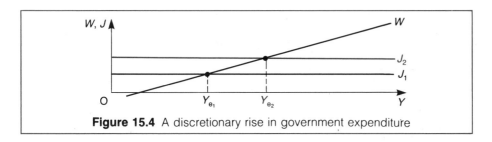

Figure 15.4 A discretionary rise in government expenditure

 Show the effect of an increase in government expenditure by using the income/expenditure diagram.

Discretionary fiscal policy: changing T

Cutting taxes by £1 million will have a smaller effect on national income than raising government expenditure on goods and services by £1 million. The reason is that cutting taxes increases people's *disposable* incomes, of which only *part* will be spent. Part will be withdrawn into extra savings, imports and other taxes. In other words, not all the tax cuts will be passed on round the circular flow of income as extra expenditure.

The proportion of the cut in taxes that will be withdrawn is given by the mpw, and the proportion that will circulate round the flow is given by the mpc_d. Thus if the mpc_d were 4/5, the tax multiplier would only be 4/5 of the normal multiplier. If the mpc_d were 2/3, the tax multiplier would only be 2/3 of the normal multiplier, and so on. The formula for the tax multiplier (k_t) becomes:[1]

$$k_t = mpc_d \times k$$

Thus if the normal multiplier was 5 (given an mpc_d of 4/5), the tax multiplier would be $4/5 \times 5 = 4$. If the normal multiplier was 4 (given an mpc_d of 3/4), the tax multiplier

---

[1] Strictly speaking, the tax multiplier is negative, since a *rise* in taxes causes a *fall* in national income.

Box 15.2

The Balanced Budget Multiplier
How to boost demand without increasing the budget deficit

Suppose that the government raised its expenditure by £1 million and at the same time raised taxes by £1 million in order to finance it. What would happen to aggregate demand?

At first sight the answer would seem to be 'nothing'. After all, injections have been raised by £1 million but withdrawals would seem also to have been raised by £1 million.

But this is not so. Although taxes have risen by £1 million, *net* withdrawals have risen by *less* than £1 million. The reason is that part of the extra taxes is met by reductions in savings and imports. Consumption of domestic product therefore does not fall by the full £1 million that government expenditure has risen. There is thus a net boost to the economy given by the amount that the net withdrawals fall short of the increase in government expenditure. This boost will then be multiplied by the size of the full multiplier.

How much will national income rise? The answer is £1 million. In other words, the *balanced budget multiplier* has a value of 1. But why?

If the *mpw* is 1/5, for example, the full multiplier is 5. If G and T both rise by £1 million, 1/5 of the rise in taxes

will be financed from reduced withdrawals: i.e. £200 000. This boost to demand will then be multiplied by the full multiplier of 5, giving a total rise in income of £200 000 × 5 = £1 million.

Algebraically, the formula for the balanced budget multiplier (k_b) is:

$$k_b = mpw \times k$$
$$= mpw \times 1/mpw$$
$$= 1$$

Thus it is possible for a government committed to maintaining a balanced budget to boost demand without unbalancing its budget. The problem is that, with such a small multiplier, it would need a much larger increase in G and T to achieve the same result as by increasing G alone.

? Suppose that the economy is in recession and that the government wishes to maintain a balanced budget and not to increase the size of the public sector. Is it possible for it to use fiscal policy to reflate the economy?

---

would be 3/4 × 4 = 3. If the normal multiplier were 3 (given an mpc_d of 2/3), the tax multiplier would be 2/3 × 3 = 2, and so on. It should be obvious from this that the tax multiplier is always 1 less than the normal multiplier. I.e.:

$$k_t = k - 1$$

The effect of cutting taxes is to shift the W line down, but not by the *full* cut in taxes. The fall in withdrawals is given by:[2]

$$\Delta W = \Delta T \times mpc_d$$

For example, if taxes were cut by £100 and the mpc_d was 3/4 and the mpw was 1/4, the consumption of domestic goods would rise by £75 and other withdrawals would rise by £25. The *net* fall in withdrawals would thus be £100 – £25 = £75:

$$£75(\Delta W) = £100(\Delta T) \times 3/4(mpc_d)$$

The effect is illustrated in Figures 15.5 and 15.6.

Figure 15.5 shows the effect of a cut in lump-sum taxes (i.e. taxes like the community charge, which do not depend on income). There is a parallel shift downward of the W line by an amount $\Delta T \times mpc_d$.

[2] To be accurate, the cut in taxes (ΔT) should be given as the *gross* income equivalent. Thus if the rate of income tax was cut to 20%, and as a result a person paid £80 less income tax per year, this would be equivalent to a gross income increase of £100: i.e. disposable income would rise by £80. The mpc_d and mpw terms are based on gross income not disposable income.

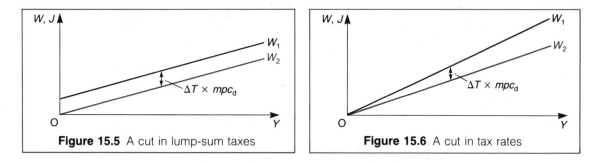

Figure 15.5 A cut in lump-sum taxes

Figure 15.6 A cut in tax rates

Figure 15.6 shows the effect of a cut in taxes that vary with income (e.g. income tax). If the income tax rate is cut, it will have the effect of making the W line less steep. The vertical difference between W_1 and W_2 is still given by the formula $\Delta T \times mpc_d$, only in this case ΔT will vary with the level of income: the higher the level of income, the bigger the absolute cut in tax revenues for a given cut in the tax rate.

The tax multiplier is smaller than the government expenditure multiplier. To achieve a given rise in income through tax cuts would therefore require a bigger budget deficit than if it were achieved through increased government expenditure. In other words, the required tax cut would be bigger than the required government expenditure increase. This poses a dilemma for a government which at one and the same time wants to boost aggregate demand and yet to minimize the size of the budget deficit and the size of the public sector. Wishing to minimize the size of the public sector, it would prefer to achieve the rise in aggregate demand by cutting taxes. But this would require a bigger rise in the budget deficit than if the government had used increased government expenditure instead.

> **?** Why will the multiplier effect of government transfer payments such as child benefit, pensions and social security be less than the *full* multiplier effect given by government expenditure on goods and services. Will this 'transfer payments multiplier' be the same as the tax multiplier? (Clue: will the recipients of such benefits have the same mpc_d as the average person?)

▲ SUMMARY

1. The government's fiscal policy will determine the size of the budget deficit or surplus and the size of the PSBR or PSDR. The size of these alone, however, is a poor guide to the government's fiscal stance. A large deficit, for example, may simply be due to the fact that the economy is in recession and therefore tax receipts are low. A better guide is whether the change in the deficit or surplus will be reflationary or deflationary.

2. Automatic fiscal stabilizers are tax revenues that rise and government expenditures that fall as national income rises. They have the effect of reducing the size of the multiplier

and thus reducing cyclical upswings and downswings.

3. Discretionary fiscal policy is where the government deliberately changes taxes or government expenditure in order to alter the level of aggregate demand. Changes in government expenditure on goods and services will have a full multiplier effect. Changes in taxes and benefits will have a smaller multiplier effect as some of the tax/benefit changes will merely affect other withdrawals and thus have a smaller net effect on consumption of domestic product. The tax multiplier will have a value 1 less than the full multiplier.

15.2 The effectiveness of fiscal policy

How successful will fiscal policy be? Will it be able to 'fine tune' demand? Will it be able to achieve the level of national income that the government would like it to achieve? Will it be able to give full employment without inflation? Will the government know just how much to change taxes and/or government expenditure?

The effectiveness of fiscal policy will depend on a number of factors, including the following:

- The accuracy of forecasting. Governments would obviously like to act as swiftly as possible to prevent a problem of excess or deficient demand. The more reliable are the forecasts of what is likely to happen to aggregate demand, the more able will the government be to intervene quickly.
- The extent to which changes in government expenditure and taxation will affect total injections and withdrawals. Will changes in G or T be partly offset by changes in *other* injections and withdrawals? If so, are these changes predictable?
- The extent to which changes in injections and withdrawals affect national income. Will it be possible to predict the size of the multiplier and accelerator effects?
- The timing of the effects. It is no good simply being able to predict the *magnitude* of the effects of fiscal policy. It is also necessary to predict how long they will take. If there are long time lags with fiscal policy, it will be far less successful as a means of reducing fluctuations.
- The extent to which changes in aggregate demand will have the desired effects on output, employment, inflation and the balance of payments.
- The extent to which fiscal policy has undesirable side-effects, such as higher taxes reducing incentives.

The effectiveness of fiscal policy also depends on the *type* of policy that is used. Does the government rely heavily on automatic stabilizers, or does it put a great deal of reliance on discretionary policy? If it uses discretionary policy, does it prefer to rely on tax changes, or changes in government expenditure, or some combination of the two? Which particular taxes or government expenditure will it prefer to change?

The effectiveness of automatic stabilizers

Automatic stabilizers have the obvious advantage that they act instantly as soon as aggregate demand fluctuates. By contrast, it may take some time before the government can institute discretionary changes in taxes or government expenditure, especially if forecasting is unreliable.

Nevertheless automatic stabilizers can never be the complete answer to the problem of fluctuations. Their effect is merely to reduce the multiplier – to reduce the severity of fluctuations, not to eliminate them altogether.

In addition they tend to suffer two specific drawbacks: adverse effects on aggregate supply and the problem of 'fiscal drag'. Let us examine each in turn.

Adverse supply-side effects
High tax rates may discourage effort and initiative. The higher the *mpt*, the greater the stability provided by the tax system. But the higher tax rates are, the more likely they are to create a disincentive to work and to invest. For example, steeply progressive income taxes may discourage workers from doing overtime or seeking promotion. A rise in the marginal rate of income tax is equivalent to a rise in the marginal cost of working. People may prefer to work less and substitute leisure for income. The

substitution effect of more progressive taxes may thus outweigh the income effect. These issues were examined in detail in section 9.2.

To the extent that steeply progressive income taxes discourage the growth of production, they will also tend to increase the rate of inflation. For any given growth in aggregate demand, the smaller the growth in aggregate supply, the higher will be the rate of inflation.

> **?** What is meant by the *income effect* of a rise in tax rates? (Refer back to Chapter 9 if you have forgotten.) What will steeply progressive income taxes do to the position and shape of the aggregate supply curve?

High unemployment benefits may increase equilibrium unemployment. High unemployment benefits, by reducing the hardship of being unemployed, may encourage people to spend longer looking for the 'right' job rather than taking the first job offered. This has the effect of increasing unemployment and may thus partly, or wholly, offset the beneficial effect on employment of the automatic stabilizer. It will have the effect of shifting the Phillips curve to the right – of increasing the amount of unemployment for any given level of inflation. This is because a longer average period of job search represents a higher level of *friction* in the economy and thus a higher *natural* (or *equilibrium*) level of unemployment.

To the extent, however, that such unemployment is *voluntary* (people choosing not to take the first job offered), rather than involuntary (lack of jobs available due to insufficient demand), the unemployment *problem* can be said to have been eased.

High income-related benefits may create a poverty trap. The higher the level of income-related benefits and the more steeply they taper off, the greater will be the problem of the 'poverty trap'. What is the point in unemployed people seeking jobs, or people in very low-paid jobs seeking better ones, if as a result they lose their benefits and end up being little or no better off than before? The more that people are discouraged in this way, the lower will be the level of aggregate supply. (The question of the poverty trap was also examined in Chapter 9 (see pages 358–60).)

The problem of fiscal drag

Automatic stabilizers help to reduce upward and downward movements in national income. This is fine if the current level of income is the *desirable* level. But suppose that there is currently a deep recession in the economy, with mass unemployment. Who would want to stabilize the economy at this level?

In these circumstances, if the economy began to recover, the automatic stabilizers would act as a drag on the expansion. This is known as fiscal drag. By reducing the size of the multiplier, the automatic stabilizers reduce the magnitude of the recovery. Similarly, they act as a drag on discretionary policy: the more powerful the automatic stabilizers are, the bigger the change in G or T that would be necessary to achieve a given change in national income.

> **Fiscal drag**
> The tendency of automatic fiscal stabilizers to reduce the recovery of an economy from recession.

Discretionary fiscal policy: problems of magnitude

Before changing government expenditure or taxation the government will need to calculate the effect of any such change on national income, employment and inflation. The magnitude of these effects will depend on (a) the extent to which changes in G or T will affect *net* injections and withdrawals and (b) the extent to which the changes in injections and withdrawals will affect final national income. If the magnitude of these effects could be forecast with relative accuracy, then fiscal policy could be a relatively

Box 15.3

Fiscal Drag in the Late 1980s
Tax cuts and budget surpluses

In the March 1988 Budget the Chancellor at the time, Nigel Lawson, made substantial cuts in taxes. The standard rate of income tax was cut from 27 per cent to 25 per cent. The top rate of income tax was cut from 60 per cent to 40 per cent. Personal allowances were increased by more than the rate of inflation. At the same time government expenditure was planned to increase in real terms.

With a seemingly reflationary Budget like this, it might be thought that the Chancellor was planning for a massive public-sector deficit.

In fact he was planning for a public-sector surplus of £3.2 billion. So how was this so? The answer is that he anticipated rapid economic growth in national income: growth that would bring in extra tax revenues despite the cut in tax rates. In his Budget speech he said:

> We have secured an enviable virtuous circle in public finance: lower borrowing and lower tax rates create both the scope and incentive for the private sector to expand. And the private sector then generates higher revenues which permit further reductions in borrowing or tax.

In the event, the public-sector debt repayment (the public-sector *surplus*) for 1988/89 turned out to be over £14 billion!

So how was this possible? The answer is 'fiscal drag'. Although the Chancellor was making discretionary cuts in tax *rates*, the growth in the economy was so strong that tax revenues actually increased. At the same time unemployment was falling rapidly and hence government spending on unemployment benefits also fell.

This had also been the pattern in the previous year. The Chancellor had planned for a PSBR of £3.9 billion

and ended up with a PSDR of £3.4 billion. Commenting on this, he said:

> Some two-thirds of this substantial undershoot of the PSBR I set at the time of last year's Budget is the result of the increased tax revenues that have flowed from a buoyant economy; while the remaining one-third is due to lower than expected public expenditure, again the outcome of a buoyant economy: less in benefits for the unemployed, higher receipts from council house sales and improved trading performance by the nationalized industries.

A word of caution. The cuts in tax rates alone would not have been sufficient to increase tax revenues. The reduced tax rates only stimulated an *already* strongly growing economy.

? 1. If the Chancellor had foreseen how rapidly aggregate demand would grow, and the inflation and balance of payments problems that would follow, what should he have done? What would this have done to the PSDR?

2. In his 1988 Budget statement he also argued: 'A balanced budget is a valuable discipline for the medium term. It represents security for the present and an investment for the future. Having achieved it, I intend to stick to it. In other words, henceforth a zero PSBR will be the norm.' Assuming that he had adjusted taxes and government expenditure throughout the year by whatever was necessary to keep a balanced budget, what would this have done to aggregate demand?

powerful tool for controlling the economy. Forecasting, however, is often very unreliable for a number of reasons.

First, a rise in government expenditure of £*x* may lead to a rise in injections (relative to withdrawals) that is smaller or larger than £*x*. The rise in injections will be *smaller* than £*x* if the rise in government expenditure *replaces* a certain amount of private expenditure. Examples include the following:

- A rise in government expenditure on social services could lead to a fall in private consumer expenditure. For example, a rise in expenditure on state education may dissuade some parents from sending their children to private schools. Similarly, an improvement in the National Health Service may lead to fewer people paying for private treatment.
- An increase in government expenditure on research and development or training may make firms feel less need to invest in these areas themselves.

- Crowding out. If the government relies on pure fiscal policy – that is, if it does not finance an increase in the budget deficit by increasing the money supply, it will have to borrow the money from individuals and firms. It will thus be competing with the private sector for finance and will have to offer higher interest rates. This will force the private sector also to offer higher interest rates. The higher interest rates may discourage firms from investing and individuals from buying on credit. Thus government borrowing *crowds out* private borrowing. In the extreme case, the fall in consumption and investment may completely offset the rise in government expenditure, with the result that aggregate demand does not rise at all.

Pure fiscal policy
Fiscal policy which does not involve any change in money supply.

The problem in each of these three cases is not whether the rise in government expenditure will or will not simply replace private expenditure. The problem is in predicting the extent to which this will happen.

 How do people's expectations influence the outcome?

The second problem in forecasting the effects of fiscal policy is that a rise in taxes, by reducing people's real disposable income, will reduce not only the amount they spend but also the amount they save. (This is why the tax multiplier is less than the full multiplier.) The problem is that it is not easy to predict just how much people will cut down on their spending and how much on their saving. In part it will depend on whether people feel that the rise in tax is only temporary, in which case they may well cut savings in order to maintain their level of consumption, or permanent, in which case they may well reduce their consumption.

 Do theories of the long-run and short-run consumption functions help us to understand consumer reactions to a change in taxes?

Thirdly, even if the government *could* predict the net initial effect on injections and withdrawals, the extent to which national income will change is still hard to predict for the following reasons:

- The size of the multiplier may be difficult to predict. This is because the mpc_d and mpw may fluctuate. For example, the amount of a rise in income that households save or consume will depend on their expectations about future price and income changes. The amount of a rise in income spent on imports will depend on the exchange rate, which may fluctuate considerably.
- Induced investment through the accelerator is also extremely difficult to predict. It may be that a relatively small fiscal stimulus will be all that is necessary to restore business confidence, and that induced investment will rise substantially. In such a case fiscal policy can be seen as a 'pump primer'. It is used to *start* the process of recovery, and then the *continuation* of the recovery is left to the market. But for pump priming to work, businesspeople must *believe* that it will work. If they are cautious and fear that the recovery will falter, they may hold back from investing. This lack of investment will probably mean that the recovery *will* falter, and that the effects of the fiscal expansion are therefore very modest. The problem is in predicting just how the business community will react. Business confidence can change very rapidly and in ways that could not have been foreseen a few months earlier.
- Multiplier/accelerator interactions. If the initial multiplier and accelerator effects are difficult to estimate, their interaction will be virtually impossible to estimate. Small divergences in investment from what was initially predicted will become magnified as time progresses.

Fourthly, there is the problem of random shocks. Forecasts cannot take into account the unpredictable. Unfortunately, unpredictable events do occur and may seriously undermine the government's fiscal policy.

 Give some examples of these random shocks.

Discretionary fiscal policy: problems of timing

Fiscal policy can involve considerable time lags. If these are long enough, fiscal policy could even be *de*stabilizing. Reflationary policies that are taken to cure a recession may only come into effect once the economy has *already* recovered and is experiencing a boom. Under these circumstances reflationary policies will be quite inappropriate: they will simply worsen the problems of overheating. Similarly, deflationary policies that are taken to prevent excessive expansion and the resulting rise in inflation and balance of payments deficits may only start taking effect once the economy has peaked and is already plunging into recession. The deflationary policies will only deepen the recession.

This problem is illustrated in Figure 15.7. Path (a) shows the course of the trade cycle without government intervention. Ideally, with no time lags, the economy should be deflated in stage 2 and reflated in stage 4. This would make the resulting course of the trade cycle more like path (b), or even, if the policy were perfectly stabilizing, a straight line. With the presence of time lags, however, deflationary policies taken in stage 2 may not come into effect until stage 4, and reflationary policies taken in stage 4 may not come into effect until stage 2. In this case the resulting course of the trade cycle will be more like path (c). Quite obviously, in these circumstances 'stabilizing' fiscal policy actually makes the economy less stable.

There are five possible lags associated with fiscal policy.

Time lag to recognition. Since the trade cycle can be irregular and forecasting unreliable, governments may be unwilling to take action until they are convinced that the problem is serious. This is illustrated in Figure 15.8, which shows an imaginary trade cycle with no government intervention.

Let us compare points *a* and *b*. In both cases the level of output is falling. In the first case this is only temporary. If the government pursues a reflationary fiscal policy at this stage, it will end up only stimulating the impending renewed expansion. As a result the economy will quickly overheat. So what does the government do at point *b*?

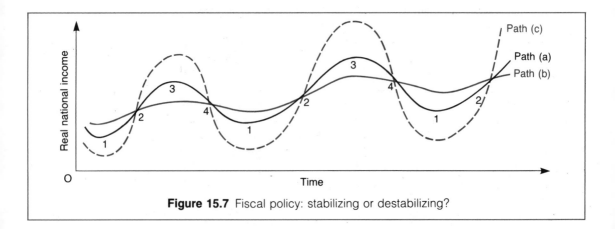

Figure 15.7 Fiscal policy: stabilizing or destabilizing?

Figure 15.8 An irregular trade cycle

Having learned the lesson from last time, it may be reluctant to reflate the economy before it is convinced that this time the economy really is going into recession. It thus chooses to wait and see. But in doing so it ends up allowing the economy to go into a deep recession!

Obviously, better forecasting would help the government to be less cautious and would thus help to remove the first time lag.

Time lag between recognition and action. Most significant changes in government expenditure have to be planned well in advance. The government cannot overnight increase spending on motorways or suddenly start building new hospitals. These projects have to be planned, tenders have to be made and contracts signed. Then the building programme has to be organized by the various contractors.

Changes in taxes and benefits cannot be introduced overnight either. They normally have to wait to be announced in the Budget, and will not be instituted until the new financial year or at some other point in the future. As Budgets normally occur annually, there could be a considerable time lag if the problems are recognized a long time before the Budget. Second or 'mini' Budgets might help, but governments prefer to avoid them if possible, in case they are seen as a sign of government incompetence in managing the economy.

Time lag between action and changes taking effect. A change in tax rates may not immediately affect tax payments. Income tax PAYE codings take two or three months to be changed by the Inland Revenue. A change in corporation tax will not affect payments until the *end* of the financial year – a full twelve months' delay. Not all taxes suffer this delay, however. New rates of excise duty on petrol, for example, come into effect immediately they are announced in the Budget.

Time lag between changes in government expenditure and taxation and the resulting change in national income, prices and employment. The multiplier round takes time. Accelerator effects take time. The multiplier and accelerator go on interacting. It all takes time.

Consumption may respond slowly to changes in taxation. The short-run consumption function tends to be flatter than the long-run function.

If the fluctuations in aggregate demand can be forecast, and if the lengths of the time lags are known, then all is not lost. At least the fiscal measures can be taken early and their delayed effects can be taken into account. Keynesians admit that problems of

Box 15.4

Riding a Switchback
A parable for Chancellors

Imagine that you are driving a car along a straight but undulating road. These undulations are not regular: some of the hills are steep, some are gentle; some are long, some are short.

You are given the instruction that you must keep the car going at a constant speed. To do this you will need to accelerate going up the hills and brake going down them.

There is a serious problem, however. The car is no ordinary car. It has the following distinctly unusual features:

- The front windscreen and side windows are blacked out, so you cannot see where you are going! All you can see is where you have *been* by looking in your rear-view mirror.
- The brake and accelerator pedals both work with a considerable and unpredictable delay.
- The car's suspension is so good that you cannot feel whether you are going up or downhill. You can only judge this by looking in your mirror and seeing whether the road behind you is higher or lower than you are.
- Finally (you are relieved to know), the car has a special sensor and automatic steering that keep it in the correct lane.

As you are going along, you see that the road behind you is higher, and you realize that you are going downhill. The car gets faster and faster. You brake – but nothing happens. In your zeal to slow the car down, you put your foot down on the brake as hard as you can.

When the brake eventually does come on, it comes on very strongly. By this time the car has already reached the bottom of the hill. As yet, however, you do not realize this

and are still braking.

Now the car is going up the hill the other side, but the brakes are still on. Looking in your mirror, you eventually realize this. You take your foot off the brake and start accelerating. But the pedals do not respond. The car is still slowing down rapidly, and you only just manage to reach the top of the hill.

Then, as you start going down the other side, the brakes eventually come off and the accelerator comes on . . .

This famous parable – first told by Frank Paish, Professor of Economics at the LSE, over twenty years ago – demonstrates how 'stabilizing' activity can in fact be destabilizing. When applied to fiscal policy, long and uncertain time lags can mean that the government can end up stimulating the economy in a boom and contracting it in a slump.

So what should be done? One alternative, of course, would be to try to reduce the time lags and to improve forecasting. But failing this, the best policy may be to do nothing: to take a 'steady as you go' or 'fixed throttle' approach to running the economy. Going back to the car analogy, a fixed throttle will not prevent the car from going faster downhill and slower uphill, but at least it will not make the speed even *more* irregular.

 1. Could you drive the car at a steady speed if you knew that all the hills were the same length and height, and if there were a constant 30 second delay on the pedals?

2. What would a fixed throttle approach to fiscal policy involve?

magnitude and time lags make stabilization less than perfect: a completely stable growth in demand could never be achieved. But at least, they argue, intervention is better than doing nothing. Fiscal policy will go *some* way to reducing fluctuations, especially if forecasting techniques are improved and measures are used which involve the minimum of time lags.

Side-effects of discretionary fiscal policy

The purpose of fiscal policy is to control aggregate demand. In doing so, however, it may create certain undesirable side-effects.

Cost inflation. If the economy is overheating and inflation is rising, the government may raise taxes. Although this will lower aggregate demand, a rise in expenditure taxes and corporation taxes will usually be passed on in full or in part to the consumer in higher prices. This in turn could lead to higher wage claims, as could a rise in income tax.

Welfare and distributive justice. The use of fiscal policy may conflict with various social programmes. The government may want to introduce cuts in public expenditure in order to reduce inflation. But where are the cuts to be made? Cuts will often fall on people who are relatively disadvantaged. After all, it is these people who are the most reliant on the welfare state and other public provision (such as state education).

Incentives. As with automatic stabilizers in the form of steeply progressive income taxes, discretionary rises in taxes could be a disincentive to effort. People may substitute leisure for income – the substitution effect may outweigh the income effect. On the other hand, it could work the other way: people may work harder or longer in an attempt to maintain their previous level of disposable income – the income effect may outweigh the substitution effect.

Postscript: the relative merits of changing government expenditure and changing taxes

Let us assume that despite all the problems of fiscal policy the government still wants to go ahead and use it to control aggregate demand. Which should it change: government expenditure, taxation or some combination of the two? There are various things it will need to take into account in making this decision.

The first consideration will probably be its overall political objectives. Does it generally favour a larger or smaller public sector?

The political left tends to argue that market economies like the UK suffer from too little public expenditure. While private expenditure by the relatively wealthy on fast cars, designer jeans, junk food and home security continues to grow rapidly, the public sector is deprived of resources. State education is squeezed; the streets are dirty; the environment is threatened; crime increases; the lot of the poor and homeless deteriorates. Private affluence goes side by side with public poverty.

The political right argues that the solution to social and economic problems does not lie in a growth of the 'nanny state', which stifles individual initiative. It is better, so the argument goes, to encourage attitudes where people take responsibility for the social consequences of their own actions, rather than leaving it up to the state.

Even if left and right agree on how much to deflate or reflate the economy by fiscal policy, they will disagree over the means. The left will tend to favour increasing government expenditure as the means of stimulating demand, and increasing taxes as the means of reducing it. The right, by contrast, will tend to favour cutting taxes as the means of stimulating aggregate demand, and cutting government expenditure as the means of reducing it.

Apart from ideological considerations, there are the practical questions of which policies are the most effective and which suffer the fewer drawbacks.

Changing government expenditure has the advantage that it affects aggregate demand directly and has a bigger multiplier effect. Changes in government expenditure can be more specifically targeted than changes in taxation. For example, government expenditure can be directed to regions of high unemployment or to specific industries that either need government support to prevent them going bankrupt or have potential for growth that could be more easily exploited with government aid. Taxes cannot be used so selectively.

Nevertheless the government can alter the balance between income and expenditure tax, or between personal income tax and corporation tax. Also the government can use taxes to alter the distribution of income. What is more, changes in taxes can usually be brought about more speedily than changes in government expenditure, and are thus more suitable for stabilizing the economy.

> **[?]** Compare the benefits of using changes in government expenditure on goods and services with those of using government transfer payments as means of stabilizing aggregate demand.

◢ SUMMARY

1. The effectiveness of fiscal policy depends on the accuracy of forecasting. It also depends on the predictability of the outcome of the fiscal measures: the effect of changes in G and T on other injections and withdrawals, the size and timing of the multiplier and accelerator effects, the relative effects of changes in aggregate demand on the various macroeconomic objectives, and whether there are any side-effects. It also depends on whether there are any random shocks.
2. Automatic stabilizers take effect as soon as aggregate demand fluctuates, but they can never remove fluctuations completely. They also create disincentives and act as a drag on recovery from recession.
3. There are problems in predicting the magnitude of the effects of discretionary fiscal policy. Expansionary fiscal policy can act as a pump primer and stimulate increased private expenditure, or it can crowd out private expenditure. The extent to which it acts as a pump primer depends crucially on business confidence – something that is very difficult to predict beyond a few weeks or months. The extent of crowding out depends on monetary conditions

and the government's monetary policy.
4. There are five possible time lags involved with fiscal policy: the time lag before the problem is diagnosed, the lag between diagnosis and new measures being announced, the lag between announcement and implementation, the lag while the multiplier and accelerator work themselves out, and the lag before consumption fully responds to new economic circumstances.
5. Discretionary fiscal policy can involve side-effects, such as disincentives, higher costs and adverse effects on social programmes.
6. The choice of which to change – government expenditure, taxation or a bit of both – depends partly on the government's political objectives: whether it wants to increase or decrease the size of the public sector. It also depends on their relative effectiveness in changing aggregate demand. Changes in G tend to have a bigger multiplier effect than changes in T. Changes in T, however, can usually be implemented more quickly than changes in G.

Money and Interest Rates 16

For the next two chapters we are going to look at the special role that *money* plays in the economy.

In this chapter we start by having a general look at the relationship between the amount of money in the economy and the level of economic activity. What effect do changes in the amount of money have on the four macroeconomic objectives? Right from the start we shall see that there is considerable disagreement between economists about just what the effects are.

Before going any further we next have to define precisely what we mean by 'money' – not as easy a task as it sounds. Money is more than just notes and coin. It includes a number of other items as well. In fact the main component of a country's money supply is not cash but deposits in banks and other financial institutions. Only a very small proportion of these deposits are kept by the banks in their safes or tills in the form of cash. The bulk of the deposits appear merely as bookkeeping entries in the banks' accounts. This may sound very worrying. Will a bank have enough cash to meet its customers' demands? The answer is yes. Only a small fraction of a bank's total deposits will be withdrawn at any one time, and banks always make sure that they have the ability to meet their customers' demands. The chances of banks running out of cash are practically nil.

If the main components of money supply are various deposits in financial institutions, we must examine these institutions and the various types of deposit if we are to going to get a clear definition of money. Section 16.2 looks at the key institutions and their role in the UK financial system.

This enables us in section 16.3 to understand the definitions of money that are officially used in the UK. Unfortunately there is not just one definition but seven! The reason is that there is no clear border line between what should and what should not count as money. Thus certain items (such as building society deposits) are included in some definitions but not in others. Having looked at the various definitions of money supply, section 16.3 goes on to consider what causes the money supply to change. What causes it to rise? What causes it to fall?

In section 16.4 we turn to why people demand money – not the silly question it may seem. We are not asking why people want to obtain money: that is obvious. What we are asking is what determines the amount of money people want to *hold*, whether in cash or in some form of account. If people choose to *hold* money, they are thereby choosing *not* to spend it on goods and services or on acquiring some other form of asset such as stocks and shares or property.

Having looked at what determines the supply and demand for money, we then put

Box 16.1

Money Supply and National Income and Wealth

Don't confuse them

Don't confuse the supply of money with the money value of national income. National income is a *flow* concept. It measures the value of the nation's output *per* year. Money supply, by contrast, is a *stock* concept. At any one *point* in time there is a given amount of money in the economy.

But what if the money supply increases? Will the national income increase by that amount? There are two reasons why the answer will be no.

● Not all the extra money will be spent. Some may simply be held.
● Not all the extra spending that does take place will be on *extra* goods and services. Some of the extra spending may simply lead to higher prices. *Real* national income will thus rise by less than the rise in spending.

So if money supply is not the same as national *income*, is it the same as national *wealth*? After all, wealth is a stock concept. Again the answer is no. The nation's wealth consists of its *real* assets such as land, buildings, capital equipment and various treasures such as works of art. People may well hold part of their wealth in the form of money, it is true, but this is not wealth as far as the nation is concerned: if it were, the government could make us all wealthier by simply printing more money! Money only represents wealth to the individual to the extent that it represents a claim on *real* goods and services. It has nothing to do with national wealth.

them together and see what determines equilibrium in money markets.

Chapter 17 then looks at how the government alters the supply of money in the economy and influences the money market.

16.1 The role of money in the economy

The amount of money in the economy can have a major effect on aggregate demand. Changes in aggregate demand will affect any or all of the four macroeconomic problems: the rate of growth of output, the rate of inflation, the level of unemployment and the balance of payments.

The way in which changes in money supply influence the economy is a fiercely debated subject in macroeconomics.

Monetarists argue that changes in money supply have a large effect on aggregate demand. This in turn has a large effect on inflation and the balance of payments, but in the long run little or no effect on output and employment.

Keynesians argue that changes in money supply have a rather uncertain effect on aggregate demand. Any changes in aggregate demand that do occur, however, will affect output and employment as well as inflation and the balance of payments, depending on the amount of slack in the economy. Because of the rather uncertain link between money supply and aggregate demand, Keynesians argue that the government should try to influence aggregate demand directly through *fiscal* policy.

Money supply and aggregate demand

If money supply changes, what is the mechanism by which it will affect aggregate demand? Monetarists argue that there is a direct mechanism. As such, if the government's monetary policy involves expanding the supply of money, aggregate demand will rise directly. Keynesians, however, argue that the mechanisms are indirect and unreliable. As such the effects of changing the money supply will be uncertain.

The direct transmission mechanism

People desire to hold a certain proportion of their assets in money form. This creates a demand for money (M_d). If the supply of money in the economy (M_s) increases, there will be more money available than people require to hold ($M_s > M_d$). They will therefore spend the surplus, thus increasing aggregate demand:

$$M_s \uparrow \; \to M_s > M_d \to AD \uparrow$$

There is thus a direct transmission mechanism from an increase in money supply to an increase in aggregate demand.

 Why will aggregate demand fall if the supply of money falls?

Direct monetary transmission mechanism

A change in money supply having a direct effect on aggregate demand.

Indirect transmission mechanisms

An indirect transmission mechanism is where a change in money supply first affects some intermediate variable. This intermediate variable then affects aggregate demand. There are two main indirect mechanisms. The first is via changes in interest rates. The second is via changes in the exchange rate.

Indirect monetary transmission mechanism

A change in money supply affecting aggregate demand indirectly via some other variable.

Via changes in interest rates. An alternative to spending money on goods and services is to purchase securities (e.g. government bonds, company shares). Thus with an increase in money supply, the demand for securities will rise above their supply. This will cause their price to rise.

These securities yield a given interest or dividend which is payable on the *original face value* of the security, not on its current market price. For example, the government may issue some bonds today with a face value of £100 which pay £10 interest per year. (The interest that the government has to pay will reflect the market rate of interest at the time when the bonds are issued.) These bonds will be redeemed by the government at their face value at some specified date in the future, say in twenty years' time. In other words, the holders of the bonds will be paid £100 on that date (known as the 'maturity date'). In the meantime, of course, the holders of the bonds may want to sell them. This they can do through a stockbroker, who will sell them via the stock market to people who want to buy such bonds. The current market price of such bonds will be determined by demand and supply. It may be above or below the face value. But whatever the current price of the bond, the government will continue to pay the same fixed sum, year in, year out. The higher the current market rate of interest, the lower will be the market price of existing bonds. This has to be so otherwise no one would be willing to buy old bonds. For example, if the current rate of interest were 20 per cent, no one would be willing to pay £100 for a bond that only yielded £10 per year. The bond's market value would have to fall to around £50. At that price an annual payment of £10 would be equivalent to a 20 per cent rate of interest. Table 16.1 shows how the market price and the market rate of interest vary with each other for a bond yielding £5 per year.

Government bonds or 'gilt-edged securities'

A government security paying a fixed sum of money each year. It is redeemed by the government on its maturity date at its face value.

 Complete a similar table showing the market price for a bond yielding £6 per year when current market rates of interest are 6 per cent, 4 per cent and 8 per cent.

So let us return to what happens when money supply rises. People will buy more securities. This will drive up the price of securities and hence will drive *down* their

Table 16.1 The relationship between bond prices and market rates of interest

Face value	Annual interest payment (nominal 5%)	Current market rate of interest	Market price
£100	£5	5%	£100
£100	£5	4%	£125
£100	£5	10%	£50

current market rate of interest. It is the same story with company shares (or equities as they are called). A rise in money supply causes more shares to be purchased. This drives up share prices. But given that companies pay a dividend (based on current profit) *per share*, the higher the price of the shares, the lower the dividend will be as a percentage of that price.

Equities

Company shares. Holders of equities are owners of the company and share in its profits by receiving dividends.

Thus an increase in money supply will lower interest rates. Lower interest rates will make it cheaper for firms and individuals to borrow. Borrowing and hence spending will thus increase:

$$M_s \uparrow \; \rightarrow M_s > M_d \rightarrow r \downarrow \; \rightarrow I \uparrow, C_d \uparrow \; \rightarrow AD \uparrow$$

The question is, will interest rates be strongly or only slightly affected by changes in money supply, and will aggregate demand be strongly or only slightly affected by changes in interest rates? Keynesians and monetarists do not agree on this. We will examine their disagreement in Chapter 18.

Via changes in the exchange rate. In recent years many economists have argued that there is another important indirect mechanism through which changes in money supply affect aggregate demand. This is the exchange rate. This is an important mechanism if a country (a) has a high proportion of imports and exports to national income and (b) operates under a system of floating exchange rates.

A rise in money supply will cause an increase in the demand for imports and for foreign assets. There will thus be an increase in the supply of pounds coming on to the foreign exchange market. This will cause a fall in the exchange rate (a depreciation). Less foreign currency will be obtained for a pound; or put another way, more pounds will be obtained for a given amount of foreign currency. For exporters who price their exports in foreign currency, a fall in the exchange rate will mean that they earn more pounds per unit sold. This will encourage them to sell more exports. At the same time imports will now be more expensive. Less will therefore be purchased.

The effect of more exports and less imports is to increase aggregate demand:

$$M_s \uparrow \; \rightarrow er \downarrow \; \rightarrow X \uparrow, M \downarrow \rightarrow AD \uparrow$$

(Where *er* is the exchange rate, *X* is expenditure on exports and *M* is expenditure on imports.)

Whether in the long term this will lead to a permanent increase in output, or whether it will simply lead to higher prices, is again a fiercely debated question. Certainly prices can be expected to rise somewhat. This is due directly to the higher price of imported goods and imported raw materials, and indirectly to the rise in wages that will be necessary to maintain workers' standard of living.

We will examine this mechanism in detail in Chapter 22, when we focus on the balance of payments and exchange rates.

Box 16.2

Is Plastic Money Really Money?

Credit cards are often referred to as 'plastic money'. On the surface this seems quite a good description. After all, we can use them to obtain goods and services in much the same way as we use cash. But are they really money?

The answer is no. They are no more money than is a cash machine or a bank clerk. These are all ways of obtaining *access* to money, but they are not money itself. When you use a credit card it is enabling you to transfer money from your account to that of the shop, but the card itself is not the money. It is similar with cheques. They are not money either. They too are merely a means of giving someone else access to the money in your account.

The functions of money

If changes in money supply have a major effect on the economy, and if the government therefore attempts to control the supply of money, it is important to have a clear understanding of (a) the purposes of money and (b) the definition of money.

The main purpose of money is as a 'medium of exchange'. It also has three other important fuctions.

A medium of exchange

In a subsistence economy where individuals make their own clothes, grow their own food, provide their own entertainments, etc., people do not need money. If people want to exchange any goods, they will do so by barter. In other words, they will do swaps with other people.

The complexities of a modern developed economy, however, make barter totally impractical for most purposes. Someone else may have something you want, but there is no guarantee that they will want what you have to offer them in return. What is more, under a system of capitalism where people are employed by others to do a specialist task, it would be totally impractical for people to be paid in food, clothes, cars, electrical goods, tickets to entertainments of various kinds and so on. What is necessary is a medium of exchange which is generally acceptable as a means of payment for goods and services and as a means of payment for labour and other factor services. 'Money' is any such medium.

Medium of exchange
Something that is acceptable in exchange for goods and services.

 Have you ever engaged in any form of barter? (Have you ever swapped things?) If so, why did you do this rather than selling your unwanted items and then buying the items you wanted? Are there any circumstances in which barter is superior to the use of money?

Money may be in the form of some physical item that is actually handed from one person to another: for example, gold, silver, other coin, banknotes, or even something like cigarettes. To be a suitable physical means of exchange, money must be light enough to carry around, must come in a number of denominations, large and small, and must not be easy to forge (see Box 16.3). Alternatively, money must be in a form that enables it to be transferred *indirectly* through some acceptable mechanism. For example money in in the form of bookkeeping entries in bank accounts can be transferred from one account to another by the use of such mechanisms as cheques, standing orders and direct debits.

 How does money aid the specialization and division of labour?

A means of storing wealth

People need a means whereby the fruits of *today's* labour can be used to purchase goods and services in the *future*. People need to be able to store their wealth: they want a means of saving. Money is one such medium in which to hold wealth. It can be saved.

A means of evaluation

Money is the unit used to value goods, services and assets. It allows the value of one good to be compared with that of another. In other words, the value of goods is expressed in terms of prices, and prices are expressed in money terms. It also allows dissimilar things to be added up. Thus a person's wealth or a company's assets can best be expressed in money terms. Similarly, a country's national income is expressed in money terms. There are, however, serious problems with relying on money prices as the means of evaluating income and wealth:

- Money prices may be distorted by monopoly power.
- They will ignore externalities.
- Simply adding up the money incomes of individuals in order to get a measure of their total incomes ignores questions of the *distribution* of income.

 Why else may money prices give a poor indication of the value of goods and services?

A means of establishing the value of future claims and payments

People often want to agree *today* the price of some *future* payment. Thus workers and managers will want to agree the wage rate for the coming year. Firms will want to sign contracts with their suppliers specifying the price of raw materials and other supplies. When people employ a builder to repair their house, they will probably want to agree a price beforehand. The use of money prices is the most convenient means of measuring future claims.

What should count as money?

What items, then, should be included in the definition of money? Must an item be able to fulfil all four functions of money to be able to be classed as money? Unfortunately, there is no clear answer to this. There is no sharp border line between money and non-money.

Cash (notes and coin) obviously counts as money. It readily meets all the functions of money. Goods (fridges, cars and cabbages) do not count as money.

But what about various financial assets such as bank accounts, building society accounts and stocks and shares? Do they count as money? The answer is 'It depends': it depends on how narrowly money is defined.

Narrow definitions of money

Items of money that can be spent directly (cash and money in cheque-book/debit-card accounts).

Narrow definitions of money only include items that can be spent directly: items such as cash and current accounts in banks (since they can be spent directly by using cheques). Note that cheques and credit cards, although they are used to pay for goods directly, do not themselves count as money. Rather it is the balance (or credit limit) in the account on which they are drawn that counts as money.

Broad definitions of money

Items in narrow definitions plus other items that can be readily converted into cash.

Broad definitions of money also include various items such as deposit accounts in banks that cannot be spent directly but which can nevertheless be readily converted into cash.

 In terms of the broad definition of money would a deposit account passbook count as money?

Box 16.3

The Attributes of Money

Virtually all societies throughout the ages have used money. It has come in many forms, however. Pigs, cattle, jewels, ornaments and shells are just a few examples. On the South Pacific island of Yap, giant stone wheels are the local currency – hardly suitable as 'small' change! In times of war or in times of rampant inflation, cigarettes, nylon stockings, sugar, coffee and various other commodities have been used as money.

With the possible exception of Yapese stones, these items are all examples of *commodity money*. That is, they have value in themselves. Animals can be slaughtered for food; jewellery can be worn; coffee can be drunk, and so on. But although they can all be used as a medium of exchange, in most cases they are far from ideal.

So what are the features of an ideal form of money?

Acceptability
If money is to act as a medium of exchange, it must be generally acceptable as a means of payment. If commodity money is to be generally acceptable, it must have a recognized intrinsic value.

Durability
Money must last a reasonable length of time before deteriorating, certainly if it is to be used as a means of storing wealth. Stone wheels are very good in this respect. Fresh fish aren't.

Convenience
It must be easy to use. In the case of money that physically changes hands, this means that it must be light and small to carry around and to hand over. In the case of bank accounts (or Yapese stone wheels), it must be easy to transfer ownership. This can be done conveniently by the use of cheques, standing orders, etc.

Divisibility
Money must come in different denominations so as to be able to pay for an item of any value, however large or small. Thus there is use for a 1p coin, for £10 notes and for the ability to transfer any amount from a bank account. In other words, money must come in a number of different denominations and forms. In this respect,

animals are a poor form of money. You could not exchange half a (live) pig.

Uniformity
Money of the same value must be of uniform quality. This applies particularly to the case where money has intrinsic value. People would be unwilling to accept an old thin cow as payment if it only had the same value as a young fat one.

Hard for individuals to produce themselves
This is an obvious requirement of paper money. It must be hard to forge.

 Would it matter if it was easy to forge a £10 note but cost £15 to do so?

In terms of commodity money, there would only be a problem of individuals producing it themselves if the monetary value of the item exceeded its intrinsic value.

Stability of value
If money is to fulfil its various functions (especially as a store of wealth and as a means of evaluating future payments), it must retain its value. Inflation, as we have seen, can be highly damaging to the economy. In terms of money produced by the state, the requirement here is that the government keeps its supply under control. In terms of commodity money, it must not be subject to violent fluctuations in supply. This is one reason why animals would be a poor form of money in many countries, especially those that are subject to drought.

? 1. How well do each of the following meet the seven requirements listed above: grain, strawberries, strawberry jam, gold, diamonds, luncheon vouchers, ICI share certificates, a savings account requiring one month's notice of withdrawal?
2. Do notes and coin perfectly fulfil all these requirements?

In the UK there are several different measures of money supply – some narrow, some broad. In order to understand their significance and the ways in which money supply can be controlled, it is first necessary to look at the various types of account in which money can be held and at the various financial institutions involved. This we do in section 16.2.

Box 16.4

The Evolution of Bank Deposit Money
From coins to banknotes to bank deposits

Precious metals have been used as money for thousands of years. Even as lumps of metal carried around in sacks they still functioned quite well as money.

 Go through the requirements of money listed in Box 16.3 and check the extent to which lumps of metal meet these requirements.

Coins made from these precious metals were an early improvement introduced by many societies including the Greeks and Romans. Coins had the clear advantage that they did not have to be weighed out each time they were used. But despite this gain in simplicity and uniformity, the use of coins enabled many rulers to increase their spending by adding base metals to the coins and thereby increasing the number of coins. This debasement of the coinage frequently led to problems of inflation as money supply increased too rapidly.

Paper money has a much more recent origin. The first paper money was issued by goldsmiths. Wealthy merchants and individuals would deposit their gold with goldsmiths whose businesses required them to have safe storage facilities. The goldsmith would issue a receipt for the gold, much as you are given a receipt at a disco when you deposit your coat!

It was soon realized that it was much easier to use these receipts for the purchase of goods than for the purchaser to have to go along to the goldsmith, withdraw the necessary amount of gold and hand it over to the seller of the goods, and for the seller then to redeposit it with the goldsmith. It was easier still if these receipts were issued in fixed denominations. Thus goldsmiths' receipts became very much like modern banknotes.

The alternative was for a purchaser to write a note instructing the goldsmith to transfer a certain amount of gold to the seller. These notes were very much like modern cheques.

Goldsmiths also realized that only a small fraction of the gold in their vaults would be withdrawn at any one time, and even then there would be other people who were making new deposits. So why not *lend out* some of the gold and make money by charging interest? This is precisely what they did. When these loans of gold were redeposited back with goldsmiths, *new* notes were issued in addition to the original ones. A proportion of these gold deposits would again be lent out and yet more notes issued when the gold once more returned to the goldsmiths' vaults.

Of course, goldsmiths had to keep a fraction back each time to cover the possibility of depositors actually withdrawing their gold rather than relying on the notes. Nevertheless the total value of the notes issued considerably exceeded the total value of the gold! The notes were only *partly* backed by gold. This is known as a system of *fractional backing*.

It was a short step from goldsmiths' notes to banknotes and bank loans. Banks, often originally operating as goldsmiths, issued their own banknotes in excess of the gold in their vaults, just as the goldsmiths had done.

Today banks in England do not issue their own notes, but their loans still exceed their deposits of cash. For every £1 in cash deposited in the banking system, loans considerably in excess of £1 can be created, and these loans come back as additional deposits. This process of *credit creation* is examined in section 16.3. Today it is bank deposits that form the bulk of money supply. Only a fraction of these deposits are in cash. The rest are simply bookkeeping entries created by the banks.

But what of modern banknotes? If these are used to back bank loans, what backs the banknotes? What does the promise on a ten pound note mean when it says, 'I promise to pay the bearer on demand the sum of ten pounds'? It does *not* mean that if you take the note along to the Bank of England you will be given £10 worth of gold. Today's currency is not backed by gold. The amount of gold in the Bank of England is only a tiny fraction of the total amount of currency in circulation.

A currency not backed by gold (and no currencies in the world today are), is known as a *fiat* currency: a currency whose supply depends on the will of government. The issuing of currency not backed by gold is known as *fiduciary issue*. This means currency issued on trust. The point is that if the government is prepared and able to match the supply of currency to the requirements of the economy, and if the public has confidence in the government's willingness and ability to do this, then this will be adequate to ensure the stability of the currency. The backing of gold will be unnecessary.

 1. If money is not backed by gold, what gives it its value?
2. If the money that banks have created vastly exceeds the amount of cash in the economy, does this mean that there is too much money in the economy?

▲ SUMMARY

1. How changes in money supply affect aggregate demand is a highly controversial issue. Monetarists argue that changes in money supply have a direct and powerful effect. Keynesians argue that they have an indirect and uncertain effect.

2. The direct mechanism is where an increase in money supply leads people directly to spend the resulting excess of money supply over money demand.

3. The indirect mechanism operates via interest rates or exchange rates. In the former, a rise in money supply leads to a fall in interest rates, which in turn leads to an increase in consumption and investment. In the latter, a rise in money supply leads to a fall in the exchange rate, which leads to a rise in exports and a fall in imports.

4. Money's main function is as a medium of exchange. In addition it is a means of storing wealth, a means of evaluation and a means of establishing the value of future claims and payments.

5. Narrow definitions of money include items that can be directly spent: cash and money in cheque-book and debit-card accounts. Broad definitions of money also include items that can readily be converted into cash.

16.2 The financial system in the UK

The role of the financial sector

There are many different types of institution that make up the financial sector, from banks to building societies to various institutions in the City of London. They are jointly known as financial intermediaries. They all have the common function of providing a link between those who wish to lend and those who wish to borrow. In other words, they act as the mechanism whereby the supply of funds is matched to the demand for funds.

As financial intermediaries these institutions provide four important services.

Financial intermediaries

The general name for financial institutions (banks, building societies, etc.) which act as a means of channelling funds from depositors to borrowers.

Expert advice
Financial intermediaries can advise their customers on financial matters: on the best way of investing their funds and on alternative ways of obtaining finance. This should help to encourage the flow of savings and the efficient use of them.

Expertise in channelling funds
Financial intermediaries have the specialist knowledge to be able to channel funds to those areas that yield the highest return. This too encourages the flow of savings as it gives savers the confidence that their savings will earn a good rate of interest. Financial intermediaries also ensure that projects that are potentially profitable will be able to obtain finance. They help to increase allocative efficiency.

Maturity transformation
Many people and firms want to borrow money for long periods of time, and yet many depositors want to be able to withdraw their deposits on demand or at short notice. If people had to rely on borrowing directly from other people, there would be a problem here: the lenders would not be prepared to lend for a long enough period. If you had £100 000 of savings, would you be prepared to lend it to a friend to buy a house if the friend was going to take 25 years to pay it back? Even if there was no risk whatsoever of your friend defaulting, most people would be totally unwilling to tie up their savings for so long. This is where a building society comes in. It borrows money from a vast number of small savers, who are able to withdraw their money on demand or at short notice. It then lends the money to house purchasers for a long period of time by granting mortgages (typically these are paid back over 20 to 30 years). This process

Maturity transformation

The transformation of deposits into loans of a longer maturity.

whereby financial intermediaries lend for longer periods of time than they borrow is known as maturity transformation. They are able to do this because with a large number of depositors it is highly unlikely that they would all want to withdraw their deposits at the same time. On any one day, although some people will be withdrawing money, others will be making new deposits.

Risk transformation

You may be unwilling to lend money directly to another person in case they do not pay up. You are unwilling to take the risk. Financial intermediaries, however, by lending to large numbers of people, are willing to risk the odd case of default. They can absorb the loss because of the interest they earn on all the other loans. This spreading of risks is known as risk transformation. What is more, financial intermediaries may have the expertise to be able to assess just how risky a loan is.

Risk transformation

The process whereby banks can spread the risks of lending by having a large number of borrowers.

 Which of the above are examples of economies of scale?

In addition to channelling funds from depositors to borrowers, certain financial institutions have another important function. This is to provide a means of transmitting payments. Thus by the use of cheques, credit cards, standing orders, etc., money can be transferred from one person or institution to another without having to rely on cash.

Financial institutions in the UK

The different financial intermediaries can be grouped according to the types of deposit taking and lending in which they specialize.

Commercial banks

These include the familiar high street banks such as Barclays and the National Westminster. They specialize in providing branch banking facilities to individuals. They operate current (cheque-book) accounts, on most of which overdraft facilities can be arranged, and deposit accounts, which by offering a higher interest rate but no cheque book are designed to encourage savers. They also provide personal loan facilities and financial advice to their customers. Unlike most other financial institutions, they are involved in operating the *payments* system: the transmission of money through cheques, standing orders, direct debits, etc.

The category of commercial banks also includes overseas banks. These have grown enormously in recent years, especially since the abolition of foreign exchange controls in 1979. Although they have made some ventures into the high street, their major specialism is the finance of international trade and they deal extensively in the foreign exchange market.

Merchant banks

These specialize in receiving large deposits from and making large loans to industry. They often act as 'brokers', arranging loans for companies from a number of different sources. They also offer financial advice to industry and 'accept' *bills of exchange* (see pages 660–4). They provide assistance to firms in raising new capital through the issue of new shares. Examples of merchant banks are Rothschilds and Hambros.

Savings banks

These were originally set up to provide savings facilities rather than current account and clearing facilities. The Trustee Savings Banks were one of the best known of such institutions. Today, however, the TSB is just another high street bank, offering the same facilities as all the others. The one remaining example of savings banks in the UK is the National Savings Bank (NSB). This is a government-run institution and operates through post offices. The savings deposited in the NSB are called 'national savings' and are lent to the government.

Building societies

These specialize in granting loans (mortgages) for house purchase. They compete for the savings of the general public through a network of high street branches. They include many familiar names such as the Halifax, the Woolwich and the Nationwide Anglia. Unlike commercial banks they are not public limited companies, their 'shares' being the deposits made by their investors.

Finance houses

These specialize in providing hire-purchase finance for the purchase of consumer durables such as cars and electrical goods. This is normally arranged through the retailer, which will offer credit to its customers. Finance houses also lease out capital equipment to firms. Their main source of funds are banks, but they do also receive deposits from the general public. Several finance houses are subsidiaries of commercial banks.

Discount houses

These institutions, unique to the UK, play an absolutely central role in the monetary system. Their specialism is in lending and borrowing for very short periods of time – from one day to up to about three months. There are nine discount houses, all members of the London Discount Market Association. Despite their importance they are not household names as they do not deal with the general public. (Have you heard of King & Shaxson or Gerrard & National?)

We will examine these various institutions in more detail later, as we see just how the financial system operates. At this stage, however, it is worth noting an important trend in recent years. Increasingly, the boundaries between the different financial institutions are becoming less clear cut. For example, in the past there was a clear distinction between banks and building societies. Today, however, they have become much more similar, with building societies now offering current account facilities and cash machines, and commercial banks granting mortgages. In fact, in 1989 the Abbey National Building Society became a public limited company and thereby ceased to be a building society, becoming instead a bank.

This is all part of a trend away from the narrow specialization of the past and towards the offering of a wider and wider range of services. Inevitably, as this trend continues the services offered by the various institutions will increasingly overlap.

At the heart of the financial system of a country is the central bank. In the case of the UK this is the Bank of England. Its role is to oversee and regulate the activities of the different financial institutions. It has the task of ensuring the stability and efficiency of the financial system. It also has the task of carrying out the government's monetary policy.

Central bank
Banker to the banks and the government.

In order to understand how these various institutions affect the economy and the part they play in the operation of monetary policy, we need to examine some of their activities and functions in more detail.

Deposit taking and lending: liabilities and assets

Liabilities

Customers' deposits in banks and other deposit-taking institutions such as building societies are liabilities to these institutions. This means simply that the customers have the claim on these deposits and thus the institutions are liable to meet the claims.

There are two major types of deposit: *sight deposits* and *time deposits*.

Sight deposits. Sight deposits are any deposits that can be withdrawn on demand by the depositor without penalty. They are sometimes called 'demand deposits'. In the past, sight deposits did not pay interest. In recent years, however, banks have introduced various types of interest-bearing sight account.

The most familiar form of sight deposit are current accounts at banks. Depositors are issued with cheque books which enable them to spend the money directly without first having to go to the bank and draw the money out in cash. Cheque guarantee cards facilitate the process. A recent development with current accounts has been the introduction of debit cards. These cards are used rather like credit cards. You hand them to the shop assistant when making a purchase and your current account is automatically debited by the amount of your purchase. This process is usually done electronically via a machine at the shop's cash till (see Box 16.5). Banks hope that in time the use of these cards will substantially reduce the number of cheques that are written, since debit-card transactions are much cheaper for the banks to process than transactions by cheque.

An important feature of current accounts is that banks often allow customers to be overdrawn. That is, they can draw on their account and make payments to other people in excess of the amount of money they have deposited. This facility is a crucial ingredient in the process whereby the money supply expands. If person A is given an overdraft and then draws a cheque on the account and pays it to person B, person B's bank account has been credited and he or she can draw this money even though person A never deposited the money in the first place.

Time deposits. These deposits require notice of withdrawal. They pay interest. With some types of account a depositor can withdraw a certain amount of money on demand, but will have to pay a penalty of so many days' interest. They are not cheque-book accounts. The most familiar form of time deposits are the deposit and savings accounts in banks and the various savings accounts in building societies. No overdraft facilities exist with time deposits.

The distinction between sight and time deposits has become increasingly blurred in recent years, with interest being paid on current accounts and with instant-access, no-penalty, high-interest accounts.

Assets

A financial institution's assets are items it owns and its claims on others.

Banks and certain other financial institutions, such as building societies, need to hold a certain amount of their assets as notes and coin. This is largely used as 'till money' to meet the day-to-day demands by customers for cash.

Liabilities

All legal claims for payment that outsiders have on an institution.

Sight deposits

Deposits that can be withdrawn on demand without penalty.

Debit card

A card that has the same use as a cheque. Its use directly debits the person's current account.

Assets

Possessions, or claims held on others.

Box 16.5

Are the Days of Cash Numbered?
EFTPOS versus ATMs

Banking is becoming increasingly automated, with computer debiting and crediting of accounts replacing the moving around of pieces of paper. What was once done by a bank clerk is often now done by computer.

One possible outcome of this replacement of labour by computers is the gradual elimination of cash from the economy – or so some commentators have claimed.

The most dramatic example of computerization in recent years has been *EFTPOS* - (electronic funds transfer at the point of sale). This is where you pay for goods in the shops by means of a card – either a credit card (like Access or Visa) or a 'debit' card (a card which allows the transaction directly to debit your current account). The card is simply 'swiped' across a machine at the till which may then require you to enter your PIN (personal identification number). The details of the transaction (the amount, the retailer and your card number) are then transmitted down the line to the EftPos UK processing centre. If necessary, the information is then directed down the line to the card issuer for authorization. If the card is valid and the transaction acceptable, then within seconds the machine will issue a slip for you to sign and the purchase is complete. Subsequently your account will be automatically debited and the retailer's account automatically credited.

The advantage of this system is that it does away with the processing by hand of pieces of paper. In particular it does away with the need for (a) credit-card slips when used in conjunction with credit cards and (b) cheques when used in conjunction with debit cards. Both cheques and credit-card slips have to be physically moved around and then read and processed by *people*. If this EFTPOS system were to become widely used for *small* transactions, it could well reduce the need for cash. But reducing the need for cash is *not* the prime purpose of EFTPOS. Its prime purpose is to do away with cheques and credit-card slips.

So are we moving towards a cashless society? Probably not. Cash is still the simplest and most efficient way of paying for a host of items, from your bus ticket to a newspaper to a packet of mints. What is more, another technical innovation is moving us in the direction of using *more* cash not less! This is the cash machine – or *ATM* (automated teller machine), to give it its official title. The spread of cash machines to virtually every bank and building society branch and to many larger stores has been rapid in recent years. The sheer simplicity of obtaining cash at all hours from these machines, not only from your current account but also on your credit card, is obviously a huge encouragement to the use of cash.

So are we using more cash or less cash? The evidence suggests a gradual decline in cash in circulation as a proportion of GDP. It fell from just over 5 per cent of GDP in 1980 to just under 4 per cent in 1990.

But although the effects of EFTPOS and ATMs may be quite different in terms of the use of cash, they both have the same advantage to banks: they reduce the need for bank staff and thereby reduce costs.

? Under what circumstances are cheques more efficient than cash and vice versa? Would you get the same answer from everyone involved in transactions: individuals, firms and banks?

Cash, however, earns no interest for banks. The vast majority of banks' assets are therefore in the form of various types of loan – to individuals and firms, to other financial institutions and to the government. These are 'assets' since they represent claims that the banks have on other people. Some of these loans are for short periods. Overdrafts to customers are often granted for a few days or weeks. Some loans to other financial institutions may be loans 'at call'. These are loans that the banks can reclaim on demand. Some institutions, such as building societies, have few if any short-term assets. Others, such as the discount houses (as we shall see later), have assets that are almost entirely short term.

Other loans are for much longer periods. For example, banks grant personal loans to customers to be repaid in instalments over a set number of years (typically six months to five years). Building societies' major assets are mortgage loans. These are very long-term and are typically paid back over 25 years.

Deposit taking and lending: retail and wholesale deposits and loans

An important distinction is that made between *retail* and *wholesale* deposits and loans.

Retail deposits and loans

Deposits and loans made through bank/building society branches at published interest rates.

Retail deposit taking and lending are the familiar type done by the high street banks, the National Savings Bank and the building societies, through their various branches. The terms of deposits and loans are published and are at standard rates of interest for each category. Interest rates are adjusted from time to time to reflect market conditions, and will be chosen to balance long-term inflows of deposits with the demand for loans: higher interest rates attracting more deposits and reducing the demand for loans.

Wholesale deposits and loans

Large-scale deposits and loans made by and to firms at negotiated interest rates.

Wholesale deposits and loans are those by and to firms who want to deposit or borrow large sums of money. These may be for short periods of time to account for the non-matching of the firm's payments and receipts from its business. They may be for longer periods of time, for various investment purposes. These wholesale deposits and loans are very large sums of money. Banks thus compete against each other for them and negotiate individual terms with the firm to suit the firm's particular requirements. The rates of interest negotiated will reflect the current market rates of interest and the terms of the particular loan/deposit. Very large loans to firms are often divided ('syndicated') between several banks.

Liquidity and profitability

Financial institutions keep a range of liabilities and assets. The balance of items in this range is influenced by two important considerations: profitability and liquidity.

Profitability. Profits are made by lending money out at a higher rate of interest than that paid to depositors.

Liquidity

The ease with which an asset can be converted into cash without loss.

Liquidity. The liquidity of an asset is the ease with which it can be converted into cash without loss. Cash itself, by definition, is perfectly liquid.

Some assets, such as money lent at call to other financial institutions, are highly liquid. Although not actually cash, these assets can be converted into cash on demand with no financial penalty.

Other assets, however, are much less liquid. Personal loans to the general public or mortgages for house purchase can only be redeemed by the bank as each instalment is paid. Other advances for fixed periods are only repaid at the end of that period.

Other assets, such as government bonds – i.e. loans to government for a fixed number of years – are somewhere in the middle. They can be sold quickly on the Stock Exchange if banks are short of cash. But their price fluctuates with market conditions and the banks may be unwilling to sell them if their current market price is too low. In other words, they can easily be converted into cash but may involve some loss.

Financial institutions must maintain sufficient liquidity in their assets to meet the demands of depositors.

Profitability is the major aim of banks and most other financial institutions. However, the aims of profitability and liquidity tend to conflict. In general, the more liquid an asset, the less profitable it is, and vice versa. Advances to customers are profitable to banks but highly illiquid. Cash is totally liquid, but earns no profit.

Thus financial institutions like to hold a range of assets with varying degrees of liquidity and profitability.

To economize on cash holdings (which earn no interest), financial institutions hold other highly liquid assets which act as reserves, but which nevertheless earn them

Box 16.6

Secondary Marketing
Or how to make illiquid assets liquid

Banks have the two conflicting aims of liquidity and profitability. They must hold sufficient liquid assets to be able to meet any demands from their customers and avoid a crisis of confidence. But they want to hold illiquid assets in order to make a profit – after all, the less liquid the asset, the greater the interest the bank is likely to be able to charge. The greater their ratio of illiquid assets to liquid ones, the greater their profit.

This conflict can be put another way. This is in terms of the size of the gap between the average maturity of a bank's assets and liabilities.

For reasons of profitability, the banks will want to 'borrow short' and 'lend long'. In other words, they will want to receive deposits that can be withdrawn instantly (like current accounts) or at only short notice. The benefits of liquidity to their customers will involve banks only having to pay out low rates of interest (or in the case of certain types of current account, none at all). But banks will want to grant *loans* with a much longer maturity (e.g. two-year personal loans), since these are charged at much higher interest rates than banks have to pay to their depositors.

As we saw in section 16.2, this process of borrowing short and lending long is known as *maturity transformation*: short-term deposits are turned into longer-term loans. The difference in the average maturity of loans and deposits is known as the *maturity gap*.

For reasons of *profitability*, the banks will want a large maturity gap between loans and deposits. For reasons of *liquidity*, however, banks will want a relatively small gap: if there is a sudden withdrawal of deposits, banks will need to be able to call in enough loans.

The obvious way of reconciling the two conflicting aims of liquidity and profitability is by compromise: to hold a mixture of liquid and illiquid assets – to have a 'reasonable' maturity gap.

There is another way, however, whereby banks can reconcile these aims, whereby they can close the gap for

liquidity purposes, but maintain the gap for *profitability* purposes. This is by the *secondary marketing* of assets.

Certificates of deposit (CDs) are a good example of secondary marketing. CDs are issued for fixed-period deposits in a bank (e.g. one year) at an agreed interest rate. The bank does not have to repay the deposit until the year is up. CDs are thus illiquid liabilities for the bank, and they allow it to increase the proportion of illiquid assets without having a dangerously high maturity gap. But the holder of the CD in the meantime can sell it to someone else (through a broker). It is thus liquid to the holder.

Because CDs are liquid to the holder, they can be issued at a relatively *low* rate of interest and thus allow the bank to increase its profitability.

Another example is when a bank sells some of its assets to another bank. The advantage to the first bank is that it gains liquidity. The advantage to the second bank is that it gains profitable assets (assuming that it has spare liquidity).

The effect of secondary marketing is to reduce the liquidity ratio that banks feel they need to keep. It has the effect of increasing their maturity gap.

There are dangers to the banking system, however, from secondary marketing. To the extent that banks individually feel that they can operate with a lower liquidity ratio, so this will lead to a lower *national* liquidity ratio. This may lead to an excessive expansion of credit (illiquid assets) in times of economic boom. Also there is an increased danger of banking collapse. If one bank fails, this will have a knock-on effect on those banks which have purchased its assets.

? Is it possible to argue that secondary marketing allows a lower *safe* average liquidity ratio? (Clue: the answer has to do with risk transformation.)

---

some interest (see pages 658–60). The greater the liquidity of its liabilities, and the more volatile the demands of depositors are for cash, the greater the proportion of liquid assets the institution must hold.

The ratio of an institution's liquid assets to illiquid assets is known as its liquidity ratio. For example, if a bank had £100 million of assets, of which £10 million were liquid and £90 million were illiquid, the bank would have a 10 per cent liquidity ratio. If a financial institution's liquidity ratio is too high, it will make too little profit. If the ratio is too low, there will be the risk that customers' demands may not be able to be met: this would cause a crisis of confidence and possible closure. Institutions thus

Liquidity ratio

The proportion of a bank's total assets held in liquid form.

have to make a judgement as to what liquidity ratio is best – one that is neither too high nor too low. They are guided and persuaded in this process by the Bank of England.

Commercial banks

By far the largest element of money supply is bank deposits. It is not surprising, then, that banks play an absolutely crucial role in the monetary system.

Monetary sector

Those financial institutions whose activities are supervised by the Bank of England.

Under the 1979 and 1987 Banking Acts, a monetary sector was defined. This consists of a series of financial institutions whose activities are supervised by the Bank of England. The largest group of institutions in the monetary sector are the recognized banks. (Also included are the National Girobank, the discount houses and the banking department at the Bank of England.) To be a recognized bank, a bank must be granted a licence by the Bank of England. This requires it to have paid-up capital of at least £5 million and to meet other requirements about its asset structure and the range of banking services it offers. If a bank is not recognized, it cannot use the word 'bank' in its title (unless it is an overseas bank operating in the UK and it is made clear that it is using the title 'bank' because it is entitled to do so in its country of origin). All the major banks in the UK and most of the larger foreign ones are in fact recognized by the Bank of England.

Recognized banks

Those commercial banks whose activities are supervised by the Bank of England.

The most important of the recognized banks in the UK for the functioning of the economy and for the implementation of monetary policy are the clearing banks. These are the main retail banks in the UK and include the familiar high street names: Barclays, Lloyds, Midland, National Westminster, Co-operative Bank, Abbey National, Royal Bank of Scotland, TSB, Bank of Scotland, Clydesdale Bank and Standard Chartered.

Clearing banks

The main UK retail banks: members of the Clearing House Association.

Banks and the transmission of payments: the clearing system

Clearing house

An institution where inter-bank debts are settled.

The clearing banks are so called because they operate a central clearing house in London. This is a means of settling banks' debts with each other on a daily basis. It enables cheques, standing orders and other means of payment to be cleared rapidly. But how does it work?

Let us examine the case of just two banks, say Lloyds and Midland. Each day all the cheques written by Midland customers that Lloyds customers have received and paid into their accounts are sent by Lloyds branches to its head-office clearing department and are added up. Likewise all the cheques that Lloyds customers have written and have been deposited in Midland accounts are sent to Midland head office and are added up. Every day the two banks take the bundles of each other's cheques along to the clearing house and exchange them. The values of the two bundles are compared. If Midland customers have paid, say, £1 million more to Lloyds customers than Lloyds customers have to Midland customers, Midland makes a *single* payment of £1 million to Lloyds, drawn on Midland's account in the Bank of England. A simple bookkeeping entry adjustment is made. (As we shall see, all recognized banks keep accounts with the Bank of England.) The debt has been settled. The cheques are then passed back to the branches on whose accounts they are drawn. The two banks then make the necessary adjustments to all their individual customers' accounts.

This procedure is carried out for each pair of banks. When customers of one branch deposit cheques from customers of a different branch of the *same* bank, the clearing house is not involved. Clearing simply takes place within the bank.

Increasingly, the process of clearing is done electronically rather than manually, the information to debit or credit individuals' accounts being sent down the line to the various branches by computer. Direct debits, standing orders and debit-card payments are cleared entirely by computer.

The clearing system, being nationwide and increasingly computerized, makes for a very efficient system of transmitting payments. It is a long way from barter!

> **?** Would there be any drawbacks of a completely automated system of clearing, whereby the branch of a bank into which a cheque was paid simply fed the information into a nationwide computer and the computer then (a) debited the account at the branch on which it was drawn and (b) for clearing purposes added the amount to the total paid from the one bank to the other on that day?

Banks and the transformation of maturity: liabilities and assets

Apart from providing a mechanism for the transmission of payments, the other important role of the banks is to provide financial intermediation. As we have seen, this involves maturity transformation. In other words, the average liquidity of bank deposits is greater than that of bank loans. Banks borrow short and lend relatively long. That is how they make their profit.

To understand this process in more detail and to prepare the way for showing how money supply expands or contracts, we must examine the particular types of deposit and loan (of liability and asset). Table 16.2 shows the total liabilities and assets of UK recognized banks at the end of January 1990. They are set out in the form of a balance sheet.

Sterling liabilities

Time deposits form the largest item, accounting for around 50 per cent of the total. *Sight deposits* are the other major item, accounting for around 28 per cent.

Up to the mid-1980s, there was a sharp distiction between most time and sight accounts as far as personal customers were concerned (i.e. at the *retail* level): time accounts paid interest whereas sight accounts did not. Today the distinction is more blurred. Some sight accounts still do not pay interest. These types of account normally have more extensive overdraft facilities or involve smaller overdraft charges. Other sight accounts, however, do pay interest at a rate only slightly below that on time accounts. This development has made sight accounts more popular with many customers, offering as they do the benefits of a time account (namely, interest) but with instant access with no loss of interest, and cheque-book and debit-card facilities.

As you can see from the figures, the bulk of sight deposits are from the *private sector*: individuals and firms. In the case of time deposits, although private-sector deposits are the largest component, a substantial proportion are from the *monetary sector*: in other words, from other banks and other financial institutions. Inter-bank lending has grown over the years as money markets have become deregulated and as deposits are moved from one currency to another to take advantage of different rates of interest between different countries. A large proportion of overseas deposits are inter-bank deposits (from foreign banks).

Certificates of deposit (CDs) are certificates issued by banks to customers (usually firms) for large deposits of a fixed term (e.g. £100 000 for eighteen months). These certificates can be sold by one customer to another, thereby transferring ownership, and are thus relatively liquid to the depositor but illiquid to the bank (see Box 16.6). The use of CDs has grown rapidly in recent years. Their use by firms has meant that, at a wholesale level, sight accounts have become *less* popular.

Certificates of deposit

Certificates issued by banks for fixed-term interest-bearing deposits. They can be re-sold by the owner to another party.

Items in suspense and transmission are funds in the process of being transferred from one customer's account to another.

Capital and other funds include shareholders' funds and internal funds of the banks themselves.

The Bank of England oversees the activities of the banks. It must ensure that the banking system is stable and that therefore banks have adequate liquidity. It also has the responsibility for controlling the money supply, which largely consists of bank deposits. For both these reasons the Bank of England will need to monitor and if necessary influence the level of bank deposits. Those deposits which the Bank of England considers important for these purposes are known as eligible liabilities. These are total sterling deposits less (a) those having an original maturity in excess of two years, (b) various inter-bank deposits, since to count these would essentially be double counting, and (c) 40 per cent of items in transit.

Eligible liabilities

The sterling liabilities of banks that the Bank of England monitors for purposes of monetary policy.

Sterling assets

In order to fulfil the twin aims of liquidity and profitability banks hold a whole range of assets. Ideally they would like these assets to be as illiquid as possible, since the less the liquidity, the higher the rate of interest they can charge. But they must always have sufficient liquidity to cover the possibility of any withdrawals. The shorter the average maturity of their deposits, the greater will have to be the liquidity of their assets. The balance sheet in Table 16.2 shows the various sterling assets of the recognized banks in descending order of liquidity.

Notes and coin by definition are totally liquid. This is the money that banks keep in their safes or tills for everyday use.

Operational balances in the Bank of England are like the banks' own current accounts and are used for clearing purposes. They can be withdrawn in cash on demand and are thus also totally liquid. They do not earn interest.

The amount that banks hold in cash and operational balances is up to them and depends on the demand for cash that they expect from their customers. Since they earn no interest, the banks like to keep as little as possible of their assets in these two forms. As you can see from Table 16.2, they account for a tiny fraction of total assets.

All recognized banks (and all other institutions within the officially defined monetary sector) are required to keep cash balances in the Bank of England to the value of ½ per cent of their eligible liabilities. These *cash ratio deposits* are non-operational: in other words, the banks cannot withdraw them.

Even though banks hold only very small amounts of cash, they nevertheless hold a large amount of other relatively liquid assets which act as reserves, but which at the same time earn interest. The largest category of these is market loans.

Market loans consist of a variety of different loans from a few hours to a few weeks, mainly to other banks or to financial institutions such as the discount houses which specialize in short-term lending and borrowing. The market for short-term loans and deposits is known as the money market.

Money market

The market for short-term loans and deposits.

The most liquid of the market loans are money at call and short notice lent to the discount houses. Money at call is money which can be withdrawn at only a few hours' notice. It is sometimes referred to as 'overnight money'. Money at short notice is money lent for up to fourteen days. Money at call is the main reserve that banks draw on if they are short of cash. It is obvious, then, that the discount houses play a crucial role in the UK monetary system. Recognizing this importance, the Bank of England requires the banks to keep deposits with the discount houses of at least 2½ per cent of their eligible liabilities.

Money at call and short notice

Money lent by the banks to the discount houses from overnight to fourteen days.

Other UK market loans are primarily short-term loans to, or assets in, other banks.

Table 16.2 Balance sheet of UK recognized banks: January 1990

Sterling liabilities	£bn	%	Sterling assets	£bn	%
Sight deposits		(27.7)	Notes and coin	2.9	(0.5)
UK monetary sector	13.1				
UK public sector	2.3		Balances with Bank		(0.3)
UK private sector	122.6		of England		
Overseas	13.2		Operational deposits	0.1	
			Cash ratio deposits	1.5	
Time deposits		(50.7)	Market loans		(25.6)
UK monetary sector	77.9		Discount houses	10.5	
UK public sector	6.4		Other UK (CDs, etc.)	103.7	
UK private sector	133.6		Overseas	25.5	
Overseas	58.0				
			Bills of exchange		(2.6)
Certificates of			Treasury bills	2.0	
deposit, etc.	49.5	(9.1)	Local authority bills	0.1	
			Commercial bills	11.4	
Items in suspense	9.6	(1.8)	Investments		(4.4)
and transmission			Public sector	4.7	
			Other	19.2	
Capital and other	56.7	(10.4)	Advances		(61.6)
funds			UK public sector	1.6	
			UK private sector	319.5	
Notes outstanding	1.4	(0.3)	overseas	15.3	
			Misellaneous	27.0	(5.0)
			Special deposits with	0.0	(0.0)
			the Bank of England		
Total sterling	544.00	(100.0)	**Total sterling assets**	547.3	(100.0)
liabilities (Of which:					
Eligible liabilities)	(285.9)	(64.1)			
Liabilities in other	674.0		Assets in other	670.7	
currencies			currencies		
Total liabilities	1218.0		Total assets	1218.0	

Source: *Financial Statistics* (CSO).

For example, if one bank has excess cash and another a shortage of cash, the first bank could make a short-term loan to the second. Certificates of deposit are an important part of other UK market loans. The bank with surplus cash could buy CDs on the money market that had been issued by another bank. In addition to loans to other banks, the category of 'other market loans' also includes short-term loans to local authorities and building societies.

 If a bank has a surplus of cash, why might it choose to make a market loan with it rather than giving extra personal loans or mortgages to its customers?

Market loans account for some 26 per cent of banks' sterling assets and are thus a major source of liquidity to individual banks. Note, however, that although short-term loans from one bank to another may provide an *individual* bank with liquidity, they do not provide the banking system as a whole with liquidity.

 Suppose there was a sudden surge in demand for cash from the general public. Would the existence of inter-bank market loans help to meet the demand in any way? (We will look at the answer to this problem later on.)

Bill of exchange

A certificate promising to repay a stated amount on a certain date, typically three months from the issue of the bill. Bills pay no interest as such, but are sold at a discount and redeemed at face value, thereby earning a rate of discount for the purchaser.

Bills of exchange are of three types: Treasury bills, local authority bills and commercial bills.

A bill of exchange is a certificate whereby the issuer (the borrower) promises to pay a certain amount of money on some specified future date. The purchaser of the bill is thus giving the issuer of the bill a loan from the date of purchase until the date of maturity.

Bills pay no interest. In order to make it worthwhile for people to buy bills, therefore, they must be sold below their face value (i.e. at a *discount*). The discount price will depend on current short-term rates of interest on comparable investments in other assets. The higher the rates of interest on other assets, the lower will be the price that people will be prepared to pay for bills (and hence the higher their *rate of discount*). For example, if interest rates are currently 12 per cent on other equivalent assets, a £100 000 bill will be sold for approximately £97 000, which will earn the purchaser an approximately 3 per cent rate of discount over the three months, which is equivalent to approximately 12 per cent per annum.

(Note that a rate of discount is calculated on the *face value* not the purchase price. This is different from the way that rates of *interest* are calculated. Interest rates are based on the *initial* sum, not the sum at the end of the period. So, for example, £3000 interest for an investment of £97 000 is somewhat more than 3 per cent: it is $3/97 \times 100 = 3.09$ per cent.)

Treasury bills

Bills of exchange issued by the Bank of England on behalf of the government. They are a means whereby the government raises short-term finance.

Treasury bills are issued by the Bank of England on behalf of the government. They are, in effect, loans to the government. They are issued for three months (91 days) at a weekly tender (an auction where bids are submitted in writing). The price that they are sold for, and hence their rate of discount, will depend on demand and supply. Demand and supply will ensure that the rate of discount will reflect market rates of interest. But the Bank of England can nevertheless influence the rate of discount by altering the amount of Treasury bills it sells. In fact this is the major way in which the government seeks to *alter* market rates of interest. (This is examined in Chapter 17.) They are thus of great importance in the management of the economy despite their small total in banks' balance sheets.

Local authority bills are also three-month bills and provide an important source of short-term finance to local authorities.

Commercial and local authority bills

Bills of exchange issued by firms and local authorities respectively.

Commercial bills are issued by firms. They have grown in importance in recent years as a way of financing trade, and in particular of tiding firms over the period from when they have to buy inputs to when they are able to sell the finished output. They are issued for anything from one month to twelve, but three months is typical.

The main purchasers of bills are the discount houses, which then sell many of them at a slightly higher price, to the banks. The banks do not buy bills directly from the issuers. They only buy them from discount houses, and then only after the bills are a few weeks old. Bills can be very easily bought and sold, and their market price steadily rises throughout the three months, with little fluctuation, until the face value is reached on maturity date. They therefore provide a secure and highly liquid asset for the banks.

 If a discount house buys a £50 000 Treasury bill for £48 000 at roughly what price will it sell it to a bank after six weeks?

Investments are of two major types. *Investments in public-sector stock* are mainly in short-dated government bonds (see Table 16.3). As explained in section 16.1, their price fluctuates inversely with the current market rate of interest. Since a rise in interest rates can cause quite a severe fall in the price of bonds, banks could make a

Table 16.3 Selected UK government bond prices ('British funds'): 17 April 1990

High	Low	Stock			Price	Ch'ge	Int only yld%	Gross Red yld%
		British Funds						
1990								
Shorts (under five years)								
84¾	82	Treas	3%	1992	83¼	. .	3.8	12.030
91⅞	85½	Treas	8%	1992	89⅜	−½	8.9	14.154
95½	90¾	Treas	10%	1992	93¼	−½	10.7	14.244
97⅛	88	Treas C	10½%	1992	93¾	−¼	10.6	11.243
100½	92	Exch	12¼%	1992	96⅜	−¼	12.6	14.054
101	97⅜	Treas	12⅔%	1992	97⅜	−½	13.0	14.203
103¾	94⅞	Exch	13½%	1992	99	−¼	13.6	13.898
85⅞	81½	Fund	6%	1993	82⅞	−½	7.2	12.247
91¼	86⅔	Treas	8¼%	1993	87⅔	−½	9.4	13.645
96½	87	Treas	10%	1993	91⅝	−½	10.9	13.510
102⅞	96⅔	Treas	12½%	1993	97⅛	−⅔	12.8	13.593
107⅛	100½	Treas	13⅔	1993	100⅞	−⅓	13.6	13.437
Five to fifteen years								
96½	83⅞	Conv	10%	1996	87¾	−⅜	11.4	12.918
110¾	96	Exch	13½%	1996	101½	−½	13.1	13.030
112⅜	102⅜	Treas	14%	1996	103½	·	13.5	13.188
119½	102½	Treas	15¼%	1996	109¼	−⅜	13.9	13.048
90	81	Treas	8¾%	1997	81½	−⅜	10.7	12.664
98¾	89½	Exch	10½%	1997	89½	−½	11.7	12.852
111⅜	100⅞	Treas	13¼%	1997	101	−½	13.1	13.019
120⅜	102½	Exch	15%	1997	108⅞	−½	13.7	13.108
88½	78	Treas	8½%	2000	78½	−½	10.8	12.388
91⅞	80⅜	Conv	9%	2000	80⅞	−½	11.1	12.408
114⅞	101½	Treas	13%	2000	101½	−⅔	12.8	12.828
91¼	76	Exch	9%	2002	79½	−½	11.3	12.278
96½	83⅝	Treas	9⅜%	2002	83%	−⅔	11.6	12.366
97¾	84½	Conv	10%	2002	87¼	. .	11.5	12.213
107	102½	Exch	12%	1999–02	102½	. .	12.6	13.061
98⅔	85½	Treas	10%	2003	85⅝	−½	11.6	12.200
118⅔	105	Treas	13⅜%	2000–03	105	−¼	13.1	12.876
Over fifteen years								
84½	72	Treas	8%	2002–08	72	−½	11.1	11.908
89⅔	76¼	Treas	8½%	2007	76¼	−¾	11.1	11.748
111	96⅔	Treas	11¾%	2003–07	96⅜	−½	12.1	12.289
93¾	78½	Treas	9%	2008	80	−½	11.2	11.647
125	108½	Treas	13½%	2004–08	108½	−½	12.4	12.212
85¼	72¾	Treas	8%	2009	72¾	−½	11.0	11.607
94	80	Conv	9%	2011	80	−½	11.2	11.554
63½	52¼	Treas	5⅝%	2008–12	52¼	−¼	10.4	11.348
82½	69¼	Treas	7¼%	2012–15	69¾	−½	11.1	11.474
Undated								
25⅞	21¾	Console	2½%		21½	. .	. .	. .
61¾	56⅞	Console	3½%		56½	. .	6.2	. .
41	34¾	Console	4		34⅞	. .	. .	. .
25½	21½	Treas	2½%		21½	. .	. .	. .
32⅔	28	Treas	3%		28½	−½	. .	. .
36¾	30⅞	War Ln	3½%		30½	. .	. .	. .

Source: *The Times*, 18 April 1990.

considerable capital loss if they were forced to sell them at such times. Thus although they can *easily* be sold, they are not very *liquid*. If, however, a bond only has a short time left to maturity, it will be much more liquid: its market price will be near its face value. Thus banks are very willing to hold these 'short-dated' bonds. Banks normally do not hold bonds with more than five years to maturity and a large proportion of their bonds have less than one year to maturity.

 Examine the bond prices given in Table 16.3. How do the prices relate to (a) their interest payments (on face value) and (b) their closeness to maturity?

Other investments are largely in subsidiary banks in the UK or abroad. Banks do not invest in company shares (equities) or company bonds (debentures).

Advances are the major profit-earning asset for the banks and account for over 60 per cent of their sterling assets. Advances include all the various forms of loan to households and firms. The three major categories at retail level are overdrafts, personal loans for fixed periods, and mortgages.

Miscellaneous assets largely consist of payments owed but not yet received from other banks.

Special deposits

Deposits that the banks can be required to make in the Bank of England. They remain frozen there until the Bank of England chooses to release them.

The Bank of England has the power to require banks to make 'special deposits' in the Bank of England. These deposits are then frozen – they cannot be withdrawn by the banks. They are thus a simple mechanism of reducing banks' liquidity and hence the amount of lending that banks can safely do. The special deposits are only released when the Bank of England feels that the time is right to allow credit to expand again. The government after 1980 chose not to use this method of controlling bank lending and hence the figure for special deposits in Table 16.2 is zero. The facility still remains for them to be used should the government so choose.

As we have seen, it is important for banks to maintain adequate liquidity. This means that the banks must hold enough cash and assets that can be readily turned into cash to be able to meet any demands from their customers. The following assets are defined by the Bank of England as being liquid:

- Operational balances with the Bank of England.
- Money at call and short notice with the discount houses.
- Bills of exchange: Treasury, local authority and certain commercial bills.
- Government bonds with less than a year to maturity.

Before 1981, these assets were known as 'reserve assets' and banks were required to hold a 12½ per cent 'reserve assets ratio'. This meant that reserve assets had to be at least 12½ per cent of eligible liabilities. Today the only *statutory* requirement is the ½ per cent cash ratio that banks must keep with the Bank of England. It is largely up to the banks themselves to decide on the ratio that they consider to be 'prudent': i.e. the ratio that provides them with enough liquid assets to enable them to meet any demands for cash.

Nevertheless the Bank of England still requires banks (and other institutions in the monetary sector) to maintain sufficient liquidity, and from time to time it can order them to increase their liquidity ratio if it feels that this is necessary. The actual ratio that the Bank of England considers to be prudent will depend on the type of bank and its proportion of sight deposits to demand deposits.

(Note that the Bank of England does not regard cash in tills as a reserve asset. The reason is that this is cash that banks are likely to need anyway, and which cannot therefore be used to meet an *increase* in demand for cash.)

 Why are government bonds which still have eleven months to run regarded as liquid, whereas overdrafts granted for a few weeks are not?

The role of the London money market

It is through the London money market that the Bank of England exercises its control of the economy. The market deals in short-term lending and borrowing. It is normally divided into the 'classical' or 'discount' market and the 'parallel' or 'complementary' market.

The discount market

There are three groups of participants in the discount market: (a) the Bank of England and other issuers of bills, (b) the discount houses and (c) the banks. Central in the relationship are the discount houses. They lend money short term to the government (through the Bank of England), to local authorities and to firms by buying bills of exchange. To do this they obtain money from the banks by borrowing money at call and short notice and by selling them bills. This relationship is illustrated in Figure 16.1.

Figure 16.1 The position of the discount houses

The discount houses provide an important service to the banks by allowing them to hold extremely liquid assets (money at call) which nevertheless earn interest. They also provide an important service to issuers of bills by offering a specialist market for such bills. In recent years the discount houses have not only borrowed from banks, but also lent to them by purchasing certificates of deposit.

Like banks, the discount houses make their profit by a process of maturity transformation: by borrowing short and lending long – or to be more precise, by borrowing very short indeed and lending slightly less short. They borrow from the banks for as little as a few hours' notice of recall by the banks (money at call), and lend to the government, local authorities and firms for typically three months (bills of exchange). They pay a slightly lower rate of interest on money at call than they earn by discounting bills. The liability and asset structure of the discount houses can be illustrated by looking at their balance sheet. Table 16.4 shows the combined balance sheet of the nine discount houses at the end of January 1990.

As we have seen, if banks are short of cash they can call in loans from the discount houses. But then the discount houses in turn may be short of liquid assets to meet this demand. What can the discount houses do?

In such circumstances (known as 'the last resort') the Bank of England will always step in and lend to the discount houses, or purchase bills of exchange from them

Table 16.4 Balance sheet of the discount houses: January 1990

Sterling liabilities		£m	Sterling assets	£m
Money at call		13 453	Cash ratio deposits with the B. of E.	13
Other		2 069	Treasury bills	836
			Local authority bills	2
			Commercial bills	5 511
(Of which:			Short-term loans to banks, etc.	479
Banks and other UK			Short-term loans to local authorities	12
monetary sector	10 931		Certificates of deposit	6 225
Other UK	4 574		Other UK	2 415
Overseas	16)		Overseas	87
			Investments	219
			Other assets	47
Total sterling liabilities		15 522	Total sterling assets	15 846
Liabilities in other currencies		379	Assets in other currencies	376

Source: *Financial Statistics* (CSO).

before the bills have reached maturity. The preferred method in recent years has been to purchase commercial bills. (The Bank of England is normally only prepared to buy commercial bills if they have been accepted, i.e. insured against default ('underwritten') by an acceptance house or other recognized bank. These are called *fine bills*.) The process of purchasing bills by the Bank of England is known as rediscounting.

Rediscounting bills of exchange
Buying bills before they reach maturity.

In being prepared to lend to the discount houses or to buy bills from them, the Bank of England is the ultimate guarantor of sufficient liquidity in the monetary system and is known as lender of last resort. The rate of rediscount, however, will be a penal one. It will be higher than the Treasury bill rate. The discount houses will therefore not like to sell bills to the Bank of England unless they are forced to. If they *are* forced to, they are said to be 'in the Bank'. This is not as uncommon as you might at first think. In fact it is often a deliberate policy of the Bank of England to create a shortage of liquidity in the economy to force discount houses to be in the Bank. But why should the Bank of England do this? It does it if it wishes to force up interest rates. If the Bank of England puts up its rediscount rate, discount houses will have to put up *their* rate of discount on bills (i.e. pay a lower price for them). This will have a knock-on effect throughout the economy, and will drive up interest rates generally. Just how the Bank of England does this, we will examine in Chapter 17.

Lender of last resort
The role of the Bank of England as the guarantor of sufficient liquidity in the monetary system.

The parallel money markets
The parallel money markets include the following:

- The inter-bank market (loans from one bank to another from one day to up to several months).
- The market for certificates of deposit.
- The local authorities market (local authority bills, short-term bonds and other short-term local authority borrowing or deposits).
- The inter-companies deposit market (short-term loans from one company to another arranged through the market).
- The foreign currencies market (dealings in foreign currencies deposited short term in London).
- Finance house borrowing (short-term borrowing to finance hire purchase).

The parallel markets have grown in size and importance in recent years. The main reasons for this have been (a) the opening-up of markets to international dealing, given the abolition of exchange controls in 1979, (b) the deregulation of banking and money market dealing and (c) the volatility of interest rates and exchange rates, and thus the desire of banks to keep funds in a form that can be readily switched from one form of deposit to another, or from one currency to another. The main areas of growth have been in inter-bank deposits, certificates of deposit and the foreign currency markets.

Although the Bank of England does not deal directly in the parallel markets and does not provide 'last resort' lending facilities, it nevertheless closely monitors the various money market rates of interest and if necessary seeks to influence them, either by its dealings in the discount market or by 'indicating' the direction it would like to see interest rates move.

> **?** 1. Why should Bank of England intervention to influence rates of interest in the discount market also influence rates of interest in the parallel markets?
> 2. If the Bank of England indicates that it would like to see interest rates rise, why should dealers in the parallel markets take any notice?

The Bank of England

We end this section by having a closer look at the Bank of England, the UK's central bank. All countries have a central bank and they fulfil two vital roles in the economy. The first is to oversee the whole monetary system and ensure that banks and other financial institutions operate as stably and as efficiently as possible. The second is to act as the government's agent, both as its banker and in carrying out monetary policy. Just how closely a central bank works with the government will vary from country to country. In the UK the Bank of England works in very close liaison with the Treasury, and although it may privately disagree with Treasury policy it is always obliged to carry it out. This requirement was made explicit in 1946 when the Bank of England was nationalized. In some other countries central banks are more independent of the government and can take much more initiative in deciding monetary policy.

Within these two broad roles the Bank of England has a number of different functions. We have already come across some of these in looking at other institutions. We can now give a complete list.

It issues notes

The Bank of England is the sole issuer of banknotes in England and Wales. (In Scotland the clearing banks issue notes.) The issue of notes is done through the Issue Department, which organizes their printing. This is one of two departments of the Bank of England. The other is the Banking Department. Table 16.5 shows the balance sheets of these two departments on 17 January 1990. As you can see from the balance sheet for the Issue Department, the note issue is backed by government and other securities (such as fine bills purchased from the discount houses).

The amount of banknotes issued by the Bank of England depends largely on the demand for notes from the general public. If people draw more cash from their bank accounts, the banks will have to draw more cash from their balances in the Bank of England. These balances are held in the Banking Department. The Banking Department will thus have to acquire more notes from the Issue Department, which will simply print more in exchange for extra government or other securities supplied by the Banking Department. Thus the amount of notes in circulation is always more at Christmas time.

The size of the note issue also depends on Bank of England intervention in the money market. If the Issue Department buys government securities (either old ones

Table 16.5 Balance sheet of the Bank of England: 17 January 1990

Liabilities	£m	Assets	£m
Issue Department			
Notes in circulation	15 042	Government securities	10 527
Notes in Banking Department	8	Other securities	4 523
	15 050		15 050
Banking Department			
Public deposits	58	Government securities	1 212
Special deposits	0	Advances and other accounts	549
Bankers' deposits	1 560	Premises, equipment, etc.	1 768
Reserves and other accounts	1 920	Notes and coin from Issue	
	3 538	Department	9
			3 538

Source: *Financial Statistics* (CSO).

soon due to mature or new ones issued by the government), it will buy them with extra money that it prints.

It acts as a bank

To the government. It keeps the two major government accounts: the 'Exchequer' and the 'National Loans Fund'. Taxation and government spending pass through the Exchequer. Government borrowing and lending pass through the National Loans Fund. The government tends to keep its deposits in the Bank of England (the *public deposits* item in the balance sheet) to a minimum. If the deposits begin to build up (from taxation), the government will probably spend them on paying back government debt. If, on the other hand, it runs short of money, it will simply borrow more.

To the recognized banks. The *bankers' deposits* item in the balance sheet refers to the cash ratio and operational balances of the banks. As we have seen, the operational balances are used for clearing purposes between the banks and to provide them with a source of liquidity.

To overseas central banks. These are deposits of sterling held by overseas authorities as part of their official reserves and/or for purposes of intervening in the foreign exchange market in order to influence the exchange rate of their currency.

It manages the government's borrowing programme

Whenever the government runs a budget deficit, it will have to finance that deficit by borrowing. It can borrow by issuing either gilt-edged securities (government bonds) or Treasury bills. The Bank of England organizes this borrowing. Even when the government runs a budget surplus the Bank of England will still have to manage the national debt (the accumulated borrowing from the past). The reason is that old bonds will be maturing and new issues of bonds will probably be necessary to replace them.

When an old issue of bonds is approaching maturity, the Bank of England will probably enter the market to buy them back over a number of weeks or months, rather than waiting to the maturity date and then suddenly releasing a large amount of liquidity into the economy.

When a new issue of bonds is made, the Bank of England will set a minimum price somewhat below the £100 face value and then invite tenders for these bonds above or at the minimum price. It will allocate them in descending order from the highest-priced bid to the lowest. Any unsold bonds (known as 'tap stock') will then be released on to the market in an orderly way at a price set by the Bank of England. Any temporary shortfall of money for the government is met by issuing Treasury bills.

The issuing of bonds and bills will also depend on the government's monetary policy. This is examined in Chapter 17.

It supervises the activities of banks and other financial institutions

It advises banks on good banking practice. It discusses government policy with them and reports back to the government. It requires all recognized banks to maintain adequate liquidity: this is called prudential control. For example, it requires banks to keep money at call with the discount houses to a minimum of 2½ per cent of their eligible liabilities. It monitors the activity of banks, which are required to submit monthly reports to it, and it attempts to spot any bank that is likely to face difficulties.

Prudential control
The insistence by the Bank of England that recognized banks maintain adequate liquidity.

It provides support to prevent banks getting into difficulties

As lender of last resort to the discount houses, it ensures that there is always an adequate supply of liquidity to meet the legitimate demands of depositors in recognized banks.

It may also come to the rescue of ailing banks. For example, in 1984 the Johnson Matthey Bank collapsed. The Bank of England stepped in, took over the running of it and provided sufficient loans to cover the demands of its creditors. Of course, if the Bank of England's supervision were perfect, rescue packages such as this would be unnecessary.

It operates the government's monetary and exchange rate policy

Monetary policy. By careful management of the issue and purchase/rediscounting of government bonds and Treasury bills, the Bank of England can manipulate interest rates and influence the size of the money supply. Details of this are given in Chapter 17.

Exchange rate policy. The Bank of England manages the country's gold and foreign currency reserves. This is done through the exchange equalization account. By buying and selling foreign currencies on the foreign exchange market, the Bank of England can affect the exchange rate. For example, if there were a sudden selling of sterling (due, say, to bad trade figures and a resulting fear that the pound would depreciate), the Bank of England could help to prevent the pound from falling by using reserves to buy up pounds on the foreign exchange market. Intervention in the foreign exchange market is examined in detail in Chapter 22.

Exchange equalization account
The gold and foreign exchange reserves account in the Bank of England.

? 1. Would it be possible for an economy to function without (a) a central bank; (b) discount houses?
2. What effect would a substantial increase in the sale of government bonds and Treasury bills have on interest rates?

▲ SUMMARY

1. Financial intermediaries include commercial banks, merchant banks, the National Savings Bank, building societies, finance houses and discount houses. Between them they provide the following important functions: giving expert advice, channelling capital to areas of highest return, maturity transformation, risk transformation and the transmission of payments.

2. Banks aim to make profits, but they must also maintain sufficient liquidity. Liquid assets, however, tend to be unprofitable and profitable assets tend to be illiquid. Banks therefore hold a range of assets of varying degrees of profitability and liquidity.

3. Commercial banks' liabilities include both sight and time deposits. They also include certificates of deposit. Their

assets include in descending order of liquidity: notes and coin, balances with the Bank of England, market loans (including money at call with the discount houses), bills of exchange (Treasury, commercial and local authority), investments (government bonds and inter-bank investments) and advances to customers (the biggest item, including overdrafts, personal loans and mortgages).

4. The money market is the market in short-term deposits and loans. It consists of the discount market and the parallel money markets. The discount market centres on the activities of the discount houses. They lend money to the government, firms and local authorities by discounting bills of exchange and to banks by purchasing certificates of deposit. They borrow from the banks at call and short notice. They also receive finance from the banks by selling them bills they have purchased. The Bank of England operates in the discount market by buying (rediscounting) and selling bills. It thereby seeks to manipulate interest rates. It is always prepared to lend to the discount houses in the *last resort* in order to ensure adequate liquidity in the economy.

5. The parallel money markets consist of various markets in short-term finance between various financial institutions.

6. The Bank of England is the UK's central bank. It issues notes; it acts as banker to the government, to the commercial banks, to various overseas central banks and to certain private customers; it manages the government's borrowing programme; it supervises the activities of banks and other financial institutions; it provides support to prevent banks getting into difficulties; it operates the government's monetary and exchange rate policy.

16.3 The supply of money

Definitions of the money supply in the UK

Monetarists argue that changes in the supply of money have a crucial effect on the economy. If inflation is to be controlled, they maintain, then the money supply must be controlled. Keynesians see money supply as less important, but even they do not believe that money supply can be ignored.

If money supply is to be monitored and possibly controlled, it is obviously necessary to measure it. But what should be included in the measure? As we have seen in section 16.2, money does not just include cash. It also includes bank deposits. But *which* deposits? Herein lies a problem. There are several different ways we can define money supply, depending on which types of deposit we include and which types we exclude from our definition. In the UK, until July 1989, there were no fewer than *seven* different definitions! Now these have been reduced to five. The definitions can be put into two groups: narrow money and broad money (see Table 16.6).

Narrow money

M0. This is the narrowest definition of money. It consists of notes and coin (both in circulation and in banks' tills), and the operational balances that banks hold in the Bank of England. It is sometimes referred to as the 'broad monetary base' ('broad' because it includes operational balances in the Bank of England as well as cash). This is a relatively new measure of money supply, first introduced in 1982. It is one of the easiest measures for the government to control, but it has been frequently criticized as being of little use as an indicator of spending power in the economy since it excludes the most important component of money supply, namely bank deposits, and includes money in banks' tills which is the money that banks need to *keep* in their tills as a 'float'.

M1. This was an older narrow definition, in fact the only one until a few years ago. It included notes and coin in circulation with the general public (but not in banks' tills), and sterling private sector *sight* deposits in banks.

This measure was dropped in 1989. There were three reasons for this:

- Increasingly, sight deposits pay interest. The amount of these deposits will therefore vary with the rate of interest. Such accounts are frequently used by firms

Table 16.6 UK monetary aggregates

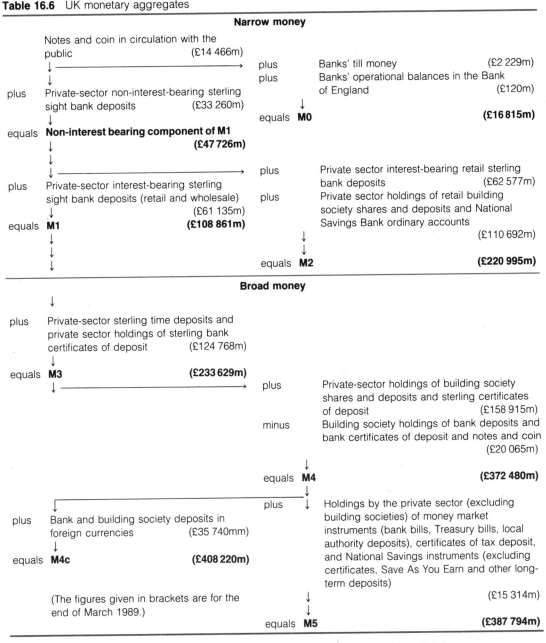

Sources: *Economic Progress Report* (HM Treasury, August 1988); *Bank of England Quarterly Bulletin.*

to make short-term large deposits – when, for example, they have a temporary surplus of funds. They are not therefore directly related to people's requirements to hold a medium of exchange. They are *wholesale* not *retail* deposits, and yet they were still included in M1.

- On the other hand, there are various time deposits that earn interest in banks, building societies and the National Savings Bank which are used by the public as an alternative means of holding money that *is* used for expenditure purposes. These retail deposits were not included in M1.

- In July 1989 the Abbey National Building Society became a retail bank. Had M1 been retained as a narrow measure of money supply, it would have shown a sudden increase as the sight deposits in the Abbey National would now have been included. Given the blurring of the distinction between banks and building societies, it was felt that now was the time to drop those measures (M1 and M3) which included bank deposits but not building society deposits.

M2. To take account of the weaknesses of M1 as a definition of narrow money, a new definition, M2, was introduced in 1982. This is M1 minus the wholesale sight deposits but including all retail deposits (both sight and time).

Broad money

In addition to retail deposits, broad definitions also include wholesale deposits. M3 (now abandoned) only included *bank* deposits. M4 and M5, however, include building society deposits too. M5 also includes various money market instruments. Each of the broad measures includes all those items contained in M1. So let us see how each of the broad measures builds up from there.

M3. This consisted of M1 plus all sterling private-sector *time* deposits in *banks* (but not building societies), plus private-sector holdings of *bank* certificates of deposit. Along with M1 this was the oldest definition of money.

M4. This is M3 plus private-sector deposits in building societies and private-sector holdings of certificates of deposit in building societies. To avoid double counting, it is necessary to *subtract* building society deposits in banks and building society holdings of bank certificates of deposit. Otherwise if, say, £1 million was deposited in a building society and the building society then deposited the £1 million in a bank, it would count as £2 million – a clear case of double counting.

M4c. All the other measures of money supply only include sterling. M4c, by contrast, includes both sterling *and* foreign currency private-sector deposits. In other respects the definition is the same as M4.

M5. This is M4 plus various other holdings of liquid assets. These include bills of exchange eligible for rediscount at the Bank of England, short-term loans to local authorities, short- and medium-term deposits in the National Savings Bank and certificates of tax deposit.

? 1. Why would the inclusion of money deposited at call with the discount houses in any of the definitions be a case of 'double counting'?

2. None of the measures includes *public-sector* deposits. Why do you think this is?

The proliferation of measures gives some indication of just how ambiguous the term 'money supply' is. To talk about controlling *the* money supply is too vague. A major problem is that the measures do not all move together. For example, if people switched deposits from time deposits to sight deposits, M1 would rise but M4 would remain unchanged.

The government, recognizing this problem, tries to gain an *overall* impression of the growth of money supply rather than concentrating on one measure alone. In recent years it has paid particular attention to M0, M4 and M5.

With the exception of M0, all the definitions of money supply include bank deposits as the major item. When governments attempt to control the money supply, therefore, they must seek to control the size of bank deposits and thereby control the amount of bank lending and hence total expenditure in the economy (aggregate demand).

To understand how money supply expands and contracts, and how it can be controlled, it is thus necessary to understand what determines the size of bank deposits. Banks can themselves expand the amount of bank deposits, and hence the money supply, by a process known as 'credit creation'.

The creation of credit: the simplest case

To illustrate this process in its simplest form, assume that banks have just one type of liability – deposits – and two types of asset – balances with the Bank of England (to achieve liquidity), and advances to customers (to earn profit).

Banks want to achieve profitability whilst maintaining sufficient liquidity. Assume that they believe that sufficient liquidity will be achieved if 10 per cent of their assets are held as balances with the Bank of England. The remaining 90 per cent will then be in advances to customers. In other words, the banks operate a 10 per cent liquidity ratio.

Assume initially that the combined balance sheet of the banks is as shown in Table 16.7. Total deposits are £100 billion, of which £10 billion (10 per cent) are kept in balances with the Bank of England. The remaining £90 billion (90 per cent) are lent to customers.

Table 16.7 Banks' original balance sheet

Liabilities	£bn	Assets	£bn
Deposits	100	Balances with the B. of E.	10
		Advances	90
Total	100	Total	100

Now assume that the government spends more money – £10 billion say, on roads or the National Health Service. It pays for this with cheques drawn on its account with the Bank of England. The people receiving the cheques deposit them in their banks. Banks return these cheques to the Bank of England and their balances correspondingly increase by £10 billion. The combined banks' balance sheet now is shown in Table 16.8.

Table 16.8 The initial effect of an additional deposit of £10 billion

Liabilities	£bn	Assets	£bn
Deposits (old)	100	Balances with the B. of E. (old)	10
Deposits (new)	10	Balances with the B. of E. (new)	10
		Advances	90
Total	110	Total	110

But this is not the end of the story. Banks now have surplus liquidity. With their balances in the Bank of England having increased to £20 billion, they now have a liquidity ratio of 20/110. If they are to return to a 10 per cent liquidity ratio, they need only retain £11 billion as balances at the Bank of England (£11 billion/£110 billion = 10 per cent). The remaining £9 billion they can lend to customers.

But then when customers spend this £9 billion in shops and the shopkeepers deposit the cheques back in the banks, thereby crediting the banks' Bank of England accounts again, the banks can make *further* loans based on these new deposits. 10 per cent (i.e. £0.9 billion) must be kept back in the Bank of England, but the remaining 90 per cent (i.e. £8.1 billion) can be lent out again. When this is deposited back in banks,

Table 16.9 The full effect of an additional deposit of £10 billion

Liabilities	£bn	Assets	£bn
Deposits (old)	100	Balances with the B. of E. (old)	10
Deposits (new: initial)	10	Balances with the B. of E. (new)	10
(new: subsequent)	90	Advances (old)	90
		Advances (new)	90
Total	200	Total	200

again 10 per cent must be retained and the remaining 90 per cent can be lent out. This process goes on and on until eventually the position is as shown in Table 16.9.

The initial increase in balances with the Bank of England of £10 billion has allowed banks to create new advances (and hence deposits) of £90 billion, making a total increase in money supply of £100 billion.

Money (or bank) multiplier

The number of times greater the expansion of money is than the additional liquidity that caused it: money multiplier = 1/*L*.

This effect is known as the money (or bank) multiplier. In this simple example with a liquidity ratio of 1/10 (i.e. 10 per cent), the money multiplier is 10. An initial increase in deposits of £10 billion allowed total deposits to rise by £100 billion. In this simple world, therefore, the money multiplier is the inverse of the liquidity ratio (*L*).

Money multiplier = 1/*L*

If banks choose to operate a 20 per cent liquidity ratio and receive extra cash deposits of £10 million:
(a) How much credit will ultimately be created?
(b) By how much will total deposits have expanded?
(c) What is the size of the money multiplier?

The creation of credit: the real world

In practice the creation of credit is not as simple as this. There are two major complications.

Banks' liquidity ratio may vary

Banks may choose a different liquidity ratio. At certain times, banks may decide that it is prudent to hold a bigger proportion of liquid assets. Their 'prudent' liquidity ratio has risen. The prudent ratio depends very much on how banks see their requirements for liquidity changing in the near future. If Christmas or the Summer holidays are approaching and people are likely to make bigger cash withdrawals, banks may decide to hold more liquid assets. They may also do so if they anticipate that their liquid assets may soon be squeezed by government monetary policy.

Customers may not want to take up the credit on offer. Banks may wish to make additional loans, but customers may not want to borrow. There may be insufficient demand. But will the banks not then lower their interest rates, thus encouraging people to borrow? Possibly, but it is not as simple as this. Banks must keep all their interest rates in line with other financial institutions in order to remain competitive. If banks lower the interest rates they charge to borrowers, they must also lower the rate they pay to depositors. But then depositors may switch to other institutions such as building societies.

Thus, just because banks have acquired additional liquid assets, it does not automatically follow that they will create credit on the basis of it.

Just as a change in liquid assets may lead to little or no change in credit, so a change

Box 16.7

Making Money Grow
A touch of banking magic

Let us examine in a bit more detail the way banks create money. First, it is worth noting that most bank managers would claim that they do no such thing. Their business is to balance their books; to lend out money that has *already* been deposited, not to create things out of thin air. But, unbeknown to them perhaps, the creation of money is precisely what they *initiate* when they grant a loan.

This time, rather than assuming that the government spends extra money and issues cheques drawn on its account in the Bank of England, let us do some magic of our own. Let us assume that while digging your garden you unearth a chest containing £1000. Delighted, you rush down to your bank (Lloyds) and deposit it before it gets stolen or the police start asking awkward questions.

Your Lloyds bank manager, only slightly less delighted than you, realizes that most of it can be lent to other customers and hence earn interest for the bank (more than the bank pays you!). First, though, the bank deposits the bulk of the cash with the Bank of England, thus swelling its operational balances there. Assuming, for simplicity, that all banks operate a 10 per cent liquidity ratio, the bank will only need to retain £100 in cash for any withdrawals you are likely to make. But the bank now has £900 worth of balances in the Bank of England above what it needs to maintain. It thus grants loans of £900.

Assume that the £900 is lent to Amanda to buy a set of golf clubs. The sports shop, on receiving her cheque for £900, deposits it in its account in, say, the Midland. When the cheque is cleared, the Midland's balances in the Bank of England will have risen by £900. The Midland bank can now use this increased liquidity to make additional loans itself. Duly keeping 10 per cent back (i.e. £90), it grants a loan of £810 to Jason to buy a luxury hamster cage and a pair of very rare Mongolian crested hamsters from the local pet shop.

The pet shop banks Jason's cheque in its branch of Barclays. When it is cleared, Barclays lends 90 per cent

Bank	New deposits	Extra balances required at Bank of England	New loans granted
Your bank (Lloyds)	£1 000.00	£100.00	£900.00
Amanda's bank (Midland)	£900.00	£90.00	£810.00
Jason's bank (Barclays)	£810.00	£81.00	£729.00
Charlene's bank (Nat. West.)	£729.00	£72.90	£656.10
Totals	£10 000.00	£1 000.00	£9 000.00

(i.e. £729) of it to Charlene to buy a mountain bike. The bike shop deposits Charlene's cheque in its branch of the National Westminster, which duly makes a loan (or loans totalling) £656.10. And so on and so on . . .

This process is shown in the diagram.

1. 'Surely, when people deposit money in bank accounts, they often demand all or nearly all of it out in cash. Isn't it very dangerous, then, for banks to keep only a small percentage of it in cash or in their operational balances in the Bank of England?' How would you answer this worry?

2. How long will the process of credit creation we have described in this box take before the totals line is reached? Does this indicate that there would be a problem in controlling the money supply simply by controlling the amount of cash or other liquid assets in the economy?

in credit may occur with little or no change in liquid assets. For example, if there is an upsurge in consumer demand for credit, banks may be very keen to grant additional loans and thus make more profits, even though they have acquired no additional liquid assets. They may simply go ahead and expand credit, and accept a lower liquidity ratio. Obviously they will be much more willing to do this if they already have plenty of spare liquidity.

Why might a bank with a given amount of liquid assets be more willing to expand its mortgage loans for house purchase than to expand its personal loans for the purchase of consumer goods?

Banks may not operate a simple liquidity ratio

The fact that banks hold a number of fairly liquid assets, such as money at call, bills of exchange and short-dated bonds, makes it difficult to identify a simple liquidity ratio. Which items should count as liquid?

To illustrate the problem consider the following case. Assume (a) that banks hold just three types of asset: cash, bills and advances; (b) that they operate a 10 per cent liquidity ratio; and (c) that they acquire additional cash deposits of £1 million.

If bills are counted as liquid, then the banks can purchase up to £1 million of extra bills and *still* create the full £9 million of credit. The bills are equivalent to cash.

If, however, bills are not counted as liquid, then for each extra £1 worth of bills they purchase, they can grant £10 worth less credit (£9 less created, and £1 displaced by the (non-liquid) bills).

Thus whether near money assets such as call money, bills and short-dated bonds count as liquid may affect the amount of credit created.

In the past, the Bank of England has required banks to hold a certain liquidity ratio and has *specified* those assets that were to count as liquid (see page 662). Since 1981, however, there has no longer been any statutory reserve ratio (other than the requirement that banks must hold deposits at call with the discount houses of at least 2½ per cent of their eligible liabilities).

There is therefore no simple universal money multiplier applying to all banks.

Of course, banks still have to maintain adequate liquidity, but in practice they do not see a clear-cut dividing line between liquid and non-liquid assets. They try to maintain a rough balance across the liquidity range, but the precise composition of assets will vary as interest rates on the various assets vary, and as the demands for liquidity vary.

In practice, therefore, the size of the money multiplier will vary and is thus difficult to predict in advance.

Near money

Highly liquid assets (other than cash).

 Is the following statement true: 'The greater the number of types of asset that are counted as being liquid, the smaller will be the money multiplier'?

What causes money supply to rise?

There are four sets of circumstances in which the money supply can rise.

Banks choose to hold a lower liquidity ratio

If banks choose to hold a lower liquidity ratio, they will have surplus liquidity. The banks have tended to choose a lower liquidity ratio over the years, and certainly a lower cash ratio. A major reason for this has been the move by customers away from cash transactions to cheque and credit card transactions.

 What effects do EFTPOS and ATMs (see Box 16.5) have on (a) banks' prudent liquidity ratios; (b) the size of the money multiplier?

The surplus liquidity can be used to expand advances. As these loans are spent and find their way back to the banks as additional deposits, so the money supply expands. The impetus to expand advances may come from the banks themselves. The aggressive promotion of credit cards and the advertising of personal loans are familiar examples. The impetus may come from the customer. As an economy pulls out of recession, the demand for loans is likely to rise. Banks with surplus liquidity will normally be happy to meet this demand.

An inflow of funds from abroad

If the government intervenes in the foreign exchange market to maintain a rate of exchange below the equilibrium, there will be an excess demand for sterling. The government may do this in order to help exporters, since a low exchange rate will make exports cheaper for foreigners to buy.

The excess demand is illustrated in Figure 16.2. It is equal to $Q_d - Q_s$ at an exchange rate of er_1. To maintain the exchange rate at this level the Bank of England will have to supply sufficient pounds on to the foreign exchange market to close the gap. In other words, it will have to buy up the excess foreign currencies on offer with *extra* pounds – pounds it has created, thereby building up the foreign currency reserves. The money supply will thus increase. When this sterling is used to pay for UK exports and is then deposited back in the banks by the exporters, credit will be created on the basis of it, leading to a *multiplied* increase in money supply.

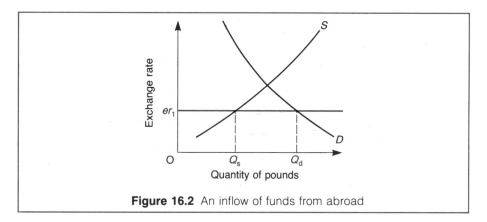

Figure 16.2 An inflow of funds from abroad

What we have been describing here is a total currency flow surplus. This is a net surplus on all elements of the balance of payments (current plus capital) but excluding the reserves. As we saw back in section 12.5, the building-up of reserves counts as a *deficit* (an *outflow* from the balance of payments account to the reserves account). This deficit on the reserves part of the balance of payments account will exactly match the surplus on the remainder of the account.

Changes in money supply from this source are likely to be much greater under a fixed than a floating exchange rate.

Under a fixed exchange rate a currency flow surplus is likely to persist for some time. The money supply will thus continue to grow. Eventually, however, the rise in money supply will eliminate the surplus. The reason is that the increase in money supply will raise aggregate demand. This in turn will lead to more imports. It may also lead to higher inflation, which, if pushed above that of the UK's overseas competitors, will reduce exports and increase imports. The net effect will be to eliminate the currency flow surplus. The demand curve for sterling will shift to the left and the supply curve will shift to the right until they intersect at the fixed rate of exchange. At that point the money will stop rising (at least from this source).

Under a totally free floating rate, total currency flow surpluses will be eliminated by an appreciation of the exchange rate. If, however, the Bank of England attempts to maintain an exchange rate below the equilibrium, it must continue to supply extra sterling to meet the shortfall and thus continue to expand the money supply.

A similar effect to the above will be experienced if depositors in foreign currencies wish to switch their deposits into sterling in the UK – in response, say, to higher

Total currency flow on the balance of payments

The current plus capital account balance but excluding the reserves.

interest rates in the UK. The demand for sterling will shift to the right. (Of course, if the exchange rate is allowed to appreciate, this effect will be eliminated.)

The money supply will also expand, but not via the balance of payments, if depositors of *sterling* in banks overseas redeposit their sterling in the UK. This is a direct inflow of sterling and hence a direct increase in the money supply.

In an open economy like the UK, with an absence of exchange controls, movements of sterling and other currencies into and out of the country can be very large, leading to large fluctuations in the money supply.

 Describe the process whereby a currency flow deficit will lead to a fall in the money supply.

The government can take deliberate steps to offset the monetary effects of currency flow surpluses or deficits. This process is known as sterilization. It is examined in Chapter 22.

A public-sector deficit: a PSBR

As we have seen before, the public-sector borrowing requirement is the deficit of the whole public sector (central government, local government and the nationalized industries): it is the difference between public-sector expenditure and public-sector receipts (from taxes, national insurance, rates and nationalized industry sales). To meet this deficit the government has to borrow money.

This borrowing is likely to affect the money supply. In general, the bigger the PSBR, the greater will be the growth in the money supply. Just how the money supply will be affected, however, depends on the form the borrowing takes. There are six possible forms. Assume in each case a PSBR of £1 billion.

1. The government sells securities to the Bank of England. The Bank of England purchases £1 billion of government securities, and credits the government's account at the Bank of England by £1 billion. The government, when it spends this £1 billion, pays with cheques drawn on its account at the Bank of England. When the recipients of these cheques pay them into their banks, the banks will present the cheques to the Bank of England, and their own balances at the Bank of England will rise by £1 billion. Thus banks' liabilities (customers' deposits of government payments) and assets (balances with the Bank of England) have both increased by £1 billion. Money supply has therefore increased by £1 billion.

Since banks' balances with the Bank of England are liquid assets, credit will probably be created. A multiplied process of money expansion will occur.

2. The government sells securities to overseas purchasers. This will lead to an inflow of foreign currency. A multiplied process of money expansion will occur just as in the case of a total currency flow surplus outlined above. (This assumes that the government does not allow the exchange rate to appreciate.)

3. The Bank of England, on behalf of the government, sells Treasury bills to the banking sector. If £1 billion of Treasury bills are sold to the discount houses, the discount houses will borrow money at call from the banks, or sell bills to the banks, to pay for these Treasury bills. Banks will thus acquire £1 billion of extra call notes and bills, but their cash or balances at the Bank of England will be reduced by £1 billion.

When, however, the government spends the £1 billion and the money finds its way back to the banks, the banks' balances at the Bank of England will rise back again by £1 billion.

There has thus been no overall change in balances at the Bank of England, but banks' holdings of call notes and bills have risen. To the extent that these are regarded as liquid assets, they can be used as the liquidity base for additional loans to customers. A multiplied process of money expansion will occur.

4. The government sells bonds to the banks. If £1 billion of bonds are sold to the banks, the banks' balances at the Bank of England will be reduced by £1 billion. When the government spends the money and it is deposited in the banks, the banks' balances at the Bank of England will be restored. Banks have thus had an increase of £1 billion deposits (new money) on their liabilities side, and £1 billion of government bonds on their assets side.

The liquidity ratio, however, has now been reduced, since bonds (except for very short-dated ones) are regarded as illiquid. If banks are already operating at their minimum prudent liquidity ratio, they must reduce advances (and hence deposits) by £1 billion, which will exactly match the £1 billion increase in deposits from the PSBR. In this case there will have been *no* expansion of the money supply at all.

5. The government sells bonds and Treasury bills to the general public and non-bank firms (collectively known as the 'non-bank private sector'). This will have no effect on the money supply. When the public buy the bonds or bills they will draw money from their banks. When the government spends the money it will be redeposited in banks. There is no new money. It is just a case of existing money changing hands.

6. The government borrows foreign currency, thereby directly financing government imports. This will not affect money supply since it involves no *sterling* transactions and hence will not affect banks' sterling deposits.

Thus financing the PSBR by methods 1, 2 and 3 will lead to a multiple growth in money supply (assuming sufficient demand for credit). Financing it by method 4 will lead to little or no growth in the money supply. Financing it by methods 5 and 6 will lead to no growth in the money supply at all.

Note that if there is a public sector *surplus* (public-sector debt repayment or PSDR), this will either reduce the money supply or have no effect, depending on what the government does with the surplus.

The fact that there is a surplus means that the public sector is spending less than it receives in taxes, etc. The initial effect, therefore, is to reduce the money in the economy: it is being 'retired' in the Bank of England. If the government then uses this money to repay the national debt by buying back more bonds and Treasury bills than it issues, this will release the money back into the economy again. If the bonds and bills are bought from the general public (the 'non-bank private sector'), the net effect is zero. The money paid by taxpayers over and above government expenditure merely returns to taxpayers again (albeit differently distributed).

If, however, the government buys back Treasury bills from the banking sector or bills or bonds from the Bank of England, there will be a net reduction in the money supply. As far as the banks are concerned, they have no change in their balances in the Bank of England (the government spends less money but then returns it to the banks by buying bills), but banks have fewer bills and hence fewer liquid assets. If banks' liquidity ratios are now below the prudent minimum, they will have to make a multiplied *contraction* in credit. If the government buys back bonds from the Bank of England, the money is not released: it remains retired.

Whether there is a PSBR or a PSDR, it is clear that the method the government uses to borrow or pay back debt will affect how much the money supply changes. In general, money supply growth will be higher (or its decline lower), the more the government borrows from the banking sector rather than the non-bank private sector (or repays to the non-bank private sector rather than the banking sector).

Here, then, is a fourth source of monetary growth.

A change in the method of financing the national debt

Even if there is no change in the level of the PSBR, the rate of change of money growth will be affected by the way in which government finance is raised.

The government's choice of how to raise finance depends on its monetary policy (which we will consider in the Chapter 17). In practice the government's choice is somewhat limited. Although it can choose whether to sell bonds or Treasury bills, it cannot decide just who is to purchase them – banks/discount houses, the general public or foreigners.

> **?** 1. If the government borrows *but does not spend the proceeds*, what effect will this have on the money supply if it borrows from (a) the banking sector; (b) the non-bank private sector?
> 2. If the government buys back £1 million of maturing bonds from the general public and then, keeping the total amount of its borrowing the same, raises £1 million by selling Treasury bills to the discount houses, what will happen to the money supply?

The flow-of-funds equation

Flow-of-funds equation

The various items making up an increase (or decrease) in money supply.

All these effects on money supply can be summarized using a flow-of-funds equation. This shows the components of a *change* in money supply. A change in money supply is a flow into (increase) or out of (decrease) the money stock. (Remember the distinction between stocks and flows.) In other words, if we want to compare the size of the money stock at one point in time (M_{s_t}) with that of a previous point in time ($M_{s_{t-1}}$), we have to look at the flow (change) of money between those two points (ΔM_s).

$$M_{s_t} = M_{s_{t-1}} + \Delta M_s$$

So what does ΔM_s consist of? The answer is given in the flow-of-funds equation, which consists of four major items (or 'counterparts' as they are known). The following flow-of-funds equation is the one most commonly used, that for M4:

ΔM_s	*equals*	PSBR (Item 1)
	minus	Sales of public-sector debt to (or *plus* purchases of public sector debt from) the non-bank private sector (Item 2)
	plus	Banks' and building societies' sterling lending to UK private sector (Item 3)
	plus	External effect (Item 4)

Public-sector borrowing (item 1) will lead to a direct increase in the money supply, but not if it is funded by selling bonds and bills to the non-bank private sector. Such sales (item 2) have therefore to be subtracted from the PSBR. But conversely, if the government buys back old bonds from the non-bank private sector, this will further increase the money supply.

The initial increase in liquidity from the sale of government securities to the banking sector is given by item 1. This increase in their liquidity will enable banks to create credit. To the extent that this extra lending is to the UK private sector (item 3), money supply will increase, and by a multiple of the initial increase in liquidity (item 1). Bank lending may also increase (item 3) even if there is no increase in liquidity or even a reduction in liquidity (item 1 is zero or negative), if banks respond to increases in the demand for loans by accepting a lower liquidity ratio.

Finally, if there is a currency flow surplus and hence a net inflow of funds from abroad (item 4), this too will increase the money supply. A currency flow deficit will appear as a negative figure. Also included in item 4 is that part of the PSBR that is funded by borrowing in *foreign* currency. Since, as we saw when looking at the financing of the PSBR, such borrowing does not increase the money supply, it reduces the otherwise expansionary effect on the money supply of the PSBR. It thus enters item 4 with a negative value.

The flow-of-funds equation we have just described is a simplified version of the one actually used in official statistics to analyze the components of changes in M4. The equation can easily be modified to show changes in M2 or M5.

Table 16.10 shows the components of changes in M4 for 1986 and 1989. It is

Table 16.10 Counterparts to changes in M4 (£m)

	PSBR(+) PSDR(−)	Sales of (−) / purchases of (+) public-sector debt to/from non-bank private sector	Banks'and building societies' sterling lending to UK private sector (less increases in banks' capital)	External effect: inflows (+) outflows (−)	Total ΔM4
	(1)	(2)	(3)	(4)	
1986	+ 2497	− 5967	+ 41 143	− 2 957	= + 34 716
1989	− 9082	+ 12 974	+ 76 385	− 15 318	= +64 959

Source: *Financial Statistics* (CSO).

interesting to compare the two years. In 1986 there was a public-sector deficit (PSBR), which therefore had the effect of increasing the money supply. In 1989, however, there was a public-sector surplus (PSDR), which, other things being equal, would have reduced the money supply. But as you can see quite clearly from the table, other things were not equal: there was a massive release of liquidity to the private sector from the repayment of public debt (item 2) and an even more massive increase in bank lending (item 3), although this was to some extent offset by a large increase in the currency flow deficit (an outflow of funds under item 4).

The relationship between money supply and the rate of interest

Simple monetary theory often assumes that the supply of money is totally independent of interest rates. This is illustrated in Figure 16.3.

The money supply is 'exogenous'. The supply of money is assumed to be determined by government: what the government chooses it to be, or what it allows it to be by its choice of the level and method of financing the PSBR.

More complex models, and especially Keynesian models, assume that higher interest rates will lead to higher levels of money supply, as in Figure 16.4. The reasons for this are as follows:

● Increases in money supply may occur as a result of banks expanding credit in response to the demand for credit. This assumes that banks have surplus liquidity

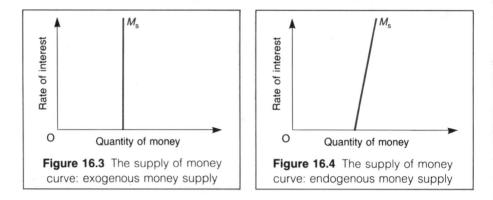

Figure 16.3 The supply of money curve: exogenous money supply

Figure 16.4 The supply of money curve: endogenous money supply

in the first place. Higher demand for credit will drive up interest rates, making it more profitable for banks to supply more credit.

- Higher interest rates may encourage depositors to switch their deposits from sight accounts (earning little or no interest) to time accounts. Since money is less likely to be withdrawn quickly from time accounts, banks may feel the need to hold less liquidity, and therefore may decide to increase credit, thus expanding the money supply.
- Higher interest rates attract deposits from overseas. This increases the money supply in the same way as does a balance of payments surplus.

An upward-sloping supply curve assumes that interest rates are determined by the market: by the interaction of supply and demand for money. An increase in demand for money raises interest rates, which in turn increases the supply of money (see sections 16.4 and 16.5).

If, however, the authorities were to *control* interest rates, the supply curve might become downward sloping. The sequence is as follows. If the authorities raise interest rates, this will reduce the demand for credit and this in turn will reduce the credit that banks create. In these circumstances, raising interest rates *reduces* the supply of money.

In both cases, supply is merely reflecting demand and is thus endogenously determined. With the upward-sloping supply curve, higher demand leads to higher interest rates and higher supply. With the downward-sloping supply curve, higher interest rates lead to lower demand and lower supply.

▲ SUMMARY

1. Money supply can be defined in a number of different ways, depending on what items are included. M0, the narrowest definition, only includes cash and banks' operational balances in the Bank of England. M1 is cash in circulation plus all sight bank deposits (both wholesale and retail). M2 is cash in circulation plus all retail deposits (including time deposits and building society deposits). M3 is M1 plus bank time deposits and certificates of deposit. M4 is M3 plus building society deposits. M5 is M4 plus various money market instruments (e.g. bills). M1 and M3 were dropped from official statistics after July 1989.

2. Bank deposits are a major proportion of money supply (except M0). The expansion of bank deposits is the major element in the expansion of the money supply.

3. Bank deposits expand through a process of credit creation. If banks' liquid assets increase, they be can used as a base for increasing loans. When the loans are redeposited in banks, they form the base for yet more loans, and thus takes place a process of multiple credit expansion. The ratio of the increase of money to an expansion of the liquidity base is called the 'money multiplier'. It is the inverse of the liquidity ratio.

4. In practice it is difficult to predict the precise amount by which money supply will expand if there is an increase in banks' liquidity. The reasons are that banks may choose

to hold a different liquidity ratio; customers may not take up all the credit on offer; and there may be no simple liquidity ratio given the range of near money assets.

5. Money supply will rise if (a) banks choose to hold a lower liquidity ratio and thus create more credit for an existing amount of liquidity; (b) there is a total currency flow surplus; (c) the government runs a PSBR and finances it by borrowing from the banking sector or from abroad; (d) the government switches its method of financing the national debt to borrowing from the banking sector or from abroad.

6. The flow-of-funds equation shows the components of any change in money supply. A rise in money supply equals the PSBR *minus* sales of public-sector debt to the non-bank private sector, *plus* banks' lending to the private sector (less increases in banks' capital), *plus* inflows of money from abroad.

7. Simple monetary theory assumes that the supply of money is independent of interest rates. In practice, a rise in interest rates will often lead to an increase in money supply. But conversely if the government raises interest rates, the supply of money may fall in response to a lower demand for money.

16.4 The demand for money

The motives for holding money

The demand for money refers to the desire to *hold* money: to keep your wealth in the form of money, rather than spending it on goods and services or saving it by purchasing financial assets such as bonds or shares. It is usual to distinguish three reasons why people want to hold their assets in the form of money.

The transactions motive. Since money is a medium of exchange, it is required for conducting transactions. But since people only receive money at intervals (e.g. weekly or monthly) and not continuously, they require to hold balances of money in cash or in sight accounts.

The precautionary motive. Unforeseen circumstances can arise, such as a car breakdown. Thus individuals often hold some additional money as a precaution. Firms too keep precautionary balances because of uncertainties about the timing of their receipts and payments. If a large customer is late in making payment, a firm may be unable to pay its suppliers unless it has spare liquidity.

The speculative or assets motive. Certain firms and individuals who wish to purchase financial assets such as bonds, shares or other securities, may prefer to wait if they feel that their price is likely to fall. In the meantime they will hold idle money balances instead. This speculative demand can be quite high when the price of securities is considered certain to fall. Money when used for this purpose is a means of temporarily storing wealth.

Similarly, people who at some time in the future will require foreign currency (people such as importers, holiday makers, or those thinking of investing abroad or in foreign securities) may prefer to wait before exchanging pounds into the relevant foreign currencies if they believe that the sterling price of these currencies is likely to fall (the pound is likely to *appreciate*).

The transactions and precautionary demand for money: L_1

The transactions plus precautionary demand for money is termed L_1. 'L' stands for liquidity preference: that is, the desire to hold assets in liquid form. Money balances held for these two purposes are called active balances: money to be used as a medium of exchange. What determines the size of L_1?

The major determinant of L_1 is *national income* (Y). The bigger people's income, the more their purchases and the bigger their demand for active balances.

Liquidity preference

The demand for holding assets in the form of money.

Active balances

Money held for transactions and precautionary purposes.

The *frequency with which people are paid* also affects L_1. The less frequently they are paid, the greater the level of money balances they will tend to hold. For example, people paid £100 per week, whose expenditure is spread evenly over the week and who spend all the £100 by the end of the week, will have roughly £50 (in the bank or in cash) on average: that is, mid-way between pay days. People paid £400 per month will have roughly £200 on average: that is, mid-month. Income is the same in both cases, but monthly paid people will have a much higher demand for active balances.

 Will students in receipt of a grant or an allowance who are paid once per term have a high or a low transactions demand for money relative to their income?

The *rate of interest* has some effect on L_1, albeit rather small (see Figure 16.5). At high rates of interest, people may feel it worthwhile to put some of their income in a savings account on pay day and draw it out again as they need it later in the month. The inconvenience of doing this makes the effect on transactions demand rather limited. The effect is likely to be bigger on the precautionary demand: a higher interest rate may encourage people to risk tying up their money. Firms' active balances are more likely to be sensitive to changes in r than individuals'.

Figure 16.5 The transactions-plus-precautionary demand for money: L_1

The elasticity of L_1 with respect to changes in the rate of interest will also depend on how money is defined. The demand for narrow money M0 or M1 is likely to be more elastic than the demand for broad money M3, M4 or M5. A rise in the rate of interest may encourage people to switch from sight to time deposits. The demand for narrow money will fall, but the demand for broad money (which includes both sight *and* time deposits) will remain the same.

Other determinants of L_1 include the season of the year: people require more money balances at Christmas, for example. Also, any other factors that affect consumption will affect L_1.

The increased use of credit cards in recent years has reduced both the transactions and precautionary demands. Paying once a month for goods requires less money on average than paying separately for each item purchased. Also the possession of a credit card reduces or even eliminates the need to hold precautionary balances for many people.

The speculative (or assets) demand for money: L_2

Idle balances

Money held for speculative purposes: money held in anticipation of a fall in asset prices.

The speculative demand for money balances is termed L_2. Money balances held for this purpose are called idle balances.

People who possess wealth, whether it be wealthy people or simply small savers, have to decide the best form in which to hold that wealth. Do they keep it in cash in a piggy bank, or in a current account in a real bank; or do they put it in some interest-bearing time account; or do they buy stocks and shares or government bonds; or do they buy some physical asset such as a car or property?

In making these decisions, people will have to weigh up the relative advantages and disadvantages of the various alternative assets. Assets can be compared according to two criteria: *liquidity* and the *possibility of earning income*. Just as we saw in the case of a bank's assets, these two criteria tend to conflict. The more liquid an asset is, the lower is likely to be the income earned from holding it. Thus cash is totally liquid to the holder: it can be used to buy other assets (or spent on goods) instantly, but it earns no interest. Stocks and shares, on the other hand, are not very liquid since they cannot be sold instantly *at a guaranteed price*. (They *can* be sold pretty well instantly, but if share prices are depressed, a considerable loss may be incurred in so doing.) But stocks and shares have the *potential* of earning quite a high income for the holder, not only in terms of the dividends paid out of the firms' profits, but also in terms of the capital gain from any increase in the shares' prices.

? Buying something like a car is at the other end of the spectrum from holding cash. A car is highly illiquid, but yields a high return to the owner. In what form is this 'return'?

The major determinant of L_2 is expectations of changes in the earning potential of securities and other assets. If the earning potential of an asset goes up, people will be likely to switch to that asset from others with a lower earning potential. Thus, for example, if people believe that the stock market is about to go through a period of 'boom' with share prices going up rapidly, they will switch some of their wealth into stocks and shares. Thus the greater the earning potential of non-money assets, the less will be the demand for money (with its zero earning potential in the case of M0 and much of M1, and with only a relatively low earning potential in the case of broader definitions).

The major determinants of expectations of assets' earning potential are (a) expectations about changes in security prices and interest rates, and (b) expectations about changes in the exchange rate.

Security prices and interest rates

If the market price of securities is high, the rate of interest (i.e. the rate of return) on these securities will be low (see section 16.1). Potential purchasers of these securities will probably wait until their prices fall and the rate of interest rises. Similarly, existing holders of securities will probably sell them while the price is high, hoping to buy them back again when the price falls, thus making a capital gain. *In the meantime, therefore, large speculative balances of money will be held. L_2 is high.*

If, on the other hand, the rate of interest is high, then L_2 is likely to be low. To take advantage of the high rate of return on securities, people buy them now instead of holding on to their money.

? Would the demand for securities be low if their price was high, but was expected to go on *rising*?

The relationship between L_2 and the rate of interest (r) is shown in Figure 16.6. The inverse relationship between r and L_2 gives a downward-sloping curve.

Keynes recognized the possibility of a minimum below which the rate of interest would not fall, since below such levels the rate of interest on securities would not cover the costs and risks of holding them. If the rate of interest approached this

Figure 16.6 The speculative demand for money: L_2

minimum level, no speculators would wish to buy securities. Instead they would prefer to hold idle money balances in the knowledge that, if they wait, the rate of interest will go up again. The speculative demand becomes virtually infinite at this minimum rate of interest. According to Keynesian theory, any extra money people have at this interest rate will simply go into idle balances. This is known as the liquidity trap. Expansion of the money supply in these circumstances may lead to no additional expenditure, only additional idle balances.

As with L_1, the elasticity of L_2 depends on how money is defined. Only this time it is the other way round. Only very short-term speculative balances will be held in sight deposits: they will be held mainly in time deposits which earn some interest, but which are still totally risk free. Thus it is the demand for time deposits, and hence broad money, that varies with speculative demand and hence interest rates.

Liquidity trap

The absorption of any additional money supply into idle balances at very low rates of interest, leaving aggregate demand unchanged.

Speculative demand and the exchange rate

In an open economy like the UK where large-scale movements of currencies across the foreign exchanges take place, expectations about chages in the exchange rate are a major determinant of the speculative demand for money.

If people believe that the pound is likely to appreciate, they will want to hold sterling until it does appreciate. For example, if the current exchange rate is £1 = \$1.50 and speculators believe that it will shortly rise to £1 = \$1.75, then if they are correct they will make a 25c per £1 profit by holding sterling. The more quickly people believe that the exchange rate will rise, the more they will want to hold sterling (as money). If, however, people believe that it will be a slow rise over time, they will want to buy sterling assets (such as UK government bonds) rather than money, since such assets will also earn the holder a rate of interest.

Conversely, if people believe that the exchange rate is likely to fall in the near future, they will economize on their holdings of sterling, preferring to hold their liquid assets in some other currency – the one most likely to appreciate against other currencies.

Graphically, changes in expectations about the exchange rate will have the effect of shifting the L_2 curve in Figure 16.6.

There is a further complication here. Expectations about changes in the exchange rate will themselves be influenced by the interest rate (relative to overseas interest rates). If the UK rate of interest goes up, people will want to deposit their money in the UK. This will increase the demand for sterling on the foreign exchange market: there will be a short-term capital inflow into the UK (the capital account of the balance of payments will go into surplus). The effect will be to drive up the exchange rate. Thus if people believe that the UK rate of interest will rise, they will *also* believe that the rate of exchange will appreciate, and they will want to hold larger speculative balances of sterling.

The introduction of the 'foreign exchange dimension' into our analysis will have two effects on the L_2 curve. First, the curve will become more elastic. We have already seen that, if the rate of interest is high, people will tend to believe that it is likely to fall and will thus not wish to hold speculative balances of money; instead they will buy securities while their price is low and their rate of interest is still high. Now we add another reason for not holding speculative balances: if the rate of interest is currently high and is likely to fall, the exchange rate will also be likely to fall. People will thus choose to keep their liquid assets in other currencies. Conversely, if the rate of interest is low and is thought likely to rise, the speculative demand is likely to be *very* high. Not only will people hold money in anticipation of a fall in security prices, but they will also hold money (sterling) in anticipation of an appreciation of the exchange rate.

Secondly, the curve will become more unstable. Expectations of changes in the exchange rate do not just depend on current domestic interest rates. They depend on the current and anticipated future state of the balance of trade, the rate of inflation, the current and anticipated levels of interest rates in other major trading countries, the price of oil, and so on. If any of these cause people to expect a lower exchange rate, the speculative demand for money will fall: L_2 will shift to the left.

? Which way is the L_2 curve likely to shift in the following cases?

(a) The balance of trade moves into deficit.
(b) People anticipate that foreign interest rates are likely to rise substantially relative to domestic ones.
(c) The domestic rate of inflation falls below that of other major trading countries.
(d) Which way will the L_2 curve shift if people believe that the pound is about to depreciate?

The total demand for money: $L_1 + L_2$

Figure 16.7 shows the total demand for money (L) plotted against the rate of interest (r). This is found by the horizontal addition of curves L_1 and L_2 in Figures 16.5 and 16.6. This curve is known as the 'liquidity preference curve'.

Any factor, other than a change in interest rates, that causes the demand for money to rise will shift the L curve to the right. For example, a rise in national income will cause L_1 to increase, and thus L will shift to the right. An increased use of credit cards will shift L_1 to the left, and hence also L.

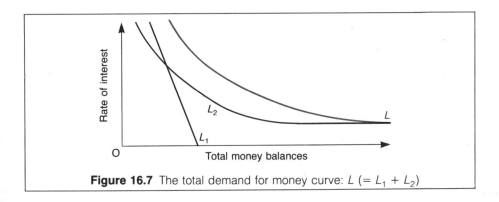

Figure 16.7 The total demand for money curve: L ($= L_1 + L_2$)

? Which way would the liquidity preference curve shift (or 'swing') in the following
   two cases?

(a) A general movement of employers towards paying people monthly rather than weekly.
(b) The inclusion of time deposits in the definition of the money supply.

Additional effects of expectations

We have talked about expectations and their importance in determining the speculative demand for money. In particular we have looked at (a) the effect of interest rates on people's anticipations of future security prices and (b) the effect of expectations about exchange rate movements. There are two other ways in which expectations can influence the demand for money, and make it more unstable.

Expectations about prices. If people expect prices to rise, they may reduce their money balances and purchase goods and assets now, before prices do rise. This will tend to shift L to the left. (Note, though, that once prices *have* risen, people will need more money to conduct the same amount of transactions.)

Expectations of interest rate levels over the longer term. If people come to expect that interest rates will normally be higher than they used to be, then any given interest rate will seem lower relative to the 'normal' rate than it used to be. People will be more inclined to hold speculative balances of money in anticipation of a rise in interest rates. This will tend to shift L upwards.

Since both of these effects are likely to occur during a period of higher inflation, the two of them will be working in opposite directions.

In an era of uncertainty about inflation and interest rates, people's expectations will be hard to predict. They will be volatile and susceptible to rumours and political events. In such circumstances, the L curve itself will be hard to predict and will be subject to considerable shifts.

Generally, it is likely that the greater the uncertainty, the greater will be the preference for liquidity, and the greater the risk of tying money up in risky assets.

Keynesian and monetarist views on the demand for money

Keynesians and monetarists disagree over the shape and stability of the liquidity preference curve (the demand for money curve). In fact this is one of the most crucial areas of disagreement between them. Keynesians argue that the L curve is relatively elastic and unstable, as in Figure 16.8(a). Monetarists argue that it is relatively inelastic and stable, as in Figure 16.8(b).

The shape of the demand for money curve

The disagreement here is over the substitutability of assets. Are other assets a close substitute for money? Are non-money assets such as stocks and shares, bonds and property close substitutes for each other?

Portfolio balance

The balance of assets according to their liquidity that people choose to hold in their portfolios.

To understand the debate we must introduce the concept of portfolio balance. People hold a whole range (or 'portfolio') of assets, from money at one end of the spectrum of liquidity to physical assets such as property and consumer durables at the other. Between the two extremes come the various financial assets such as bonds and shares. The balance of assets in people's portfolios will depend on the relative returns on these assets. If the return on one type of asset goes up, people will switch to holding more of that asset in their portfolios. The more substitutable one asset is for another, the more readily people will switch.

Figure 16.8 Keynesian and monetarist views on the demand for money curve

For simplicity let us group assets into just three types: money, financial assets and physical goods.

Keynesians. Keynesians argue that money and financial assets are relatively close substitutes for each other. They are alternative means of holding wealth. Money has the advantage of liquidity and hence lack of risk. Financial assets have the advantage of earning income. People thus switch between them as the balance of advantage changes. As interest rates go up, the balance of advantage shifts towards holding financial assets which earn these higher interest rates. People thus hold less of their wealth in the form of money. The demand for money falls significantly. *The L curve is elastic.*

Physical goods, by contrast, are not seen by Keynesians as being close substitutes for financial assets (and certainly not for money). They are far too illiquid.

Thus the stress on money as a *means of storing wealth* and the close substitutability of money and other financial assets give an elastic liquidity preference curve.

Monetarists. Monetarists stress the function of money as a *medium of exchange* and play down its role as a store of wealth. It is thus not a close substitute for financial assets. If the rate of interest changes, there will be relatively little shifting between money and financial assets. *The L curve is inelastic.*

At the same time monetarists argue that physical goods *are* a relatively close substitute for financial assets. If, therefore, the rate of interest falls on financial assets, then people, rather than shifting away from financial assets toward money, will buy more physical goods instead.

The stability of the demand for money curve

Keynesians argue that expectations about inflation, exchange rates and interest rates frequently change and have significant effects on the holding of speculative balances of money. Given the importance of money as a means of storing wealth, these balances can be sizeable. As a result any given percentage change in speculative balances will cause a relatively large percentage change in the overall demand for money. The *L* curve is thus likely to shift around and be hard to predict.

Monetarists argue that the *L* curve does not shift very much. The reason is that they deny the significance of speculative balances and argue that overwhelmingly money is held as a medium of exchange. Any shifts in the *L* curve are therefore likely to be gradual in response to longer-run changes in income or institutional influences on holding money (such as credit cards and cash machines).

Evidence

Evidence suggests that the *L* curve is relatively elastic. The degree of elasticity depends on which measure of money is chosen. The demand for narrow money is less interest elastic than the demand for broad money.

 Why would the demand for M0 be very inelastic indeed?

Evidence is far less clear on the stability of the *L* curve. It depends very much on which measure of money is chosen, which period of history is examined, and what form of monetary policy the government is operating.

The implications of the Keynesian and monetarist views for monetary policy, and the evidence supporting them, are examined in subsequent chapters.

▲ SUMMARY

1. The three motives for holding money are the transactions, precautionary and speculative (or assets) motives.
2. The transactions-plus-precautionary demand for money (L_1) depends primarily on the level of national income, the frequency with which people are paid and institutional arrangements (such as the use of credit or debit cards). It also depends to some degree on the rate of interest. The transactions-plus-precautionary demand for narrow money is more interest elastic than for broad money.
3. The speculative demand for money (L_2) depends primarily on anticipations about future movements in security prices (and hence their rate of return) and future movements in exchange rates. If security prices are anticipated to fall or the exchange rate to rise, people will demand to hold more (domestic) money balances.
4. The demand for money is also influenced by expectations

of price changes and the levels of interest rates over the longer term.
5. Keynesians argue that the demand for money is elastic with respect to interest rates and also unstable. They stress the importance of money as a means of storing wealth, and argue that (broad) money is a close substitute for financial assets. Thus people will readily switch back and forth from money to other assets.
6. Monetarists argue that the demand for money is inelastic with respect to interest rates and also fairly stable over time. They stress the importance of money as a medium of exchange, and argue that money is not a close substitute for financial assets. Thus people will not switch back and forth, but will hold a relatively constant amount of money.

16.5 Equilibrium

Equilibrium in the money market

Equilibrium in the money market will be where the demand for money (*L*) is equal to the supply of money (M_s). This equilibrium will be achieved through changes in the rate of interest and the exchange rate. For the moment let us ignore the exchange rate and concentrate on changes in the rate of interest.

In Figure 16.9, equilibrium is achieved with a rate of interest r_e and a quantity of money M_e. If the rate of interest were above r_e, people would have money balances surplus to their needs. They would use this to buy securities and other assets. This would drive up the price of securities and drive down the rate of interest. As the rate of interest fell, so there would be a contraction of the money supply (a movement down along the M_s curve) and an increase in the demand for money balances – especially speculative balances, since people would increasingly judge with lower interest rates that now was not the time to buy securities (there is a movement down along the liquidity preference curve). The interest rate would go on falling until it reached r_e. Equilibrium would then be achieved.

Figure 16.9 Equilibrium in the money market

Similarly, if the rate of interest were below r_e, people would have insufficient money balances. They would sell securities, thus lowering their prices and raising the rate of interest until it reached r_e.

A shift in either M_s or L will lead to a new equilibrium quantity of money and rate of interest at the new intersection of the curves.

? What effects will the following have on the equilibrium rate of interest? (You should consider which way the demand and/or supply curves of money shift.)
(a) Banks find that they have a higher liquidity ratio than they need.
(b) A rise in incomes.
(c) A growing belief that interest rates will rise from their current level.

In practice there is no *one* single rate of interest. Different assets have different rates of interest. Table 16.11 gives examples of the rates of interest on various assets at the end of January 1990.

Table 16.11 Selected rates of interest: 26 January 1990

Asset	Period of loan	Rate of interest (% per annum)
Call money	Overnight	14.75
Bank deposit account	7 days' notice	6.59
Treasury bills	3 months	14.63
Inter-bank loans	Overnight	14.78
Inter-bank loans	7 days	14.88
Inter-bank loans	1 month	15.05
Inter-bank loans	3 months	15.16
Certificates of deposit	3 months	15.13
Short-dated government bonds	Up to 5 years	11.62
Medium-dated government bonds	5–10 years	10.89
Building society shares	No notice	10.02
Building society mortgage	Variable (25 years typical)	14.43

Source: *Financial Statistics* (CSO).

Equilibrium in the money markets, therefore, will be first where the *total* demand for and supply of money are equal. This is achieved by adjustments in the average rate of interest. Secondly, it will be where demand and supply of *each type* of financial asset separately balance. This is achieved by changes in relative interest rates in the different parts of the market. If, for example, there was excess demand for short-term loans (like money at call) and excess supply of money to invest in long-term assets (like bonds), short-term rates of interest would rise relative to long-term rates.

Equilibrium in both the money market and in national income

Changes in money supply (or demand) will affect national income via changes in the rate of interest. It is a three stage process. This is illustrated in Figure 16.10:

- In diagram (a) a rise in money supply (M_s) will lead to a fall in the rate of interest (r): this is necessary to restore equilibrium in the money market.
- In diagram (b) the fall in r will lead to a rise in investment and other forms of borrowing (I). Since borrowing money will be cheaper, investment will cost less.
- In diagram (c) the rise in investment (being an injection) will lead to a multiplied rise in national income (Y) and aggregate demand (AD).

The rise in income will be less than that shown in diagram (c), however, since any rise in income will lead to a rise in the transactions demand for money, L_1. L will shift to the right in diagram (a), and thus r will not fall as much as illustrated. Thus investment (diagram (b)) and income (diagram (c)) will not rise as much as illustrated either.

 Trace through the effect of a rise in the demand for money.

Learn

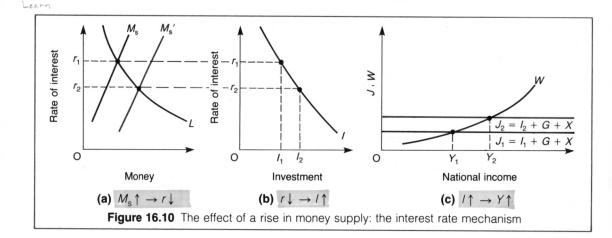

(a) $M_s\uparrow \rightarrow r\downarrow$ **(b)** $r\downarrow \rightarrow I\uparrow$ **(c)** $I\uparrow \rightarrow Y\uparrow$

Figure 16.10 The effect of a rise in money supply: the interest rate mechanism

How big will the effect of changes in money supply be on output, employment and prices?

The effect on national income will be bigger:

a - The less elastic the liquidity preference curve: this will cause a bigger change in the rate of interest.
b - The more interest elastic is the investment curve: this will cause a bigger change in investment.
c - The lower the marginal propensity to withdraw (*mpw*), and hence the flatter the withdrawals function: this will cause a bigger multiplied change in national income and aggregate demand.

The change in aggregate demand will have a bigger effect on output and employment, the more elastic is the aggregate supply curve. This is illustrated in Figure 16.11. Aggregate demand rises from *AD* to *AD'*. With the more elastic aggregate supply curve AS_2, national output rises to Y_2. With the less elastic curve AS_1, output only rises to Y_2.

All these issues – the shape and stability of the *L* curve, the shape and stability of the *I* curve and the shape of the *AS* curve – are highly controversial.

Generally, Keynesians argue that increases in money supply have a small and uncertain effect on aggregate demand because the *L* curve is elastic and unstable and because investment is not very responsive to changes in interest rates; but that any increase that does occur in aggregate demand is likely to affect output and employment if there is demand-deficient unemployment: *AS* is relatively elastic until full employment is approached.

Monetarists argue that increases in money supply have a large effect on aggregate demand (certainly in the long run) because the *L* curve is inelastic and investment is responsive to changes in interest rates; but that this increase in aggregate demand will simply be reflected in the long run in higher prices: the *AS* curve is vertical.

These arguments will be examined in Chapters 18 and 19.

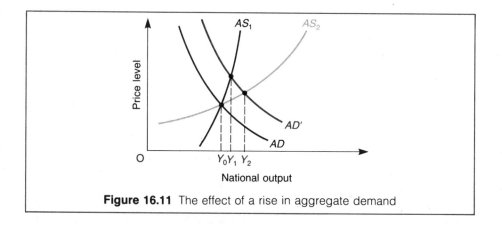

Figure 16.11 The effect of a rise in aggregate demand

Equilibrium when interest rates are controlled

If the government controls interest rates and the supply of money reflects the demand, then the analysis becomes somewhat different. As explained on page 680, the supply of money curve will be downward sloping.

In the extreme case, the supply will depend exclusively on demand. Banks will merely supply whatever is demanded: in this case the supply curve is the same as the demand curve. In Figure 16.12 the supply curve, M_{s_1}, equals the demand curve, *L*. A rise in interest rates from r_1 to r_2 will reduce both the demand and supply of money from Q_1 to Q_2.

In the less extreme case, the supply of money depends to some extent, but not exclusively, on demand. The supply of money curve will be steeper than the demand curve: like M_{s_2} in Figure 16.12. If the authorities raise interest rates to r_2, there will be a disequilibrium. There will be excess liquidity in the economy $(Q_3 - Q_2)$. In this case either there will be downward pressure on interest rates, or the authorities will have to take other measures to reduce this liquidity.

Figure 16.12 Equilibrium in the money market when money supply depends on demand

The whole question of controlling money supply and interest rates is the subject of Chapter 17.

Equilibrium in an open economy

Finally let us see what happens when money supply changes in an open economy with floating exchange rates. How does the change in the supply of money affect the exchange rate, and how in turn does this affect equilibrium in the money market and in the real economy?

Let us assume that initially the exchange rate was in a stable equilibrium with no shifts in the demand for and supply of sterling. Now let us assume that the money supply increases. The supply of money will thus exceed the demand. This has three direct effects:

- *Part* of the excess balances will be used to purchase foreign assets. This will therefore lead to an increase in the supply of pounds coming on to the foreign exchange markets.
- The excess supply of money in the domestic money market will push down the rate of interest. This will reduce the return on UK assets below that on foreign assets. This, like the first effect, will lead to an increased demand for foreign assets and thus an increased supply of pounds on the foreign exchange market.
- Speculators will anticipate that the higher supply of sterling will cause the exchange rate to depreciate. They will therefore sell sterling and buy foreign currencies.

The effect of all three is to cause the exchange rate to depreciate. This will have two effects on aggregate demand:

- Imports will be more expensive relative to home-produced goods. People will thus buy fewer imports and more home-produced goods. Withdrawals (W) will thus fall and consumption of domestic goods (C_d) will rise.
- The initial effect on exporters depends on how exports are priced. If they are priced in dollars, D-Marks or some other foreign currency, they will now earn more pounds and will therefore be more profitable for exporters. Exporters will thus increase their production. If exports are priced in *pounds*, they will now be cheaper in foreign currency terms for foreigners to buy. The demand for UK exports will thus increase.

Either way, a rise in exports, being an injection into the circular flow of income, will raise aggregate demand and hence lead to a multiplied rise in income.

Figure 16.13 The effect of a rise in the money supply: the exchange rate mechanism

The various effects are illustrated in Figure 16.13:

- In diagram (a) a rise in money supply will cause the rate of interest to fall from r_1 to r_2.
- In diagram (b) the rise in money supply plus the fall in the rate of interest will cause the exchange rate to depreciate from er_1 to er_2.
- In diagram (c) the fall in the exchange rate will cause a fall in imports and a rise in exports. This, coupled with the effect on investment of a fall in interest rates, will cause a multiplied rise in national income from Y_1 to Y_2.

Note that the lower interest rate causes a capital account deficit on the balance of payments as people buy foreign assets. This is matched (as it must be if the government does not use the reserves to support the pound) by a current account surplus as exports rise and imports fall.

The full effect will not be as large as that illustrated. This is because the increased national income will cause an increased *transactions* demand for money. This will shift the L curve to the right in diagram (a), and thus lead to a smaller fall in the rate of interest than that illustrated.

 Trace through the effects of a *fall* in the supply of money.

In the extreme case where the aggregate supply curve is vertical, the increased money supply will simply lead to higher prices. In such a case the rise in the transactions demand for money will match the rise in the supply of money. Interest rates will rise back up to the original level. The exchange rate depreciation will then simply match the rise in prices.

Monetarists take this extreme view. Any increase in the money supply, they argue, will simply lead to higher prices and a lower exchange rate. A 10 per cent rise in money supply will lead to a 10 per cent rise in prices and a 10 per cent depreciation of the exchange rate (assuming no inflation abroad).

 If foreign prices rose on average by 4 per cent and UK prices rose by 10 per cent, how much would the pound have to depreciate?

We will examine the relationship between money and exchange rates in more detail in Chapter 22.

◭ SUMMARY

1. Equilibrium in the money market is where the supply of money is equal to the demand. Equilibrium is achieved through changes in the interest rate and the exchange rate.
2. The interest rate mechanism works as follows: (a) a rise in money supply causes money supply to exceed money demand; interest rates fall; (b) this causes investment to rise; (c) this causes a multiplied rise in national income; but (d) as national income rises so the transactions demand for money will rise, thus preventing quite such a large fall in interest rates.
3. Keynesians argue that effects (a) and (b) are weak and unreliable, making monetary policy an unreliable weapon for controlling aggregate demand. Monetarists argue that they are much stronger and more predictable, but that any change in aggregate demand will (in the long run) simply affect prices and not output and employment.
4. The exchange rate mechanism works as follows: (a) a rise in money supply causes interest rates to fall; (b) the rise in money supply plus the fall in interest rates causes an increased supply of domestic currency to come on to the foreign exchange market; this causes the exchange rate to fall; (c) this will cause increased exports and reduced imports, and hence a multiplied rise in national income.

Monetary Policy

17

17.1 Attitudes towards monetary policy

Monetary policy is the deliberate attempt by the authorities (a) to control the supply of money, or (b) to control interest rates, or (c) to ration the amount of credit granted by banks.

Monetary policy is highly controversial. Economists are not agreed (nor are politicians for that matter) on how effective it has been or can be, or on what form it should take.

Government attitudes towards monetary policy have undergone enormous changes since 1945. In the Keynesian era from 1945 to the end of the 1960s, *fiscal* policy was seen as the major weapon for controlling the economy. Monetary policy was relegated to the fairly minor role of preventing excessive fluctuations in interest rates. For most of this period, this simply meant allowing money supply to expand to accommodate increases in aggregate demand associated with expansionary fiscal policy (otherwise the shortage of money would have driven up interest rates). It also meant allowing money supply to contract, or grow less rapidly, when deflationary fiscal policies were pursued.

During the 1970s there was a major swing in the attitudes of many economists and politicians. The rise of monetarism was accompanied by increased importance being attached to monetary policy. There were a number of factors leading to this. The main ones were as follows:

- The failure of Keynesianism to account for and provide solutions to the growing problem of stagflation. Fiscal policy had failed, perhaps monetary policy could provide the answer.
- Increased academic interest in monetary economics, and in particular increased evidence, most notably that of Milton Friedman and Anna Schwartz in their *Monetary History of the United States*, that there is a direct causal link between growth in the money supply and inflation.
- The growth of the radical right in politics, and the subsequent elections of Reagan, Thatcher, Kohl and others. The radical right is committed to *laissez-faire* policies, with the main economic role of the government reduced to that of providing 'sound money'. This means controlling the money supply to control inflation. Stable prices will then allow the market mechanism to give clear, unambiguous signals of relative scarcities. This will help enterprise to flourish, and output and employment should grow.

The high point of monetarism came in the early 1980s. Governments round the world made the control of inflation the number one short-term macroeconomic objective. To achieve this they pursued tight monetary policies which in many cases involved setting targets for the growth in money supply. In the UK the Conservative government adopted a medium-term financial strategy (MTFS). This involved setting targets each year for the growth of money supply over the following four years: the targets got progressively tighter over the four years, thus 'putting the squeeze on inflation'. To achieve these money supply targets the MTFS also included targets for cutting the public sector borrowing requirement.

Medium-term financial strategy

The policy of the Conservative government in the UK during the 1980s of setting targets for the PSBR and the growth of money supply for the following four years.

From the mid-1980s the UK, along with several other countries, began to adopt a more pragmatic approach to monetary policy. It had been found difficult to control money supply and to keep it within target ranges. Anyway, as elections approached it was not always politically desirable to have a tight monetary policy. It is easier to win elections if the economy is growing rapidly – a government can cope with any resulting inflation *after* the election! But perhaps one of the main reasons for abandoning monetary targets was the desire to prevent exchange rate fluctuations, and the use of changes in interest rates to achieve this. As we shall see, if the interest rate is used to control exchange rates, it cannot at the same time be used to achieve money supply targets.

What form should monetary policy take?

In framing its monetary policy, a government must address itself to a number of important questions:

● What are the goals of monetary policy? Is the aim simply to control inflation, or does the government wish also to affect output and employment, or does it want to control the exchange rate?

● Where does monetary policy fit into the total package of macroeconomic policies? Is it seen as the major or even sole macroeconomic policy weapon, or is it merely one of several policy weapons, and possibly a minor one at that?

● What element of the monetary system should the government seek to control? Should it be the supply of money, and if so which measure? Should it be the demand for money, and if so how should that be measured? Or should it be the rate of interest, and if so at what level?

● Should the government take a long-term perspective or a short-term perspective? Should it adopt a target for money supply growth, say, and stick to it come what may? Or should it adjust its policy as circumstances change and attempt to 'fine-tune' the economy?

● How reliable is monetary policy in controlling monetary variables? Just how successfully can a government control money supply or interest rates?

Keynesian and monetarist attitudes towards monetary policy

Keynesians and monetarists give very different answers to these questions. Keynesians see the prime role of macroeconomic policy as stabilizing aggregate demand at or near 'full employment' income. The prime weapon for managing demand is discretionary *fiscal* policy, with monetary policy being used merely as a back-up to this. If stagflation becomes a problem, then demand management policies (both fiscal and monetary) should be used to eliminate demand-deficient unemployment, with back-up 'supply-side' policies being used to cure the remaining unemployment. Such policies would involve government intervention to provide better training and job information to reduce occupational immobility, and grants to firms to set up in areas of high unemployment to reduce regional imbalances. Inflation *not* resulting from excess demand could possibly be controlled by a prices and incomes policy.

Keynesians see monetary policy, therefore, as merely one part of a much larger package of policies. What is more, they see monetary policy as rather ineffective. They make three points here:

- It is difficult to control money supply, and impossible to control it precisely.
- The link between money supply and aggregate demand is weak and unpredictable. Thus if it is aggregate demand that requires controlling, monetary policy is a poor weapon to do this.
- If monetary policy is to be used to control aggregate demand, it will be through interest rate changes. Thus it is best to control interest rates directly, rather than relying on changes in money supply to affect them.

Monetarists see the prime role of macroeconomic policy as providing an environment conducive to private enterprise and investment. This is the way, they claim, to bring long-term increases in output and employment. To create this environment, two types of policy must be pursued: monetary policy and free-market-orientated supply-side policies.

They reject the Keynesian approach to monetary and fiscal policies which sees them as discretionary, essentially short-term, demand management policies. Both policies, monetarists argue, involve considerable time lags, which can make them destabilizing. Instead a much longer-term perspective should be taken. There is a strong causal link, they claim, between money and prices. Long-run price stability therefore requires long-run control over the money supply. This involves setting targets for money supply into the future, and then using monetary policy to ensure that these targets are met. Monetary policy, they argue, providing it is carefully designed and executed, *can* control the money supply.

Supply-side policies, they say, should be geared (a) to removing impediments to the working of the market – impediments such as restrictive practices and nationalization – and (b) to fostering competition, by creating incentives, reducing taxes and removing bureaucratic obstacles to small businesses.

▲ SUMMARY

1. During the 1970s and 1980s governments around the world attached increasing importance to monetary policy and less importance to fiscal policy. This was due to an increased acceptance of monetarist arguments and a rejection of Keynesian ones.
2. Keynesians argue that monetary policy is an unreliable means of controlling aggregate demand. Instead governments should use fiscal policy combined with a policy of relatively stable interest rates.

3. Monetarists argue that monetary policy is a powerful weapon. A stable economy is best achieved by ensuring a steady and low rate of growth in the money supply.
4. In framing its monetary policy a government must have a clear idea of what the goals of the policy are, which monetary variable it is going to attempt to control and by what means, whether to take a long-term or short-term perspective, and how the policy fits in with other policies.

17.2 Varieties of monetary policy

Control of the money supply over the medium and long term

As explained in Chapter 16, there are four possible sources of monetary growth: (a) banks choosing to hold a lower liquidity ratio (probably in response to an increase in the demand for loans); (b) a balance of payments surplus; (c) public sector borrowing; (d) a change in the method of financing the national debt. If the government wishes to restrict monetary growth over the longer term, it could in theory attempt to control any of these four.

Banks' liquidity ratio

The authorities (the government operating through the Bank of England) could impose statutory minimum reserve requirements on the banks to prevent them choosing to reduce their liquidity ratio and choosing thereby to create more credit.

A major problem with imposing restrictions of this kind is that banks may find ways of getting round them. After all, banks would like to lend and customers would like to borrow. It would be very difficult for the Bank of England to regulate and police every single part of the UK's complex financial system. If it succeeds merely in regulating *part* of the system, then something called Goodhart's law is likely to come into operation. This law (named after Charles Goodhart, formerly of the Bank of England) states that attempts to regulate *one* part of the financial system will merely divert business to *other* parts which are unregulated (see Box 17.1). Total borrowing may thus continue to increase.

Monetarists are opposed to this form of monetary control, arguing that banks, like any firm, ought to be free to compete in the market, free from government restrictions. Imposing reserve requirements on banks is 'anti-market' and could lead to banks becoming inefficient.

So how else can the government discourage banks from increasing their lending if the banks are only too willing to expand credit and accept a lower liquidity ratio? The answer is to curb the long-run *demand* for money. This will normally involve keeping interest rates high. The problem with this is that it will drive up the exchange rate and thus make it harder for firms to export.

> **Goodhart's law**
>
> Controlling a symptom of a problem or only one part of the problem will not *cure* the problem: it will simply mean that the part that is being controlled now becomes a poor indicator of the problem.

A total currency flow surplus

Total currency flow surpluses will only occur if the government keeps the exchange rate below the equilibrium by continuing to sell the domestic currency on the foreign exchange market. Since governments are unlikely to do this over the long term, this will not be a long-term source of excessive monetary growth.

The PSBR and its method of financing

If the public-sector borrowing requirements (PSBR) is financed by borrowing from the Bank of England or by the sale of Treasury bills to the banking sector, the money supply will increase.

If it is financed by selling bills or bonds outside the banking sector or by selling bonds to the banks, the money supply will not increase. If there is no increase in money supply, however, the increased demand for loans by the government will 'crowd out' lending to the private sector. To attract money the government will have to offer higher interest rates on bonds. This will force up private sector interest rates and reduce private-sector borrowing and investment.

This financial crowding out, as it is called, could be offset to some extent by an increase in the speed at which money circulates – the velocity of circulation. If existing money circulates faster, there will be less shortage of money and less upward pressure on interest rates. The velocity of circulation will rise if there is a reduction in idle balances. The more idle balances fall, the more money will be available for spending. But why should idle balances fall? This is simply the result of a downward-sloping liquidity preference curve. As interest rates begin to rise, so people choose to hold less idle balances. The more elastic the liquidity preference curve, the more idle

> **Financial crowding out**
>
> Where an increase in government borrowing diverts money away from the private sector.
>
> **Velocity of circulation**
>
> The speed with which money circulates: the number of times on average it is spent per period of time.

Box 17.1

Goodhart's Law
'To control is to distort'

'If you want to tackle a problem, it's best to get to the root of it.'

This is a message that economists are constantly preaching. If you merely treat the *symptoms* of a problem rather than its *underlying causes*, the problem may simply manifest itself in some other form. What is more, the symptoms (or lack of them, if the treatment makes them go away) will now be a poor indicator of the problem. Let's illustrate this with a medical example.

Assume that you suffer from deteriorating eyesight. As a result you get increasingly bad headaches. The worse the headaches become, the worse it suggests your eyesight is getting. The headaches are thus a symptom of the problem and an indicator of the problem's magnitude. So what do you do? One approach is to treat the symptoms. As a result you regularly take aspirins and the headaches go away. But you haven't treated the underlying problem – by, for example, getting stronger glasses, or perhaps even having eye surgery – all you have done is to treat the symptoms. As a result, headaches (or rather the lack of them) are now a poor indicator of your eyesight.

If you control the indicator rather than the underlying problem, the indicator then ceases to be a good indicator. 'To control [the indicator] is to distort [its use as an indicator].' This is Goodhart's law.

Goodhart's law has many applications in economics, especially in the field of monetary policy. There are three common examples.

Money as an indicator of aggregate demand

Monetarists argue that the level of money supply determines the level of aggregate demand and prices. They therefore argue in favour of setting targets for the growth of money supply. Critics, however, argue that the level of money supply is only an *indicator* of the level of aggregate demand (and a poor one at that). As soon as you start to *control* money supply, they say, the relationship between them breaks down. If, for example, you restrict the amount of money and yet people still want to borrow, money will simply circulate faster, and hence aggregate demand may not decline.

The choice of money supply target

If targets for the growth of money supply are to be set, which measure of money supply should be chosen? Goodhart's law suggests that whichever measure is chosen it will, by virtue of its choice, become a poor indicator. For example, if the government targets M0 and directs its policy to reducing the amount of notes and coin in the economy, banks may try to reduce their customers' demand for cash by, say, increasing the charges for cash advances on credit cards. As a result, M0 may well be constrained, but all the other measures of money supply are likely to go on increasing.

The choice of institutions

If bank advances are a good indicator of aggregate demand, the government may choose to control bank lending. But as soon as it does so, bank lending will become a poor indicator. If people's demand for loans is still high and *bank* loans are becoming difficult to obtain, people will simply go elsewhere to borrow money. If you regulate *part* of the financial system, you are likely to end up merely diverting business to other parts which are unregulated.

? Give some everyday examples of Goodhart's law (cases where controlling an indicator or symptom of a problem merely distorts its accuracy in measuring the problem).

balances will fall. Nevertheless, unless the liquidity preference curve is totally elastic, *some* financial crowding out will occur. (Crowding out is examined in detail in Chapter 18.)

If governments wish to reduce monetary growth and yet avoid financial crowding out, they must therefore reduce the level of the PSBR.

Monetarists argue that governments should make reductions in the PSBR (as a proportion of national income) the central part of their medium- and longer-term monetary strategy. Not only is this desirable as a means of restricting monetary growth, but, if it involves cutting government expenditure (as opposed to increasing taxes), it will also increase the size of the private sector relative to the public sector –

and it is the private sector that monetarists see as the main source of long-term growth in output and employment.

In the UK, the Conservative government's medium-term financial strategy introduced in 1980 attempted to do just this. As well as setting targets for the growth of money supply, it also gave targets for the PSBR as a percentage of GDP.

Table 17.1 Medium-term financial strategy: April 1980

	1980/81	1981/82	1982/83	1983/84
Target growth of M3 (annual %)	7–11	6–10	5–9	4–8
Target PSBR as % of GDP	3¾	3	2½	1½

Source: *Financial Statement and Budget Report: The 'Red Book'* (HM Treasury, 1980).

The original MTFS is shown in Table 17.1. As it turned out, actual PSBR was considerably higher than the target figures. Nevertheless the government continued setting targets for a reduction in PSBR. The April 1985 figures are shown in Table 17.2.

Table 17.2 Medium-term financial strategy: April 1985

	1985/86	1986/87	1987/88	1988/89
Target growth of M0 (annual %)	3–7	2–6	1–5	0–4
Target growth of M3 (annual %)	5–9	4–8	3–7	2–6
Target PSBR as % of GDP	2	2	1	1

Source: *Financial Statement and Budget Report: The 'Red Book'* (HM Treasury, 1985).

 How could long-term monetary growth come about if the government persistently ran a public-sector surplus (public-sector debt repayment, PSDR)?

Short-term monetary control: what should governments attempt to control?

Monetary policy may be off target. Alternatively, the government may wish to alter its monetary policy. Assume, for example, that the government wishes to operate a tighter monetary policy in order to reduce aggregate demand. What can it do?

For any given supply of money (M_s) there will be a particular equilibrium rate of interest at any one time: where the supply of money (M_s) equals the demand for money (L). This is shown as r_1 in Figure 17.1.

Thus to operate a tighter monetary policy the authorities can do the following:

- Reduce money supply and accept whatever equilibrium interest rate results. Thus if money supply is reduced to Q_2 in Figure 17.1, a new higher rate of interest, r_2, will result.
- First raise interest rates to r_2 and then manipulate the money supply to reduce it to Q_2.
- Keep interest rates low (at r_1) in order, say, to keep down the costs of investment, but also reduce money supply to a level of Q_2. The trouble here is that the government cannot both control the money supply *and* keep interest rates down without running into the problem of disequilibrium. Since the demand for money now exceeds the supply by $Q_1 - Q_2$ some form of credit rationing will have to be applied.

There is a fourth possibility, but this is not primarily monetary policy. This would be to reduce the demand for money (i.e. *shift* the demand for money curve (L) to the

Figure 17.1 The demand for and supply of money

left). A contractionary fiscal policy would probably be necessary here. This would reduce aggregate demand directly and thus reduce the transactions demand for money. This would allow money supply to be reduced without raising interest rates or having to resort to credit rationing.

The following sections look at various techniques of monetary policy in each of the three categories: (a) controlling the money supply, (b) controlling interest rates and (c) rationing credit.

Techniques to control the money supply

The possible techniques available to the authorities have one major feature in common: they involve manipulating the liquid assets of the banking system. The aim is to influence the total money supply by affecting the amount of credit that banks can create.

Suppose, in the simplest possible case, banks operate a rigid 10 per cent cash ratio and just have two types of asset: cash and advances. Suppose that the government is able to reduce cash by £1 million; then with a money multiplier of 10 (= 1/cash ratio), advances must be reduced by £9 million, bringing a total £10 million reduction in deposits and hence in money supply. This is illustrated in Table 17.3.

Table 17.3

Liabilities		Assets	
Deposits	£10m ↓	Cash	£1m ↓
		Advances	£9m ↓

? If banks operated a rigid 12½ per cent cash ratio and the government reduced the supply of cash by £1 million, how much must *credit* contract? What is the money multiplier?

Before they can actually apply techniques of monetary control, there are two preliminary decisions the authorities must make:

- Should a statutory liquidity ratio be imposed on the banks, or should the banks be allowed to choose whatever ratio they consider to be prudent?
- Should the authorities attempt to control a range of liquid assets, or should they focus on controlling just the monetary base - either the narrow monetary base

(banks' balances with the Bank of England) or the broad monetary base, M0 (banks' balances with the Bank of England plus notes and coin)?

Before 1981 statutory liquidity ratios were imposed on the banks. Since 1981, however, banks have been left to decide their own prudent liquidity ratios.

Before 1981 the authorities concentrated on a whole range of liquid assets and on broad measures of money supply, like M3: the argument being that it is broad liquidity that determines credit creation and broad measures of money that influence aggregate demand. After 1981 government opinion shifted in favour of focusing on the monetary base, as this is more easily controlled by the authorities, and after 1984 the government started targeting M0 as well as M3 in its medium-term financial strategy.

In 1985 all targets except for M0 were abolished. This, it might seem, meant that the government was from that point firmly committed to controlling the monetary base rather than broader liquidity. In reality it was simply a recognition that the government had abandoned any serious attempt to keep monetary growth within targets. The government was still *monitoring* all measures of money and a whole range of liquid assets. It was just that monetary policy was now more directed to managing aggregate demand or to influencing the exchange rate, depending on whatever was the most politically pressing. Thus targeting was abandoned, but the government still continued to use various techniques of monetary control.

There are three techniques that have been used to control money supply. Each one affects banks' liquidity.

Open-market operations

Open-market operations

The sale (or purchase) by the authorities of government securities in the open market in order to reduce (or increase) money supply.

Open-market operations are the purchase or sale by the Bank of England of government securities (bonds or Treasury bills) in the open market. These purchases or sales are *not* in response to changes in the PSBR or PSDR, and are best understood, therefore, in the context of an unchanged PSBR or PSDR.

If the government wished to *reduce* the money supply, the Bank of England would sell more securities. When people buy these securities, they pay for them with cheques drawn on banks. Thus banks' balances with the Bank of England are reduced. If this brings bank reserves below their prudent ratio (or statutory ratio, if one is in force), banks will reduce advances. There will be a multiple contraction of credit and hence of money supply.

The effect will be limited if the extra securities are Treasury bills (as opposed to bonds) and if some are purchased by discount houses and banks. The reduction in one liquid asset (balances with the Bank of England) will be offset to some extent by an increase in another liquid asset (Treasury bills). Open-market operations are more likely to be effective in reducing the money supply, therefore, when conducted in the bond market.

If the government wishes to *increase* the money supply, the Bank of England would purchase back securities. When people pay these Bank of England cheques into their banks, the banks' balances with the Bank of England will rise. Credit creation can take place.

? 1. Assume that a bank has the following simplified balance sheet.

Liabilities	(£m)	Assets	(£m)
Deposits	100	Balances with B. of E.	10
		Advances	90
	100		100

Now assume that the Bank of England repurchases £5 million of government bonds on the open market. Assume that the people who sell the bonds all have their accounts with this bank. Draw up the new balance sheet directly after the purchase of the bonds. Then draw up the eventual balance sheet after credit creation has taken place.
2. Why would it be difficult for the Bank of England to predict the precise effect on money supply of open-market operations?

Funding

Funding is where the Bank of England, if it wishes to reduce the money supply, issues more government bonds, but at the same time fewer Treasury bills. Banks' balances with the Bank of England will be little affected, but to the extent that banks hold fewer bills, there will be (*ceteris paribus*) a reduction in their liquidity. Funding is thus the conversion of one type of government debt into another.

In the mid-1980s the government engaged in overfunding. This is where the government makes a net issue of bonds to the (non-bank) private sector *in excess* of the total PSBR. As with open-market operations and ordinary funding, the sale of securities to the private sector leads to a squeeze on banks' balances at the Bank of England. As a result banks may have to call in money from the discount houses, which, in turn being short of liquidity, have to sell bills back to the Bank of England (acting as lender of last resort). If there are insufficient Treasury bills to be rediscounted by the Bank of England, the discount houses will have to sell other bills, such as commercial bills that have been accepted by an acceptance house or bank. In 1984 the Bank of England built up a 'commercial bill mountain' through overfunding (see Box 18.5).

? If the government issues £1 million worth of extra bonds and buys back £1 million worth of Treasury bills, will there automatically be a reduction in credit (by a multiple of £1 million)?

Special deposits

Banks can be required to deposit a given percentage of their deposits in a special account at the Bank of England. These special deposits are frozen, and cannot be drawn on until the authorities choose to release them. They are thus illiquid. They provide a simple means of reducing banks' liquidity and hence their ability to create credit. Releasing special deposits allows banks to create more credit.

A particular variant of special deposits, used on and off during the 1970s, was supplementary special deposits ('the corset'). The authorities set limits to the expansion of bank deposits. Whenever these limits were exceeded, banks were required to place a proportion of them in special deposits. The more the limits were exceeded, the bigger was this proportion. This was a form of automatic, as opposed to discretionary, monetary policy. In theory it was a very simple way of keeping money supply within limits: within a corset. The more that deposits expanded, the tighter would become the corset.

Although all three techniques have been used in the past, they have not been used as the prime form of monetary policy. Instead the authorities have tended to concentrate on controlling interest rates and hence the demand for money.

Techniques to control interest rates

If in Figure 17.2 the authorities wished to reduce the demand for money to Q_2, they would raise interest rates to r_2. How, then, can the authorities control interest rates?

Funding
Where the authorities alter the balance of bills and bonds for any given level of government borrowing.

Overfunding
Where the issue of bonds (minus those maturing) exceeds the PSBR.

Supplementary special deposits ('the corset')
Where banks were automatically required to place a proportion of an increase in customers' deposits above a specified limit in special deposits (frozen deposits) in the Bank of England.

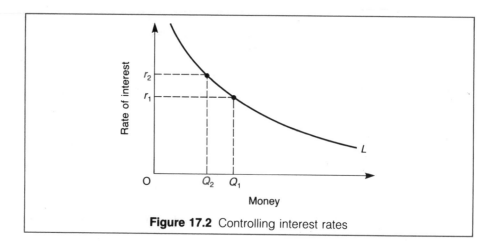

Figure 17.2 Controlling interest rates

Interest rates are controlled by the Bank of England, through its operations in the discount market.

The Bank of England ('the Bank') is the lender of the last resort. If commercial banks are short of liquid assets, they will have to call in money from the discount houses. The discount houses, as a result, may themselves become short of liquid assets. They will be forced to borrow from the Bank, as lender of last resort, or get the Bank to rediscount (buy) bills of exchange. The Bank can *choose what rate of interest or rediscount to charge the discount houses*. This in turn will affect interest rates generally throughout the economy.

Until 1972 this rate of interest was called *Bank rate*. The clearing banks used to change their interest rates on advances and deposits *automatically* by the same amount that Bank rate changed. Thus by changing Bank rate the authorities could directly change banks' interest rates. This would then stimulate other institutions to change their rates too, in order for them to remain competitive with the clearing banks.

From 1972 to 1981 Bank rate was replaced by *minimum lending rate* (MLR). This too was the rate at which the Bank of England would lend to the discount houses in the last resort. Unlike with Bank rate, however, the clearing banks were not obliged to change their rates when MLR changed. Nevertheless, they usually did. There were two reasons for this.

First the Bank of England would usually back up any change in MLR with *open-market operations* in the bond or more likely the bill market. If, for example, the authorities wished to pursue a tighter monetary policy, they would raise MLR and at the same time sell more government bonds and Treasury bills. These open-market sales would lower the price of bonds and bills, and hence raise their rate of interest to match the rise in MLR.

Further, purchases of these securities by the general public would reduce banks' liquidity, as people paid with cheques drawn on their bank accounts. The banks might then be obliged to call in money from the discount houses. This, plus direct purchases of some of the bills by the discount houses, would reduce the liquidity of the discount houses, which then would be forced to borrow from the Bank of England at the new higher MLR. Before 1981 the Bank of England as a matter of course deliberately sold sufficiently large amounts of Treasury bills to keep the discount houses short of liquidity. Discount houses are obliged to purchase any Treasury bills not purchased by other people or institutions.

Having to pay this new higher MLR would force the discount houses to tender a lower price for bills, in order to get a higher rate of discount. Higher rates of discount on bills would in turn drive up interest rates on other types of borrowing and lending that compete with bills (e.g. short-term bank loans). At the same time, if discount houses ran the risk of borrowing at a new higher MLR they would try to borrow more money at call and would be prepared to pay a higher rate of interest to do so. Banks would then divert assets from advances to call money, which would create a shortage of money for advances and drive up their rate of interest.

In other words, a rise in MLR had a knock-on effect on interest rates throughout the economy.

Secondly, MLR was seen as a *signal of government intention*. A rise in MLR was a sign that the authorities wanted to pursue a tighter monetary policy. As a result banks would tend to raise their rates in anticipation of a general rise in rates.

Since 1981 a formally announced MLR has been abandoned, and the Bank of England no longer keeps discount houses deliberately short of liquidity as a matter of course. Nevertheless the Bank still actively intervenes to affect interest rates.

It does this by altering the supply of Treasury bills on offer, at times when it is trying to reduce liquidity; or by altering the amount of bills (eligible commercial bills and local authority bills as well as Treasury bills) it is prepared to buy, at times when it is trying to provide more liquidity. In other words, it conducts *open-market operations* in the bill market with the intention of achieving a particular *interest rate* rather than a particular supply of liquid assets.

Assume that the Bank of England wishes to raise interest rates. Assume also that the discount houses have *surplus* liquidity and that the Bank of England is selling Treasury bills. The greater the supply of Treasury bills on offer by the Bank, the lower the price the discount houses will be prepared to pay for them, and hence the higher the rate of discount (r) they must receive. Thus in Figure 17.3(a), a rise in Treasury bill issue from S_1 to S_2 will raise the discount rate from r_1 to r_2. Thus the Bank of England can alter the discount rate by altering the supply of Treasury bills.

Now assume that discount houses have *insufficient* liquidity and are forced to borrow from the Bank of England. Since 1981 the Bank prefers not to lend as such, but rather to purchase ('rediscount') bills from the discount houses. The Bank does not announce its rediscount rate, but instead invites the discount houses to offer it bills. If the price asked by the discount houses is thought to be too high, the Bank will refuse to purchase them. This will drive down the price and hence drive up the rate of rediscount (r). The discount houses will thus try to economize on the bills they offer

(a) The Bank of England sells more bills   **(b)** The Bank of England buys fewer bills

Figure 17.3 Bank of England operations in the bill market to affect interest rates to the Bank by, say, offering a higher rate of interest on money at call, and thus encouraging further such deposits from the banks. Thus in Figure 17.3(b), the supply of bills on offer by the discount houses to the Bank falls as the rate of rediscount rises (the supply curve of bills by the discount houses is upward sloping). The Bank, by rejecting offers at r_1, is in effect reducing its demand for bills (D_1 to D_2), and thereby drives up the rediscount rate to r_2.

In either case (the Bank selling more or buying fewer bills), there will be a knock-on effect on interest rates throughout the economy, just as there used to be with MLR.

In recent years the government has returned to announcing interest rate changes, and thus the current system is similar to the old MLR system.

Note that, although the current approach to monetary policy focuses on the rate of interest in order to affect the demand for money, this approach is still backed up by measures to control the money *supply*. Thus in Figure 17.4, if the authorities want to raise the rate of interest from r_1 to r_2, their actions in the discount market outlined above will reduce money supply from Q_1 to Q_2, to ensure that r_2 is an *equilibrium* rate of interest.

Apart from wanting to control the domestic demand for money, there is another reason why the Bank of England sometimes alters interest rates. This is to influence the rate of exchange. If it raises interest rates, using the techniques described above, this will encourage people overseas to deposit their money in the UK. This will increase the demand for sterling on the foreign exchange markets and hence cause an appreciation of the exchange rate. As we shall see later in the chapter, however, there is a potential conflict between using interest rates to control the demand for money and using them also to control the exchange rate.

Techniques to ration credit

In the past, and particularly in the late 1960s, governments attempted to keep interest rates low so as not to discourage investment. This frequently meant that the demand for money exceeded the supply of money that the authorities were prepared to permit. Thus in Figure 17.5, if the authorities keep interest rates at r_1, and yet do not allow money supply to expand beyond Q_2, there will be excess demand for money of $Q_1 - Q_2$. Faced with this excess demand, the authorities had to ration credit. There were three possible techniques open to the authorities.

Suggestion and request (sometimes called 'moral suasion'). This could be *qualitative*

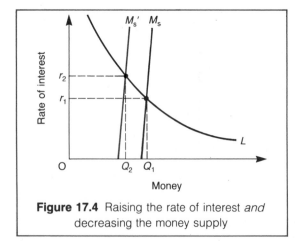

Figure 17.4 Raising the rate of interest *and* decreasing the money supply

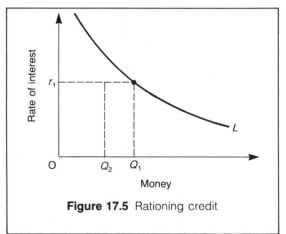

Figure 17.5 Rationing credit

where the Bank of England requested the banks to discriminate between borrowers. For example, they might be asked to restrict the amount of credit granted to private individuals for consumption, or to property speculators. It could also be *quantitative*. This was where the Bank of England requested banks to restrict *total* lending. This most frequently involved the use of ceilings: banks being told not to allow advances to expand by more than a certain percentage compared with the previous year.

Directives. The Bank of England has the legal power to order banks to obey its requests. In practice it has never had to invoke this law.

Hire-purchase controls. The authorities could restrict hire purchase credit by specifying minimum deposits or maximum repayment periods.

One technique of monetary control, which amounts to a form of credit rationing, is to vary the statutory reserve ratio that banks must adhere to. Clearly this policy option would not be open in the UK as long as there effectively are no statutory reserve requirements and it is up to banks to decide their own prudent ratio.

If, however, the central bank sets the reserve ratio, then by simply increasing it, it can force banks to reduce their non-reserve assets (mainly credit). Table 17.4 illustrates the effect of raising the ratio from 20 per cent to 25 per cent. Initially the

Table 17.4 The effect of raising the minimum reserve ratio from 20% to 25%

Initial position: 20% reserve ratio				New position: 25% reserve ratio			
Liabilities		Assets		Liabilities		Assets	
Deposits	£50bn	Reserve assets	£10bn	Deposits	£40bn	Reserve assets	£10bn
		Advances, etc.	£40bn			Advances, etc.	£30bn
Total	£50bn	Total	£50bn	Total	£40bn	Total	£40bn

banks have reserve assets of £10 billion and advances, etc. of £40 billion, giving total assets of £50 billion (of which £10 is 20 per cent). Increasing the reserve ratio to 25 per cent forces banks to reduce their advances, etc. to £30 billion, giving total assets of £40 billion (of which £10 billion is 25 per cent). This is equivalent to credit rationing because banks would *like* to continue lending the £40 billion (or even more), but are being prevented from doing so by the authorities.

Minimum reserve ratios are widely used around the world to restrict credit, including in the USA, Japan, Canada and all the EC countries other than the UK and Luxembourg (see Box 17.3).

 # SUMMARY

1. In the medium and long term, the major sources of monetary growth are banks choosing to operate with a lower liquidity ratio and government borrowing.
2. Banks choosing to operate with a lower liquidity ratio could be prevented by the authorities imposing statutory reserve requirements on banks. Although this practice is commonplace throughout the world, the authorities in the UK have preferred not to use this method, regarding it as 'anti-market'. Instead they have chosen to rely on using interest rates to curb the *demand* for credit.
3. In the UK, the government has tried to limit the size of the PSBR, or even to run a PSDR, in order to keep monetary growth in check.

4. In the short term, the government can use monetary policy to restrict the growth in aggregate demand in one of three ways: (a) reducing money supply directly, (b) reducing the demand for money by raising interest rates, or (c) rationing credit.
5. The money supply can be reduced directly by using open market operations. This involves selling more government securities and thereby reducing banks' reserves when their customers pay for them from their bank accounts. Alternatively, funding can be used. This is where the government increases the ratio of bonds to bills. Since bills are a reserve of banks, this too will reduce banks' liquidity. Finally, banks' liquidity can be

reduced directly by techniques such as special deposits.

6. Interest rates can be controlled by order of the central bank. This used to be the system operated in the UK when banks had to set their interest rates in line with Bank rate. Today the Bank of England influences interest rates by its operations in the discount market. By selling more bills or buying back fewer, it can force down their price and hence force up the rate of discount. This then has a knock-on effect on interest rates throughout the economy.

7. Credit rationing in the UK has not been favoured by the Conservative government of the 1980s and early 1990s. In the past, rationing took the form of requests to the banks by the Bank of England, and hire-purchase controls. The manipulation of statutory reserve requirements is another form of credit rationing which is used in many countries.

17.3 Problems of monetary policy

Medium- and long-term control over the money supply

A government committed to a sustained reduction in the growth of the money supply over a number of years will find this very difficult unless it restricts the size of the public-sector deficit. The Thatcher government in the 1980s recognized this and made reducing the PSBR the central feature of its medium-term financial strategy. There are serious problems, however, in attempting to reduce the PSBR.

Automatic fiscal stabilizers

Reducing the PSBR must involve either reducing government expenditure or raising taxes, or some combination of the two. This is deflationary and may lead to a recession. But in a recession automatic fiscal stabilizers come into force which will tend to push the PSBR back up again. Lower incomes and lower expenditure will mean that less taxes are paid. At the same time, higher unemployment will involve increased government expenditure on unemployment benefits. This was a major problem for the Thatcher government in the early 1980s, when despite efforts to cut government expenditure the PSBR remained high.

The desire to cut taxes

Governments gain popularity by cutting taxes, not by increasing them. The Thatcher government in particular, throughout its terms of office, repeatedly committed itself to cutting the burden of taxation, and thereby to increasing incentives and encouraging enterprise and initiative. But cutting taxes raises the PSBR.

The difficulty in cutting government expenditure

Cuts in government expenditure are politically unpopular. The Thatcher government as soon as it came into office met considerable opposition in Parliament, from public opinion, from local authorities and from various pressure groups, to 'cuts'. What is more, much of government expenditure is committed a long time in advance and cannot easily be cut. As a result the government may find itself forced into refusing to sanction *new* expenditure. But this will mean a decline in capital projects such as roads, housing, schools and sewers, with the net result that there is a decline in the country's infrastructure and long-term damage to the economy.

The less successful a government is in controlling the PSBR, the more it will have to borrow through bond issue to prevent money supply from growing too fast. This will mean high interest rates and the problem of crowding out.

President Reagan found it difficult to reduce the US budget deficit for the same

Box 17.2

The Credit Boom of the 1980s

The abandonment of all forms of credit rationing in the early 1980s contributed to a subsequent boom in consumer credit.

Between 1981 and 1989 consumer credit increased by some 17 per cent per year. Average (nominal) earnings grew by only 8 per cent per year over the same period. By 1989 £48 billion was owed. This amounted to 14 per cent of total personal disposable income (compared with 7.5 per cent in 1981). The table highlights the massive credit expansion.

As the economy pulled out of the recession of the early 1980s, so this rapid rise in credit helped to fuel the recovery. But there were two macroeconomic problems with this credit boom. The first was that spending was going ahead of the ability to produce, and so inflation began to rise after 1986. The second was that a large proportion of the goods bought on credit were imported: foreign cars, Japanese hi-fi, Taiwanese sports goods and so on. Consequently, the balance of payments on current account began to 'dive into the red' (see Figure 12.23 on page 509).

But it was not only an economic problem for the nation as a whole. It was also a very serious problem for those individuals who, tempted by easy credit and the promise of instant consumption, found that they could not afford the repayments. Their problem was compounded in 1988 when there were substantial rises in the rate of interest. Many people were forced into borrowing more in order to pay the interest on existing loans, thus getting even deeper into debt.

And it was not just consumer credit that boomed. Mortgages too were readily available, with various schemes to tempt the first-time buyer to enter the housing market. As more and more money was lent out, so this fuelled the demand for houses, and hence drove up their prices. This meant that people had to take out bigger and bigger mortgages. When mortgage interest rates were then raised in 1988, many people had real difficulties in making ends meet.

1. How does the easy availability of credit affect the problem of inequality?
2. Why might there be a rapid rise in credit during a *recession*?

The rapid growth in credit: 1981–89

	1981	1982	1983	1984	1985	1986	1987	1988	1989
Outstanding credit (£bn)	13.4	16.0	18.9	22.3	26.1	30.2	36.2	42.5	48.2
Growth of credit (%)	21.2	19.4	18.1	18.0	17.0	15.7	13.2	17.4	13.4
Earnings growth (%)	11.2	7.9	8.0	7.1	7.8	7.4	7.8	8.7	9.1
Price inflation (%)	11.9	8.6	4.6	5.0	6.1	3.4	4.2	4.9	7.8

Sources: *Financial Statistics and Economic Trends* (CSO).

reasons. As a result US interest rates had to be kept at a high level. This tended to crowd out investment in the rest of the world, as other countries raised their interest rates too to prevent an excessive outflow of money to the USA and the resulting depreciation of their currency against the US dollar.

There is a further reason why it is difficult to restrain the growth of the money supply over the longer term. Over the years, individuals have increasingly used cheques and credit cards for transactions, and firms have increasingly used various forms of trade credit. Thus people's cash requirements have proportionately reduced (see Box 16.5). Banks therefore require to hold a lower liquidity ratio, and can create more credit. Thus, over time, for any given PSBR, the money supply will tend to rise.

In the mid-1980s, as the UK pulled out of recession, so automatic stabilizers worked in reverse. The fall in unemployment meant a fall in government expenditure on unemployment benefits. The rapid rise in incomes meant a substantial rise in tax revenues, despite cuts in tax *rates*. The effect on the PSBR was dramatic. It disappeared and from 1987 was replaced by a public-sector surplus (PSDR).

A PSDR should have made it easier to restrain the growth of the money supply. But the problem here was that, with the buoyant economy, the demand for credit was high. Banks, being prepared to operate with a lower liquidity ratio, were only too pleased to supply the credit being demanded.

The conclusion from all this is that the state of the economy will have a crucial effect on the demand for and supply of money. If, therefore, the government wishes to *control* the demand for and supply of money, it must actively intervene in money markets. For the remainder of this section we will look at the problems associated with such intervention.

Practical difficulties in controlling money supply in the short run

The authorities may experience considerable difficulties in controlling the money supply. Difficulties occur whether they focus on the monetary base or on a wider range of liquid assets, and whether they impose statutory ratios or allow banks to determine their own prudent ratios.

Problems with monetary base control

Assume that the authorities seek to control M0, the broad monetary base. This could be done by imposing a statutory 'cash' ratio on banks (where 'cash' is M0: i.e. notes and coin and banks' balances with the Bank of England). Assume that a statutory ratio of 10 per cent is imposed. Then provided the authorities control the supply of 'cash' by, say, open-market operations, it would seem that they can thereby control the creation of credit and hence deposits. There would be a money multiplier of 10. For every £1 million decrease in cash, money supply would fall by £10 million. There are serious problems, however, with this form of monetary base control:

Monetary base control

Monetary policy that focuses on controlling the monetary base (as opposed to broad liquidity).

- Banks could hold cash in excess of the statutory minimum. For a time, therefore, they could respond to any restriction of cash by the authorities by simply reducing their cash ratio toward the minimum, rather than having to reduce credit.
- Goodhart's law. Unless cash ratios were imposed on every single financial institution, the control of certain institutions' lending would merely shift business to other uncontrolled institutions.
- Alternatively, if those banks subject to statutory cash requirements were short of cash, they could attract cash away from the uncontrolled institutions.
- Similarly, banks could encourage the general public to withdraw less cash: for example, by making time deposits more attractive than sight deposits or by encouraging a greater use of credit cards.

Problems would also be experienced if the authorities sought to control the *narrow* monetary base: namely, banks' balances with the Bank of England (but not cash in tills). Monetary base control is often discussed in the context of controlling the narrow base.

These problems could be eased by (a) bringing as many institutions as possible under control and (b) backing up open market operations with a rigorous use of special deposits applied across the range of financial institutions.

Disintermediation

The diversion of business away from financial institutions which are subject to controls.

The problems of the switching of business away from the banks is known as disintermediation. To avoid this problem and to allow the greatest freedom of competition between financial institutions, the alternative is to use monetary base control with no *statutory* cash ratio. But this too has problems, some of which are the same as with a statutory cash ratio:

- Banks may vary their prudential ratio, depending on how much cash they anticipate customers are likely to need in the near future.
- When the base is squeezed by open-market operations, etc., the banks may be able to economize on cash balances by encouraging customers to switch to time accounts which have less risk of large cash withdrawals.
- Banks may keep cash balances surplus to their requirements in times of 'easy' money to enable them later to resist open market operations when the authorities are attempting to squeeze the base.
- Goodhart's law may still apply. There may still be disintermediation. Even though open-market operations may be effective in reducing bank lending, people may still be able to borrow money from other financial institutions at home or abroad: institutions which may have surplus liquidity. If, for example, banks refuse overdrafts, people may well borrow from building societies by extending their house mortgages. Some of this money may find its way back to building societies, which can then lend it out again to other customers. Thus although the monetary base is controlled, spending still expands. Alternatively, banks, unable to lend at home, may encourage business customers to take a loan in a foreign currency from one of their overseas branches and then convert the currency into sterling. With an absence of foreign exchange controls this is not difficult.

There is one major problem with monetary base control, with or without a statutory cash ratio, that is perhaps the most serious of all. The Bank of England, as lender of the last resort, *is always prepared to lend cash if it is demanded*. This makes it virtually impossible to have a precise control of the monetary base.

> **?** Trace through the effects of a squeeze on the monetary base from an initial reduction in cash to banks' liquidity being restored by the rediscounting of bills. Will this restoration of liquidity by the Bank of England totally nullify the initial effect of reducing the supply of cash? (Clue: what is likely to happen to the rate of interest?)

Thus despite the fact that the Thatcher government in the early 1980s was committed to a tight control of money supply and set targets for the broad monetary base M0, and despite the fact that the authorities have expressed interest in monetary base control, this has not been the form of policy pursued.

> **?** 1. Why is increasing the monetary base a less reliable means of increasing the money supply than decreasing the monetary base is of decreasing the money supply?
> 2. Given the difficulties of monetary base control, would you expect M0 and broader measures of the money supply, such as M4, to rise and fall by the same percentage as each other? Explain.

Problems with controlling broad liquidity

One solution to the problems of monetary base control would be for the authorities to attempt to control *broader* measures of liquidity. Targets for M3 were an important part of monetary policy from 1976 to 1985, and for part of the time other broader measures (similar to the modern definition of M5) were targeted.

How would such a policy work? Assume that the authorities want to operate a tight monetary policy. They sell bonds on the open market. Banks, now short of cash, call in money from the discount houses, which are in turn forced to borrow from the Bank of England. The Bank of England lends by rediscounting bills. Thus although the Bank of England has been obliged to restore the amount of cash it had withdrawn from the system, there has been an equal and opposite decrease in bills plus money at call held by the banks. Banks' *overall* liquidity has thus been reduced.

Open-market operations should therefore be much more effective in reducing general liquidity than in reducing the monetary base. Note here that open-market operations must be conducted in the bond market not the bill market, since selling Treasury bills would merely exchange one liquid asset for another!

Focusing on the control of broad liquidity also allows another method of control, namely funding, to be used. By merely converting short-term debt (Treasury bills) into long-term debt (bonds), the authorities can reduce liquidity without increasing the size of the national debt – a problem with open-market operations.

Just as with a cash ratio, the authorities could impose a statutory liquidity ratio or they could merely allow banks to set their own prudent liquidity ratio. An example of a statutory liquidity ratio was the minimum 12½ per cent reserve assets ratio imposed on banks from 1971 to 1981. These reserves included balances with the Bank of England, money at call, bills of exchange and government bonds with less than one year to maturity.

But despite the advantages of focusing on broad liquidity, there were considerable problems in operating statutory reserve requirements:

- As with cash ratios, banks could hold reserve assets above the statutory minimum, thus helping them to resist a squeeze on reserves (but not indefinitely).
- Goodhart's law again! Business could switch to uncontrolled institutions.
- Not all reserve assets were under government control. If, for example, the authorities attempted to reduce Treasury bills through funding, the banks could increase their holdings of *other* types of bill instead.
- Even those assets whose supply *is* controlled by the authorities are not all held by the controlled institutions. Thus if more bonds and fewer Treasury bills were issued, the banks could still obtain the same amount of bills as before (by paying a higher price), with other buyers getting less. Similarly, they can persuade other holders of bills to exchange them for time deposits in banks, by offering a higher rate of interest on time deposits; something they can do if the demand for advances is high and hence higher interest rates can be charged on advances.

Even if there is no statutory reserve ratio, it is still difficult to control liquidity:

- Banks may vary their prudent liquidity ratios.
- Banks may keep surplus liquidity to help them resist a squeeze.
- Disintermediation may still occur as customers turn to institutions such as finance houses which, by specializing in longer-term loans, are prepared to operate with less liquidity.

 'It is easier to control the monetary base than broader money, but it is less relevant to do so.' Do you agree with this statement?

The effect on interest rates

A policy of controlling money supply can lead to severe fluctuations in interest rates. This can cause great uncertainty for business and can be very damaging to long-term investment and growth.

The problem is more acute if the overall demand for money is inelastic and is subject to fluctuations. Thus in Figure 17.6, with money supply controlled at M_s, even a fairly moderate increase in demand from L to L' has led to a large rise in interest rates from r to r_1.

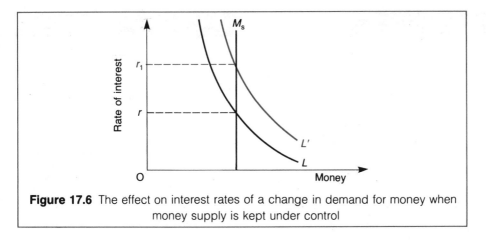

Figure 17.6 The effect on interest rates of a change in demand for money when money supply is kept under control

And yet, if the authorities are committed to controlling money supply, they will have to accept that equilibrium interest rates may well fluctuate in this way.

Difficulties in selling bonds

The use of open-market operations or funding to reduce money supply involves selling more bonds. The authorities may find it difficult to do this. If potential purchasers believe interest rates will rise in the future (highly likely when the government is attempting to operate a tighter monetary policy), they will hold off buying bonds now and may even attempt to sell bonds before bond prices fall. Thus the authorities may be forced into a large immediate increase in bond interest rates.

Problems with credit rationing

To overcome many of the above problems, governments in the past, and particularly in the late 1960s, have resorted to various forms of credit rationing, such as ceilings on bank lending, requests to banks to discriminate between customers, and hire-purchase controls. There are three potential advantages of credit rationing:

● It allows interest rates to be kept lower. For example, in Figure 17.7, if interest rates are to be kept at r and money supply at Q_2, the excess demand for money $Q_1 - Q_2$ can be eliminated by rationing.

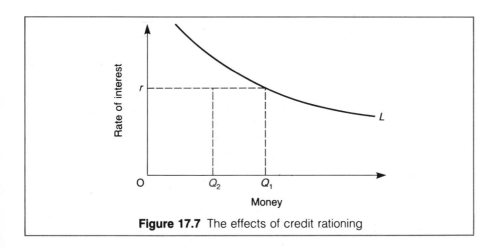

Figure 17.7 The effects of credit rationing

Box 17.3

Views on Credit Control
A comparison of German and UK attitudes

The following are extracts from an article appearing in the *Guardian* on 11 April 1990.

The view of the Bundesbank (the German central bank)

'Minimum reserves, or closely related arrangements, have long been an integral part of the monetary armoury of Western industrialized countries. In the European Community, for instance, minimum reserves are used, or at least available, as monetary policy instruments in all the EC member states except the United Kingdom and Luxembourg. The same applies to the major non-European industrialized countries, i.e., the United States, Japan and Canada.'

Reserve ratios are different between countries, and there is a host of factors, not least the globalization of financial markets and varying legal regimes, that account for the variations; but, says the Bundesbank, 'it would be wrong to infer that the minimum reserve instrument is increasingly being abandoned. No major country in which this instrument is available has abolished the right to maintain minimum reserves; on the contrary, in Belgium it was not until 1988 that the legal framework for introducing minimum reserve requirements was established, even though this instrument has not yet been used.' . . .

The Bundesbank recognizes that there has been a worldwide trend towards more free market monetary management systems, and that changing reserve ratios has become less popular a means of managing the financial systems' liquidity than open market operations . . . But in

a key passage the Germans insist that even in these circumstances minimum reserve requirements 'ensure the effectiveness of monetary policy.'

For if the banks are given a completely free hand, then they will lend as much as they can, converting all their former deposits with the central bank into interest-bearing assets.

In this case 'the central bank would then be faced with the problem of having to refuse to provide liquidity assistance if pressure was building up in the money market – which in all probability would give rise to extreme interest rate swings in the money market or, conversely, the central bank would run the risk of being "dragged along" by excessive funding requests from banks and thus losing control over monetary expansion.'

'Hence most central banks still regard the minimum reserve instrument as an integral part of their monetary management system. Any proposals drastically to lower minimum reserve requirements or to lift them altogether that are based solely on the grounds of the side-effects on interest rates or the potential competitive impact of the instrument therefore miss the point.'

The view of the UK Treasury

In his Budget speech [20 March 1990], the Chancellor John Major said: 'I know many people favour direct controls on lending, hire purchase and consumer credit. I do understand that . . .

'But having looked at the matter, I have concluded that it is extremely unlikely that credit controls would

- It affects lending *directly*. It thus tackles head on the problem of excess or deficient aggregate demand. Altering banks' liquidity or the rate of interest are *indirect* methods of controlling spending.
- It allows the authorities to discriminate between loans for productive investment and loans merely for consumption or speculation.

However, the problems of credit rationing can be serious:

- Given that there is surplus liquidity that banks are prevented from using to grant loans, Goodhart's law may apply quite severely. Credit rationing is unlikely to apply to *all* financial institutions. In the late 1960s it only applied to the clearing banks. Other financial institutions (foreign banks, finance companies, clearing banks' subsidiaries, etc.) expanded their activities. Given plenty of liquidity in the economy, these institutions, by offering higher interest rates than the clearing banks, attracted deposits and were thus able to expand their loans. To avoid this, credit rationing would have to extend to all institutions. The more complex the banking system, the more difficult it is to do this.

Box 17.3 (cont'd)

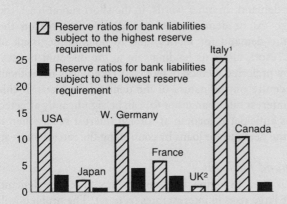

Notes: 1 Uniform incremental reserve ratio: in Italy minimum reserves carry interest.

2 Uniform reserve ratio: in the UK the minimum reserve instrument does not serve monetary policy purposes.

Minimum reserve ratios in major countries

work in the modern world in anything other than the very short term.'

'They were becoming less and less effective even before exchange controls were abolished over 10 years ago. Their main impact now would be to replace domestic borrowing. These days it would, for example, be a simple matter for any High Street bank to arrange its lending through an overseas branch . . .

'It is for this reason that governments of all persuasions throughout the Western world are abolishing credit controls and are relying on interest rates to control money – and thus inflation.'

The Treasury's 'Red Book' published on Budget day explained the government's view that reserve ratios are no more than a means of ensuring that the State's chosen interest rate percolates efficiently through the monetary system; they are not, in the Treasury's view, a means of controlling credit in their own right.

'Because interest rates are the essential instrument of monetary policy, the monetary authorities must be in a position to exercise a high degree of influence over their movements. That means they need to ensure that the financial system is dependent on funds provided by the central bank so that its own lending rate is transmitted more widely into market rates.

'To achieve this result, a number of other countries – France and Germany for example – impose minimum reserve assets ratios on their banks. The operation of the ratio increases the banking system's need for funds from the central bank, and thereby helps to ensure that market rates will reflect the rate of interest at which the central bank provides the supply. Only the central bank can meet these needs. It is thus mistaken to see reserve requirements as an alternative monetary instrument to interest rates.

'In particular, reserve requirements do not serve as a direct credit control. Rather, they provide a means whereby official influence on interest rates is made effective.'

1. On what points do the UK and German authorities agree and disagree concerning the role of minimum reserve ratios?
2. 'It is not the mere existence of minimum reserve ratios that constitutes a form of credit rationing, rather it is the deliberate *increasing* of the ratios.' Do you agree with this statement?

- Banks may resist the attempts at rationing. They would *like* to lend and have the liquidity to do so. They may thus find ways to get round the controls.
- Credit rationing stifles competition between banks. It prevents efficient banks from expanding. Customers may be forced to borrow from inefficient banks or other financial institutions, probably charging higher interest rates.
- Banks may favour their established customers, especially the larger ones. This would discriminate against the growth of small, new firms, which may rely on bank loans to finance their investment.
- Hire-purchase controls may have serious disruptive effects on certain industries (e.g. cars and other consumer durables), whose products are bought largely on hire-purchase credit.

The Thatcher government was always very much opposed to the use of credit rationing, since it prevents free competition in financial markets.

 Is credit rationing easier to implement if banks operate as a cartel or if they are highly competitive?

Problems with controlling interest rates

As long as people want to borrow, banks and other financial institutions will normally try to find ways of meeting the demand. In other words, in the short run at least, the supply of money is to a large extent demand determined. For this reason the authorities prefer to control the demand for money, and to do this the Bank of England, as lender of the last resort, alters its lending rate to the discount houses.

Even though this is the current preferred method of monetary control it is not without its difficulties. The problems centre on the nature of the demand for loans. If this demand (a) is unresponsive to interest rate changes or (b) can be significantly affected by other determinants (such as anticipated income or foreign interest rates), then it will be very difficult to control the demand for loans by controlling the rate of interest.

Problem of an inelastic demand for loans

If the demand for loans is inelastic, as in Figure 17.8, any attempt to reduce demand (e.g. from Q_1 to Q_2) will involve large rises in interest rates (r_1 to r_2). The problem will be compounded if the demand curve shifts to the right, due, say, to a consumer spending boom.

High interest rates lead to the following problems:

- They may discourage investment plans and hence long-term growth. Governments might prefer 'less important' borrowing to be curtailed.
- They add to the costs of production, to the costs of house purchase and generally to the cost of living. They are thus cost inflationary.
- They are politically unpopular, since the general public do not like paying higher interest rates on overdrafts, credit cards and mortgages.
- The necessary bond issue to restrain liquidity will commit the government to paying high rates on these bonds for the next twenty years or so.
- High interest rates encourage inflows of money from abroad. This makes it even more difficult to restrain bank lending.
- Inflows of money from abroad drive up the exchange rate. This can be very damaging for export industries and industries competing with imports. Many firms suffered badly in 1980 when as a result of a high interest rate policy (plus North Sea oil's effect on the balance of payments) the exchange rate soared to over £1 = $2.30 (from only £1 = $1.60 some three years earlier).

Figure 17.8 An inelastic demand for loans

Box 17.4

Using Interest Rates to Control Both Aggregate Demand and the Exchange Rate
A problem of one instrument and two targets

We have assumed up to now that the government is using interest rates to control aggregate demand and hence output (and employment) and/or inflation. Let us assume that inflation is rising and therefore the government wants to raise interest rates to dampen the demand and supply of money, and thereby the level of aggregate demand.

But what if the government wants also to manage the *rate of exchange*? Let us assume that the government considers that the rate of exchange (currently, say, at £1 = DM3.10) is too high. Perhaps this has been caused by the high rates of interest in the UK attracting foreign capital and causing a surplus on the capital account of the balance of payments. This, of course, must be matched by a deficit on the current account. Assume that the government is worried about the damaging effect this is having on exports and wants to reduce the exchange rate to £1 = DM2.85.

If it uses interest rates as the means of achieving this, it will have to *lower* them: lower interest rates will cause capital to flow out of the UK, and this will cause the rate of exchange to depreciate.

But there is a dilemma here. The government wants *high* interest rates to contain inflation, but *low* interest rates to help exporters. But of course it cannot have both

high and low interest rates at the same time! If interest rates are the government's only weapon, one objective will have to be sacrificed for the other.

This is an illustration of a rule in economic policy: you must have at least as many instruments as targets. If you have two targets (e.g. low inflation and a low exchange rate) you must have at least two policy instruments (e.g. interest rates and one other).

Another example we have come across is the two targets of low inflation and low unemployment in the Keynesian model. Changes in aggregate demand cannot be used to achieve both objectives simultaneously. Lower unemployment would require a more rapid growth in aggregate demand, whereas lower inflation would require a less rapid growth in aggregate demand. That is why Keynesians argue that you require *another* instrument of policy as well – such as a prices and incomes policy.

? 1. Give some other examples of the impossibility of using one policy instrument to achieve two policy objectives simultaneously.

2. If the government wanted to achieve a lower rate of inflation and also a *higher* exchange rate, could it under these circumstances rely simply on the one policy instrument of interest rates?

Evidence suggests that the demand for loans may indeed be quite inelastic. The reasons include the following:

- A rise in interest rates, particularly if it deepens a recession, may force many firms into borrowing merely to survive. This increase in 'distress borrowing' may largely offset any decline in borrowing by other firms or individuals.
- Although investment *plans* may be curtailed by high interest rates, *current* borrowing by many firms cannot easily be curtailed. Similarly, high interest rates may discourage householders from taking on *new* mortgages, but existing mortgages are unlikely to be reduced.
- High interest rates may discourage many firms from taking out long-term fixed-interest loans. Instead they may borrow from banks whose loans are shorter-term variable-interest loans. This extra borrowing from banks will reduce the overall fall in demand for bank loans, thus making the demand less elastic.

Problem of an unstable demand
Accurate monetary control requires the authorities to be able to predict the demand curve for money. Only then can they set the appropriate level of interest rates.

Unfortunately, the demand curve may shift unpredictably, making control very

Box 17.5

Effective Monetary Policy Versus Banking Stability and Efficiency

A problem for the Bank of England?

The Bank of England has three potentially conflicting aims.

The first aim is to maintain a *stable banking system*: to make sure that banks do not fail, do not take undue risks and do not undermine public confidence in the whole financial system. Two examples of the Bank of England's attempt to meet this objective are (a) its role as lender of last resort, whereby it guarantees sufficient liquidity to the banking system via the discount houses, and (b) the requirement that banks should keep ½ per cent of their eligible liabilities in cash at the Bank of England.

The second aim is to encourage *efficient banking*. Banking is potentially oligopolistic. This can lead to lower 'output' (i.e. a smaller number of loans), collusion over interest rates (keeping them low to depositors and high to borrowers) and a lack of innovation as banks feel no urgency to compete. To achieve the aim of efficiency, therefore, the Bank of England may wish to break down collusion, remove barriers to the entry of new banks and new banking practices, and not to regulate banks' behaviour excessively. Deregulation of banking and the opening-up of banking to competition has been a major part of government policy in recent years.

The third aim is to *carry out the government's monetary policy* efficiently and effectively. To do this the Bank of England will need to be able to carry out measures that force banks to change interest rates and/or alter their lending/borrowing behaviour swiftly and by the amount desired by the government.

So how are these three aims likely to conflict?

Conflicts between stability and efficiency

The more the competition between the banks, the greater will be the risk of bank failure. Supernormal profits will be eroded; banks may feel forced to grant riskier loans in order to retain market share; a failure of one bank could more easily lead to failures of other banks once public confidence was shaken.

Putting it the other way round, if the Bank of England

guarantees the stability of the system, it may make banks more complacent and less concerned to be efficient.

Conflicts between stability and the operation of monetary policy

If monetary policy is to be effective, banks must fear the risk of failure. If they do, then any squeeze on their liquidity by the Bank of England will force them to cut back on their lending. If, by contrast, there is little competition between the banks and they thus operate with high profit margins and plenty of surplus liquidity, it will be harder for the Bank of England to engineer a liquidity shortage.

More importantly, if the Bank of England acts as lender of last resort, this will remove altogether the fear of a liquidity shortage. The Bank of England will have to rely much more on high interest rates to deter the *demand* for credit.

To summarize: the aim of stability requires banks to be invulnerable; an effective monetary policy requires banks to be vulnerable.

Conflicts between efficiency and the operation of monetary policy

Competition between banks makes it more difficult for the Bank of England to impose credit controls on the banks. If it tries to impose ceilings on clearing bank credit, this will simply encourage the growth of credit through non-clearing banks.

A lack of competition between banks makes it easier for the Bank of England. It is easier to deal with a cartel and to impose rules on its behaviour than it is to influence a highly diverse and competitive banking sector that is open to international movements of capital.

? Does increased bank competition necessarily make it harder for the Bank of England to force through changes in interest rates (a) by decree; (b) by dealings in the money market?

difficult. The major reason for unpredictable shifts is *speculation*: speculation against changes in interest rates, exchange rates and the inflation rate, and changing business confidence in the prospects of economic growth.

- If people think interest rates will rise and bond prices fall, in the meantime they will demand to hold their assets in liquid form. The demand for money will rise.
- If people think exchange rates will rise, they will demand sterling while it is still relatively cheap. The demand for money will rise.

- If people think inflation will rise, the transactions demand for money may rise. People spend now while prices are still relatively low.
- If people think the economy is going to grow faster, the demand for loans will increase as firms seek to increase their investment.

In all these cases, it is very difficult for the authorities to predict what people's speculation will be. Speculation depends so much on world political events, rumour and 'random shocks' (such as a coal strike or worse than expected trade, unemployment, PSBR or inflation statistics).

If the demand curve shifts very much, and if it is inelastic, then monetary control will be very difficult. Furthermore, it will mean that the authorities will have to make frequent and sizeable adjustments to interest rates. These fluctuations can be very damaging to business confidence and may discourage long-term investment.

 Why does an unstable demand for money make it difficult to control the *supply* of money?

Conclusions

It is impossible to use monetary policy as a precise means of controlling aggregate demand. It is especially weak when it is pulling against the expectations of firms and consumers, and when it is implemented too late.

Nevertheless, if the authorities operate a tight monetary policy firmly enough and long enough, they should eventually be able to reduce lending and aggregate demand. But there will inevitably be time lags and imprecision in the process.

An expansionary monetary policy is even less reliable. If the economy is in recession, no matter how low interest rates are driven, people cannot be forced to borrow if they do not wish to.

Few economists, therefore, argue that monetary policy can be used to 'fine tune' the economy. Even monetarists would accept that monetary policy is best regarded as the means of keeping monetary growth within fairly broad medium- or long-term target ranges. This was very much the approach of the Thatcher government's medium-term financial strategy in the early and mid-1980s.

▲ SUMMARY

1. It is difficult to control the growth of the money supply over the longer term without controlling the growth of the PSBR. This will be difficult to do in a period of stagflation. In a recession, automatic fiscal stabilizers will cause a growth in government expenditure and a cut in tax revenues. What is more, tax increases or cuts in government expenditure are politically unpopular. Even if the PSBR *is* reduced, this may be insufficient to prevent the growth of credit, especially if banks are prepared to operate with a lower liquidity ratio.

2. All forms of short-term monetary policy involve problems. Controlling either the monetary base or broad liquidity is difficult given that the Bank of England is always prepared to provide liquidity to the discount houses as lender of last resort. Also there are the problems of disintermediation, as customers switch their borrowing away from those banks short of liquidity, and the problem of banks

resisting the squeeze on liquidity by operating with a lower liquidity ratio. If the government is successful in controlling the money supply, there then arises the problem of severe fluctuations in interest rates if the demand for money fluctuates and is relatively inelastic.

3. Credit rationing provides a means of directly reducing aggregate demand without having to raise interest rates. It stifles competition between banks, however, and encourages banks to discriminate (perhaps unfairly) between customers. Banks may also try to evade the controls, and disintermediation is likely to occur towards those institutions that are not controlled.

4. The form of monetary policy that has been favoured in recent years is the control of interest rates. Higher interest rates, by reducing the demand for money, effectively also reduce the supply. Nevertheless there are problems with this approach too. With an inelastic

demand for loans, interest rates may have to rise to very high levels in order to bring the required reduction in monetary growth. They are politically unpopular and discriminate against those with high borrowing commitments, such as those with large mortgages. Also high interest rates have the effect of driving up the exchange rate, which in turn can be damaging to exports. Controlling aggregate demand through controlling interest rates is made even more difficult as a result of fluctuations in the demand for money. These *fluctuations* are made more severe by speculation against changes in interest rates, exchange rates, the rate of inflation, etc.

5. It is impossible to use monetary policy as a precise means of controlling aggregate demand in the short term. Nevertheless in the long term, if the policy is pursued rigorously enough, many economists argue that it is the most effective way of keeping inflation under control.

Keynesian and Monetarist Controversies I: The Control of Aggregate Demand

18

There is no current orthodoxy in macroeconomics. The debate between Keynesians and monetarists shows no signs of being settled. What is more, there are not just two clear-cut sets of theories and policies in this debate. There are different varieties of Keynesians and monetarists. For example, one of the most influential developments in macroeconomics in recent years has been the rise of the new classical school – an extreme form of *laissez-faire* monetarism.[1]

Furthermore, the debate is not just between Keynesians and monetarists. At the other end of the political spectrum from the new classical school are the various Marxist schools. The stagflation of the 1970s and the recessions of the early 1980s and early 1990s are seen by such economists as symptoms of a growing crisis of the capitalist system. Then there are many economists who shun labels and who do not wholeheartedly embrace any one school. These 'eclectic' economists prefer to look at each element of the debate and assess it as dispassionately as possible in the light

At the centre of these debates are the key questions of how well does a free-market economy meet the various macroeconomic objectives, and to what extent can government intervention improve things?

The market economy involves both demand and supply. The debate correspondingly branches into two. One part of the debate focuses on aggregate demand. What are the determinants of aggregate demand? What is the relationship between money supply and aggregate demand? How does aggregate demand respond to changes in interest rates? How effectively can the government control aggregate demand through either fiscal or monetary policy?

The other part of the debate focuses on aggregate supply. What is the shape of the aggregate supply curve? How responsive is it to changes in aggregate demand? What are the determinants of aggregate supply? Can the government influence aggregate supply, and how?

We will consider aggregate supply and supply-side policies in Chapters 19 and 20. This chapter looks at the debate over aggregate demand.

---

[1] Members of the new classical school might well object to being termed 'extreme monetarists', but it is useful categorization for the present. We examine their views in Chapter 19.

18.1 Monetary policy and aggregate demand

The quantity theory of money

A simple illustration of the controversy over the effects of monetary policy on aggregate demand is provided by the *quantity theory of money* (see page 536). One version of this theory is expressed in the following equation:

$$MV = PQ$$

where M = the supply of money
Q = the quantity of national output sold in a year
P = the average level of prices
V = the income velocity of circulation: that is, the average number of times money is spent on national output in a year.

PQ will thus be the money value of national output sold (i.e. national income, Y). MV will be the total spending on national output, and therefore must be equal to PQ. For example, if money supply were £10 billion, and money as it passed from one person to another was spent on average eight times a year on national output, then total spending (MV) would be £80 billion a year. And thus the value of goods sold (PQ) must also equal £80 billion.

 Refer back to the version of the quantity equation we looked at in Chapter 13 (page 536). What is the relationship between the term k in that version and the term V in the version we have just looked at?

The quantity *equation* is true by definition. MV is *necessarily* equal to PQ because of the way the terms are defined. The equation itself, therefore, is not the subject of debate: it is simply an identity. What a change in M does to P, however, *is* a matter of debate. The controversy centres on the assumptions made about two of the terms, V and Q: whether and how they are affected by changes in the money supply (M). How a change in M affects V and Q will determine what happens to P.

The velocity of circulation (V)

Monetarists argue that variations in the velocity of circulation (V) are predictable and moderately small, especially over the longer run. More importantly, they argue that over the longer run V is determined *totally independently* of the money supply (M). Thus an increase in M will leave V unaffected, and there will be a corresponding rise in MV. In other words, a change in money supply (M) brings a corresponding change in expenditure (MV):

$$M\uparrow, \bar{V} \rightarrow MV\uparrow$$

where the bar over the V term means that it is exogenously determined: i.e. determined *independently* of M.

Monetarists therefore claim that monetary policy is an extremely powerful weapon for controlling aggregate demand.

 If V is constant, will (a) a £10 million rise in M give a £10 million rise in MV; (b) a 10 per cent rise in M give a 10 per cent rise in MV? (Test your answer by fitting some numbers to the terms.)

Keynesians argue that V tends to vary inversely with M, but also rather unpredictably. An increase in money supply will not necessarily have much effect on spending; instead people may simply increase their holdings of idle speculative balances, with a corresponding decline in the speed with which money circulates (V). How much extra idle balances people will hold will depend on their expectations of changes in interest rates, prices and exchange rates. Since expectations are difficult to predict, the amount by which V will fall is also difficult to predict:

$$M\uparrow \rightarrow V\downarrow (?) \rightarrow MV?$$

Keynesians therefore claim that monetary policy is an extremely unreliable weapon for controlling aggregate demand.

The quantity of national output (Q)

Monetarists argue that aggregate supply is inelastic in the long run (see Figure 18.1 (a)), and therefore output (Q) is determined independently of aggregate demand. Any rise in MV will be totally reflected in a rise in prices (P):

$$MV\uparrow \rightarrow P\uparrow, \overline{Q}$$

The stock of money therefore determines the price level, and the rate of increase in money supply determines the rate of inflation. Thus monetary policy is the means of controlling inflation, and in the long run, control of the money supply will not affect output (Q) and employment. It is this emphasis on controlling the money supply that has led to the title 'monetarist'.

 If both V and Q are constant, will (a) a £10 million rise in M lead to a £10 million rise in P; (b) a 10 per cent rise in M lead to a 10 per cent rise in P? (Again, try fitting some numbers to the terms.)

Keynesians argue that aggregate supply is relatively elastic except when full employment is approached (see Figure 18.1(b)). Thus Q is variable. A tight monetary policy therefore, to the extent that it does affect aggregate demand, is likely to reduce Q as well as P, especially when there is resistance from monopolistic firms and unions to price and wage cuts:

$$MV\downarrow \rightarrow P\downarrow \ and \ Q\downarrow$$

If monetary policy is successful in reducing aggregate demand, it can lead to a lasting recession.

The variability of V is the subject of this section. The variability of Q is the subject of Chapter 19.

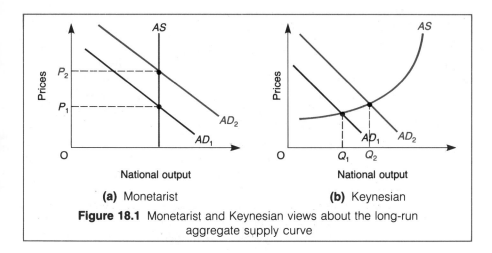

(a) Monetarist   **(b)** Keynesian

Figure 18.1 Monetarist and Keynesian views about the long-run aggregate supply curve

Monetary policy's effect on aggregate demand: the traditional Keynesian transmission mechanism

In order to assess the arguments over the variability of V it is necessary to see just how a change in money supply is transmitted through to a change in aggregate demand.

Keynesians stress that transmission mechanisms are indirect: changes in money supply affect aggregate demand *indirectly* via changes in interest rates or exchange rates. We looked at these mechanisms in Chapter 16. Here we focus on the interest rate mechanism. Shortly we will look at the role of exchange rates.

Recall Figure 16.10: it is reproduced as Figure 18.2. Changes in money supply affect aggregate demand in three stages:

1. A rise in money supply from M to M' will lead to a fall in the rate of interest from r_1 to r_2.
2. A fall in the rate of interest will lead to more investment and any other interest-sensitive expenditures (from I_1 to I_2)
3. A rise in investment will lead to a multiplied rise in national income (from Y_1 to Y_2).

The problem, though, according to Keynesians is that stages 1 and 2 are unpredictable and perhaps rather weak.

(a) Stage 1: $M\uparrow \rightarrow r\downarrow$ **(b)** Stage 2: $r\downarrow \rightarrow I\uparrow$ **(c)** Stage 3: $I\uparrow \rightarrow J\uparrow \rightarrow Y\uparrow$

Figure 18.2 The traditional Keynesian transmission mechanism

Problems with stage 1: the money–interest link

The problem of an interest-elastic demand for money. According to Keynesians, the speculative demand for money is highly responsive to changes in interest rates. The speculative demand can be quite large. Keynesians point to the large sums of money that move around the money market as firms and financial institutions anticipate changes in interest rates. If people believe the rate of interest will rise, and thus the price of bonds and other securities will fall, few people will want to buy them. Instead there will be a very high demand for liquid assets (money and near money). The demand for money will therefore be very elastic in response to changes in interest rates. The demand for money curve (the liquidity preference curve, L) will be shallow and may even be infinitely elastic at some minimum interest rate. This is the point where everyone believes interest rates will rise, and therefore no one wants to buy bonds. Everyone wants to hold their assets in liquid form.

With a very shallow L curve (as in Figure 18.3), a rise in money supply from M to M' will only lead to a small fall in the rate of interest from r_1 to r_2. Once people believe that the rate of interest will not go any lower, any further rise in money supply will

Figure 18.3 An elastic liquidity preference curve

have no effect on *r*. The additional money will be lost in the 'liquidity trap'. People simply hold the additional money as idle balances.

Keynes himself saw the liquidity trap as merely a special case: the case where the economy is in deep recession. In such a case, an expansion of money supply would have no effect on the economy. In more normal times, an expansion of money supply would be likely to have some effect on interest rates.

The problem of an unstable demand for money. A more serious Keynesian criticism is that the liquidity preference curve (*L*) is *unstable*. People hold speculative balances of money when they anticipate that interest rates will rise (security prices will fall). But it is not just the current interest rate that affects people's expectations of the future direction of interest rates. There are many factors that could affect such expectations:

● Changes in foreign interest rates. UK interest rates would have to follow suit if the authorities wished to maintain a stable exchange rate.
● Changes in exchange rates. With a falling exchange rate, the authorities may raise interest rates to protect sterling.
● Statements of government intentions on economic policy.
● Good or bad industrial news. With good news, people tend to buy shares.
● Newly published figures on inflation or money supply. If inflation or the growth in money supply are higher than anticipated, people will expect a rise in interest rates in anticipation of a tighter monetary policy.
● Similarly, a consumer boom, to the extent that it increases the transactions demand for money and increases imports, will encourage the authorities to increase interest rates in order to keep money supply on target.

Thus the *L* curve can be highly volatile. With an unstable demand for money, it is difficult to predict the effect on interest rates of a change in money supply.

 Go through each of the above six factors that affect expectations and consider what would cause people to anticipate a *fall* in interest rates.

A policy of *targeting* money supply is also criticized by Keynesians for similar reasons. A volatile demand for money that shifts about as expectations change can cause severe fluctuations in interest rates if the supply of money is kept constant. These fluctuations in interest rates will cause further uncertainty and further shifts in the speculative demand for money. A policy of targeting money supply can therefore add to the volatility of the velocity of circulation (*V*).

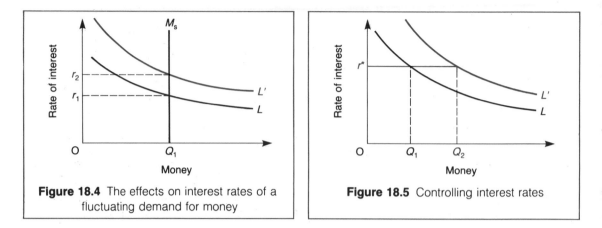

Figure 18.4 The effects on interest rates of a fluctuating demand for money

Figure 18.5 Controlling interest rates

The effect on interest rates of a shift in the demand for money when money supply is kept to a target is illustrated in Figure 18.4.

Keynesians argue that it is best to focus on controlling interest rates, and to adjust money supply to whatever level is necessary to meet the target interest rate. Thus if the target rate of interest in Figure 18.5 is r^*, and the authorities estimate the demand for money to be L, they should allow the money supply to be Q_1. If demand increases to L', then the authorities should allow the money supply to rise to Q_2.

A policy of controlling interest rates is likely to cause a more stable demand for money, with fewer shifts in the speculative demand. This in turn will further aid the process of controlling interest rates.

Although the authorities in the UK have sought to control interest rates by their operations in the discount market, this relates much more to Figure 18.4 than Figure 18.5, especially during the first part of the 1980s. For any given demand for money, they seek to adjust interest rates so as to make the demand for money equal to the target money supply. Thus in Figure 18.4, if the demand for money increased to L', and the money supply target was Q_1, the authorities would raise interest rates to r_2.

This policy necessarily involves the interest rate fluctuating with the demand for money. Keynesians are critical of this policy, arguing that the uncertainty over interest rates, combined with a generally too restrictive monetary policy and a correspondingly too high average interest rate, is very damaging to business investment and hence long-term growth.

Problems with stage 2: the interest rate–investment link
Again there are two types of criticism that Keynesians make about this link. The first is that investment is insensitive to changes in interest rates. The second is that investment is volatile and unpredictable.

The problem of an interest-inelastic investment demand. After the war many Keynesians argued that investment was unresponsive to interest rate changes: that the I curve in Figure 18.2(b) was steep. In these circumstances a very large change in interest rates would be necessary to have any significant effect on investment and aggregate demand.

Investment, it was argued, depends on confidence of future markets. This relationship is explained by the accelerator theory or similar theories. If confidence is high, firms will continue to invest even if interest rates are high. They can always pass the higher costs on to the consumer. If confidence is low, firms will not invest even if interest rates are low and borrowing is cheap. Evidence seemed to confirm the interest inelasticity of investment demand.

Few Keynesians hold this extreme position today. The evidence for an inelastic investment demand has been challenged. Just because investment was not significantly lower on occasions when interest rates were high, it does not follow that investment is unresponsive to interest rate changes. The high interest rates might well have depressed investment *if other things had remained equal*, but there may have been changes in *other* factors that helped to *maintain* investment: in other words, the *I* curve shifted to the right. The most obvious example is changes in consumer demand. If consumer demand rose, this would both cause the high interest rate *and* encourage higher investment.

> **?** Figure 18.6 shows a steep investment demand curve. If the rate of interest rises from r_1 to r_2, there is only a small fall in investment from I_1 to I_2. Now draw a much more elastic *I* curve passing through point *a*. Assume that this is the true *I* curve. Show how the rate of interest could still rise to r_2 and investment still only fall to I_2 if this curve were to shift.

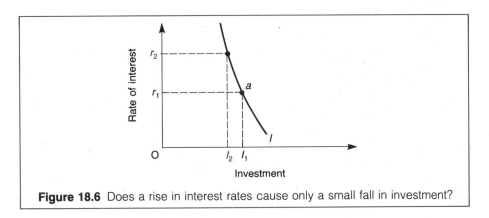

Figure 18.6 Does a rise in interest rates cause only a small fall in investment?

Even if fixed investment in plant and machinery is not very interest sensitive, there are other components of aggregate demand that may well be: for example, investment in stocks, consumer demand financed through credit cards, bank loans or hire purchase, and the demand for houses financed through mortgages.

The problem of an unstable investment demand. Today the major worry about the interest–investment link is not that the investment curve is inelastic, but rather that it shifts erratically with the confidence of investors. Such confidence is highly volatile.

For example, assume in Figure 18.7 that the authorities increase money supply and this lowers interest rates from r_0 to r_1. Other things being equal, the level of investment will rise from Q_0 to Q_1. If, however, firms believe that the economy will now pull out of recession, their confidence will increase. The investment curve will shift to I_2 and investment will increase quite markedly to Q_2. If, on the other hand, firms believe that inflation will now rise, which in turn will later force the authorities to pursue a tighter monetary policy, their confidence may well decrease. The investment curve will shift to I_3 and the level of investment will actually fall to Q_3.

Monetary policy is only likely to be effective, therefore, if the government can 'sell' it to the people, so that people have confidence in its effectiveness. This *psychological* effect can be quite powerful. It demands considerable *political* skill, however, to manipulate it.

Figure 18.7 The effects of interest rate changes given an unstable investment demand curve

The Keynesian analysis of the exchange rate transmission mechanism

The traditional Keynesian mechanism can be extended to an open economy to take into account international capital flows and movements in the exchange rate. The mechanism is still indirect. But this time it includes the exchange rate as an intermediate variable between changes in the money supply and changes in aggregate demand. There are four stages in the mechanism:

1. A rise in money supply will cause a fall in interest rates.
2. A fall in interest rates will lead to an outflow of short-term capital from the country. This will cause a depreciation of the exchange rate (assuming the authorities allow it to).
3. This will cause a rise in demand for exports and a fall in demand for imports.
4. This will cause a multiplied rise in national income.

The four stages are illustrated in Figure 18.8.

Stage 1 will tend to be more powerful than in a closed economy. The liquidity preference curve will tend to be less elastic. The reason is that, as interest rates fall, although people may buy fewer *UK* securities, they will not simply switch to holding idle balances of sterling. Instead, fearing a depreciation of sterling, they may well switch to holding other currencies.

Just how much people will switch out of sterling depends on *how much* they think the exchange rate will depreciate. But these expectations are highly unpredictable. Thus stage 1 may be relatively strong, but just how strong is very difficult to predict.

Stage 2 is likely to be very strong indeed. Given the openness of international financial markets, the ease of transferring large amounts of capital from one country to another and the huge amounts of short-term capital in the international monetary system, international capital flows can be enormous in response to interest rate changes. Thus only a relatively small change in interest rates is necessary to cause a relatively large capital flow.

Stage 3 may be quite strong in the long run. Given time, the demand by consumers abroad for UK exports and demand in the UK for imports may be quite elastic. In the short run, the effect may be rather limited. But here again, the size of the effect is uncertain and *could* be quite large. It depends on people's expectations of exchange rate movements. If people think that the exchange rate will fall further, importers will

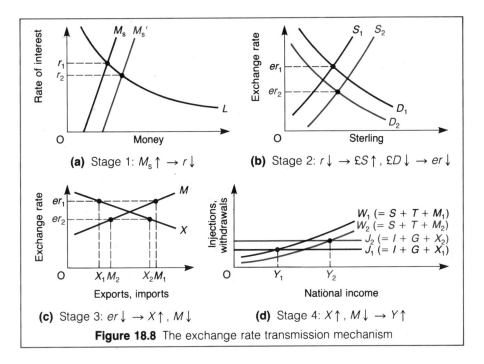

(a) Stage 1: $M_s \uparrow \rightarrow r \downarrow$

(b) Stage 2: $r \downarrow \rightarrow £S \uparrow, £D \downarrow \rightarrow er \downarrow$

(c) Stage 3: $er \downarrow \rightarrow X \uparrow, M \downarrow$

(d) Stage 4: $X \uparrow, M \downarrow \rightarrow Y \uparrow$

Figure 18.8 The exchange rate transmission mechanism

buy *now* before the rate does fall and they have to pay more for the imports. Exporters, on the other hand, will hold back as long as possible before shipping their exports: if the rate does fall, they will earn more sterling per dollar's worth of exports. These actions will tend to push the exchange rate down. This will tend to 'hasten' the long run. But such speculation is very difficult to predict as it depends on often highly volatile expectations.

? If importers and exporters believe that the exchange rate has 'bottomed out', what will they do?

Stage 4 is the familiar multiplier, only this time triggered off by a change in imports and exports.

To summarize: the effects of a change in the money supply might be quite strong, but their precise magnitude is usually highly unpredictable.

The effects of changes in money supply will depend also on just how free the exchange rate is. If the government intervenes to 'peg' (i.e. fix) the exchange rate or even to prevent excessive fluctuations, the transmission mechanism will not work in the same way as we have described. Alternative exchange rate systems (or 'regimes', as they are called) are examined in Chapter 22.

Monetary policy's effect on aggregate demand: the monetarist transmission mechanism

The direct mechanism

Monetarists stress the direct transmission mechanism. If money supply increases, people will have more money than they require to hold. They will spend this surplus. Much of this spending will go on goods and services, thereby directly increasing aggregate demand:

$$M_s \uparrow \; \rightarrow \; M_s > M_d \; \rightarrow \; AD \uparrow$$

The theoretical underpinning for this is given by the *theory of portfolio balance*. People have a number of ways of holding their wealth. They can hold it as money, or as financial assets such as bills, bonds and shares, or as physical assets such as houses, cars and televisions. In other words, people hold a whole portfolio of assets of varying degrees of liquidity – from cash to central heating.

Now assume that money supply expands. People will find themselves holding more money than they require: their portfolios are unnecessarily liquid. Some of this money will be used to purchase financial assets, and some to purchase *goods and services*. As more assets are purchased, this will drive up their price. This will effectively reduce their 'yield'. For bonds and other financial assets, this means a reduction in their rate of interest. For goods and services, this means a reduction in their marginal utility/price ratio: a higher level of consumption will reduce their marginal utility and drive up their price. The process will stop when a balance has been restored in people's portfolios.

 Do you think that this is an accurate description of how people behave when they acquire extra money?

This mechanism has been criticized by Keynesians. Just how is the extra money injected into people's portfolios in the first place? There are two possible means in the short term.

An expansionary fiscal policy financed by an increased money supply. In this case, people receive the extra money either through tax cuts or through increased government expenditure. But in these circumstances, claim Keynesians, it is *fiscal* policy that is causing the resulting increase in aggregate demand through its effect on people's real incomes.

The use of monetary techniques. If credit rationing has been in force, then a relaxation of controls *will* increase borrowing and spending. But monetarists frown on the use of credit rationing as being 'anti-market'. If the monetarists' preferred method of control is used – namely, open market operations – the working of the direct mechanism is unclear. An open-market operation involves people exchanging bonds and bills for money. Therefore the resulting extra money in their portfolios has not involved any increase in wealth. People have more money but fewer bonds and bills. Any increase in the ratio of shares and physical assets in people's portfolios will be due simply to the new lower interest rates on bonds. Certainly in the short run, therefore, the direct mechanism may be weak if working through open-market operations.

The indirect mechanisms
Monetarists also see monetary policy operating through the indirect mechanisms.

The traditional interest rate mechanism. This, they argue, is more powerful than in traditional Keynesian theory, because stages 1 and 2 are much stronger.

1. The liquidity preference curve (L) (Figure 18.2(a)) is relatively inelastic. This is because of the much smaller role played by speculative balances. A reduction in the rate of interest (r) following an increase in money supply may well make bond holding less attractive, but this does not mean that the extra money will be mainly held in idle balances. Again, it can be used to purchase other assets such as houses.

2. The investment demand curve (*I*) (Figure 18.2(b)) is relatively elastic. Monetarists criticize Keynesians for concentrating merely on investment. Instead they stress the wide range of expenditures that are interest sensitive, such as expenditure on consumer durables.

With a steep *L* curve and a shallow *I* curve, the effect on aggregate demand will be much greater.

 Redraw the three diagrams of Figure 18.2 with a steeper *L* curve and a shallower *I* curve. Show how an increase in money supply will have a larger effect on national income.

The exchange rate transmission mechanism. Monetarists argue that, in an open economy with free-floating exchange rates, the effect of an increase in the money supply is stronger still. Any fall in interest rates will have such a strong effect on international capital flows and the exchange rate that the rise in money supply will be relatively quickly and fully transmitted through to aggregate demand.

Short-run variability of V. Even though monetarists stress the direct mechanism and a relatively inelastic *L* curve, they do admit to some variability of the velocity of circulation (*V*) in the short run. To the extent that interest rates and yields do fall with an expansion of the money supply, people may well hold larger money balances: after all, the opportunity cost of holding that liquidity (i.e. the interest sacrificed by not holding bonds, etc.) has been reduced. If people hold relatively more money, the velocity of circulation is thereby reduced, thus reducing the effect on aggregate demand. Furthermore, the direct mechanism may take time to operate. In the meantime *V* will fall.

Monetarists also recognize that the demand for money can shift unpredictably in the short run with changing expectations of prices, interest rates and exchange rates. Thus *V* is unpredictable in the short run, and hence the effect of monetary policy on aggregate demand is also unpredictable in the short run. For these reasons monetarists argue that monetary policy cannot be used for short-run demand management. Here at least, then, there is a measure of agreement between Keynesians and monetarists.

Long-run stability of V. The main claim of monetarists is that the velocity of circulation (*V*) is relatively stable over the longer run, and any changes that do occur are the predictable outcome of institutional changes, such as the increased availability and use of credit cards.

One reason why *V* remains relatively stable in the long run, despite an increase in money supply, is that sufficient time has elapsed for the direct mechanism to have worked fully through. The other reason is the effect on inflation and consequently on interest rates. This works as follows.

Assume an initial increase in money supply. Interest rates fall. *V* falls. But if money supply goes on rising and hence expenditure goes on rising, inflation will rise. This will drive up *nominal* interest rates (even though *real* interest rates will stay low). But in choosing whether to hold money or to buy assets, it is the *nominal* rate of interest that people look at, since that is the opportunity cost of holding money. Thus people economize on money balances and *V* rises back again.

(Note that in extreme cases *V* will even rise to levels higher than before. This is likely if people start speculating that prices will rise further. People will rush to buy goods and assets before their prices rise further. This action will help to push the prices up even more. This form of destabilizing speculation took place in the hyper-

---

Box 18.1

Flying the Economic Kite

Monetary policy with statutory reserves is rather like operating via a piece of string. Pull on the string (a contractionary policy) and once it goes taut (banks are at their minimum level of reserves) the economy will respond. Push on the string (an expansionary policy) and the economy will only respond if it wanted to anyway (if aggregate demand was already high).

It's a bit like flying a kite. Pull on the string and once it goes taut the kite will come towards you. Let the string out and the kite will only go higher if the wind takes it.

---

inflation of Germany in the 1920s, as people spent their money as quickly as possible.)

With a predictable V in the longer run, monetary policy then becomes the essential means of controlling the long-term path of aggregate demand. For this reason monetarists favour a longer-term approach to monetary policy. This involves setting targets for the growth of the money supply: the approach adopted in the Thatcher government's medium-term financial strategy of the early 1980s that we looked at in Chapter 17.

Is money supply exogenous or endogenous?

Exogenous money supply

Money supply that does not depend on the demand for money but is set by the authorities.

Endogenous money supply

Money supply that is determined (at least in part) by the demand for money.

Money supply is exogenous (independently determined) if it can be fixed by the authorities and if it does not vary with aggregate demand and interest rates. In Figure 18.2(a) the M 'curve' would be vertical. It would only shift if the government *chose* to alter the money supply. Money supply is endogenous (determined within the model) if it is determined by aggregate demand and hence the demand for money: banks simply expanding or contracting credit in response to customer demand.

The extreme monetarist position is that money supply is wholly exogenous. The extreme Keynesian position is that money supply is wholly endogenous.

In reality money supply is partly exogenous and partly endogenous. The authorities are able to influence money supply by the policies examined in Chapter 17, but also banks and other financial institutions have considerable scope for creating credit in response to demand. If monetarism is adopted as the basis for policy, the authorities must reduce the endogenous element to a minimum.

One approach is to impose statutory reserve or cash requirements on banks and all other financial institutions, and then engage in tough open-market operations, possibly backing them up with special deposits (again applied to all financial institutions). Eventually, a contractionary monetary policy of this form must work. There is much more of a problem, however, if the authorities wish to expand the money supply. They can increase the monetary base through open market operations or the release of special deposits, but they cannot force banks to lend if customers do not want to borrow.

Many monetarists reject statutory ratios as being anti-market. Relying on banks' prudent ratios, however, which can vary considerably, makes precise control of the money supply very difficult indeed.

As we saw in Chapter 17, the authorities in the UK recognize the difficulties in controlling the money supply directly. They therefore influence the supply of money indirectly by controlling interest rates and hence the demand for money.

Box 18.2

Choosing the Exchange Rate or Choosing the Money Supply
You can't have it both ways

If the government expands the money supply, then interest rates will fall and aggregate demand will tend to rise. With a floating exchange rate this will cause the currency to depreciate.

But what if the government attempts to maintain a fixed exchange rate? To do this it must keep interest rates comparable with world rates. This means that it is no longer free to choose the level of money supply. The money supply has become endogenous.

The government can't have it both ways. It can choose the level of the money supply (providing it has the techniques to do so) and let interest rates and the exchange rate be what they will. Or it can choose the exchange rate, but this will then determine the necessary rate of interest and hence the supply of money.

? Can the government choose both the exchange rate *and* the money supply if it is prepared to use the reserves to support the exchange rate?

These issues are explored in Chapter 22.

▲ SUMMARY

1. The quantity equation $MV = PQ$ can be used to analyze the possible relationships between money and prices. Monetarists argue that the velocity of circulation (V) and the level of output (Q) are independent of money supply (M), and that therefore increases in money supply will simply raise prices (P).

2. Keynesians argue that V varies inversely, but unpredictably, with M and that Q will depend on aggregate demand (MV) according to the degree of slack in the economy.

3. Keynesians argue that the interest rate transmission mechanism between changes in money and changes in national income is unreliable and possibly weak. The reasons are (a) an unstable and possibly elastic demand for money and (b) an unstable and possibly inelastic investment demand.

4. They argue that the exchange rate transmission mechanism is stronger but still very unpredictable.

5. Monetarists argue that the transmission mechanisms are strong and relatively stable in the long run. If people have an increase in money in their portfolios, they will attempt to restore portfolio balance by purchasing assets, including goods. Thus an increase in money supply is transmitted directly into an increase in aggregate demand. The interest rate and exchange rate mechanisms are also argued to be strong. The demand for money is seen to be stable in the long run. This leads to a long-run stability in V (unless it changes as a result of other factors, such as institutional arrangements for the handling of money).

6. Money supply is exogenous if it is wholly determined by the authorities. In practice it is in part endogenously determined: it depends on aggregate demand. This makes it more difficult to have a precise control over the money supply.

18.2 Fiscal policy and aggregate demand

Fiscal policy is favoured by Keynesians as the prime means of controlling aggregate demand. Monetarists argue that, at best, fiscal policy can only have any lasting effect if it is accompanied by monetary policy; in which case, it is really the monetary policy that is affecting aggregate demand. At worst, fiscal policy is positively damaging, causing greater fluctuations in demand than would otherwise have occurred. Possible problems of controlling aggregate demand through fiscal policy were examined in Chapter 15. The most important are as follows:

- Predicting the extent to which changes in government expenditure or taxation will affect other injections and withdrawals. What effect will fiscal policy have on confidence? Will it crowd out private investment? How much of a tax cut will be saved or spent on imports? To what extent will the government provision of goods and services merely replace private consumption?
- Predicting the size of the multiplier and accelerator.
- The time lags involved.

Monetarists argue that these problems are so severe as to rule out the use of fiscal policy. Keynesians argue that the problems can to a large extent be overcome. Their respective arguments are examined below.

The Keynesian view: fiscal policy to cure fundamental disequilibria

Fiscal policy can be used in either of two contexts: either to cause substantial shifts in aggregate demand to cure a sizeable and persistent deflationary or inflationary gap; or to 'fine tune' the economy, by smoothing out cyclical fluctuations. Here we look at the use of fiscal policy to close a substantial and persistent deflationary or inflationary gap.

Persistent deflationary gap

If the economy is in a deep and lasting recession – as in the 1920s and 1930s, or in the early 1980s – Keynesians argue that fiscal policy is a simple and direct method of curing the problem. Whether aggregate demand is boosted by tax cuts or by increased government expenditure, the policy is likely to prove popular with the electorate. Both tax cuts and increased government expenditure have advantages and disavantages.

Advantages of tax cuts and benefit increases. Tax cuts and benefit increases (pensions, child benefit, social security, etc.) can provide a quick and general boost to the economy. There are only small time lags between tax or benefit changes being announced in the budget and the measures actually being implemented. Tax cuts that lower the marginal rate of taxation also have the advantage of increasing take-home pay or after-tax profit, and can thus increase incentives. This in turn can stimulate output, investment and growth. These *supply-side* effects are considered in Chapter 20.

Problems with tax cuts and benefit increases. It may be difficult to estimate exactly how much of the tax cuts or benefit increases will be spent, but if the problem is one of a persistent and deep recession, the exact size of the effect is of secondary importance to 'getting the economy moving'.

There may be a large resulting increase in imports. If there is a high marginal propensity to import, the multiplier effect will be lower and there may be a significant deterioration in the current account of the balance of payments.

> **?** Will there be any difference in the size of the multiplier effect from a change in taxes and a change in benefits? Will all types of tax change have the same-size multiplier?

Advantages of increased government expenditure. Government expenditure directly increases aggregate demand, and there is therefore the full multiplier effect. Government expenditure can be used more selectively than tax cuts. For example, money can be put into building roads, power stations, airports and other infrastructural projects, which will lead not only to higher demand but also to higher productive potential for the economy. Projects can be chosen which bring the maximum desired effect: for example, labour-intensive projects (to reduce unemployment as much as possible), projects with a low import content, and projects in particularly depressed regions of the economy.

Problems with increased government expenditure. The main problem is the time lag involved. Infrastructure projects may take a long time to plan and execute. Nevertheless in dealing with a *long-term* recession, this problem may not be too serious.

The main monetarist objection to fiscal policy as a cure for recession is that it simply will not work to increase *output*, and to the extent that it does increase demand (because of a simultaneous expansion of the money supply), inflation will be the sole long-term result. This is especially likely in the context of a floating exchange rate: the expansion of demand from the fiscal measures (given an accompanying increase in money supply) will simply lead to a depreciation of the exchange rate. This will directly fuel inflation by raising the price of imported goods and materials.

Persistent inflationary gap

If the economy experiences persistent demand-pull inflation accompanied by near full employment, then Keynesians argue that *deflationary* fiscal policy should be used.

There have been no periods since the war when such a situation has existed, other than on a temporary basis. The persistently high inflation of the 1970s was accompanied by rising unemployment. Keynesians explain this stagflation in terms of a leftward shift in the aggregate supply curve (from AS_1 to AS_2 in Figure 18.9). A contraction in aggregate demand under these circumstances (from AD_1 to AD_2) may offset the inflationary effect, but there will be a further decline in output (to Y_3) and a corresponding rise in unemployment.

Only during the two wars have there been persistent inflationary gaps, due to the high level of wartime government spending. Obviously under these circumstances it is difficult to cut government spending. Raising taxes sufficiently is also difficult, although the war spirit helps. Keynes himself advocated the additional use of special savings schemes and a form of hybrid between taxation and savings called 'post-war credits'. These were compulsory loans to the government to be repaid at some time after the war.

One of the major problems with tough deflationary policies is their political unpopularity. No one likes paying higher taxes. Few people like substantial cuts in public services.

What is more, there may be adverse supply-side effects. Tax increases may reduce incentives. They may also stimulate cost-push inflation. Cuts in government expenditure can have serious effects on particular sections of the economy – health, education,

Figure 18.9 Keynesian explanation of stagflation

public transport, etc. Damage to the infrastructure may damage long-term growth.

Perhaps the most serious question is whether deflation can squeeze out the inflation from the economy without causing a severe recession. This depends on the shape of the aggregate supply curve and people's expectations of prices and markets. These are the subject of Chapter 19.

 If people expect lower inflation, what will this do to pay claims by workers and price setting by firms? What does this suggest about the *public relations* side of persuading people that an anti-inflationary policy will actually work?

The Keynesian view: fine tuning

During the 1950s and 1960s governments and most economists believed that the fluctuations of the trade cycle could be considerably lessened by demand management policy. This involved both fiscal and monetary policy, but of the two fiscal policy was regarded as the more important.

By reflating the economy when in recession and deflating when in boom, economists believed that the growth path of the economy could be stabilized. Between points *a* and *b* in Figure 18.10, the government would pursue a reflationary fiscal policy. Between points *b* and *c* it would pursue a deflationary one. Instead of being like path I, therefore, the growth path would become more like path II. No one, however, went as far as saying that fluctuations could be removed completely.

Stabilization policy was helped by automatic fiscal stabilizers. These reduce the size of the multiplier and thus help to reduce the severity of the fluctuations. The main weapons, however, were the discretionary changes in taxation and benefits announced each year in the Budget, or sometimes more frequently; and to a lesser extent changes in other forms of government expenditure.

 Why are automatic fiscal stabilizers rather limited in their effect? (Refer back to Chapter 15.)

The advantages claimed for stabilization policy were as follows:

- The avoidance of alternating periods of unemployment and stagnation followed by periods of inflation and balance of payments deficits.
- The creation of a more stable and certain environment for businesses to plan and invest, thereby encouraging faster long-term growth.

Figure 18.10 Keynesian fine tuning

The main problems of these attempts to fine tune the economy centred on timing. If time lags are long enough, 'stabilization' policy can actually be *destabilizing*. If reflationary policies, initiated in a recession, do not take effect until a boom has already occurred, they will end up making the inflation and balance of payments problems of the boom worse. Similarly, if deflationary policies, initiated in a boom, do not take effect until a recession has occurred, they will simply deepen that recession.

The following are therefore the main requirements for successful stabilization:

- Accurate forecasting, so that appropriate policies can be introduced early.
- Policies that can be introduced quickly. Government expenditure programmes often take a long time to plan. Many taxes and benefits, however, can be changed simply and quickly. Governments have therefore relied much more on tax and benefit changes when attempting to fine tune the economy.
- Policies that have a predictable effect on aggregate demand.
- Policies that can be readily reversed: essential as the economy moves from one part of the trade cycle to another. Here again, taxes are far easier to increase or decrease than government expenditure. It is difficult to cut government expenditure or welfare benefits.

Keynesians argue that, although fiscal policy can never remove all fluctuations, combinations of good forecasting, appropriately designed measures and swift action can go a long way to creating relatively stable growth.

 Do you think it is more difficult to stabilize an open economy like the UK than one that engages far less in international trade?

The monetarist view

Monetarists make this clear distinction:

- Pure fiscal policy. This is where fiscal policy operates with *no* change in the money supply.
- Fiscal policy operating alongside a change in money supply. This could be due either to active fiscal and monetary policies being pursued at the same time, or to a passive expansion (contraction) of money supply to accommodate an expansionary (contractionary) fiscal policy.

In the case of pure fiscal policy, monetarists argue that it may have some short-term effects on demand, but due to time lags, the difficulties in predicting people's reactions to the policy, and the problem of random unexpected shocks to the economy, such policy cannot be used to control demand with any precision, and certainly cannot be used for fine tuning. In the long run, pure fiscal policy is totally ineffective: it will simply lead to *crowding out*. Increases in government expenditure will lead to corresponding decreases in private expenditure.

Fiscal policy operating alongside a change in money supply *will* affect demand. But here it is the change in the money supply that is causing the effect, not the fact that the monetary change was accompanied by fiscal policy.

To assess these arguments, it is necessary to examine the monetary effects of fiscal policy.

The monetary effects of fiscal policy

Fiscal and monetary policy are closely interrelated. Any fiscal policy that a government adopts will have monetary implications. Likewise any specific monetary policy will have implications for the conduct of the government's fiscal policy.

Assume that previously the government has had a balanced budget, but that now it chooses to adopt a reflationary fiscal policy. As a result it runs a budget deficit ($G > T$). But this deficit will have to be financed by borrowing. The resulting public-sector borrowing requirement will, in turn, lead to an increase in the money supply if it is financed by borrowing from the Bank of England or by the sale of Treasury bills to the banking sector. Alternatively, if it is financed by selling bills or bonds outside the banking sector or by selling bonds to the banks, there will be no increase in the money supply.

At the same time, the increase in aggregate demand that results from the budget deficit will lead to an increased transactions demand for money.

These effects are illustrated in Figure 18.11. Assume that the budget deficit arises from an increase in government expenditure. In Figure 18.11(a), injections will rise to J_2 and, other things being equal, national income will rise to Y_2. But this increase in national income will lead to a rise in the demand for money. This is illustrated in Figure 18.11(b) by a shift in the demand for money curve from L to L'. If the PSBR is financed in such a way as to allow money supply to expand to M_s', there will be no change in the interest rate and no crowding-out effect. If, however, the money supply is not allowed to expand, interest rates will rise to r_2. This in turn will reduce investment. Crowding out will occur. Thus injections will fall back again below J_2. In the extreme case, injections could even fall back to J_1 and thus national income return to Y_1.

 Assume that the government cuts its expenditure and thereby runs a public-sector surplus.
(a) What will this do initially to equilibrium national income?
(b) What will it do to the demand for money and initially to interest rates?
(c) Under what circumstances will it lead to (i) a decrease in money supply; (ii) no change in money supply?
(d) What effect will (i) and (ii) have on the rate of interest compared with its original level?

Keynesian and monetarist analyses of crowding out

Just how much crowding out will occur when there is an expansionary fiscal policy, but when money supply is *not* allowed to expand, depends on two things.

The responsiveness (elasticity) of the demand for money to a change in interest rates. Keynesians argue that the demand is relatively *elastic* (as in Figure 18.12(a)). In this case the increase in demand from L to L' will only lead to a small rise in interest rates.

(a) The goods market   **(b)** The money market

Figure 18.11 The monetary effects of fiscal policy

Figure 18.12 Different views on the demand for money

Monetarists argue that the demand is relatively *inelastic* (as in Figure 18.12(b)). In this case there will be a bigger rise in interest rates.

The responsiveness (elasticity) of investment to a change in interest rates. Keynesians argue that investment is relatively *unresponsive* to changes in interest rates. Business-people are much more likely to be affected by the state of the market for their product rather than by interest rates: if demand is expanding, they are likely to invest even if interest rates go up. Thus in Figure 18.13(a), there is only a small fall in investment. Monetarists argue that investment is relatively *responsive* to changes in interest rates. Thus in Figure 18.13(b), there is a bigger fall in investment.

In the Keynesian case, therefore, the rise in demand for money arising from an expansionary fiscal policy will have only a small effect on interest rates and an even smaller effect on investment. Little or no crowding out takes place. In fact the opposite might occur. The expansion of demand causes an increase in investment through the accelerator effect.

Monetarists argue that interest rates will rise significantly and that there will be an even more severe effect on investment. Crowding out is substantial. For this reason they argue that it is vital for governments to reduce the size of their budget deficit. They argue that in the long run crowding out is total, given the long-run stability of the velocity of circulation.

 Using diagrams like Figures 18.12 and 18.13, compare the Keynesian and monetarist analyses of a *contractionary* fiscal policy.

Figure 18.13 Different views on the demand for investment

Box 18.3

Crowding Out in an Open Economy
Taking exchange rate effects into account

Will fiscal policy be crowded out in an open economy with floating exchange rates?

Assume that the government increases its expenditure but does not allow the money supply to expand: a case of pure fiscal policy. What will happen?

- As in Figure 18.12, the increased government expenditure will increase the demand for money.
- This will drive up interest rates – the amount depending on the elasticity of the liquidity preference curve.
- This will lead to an inflow of capital from abroad, which in turn will lead to an appreciation of the exchange rate.
- The higher exchange rate will reduce the level of exports (an injection) and increase the level of imports

(a withdrawal). This will add to the degree of crowding out.

Thus in an open economy with floating exchange rates an expansionary fiscal policy will be crowded out not only by higher interest rates but also by a higher exchange rate.

? We have argued that the short-term capital inflow following a rise in the rate of interest will drive up the exchange rate. Are there any effects of higher interest rates on the demand for imports (and hence on the current account) which will go some way to *offsetting* this?

Postscript: fiscal and monetary policies together

If fiscal policy is financed by increasing the money supply, there will be no rise in interest rates. Money supply is increased to M_s' in Figure 18.11(b). There will be no crowding out, and the policy will therefore have a powerful effect on aggregate demand. Whether this leads to an increase in output or simply a rise in prices will depend on the shape of the aggregate supply curve. That is something we will analyze in Chapter 19.

▲ SUMMARY

1. Keynesians argue that persistent inflationary or deflationary gaps can be closed by fiscal policy. Monetarists argue that, if there is a significant change in aggregate demand as a result of the policy, it will only be because money supply has changed, in which case the so-called fiscal policy is really only monetary policy.

2. Many Keynesians also argue that fiscal policy can help to reduce (but not eliminate) cyclical fluctuations, provided that forecasting is reasonably accurate and that the appropriate changes in G or T can be made swiftly and with predictable effects.

3. Any fiscal changes will have monetary implications. If there is a fiscal expansion and *no* change in the money supply, the increased demand for money will drive up the interest rate and drive down the exchange rate. This will to some extent crowd out private expenditure and thus reduce the effectiveness of the fiscal policy.

4. The extent of crowding out will depend on the shape of the liquidity preference curve and the investment demand curve. The less interest elastic is the liquidity preference curve, the more will a fiscal expansion drive up the interest rate. The more elastic the investment demand curve, the more will a rise in interest rates reduce investment. Thus the less elastic the demand for money, and the more elastic the investment demand, the more crowding out will take place, and the less effective will fiscal policy be.

5. If the demand for and supply of sterling on the foreign exchange markets are responsive to interest rate changes, then the higher interest rates from an expansionary fiscal policy will drive up the exchange rate and lead to fewer exports and more imports, thereby leading to additional crowding out.

*18.3 ISLM analysis: the integration of the goods and money market models

The goods and money markets

In this chapter we have shown that there are two key markets through which both fiscal and monetary policy operate. The first is the goods market; the second is the money market. Each of these two markets has been analyzed by using a model.

In the case of the goods market, the model is the Keynesian injections/withdrawals model. Fiscal policy operates directly in this market. For example, a rise in government expenditure shifts the J line upwards and causes a rise in equilibrium national income. In other words, an increase in the demand for goods causes a (multiplied) rise in the output of goods (assuming that there are sufficient idle resources).

In the case of the money market, the model is the one showing the demand for money (L) and the supply of money (M) and their effect on the rate of interest. Monetary policy operates directly in this market, either by affecting the supply of money or by operating on interest rates.

What we have shown in this chapter is that the two markets *interact*: that changes in one market cause changes in the other. Take the case of an expansionary fiscal policy: it has a direct effect in the goods market but also an indirect effect in money markets. We illustrated this in Figure 18.11. The goods market effect was shown in Figure 18.11(a). The rise in injections led to a multiplied rise in income to Y_2. The money market effect was shown in Figure 18.11(b). The rise in income led to a rise in the transactions demand for money and a resulting rise in interest rates to r_2. This in turn had an effect back in the goods market, with a higher interest rate dampening investment somewhat and reducing the final rise in income.

The effects of monetary policy in the two markets was shown in Figures 18.2 and 18.8. An expansionary monetary policy, by increasing the money supply, will reduce interest rates. This will then, via an increase in investment (or a reduction in the exchange rate and a resulting increase in exports and a reduction in imports), lead to a multiplied rise in income in the goods market. This in turn has an effect back in the money market, with a higher income leading to a higher demand for money, thus limiting the fall in interest rates.

The trouble with our analysis so far is that we have needed at least two diagrams. What we are going to look at in this section is a model which *combines* these two markets, which means that we will need only one diagram. The model is known as the ISLM model.

The model allows us to examine the effects of fiscal and monetary policy on both national income *and* interest rates: it shows what the equilibrium will be in both the goods and the money markets simultaneously. The model, as its name suggests, consists of two curves: an *IS* curve and an *LM* curve. The *IS* curve is based on equilibrium in the goods market; the *LM* curve is based on equilibrium in the money market.

Let us examine these two curves in turn.

ISLM model
A model showing simultaneous equilibrium in the goods market ($I = S$) and the money market ($L = M$).

The IS curve

Deriving the IS curve

To explain how the *IS* curve is derived let us examine Figure 18.14, which as you can see is in two parts. The top part shows the familiar Keynesian injections and

Figure 18.14 Goods market equilibrium: deriving the *IS* curve

withdrawals diagram, only in this case, for simplicity, we are assuming that savings are the only withdrawal from the circular flow of income, and investment the only injection. Thus in equilibrium $I = S$ (i.e. $J = W$). The bottom part of the diagram shows the *IS* curve. This shows all the various combinations of interest rates (r) and national income (Y) at which $I = S$.

Let us assume that initially interest rates are at r_1. Both investment and savings are affected by interest rates, and thus, other things being equal, an interest rate of r_1 will give particular investment and savings schedules. Let us say that in the top part of the diagram these are shown by the curves I_1 and S_1. Equilibrium national income will be where $I = S$, i.e. at Y_1. Thus in the lower part of the diagram, an interest rate of r_1 will give a level of national income of Y_1. Thus point a is one point on the *IS* curve. At an interest rate of r_1 the goods market will be in equilibrium at an income of Y_1.

Now what will happen if the rate of interest changes? Let us assume that it falls to r_2. This will cause a rise in investment and a fall in savings. A rise in investment is shown in the top part of Figure 18.14 by a shift in the investment line to I_2. Likewise a fall in savings is shown by a shift in the savings curve to S_2. This will lead to a multiplied rise in income to Y_2 (where $I_2 = S_2$). This corresponds to point b in the lower diagram.

Thus *lower* interest rates are associated with *higher* national income, if equilibrium is to be maintained in the goods market ($I = S$).

The elasticity of the IS curve
The elasticity of the *IS* curve (i.e. the responsiveness of national income to changes in interest rates) depends on two factors.[2]

The responsiveness of investment and savings to interest rate changes. The more investment and savings respond, the bigger will be the vertical shift in the I and S curves in the top part of the diagram, and thus the bigger will be the effect on national income. The bigger the effect on national income, the more elastic will be the *IS* curve.

---

[2] Note that, as with demand and supply curves, the elasticity of the *IS* curve will vary along its length. Therefore we should really talk about the elasticity at a particular point on the curve, or between two points.

The size of the multiplier. This is given by the *mps* (i.e. the *mpw*). The larger the value of the multiplier, the bigger will be the effect on national income of any rise in investment and fall in savings, and the more elastic therefore will be the *IS* curve.

> **?** In a complete model where there were three injections (*I*, *G* and *X*) and three withdrawals (*S*, *T* and *M*), what else would determine the shape of the '*JW*' curve?

Keynesians argue that the *IS* curve is likely to be fairly inelastic. The reason they give is that investment is unresponsive to changes in interest rates: the demand for investment curve in Figure 18.2(b) is relatively inelastic. Savings also, claim Keynesians, are unresponsive to interest rate changes. The effect of this is that there will only be a relatively small shift in the *I* and *S* curves in response to a change in interest rates, and thus only a relatively small change in national income.

Monetarists, by contrast, argue that investment and savings are relatively responsive to changes in interest rates and that therefore the *IS* curve is relatively elastic.

Shifts in the IS curve

A change in interest rates will cause a movement *along* the *IS* curve. As we saw in Figure 18.14, a reduction in interest rates from r_1 to r_2 causes a movement *along* the *IS* curve from point *a* to point *b*.

A change in any *other* determinant of investment or savings, however, will *shift* the whole curve. The reason is that it will change the equilibrium level of national income at any given rate of interest.

An increase in investment, other than as a result of a fall in interest rates, will shift the *IS* curve to the *right*. This could happen, for example, if there were an increase in business confidence. A rise in business confidence *at the current interest rate* will cause an upward shift of the *I* curve in the top diagram of Figure 18.14, which will cause a multiplied rise in income. Thus in the lower part of the diagram a higher equilibrium income is now associated with each level of the interest rate: the *IS* curve has shifted to the right.

Likewise, for any given interest rate, a fall in savings, and hence a rise in consumption, would also shift the *IS* curve to the right. This would happen, for example, in a pre-Christmas spending spree. In the top part of the diagram, the *S* curve would shift downwards. This would cause a multiplied rise in income. Thus again in the lower part of the diagram a higher equilibrium income would now be associated with each level of the interest rate: again the *IS* curve would shift to the right.

In a complete model (with three injections and three withdrawals), where the *IS* curve was a '*J* = *W*' curve rather than a simple '*I* = *S*' curve, similar shifts would result from changes in other injections or withdrawals. Thus an expansionary fiscal policy that increased government expenditure (*G*) or cut taxes (*T*) would shift the '*IS*' curve (i.e. the *JW* curve) to the right.

> **?** In a complete *JW* model, what else would cause the *JW* curve (a) to shift to the right; (b) to shift to the left?

The LM curve

The *IS* curve is concerned with equilibrium in the goods market. The *LM* curve is concerned with equilibrium in the money market. The *LM* curve shows all the various combinations of interest rates and national income at which the demand for money equals the supply ($L = M$).

Deriving the LM curve

To explain how the *LM* curve is derived we again use a diagram in two parts, only this time they are side by side (the reason being that we use the same *vertical* axis (r) this time, whereas in Figure 18.14 we used the same horizontal axis (Y)). The left-hand part of the diagram is the familiar money market diagram, showing a liquidity preference (demand for money) curve (L) and a supply of money curve (M). The liquidity preference curve consists of two elements: the transactions-plus-precautionary demand for money and the speculative demand for money. The transactions-plus-precautionary demand depends primarily on the level of national income, whereas the speculative demand depends primarily on the rate of interest. In equilibrium the demand for money (L) equals the supply (M).

At any given level of national income there will be a particular level of transactions-plus-precautionary demand for money, and hence a given overall demand for money curve (L). Let us assume that, when national income is at a level of Y_1 in the right-hand diagram of Figure 18.15 the demand for money curve is L'. With the given money supply curve M_s, the equilibrium rate of interest will be r_1. Thus point c is one point on the *LM* curve. At a level of national income Y_1, the money market will be in equilibrium at a rate of interest of r_1.

Now what will happen if the level of national income changes? Let us assume that national income rises to Y_2. The effect is to increase the transactions-plus-precautionary demand for money. The L curve shifts to the right: to, say, L''. This will cause the rate of interest to rise to the new equilibrium level of r_2. This therefore gives us a second point on the *LM* curve (point d).

Thus *higher* national income will lead to a greater demand for money and hence *higher* interest rates if equilibrium is to be maintained in the money market. The *LM* curve will therefore be upward sloping.

Figure 18.15 Money market equilibrium: deriving the *LM* curve

The elasticity of the LM curve

The elasticity of the *LM* curve (i.e. the responsiveness of interest rate changes to a change in national income)[3] again depends on two factors.

The responsiveness of the demand for money to changes in national income. The greater the marginal propensity to consume, the more will the transactions demand for money rise as national income rises, and thus the more will the L curve shift to the

---

[3] Note this time that the rate of interest is the dependent variable and the level of national income is the independent variable. Thus the more elastic is the *LM* curve (i.e. the more responsive interest rates are to changes in national income), the *steeper* will be the curve.

right. Hence the more will the equilibrium interest rate rise, and the steeper will be the *LM* curve.

The responsiveness of the demand for money to changes in interest rates. The more the demand for money responds to a change in interest rates, the flatter will be the liquidity preference curve in the left-hand diagram. The flatter the *L* curve, the less will the equilibrium interest rate change for any given horizontal shift in the *L* curve (arising from a change in *Y*). The less the equilibrium interest rate changes, the flatter will be the *LM* curve.

The Keynesian and monetarist views on the shape of the *LM* curve reflect their views on the elasticity of the *L* curve. Keynesians argue that the *L* curve is likely to be relatively flat given the responsiveness of the speculative demand for money to changes in interest rates. They thus argue that the *LM* curve is correspondingly flat (depending, of course, on the scales of the axes). Monetarists, on the other hand, argue that the *LM* curve is relatively steep. This is because they see the demand for money as insensitive to changes in interest rates.

Shifts in the LM curve

A change in national income will cause a movement *along* the *LM* curve to a new interest rate. Thus in Figure 18.15 a rise in national income from Y_1 to Y_2 leads to a rise in the rate of interest from r_1 to r_2.

A change in any *other* determinant of the demand and supply of money will *shift* the whole curve. The reason is that it will change the equilibrium level of interest associated with any given level of national income.

An increase in the demand for money, other than as a result of a rise in income, will shift the *L* curve to the *right*. This could be due to people being paid less frequently, or a greater use of cash machines, or increased speculation that the price of securities will fall. This increased demand for money will raise the equilibrium rate of interest at the current level of national income. The *LM* curve will shift upwards.

An increased supply of money will shift the M_s curve to the right. This will lower the rate of interest (in the left-hand part of Figure 18.15). This will shift the *LM* curve downwards: a lower rate of interest will be associated with any given level of national income.

? Draw a diagram like Figure 18.15, only with just one *L* curve. Assume that the current level of national income is Y_1. Now assume that the supply of money decreases. Show the effect on (a) the rate of interest; (b) the position of the *LM* curve.

Equilibrium

The *IS* curve shows all the combinations of the rate of interest (*r*) and national income (*Y*) at which the *goods* market is in equilibrium. The *LM* curve shows all the combinations of *r* and *Y* at which the *money* market is in equilibrium. *Both* markets will be in equilibrium where the curves intersect. This is at r_e and Y_e in Figure 18.16.

But what would happen if both markets were not simultaneously in equilibrium? How would equilibrium be achieved?

Let us suppose that the current level of national income is Y_1. This will create a demand for money which will lead to an equilibrium interest rate of r_1 (point *a* on the *LM* curve). But at this low interest rate the desired level of investment and savings would generate an income of Y_2 (point *b* on the *IS* curve). Thus national income will rise. But as national income rises, there will be a movement up along the *LM* curve

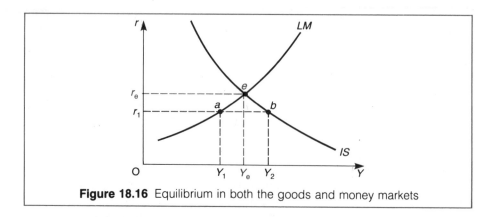

Figure 18.16 Equilibrium in both the goods and money markets

from point *a*, since the higher income will generate a higher demand for money and hence push up interest rates. And as interest rates rise, so the desired level of investment will fall and the desired level of savings will rise so as to reduce the equilibrium level of national income below Y_2. There will be a movement back up along the *IS* curve from point *b*. Once the interest rate has risen to r_e, the actual level of income will be at the equilibrium level (i.e. *on* the *IS* curve). Both markets will now be in equilibrium.

> 1. In describing the movement to overall equilibrium we have been assuming that initially there is equilibrium in the money market but disequilibrium in the goods market. Why would this be more likely than equilibrium in the goods market and disequilibrium in the money market? (Clue: the answer has to do with the relative speed with which *r* and *Y* adjust to disequilibria.)
> 2. Assume that national income is initially at Y_2 in Figure 18.16. Describe the process whereby equilibrium in both markets will be achieved.
> 3. Assume that business confidence rises and firms decide to increase their investment. Trace through the effects of this in the ISLM model. (One of the curves shifts.)

Fiscal and monetary policy

ISLM analysis can be used to examine the effects of fiscal and monetary policy. Assume that the economy is in recession and that the government wishes to raise the level of national income. Figure 18.17 illustrates the policy alternatives.

Figure 18.17(a) shows the effect of an increase in government expenditure (*G*) or a cut in taxes (*T*), but with no increase in money supply. The *IS* curve shifts to the right. Income rises to Y_2, but interest rates also rise (to r_2). Thus some crowding out occurs.

Figure 18.17(b) shows the effect of an increase in money supply. The *LM* curve shifts to the right. Interest rates fall to r_3 and this encourages an increase in investment. As a result of this, income rises to Y_3.

Figure 18.17(c) shows what happens when the government finances higher government expenditure or lower taxes by increasing the money supply. There is no rise in interest rates, and thus no crowding out. National income rises by a greater amount than in (a) or (b), to Y_4.

The effectiveness of fiscal and monetary policy depends on the slope of the two curves. Fiscal policy is most effective when the *LM* curve is shallow and the *IS* curve is steep. When *LM* is shallow, a rightward shift in *IS* will only lead to a small rise in the rate of interest (*r*). If *IS* is steep, this rise in *r* will only lead to a small curtailing of

Box 18.4

Sir John Hicks (1906–89)
Person profile

With more than twenty books and fifty articles to his credit, John Hicks ranks high in the list of 'great economists'. His first book, *The Theory of Wages*, was published in 1932, but he was still writing actively before his death 57 years later.

He was born in Warwick in 1904 and entered Oxford as a student in 1922. Shortly after graduating he became a lecturer at the London School of Economics, where he stayed until 1935. After three years as a fellow at the University of Cambridge, he became Professor of Economics at Manchester University. He then moved to Nuffield College, Oxford, in 1946, where he remained for the rest of his career.

He was knighted in 1966, and then in 1972 he received perhaps the highest recognition the economics world can bestow: the Nobel prize in economics. The award was for his outstanding contribution to the development of economic theory in both the micro and macro fields. This says a lot about Hicks' place in the history of economics. His contributions were not confined to just one area, but covered a whole range of issues.

Perhaps his major contribution was as a synthesizer. He had the happy knack of being able to develop models and techniques that brought out the essence of theories developed by other economists, or brought together in one theory ideas developed by different economists.

With R. G. D. Allen in a work entitled 'A reconsideration of the theory of value' (*Economica*, 1934), he developed indifference curve analysis. This, as we saw in Chapter 3, replaced marginal utility analysis as the standard way of explaining consumer behaviour.

Perhaps his most famous contribution to the field of macroeconomics came in his article 'Mr Keynes and the classics' (*Econometrica*, 1937). It was in this work that ISLM analysis was born. The analysis was used by Hicks to provide a graphical interpretation of Keynes' *General Theory*, and to show how Keynes' policy prescriptions differed from his predecessors'. Subsequently, Hicks' ISLM approach became widely adopted throughout the economics profession, and it is now a core element in macroeconomic theory.

It is these contributions to fundamental economic theory, contributions which have changed the way the subject is taught, which set Hicks apart from his contemporaries and ensure that his work will have a lasting impression on all those who study the discipline of economics.

investment. In these two circumstances, crowding out is minimized. There will be a large increase in national income (Y).

Monetary policy, by contrast, is most effective when the LM curve is steep and the IS curve is shallow. When LM is steep, a rightward shift in LM will lead to a relatively large fall in r. When IS is shallow, this fall in r will lead to a relatively large increase in investment and hence Y.

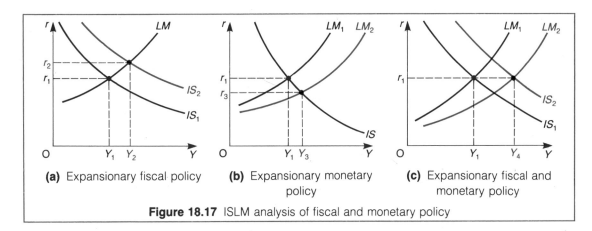

(a) Expansionary fiscal policy

(b) Expansionary monetary policy

(c) Expansionary fiscal and monetary policy

Figure 18.17 ISLM analysis of fiscal and monetary policy

Fiscal and monetary policies will be most effective when applied simultaneously, as in Figure 18.17(c).

The Keynesian position

The Keynesian analysis makes the following assumptions.

The LM curve is relatively shallow. This is because the liquidity preference curve (*L*) is relatively shallow, due to the important role of the speculative demand for money (see Figure 18.2(a)).

The IS curve is relatively steep. This is because the investment demand curve is relatively inelastic, due to the unresponsiveness of investment to changes in interest rates (see Figure 18.2(b)). Also savings are relatively unresponsive to interest rate changes.

Under these circumstances fiscal policy is more effective than monetary policy in controlling aggregate demand. Figure 18.18(a) shows a bigger increase in national income with expansionary fiscal policy, than does Figure 18.18(b) with expansionary monetary policy. Monetary policy is weak because increases in money supply lead to substantially increased holdings of idle balances and a corresponding reduction in the velocity of circulation.

?   According to Keynesians, which will have a bigger effect on national income and employment: (unforeseen) fluctuations in investment or (unforeseen) fluctuations in the money supply?

If money supply is endogenous, fiscal policy will be more effective still. A relatively elastic supply of money curve in the left-hand diagram of Figure 18.15 will give an even shallower *LM* curve.

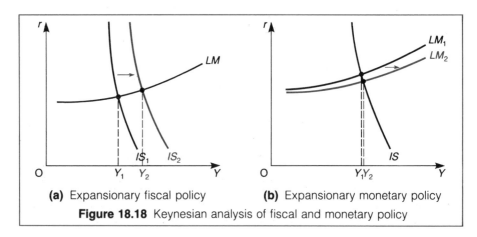

(a) Expansionary fiscal policy   **(b)** Expansionary monetary policy

Figure 18.18 Keynesian analysis of fiscal and monetary policy

The monetarist position

The monetarist analysis makes the following assumptions.

The LM curve is relatively steep. This is because the *L* curve is relatively steep, due to the relatively small role of speculative balances of money, and the general interest inelasticity of the demand for money.

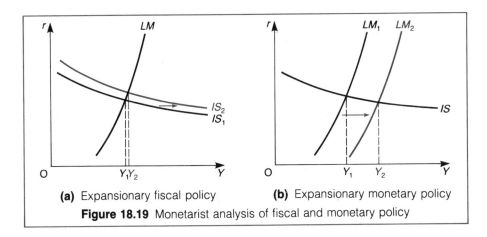

(a) Expansionary fiscal policy   **(b)** Expansionary monetary policy

Figure 18.19 Monetarist analysis of fiscal and monetary policy

The IS curve is relatively shallow. This is because the *I* curve is relatively shallow, due to the wide range of interest-sensitive expenditures.

Under these circumstances monetary policy is more effective than fiscal policy. Figure 18.19(b) shows a bigger increase in income with expansionary monetary policy than does Figure 18.19(a) with expansionary fiscal policy.

According to monetarists, fiscal policy is weak because of crowding out. This is illustrated in Figure 18.19(a) by the steepness of the *LM* curve. The increased transactions demand resulting from a rise in income will lead to a large rise in interest rates. The reason is that there are few speculative holdings of money, and therefore a large rise in interest rates will be necessary to release sufficient money balances to meet the new higher transactions demand.

? How would monetarists analyze the effects of a contractionary fiscal policy?

A compromise

Using both fiscal and monetary policy together has a stronger effect than using either separately (see Figure 18.17(c)).

In the Keynesian era of the 1950s, 1960s and early 1970s, expansionary fiscal policy was normally 'accommodated' by keeping interest rates low and allowing the money supply to expand. Similarly, periods of deflationary fiscal policy were not allowed to be undermined by a too loose monetary policy. This all fitted in with the view that money supply is endogenous: that it is determined by the demand for money. Therefore, if the government used fiscal policy to boost aggregate demand, the money supply would to a large extent expand automatically, as banks expanded credit to meet the new higher demand.

The early 1980s, with monetarism in the ascendant, saw the emphasis being placed on monetary policy, but with the means of controlling the money supply over the medium term being a progressive reduction in the PSBR. Thus a tight fiscal policy was to be the means of achieving a tight monetary policy. Again, fiscal and monetary policy were in relative harmony.

The mid-1980s saw an imbalance emerging. A more relaxed monetary policy was adopted in order to achieve economic growth, but fiscal policy was being kept very tight. So did this period support the monetarist hypothesis that monetary policy is more powerful than fiscal policy? The answer depends on what caused the growth in the economy. Was it *caused* by the loose monetary policy? If it was, then this would seem to support the monetarist position. But if the growth was simply the natural re-emergence of the economy after a recession, then this fits with Keynesian trade cycle theory. The relatively tight fiscal policy simply prevented the economy from overheating any more than it did. The expansion of the money supply was simply an *endogenous* expansion in response to the buoyant consumer demand.

▲ SUMMARY

1. The ISLM model allows equilibrium to be shown in both goods and money markets simultaneously. The model shows the relationship between national income and interest rates. The rate of interest is plotted on the vertical axis; the level of national income on the horizontal axis.
2. Equilibrium in the goods market is shown by the *IS* curve. This shows all the combinations of the rate of interest and national income where investment (*I*) equals savings (*S*) (or, in a complete Keynesian model, where injections equal withdrawals). As the rate of interest rises, so investment will fall and savings will rise: thus equilibrium national income will fall. The *IS* curve is thus downward sloping.
3. A change in interest rates will cause a movement along the *IS* curve. A change in anything else that affects national income (i.e. a change in injections or withdrawals other than as a result of a change in interest rates) will cause a shift in the *IS* curve.
4. Equilibrium in the money market is shown by the *LM* curve. This shows all the combinations of national income and the rate of interest where the demand for money (*L*) equals the supply (*M*). As national income rises, so the demand for money will rise: thus the equilibrium rate of interest in the money market will rise. The *LM* curve is thus upward sloping.
5. A change in national income will cause a movement along the *LM* curve. A change in anything else that affects interest rates (i.e. a change in the demand or supply of money other than as a result of a change in national income) will shift the *LM* curve.
6. Simultaneous equilibrium in both goods and money markets (i.e. the equilibrium national income *and* the equilibrium rate of interest) is where *IS* = *LM*.

7. Fiscal policy will shift the *IS* curve. An expansionary fiscal policy will shift it to the right. This will cause a rise in both national income and the rate of interest. The rise in income will be bigger and the rise in the rate of interest smaller, the steeper the *IS* curve and the flatter the *LM* curve.
8. Keynesians argue that fiscal policy is relatively effective and that there will be relatively little crowding out because the *IS* curve is relatively steep (due to an inelastic investment demand schedule) and the *LM* curve is relatively shallow (due to an elastic liquidity preference curve).
9. Monetarists argue the opposite: that fiscal policy is relatively ineffective and that there will be substantial crowding out because the *IS* curve is relatively shallow (due to the wide range of interest-sensitive expenditures) and the *LM* curve is relatively steep (due to the small role of speculative balances).
10. Monetary policy will shift the *LM* curve. An expansionary monetary policy will shift it to the right. This will cause a fall in interest rates and a rise in national income. The rise in national income will be larger, the steeper the *LM* curve and the flatter the *IS* curve. This means that monetarists argue that monetary policy is relatively effective, whereas Keynesians argue that it is relatively ineffective.
11. Fiscal and monetary policy operating together will have the most powerful effect. An expansionary fiscal policy accompanied by a rise in money supply can lead to an increase in national income with no rise in interest rates and thus no crowding out irrespective of the shapes of the *IS* and *LM* curves.

18.4 The control of aggregate demand in practice

Attitudes towards demand management

The debate between Keynesians and monetarists over the control of demand has shifted ground somewhat in recent years. There is less debate today over the relative merits of fiscal and monetary policy. There is general agreement now that a *combination* of fiscal and monetary policies will have a powerful effect on demand.

The debate today is much more concerned with whether the government ought to pursue an active demand management policy at all, or whether it ought merely to adhere to a set of policy rules.

Keynesians believe that governments should manage the level of aggregate demand, both to remove persistent inflationary and deflationary gaps, and to smooth out cyclical fluctuations in national income. This is centred on the belief that:

- The market system cannot be relied upon to generate full employment and can experience deep recessions.
- The market system is inherently unstable and can experience trade cycles of considerable magnitude.
- The management of aggregate demand by the government through fiscal policy, preferably supported by monetary policy, can considerably improve the situation.

Monetarists believe that governments should not engage in demand management policies. This is centred on the belief that:

- The market system will generate high employment in the long run. Demand management would not be able to achieve any higher long-term employment.
- Fluctuations in aggregate demand are due to fluctuations in the money supply. Fluctuations in money supply are the responsibility of government.
- Stability can best be achieved by the government setting targets for the growth of money supply and not deviating from them.
- Fiscal policy is best used for providing supply-side incentives (e.g. through low rates of income tax). It should not be used for demand management purposes.

In summary: Keynesians prefer discretionary policy – changing policy as circumstances change. Monetarists prefer to set firm rules and then stick to them.

The Keynesian case for discretionary policy

The Keynesian case for active intervention is based on the Keynesian analysis of national income and the trade cycle, explained in Chapter 14.

The economy is subject to exogenous changes in aggregate demand. These could be changes in investment, consumption, savings, exports or imports. They could be caused by changes in expectations, by political events (such as an impending election), by industrial events (such as a miners' strike), by world economic factors (such as a change in US interest rates), by world political events (such as a war), or by many other factors. These shifts in injections or withdrawals cause the economy to deviate from a stable full employment growth path.

Any change in injections or withdrawals will lead to a cumulative effect on national income via the multiplier and accelerator and via changing expectations. These endogenous effects take time and interact with each other, and so a process of expansion or contraction can last many months before a turning point is eventually reached.

Since the exogenous changes in demand occur at irregular intervals and are of different magnitudes, the economy is likely to experience cycles of irregular duration and of varying intensity.

Given that the economy is inherently unstable and is buffeted around by various exogenous shocks, Keynesians argue that the government needs actively to intervene to stabilize the economy. Otherwise, the uncertainty caused by unpredictable fluctuations would be very damaging to investment and long-term growth (quite apart from the short-term effects of recessions on output and employment).

Keynesian policy in action: demand management in the 1950s and 1960s

During the 1950s and 1960s both Labour and Conservative governments embraced Keynesian ideas. They pursued active demand management policies in an attempt to smooth out cyclical fluctuations and to keep national income as close as possible to the full employment level.

The main weapon for this was changes in tax rates. But use was also made of government expenditure changes. Monetary policy was generally thought to be ineffective, both because of the insensitivity of demand to interest rate changes, and the difficulties in controlling overall liquidity through open market operations. In the 1960s, however, increasing use was made of credit rationing to back up fiscal policy and to keep interest rates down. As a result, a 'package deal' of policies was frequently adopted.

The overall performance of the economy

Economic performance during the 1950s and 1960s compares very favourably with the periods both before and after. This is illustrated in Figure 18.20 and Table 18.1.

Table 18.1 UK macroeconomic performance: 1921–89

	Unemployment (% of labour force)[1]	Inflation (% increase in RPI)[2]	Growth (% increase in real GDP)[2]
1921–38	13.4	−1.5	2.1
1950–69	1.6	4.0	2.8
1970–79	3.3	12.7	2.4
1980–89	9.2	7.4	2.2

[1] Average.
[2] Average annual.

Unemployment was considerably lower in the 1950s and 1960s than either before or after. By the early 1980s unemployment at over 10 per cent was approaching the average of the inter-war period. Although it subsequently fell, it has remained well above the levels of the 1950s and 1960s.

Figure 18.20 UK growth, inflation and unemployment: 1920–89

Note: $\dot{Y}$ = growth (% rise in real GDP); $\dot{P}$ = inflation (% rise in RPI); U = unemployment (%).

Sources: *British Economy Key Statistics in 1900–1964* (Time Publishing Co.); *Economic Trends* (CSO, various issues).

Inflation, although averaging 4 per cent, and thus above the negative rates of the inter-war years, was nevertheless very modest by recent standards. Even the lowest inflation recorded in the period 1970–85 (4.6 per cent in 1983) was still above the 4 per cent average for 1950–69; and even since 1985 there has only been one year (1986) when inflation dipped below this average.

Growth in the 1950s and 1960s was at a higher level than in the periods before or up to the mid-1980s. Also there was no deep or prolonged recession like those of the early 1920s, the early 1930s, 1979–82 and 1990–92.

Despite these successes, there were still fluctuations in the economy, albeit of shorter duration and lower intensity than before or since. Also, although growth was relatively high by UK standards, it was low by international standards, and significantly lower than in West Germany, France and Japan.

The balance of payments

Throughout the 1950s and 1960s, the UK was operating on a fixed exchange rate system. The exchange rate was pegged at $2.80 to the pound from 1949 until 1967 when it was devalued to $2.40. A fixed exchange rate constrained the government in its demand management policy. If the economy expanded too fast, the balance of payments went into deficit. This was seen as a red light to the government. It would therefore pursue a deflationary policy, both to reduce the demand for imports directly, and to reduce inflation in order to increase the competitiveness of UK goods. Similarly, if the balance of payments went into surplus, this was seen as a green light and the government would reflate the economy. As a result of this, demand management was often referred to as stop–go policy.

Stop–go policies
Alternate deflationary and reflationary policies.

The most common weapon used in times of balance of payments crisis was Bank rate. On several such occasions there were quite steep rises in Bank rate.

To the extent that balance of payments swings mirrored the cyclical movements of aggregate demand, it was quite consistent to use demand management policies for stabilizing both the balance of payments and national income. Figure 18.21 illustrates how the two fluctuated over the period, and it can be seen that there was a close inverse relationship between them.

During the 1960s, however, the maintenance of balance of payments equilibrium and of growth at full employment became increasingly incompatible objectives. Stop–go policy was thus perceived as swinging from one objective (correction of balance of payments deficits with 'stop' policy) to the other (stimulating growth and employment

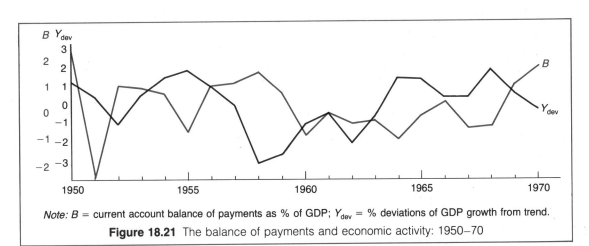

Note: B = current account balance of payments as % of GDP; Y_{dev} = % deviations of GDP growth from trend.

Figure 18.21 The balance of payments and economic activity: 1950–70

with 'go' policy). The underlying problem was that UK goods were becoming increasingly uncompetitive in world markets. This was due partly to a decline in the relative quality of UK goods, and partly to their higher relative prices.

Under a fixed exchange rate system there was therefore a long-term tendency for the balance of payments to deteriorate, and for governments to deflate. Eventually in 1967, with mounting pressure on sterling, the UK was forced to devalue the pound.

Monetarist criticisms of the policies of the 1950s and 1960s

Monetarists, in judging the record of the Keynesian policies pursued during the 1950s and 1960s, make two major criticisms.

Firstly, the policies pursued actually served to make the economy more unstable for the following reasons:

- Forecasting was bad. Frequently the forecasters had not foreseen the exogenous changes to demand. Even when the shocks had occurred, forecasters wrongly predicted the magnitude and timing of their effects.
- Governments as a result were hesitant to take action until the economy was clearly either booming (or in balance of payments crisis) or in recession.
- When governments did take action, they tended to over-react in their attempt to speed up the correction of the problem.

To summarize: governments did too much and too late.

Secondly, inflation was kept fairly low in this period *despite* attempts to fine tune the economy. The reason for this was the fixed exchange rate that forced governments to deflate whenever inflation threatened the balance of payments. In other words, it was the existence of an exchange rate *rule* that forced constraint of the money supply, which in turn led to low inflation. If there had been no such constraint, Keynesian governments would have pursued much more expansionist policies, which would have driven up the rate of inflation.

 Would a floating exchange rate have imposed no constraint at all on expansionist policies?

(Note that, despite these arguments, monetarists do not favour a fixed exchange rate or targeting the exchange rate. They argue that it is better for the government to make the control of the money supply a deliberate act of policy rather than simply being forced to control money supply in order to maintain a fixed exchange rate.)

The Keynesian response

Keynesians argue that the record speaks for itself. The economy was much more stable, and there was a better record of achieving the various macroeconomic objectives.

Nevertheless they do admit that the performance of the economy could have been better if there had been more flexibility in the exchange rate, or at least an earlier devaluation. This would have reduced the need for stop–go measures. There could then have been a more sustained expansion of the economy. This in turn would have boosted business confidence, increased investment and thereby increased long-term growth potential.

Provided demand was prevented from expanding too rapidly so as to open up an inflationary gap, any tendency for inflation to increase would be more due to cost-push or structural factors. These would be much better dealt with by using interventionist supply-side policies, such as prices and incomes policy to prevent cost-push inflation, and selective investment grants and infrastructure projects to relieve bottlenecks.

Finally, improvements in forecasting techniques and the swifter implementation of policies would help to reduce time lags and allow finer tuning. In other words, if fine tuning has not worked very well, Keynesians argue that governments should try to do better.

 Answer these points from a monetarist perspective.

The demise of fine tuning in the 1970s: the problem of stagflation

Fine tuning became impossible in the 1970s because of the rising problem of stagflation. Figure 18.22 illustrates this.

Demand management policies were still extensively used throughout the period, but alone they could no longer achieve an acceptable combination of inflation and unemployment. The Phillips curve had broken down.

Sometimes reflationary policies were used to get a modest reduction in unemployment, but then inflation would be very high. At other times deflationary policies were used to reduce inflation, but then unemployment rose very rapidly.

Economists are not agreed on the causes of the stagflation of the 1970s and early 1980s, but there were a number of possible contributing factors.

The approach to monetary control. With the publication of the Bank of England document *Competition and Credit Control* in 1971, the authorities introduced new measures to control the money supply. Although part of the aim was to rely more on open market operations and if necessary to allow interest rates to rise in line with policies on restraining the growth in money supply, another part was to encourage more competition between banks. As a result, ceilings on bank credit were abandoned; the liquidity ratio that banks were required to hold was reduced; all special deposits were released; and banks were no longer required to set their interest rates in accordance with Bank rate (which was subsequently renamed *minimum*

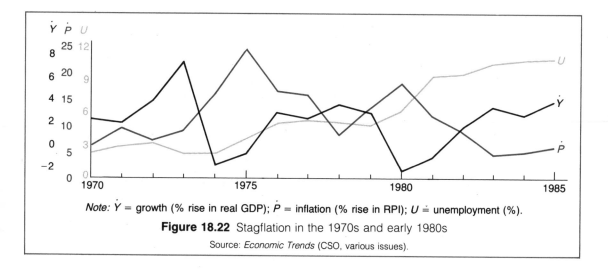

Note: $\dot{Y}$ = growth (% rise in real GDP); $\dot{P}$ = inflation (% rise in RPI); $U \doteq$ unemployment (%).

Figure 18.22 Stagflation in the 1970s and early 1980s

Source: *Economic Trends* (CSO, various issues).

lending rate (MLR)). The effect was to make it much more difficult to prevent an expansion of credit and there was a mushrooming of new banks and credit institutions.

Highly reflationary budgets in 1972 and 1973. The Heath government (1970–74) was committed to a rapid rate of economic growth. This was to be achieved by sharply expansionary fiscal policy. Sizeable tax cuts were given, especially in the 1972 budget. The effect was a rapid increase in the PSBR. This, combined with the 1971 monetary measures, led to a very rapid growth in money supply in 1972 and 1973 (over 50 per cent in these 2 years). The accompanying growth in aggregate demand could only in small part be met by increased output and employment. Inflation soared.

The adoption of floating exchange rates. In June 1972 a fixed exchange rate with the dollar was abandoned. A floating pound reduced the need to pursue deflationary policies in response to a balance of payments deficit. Instead the exchange rate could be allowed to depreciate. This removed a major constraint on the growth in money supply. This applied not just in the UK but throughout the world as countries moved over to floating exchange rates.

Oil prices. OPEC raised oil prices steeply in two periods. Between 1973 and 1974 the price of oil rose from $3 to $12 per barrel, and between 1978 and 1980 it rose from $13 to $31 per barrel. This not only raised costs and thus caused cost-push inflation, but also caused recessions in 1975 and 1979–81 as governments throughout the world deflated in response to the inflation and balance of payments crises. There were also significant rises in other world commodity prices during these two periods.

Domestically generated cost-push pressures. The following have been highlighted by various economists as significantly contributing to stagflation:

● Growing union power and militancy causing wages to rise independently of aggregate demand.
● The desire for real wage increases each year in excess of the economy's real growth.
● Increasing monopoly/oligopoly power of firms with an increase in mergers and industrial concentration.
● Low productivity growth and hence a lack of price competitiveness of UK goods compared with foreign goods.

Increased import penetration and a decline in the UK's share of world exports. Increasing competition from foreign imports combined with a lack of quality of UK goods have been blamed for poor balance of payments, low growth, structural unemployment in the poor performance industries, and inflation caused by a falling exchange rate (necessary to restore price competitiveness of UK exports).

Technological change. The microchip revolution and other labour-displacing technology created unemployment. There was insufficient aggregate demand to create new jobs in other sectors of the economy.

Expectations of inflation. High and volatile inflation rates fuelled expectations of high inflation, which then made inflation worse.

 Go through each of the above causes of the stagflation of the 1970s and early 1980s and consider whether there would have been any policies that the government could realistically have adopted to deal with each one.

The response to stagflation

Several of these problems were problems of cost and supply, rather than problems of excess or deficient demand. Not surprisingly, therefore, it was increasingly realized that in addition to fiscal and monetary policies there would have to be significant 'supply-side' policies.

The Keynesian response was to recommend supplementing demand management with interventionist supply-side policies, such as prices and incomes policy, regional policy, import restrictions and retraining policies.

The monetarist response was to recommend abandoning discretionary demand management of the stop–go variety altogether, and moving to a 'steady-as-you-go' policy of sticking to monetary targets. In addition market-orientated supply-side policies should be pursued. Such policies would include tax reform so as to increase the incentives for work and investment, legislation to reduce the monopoly power of unions, abandoning minimum wages (set by such government bodies as wages councils) and reducing the level of unemployment benefits.

Chapters 19 and 20 look at the supply side of the economy. The remainder of this chapter looks at the changing role of demand management in recent years.

Demand management in the 1970s

The Conservative government under Heath: 1970–74

1970–71. Under the previous Labour administration there had been a tight monetary and fiscal policy. This was designed (a) to help make the 1967 devaluation of sterling more effective and (b) to help reduce the rapid wage increases following the relaxing of the incomes policy it had pursued since 1966.

The Heath administration continued to squeeze demand. But unemployment rose rapidly and there was growing industrial unrest with a damaging miners' strike in the winter of 1971–2. Wage inflation continued to rise.

1972–73. The growing problem of stagflation led to a 'U-turn' in 1972. There were very expansionary budgets in 1972 and 1973 as the government went on a 'dash for growth'. The large budget deficits, plus the new less constraining monetary reforms of 1971, led to large increases in money supply. The floating of the pound in 1972 reduced the need for monetary restraint. A prices and incomes policy was introduced in November 1972 in an attempt to bring inflation down despite this huge stimulus to demand.

Although growth was now very rapid (7.3 per cent in 1973), there was no way it could be sustained. Inflationary pressures were building up. When world commodity prices rose sharply in 1972/73, and when the oil price shot up in late 1973, it was inevitable that inflation would soar.

By 1973 the authorities were becoming concerned at the rate of growth of the money supply. Open-market operations and special deposits were used to reduce the growth in liquidity, and these were supported by the raising of MLR, not just in response to a rise in market interest rates, but in an attempt to *force them up*.

However, these measures were inadequate. Part of the problem was that, although nominal rates of interest (the actual rate paid) were rising, *real* rates (the nominal rate minus the rate of inflation) were falling and then became negative (see Table 18.2). People's savings were declining in value. Thus people were encouraged to save less and borrow more. But the authorities were unwilling to see nominal rates of interest soar.

And so, in order to restrain monetary growth, the authorities abandoned the spirit

Table 18.2 Selected monetary indicators: 1969–89

	Change in M3 (%)	Change in M4 (%)	PSBR (£m)	Inflation (% rise in RPI)	Nominal interest rate (av. on 20-year bonds)	Real interest rate (5) –(4)
	(1)	(2)	(3)	(4)	(5)	(6)
1969	18.2	5.1	−534	5.4	9.1	3.7
1970	8.2	11.5	−51	6.3	9.3	3.0
1971	10.9	16,0	1 320	9.4	8.9	−0.5
1972	26.0	23.7	1 950	7.3	9.0	1.7
1973	27.0	22.3	4 093	9.1	10.8	1.7
1974	12.3	11.1	6 452	16.0	14.8	−1.2
1975	10.4	12.4	10 161	24.2	14.4	−9.8
1976	8.5	11.2	9 000	16.5	14.4	2.1
1977	7.7	14.7	5 466	15.9	12.7	−3.2
1978	12.7	15.0	8 195	8.3	12.5	4.2
1979	11.1	14.1	12 551	13.4	13.0	−0.4
1980	16.2	17.2	11 786	18.0	13.8	−4.2
1981	12.3	20.9	10 507	11.9	14.7	2.8
1982	8.8	12.1	4 880	8.6	12.9	4.3
1983	10.2	13.2	11 605	4.6	10.8	6.2
1984	9.7	13.6	10 281	5.0	10.7	5.7
1985	13.4	13.1	7 474	6.1	10.6	4.5
1986	19.0	15.4	2 497	3.4	9.9	6.5
1987	22.8	16.3	−1 432	4.2	9.5	5.3
1988	20.5	17.6	−11 611	4.9	9.4	4.5
1989	n/a	18.2	−9 147	7.8	9.6	1.8

Source: *Economic Trends* (CSO).

of 'Competition and Credit Control' and reintroduced various forms of selective control. Moral suasion was therefore extensively used to try to restrain the growth of bank lending, and the corset (first introduced in 1973) was applied with varying degrees of ferocity.

The miners' strike in the winter of 1973–4 was a direct challenge to the government's incomes policy. The government called an election in February 1974 to get a mandate for its economic policies. It lost the election.

The Labour governments under Wilson and Callaghan: 1974–79

1974–75. The Labour government abandoned the incomes policy. There was a resulting pay explosion fuelled by the excess demand and the oil and other commodity price increases. By 1975 wage inflation was over 30 per cent. Firms shed labour in response to the rapid rise in their costs. There was a resulting recession in 1975: a worldwide phenomenon.

Given the rise in both unemployment and inflation, discretionary demand management policy was not clearly deflationary or reflationary. Budget deficits were high, but this was largely due to the higher costs of government expenditure and the automatic fiscal stabilizers brought into play by the recession (e.g. increased government expenditure on unemployment benefit). Nevertheless the government tolerated these high deficits.

In the summer of 1975 the government resorted to a tough prices and incomes policy to try to reduce inflation.

1976–79. Inflation began to fall in 1976 and growth re-emerged. The government allowed the exchange rate to fall to help stimulate the demand for exports. But the falling pound caused speculation of further falls, and a sterling crisis resulted in late

1976. The government was forced to borrow from the International Monetary Fund to support the pound, and in return had to pursue tighter demand management policies.

For the first time, targets were adopted for money supply (M3). This shift in a monetarist direction was only partial, however, since prices and incomes policy was still seen as the major weapon against inflation.

From 1976 to 1979 growth was steady at between 2½ and 3 per cent, unemployment was steady at between 5 and 5½ per cent, and inflation was falling. But growing resentment at incomes restraint led to the 'winter of discontent' of 1978–9, when several groups of workers attempted to defy the incomes policy. The government subsequently lost the 1979 election.

Monetarism under Thatcher

With the election of the Conservatives in 1979, the UK for the first time had a government committed to monetarist policies. There were two main features to this.

On the supply side, the government pursued policies to free up the market. The prices and incomes policy was abandoned; legislation was introduced to curb trade union power; foreign exchange controls were lifted; in order to increase incentives the standard rate of income tax was cut from 33 per cent to 30 per cent (with VAT being raised to compensate for the loss of revenue); the government made it clear that it would not bale out 'lame duck' industries that were unable to survive the rigours of the market; and later on it pursued a comprehensive policy of privatization.

On the demand side, the cornerstone of the government's policy on inflation was the medium-term financial strategy. Discretionary demand management in an attempt to fine tune the economy was totally abandoned. Instead targets were adopted for money supply. By setting a clear target for money supply, a target that the government was committed to achieving, it was hoped to convince people of the seriousness of the government's purpose in reducing inflation. This, combined with statements that inflation was 'public enemy number one', was designed to reduce people's expectations of inflation, and hence the level of wage settlements. The way in which money supply was to be kept on target in the short term was by changes in interest rates. The Bank of England would achieve intrest rate changes by its operations in the discount market. All other forms of monetary control were abandoned. Foreign exchange controls were abolished in 1979 as were all forms of credit rationing; the corset was abandoned in 1980; statutory reserve requirements were abolished in 1981. The special deposits scheme was retained as an option, but from 1981 the banks were not required to make any.

In the medium term the achieving of the targets would require a progressive reduction in the PSBR as a proportion of GDP (if crowding out was to be avoided). Thus although the government considered *pure* fiscal policy to be ineffective, tight fiscal policy was to be the means of reducing the PSBR and hence keeping money supply under control. In the public mind, therefore, the government's monetarist policy became synonymous with 'cuts'.

Demand-side policies in the early 1980s

1979–81

The UK experienced its deepest recession since the 1930s. What is more, unlike in the 1930s there was also high inflation.

The abandoning of incomes policy, the rise in oil prices from 1979 to 1981 and the rise in VAT from 7 per cent to 15 per cent led to a rise in inflation from 8.3 per cent in 1978 to 18 per cent in 1980. At the same time fiscal and monetary policy had a highly deflationary effect. Interest rates rose rapidly, with MLR reaching 17 per cent in late 1979. The high interest rates, plus an improving balance of payments due to North Sea oil, led to a rapid rise in the exchange rate, fuelled by speculation of further rises.

The combination of low demand, high interest rates, a high exchange rate and rapidly rising costs led to a severe recession, and unemployment rocketed from 4.7 per cent in 1979 to nearly 10 per cent in 1981.

1982–85

The continuing tight monetary policy with high real interest rates allowed only a slow recovery from recession. Recovery was, however, helped somewhat by a fall in the exchange rate between 1981 and 1985. This was in part a response to the strength of the dollar, which was due to high US interest rates resulting from the large and growing US budget deficit. Growth re-emerged from 1982 and inflation fell back to around 5 per cent (albeit with a small increase in 1985). The growth in demand, however, was insufficient to prevent the continuing rise in unemployment.

Although exogenous factors such as consumer and business expectations made it difficult to keep money supply on target, there was a relatively consistent attempt throughout to pursue a steady-as-you-go demand management policy.

Rules had replaced discretion. (Section 18.5 looks at the relative advantages and disadvantages of rules versus discretion.)

A return to discretionary policies after 1985

Assessing the monetarist experiment

Was the government able to carry through its monetarist intentions? On the plus side, after an initial upsurge (1979–81) the growth of money supply was reduced and inflation fell. But despite this there were a number of problems. Some of these are illustrated in Table 18.3.

- The PSBR proved very difficult to control and was above target in several years.
- From 1983 onwards the recorded level of the PSBR was artificially reduced by the sale of public-sector assets (British Telecom, British Gas, etc.). These sales were recorded as a reduction in public-sector expenditure and thus made the PSBR seem smaller than it really was. Critics of the government have referred to this as 'fudging' or 'massaging' the statistics. It allowed the government to pursue a more expansionary fiscal policy whilst *appearing* to maintain a tight monetary policy.
- The growth in M3 was also above target in several years despite a wide target range, and the eventual reduction in its growth after 1981 was achieved at the cost of very high real interest rates.
- The government was forced to raise the target ranges in 1982, despite its commitment in the MTFS to a progressive lowering of them.
- In its search for the best measure of money supply – or the easiest to control – the government, in addition to M3 which it targeted throughout, first targeted M1 and M5. (At that time M5 was known as 'PSL2', where PSL stood for 'private sector liquidity'.) It then abandoned targeting M1 and M5, and instead targeted M0 (see Table 18.3). This makes it very difficult to assess the success of the policy.
- Whenever one measure of money supply is targeted and measures are adopted to

Box 18.5

Overfunding and Goodhart's Law
Successful monetary policy or 'fudging'?

According to Goodhart's law (see Box 17.1), 'If one particular measure of money supply is targeted and measures are adopted to control it, it will cease to be a good indicator of monetary conditions. Other measures are still likely to go on expanding.'

A good example of this is the case of 'overfunding' – a practice pursued after 1980, and vigorously between 1983 and the first part of 1985. The government sold very large quantities of bonds: more than enough to cover the PSBR. With no further action by the Bank of England, this would normally slow down the growth of money supply.

But to provide the private sector with adequate liquidity, the Bank of England purchased huge quantities of commercial bills. In the financial year 1983/84 the Bank of England purchased over £80 billion worth of such bills. A 'commercial bill mountain' was built up. This provided finance direct to industry without firms having to borrow from the banks. The bills accumulated by the Bank of England are not included in M3, and thus, given the overfunding, the growth of M3 slowed down despite this injection of liquidity. You can see this by looking at

Table 18.3. This was referred to by critics at the time as a form of fudging.

M5, which ceased to be targeted after 1983/84, actually grew *more* rapidly between 1983/84 and 1985/86 (see Table 18.3). This was the only time in the 1980s when M5 growth was more rapid than M3 growth. So why did the growth in M5 not slow down along with M3? The reason is that the bills purchased by the Bank of England *are* included in M5. Given that the purchase of these bills was providing large increases in liquidity, M5 was probably a better indication of 'true' monetary growth than M3. Hence Goodhart's law: 'To control is to distort'.

At the end of 1985 the government reversed its policy and began running down the bill mountain. M3 began to rise rapidly and probably gave a much truer indication of monetary conditions.

? Why, do you think, did the growth of M1 not slow down along with the growth in M3? (See Table 18.3 for details.)

Table 18.3 Monetary indicators: 1979/80–1985/86

	1979/80	1980/81	1981/82	1982/83	1983/84	1984/85	1985/86
PSBR target (% of GDP)	–	3.25	4.25	3.5	2.75	2.25	2.0
PSBR actual (% of GDP)	4.9	5.4	3.4	3.1	3.2	3.2	
M3 target (% growth)	–	7–11	6–10	8–12	7–11	6–10	5–9
M3 actual (% growth)	15.2	19.4	12.8	11.2	9.5	9.7	13.6
M1 target (% growth)	–	–	6–10	8–12	7–11	–	–
M1 actual (% growth)	5.3	11.9	7.2	12.3	14.0	14.6	17.4
M5 target (% growth)	–	–	6–10	8–12	7–11	–	–
M5 actual (% growth)	12.5	14.8	12.0	11.5	12.6	15.2	14.6
M0 target (% growth)	–	–	–	–	–	4–8	3–7
M0 actual (% growth)	9.2	6.2	2.7	4.6	5.8	5.3	3.0
Sterling index (weighted average exchange rate)	89.9	98.3	92.3	87.9	83.5	76.3	79.8

Note: The targets are the new targets set at the beginning of each financial year.

Sources: *Midland Bank Review* (Autumn 1984); *Economic Trends* (CSO: various issues).

control it, other measures of the money supply are still likely to go on expanding if the demand for money is buoyant: Goodhart's law again. This happened from 1983 to 1985. M3 was targeted and brought under control, but other measures of money supply went on growing (see Table 18.3 and Box 18.5).

Box 18.6

MTFS – RIP
The life history of the medium-term financial strategy

March 1980: Birth and childhood

The government considers that a progressive reduction in the rate of growth of the money stock is essential to achieving a permanent reduction in inflation.

The government believes that its monetary policy can best be formulated if it sets targets for the growth of one of the aggregates, against which progress can be assessed. This gives the clearest guidance to those concerned in both financial markets and domestic industry, on which to . . . formulate expectations.

There seems to be considerable agreement that [sterling] M3 best suits the present circumstances of the United Kingdom. It is well understood in the markets. It indicates links with the other policies. It is also relatively easy to define in terms of the banking system.'[1]

March 1981: Youth and growing pains

Taken on its own, £M3 has not been a good indicator of monetary conditions in the past year. However, over the medium term its velocity of circulation has been broadly stable, and for such a period the growth of £M3 can be more readily related to the growth of nominal income and overall fiscal stance . . .

£M3 is accordingly being retained as the main target variable in the medium-term financial strategy, though as in the past year, the significance of short-run movements

for interest rate policy will be interpreted in the light of other financial developments as well.[2]

March 1982: Troublesome adolescence

The case for looking at a range of measures is especially strong when the financial system is undergoing rapid change. For example £M3 . . . has been affected by the . . . ending of the supplementary special deposits scheme [the corset], while M0 and the non-interest bearing component of M1 may have been influenced by changes in payments mechanisms.

The growth in £M3 over the year to February 1982 is now put at 14½ per cent compared with a target of 6–10 per cent . . .

Despite the relatively rapid growth in broad money, the balance of the evidence suggests that, as intended, financial conditions have been moderately restrictive during the past year.[3]

March 1983: Maturity

Government policies have helped to bring about a rate of inflation that is already in single figures . . .

Control of the money supply is a central part of this strategy. In judging the rate of monetary growth needed to reduce inflation, the Government will continue to take account of structural influences on the different monetary

---

- The policy of allowing sterling to float more freely brought problems. High interest rates and North Sea oil caused the pound to soar in 1980, with consequent damage to the export sector. Exporting firms simply could not sell their products at such high foreign currency prices, or make sufficient sterling profits if their goods were priced in foreign currency terms. And yet the government was afraid of intervening to lower the exchange rate because that would have increased the money supply (through either having to lower interest rates or running a total currency flow surplus).
- The opposite problem was faced in January/February 1985. The pound was falling dramatically against a strong US dollar. As the pound approached $1, the government felt obliged to intervene. Interest rates were raised dramatically, and on 14 January a formally announced MLR was reintroduced for one day to drive interest rates up by 2 per cent.

Despite all these difficulties – and as you can see they were considerable – monetary policy was nevertheless more consistent in the early 1980s than before or since. At least inflation was seen as 'public enemy number one', and the means of getting it down was seen to be a tight monetary policy and the adherence to monetary targets.

As the 1980s progressed, however, although monetary targets (M3) were almost being achieved, their importance was waning as far as the government was concerned.

Box 18.6 (cont'd)

aggregates, as well as the behaviour of other financial indicators . . .[4]

March 1984: Comfortable middle age

Inflation has come down to levels not experienced in the UK since the 1960s. There has been a steady recovery in output for almost three years. The aim over the medium term is to continue reducing inflation and to build on recent improvements in the performance of the economy. The government therefore intends to continue with present policies. The medium-term financial strategy sets out the framework within which policy operates.

M1 grew by 11 per cent . . . the top of the target range. But the increasing share of interest bearing deposits within the total has complicated interpretation, and made M1 an increasingly inadequate measure of transactions balances . . .

Other measures of narrow money, such as M0, are likely to be more satisfactory indicators of financial conditions.

In the year to mid-February £M3 grew by 9¾ per cent, well within the target range.

Broad and narrow money will have equal importance in the assessment of monetary conditions and interest rates. As in the past the authorities will take into account all the available evidence, including exchange rates.[5]

March 1986: Decline

Measures of broad money have persistently grown faster than money GDP over the last six years . . .

For £M3, the target range has been raised to 11–15 per cent reflecting the rapid fall in velocity observed in recent years. Illustrative ranges for future years are not given for £M3 because the uncertainties surrounding its velocity trend are at present too great.[6]

October 1986: Old age

Only two of the past six annual targets of growth for £M3 have been achieved and, of these two, that for 1982–83 was achieved only after the target range indicated in the previous MTFS had been raised in the 1982 Budget.

It is perfectly fair to ask whether in these circumstances a broad money target continues to serve a useful purpose . . . [and whether] we would do better to dispense with monetary targetry altogether.[7]

March 1987: Death

For broad money (£M3) . . . it is probably wiser to eschew an explicit target altogether.[8]

[1] Government green paper, *Monetary Control* (HMSO, 1980).
[2] *Financial Statement and Budget Report 1981/82* (HM Treasury).
[3] *Financial Statement and Budget Report 1982/83* (HM Treasury).
[4] *Financial Statement and Budget Report 1983/84* (HM Treasury).
[5] *Financial Statement and Budget Report 1984/85* (HM Treasury).
[6] *Financial Statement and Budget Report 1985/86* (HM Treasury).
[7] Governor of the Bank of England, Loughborough University Banking Centre Annual Lecture in Finance.
[8] 1987 Budget speech.

With unemployment over 3 million, the government was putting less emphasis on the desirability of a generally tight monetary policy and instead was becoming more pragmatic. It wanted to allow monetary growth, and with it the growth of private-sector activity, to be as fast as possible without causing a resurgence of inflation or a run on the pound. Interest rate policy was thus becoming increasingly determined by short-run considerations of managing the exchange rate or responding to upward pressures on inflation: interest rates were no longer to be used primarily to keep monetary growth within a previously set target range.

With the effective abandonment of money supply targets after 1985, demand management policy reverted to a more traditional stop–go pattern. Discretion seemed to be replacing rules.

The period from 1985 to 1988 can be summarized as a period of unbalanced fiscal and monetary policy.

Monetary policy was expansionary. With inflation still relatively low after the recession of the early 1980s, and the pound relatively strong on the foreign exchange market, interest rates were lowered in order to stimulate economic growth, reduce unemployment and prevent further rises in the exchange rate (and the consequent damage to exports).

Fiscal policy, on the other hand, remained relatively tight. Although the government made several cuts in tax rates, these were not enough to prevent considerable

Box 18.7

Targeting the Exchange Rate as a Means of Controlling Inflation
A justification for the UK's entry to the ERM?

In an open economy like the UK, the exchange rate is an important part of the transmission mechanism between changes in money supply and changes in the level of prices.

A rise in the money supply will cause a fall in the rate of interest. A fall in the rate of interest will cause an outflow of capital from the country and hence a depreciation of the exchange rate. This will cause a direct rise in prices as imports become more expensive. It will also cause an increase in the production and sales of exports. This will put further upward pressure on prices. The resulting rise in the transactions demand for money will push the rate of interest back up again until the outflow of money ceases and equilibrium is restored. Thus a rise in money supply will raise prices via its effect on the exchange rate.

So what would happen if the *exchange rate* were targeted (rather than the money supply)? In other words, what would happen if the government used interest rates to maintain the exchange rate at some target level?

If the supply of money rose, the rate of interest would fall. This would put downward pressure on the exchange rate. To prevent the exchange rate falling, the government would have to raise the interest rate. But this would

help to arrest the increase in money supply and dampen aggregate demand. The result would be that inflation would be kept under control *because the fixed exchange rate would nip any excessive expansion of money supply in the bud.*

Thus, say its advocates, targeting the exchange rate is a way of controlling inflation. It also has the added advantage of providing the stability that businesspeople like. If they know what the exchange rate will be in advance, it makes it much easier to predict import costs and export revenues *in sterling*: the resulting reduction in uncertainty will aid business planning and make firms more willing to engage in foreign trade.

There is a major qualification to these arguments, however. Fixing the exchange rate to other countries' currencies effectively means accepting their average rate of inflation. This may be fine if the countries are like Germany and have a low rate of inflation. But if the countries *collectively* increase money supply, inflation will rise without any exchange rate pressures between them to prevent it.

? How might targeting the exchange rate possibly be damaging (a) to exporters; (b) to domestic producers competing with foreign imports?

fiscal drag: tax *revenues* increased. At the same time the government continued to try to reduce government expenditure as a proportion of national income. The net result was that a PSBR of over £11bn in 1983 was turned into a PSDR of over £11bn by 1988.

The result of the imbalance in policy was an imbalance in the impact of the policy. The extra money was spent largely on property and consumer durables (a large proportion of which were imported). House prices soared as mortgages were easy to obtain. Car sales boomed, as did the sales of electrical goods, furniture and foreign holidays.

Monetary policy was relatively expansionary throughout the world, and part of the extra money went into stocks and shares. The resulting increase in share prices was faster than the increase in profits and dividends. Eventually, in October 1987, 'the bubble burst' and share prices crashed. Worried that this collapse in share prices would lead to a collapse of confidence by firms and hence a collapse of investment and a plunge into recession, monetary policy was further relaxed.

Despite the monetary boost of 1987 and early 1988, UK interest rates were still high by international standards, and the pound appreciated during early 1988. As a result the government, wishing to avoid repeating the damage done to exports by the high pound of the early 1980s, reduced interest rates. Aggregate demand thus grew more rapidly. Unemployment fell more rapidly and output grew more rapidly; but inflation began to rise rapidly and the balance of payments on current account plunged into a record deficit.

In response to this crisis, interest rates were raised several times in the last part of 1988 and during 1989. Banks' base rate rose from 7.5 per cent in May 1988 to 15 per cent by October 1989, and then remained at this level until October 1990 when the UK joined the exchange rate mechanism (ERM) of the European Monetary System (see section 22.7). It was clear that the government was pursuing a stop–go monetary policy, depending on how bad were the problems of inflation, the balance of payments and a depreciating exchange rate.

 In what way was the stop–go policy of the late 1980s different from the stop–go policies pursued during the 1950s and 1960s?

Targets were not completely abandoned after 1985. There was a growing belief that, with closer links being forged with Europe, and with the desirability of a stable exchange rate between the pound and other European currencies, the exchange rate ought to be targeted. But as we saw in Chapter 17 and in Box 17.4, the problem with effectively having only one instrument (interest rates) was that the government could not use it at one and the same time to control both the level of aggregate demand (and hence inflation) *and* the rate of exchange. If the two goals of policy were in conflict, a choice would have to be made between them. Such a conflict occurred in 1988. High interest rates were required to control the rapidly expanding credit. Low interest rates were required to prevent the exchange rate from rising above its target level of around £1 = DM3.00: a rise that would be damaging to exports. Which to choose was a matter of fierce political debate – not least between the Prime Minister, Margaret Thatcher, who saw control of inflation as the immediate objective, and the Chancellor (Nigel Lawson), who saw control of the exchange rate as the immediate objective, albeit as a means, amongst other things, of controlling inflation. The debate, however, resolved itself. With a *falling* pound in 1989, high interest rates were desirable for both exchange rate and counter-inflationary reasons.

 Will targeting the exchange rate help to reduce inflation? Does it depend on the rate of inflation in the countries to whose currencies the pound is fixed?

But what about fiscal policy? What was its role? Fiscal policy was largely confined to the role of improving the *supply* side of the economy. This would be achieved by reducing the size of the public sector (which was seen by the government to be less productive than the private sector), and by giving tax cuts to improve incentives. So did fiscal policy have no demand management role at all? It did, but only to the extent that the amount of tax cuts was influenced by demand considerations. In the 1989 and 1990 Budgets, for example, despite large public-sector *surpluses*, there were no cuts in tax rates because of the problem of rising inflation and balance of payments deficits, and hence the need to restrain the growth of aggregate demand.

From October 1990 a new element was introduced into demand management policy. With UK entry to the ERM, the pound has now to be kept within an exchange rate band. This has considerably reduced the government's room for manoeuvre: discretion has been reduced. These issues are explored in Chapter 22.

▲ SUMMARY

1. In the 1950s and 1960s, both Labour and Conservative governments pursued active demand management policies. The dominating constraints on these policies were the balance of payments and electoral considerations. As a result demand management, rather than being governed by the long-term objective of smoothing out the trade cycle, was instead little more than stop–go policy dictated by the state of the balance of payments and the need to win elections.

2. Nevertheless the experience of the 1950s and 1960s was one of relative economic success compared with either earlier or later periods. But whether this was due to the pursuit of Keynesian demand management policies or to other factors such as a buoyant world economy and economic optimism is a matter of debate.

3. The 1970s were less successful. Stagflation became a major problem, a problem that simple demand management could not solve. Stagflation was due to a number of factors, including expansionary fiscal and monetary policies in the early 1970s, the adoption of floating exchange rates, a large rise in oil prices, growing domestically generated cost-push pressures, a decline in the competitiveness of UK exports, technological change and increasingly pessimistic expectations.

4. As a result of the dilemma of rising inflation *and* rising unemployment, government policy swung violently over the period from a 'dash for growth' in the early 1970s, to two sets of prices and incomes policies, to a tight monetary policy towards the end of the decade.

5. The Conservative government in the 1980s initially pursued a tight monetary policy and targeted the PSBR and the growth in the money supply. The exchange rate rose and the economy plunged into a deep recession. The economy started to grow again after 1982, but for a time a tight monetary policy was retained (along with monetary targets) in order to keep a downward pressure on inflation. Then, after 1985, targets for monetary growth were abandoned and for a time targeting the exchange rate became the main focus of monetary policy. But with only one instrument (interest rates) there was a conflict between keeping exchange rates down and controlling inflation. This conflict disappeared after 1988 when high interest rates were required both for keeping inflation down and for preventing a fall in the exchange rate.

6. Pure fiscal policy was seen as irrelevant as a means of macroeconomic control. Instead the control of the PSBR was seen as a means of reducing *monetary* growth and of preventing crowding out.

18.5 Rules versus discretion

Central to the debate between Keynesians and monetarists over the control of demand is the question of rules versus discretion. Should monetary (and fiscal) rules be adhered to, or should governments exercise the discretion to change the policies as economic circumstances change? Monetarists favour rules. Keynesians favour discretion. We finish this chapter by having a look at the arguments on each side.

The monetarist case against discretion and in favour of rules

Monetarists are highly critical of discretionary policy, both fiscal and monetary. Such policy can involve long and variable time lags, which can make the policy at best ineffective or at worst destabilizing. Taking the measures *before* the problem arises, and thus lessening the problem of lags, is no answer since forecasting tends to be unreliable.

Given the lags, the government may *over*-correct the level of demand in order to speed up the effects of the policy. This may not create too much of a problem in the short term. Growth may rise and unemployment fall. But long-term effects will be undesirable as inflationary expectations rise. Governments may be tempted to ignore the long run, however, and, for example, engineer a pre-election boom in order to win votes.

By setting and sticking to rules, and then not interfering further, the government can provide a sound monetary framework in which there is maximum freedom for individual initiative and enterprise, and in which firms are not cushioned from market forces and are therefore encouraged to be efficient. By the government declaring medium-term targets for a steady reduction in the growth of money supply, and then resolutely sticking to them, people's expectations of inflation will be reduced. This will help further to reduce inflation. This sound and stable monetary environment, with no likelihood of sudden deflations or reflations, will encourage firms to take a longer-term perspective and to plan ahead. This could then lead to increased capital investment and long-term growth.

The optimum situation is for all the major countries to adhere to mutually consistent rules, so that their economies do not get out of line. This will create more stable exchange rates and provide the climate for world growth.

? Would it be desirable for all countries to stick to the *same* money supply targets?

The Keynesian case against rules and in favour of discretion

Keynesians reject one of the central points of the monetarist argument: that rules provide the environment for high and stable growth. Demand, argue Keynesians, is subject to many and sometimes violent exogenous shocks. If the demand for money thereby fluctuates, so must interest rates if a money supply rule is to be adhered to. Excessive fluctuations in interest rates will discourage long-term business planning and investment. What is more, the government may find it difficult to keep to its targets (see Table 18.3). This too may cause uncertainty and instability.

If the government is to adopt a rule, which rule should it choose? If a monetary measure is to be chosen, which one? M0? M2? M4? M5? They frequently do not grow at the same rate. What is more, the adoption of one measure as the target may lead to distortions as people switch the form of their holdings of liquidity and wealth (Goodhart's law).

Economic circumstances may change. The rules adopted in the past may no longer be relevant. For example, a faster growth in productivity or a large increase in oil revenues may increase potential growth and thus warrant a faster growth in money supply. The government must at least have the discretion to *change* the rules, even if only occasionally.

The short-term costs of sticking to previously set rules may be too high. If expectations are slow to adjust downward and inflation remains high, then adherence to a tight monetary rule may lead to a very deep and unacceptable recession. This was a criticism made by many economists of monetarist policies between 1979 and 1982.

But if rules should not be stuck to religiously, does this mean that the government can engage in fine tuning? Keynesians recognize that fine tuning may not be possible; nevertheless, significant and persistent excess or deficient demand *can* be corrected by demand management policy. For example, the deep recession of 1980–1 could have been substantially relieved by a more expansionary fiscal and monetary policy.

Improvements in forecasting, a willingness of governments to act quickly and the use of quick-acting policies can all help to increase the effectiveness of discretionary demand management.

 Under what circumstances would adherence to money supply targets lead to (a) more stable interest rates and (b) less stable interest rates than pursuing discretionary demand management policy?

Box 18.8

Which Target to Aim For?
A choice of bull's-eyes

Money supply targets are not the only ones that governments can choose. There are several other possible targets, each having arguments to recommend it, but each having drawbacks.

Interest rate targets

A major problem with sticking to money supply targets is that interest rates will fluctuate with fluctuations in economic activity and hence in the demand for money. For this reason many economists have argued that it is best to target interest rates. Stable interest rates will provide an environment of certainty in which businesses can make long-term investment plans. In the Keynesian era of the 1950s and 1960s governments were more concerned to achieve relatively stable interest rates than a stable growth in money supply.

The problem with targeting interest rates is that the money supply will fluctuate with demand and hence feed those fluctuations. For example, if aggregate demand grows rapidly and inflation begins to soar, then to keep interest rates down to the target level, money supply will have to be allowed to expand. But this will feed the inflation. People will come to expect higher and higher inflation, and prices and expectations will chase each other in an upward spiral. Discretionary fiscal policies or prices and incomes policies will then be needed to break the spiral.

Exchange rate targets

Provided the rest of the world is relatively stable, an exchange rate target can provide a useful brake on domestic policy. If the government were to allow the money supply to expand too fast and/or the interest rate to fall, the resulting increase in demand and outflow of capital would lead to a depreciation of the exchange rate. To get it back to target, therefore, the government would have to raise interest rates and reduce the growth in money supply.

In addition, an exchange rate target (a fixed exchange rate) is usually preferred by firms, which are thereby given the certainty to plan their imports and exports and investment abroad.

The main problem with exchange rate targets comes when the rest of the world is *not* stable. If, for example, US or German interest rates fluctuate, then UK interest rates will have to follow suit in order to prevent capital flows and the resulting change in the exchange rate. But these changes in interest rates may not be consistent with domestic demand-side policies. For example, if world interest rates fall at a time when UK inflation is rising, UK interest rates would have to fall in order to maintain the target exchange rate. But this would tend to fuel the inflation by boosting domestic demand. (This is precisely what happened in the spring of 1988 when the government attempted to maintain a target exchange rate of £1 = DM3.00.)

PSBR/PSDR targets

Part of the medium-term financial strategy of the early 1980s consisted of setting PSBR targets (as a percentage

Conclusions

The resolution of this debate will depend on the following factors:

- The confidence of people in the effectiveness of either discretionary policies or rules.
- The degree of self-stabilization of the economy (in the case of rules), or conversely the degree of inherent instability of the economy (in the case of discretion).
- The ability and determination of governments to stick to rules.
- The ability of government to adopt and execute appropriate discretionary policy.
- The speed with which such policies can be effected.
- The accuracy of forecasting.
- The size and frequency of exogenous shocks to demand.

Box 18.8 (cont'd)

of GDP). Even after the abandoning of money supply targets after 1986, the government still set targets for the PSBR and later for the PSDR, with the long-term aim of running a balanced public-sector budget (PSBR = 0).

To the extent that the size of the PSBR (or PSDR) determines the growth of the money supply, then a PSBR target can be seen as a form of money supply target.

The problem is that the correlation between the PSBR and money supply is not very close (as Chapter 16 showed): after 1987 there was a growing public-sector surplus accompanied by a rapid growth in the money supply.

Also if the government aims for a set PSBR/PSDR, this removes the automatic stabilizing property of fiscal policy. If, for example, there is an economic recession, tax revenues will fall and benefit payments will rise. This will increase the PSBR. To bring it back to target, therefore, the government would have to raise taxes or cut government expenditure, either of which would deepen the recession.

Final goal targets

The problem with all the targets we have looked at so far – money supply, interest rate, exchange rate and PSBR targets – is that they are all *intermediate targets*: that is, they are not the ultimate goals of policy but merely means of achieving them. Thus, for example, control of the money supply is not the ultimate goal of monetarist economic policy, but rather the *means* of achieving low inflation and an environment conducive to the flourishing of private enterprise.

Some economists argue that it is better to target the final goals themselves, given the problems we have looked at of targeting the means. For example, the government could target physical goals such as economic growth or unemployment, or financial goals such as inflation.

 Should low inflation be regarded as a final goal or merely an intermediate one?

The problem with final goals is that they may be inconsistent with each other. For example, low unemployment may be inconsistent with low inflation (the Phillips curve trade-off). Thus governments may swing from aiming for one target to aiming for another – and that is hardly consistent with the idea of targets being something you set and then stick to, come what may.

Also there is the problem of how you achieve the targets. The longer the transmission mechanism is from the 'levers' to the target, the more difficult it will be to achieve the target with any degree of accuracy. Thus it is relatively easy to achieve an interest rate target since the Bank of England has direct control over interest rates. But to achieve an inflation target or an unemployment target may involve frequent *adjustments* to policy depending on how successful previous policies have been. Thus a final goal target relates less to the 'steady as you go', 'fixed throttle' policies of intermediate targets, and more to discretionary policies.

 Make a list of other possible targets the government could aim for. Are they intermediate or final targets? What problems might the government have in achieving them? Would there be any other problems if the government did achieve them?

▲ SUMMARY

1. The monetarist case against discretionary policy is that it involves unpredictable time lags which can make the policy destabilizing. The government may as a result *over*-correct. Also the government may ignore the long-run adverse consequences of policies designed for short-run political gain.
2. The monetarist case in favour of rules is that they help to reduce inflationary expectations and thus create a stable environment for investment and growth.
3. The Keynesian case against sticking to money supply rules is that they may cause severe fluctuations in interest rates and thus create a less stable economic environment for business planning. Also, given Goodhart's law, it is not clear which rule should be chosen. Given the changing economic environment in which we live, rules adopted in the past may no longer be suitable for the present.
4. Although perfect fine tuning may not be possible, Keynesians argue that the government must have the discretion to change its policy as circumstances demand.

19 Keynesian and Monetarist Controversies II: Aggregate Supply, Unemployment and Inflation

19.1 Aggregate supply

What will be the effect of an increase in aggregate demand? Will output and employment increase? Or will the effect be simply a rise in prices with no change in output and employment? Or will there be some rise in output and employment and some rise in prices?

The answer to these questions is crucial to macroeconomic policy and is at the heart of the current Keynesian/monetarist/new classical debate. The debate hinges on the shape of the aggregate supply curve.

To put the debate in its starkest form, consider the extreme Keynesian and extreme monetarist positions. These are illustrated in Figure 19.1.

Extreme Keynesians argue that up to full employment (Y_f), the aggregate supply (*AS*) curve is *horizontal*. A rise in aggregate demand from AD_1 to AD_2 will raise output from Y_1 to Y_2, but there will be *no effect on prices*. This is the equivalent of reducing a deflationary gap in the Keynesian 45° model. Only when full employment is reached will prices rise. Thus in the extreme Keynesian model, aggregate supply up to the full employment level is determined entirely by the level of aggregate demand. But there is no guarantee that aggregate demand will intersect aggregate supply at full

Figure 19.1 Contrasting views of the aggregate supply curve

employment. Therefore governments should manage aggregate demand by appropriate fiscal and monetary policies in order to ensure production at Y_f.

Extreme monetarists argue that the aggregate supply curve is *vertical*. Any rise in aggregate demand will have *no effect on output and employment*. It will merely lead to higher prices. Thus it is essential to control demand if *prices* are to be kept under control. On the other hand, increasing demand in an attempt to raise output and employment is useless. To raise output and employment, *other* policies must be adopted. These are supply-side policies to shift the *AS* curve to the right (e.g. policies to encourage a more efficient use of resources).

If *AS* is somewhere between these two extremes, an increase in *AD* will have some effect on prices and some effect on output and employment. This is illustrated in Figure 19.2.

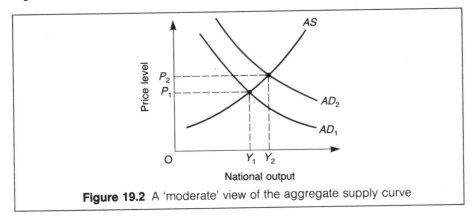

Figure 19.2 A 'moderate' view of the aggregate supply curve

Just what is the shape of the *AS* curve in practice, and what implications follow for policies to cure inflation and unemployment? How do Keynesians and monetarists differ in their answers to these questions? These are the topics for this chapter.

? 1. In the extreme Keynesian model, is there any point in supply-side policies?
2. In the extreme monetarist model, is there any point in using supply-side policies as a weapon against *inflation*?

Let us now look at the aggregate supply curve in a bit more detail. We start by distinguishing between short-run and long-run aggregate supply curves.

Short-run aggregate supply

To understand the shape of the short-run *AS* curve, it is necessary to look at its microeconomic foundations. How will *individual* firms and industries respond to a rise in demand? What shape will their individual supply curves be?

Take the short run first. Assume that firms respond to the rise in demand for their product without considering the effects of a general rise in demand on their suppliers or on the economy as a whole.

In the case of a profit-maximizing firm under monopoly or monopolistic competition, there will be a rise in price and a rise in output. This is illustrated in Figure 19.3. Profit-maximizing output rises from where $MC = MR_1$ to where $MC = MR_2$. (If necessary, refresh your memory of this analysis by re-reading Chapters 4 and 5.) Just how much price changes compared with output depends on the shape of the marginal cost (MC) curve. The steeper the curve (and hence the more rapidly costs rise as

Figure 19.3 Short-run response of a profit-maximizing firm or industry to a rise in demand

output rises), the bigger will be the rise in price, and the smaller the rise in output.

The nearer the firm is to full capacity, the steeper the *MC* curve is likely to be. To increase output the firm is likely to find diminishing returns setting in rapidly, and it is also likely to have to use more overtime with correspondingly higher unit labour costs. If, however, the firm is operating well below capacity, and especially if it has plentiful stocks of raw materials and finished goods, it can probably respond to an increased demand by supplying more with little or no increase in price. Its *MC* curve may thus be horizontal at lower levels of output.

Under oligopoly, where there is a tendency for prices to be more stable, firms may respond to an increase in demand without raising prices, even if their costs rise somewhat.

When there is a general rise in demand in the economy, the *aggregate* supply response in the short run can be seen as simply the sum of the responses of all the individual firms.

The short-run *AS* curve will therefore look something like that in Figure 19.4. If there is generally plenty of spare capacity, a rise in aggregate demand (e.g. from AD_1 to AD_2) will have a big effect on output and only a small effect on prices. However, as more and more firms find their costs rising as they get nearer to full capacity, so the *AS* curve becomes steeper. Further increases in aggregate demand (e.g. from AD_2 to AD_3) will have bigger effects on prices and smaller effects on output.

Figure 19.4 The short-run aggregate supply curve

Long-run aggregate supply

Three important factors operate in the longer run. These will affect the *AS* curve in different ways.

The interdependence of firms

A rise in aggregate demand will lead firms throughout the economy to raise their prices (in accordance with the short-run *AS* curve). But this is not the end of the story. As raw material and intermediate good producers raise their prices, so this will raise the costs of production further up the line. A rise in the price of steel will raise the costs of producing cars and washing machines. At the same time, workers, seeing the prices of goods rising, will demand higher wages. Firms will be relatively willing to grant these wage demands, given that they are experiencing a buoyant demand from their customers.

The effect of all this is to raise firms' costs, and hence their prices. As prices rise for any given level of output, so the short-run *AS* curve will shift upward. This is shown by a move to AS_1 in Figure 19.5.

The long-run effect of a rise in aggregate demand can now be shown. Aggregate demand shifts to AD_1. The economy moves from point *a* to point *b* along the short-run *AS* curve. As costs rise and are passed on throughout the economy, the short-run *AS* curve shifts to AS_1, and the economy moves to point *c*. Thus the long-run *AS* curve passing through points *a* and *c* is steeper than the short-run *AS* curve. A rise in aggregate demand will therefore have a smaller effect on output and a bigger effect on prices in the long run than in the short run.

> **?** Under what circumstances would this interdependence of firms give a vertical long-run aggregate supply curve?

Investment

With a rise in demand, firms may be encouraged to invest in new plant and machinery (the accelerator effect). In so doing they may well be able to increase output significantly in the long run with little or no increase in their prices. Their long-run *MC* curves are much flatter than their short-run *MC* curves.

In Figure 19.6 the short-run *AS* curve shifts to the right. Equilibrium moves from point *a* to *b* to *d*. In this case the long-run *AS* curve joining points *a* and *d* is much more elastic than that in Figure 19.5. There is a relatively large increase in output and a relatively small increase in price.

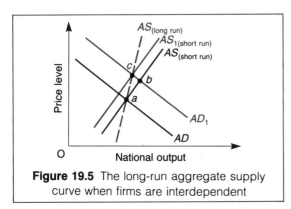

Figure 19.5 The long-run aggregate supply curve when firms are interdependent

Figure 19.6 The effect of investment on the long-run aggregate supply curve

The long-run *AS* curve will be flatter and possibly even downward sloping if the investment involves the introduction of new cost-reducing technology. It will be steeper if the extra investment causes significant shortages of materials, machinery or labour. This is more likely when the economy is already operating near its full potential.

> **?**
> 1. Will the shape of the long-run *AS* curve here depend on just how the 'long' run is defined?
> 2. If a shift in the aggregate demand curve from *AD* to *AD₁* in Figure 19.6 causes a movement from point *a* to point *d* in the long run, would a shift in aggregate demand from *AD₁* to *AD* cause a movement from point *d* back to point *a* in the long run?

Expectations

The effect of a rise in aggregate demand on output and prices will depend crucially on what effect people *expect* it will have.

If firms believe that it will lead to rapid economic growth, they will invest. The short-run *AS* curve will shift to the right.

If, on the other hand, people expect that a rise in demand will simply lead to higher prices, firms will not invest. Workers will demand higher wages to compensate for the higher cost of living. Firms will grant wage rises, knowing that they can pass on the rise in labour costs to the consumer. After all, if other firms raise their prices, a firm will not lose market share by raising its prices too. In these circumstances the short-run aggregate supply curve will shift upward (to the left).

If there is a fall in aggregate demand, the above three factors will operate in reverse; and again they will affect aggregate supply in different ways:

- The general reduction in costs will lead to the short-run *AS* curve shifting downward (to the right).
- A fall in investment may lead to a decline in the capital stock and a leftward shift in the short-run *AS* curve.
- People may expect a recession and falling output (*AS* shifts to the left), or merely that prices will fall (*AS* shifts downward to the right).

Depending on the relative strength of these three factors, the long-run *AS* curve could be steep or shallow. A fall in *AD* could thus lead to a deep recession with little effect on prices, or there could be little or no long-run reduction in output, but a significant reduction in prices.

Keynesians and monetarists put very different emphases on the three factors, and as a result draw very different conclusions about the shape of the long-run *AS* curve. In particular their analyses of the role and formation of expectations is very different. This is examined in detail in sections 19.3 to 19.5.

We now turn to examine in more detail how aggregate supply and demand analysis can be used to analyze inflation and unemployment. We start by looking at inflation.

Aggregate demand and supply, and inflation

Aggregate demand and supply analysis can be used to distinguish between demand-pull and cost-push inflation.

Demand-pull inflation

Assume that the economy is operating near the full employment potential. Aggregate demand now rises: the *AD* curve shifts to the right.

The initial effect is illustrated in Figure 19.7(a). There is some increase in output,

Figure 19.7 Demand-pull inflation

and the price level rises from P_0 to P_1. If demand goes on rising, so that the *AD* curve goes on shifting to the right, the price level will go on rising and there will be demand-pull inflation. There will be a movement from point *a* to *b* to *c* in Figure 19.7(b).

But sooner or later the short-run aggregate *supply* curve will start shifting. If the effects of rising costs and rising price expectations offset any stimulus to investment, the short-run *AS* curve will shift upward. This will lead to a falling back of output but a further rise in prices as the economy moves to point *d*. If the government responds by giving a further boost to demand in order to keep expansion going, there will be a movement outward again to point *e*, but a further rise in prices. Then the *AS* curve will probably continue shifting upward and the economy will move to point *f*.

If, at this stage, the government makes the control of inflation its main policy objective, it may stop any further increases in aggregate demand. Aggregate supply may continue to rise for a while as cost increases and expectations feed through. The economy moves to point *g*. In the extreme case, point *g* may be vertically above point *a*. The only effect of the shift in *AD* to AD_3 has been inflation.

If investment has increased output or if there are other exogenous increases in aggregate supply (e.g. the discovery of new North Sea oil fields), the *AS* curve will not shift upwards so far and the rise in prices will not be so great.

Note that, although costs in Figure 19.7(b) have increased and hence the *AS* curves have shifted upward, this is not *cost-push* inflation. It is *demand-pull* inflation because the rise in costs was the result of the rise in demand.

? If point *g* is vertically above point *a*, does this mean that the long-run *AS* curve is vertical? Are there any circumstances where point *g* might be to the left of point *a*?

Cost-push inflation

Assume that there is now some exogenous increase in costs: a sharp increase in world oil prices, or an increase in wages due to increased trade union militancy or an increased expectation of inflation (following, say, the abandonment of an incomes policy).

The initial effect is illustrated in Figure 19.8(a). The short-run *AS* curve shifts to AS_1. Prices rise to P_1 and there is a fall in national output.

If these increases in costs continue for some time, the *AS* curve will go on shifting upward. Price rises will continue and there is cost-push inflation. The economy will move from point *a* to *b* to *c* in Figure 19.8(b).

Box 19.1

Inflation and Price Increases
Don't get confused

The Chancellor raises VAT. 'This will put up prices in the shops', claim his critics, 'and cause inflation.' Similar worries are voiced when oil prices rise, or if the European Community puts up intervention prices for various foodstuffs. But are these worries justifed?

It is important to distinguish a *single* supply shock, such as the rise in oil prices in 1973 and the increase in VAT from 7 per cent to 15 per cent in 1979, from a continuing upward pressure on costs, such as workers continually demanding increases in real wages above the level of labour productivity.

A single supply shock will give a *single* upward movement in the *AS* curve. Prices will move to a new higher equilibrium. Cost-push inflation in this case is a *temporary* phenomenon. Once the new higher price level has been reached, the cost-push inflation disappears. If, however, there is a continuous upward pressure on costs, cost-push inflation is likely to continue. It will get worse if the cost pressure intensifies.

After a time aggregate demand is likely to rise. This may be due to the government using expansionary fiscal and monetary policies to halt the falling output and employment. Or it may be due to money supply expanding endogenously in response to a higher demand for money as workers and firms need more money to pay for increasingly costly transactions. Aggregate demand shifts to AD_1 and there is a movement to point *d*. There may then be a further increase in costs and a movement to point *e*, and then a further increase in aggregate demand and so on.

Note again that, although demand has increased, this is still *cost-push* inflation because the rise in demand is the result of the upward pressure on costs.

What causes inflation in practice?
Monetarists blame exogenous rises in money supply. For them inflation is of the demand-pull variety.

Some Keynesians also blame rises in demand, but tend to focus on excessive fiscal expansion rather than monetary expansion. Other Keynesians tend to highlight cost-push factors and especially wage-push inflation, and thus call for incomes policies to restrain wage increases. Most Keynesians argue that there are a mixture of causes.

Does the evidence support a demand-pull or a cost-push view of the world?

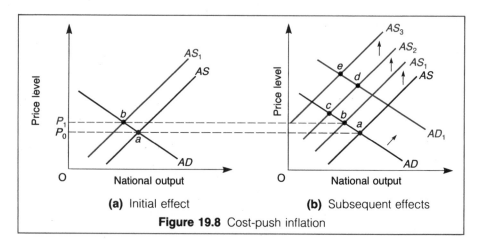

(a) Initial effect **(b)** Subsequent effects

Figure 19.8 Cost-push inflation

Box 19.2

The Evidence on Inflation: 1971–1977
Seeing what you want to see

UK price and output indices: 1971–77

	1971	1972	1973	1974	1975	1976	1977
Output index[1]	78.8	81.2	86.0	84.7	83.1	84.8	87.2
Price index[2]	21.4	23.0	25.1	29.1	36.1	42.1	48.8

[1] GDP (1985 = 100).
[2] RPI (1985 = 100).

Source: *Economic Trends Annual Supplement* (CSO).

The table shows price and output indices for the years 1971 to 1977. These figures are plotted in the two diagrams. By selecting just part of the period, the figures can be made to support a particular view of the causes of inflation.

Evidence used to support the monetarist case

Monetarists could cite the period from 1971 to 1975 to support their view that inflation is of the demand-pull variety caused by a too rapid expansion of the money supply. Diagram (a) shows the price level and national output (measured as indices) between these years.

(a) Evidence used to support the demand-pull case

A rapid expansion of money supply, associated with the Heath government's reflationary policies, led to an increase in aggregate demand and thus initially to increased output.

Then, as expectations of inflation rose, the aggregate supply curve shifted upwards, and thus the long-term effect of the rise in aggregate demand was simply higher prices. Diagram (a) corresponds to Figure 19.7(b).

Evidence to support the cost-push case

Cost-push economists argue that there was a major exogenous supply shock in December 1973, when after the Middle East war OPEC raised the oil price substantially. This was followed in February 1974 by the defeat of the Heath government and hence the collapse of its incomes policy. The cost-push school argue that these were largely exogenous supply-side factors. The *AS* curve shifted upward, and hence both inflation and recession were experienced.

(b) Evidence used to support the cost-push case

This was later followed by some reflation of the world economy to offset the effects of world recession. This led to a rightward shift in the aggregate demand curve. Diagram (b) corresponds to Figure 19.8(b).

> **?** If shifts in aggregate demand cause shifts in aggregate supply, and if shifts in aggregate supply cause shifts in aggregate demand, is it even theoretically possible to separate 'original' demand-pull factors from 'original' cost-push factors?

Unfortunately, as in much of economics, the evidence is ambiguous. Economists tend to use evidence selectively to support their case, picking those periods most favourable to their point of view (see Box 19.2). Probably inflation is a mixture of demand-pull and cost-push, since there are a number of factors that can cause exogenous rises in demand and a number of others that can cause exogenous rises in supply. Sometimes they occur at different times; sometimes they occur simultaneously.

Aggregate supply, the labour market and unemployment: short run

What is the relationship between aggregate supply and unemployment? To answer this it is necessary to distinguish between the short run and the long run. In the short run the following assumptions will be made:

- Labour productivity is constant. There is therefore a constant labour/output ratio in the economy. Any rise in national output must therefore be accompanied by a rise in employment and vice versa. A rise in the aggregate demand for goods will therefore lead to a rise in the aggregate demand for labour.
- Individual labour markets operate independently. This assumption means that workers and employers in any given labour market respond to a change in demand in their market only, *without* considering the effects of similar changes in demand on wages, prices, output and employment in the rest of the economy.

Two cases will be considered: (a) markets which are competitive and where wages are flexible, and (b) markets where wages are determined by a process of collective bargaining and where, therefore, there is much greater rigidity in wages.

Competitive labour markets (flexible wages)

Here it is assumed that there are no unions to maintain wages above equilibrium. Wages will adjust quickly to equate the demand for labour with the supply of those willing to work. This is illustrated in Figure 19.9.

The vertical axis measures money wage rates. In the short run, a rise in money wages is seen by workers as a rise in *real* wages. The reason for this is that workers are assumed only to look at wages in their particular labour market, and do not consider the fact that higher wages generally may simply lead to higher prices.

Higher wages will encourage more people to enter the labour market. For example, if wages go up, more married women may seek employment. Thus the total labour force increases as wages rise. This is the *gross supply of labour* (N). The curve gets steeper as the limit of the potential labour force is reached.

There will, however, be some frictional and structural unemployment. Some workers will be searching for better jobs, and others will have the wrong qualifications or live in the wrong location. Therefore the number of workers willing and able to accept jobs – the *effective supply of labour* (AS_L) will be less than the gross labour supply (N).

Assume that the aggregate labour demand curve is AD_{L_1}. The equilibrium wage will be W_1, with Q_1 workers employed. Because the market clears, there is no disequilibrium unemployment. Equilibrium or 'natural' unemployment (i.e. frictional plus structural unemployment) is $b - a$.

Assume now that the aggregate demand for goods rises so that the aggregate labour demand shifts to AD_{L_2}. Wages will rise to W_2 and employment to Q_2.

The shape of the short-run aggregate supply (of goods) curve will thus depend on the shape of the short-run effective labour supply curve. The steeper the latter, the steeper the former.

Figure 19.9 Short-run response of labour supply to a rise in the aggregate demand for labour

Figure 19.10 Short-run response to a fall in the aggregate demand for labour: sticky wages

Note that, as wages rise, the gap between the gross and effective labour supply curves narrows: $(d - c) < (b - a)$. This is because at higher wages frictional unemployment is likely to be reduced as workers searching for jobs find ones more rapidly that pay acceptable wages. (In Figure 12.16 on page 494, the W_0 curve has shifted upward.) Thus in this competitive model, although there is no demand-deficient unemployment because the labour market is always in equilibrium, a rise in aggregate demand can still reduce unemployment, by reducing frictional unemployment. What is more, if the government directs aggregate demand into areas of high unemployment, it may reduce structural unemployment. This is shown by a rightward shift of the effective supply of labour curve (AS_L) and a narrowing of the gap $d - c$.

Similarly, a fall in aggregate demand will lead to an increase in frictional unemployment and possibly structural unemployment.

 If there were no frictional or structural unemployment, how would a rise in aggregate demand in competitive markets affect employment, unemployment and output?

Labour markets with 'sticky' wages

In practice many labour markets have considerable wage inflexibility. Employers bargain with unions and set wage rates usually for a whole year. If there is a fall in consumer demand, firms usually respond *not* by cutting wages, but rather by laying off workers, or by instituting early retirement, or by not replacing workers when they leave.

In the short run, therefore, wages in many sectors of the economy are insensitive to a fall in demand. The effect of this is illustrated in Figure 19.10.

Assume initially that, with aggregate demand for labour at AD_{L_1}, the labour market is in equilibrium. The only unemployment is equilibrium unemployment of $b - a$. Now assume there is a fall in the aggregate demand for goods. The demand for labour falls to AD_{L_2}. But wages do not fall. Instead, firms reduce their labour force from Q_1 to Q_2. There is now disequilibrium (demand-deficient) unemployment of $a - c$. *Total* unemployment is $b - c$.

This will give a short-run aggregate supply (of goods) curve that is highly elastic below the current wage. A fall in aggregate demand will lead to a large fall in output and only a small fall in prices. Any reductions in prices that do occur will be due to firms being prepared to accept smaller profit margins in order to sell their goods.

If demand now rises again, there is no guarantee that equilibrium will return to

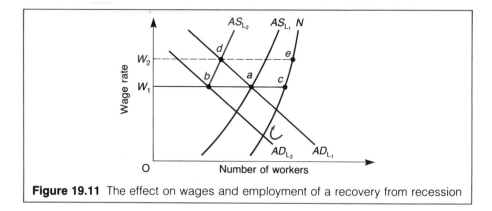

Figure 19.11 The effect on wages and employment of a recovery from recession

point *a*. Those previously laid off may not be readily re-employable, especially if they have been out of work for some time. In Figure 19.11, if demand shifts back to AD_{L_1}, wages may now be bid up to W_2 as the economy moves up a new effective supply of labour curve AS_{L_2}. Unemployment will now be $e - d$. As an economy pulls out of recession, therefore, unemployment may not fall back to the levels of the previous boom.

Of course, not every individual labour market is like this. Some are more competitive and exhibit greater downward flexibility of wages. When the economy contains both types of market, there will be some net downward flexibility of wages, but nevertheless there will still be some disequilibrium unemployment when *AD* falls.

Monetarists tend to argue that labour markets exhibit more wage flexibility; Keynesians that they exhibit less.

> 1. What implications follow from the analysis of inflexible wages for the length and depth of a recession resulting from severely deflationary monetary policies like those pursued in 1979–82?
> 2. How will (price) inflation affect the position of the AS_L curve?

Aggregate supply, the labour market and unemployment: long run

The effective aggregate supply curve of labour is likely to be steeper in the long run than in the short run. There are two reasons for this.

The interdependence of markets

A rise in aggregate demand will lead to a rise in the demand for labour. This will raise wages and employment along the short-run aggregate effective supply of labour curve (AS_{L_1}), from point *a* to point *b* in Figure 19.12. But this rise in wages will be passed on to the consumer in higher prices. Thus the purchasing power of these higher money wages is reduced. The *real* wage (W/P) falls as prices rise. Thus at any given (money) wage, the effective supply of labour will be reduced. The short-run effective supply of labour curve shifts to the left. Put another way, workers will need wage rises to compensate for the price rises, and this will shift the short-run AS_L curve upward. Either way, the short-run AS_L curve shifts from AS_{L_1} to AS_{L_2}. Equilibrium now moves to point *c*. There is a higher wage, but less employment than at *b*. The long-run effective aggregate supply curve of labour (going through points *a* and *c*) is much steeper than the short-run curve.

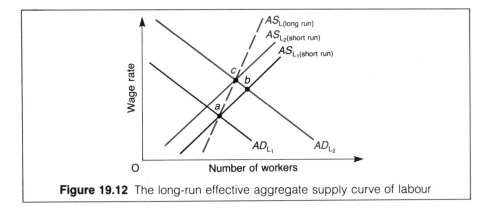

Figure 19.12 The long-run effective aggregate supply curve of labour

Expectations

If workers and firms expect higher demand to lead to higher prices, workers will demand higher wages and firms will be prepared to pay them. The short-run AS_L curve shifts upward.

If, however, there is high unemployment already and plenty of slack in the economy, people may expect an increase in aggregate demand to raise output and employment, with only small price and wage increases. In this case the short-run AS_L curve will shift up by a smaller amount, and the long-run AS_L curve, although steeper than the short-run curve, will be less steep than that illustrated in Figure 19.12.

At the other extreme, if people expect that increases in aggregate demand will lead solely to inflation, the long-run effective supply of labour (AS_L) curve will be vertical. This is more likely if the economy is near full employment. The level of unemployment corresponding to a vertical long-run AS_L curve is sometimes referred to as the natural level of unemployment. This concept is used widely by monetarists.

If *labour productivity* is unchanged by shifts in aggregate demand, then a relatively steep long-run AS_L curve will give a relatively steep long-run AS (of goods) curve. In the extreme case of a vertical long-run AS_L, the AS curve will also be vertical. The point where it crosses the horizontal axis is referred to as the natural level of output.

The effects of interdependence and expectations are mitigated, however, if the increase in aggregate demand leads to *investment* that increases labour productivity. Even though the long-run AS_L curve may be vertical, the long-run AS curve will not be. If an increase in demand causes investment, which in turn causes a rise in output, then for any given employment there is no such thing as a 'natural level of output'.

What if there is a long-run *fall* in aggregate demand? Will the effect of lower prices reduce the wage at which workers are prepared to work? In other words, will the long-run AS_L curve be steep or vertical downwards as well as upwards? The answer is that workers may still resist money wage cuts even though prices are falling.

This is partly due to what is called money illusion. This is where people believe that they will be worse off with a wage cut even though prices are lower. They simply focus on the fact that there are fewer pounds in their pay packets. It is also partly due to the fear that the price fall may be temporary, and thus workers want to hang on to wage rates that management have already agreed to in the past.

The resulting long-run AS_L curve is thus kinked at the current wage (see Figure 19.13). This will give a similarly kinked long-run AS curve.

 If there is money illusion also about the effects of an *increase* in money wages, what effect will this have on the 'kink' in Figure 19.13?

Natural level of unemployment

The level of equilibrium unemployment in monetarist analysis measured as the difference between the (vertical) long-run gross labour supply (*N*) and the (vertical) long-run effective labour supply (AS_L).

Natural level of output

The level of output in monetarist analysis where the vertical long-run aggregate supply curve cuts the horizontal axis.

Money illusion

The belief that a *money* change in wages or prices represents a *real* change.

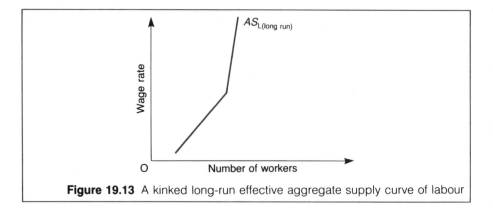

Figure 19.13 A kinked long-run effective aggregate supply curve of labour

Aggregate supply, unemployment and inflation

The above analysis has looked at the relationship between aggregate supply, unemployment and the *level* of prices. The modern world, however, is characterized not by single rises in demand and single price rises. It is not characterized by rising unemployment accompanied by actual falls in the price level. Instead there are the problems of both inflation (*continuously* rising prices) *and* unemployment.

How can the above analysis be extended to cope with the relationship between aggregate supply, unemployment and the *rate of inflation* (rather than the *level* of prices)? The answer lies in theories that develop the old Phillips curve.

The remainder of the chapter, therefore, looks at the ways in which the different schools of thought have modified the Phillips curve to fit in with their assumptions.

▲ SUMMARY

1. Keynesians argue that the aggregate supply curve is relatively elastic up to the full employment level of output. Monetarists argue that it is relatively inelastic, and that in the long run it is vertical.

2. The short-run aggregate supply curve depends on firms' short-run marginal cost curves. The more rapidly costs rise as output increases, the less elastic will the *AS* curve be.

3. The long-run *AS* curve will be less elastic (a) the more that cost increases are passed on from one part of the economy to another, (b) the less that increases in aggregate demand stimulate cost-reducing investment and (c) the more that people expect prices to rise as a result of the increase in demand.

4. Demand-pull inflation occurs where there is a continuous rightward shift in the *AD* curve. There may also be (upward) shifts in the *AS* curve (e.g. as a result of higher wages), but if these are in response to the higher demand it still constitutes demand-pull inflation.

5. Cost-push inflation occurs where there is a continuous upward shift in the *AS* curve. There may also be rightward shifts in the *AD* curve (e.g. the government responding to higher costs and the resulting higher unemployment by increasing the money supply), but again if these are in response to the higher costs it still

constitutes cost-push inflation.

6. In practice it is difficult to separate demand-pull and cost-push inflation as there are often exogenous and endogenous factors affecting both demand and costs simultaneously.

7. The aggregate supply of goods depends on the aggregate supply of labour. The more flexible is the effective aggregate supply of labour to a change in wages, the more elastic will be the *AS* (of goods) curve. In the short run, if wages are 'sticky' downwards, the effect of a fall in aggregate demand and hence in the aggregate demand for labour will be to reduce employment and output. A recession could result. If demand subsequently increases, the resulting rise in wages may result in only a slow reduction in unemployment.

8. In the long run, the effective aggregate supply of labour will be less elastic: (a) the more that wage increases are passed on by firms in higher prices and (b) the higher the prices that workers expect to result from a given increase in aggregate demand.

9. If wages are sticky downwards in the long run, the long-run AS_L curve will be kinked at the current level of wages, and the long-run *AS* curve will be kinked at the current level of prices.

19.2 Inflation and unemployment: the Phillips curve and its modifications

The original Phillips curve

Phillips' article was published in 1958 (see section 12.6). The inverse relationship that it illustrated between wage inflation ($\dot{W}$) and unemployment is shown in Figure 19.14. It was generally accepted at the time that the Phillips curve lent weight to the Keynesian analysis of inflation and unemployment in terms of excess and deficient demand respectively.

If, however, inflation and unemployment were solely due to excess or deficient demand, then by getting aggregate demand just right, the economy could operate at point c with no wage inflation and no unemployment. It was argued, therefore, that there was some underlying non-demand inflation and some equilibrium (frictional, structural, etc.) unemployment. This would allow both inflation and unemployment to occur at the same time: say, at point a.

Nevertheless, Phillips found that the curve was fairly stable over time, which suggested that changes in inflation and unemployment were due not to changes in these underlying factors, but rather to changes in aggregate demand. If, for example, the economy was operating at point a, then, if aggregate demand rose more rapidly than previously compared with aggregate supply, the economy would move to point b. Demand-pull inflation would have risen. Unemployment would have fallen.

This seemed to present governments with a simple policy choice. By demand management policy they could trade off inflation against unemployment.

Let us now look in more detail at explanations given for (a) the shape of the curve – why it slopes downwards, why it is bowed in and whether it is smooth or kinked – (b) the position of the curve – what causes it to shift.

The shape of the curve

A more usual version of the Phillips curve has price inflation ($\dot{P}$) on the vertical axis. This curve can be expressed as follows:

$$\dot{P} = a + b(1/U) \tag{1}$$

where $\dot{P}$ is the rate of price inflation, U is the level of unemployment, and a and b are constants. A fall in unemployment (a rise in $1/U$) will lead to a rise in inflation. There is a movement up along the Phillips curve.

Figure 19.14 The original Phillips curve

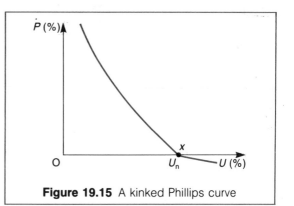

Figure 19.15 A kinked Phillips curve

The justification for this equation is that both inflation *and* unemployment depend on the level of aggregate demand relative to aggregate supply. Let us take a look at each in turn.

Inflation

If there is excess demand in any industry i ($D_i > S_i$), prices in that industry will rise. The rate of increase in prices is assumed to depend on the magnitude of the excess demand. The proportionately more that demand exceeds supply, $(D_i - S_i) \div S_i$, the more rapidly will price rise:

$$\dot{P}_i = f\frac{(D_i - S_i)}{S_i} \tag{2}$$

Similarly, on a national scale, the more that aggregate demand exceeds aggregate supply, the more rapidly will prices rise:

$$\dot{P} = g\frac{(AD - AS)}{AS} \tag{3}$$

Unemployment

Higher demand for goods will be reflected in higher demand for labour. If there is excess demand for labour in any labour market, wages will rise and frictional unemployment will be lower as people take jobs more readily. The same will apply to the economy as a whole.

$$U = h + j\frac{(AD - AS)^{-1}}{AS} \tag{4}$$

In other words, the greater the excess demand, the lower the unemployment. But unemployment will never reach zero: hence the constant term h.

 Why is the excess demand term, $(AD - AS) \div AS$, expressed to the power of -1 in equation (4)?

If wages are sticky downwards, the Phillips curve will have a more complex formulation and will have a kink in it. Equation (4) will then only apply when there is *excess* demand: when $(AD - AS) \div AS > 0$.

Assume that $AD = AS$, and that there is therefore no demand-pull inflation. Assume also that there is no cost-push inflation either. The economy will be at point x in Figure 19.15. Unemployment is purely equilibrium unemployment. This is often referred to as the natural rate of unemployment (U_n).

Assume now that aggregate demand falls. If wages are sticky downwards, unemployment will rise significantly, but prices will fall only slightly, if at all. The curve is therefore much less steep to the right of point x. It is kinked.

Natural rate of unemployment

The rate of unemployment at which there is no excess or deficiency of demand for labour.

 Under what circumstance might the kink be above a zero inflation level? (For the answer, read on.)

The position of the curve

The *position* of the Phillips curve is given by the constant term a in equation (1) above. The size of this term depends on the *other* factors contributing to inflation:

- Long-run cost-push factors, such as unions consistently bargaining for real wage increases in excess of growth in labour productivity.

- Short-run cost-push factors. These are supply shocks due, say, to sharp increases in world commodity prices or changes in VAT.
- Expectations of inflation. The higher that workers and firms expect inflation to be, the higher will their wage and price increases be.
- The rapidity with which demand is shifting from one sector of the economy to another. The greater the demand shift and the less mobile is labour, the greater will be the excess demand in some sectors and the greater the deficiency of demand in others. Given the kinked nature of the Phillips curve in individual markets as well as nationally, the rise in prices in the excess demand sectors will more than offset any fall in prices in the deficient demand sectors. Note that *aggregate* demand can still equal *aggregate* supply.

A rise in any of these types of inflation will increase the *a* term and thereby shift the Phillips curve upward.

The size of the *a* term also depends on the amount of equilibrium unemployment. If equilibrium unemployment rises – due, say, to increased unemployment benefits encouraging people to spend longer looking for jobs - the value of *a* will increase. In other words, any given level of inflation will now be associated with a higher level of unemployment. The Phillips curve will shift to the right.

Shifts and movements along the curve are illustrated in Figure 19.16.

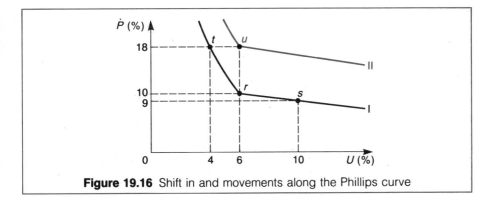

Figure 19.16 Shift in and movements along the Phillips curve

Assume that the non-demand *a* term is contributing 10 per cent to inflation. Assume at first that *AD = AS*: that there is no excess or deficient demand. The economy will be at point *r* on curve I, with 10 per cent inflation. Equilibrium unemployment is 6 per cent. There is no disequilibrium unemployment.

Assume there is no underlying growth in *real* aggregate supply. Nevertheless, aggregate supply in *money* terms is growing at 10 per cent because of inflation. Thus for the economy to be at point *r*, aggregate demand has also to increase by 10 per cent in money terms in order to keep its real value constant. This increase in aggregate *monetary* demand 'validates' the 10 per cent non-demand inflation.

To distinguish the different types of shifts and movements along the Phillips curve let us examine four different scenarios: each is illustrated in Figure 19.16.

Aggregate monetary demand rises by less than 10 per cent (real AD falls)

The economy moves to point *s*. Non-demand factors are still contributing 10 per cent to inflation, but the deficiency of demand causes a downward pressure on inflation of, say, 1 per cent. Inflation will thus be reduced to 9 per cent. The curve is shallow to the right of point *r*, since *real* wages are sticky downwards. This means that workers will resist wage rises below the current 10 per cent rate of inflation. Considerable demand-deficient unemployment may be necessary to bring a mere 1 per cent reduction in inflation. In this example, unemployment rises to 10 per cent.

 If it was *money* wages that were sticky downwards (rather than *real* wages) and the economy was currently at point *r*, what shape would the Phillips curve have?

Aggregate monetary demand rises by more than 10 per cent (real AD rises)

The economy moves to point *t*. Non-demand factors are still contributing 10 per cent to inflation, but there is now demand-pull inflation of 8 per cent. Total inflation is thus 18 per cent. There is a fall in unemployment due to a reduction in equilibrium unemployment. This consists partly of a fall in frictional unemployment as workers take jobs more readily, and partly of a fall in structural unemployment due to a re-emergence of some demand in depressed regions or in declining industries. In this example, unemployment falls to 4 per cent.

A rise in non-demand inflation by 8 per cent

This will shift the whole curve upward by 8 percentage points. It is shown by curve II. If this rise in inflation is validated by an increase in aggregate monetary demand (i.e. if *real AD* stays the same), the economy will move from point *r* to point *u*.

Three examples of a rise in non-demand inflation are as follows:

A short-run supply shock. An example of this is a sudden oil price increase that raises the price level by 8 per cent. Note here that, if it is a *single* increase in oil prices, then once its effects have worked through into higher prices, inflation will return to its previous level (if real *AD* stays constant). The curve shifts back again to curve I and the economy moves back to point *r*.

A long-run change in supply conditions. An example of this would be a growth in the power of unions and firms, which leads unions to attempt to push up the real wage (*W/P*) more rapidly, and firms to attempt to push up prices even faster (i.e. raising *P/W*) in order to raise profits. This leads to a greater 'leap-frogging' of wages and prices.

Changes in these cost-push factors are likely to occur relatively slowly. Thus the shift to curve II, although possibly a permanent shift, may take a relatively long time.

 Might a short-run supply shock in practice develop into a long-run change in supply conditions? Give examples.

Changes in expectations. If expectations of inflation rise, workers will demand higher wage increases than previously and firms will be willing to grant them, knowing that they can put their prices up more than previously. If workers and firms expect an inflation rate of 10 per cent, the curve will remain at position I. If they now expect inflation to rise to 18 per cent, the curve will move to position II.

A rise in equilibrium unemployment

This could be caused by greater unemployment benefits increasing the amount of time that people are prepared to search for a job. It could be caused by the removal of trade barriers, which causes structural unemployment in those sectors unable to compete with imports. Assume that equilibrium unemployment rises by 3 per cent. The Phillips curve will shift 3 per cent points to the right. This is given by curve III in Figure 19.17. Real aggregate supply has fallen. If inflation is to stay constant, real aggregate demand must fall in order to stay equal to real aggregate supply. The economy will move from point *r* to point *v*.

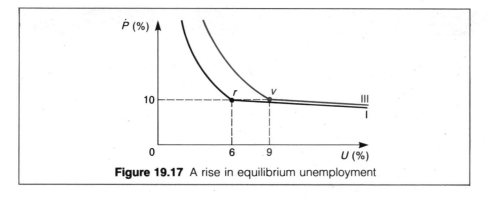

Figure 19.17 A rise in equilibrium unemployment

? What factors would cause (a) a leftward shift of the Phillips curve; (b) a downward shift of the Phillips curve?

What actually happened to the Phillips curve after 1966?

The one thing economists agree on about the Phillips curve is that it no longer exists in its original position. The 1970s and 1980s saw higher unemployment *and* higher inflation than the 1950s and 1960s.

Does a curve exist today at all? If it does, where does it lie? What caused it to shift? Has it changed shape? Is there a difference between a long-run and a short-run Phillips curve? In short, just what is the relationship between inflation and unemployment? Different answers to these questions are given in the following sections.

▲ SUMMARY

1. The Phillips curve can be expressed in terms of the equation: $\dot{P} = a + b(1/U)$. Both inflation and unemployment can be seen to depend on the level of excess demand: inflation directly and unemployment inversely. It is this that relates them in the Phillips curve.

2. The Phillips curve is likely to be kinked if wages are sticky downwards.

3. The position of the curve depends on the *a* term. This in turn depends on non-demand factors contributing to inflation or unemployment. If these non-demand factors change, the value of *a* will change and the curve will shift. A rise in non-demand inflationary factors, such as a rise in costs or inflationary expectations, will shift the curve upwards. A rise in equilibrium unemployment will shift the curve rightwards.

19.3 Inflation and unemployment: the moderate monetarist position

The main contribution of monetarists to the theory of unemployment and inflation is the incorporation of expectations into the Phillips curve. In its simplest form this expectations-augmented Phillips curve may be expressed as:

$$\dot{P} = f(1/U) + \dot{P}^e \tag{5}$$

where $\dot{P}^e$ is the expected rate of inflation.

Thus if people expected a 5 per cent inflation ($\dot{P}^e = 5$ per cent) and if excess demand were causing demand-pull inflation of 3 per cent ($f(1/U) = 3$ per cent), actual inflation would be 8 per cent.

Expectations-augmented Phillips curve

A (short-run) Phillips curve whose position depends on the expected rate of inflation.

Box 19.3

Milton Friedman on Adaptive Expectations

[The adaptive expectations hypothesis] states that anticipations are revised on the basis of the difference between the current rate of inflation and the anticipated rate. If the anticipated rate was, say, 5 per cent but the current rate 10 per cent, the anticipated rate will be revised upward by some fraction of the difference between 10 and 5. As is well known, this implies that the anticipated rate of inflation is an exponentially weighted average of past rates of inflation, the weights declining as one goes further back.[1]

In the simplest adaptive expectations model ($\dot{P}^e_t = \dot{P}_{t-1}$), the 'fraction' referred to by Friedman is 1. More sophisticated versions are examined in Box 19.4.

[1] M. Friedman, 'Unemployment versus inflation', *IEA Occasional Paper*, no. 51 (Institute for Economic Affairs, 1977), p.25.

Monetarists develop their model in the framework of market clearing. Wages are not sticky downward, at least not in the long run. There can be no long-run disequilibrium unemployment: no long-run deficiency of demand.

Adaptive expectations

Adaptive expectations hypothesis

The theory that people base their expectations of inflation on past inflation rates.

What determines the expected rate of inflation ($\dot{P}^e$)? The moderate monetarist position is that it depends on inflation rates *in the past*. This is known as the adaptive expectations hypothesis. What this means is that people learn from experience. If last year they underpredicted the rate of inflation, then this year they will adapt: they will revise their expectations of inflation upwards.

In its simplest form the adaptive expectations hypothesis assumes that the expected rate of inflation this year ($\dot{P}^e_t$) will be the rate that inflation actually was last year ($\dot{P}_{t-1}$):

$$\dot{P}^e_t = \dot{P}_{t-1} \tag{6}$$

To keep the analysis straightforward we will stick to this simple version of the adaptive expectations hypothesis.

Shifts in the short-run Phillips curve and the accelerationist theory

Let us trace the course of inflation and expectations over a number of years in an imaginary economy. To keep the analysis simple, assume there is no growth in the economy.

Year 1. Assume that at the outset, in year 1, there is no inflation of any sort; that none is expected; that $AD = AS$; and that equilibrium unemployment is 8 per cent. The economy will be at point *a* in Figure 19.18 and Table 19.1.

Year 2. Now assume that the government expands aggregate demand in order to reduce unemployment. Unemployment falls to 6 per cent. The economy moves to point *b* along curve I. Inflation has risen to 4 per cent, but people, basing their expectations of inflation on year 1, still expect a zero inflation. There is therefore no shift as yet in the Phillips curve. Curve I corresponds to an expected rate of inflation of zero.

*Box 19.4

Basing Expectations on the Past
More sophisticated adaptive expectations models

More complex adaptive expectations models assume that $\dot{P}^e$ is a weighted average of past rates of inflation:

$$\dot{P}^e_t = a\dot{P}_{t-1} + b\dot{P}_{t-2} + c\dot{P}_{t-3} \ldots + m\dot{P}_{t-n} \qquad (7)$$

where $a + b + c \ldots + m = 1$, and where $a > b > c$, etc.

In other words, people will base their expectations of inflation on the actual inflation rates over the last few years, but with last year's inflation having a bigger influence on people's expectations than the previous year's and so on.

In times of rapidly *accelerating* inflation, people may adjust their expectations of inflation upward by the amount that inflation *rose* last year ($\Delta\dot{P}_{t-1}$). This gives:

$$\Delta\dot{P}^e_t = \Delta\dot{P}_{t-1} \qquad (8)$$

? Under what circumstances will term a in equation (7) be large relative to terms b, c, etc.?

Table 19.1 The accelerationist theory of inflation and inflationary expectations

Year	Point on graph	$\dot{P}$	$= f(1/U) +$	$\dot{P}^e$
1	a	0	= 0 +	0
2	b	4	= 4 +	0
3	c	4	= 0 +	4
4	d	8	= 4 +	4
5	e	12	= 4 +	8
6	f	16	= 4 +	12

Year 3. People now revise their expectations of inflation to the level of year 2. The Phillips curve shifts up by 4 percentage points to position II. If aggregate *monetary* demand continues to rise at the same rate, the whole of the increase will now be absorbed in higher prices. *Real* aggregate demand will fall back to its previous level and the economy will move to point *c*. Unemployment will return to 8 per cent. There is no *demand-pull* inflation now, ($f(1/U) = 0$), but inflation is still 4 per cent due to expectations ($\dot{P}^e = 4$ per cent).

Figure 19.18 The accelerationist theory of inflation and inflationary expectations

Year 4. Assume now that the government expands *real* aggregate demand again so as to reduce unemployment once more to 6 per cent. This time it must expand aggregate *monetary* demand by *more* than it did in year 2, because this time, as well as reducing unemployment, it also has to validate the 4 per cent expected inflation. The economy moves to point d along curve II. Inflation is now 8 per cent.

Year 5. Expected inflation is now 8 per cent (the level of actual inflation in year 4). The Phillips curve shifts up to position III. If the government now tries to keep unemployment at 6 per cent it must expand aggregate monetary demand 4 per cent faster in order to validate the 8 per cent expected inflation. The economy moves to point *e* along curve III. Inflation is now 12 per cent.

Year 6. To keep unemployment at 6 per cent, the government must continue to increase aggregate monetary demand by 4 per cent more than the previous year. As the expected inflation rate goes on rising, the Phillips curve will go on shifting up each year.

Thus in order to keep unemployment below the initial equilibrium rate, inflation must go on *accelerating* each year. For this reason, the adaptive expectations theory of the Phillips curve is sometimes known as the accelerationist theory

The more the government reduces unemployment, the greater the rise in inflation that year, and the more the rise in expectations the following year and each subsequent year; and hence the more rapidly will inflation accelerate. Thus the true longer-term trade-off is between unemployment and the rate of *acceleration* in inflation.

$$\Delta\dot{P} = f(1/U) \tag{9}$$

($\Delta\dot{P}$ may be written $\ddot{P}$)

Note that the upward shift in the Phillips curve will be less rapid if expectations do not fully adjust to last year's inflation rate. The upward shift will be more rapid if expectations adjust to the rate of *increase* in inflation last year ($\Delta\dot{P}_{t-1}$).

 Construct a table like Table 19.1, only this time assume that the government wishes to reduce unemployment to 5 per cent. Assume that every year from year 1 onwards the government is prepared to expand aggregate demand by whatever it takes to do this. If this expansion of demand gives $f(1/U) = 7$ per cent, fill in the table for the first six years. Do you think that after a couple of years people might begin to base their expectations differently?

The long-run Phillips curve and the natural rate of unemployment

As long as there are demand-pull pressures ($f(1/U) > 0$), inflation will accelerate as the expected rate of inflation ($\dot{P}^e$) rises. In the long run, therefore, the Phillips curve will be vertical (see Figure 19.19) at the rate of unemployment where real aggregate demand equals *real* aggregate supply. This is the rate of unemployment that monetarists call the *natural rate* (U_n). It is sometimes also known as the non-accelerating-inflation rate of unemployment (NAIRU).

The implication for government policy is that expansionary monetary and fiscal policy can only reduce unemployment below U_n in the *short* run. In the long run, the effect will be purely inflationary.

 What will determine the speed at which inflation accelerates?

Accelerationist theory

The theory that unemployment can only be reduced below the natural rate at the cost of accelerating inflation

Natural rate of unemployment or non-accelerating-inflation rate of unemployment (NAIRU)

The rate of unemployment consistent with a constant rate of inflation: the rate of unemployment at which the vertical long-run Phillips curve cuts the horizontal axis.

Figure 19.19 The long-run Phillips 'curve'

The effects of deflation

Let us now move on a few years from Table 19.1. Assume that the economy has returned to the natural level of unemployment: $f(1/U) = 0$. The economy is therefore on the long-run Phillips curve. But, due to past excess demand, the expected rate of inflation is 20 per cent. The economy is thus at point j on short-run Phillips curve X in Figure 19.20.

The government now decides to make the control of inflation its main priority. It therefore reduces the growth of aggregate monetary demand *below* the rate of inflation. Real aggregate demand falls. Let us assume that there is a 2 per cent downward pressure on inflation: $f(1/U) = -2$. Inflation thus falls to 18%. But unemployment rises from 8 per cent to 13 per cent. The economy moves along curve X to point k.

Next year the expected rate of inflation will fall to 18 per cent to match, and if real demand is still being deflated by the same amount ($f(1/U) = -2$), actual inflation will fall to 16 per cent. The economy moves to point l on curve XI.

If the government maintains unemployment at 13 per cent, inflation will continue to fall by 2 per cent a year. After ten years of unemployment at 13 per cent the economy could return to point a, with unemployment falling back to U_n.

Figure 19.20 The effects of deflation

> **?** Construct a table like Table 19.1, only this time assume that in year 1 the economy is in recession with high unemployment, but also high inflation due to high inflationary expectations as a result of past excess demand. Assume that in year 1 $\dot{P} = 30$ per cent, $f(1/U) = -6$ per cent and $\dot{P}^e = 36$ per cent. Continue the table for as many years as it takes for inflation to be 'squeezed out' of the economy (assuming that the government keeps aggregate demand at a low enough level to maintain $f(1/U) = -6$ per cent throughout).

How quickly can inflation be eliminated?

The short-run Phillips curve is relatively shallow to the right of U_n. Thus to get a relatively rapid fall in inflation, unemployment may have to be very high indeed.

Moderate monetarists therefore present two alternative routes to eliminating inflation:

The quick route. This involves a *severe* deflation. Unemployment rises to very high rates and the economy is plunged into a deep recession. However, the short-run Phillips curve shifts down fairly rapidly as the expected rate of inflation ($\dot{P}^e$) falls quite quickly. Inflation may be squeezed out of the economy within two or three years. This approach could be called the 'short, sharp shock'.

The slow route. This involves a *mild* deflation. Unemployment rises perhaps one or two percentage points above the natural rate. Inflation falls only slightly in the first year, and thus $\dot{P}^e$ falls only slowly the next year and each subsequent year. Although less painful, this approach may take many years to eliminate inflation.

Explanations of stagflation

The moderate monetarist explanation of stagflation – the simultaneous rise in both unemployment and inflation – can now be presented quite simply. There are two possibilities: clockwise loops and rightward shifts in the long-run Phillips curve.

Clockwise Phillips loops

Consider a ten-year cycle. This is illustrated in Figure 19.21. The economy starts at position *a* in year 0. There is no inflation and the economy is at the natural rate of unemployment. The government over the next three years pursues an expansionary policy in order to reduce unemployment. The economy moves up through points *b*, *c* and *d*.

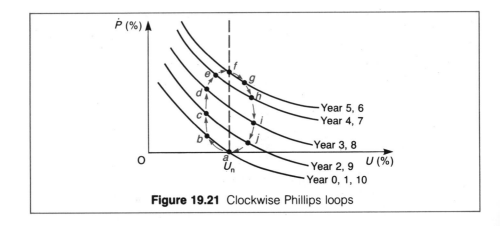

Figure 19.21 Clockwise Phillips loops

Box 19.5

The Political Trade Cycle (Part II)
The art of looping the loop
(see Box 12.11 for Part I)

Imagine that a politically naïve government has been fulfilling election promises to cure unemployment, cut taxes and increase welfare spending. In Figure 19.21 this is shown by a move from points *a* to *b* to *c*.

To its dismay, by the time the next election comes, inflation is accelerating and unemployment is rising again. The economy is moving from point *d* to *e* to *f*. You would hardly be surprised to learn that it loses the election!

But now suppose a much more politically adroit government is elected. What does it do? The answer is that it does politically unpopular things at first, so that before the next election it can do nice things and curry favour with the electorate.

The first thing it does is to have a tough Budget and to raise interest rates. 'We are having to clear up the economic mess left by the last government.' It thus engineers a recession and begins to squeeze down inflationary expectations. The economy moves from point *f* to *g* to *h*.

But people have very short memories (despite opposition attempts to remind them). After a couple of years of misery, the government announces that the economy has 'begun to turn the corner'. Things are looking up.

Inflation has fallen and unemployment has stopped rising. The economy has moved from point *h* to *i* to *j*.

'Thanks to prudent management of the economy', claims the Chancellor, 'I am now in a position to reduce taxes and to allow modest increases in government expenditure.' Unemployment falls rapidly; the economy grows rapidly; the economy moves from point *j* to *a* to *b*.

The government's popularity soars; the pre-election 'give-away' Budget is swallowed by the electorate who trustingly believe that similar ones will follow if the government is returned to office. The government wins the election.

Then comes the nasty medicine again. But who will be blamed this time?

? 1. Why might a government sometimes 'get it wrong' and find itself at the wrong part of the Phillips loop at the time of an election?
2. Which electoral system would most favour a government being re-elected: the US fixed term system with presidents being elected every four years, or the UK system where the government can choose to hold an election any time within five years of the last one?

The government then starts worrying about inflation. It allows unemployment to rise somewhat, but being still below U_n, there is still demand-pull inflation. The economy moves to point *e*. The government now allows unemployment to rise to U_n, but the Phillips curve still shifts up as expectations catch up with last year's inflation. The economy moves from point *e* to point *f*.

Thereafter the government allows unemployment to rise further, and the economy eventually returns to point *a*, via points *g*, *h*, *i* and *j*. The economy has thus moved through a clockwise loop.

Stagflation is easy to see. From points *d* to *f*, both unemployment *and* inflation are rising. What is more, several points are to the 'north-east' of other earlier points. For example, point *g* is north-east of point *c*. In other words, inflation *and* unemployment in year 6 (point *g*) are worse than in year 2 (point *c*).

? Under what circumstances would a Phillips loop be (a) tall and thin; (b) short and wide?

Rightward shifts in the long-run Phillips curve
If frictional or structural unemployment rise (due, say, to increased unemployment benefits), U_n will increase. The long-run Phillips curve will shift to the right.

Assume that the economy was initially on the long-run Phillips curve with $U_n = 10$ per cent and a stable inflation rate of 5 per cent. U_n now rises to 15 per cent. The government uses demand management policy to keep the rise in unemployment to only 13 per cent. But this is now *below* U_n and thus inflation will increase. Thus both inflation *and* unemployment have risen.

Evidence

The evidence since 1971 fits in with the above moderate monetarist explanation. (But note that it also fits in with other explanations too!) In Figure 19.22 loops can clearly be seen. At the same time, U_n would seem to be increasing from about 2.5 per cent in 1972/73 to about 4.4 per cent in 1978 to over 10 per cent in 1985, and then falling to about 8 per cent in the late 1980s.

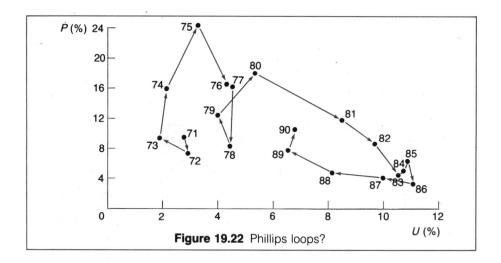

Figure 19.22 Phillips loops?

Policy implications

Monetarists make a sharp distinction between demand-side policies (which for them means monetary policy) and supply-side policies.

Monetary policy in the long run can only be used to control inflation and not unemployment. It will merely move the economy up or down the long-run Phillips curve. Given that inflation is undesirable, monetarists argue for a tight control over money supply. Expansionary monetary policy could only ever bring a *temporary* reduction in unemployment below U_n. But likewise a deflationary monetary policy will only bring a temporary rise in unemployment above U_n.

To reduce unemployment permanently, *supply-side* policies should be used. For monetarists this means policies to reduce impediments to the working of the free market. By reducing frictional and/or structural unemployment, such policies will shift the long-run Phillips curve back to the left.

▲ SUMMARY

1. The moderate monetarist analysis of the relationship between inflation and unemployment is based on the adaptive expectations hypothesis. In its simplest form the hypothesis states that the expected rate of inflation this year is what it actually was last year: $P^e_t = P_{t-1}$.

2. If there is excess demand in the economy, producing upward pressure on wages and prices, initially unemployment will fall. The reason is that workers and firms will believe that wage and price increases represent *real* wage and price increases. Thus workers are prepared to take jobs more readily and firms choose to produce more. But as people's expectations adapt upwards to these higher wages and prices, so ever increasing rises in demand will be necessary to maintain unemployment below the natural rate. Price and wage rises will accelerate: i.e. inflation will rise.

3. The Phillips curve, according to monetarist analysis, is thus vertical at the natural rate of unemployment.

4. If an economy suffering from high inflation is deflated, initially unemployment will rise above the natural rate. But as expectations adapt downwards, so the short-run Phillips curve will shift downwards and inflation will fall. Eventually the economy will return to zero inflation at the natural rate of unemployment.

5. This position can be reached more quickly if the government deflates sharply, but then in the short run the rate of unemployment may rise substantially above the natural rate.

6. Stagflation can be explained in this model either by a movement from 9 o'clock to 12 o'clock round a clockwise Phillips loop, or by a rightward shift in the vertical Phillips curve combined with a mild reflationary policy.

7. The evidence since 1970 is consistent with clockwise Phillips loops.

19.4 Inflation and unemployment: the new classical position

Over the last 10–15 years a new more extreme version of monetarism has gained a considerable following. This is the new classical school. Leading exponents of new classical macroeconomics include Robert Lucas and Thomas Sargent in the USA and Patrick Minford in the UK.

The *moderate* monetarists argue that the aggregate supply and Phillips curves are vertical in the long run. The policy implication of this is that demand management can have no effect on *long*-run output and employment.

The *new classical* economists take a more extreme view. They argue that the aggregate supply and Phillips curves are vertical also in the *short run*. There is, therefore, no role for demand management policy at all – even in the short run. The only effect of a rise in aggregate demand will be to raise prices.

There are two crucial assumptions in new classical macroeconomics:

● Prices and wages are flexible, and thus markets clear very rapidly.
● Expectations are 'rational', but are based on imperfect information.

Let us examine these.

New classical school

The school of economists which believes that markets clear virtually instantaneously and that expectations are formed 'rationally'.

Flexible wages and prices

The moderate monetarists assume that markets have a tendency to clear. Prices and wages are fairly flexible, and therefore disequilibrium unemployment is merely a temporary phenomenon. This was also the position of the classical economists of the 1920s and 1930s.

The new classical economists take this further. They assume that markets clear virtually instantaneously. There is thus no disequilibrium unemployment, even in the short run. All unemployment, therefore, is *equilibrium* unemployment, or 'voluntary

---

Box 19.6

The Rational Expectations Revolution
Trying to 'unfool' the economics profession

The rational expectations revolution swept through the economics profession in the 1970s in a way that no other set of ideas had done since Keynes. Although largely associated with the free-market, non-interventionist wing of economics, the rational expectations revolution has been far more wide reaching. Even economists implacably opposed to the free market have nevertheless incorporated rational expectations into their models.

The rational expectations revolution is founded on a very simple idea. People base their expectations of the future on the information they have available. They don't just look at the past, they also look at current information, including what the government is saying and doing and what various commentators have to say.

The new classical economists use rational expectations in the following context. If the *long-run* Phillips curve is vertical, so that an expansionary policy will in the end merely lead to inflation, it will be difficult for the government to fool people that this will not happen. If employers, unions, city financiers, economic advisers, journalists, etc. all expect this to happen, then it will do: and it will happen in the *short run*. Why should firms produce more in response to a rise in demand if their costs are going to rise by just as much? Why should higher wages attract workers to move jobs, if wages everywhere are going up? Why should firms and unions not seek price and wage rises fully in line with the expected inflation?

But can the government not surprise people? The point here is that 'surprising' people really only means 'fooling' them – making them believe that an expansionary policy really *will* reduce unemployment. But why should

the public be fooled? Why should people believe smooth-talking government ministers rather than the whole host of critics of the government, from the opposition, to economic commentators, to the next-door neighbour?

The rational expectations school revised the old saying, 'You can't fool all the people all the time' to 'You can hardly fool the people at all.' And if that is so, argue the new classical economists, unemployment can only momentarily be brought below its natural level.

Two of the most famous rational expectations economists are Robert Lucas and Thomas Sargent. Robert Lucas, like Milton Friedman and many other famous conservative economists, has his academic base in the University of Chicago, where he has been a professor since 1974. Tom Sargent is professor at the University of Minnesota.

Both have written extensively on the subject and have developed highly complex models: complex in the way in which the expectations themselves are modelled, and complex in the way in which they are incorporated into the models of the economy. They have both undertaken extensive testing of their models, involving sophisticated econometric techniques – far too sophisticated (you will be relieved to know) for beginning students!

In recent years they have gone beyond the simple context of the new classical world of perfect markets with instant market clearing, and have considered the role of rational expectations when markets are distorted. In this context, government policy *can* be effective. For example, supply-side policies can be directed to removing market distortions.

---

unemployment' as new classical economists tend to call it. Increases in unemployment are therefore due to an increase in the natural level of unemployment, as people choose not to take jobs due to a lack of incentives to do so.

Rational expectations

Rational expectations

Expectations based on the *current* situation. These expectations are based on the information people have to hand. Whilst this information may be imperfect and therefore people will make errors, these errors will be random.

The moderate monetarist analysis is based on *adaptive* expectations. Expectations of inflation are based on *past* information and therefore take a time to catch up with changes in aggregate demand. Thus for a short time a rise in aggregate demand will raise output and employment above the natural level, while prices and wages are still relatively low.

The new classical analysis is based on rational expectations. Rational expectations are not based on past rates of inflation. Instead they are based on the current state of the economy and the current policies being pursued by the government. Workers and firms look at the information available to them – at the various forecasts that are

Box 19.7

Forecasting the Weather:
An Example of Rational Expectations
Getting it right 'on average'

'What's the weather going to be like tomorrow?' If you are thinking of having a picnic, you will want to know the answer before deciding.

So what do you do? You could base your assessment on past information. Yesterday was fine; so was the previous day. Today is glorious. So, you think to yourself, it's a good bet that tomorrow will be fine too. If, on the other hand, the weather has been very changeable recently, you may feel that it's wiser not to take the risk. These 'forecasts' are examples of *adaptive* expectations: your forecasts are based on the actual weather over the last few days.

But would you really base such a crucial decision as to whether or not to have a picnic on something so unreliable? Wouldn't you rather take on board more information to help you make up your mind?

The first thing that might come to mind is the old saying that a British summer is three fine days and a thunder storm. We've just had the three fine days, you think to yourself, so perhaps we'd better stay at home tomorrow.

Or, being a bit more scientific about it, you turn on the weather forecast. Seeing loads of sunshine symbols all over the map you decide to take a chance.

Basing your expectations this way on current information (including even seeing whether there is a red sky that night) is an example of *rational* expectations.

So you go on your picnic, and, guess what, it rains!

'I bet if we had decided to stay at home it would have been fine', you grumble, as you eat your soggy sandwiches.

What you are acknowledging is that your decision was made on *imperfect* information. But the decision was still rational. It was still the best decision you could have made on the information available to you.

Weather forecasters make mistakes. But they are just as likely to get it wrong in predicting a sunny day as in predicting a wet day. It is still rational to base your decisions on their forecasts provided they are reasonably accurate.

? Under what circumstances might weather forecasters have a tendency to err on the side of pessimism or optimism? If you knew this tendency, how would this affect your decisions about picnics, hanging out the washing or watering the garden?

---

published, at various economic indicators and the assessments of them by various commentators, at government pronouncements, etc. Then, on the basis of this information, they predict as well as they can what the rate of inflation will be. It is in this sense that the expectations are 'rational': people use their reason to assess the future on the basis of current information.

But forecasters frequently get it wrong, and so do economic commentators! And the government does not always do what it says it will. Thus workers and firms will be basing expectations on *imperfect information*. Some versions of rational expectations theory assume that workers and firms will make the best forecasts possible on the basis of this imperfect information. Other versions assume that they may make very poor use of this information. But either way, people will frequently forecast incorrectly.

The crucial point about the rational expectations theory is that these errors in prediction are *random*. People's predictions of inflation are just as likely to be too high as too low. Thus, on *average*, it is assumed that people will forecast correctly.[2]

---

[2] The rational expectations hypothesis can be stated as:

$$\dot{P}^e_t = \dot{P}_t + \epsilon_t \qquad (\sum_{l=1}^{l=n} \epsilon = 0)$$

In other words, the expected rate of inflation for any time period ($\dot{P}^e_t$) will be the actual rate of inflation that will be experienced in that time period ($\dot{P}_t$) plus an error term (ϵ_t). This error term may be quite large but is equally likely to be positive or negative. (Thus when you sum (Σ) the error terms over the years, the positive and negative values will cancel each other out and the sum will therefore be zero.) In other words, people have no systematic tendency to underpredict or overpredict the rate of inflation.

Aggregate supply and the Phillips curve when expectations are correct

If people are correct in their expectations, and if the long-run aggregate supply and Phillips curves are vertical, so too will be the short-run curves. In the moderate monetarist (adaptive expectations) model, the short-run *AS* curve is upward sloping (and the short-run Phillips curve downward sloping) only because expectations lag behind any changes in aggregate demand. Once expectations have adapted, the effect is felt purely in terms of price changes. Output and employment stay at the natural level in the long run.

In the new classical (rational expectations) model, there is *no* lag in expectations. If their information is correct, people will rationally predict that output and employment will stay at the natural level. They predict that any change in aggregate *monetary* demand will be reflected purely in terms of changes in prices, and that real aggregate demand will remain the same. If real aggregate demand remains the same, so will the demand for and supply of labour and the demand for and supply of goods. Thus, even in the *short* run, output and employment will stay at the natural level.

Let us see how the adaptive expectations and the rational expectations models analyze the effects of an increase in aggregate demand. Figure 19.23 uses simple aggregate demand and supply curves. Diagram (a) gives the adaptive expectations analysis. Diagram (b) gives the rational expectations analysis.

In both diagrams there is an initial equilibrium at point *a*. This is a long-run equilibrium, where aggregate demand (AD_1) equals long-run aggregate supply (*LRAS*). Price is stable and is at the level of P_1. The short-run supply curve with P_1 as the *expected* price level is given by $SRAS_1$. Note that this is upward sloping in *both* diagrams because it shows how much will be supplied *if* (and only if) people expect price to remain at P_1.

Now assume that the government raises aggregate demand to AD_2. What will happen to prices and output?

In Figure 19.23(a), people base their expectations of prices on the past. In other words, at first they expect the price level to stay at P_1. The economy thus moves to point *b*, where $AD_2 = SRAS_1$. Output rises to Q_2 and the price level rises to P_2. Then over time, as price expectations rise, the short-run aggregate supply curve shifts upwards, eventually reaching $SRAS_2$. Long-run equilibrium is thus at point *c*, where $AD_2 = LRAS$. In the short run, therefore, if the government expands aggregate demand there will be a rise in output and employment. It is only in the long run that

Figure 19.23 The effects of an increase in aggregate demand

the effect is confined to higher prices. The actual length of time it takes to reach point c will depend on how quickly expectations adjust upwards.

In Figure 19.23(b), people correctly anticipate the full price effects of any increase in aggregate demand. The short-run aggregate supply curve based on a particular price (e.g. $SRAS_1$ based on a price level P_1) cannot be moved along. The moment aggregate demand shifts to the right, people will correctly anticipate a rise in the price level. Thus the moment the economy begins to move up along $SRAS_1$ from point a, the whole $SRAS$ curve will shift upwards. As a result the economy moves *directly* to point c. Thus the *actual* short-run supply curve is vertical and, assuming expectations are correct, will be identical to the long-run 'curve'.

? Show these effects of an increase in aggregate demand from both the adaptive expectations and rational expectations points of view, only this time show the effects on Phillips curves.

Aggregate supply and the Phillips curve when expectations are incorrect

Although over the years people's expectations are assumed to be correct on average, it is more than likely that in any one year they will be wrong. What implication does this have for output and employment?

The goods market

Assume that aggregate demand increases but that firms *under*predict the resulting rate of inflation: $\dot{P}^e < \dot{P}$. Firms do not realize that the increased expenditure on their product will be offset by an increase in costs. As a result, as profit maximizers, they decide to produce more. Thus if the government catches people unawares and unexpectedly boosts demand, then output will rise as firms, underpredicting the rate of inflation, believe that *real* demand has risen.

But in a rational expectations framework, this is just luck on the government's side. Firms might just as well have thought the government would give an even bigger boost to aggregate demand than it actually did. In this case firms would have *over*predicted the rate of inflation, and as a result would have cut their output, believing that real demand had fallen. This is illustrated in Figure 19.24.

As in Figure 19.23, aggregate demand is initially at AD_1 and the short-run

Figure 19.24 How a rise in aggregate demand could cause a fall in national output

aggregate supply curve based on an expected price of P_1 is given by $SRAS_1$. The long-run aggregate supply curve is vertical at the natural level of output.

Now assume that the government boosts aggregate demand in an attempt to raise output and employment. But let us assume that people *overpredict* the amount by which demand will rise. They *believe* that the government will raise aggregate demand to AD_2. They therefore adjust their price expectations upwards to P_2, with the effect that the short-run aggregate supply curve shifts up to $SRAS_2$. In practice, however, the government only raises demand to AD_3. The result is that the price level only rises to P_3 and the level of output actually *falls*, to Q_3.

 Show diagrammatically how an *underprediction* of inflation would lead to a *rise* in output if the government raised aggregate demand.

The labour market

As before, let us assume that the government raises aggregate demand more than people expect so that people underpredict the rate of inflation: $\dot{P}^e < \dot{P}$.

This means that workers will believe that they are getting a higher real wage (W/P) than they really are: $(W/P)^e > W/P$. They will supply more labour. In Figure 19.25, the labour supply curve shifts from S_1 to S_2. Employment rises above the natural level Q_1 (where expectations are correct), to Q_2. If only labour underpredicts the rate of inflation, this rise in employment to Q_2 is the only short-run effect.

If, however, firms underpredict the rate of inflation too, the effect on employment will be more complicated. On the one level, as explained above, firms will want to produce more, and thus the demand for labour will tend to increase. For example, it might shift to D_2 in Figure 19.25, and thus employment would rise to Q_3. On the other hand, given that they are underpredicting the rate of inflation, they will believe that any given level of money wages (W) represents a higher level of *real* wages $(W/P)^e$ than it really does (W/P). They will tend, therefore, to employ fewer people at each wage rate, and the demand curve will shift to the left. Thus, depending on which way the demand curve shifts, firms could employ more or less labour than Q_2.

If people *over*predict the rate of inflation, employment will fall as workers believe that their real wage is lower than it really is and therefore work less; and output will fall as firms believe their product's relative price has fallen.

Thus output and employment can vary from their natural level when people make errors in their predictions of inflation. But the short-run AS and Phillips curves will still be vertical because these errors are random. Errors in prediction simply shift the curves. Underprediction of inflation shifts the short-run Phillips curve to the left (and

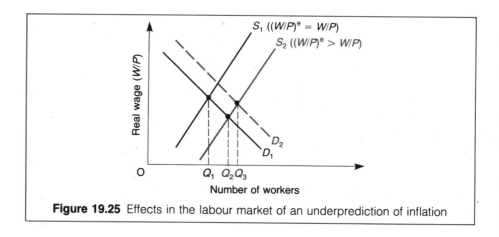

Figure 19.25 Effects in the labour market of an underprediction of inflation

Figure 19.26 Short-run Phillips curves

the *AS* curve to the right) as unemployment temporarily falls below the natural level (and output rises above its natural level). Overprediction of inflation shifts the Phillips curve to the right (and the *AS* curve to the left). This is shown in Figure 19.26. The average position for the short-run Phillips curve will be at U_n.

 Should the government therefore simply give up as far as curing unemployment is concerned? (For the answer, see below.)

'Sticky' wages and prices

If people do make mistakes in their predictions, they will attempt to rectify them. If wages and prices are highly flexible, they will rapidly adjust as people realize their mistakes. Deviations from the natural level of output and employment will be quickly eliminated.

In most labour markets, however, wages change only at intervals. Typically, wage negotiations take place annually and fix the wage rate for the whole year. Thus if workers underpredict the rate of inflation, the wage cannot be corrected until next year's negotiations.

Similarly, in many goods markets, prices are changed relatively infrequently. This may be due to the administrative costs of changing price lists, or the desire not to upset customers, or the desire to collude with other firms.

In either case, an unanticipated rise in aggregate demand will not fully feed through into inflation until these lags in wage and price changes have worked through. In the meantime there may be a temporary disequilibrium, a shortage of labour and goods, and a resulting rise in employment and output.

In the case of an unanticipated *fall* in aggregate demand, there will be a temporary surplus of labour and goods until wages and prices can adjust downwards. In other words, there will be some temporary disequilibrium unemployment.

(Note that under strict new classical assumptions this cannot arise as there is total flexibility of wages and prices.)

Policy implications

If the new classical analysis is correct, anticipated changes in aggregate demand will have no effect on output and employment. *Un*anticipated changes in aggregate demand will have some effect, but only for as long as it takes people to realize their mistake and for their wages and prices to be corrected. Given rational expectations, people can only be fooled in this way by luck. There is no way that a government can

Box 19.8

The Boy Who Cried Wolf
A government had better mean what it says

Do you remember the parable of the boy who cried, 'Wolf!'?

There was once this little village on the edge of the forest. The villagers used to keep chickens, but, when no one was around, wolves would come out of the forest and carry off the chickens. So one of the boys in the village was given the job of keeping a lookout for wolves.

One day for a joke the boy called out, 'Wolf, wolf! I see a wolf!' even though there was none. All the villagers came rushing out of their houses or back from the fields to catch the wolf. As you might expect, they were very angry to find that it was a false alarm.

The next day, thinking that this was great fun, the boy played the same trick again. Everyone came rushing out, and they were even more angry to find that they had been fooled again. But the boy just grinned.

The next day, when everyone was away in the fields, a wolf stalked into the village. The boy, spotting the animal, cried out 'Wolf, wolf! I see a wolf!' But the people in the fields said to each other, 'We're not going to be fooled this time. We've had enough of his practical jokes.' And so they carried on working.

Meanwhile, back in the village, the wolf was killing all the chickens. But the boy was too small to stop it on his own. So he carried on shouting at the top of his voice, 'Wolf, wolf! The wolf is killing the chickens! Come quick!' But as you can guess, still no one came.

You can probably also guess what the villagers said when they returned in the evening to find just a large pile of feathers.

A government says, 'We will take tough action to bring the rate of inflation down to 2 per cent.' Now of course this might be a 'joke' in the sense that the government doesn't really expect to succeed or even seriously to try, but is merely attempting to persuade unions to curb their wage demands. But if unions *believe* in both the government's intentions and its ability to succeed, the 'joke' may pay off. Some unions may well moderate their pay demands.

But some may not. What is more, the government may decide to give tax cuts to boost its popularity and stimulate growth, knowing that union pay demands are generally quite moderate. As a result inflation soars.

But can the government get away with it a second or third time? It's like the boy who cried, 'Wolf!' After a time people will simply not believe the government. If they see the government boosting aggregate demand, they will say to themselves, 'Here comes inflation. We'd better demand higher wages to compensate.'

? Does this parable support the adaptive or the rational expectations hypothesis?

systematically use demand management policy to keep output and employment above the natural level.

The new classical economists therefore totally reject Keynesian demand management policy, even in the short run. Monetary policy should be used to control inflation, but neither fiscal nor monetary policy can be used to increase output and employment. Similarly, there is no fear of a deflationary monetary policy reducing output and employment and leading to a recession. The reduction in aggregate demand will simply lead to lower inflation. Output and unemployment will remain at the natural level.

Thus for new classicists, the problems of inflation and unemployment are totally separate. Inflation is caused by excessive growth in the money supply and should be controlled by monetary policy. Unemployment is due to shifts in the natural rate of unemployment and should be controlled by supply-side policies designed to increase the incentives to work.

To prevent unanticipated changes in aggregate demand and thus to prevent unemployment deviating from its natural level, new classical economists, like moderate monetarists, advocate the announcement of clear monetary rules and then sticking to them.

If the government announced that it would, come what may, reduce the growth of money supply to *zero* next year, what (according to new classical economists) would happen? How might their answer be criticized?

▲ SUMMARY

1. The new classical theory assumes flexible prices and wages in the short run as well as in the long run. It also assumes that people base their expectations of inflation on a rational assessment of the *current* situation.
2. People may predict wrongly, but they are equally likely to underpredict or to overpredict. On average over the years they will predict correctly.
3. The rational expectations theory implies that not only the long-run but also the short-run *AS* and Phillips curves will be vertical. If people correctly predict the rate of inflation, they will correctly predict that any increase in aggregate *monetary* demand will simply be reflected in higher prices. Total output and employment will remain the same: at the natural level.
4. If people underpredict the rate of inflation, they will believe that there has been a *real* increase in aggregate

demand, and thus output and employment will increase. But they are just as likely to overpredict the rate of inflation, in which case they will believe that real aggregate demand has fallen. The result is that output and employment will fall.
5. When the government adopts fiscal and monetary policies, people will rationally predict their effects. Given that people's predictions are equally likely to err on either side, fiscal and monetary policies are useless as means of controlling output and employment.
6. If, contrary to new classical assumptions, wages and prices are sticky, then even if expectations are rationally based, there will be *temporary* changes in output and employment as a result of any changes in aggregate demand. When prices and wages have adjusted, however, output and employment will return to the natural level.

19.5 Inflation and unemployment: the modern Keynesian position

Keynesians in the 1950s and early 1960s looked to aggregate demand to explain inflation and unemployment. Their approach was typically that of the inflationary/deflationary gap model. Although they recognized the existence of some cost-push inflation and some equilibrium unemployment, these factors were seen as relatively constant. As a result there was thought to be a relatively stable inverse relationship between inflation and unemployment, as depicted by the Phillips curve. Governments could trade off inflation against unemployment by manipulating aggregate demand.

Modern developments of the Keynesian model

Keynesians still see aggregate demand as playing the crucial role in determining the level of inflation, output and employment. They still argue that the free market works inefficiently: it frequently does not clear; price signals are distorted by economic power; most wages and many prices are 'sticky'; and most importantly, the free market is unlikely to settle at full employment.

They still argue, therefore, that it is vital for governments to intervene actively to prevent either a slump in demand or an over-expansion of demand.

Nevertheless the Keynesian position has undergone three major modifications in recent years. This has been in response to the problem of stagflation and the inability of the traditional Keynesian model to explain it. The three modifications are as follows:

- An increased importance attached to cost-push factors.
- An increased importance attached to equilibrium unemployment.
- The incorporation of the theory of expectations: either adaptive or rational.

Cost-push explanations: growth in monopoly power

Most Keynesians argue that the Phillips curve has shifted to the right. A major explanation for this is the increased exercise of monopoly power at home and abroad.

The breakdown of the original Phillips curve in the late 1960s and early 1970s was accompanied by growing industrial unrest, with an increased number of strikes and other forms of industrial action. At the same time there was growing concentration of monopoly power in industry, with a large number of mergers and take-overs. Oil price and other commodity price increases provided a further supply shock.

Many economists saw these developments as the major cause of the stagflation of the 1970s and early 1980s. Governments, faced by higher inflation, attempted to deal with the problem by using (amongst other things) deflationary policies. This is illustrated in Figure 19.27.

Figure 19.27 A cost-push shift in the Phillips curve

Assume that the economy is initially at point a on Phillips curve I. There is a politically acceptable level of unemployment U_1 and inflation $\dot{P}_1$.

Now assume that, as a result of cost-push pressures, the Phillips curve shifts to position II. The government responds to the new cost inflation by pursuing mildly deflationary policies. Unemployment rises and the economy moves to point b. The movement from a to b represents stagflation. The growth in unemployment is due to the government's refusal to validate the increases in costs. The unemployment level *could* be reduced back to U_1 by expanding aggregate monetary demand sufficiently, but then the economy would move to point c with inflation of $\dot{P}_3$.

The preferred solution to this stagflation would be to try to shift the Phillips curve back again. For this reason, many Keynesians advocate some form of prices and incomes policy (see section 20.3). If such a policy succeeded in reducing cost inflation, aggregate demand could be expanded again, and the economy could move back from point b to point a.

> **?** Assume that the Phillips curve has shifted from position I to II in Figure 19.27.
> Assume that the government blames the cost-push inflation on a growth in the power and militancy of trade unions. Its long-term goal is to reduce this power by passing anti-union legislation, and hence to get the Phillips curve to shift back again. However, it believes that it will only be able to do this if it can weaken unions' resistance to the government in the short term by having a large rise in unemployment. Trace out the path from point a in the beginning and eventually back to point a at the end.

Target real wage theory

The theory that unions bargain for target real wage increases each year irrespective of the level of real growth in the economy.

Cost-push explanations: target real wages

A major development in Keynesian theory in the 1970s was the theory of the target real wage Evidence was used to show that unions bargain for a given *real* wage

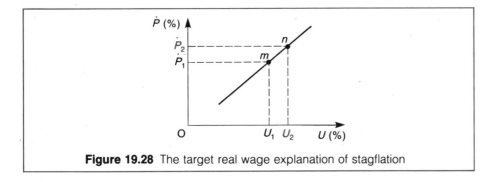

Figure 19.28 The target real wage explanation of stagflation

increase each year. If the growth in the economy is sufficient to pay this increase, there will be no cost inflation. But if workers start bargaining for a higher real wage increase (perhaps due to their increased monopoly power), or alternatively if the growth in the economy slows down, then there will be increased cost pressures as the demands for real wage increases cannot be met.

In its extreme form, this theory can give an upward-sloping Phillips curve. In Figure 19.28, the economy is initially at point *m*. Assume that real aggregate demand now falls. Output and employment fall. Unemployment rises from U_1 to U_2 and the growth in real wages falls. Unions use their monopoly power to attempt to maintain the target growth in their wages. But with no growth in output the effect is merely to fuel inflation. Inflation rises from P_1 to P_2, and the economy moves from point *m* to point *n*. This is a movement *along* the curve because the higher unemployment (and lower output) has caused the higher inflation.

> **?** 1. If trade unions decide to bargain for higher real wage increases, what effect will this have on the curve?
>
> 2. What will determine the *slope* of the curve?

A more moderate version of this theory accepts that the power of unions to force through such wage increases is limited when they are faced with growing unemployment. The more moderate version, therefore, simply argues that the attempt to maintain target real wage increases will make the downward-sloping Phillips curve less steep.

The growth in equilibrium unemployment

Most Keynesians include growth in equilibrium unemployment as part of the explanation of a rightward shift in the Phillips curve. In particular, Keynesians highlight the considerable structural rigidities in the economy in a period of rapid industrial change. The changes include the following:

- Dramatic changes in technology. The microchip revolution, for example, had led to many traditional jobs becoming obsolete.
- Competition from abroad. The introduction of new products from abroad, often of superior quality to UK goods, or produced at lower costs, had led to the decline of many older industries: e.g. the textile industry.
- Shifts in demand away from the products of older labour-intensive industries to new capital-intensive products.

Keynesians argue that the free market simply cannot cope with these changes without a large rise in structural/technological unemployment. Labour is not sufficiently mobile – either geographically or occupationally – to move to areas where there are labour shortages or into jobs where there are skill shortages.

One of the worst manifestations of this problem is regional unemployment and regional decline: a problem made worse when the declining industries are concentrated in already depressed geographical regions. Keynesians argue that the free market does not provide enough incentives for new firms to move into these regions.

1. What effect will these developments have had on (a) the Phillips curve; (b) the aggregate supply curve?
2. What policy implications follow from these arguments?

The incorporation of expectations

Some Keynesians incorporate adaptive expectations into their models. Others incorporate rational expectations. Either way their models differ from monetarist models in two important respects:

● Prices and wages are not perfectly flexible. Markets are characterized by various rigidities.
● Expectations influence *output* and *employment* decisions, not just pricing decisions.

Price and wage rigidities are likely to be greater downwards than upwards. It is thus necessary to separate the analysis of a decrease in aggregate demand from that of an increase.

Expansion of aggregate demand

Unless the economy is at full employment or very close to it, Keynesians argue that an expansion of demand *will* lead to an increase in output and employment, even in the long run after expectations have fully adjusted.

In Figure 19.29, assume that the economy is at the bottom of a recession, with high unemployment (U_1) but at the same time some cost inflation. Inflation is constant at $\dot{P}_1$, with expectations of inflation at $\dot{P}_1$ also. The economy is at point *a*.

Now assume that the economy begins to recover. Aggregate demand rises. As there is plenty of slack in the economy, output can rise and unemployment fall. The economy moves to point *b* on short-run Phillips curve I. The rise in inflation will feed through into expectations. The short-run Phillips curve will shift upwards. With adaptive expectations, it will initially shift up, say, to curve II.

But will the short-run Phillips curve not go on shifting upwards as long as there is any upward pressure on inflation, with this feeding through into higher and higher

Figure 19.29 The Keynesian analysis of reflationary policies

unemployment? Will the long-run Phillips curve not be vertical at the natural level of unemployment, and will this natural level not be U_1: the level where there was constant inflation?

Keynesians reject the concept of a natural level for two reasons:

- If there is a gradual but sustained expansion of aggregate demand, firms, seeing the economy expanding and seeing their orders growing, will start to invest more and make longer-term plans for expanding their labour force. People will generally *expect* a higher level of output, and this optimism will cause that higher level of output to be produced. In other words, expectations will affect output and employment as well as prices.

  Graphically, the increased output and employment from the recovery in investment will shift the Phillips curve to the left, offsetting (partially, wholly or more than wholly) the upward shift from higher inflationary expectations.

- If U_1 includes a considerable number of long-term unemployed, then the expansion of demand may be *initially* inflationary since many of the newly employed will require some retraining (a costly exercise). But as these newly employed workers become more productive, their lower labour costs may offset any further upward pressure on wages from the expansion of demand. At the same time, the higher investment may embody new more efficient techniques which will also help to prevent further acceleration in costs.

It is quite likely that these effects can prevent any further rises in inflation. Inflation can become stable at, say, $\dot{P}_2$, with the economy operating at point c. The short-run Phillips curve settles at position Z. There is thus a long-run downward-sloping Phillips curve passing through points a and c.

> **?** Would it in theory be possible for this long-run Phillips curve to be horizontal or even upward sloping over part of its length?

If expectations are formed rationally rather than adaptively, there will merely be a quicker movement to this long-run equilibrium. If people rationally predict that the effect of government policy will be to move the economy to point c, then their predictions will bring this about. All rational expectations do is to bring the long run about much sooner! The theory of rational expectations on its own does not provide support specifically for either the new classical or the Keynesian position.

Contraction of aggregate demand

Most Keynesians argue that the short-run Phillips curve is kinked at the current level of real aggregate demand. A reduction in real aggregate demand will only have a slight effect on inflation, since real wages are sticky downwards. Unions may well prefer to negotiate a reduction in employment levels, preferably by natural wastage (i.e. not replacing people when they leave), rather than accept a reduction in real wages. Thus in Figure 19.30, to the right of point a, the short-run Phillips curve is very shallow.

As long as this curve is not totally horizontal to the right of a, the introduction of expectations into the analysis will cause the short-run curve to shift downward over time (if unemployment is kept above U_1) as people come to expect a lower rate of inflation.

With *adaptive* expectations, however, the curve could shift downward very slowly indeed. If a movement from point a to point d only causes a 1 per cent reduction in inflation, and if it takes, say, two years for this to be fully reflected in expectations, then if unemployment is kept at U_2, inflation will only reduce (i.e. the curve shift

Figure 19.30 The Keynesian analysis of deflationary policies

downward) by ½ per cent a year. This may be totally unacceptable politically if inflation is already at very high levels, and if U_2 is also very high.

Even with *rational* expectations the response may be too slow. If there is a resistance from unions to receiving increases in wages below the current rate of inflation, or if they are attempting to 'catch up' with other workers, then even if they rationally predict the correct amount by which inflation will fall, inflation will only fall slowly. People will rationally predict the *resistance* to wage restraint, and sure enough, therefore, inflation will only fall slowly.

The worst scenario is when the government, in its attempt to eliminate inflation, keeps unemployment high for a number of years. As the core of long-term unemployed workers grows, there will be an increasing number of workers who become deskilled and therefore effectively unemployable. The effective labour supply is reduced, and firms no longer find there is a surplus of employable labour *despite* high unemployment. A long-term equilibrium is reached at, say, point *e* with still substantial inflation. The long-run Phillips curve too may thus be relatively shallow to the right of point *a*.

The Keynesian criticisms of non-intervention

Keynesians are therefore highly critical of the new classical conclusion that governments should not intervene other than to restrain the growth of money supply. High unemployment may persist for many years and become deeply entrenched in the economy if there is no deliberate government policy of creating a steady expansion of demand.

 Why is it important in the Keynesian analysis for there to be a *steady* expansion of demand?

◭ SUMMARY

1. Modern Keynesians incorporate expectations into their analysis of inflation and unemployment. They also see an important role for cost-push factors in inflation, and in particular the bargaining by unions for a target real wage increase. They also, like the monetarists, accept that equilibrium unemployment has increased since the 1950s and 1960s.

2. An increase in cost-push inflation will shift the Phillips

curve upwards. A moderate deflation will then bring increased unemployment as well: i.e. stagflation.

3. If unions seek to maintain a target real wage irrespective of the real growth in the economy, this will lead to higher cost-push inflation the lower the rate of growth (and the higher the level of unemployment). The Phillips curve will slope upwards.

4. The growth in equilibrium unemployment has been

caused by more rapid changes in technology, greater competition from abroad and more rapid changes in demand patterns. The effect of increased equilibrium unemployment is to shift the Phillips curve to the right.

5. If expectations are incorporated into Keynesian analysis, the Phillips curve will become steeper in the long run (and steeper in the short run too in the case of rational expectations). It will not become vertical, however, since people will expect changes in aggregate demand to affect output and employment as well as prices.

6. If people expect a more rapid rise in aggregate demand to be sustained, firms will invest more, thereby reducing unemployment in the long run and not just increasing the rate of inflation. The long-run Phillips curve will be downward sloping.

7. The short- and long-run Phillips curves may be kinked. Reductions in real aggregate demand may only have a slight effect on inflation if wages are sticky downwards. Expectations of inflation may only fall slowly even at quite high levels of unemployment. In the extreme case, a reduction in real aggregate demand may substantially increase equilibrium unemployment if significant numbers of people become deskilled.

19.6 Postscript: the importance of expectations

Expectations are crucial in determining the success of government policy on unemployment and inflation. Whatever people expect to happen, their actions will tend to make it happen.

If people believe that an expansion of money supply will merely lead to inflation (the monetarist position), then it will. Firms and workers will adjust their prices and wages upward. Firms will make no plans to expand output and will not take on any more labour. If, however, people believe that an expansion of demand will lead to higher output and employment (the Keynesian position), then, via the accelerator mechanism, it will.

Similarly, just how successful a deflationary policy is in curing inflation depends in large measure on people's expectations (but, as explained above, it also depends on the downward stickiness of real wages). If people believe that a deflationary policy will cause a recession, then firms will stop investing and will cut their workforce. If they believe that it will cure inflation and restore firms' competitiveness abroad, firms may increase investment.

To manage the economy successfully, therefore, the government must convince people that its policies will work. This is as much a job of public relations as of pulling the right economic levers.

? 1. If constant criticism of governments in the media makes people highly cynical about any government's ability to manage the economy, what effect will this have on the performance of the economy?

2. Suppose that, as part of the government's desire to introduce a national curriculum, everyone in the country had to study economics up to the age of sixteen. Suppose also that the reporting of economic news by the media became more thorough (and interesting!). What effects would these developments have on the government's ability to manage the economy? How would your answer differ if you were a Keynesian from if you were a new classicist?

20 Supply-Side Policies

20.1 The supply-side problem

Lack of aggregate demand is only one of the causes of unemployment and lack of growth. Excess aggregate demand is only one of the causes of inflation and balance of payments deficits. Many of the causes of these problems lie on the supply side.

This chapter examines various policies that can be adopted to influence aggregate supply.

Unemployment and supply-side policies

Equilibrium unemployment – frictional, structural, etc. – is caused by various rigidities or imperfections in the market system. There is a mismatching of aggregate supply and demand. Vacancies are not filled despite the existence of unemployment. Perhaps workers have the wrong qualifications, or are poorly motivated, or are living a long way away from the job, or are simply unaware of the jobs that are vacant. Generally, the problem is that labour is not sufficiently mobile, either occupationally or geographically, to respond to changes in the job market. Labour supply for particular jobs is too inelastic.

Supply-side policies aim to influence labour supply. They aim to make workers more responsive to changes in job opportunities. Alternatively, they may aim to make employers more adaptable and willing to operate within existing labour constraints.

Disequilibrium unemployment may well be caused by demand-side problems: i.e. a decline in aggregate demand. In this case, demand management policies may be called for. But disequilibrium unemployment *may* be caused by wage rates being forced above the equilibrium by the monopoly power of trade unions in supplying labour. In this case, the government may impose some form of supply-side policy: either a policy to reduce the power of labour (e.g. banning closed shops), or alternatively an *incomes policy* to prevent unions from exercising their power.

Inflation and supply-side policies

Inflation may be caused by cost-push pressures. Cost-push inflation is usually caused by an exercise of economic power. Unions exercise power in the supply of labour and drive up wages. Firms exercise power in the supply of goods and drive up prices. Governments may put up taxes and thereby raise prices.

Supply-side policies can reduce cost-push inflation in two ways:

- By reducing the power of unions and/or firms (e.g. anti-monopoly legislation) and thereby encouraging more competition in the supply of labour and/or goods.
- By preventing people from exercising that power by some form of prices and incomes policy.

Growth and supply-side policies

Traditional Keynesian economics tends to assume that there is a given potential national income. The actual level of income within that potential is determined by aggregate demand. This focus, then, is a *demand-side* focus.

In the *short run*, demand-side policy is designed to take up any slack in the economy. Aggregate demand is expanded so that actual income rises to meet full employment potential income.

In the *long run*, demand-side policy can be used to expand aggregate demand so that actual income expands to match any increases in potential income.

Supply-side economics focuses on *potential* income. Supply-side policies aim to shift the production possibility curve itself outward and, similarly, to shift the full employment level of national income to the right.

Supply-side policies can be used to increase the total quantity of factors of production: e.g. tax concessions to oil companies to encourage prospecting for new oil supplies, or policies designed to encourage the building of new factories. Alternatively, they can be used to encourage greater productivity of factors of production: e.g. policies to encourage the training of labour, or incentives for people to work harder.

> **?** Why do Keynesians argue that even in the long run demand-side policies will be still be required?

The monetarist approach to supply-side policy

Monetarists argue that a very clear distinction needs to be made between demand-side and supply-side policies.

Demand-side policy (and this, for a monetarist, means monetary policy) is only suitable as a weapon against inflation. It cannot be used to influence growth and employment in the long run.

For a monetarist, then, supply-side policy is the appropriate policy to increase output and reduce the level of unemployment. It can also have the benefit of reducing the level of prices associated with any given level of the money supply. In the equation $M\overline{V} = PT$, an increase in aggregate supply will raise the number of transactions that can take place (T), and therefore lower the price level (P) for any given level of the money supply (M).

Supply-side policy can be used to shift the aggregate supply curve to the right: to increase the amount that firms wish to supply at any given price. In Figure 20.1, output rises to Q_2 and prices fall to P_2.

Supply-side policies, if directed to the labour market, can also reduce the natural level of unemployment, and thus shift the vertical long-run Phillips curve to the left. In Figure 20.2, unemployment falls from U_{n_1} to U_{n_2}.

The term 'supply-side policy' is often associated with monetarism. Monetarists advocate policies to 'free up' the market: policies that encourage private enterprise, risk taking and competition; policies that provide incentives and reward initiative, hard work and productivity. It is this part of monetarism, more than any other, that associates it with the political right. Section 20.2 examines these market-orientated supply-side policies

Market-orientated supply-side policies

Policies to increase aggregate supply by freeing up the market.

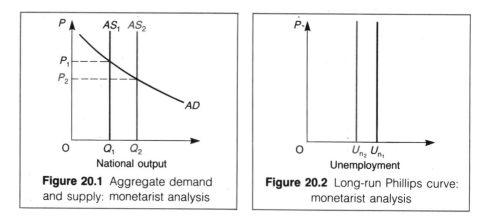

Figure 20.1 Aggregate demand and supply: monetarist analysis

Figure 20.2 Long-run Phillips curve: monetarist analysis

The Keynesian approach to supply-side policy

Although the term 'supply-side policy' is often used to refer specifically to free-market-orientated policies, there are other supply-side policies that are advocated by Keynesians and economists on the political left, which are interventionist in nature and designed to counteract the deficiencies of the free market.

Keynesians today do not focus exclusively on demand. They too argue for policies to shift the aggregate supply curve to the right and the Phillips curve to the left. If there is a lot of slack in the economy, however, increasing the quantity or productivity of factors of production will only create more slack.

Thus in Figure 20.3, if output is at Q_1 with aggregate demand at AD_1, the appropriate policy is to increase aggregate *demand* rather than aggregate supply. If, however, the economy is approaching full employment with aggregate demand at AD_2, and output at Q_2, there is little scope for further increases in output. Here the most appropriate policy to increase output is a supply-side policy. This will shift the AS curve to the right (e.g. to AS_2) and raise output (e.g. to Q_3).

 If Keynesians are correct, does this mean that supply-side policies should only be used at times of full employment?

Keynesians also advocate supply-side policies to improve the inflation–unemployment trade-off: to shift the Phillips curve to the left. If successful, such policies could lead

Interventionist supply-side policies

Policies to increase aggregate supply by government intervention to counteract the deficiencies of the market.

Figure 20.3 Aggregate demand and supply: Keynesian analysis

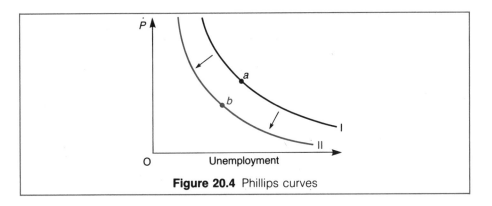

Figure 20.4 Phillips curves

simultaneously to both lower unemployment and lower inflation. The economy could move from, say, point *a* to point *b* in Figure 20.4.

Some Keynesian supply-side policies are more specifically concerned with output and employment (e.g. policies to set up training schemes, or regional policies to encourage firms to set up in areas of high unemployment). Such policies would shift the *AS* curve to the right and the Phillips curve to the left. Other Keynesian supply-side policies are more specifically concerned with production costs (e.g. prices and incomes policies). Such policies would shift the Phillips curve downwards, and aim to prevent the *AS* curve shifting upwards.

The link between demand-side and supply-side policies

Although demand-side and supply-side policies are often presented as being totally separate, many policies have both demand-side and supply-side effects.

For example, many supply-side policies involve increased government expenditure: whether it be on retraining schemes, on research and development projects, or on industrial relocation. Unless the government fully offsets any rise in government expenditure by a reduction in private expenditure (through higher taxes), there will also be a rise in aggregate demand. Similarly, supply-side policies of tax cuts designed to increase incentives will also lead to an increase in aggregate demand unless accompanied by a cut in government expenditure. It is thus important to consider the consequences for demand when planning various supply-side policies.

Likewise, demand management policies often have supply-side effects. If a cut in interest rates boosts investment, there will be a multiplied rise in national income: a demand-side effect. But that rise in investment will also create increased productive capacity: a supply-side effect.

A big problem with policies to stimulate investment is in trying to match these demand and supply effects. A rise in investment could even be 'deflationary' if the rise in productive potential (the supply effect) is bigger than the rise in actual income (the demand effect)! This was indeed the hope of the Heath administration in 1972–3 during its 'dash for growth' (see page 757). It was hoped that maintaining a high level of aggregate demand would encourage a high level of investment, and that this in turn would cause a rise in aggregate supply sufficiently large to offset any inflationary effects of the higher demand. As it turned out, demand soon outstripped supply.

? Define 'demand-side' and 'supply-side' policies. Sometimes it is said that Keynesians advocate demand-side policies and monetarists advocate supply-side policies. Is there any accuracy in this statement?

▲ SUMMARY

1. Whereas demand-side policies (fiscal and monetary) may be suitable for controlling demand-pull inflation or demand-deficient unemployment, supply-side policies will be needed to control the other types of inflation and unemployment.
2. Demand-side policies can be used to increase the actual rate of economic growth if there is slack in the economy. In the long term, however, economic growth can only be increased if there is an increase in the *potential* rate of economic growth. To achieve this the government will require supply-side policies.
3. Supply-side policies, if successful, will shift the aggregate supply curve to the right, and possibly the Phillips curve downwards/to the left.
4. Monetarists favour market-orientated supply-side policies. Keynesians favour interventionist supply-side policies.
5. Supply-side policies often have demand-side effects, and demand-side policies often have supply-side effects. It is important for governments to take these secondary effects into account when working out their economic strategy.

20.2 Market-orientated supply-side policies

Supply-side policies in the 1980s

Margaret Thatcher and Ronald Reagan both had two major elements in their economic strategy. The first, on the demand side, was to pursue a policy of firm monetary control in order to reduce inflation. The second was to pursue radical market-orientated supply-side policies.

The essence of these supply-side policies was to encourage and reward individual enterprise and initiative, and to reduce the role of government; to put more reliance on market forces and competition, and less on government intervention and regulation. The policies were thus associated with the following:

- Reducing government expenditure so as to release more resources for the private sector.
- Reducing taxes so as to increase incentives.
- Reducing the monopoly power of trade unions to keep wages above market equilibrium levels.
- Reducing the automatic entitlement to certain welfare benefits so as to encourage greater self-reliance.
- Reducing red tape and other impediments to investment and risk taking.
- Encouraging competition through policies of deregulation and privatization.
- Abolishing exchange controls and other impediments to the free movement of capital.

Reducing government expenditure

Monetarism is often associated with 'cuts'. The desire of monetarists to cut government expenditure is not just to reduce the PSBR (or increase the PSDR) and hence reduce the growth of money supply; it is also an essential ingredient of their supply-side strategy.

The size of the public sector in the UK, relative to national income, had grown substantially since the 1950s (see Table 20.1). A major aim of the Thatcher government was to reverse this trend. The public sector was portrayed as more bureaucratic and less efficient than the private sector. What is more, it was claimed that a growing proportion of public money was being spent on administration and other 'non-productive' activities, rather than on the direct provision of goods and services.

Box 20.1

The Supply-Side Revolution in the USA
'Reaganomics'

In both the UK and the USA the 1980s proved to be years of radical political and economic change. Traditional economic and political practices were replaced by new and often controversial policies, although in theory many of the ideas advocated were based on old principles of *laissez-faire* capitalism.

In the USA the era of 'Reaganomics', as it has been called, began in January 1981 when Ronald Reagan became President. With this new administration came a radical shift in policy aimed at directly tackling the supply side of the economy. As Reagan was to remark to Congress:

> The new policy is based on the premise that ... government [should] provide a stable and unfettered environment in which private individuals can ... make appropriate decisions.

This policy strategy involved four key strands:

● A reduction in the growth of Federal (central government) spending.

● A reduction in individual and corporate tax rates.

● A reduction in Federal regulations over private enterprise.

● A reduction in inflation through tight monetary policy.

On all four points President Reagan was to achieve a degree of success. Federal spending *growth* was reduced even though military spending rocketed. Tax rates fell dramatically. Deregulation was speeded up. Inflation at first was stabilized and then fell sharply.

These supply-side measures were hailed as a great success by Republicans, and followers in both the UK and the USA were quick to advocate an even bigger reduction in the government's role.

Critics, on the other hand, have remained sceptical and point to the costs of Reaganomics. The huge budget deficits (the largest in US history) plagued the Reagan administration and the Bush administration that followed. The problem was that the massive tax cuts were not matched by an equivalent cut in public expenditure; nor did they produce a sufficiently high rate of economic growth, through which additional tax revenues were to balance the budget. In particular, 'civilian' or welfare spending was cut repeatedly in preference to the huge military budget. This led to increasing social hardship.

Table 20.1 Government expenditure (central plus local) as a percentage of GDP at market prices: 1950–89

	1950	1960	1970	1975	1979	1981	1982	1983	1985	1987	1989
Final consumption	16.5	16.4	17.6	21.8	19.8	21.9	21.8	21.9	21.1	20.4	19.4
Investment	3.4	3.3	4.8	4.7	2.6	1.8	1.6	2.0	2.0	1.6	1.6
Transfers, etc.	14.8	15.0	18.3	22.0	21.0	22.5	23.0	22.2	21.8	18.2	17.5
Total	34.7	34.7	40.7	48.5	43.4	46.2	46.4	46.1	44.9	40.2	38.5

Source: *Economic Trends* (CSO, various issues).

Two things were needed: (a) a more efficient use of resources within the public sector and (b) a reduction in the size of the public sector. This would allow private investment to increase with no overall rise in aggregate demand. Thus the supply-side benefits of higher investment could be achieved without the demand-side costs of higher inflation. A number of measures were adopted:

● Cash limits were imposed on various government departments and local authorities. It was hoped thereby to force them to become more efficient. Local authorities which planned to spend beyond their limits became subject to rate capping (later, charge capping): a process whereby they were prevented from raising additional rates (poll tax) to finance 'excess' expenditure.

- Grants and subsidies were reduced. The rate support grant from the government to local authorities was reduced from 61 per cent of local authority expenditure in 1979, to 54 per cent in 1986 and to 50 per cent in 1989. Subsidies to nationalized industries (e.g. British Rail) were reduced. Many nationalized industries were forced to raise their prices.
- Tough managers (e.g. Ian MacGregor in first British Steel and then the National Coal Board) were appointed in several nationalized industries, in order to bring about radical reorganization and substantial increases in efficiency. In several cases this meant redundancies. The government was prepared to withstand lengthy industrial disputes in the pursuit of this policy: for example, the bitter miners' dispute in 1984–5 over pit closures.
- The civil service was cut from 484 000 full-time equivalent staff in 1979 to 424 800 in 1984.
- The government pursued a tough line on public-sector pay. Here too it was prepared to withstand union action.

These policies were not without problems, however:

- In some sectors the effect was to cut services rather than increase efficiency.
- It was found much easier to cut long-term capital expenditure than current expenditure (e.g. wages). Thus there was a sharp decline in new roads, schools, public-sector housing, etc. This decline in public investment was a major disadvantage of a policy designed to increase overall investment in the economy. Public investment was cut from 2.6 per cent of GDP in 1979, to 1.8 per cent in 1981 and to 1.6 per cent in 1989 (see Table 20.1).
- Reducing the overall size of the public sector was very difficult when the government was also trying to reduce inflation by tight monetary policy. The dramatic rise in unemployment after 1979 led to large increases in expenditure on unemployment and other social security benefits. Table 20.1 shows that up to 1982 government expenditure actually rose as a proportion of GDP. On the other hand, high unemployment and the recession weakened trade union resistance to many of the measures.

? Why might a recovering economy (and hence a fall in government expenditure on social security benefits) make the government feel even more concerned to make discretionary cuts in government expenditure?

Tax cuts: the effects on labour supply and employment

Cutting the marginal rate of income tax was a major objective of the Thatcher government (as it was of the Reagan administration). Cuts in the marginal rate of income tax are claimed to have five beneficial effects: people work longer hours; more people wish to work; people work more enthusiastically; unemployment falls; employment rises. These are big claims. Are they true?

People work longer hours

A cut in the marginal rate of income tax has a *substitution effect* inducing people to work more and also an *income effect* causing people to work less. (At this point you should review the arguments about the incentive effects of tax cuts which were examined in detail in section 9.2, pages 349–53, and in Box 9.7.)

A cut in income tax can therefore work either way. Evidence suggests that the two effects will roughly cancel each other out. Anyway, for many people there is no such choice in the short run. There is no chance of doing overtime or working a shorter week. The job is a set number of hours. In the long run, however, there may be some flexibility in that people can change jobs.

More people wish to work

This applies largely to second income earners in a family, mainly women. A rise in after-tax wages may encourage more women to look for jobs. It may now be worth the cost in terms of transport, child minders, family disruption, etc. The effects of a 1 or 2 per cent cut in income tax rates, however, are likely to be negligible. A more significant effect may be achieved by raising tax allowances. Part-time workers, especially, could end up paying no taxes. Whether more people seeking employment is seen by the government as desirable depends on the level of unemployment. If unemployment is already high, the government will not want to increase the labour force.

People work more enthusiastically

There is little evidence to test this claim. The argument, however, is that people will be more conscientious and more willing to put effort into their work if they can keep more of their pay.

Unemployment falls

One of the causes of natural unemployment highlighted by monetarists is the cushioning provided by unemployment benefit. If income taxes are cut, there will be a bigger difference between after-tax wages and unemployment benefits. More people will be motivated to 'get on their bikes' and look for work.

This is illustrated in Figure 20.5. The diagram shows two curves. The total labour force curve (N) shows the total number of people who are either working or unemployed. The aggregate supply of labour curve (AS_L) shows the number of people who are actually qualified and willing to do the specific jobs they are offered at each wage rate. The gap between the two curves shows *equilibrium* unemployment (i.e. the unemployment due to mismatching at a micro level, not the unemployment due to wages generally being set above the point where *aggregate* demand and supply of labour are equal).

As tax rates are cut, after-tax wages will rise. There will thus be a movement up along the two curves. As the gap between them narrows, so equilibrium unemployment will fall: more of the unemployed will be willing to take jobs.

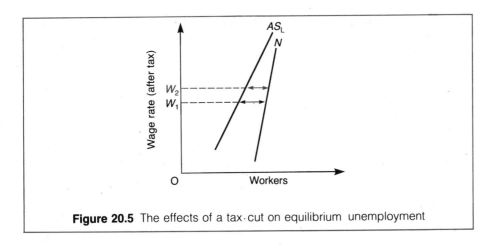

Figure 20.5 The effects of a tax cut on equilibrium unemployment

The argument is only valid if (pre-tax) wage rates are flexible. Firms must be willing to take on the extra labour now willing to accept jobs. This means that *some* of the benefit of the tax cuts must be filtered through into *lower* pre-tax wages and hence lower wage costs for firms (but not enough, of course, to eliminate the benefit to the workers). If *pre-tax* wages are sticky downwards, however, the extra labour supply will simply not be employed. Workers will not 'price themselves into jobs'. There will be no extra jobs for them to go to. Disequilibrium unemployment will simply replace equilibrium unemployment!

1. Why do the two curves in Figure 20.5 get closer together at higher wage rates?
2. What would happen to the two curves if the level of unemployment benefits was increased?

Employment rises

If wages are flexible, then not only will equilibrium unemployment fall, but total employment will rise. This is illustrated in Figure 20.6. Assume an initial income tax per worker of $a - b$. The equilibrium employment will be Q_1. Workers receive an after-tax wage W_1 and thus supply Q_1 labour. Employers' labour cost is the pre-tax wage lc_1. At this wage they demand Q_1 labour.

If the income tax per worker now falls to $c - d$, equilibrium employment will rise to Q_2. Firms will employ more workers because their labour costs have fallen to lc_2. More workers will take up jobs because their after-tax wages have risen to W_2.

Assuming that unemployment benefits do not change, equilibrium unemployment will fall from $e - b$ to $f - d$.

Whilst marginal income tax rates were cut during the 1980s, these were offset by increases in VAT and national insurance contributions (see Tables 9.15 and 9.16 on pages 344 and 345). Total taxes and national insurance contributions as a proportion of GDP rose from 34.2 per cent in 1979 to 38.0 per cent 1985, and then fell back somewhat to 36.9 per cent in 1989.

Does this mean that there were *no* positive incentive effects from the Thatcher government's tax measures?

To the extent that tax cuts do succeed in increasing take-home pay, there is a danger of 'sucking in' imports. Consumers may have a high marginal propensity to import: spending their money on Japanese videos and hi-fi, Japanese or European cars, holidays abroad and so on. Tax cuts can therefore have a serious effect on the balance of payments.

Tax cuts for business and other investment incentives

There are a number of financial incentives that can be given to encourage investment. Selective intervention in the form of grants for specific industries or firms is best classified as an interventionist policy and will be examined later in this chapter. Market-orientated policies seek to reduce the general level of taxation on profits, or to give greater tax relief to investment. There is no discrimination between different types of firm or different types of investment. The pattern of investment is left to the market.

A cut in corporation tax will increase after-tax profits. This means that more money will be available for ploughing back into investment and also that the higher after-tax return on investment will encourage more investment to take place. In 1984 the main rate of corporation tax in the UK was reduced from 52 per cent of profits, the amount of the reduction depending on the size of the company. By 1989 the rate of corporation tax was 35 per cent for large companies and 25 per cent for small.

An alternative policy would be to increase investment allowances. Investment allowances are the system whereby the cost of investment can be offset against pre-tax profit, thereby reducing a firm's tax liability.

Until 1984 the UK system of investment and other allowances for firms and various subsidies had been quite complex, and discriminated seemingly arbitrarily between different types of investment. After 1984 the whole system was simplified in order to reduce these distortions and allow investment to be more 'market determined'. Nevertheless, as previously, better allowances were given for plant and machinery than for industrial buildings, and no allowances were given for most commercial buildings. The overall level of allowances, however, was reduced.

Reducing the power of labour

In Figure 20.7, if the power of unions to push wages up to W_1 were removed, then (assuming no change in the demand curve for labour) wages would fall to W_e. Disequilibrium unemployment $(Q_2 - Q_1)$ would disappear. Employment would rise from Q_1 to Q_e.

Equilibrium unemployment, however, will rise somewhat as the gap between gross and effective labour supply widens. With the reduction in wages, some people may now prefer to remain 'on the dole'.

If labour costs to employers are reduced, their profits will probably rise. This could encourage and enable more investment and hence economic growth. If the monopoly power of labour is reduced, then cost-push inflation will also be reduced.

But what will be the effect on aggregate demand? Will a policy that reduced wages not also reduce aggregate demand? If so, the demand curve for labour will shift to the left. If that is the case, then will wage-push unemployment not merely be replaced by demand-deficient unemployment? The answer depends on the government's demand management policy. If aggregate demand is maintained by fiscal and/or monetary policies, demand-deficient unemployment need not arise.

The Thatcher government took a number of measures to weaken the power of labour. These included restrictions on union closed shops, restrictions on secondary picketing, and enforced secret ballots on strike proposals (see Chapter 8). It set a lead in resisting strikes in the public sector. Unlike previous Labour governments, it did not consult with union leaders over questions of economic policy. It was publicly very

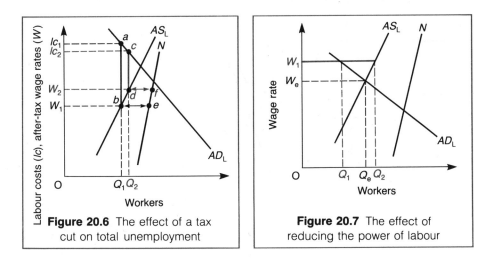

Figure 20.6 The effect of a tax cut on total unemployment

Figure 20.7 The effect of reducing the power of labour

critical of trade union militancy and blamed the unions for many of the UK's economic ills. As a result, unions lost a lot of political standing and influence.

Apart from the miners' strike in 1984–5 and the industrial action of teachers in 1986–7, most of the 1980s was a period of relative industrial calm. Despite the legislation, it can be argued that the main factor that weakened the power of unions was the very high level of unemployment that existed throughout most of the 1980s. When unemployment began to fall towards the end of the decade, the level of industrial disputes increased.

 Is the number of working days lost through disputes a good indication of (a) union power; (b) union militancy?

Reducing welfare

Monetarists claim that a major cause of unemployment is the small difference between the welfare benefits of the unemployed and the take-home pay of the employed. This causes voluntary unemployment (i.e. frictional unemployment). It is not worth people taking a job for the small amount of extra income they would receive. They are caught in a 'poverty trap': if they take a job, they lose their benefits (see pages 358–60).

A dramatic solution to this problem would be to cut unemployment benefits. Unlike policies to encourage investment, this supply-side policy would have a very rapid effect. It would shift the effective labour supply curve to the right. In Figure 20.8, equilibrium unemployment would fall from $a - b$ to $c - d$ if wages were flexible downwards; or from $a - b$ to $a - e$ if wages were not flexible. In the case of non-flexible wages, the reduction in equilibrium unemployment would be offset by a rise in disequilibrium unemployment ($e - b$).

Because workers would now be prepared to accept a lower wage, the average length of job search by the unemployed would be reduced. In Figure 20.9, the average duration of unemployment would fall from T_1 to T_2. (see pages 494–5).

 Would a cut in benefits affect the W_o curve. If so, with what effect?

What happened in practice? The gap between take-home pay and welfare benefits to the unemployed had actually widened up to 1979. This suggests that too high benefits were not a cause of the growing unemployment up to that time. After 1979

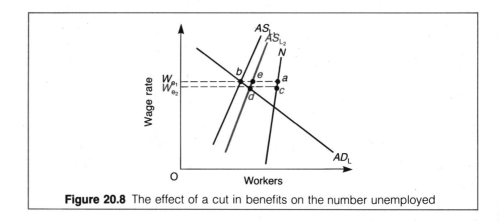

Figure 20.8 The effect of a cut in benefits on the number unemployed

Box 20.2

The Labour Market and Oranges
A radical-right view of unemployment

The labour market is just like any other market, except that it's the most interfered market we've got in the economy . . .

First there are minimum wages. Secondly, there are unions that restrict the supply of labour in very many areas of the economy. Thirdly, the government sets a minimum social wage in the form of social security benefits . . .

These things constitute massive interference in the market. If we were to take the market for oranges . . . and to do these things . . . we would not be surprised if certain things happened to the quantity of oranges sold and the price of oranges.

Unemployment is a response to the interaction of basic supply forces and basic demand forces . . . Therefore the way to get unemployment down, and to get demand up, is to tackle the underlying causes of the market distortion . . . to get at the reasons why wages will

not fall to levels at which labour will be more competitive [or] why working practices [are not] flexible to get efficiency up.

If you try and stimulate demand by engineering a rise in public expenditure, you will not have changed the underlying situation . . . Unemployment will go back up.

Patrick Minford, Professor of Economics, Liverpool University[1]

? 1. If these arguments are correct, what specific policies could be introduced to 'cure' these labour market distortions?

2. Provide a critique of these arguments.

[1] Part of an interview appearing in the Open University series D284, programme 6, 'Unemployment'.

the gap continued to widen, but unemployment rose dramatically. Nevertheless, the claim that there was too little incentive for people to work was still a major part of the Thatcher government's explanation of growing unemployment.

A major problem is that, with changing requirements for labour skills, many of the redundant workers from the older industries are simply not qualified for new jobs that are created. What is more, the longer people are unemployed, the more demoralized they become. If employers were to take such workers on, they would probably be prepared to pay only very low wages. To persuade these unemployed people to take such low-paid jobs, the welfare benefits would have to be slashed to very low levels. A 'market' solution to the problem, therefore, may be a very cruel solution. A fairer solution would be an interventionist policy: a policy of retraining labour.

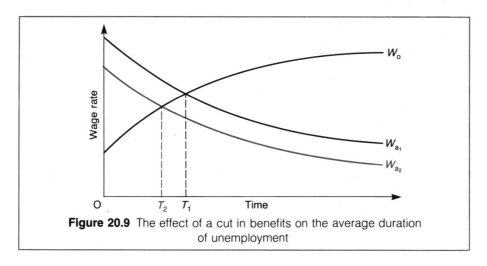

Figure 20.9 The effect of a cut in benefits on the average duration of unemployment

Policies to encourage competition

Under this heading, the Thatcher government concentrated its attention mainly on the public sector. There were two elements in this policy: privatization of various forms and deregulation. It was hoped that the increased competition that would result would increase efficiency. At a macro level, this would help increase national output and reduce inflation.

Privatization

This can involve the sale of a public enterprise (e.g. British Telecom, British Gas, British Airways and the twelve water authorities). If this simply involves the transfer of a natural monopoly to private hands, the scope for increased competition is limited. However, where there is genuine scope for competition (e.g. in the sale of telephones), privatization can lead to increased efficiency, more consumer choice and lower prices. Whether it would have been possible to have just as much competition under nationalization – for example, nationalized industries being forced to compete on the open market for investment funds, or British Airways competing openly with other airlines – is a matter of debate.

Alternatively, privatization can involve the introduction of private services into the public sector (e.g. private contractors providing cleaning services in hospitals, or catering on British Rail, or refuse collection for local authorities). Private contractors may compete against each other for the franchise. This may well lower the cost of provision of these services, but the quality of provision may also suffer unless closely monitored. The effects on unemployment are uncertain. Private contractors may offer lower wages and thus may use more labour. But if they are trying to supply the service at minimum cost, they may employ less labour – especially if previous agreements favourable to labour are no longer honoured.

 What are the arguments for and against privatization as a means of encouraging greater competition and greater efficiency? Are these the most important considerations in the nationalization/privatization debate?

Deregulation

This involves the removal of monopoly rights: again, largely in the public sector. In 1979 the National Bus Corporation lost its monopoly of long-distance coach haulage. Private operators were now allowed to compete. This substantially reduced coach fares on a number of routes. In 1986 competition was allowed in providing local bus services. (See Box 20.3.)

An example in the private sector was the so-called 'Big Bang' on the Stock Exchange in 1986. Under this, the monopoly power of jobbers to deal in stocks and shares on the Stock Exchange was abolished. In addition, stockbrokers now compete with each other in the commission rates they charge. Previously there had been uniform rates.

Another form of competition policy would be to extend the scope and activity of the Monopolies and Mergers Commission. This was not favoured by the Thatcher government, which preferred to intervene as little as possible in the private sector – even if that 'intervention' should be market orientated.

Free trade and free capital movements

The Thatcher government was very much in favour of free trade and free movements of capital right from the outset. In October 1979, soon after coming to office, the

Box 20.3

Deregulating the Bus Industry

Since the 1950s, with the rapid growth of the car industry, bus services in the UK have been having a difficult time. Between 1953 and 1983, passenger kilometres travelled by all types of transport grew by 154 per cent. However, the bus industry saw its share of total passengers decline from 42 per cent to a mere 8 per cent. Somewhat surprisingly, bus fares increased rapidly: between 1972 and 1983 by almost 30 per cent in real terms compared to an increase of just 3 per cent in private motoring costs. Over the same period, government subsidies and grants rose from £71 million to £897 million which in real terms is a 238 per cent increase.

In the light of this position, when the Conservative Party came to power in 1979, with its supply-side ideology, it was not long before it introduced measures to deregulate the industry.

The 1980 Transport Act took the first steps towards removing the Road Service Licence (RSL), which had been used by the Traffic Commissioners to maintain both price and quality control over the bus industry. Its full removal came in the 1985 Transport Act, along with the privatization of the National Bus Company and the introduction of competitive tendering for unprofitable bus services.

What effects have such deregulatory measures had? The year after the 1985 Act saw the number of private bus operators increase by 6.5 per cent and the number of vehicle-kilometres increase by 13 per cent. On the other hand, passenger numbers fell by 5.6 per cent, and many evening, Sunday and rural services were cut, although not to the extent that critics had predicted.

It appears that the prime deregulation objective (i.e. to stimulate competition) has not been fully realized. Existing operators have tended to channel resources into pre-deregulated networks rather than expand services. What competition there is tends to be in the form of increased service frequency rather than a reduction in fares.

The quality of service is a key topic of debate. A recent survey by the Transport and Road Research Laboratory found that 45 per cent of bus users consider the service to have deteriorated, while only 15 per cent consider it to have improved. Thus the bus service today appears to be neither the success nor the failure that either end of the political spectrum predicted.

?
1. Under what circumstances would it be wise for a bus company to put up fares when faced by falling numbers of passengers? Would deregulation make any difference to this decision?
2. How has the introduction of mini-buses affected the viability of urban bus routes? Do they affect the case for or against deregulation?

government removed all exchange controls. This deregulation permitted free inflows and outflows of capital, both long term and short term. The arguments for and against free trade are examined in Chapter 21.

Conclusions

In the period 1979–82, although a number of supply-side measures were taken by the government, unemployment rose dramatically and industrial output fell as the economy plunged into the deepest recession since the 1930s. The main causes of this recession are to be found on the demand side: a restrictive monetary policy combined with a high exchange rate and later a world recession.

This recession, however, had supply-side as well as demand-side effects. Much of UK industrial capacity was lost for ever. Many of the redundant became deskilled and demoralized as they became long-term unemployed. On the other hand, many of those companies that survived were only able to do so by considerable increases in efficiency. Resistance from unions to the introduction of new labour-saving technology was weakened by high unemployment and the fear that without the new technology firms might be forced to close.

Thus many of the supply-side effects were the result of changes in demand. When demand was expanded in the late 1980s and unemployment began to fall, so inflation rose and the balance of payments went into record deficit. This cast serious doubt on the ability of the economy to maintain sustained high economic growth and on whether the supply-side measures were as successful as the government maintained. The rate of increase in productivity was higher in the 1980s than in the 1960s and 1970s. But to what extent this is attributable to the government's supply-side measures rather than to other factors, such as international competition and a more rapid rate of technological advance, is not clear.

 If supply-side measures led to a 'shake out' of labour and a resulting reduction in overstaffing, but also to a rightward shift in the Phillips curve, would you judge the policy as a success?

▲ SUMMARY

1. Market-orientated supply-side policies aim to increase the rate of growth of aggregate supply by encouraging private enterprise and the freer play of market forces.
2. Reducing government expenditure as a proportion of GDP is a major element of such policies. This can involve the use of cash limits on government departments and local authorities, reducing grants and subsidies, reducing the number of civil servants and other public employees, resisting pay increases in the public sector, and reorganizing public-sector industries and departments in order to achieve greater efficiency.
3. Tax cuts can be used to encourage more people to take up jobs, and people to work longer hours and more enthusiastically. They can be used to reduce equilibrium unemployment and encourage employers to take on more workers. Likewise tax cuts for businesses or increased investment allowances may encourage higher investment. The effects of tax cuts will depend on how people

respond to incentives. For example, people will only work longer hours if the substitution effect outweighs the income effect.
4. Reducing the power of trade unions by legislation could reduce disequilibrium unemployment and cost-push inflation. It could also lead to a redistribution of income to profits, which could increase investment and growth (but possibly also lead to greater inequality).
5. A reduction in welfare benefits, especially those related to unemployment, will encourage workers to accept jobs at lower wages and thus decrease equilibrium unemployment.
6. Privatization and deregulation are two examples of policies that could be used to encourage greater competition. In practice, there will be little or no gain in competition from privatization if industries are sold as monopolies.
7. A policy of free trade and free capital movements can be used to encourage greater competition from abroad.

20.3 Prices and incomes policy

On a number of occasions since the Second World War, governments have attempted to control prices, wages and perhaps other incomes directly. The aim of these prices and incomes policies has been to reduce inflation: to get price and wage increases below what they would otherwise have been.

Prices and incomes policies have taken a number of different forms. A policy may be *comprehensive* in scope: designed to control *all* prices and *all* incomes (wages, salaries, dividends, rent, etc.). Alternatively, it may be a *partial* policy: a wages policy, or a prices policy, or a policy to control certain wages (e.g. those of public-sector workers, or basic wages rather than total pay), or certain prices (e.g. nationalized industry prices).

A policy may be *voluntary*, where the government either simply asks for unions' and/or firms' support or where it offers something in exchange (e.g. tax cuts and/or increased government spending). Alternatively, a policy may be *statutory* where it is backed by law.

A policy may take the form of a complete freeze on wages and/or prices, with or without certain limited exceptions. Alternatively, there may be a ceiling to increases in wages, prices, profits, etc., or there may be some norm (e.g. 10 per cent) which people might typically expect to receive, but more may be allowed for some people who are judged as 'special cases'.

Most of these varieties were tried in the UK at one time or another during the 1960s and 1970s. As a result it is difficult to judge whether prices and incomes policies *in general* are effective. Some types might be effective. Other types might not.

Attitudes towards prices and incomes policy

What do the various schools of thought feel about prices and incomes policy?

New classical economists (extreme monetarists)

New classicists argue that prices and incomes policy should not be used. Inflation, they say, is caused purely by excessive monetary growth, and expectations adjust quickly, if not immediately, to changes in money supply. The short-run Phillips curve is vertical. Thus the cure for inflation is a reduction in the growth of money supply, and there will be no adverse effects on unemployment.

If a prices and incomes policy is imposed, at most it may temporarily suppress inflation, but the excess demand will soon lead to black markets and people getting round wage and price controls (see below). Furthermore, by interfering with the market, prices and incomes policies may have very damaging effects and may lead to falling output and employment. Whilst in operation, then, they will shift the (vertical) Phillips curve to the right.

Moderate monetarists

Moderate monetarists too are generally critical of prices and incomes policies. Like the new classicists they argue that such policies interfere with markets and can lead to lower output and employment. Nevertheless some monetarists argue that there may be a place for a temporary prices and incomes policy.

If inflation is high and the government pursues a tight monetary policy, inflation will eventually fall, and once expectations of inflation have adjusted downwards, unemployment will fall back to the natural level. But to get expectations to adjust downwards fairly rapidly, unemployment may have to rise to unacceptably high levels.

If a prices and incomes policy is imposed, it may cause people to adjust their expectations downwards quite rapidly. The short-run Phillips curve will shift downwards and inflation will be reduced without the need for such high unemployment.

Prices and incomes policy is here only being used to *supplement* monetary policy: to bring the long-run equilibrium about more quickly. It should never, say monetarists, be used to *replace* monetary policy.

Even moderate monetarists frequently reject prices and incomes policy altogether. Only some are in favour of its (temporary) use.

Keynesians

Keynesians generally are much more sympathetic towards prices and incomes policy. They differ, however, over the extent to which they would use it. Some Keynesians, like some moderate monetarists advocate prices and incomes policy primarily as a temporary weapon, to reduce expectations and hence bring a sharp initial reduction in inflation. Then for the longer run, they advocate reliance on fiscal and monetary policies and alternative supply-side policies.

Box 20.4

Prices and incomes policy in the UK
The experience of the 1970s

The Conservative government when elected in June 1970 was opposed to prices and incomes policy. It was felt to be damaging to the working of the market economy, and ineffective as a remedy for inflation. The government initially relied on relatively tight fiscal policy to contain inflation.

But continuing high inflation and growing unemployment led to a U-turn in 1972. Aggregate demand was expanded massively in order to increase growth and reduce unemployment, and a prices and incomes policy was introduced in order to restrain inflation.

There were three stages in the policy. The first stage (November 1972 – April 1973) was a five-month statutory freeze on prices and incomes. The second stage (April 1973 – November 1973) and third stage (November 1973 – February 1974) were also compulsory, and two bodies were set up to enforce the details of the policy. A Price Commission was responsible for administering a Price Code. All large firms needed the permission of the Price Commission before they could raise prices. Similarly, a Pay Board was responsible for administering the wages policy and ensuring its observance.

 Imagine that you are responsible for administering a Price Commission. Under what circumstances would you allow a firm to raise its prices? How would you check that these circumstances were genuine?

Initially the policy seemed to be moderately successful. Inflation was relatively stable at around 9 per cent for most of 1973. There were, however, serious problems with the policy.

Inflationary pressures were increasing. The government was pursuing a highly expansionary monetary and fiscal policy in a 'dash for growth'. In these circumstances, a prices and incomes policy could do little more than temporarily suppress inflation. In addition, world commodity prices, and in particular oil prices, were rising rapidly in 1973 and 1974.

Also many workers were unwilling to accept the policy. The miners' strike in the winter of 1973–4 was a direct challenge to the government. The shortage of fuel led to electricity cuts and the introduction of a three-day working week. The government called a general election asking for public endorsement of its policies. It was defeated, and as a result the policy collapsed and there was, therefore, a wage and price explosion.

Thresholds aggravated the problem. A 'threshold' clause in stage 3 allowed all workers a 40p per week rise for each 1 per cent that price rises exceeded 7 per cent above their October 1973 level. This was therefore a form of indexation: wages would *automatically* rise with inflation. The government hoped that the incomes policy would keep inflation below 7 per cent and that unions would not seek excessive wage increases with this threshold 'safety net'.

As it turned out, price rises soon exceeded the 7 per cent mark. The incoming Labour government felt obliged to keep this part of the policy in force for the full twelve months originally envisaged. It thus found threshold payments rising month by month, right up to the end of

---

Other Keynesians argue that prices and incomes policy should be part of a much longer-term 'social contract' where, in return for various promises by the government, unions and firms agree not to exercise their monopoly power. If the long-run Phillips curve can thereby be shifted to the left, the government should be able to run the economy at a lower level of unemployment.

 What promises might a government make to unions to persuade them to settle for lower wage increases? Would these promises when carried out lead to any harmful economic consequences?

Problems with prices and incomes policy: harmful side-effects

Even if a prices and incomes policy is successful in controlling prices and incomes, there may be undesirable side-effects. In a market economy, factors of production are encouraged to move to more efficient uses by the incentives of the price mechanism. The movement of factors of production is likely to be reduced if a prices and incomes

Box 20.4 (cont'd)

the period. These automatic wage rises then fuelled further price rises.

? Under what circumstances will indexation (a) help to reduce inflation; (b) make inflation worse?

The Labour government was committed to free collective bargaining. It thus abolished the Pay Board. The Price Commission was retained but the Price Code was relaxed somewhat in December 1974 in the light of falling company profits.

Worried about rising wage inflation, the government relied on a voluntary 'Social Contract' with the TUC. In return for unions ensuring that wage rises did not exceed the rate of inflation, the government agreed to introduce various social policies approved of by the unions.

This policy was not enforced, and by early 1975 wage inflation was approaching 30 per cent. The crisis forced the government to introduce a full prices and incomes policy in August 1975. The Price Commission continued to control prices, and a semi-voluntary incomes policy was adopted. The policy was known as 'Social Contract Mark II'. This prices and incomes policy consisted of four phases and lasted nearly four years.

As with the previous Conservative government's policy, this policy seemed initially successful. Inflation fell from 24 per cent in 1975 to 16 per cent in 1976, despite slightly expansionary fiscal and monetary policies (although this could equally have been due to the effects of the huge expansion in aggregate demand from 1972 to 1974 having finished working through into prices).

Given the crisis of 1975, the policy was initially acceptable to the unions. By phase 3, however, agreement with the unions had broken down. Despite the work of the Price Commission, prices were rising faster than wages, and unions were not prepared to accept further restraint. The government had to resort to putting pressure on *firms* to stick to the wages policy: the public sector would cease to do business with firms that paid wage increases above the norm. Not surprisingly, firms too were reluctant to accept this policy, and increasingly sought ways to evade price restraint in order to protect profits. Nevertheless inflation was still falling, reaching a low of 8 per cent in 1978.

By phase 4 the policy was in ruins. Many unions sought and obtained wage increases substantially above that phase's 5 per cent norm, in what became known as the 'winter of discontent'.

The government lost the general election of May 1979, and the incoming Conservative government abandoned prices and incomes policy. Such policies have not been used since. The Thatcher government saw them as at best useless, and at worst positively harmful, preventing markets from functioning so well.

? In 1989 and 1990, with inflation rising and pay settlements on average several percentage points above those of the mid-1980s, the Conservative government warned of the inflationary consequences of excessive wage demands. It tried to keep pay increases down in the public sector and faced industrial action from the rail unions, ambulance staff and other public-sector workers. What does this tell us about the its perceptions of the causes of inflation?

policy prevents relative wages, profits, rents, etc. from changing according to demand and supply.

Thus, for example, growth industries and more efficient firms cannot attract labour by offering higher wages. Contracting industries and less efficient firms may feel obliged to pay the wage norm, and may therefore be forced to reduce their labour force. Alternatively, if prices are frozen or controlled, firms will have the incentive to lower costs, but they may do this by a reduction in quality, or in research and development, or in employment.

A prices and incomes policy may reduce growth, reduce efficiency and increase unemployment. If aggregate supply is thereby reduced, the resulting excess of demand over supply in the economy (*ceteris paribus*) will increase demand-pull pressures.

These side-effects can be somewhat reduced if wage increases allow for increased productivity thereby providing an incentive for increased efficiency. In many cases, however, productivity is very difficult to measure, especially for white-collar or public-sector workers and in some cases workers may be unable to increase productivity by the very nature of their jobs. Some groups of workers will feel they

| Box 20.5 |

Urging Restraint on Top Salary Earners
A voluntary incomes policy with too few volunteers?

The open and often hostile opposition to any form of prices and incomes policy by the Thatcher government was hardly surprising given its emphasis on the operation of free-market forces. But free-market forces during the boom at the end of the 1980s led to rising wage inflation. As a result the government felt it necessary to condemn large pay settlements and to urge pay restraint.

A dramatic example of this was the rapid rise of top salaries. Cries of restraint from the Prime Minister and her colleagues fell on stony ground. 'Moderation' and the 'setting of a shining example' to the labour movement failed to impress those at the top of industry whose salaries increased by 33 per cent in 1989.

The following article appeared in the *Guardian* on 3 May 1990:

The evidence of a lack of pay restraint at the top of British companies comes as the Government is seeking to persuade workers to peg wage demands in an attempt to slow inflation. The rises fly in the face of directors' own warnings that large increases will mean fewer jobs and less investment.

The annual reports of 27 of the country's 100 biggest companies disclosing executive salaries for 1989 show that annual rises are substantially higher than the previous year, at 33 per cent. That is four times the rate of inflation and almost four times the current increase in average earnings.

The latest increases follow average rises for the best paid in Britain's top 100 companies of nearly 28 per cent last year – an increase that prompted the Prime Minister to urge business leaders to set an example.

But there is, so far, little evidence that directors have heeded government warnings. They argue that their pay is related to company performance, which was buoyant last year, in contrast to early indications for 1990 results.

Salaries for the highest-paid directors in Britain's largest 100 companies have risen by 120 per cent since 1985, in contrast to a growth in corporate earnings of 83 per cent. Highly-paid executives have also benefited from a reduction in the top rate of tax.

The next day the same paper reported that:

Sir Geoffrey Howe, Leader of the Commons, said industry leaders should show salary moderation themselves as well as demanding it from their employees.

He added that restraint was needed at a time when unit labour costs must be controlled and when the effective competitiveness of industry and its profitability are under pressure.

'Those in charge of companies and businesses should certainly take account of the need for moderation for themselves as well as those whom they employ,' he told the Commons.

Not surprisingly, this voluntary incomes policy like all the rest failed to persuade people. As Margaret Thatcher once remarked, 'You cannot buck market forces.'

---

warrant increases larger than the norm. Others will feel it to be unfair if they are paid less than similar workers elsewhere. The more the authorities have to look at individual cases, however, the more expensive the policy becomes to administer.

 Assume that you are an ambulance driver, a teacher or a doctor. Make out a case why you should be paid more than the norm allowed by a current prices and incomes policy.

Problems with prices and incomes policy: difficulties in controlling prices and incomes

Prices and incomes policy may fail to control inflation for several reasons.

Some workers and firms may be able to evade government controls.

Wage drift

Where total pay including overtime, bonuses, etc. increases more rapidly than basic pay.

If basic wage rates are controlled, wage drift may occur. This is where total pay increases by more than basic rates. This could be due to promotion, job-changing, job reclassification, more bonuses, more overtime (without necessarily any increase in output), more perks, etc. This problem is particularly serious for the government if firms are very willing to grant such wage increases and thereby to assist workers in evading the policy.

The problem could be reduced if the government controlled the total amount of wages that firms pay out. If, however, the government wished to allow productivity deals, there would be the problem of checking whether there was a genuine increase in productivity.

Firms can get round price controls by redefining their product, so that it becomes a new product and thus has a new price. Sunshine washing powder could have extra added brightness and become 'New Sunshine'. Firms may be able to reduce quality, contents, size, etc. If firms are allowed to pass increases in costs on to the consumer in higher prices, they may exaggerate cost increases in order to obtain larger price increases.

If enough powerful groups resist a prices and incomes policy, the government may not have sufficient power to enforce it. If the government resorts to legal sanctions, this may create a confrontation from which the government may feel forced to back down.

If a prices and incomes policy is initially successful in reducing inflation, the government may feel less constrained to control aggregate demand. The government may even be obliged to expand aggregate demand (e.g. by increasing social services or by cutting taxes) in order to gain unions' acceptance of pay restraint. Increased demand will increase expenditure on imports. If the exchange rate is flexible, it will tend to depreciate and thus drive up the price of imports.

Increased demand will encourage firms and unions to evade the policy. Firms, facing increased orders, will be keen to maintain good industrial relations and high productivity. They may thus be willing to collude with unions to find ways to pay more than is currently allowed by the policy.

Governments which have resorted to prices and incomes policy have tended (initially) to see it as a temporary measure, since distortions to the price mechanism, evasion and resistance to the policy are likely to grow with time. When the controls are removed, however, there may be a wage/price explosion as people try to make up for what they feel they lost while the policy was in operation. If people expect such an explosion, the expected rate of inflation will rise, thus further fuelling inflation.

 How may a government attempt to keep the expected rate of inflation down as an incomes policy is drawing to an end?

Lessons from past experience

Although prices and incomes policy suffers from serious disadvantages, these can be lessened if the policy is appropriately designed:

- The policy is more likely to succeed if the government can obtain the co-operation of unions and firms. The government thus may need to persuade people that the policy is in their interest.
- It should be used to *supplement* demand management policies, not *replace* them.
- The government may increase people's willingness to accept lower wage rises if it reduces taxes or increases benefits. The problem here, though, is that aggregate demand is likely to increase as a result.
- The government must set the norm sufficiently low so as to have the desired effect on inflation, but not so low that resistance becomes so great that the policy breaks down.
- As an emergency measure (in an inflationary crisis), a simple and clear policy may be more politically acceptable. If the policy is perceived to be fair, people may be more willing to accept it.
- If the policy is continued beyond, say, six months to a year, sufficient flexibility may have to be built in to allow for productivity increases and the consideration of

Box 20.6

Prices and Incomes Policy Latin American Style
King Canute against a tidal wave?

Hyperinflation has been commonplace in Latin America. In many countries inflation has frequently been over 100 per cent. In some cases it has been over 1000 per cent.

Such inflations are invariably accompanied by similar increases in money supply, but the underlying causes of such increases are to be found in the broader political and economic environment. Rising raw material costs (e.g. the quadrupling of oil prices in the early 1970s), the steep rise in interest rates in the early 1980s, various natural disasters, ambitious expenditure programmes by governments and an unwillingness to raise taxes have all been blamed as contributing factors.

In this environment, Latin American governments have frequently resorted to direct controls over prices and incomes. The Argentinian Austral Plan (1985) and the Brazilian Cruzado Plan (1986), Bresser Plan (1987), Plano Verao (1989) and Collor Plan (1990) have all had wage and price controls as a major element (although in the Collor Plan a massive reduction in money supply and a freezing of savings accounts was the dominant element).

In Brazil the use of prices and incomes policy has tended to be more extensive than in other Latin American countries. The indexation of wages, prices, interest rates and rents has tended to alternate with periodic freezes. The Cruzado Plan, for example, involved a general price freeze and a partial freeze on wages and other earnings.

As with most prices and incomes policies attempted elsewhere, assessing the success or otherwise of such strategies has been difficult. On face value they appear to have had little long-term impact on inflationary trends. For example, the Argentinian Austral Plan ended in

disarray after direct controls on wages had been first imposed, then lifted and then, as inflation soared above 150 per cent, reimposed.

The Brazilian Cruzado Plan equally ran into problems. It attempted to freeze wages and prices, but with growing shortages of basic items like meat and milk, the government was forced to raise the price of many of these goods. This set in motion a rise in wages, which were frozen only so long as inflation remained below 20 per cent. With wage levels re-adjusted as prices soared above the trigger level, the whole process began to repeat itself and the plan was abandoned. The imposition of the plan in 1986 had contributed to a fall in inflation from 235 per cent in 1985 to 65 per cent in 1986. But by 1987 inflation was reaching hyperinflation levels. The rate was 416 per cent in 1987, just over 1000 per cent in 1988 and over 1500 per cent in 1989.

Even given what appears to be a series of highly unsuccessful attempts at prices and incomes policy, the use of direct controls on prices and incomes remains a crucial part of Latin American anti-inflationary strategy. Assessment of their success or otherwise is extremely difficult, however, given that they are frequently only one strategy used amongst others and given the unstable international environment these countries have faced in recent years with high and fluctuating interest rates and the burden of huge foreign debts.

? Make out a case for and against using indexation as part of an anti-inflationary strategy during a period of hyperinflation.

questions of comparability. It should not be so flexible, however, that everyone becomes a special case. There must be some way of preventing phoney productivity deals, but with the minimum of administrative costs.

Prices and incomes policy in the future

In the past, prices and incomes policies have been introduced at times of inflationary and/or balance of payments crises. As a result they have been able to do little more than temporarily suppress inflation. Eventually, the forces of excess demand have come through into higher prices.

An alternative approach, advocated by many Keynesians and by some centrist politicians, is for a prices and incomes policy to be introduced in a time of recession, when there is plenty of slack in the economy. A recovery of demand, they argue, without a prices and incomes policy, will lead to rising inflation with probably only a modest reduction in unemployment. As soon as unemployment begins to fall, there will be a renewed upward pressure on wages and prices. With a prices and incomes policy, however, the growth in demand could lead to increases in output and employment *without* producing a rise in inflation. Workers may be quite willing to accept restraint in *money* wage increases if this means bigger *real* wage increases. Trade unions may be more willing to accept a prices and incomes policy if they see it as part of a package of growth and recovery, rather than as a means of suppressing real wages.

To back up such policies, many economists have advocated the use of tax penalties. Pay increases above the norm would be subject to higher levels of tax. These taxes might be levied on the workers themselves or more probably on their employers.

▲ SUMMARY

1. Prices and incomes policies differ in terms of their scope, their degree of compulsion and the levels of price and income changes that are permitted.
2. New classicists and moderate monetarists too are generally opposed to prices and incomes policy, arguing that at best it can merely suppress inflation for a short period of time. Over the longer term it will reduce aggregate supply by interfering in the working of the market. Many Keynesians, however, see it as playing an important role especially in the short run as a means of making rapid and substantial reductions in inflation. In the longer term it can be part of a social contract.
3. Prices and incomes policy can have harmful side-effects in that, by freezing wage and price differentials, incentives to the movement of factors of production are reduced.
4. It may also fail to control inflation if people can evade the policy, if the government finds difficulty in enforcing it, if

the government feels less constrained to control aggregate demand, or if there is a wage/price explosion when the policy ends.

5. There have been three major attempts in the UK to operate a prices and incomes policy: 1964–70, 1972–74 and 1975–79. In each case there were initial successes, but then resistance and evasion grew.
6. The disadvantages can be lessened if there is co-operation between government, industry and the unions, if the policy is used as part of a package of policies, if it is perceived to be fair, if it is flexible enough to allow for special cases but not so flexible that everyone becomes a special case, and if it is introduced at a time of recovery from recession and when, therefore, there is scope for *real* wage increases.
7. One form of incomes policy is to impose tax penalties on firms paying above the norm.

20.4 Regional policy

Unemployment is not evenly distributed around the country. Northern Ireland and parts of the north and west of England, parts of Wales and parts of Scotland have unemployment rates two or three times that in the south-east of England. What is more, regional disparities in unemployment increased substantially during the 1980s. This is illustrated in Table 20.2.

Similarly, there are regional disparities in average incomes, rates of growth and levels of prices, as well as in health, crime, housing, etc. Many of these disparities too have grown wider in recent years. The magnitude of the problem in many parts of the north has led to the 'north–south divide' becoming a major political issue.

Causes of regional imbalance and the role of regional policy

Many industries are concentrated in certain areas, to take advantage of some natural resource or of external economies of scale. With the decline and/or rationalization of many of the older industries (mining, textiles, steel, shipbuilding) and the concentration

Table 20.2 Regional unemployment: selected years

Region	Unemployment (%)		
	January 1979	January 1987	January 1989
UK (average)	4.2	10.9	5.7
South-East	2.9	7.9	3.6
East-Anglia	3.5	8.2	3.4
South-West	4.5	9.0	4.1
East Midlands	3.5	9.9	4.9
West Midlands	3.8	12.5	5.9
Yorks & Humberside	4.1	12.3	6.8
North-West	5.3	13.4	7.6
Wales	5.6	13.1	6.7
Scotland	5.8	13.8	8.3
North	6.2	15.1	8.6
Northern Ireland	7.9	17.6	14.0

Source: *Economic Trends* (CSO).

of many of the newer industries in the south, structural and technological unemployment and demand-shift inflation result.

If the market functioned perfectly, there would be no regional problem. If wages were lower and unemployment were higher in the north, people would simply move to the south. This would reduce unemployment in the north and help to fill vacancies in the south. It would drive up wages in the north and reduce wages in the south. The process would continue until regional disparities were eliminated.

The capital market would function similarly. New investment would be located in the areas offering the highest rate of return. If land and labour were cheaper in the north, capital would be attracted there. This too would help to eliminate regional disparities.

In practice the market does not behave as just described. Labour may be geographically immobile. The regional pattern of industrial location may change more rapidly than the labour market can adjust to it. Thus jobs may be lost in the depressed areas more rapidly than people can migrate.

Is capital similarly immobile? Existing capital stock is highly immobile. Buildings and most machinery cannot be moved to where the unemployed are! *New* capital, however, is much more mobile. The problem here, though, is that there may be insufficient new investment, especially during a recession, to halt regional decline, even if some investors are attracted into the depressed areas by low wages and cheap land.

The continuing shift in demand may in part be due to regional multiplier effects

In the south, the new industries and the new workers attracted there create additional demand. This in turn creates additional output and jobs and hence more migration. There is a multiplied rise in income. In the north, the decline in demand and loss of jobs causes a multiplied downward effect. Loss of jobs in manufacturing leads to less money being spent in the local community; transport and other service industries lose custom. The whole region becomes more depressed.

Differences in regional unemployment and incomes cannot be eliminated by general demand management policies. They are not symptoms of disequilibrium of *aggregate* demand and supply. Rather they reflect imbalances *between* markets that have not been corrected. There may be persistent excess demand in London and the south-east, while at the same time there is persistent deficient demand in the north.

Regional multiplier effects

When a change in injections into or withdrawals from a particular region causes a multiplied change in income in that region. The regional multiplier (k_r) is given by $1/mpw_r$, where the import component of mpw_r consists of imports into that region either from abroad or from other regions of the economy.

In theory, regional policy could aim to increase consumer demand for the goods produced in the depressed regions, and reduce consumer demand for goods produced in the prosperous ones. In practice, however, regional policy concentrates on the supply side. It aims to encourage industries to move to the depressed regions.

Radical-right policies

If the regional problem is due to a failure of markets, then should markets be made more perfect, or should the government intervene to influence directly the movement of labour or the location of industry? The radical right favours the first of these approaches: making the market more perfect.

The radical right argues that firms are the best judges of where they should locate. Government intervention would impede efficient decision taking by firms. It is better, they argue, to remove impediments to the market achieving regional balance. For example, they favour the following:

Locally negotiated wage agreements. Nationally negotiated wage rates mean that wages are not driven down in the north and up in the south. This in turn means that firms are discouraged from locating in the north. At the same time firms find it difficult to recruit labour in the south, where wages are not high enough to compensate for the higher cost of living there. Thus the Thatcher government in the mid-1980s advocated that locally negotiated wages should replace nationally negotiated wages.

Control of local authority taxes. Many Labour-led local authorities in depressed areas in the past sought to protect services by putting up the rates (both to individuals and to businesses). This could discourage firms from moving into the area and might encourage others to leave. The Thatcher government introduced measures to prevent such increases and thereby to remove this impediment to regional balance. In the early and mid-1980s many of the higher spending local authorities were 'rate capped' (and later 'charge capped' or 'poll tax capped'). They were given limits to the rates they could set (for both individuals and businesses). The introduction of a uniform business rate in 1990 meant that business rates were set *nationally* not locally.

Reducing unemployment benefits. A general reduction in unemployment benefits and other welfare payments would encourage the unemployed in the north to migrate south, or enable firms to offer lower wages in the north without people preferring to stay 'on the dole'.

The problem with these policies is that they attempt initially to *widen* the economic divide between workers in the north and south in order to encourage capital and labour to move. Such policies would hardly be welcomed by workers in the north!

1. Think of some other 'pro-market' solutions to the regional problem.
2. Do workers in the north benefit from pro-market solutions?

Interventionist policies

The political centre and left argue in favour of an *interventionist* approach. In theory, this could involve policies to encourage *migration*. For example, people could be given grants to move, or retraining programmes could be devised for potential migrants to enable them to take up the jobs in the south. The problem with this approach is that, via regional multiplier effects, it could exacerbate the problem. The north could become more depressed; the south more overcrowded. Interventionists therefore favour policies to encourage *firms* to move. There are four ways that this can be done.

Subsidies and tax concessions in the depressed regions

These can have two beneficial effects: an *income* effect and a *substitution* effect. The income effect is where higher income for firms, as a result of subsidies, encourages them to produce more output and hence to employ more people. The substitution effect is where firms are encouraged to substitute labour for capital: in other words, to use more labour-intensive techniques.

General subsidies. Grants or concessions for buildings, reduced rates of corporation tax, grants for firms to move, rate relief, etc. would lead to an income effect as firms were attracted into the region. There would be more employment. But the firms would not thereby be encouraged to use more labour-intensive techniques. There would be no substitution effect.

Employment subsidies. Subsidies for employment, or reduced employers' national insurance contributions, would lead to both an income effect *and* a substitution effect. Firms would be attracted into the region and there would also be an encouragement to substitute (now cheaper) labour for capital. Even if many firms have little scope for substituting labour for capital, employment subsidies would have the advantage of attracting into the area firms which *already* use labour-intensive techniques.

Capital subsidies. Grants for investment or other measures which reduce the cost of capital would lead to a positive income effect. The substitution effect, however, would be *negative*. Firms attracted to the area would be encouraged to use capital-intensive techniques, and would thus provide little employment.

In the short run, therefore, employment subsidies will have the largest effect on employment. In the long run, however, it is not so clear cut. Capital-intensive industries may require the services of local *labour*-intensive industries. Also capital-intensive industries may be more profitable and have a higher rate of growth, thus generating more employment in the future.

> **?** If a Japanese car manufacturer were attracted into an unemployment blackspot and opened up a highly capital-intensive 'robot-line' car assembly plant, in what other local industries might employment be stimulated?

The provision of facilities in the depressed regions

The government or local authorities could provide facilities directly to incoming firms – facilities such as land and buildings. Alternatively, government could improve the infrastructure of the region, such as roads and communications, and local technical colleges. Another alternative is for the government to move some of its own departments out of London and locate them in areas of high unemployment. The siting of the vehicle licensing centre in Swansea and the National Savings Bank in Durham are examples of this.

Restrictions on the expansion of firms in the prosperous regions

In contrast to the two types of measure above, the government could restrict expansion of firms in prosperous regions, thereby encouraging firms to move to the depressed regions. There are two ways this could be done.

Taxes. The government could tax company income, employment or new building at higher rates in prosperous regions. A tax on income or buildings is probably preferable to a tax on employment. If employment is taxed, it might simply encourage firms in prosperous areas to substitute capital for labour, rather than move to depressed areas. On the other hand, the firms most likely to be forced to move by employment taxes would be the labour-intensive firms – the firms capable of providing the most employment in the depressed regions. It depends, therefore, on the elasticity of substitution of capital for labour. The more readily capital can be substituted, the less likely will the firms be to move.

Regulation. The government could simply prevent firms from setting up or expanding in the prosperous regions. The old Industrial Development Certificate (IDC) system comes under this heading. Before 1972 an IDC was required in all areas for new industrial buildings over a certain size. From 1972 they were only required in non-assisted areas. By refusing an IDC in a prosperous region the government would hope to force the firm concerned to move to a depressed region. The IDC system was suspended in 1982.

There is a major problem with both of these measures. If firms are prevented or discouraged from expanding in the south, they may not expand at all, or may go abroad.

In comparing the different types of interventionist policy it is important to distinguish policies that merely seek to *modify* the market by altering market signals, from policies that *replace* the market.

Regulation replaces the market, and unless very carefully devised and monitored may lead to ill-thought-out decisions being made. Either there must be simple rules about which firms are to be denied permission to set up in the south, in which case there may be many firms which will not expand at all; or alternatively, discretion must be given to government officials to grant or deny permission as they see fit, in which case the administration of the policy may become bureaucratic and arbitrary.

Subsidies and *taxes* merely modify the market, leaving it to individual firms to make their final location decisions. Taxes and subsidies in theory can internalize externalities: charging firms in the south for the external costs they impose on society, and rewarding firms in the north for the external benefits they confer on society. Taxes and subsidies can make actual prices reflect opportunity costs rather than market power. Again, ill-thought-out decisions can be made about the rates of tax or subsidy. If there are uniform tax or subsidy rates throughout a region, then they will be higher than necessary in some cases and lower in others.

> **?** 1. If you were the government, how would you set about deciding the rate of subsidy to pay a firm thinking of moving to the north?
> 2. Should firms already located in the north be paid a subsidy?

Regional policy in the UK

Certain areas are identified as requiring government financial assistance. UK regional policy has focused on *development areas* and *intermediate areas. Development areas* cover the bulk of Scotland, South Wales, parts of North Wales, the north-east and north-west of England, and the far south-west of England, plus other smaller areas severely affected by industrial closures. (Until 1984 *special development areas* were also defined. They were small areas suffering from severe economic decline and received higher levels of financial assistance.) *Intermediate areas* lie outside the development areas, often adjacent to them. Although they suffer similar problems to the development areas, these are not so acute, and intermediate areas therefore qualify for less assistance than the development areas. The particularly acute economic problems of Northern Ireland qualify it for more generous assistance than the development areas.

Regional development grants (RDGs) were the major form of regional assistance for many years. In March 1988, however, the government decided not to grant any new RDGs, and thus the scheme was to be gradually phased out. RDGs covered 15 per cent of the costs of buildings and machinery (with a maximum of £10 000 per job created in large firms). They were *automatically* available to manufacturing firms and certain service-sector firms locating in development areas. They were not available in intermediate areas.

Regional selective assistance (RSA) is in the form of *discretionary* grants given for certain projects. The main basis for their award is job creation. They are available in both development and intermediate areas. The amount awarded is normally that judged to be the minimum necessary for the project to proceed (subject to certain maxima).

RDGs and RSA can be supplemented by grants from the *European regional development fund (ERDF)*. Since 1985 it has provided grants up to 50 per cent for job-creating projects and projects to develop infrastructure. The money is available for use in the development and intermediate areas and in Northern Ireland. The Department of Trade and Industry deducts the amount of any ERDF grant from any selective assistance that it gives.

Assistance for small businesses is provided as grants in development areas to firms that employ fewer than 25 people. These involve new investment grants of 15 per cent of capital expenditure and new innovation grants of 50 per cent. *Enterprise initiative grants* are available in both development and intermediate areas to encourage the launching of new enterprises. Grants of two-thirds of the cost of business consultancy schemes are available.

During the 1980s several new geographical areas were identified. *Enterprise zones* are very small districts in urban areas suffering acute industrial decline. Substantial incentives are given to firms setting up in enterprise zones: 100 per cent capital allowances on property, exemption from rates and land tax, fewer planning regulations and less bureaucratic intervention generally.

Urban Development Corporations (UDCs) were first established in the early 1980s and were designed to tackle inner-city decay. Their brief was to combat this decay by the physical renewal of land and buildings with the aim of attracting private-sector investment and development into the area. By the end of the 1980s there were ten such UDCs in operation, with control over approximately 40 000 acres of land and in receipt of funding in the region of £200 million per annum from central government. The UDCs have a pump-priming role: i.e. to stimulate private-sector-led regeneration of inner-city areas. They have considerable powers to enable them to do this, many of which override local authority powers. For example, they can grant planning permission; acquire, hold and manage land and property (including making compulsory purchases); and provide grants and other assistance to firms.

The government also provides grants directly for various enterprise schemes in certain inner-city areas which are subject to high levels of deprivation.

The Thatcher government's attitude towards regional policy

There were substantial changes in regional policy under the Thatcher government. There were two main elements in these changes.

Reducing the total amount of money spent on regional assistance

After considerable growth in government expenditure on regional policies in the late

Table 20.3 Regional development grants plus regional selective assistance: selected years 1975–88

	1975/76	1978/79	1981/82	1983/84	1985/86	1987/88
Total RDG plus RSA						
At current prices (£m)	348	516	693	588	534	419
At 1975 prices (£m)	348	353	317	237	193	140
As % of GDP						
factor cost	0.35	0.38	0.31	0.24	0.17	0.11

Sources: *Regional Trends* (CSO); *Reports of the Industrial Development Act 1982* (HMSO).

1960s and mid-1970s, there were substantial cuts in regional assistance in the 1980s under the Thatcher government. This is illustrated in Table 20.3.

In part this stemmed from its general desire to cut the size of public expenditure, in order to reduce the PSBR and give scope for tax cuts; and in part it stemmed from its particular desire to allow regional disparities to be corrected, wherever possible, by market forces.

To achieve these goals, the following measures were introduced in 1984:

- The special development area category was abolished (with its higher RDG rate).
- The portion of the country eligible for (automatic) RDGs was reduced from 23 per cent of the working population of Great Britain in 1979 to 15 per cent in 1984.
- The basis on which RDGs were given was redefined in 1984. This substantially reduced their amount. By 1987/88, the first year in which the new arrangements were fully in force, RDGs were less than half what they would have been under the old arrangements.
- Intermediate areas now accounted for a larger proportion of the total assisted areas. These only receive modest government support through RSA, but are still eligible for support from the European Regional Development Fund.

Making regional assistance more cost-effective
The Thatcher government was highly critical of the RDG system:

- Regional development grants were paid automatically to firms moving into development areas, even if they would have moved there anyway.
- RDGs were paid for replacement of plant and machinery, as well as for new investment. But replacement investment creates little if any jobs.
- RDGs were largely confined to manufacturing industry, even though service industries are generally more labour intensive.
- Some RDGs were paid automatically: they did not discriminate between efficient and inefficient firms.
- RDGs were essentially *capital* grants: they thus encouraged firms to become more capital intensive.

Not surprisingly, the government claimed that the system was not a cost-effective means of creating new jobs. As a result RDGs were severely restricted in 1984 and phased out completely after 1988 (see Box 20.7). Henceforth regional assistance would be mainly in the form of regional selective assistance.

RSA is not automatic. It is given at the discretion of the Department of Trade and Industry. The government intended that it would only be awarded to projects that were cost-effective in creating jobs. But given the substantial reduction in total government expenditure on regional assistance (see Table 20.3), there would have to

Box 20.7

Regional Development Grants (Termination) Bill (10 March 1988)

An excerpt from the House of Commons debate

The Minister of State, Scottish Office (Mr Ian Lang):

The ending of the regional development grant scheme is part of a group of measures by which the Government aim to strengthen regional policy and to make it more cost-effective. At present regional development grant is available for a wide range of projects in development areas. The scheme involves virtually automatic grant payments at standard rates. This mechanistic nature of the scheme make it unsatisfactory in a number of respects. The grant is available to companies of any size and there is no assessment made at the time of application of whether a project really needs to be grant-aided before it can proceed or whether is based on a viable business plan. A large number of projects therefore receive aid which would have gone ahead in the same location in any case. The waste of scarce public resources that arises cannot be justified. A less automatic approach to regional assistance is necessary. In this way we shall ensure that projects are properly evaluated in advance and that only those where need is demonstrated receive assistance. That is the basis on which regional assistance will be administered in future.

The changes that we are making are positive. Regional selective assistance continues, and funding provision for it has increased. New grants to assist small firms in development areas to pursue investment and innovation projects will come into effect on 1 April.

These policies show our determination to use public funds wisely and effectively to strike at the root of the problem of regional disadvantage. No longer will money be thrown at companies in a wasteful and unnecessary attempt to ensure that they do what they had all along intended to do.

Mr Austin Mitchell (Great Grimsby):

A point that we emphasise constantly in Committee but which we still have not got across to Ministers is that the great advantage of regional development grants is that they are automatic. They are given automatically to firms going to development areas. Firms know that the grant is there and can take it into account. Firms pay less tax because of the automatic nature of those grants than they would pay under regional selective assistance. Because the grants are automatic it is easier to attract foreign firms.

Surely it must be easier to attract footloose international industry if we can offer it the automatic guarantee of a regional development grant.

It is the automatic nature of these grants that is their strength, but it is also the reason why the Government object to these grants. They do not like the automatic nature. Specifically, the Treasury does not like anything that is demand-led, as this is, because, if a firm goes to a region, it gets the grant. That is what rankles with the Treasury. It wants the power to control those grants, it can cut regional selective assistance or impose cash limits on it ... That cannot happen with demand-led grants such as regional development grants.

Regional strategies, economic policies and incentives to attract industry to the regions are not only a matter of social justice and fairness between regions but make

have been a huge increase in cost-effectiveness in the move from RGDs to RSA, if as many jobs were to have been created as before.

 What are the arguments for and against relying entirely on *discretionary* regional grants?

Conclusions

Regional unemployment disparities in the UK have not narrowed in recent years. Does this mean, then, that regional policy is a failure? To answer this question it would be necessary to know (a) what unemployment rates would have been in the absence of regional policy (they might have been much worse) and (b) whether alternative regional policies would have been more successful. These questions could only be answered with a model of the national and regional economies. Unfortunately, there is no one universally agreed model.

Box 20.7 (cont'd)

economic sense. This is a Government of the country by the south-east, for the south-east. The south-east is better off, yet it is the area that is producing the pressures and the inflation which the Government are using as an excuse to damp down economic expansion. Where does the pressure of skill shortages come? It comes in the south-east. Where is the pressure of rising house prices, which has an effect on inflation? It is in the south-east. Where are house prices being used as a lever to get more and more credit to spend more and more? It is in the south-east, not in the north.

In other words, all those pressures of inflation from London are being used as an excuse to damp down the economy in a way that hits the rest of the country quite disproportionately. It hits the areas of the country that are represented by Labour Members, and the Minister is compounding that with this legislation. It is no good telling people in the north that there will be a trickle-down effect from the prosperity of the south-east. I do not know whether we are supposed to buy their second-hand Porsches or Gucci shoes or whether we are supposed to have the wet back economy of people travelling down the M1 to obtain work in the building trade because no jobs are available in their own areas.

It makes sense to use the social capital and facilities of the north by attracting industry to the area. To do so we need weapons such as automatic regional development grants.

Mr Anthony Coombs (Wyre Forest):

In welcoming the Bill, let me say first that the abolition of regional development grant and the subsequent changes in regional policy are long overdue. I say that not only because I come from the West Midlands, which had to undergo its industrial re-structuring without any benefit of regional development grant, but because generally regional development grants have not managed – in the words of the Hon. Member for Fife Central (Mr McLeish) during the Committee stage – to 'equalise opportunities

for our firms and businesses so that some day they can take part in the great enterprise culture which seems to be sweeping the nation' (*Official Report*, Standing Committee D, 16 February 1988, c. 25).

Too often in the past, they have been inefficient and wasteful, and have distorted the regional economies and damaged the job prospects of precisely the people they were designed to help.

That the grants have been costly is beyond doubt. Over the past 20 years, the 600,000 jobs have been bought at the cost of some £35,000 per job. Even the Labour-controlled city council in Birmingham, through its job creation scheme, spends a maximum of £10,000 per job. An average enterprise agency would not consider spending more than £5,000 per job, and the French system of regional assistance mentioned by the Hon. Member for Great Grimsby (Mr Mitchell) in Committee spends about £5,000 per job. The costliness of our sort of regional policy is evident for all to see. It is small wonder that the Public Accounts Committee said in 1987 that there were serious questions about the cost-effectiveness of this kind of assistance.

Mr Henry McLeish (Fife, Central):

Clearly, we are witnessing not just the termination of regional development grant but the abandonment of any serious semblance of regional industrial strategy. This is a step-by-step process. The Government know from experience and, as my Hon. Friends appreciate, they do not do things overnight. Step by step we are seeing the abandonment of any policy for effective regional aid.[2]

? 1. Summarize the arguments of the two sides.
2. If automatic regional grants were reintroduced, is there any way they could be redesigned to make them more cost-effective?

[2] *Hansard*, 10 March 1988.

Nevertheless, some tentative conclusions can be reached:

- A more carefully targeted policy, which focuses on job creation (subject to efficiency criteria), is likely to be more cost-effective than general investment grants. Similarly, a policy that does not discriminate against the service sector, or small firms, is likely to be more cost-effective than one that concentrates on manufacturing (and often large-scale, capital-intensive manufacturing at that). The measures of 1984 and 1988 were a move in this direction.
- The government could focus its national expenditure more specifically on the depressed regions. The relocation of more government offices might help, but so too would the deliberate location of much of the spending of the various government departments and the targeting of infrastructure construction – roads, hospitals, schools, etc. – in the depressed regions.
- Given the magnitude of the regional problem, there is a strong case for a substantial *increase* in regional assistance, not the substantial *decrease* that has actually occurred.

Box 20.8

'Will the Last One in Consett Please Turn Out the Lights'[3]

When the steelworks in Consett finally stopped production in September 1980, making 3700 steelworkers redundant, this small town of 30 000 inhabitants was devastated. Over the following months a further twenty local firms closed down and by 1982 Consett had lost half its traditional manufacturing industry. Unemployment and despondency were high. But despite this, a wholesale exodus of Consett residents did not occur and the picture today presents a dramatic change in fortunes. Rush-hour traffic jams and wine bars signify the area's new-found prosperity. Since 1980 some 3900 jobs have been created, reducing unemployment back to its 1979 level.

But what have been the causes of this turnabout? Has it been due to the operation of the free market, or to government intervention?

Private enterprise certainly played a decisive role in the area's redevelopment, with capital being attracted by low costs and a relatively skilled pool of labour. But there were also key organizational, financial and infrastructural inputs from the public sector. Regional grants were co-ordinated by the Derwentside Development Agency, and British Steel helped in re-establishing the local economy by encouraging the setting-up of new businesses.

Consett seems to be a successful case of co-ordinated public and private enterprise.

? 1. Why is there not necessarily a mass exodus from towns experiencing exceptionally high rates of local unemployment?
2. What sort of industries would be most likely to be attracted into a town like Consett?

[3] Graffiti on a door of the derelict steelworks.

The problem of high regional unemployment in the 1980s is in part a manifestation of the much higher levels of *national* unemployment than in the past. A general expansion of economic activity throughout the whole country, while perhaps not removing regional *disparities*, goes a long way towards easing the problems of the depressed regions.

▲ SUMMARY

1. Regional disparities arise from a changing pattern of industrial production. With many of the older industries concentrated in the north and the newer ones in the south, and with an acceleration in the rate of industrial change, so the gap between north and south has widened.
2. Regional disparities can in theory be corrected by the market, with capital being attracted to areas of low wages and workers being attracted to areas of high wages.
3. In practice, regional disparities persist because of capital and labour immobility and regional multiplier effects.
4. The radical-right solution is to remove impediments to the market achieving regional balance. They favour such policies as local rather than national pay bargaining, reducing unemployment benefits, adopting uniform business rates and charge capping local authorities.
5. Interventionist solutions focus on measures to encourage

firms to move to areas of high unemployment. These measures might include subsidies or tax concessions for firms which move, the provision of facilities and improved infrastructure in the depressed regions, the siting of government offices in the depressed regions and the prevention of firms expanding in the prosperous regions. In the case of financial incentives, employment subsidies will create more jobs than general subsidies, which in turn will create more jobs than capital subsidies.

6. In the UK there has been a movement away from general grants to firms in development areas (RDGs) to discretionary grants (RSA) based on job creation in both development and intermediate areas. There are also regional grants from the EC and grants and incentives for enterprise zones and inner cities.

20.5 Industrial policy

The poor performance of UK industry

For decades, the UK has had a lower level of investment relative to national income than other industrialized countries. This is illustrated in Table 20.4.

Table 20.4 Gross fixed capital formation as a percentage of GDP: 1960–89

Year (average)	UK	W. Germany	Japan	OECD[1] (total)
1960–67	17.7	25.2	31.0	21.0
1968–73	19.1	24.4	34.6	22.3
1974–79	19.3	20.8	31.8	22.3
1980–84	16.3	21.1	29.6	21.0
1985–89	16.3	19.1	30.1	20.5

[1] OECD: Organization for Economic Co-operation and Development (the developed capitalist economies).

Sources: *Historical Statistics 1960–87* (OECD, 1988); *Main Economic Indicators* (OECD, 1990).

This low level of investment has been a major reason for the UK's poor growth performance. It has also meant that in many industries there has emerged a widening technological gap between the UK and her major competitors, such as Japan and Germany. In many industries the UK's productivity lags well behind these other countries. This, in turn, is reflected in the poor quality and high cost of many UK products. The fact that wages in the UK have been lower than in competing countries has not been sufficient to offset this.

As a result there has been a growing import penetration of the UK market. Imports of manufactured products have grown more rapidly than UK manufactured exports. The result has been that the UK in recent years has become a net importer of manufactured products. This is illustrated in Table 20.5.

Table 20.5 UK balance of trade in manufactures: selected years 1974–89

	1974	1978	1980	1982	1984	1986	1988	1989
Exports of manufactures (£bn)	13.3	28.0	34.8	37.3	46.7	54.5	66.0	76.3
Imports of manufactures (£bn)	11.7	24.4	31.2	37.1	53.0	62.8	83.3	95.1
Balance of trade in manufactures (£bn)	+1.6	+3.6	+3.6	+0.2	−6.3	−8.2	−17.3	−18.8

Sources: *Monthly Digest of Statistics* (CSO); *Annual Abstract of Statistics* (CSO).

Three vicious circles have existed:

- Low investment leads to low productivity, low quality and hence a lack of competitiveness of UK goods. This leads to balance of trade deficits. This leads to deflationary policies with higher interest rates. This leads to low investment.
- Low investment leads to low growth of profits. This leads to low investment.
- Low investment leads to low productivity growth. This leads to low growth in real wages. But unions, seeking to achieve an increase in living standards, demand real

wages that cannot be met. This causes cost-push inflation. This may cause deflationary policies to be pursued, uncertainty for firms and an erosion of profits. This leads to low investment.

De-industrialization

Not only has the competitiveness of UK industry declined, but industrial production in the UK has grown much more slowly than in other industrialized countries. Manufacturing industry hardly grew at all until the end of the 1980s. Manufacturing output in the UK in 1986 was only 1 per cent higher than in 1970, whereas in the developed world as a whole it was 50 per cent higher. The growth of industrial and manufacturing production is illustrated in Table 20.6.

 Why, do you think, was the UK's performance in *industrial* production in the early 1980s better than in *manufacturing* production?

Table 20.6 Industrial and manufacturing production in the UK and the OECD countries: selected years 1970–89

	Industrial production (1970 = 100)		Manufacturing production[1] (1970 = 100)	
	UK	OECD (total)	UK	OECD (total)
1970	100	100	100	100
1974	109	120	109	120
1975	103	110	102	109
1978	115	129	106	129
1980	111	135	97	134
1982	109	131	91	128
1984	115	145	97	143
1986	123	153	101	150
1988	131	164	114	165
1989	132	171	120	172

[1] Industrial production less mining, oil, energy and water.

Sources: *Indicators of Industrial Activity* (OECD); *Monthly Digest of Statistics* (CSO).

Policy alternatives

How may investment be increased? How may efficiency be increased? How may de-industrialization be halted or slowed down? There are two approaches: a demand-side approach and a supply-side approach.

One part of the *demand-side* approach has already been examined. It is the Keynesian approach of trying to maintain a high level of activity in the economy by demand management policy. It is based on the premise that the major determinant of investment is consumer demand.

Another approach on the demand side is to reduce the demand for imports by import control. This would then allow aggregate demand to be maintained at high levels without causing balance of payments deficits. Investment could thus be sustained with no fear of impending deflationary policies.

Supply-side approaches aim to provide more incentives to invest for any given level of aggregate demand. They also attempt to improve industrial efficiency and competitiveness for any given level of investment.

The advocates of such policies highlight a number of supply-side weaknesses of

Box 20.9

Oiling the Wheels of British Industry?
The effects of the North Sea

When the UK oil production was at its peak in 1985, some 2½ million barrels a day were being pumped from the North Sea. This made the UK the world's sixth largest oil producer, accounting for some 5 per cent of total production.

Not surprisingly, this has had a major impact on the UK economy. The government raised £12.2 billion in revenue in 1985/86, and oil contributed £16 billion to the value of exports in 1985. This enabled the government to reduce the public-sector borrowing requirement, which in turn allowed the government to make substantial cuts in tax rates.

Surely, then, North Sea oil has been a bonanza – a free gift of nature which has made everyone in the UK better off? But has it been an unmixed blessing? Or has the way in which the oil revenues have been used actually contributed to the country's economic problems?

From the late 1970s to the mid-1980s, the time when oil was beginning to bring in substantial revenues, the government pursued strong anti-inflationary policies. These involved high interest rates and thus led to a high exchange rate. This made it difficult for UK exporters to compete abroad. Oil, rather than helping alleviate the problem, only compounded it. Oil revenues led to a current account surplus, and this drove up the exchange rate even further, thereby further squeezing UK industry's

international competitiveness.

North Sea oil, then, in the early part of the 1980s effectively *crowded out* traditional UK exports. Rather than being used to pay for more imports of capital goods, which could have been used to refurbish UK industry, it was used to soften the blow of deflationary policies by helping to keep taxes low.

By the time of the late 1980s, when oil was selling for a much lower price and thus making a much smaller contribution to the balance of payments, the current account had moved into severe deficit (see Box 22.1). A consumer boom, fuelled by a rapid expansion of money supply and by tax cuts, had sucked in vast quantities of imports. UK industry had simply not been able to meet this demand.

Critics of the Thatcher government argue that North Sea oil revenues should have been spent on long-term investment in the export and import-substituting industries and on improving the nation's infrastructure.

? 1. Would the UK have been better off without North Sea oil, or would balance of payments crises and the relative decline of UK manufacturing industry have been even worse?
2. How could the crowding-out effect of North Sea oil have been avoided?

---

the UK economy: overstaffing, union restrictive practices, an outdated educational and training system insufficiently geared to industry's needs, too little research and development, misdirected research and development, and a poor management that is unwilling to go out into world markets and compete aggressively, and that is generally lacking the professionalism of managers in other industrial countries. The list is long and it is impossible to examine all these weaknesses in depth here.

Supply-side policies to tackle them can be interventionist or non-interventionist. Radical-right non-interventionist supply-side policies have been examined in section 20.2. The remainder of this chapter considers interventionist policies. In particular, it focuses on industrial policies: policies to reverse the relative decline of industry by providing government incentives or encouragement to invest.

Industrial policies

Policies to encourage industrial investment and greater industrial efficiency.

The case against the market

There are potentially large external benefits from research and development. Firms investing in developing and improving products, and especially firms engaged in more general scientific research, may produce results that provide benefits to many other firms. Thus the social rate of return on investment may be much higher than the private rate of return. Investment that is privately unprofitable for a firm may therefore still be economically desirable for the nation.

Similarly, investment in training may yield benefits to society which are lost to the firms providing the training when the workers leave.

Investment often involves risks. Firms may be unwilling to take those risks, even though there is a reasonable probability of the investment yielding a profit: the costs of possible failure may be too high. When looked at nationally, however, the benefits of investment might well have substantially outweighed the costs, and thus it would have been socially desirable for firms to have taken the risk. Successes would have outweighed failures.

Markets in the real world may be highly monopolistic. This lack of competition may discourage investment. What is the point of investing if profits are quite satisfactory already? These monopoly profits may allow management and labour to continue to be inefficient without their firms being driven out of business – at least until there is an economic recession. Then they may not have the strength to survive.

The *capital* market may be imperfect. This may result in even privately profitable investment not being financed. The banks in the UK have frequently been accused of being too concerned with firms' short-run profitability. Unlike banks in France, Germany and Japan they have been reluctant to lend to firms for long-term investment. Similarly, if firms rely on raising finance by the issue of new shares, this makes them very dependent on the stock market performance of their shares, which depends on current profitability and expected profitability in the near future, not on long-term profitability. This all leads to the UK disease of 'short-termism': the obsession with short-term profits and the neglect of investment that yields profits only after a number of years.

Finally, in the case of ailing firms, if the government does not help finance a rescue investment programme, there may be substantial social costs from job losses. The avoidance of these social costs may make the investment socially profitable even if it is not privately profitable.

Thus the free market is likely to provide too little investment, too little research and development, and too little training. This, then, is the basis of the case for government intervention.

? How would the radical right reply to these arguments?

The forms of intervention

Nationalization. This is the most extreme form of intervention. The nationalization of Rolls Royce in 1971 and British Leyland in 1975 are examples. As in these two cases, nationalization may initially be a means of rescuing firms in financial difficulties – firms that are probably considered to be of strategic importance. Once nationalized, however, the government may then choose to invest public money in them with the aim of making them profitable in the long run. By the time it was privatized in 1987, BL had become profitable again, thanks largely to a major programme of investment in new models (the Metro, Maestro and Montego) and new production-line techniques.

Grants. The government may sponsor research and development in certain industries (e.g. aerospace) or in specific fields (e.g. microprocessors). It may back investment programmes considered to benefit the economy, but which are unlikely to be initiated by private industry on its own.

Rationalization. The government may encourage mergers or other forms of industrial reorganization that will lead to greater efficiency and/or higher levels of investment. This could be done through government agencies (e.g. the IRC: see below) or government departments.

Advice and persuasion. The government may engage in discussions with private firms in order to find ways to improve efficiency and innovation. It may bring firms together to exchange information so as to co-ordinate their decisions and create a climate of greater certainty. It may bring firms and unions together to try to create greater industrial harmony.

Information. The government may provide various information services to firms: technical assistance, the results of public research, information on markets, etc.

Direct provision. Improvements in infrastructure – such as a better motorway system – can be of direct benefit to industry. Alternatively, the government could provide factories or equipment to specific firms.

The measures the government adopts will not only be governed by its approach to improving industrial performance. There are also policies designed to achieve other objectives which may involve similar measures. For example, regional policy involves grants to firms and provision of infrastructure. Fiscal policies to stimulate demand may also involve increased government expenditure on infrastructure.

Planning

The most comprehensive approach to industrial policy is for the government to engage in national economic planning. This is not the 'command planning' of the Soviet Union, where factories were, until recently, issued with instructions on what to produce, what inputs to use and how much to invest. Rather, it is 'indicative planning'. Indicative planning works alongside the market. It does not replace it.

In a free market there are likely to be many uncertainties for firms. Firms are often highly interconnected. Firms supply other firms, which supply other firms, and so on. If the car industry plans to expand, there must be enough steel available to build the cars, and dealers must be willing to take extra cars. If more steel is to be produced, there must be enough coal available, and enough blast furnace capacity. Similarly, if there is a growth in demand for computers, there must be a sufficient supply of computer chips.

If individual firms' and industries' plans do not match, there will be either bottlenecks or idle capacity. Unless, therefore, firms can know the plans of other firms – supplying firms, consuming firms and even rival firms – they may be cautious about taking investment decisions.

Indicative planning is where the government consults with industrialists to find out their intentions. It then seeks to co-ordinate the plans of firms, industries and sectors, and to recommend realistic and mutually consistent targets for output and investment. If firms' plans do not match, the government hopes that, in the light of the better information the planning exercise provides, the firms will adjust their plans. In addition, the government could use persuasion or various financial incentives – such as grants for investment – in order to obtain a consistent plan.

The nearest the UK came to full-scale indicative planning was the National Plan of 1965. This was strongly influenced by French experience. France had used national planning since shortly after the war. 'Le Plan' is administered by civil servants. Industrialists are given information on national economic priorities. They, in turn, give information on their plans and what the national goals will mean for their particular firms and industries. In the light of all this information, recalculations are made to make the plan realistic and internally consistent. Planning in France, up to the late 1970s, is generally considered to have been a success. Investment and growth were higher than in the UK.

In the UK in 1962, in a preliminary attempt at planning, the National Economic Development Council (NEDC or 'Neddy') was set up.

This is a body with representatives of employers, trade unions and the government. Also 21 Economic Development Committees (EDCs or 'Little Neddies') were set up, each for a specific industry. The purpose of these bodies was for exchanging information on plans and priorities.

The National Plan of 1965 was the brainchild of the Department of Economic Affairs, set up by the newly elected Labour government to administer industrial policy. Both the earlier NEDC reports and the plan itself explored the implications for industry of a 4 per cent target growth rate.

But the plan was a failure. The 4 per cent growth target was far too optimistic, and the plan was rapidly overtaken by a balance of payments crisis and the adoption of deflationary fiscal and monetary policy. Planning was discredited. It was abandoned. The NEDC, however, along with the EDCs, still continued to provide reports and encouraged the exchange of information.

A modified form of planning was resurrected in the mid-1970s. When Labour returned to power in 1974, they stressed the role of the NEDC in implementing an 'industrial strategy'. Sector working parties (SWPs) were established (like the NEDC on a tripartite basis), to identify bottlenecks and obstacles to economic growth in specific industries. The sectors selected were those felt to have the greatest long-term growth potential.

The SWPs produced reports and made recommendations on increasing efficiency, training, research and development, marketing, etc.; and grants were provided by the government to support their recommendations. For example, the Microprocessor Application Project (MAP) was set up: a project funded by the government to promote understanding and use of computers, and to develop various uses for computers in industry. Another scheme emanating from the work of the SWPs was the Market Entry Guarantee Scheme (MEGS), which provided funds for projects designed to enable firms to break into new markets. The government representatives on the SWPs had the task of ensuring that the recommendations were co-ordinated nationally.

The industrial strategy of the Labour government led also to the establishment of the National Enterprise Board (NEB) in 1975 as a state industrial holding company. In other words, the NEB provided financial assistance to firms in exchange for shares. This shareholding then enabled it to take part in the decision making of the firms. Originally, it was intended that the £1 billion allocated to the NEB would enable it to have a wide share ownership and hence a wide influence across the country. As it turned out, it was mainly occupied with supervising British Leyland and Rolls Royce, and the majority of its resources were used to finance these two companies.

When the Conservatives were elected in 1979, they abandoned completely the idea of national planning, preferring to rely on the market for the co-ordination of the various sectors of the economy. The NEDC, although retained, was virtually ignored by the government. The NEB was wound up in its original form.

1. Are bodies like the SWPs better able to forecast a firm's markets than the firm itself? Explain why or why not.
2. What instruments might a government use to 'persuade' firms to abide by a national plan? What are their advantages and disadvantages?

Box 20.10

Planning Italian Style
The public/private compromise

Italy is famous for a particular form of intervention in the economy. It began in 1933 under the dictatorship of Mussolini. With the depression of the 1930s, many companies were facing financial ruin. To help prevent a collapse of the economy and to shape its future development, the government set about acquiring shares in many of the key companies. It was from these roots that the *state holding sector* was to grow, a sector that was to play a crucial role in the Italian economy.

The state holding sector is composed of six state holding groups, each of which controls or influences a number of different companies by owning shares in them. The two largest groups are IRI (Instituto per la Riconstruzione Industriale) and ENI (Ente Nazionale Idrocarburi). IRI's main areas of activity include steel, engineering, electronics, shipbuilding, telecommunications and banking. ENI's area of concern is largely restricted to oil and gas production.

Each state holding group is responsible for implementing directives issued by the Ministry of State Holdings. They achieve these directives by having either a direct or an indirect controlling interest in a range of companies. IRI was composed of over 1000 companies in 1985. Unlike full-scale nationalization of industry, as was used in the UK after the war, Italian intervention is a compromise: it is *partial* state ownership and state influence in key parts of the private sector.

The benefits to the Italian economy from this system of state management have been immense:

● The state holding sector has created rapid growth in those parts of the economy in which it has been involved. It has done this by encouraging high levels of investment. In many cases this has led to improved efficiency and increased technological competitiveness.

● It has generally taken a more socially responsible attitude than the purely private sector. Employment and welfare objectives have often been given priority over profits.

● It has injected competition into the Italian economy, challenging many established monopolies (e.g. in fertilizer, cement and car production). It has helped to prevent oligopolistic collusion by itself refusing to collude.

● It has helped the government to pursue its regional policy by concentrating much of its investment in the poorer south of the country.

● It has been used by the government as a means of managing aggregate demand. By varying the levels of expenditure in the state holding sector, the government has better been able to operate its counter-cyclical policy.

But despite their historical successes, in recent years the place of the state holding companies has been increasingly questioned. Huge financial losses, plus a shift in political thinking towards the right, have led to an increased belief that free-market forces and privatization are what is required to put the Italian economy back on track. Several of IRI's assets have been sold off. Nevertheless the state holding sector remains large, as does the degree of government involvement in it.

? What problems are there in a system of state holding companies?

Selective intervention

Conservative governments have never favoured the type of comprehensive industrial strategy advocated by the Labour Party. Nevertheless, governments of both parties have intervened selectively in areas where they have felt that the market has provided inadequate investment.

Research and development

Slightly more than half of UK research and development is financed by the government, but this is highly concentrated in the fields of defence, aerospace and the nuclear power industry. As a result, there has been little government sponsorship of research in the majority of industry. Since the mid-1970s, however, there have been a number of government initiatives in the field of information technology. Funds have been provided for various educational programmes in schools, higher education and

Box 20.11

Industrial Policy in Japan
Helping the sunrise industries shine

The UK, once known as the 'workshop of the world', has lost its crown to Japan. Japan is now the world's largest manufacturer of steel, ships, cars and lorries, motor cycles, engines, cameras, calculators, big memory chips, televisions, video tape recorders and photocopiers. Between 1975 and 1982 industrial output in Japan grew by 50 per cent, investment averaged 33 per cent of GDP and the rate of automation outpaced all her economic rivals.

Japanese industries' willingness to develop new products and put new life into old products and processes has been actively encouraged by the Japanese government.

Industrial policy in Japan is guided by the Ministry of International Trade and Industry (MITI), whose role is to encourage co-operation between private companies and to help stimulate investment in new technology and product development. Using a mixture of state aid and legislative power, MITI wields a considerable amount of influence. However, this power is seldom in evidence as most Japanese industry is only too willing to take advantage of the services MITI can offer.

The computer industry and MITI
The computer industry took off in Japan in the late 1970s, although MITI had been active in organizing its structure as early as 1957. It established in 1961 a computer leasing firm, enabling firms to reduce their capital outlay on renting computers. This was superseded in 1971 by various research associations which were set up and partly financed by MITI. Companies large and small were encouraged to work together on a set project (usually on different aspects) for a given period of time; then findings were pooled. The research, once completed, would then be available to the participating firms, which would then compete with each other in making use of it.

The extent of MITI's active role was highlighted in 1981 with the announcement of a ten-year project of research into 'next-generation computer technology'. This encompassed twelve distinct projects, covering investigations into new materials, bio-technology and semi-conductors.

Long-term industrial policy on this scale is certain to give Japanese computer firms and many other industries a superior market position for a long time to come. Co-operation, organization and state aid have proved a successful recipe for Japanese industry in the past and look set to continue that way in the future.

? Compare and contrast the Japanese attitude towards industrial policy with that of the current and previous UK governments.

industry, and for research into computers and their applications. Even so, the amount of government support in this field has been very small compared with Japan, France and the USA. What is more, the amount of support has declined since the mid-1980s.

Industrial reorganization
Labour governments have been concerned with encouraging efficiency and investment via rationalization. The Industrial Reorganization Corporation (IRC) was set up in 1967 to provide loans to industry, and to arrange and finance mergers, where these were felt to lead to economies of scale and greater scope for investment. The Industrial Expansion Act of 1968 provided additional funds for encouraging industrial reorganization and investment.

Although the 1970 Conservative government abolished the IRC, its Industry Act of 1972 enabled the government to provide finance to firms for reorganization and investment. This Act was used extensively by the 1974 Labour government. It was used in particular to help ailing companies: e.g. British Leyland and Alfred Herbert (the machine-tool producer).

Assistance to small firms

Conservative governments have been concerned to assist small firms. The 1970 Conservative government set up small firms' advisory centres and introduced various forms of tax relief. The 1979 Conservative government extended this policy and introduced a number of new tax concessions. Small firms pay a 25 per cent rate of corporation tax compared with 35 per cent for larger ones. It also relaxed various planning and other bureaucratic controls. In 1988 it introduced measures to provide financial assistance for new investment and innovation by small firms in development areas (see section 20.4).

The case against intervention

Although the Thatcher government continued to intervene selectively, particularly in the cases of small firms and certain types of research and development, it nevertheless substantially cut the overall level of industrial support. It claimed that intervention weakens market forces and in the long run reduces, not increases, industrial efficiency. The following arguments were used:

- A poor investment record may in large part be due to managerial inertia and union restrictive practices. Forcing firms and unions to face up to competition in the market may be a better way of encouraging willingness to accept change. Government subsidies, on the other hand, may simply allow firms to continue producing inefficiently.
- The knowledge that 'lame ducks' will be rescued by the government removes the ultimate incentive to efficiency: the fear of closure.
- The government may not make an efficient use of taxpayers' money by giving investment grants. The money may well go to extravagant and unprofitable projects like Concorde. Any external benefits of such investment may be small.
- The low investment record of private industry may be due to a low potential return on investment. If market opportunities were good, firms would invest without the need of government support.
- British investment has remained low in the past despite interventionist industrial policy.

If the government is to help industry, argued the Thatcher government, it is best to reduce the tax burden generally, so as to increase the return on investment. The microeconomic allocation of investment resources will still then be provided by the market, rather than by bureaucratic government.

 Provide a critique of these arguments.

◭ SUMMARY

1. The UK has had a lower rate of investment than most other industrialized countries. This has contributed towards a historically low rate of economic growth and a growing trade deficit in manufactures.
2. Those in favour of interventionist industrial policy point to failings of the market, such as the externalities involved in investment and training, the imperfections in the capital market and the short-term perspective of decision makers.
3. Intervention can take the form of nationalization of ailing industries, grants, the encouragement of mergers and other forms of rationalization, advice and persuasion, the provision of information and the direct provision of infrastructure.

4. The government could engage in indicative planning, where the government seeks a partnership with industry to co-ordinate investment decisions throughout the economy. Such planning met with a great deal of success in France in the 1950s, 1960s and 1970s. The UK's one major attempt at national planning in 1965, however, was a failure.

5. Selective intervention in the UK has taken the form of grants for research and development (but concentrated in a narrow range of industries), encouragement of reorganization and assistance to small firms. Apart from the last of these, the Thatcher government has generally been against intervention, preferring to use market-orientated supply-side policies.

International Trade $\boxed{21}$

Without international trade we would all be much poorer. There would be some items like bananas, pineapples, coffee, cotton clothes, foreign holidays and uranium that we would simply have to go without. Then there would be other items like wine and spacecraft and space exploration that we could only produce very inefficiently.

International trade has the potential to benefit *all* participating countries. This chapter explains why.

Totally free trade, however, may bring problems to countries or to groups of people within those countries. Many people argue strongly for restrictions on trade. Textile workers see their jobs threatened by cheap imported cloth. Car manufacturers worry about falling sales as customers switch to Japanese models or to cheap Eastern European ones. The chapter therefore also examines the arguments for restricting trade. Are people justified in fearing international competition, or are they merely trying to protect some vested interest at the expense of everyone else?

The third part of the chapter considers the arguments for a *partial* form of free trade. This is where a group of countries agree to have free trade between themselves, but still impose trade restrictions on the rest of the world. We will have a look at the general arguments for and against such arrangements, which go under the various titles of *customs unions, free trade areas* and *common markets*.

The most famous of common markets is that of the European Community, and the chapter finishes by looking at its arrangements and evolution, from its founding in 1957 to the enactment at the end of 1992 of the 1986 Single European Act.

21.1 The advantages of trade

Specialization as the basis for trade

Why do countries trade with each other, and what do they gain out of it? The reasons for international trade are really only an extension of the reasons for trade *within* a nation. Rather than people trying to be self-sufficient and do everything for themselves, it makes sense to specialize.

Individuals specialize in the jobs they do, and with the money they earn from selling their labour they buy the goods they need: goods that other people have specialized in producing. We examined the advantages of the specialization and division of labour back in Chapter 4.

Firms specialize in producing certain goods. This allows them to gain economies of scale and to exploit their entrepreneurial and management skills and the skills of their labour force. It also allows them to benefit from their particular location and from the ownership of any particular capital equipment or other assets they might possess. With the revenues firms earn, they buy in the inputs they need from other firms and the labour they require. Firms thus trade with each other.

Countries also specialize. They produce more than they need of certain goods. What is not consumed domestically is exported. The revenues earned from the exports are used to import goods which are not produced in sufficient amounts at home.

> [?] Why does the USA not specialize as much as General Motors or Texaco? Why does the UK not specialize as much as ICI? Is the answer to these questions similar to the answer to the questions, 'Why does the USA not specialize as much as Luxembourg', and 'Why does ICI or Unilever not specialize as much as the local butcher?'

But which goods should a country specialize in? What should it export and what should it import? The answer is that it should specialize in those goods in which it has a *comparative advantage*. Let us examine what this means.

The law of comparative advantage

Countries have different endowments of factors of production. They differ in population density, labour skills, climate, fertility, raw materials, capital equipment, etc. These differences tend to persist because factors are relatively immobile between countries. Obviously land and climate are totally immobile, but even with labour and capital there are more restrictions on their international movement than on their movement within countries. Thus the ability to supply goods differs between countries.

What this means is that the relative costs of producing goods will vary from country to country. For example, one country may be able to produce 1 fridge for the same cost as 6 tonnes of wheat or 3 compact disc players or 100 tonnes of coal, whereas another country may be able to produce 1 fridge for the same cost as only 3 tonnes of wheat but 4 CD players and 200 tonnes of coal. It is these differences in relative costs that form the basis of trade.

At this stage we need to distinguish between *absolute advantage* and *comparative advantage*.

Absolute advantage

Absolute advantage
A country has an absolute advantage over another in the production of a good if it can produce it with less resources than the other country.

When one country can produce a good with less resources than another country it is said to have an 'absolute advantage' in that good. If France can produce wine with less resources than the UK, and the UK can produce gin with less resources than France, then France has an absolute advantage in wine and the UK an absolute advantage in gin. Production of both wine and gin will be maximized by each country specializing and then trading with the other country. Both will gain.

Comparative advantage

The above seems obvious, but trade between two countries can still be beneficial even if one country could produce *all* goods with less resources than the other, providing the *relative* efficiency with which goods can be produced differs between the two countries.

Take the case of a developed country that is absolutely more efficient than a less developed country at producing both wheat and cloth. Assume that with a given amount of resources (labour, land and capital) the alternatives shown in Table 21.1 can be produced in each country.

Despite the developed country having an absolute advantage in both wheat and

Table 21.1 Production possibilities for two countries

		Kilos of wheat		Metres of cloth
Less developed country	Either	2	or	1
Developed country	Either	4	or	8

cloth, the less developed country (LDC) has a comparative advantage in wheat, and the developed country has a comparative advantage in cloth.

This is because wheat is relatively cheaper in the LDC: only 1 metre of cloth has to be sacrificed to produce 2 kilos of wheat, whereas 8 metres of cloth would have to be sacrificed in the developed country to produce 4 kilos of wheat. In other words, the opportunity cost of wheat is four times higher in the developed country (8/4 compared with 1/2).

On the other hand, cloth is relatively cheaper in the developed country. Here the opportunity cost of producing 8 metres of cloth is only 4 kilos of wheat, whereas in the LDC 1 metre of cloth costs 2 kilos of wheat. Thus the opportunity cost of cloth is four times higher in the LDC (2/1 compared with 4/8).

> **?** Draw up a similar table to Table 21.1, only this time assume that the figures are: LDC 6 wheat or 2 cloth; DC 8 wheat or 20 cloth. What are the opportunity cost ratios now?

To summarize: countries have a comparative advantage in those goods that can be produced at a lower opportunity cost than in other countries.

If countries are to gain from trade, they should export those goods in which they have a comparative advantage and import those goods in which they have a comparative disadvantage. Given this we can state a law of comparative advantage: provided opportunity costs of various goods differ in two countries, both of them can gain from mutual trade if they specialize in producing (and exporting) those goods that have relatively low opportunity costs compared with the other country.

But why do they gain if they specialize according to this law? And just what will that gain be? We will consider these questions next.

The gains from trade based on comparative advantage

Before trade, unless markets are very imperfect, the prices of the two goods are likely to reflect their opportunity costs. For example, in Table 21.1, since the less developed country can produce 2 kilos of wheat for 1 metre of cloth, the *price* of 2 kilos of wheat will roughly equal the price of 1 metre of cloth.

Assume, then, that the pre-trade exchange ratios of wheat for cloth are as follows:

LDC   :   2 wheat for 1 cloth
Developed country :   1 wheat for 2 cloth (i.e. 4 for 8)

Both countries will now gain from trade, provided the exchange ratio is somewhere between 2:1 and 1:2. Assume, for the sake of argument, that it is 1:1, that 1 wheat trades internationally for 1 cloth. How will each country gain?

The LDC gains by exporting wheat and importing cloth. At an exchange ratio of 1:1, it now only has to give up 1 kilo of wheat to obtain a metre of cloth, whereas before trade it had to give up 2 kilos of wheat.

Comparative advantage

A country has a comparative advantage over another in the production of a good if it can produce it at a lower opportunity cost: i.e. if it has to forgo less of other goods in order to produce it.

The law of comparative advantage

Trade can benefit all countries if they specialize in the goods in which they have a comparative advantage.

Box 21.1

Sharing Out the Jobs
or we can't all be brilliant

Imagine that you and a group of friends are fed up with the rat race and decide to set up a self-sufficient community. So you club together and use all your savings to buy an old run-down farmhouse with 30 acres of land and a few farm animals.

You decide to produce all your own food, make your own clothes, renovate the farmhouse, make all the furniture, provide all your own entertainment and set up a little shop to sell the things you make. This should bring in enough income to buy the few items you cannot make yourselves.

The day comes to move in, and that evening everyone gathers to decide how all the jobs are going to be allocated. You quickly decide that it would be foolish for all of you to try to do all the jobs. Obviously it will be more efficient to specialize. This does not necessarily mean that everyone is confined to doing only one job, but it does mean that each of you can concentrate on just a few tasks.

But who is to do which job? The answer would seem to be obvious: you pick the best person for the job. So you go down the list of tasks. Who is to take charge of the renovations? Pat has already renovated a cottage, and is brilliant at bricklaying, plastering, wiring and plumbing. So Pat would seem to be the ideal person. Who is to do the cooking? Everyone agrees on this. Pat makes the best

cakes, the best quiches and the best Irish stew. So Pat is everyone's choice for cook. And what about milking the sheep? 'Pat used to keep sheep', says Tarquin, 'and made wonderful feta cheese.' 'Good old Pat!' exclaims everyone.

It doesn't take long before it becomes obvious that 'clever-clogs' Pat is simply brilliant at everything, from planting winter wheat, to unblocking drains, to doing the accounts, to tie-dying. But it is soon realized that, if Pat has to do everything, nothing will get done. Even Chris, who has never done anything except market research, would be better employed milking the sheep than doing nothing at all.

So what's the best way of allocating the jobs so that the work gets done in the most efficient way? Sharon comes up with the solution. 'Everyone should make a list of all the jobs they could possibly do, and then put them in order from the one they are best at to the one they are worst at.'

So this is what everyone does. And then people are allocated the jobs they are *relatively* best at doing. Chris escapes milking the sheep and keeps the accounts instead. And Pat escapes with an eight-hour day!

 If Pat took two minutes to milk the sheep and Tarquin took six, how could it ever be more efficient for Tarquin to do it?

The developed country gains by exporting cloth and importing wheat. Again at an exchange ratio of 1:1, it now only has to give up 1 metre of cloth to obtain 1 kilo of wheat, whereas before it had to give up 2 metres of cloth.

Thus both countries have gained from trade.

 Show how each country could gain from trade if the LDC could produce (before trade) 3 wheat for 1 cloth and the developed country could produce (before trade) 2 wheat for 5 cloth, and if the exchange ratio (with trade) was 1 wheat for 2 cloth. Would they both still gain if the exchange ratio was (a) 1 wheat for 1 cloth; (b) 1 wheat for 3 cloth?

The actual exchange ratios will depend on the relative prices of wheat and cloth after trade takes place. These prices will depend on total demand for and supply of the two goods. It may be that the trade exchange ratio is nearer to the pre-trade exchange ratio of one country than the other. Thus the gains to the two countries need not be equal. (We will examine these issues below.)

 In the last question, which country gained the most from a trade exchange ratio of 1 wheat for 2 cloth?

Box 21.2

David Ricardo and the Law of Comparative Advantage

We came across David Ricardo in Chapter 13 (see Box 13.1). His most important work on economics is *On the Principles of Political Economy and Taxation* (1817). In expounding the advantages of free trade he gives the first clear analysis of the law of comparative advantage. In chapter VII he writes:

> Under a system of perfectly free commerce, each country naturally devotes its capital and labour to such employments as are most beneficial to each. This pursuit of individual advantage is admirably connected with the universal good of the whole . . . It is this principle which determines that wine shall be made in France and Portugal, that corn shall be grown in America and Poland, and that hardware and other goods shall be manufactured in England.
>
> If Portugal had no commercial connexion with other countries, instead of employing a great part of her capital and industry in the production of wines, with which she purchases for her own use the cloth and hardware of other countries, she would be obliged to devote a part of that capital to the manufacture of those commodities, which she would thus obtain probably inferior in quality as well as quantity . . .
>
> England may be so circumstanced, that to produce the cloth may require the labour of 100 men for one year; and if she attempted to make the wine, it might take the labour of 120 men for the same time. England would

therefore find it in her interest to import wine, and to purchase it by the exportation of cloth.

To produce the wine in Portugal, might require only the labour of 90 men for the same time. It would therefore be advantageous for her to export wine in exchange for cloth. This exchange might even take place, notwithstanding that the commodity imported by Portugal could be produced with less labour than in England. Though she could make the cloth with the labour of 90 men, she would import it from a country where it required the labour of 100 men to produce it, because it would be advantageous to her rather to employ her capital in the production of wine, for which she would obtain more cloth from England, than she could by diverting a portion of her capital from the cultivation of vines to the manufacture of cloth.

Thus England would give up the produce of labour of 100 men, for the produce of 90.[1]

? In Ricardo's example, what is the opportunity cost of wine in terms of cloth in (a) Portugal; (b) England? (Assume that the only costs are labour costs.)

[1] P. Sraffa (ed.), *The Works and Correspondence of David Ricardo* (Cambridge University Press, 1951), volume I, pp. 133–5.

Simple graphical analysis of comparative advantage and the gains from trade: constant opportunity cost

The gains from trade can be shown graphically using production possibility curves. Let us continue with the example of the developed and less developed countries that we looked at above in Table 21.1, where both countries produce just two goods: wheat and cloth.

For simplicity, assume that the pre-trade opportunity costs of cloth in terms of wheat in the two countries do not vary with output: i.e. there are *constant opportunity costs* of cloth in terms of wheat of 2/1 in the LDC and 1/2 in the developed country. Let us assume that the pre-trade production possibilities are as shown in Table 21.2.

? If the LDC has an *absolute* disadvantage in both goods, so that it has to use twice as many resources as the developed country to produce a kilo of wheat and eight times as many resources to produce a metre of cloth, why (in Table 21.2) can it produce almost as much wheat as the developed country?

For each 100 extra metres of cloth that the LDC produces it has to sacrifice 200 kilos of wheat. For each extra 200 kilos of wheat that the developed country produces it has to sacrifice 400 metres of cloth. Straight-line pre-trade production possibility 'curves' can thus be drawn for the two countries with slopes of 2/1 and 1/2 respectively.

Table 21.2 Pre-trade production possibilities

| | Less developed country | | | Developed country | |
	Wheat (kilos m)	Cloth (metres m)		Wheat (kilos m)	Cloth (metres m)
a	1000	0	*g*	1200	0
b	800	100	*h*	1000	400
c	600	200	*i*	800	800
d	400	300	*j*	600	1200
e	200	400	*k*	400	1600
f	0	500	*l*	200	2000
			m	0	2400

These lines illustrate the various total combinations of the two goods that can be produced and hence consumed. They are shown as the black lines in Figure 21.1.

Let us assume that before trade the LDC produces (and consumes) at point *e*: namely, 200 million kilos of wheat and 400 million metres of cloth; and that the developed country produces at point *k*: namely, 400 million kilos of wheat and 1600 million metres of cloth.

If they now trade, the LDC, having a comparative advantage in wheat, will specialize in it and produce at point *a*. It will produce 1000 million kilos of wheat and no cloth. The developed country will specialize in cloth and produce at point *m*. It will produce 2400 million metres of cloth and no wheat.

For simplicity let us assume that trade between the two countries takes place at an exchange ratio of 1:1. This means that the two countries can now consume along the red lines in Figure 21.1: at, say, points *x* and *y* respectively. At point *x* the LDC consumes 400 million kilos of wheat (a gain of 200 million kilos over the pre-trade position) and 600 million metres of cloth (a gain of 200 million metres over the pre-trade position). At point *y* the developed country consumes 600 million kilos of wheat (a gain of 200 million kilos over the pre-trade position) and 1800 million metres of cloth (a gain of 200 million metres over the pre-trade position). Thus trade has allowed both countries to increase their consumption of both goods.

(a) Less developed country   **(b)** Developed country

Figure 21.1 The effect of trade on consumption possibilities

To summarize: before trade, the countries could only consume along their production possibility curves (the black lines); after trade, they can consume along the higher red lines.

Note that in this simple two-country model the production and consumption of the two-countries must match, since one country's exports are the other's imports. Thus if the LDC consumes at point *x* the developed country must consume at point *y* and vice versa. The effects on trade of the two countries consuming at points *x* and *y* are shown in Table 21.3.

Table 21.3 The production and consumption gains from trade

	Less developed country			Developed country			Total	
	Production	Consumption	Imports (−) Exports (+)	Production	Consumption	Imports (−) Exports (+)	Production	Consumption
No trade								
Wheat (kilos m)	200	200	0	400	400	0	600	600
Cloth (metres m)	400	400	0	1600	1600	0	2000	2000
With trade								
Wheat (kilos m)	1000	400	+600	0	600	−600	1000	1000
Cloth (metres m)	0	600	−600	2400	1800	+600	2400	2400

As complete specialization has taken place in our example, the LDC now has to import all its cloth and the developed country has to import all its wheat. Thus, given the exchange ratio of 1:1, the LDC exports 600 million kilos of wheat in exchange for imports of 600 million metres of cloth. (These imports and exports are also shown in Figure 21.1.)

The final two columns of Table 21.3 show that trade has increased the total production and consumption of the two countries.

1. If the opportunity cost ratio of *wheat* for *cloth* is 1/2 in the LDC, why is the slope of the production possibility curve 2/1? Is the slope of the production possibility curve always the reciprocal of the opportunity cost ratio?
2. Show (graphically) that, if the (pre-trade) opportunity cost ratios of the two countries were the same, there would be no gain from trade – assuming that the production possibility curves were straight lines and did not shift as a result of trade.

International trade and its effect on factor prices

Countries will tend to have a comparative advantage in goods that are *intensive in their abundant factor*. Canada has abundant land and hence it is cheap. Therefore Canada specializes in grain production since grains are land intensive. South-East Asian countries have abundant supplies of labour with low wages, and hence specialize in clothing and other labour-intensive goods. Europe, Japan and the USA have relatively abundant and cheap capital, and hence specialize in capital-intensive manufactured goods.

The effect of trade between such countries will tend to lead to greater equality in factor prices. For example, the demand for labour will rise in labour-abundant countries like Hong Kong if they specialize in labour-intensive goods. This will push up wages in these low-wage countries, thereby helping to close the gap between wages in these countries and the developed world. Without trade, wages would tend to be even lower.

Box 21.3

Do We Exploit Foreign Workers by Buying Cheap Foreign Goods?

People sometimes question the morality of buying imports from countries where workers are paid 'pittance' wages. 'Is it right', they ask, 'for us to support a system where workers are so exploited?' As is often the case with emotive issues, there is some truth and some misunderstanding in a point of view like this.

First the truth. If a country like the UK trades with a regime which denies human rights, and treats its workers very badly, then we may thereby be helping to sustain a corrupt system. We might also be seen to be lending it moral support. In this sense, therefore, trade may not help the cause of the workers in these countries. It is arguments like these that have been used to support the imposition of trade sanctions against South Africa.

Now the misunderstanding. If we buy goods from countries that pay low wages, we are *not* as a result contributing to their low-wage problem. Quite the reverse. If countries like India export textiles to the West, this will help to *increase* the wages of Indian workers. If India has a comparative advantage in labour-intensive goods, these goods will earn a better price by being exported than by being sold entirely in the domestic Indian market. Provided *some* of the extra revenues go to the workers, they will gain from trade.

? Under what circumstances would a gain in revenues by exporting firms *not* lead to an increase in wage rates?

Increasing opportunity costs and the limits to specialization and trade

In practice, countries are likely to experience increasing opportunity costs (and hence have bowed-out production possibility curves). The reason for this is that, as a country increasingly specializes in one good, it will have to use resources that are less and less suited to its production and which were more suited to the other good. Thus ever increasing amounts of the other good will have to be sacrificed. For example, as a country specializes more and more in grain production, it will have to use land that is less and less suited to growing grain.

These increasing costs from specialization will lead to the disappearance of a country's comparative cost advantage. When this happens, there will be no point in further specialization. Thus whereas a country like Germany has a comparative advantage in capital-intensive manufactures, it does not produce only manufactures. It would make no sense not to use its fertile lands to produce food or its forests to produce timber. The opportunity costs of diverting all agricultural labour to industry would be very high.

Thus increasing opportunity costs limit the amount of a country's specialization and hence the amount of its trade. There are other limits to trade also:

- Transport costs may outweigh any comparative advantage. A country may be able to produce bricks more cheaply than other countries, but their weight may make them too expensive to export.
- It may be the factors of production, rather than the goods, that move from country to country. Thus developed countries, rather than exporting finished goods to LDCs, may invest capital in LDCs to enable manufactures to be produced there. Labour may migrate from low-wage to high-wage countries.
- Governments may restrict trade (see section 21.2).

? 1. Are there any social or cultural factors that limit trade between countries?
2. If capital moves from developed to less developed countries, and labour moves from less developed to developed countries, what effects will these factor movements have on wage rates and the return on capital in the two types of country?

The terms of trade

What price will our exports fetch abroad? What will we have to pay for imports? The answer to these questions is given by the *terms of trade*.

To simplify matters, let us assume to start with that there is only one exported good and only one imported good. In this case the terms of trade are defined as P_x/P_m, where P_x is the price of the exported good and P_m is the price of the imported good. This is the reciprocal of the exchange ratio: for example, if 2x exchange for 1m (an exchange ratio of 2/1), the price of x will be half the price of m. The terms of trade will be 1/2.

 1. If 4x exchange for 3m, what are the terms of trade?
2. If the terms of trade are 3, how many units of the imported good could I buy for the money earned by the sale of 1 unit of the exported good? What is the exchange ratio?

In the real world where countries have *many* exports and imports, the terms of trade are given by:

Average price of exports
─────────────────────────
Average price of imports

expressed as an index, where price changes up or down are measured against a base year in which the terms of trade are assumed to be 100.

If the terms of trade rise (export prices rising relative to import prices), they are said to have 'improved', since less exports need now be sold to purchase any given quantity of imports. Changes in the terms of trade are caused by changes in the demand for and supply of imports and exports, and by changes in the exchange rate.

> **Terms of trade**
>
> The price index of exports divided by the price index of imports. This means that the terms of trade will be 100 in the base year.

The terms of trade and comparative advantage

Assuming there are two goods x and m, trade can be advantageous to a country as long as the terms of trade P_x/P_m are different from the opportunity cost ratios of the two goods, given by MC_x/MC_m. For example, if the terms of trade were greater than the opportunity cost ratio ($P_x/P_m > MC_x/MC_m$), it would benefit the country to produce more x for export in return for imports of m, since the relative value of producing x (P_x/P_m) is greater than the relative cost (MC_x/MC_m).

With increasing opportunity costs, however, increasing specialization in x will lead to MC_x rising (and MC_m falling), until $P_x/P_m = MC_x/MC_m$. At this point there can be no more gain from further specialization and trade: the maximum gain has been achieved: comparative cost advantages have been exhausted.

Simple graphical analysis of the determination of the terms of trade

When countries import and export many goods, the terms of trade will depend on the prices of all the various exports and imports. These prices will depend on the demand and supply of each traded good and their elasticities in the respective countries. Take the case of good g in which country A has a comparative advantage with respect to the rest of the world. This is illustrated in Figure 21.2.

Demand and supply curves of good g can be drawn for both country A and the rest of the world. (The upward-sloping supply curves imply increasing opportunity costs of production.) Before trade, country A has a low equilibrium price of P_1 and the rest of the world a high equilibrium price of P_2. After trade, price will settle at P_3 in both countries (assuming no transport costs), where total demand by both country A and the rest of the world together equals total supply, and thus where the imports of g into

Figure 21.2 Determination of the price of an individual traded good

the rest of the world ($d - c$) equal the exports from country A ($b - a$). The position of P_3 relative to P_1 and P_2 will depend on the elasticities of demand and supply.

A similar analysis can be conducted for all the other traded goods – both exports and imports of country A. The resulting prices will allow country A's terms of trade to be calculated.

 Draw a similar diagram to Figure 21.2 showing how the price of an individual good imported into country A is determined.

The analysis is complicated somewhat if different national currencies are involved, since the prices in each country will be expressed in its own currency. Thus to convert one country's prices to another currency will require knowledge of the rate of exchange: e.g. for the USA and the UK it might be $2 = £1. But under a floating exchange rate system the rate of exchange will depend in part on the demand for and supply of imports and exports. If the rate of exchange were to depreciate – say, from $2 = £1 to $1.50 = £1 – the UK's terms of trade will worsen. Exports will earn less foreign currency per pound: e.g. £1 worth of exports will now be worth only $1.50 rather than $2. Imports, on the other hand, will be more expensive: e.g. $6 worth of imports previously cost £3; they now cost £4.

 Why will exporters probably welcome a 'deterioration' in the terms of trade?

In a world of many countries and many goods, an individual country's imports and exports may have little effect on world prices. In the extreme case it may face prices totally dictated by the external world demand and supply. The country in this case is similar to an individual firm under perfect competition. The country is too small to influence world prices, and thus faces a horizontal demand curve for its exports and a horizontal supply curve for its imports. In foreign currency terms, therefore, the terms of trade are outside its control. Nevertheless, these terms of trade will probably be to its benefit in the sense that the gains from trade will be virtually entirely received by this small country rather than the rest of the world. It is too small for its trade to depress the world price of its exports or drive up the price of its imports.

 Draw two pairs of diagrams like Figure 21.2, one for an exported good and one for an imported good, only this time make the 'small country' assumption that country A is too small to affect the world price. (The scales of the horizontal axes will need to be quite different for country A and the rest of the world.)

In general a country's gains from trade will be greater the less elastic its own domestic demand and supply of tradable goods, and the more elastic the demand and supply of other countries. You can see this by examining Figure 21.2. The less elastic the domestic demand and supply, the bigger will be the effect of trade on prices faced by that country. The more the trade price differs from the pre-trade price, the bigger the gain.

∗ Intermediate graphical analysis of comparative advantage and the gains from trade: increasing opportunity costs

The analysis of section 10.1 can be used to demonstrate the welfare gains from trade and the limits to specialization under conditions of increasing opportunity cost. A simple two-good model is used, and the pre-trade position is compared with the position with trade.

Pre-trade
Let us make the following simplifying assumptions:

- There are two goods, x and m.
- Country A has a comparative advantage in the production of good x.
- There are increasing opportunity costs in the production of both x and m. Thus the production possibility curve is bowed out.
- Social indifference curves can be drawn, each one showing the various combinations of x and m that give society in country A a particular level of utility.

Figure 21.3 shows the pre-trade position in country A. Production and consumption at P_1C_1 will give the highest possible utility. (All other points on the production possibility curve intersect with lower indifference curves.)

If there is perfect competition, production will indeed be at P_1C_1. There are four steps in establishing this:

- The slope of the production possibility curve $(-\Delta m/\Delta x)$ is the marginal rate of transformation (*MRT*), and equals MC_x/MC_m. For example, if the opportunity cost of producing 1 extra unit of x (Δx) was a sacrifice of 2 units of m $(-\Delta m)$, then an extra unit of x would cost twice as much as an extra unit of m: i.e. $MC_x/MC_m = 2/1$, which is the slope of the production possibility curve, $-\Delta m/\Delta x$.
- The slope of each indifference curve $(-\Delta m/\Delta x)$ is the marginal rate of substitution in consumption (*MRS*), and equals MU_x/MU_m. For example, if x had three times the marginal utility of m $(MU_x/MU_m = 3)$, consumers would be willing to give up 3m for 1x $(-\Delta m/\Delta x = 3)$.
- Under perfect competition: $\dfrac{MC_x}{MC_m} = \dfrac{P_x}{P_m} = \dfrac{MU_x}{MU_m}$
- Thus the domestic pre-trade price ratio P_x/P_m under perfect competition must equal the slope of the production possibility curve (MC_x/MC_m) and the slope of the social indifference curve (MU_x/MU_m). This is the case at P_1C_1 in Figure 21.3.

? 1. If production was at point *a* in Figure 21.3, describe the process whereby equilibrium at point P_1C_1 would be restored under perfect competition.
2. Why would production be unlikely to take place at P_1C_1 if competition were not perfect?

With trade
If country A has a comparative advantage in good x, the price of x relative to m is likely to be higher in the rest of the world than in country A: i.e. world $P_x/P_m >$ pre-trade domestic P_x/P_m. This is shown in Figure 21.4. The world price ratio is given by

Figure 21.3 Equilibrium before trade

Figure 21.4 Equilibrium with trade

the slope of the line *ww*. With this new steeper world price ratio the optimum production point will be P_2 where *MRT* (the slope of the production possibility curve) = world P_x/P_m (the slope of *ww*).

With production at P_2, the country can by trading consume *anywhere* along this line *ww*. The optimum consumption point will be C_2 where *MRS* (the slope of the indifference curve) = world P_x/P_m (the slope of *ww*). Thus trade has allowed consumption to move from point C_1 on the lower indifference curve I_1 to point C_2 on the higher indifference curve I_2. There has thus been a gain from trade. Perfect competition will ensure that this gain is realized, since production at P_2 and consumption at C_2 meet the equilibrium condition that:

$$\frac{MC_x}{MC_m} = \frac{P_x}{P_m} = \frac{MU_x}{MU_m}$$

How much will be imported and how much will be exported? With production at P_2 and consumption at C_2, country A will import $C_2 - D$ of good m in exchange for exports of $P_2 - D$ of good x.

A similar diagram can be drawn for other countries. Such diagrams are known as general equilibrium diagrams, since they show equilibrium for both imports and exports on the one diagram.

General equilibrium diagrams (in trade theory)

Indifference curve/ production possibility curve diagrams that show a country's production and consumption of both imports and exports.

? 1. Draw a similar diagram to Figure 21.4, only this time assume that the two goods are good a measured on the vertical axis and good b measured on the horizontal axis. Assume that the country has a comparative advantage in good a. (Note that the world price ratio this time will be shallower than the domestic pre-trade price ratio.) Mark the level of exports of a and imports of b.

2. Is it possible to gain from trade if competition is not perfect?

Other reasons for gains from trade

Decreasing costs. Even if there are no initial comparative cost differences between two countries, it will still benefit both to specialize in industries where economies of scale can be gained, and then to trade. Once the economies of scale begin to appear, comparative cost differences will also appear, and thus the countries will have gained a comparative advantage in these industries.

These decreasing costs could be due to firms achieving economies of large-scale production (internal economies of scale), or they could be due to the development of specialized facilities for the industry – transport, finance, training schemes, etc. – that are external to the individual firm (external economies of scale). They could be due simply to the development of a skilled and efficient labour force as people learn on the job – 'learning by doing'.

This reason for trade is particularly relevant for small countries where the domestic market is not large enough to support large-scale industries. Thus exports form a much higher percentage of GNP in small countries such as Switzerland than in large countries such as the USA.

 Would it be possible for a country with a comparative disadvantage in a given product at *pre*-trade levels of output to obtain a comparative advantage in it by specializing in its production and exporting it?

Differences in demand. Even with no comparative cost differences and no potential economies of scale, trade can benefit both countries if demand conditions differ.

If people in country A like beef more than lamb, and people in country B like lamb more than beef, then rather than A using resources better suited for lamb to produce beef and B using resources better suited for producing beef to produce lamb, it will benefit both to produce beef *and* lamb and to export the one they like less in return for the one they like more.

Increased competition. If a country trades, the competition from imports may stimulate greater efficiency at home. This extra competition may prevent domestic monopolies/ oligopolies from charging high prices. It may stimulate greater research and development and the more rapid adoption of new technology. It may lead to a greater variety of products being made available to consumers.

Trade as an 'engine of growth'. In a growing world economy, the demand for a country's exports is likely to grow over time, especially when these exports have a high income elasticity of demand. This increase in injections will provide a stimulus to aggregate demand and allow a country to purchase additional imports. This argument is particularly relevant when countries have an abundance of a certain commodity, such as oil or uranium.

Non-economic advantages. There may be political, social and cultural advantages to be gained by fostering trading links between countries.

▲ SUMMARY

1. Countries can gain from trade if they specialize in producing those goods in which they have a comparative advantage: i.e. those goods that can be produced at relatively low opportunity costs. This is merely an extension of the argument that gains can be made from the specialization and division of labour.

2. If two countries trade, then, provided that the trade price ratio of exports and imports is somewhere between the pre-trade price ratios of these goods in the two countries, both countries can gain. They can both consume *beyond* their production possibility curves.

3. Trade will tend to have the effect of equalizing factor prices between countries.

4. With increasing opportunity costs there will be a limit to specialization and trade. As a country increasingly specializes, its (marginal) comparative advantage will eventually disappear. Trade can also be limited by transport costs, factor movements and government intervention.

5. The terms of trade give the price of exports relative to the price of imports. Additional trade can be beneficial if the terms of trade (P_x/P_m) are greater than the relative

marginal costs of exports and imports (MC_x/MC_m).

6. A country's terms of trade are determined by the demand and supply of imports and exports and their respective elasticities. This will determine the prices at which goods are traded and also the rate of exchange. A country's gains from trade will be greater $(P_x/P_m$ greater) the less elastic its own domestic demand and supply of tradable goods, and the more elastic the demand and supply of other countries.

* 7. Trade allows countries to achieve a higher level of utility by consuming on a higher social indifference curve. The maximum gain from trade is achieved by consuming at the point where the world price ratio is tangential to both the production possibility curve and a social indifference curve. This would be achieved under perfect competition.

8. Gains from trade also arise from decreasing costs (economies of scale), differences in demand between countries, increased competition from trade and the transmission of growth from one country to another. There may also be non-economic advantages from trade.

21.2 Arguments for restricting trade

We have seen how trade can bring benefits to all countries. But when we look around the world we see countries frequently erecting barriers to trade. It is clear to their politicians, therefore, that trade involves costs as well as benefits. In this section we will attempt to identify what these costs are, and whether they are genuine reasons for restricting trade.

In looking at the costs and benefits of trade, the choice is not the stark one of whether to have free trade or no trade at all. Although countries may sometimes contemplate having completely free trade, typically countries limit their trade. However, they certainly do not ban it altogether. The sorts of questions, therefore, that governments pose are (a) should they have freer or more restricted trade and (b) in which sectors should restrictions be tightened or relaxed. If these marginal decisions are to be made rationally, countries should weigh up the marginal benefits against the marginal costs of altering restrictions.

Before we look at the arguments for restricting trade, we must first see what types of restriction governments can employ.

Methods of restricting trade

Ad valorem tariffs

Tariffs levied as a percentage of the price of the import.

Tariffs (customs duties). These are taxes on imports and are usually ad valorem: i.e. a percentage of the price of the import. Tariffs that are used to restrict imports will be most effective if demand is elastic (e.g. when there are close domestically produced substitutes). Tariffs can also be used as a means of raising revenue. Here they will be more effective if demand is inelastic (see pages 97–100 on the incidence of taxation). They can also be used to raise the price of the imported good up to a certain level to prevent 'unfair' competition for domestic producers of the good. In this case the rate of tariff would have to be variable, rising as the world price fell and vice versa. The variable import levies of the European Community on imported foodstuffs are an example of this type of tariff.

Quotas. This is where there is a limit imposed on the quantity of a good that can be imported. The quotas can be imposed by the government, or they can be negotiated with importing countries which agree 'voluntarily' to restrict the amount of imports (see Box 21.4).

Exchange controls. These include limits on the amount of foreign exchange made available to importers (financial quotas), or to citizens travelling abroad, or for investment. Alternatively, they can be in the form of charges made on people purchasing foreign currencies.

Import licensing. The imposition of exchange controls or quotas will often involve importers obtaining licences so that the government can better enforce its restrictions.

Embargoes. This is where the government completely bans certain imports (e.g. drugs) or exports to certain countries (e.g. to enemies during war).

Export taxes. These can be used to increase the price of exports when the country has monopoly power in their supply.

Dumping

Where exports are sold at prices below marginal cost – often as a result of government subsidy.

Subsidies. These can be on goods made at home for the home market to prevent competition from otherwise lower-priced imports. They can also be on exports. Here trade is artificially increased. This is known as dumping. The goods are 'dumped' at artificially low prices in the foreign market.

Box 21.4

Unwilling Volunteers: The Acceptance of Voluntary Quotas
The USA and the use of 'voluntary restraint arrangements'

Much of US industry was having a hard time in the 1980s. With high interest rates causing a high exchange rate for the dollar against other currencies, US exporters found themselves unable to compete in overseas markets. In the home market too, European, Japanese and Korean imports were eroding US companies' market share. And it was not just a problem of the low price of foreign goods, it was also often a question of their superior quality.

The huge and growing US balance of trade deficit prompted the government to take tough action to cut down on foreign imports, especially in certain key industries like automobiles, steel and computer chips. Many politicians wanted the US administration to go much further, but despite the free trade rhetoric of Presidents Reagan and Bush, protectionism still grew inexorably during the 1980s.

In particular there was a growth of special protective measures given to politically sensitive industries. The proportion of imports facing specific protective barriers rose from around 10 per cent at the beginning of the 1980s to nearly 25 per cent at the end.

One of the most widely used protective measures has been the VRA – voluntary restraint arrangement. This is where an importing country such as Japan agrees to limit its imports to a quota. Two major examples of VRAs have been in steel and automobiles.

Steel
In the early 1980s, US steel companies were making huge losses. A combination of gross inefficiency and intense foreign competition had seen the USA's share of the world steel market fall from over 50 per cent after the Second World War to under 10 per cent by the beginning of the 1980s.

In 1984, after intense lobbying by the industry, the US government decided to try to cut steel imports to 20 per cent of the home market (import penetration by that time had reached 26 per cent). The method adopted was the voluntary restraint agreement. VRAs were negotiated for a five-year period with 29 other countries, and as a result

the level of import penetration began to fall. The 20 per cent target was eventually reached in 1988, shortly before the VRAs were due to expire. By that time, however, the US steel industry had been transformed. Employment had fallen dramatically, old plant had been closed, productivity had increased and costs had fallen. .

In arguing for an extension of VRAs in 1989, the steel companies claimed that the dramatic increases in efficiency had only been possible with the protection of the VRAs. Without the protection, they would not have been able to afford the investment that had been necessary to transform the industry. Without a continuation of VRAs, they claimed, they would face unfair competition from countries which subsidized their steel industries.

Critics, however, claimed that an extension of VRAs would discourage further cost reductions and encourage other countries to protect *their* steel industries more heavily. What is more it would simply encourage US firms to import steel components from abroad, rather than importing the steel and then manufacturing the components in the USA.

Automobiles
With large increases in the sales of Japanese and European cars, the US car companies were also calling for protection in the early 1980s. VRAs were first 'negotiated' with Japan in 1981 and were successful to the extent that Japan accepted the arrangement and imports were cut to the agreed level (in some years even below it). As with steel, the VRAs helped the US automobile industry to survive a very difficult period.

But critics claim that the costs to the US consumer have been high. Various studies have estimated that VRAs have pushed up the price of imported Japanese cars by between $1000 and $3000 per car, and that they have also, by reducing foreign competition, pushed up the price of US cars by between $500 and $1000 per car.

? Are there any possible benefits that the US consumer might gain from VRAs?

Administrative barriers. This is where various restrictions are placed on the type of good that can be sold on the home market or on the methods used in its manufacture. These regulations may be designed in such a way as to exclude imports. For example, in Germany all lagers not meeting certain purity standards could be banned. The Germans effectively excluded foreign brands by such measures. Taxes may be

Box 21.5

Friedrich List (1789–1846)
Person profile

Friedrich List is probably the most famous representative of the *German historical school*, but is perhaps best known as the 'inventor' of the infant industry argument for protectionism.

The German historical school was fundamentally opposed to British classical economics with its stress on the benefits of the market and its advocacy of *laissez-faire* and free trade. List criticized Adam Smith and Jean-Baptiste Say for arguing in the abstract and ignoring the political, institutional and social environment in which the economy functions.

Countries, he argued, go through a series of historical stages, and it is the function of economists to identify these stages and devise appropriate policies for each one. Classical theory, argued List, might have been relevant to an industrially advanced country like Britain, but it was inapplicable to countries like Germany and the USA which had not yet reached that stage. These countries could not hope to compete internationally without some

degree of protection by the state.

After an illustrious early career in Germany, being made professor at the age of 31, he fled to the United States in 1825 to escape a gaol sentence for advocating reforms to the German legal and administrative system. There he quickly gained considerable influence in political circles, and his protectionist views were very popular amongst politicians and the business community alike. He is sometimes referred to in the USA as the 'father of American protectionism'. After lending support to Andrew Jackson's presidential election campaign in 1832, he returned to Germany as US consul.

But his problems were not over. In 1837 he once more had to flee Germany, this time because of a business scandal. After three years in Paris he returned to Germany, and in 1841 he published his best-known work, *The National System of Political Economy*, which was generally well received. Later, in 1846, being deeply depressed by serious business problems, he took his own life.

imposed which favour locally produced products or ingredients. A country may prevent foreign companies from setting up certain types of business in certain or all parts of the country. The seriousness of this last barrier depends on whether transport costs or other barriers are high enough to prevent the foreign companies from importing the finished products into the country instead. (See also Box 21.11)

Economic arguments having some general validity

Free trade can bring costs. The following arguments for restricting or influencing trade highlight particular costs.

The infant industry argument. There may be industries in a country that are in their infancy, but which have a potential comparative advantage. This is particularly likely in developing countries. These industries are too small yet to have gained economies of scale; workers are as yet inexperienced; there is a lack of back-up facilities – communications networks, specialist research and development, suppliers of specialist parts, etc. Without protection, these infant industries will not survive competition from abroad.

Infant industry

An industry which has a potential comparative advantage, but which is as yet too underdeveloped to be able to realize this potential.

Protection from foreign competition, however, will allow them to expand and become more efficient. Once they have achieved a comparative advantage, the protection can then be removed to enable them to compete internationally.

Sometimes it is argued that the infant industry argument for intervention is only valid if the potential could not be realized by the firms themselves: in other words, if the economies of scale are *external* to the firm. This would be true in a world of perfect competition and perfect capital markets: in such a situation, any firm with a *potential* comparative advantage could simply borrow enough to tide it over the period where it was too small and inexperienced to compete internationally. In practice, of course, capital and other markets are often highly distorted, especially in the Third World, and thus some form of government intervention is justified if industries are genuine infants with a potential comparative advantage.

 It is often argued that, if the market fails to develop infant industries, then this is an argument for government intervention, but not necessarily in the form of restricting imports. What *other* ways could infant industries be given government support?

Similar to the infant industry argument is the *senile industry argument*. This is where industries with a potential comparative advantage have been allowed to run down and can no longer compete effectively. Some of these industries have little or no chance of ever competing internationally, and the infant/senile industry argument does not apply to them. Other industries, however, may have considerable potential, but be simply unable to make enough profit to afford the necessary investment without some temporary protection. This is one of the most powerful arguments used to justify the use of special protection for the automobile and steel industries in the USA (see Box 21.4).

 How would you set about judging whether an industry had a genuine case for infant/senile industry protection?

Changing comparative advantage and the inflexibility of markets. Comparative advantage can change over time, either naturally (e.g. new raw materials may be discovered) or as a result of deliberate policies (e.g. in the field of education, capital investment or technological research). Due to factor immobility, production may respond fairly slowly to these changing conditions. Thus free trade may reflect *past* comparative advantage rather than present. These industries could be regarded as infants and thus warranting protection.

To prevent 'dumping' and other unfair trade practices. A country may engage in dumping by subsidizing its exports. Alternatively, firms may practise price discrimination by selling at a higher price in home markets and a lower price in foreign markets in order to increase their profits. (It is assumed that their price elasticity of demand differs in the two markets: see section 6.3.) Either way, prices may no longer reflect comparative costs. A country may even export goods in which it has a comparative *disadvantage*. Thus the world would benefit from tariffs being imposed by importers to counteract the subsidy.

 Does the consumer in the importing country gain or lose from dumping?

It can also be argued that there is a case for retaliating against countries which impose restrictions on your exports. In the *short* run, a 'tit for tat' policy will probably benefit no one. Both countries are likely to be made worse off by a contraction in trade. But if the retaliation can 'bring the other country to its senses' and persuade it to remove its restrictions in return for you removing yours, then the retaliation may have a longer-term benefit.

In some cases, merely the threat of retaliation may be enough to get another country to remove its protection.

To prevent the establishment of a foreign-based monopoly. Competition from abroad, especially when it involves dumping, could drive domestic producers out of business.

Box 21.6

Super 301

The USA used the 'retaliation to stop unfair practices' argument to justify the 'super 301' clause of its 1988 Trade Act. This involves the naming of 'priority foreign countries' (PFCs) which are suspected of practices such as erecting barriers to US exports and dumping their products on the US market. If during subsequent negotiations these practices are not ended, then the USA, under the Act, must take retaliatory action against the offending country.

The foreign company, now having a monopoly of the market, could charge high prices with a resulting misallocation of resources.

To reduce reliance on goods with little dynamic potential. Many developing countries have traditionally exported primaries: foodstuffs and raw materials. The world demand for these, however, is fairly income inelastic. World demand for food grows relatively slowly compared with that for manufactures. Likewise the demand for many raw materials has grown slowly due to the development of synthetic substitutes in industrialized countries. In such cases, free trade is not an engine of growth. Instead, if it encourages countries' economies to become locked into a pattern of primary production, it may prevent them from expanding in sectors like manufacturing which have a higher income elasticity of demand. There may thus be a valid argument for protecting or promoting manufacturing industry.

To spread the risks of fluctuating markets. A highly specialized economy – Zambia with copper, Cuba with sugar – will be highly susceptible to world market fluctuations. Greater diversity and greater self-sufficiency, although perhaps leading to less efficiency, can reduce these risks.

To reduce the influence of trade on consumer tastes. The assumption of fixed consumer tastes dictating the pattern of production through trade is false. Multinational companies through their advertising and other forms of sales promotion may influence consumer tastes. Thus some restriction on trade may be justified in order to reduce this 'producer sovereignty'.

 In what ways may free trade have harmful cultural effects on developing countries?

To prevent the importation of harmful goods. A country may want to ban or severely curtail the importation of things such as drugs, pornographic literature and live animals (where there is a risk of rabies or other disease).

To take account of externalities. Free trade will tend to reflect private costs. Both imports and exports, however, can involve externalities. The mining of many minerals for export may adversely affect the health of miners; the production of chemicals for export may involve pollution; the importation of juggernaut lorries may lead to structural damage to houses.

Economic arguments having some validity for specific groups or countries

The following can be seen as 'beggar my neighbour' arguments: that is, they are arguments for restricting trade to enable some groups to benefit at the expense of others. Whether there would be a *net* gain in welfare is difficult to assess, as it would involve weighing up one group's gains against another's losses.

To improve a country's terms of trade by exploiting its market power. If a country, or a group of countries, has market power in the supply of exports (e.g. Brazil with coffee, South Africa with diamonds, OPEC with oil) or market power in the demand for imports (e.g. the USA or other large wealthy countries), it can exploit this power by intervening in trade. By imposing taxes or quotas on exports, or tariffs or quotas on imports, the country can improve its terms of trade.

Let us first take the case of a country, or a group of countries acting as a cartel, which has monopoly power in the sale of a particular export: for example, West African countries in the sale of cocoa. But let us assume that there are many individual producers which are therefore price takers and are thus not in a position to exploit the country's overall market power. This is illustrated in Figure 21.5. If all the firms in the country are price takers, they will collectively produce at point *a* where $P = MC$. Market equilibrium will thus be at a trade price of P_1 and an output of Q_1.

The country's profit, however, would be maximized at point *b* where $MC = MR$, with output at the lower level of Q_2. By imposing an export tax of $P_2 - P_3$, therefore, the country can maximize its gain from this export. Producers will receive P_3 and will therefore supply Q_2. Market price will be P_2.

  1. How much would be the total tax revenue for the government?
2. Will the individual producers gain from the export tax?

Now let us take the case of a country which has *monopsony* power in the demand for an import. This is illustrated in Figure 21.6. Without intervention, equilibrium will be at point *d* where demand equals supply. Q_1 would be purchased at a price of P_1.

But the marginal cost of imports curve will be *above* the supply curve. The reason for this is that, given the country's size, the purchase of additional imports would drive up their price. This means that the cost of additional imports would be the new higher price (given by the supply curve) *plus* the rise in expenditure on the imports that would previously have been purchased at a lower price. Given this *MC* curve, the country will maximize its gain from trade at point *f* by importing Q_2, where demand equals marginal cost. (This assumes that there are no externalities and that therefore the demand curve gives marginal *social* benefit and the marginal cost curve gives marginal *social* cost.) Consumption can be reduced to Q_2 if the government imposes a tariff of $P_3 - P_2$. This is known as the optimum tariff. The country now only pays P_2

Optimum tariff

A tariff that reduces the level of imports to the point where marginal social cost equals marginal social benefit.

Figure 21.5 A country with a monopoly supply of an export

Figure 21.6 A country with a monopsony demand for an import

The Optimum Tariff or Export Tax
Using calculus

How big is the optimum export tax in Figure 21.5? In other words, what tax rate gives the maximum gain from the sale of a given export?

You can see, if you imagine rotating the demand curve (and hence the MR curve too), that the size of the optimum tax (t) will depend on the price elasticity of demand ($P\epsilon_d$). The less elastic it is, the bigger will be the optimum export tax.

The formula for the optimum export tax rate is:

$$t = 1/P\epsilon_d$$

The proof of this is as follows.

In Figure 21.5, the optimum tax rate is:

$$(P_2 - P_3) \div P_2 \qquad (1)$$

From the point of view of the country (as opposed to individual producers) this is simply:

$$(P - MR) \div P \qquad (2)$$

Remember from Box 2.5 that price elasticity of demand is given by:

$$P\epsilon_d = \frac{-dQ}{dP} \times \frac{P}{Q} \qquad (3)$$

Remember also, from Box 4.11, that:

$$MR = \frac{dTR}{dQ} = \frac{d(P.Q)}{dQ} \qquad (4)$$

From the rules of calculus:

$$\frac{d(P.Q)}{dQ} = \frac{dP.Q + dQ.P}{dQ} \qquad (5)$$

$$\therefore \quad P - MR = P - \frac{(dP.Q + dQ.P)}{dQ} \qquad (6)$$

and

$$\frac{P}{P - MR} = \frac{P}{P - \frac{(dP.Q + dQ.P)}{dQ}} \qquad (7)$$

$$= 1 - \frac{P}{\frac{dP.Q + dQ.P}{dQ}} \qquad (8)$$

Again from the rules of calculus:

$$= 1 - \left(\frac{dQ.P}{dP.Q} + \frac{dQ.P}{dQ.P}\right) \qquad (9)$$

$$= 1 - \frac{dQ.P}{dP.Q} - 1 \qquad (10)$$

$$= \frac{-dQ.P}{dP.Q} = P\epsilon_d \qquad (11)$$

$\therefore$ from equations (2) and (11):

$$\frac{P - MR}{P} = optimum\ tax\ rate = \frac{1}{P\epsilon_d}$$

? See if you can devise a similar proof to show that the optimal import tariff, where a country has monopsony power, is $1/P\epsilon_s$ (where $P\epsilon_s$ is the price elasticity of supply of the import).

to importers. Consumers have to pay P_3, but $P_3 - P_2$ will be revenue to the government.

The country gains from such intervention, but only at the expense of the other countries with which it trades.

To protect declining industries. An industry may lose its comparative advantage. If labour and capital could move with no cost to expanding industries, the country would gain by allowing this industry to decline. Factors, however, are often highly immobile and factor movement can be costly. The human costs of sudden industrial closures can be very high. In such circumstances, temporary protection may be warranted to allow the industry to decline more slowly, thus avoiding excessive structural unemployment. Such policies will be at the expense of the consumer, who will be denied access to cheaper foreign imports.

To improve the balance of payments. Under certain special circumstances, when other methods of balance of payments correction are unsuitable, there may be a case for resorting to tariffs (see Chapter 22).

'Non-economic' arguments

A country may be prepared to forgo the dircet economic advantages of free trade – consumption at a lower opportunity cost – in order to achieve objectives that are often described as 'non-economic':

- It may wish to maintain a degree of self-sufficiency in case trade is cut off in times of war. This may apply particularly to the production of food and armaments.
- It may decide not to trade with certain countries with which it disagrees politically.
- It may wish to preserve traditional ways of life. Rural communities or communities built round old traditional industries may be destroyed by foreign competition.
- It may prefer to retain as diverse a society as possible, rather than one too narrowly based on certain industries.

These may all be perfectly valid objectives. The economist is not able to pronouce on the 'correct' set of objectives a society should have. The economist has no superior right to make such normative judgements.

Nevertheless, pursuing such objectives will involve costs. Preserving a traditional way of life, for example, may mean that consumers are denied access to cheaper goods from abroad. Society must therefore weigh up the benefits against the costs of such policies.

 If economics is the study of choices of how to use scarce resources, can these other objectives be legitimately described as 'non-economic'?

Fallacious arguments for restricting trade

Some arguments for protection simply do not stand up to close inspection. Typical of such arguments are the following.

'Imports should be reduced since they lower the standard of living. The money goes abroad rather than into the domestic economy.' Imports are consumed and thus add directly to consumer welfare. Also, provided they are matched by exports, there is no net outflow of money. Trade, because of the law of comparative advantage, allows countries to increase their standard of living: to consume beyond their production possibility curve (see Figures 21.1 and 21.4).

True, money is *spent* on imports, whereas money is *earned* from exports. But this does not make exports 'better' than imports. Money earned is not useful for its own sake, only for what it can buy. There is thus no long-term advantage in having an excess of exports over imports (beyond that necessary to maintain adequate foreign currency reserves).

'Protection is needed from cheap foreign labour.' This argument is certainly fallacious when applied to total consumption. Importing cheap goods from, say, Hong Kong, allows more goods to be consumed. The UK uses less resources by buying these goods through the production and sale of exports than by producing them at home. Nevertheless there will be a cost to *certain* UK workers whose jobs are lost through foreign competition. Policy makers must weigh the benefits of trade to consumers and export industries against the costs to specific workers.

'Protection reduces unemployment.' At a microeconomic level this may be true. Protecting industries from foreign competition may well allow workers in those industries to retain their jobs. On the other hand, if foreigners sell fewer goods to the UK, they will not be able to buy so many UK exports. Thus unemployment will rise in UK export industries. Overall unemployment, therefore, is little affected, and in

the meantime the benefits from trade to consumers are reduced. Resources are being used inefficiently.

Nevertheless there is some truth in the unemployment argument in certain circumstances: e.g. when temporary protection is given to declining industries.

'Dumping is always a bad thing, and thus a country should restrict subsidized imports.'
Dumping may well reduce world economic welfare: it goes against the law of comparative advantage. The importing country, however, may well *gain* from dumping. Provided the dumping is not used to drive domestic producers out of business and establish a foreign monopoly, the consumer gains from lower prices. Dumping is essentially a transfer of resources from the 'dumper' to the 'dumped on'. The losers, therefore, are the taxpayers in the foreign country – and also the workers in competing industries in the home country.

Problems with protection

Tariffs and other forms of protection impose a cost on society. This is illustrated in Figure 21.7. It illustrates the case of a good that is partly home produced and partly imported. Domestic demand and supply are given by D_{dom} and S_{dom}. It is assumed that firms in the country produce under perfect competition and that therefore the supply curve is the sum of the firms' marginal cost curves.

The world price is given, at P_w, and hence world supply (S_{world}) is perfectly elastic: the country is a price taker. At P_w, Q_2 is demanded, Q_1 is supplied by domestic suppliers and hence $Q_2 - Q_1$ is imported.

Now a tariff is imposed. This shifts up the world supply curve by the amount of the tariff. Price rises to $P_w + t$. Domestic production increases to Q_3, consumption falls to Q_4, and hence imports fall to $Q_4 - Q_3$.

This imposes a cost on society. Consumers are having to pay a higher price, and hence consumer surplus falls from *ABC* to *ADE*. The cost to consumers in lost consumer surplus is thus EDBC (i.e. areas 1 + 2 + 3 + 4). *Part* of this cost, however, is redistributed as a *benefit* to other sections in society. *Firms* face a higher price, and thus gain extra profits (area 1): where profit is given by the area between the price and the *MC* curve. The *government* receives extra revenue from the tariff payments (area 3): i.e. $Q_4 - Q_3$ × tariff. These revenues can be used, for example, to reduce taxes.

But *part* of this cost is not recouped elsewhere. It is a net cost to society (areas 2 and 4).

Figure 21.7 The cost of protection

Area 2 represents the extra costs of producing $Q_3 - Q_1$ at home, rather than importing it. If $Q_3 - Q_1$ were still imported, the country would only be paying S_{world}. By producing it at home, however, the costs are given by the domestic supply curve ($= MC$). The difference between MC and S_{world} (area 2) is thus the efficiency loss on the production side.

Area 4 represents the loss of consumer surplus by the reduction in consumption from Q_2 to Q_4. Consumers have saved area FBQ_2Q_4 of expenditure, but have sacrificed area DBQ_2Q_4 of utility in so doing – a net loss of area 4.

The government should ideally weigh up such costs against any benefits that are gained from protection.

 In this model, where the country is a price taker and faces a horizontal supply curve (the small country assumption), is any of the cost of the tariff borne by the overseas suppliers?

There are other specific problems with protection.

Protection as 'second best'. Many of the arguments for protection amount merely to arguments for some type of government intervention in the economy. Protection, however, may not be the best way of dealing with the problem, since protection may have undesirable side-effects. There may be a more direct form of intervention that has no side-effects. In such a case, protection will be no more than a *second-best* solution.

For example, using tariffs to protect old inefficient industries from foreign competition may help prevent unemployment in those parts of the economy, but the consumer will suffer from higher prices. A better solution would be to subsidize retraining and investment in those areas of the country in *new efficient* industries – industries with a comparative advantage. In this way, unemployment is avoided, but the consumer does not suffer.

Even if the *existing* industries were to be supported, it would still be better to do this by paying them subsidies than by putting tariffs on imports. This argument can be expressed in terms of Figure 21.7. As we have seen, a tariff imposes costs on the consumer of areas $1 + 2 + 3 + 4$. In the current example, area 2 may be a cost worth paying in order to increase domestic output to Q_3 (and hence reduce unemployment). Areas 1 and 3, as argued above, are merely *redistributed* elsewhere (to firms and the government respectively). But this still leaves area 4. This is a side-effect cost *not* recouped elsewhere.

A *subsidy*, on the other hand, would not have involved this side-effect cost. In order to raise output to Q_3, a rate of subsidy the same as the tariff rate would have to be given to producers. This would raise the amount they receive per unit to $P_w + t$. They would choose to supply Q_3. The price to the consumer, however, would *remain at the world price P_w*. There would thus be no cost to the consumer. The cost of the subsidy to the taxpayer would be areas $1 + 2$. Area 1 would be redistributed to firms as extra profit. Area 2, as argued above, may be worth paying in order to bring the desirable output and employment consequences.

If the aim is to increase output, a *production* subsidy is the best policy. If the aim is to increase employment, an *employment* subsidy is the best policy. In either case, *protection* is no more than second best, since it involves side-effects.

To conclude: the best policy is to tackle the problem directly. Unless the aim is specifically to reduce imports (rather than help domestic industry), protection is an indirect policy, and hence never more than second best.

 What would be the 'first-best' solution to the problem of an infant industry not being able to compete with imports?

Box 21.8

The Uruguay Round
'We will liberalize, but only if you will too'

In September 1986 in the town of Punta del Este, in Uruguay, the members of GATT, the General Agreement on Tariffs and Trade, began a new round of trade negotiations. The 'Uruguay round' was set to last until December 1990 and was the most ambitious of all eight rounds that had taken place since GATT was signed in 1947. In all, 105 countries participated in the Uruguay round: the 96 members of GATT plus countries which had applied for membership before April 1987.

On the agenda was the extensive liberalization of trade in virtually all goods and services. One means of achieving this was to reduce tariffs, but these had already been reduced substantially in previous rounds. By the end of the 1980s the average tariff rate for developed countries was only around 5 per cent, compared with around 40 per cent back in 1947. Tariff rates in developing countries, however, were considerably higher.

Tariffs are the only form of trade restriction permitted under GATT, and yet, as tariffs have fallen, so other forms of trade restriction have grown, in many cases quite dramatically. If there was to be a significant movement towards free trade, therefore, these non-tariff barriers would have to be substantially reduced. The major goals of the Uruguay round are shown in the table.

The success or otherwise of the Uruguay round was crucially dependent on the USA. President Bush, on a number of occasions, stressed the USA's commitment to the principles of free trade, and the US negotiators in the Uruguay round of talks frequently called for tougher GATT rules and the strengthening of GATT's powers to enforce its rulings. The USA made several major liberalizing proposals, such as the abolition of virtually all farm support within ten years and the abolition of many restrictions on foreign investment:

> 'We are totally committed to the maintenance of an open and fair trade policy', insists Mr Rufus Yerxa, America's ambassador to GATT, adding that the task of the Uruguay round is to create the conditions which would make resort to unilateral and bilateral solutions unnecessary. Mr Yerxa also claims that America is one of the most open economies in the world. It takes over 50% of the manufactured exports of developing countries, for example, compared with less than 30% for the EC and 8% for Japan.[2]

And yet the USA was not prepared to liberalize its restrictions on imports while it saw other countries maintaining or increasing theirs. With the passing of the 1988 Trade Act with its section 301 (see Box 21.6), the USA was prepared to flout GATT rules and retaliate unilaterally against countries it accused of unfair trade practices. At the same time Congress, worried about the threats to many US industries from cheap foreign imports, was becoming increasingly protectionist in sentiment:

World multiplier effects. If the UK imposes tariffs or other restrictions, imports will be reduced. But these imports are other countries' exports. A reduction in their exports will reduce the level of injections into the 'rest-of-the-world' economy, and thus lead to a multiplied fall in rest-of-the-world income. This in turn will lead to a reduction in demand for UK exports. This, therefore, tends to undo the benefits of the tariffs.

? What determines the size of this world multiplier effect?

Retaliation. If the UK imposes restrictions on, say, Japan, then Japan may impose restrictions on the UK. Any gain to UK firms competing with Japanese imports is offset by a loss to UK exporters. What is more, UK consumers suffer since the benefits from comparative advantage have been lost.

The increased use of tariffs and other restrictions can lead to a trade war: each country cutting back on imports from other countries. In the end, everyone loses.

Protection may allow firms to remain inefficient. By removing or reducing foreign competition, protection may reduce firms' incentive to reduce costs. Thus if protection is being given to an infant industry, the government must ensure that the

Box 21.8 (cont'd)

Uruguay round negotiating goals

1 **Tariffs:** Overall cut of one-third.
2 **Non-tariff measures:** Reduction and elimination.
3 **Natural resource-based products:** Liberalisation of trade in fisheries, forestry, non-ferrous metals and minerals products.
4 **Textiles and clothing:** Phase out the multi-fibre arrangement and bring textiles trade within normal GATT rules.
5 **Agriculture:** Reduce farm subsidies and other forms of support tied to production and open up domestic markets.
6 **Tropical products:** Tariff cuts and elimination of non-tariff barriers.
7 **GATT articles:** Redrafting of some rules such as third-world exemption from the ban on import controls for balance-of-payments reasons.
8 **GATT codes:** Strengthening GATT's voluntary codes such as those on anti-dumping and technical barriers to trade.

9 **Safeguards:** New rules governing emergency protection against imports, including disciplines on (or elimination of) 'grey area' measures such as voluntary export restraints.
10 **Subsidies and countervailing measures:** Tightening disciplines on subsidies and measures taken to counteract them.
11 **Intellectual property:** A comprehensive agreement covering standards and principles of protection for trade in ideas.
12 **Investment measures:** Possible new disciplines to curb trade-restricting conditions on foreign investment.
13 **Disputes settlement:** Measures to make the process speedier and more effective.
14 **Functioning of the GATT system:** Trade-policy review of members already instituted, more frequent ministerial meetings, better co-operation with the International Monetary Fund and the World Bank.
15 **Services:** A general agreement applying fair-trade rules to trade in services.[1]

What Mr Yerxa fails to point out is that while other countries are moving fast in the direction of liberalizing trade, America is going into reverse. A report ... on American trade policy compiled by GATT economists noted that American barriers had increased over the past decade, despite presidential resistance to more extreme measures. On one estimate, the proportion of America's imports affected by significant barriers has doubled to nearly 25% since 1980.[3]

The biggest stumbling block to agreement in the Uruguay round was agriculture. The USA proposed a 75 per cent cut in agricultural support. The EC was not prepared to consider cuts much above 30 per cent. As the 7 December deadline approached, Third World countries, desperate to gain entry to European and North American markets, could do little but stand by and watch the two Titans – the USA and the EC – refusing to budge. The result was that the negotiations collapsed. It was agreed, however, to resume talks early in 1991.

[1] *The Economist*, 21 April 1990.
[2] *Ibid.*
[3] *Ibid.*

lack of competition does not prevent it 'growing up'. Protection should not be excessive and should be removed as soon as possible.

Bureaucracy. If a government is to avoid giving excessive protection to firms, it should examine each case carefully. This can lead to large administrative costs.

Corruption. Some countries that have an extensive programme of protection suffer from corruption. Home producers want as much protection as possible. Importers want as much freedom as possible. It is very tempting for both groups to bribe officials to give them favourable treatment.

World attitudes towards trade and protection

Pre-war growth in protectionism

After the Wall Street crash of 1929, the world plunged into the Great Depression. Countries found their exports falling dramatically, and many suffered severe balance of payments difficulties. The response of many countries was to restrict imports by the use of tariffs and quotas. Of course, this reduced other countries' exports, which encouraged them to resort to even greater protectionism. The net effect of the Depression and the rise in protectionism was a dramatic fall in world trade. The volume of world trade in manufactures fell by more than a third in the three years following the Wall Street crash. Clearly there was a net economic loss to the world from this decline in trade.

On the other hand, the protectionism allowed countries to build up their own home industries behind the trade barriers. This helped to offset the effects of the Depression and lessened the fall in demand for imports. Nevertheless, world trade was still 14 per cent lower in real terms in 1937 than in 1929.

Post-war reduction in protectionism and the role of GATT

After the war there was a general desire to reduce trade restrictions, so that all countries could gain the maximum benefits from trade. There was no desire to return to the beggar-my-neighbour policies of the 1930s.

In 1947, 23 countries got together and signed the General Agreement on Tariffs and Trade (GATT): today there are over 100 member countries, between them accounting for over 90 per cent of world trade. The aims of GATT were and are to liberalize trade, and under GATT arrangements, member countries have met periodically to negotiate reductions in tariffs and other trade restrictions. There have been eight 'rounds' of such negotiations since 1947. The three major ones were the Kennedy round (1964–7), the Tokyo round (1973–9) and the Uruguay round (1986–90). The Kennedy round led to tariff reductions averaging 35 per cent. The Tokyo round involved agreements for tariff reductions of about 33 per cent, but many of the reductions in the event were less than those agreed. The Uruguay round is examined in Box 21.8.

The lesson from the negotiations is that countries are very quick to complain about the protectionist measures used by their rivals. They thus pay lip service to the general removal of trade restrictions. But when it comes to agreeing to remove their *own* trade restrictions, they are much less willing, and find all sorts of reasons to justify them.

In addition to the negotiated reductions in trade restrictions, GATT provides various rules governing trade:

- *Most favoured nation* clause. This requires that any trade concession that a country makes to one member must then be granted to *all* signatories. There is an exception to this, however, in the case of free trade areas and customs unions. In such cases, trade restrictions can be eliminated between the countries involved and yet still be maintained with the rest of the world – provided this does not involve *raising* them with the rest of the world.
- The general prohibition of quotas (but with notable exceptions: e.g. agricultural imports).
- Special arrangements for developing countries, to permit them a greater use of protection than developed countries.
- The forbidding of any member from taking retaliatory action against countries it suspects of unfair trade practices. Under GATT procedures, the case can be referred to a disputes panel which will decide whether GATT rules have been broken. If they have and the offending country continues to break them, the aggrieved country can be compensated. In practice this procedure is rarely used.

Recent re-emergence of protectionist sentiments

The balance of payments problems that many countries experienced after the oil crisis of 1973 and the recession of the early 1980s led many politicians round the

Box 21.9

Strategic Trade Theory
An argument for protection?

Lester Thurow is Dean of the Sloan School of Management at the Massachusetts Institute of Technology (MIT). He is also one of the USA's best-known and most articulate advocates of 'managed trade'.

Thurow (and others) have been worried by the growing penetration of US markets by imports from Japan, Europe and many Third World countries. Their response is to call for a carefully worked-out strategy of protection for US industries. What they want is a package of protectionist measures, from tariffs and quotas to administrative and legal barriers.

The *strategic trade theory* that they support argues that the real world is complex. It is wrong, they claim, to rely on free trade and the law of comparative advantage. Particular industries will require particular policies of protection or promotion tailored to their particular needs:

● Some industries will require protection against unfair competition from abroad – not just to protect the industries themselves, but also to protect the consumer from the oligopolistic power that the foreign companies will gain if they succeed in driving the domestic producers out of business.

● Other industries will need special support in the form of subsidies to enable them to modernize and compete effectively with imports.

● New industries may require protection to enable them to get established.

● If a particular foreign country protects or promotes its *own* industries, it may be desirable to retaliate in order to persuade the country to change its mind.

Thurow claims that Japan has been following a policy of managed trade for years – and look how successful it has been!

But, despite the enthusiasm of the strategic trade theorists, their views have come in for concerted criticism from economic liberals. If the USA is protected from cheap Japanese imports, they claim, all that will be achieved is a huge increase in the shopping bill of the US consumer. The car, steel, telecommunications and electrical goods industries might find their profits bolstered, but this is hardly likely to encourage them to be more efficient.

Another criticism of managed trade is the difficulty of identifying just which industries need protection, how much and for how long. Governments do not have perfect knowledge. What is more, the political lobbyists from various interested groups are likely to use all sorts of tactics – legal or illegal – to persuade the government to look favourably on them. In the face of such pressure will the government remain 'objective'? No, say the liberals.

So how do the strategic trade theorists reply? If it works for Japan, they say, it can work for the USA. What is needed is a change in attitudes. Rather than industry looking on the government as either an enemy to be outwitted or a potential benefactor to be wooed, and government looking on industry as a source of votes or tax revenues, both sides should try to develop a partnership – a partnership from which the whole country can gain.

But whether sensible, constructive managed trade is possible in the US democratic system, or the UK for that matter, is a highly debatable point. 'Sensible' managed trade, say the liberals, is just pie in the sky.

? In what ways might the *consumer* gain from 'sensible' managed trade?

---

world to call for trade restrictions. For example, some Democrat politicians in the USA saw trade restrictions, especially against Japanese and European imports, as the best way of dealing with the chronic US balance of payments deficit. This was resisted by Presidents Reagan and Bush, who were committed to a policy of free trade and a reliance on markets.

A tariff war has so far been averted, but there has been a gradual increase in non-tariff barriers, such as subsidies on domestic products, the prohibition of imports that do not meet precise safety or other specifications, administrative delays in customs clearance, limits on investment by foreign companies and governments favouring domestic firms when purchasing supplies.

Quotas have been increasingly used in recent years, especially against Japanese imports. In most cases these have been 'voluntary' agreements (see Box 21.4). Japan, on a number of occasions, has agreed to restrict the number of cars it exports to various European countries. Similar restrictions have applied to Japanese televisions and videos. Over 200 VRAs were in force around the world in 1990.

The problem of increasing non-tariff barriers was recognized in the Uruguay round of GATT negotiations, and agreements were sought to dismantle many of them (see Box 21.8).

▲ SUMMARY

1. Countries use various methods to restrict trade, including tariffs, quotas, exchange controls, import licensing, export taxes, and legal and administrative barriers. Countries may also promote their own industries by subsidies.

2. Reasons for restricting trade that have some validity in a world context include the infant industry argument, the inflexibility of markets in responding to changing comparative advantage, dumping and other unfair trade practices, the danger of the establishment of a foreign-based monopoly, the problems of relying on exporting goods whose market is growing slowly or even declining, the need to spread the risks of fluctuating export prices, and the problems that free trade may adversely affect consumer tastes, may allow the importation of harmful goods and may not take account of externalities.

3. Often, however, the arguments for restricting trade are in the context of one country benefiting even though other countries may lose more. Countries may intervene in trade in order to exploit their monopoly/monopsony power. In the case of imports, the optimum tariff would be that which would reduce consumption to the level where price was equal to the country's marginal cost. In the case of exports, the optimum export tax would be that which reduced production to the level where the country's marginal revenue was equal to marginal cost. Other 'beggar-my-neighbour' arguments include the protection of declining industries and improving the balance of payments.

4. Finally, a country may have other objectives in restricting trade, such as remaining self-sufficient in certain strategic products, not trading with certain countries of which it disapproves, protecting traditional ways of life or simply retaining a non-specialized economy.

5. Arguments for restricting trade, however, are often fallacious. In general, trade brings benefits to countries, and protection to achieve one objective may be at a very high opportunity cost. Other things being equal, there will be a net loss in welfare from restricting trade, with any gain in government revenue or profits to firms being outweighed by a loss in consumer surplus. Even if government intervention to protect certain parts of the economy is desirable, restricting trade is unlikely to be a first-best solution to the problem, since it involves side-effect costs. What is more, restricting trade may have adverse world multiplier effects; it may encourage retaliation; it may allow inefficient firms to remain inefficient; it may involve considerable bureaucracy and possibly even corruption.

6. Most countries of the world are signatories of GATT and in theory are in favour of moves towards freer trade. The Uruguay round sought significant reductions in trade restrictions, both tariff and non-tariff. In practice, however, countries have been very unwilling to abandon restrictions if they believe that they can gain from them, even though they might be at the expense of other countries.

21.3 Preferential trading

Types of preferential trading arrangement

A partial move towards free trade is for a country to remove trade restrictions with selected other countries. There are three possible forms of such trading arrangements.

Free trade areas

Free trade area

A group of countries with no trade barriers between themselves.

A free trade area is where member countries remove tariffs and quotas between themselves, but retain whatever restrictions *each member chooses* with non-member countries. Some provision will have to be made to prevent imports from outside coming into the area via the country with the lowest external tariff.

Customs union

A free trade area with common external tariffs and quotas.

Customs unions

A customs union is like a free trade area, but in addition members must adopt common external tariffs and quotas with non-member countries.

Common markets

A common market is where member countries operate as a *single* market. Like a customs union there are no tariffs and quotas between member countries and there are common external tariffs and quotas. But a common market goes further than this. A full common market includes the following features:

Common market

A customs union where the member countries act as a single market with free movement of labour and capital, common taxes and common trade laws.

A common system of taxation. In the case of a *perfect* common market this will involve identical rates of tax in all member countries.

A common system of laws and regulations governing production, employment and trade. For example, in a perfect common market there would be a *single* set of laws governing the following:

- Product specification (e.g. permissible artificial additives to foods, or levels of exhaust emissions from cars).
- Industrial technology (e.g. standard sizes of equipment, or the composition of various inputs).
- Health and safety at work.
- The employment and dismissal of labour.
- The rights of trade unions and their members.
- Mergers and take-overs.
- Monopolies and restrictive practices.
- The setting-up of new companies.

Free movement of labour, capital and materials and of goods and services. In a perfect common market this will involve a total absence of border controls between member states (except perhaps to prevent the movement of drugs or other illegal items), the freedom of workers to work in any member country, the freedom of firms to expand into any member state, and the absence of administrative barriers such as the requirement for firms to fill in separate forms for each country in the market to which it exports.

The absence of special treatment by member governments of their own domestic industries. For example, governments are large purchasers of goods and services. In a perfect common market they should buy from whichever companies within the market offer the most competitive deal and not show favouritism towards domestic suppliers: they should operate a *common procurement policy*.

The definition of a common market is sometimes extended to include the following two features of *economic and monetary union*.

A fixed exchange rate between the member countries' currencies. In the extreme case this would involve a *single currency* for the whole market.

Common macroeconomic policies. To some extent this must follow from a fixed exchange rate, but in the extreme case it will involve a single macroeconomic management of the whole market, and hence the abolition of separate fiscal or monetary intervention by individual member states.

The best-known example of a preferential trading system is that of the European Community. We will examine the EC and its advantages and disadvantages in section 21.4. For now, however, we concentrate on *theoretical* advantages and disadvantages of preferential trading. We will look at these arguments in the context of forming a customs union (rather than a common market), i.e. on the effects of removing tariff barriers between the member countries. (The advantages and disadvantages of a full common market are examined in section 21.4 in the context of 1992.)

The static effects of a customs union: trade creation and trade diversion

By joining a customs union (or free trade area), a country will find that its trade patterns change. Two such changes can be distinguished: trade creation and trade diversion.

Trade creation

Trade creation

Where a customs union leads to greater specialization according to comparative advantage and thus a shift in production from higher-cost to lower-cost sources.

Trade creation is where consumption shifts from a high-cost producer to a low-cost producer. The removal of trade barriers allows greater specialization according to comparative advantage. Instead of consumers having to pay high prices for domestically produced goods in which the country has a comparative disadvantage, the goods can now be obtained more cheaply from other members of the customs union. In return, the country can export goods to them in which it has a comparative advantage.

For example, suppose that the most efficient producer in the world of good x is France. Assume that, before it joined the EC, the UK had to pay tariffs on good x from France. After joining the EC, however, it was then able to import good x from France without paying tariffs. There was a gain to UK consumers. This gain is illustrated in Figure 21.8. The diagram assumes for simplicity that the UK is a price taker as an importer of good x from France: the EC price is given.

The diagram shows that, before joining the EC, the UK had to pay the EC price *plus* the tariff (i.e. P_1). At P_1 the UK produced Q_2, consumed Q_1 and thus imported $Q_1 - Q_2$. With the removal of tariffs, the price falls to P_2. Consumption increases to Q_3 and production falls to Q_4. Imports have thus increased to $Q_3 - Q_4$. Trade has been created. Similar diagrams can be drawn for other goods in which the UK has a comparative advantage, and where therefore exports to the EC increase after the removal of tariff barriers.

The gain in welfare from the removal of the tariff is also illustrated in Figure 21.8. It is the same as the loss in welfare from the *imposition* of a tariff that we illustrated in Figure 21.7. A reduction in price from P_1 to P_2 leads to an increase in consumer surplus of areas $1 + 2 + 3 + 4$. On the other hand, there is a loss in profits to domestic producers of good x of area 1 and a loss in tariff revenue to the government of area 3. There is still a net gain, however, of areas $2 + 4$.

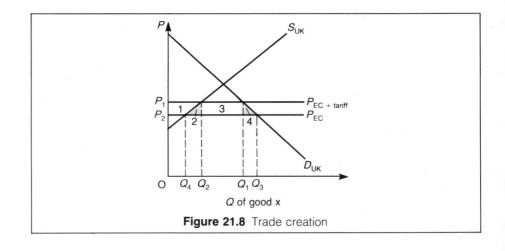

Figure 21.8 Trade creation

The increased consumption of wine in the UK after joining the EC may be seen as trade creation.

Trade diversion

Trade diversion is where consumption shifts from a lower-cost producer outside the customs union to a higher-cost producer within the union.

Assume that the most efficient producer of good y in the world is New Zealand – outside the EC. Assume that, before membership, the UK pays a similar tariff on good y from any country, and thus imports the product from New Zealand rather than the EC.

After joining the EC, however, the removal of the tariff makes the EC product cheaper, since the tariff remains on the New Zealand product. Consumption has thus switched to a higher-cost producer. Consumers still gain, since they are paying a lower price than before, but this time the loss in profits to domestic producers and the loss in tariff revenue to the governments may be larger.

These benefits and costs are shown in Figure 21.9. For simplicity it assumes a constant New Zealand and EC price (i.e. that their supply curves are infinitely elastic). The domestic supply curve (S_{UK}) is upward sloping, and is assumed to be equal to marginal cost.

Before joining the EC, the UK was importing good y from New Zealand at a price P_1 (i.e. the New Zealand price plus the tariff). The UK thus consumed Q_2, produced Q_1 domestically, and thus imported the remainder, $Q_2 - Q_1$. On joining the EC it was now able to consume at the EC (tariff-free) price of P_2. (Note that this is above the tariff-free New Zealand price, P_3.) What are the gains and losses?

> Consumers' gain: consumer surplus rises by areas 1 + 2 + 3 + 4.
> Producers' loss: UK producer surplus (profit) falls by area 1.
> Government's loss: previously tariffs of areas 3 + 5 were paid.
>   Now no tariffs are paid. The government thus loses this revenue.

There is thus a net gain of areas 1 + 2 + 3 + 4 minus areas 1 + 3 + 5, i.e. areas 2 + 4 minus area 5. If, however, area 5 is bigger than areas 2 + 4, there is a net loss.

When trade *diversion* takes place, therefore, there may still be a net gain, but there may be a net loss. It depends on circumstances.

Trade diversion
Where a customs union diverts consumption from goods produced at a lower cost outside the union to goods produced at a higher cost (but tariff free) within the union.

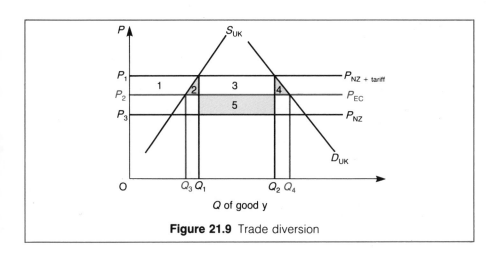

Figure 21.9 Trade diversion

> **?** Under which of the following circumstances is there likely to be a net gain from trade diversion? (Refer to Figure 21.9.)
> (a) A small difference between the EC price and the New Zealand pre-tariff price, and a large difference between the EC price and the New Zealand price with the tariff, or vice versa.
> (b) Elastic or inelastic UK demand and supply curves.
> (c) The UK demand and supply curves close together or far apart.

A customs union is more likely to lead to trade diversion rather than trade creation:

- When the union's external tariff is very high. Under these circumstances the abolition of the tariff within the union is likely to lead to a large reduction in the price of goods imported from other members of the union.
- When there is a relatively small cost difference between goods produced within and outside the union. Here the abolition of even relatively low tariffs within the union will lead to internally produced goods becoming cheaper than externally produced goods.

Dynamic effects of a customs union

The problem with the above analysis is that it assumes *static* demand and supply curves: in other words, supply and demand curves that are unaffected by changes in trading patterns. In reality, if a country joins a customs union, the curves are likely to shift. Membership itself affects demand and supply – perhaps beneficially, perhaps adversely. These are the dynamic effects of membership.

Dynamic advantages (economic)

- Increased market size may allow a country's firms to exploit *(internal) economies of scale*. This argument is more important for small countries, which have therefore more to gain from an enlargement of their markets.
- *External economies of scale*: increased trade may lead to improvements in the infrastructure of the members of the customs union (better roads, railways, financial services, etc.). This in turn could then bring bigger long-term benefits from trade between members, by making the transport and handling of imports and exports cheaper.
- The bargaining power of the whole customs union with the rest of the world may allow member countries to gain *better terms of trade*. This, of course, will necessarily involve a degree of political co-operation between the members.
- *Increased competition* between member countries may stimulate efficiency, encourage investment and reduce monopoly power. Of course, a similar advantage could be gained by the simple removal of tariffs with any competing country.
- Integration may encourage a *more rapid spread of technology*.

Dynamic disadvantages (economic)

- *Resources may flow from the country* to more efficient members of the customs union, or to the geographical centre of the union (so as to minimize transport costs). This can be a major problem for a *common market* (where there is free movement of labour and capital). The country could become a depressed 'region' of the community, with adverse regional multiplier effects.
- If integration encourages greater co-operation between firms in member countries, it may also encourage *greater oligopolistic collusion*, thus keeping prices higher to the consumer. It may also encourage mergers and take-overs which would increase monopoly power.

- *Diseconomies of scale*: if the union leads to the development of very large companies, they may become bureaucratic and inefficient.
- The *costs of administering* the customs union may be high. These costs may increase over time if the member countries have inadequate controls over the union's expenditure. This problem is likely to be worse the more the intervention in the affairs of individual members. This will encourage members to press for higher expenditure when it benefits them specifically, knowing that the costs will be met by the members collectively.

It is extremely difficult to assess these arguments. To decide whether membership has been beneficial to a country requires a prediction of what things would have been like if it had not joined. No *accurate* predictions of this sort can be made, and they can never be tested. Also, many of the advantages and disadvantages are very long term, and depend on future attitudes, institutions, policies and world events, which again cannot be predicted.

In addition, some of the advantages and disadvantages are distinctly political, such as 'greater political power' or 'loss of sovereignty'. Assessment of these arguments cannot be made by economists.

 How would you set about assessing whether or not a country had made a net dynamic gain by joining a customs union? What sort of evidence would you look for?

Preferential trading in practice

There have been several examples of preferential trading arrangements in different parts of the world. An example in the developed world is the European Free Trade Area (EFTA), which consists of Austria, Finland, Iceland, Norway, Sweden and Switzerland. The UK, Denmark and Portugal were also members before they joined the EC. EFTA is concerned with free trade in industrial products: agricultural products and services are excluded. Another example of a free trade area in many products is that of the USA and Canada.

Preferential trading has the greatest potential to benefit countries whose domestic market is too small, taken on its own, to enable them to benefit from economies of scale, and where they face substantial barriers to their exports. Many smaller developing countries fall into this category and as a result many countries throughout the Third World have attempted to form preferential trading arrangements. Examples include or have included the eleven-member Latin American Free Trade Area (LAFTA) (now the Latin American Integration Association), the Andean Pact, the Central American Common Market, the Caribbean Community (CARICOM) and the Economic Community of West African States (ECOWAS).

By far the most famous and powerful of all preferential trading arrangements is the European Community. Despite being referred to as 'The Common Market', it has not in fact been a true common market, but rather a customs union, and an imperfect one at that. For most of the 1970s and 1980s the number and variety of non-tariff barriers increased. Member countries adopted all sorts of laws and administrative restrictions to prevent the free flow of goods and resources within the EC, and to favour their own domestic industries over those of other members.

By the mid-1980s, however, the tide of opinion was turning in the Community. Member governments were becoming much more wedded to the idea of free markets and free trade. In this atmosphere of encouraging competition the member countries signed the 'Single European Act'. This committed the twelve countries to the establishment of a true common market – 'the single market' as it is called – by the end of 1992.

Section 21.4 focuses on the EC as an example of a preferential trading system, and looks at the costs and benefits of its move towards being a full common market.

▲ SUMMARY

1. Countries may make a partial movement towards free trade by the adoption of a preferential trading system. This involves free trade between the members, but restrictions on trade with the rest of the world. Such a system can be either a simple free trade area, or a customs union (where there are common restrictions with the rest of the world), or a common market (where in addition there is free movement of capital and labour, and common taxes and trade laws).

2. A preferential trading area can lead to trade creation where production shifts to low-cost producers within the area, or to trade diversion where trade shifts away from lower-cost producers outside the area to higher-cost producers within the area.

3. There is a net welfare gain from trade creation: the gain in consumer surplus outweighs the loss of tariff revenue and the loss of profit to domestic producers. With trade

diversion, however, these two losses may outweigh the gains to consumers: whether they do depends on the size of the tariffs and on the demand for and supply of the traded goods.

4. Preferential trading may bring dynamic advantages of increased economies of scale (both internal and external), improved terms of trade from increased bargaining power with the rest of the world, increased efficiency from greater competition between member countries and a more rapid spread of technology. On the other hand, it can lead to increased regional problems for members, greater oligopolistic collusion and various diseconomies of scale. There may also be large costs of administering the system.

5. There have been several attempts around the world to form preferential trading systems, but by far the most powerful one has been the European Community.

21.4 The European Community

Historical background

The European Economic Community was formed by the signing of the Treaty of Rome in 1957 and came into operation on 1 January 1958.

The original six member countries of the EEC (Belgium, France, Italy, Luxembourg, Netherlands and West Germany) had already made a move towards integration with the formation of the European Coal and Steel Community in 1952. This had removed all restrictions on trade in coal, steel and iron ore between the six countries. The aim had been to gain economies of scale and allow more effective competition with the USA and other foreign producers.

The European Economic Community extended this principle and aimed eventually to be a full common market with completely free trade between members in all products, and with completely free movement of labour, enterprise and capital. By uniting many of the countries of Western Europe it was hoped too that the conflicts of the two world wars would never be repeated, and that acting together the countries of the EEC could be an effective political and economic force in a world dominated by political giants such as the USA and the USSR, and by economic giants such as the USA (and later Japan).

All internal tariffs between the six members had been abolished and common external tariffs established by 1968. But this still only made the EEC a *customs union* since a number of restrictions on internal trade remained (legal, administrative, fiscal, etc.). Nevertheless the aim was eventually to create a full common market.

In 1973 the UK, Denmark and Ireland joined the EEC. Greece joined in 1981, and Spain and Portugal in 1986.

The institutions of the European Community

The goal of some politicians is for the European Community (as it is now called) to become a complete political union, with a central federal government: a 'United States of Europe'. Although this is unlikely in the immediate future, there are some political and legal institutions that affect life in member countries.

European Commission. This consists of seventeen commissioners appointed by the member countries, two each from the five large countries, and one each from the small. The commissioners administer existing Community policy and propose new policies. They are backed up by a secretariat of some 3000 people in Brussels.

European Council of Ministers. This consists of twelve senior ministers, one from each country. It receives proposals from the Commission, and has the power to decide on all EC issues. Which ministers are represented on the Council depends on the purpose of the meeting. Thus finance ministers would represent their country on economic issues, agricultural ministers on farm policy, foreign ministers on Community external relations and so on.

European Parliament. Constituencies in the member countries elect MEPs to serve in the European Parliament in Strasbourg. Its powers are rather limited in practice, but in theory both the Commission and the Council are answerable to it.

The European Court of Justice. This meets in Luxembourg and decides on areas of legal dispute arising from the Rome Treaty, whether between governments, institutions or individuals. Sometimes its decisions have far-reaching effects (see Box 21.12).

Customs union or common market? The economic nature of the European Community

The European Community is clearly a customs union. It has common external tariffs and no internal tariffs. But is it more than this? Is it also a common market? The answer is that for years there have been *certain* common economic policies in the EC. In other respects the Community of the 1970s and 1980s was far from a true common market: there were all sorts of non-tariff barriers. Although these were often erected for other reasons (e.g. health and safety), they had the effect of restricting trade within the EC and favouring domestic producers.

We need to answer three questions: (a) In what areas has the EC had common economic policies? (b) What have been the non-tariff barriers preventing the EC from operating as a single market? (c) How are things changing? These questions are answered in the following pages.

Common economic policies of the EC

There are six major areas where the EC has operated economic policies with at least some common element throughout the Community.

The Common Agricultural Policy (CAP). As you will recall from section 11.1, the Community sets common high prices for farm products. In the case of food imported into the EC, this will involve charging variable import duties to bring foreign food imports up to EC prices. In the case of food produced within the EC, the policy will involve intervention to buy up the surpluses that will result if the price is set above the equilibrium.

Regional policy. The EC regional policy provides grants to firms and local authorities in depressed regions of the Community (see section 20.4).

Monopoly and restrictive practice policy. EC policy here has applied primarily to companies operating in more than one member state (see section 11.2). For example, Article 85 of the Treaty of Rome prohibits agreements between firms (e.g. over pricing or sharing out markets) which will adversely affect competiton in trade between member states. In practice, relatively few cases have been taken to the European Court of Justice.

Harmonization of taxation. VAT is the standard form of indirect tax throughout the EC. Thus when the UK joined the EEC it had to abandon its old form of indirect taxation (purchase tax) and adopt VAT instead. Throughout the 1970s and 1980s, however, there were substantial differences in VAT rates between member states as Table 21.4 shows. Governments have been reluctant to give up their right to choose their own forms and rates of tax.

Table 21.4 Percentage VAT rates in the EC: 1988

	Reduced rate	Standard rate	High rate
Belgium	1 and 6	19	25 and 33
Britain	0	15	–
Denmark	–	22	–
France	1–7	18.6	33⅓
Greece	6	18	36
Holland	6	20	–
Ireland	4 and 10	25	–
Italy	2 and 9	18	38
Luxembourg	3 and 6	12	–
Portugal	8	16	30
Spain	6	12	33
W. Germany	7	14	–

? What would be the economic effects of (a) different rates of VAT, (b) different rates of personal income tax and (c) different rates of company taxation between member states if in all other respects there were no barriers to trade or factor movements?

Transport policy. Given that transport costs account for around 25 per cent of firms' costs, differences in taxes and subsidies on transport can considerably affect the pattern of trade. The importance of a common transport policy was recognized early on by the Community in Article 3 of the Treaty of Rome. Articles 74–84 outline the features of such a policy, including free competition between carriers of all Community countries within any one country, common regulations for the crossing of frontiers, and the regulation of state financial assistance to their domestic transport industries. After many years of negotiations, however, many different restrictions remained throughout the Community on all parts of the transport industry – road, rail, sea and air. No common transport policy existed in practice. Member governments were too unwilling to expose their own transport industries to free competition from other member countries. But with the advent of the single market in 1992, the search for such a policy quickened.

Box 21.10

Social Charter Rights

The following summary of the main elements of the social charter appeared in the journal *Industrial Relations* (11 July 1989).

  Freedom of movement: Measures to ease free movement of labour between EC states, including recognition of qualifications, host country 'social protection' for employees from one EC state working in another.
  Employment and remuneration: rights to 'decent' wages; freedom to pursue an occupation; access to placement services free of charge.
  Living and working conditions: commitment to improvements, including establishment of maximum weekly hours of work and rights to annual paid leave and a weekly rest period; improvements relating to fixed-term contracts, temporary work, weekend work, night work and shift work.
  Social protection: rights to a minimum income for those 'excluded from the labour market'.
  Freedom of association and collective bargaining: the right to belong to any professional or union organization of one's choice; to negotiate collective agreements; and to resort to collective action.
  Vocational training: covers training opportunities, training and retraining systems and the freedom for every EC citizen to enrol for occupational training on the same terms as any national of the member state where the course is to take place.
  Equal treatment: guarantees 'intensification' of measures to ensure equal treatment between men and women in matters such as remuneration, employment, training and career development.
  Information, consultation and participation of workers: to be developed along lines that take practice in member states into account – particularly applicable to technological change; company restructuring and mergers; and 'transfrontier' employees.
  Health and safety: covers further harmonization in this area, with particular regard to public works.
  Children and adolescents: covers minimum employment age (16), equitable remuneration, training and labour regulations.
  Elderly: covers living standards, minimum income and social protection.
  Disabled: covers integration into working life, including training, accessibility, transport and housing.

? Which of these elements of the social charter would, if implemented, be likely to affect employment and in what way?

Social policy. Articles 117–128 of the Treaty of Rome refer to social policy. For example, Article 118 calls for collaboration between member states on laws relating to employment, health and safety at work and collective bargaining rights, and on the provision of social security and training. Article 119 refers to equal pay for men and women for doing the same work. Article 123 refers to the European Social Fund, whose objective is to provide financial assistance for training and job creation projects.

In practice during the 1980s there was little harmonization of Community social policy, with laws and provisions differing widely between member states. But with the moves towards a single market and the harmonization of trade policies, there were accelerating moves towards harmonizing social policies too.

In 1989 the European Commission presented a *social charter* to the EC heads of state. This represented the culmination of the Commission's efforts to tackle the social dimension of the single market. The social charter (see Box 21.10) spelt out a series of worker and social rights that should apply across the whole Community. These rights were grouped under twelve headings covering areas such as the guarantee of decent levels of income for both the employed and the non-employed, freedom of movement of labour between EC countries, freedom to belong to a trade union and equal treatment of women and men in the labour market. Some of the headings gave only broad indications, however. For example, there was no attempt to define a 'decent wage'.

The social charter was only a recommendation and each element had to be approved separately by the Council. The UK was unwilling to accept provisions that would guarantee minimum incomes, arguing that they would increase unemployment.

Box 21.11

How Regulations Can Reduce Imports
Two examples

Italian mineral water
Have you ever bought European mineral water? Apart from Perrier, which as the market leader has a comparatively inelastic demand, these mineral waters are sold in plastic bottles. Plastic being much lighter than glass is much cheaper to transport. This is the only sensible way of packaging them if they are to compete with local mineral water.

The Italians, realizing this simple fact, found an effective way of protecting the Italian mineral water industry. Many Italian local authorities insisted that all mineral water had to be sold in glass bottles.

French tiles
The following extract is from the journal *European Economy*. It appeared in March 1988 in an edition titled 'The economics of 1992' (p. 53).

In France, domestic tile manufacturers working through the national standardization body Afnor have created particularly stringent standards for tiles. As the Afnor specifications are not legally binding, non standard tiles can still be sold in France but they cannot be used in public construction works (about 40% of the market) and architects and engineers are reluctant to employ them for insurance reasons. The standard is linked to a conformity marking process, which reportedly can take up to one year's delay. These technical barriers have effectively curbed imports from traditional tile manufacturing countries like Italy and Spain. Spanish tiles are reckoned to be on average more than 25% cheaper than French ones. According to a study by MAC, if these standard-induced restrictions prevent the Spanish producers from gaining an incremental 10% of the market, they are costing French consumers about 3% of the value of their domestic expenditure on tiles. Indirect costs could be more pronounced as tile manufacturing lends itself to significant scale economies.

Non-tariff barriers

Tariffs were eliminated long ago between EC members (except in the case of the newest members, which were given until 1992 to eliminate all theirs). But tariffs are not the only type of trade barrier.

Quotas and other quantitative restrictions
Like tariffs, quotas have been eliminated for intra-EC trade for a long time. Nevertheless from time to time they have been imposed by *individual* members on imports from outside the EC (e.g. on the imports of cars and textiles). This then requires customs checks at the borders with other EC countries to prevent the goods coming in via them.

Cost-increasing barriers
This is where it costs more to import a good from another EC country than to buy it from a domestic supplier, even though the other country's *production* costs may be lower. Part of the reason for this may be simple geography: imported goods may have to be transported a longer distance and thus incur higher transport costs. This is particularly relevant to, say, Ireland, where transport costs from continental EC countries may be very high. But several of the reasons may be artificially created. There are three major types.

Taxation. As long as different rates of VAT and excise duties are charged in the various member states, this will affect competition. In the mid-1980s Italy, Greece, Spain, Portugal and West Germany put no excise duty on wine. The UK, Denmark and Ireland (non-wine producers) in contrast had quite high duties on wine. Not

---

Box 21.12

Mutual Recognition: The Cassis de Dijon Case
Or when is a liqueur not a liqueur?

Crème de Cassis is an alcoholic blackcurrant drink made by the French firm Cassis de Dijon. Added to white wine it makes the drink kir. It is not just the French that like drinking kir; it is also, amongst others, the Germans. In this seemingly innocent fact lay the seeds for the dismantling of some of the most serious trade barriers in Europe!

The story starts back in 1978. The West German company Rewe Zentral AG wanted to import Cassis, but found that under West German law it could not. The problem was that Cassis does not contain enough alcohol to be classed as a liqueur, and it also fell outside any other category of alcoholic drink that was permitted by West German law.

But Rewe was not to be put off. It started legal proceedings in Europe to challenge the German law. The basis of Rewe's case was that this law discriminated against non-German companies. After much legal wrangling the European Court of Justice in Luxembourg ruled that Germany had no right to prevent the importation of a product that was legitimately on sale in another member country (i.e. France). The only exceptions to this ruling would be if the product was barred for reasons of consumer protection, health or fair trade. None of

these applied to Cassis, so the Germans can now drink kir to their hearts' content without having to become smugglers.

But what of the implications of the case? These are enormous and were spelt out in the Single European Act: 'the Council may decide that provisions in force in a member state must be recognized as being equivalent to those applied by another'. In other words, individuals and firms can choose which country's sets of regulations suit them the best and then insist that they be applied in *all* member states.

'Mutual recognition' of each other's laws will tend to lead to deregulation, as people choose those countries' laws that give them the greatest freedom. This appeals to economic and political liberals. Equally it worries those who argue that regulations and laws on industrial standards have been instituted for a purpose, and should not be undone just because some other member country has not been wise enough to institute them itself.

? How does the Cassis de Dijon ruling affect the balance of power in the Community between (a) individual states and the whole community; (b) governments and the courts?

---

surprisingly, wine-producing countries claimed that this was an unfair barrier to their exports.

Customs formalities. Different rates of indirect taxation (VAT and excise duties) necessarily involve customs checks and paperwork. These add to the costs of trade within the Community.

Regulations and norms. Regulations have often been cleverly designed by countries to favour their domestic suppliers. For example, the Danes have a highly developed industry producing recycled containers. A Danish law requires that all soft drinks in Denmark are sold in recycled containers. This would add substantially to the costs of some other EC member companies wishing to export soft drinks to Denmark. In Spain, double inspection has to be made of imported spirits. This costs approximately 1 per cent of the value of these imports. (See Box 21.11.)

Barriers to entry

This is where entry to another member's market is blocked or restricted. These barriers are often more serious than cost barriers. After all, a competitor from another EC country may still be able to compete even if it has a cost handicap. If, however, its entry is blocked, there may be nothing it can do.

State procurement (government favouring domestic suppliers). The public sector is a major purchaser of goods and services. National governments, local governments and nationalized industries between them spend over 15 per cent of the Community's GDP. But whether it be for defence equipment, power stations, office equipment, railway rolling stock or official cars, governments prefer to buy from their own national industries. In fact it has been this government purchasing policy that has kept many firms afloat. Why else are there some fifteen producers of locomotives in the EC and yet only two in the USA?

Licensing and similar restrictions. In certain industries, firms may require a licence to operate. Governments may favour domestic firms in granting such licences. A classic example here is in civil aviation. National airlines are often granted sole right to operate a given domestic route (or pairs of airlines on routes between two countries).

Educational qualifications. Some professions may only recognize their own national qualifications.

Financial barriers. Up to the mid-1980s there were many barriers to financial dealing in other members' countries. Exchange controls, limited entry to stock markets, licensing of financial dealers, restrictions on the right to sell financial services across EC borders and for financial firms to operate in other EC countries, restrictions on cross-country mergers and take-overs, government control over the allocation of credit, etc. – these are all examples of barriers which were very extensive until recent years.

Regulations and norms. This category has often been cited by businesses as being the most important single barrier. In some cases (like the Danish insistence on recycled containers for soft drinks described above) the regulations merely add to the costs of imports. But in other cases the regulations can effectively block imports. In the case of many mechanical engineering and telecommunications products, technical and health and safety regulations have sometimes been so severe as to rule out foreign imports altogether.

Market-distorting barriers. These are barriers that distort the market so as to give domestic producers an unfair advantage. The most obvious example is government subsidies or tax relief, but the category also includes price controls that favour domestic suppliers and government connivance in restrictive practices operated by domestic firms.

Completing the internal market: the economics of 1992

Despite its agricultural and regional policies, the EEC even after 25 years was still little more than a customs union. Extensive barriers remained in place, and in many cases increased, for most of the 1970s and 1980s. But ever since the Treaty of Rome was signed in 1957, politicians and economists have debated ways of moving towards a true common market.

In the mid-1980s, things were changing. There had been a general movement to the right in European politics and a growing belief in the merits of free markets and competition. Even President Mitterrand's Socialist government in France, after an early attempt at increased intervention and reflation (1981–3), began to relax controls.

In 1984 the French finance minister, Jacques Delors, had extensive discussions with other European leaders to find the best way forward for Europe. It quickly became clear that this could now be achieved not by greater intervention or by a major extension of the political powers of European institutions, but simply by the removal of barriers to internal trade – by 'completing the internal market'.

In 1985 Delors became President of the European Commission and asked Lord Cockfield (a newly appointed commissioner from the UK) to prepare a white paper on dismantling barriers. What resulted was a proposal for 300 measures. These became the basis for the Single European Act of 1986. The Act set a date of 31 December 1992 by which its proposals should be in place. The Act did not propose the removal of *all* barriers, but was a massive move in that direction.

One of the most crucial aspects of the Act was its acceptance of the principle of mutual recognition. This is the principle whereby if a firm or individual is permitted to do something under the rules and regulations of *one* EC country, it must also be permitted to do it in all other EC countries. This means that firms and individuals can choose the country's rules that are least constraining. It also means that individual governments can no longer devise special rules and regulations that keep out competitors from other EC countries (see Box 21.12.)

Another crucial aspect of the Single European Act was the institution of *majority* voting in questions of harmonization of rules and regulations (Article 100 of the Treaty of Rome). Previously, unanimous approval had been necessary. This had meant that an individual country could veto the dismantling of barriers. This new system of majority voting, however, does not apply to the harmonization of taxes.

Mutual recognition

The EC principle that one country's rules and regulations must apply throughout the Community. If they conflict with those of another country, individuals and firms should be able to choose which to obey.

1992: The benefits and costs

When the Single European Act was passed it was very difficult to calculate its benefits and costs. There were two key reasons for this. The first is that it was not clear just how completely the barriers would be eliminated. The second is that removing barriers merely creates an opportunity. Just how far firms would exploit the opportunities of an open market and just how much one country's firms would benefit relative to another's could not be predicted with any precision.

Nevertheless many studies have been done to try and estimate the benefits and costs. These studies tend to group benefits into the following main categories.

Trade creation. Costs and prices are likely to fall from a greater exploitation of comparative advantage. Member countries can specialize in those goods and services that they can produce at a comparatively low opportunity cost.

Reduction in the direct costs of barriers. This category includes administrative costs, border delays and technical regulations. Their abolition or harmonization could lead to substantial cost savings.

Economies of scale. With industries based on a Europe-wide scale, firms can be large enough, and their plants large enough, to gain the full potential economies of scale. Yet the whole European market would be large enough for there still to be adequate competition. Such gains will vary from industry to industry depending on the minimum efficient scale of a plant or firm.

Greater competition: short run. More effective competition from other EC countries can (a) squeeze profit margins and thus bring prices more in line with costs and (b) encourage more efficient use of resources and thus reduce costs.

Greater competition: long run. In the long run, greater competition can stimulate greater innovation, the greater flow of technical information and the rationalization of production.

Box 21.13

The Benefits of Completing the Internal Market
Some empirical estimates

In March 1988 the European Commission's journal *European Economy* published a special edition entitled 'The economics of 1992'. In it were contained estimates of the benefits of the removal of all trade barriers in Europe. The estimates were based on surveys carried out in seven of the twelve EC countries (the original six plus the UK).

The journal made the following reservations:

Any estimates of the effects of a complex action like completing the internal market can only be regarded as very approximate. Apart from being subject to a number of policy conditions, such estimates are extremely difficult to make, especially as regards some of the more speculative and long-term effects.[4]

However, it then went on to list the following estimated advantages:

- The removal of frontier formalities could save some 1.8 per cent of the value of goods traded in the Community (about £6 billion).
- The removal of *all* industrial barriers (including technical regulations as well as frontier formalities) are estimated in opinion surveys of industrialists to save some 2 per cent on industrial costs (about £26 billion). Other surveys support these findings. Their estimates

of cost reductions vary from industry to industry: e.g. from 1–2 per cent in the food, construction materials and clothing industries to 5 per cent in the automobile industry.

- In addition to direct cost savings, *economies of scale* are likely to arise from a larger market. One study shows that in more than half all branches of industry at least twenty firms of efficient size can exist in the Community market, whereas the largest national markets could only have an average of four firms each. With four firms there is likely to be a problem of oligopoly power. With twenty firms there is not. Only the European internal market can therefore combine the advantages of economies of scale with those of competition. The benefits of economies of scale and rationalization could yield cost savings of between 1 and 7 per cent (some £40 billion).
- In branches of industry currently subject to entry barriers the combined savings from increased competition and economies of scale could be much greater still. This is particularly so in industries supplying government departments under contract (e.g. energy generating, transport, and office and defence equipment). Here savings of some 10–20 per cent (about £13 billion) could be expected if governments ceased to favour domestic suppliers. Savings of a similar

The Single European Act has not received universal welcome within the Community. Its critics have argued that, in a Europe of oligopolies, unequal ownership of resources, rapidly changing technologies and industrial practices, and factor immobility, the removal of internal barriers to trade merely exaggerates the problems of inequality and economic power. More specifically a number of criticisms are made.

Radical economic change is costly. Substantial economic change is necessary to achieve the full economies of scale and efficiency gains from a single European market. These changes necessarily involve redundancies – from bankruptcies, take-overs, rationalization and the introduction of new technology. The severity of this structural and technological unemployment depends on (a) the pace of economic change and (b) the mobility of labour – both occupational and geographical.

Adverse regional multiplier effects. Firms are likely to locate as near as possible to the 'centre of gravity' of their markets and sources of supply. If, before barriers are removed, a firm's prime market is the UK, it may well locate in the Midlands or the north of England. If, however, when barriers are removed, its market now becomes

Box 21.13 (cont'd)

magnitude could be expected in the financial services industry.

- Gains from reductions in 'X inefficiency' (see Box 5.5) are very hard to estimate, but they could be as high as those from economies of scale, and for several industries some two to three times higher than the direct cost savings from the removal of barriers.
- These effects could be reflected after several years in a general downward convergence of prices in the Community.
- Estimates for the total benefits range from £46 billion (or 2½ per cent of Community GDP) for the direct effects of removing barriers, to between £82 billion and £125 billion under the assumption of a much more integrated and competitive market.

Some of these benefits may take five years or more to be achieved. A lot depends on the *macroeconomic* policies that are pursued.

With a passive macroeconomic policy there are likely to be some initial costs of market integration, the most serious of which are likely to be the redundancies that arise from a process of rationalization. In the medium term, however, the benefits are likely to be substantial, even with a passive macroeconomic policy. After five to six years the cumulative increase in GDP is likely to be around 4½ per cent and the decrease in prices around 6 per cent. Even employment is likely to grow by some 2 million jobs (about 2 per cent). The budget balance and the balance of payments are both likely to improve significantly.

With a more expansive macroeconomic policy, GDP after the five to six years could be some 2½ per cent higher still (making a total of 7 per cent) without causing serious problems of inflation or balance of payments deficits. The report states:

> There should be no misunderstanding about the nature of such figures. They are the product of many sources of very approximate information, combined with economic assumptions that are defendable but also only approximate.
>
> The important conclusions are basically the following. The estimates have been assembled in an eclectic manner, using various techniques of microeconomic and macroeconomic analysis. These different approaches suggest consistent results. The potential gains from a full, competitive integration of the internal market are not trivial in macroeconomic terms. They could be about large enough to make the difference between a disappointing and very satisfactory economic performance for the Community economy as a whole.[5]

The benefits could be even greater than those estimated. The reason is that the estimates leave out the possible benefits of the following:

- An increased rate of technical progress as a result of greater competition and economies of scale.
- The increased spread of skills and information.
- The development of truly European companies with international economic power.

? If the benefits of a single internal market are so great, why have individual member governments of the EC often fiercely resisted the dismantling of particular internal barriers?

[4] *European Economy*, no. 35. (March 1988), p. 18.
[5] *Ibid.*, pp. 19–20.

Europe as a whole, it may choose to locate in the south of England or in France, Germany or the Benelux countries instead. The creation of a single European market is likely to attract capital and jobs away from the edges of the Community to its geographical centre.

In an ideal market situation, areas like Scotland, the north of England, Eire, the south of Italy or Portugal should attract resources from other parts of the Community. Being relatively depressed areas, wages and land prices are lower. The resulting lower industrial costs should encourage firms to move into the areas. In practice, regional multiplier effects may worsen the problem. As capital and labour (and especially young and skilled workers) leave the extremities of the Community, so these regions are likely to become more depressed. If, as a result, their infrastructure is neglected, they then become even less attractive to new investment.

? Is the problem of adverse regional multiplier effects likely to be made better or worse by the adoption of a single European currency? (This issue is explored in Chapter 22.) Clue: without a single currency how would the devaluation of the drachma affect a depressed Greek economy?

The development of monopoly/oligopoly power. The free movement of capital is likely to lead to the development of giant 'Euro-firms' with substantial economic power. This could lead to higher, not lower prices, and less choice for the consumer. It all depends on just how effective competition is, and whether such firms are allowed by law to pursue collusive practices.

Trade diversion. Just as increased trade creation is a potential advantage of completing the internal market, so trade diversion is a possibility too. This is more likely if *external* barriers remain high (or are even increased) and internal barriers are *completely* abolished.

 Is trade diversion more likely or less likely in the following cases?

(a) European producers gain monopoly power in world trade.
(b) Modern developments in technology and communications reduce the differences in production costs associated with different locations.
(c) The development of the internal market produces substantial economies of scale in many industries.

Perhaps the biggest objection raised against 1992 is a political one: the loss of national sovereignty. Governments would find it much more difficult to intervene at a microeconomic level in their own economies.

But what of Brussels? Does the completion of the internal market mean more intervention by the Community? Those worried about the *adverse* economic consequences of a single market argue that there will need to be much more effective regional, social and anti-monopoly policies. Large-scale increases in the various Community funds may be necessary to alleviate some of the inequalities and hardships associated with the single market.

 Why may the newer members of the Community have possibly the most to gain from 1992, but also the most to lose?

Postscript: the future of the Community

There are a number of factors which will have a major effect on the shape and performance of the Community and on the costs and benefits to the members. The first of these, as we have seen, is the extent to which the goals of the Single European Act will be realized. Will there be a genuine single market, or will governments find ways of frustrating the goals of the Act by continuing to favour their own industries?

Another factor is the extent to which there will be a monetary union with not only fixed exchange rates, but also common monetary and fiscal policies or even a common currency. These issues are examined in section 22.7. An important issue here is whether there will be the development of a two-tier Community, with some countries entering wholeheartedly into an economic and political union, and other countries – perhaps just the UK – remaining more independent.

A major issue of the 1990s is the question of new membership of the Community. With the emergence of market-based democracies in Eastern Europe and with the unification of Germany, there has been growing pressure for enlarging the Community to include some or all of these Eastern European countries. Clearly, their membership would have a profound effect on the Community.

 Look through the costs and benefits that we identified for the completion of the internal market. Do the same costs and benefits arise from a substantially enlarged Community?

▲ SUMMARY

1. The European Community is a customs union in that it has common external tariffs and no internal ones. But virtually from the outset it has also had elements of a common market, particularly in the areas of agricultural policy, regional policy, monopoly and restrictive practice policy, and to some extent in the areas of tax harmonization, transport policy and social policy.

2. Nevertheless, there have been substantial non-tariff barriers to trade within the Community: these have included cost-increasing barriers, such as different tax rates, customs formalities and various regulations over product quality; barriers to the entry of firms into other members' markets, through such practices as licensing, state procurement policies, educational qualification requirements, financial barriers and various regulations and norms; and market-distorting barriers, such as subsidies or tax relief to domestic producers and lax policies towards domestic restrictive practices.

3. The Single European Act of 1986 sought to sweep away these restrictions and to establish a genuine free market within the EC: to establish a full common market. Benefits from completing the internal market include trade creation, cost savings from no longer having to administer barriers, economies of scale for firms now able to operate on a Europe-wide scale, and greater competition leading to reduced costs and prices, greater flows of technical information and more innovation.

4. Critics of the single market point to the radical changes in industrial structure that may result, bringing problems of redundancies and closures. They also point to adverse regional multiplier effects as resources are attracted to the geographical centre of the EC, to possible problems of market power with the development of giant 'Euro-firms', and to the possibilities of trade diversion.

5. The actual costs and benefits of EC membership to the various countries vary with their particular economic circumstances – for example, the extent to which they gain from trade creation, or lose from adverse regional multiplier effects – and with their contributions to and receipts from the EC budget.

6. These cost and benefits in the future will depend on just how completely the barriers to trade are abolished, on the extent of monetary union and on any enlargements to the Community.

22 The Balance of Payments, Exchange Rates and International Economic Relationships

22.1 Alternative exchange rate regimes

Policy objectives: internal and external

Internal policy objectives

Objectives relating solely to the domestic economy.

External policy objectives

Objectives relating to the economy's international economic relationships.

Internal balance

Where the equilibrium level of national income is at the desired level.

External balance

Narrow definition: where the current account of the balance of payments is in balance (and thus also the capital account). Loose definition: where there is a total currency flow balance at a given exchange rate.

A country is likely to have various internal and external policy objectives. *Internal* objectives include such things as economic growth, low unemployment and low inflation. *External* objectives include such things as achieving balance of payments equilibrium, encouraging international trade and preventing excessive exchange rate fluctuations. Internal and external objectives may come into conflict, however.

A simple illustration of potential conflict is with the objectives of *internal balance* and *external balance*.

Internal balance. Internal balance is the term used to refer to a Keynesian *full employment* equilibrium: where Y_e (equilibrium national income) $= Y_f$ (full employment national income) (see Chapter 14).

External balance. External balance is the term used to refer to a *balance of payments* equilibrium. Sometimes it is used in the narrow sense to refer to a current account balance, and therefore also a capital account balance. Sometimes it is used more loosely to refer merely to a *total currency flow balance* (where any current account deficit is matched by an identical capital account surplus, and vice versa, with *no need for intervention from the reserves*).

Internal and external balance are illustrated in Figure 22.1. In Figure 22.1(a) internal balance is achieved where $Y_e = Y_f$ (e.g. with curves W_1 and J_1). In Figure 22.1(b) external balance (in the loose sense) is achieved where the demand for and supply of the currency intersect at the current exchange rate (e.g. S_1 and D_1 intersecting at a current exchange rate of r_1).

It may, however, be difficult to achieve internal and external balance simultaneously. Assume, for example, that there was a recession and high unemployment, and thus a deflationary gap. Withdrawals and injections are given by W_2 and J_2 in Figure 22.1(a). Equilibrium is at Y_{e_2} – below Y_f. There is no *internal* balance. Let us assume, however, that there *is external* balance in both the narrow and the loose sense. If the government expands aggregate demand to close the deflationary gap and restore internal balance, demand for imports will rise. The supply of sterling will shift to S_2 in Figure 22.1(b). There will now be a current account deficit, and external balance in the narrow sense will be destroyed. If the government maintains the exchange rate at r_1, external balance will have been destroyed in the loose sense too.

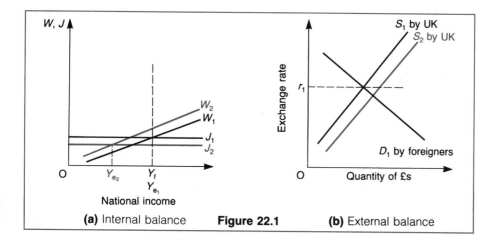

(a) Internal balance **Figure 22.1** **(b)** External balance

External balance in the loose sense could be restored if the exchange rate were allowed to depreciate, so that the demand and supply of sterling were equated at the new lower exchange rate. This, however, may conflict with internal objectives. For example, a falling exchange rate will increase the cost of imports. This can lead to higher inflation. A falling exchange rate may lead to currency speculation. People sell sterling before its dollar price drops any lower. But this leads to a further fall in the exchange rate. Finally, a falling exchange rate will boost exports (an injection) and reduce imports (a withdrawal), thus increasing aggregate demand. This will then destroy internal balance again (assuming that it had been restored).

There are a number of such potential conflicts between internal and external objectives. But in each case, the nature of the conflict depends on the exchange rate regime

 Imagine that there is an *inflationary* gap, but a balance of payments equilibrium. Describe what will happen if the government raises interest rates in order to close the inflationary gap. Assume first that there is a fixed exchange rate and then that there is a floating exchange rate.

Alternative exchange rate regimes

There are a number of possible exchange rate regimes. They all lie somewhere between two extremes. These two extreme regimes are a totally fixed rate, and a freely floating rate

In the case of a *fixed rate*, the government will almost certainly have to intervene in the foreign exchange market in order to maintain that rate, and will probably have to take internal policy measures too.

In the case of a *freely floating rate*, there is no government intervention in the foreign exchange market. Exchange rates fluctuate according to market forces – according to changes in the demand for and supply of sterling. Changes in the exchange rate may well affect internal policy objectives, however, and thus cause the government to take various internal policy measures.

 What adverse internal effects may follow from (a) a depreciation of the exchange rate; (b) an appreciation of the exchange rate?

Exchange rate regime

The system under which the government allows the exchange rate to be determined.

Totally fixed exchange rate

Where the government takes whatever measures are necessary to maintain the exchange rate at some stated level.

Freely floating exchange rate

Where the exchange rate is determined entirely by the forces of demand and supply in the foreign exchange market with no government intervention whatsoever.

Box 22.1

The UK's Balance of Payments Dive
Catastrophe or temporary 'blip'?

In the late 1980s, the UK current account balance of payments moved sharply into deficit. Opinions differed dramatically, however, as to how seriously we should have taken these figures. Not surprisingly, the government claimed that the problem was merely temporary and was not something to cause serious concern. The opposition parties (also not surprisingly) saw the figures as disastrous and a sign that the economy was badly off course.

Addressing the IMF in September 1989, in what was to be virtually his last speech as Chancellor of the Exchequer, Nigel Lawson admitted that the current account deficit for that year had been much under-forecast, but claimed that it was 'more or less flattening out as a prelude to coming down'.

But Mr Lawson stuck doggedly to his line that the current account deficit is a private sector affair, so therefore less embarrassing than a public sector one, a view that the IMF, at least, is prepared to support. Then again, said Mr Lawson, with his chief economist at his elbow, large surpluses and deficits were quite common-place in the classical gold standard days – after which the Chancellor seems to hanker more and more – without being destabilizing or inflationary. So there were no

'necessary implications for exchange rates'. It would be a 'mistake' to look at the exchange rate to resolve what he euphemistically described as Britain's 'set of circumstances'.[1]

The large deficit led to fears that the exchange rate would fall dramatically. In order to prevent this, interest rates had to be kept high and the Bank of England had to intervene frequently in the currency markets.

The Bank of England yesterday embarked on a deter-mined defence of the pound as the currency slid down sharply on the foreign exchange markets, intensifying fears that base interest rates would have to rise again . . . The pound's steep decline yesterday afternoon was inadvertently triggered by Nigel Lawson . . . whose remarks . . . were interpreted as suggesting a lack of concern for sterling.[2]

So should we worry about balance of payments deficits? What effect do they have on exchange rates, inflation, growth, unemployment, etc? What should the govern-ment do? These are questions we shall look at in this chapter.

[1] *Independent*, 28 September 1989.
[2] *Ibid.*

UK balance of payments current account: 1985–90
Source: *Economic Trends* (CSO, various issues).

Intermediate exchange rate regimes

Where the government intervenes to influence movements in the exchange rate.

Between these extremes there are a number of intermediate regimes, where exchange rates are partly left to the market, but where the government intervenes to influence the rate. These intermediate regimes differ according to the amount that the government intervenes, and thus according to how much flexibility of the exchange rate it is prepared to allow.

Correction under fixed exchange rates

Foreign exchange intervention

Unless the demand for and supply of sterling on the foreign exchange markets are equal at the fixed rate – unless, in other words, there is a total currency flow balance (i.e. a net current plus capital account balance) – the Bank of England will have to buy or sell sterling to make up the difference. This is illustrated in Figure 22.2.

Figure 22.2(a) shows the case of a currency flow deficit (an excess of pounds) of an amount $a - b$. The Bank of England thus has to purchase these excess pounds by drawing on its foreign exchange reserves, or by borrowing foreign currency from foreign banks.

In Figure 22.2(b) there is a currency flow surplus of $c - d$. In this case the Bank of England has to supply $c - d$ additional pounds on to the market, and will acquire foreign currencies in exchange. It can use these to build up reserves or to pay back foreign loans.

Foreign exchange market intervention and the money supply. Maintaining a fixed rate will cause changes in the money supply. If the rate is maintained *above* the equilibrium (Figure 22.2(a)), there is a total currency flow deficit. The Bank of England buys pounds. It thereby withdraws them from circulation and reduces the money supply.

If the rate is maintained *below* equilibrium (Figure 22.2(b)), there is a total currency flow surplus. The Bank of England supplies additional pounds (which are spent by foreigners on UK exports, etc. and are thus injected into the UK economy). It thereby increases the money supply.

If the Bank of England did not want the money supply to alter, it would have to counter these effects with other monetary measures: e.g. open-market operations. Thus when there is a deficit and money supply falls, the Bank of England could buy back government bonds from the general public, thereby restoring the money supply to its previous level.

This process of countering the effects on money supply of a balance of payments deficit or surplus is known as sterilization.

> **?** Describe the open-market operations necessary to sterilize the monetary effects of a balance of payments surplus. Would this in turn have any effect on the current or capital accounts of the balance of payments?

Sterilization

Where the government uses open market operations or other monetary measures to neutralize the effects of balance of payments deficits or surpluses on the money supply.

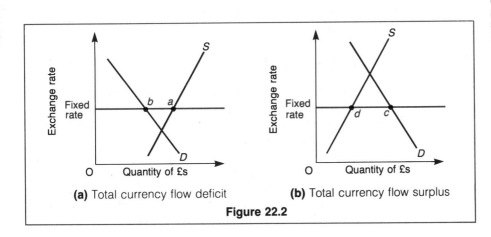

(a) Total currency flow deficit   **(b)** Total currency flow surplus

Figure 22.2

Correcting the disequilibrium

If a balance of payments deficit persists, and reserves continue to dwindle or foreign debts mount, the government will have to tackle the underlying disequilibrium. If the exchange rate is to remain fixed, it must shift the demand and supply curves so that they intersect at the fixed exchange rate.

It can use deflationary fiscal and monetary policies for this purpose. Such policies have two main effects on the current account: an income effect (expenditure reducing) and a substitution effect between home and foreign goods (expenditure switching).

Expenditure reducing. Deflationary policy will reduce national income. This will reduce expenditure, including expenditure on imports. This will shift the supply of sterling curve to the left in Figure 22.2(a). The bigger the marginal propensity to import, the larger the shift.

There is a possible conflict here, however, between external and internal objectives. The balance of payments may improve, but unemployment is likely to rise and the rate of growth fall.

> **?** Under what circumstances would (a) deflationary and (b) reflationary policies cause *no* conflict between internal and external objectives?

Expenditure switching. If deflationary policies reduce the rate of inflation, exports will become relatively cheaper compared with foreign competing goods; imports will become relatively more expensive compared with home-produced alternatives. Foreign consumers will switch to UK exports. The more elastic their demand, the bigger the switch. UK consumers will switch to home-produced goods. Again, the more elastic their demand, the bigger the switch. Demand in both cases will be more elastic the closer UK goods are as substitutes for foreign goods.

To the extent that deflation leads to expenditure switching rather than expenditure reducing, so this will reduce the conflict between balance of payments and employment objectives.

Expenditure switching could also be achieved by the use of restrictions on imports: tariffs and/or quotas, or the subsidizing of exports. But this would conflict with the objective of free trade.

To the extent that fiscal and monetary policies affect interest rates, so this will affect the capital account of the balance of payments. Higher interest rates will increase the demand for sterling and will thus lead to an improvement on the capital account. (The implications of this are explored later in the chapter.)

Correction under free-floating exchange rates

Freely floating exchange rates should automatically and immediately correct any balance of payments deficit or surplus: by depreciation and appreciation respectively. Foreign exchange dealers simply adjust the exchange rate so as to balance their books – in line with demand and supply.

As with fixed rates, an income effect and a substitution effect of the correction process can be distinguished. But the nature of the income and substitution effects of depreciation/appreciation is quite different from that of deflation. It is only the substitution effect that corrects the disequilibrium. The income effect makes the problem *worse*! First the substitution effect: expenditure switching

---

Expenditure changing (reducing) from deflation: the income effect

Where deflationary policies lead to a reduction in national income and hence a reduction in the demand for imports.

Expenditure switching from deflation: the substitution effect

Where deflationary policies lead to a reduction in inflation and thus cause a switch in expenditure away from imports and towards exports.

Expenditure switching from depreciation: the substitution effect

Where a lower exchange rate reduces the price of exports and increases the price of imports. This will increase the sale of exports and reduce the sale of imports.

Expenditure switching (the substitution effect)

The process of adjustment. Assume a higher rate of inflation in the UK than abroad. As domestic prices rise relative to the price of imports, more imports will be purchased. The supply of pounds curve will shift to the right (to S_2 in Figure 22.3). UK exports will now be relatively more expensive for foreigners. Less will be sold. The demand for pounds curve will shift to the left (to D_2 in Figure 22.3).

Foreign exchange dealers will now find themselves with a glut of unsold pounds. They will therefore lower the exchange rate (to r_2 in Figure 22.3). The amount that the exchange rate has to change will depend on:

- The amount that the curves shift. Thus large differences in international inflation rates or large differences in international interest rates will cause large shifts in the demand for and supply of currencies, and hence large movements in exchange rates.
- The elasticity of the curves. The less elastic the demand and supply curves of sterling, the greater the change in the exchange rate for any given shift in demand and supply.

The elasticity of *demand* for sterling depends on the elasticity of demand for UK *exports*.

If sterling depreciates, the foreign currency price of UK exports falls; thus more will be purchased by foreigners. The *sterling* price of these exports, however, has not changed. But since more exports are now being purchased, foreigners will require more pounds than before. Thus as long as demand is not totally inelastic the demand for sterling curve will be downward sloping. The lower the exchange rate, the more exports will be sold and the more pounds will be demanded.

The greater the elasticity of demand for exports, the more will be purchased as the exchange rate falls, and hence the more pounds will be demanded. Thus the greater the elasticity of demand for UK exports, the greater the elasticity of demand for sterling.

> **?** Under what circumstances is a country likely to have an elastic demand for its exports?

The elasticity of *supply* of sterling depends on the elasticity of demand for *imports*. The relationship, however, is different from that between the elasticity of demand for sterling and the elasticity of demand for exports.

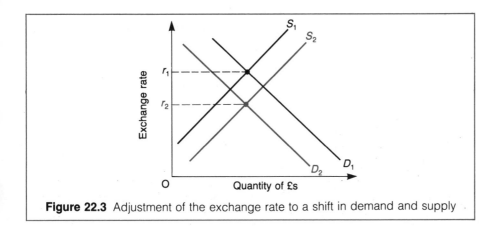

Figure 22.3 Adjustment of the exchange rate to a shift in demand and supply

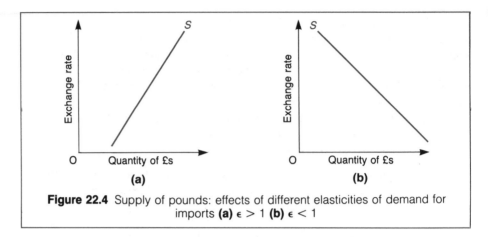

Figure 22.4 Supply of pounds: effects of different elasticities of demand for imports **(a)** $\epsilon > 1$ **(b)** $\epsilon < 1$

If sterling depreciates, the sterling price of imports rises and hence less will be purchased. However, fewer pounds will be required only if total *expenditure* on imports falls. This will only occur if the demand for imports is elastic: if it has an elasticity greater than 1.

If the demand for imports *is* elastic, there will be a 'normal' upward-sloping supply of sterling curve (as in Figure 22.4(a)). A lower exchange rate (higher import prices) leads to a lower expenditure and hence a lower quantity of sterling supplied.

If, however, the demand for imports is *in*elastic, the rise in the price of imports from the depreciation would more than offset the fall in sales. More pounds would thus be spent as the exchange rate fell. The supply of sterling curve would be downward sloping (as in Figure 22.4(b)).

Unstable equilibrium. If the supply curve were downward sloping *and* flatter than the demand curve, exchange rates would be unstable. As soon as the exchange rate fell below r in Figure 22.5 (due to a shift in demand or supply), the supply of pounds would exceed the demand. The rate would fall further and further. Similarly, if the rate went above r, it would continue rising.

In order for the exchange rate to be stable, the supply curve must be steeper than the demand curve. This is known as the 'Marshall–Lerner condition' after the two economists who analyzed it.

The Marshall–Lerner condition. We have already established that a depreciation will increase the *demand* for pounds if the demand for exports rises at all ($P\epsilon_{d_x} > 0$), and that it will reduce the *supply* of pounds if the demand for imports is elastic ($P\epsilon_{d_m} > 1$).

Figure 22.5 Unstable equilibrium

Overall, therefore, a depreciation will improve the balance of payments such as to give a stable equilibrium if:

$$(P\epsilon_{d_x} + P\epsilon_{d_m}) > 1.$$

This is the Marshall–Lerner condition. In other words, there can still be an improvement in the balance of payments *even if* $P\epsilon_{d_m} < 1$ (giving a *downward*-sloping S curve) *provided* that $P\epsilon_{d_x}$ is correspondingly greater than zero – such that the D curve is *flatter* than the S curve.

The greater the sum of the price elasticities of demand for imports and exports, the less the change in the exchange rate necessary to restore equilibrium.

 Over which time period is the Marshall–Lerner condition less likely to be met: the short run or the long run?

Expenditure changing (the income effect)

Depreciation, as well as affecting relative prices, will affect national income. This will cause expenditure changing.

We have already established that, as the exchange rate falls, so more exports will be sold and less imports purchased: this was the substitution effect. But this is only an initial effect.

Exports are an injection into, and imports a withdrawal from, the circular flow of income. There will thus be a multiplied rise in national income. This income effect (expenditure *increasing*) will reduce the effectiveness of the depreciation. Two situations can be examined.

A rise in national income and employment, but no change in prices. Assume that there are substantial unemployed resources, so that an increase in aggregate demand will raise output and employment but not prices. As national income rises, so imports rise (thereby tending to offset the initial fall), but exports are unaffected.

This is illustrated by the line $(X - M)_1$ in Figure 22.6. At low levels of national income, spending on imports is low; thus exports (X) exceed imports (M). $X - M$ is positive. As national income and hence imports rise, $X - M$ falls, and after a point becomes negative. Thus the $X - M$ line is downward sloping.

Assume an initial equilibrium national income at Y_1, where national income (Y)

Figure 22.6 The income effect (stable prices)

equals national expenditure (E_1), but with imports exceeding exports by an amount $a - b$. The exchange rate thus depreciates.

This will cause a substitution effect: exports rise and imports fall. The $X - M$ line therefore shifts upwards. But this in turn causes an income effect. Aggregate demand rises, and the E line shifts upwards.

An eventual internal and external equilibrium is reached at Y_2, where $Y = E_2$ and $(X - M)_2 = 0$.

The positive substitution effect of this depreciation is $c - b$. The negative income effect is $c - a$. The net effect is thus only $a - b$, which is the size of the initial deficit. Had it not been for this negative income effect, a smaller depreciation would have been needed.

At least in this case the income effect is having a desirable *internal* consequence: reducing unemployment.

> **?** Draw a diagram like Figure 22.6, only this time show an initial equilibrium national income with a balance of payments *surplus*. Mark the size of the surplus. Show the resulting shifts in the ($X - M$) and the E curves, and mark the eventual equilibrium. Show the size of the income and substitution effects (of the change in exchange rate). Under what circumstance will the income effect be (a) 'desirable'; (b) 'undesirable'?

A rise in prices. If, however, the economy is near full employment, the rise in aggregate demand from depreciation will make that depreciation even less effective. Not only will the higher demand lead directly to more imports, but it will also lead to higher inflation. There will thus be an adverse substitution effect too. This will partially offset the beneficial substitution effect of the depreciation. The higher inflation will have the effect of shifting the $X - M$ line back down again somewhat.

In the extreme case, where money supply expands to accommodate the rise in aggregate demand, $X - M$ may simply return to its original position. The depreciation will fail to correct the balance of payments disequilibrium. In Figure 22.3, the fall in the exchange rate to r_2 will simply lead to a further rightward shift in supply and a leftward shift in demand, until the gap between them is the same as it was at r_1.

To offset the income effect, a government may feel it necessary to back up a currency depreciation with deflationary demand management policies.

Intermediate exchange rate regimes

There are a number of possible intermediate systems between the two extremes of totally fixed and completely free-floating exchange rates.

Adjustable peg. The adjustable peg system is towards the fixed end of the spectrum. Exchange rates are fixed (or 'pegged') for a period of time – perhaps several years.

In the short and medium term, therefore, correction is the same as with a totally fixed system. Central banks have to intervene in the foreign exchange market to maintain the rate. If a deficit persists, then deflationary or other policies must be adopted to *shift* the currency demand and supply curves. This will be a problem, however, if there already exist substantial unemployed resources.

In the long term, however, if a fundamental disequilibrium occurs, the currency can be repegged at a lower or higher rate. Adjusting the peg downwards is known as devaluation. Adjusting it upwards is known as revaluation.

Alternatively, more frequent smaller adjustments could be made, thus moving the system away from the fixed end of the spectrum.

Dirty floating. The dirty floating system is towards the free-floating end of the spectrum. Exchange rates are not pegged: they are allowed to float. But the central

Adjustable peg

A system whereby exchange rates are fixed for a period of time, but may be devalued (or revalued) if a deficit (or surplus) becomes substantial.

Devaluation

Where the government repegs the exchange rate at a lower level.

Revaluation

Where the government repegs the exchange rate at a higher level.

Dirty floating (managed flexibility)

A system of flexible exchange rates, but where the government intervenes to prevent excessive fluctuations or even to achieve an unofficial target exchange rate.

bank intervenes from time to time to prevent excessive exchange rate fluctuations. It is thus a form of 'managed flexibility'.

Under such a system the central bank does not seek to maintain a long-term or even medium-term disequilibrium rate. Rather it tries to allow an 'orderly' exchange rate adjustment to major changes in demand and supply, whilst preventing the violent short-term swings that can occur with a totally free float (swings arising from currency speculation).

To back up the central bank's use of reserves, the government may also alter interest rates to prevent exchange rate fluctuations. If, for example, there were a large scale selling of pounds, the government could raise interest rates to counter this effect and prevent the exchange rate from falling.

> **?** How would raising interest rates in this way affect the balance between the current and capital accounts of the balance of payments?

The degree of currency stability sought, and hence the degree of intervention required, will vary from country to country and from government to government. At one extreme, the government may only intervene if exchange rate fluctuations become very severe; at the other extreme, the government may try to maintain the exchange rate at some unofficial target level.

Crawling peg. The crawling peg system is midway between dirty floating and the adjustable peg system. Instead of making large and infrequent devaluations (or revaluations), the government adjusts the peg by small amounts, but frequently – say, once a month, as the equilibrium exchange rate changes.

Crawling peg
A system whereby the government allows a gradual adjustment of the exchange rate.

Joint float. Under a joint float a group of countries have a fixed or adjustable peg system between their *own* currencies, but *jointly float* against all other currencies.

Joint float
Where a group of currencies pegged to each other jointly float against other currencies.

Exchange rate band. With an exchange rate band the government sets a lower and an upper limit to the exchange rate: say, £1 = \$1.40 and £1 = \$1.60. It will then allow the exchange rate to fluctuate freely within these limits. It will intervene, however, if the rate hits the floor or the ceiling. Exchange rate bands could be narrow (say ± 1 per cent) or wide (say ± 10 per cent).

Exchange rate band
Where a currency is allowed to float between an upper and lower exchange rate but is not allowed to move outside this band.

Exchange rate bands can be incorporated in other systems – the band could be adjustable, crawling or fixed. For example, Figure 22.7 illustrates a crawling peg system with an exchange rate band. The Exchange Rate Mechanism (ERM) of the European Monetary System (EMS) is an example of a joint float against non-member currencies and an exchange rate band with member currencies (see Section 22.7).

All these intermediate systems are attempts to achieve as many as possible of the advantages of both fixed and flexible exchange rates, with as few as possible of the

Figure 22.7 The crawling peg within exchange rate bands

attendant disadvantages. To assess any of these compromise systems, therefore, the advantages and disadvantages of fixed and flexible exchange rates must be examined. This is done in the next two sections.

▲ SUMMARY

1. There may be a conflict in achieving both internal and external balance simultaneously. The nature of the conflict will depend on the exchange rate regime that the country adopts.

2. Under a fixed exchange rate system, the government will have to intervene whenever the equilibrium exchange rate ceases to coincide with the fixed rate. If the equilibrium rate falls below the fixed rate, the government will have to buy in the domestic currency on the foreign exchange market. This will have the effect of reducing the money supply. Likewise selling the domestic currency in order to prevent an appreciation will increase money supply. The government can prevent these changes in money supply by the use of appropriate open market operations or other monetary measures. This is known as 'sterilization'.

3. If a deficit (or surplus) persists under a fixed rate, the government can attempt to shift the currency demand and supply curves. To cure a deficit it can use deflationary fiscal or monetary policies. These will have two effects. Deflation leads to a fall in national income (the income effect) and hence a fall in the demand for imports. It also leads to a fall in inflation and hence a switch in demand from foreign goods to home-produced goods (the substitution effect).

4. Correction under free-floating exchange rates will also involve an income and a substitution effect. If there is a deficit, the exchange rate will depreciate. This will make imports more expensive and exports cheaper, and hence there will be a substitution effect as imports fall and exports rise. The balance of payments will only improve, however, if the Marshall–Lerner condition holds: namely, that the sum of the price elasticities of demand for imports and exports is greater than 1. If the condition does not hold, the supply curve for the domestic currency will be downward sloping and flatter than the demand curve. There will be no stable equilibrium exchange rate.

5. The income effect of a depreciation will reduce its effectiveness. The rise in exports and fall in imports (i.e. the substitution effect of a depreciation) will lead to a multiplied rise in national income, which will cause imports to rise back again somewhat. The bigger this income effect, the bigger will be the depreciation necessary to achieve equilibrium in the foreign exchange market. Correction is made more difficult if any depreciation leads to increases in domestic prices and hence to a second substitution effect – only this time a negative one.

6. There are intermediate exchange rate regimes between the extremes of fixed rates and free-floating rates. The exchange rate may be fixed for a period of time (the adjustable peg); or it may be allowed to change gradually (the crawling peg); or the government may merely intervene to dampen exchange rate fluctuations (dirty floating); or the exchange rate may be allowed to fluctuate within a band, where the band in turn may be fixed, adjustable or crawling.

22.2 Fixed exchange rates

Under fixed exchange rates, it is unlikely that internal and external balance can persist for long without government intervention. Various shocks are likely to occur that will destroy either internal or external balance or both. Even with government intervention, it may still be very difficult, if not impossible, to restore both balances. Correction of balance of payments disequilibria will come into conflict with the other macroeconomic goals of growth, full employment and stable prices.

Two questions arise from this:

● In the absence of corrective fiscal and monetary policies, just how will the economy respond to shocks? Shocks may be internal, such as a rise in consumer demand; or external, such as a recession in the rest of the world.

● What sort of policy measures – fiscal or monetary – will be most effective in dealing with the resulting disequilibria?

Monetarists and Keynesians give different answers to these questions. Their answers are examined in the following pages.

Response to shocks: extreme monetarist (new classical) analysis – perfect markets

Extreme monetarists assume price and wage flexibility. This will ensure that internal balance is maintained: the Phillips curve is vertical. But will this price and wage flexibility also ensure external balance with a fixed exchange rate? Assume that there is initially both internal and external balance. Then some shock occurs.

Response to an internal shock

Let us assume, for example, that people decide to spend more and save less. This internal shock will have an effect on both the current and capital accounts.

Effect on the current account. The higher demand will push up wages and prices. Higher demand and higher prices will lead to a current account deficit. Other things being equal, central bank intervention to support the exchange rate will lead to a reduction in money supply.

 Explain why money supply will fall.

Effect on the capital account. There will be an opposite effect, however, on the capital account. The increased transactions demand for money, plus the reduction in money supply caused by the current account deficit, will put upward pressure on interest rates. Given high international capital mobility, there will be a large capital inflow. The more elastic this supply of capital, the less will interest rates have to rise. Extreme monetarists assume very high, if not infinite, capital mobility; hence very little, if any, interest rate rise will be required. Interest rates are thus virtually pegged to world rates. The effect of this is to make the money supply curve virtually infinitely elastic at world interest rates.

This is illustrated in Figure 22.8. If the demand for money rises from L to L', the upward pressure on interest rates will lead to an inflow of capital. This surplus on the capital account will lead to an increase in money supply from M_{s_1} to M_{s_2}.

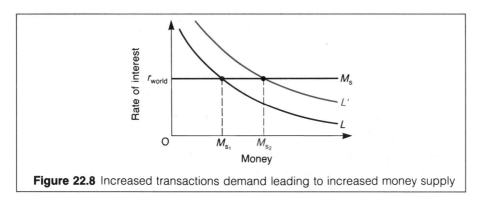

Figure 22.8 Increased transactions demand leading to increased money supply

Short-run effect on the overall balance of payments. The capital account surplus will exceed the current account deficit. For interest rates to remain at world levels, the capital inflow must match not only the current account deficit, but also the increased transactions demand for money from the initial higher consumption. There will thus be a total currency flow surplus.

Long-run position. Once money supply has expanded to M_{s_2} in Figure 22.8, *overall* external balance will be restored. Less upward pressure on interest rates will mean that the capital account surplus will now fall to match the current account deficit.

There is no mechanism, however, to restore *current* account balance.

Response to an external shock

If a shock applies directly to the balance of payments itself, the adjustment process is simpler. Let us assume, for example, that there is a fall in demand for UK exports. Again there will be an effect on both the current and capital accounts.

Effect on the current account. With a fall in demand for exports the current account will go into deficit. The lower demand will reduce wages and prices. This will make exports more competitive and imports relatively more expensive. This will therefore help to correct the current account deficit.

Effect on the capital account. Is there any change in the capital account? This will depend on whether there is any pressure on interest rates. A current account deficit will reduce the money supply, putting upward pressure on interest rates. A fall in prices, however, will reduce the transactions demand for money, putting downward pressure on interest rates. The net effect on interest rates is likely, therefore, to be small. There will thus be a correspondingly small effect on the capital account.

Long-run position. Overall external balance will be achieved. For interest rates to remain at world levels, any current account deficit must be matched by a capital account surplus. Whether current account balance is achieved, however, depends on whether wage and price reductions are sufficient to eliminate the deficit, or whether some of the previously exported goods are now diverted to home consumption.

Conclusion

Flexible prices and wages will ensure internal and *overall* external balance. The maintenance of *current account* balance, however, cannot be assured.

Response to shocks: Keynesian analysis – imperfect markets

Keynesians make three crucial assumptions:

- Prices and especially wages are inflexible downwards. There is thus no guarantee that internal equilibrium will be maintained. A depression, with disequilibrium unemployment, may persist.
- Cost-push pressures may cause persistent inflation.
- Money supply is endogenously determined. Money supply will thus expand passively to accommodate cost-inflationary pressures.

Given these assumptions, how does the economy respond to shocks under a fixed exchange rate regime?

Response to an internal shock

As before, let us assume that there is a rise in consumer demand and a fall in savings. Again there will be effects on both the current and capital accounts.

Current account. The rise in demand causes a multiplied rise in national income. The amount that wages and prices rise will depend on how close the economy is to full employment. Higher demand plus higher prices will lead to a rise in imports and a fall in exports, and hence to a current account deficit.

The deficit will lead to a fall in the money supply, as the Bank of England buys in pounds in order to maintain the exchange rate. This, however, will be more than offset by a passive expansion of the money supply as banks create more credit to meet the higher level of aggregate demand: if demand is higher than before, and if money supply responds passively to demand, then money supply will be higher than before. This will therefore allow the current account deficit to persist.

Capital account. The expansion of the money supply will prevent upward pressure on interest rates. There will thus be no capital account surplus to match the current account deficit. Overall external imbalance will persist.

Response to an external shock

Assume again a fall in demand for UK exports.

Current account. The fall in exports will cause the current account to go into deficit. The fall in exports also reduces aggregate demand. There will thus be a multiplied fall in national income. This will reduce the demand for imports: the larger the marginal propensity to import, the bigger the reduction in imports. Aggregate demand will go on falling until the lower injections (due to initially lower exports) are matched by lower withdrawals. But the current account deficit will not be eliminated, since the fall in withdrawals to match the fall in exports (injections) is only partly due to lower imports, and *partly* due to lower savings and lower tax receipts.

The reduction in demand may also put downward pressure on UK prices and wages. The greater the downward rigidity of prices and wages, however, the less will prices of exports and import substitutes fall, and hence the less will the balance of payments deficit be reduced.

It is unlikely that these combined effects will be sufficient to eliminate the deficit. Even if they did, *internal* balance would be destroyed. There would be a deflationary gap, with demand-deficient unemployment.

Capital account. As with the new classical analysis, the effects here will be relatively small because there are contradictory forces operating on interest rates. The current account deficit will reduce the supply of money, but the fall in national income will reduce the demand for money. The net effect on interest rates will depend on which of these effects is the greater.

Conclusion

Under Keynesian assumptions, shocks are thus likely to destroy both internal and external balance.

1. Making Keynesian assumptions, trace through the effects (under a fixed exchange rate) of (a) an increase in domestic savings; (b) a rise in the demand for exports.
2. How would the answer differ if you made new classical assumptions (see pages 907–8)?

Causes of balance of payments problems under fixed exchange rates

With moderately flexible prices, external balance may eventually be restored after 'one-off' shocks. Normally, however, it is a case not of just one single shock, but rather of long-term continuing shifts in demand and supply. Even with moderately flexible prices, then, balance of payments problems are likely to persist, and probably get worse, without corrective government policy.

There are several causes of these long-term shifts. Let us examine four of them.

Different rates of inflation between countries. If a country has persistently higher rates of inflation than the countries with which it trades, there will be a growing balance of payments deficit. Exports and import substitutes will be becoming continuously less competitive.

Different rates of growth between countries. If a country grows faster than the countries with which it trades, then, other things being equal, its imports will grow faster than its exports (their imports from it).

 Is Japan an exception to this rule? If so, why?

Income elasticity of demand for imports higher than for exports. If the income elasticity of demand for imports is relatively high, and the income elasticity of demand for exports is relatively low, then as world incomes grow, the country's imports will grow faster than its exports. This is a particular problem for many developing countries: they import manufactured goods and capital equipment, whose demand grows rapidly, and export primary products – food and raw materials – whose demand grows relatively slowly.

Long-term structural changes. There are a number of possible structural changes that will affect a country's balance of payments:

- Trading blocs may emerge, putting up tariff barriers to other countries. Australian and New Zealand exports were adversely affected when the UK joined the EC.
- Countries may exercise monopoly power to a greater extent than previously. The OPEC oil price increases of 1973/74 and 1978/79 are examples.
- Countries may develop import substitutes. Thus plastics and other synthetics have in many cases substituted for rubber and metals, thus worsening the balance of payments of traditional primary exporters – such as many developing countries.
- The nature and quality of a country's products may change. Thus Japan has shifted from producing low-quality simple manufactured goods in the 1950s to producing high-quality sophisticated manufactured goods today. This has helped increase its exports.

If a fixed exchange rate is to be maintained under such circumstances, governments will have to take measures to correct the disequilibria. They can use demand-side policies (fiscal and monetary), supply-side policies or protectionist policies. The effects of these various policies are examined in Box 22.2.

Advantages of fixed exchange rates

Many, if not most, economists are opposed to fixed exchange rates, for the reasons examined shortly. Nevertheless many businesspeople are in favour of relatively rigid exchange rates: if not totally fixed, then at least pegged for periods of time. The following arguments are used.

Certainty. With fixed exchange rates, international trade and investment becomes much less risky. Let us illustrate this.

Assume a UK firm correctly forecasts that its product will sell in the USA for \$1.50. It costs 80p to produce. If the rate of exchange is fixed at £1 = \$1.50, each unit will earn £1 and hence make a 20p profit. If, however, the rate of exchange were not fixed, exchange fluctuations could wipe out this profit. If, say, the rate appreciated to £1 = \$2, and if units continued to sell for \$1.50, they would now earn only 75p each, and hence make a 5p loss.

With fixed rates therefore:

- International trade is encouraged (provided the exchange rate is not excessively high). Pricing is virtually as easy for foreign trade as for domestic trade. Increased trade allows countries more fully to exploit their comparative advantage.

Box 22.2

The Effectiveness of Different Government Policies Under Fixed Exchange Rates

Monetary policy

Monetary policy will not be very effective under fixed exchange rates.

Assume a high rate of domestic inflation and a balance of payments deficit. The government now reduces money supply and raises interest rates in order to reduce aggregate demand and correct the deficit. The higher interest rates will simply encourage an inflow of capital. This capital account surplus will *increase* money supply again and reduce interest rates back towards the world level.

Overall external balance has been improved, but the rise in money supply again will cause inflation to continue and the current account to remain in deficit.

The greater the mobility of international capital, the more closely will domestic interest rates be pegged to world rates, and the less effective, therefore, will monetary policy be. In the extreme case of an infinitely elastic money supply curve (as in Figure 22.8), *monetary policy will be totally ineffective.*

Fiscal policy

Fiscal policy will be much more effective.

Assume a high rate of inflation and a resulting current account deficit. The government now raises taxes and/or reduces government expenditure. This will reduce aggregate demand and thereby help to reduce the current account deficit.

The reduction in aggregate demand will lower interest rates. This will lead to an outflow of capital and a capital account deficit. This will reduce the money supply, thereby *reinforcing* the deflationary fiscal policy. Inflation will fall, thus reducing the current account deficit further. Once money supply has fallen to match the reduced demand, interest rates can rise again, thus correcting the capital account deficit.

The greater the mobility of capital, the more will interest rates be pegged to world rates and the more, therefore, will the supply of money contract (or expand) to reinforce any contraction (or expansion) of demand through fiscal policy.

Supply-side policies

Supply-side policies can help to improve the balance of payments in two ways:

- Reducing the costs of production of exports and hence their *prices*. Examples of such policies would be tax incentives or investment grants for exporting firms.

    The effectiveness of such policies depends on how close UK exports are as substitutes for foreign goods, and hence how elastic their demand is. The closer the substitutability, and hence the more elastic the demand, the more will the sales of exports increase as their prices fall. Provided the price-elasticity of demand is greater than 1, export earnings will thus rise.

- Improving the *quality* of exports. Again tax incentives or investment grants may be ways of achieving this. Also the government may give incentives to encourage the development of new products for export.

In both cases, the effect of an increase in export revenue will be to shift the demand for sterling curve to the right: see Figure 22.2(a).

Supply-side policies can similarly help to reduce imports, by reducing the prices or increasing the quality of home-produced substitutes. This will shift the supply of sterling curve to the left: see again Figure 22.2(a).

Protectionist policies

A final alternative is to use policies that restrict imports: e.g. tariffs and quotas. Tariffs, by raising the price of imports, will reduce their demand. This in turn will reduce the supply of sterling on the foreign exchange markets. Quotas and exchange controls directly reduce the supply of sterling.

? 1. Suppose that under a *dirty floating system* the government is worried about high inflation and wants to keep the exchange rate up in order to prevent import prices rising. To tackle the problem of inflation it raises interest rates. (Similar policies have been pursued in recent years.) What will happen to the current and capital accounts of the balance of payments?

2. Why were many monetarists opposed to the UK's entry to the ERM?

- Overseas investment is encouraged. Firms will be much more willing to set up factories overseas if the uncertainty of exchange rate fluctuations is removed.

Little or no speculation. Provided the rate is *absolutely* fixed – and people believe that it will remain so – there is no point in speculating. If there is no speculative pressure on the pound, the Bank of England will need to intervene less to maintain the rate.

Automatic correction of monetary errors. If the government allows the money supply to expand too fast, the resulting extra demand and lower interest rates will lead to a balance of payments deficit. This deficit, however, will have the effect of reducing the money supply, thus going some way towards correcting the error.

Prevents governments pursuing 'irresponsible' macroeconomic policies. If a government deliberately and excessively expands aggregate demand – perhaps in an attempt to gain short-term popularity with the electorate – the resulting balance of payments deficit will force it to constrain demand again (unless it resorts to import controls).

Governments cannot allow their economies to have a persistently higher inflation rate than competitor countries without running into balance of payments crises, and hence a depletion of reserves. Fixed rates thus force governments (in the absence of protection) to keep the rate of inflation roughly to world levels.

Disadvantages of fixed exchange rates

The new classical view
As we explained earlier, in the new classical world of flexible prices and international capital mobility, the overall balance of payments will be corrected automatically if there are any shocks to the economy. Any deficit on the current account will be matched by an equal and opposite surplus on the capital account. Nevertheless, there are three crucial criticisms of fixed rates made by new classicists and monetarists.

Fixed exchange rates make monetary policy ineffective. Interest rates are pegged to world levels, and thus money supply is infinitely elastic and will depend purely on the demand for money (see Figure 22.8). As a result the government cannot control inflation by attempts to control money supply. Inflation will depend on world rates, which may be high and domestically unacceptable. If the government tries to reduce inflation by attempting to reduce money supply and raise interest rates, the current and capital account will go into surplus. Money supply will thus increase until domestic inflation rises back to world levels again.

An imbalance between current and capital account may persist. As we explained before, although an *overall* external balance may be achieved automatically under fixed rates, a current account deficit may persist. The surplus on capital account required to finance this is likely to lead to an accumulation of overseas debt. This may become a burden for the future, in terms of interest payments.

Fixed rates contradict the objective of having free markets. Why fix the exchange rate, when a simple depreciation or appreciation can correct a disequilibrium? In the new classical world where markets clear, and supply and demand are relatively elastic, why not treat the foreign exchange market like any other, and simply leave it to supply and demand?

The Keynesian view
In the Keynesian world, wages and prices are relatively 'sticky', and demand-deficient unemployment and cost-push inflation may persist. In this world there is no guarantee of achieving both internal and external balance simultaneously when exchange rates are fixed. This leads to the following problems.

Balance of payments deficits can lead to a depression. A balance of payments deficit can occur even if there is no excess demand: even though there is internal balance. For example, there can be a fall in the demand for the country's exports as a result of an external shock or because of increased foreign competition. If protectionism is to be avoided, and if supply-side policies only work over the long run, the government will be forced to deflate the economy. If wages and prices are sticky downwards, the deflation may have to be severe if the deficit is to be corrected. Reliance will have to be placed largely on lower *incomes* reducing the demand for imports. A severe recession, with high unemployment, may thus result.

Even if the price level (or at least inflation) does fall, foreigners' demand for UK exports may be relatively price inelastic, as may also the UK demand for substitutes for imports. Again, the deflation will thus have to be severe to bring the required adjustment.

The problem here is that with fixed exchange rates domestic policy is entirely constrained by the balance of payments. Any attempt to reflate and cure unemployment will simply lead to a balance of payments deficit and thus force governments to deflate again.

Competitive deflations leading to world depression. If deficit countries deflated, but surplus countries *reflated*, there would be no overall world deflation or reflation. Countries may be quite happy, however, to run a balance of payments surplus and build up reserves. Countries may thus competitively deflate – all trying to achieve a balance of payments surplus. But this is beggar-my-neighbour policy. Not all countries can have a surplus! Overall the world must be in balance. The result of these policies is to lead to general world deflation and a restriction in growth.

Problems of international liquidity. If trade is to expand, there must be an expansion in the supply of currencies acceptable for world trade (dollars, pounds, marks, gold, etc.): there must be adequate international liquidity. Countries' reserves of these currencies must grow if they are to be sufficient to maintain a fixed rate at times of balance of payments disequilibrium. Conversely, there must not be excessive international liquidity. Otherwise the extra demand that would result would lead to world inflation. It is important under fixed exchange rates, therefore, to avoid too much or too little international liquidity. The problem is whether there is adequate control of international liquidity. The supply of dollars, for example, depends largely on US policy, which may be dominated by its internal economic situation rather than by a concern for the well-being of the international community.

> **International liquidity**
> The supply of currencies in the world acceptable for financing international trade and investment.

? Why will excessive international liquidity lead to international inflation?

Inability to adjust to shocks. With sticky prices and wages, there is no swift mechanism for dealing with sudden balance of payments crises – like that caused by a sudden increase in oil prices. In the short run, countries will need huge reserves or loan facilities to support their currencies. There may be insufficient international liquidity to permit this. In the longer run, countries may be forced into a depression by having to deflate. The alternative may be to resort to protectionism, or to abandon the fixed rate and devalue.

Speculation. If speculators believe that a fixed rate simply cannot be maintained, speculation is likely to be massive. If there is a huge deficit, there is no chance whatsoever of a *re*valuation. Either the rate will be devalued or it will remain the same. Speculators will thus sell the domestic currency. After all, it is a pretty good gamble:

heads they win (devaluation); tails they stay the same (no devaluation). This speculative selling will worsen the deficit, and may itself force the devaluation.

 To what extent do Keynesians and new classicists agree about the role of fixed exchange rates?

Postscript

An argument used in favour of fixed rates is that they prevent governments from pursuing inflationary policies. But if getting inflation down is desirable, why do governments not pursue an anti-inflationary policy directly? In 1979 when Mrs Thatcher was first elected, she declared inflation to be 'public enemy number one'. Yet the UK was under a floating exchange rate regime and was thus not *forced* to follow an anti-inflationary policy. If, however, elected governments choose *not* to pursue anti-inflationary policy, is it desirable that they should be forced to?

▲ SUMMARY

1. The effects of internal and external shocks under fixed exchange rates are analyzed differently by new classical and Keynesian economists.

2. New classical economists argue that an *internal* shock will not affect internal balance (because of price flexibility), nor will it affect the *overall* external balance. Any current account imbalance will, via pressure on interest rates, lead to an equal and opposite capital account imbalance. Keynesian economists, however, argue that an internal shock can cause a persistent imbalance, both internally and externally. Inflexible prices can cause a persistent recession, and an endogenous money supply will remove the pressure on interest rates that would be necessary for capital flows to counterbalance the current account imbalance.

3. New classical economists argue that an *external* shock will have a relatively small effect on both current and capital accounts. Flexible wages and prices will restore current account balance and ensure little pressure on interest rates and thus little effect on the capital account. Keynesian economists argue that an external shock will, via the multiplier, destroy internal balance and may lead to a persistent current account imbalance given the inflexibility of prices. The effects on the capital account will be

relatively small given that endogenous changes in money supply result in little change in interest rates.

4. Under fixed exchange rates, monetary policy will not be very effective, but fiscal policy will be much more effective.

5. Fixed exchange rates bring the advantage of certainty for the business community, which encourages trade and foreign investment. They also help to prevent governments from pursuing irresponsible macroeconomic policies.

6. Both new classical and Keynesian economists, however, see important disadvantages in fixed exchange rates. New classical economists argue that they make monetary policy totally ineffective; that an imbalance between current and capital accounts may persist; and that they run counter to the efficiency objective of having free markets. Keynesians argue that fixed rates can lead to serious internal imbalance with perhaps a deep recession; that with competitive deflations a recession can be worldwide; that there may be problems of excessive or insufficient international liquidity; that there may be difficulty in adjusting to external shocks; and that speculation could be very severe if people came to believe that a fixed rate was about to break down.

22.3 Free-floating exchange rates

Floating exchange rates and the freeing of domestic policy

With a freely floating exchange rate there can be no overall balance of payments disequilibrium. Foreign exchange dealers will constantly adjust the exchange rate so as to balance their books: so that the demand for and supply of any currency are equal.

This, therefore, removes the balance of payments constraint on domestic policy that exists under a fixed exchange rate. No reserves are required since there is no central bank intervention to support the exchange rate. The government, it would seem, is free to pursue whatever domestic policy it likes. Any resulting effects on the balance of payments are simply and automatically corrected by a depreciation or appreciation of the exchange rate.

In reality, however, things are not quite so simple. Even under a totally free-floating exchange rate, there may be some constraints on domestic policy from the effects of these exchange rate movements. For example, a depreciation of the exchange rate increases the price of imports. If the demand for imports is relatively inelastic, this may lead to a higher rate of inflation.

Response to shocks under a floating exchange rate

Internal shocks

Let us assume that there is a rise in aggregate demand that causes inflation. For the moment, however, let us also assume that monetary policy maintains interest rates at international levels. For simplicity, let us assume that there is no inflation abroad. How will a floating exchange rate system cope with this internal shock of a rise in aggregate demand? The exchange rate will simply depreciate to maintain the competitiveness of UK exports and import substitutes.

For example, assume an initial exchange rate of £1 = $2. A UK product costing $2 in the USA will earn £1 for the UK exporter. If UK inflation now causes prices to double, the exchange rate will roughly halve. If it falls to £1 = $1, then the same product costing $2 in the USA will now earn £2 for the UK exporter: which in *real* terms is the same amount as before.

This is the purchasing power parity theory. This states that domestic price changes will be offset by exchange rate changes, thereby maintaining the same relative prices between countries as before. In other words, if UK goods double in price, then the resultant halving of the exchange rate will cause foreign imports into UK to double in price also, and UK exports to maintain the same *dollar* price as before.

Purchasing power parity theory

The theory that the exchange rate will adjust so as to offset differences in countries' inflation rates, with the result that the same quantity of internationally traded goods can be bought at home as abroad with a given amount of the domestic currency.

 If this is the case, need firms worry about losing competitiveness in world markets if domestic inflation is higher than world inflation?

If we now drop the assumption that interest rates are maintained at the same level as abroad, the purchasing power parity theory will break down. Let us assume that the rise in aggregate demand causes a rise in UK interest rates.

In this case, the demand for sterling will rise, as depositors choose to hold their money in pounds. The exchange rate will rise – above the purchasing power parity rate. The capital account will have moved into surplus. Under a floating rate this must be counterbalanced by an equal and opposite current account deficit. Exports will fall as exporters find it increasingly difficult to sell abroad with the higher exchange rate. Imports will rise as the lower exchange rate makes imports relatively cheaper. The net effect is that both export and import competing industries will suffer.

External shocks

Now let us assume that the rest of the world goes into recession (but with no change in international interest rates). The demand for UK exports will fall. This will lead to a depreciation of the exchange rate. This in turn will boost the demand for UK exports and substitutes for imports. This boost to demand again will help to offset the dampening effect of the world depression.

Box 22.3

The Price of a Big Mac

The Economist's guide to purchasing power parity rates

Once a year *The Economist* publishes its 'hamburger standard' exchange rates for currencies. It is a light-hearted attempt to see if currencies are exchanging at their purchasing power parity rates. The test is the price at which a 'Big Mac' McDonald's hamburger sells in different countries!

The following extract is from the 1990 Big Mac report:

> The McDonald's standard is based on the theory of purchasing power parity (PPP), which argues that in the long run the exchange rate between two currencies should equate the price of an identical basket of goods and services in the respective countries. Our 'basket' is simply a Big Mac, which has the virtue of being made locally in more than 50 countries and of tasting virtually the same from Manchester to Moscow.
>
> In America the average price of a Big Mac (including tax) is about $2.20. In Tokyo our correspondent had to fork out ¥370 for this gastronomic delight. Dividing the yen price by the dollar price gives an implied PPP for the dollar of ¥168, compared with the current exchange rate of ¥159. So even after the recent slide of the yen, the dollar still looks to be 5% undervalued against the yen on PPP grounds. It also looks 14% undervalued against the DMark, with a Mac-PPP of DM1.95.
>
> Economists who have calculated PPPs by more soph-

isticated means come up with remarkably similar results. Professor Ronald McKinnon of Stanford University, one of the leading proponents of the theory of purchasing power parity, comes up with mid-point estimates for the dollar's PPP of ¥165 and DM2.00.

> The dollar's current exchange rate against the pound ($0.61) is close to its Mac-PPP of $0.64. But that, in turn, means that the pound is undervalued by 10% against the DMark, giving British manufacturers a competitive edge. On the other hand most EMS currencies, especially the French franc and the lira, are still over-valued against the DMark on PPP grounds.
>
> Mac-currencies are now becoming truly global: the opening of the first McDonalds in Moscow has allowed us to add the rouble to our sample. Muscovites have to pay the equivalent of $6.25 (converting at the official exchange rate) for a Big Mac, which makes it the most expensive hamburger in our sample. In other words, the rouble is overvalued against the dollar to a greater degree than any other currency, with an implied PPP of 1.70 roubles compared with an official rate against the dollar of 0.60 roubles.
>
> Yet this overlooks one crucial fact: in Moscow fast food comes slow, with two-to-three hour queues. If this time is valued at average Soviet hourly wages, then the true cost of gorging on a Big Mac is roughly double the cash price. This implies a 'queue-adjusted' Mac-PPP of 3.40 roubles. Indigestion, Mikhail?[3]

Floating exchange rates thus help to insulate the domestic economy from world economic fluctuations.

> **?** 1. Will there be *any* cost to the UK economy from a decline in the demand for exports resulting from a world recession?
> 2. What will happen under floating exchange rates if there is a rapid expansion in world economic activity?

Speculation

Things are made more complicated, however, by the activities of speculators. As soon as any exchange rate change is anticipated, speculators will buy or sell the currency.

Assume, for example, that there is a rise in UK inflation above international rates. This causes a fall in the demand for exports and hence a fall in the demand for sterling (assuming a price elasticity of demand greater than 1), and a rise in imports and hence a rise in the supply of sterling. This is illustrated in Figures 22.9 and 22.10. The exchange rate depreciates from r_1 to r_2. Speculators seeing the exchange rate falling can react in one of two ways. The first is called *stabilizing speculation*; the second is called *destabilizing speculation* (see section 2.5).

Box 22.3 (cont'd)

Big MacCurrencies: hamburger prices

Country	Price in local currency[1]	Implied PPP[2] of the dollar	Actual exchange rate (30.4.90)	% over (+) or under (−) valuation of the dollar
Australia	A$2.30	1.05	1.32	+26
Belgium	BFr97	44.00	34.65	−21
Britain	£1.40	0.64	0.61	−5
Canada	C$2.19	1.00	1.16	+16
Denmark	DKr25.50	11.60	6.39	−45
France	FFr17.70	8.05	5.63	−30
Holland	FL5.25	2.39	1.88	−21
Hong Kong	HK$8.60	3.90	7.79	+100
Ireland	IR£1.30	0.59	0.63	+7
Italy	Lire3900	1773	1230	−31
Japan	¥370	168	159	−5
Singapore	S$2.60	1.18	1.88	+59
S. Korea	Won2100	955	707	−26
Soviet Union	Rouble3.75	1.70	0.60	−65
Spain	Ptas295	134	106	−21
Sweden	SKr24	10.90	6.10	−44
United States[3]	$2.20	–	–	–
W. Germany	DM4.30	1.95	1.68	−14
Yugoslavia	Dinar16	7.27	11.72	+61

[1] Prices may vary between branches.
[2] Purchasing power parity: foreign price divided by dollar price.
[3] Average of New York, Chicago, San Francisco and Atlanta.

? 1. If the pound is undervalued by 10 per cent against the D-Mark in PPP terms, what implications does this have for the interpretation of UK and German GDP statistics?

2. If the rouble is overvalued, does this mean that Muscovites can obtain imports at very low prices?

[3] *The Economist*, 5 May 1990.

Stabilizing speculation

This occurs when speculators believe that any exchange rate change will be reversed.

In our example, speculators may anticipate that the government will raise interest rates or take some other measure to reduce inflation. They thus believe that the exchange rate will appreciate again. As a result, they buy more pounds and sell fewer. But this very act of speculation causes the appreciation they had anticipated.

Figure 22.9 Stabilizing speculation

Figure 22.10 Destabilizing speculation

This is illustrated in Figure 22.9. Inflation has caused the demand for and supply of pounds to shift from D_1 and S_1 to D_2 and S_2, and the exchange rate to fall from r_1 to r_2. Stabilizing speculation then shifts the curves back again, to D_3 and S_3, and the exchange rate rises again to r_3.

The action of speculators in this case, therefore, prevents excessively large exchange rate changes.

In general, stabilizing speculation will occur whenever speculators believe that the exchange rate has 'overreacted' to the current economic situation.

 Draw a similar diagram to Figure 22.9, showing how an *appreciation* of the exchange rate would similarly be reduced by stabilizing speculation.

Destabilizing speculation

This occurs when speculators believe that exchange rate movements will continue in the same direction.

In our example, speculators may believe that the government will not succeed in getting inflation under control. They anticipate a continuing fall in the exchange rate and thus sell *now* before the exchange rate falls any further. In Figure 22.10 this speculation causes the demand and supply curves to shift further, to D_3 and S_3; and causes the exchange rate to fall further, to r_3.

Eventually, however, this destabilizing speculation could cause overshooting, with the exchange rate falling well below the purchasing power parity rate. At this point speculators, believing that the rate will rise again, will start buying pounds again. This causes the exchange rate to rise.

Obviously, governments prefer stabilizing to destabilizing speculation. Destabilizing speculation can cause severe exchange rate fluctuations. The resulting uncertainty is very damaging to trade. It is very important, therefore, that governments create a climate of confidence. People must believe that the government can prevent economic crises from occurring.

> **Exchange rate overshooting**
>
> Where a fall (or rise) in the long-run equilibrium exchange rate causes the actual exchange rate to fall (or rise) by a greater amount before eventually moving back to the new long-run equilibrium level.

Conclusion

Whatever speculators anticipate will happen to the exchange rate, their actions will help to bring it about. If they think the rate will fall, they will sell pounds, hence causing it to fall. Thus speculators as a whole will gain. This applies to both stabilizing and destabilizing speculation.

Advantages of a free-floating exchange rate

The advantages and disadvantages of free-floating rates are to a large extent the opposite of fixed rates.

Automatic correction. The government simply lets the exchange rate move freely to the equilibrium. In this way, balance of payments disequilibria are automatically and instantaneously corrected without the need for specific government policies – policies which under other systems can be mishandled.

No problem of international liquidity and reserves. Since there is no central bank intervention in the foreign exchange market, there is no need to hold reserves. A currency is automatically convertible at the current market exchange rate. International trade is thereby financed.

Insulation from external economic events. A country is not tied to a possibly

Box 22.4

The Effectiveness of Monetary and Fiscal Policy Under Floating Exchange Rates

With a fixed exchange rate, monetary policy is weak and fiscal policy is strong. With a floating rate this is reversed: monetary policy is strong and fiscal policy is weak.

Monetary policy
Assume that the government wishes to reduce aggregate demand. It reduces money supply. This pushes up interest rates. Three effects follow, each contributing to the effectiveness of the monetary policy:

1. *The tighter monetary policy directly reduces aggregate demand.* The size of the effect here depends on: the ability of the authorities to control money supply; the effectiveness of raising interest rates; and the elasticity of aggregate demand in response to changes in interest rates.

2. *The exchange rate appreciates.* Lower aggregate demand reduces national income and hence the demand for imports. Lower aggregate demand also reduces prices, and hence raises the demand for exports and reduces the demand for imports. These factors combined with the higher interest rates increase the demand for and reduce the supply of sterling. The exchange rate thus appreciates (the purchasing power parity rate has increased).

   This reinforces the reduction in domestic demand. A higher exchange rate makes exports more expensive again and therefore reduces their demand (an injection). Imports become cheaper again and therefore their demand rises (a withdrawal). There is thus a *further* multiplied fall in income.

3. *Speculation causes initial exchange rate overshooting.* Higher UK interest rates cause speculative inflows of capital, in anticipation of the appreciation. This will cause the exchange rate to rise above its eventual rate – to overshoot, thus causing a further reduction in aggregate demand.

   Speculators will only stop buying pounds when the rate has gone so high that they feel it must fall again (back towards the purchasing power parity level) sufficiently fast to offset the higher interest rates they are now getting.

Of course, this third effect on aggregate demand only applies while speculators are buying pounds. Once the exchange rate has reached its peak and starts to come down again, this effect will no longer apply. Nevertheless this exchange rate overshooting has an important *short-term* effect on aggregate demand.

The new classical view of monetary policy
In the new classical world, prices and wages are flexible. A reduction in money supply will quickly lead to a reduction in prices. Effects 1 and 2 above are thus rapid and strong. Effect 3, however, is limited or non-existent, since the rapid fall in prices quickly eliminates the excess demand for money, and thus quickly removes the upward pressure on interest rates.

The Keynesian view of monetary policy
In the Keynesian world, prices and wages are inflexible downwards, and monetary policy is generally less effective (see Chapter 18). Effects 1 and 2 are therefore weaker. Nevertheless effect 3 will be relatively strong, since higher interest rates will persist.

Fiscal policy
Fiscal policy is relatively weak under a floating rate. Again let us assume that the government wishes to reduce aggregate demand. It thus raises taxes and/or lowers government expenditure.

The lower aggregate demand will lower the transactions demand for money and hence *reduce* interest rates. These lower interest rates will lead to an outflow of capital and a *depreciation* of the exchange rate. This will reduce imports and increase exports, thus raising aggregate demand again, and reducing the effectiveness of the fiscal contraction.

 Compare the relative effectiveness of fiscal and monetary policies as means of *expanding* aggregate demand under a system of floating exchange rates.

---

unacceptably high world inflation rate, as it is under a fixed exchange rate. It is also to some extent protected against world economic fluctuations and shocks (see page 915).

 Explain how a country with a free-floating exchange rate would be protected from world economic fluctuations. Would such fluctuations cause any adverse consequences for the country at all?

Governments are free to choose their domestic policy. Under a fixed rate a government may have to deflate the economy even when there is high unemployment. Under a floating rate the government can choose whatever level of domestic demand it considers appropriate, and simply leave exchange rate movements to take care of any balance of payments effect. This is a major advantage, especially when the effectiveness of deflation is reduced by downward wage and price rigidity, and when competitive deflation between countries may end up causing a world recession.

Disadvantages of a free-floating exchange rate

Despite these advantages there are still a number of serious problems with free-floating exchange rates.

Unstable exchange rate. If the demands for imports and exports are highly inelastic, such that $(P\epsilon_{d_m} + P\epsilon_{d_x}) < 1$, equilibrium will be unstable (see Figure 22.5). The Marshall–Lerner condition is not satisfied. If there is a deficit, a depreciation will *worsen* that deficit.

In the long run, in a competitive world with domestic substitutes for imports and foreign substitutes for exports, it is highly unlikely that the sum of the elasticities *will* be less than 1. Nevertheless, in the short run, given that many firms have contracts with specific overseas suppliers or distributors, the demands for imports and exports are less elastic. Even if the Marshall–Lerner condition is satisfied, the steepness of the short-run demand and supply curves of sterling may cause severe exchange rate fluctuations.

Speculation. Short-run instability can be lessened by stabilizing speculation, thus making speculation advantageous. If, due to short-run inelasticity of demand, a deficit causes a very large depreciation, speculators will *buy* pounds, knowing that in the long run the exchange rate will appreciate again. This action of speculators will therefore help to lessen the short-run fall in the exchange rate.

Nevertheless, in an uncertain world where there are few restrictions on currency speculation, where the fortunes and policies of governments can change rapidly, and where large amounts of short-term deposits are internationally 'footloose', speculation can be highly destabilizing in the short run. Considerable exchange rate overshooting can occur. As we shall see in section 22.6, there have been violent swings in exchange rates in recent years – even under a dirty floating exchange rate system where governments have attempted to dampen such fluctuations!

The continuance of exchange rate fluctuations over a number of years is likely to encourage the growth of speculative holdings of currency. This can then cause even larger and more rapid swings in exchange rates.

Forward exchange market

Where contracts are made today for the price at which currency will be exchanged at some specified future date.

Uncertainty for traders and investors. The uncertainty caused by currency fluctuations can discourage international trade and investment. To some extent the problem can be overcome by using the forward exchange market. Here traders agree with a bank *today* the rate of exchange for some point in the *future* (say, six months' time). This allows traders to plan future purchases of imports or sales of exports at a known rate of exchange. Of course, banks charge for this service since they are taking on the risks themselves of adverse exchange rate fluctuations.

This will not help long-term investment, however. The possibility of exchange rate appreciation may well discourage firms from investing abroad.

 Why would banks not be prepared to offer a forward exchange rate to a firm for, say, five years' time?

Lack of discipline on the domestic economy. Governments may pursue irresponsibly inflationary policies. Also unions and firms may well drive up wages and prices, without the same fear of losing overseas markets or of the government imposing deflationary policies. The depreciation resulting from this inflation will itself fuel the inflation by raising the price of imports.

Conclusion

Neither fixed nor free-floating exchange rates are free from problems. For this reason governments have sought a compromise between the two, the hope being that some intermediate system will gain the benefits of both, while avoiding most of their disadvantages.

One compromise was tried after the Second World War. This was the *adjustable peg*. We will examine this system in section 22.5. Another is the system that replaced the adjustable peg in the early 1970s. This is the system of *dirty floating*. We will examine this in section 22.6.

▲ SUMMARY

1. Under a free-floating exchange rate the balance of payments will automatically be kept in balance by movements in the exchange rate. This will remove the *balance of payments* constraint on domestic policy. It will not, however, remove external constraints entirely.
2. According to the purchasing power parity theory, any changes in domestic prices will simply lead to equivalent changes in the exchange rate, leaving the international competitiveness of home-produced goods unaffected. If, however, internal shocks cause changes in interest rates, there will be a change in the *capital* account balance. This will influence exchange rates and destroy the purchasing power parity theory. The current account will go out of balance (in an equal and opposite way to the capital account).
3. External shocks will be reflected in changes in exchange rates and will help to insulate the domestic economy from international economic fluctuations.
4. Exchange rate movements are highly influenced by speculation. If speculators believe that an appreciation or

depreciation is merely temporary, their activities will help to stabilize the exchange rate. If, however, they believe that an exchange rate movement in either direction will continue, their activities will be destabilizing and cause a bigger movement in the exchange rate.
5. The advantages of free-floating exchange rates are that they automatically correct balance of payments disequilibria; they eliminate the need for reserves; and they give governments a greater independence to pursue their chosen domestic policy.
6. On the other hand, a completely free exchange rate can be highly unstable, especially when the elasticities of demand for imports and exports are low; also speculation may be destabilizing. This may discourage firms from trading and investing abroad. What is more, a flexible exchange rate, by removing the balance of payments constraint on domestic policy, may encourage governments to pursue irresponsible domestic policies for short-term political gain.

*22.4 The open economy and ISLM analysis

In this section we show how the ISLM analysis we examined in section 18.3 can be extended to incorporate the open economy. We will start by assuming a fixed rate of exchange and then later see how the analysis can be adapted to a free-floating rate.

Analysis under a fixed exchange rate

The BP curve

We start by introducing a third curve, the *BP* (balance of payments) curve. This curve, like the *IS* and *LM* curves, plots a relationship between the rate of interest (r)

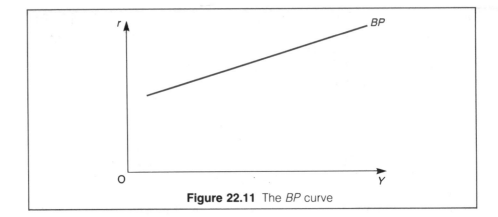

Figure 22.11 The *BP* curve

and the level of national income (*Y*). All points along the *BP* curve represent a position of *balance of payments equilibrium*.

The curve slopes upwards from left to right (see Figure 22.11). Increases in the rate of interest (*r*) will cause the capital account to move into surplus as capital is attracted into the country. Increases in national income (*Y*), in contrast, will cause the current account to move into deficit as more imports are purchased. If the overall balance of payments is to stay in equilibrium, current account deficits must be matched by capital account surpluses and vice versa. Thus a rise in *Y* must be accompanied by a rise in *r*, and reductions in *Y* must be accompanied by reductions in *r*. The *BP* curve therefore slopes upwards. Any point below the *BP* line represents a position of overall deficit; any point above the line, a position of surplus.

The slope of the *BP* curve depends on two factors.

The marginal propensity to import (mpm = $\Delta M / \Delta Y$). The higher the *mpm*, the steeper will be the *BP* curve. The reason is that with a high *mpm* there will be a correspondingly large rise in imports for any given rise in national income. This will cause a large current account deficit. To maintain an overall balance of payments equilibrium this will require a correspondingly large capital account surplus. This in turn will require a large rise in interest rates. Thus the bigger the *mpm*, the larger the rise in interest rates that will be necessary to restore balance of payments equilibrium, and hence the steeper will be the *BP* curve.

The elasticity of supply of international capital. The greater the elasticity of supply of international capital, the less will be the rise in interest rates necessary to restore balance of payments equilibrium after a rise in national income, and hence the flatter will be the *BP* curve.

Equilibrium in the model

If we now put the *BP* curve on an *ISLM* diagram, we have the position shown in Figure 22.12. Point *a* represents full equilibrium. At r_1 and Y_1, investment equals savings (point *a* is on the *IS* curve), the demand for money equals the supply (point *a* is also on the *LM* curve), and finally the balance of payments is in balance (point *a* is also on the *BP* curve).

But what is the mechanism that ensures that all three curves intersect at the same point? To answer this question, let us assume that to start with the three curves just happen to intersect at the same point, and then let us examine the effects of changes in fiscal and monetary policies, which shift the *IS* and *LM* curves respectively. Will

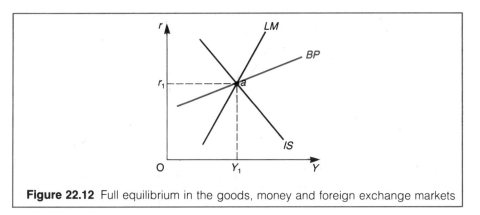

Figure 22.12 Full equilibrium in the goods, money and foreign exchange markets

equilibrium be restored? The answer is yes, via a change in the money supply. Let us examine fiscal and monetary policy changes in turn.

Fiscal policy under fixed exchange rates

An expansionary fiscal policy, i.e. a rise in government spending and/or a reduction in tax, will have the effect of shifting the *IS* curve to the right. The reason is that for any given rate of interest there will be a higher equilibrium level of national income than before. This is shown by a movement from IS_1 to IS_2 in Figure 22.13.

This will increase national income, but the extra demand for money that results will drive up interest rates. In a *closed* economy, equilibrium would now be at point *b* (r_2, Y_2), where $IS_2 = LM_1$. But in our open economy model this equilibrium is *above the BP curve*. There is a balance of payments surplus. The reason for this is that the higher interest rates have caused a capital account surplus that is bigger than the current account deficit that results from the higher national income.

Such a surplus will cause the money supply to rise as funds flow into the country. This will in turn cause the *LM* curve to shift to the right. Equilibrium will finally be achieved at point *c* (r_3, Y_3), where $IS_2 = LM_2 = BP$. Thus under these conditions, the monetary effect of the change in the balance of payments will *reinforce* the fiscal policy and lead to a bigger rise in national income.

 Why does the *LM* curve only shift as far as LM_2?

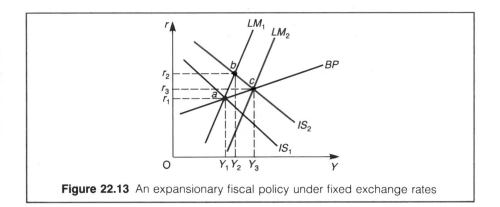

Figure 22.13 An expansionary fiscal policy under fixed exchange rates

Figure 22.14 The effects of an expansionary fiscal policy under fixed exchange rates: a steep *BP* curve

If the *BP* curve were steeper than the *LM* curve, the effect would be somewhat different. (Remember the *BP* curve will be steep if there is a high *mpm* and an inelastic supply of international capital.) This is illustrated in Figure 22.14.

Under these circumstances an initial rise in national income to Y_2 (where $IS_2 = LM_1$) will cause a balance of payments *deficit* (point *b* is *below the BP curve*). The reason is that this time the current account deficit is bigger than the capital account surplus (due to a large *mpm* and a small inflow of capital). This will reduce the money supply and cause the *LM* curve to shift to the left. Equilibrium will be achieved at point *c*, where $LM_2 = IS_2 = BP$.

When the *BP* curve is steeper than the *LM* curve, therefore, the monetary effect of the change in the balance of payments will *dampen* the effect of the fiscal policy and lead to a smaller rise in national income.

Monetary policy under fixed exchange rates

An expansionary monetary policy will cause the *LM* curve to shift to the right. This is shown by a shift from LM_1 to LM_2 in Figure 22.15.

The increased supply of money will drive down the rate of interest and increase national income. In a closed economy, equilibrium would now be at point *b* (r_2, Y_2),

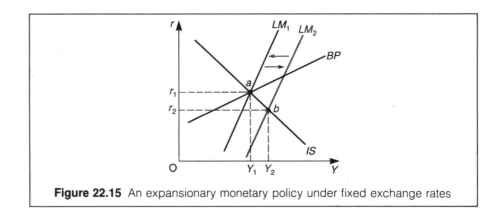

Figure 22.15 An expansionary monetary policy under fixed exchange rates

where $LM_2 = IS$. But in an open economy, this extra demand will have sucked in extra imports, and the lower interest rate will have led to less capital inflows and more capital outflows. There will be a balance of payments deficit: point *b* is below the *BP* curve.

The balance of payments deficit will cause the money stock to fall as money flows abroad. This will cause the *LM* curve to shift back again to its original position. The economy will return to its initial equilibrium at point *a*.

Thus under a fixed exchange rate regime, monetary policy alone will have *no long-term effect* on national income and employment. Only when accompanied by an expansion in aggregate demand (either through fiscal policy or through an autonomous rise in investment or a fall in savings) will an expansion of money supply lead to higher national income.

> **?** 1. Why does this conclusion remain the same if the *BP* curve is steeper than the *LM* curve?
> 2. Trace through the effects of a contractionary monetary and fiscal policy.
> 3. Trace through the effects of a fall in exports (thereby shifting the *BP* curve).
> 4. Show what will happen if there is (a) a rise in business confidence and a resulting increase in investment; (b) a rise in the demand for money balances (say, for precautionary purposes).

Analysis under free-floating exchange rates

As the exchange rate changes, the *BP* curve will shift. This is shown in Figure 22.16.

If the *IS* and *LM* curves intersect *above* the *BP* curve, there will be a balance of payments surplus. This will cause the exchange rate to appreciate. The appreciation will cause the surplus to disappear. This in turn will cause the *BP* curve to shift upwards.

Similarly, if the *IS* and *LM* curves intersect *below* the *BP* curve, the resulting balance of payments deficit will cause a depreciation and a downward shift of the *BP* curve. Thus the *BP* curve will always shift so that it intersects where the *IS* and *LM* curves intersect.

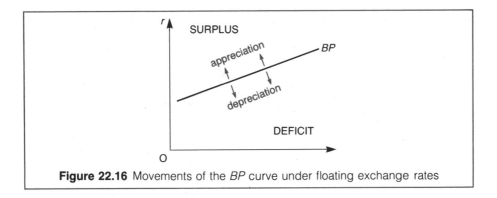

Figure 22.16 Movements of the *BP* curve under floating exchange rates

Fiscal policy under floating exchange rates

Assume that the government pursues a reflationary fiscal policy. The *IS* curve shifts to IS_2 in Figure 22.17.

At point *b*, where the *LM* curve and the new *IS* curve intersect, there is a balance of payments surplus (due to higher capital inflows attracted by the higher rate of

Figure 22.17 The effects of an expansionary fiscal policy under floating exchange rates

interest). This causes the exchange rate to appreciate and the *BP* curve to shift upwards.

But the higher exchange rate will cause a fall in exports and a rise in imports. This fall in aggregate demand will cause the *IS* curve to shift back towards the left. The new equilibrium will be at a point such as *c*. This represents only a modest change from point *a*. Thus under a floating exchange rate the effects of fiscal policy may be rather limited.

The effect will be stronger, however, the steeper the *BP* curve. In Figure 22.18, the *BP* curve is steeper than the *LM* curve. This time a rise in the *IS* curve from IS_1 to IS_2 will lead to a balance of payments *deficit* and hence a *depreciation* of the exchange rate. The *BP* curve will shift *downwards*. The depreciation will cause a rise in exports and a fall in imports. This *rise* in aggregate demand will cause the *IS* curve to shift to the *right*. The new equilibrium will be at point *c*, which is at a higher level of national income, Y_3. Under these circumstances the balance of payments effect makes fiscal policy stronger.

? 1. Under what circumstances would an expansionary fiscal policy have *no effect at all* on national income?
2. Trace through the effects of a deflationary fiscal policy.

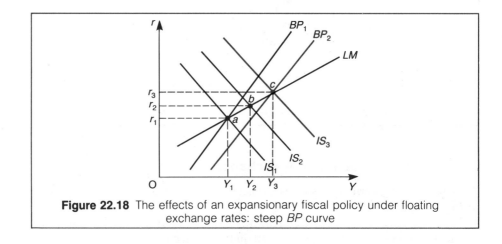

Figure 22.18 The effects of an expansionary fiscal policy under floating exchange rates: steep *BP* curve

Monetary policy under floating exchange rates

An expansionary monetary policy will shift the *LM* curve to the right, to LM_2 in Figure 22.19. In a closed economy, equilibrium would now be at point *b*.

In an open economy under a floating exchange rate, the fall in the rate of interest will cause the exchange rate to depreciate and the *BP* curve to shift downwards. The depreciation will cause exports to rise and imports to fall. This increase in aggregate demand will shift the *IS* curve to the right. The new equilibrium will thus be at a point *c*, where $LM_2 = IS_2 = BP_2$. This represents a large change from the initial point *a*.

Thus monetary policy can have a substantial effect on the level of national income under a system of floating exchange rates.

1. What will determine the size of the shift in the *BP* curve in each case?
2. Trace through the effects of a deflationary monetary policy.

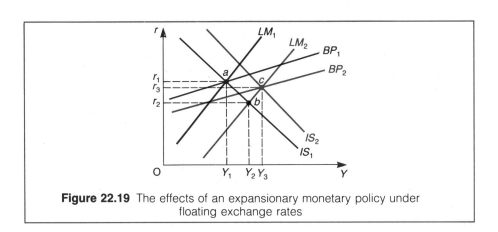

Figure 22.19 The effects of an expansionary monetary policy under floating exchange rates

---

▲ SUMMARY

1. A *BP* curve can be added to an *ISLM* diagram. It shows all the combinations of national income and interest rates at which the balance of payments is in equilibrium. The curve is upward sloping, showing that a rise in national income (causing a current account deficit) will require a rise in interest rates to give a counterbalancing capital account surplus.

2. The higher the *mpm* and the less elastic the supply of international capital, the steeper will be the *BP* curve.

3. Under a fixed exchange rate, the flatter the *BP* curve, the larger will be the effect on national income of an expansionary fiscal policy. Provided the *BP* curve is flatter than the *LM* curve, an expansionary fiscal policy will cause a balance of payments surplus (via its effect of increasing interest rates). The resulting increase in money supply will strengthen the initial effect of the fiscal policy.

4. Monetary policy under fixed exchange rates will have no effect on national income. Any expansion of money supply will, by depressing interest rates, simply lead to a balance of payments deficit and thus a reduction in the money supply again.

5. Under a floating exchange rate an appreciation will shift the *BP* curve upwards and a depreciation will shift it downwards.

6. If the *BP* curve is flatter than the *LM* curve, fiscal policy under a floating exchange rate will be dampened by the resulting changes in the exchange rate. An expansionary fiscal policy will lead to an appreciation (due to the effects of higher interest rates), which in turn will dampen the rise in aggregate demand.

7. Monetary policy will have a relatively large effect on aggregate demand under floating rates. A rise in money supply will reduce interest rates and raise aggregate demand. This will cause a balance of payments deficit and thus a depreciation. This in turn will lead to a further expansion of aggregate demand.

22.5 The adjustable peg system: 1945–71

The Bretton Woods System

After the collapse in 1931 of the fixed exchange rate system of the gold standard (see section 13.3), foreign exchange markets were pretty chaotic. The huge scale of the initial disequilibria caused wild swings in exchange rates. Many countries devalued their currencies in a beggar-my-neighbour fashion, in order to try to gain a competitive advantage over their rivals. Also many countries resorted to protectionism, given the great uncertainties associated with free trade under fluctuating exchange rates.

In 1944 the allied countries met at Bretton Woods in the USA to hammer out a new exchange rate system: one that would avoid the chaos of the 1930s and encourage free trade, but that would avoid the rigidity of the gold standard. The compromise they worked out was an adjustable peg system that lasted until 1971.

Under the Bretton Woods system there was a totally fixed dollar/gold exchange rate ($35 per ounce of gold). The USA guaranteed that it would freely convert dollars into gold. It was hoped thereby to encourage countries to hold dollars as their major reserve currency. After all, if dollars were freely convertible into gold, they were as good as gold. All other countries pegged their exchange rate to the dollar. From time to time, however, they could devalue or revalue their currency against the dollar (and hence against gold). It was thus an adjustable peg regime.

Bretton Woods system

An adjustable peg system whereby currencies were pegged to the US dollar. The US maintained convertibility of the dollar into gold at the rate of $35 to an ounce.

The Bretton Woods system allowed for different types of adjustment to balance of payments disequilibria, depending on the severity of the problem.

To prevent temporary, short-term fluctuations in the exchange rate, central banks *intervened* on the foreign exchange markets using their foreign reserves. This enabled them to maintain the pegged rate within a 1 per cent band.

If the disequilibrium became more serious, governments were supposed to pursue policies of *deflation* or *reflation*. Of course, such policies take time to work, and in the meantime, in the case of a deficit, the central bank might have insufficient reserves to maintain the exchange rate. To provide central banks with sufficient resources to maintain the pegged rate, the International Monetary Fund was set up. All countries were required to deposit a quota of funds with the IMF, depending on the size of their trade. The IMF would then lend to countries in balance of payments deficit to enable them to maintain their exchange rate. The more a country had to borrow from the IMF, the more the IMF would insist that it pursued appropriate deflationary policies to correct the disequilibrium.

If the deficit (or surplus) became severe, countries could *devalue* (or *revalue*): the pegged rate could be adjusted. They were supposed to do this in consultation with the IMF, so that the IMF could ensure that there really was a 'fundamental' disequilibrium, and so that it could prevent a self-defeating round of competitive devaluations by other countries. If the devaluation was to be greater than 10 per cent, the IMF had the right to prevent it.

 Under this system how would you expect countries to respond to a balance of payments surplus? Would a revaluation benefit such countries?

The advocates of an adjustable peg system argue that the Bretton Woods arrangement worked well for over twenty years, encouraging freer trade and a growth in trade and overseas investment. They claim that it made a significant contribution to the long boom of the 1950s and 1960s and argue that:

- Since rates were fixed for a long period of time – perhaps many years – uncertainty was reduced and trade was encouraged.

- Pegged rates, plus the overseeing role of the IMF, prevented governments from pursuing irresponsible policies, and helped to bring about an international harmonization of policies. It kept world inflation in check.
- If a deficit became severe, countries could devalue. This prevented them being forced into a depression or into adopting protectionist policies. The IMF ensured an orderly process of devaluation.

In other words, it was argued that the adjustable peg system gave the advantages of fixed exchange rates while avoiding their major disadvantage.

As it turned out, however, there were serious weaknesses with the system. These weaknesses became more and more apparent during the 1960s, and eventually led to the system's downfall. There were two main areas of weakness. The first concerned the method of adjustment to balance of payments disequilibria. The second concerned the question of liquidity and the roles of gold and the dollar.

Problems of adjustment to balance of payments disequilibria

To avoid internal policy being governed by the balance of payments, and to avoid being forced into a depression, countries with a fundamental deficit were supposed to devalue. There were several difficulties here, however.

First, there was the difficulty of identifying whether a deficit was fundamental. In practice it was not always easy to determine whether a deficit was likely to persist, or whether exports might pick up. Governments were frequently over-optimistic about the future balance of payments position.

Secondly, there was the problem that if devaluation did take place it could be very disruptive to firms. A devaluation suddenly alters the costs and revenues of importers and exporters by a substantial amount. It has a very disruptive effect, therefore, on their businesses. If a devaluation is felt to be imminent, it can cause great uncertainty and make businesses reluctant to take on new trade commitments.

 Will this uncertainty have a similar or a different effect on exporting companies and companies using imported inputs?

Thirdly, there was the danger that a devaluation might at first make a deficit *worse*: the so-called J-curve effect. The reason for this is that the price elasticities of demand for imports and exports may be low in the short run. As a result the Marshall–Lerner condition may not be initially satisfied (see pages 902–3 above). Directly after devaluation few extra exports may be sold, and more will have to be paid for imports that do not have immediate substitutes. There is thus an initial deterioration in the balance of payments before it eventually improves. This is illustrated in Figure 22.20. Devaluation takes place at time t_1. As you can see, the diagram has a J shape.

The J-curve effect

Where a devaluation causes the balance of payments first to deteriorate and then to improve. The graph of the balance of payments over time thus looks like a letter J.

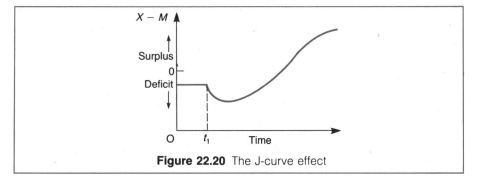

Figure 22.20 The J-curve effect

Box 22.5

Was There a J-Curve Effect After 1967?
The aftermath of the 1967 devaluation

Chronic balance of payments problems had bedevilled the UK economy for much of the 1950s and 1960s. Yet for nearly twenty years from 1949 the exchange rate was kept fixed at £1 = $2.80. Successive governments preferred *deflation* as the solution to a balance of payments crisis, rather than risking the uncertain reaction of overseas holders of sterling to a devaluation.

But finally in November 1967 the long-resisted devaluation came. The pound was devalued from $2.80 to $2.40. A current account deficit of £294 million in 1967 was transformed into a current account surplus of £463 million in 1969, £731 million in 1970 and £1111 million in 1971. The success of devaluation, however, was not immediate. It took many months before exports and imports adjusted fully to the new lower terms of trade.

But was there actually a J-curve effect? Did the balance of payments deteriorate before it improved? The facts are set out in the table.

UK balance of payments: 1967–70

	Current account (1)	Capital account (excluding official transactions) (2)	Balance of payments (1) + (2) (3)	Terms of trade (1975 – 100) (4)
1967 Q1	+22	+487	+509	122.5
Q2	−38	+26	−12	124.2
Q3	−59	−447	−506	123.9
Q4	−219	−443	−662	devaluation
1968 Q1	−149	−370	−519	116.9
Q2	−55	−466	−521	118.6
Q3	−66	+42	−24	118.3
Q4	−16	−330	−346	117.7
1969 Q1	−18	+290	+272	119.9
Q2	+165	−103	+62	118.6
Q3	+154	−234	−80	117.7
Q4	+162	+595	+433	116.4
1970 Q1	+235	+680	+915	119.0
Q2	+166	+61	+227	119.4
Q3	+88	−290	−202	121.4
Q4	+242	+105	+347	122.0

Source: *Economic Trends* (CSO).

?

1. Draw a chart with time on the horizontal axis and the balance of payments on the vertical axis. Show (a) the current account balance, (b) the capital account balance (excluding official financing, i.e. government borrowing from abroad and drawing on reserves) and (c) the total balance: (a) + (b).
2. Was there a J curve in either the current account or the capital account?
3. Why does the capital account show greater short-term fluctuations than the current account?
4. How much did devaluation affect the terms of trade?
5. If traders had accurately *predicted* both the timing and the amount of the devaluation, how would this have affected a possible J-curve effect?
6. How would the capital account have been affected by the raising of Bank rate from 6 per cent to 8 per cent between October and November 1967? (The rate stayed above 7 per cent until 1971.)

Because of these problems, countries in deficit tended to put off devaluing until they were forced to by a crisis. This applied particularly to the UK, given sterling's role as a reserve currency. Many countries, especially in the Commonwealth, held sterling as a major part of their reserves. A devaluation of sterling would, at a stroke, reduce the value of these countries' reserves. They might then lose confidence in sterling: after all, if it can be devalued once, then why not again sometime? The UK, however, had insufficient gold and dollar reserves to buy back all these pounds if the countries decided to sell them. Such selling would cause a crisis, forcing further devaluation.

The reluctance of countries to devalue caused other problems.

Stop–go policies. Countries had to rely much more on *deflation* as a means of curing deficits. The UK in particular found that, whenever the economy started to grow, the balance of payments went into deficit. This forced the government to curb demand again through fiscal and/or monetary policies. Throughout the 1950s and 1960s the UK was bedevilled by this problem, and its poor growth throughout the period was partly due to these stop–go policies.

Speculation. If countries delayed devaluing until a deficit became really severe, an eventual large devaluation became inevitable. This provided a field day for speculators: they could not lose, and there was a high probability of a substantial gain. Thus speculators who sold pounds for $2.80 just before the 1967 devaluation, and bought them back again at $2.40 just after, made a 40c gain on each pound. The losers were the UK taxpayers. The more the Bank of England tried to stave off devaluation by buying pounds for $2.80, the more it (and hence the taxpayer) lost.

Large-scale disruption. The delay in devaluing plus the build-up of speculative pressure, could cause the devaluation to be very large when it eventually came. This could be highly disruptive.

Countries' balance of payments deficits could be reduced and adjustment made easier if surplus countries were willing to revalue. There was a reluctance to do this, however, by countries such as Japan. Revaluation was strongly opposed by exporters (and producers of import substitutes), who would find it suddenly more difficult to compete. What is more, there were not the same pressures for surplus countries to revalue as there were for deficit countries to devalue. A lack of reserves can force deficit countries to devalue. Surplus countries, however, may be quite happy to carry on building up reserves.

An advantage of revaluation was that it reduced the price of imports to a country and thus helped to reduce inflation. But surplus countries were already likely to have low inflation rates, and thus further reductions in inflation were not seen as very important.

A final difficulty in adjustment concerned the USA. Unlike other countries it was not allowed to devalue when in deficit. The onus was on other countries to revalue, which they were reluctant to do. Large US deficits persisted.

The problem of these deficits was linked to the second major problem area: that of international liquidity.

Problems of international liquidity and the collapse of the system

International liquidity refers to the amount of reserves that are acceptable to central banks for intervention in the foreign exchange market. Too little liquidity will force deficit countries into frequent crises and devaluations. Too much liquidity will allow countries to continue with balance of payments deficits without correcting them. It will lead to worldwide inflation due to excess demand. An adjustable peg system therefore requires that international liquidity is controlled.

Under the Bretton Woods system there were three main sources of liquidity: gold, dollars and IMF quotas. But since IMF quotas were only in existing currencies, they were not a source of *additional* liquidity. That left dollars and gold. Dollars were acceptable as a reserve since the USA kept most of its reserves in gold and guaranteed to convert other countries' holdings of dollars into gold at a fixed price of $35 per ounce.

As world trade expanded, so deficits (and surpluses) were likely to be larger, and so more reserves were required. But the supply of gold was not expanding fast enough, so countries increasingly held dollars. After all, dollars earned interest. The willingness to hold dollars enabled the USA to run large balance of payments deficits. All the USA needed to do to pay for the deficits was to 'print' more dollars, which other countries were prepared to accept as reserves.

US balance of payments deficits in the 1960s got steadily worse. The financing of the Vietnam War, in particular, deepened the deficit. Dollars flooded out of the USA. World liquidity thus expanded rapidly, thereby fuelling world inflation. Furthermore, the rapid growth in overseas dollar holdings meant that US gold reserves were becoming increasingly inadequate to guarantee convertibility. Some countries, fearful that the US might eventually be forced to suspend convertibility, chose to exchange dollars for gold. US gold reserves fell, thus creating a further imbalance and a deepening of the crises. This growing imbalance is illustrated in Table 22.1.

Table 22.1 World gold and foreign currency reserves ($bn)

	World gold holdings	World foreign currency reserves (mainly dollars in 1960 and 1970)	US gold reserves
1950	33.8	14.7	24.4
1960	40.5	19.0	17.8
1970	37.2	44.6	11.1

Source: *UN Statistical Year Book* (UN).

Despite various attempts to rescue the system with its over-reliance on the dollar the system collapsed. In June 1972 the pound was floated. Over the following year other countries followed suit, and despite a further dollar devaluation the system was finally abandoned in 1973. The world had moved to a system of dirty floating.

 Why would the adjustable peg system have been less suitable in the world of the mid-1970s than it was back in the 1950s?

▲ SUMMARY

1. Under the adjustable peg (Bretton Woods) system that was used from 1945 to 1971, currencies were pegged to the US dollar. The rate was supported from countries' reserves and if necessary with loans from the International Monetary Fund. If there was a moderate disequilibrium, countries were supposed to use deflationary/reflationary policies. If the disequilibrium became severe, they were supposed to devalue/revalue.

2. The system was claimed to bring the advantages of fixed rates – namely, certainty for business and a constraint on governments pursuing irresponsible fiscal and monetary policies – whilst avoiding the problem of recessions if a balance of payments deficit became severe.

3. Devaluation, however, brought problems. It was some-

times difficult to identify whether a deficit was severe enough to warrant a devaluation; this plus a devaluation itself could be very disruptive for firms; and devaluation at first could make the deficit worse (the J-curve effect), thus forcing a further devaluation.

4. If a country was reluctant to devalue, as was the UK given sterling's role as a reserve currency, it could find itself having to pursue 'stop–go' policies. There could be large-scale speculation as pressure for a devaluation mounted; and the devaluation could be very large when it eventually came, causing large-scale disruption.

5. Problems for deficit countries were made worse by an unwillingness of surplus countries to revalue.

6. Dollars were the main source of international liquidity

under the Bretton Woods system. This effectively meant that the USA, by running balance of payments deficits, was able to print world currency, which would force other countries, via their balance of payments surpluses, to do likewise if they were to maintain the pegged rate. The resulting excess liquidity caused world inflation and a growing lack of confidence in US ability to maintain the fixed dollar/gold rate.

7. Attempts to patch up the system failed to solve these problems and the system was replaced by dirty floating in the early 1970s.

22.6 Dirty floating: 1972 onwards

Forms of managed flexibility

The world has been on a floating exchange rate system since the breakdown of the Bretton Woods system in the early 1970s. Some minor currencies remain pegged (but adjustable) to a major currency such as the dollar or pound, but float along with it against other currencies. Other currencies are pegged to each other, but jointly float with the rest of the world. The most notable example of this is the currencies of the exchange rate mechanism of the European Monetary System – (see section 22.7).

Except for limited periods, no country has adopted a free float. All countries manage their exchange rate and are thus under a 'dirty' floating system. Nevertheless the extent and forms of this intervention vary.

Extent of intervention

Some countries intervene a great deal, attempting to maintain what amounts to a *crawling peg* system. They attempt to prevent short-term fluctuations in exchange rates, keeping their currency within fairly narrow bands, but allow the exchange rate to adjust gradually to long-term shifts in the demand for and supply of their currency. Other countries, such as the USA for most of the period, and the UK from late 1977 to late 1981, have intervened very little, except when there has been sudden large-scale buying, or more likely selling, of their currency.

Forms of intervention

The following can be used to prevent the exchange rate falling:

- Central bank purchases of the currency on the foreign exchange market using reserves or foreign loans.
- Raising interest rates to attract short-term capital inflows.
- Exchange controls: e.g. restricting outflows of capital for investment abroad, or imposing restrictions on currency for foreign travel.
- Indirect methods: e.g. deflationary fiscal policy, or prices and incomes policy. These policies, although they will not affect imports and exports for some time, may nevertheless encourage stabilizing speculation. If speculators believe that the measures will eventually work to prevent depreciation, they will purchase the currency if it does depreciate in the meantime, thus helping to stop further depreciation.

 What could be done to stop the exchange rate *appreciating*?

Justification of dirty floating

After the breakdown of the Bretton Woods system, countries felt they had no option but to float their currencies. This was the only way at that time of achieving the following objectives:

● Allowing exchange rates to adjust to inevitable shifts in demand and supply, without the huge pressures that used to build up under the Bretton Woods system and all the attendant problems of speculation and disruption.
● Freeing the world from the need for large amounts of reserves, and the previous over-reliance on US balance of payments deficits to provide adequate liquidity.
● Preventing domestic policy from being almost wholly determined by the balance of payments situation.

Some countries hoped eventually to return to an improved adjustable peg system, where less reliance needed to be placed on the dollar for liquidity purposes and where adjustments could be made more frequently and less painfully. In the meantime, however, floating exchange rates were felt to be a definite improvement. This was confirmed as the 1970s progressed and greater exchange rate adjustments were required, given the oil crises of 1973/74 and 1979/80, and the rapid change in world trading patterns.

But why not adopt a free float? The reason has largely to do with the potential volatility of short-term exchange rates. There might be such sudden and violent shifts in demand and supply that the resulting massive depreciation or appreciation would be too disruptive to trade and investment, and to domestic prices and employment. There are two possible scenarios.

Demand and supply changes are temporary. Temporary changes might be due to a miners' strike, or to a sudden but short-term rise in interest rates caused by the desire to reduce an unexpected rise in money supply. Without intervention, speculators, lacking confidence in the government's ability to deal with the domestic situation, may destabilize the exchange rate. In these circumstances the central bank can act as a stabilizing speculator and bring the exchange rate back to its (stable) long-run equilibrium.

Demand and supply changes are long term. Long-term changes might be due to persistently higher rates of inflation, to a shift in long-term trading patterns, or to a change in oil or other commodity prices. Again, without intervention, there may be a sudden and damaging change in exchange rates, with highly destabilizing speculation and overshooting. This will be made worse by the J-curve effect. In this case the central bank can intervene to allow a gradual and orderly adjustment to the new equilibrium.

There may be political reasons too for maintaining stable exchange rates. If the exchange rate appreciates significantly, exporters complain that they cannot compete abroad. If it depreciates significantly, the public complains about higher import prices, and also the general rate of inflation is likely to increase. Maintaining the existing exchange rate thus seems the most politically expedient!

Problems with dirty floating since 1972

Managing the exchange rate involved problems, however. Governments needed to know when to intervene, what exchange rate level they should aim to maintain, and how persistently they should try to maintain that rate in the face of speculative pressure.

Predicting the long-term equilibrium exchange rate

Differing inflation rates between countries will require exchange rate adjustments to maintain purchasing power parity. It is not correct, however, for governments to

---

Box 22.6

The Importance of Capital Movements
How a current account deficit can coincide with
an appreciating exchange rate

The era of dirty floating exchange rates has seen a huge increase in short-term capital movements. Vast amounts of moneys transfer from country to country in search of higher interest rates or a currency that is likely to appreciate. This can have a bizarre effect on exchange rates.

If a country pursues a reflationary fiscal policy, the current account will tend to go into deficit as extra imports are 'sucked in'. What effect will this have on exchange rates? You might think that the answer is obvious: the higher demand for imports will create an extra supply of domestic currency on the foreign exchange market and hence drive down the exchange rate.

In fact the opposite is likely. The higher interest rates resulting from the higher domestic demand can lead to a massive inflow of short-term capital. The capital account can thus move sharply into surplus. This is likely to outweigh the current account deficit and cause an *appreciation* of the exchange rate.

Exchange rate movements, especially in the short term, are largely brought about by changes on the capital rather than the current account.

> **?** Why do high international capital mobility and an absence of exchange controls severely limit a country's ability to choose its interest rate?

---

assume that this will be the *only* cause of shifts in the long-term equilibrium exchange rate. The 1973/74 and 1979/80 oil crises caused fundamental and unpredictable changes in currency demand and supply. So too did other factors, such as UK membership of the EC and its effect on trading patterns, protectionist measures adopted in different parts of the world, changes in technology and changes in tastes.

It is therefore very difficult for the government to predict what the long-term equilibrium will be, and what proportion of any exchange rate movement is therefore due to long-term and what proportion merely to short-term phenomena.

The growth in speculative capital movements
The OPEC oil price increase in 1973/74 caused huge balance of payments deficits for oil importers. The OPEC countries could not spend all of these surpluses on additional imports since (a) they did not have the capacity to consume such a huge increase in imports and (b) the oil-importing countries did not have the capacity to supply such a huge increase in exports. The surpluses were thus largely invested in short-term dollar and to a lesser extent sterling and other Western currency assets. This created a large capacity for short-term loans by Western banks. These moneys could be rapidly shifted from one world financial centre to another, depending on which country had the most favourable interest rates and exchange rates.

This created a massive capacity for speculation, and thus made it difficult for countries to control exchange rates by currency sales alone. Reserves and access to foreign loans were simply inadequate to prevent concerted speculative selling. Governments therefore had to rely much more on using interest rates, which would enable them better to control these speculative flows.

Conflicts with internal policy
If the main weapon for controlling the exchange rate is interest rates, then interest rates cannot also be used to determine domestic money supply. The growth of

monetarism in the late 1970s, and the setting of monetary targets, therefore made it far more difficult for government to control the exchange rate (see Box 17.4 and Section 18.4).

Beggar-my-neighbour policies

The use of higher interest rates to prevent short-term capital outflows may cause other countries to raise their interest rates in competition. This could then lead to world deflation and world recession.

 Would any of these problems be lessened by the world returning to an adjustable peg system? If so, what sort of adjustable peg system would you recommend?

The UK experience of dirty floating

Figure 22.21 shows the fluctuations in UK exchange rates since 1971, both with respect to the dollar, and the more important trade-weighted average exchange rate with all other countries. As can be seen, the fluctuations have been large and often violent.

Differences in inflation between the UK and the rest of the world account for some of the exchange rate movements. But even when allowances are made for inflation, there were still major divergences from the purchasing power parity (PPP) rate. The PPP rate is the exchange rate that *would* occur if inflation rates were the *only* determinant of the exchange rate. The formula is $PPP = P_w/P_{UK} \times 100$, where P_w is a weighted index of world prices and P_{UK} is the UK price index. Prices are consumer prices and the base year is 1975.

Figure 22.22 shows divergencies between the actual exchange rate and the PPP rate, and thus shows fluctuations *not* due to inflation. Two PPP rates are used: one based on world prices and one based on the prices of the industrialized world alone. Since all-world inflation has been higher than industrialized countries' inflation, the PPP rate based on all-world figures is higher. The actual exchange rate relative to this PPP rate is therefore lower. In both cases fluctuations are sizeable, and occurred despite considerable exchange market intervention by the Bank of England, especially during 1976/1977, 1984/1985 and 1988/89.

 Are the graphs in Figures 22.21 and 22.22 of a similar pattern? What would cause their pattern to differ?

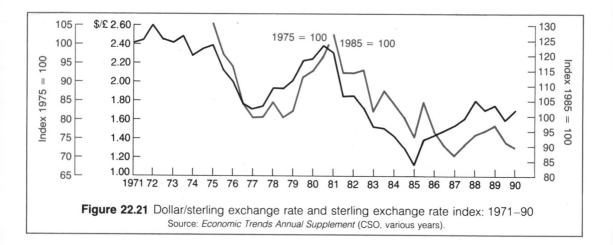

Figure 22.21 Dollar/sterling exchange rate and sterling exchange rate index: 1971–90
Source: *Economic Trends Annual Supplement* (CSO, various years).

Figure 22.22 Percentage divergence of actual exchange rate from PPP rate: 1975–87 (1975 = 0)

Sources: *Economic Trends* (CSO, various issues); *International Financial Statistics* (IMF, various issues).

Other countries experienced similarly volatile exchange rates. But why have exchange rates fluctuated so much? We will now look at the major causes of exchange rate movements since 1972.

The first oil crisis and its aftermath: 1973–76

The 1973/74 oil crisis, which followed large world commodity price increases over the previous two years, caused a major shock to the world economy. What were the UK and other industrialized countries to do?

Depreciation could not provide the solution. The demand for oil is highly price inelastic. The price increase had thus already caused a major inflationary shock to the world economy. Depreciation would have probably made things worse. It would have caused a further rise in inflation and little increase in exports (given OPEC's limited ability to absorb extra imports), and could well have sparked off beggar-my-neighbour depreciations between oil-importing countries.

Concerted deflationary policies, or a growth in protectionism, would have caused a major world recession. As it was, the oil price increase acted like a tax and reduced real spending power, causing both inflation and a moderate recession.

The solution, then, seemed to be to borrow: (a) to 'recycle' the oil revenues so as to prevent excessive deflation, and (b) to attempt to maintain reasonably stable exchange rates and avoid competitive depreciation.

Until 1975 the UK was reasonably successful in this policy. A substantial proportion of the OPEC surpluses were deposited in the UK, and the government undertook large-scale foreign borrowing. The exchange rate was thus kept up by these capital inflows, and also by using reserves.

From early 1975, however, the exchange rate began falling, despite continued intervention. In 1976 it began to plummet, as you can see from Figures 22.21 and 22.22. The reasons for this are not clear, given that the UK balance of payments deficit by this time was falling: the world economy was beginning to expand again and with it the demand for UK exports; inflation was falling, with the prices and incomes policy seeming to have a marked effect; and North Sea oil would soon be making a major contribution. Nevertheless the fall in the exchange rate in early 1976 gathered momentum and destabilizing speculation set in. Many of the short-term capital deposits were withdrawn from the UK.

A crisis was reached in November 1976, when a major loan had to be negotiated with the IMF. The resulting rescue package included an insistence on deflationary measures such as higher interest rates. The exchange rate bottomed out at the end of 1976.

The second oil crisis and the rise of monetarism: 1976–81

The measures of late 1976, helped by the growing importance of North Sea oil, caused renewed confidence in sterling. Until the autumn of 1977, the Bank of England intervened to prevent the exchange rate from rising too much. Vast amounts of sterling were sold, and the foreign exchange acquired was used to build up the reserves again and to pay off some of the foreign loans of previous years.

Then, from autumn 1977 to autumn 1981, the pound was allowed to float relatively freely. There was still some intervention from time to time (e.g. to support the pound in April 1978), but the government permitted a massive 30 per cent appreciation of the pound (a 53 per cent appreciation of the PPP rate!) from December 1976 to February 1981. There were four main reasons for this unprecedented rise in the pound.

The UK's growing oil surplus. North Sea oil was making an increasing contribution to the current account of the balance of payments.

The 1979/80 oil crisis. Oil rose from $13 to $19 per barrel during 1979 and to $31 during 1980. Since the UK was becoming a major oil exporter, and the pound was now a 'petrocurrency'. OPEC surpluses were attracted to London: after all, there were now not the same exchange rate risks attached to sterling as to the dollar, yen, D-Mark or other major currency.

The advent of monetarism. From 1977 the money supply (£M3) was targeted. When the Thatcher government came to power in 1979, these monetarist policies were more rigorously applied. But with the large capital inflow, any attempt to prevent the exchange rate rising would have caused massive balance of payments surpluses and hence unacceptable increases in the money supply. In order to keep to its monetary targets, the government drove up interest rates, with short-term interest rates reaching over 17 per cent in late 1979. Interest rates remained considerably higher than in competitor countries. But this simply encouraged further capital inflows. The exchange rate had to rise.

The government could not target both the exchange rate and the money supply. It chose to target money supply, and thus had to let interest rates and hence the exchange rate rise to very high levels.

The recession of 1980–82. The recession was caused by these highly deflationary monetary policies. The recession was earlier and deeper in the UK than elsewhere. The resulting decline in the demand for imports further contributed to a rising exchange rate.

The effects of the huge appreciation of sterling were devastating to large parts of UK industry. Many exporters simply could not compete at such high exchange rates, while imports were so cheap that they drove many firms out of business. The appreciation, therefore, contributed to the recession.

Keynesian critics of the government argue that it should have adopted a less restrictive fiscal and monetary policy. As far as fiscal policy is concerned, they argue that taxation from oil revenues could have been directly invested in infrastructure. Alternatively, significant tax cuts could have been given. (It would not matter if imports rose as a result, since that would help to lower the exchange rate.)

Box 22.7

Trying to Keep the Pound Down
The early 1980s versus the late 1980s

When there is a large balance of payments deficit, or when the exchange rate falls, this will normally hit the headlines. The government may well make bland statements such as 'You shouldn't take too much notice of one month's figures' or 'This is simply a temporary problem', but it will probably be busy taking action, such as raising interest rates or intervening in the foreign exchanges.

But what of the case when the pound is rising? Will the government heed the worries of exporters? Will it therefore intervene so as to keep the exchange rate down?

It is interesting to compare two periods when the pound was rising. The first is from April 1980 to February 1981. The second is from January 1987 to May 1988.

In the first period there was very little intervention in the foreign exchange markets, with reserves staying roughly constant. There was virtually a *clean float*. Although the government reduced interest rates, this was not enough to prevent a dramatic appreciation of the exchange rate (especially since interest rates were falling all round the world. Table (a) shows what happened to reserves and to the exchange rate index.

(a)

	Official reserves ($m)	Exchange rate index (1975 = 100)
1980 April	28 008	94.3
May	28 284	94.7
June	28 172	94.5
July	28 272	95.6
August	28 291	96.8
September	27 637	97.6
October	28 026	99.2
November	28 189	101.1
December	27 476	100.2
1981 January	28 394	103.2
February	28 434	102.5

Source: *Economic Trends* (CSO, December 1982).

In the second period, from January 1987 to March 1988, the government was effectively targeting the £/D-Mark exchange rate at around £1 = DM2.90–3.00. But UK interest rates were comparatively high, and thus there was strong upward pressure on the exchange rate. The government's response was to reduce interest rates somewhat, but it was afraid of too dramatic a fall in interest

rates for fear of triggering an explosion of credit and a rise in the rate of inflation.

As a result, by contrast with the earlier period, the government intervened actively in the foreign exchange market. The float was 'very dirty indeed'. The Bank of England sold massive amounts of sterling, and consequently bought massive amounts of foreign currencies into the reserves. The reserves more than doubled in twelve months! Table (b) gives the details.

(b)

	Official reserves ($m)	DM/£	Exchange rate index (1985 = 100)
1987 January	21 952	2.80	85.4
February	22 257	2.79	85.4
March	27 039	2.92	89.2
April	29 807	2.95	89.9
May	34 679	2.98	91.1
June	34 364	2.96	90.3
July	34 915	2.97	90.5
August	34 365	2.97	90.0
September	34 808	2.98	90.9
October	41 399	2.99	91.4
November	41 284	2.99	93.2
Decernber	44 326	2.99	93.6
1988 January	43 093	2.98	92.8
February	42 927	2.98	92.2
March	47 519	3.07	95.3
April	47 857	3.14	97.2
May	48 533	3.17	97.6

Source: *Economic Trends* (CSO, May 1989).

By early 1988 it was becoming more and more difficult to stop the pound rising. Despite the huge build-up of the reserves, the Chancellor felt it was necessary to make further reductions in interest rates. Between March and May interest rates were cut from 9 per cent to 7½ per cent (the lowest for ten years). But despite this the pound rose well above the DM3.00 level. And, much to the annoyance of the Prime Minister, there was an explosion of credit, a rise in inflation and a rapidly deteriorating current account balance of payments deficit.

? Compare the probable effects of the exchange rate policies in the two periods on money supply and inflation.

As far as monetary policy is concerned, they argue that the government should have adopted higher monetary targets. This would have kept interest rates down and would thus have lowered the exchange rate.

These policies, they claim, would have averted recession. But would they have been inflationary? Keynesians argue that they would not because North Sea oil gave the UK an increase in *potential* income. A rise in aggregate demand to match this would simply have prevented a deflationary gap from opening.

1. Were there any advantages of the high exchange rate?
2. Would there have been a danger of inflation rising if deflationary policies had not been used, even though there was a rise in potential income caused by North Sea oil?

'Reaganomics' and the US budget deficit: 1981–85

With the election of President Reagan in late 1980, the USA adopted 'Reaganomics'. This had two main features:

● Incentives. President Reagan was committed to free markets. He argued that growth would be best achieved by supply-side policies: by increasing incentives. The major element in this policy was tax cuts.
● Monetarism. Tight control was to be kept over the growth of the money supply.

Initially President Reagan had hoped to maintain a balanced budget, with tax cuts being matched by cuts in government expenditure. But he also had a major commitment to increasing defence expenditure. As a result it was simply not possible for cuts in other parts of government expenditure (e.g. welfare) to prevent a rapid increase in the overall level of government spending. Tax cuts and increased government expenditure led to a growing budget deficit increasing from $76bn in 1980 to £212bn in 1985.

Given the commitment to monetarism, the US administration was unwilling to finance the budget deficit by significantly increasing the money supply. The deficit therefore had to be financed largely by borrowing. This led to high interest rates. Although from 1982 a slightly more relaxed monetary policy was followed, the growth in aggregate demand (as the US pulled out of recession) kept interest rates well above those of other countries. This is illustrated in Table 22.2.

Table 22.2 Money market interest rates: 1981–86 (average % per annum)

	1981	1982	1983	1984	1985	1986
USA	16.38	12.26	9.09	10.23	8.10	6.81
Japan	7.43	6.94	6.39	6.10	6.46	4.79
UK	13.12	11.36	9.09	7.62	10.78	10.68
West Germany	11.26	8.67	5.36	5.55	5.19	4.57

Source: *International Financial Statistics* (IMF).

The budget deficit had a very distorting effect on the US balance of payments. High aggregate demand led to a rise in imports and a current account deficit. High interest rates, however, attracted foreign capital to the USA and thus produced a capital account surplus. These capital movements were so large that they caused the dollar to appreciate, despite the current account deficit. This appreciation, in turn, worsened the current account deficit. This is illustrated in Table 22.3.

Table 22.3 US and Japanese balance of payments: 1980–86 ($bn)

	1980	1981	1982	1983	1984	1985	1986
USA current account	+1.84	+6.37	−9.06	−46.67	−106.46	−111.65	−140.62
USA capital account	−35.91	−27.89	−25.27	+31.41	+79.73	+100.38	+80.92
Japan current account	−10.75	+4.77	+6.85	+20.80	+35.00	+49.17	+85.96
Japan capital account	+18.88	+17.32	−16.20	−21.32	−36.57	−53.53	−73.51

Source: *International Financial Statistics* (IMF).

Other industrialized economies, and especially Japan, experienced the opposite effect. Japan, with its lower rates of inflation and lower growth in domestic demand, had a growing current account surplus. But this was more than offset by a capital account deficit. The Japanese have a high propensity to save: 17 per cent of Japanese GDP is saved, compared to 6 per cent of US GDP. This too helps to maintain low Japanese interest rates. The current account surpluses plus much of these savings were deposited in the USA at high US interest rates. The effect of these huge capital account deficits was a *depreciation* of the yen relative to the dollar. This is illustrated in Table 22.4.

Table 22.4 US and Japanese exchange rates: 1980–85 (1980 = 100)

	1980	1981	1982	1983	1984	1985
US effective exchange rate (trade weighted)	100.0	112.7	125.9	133.2	143.7	150.2
Japanese exchange rate	100.0	102.6	91.0	95.1	95.2	95.4

Source: *International Financial Statistics* (IMF).

There was thus an irony: the USA had huge current account deficits and yet an appreciating dollar; Japan had huge current account surpluses and yet a depreciating yen relative to the dollar.

As the US budget deficit increased, so US interest rates continued to remain high relative to rates in other countries, and so the dollar continued to rise. The high dollar caused grave problems for US exporting industries and industries competing with imports. Large numbers of bankruptcies were suffered in both industry and agriculture. There were growing demands for protectionism – demands, however, to which President Reagan did not give in.

Sterling was particularly vulnerable as many of the OPEC oil revenues deposited in the UK were switched to the USA. As the dollar rose, so the pound fell (see Figure 22.21). Crisis was reached in January/February 1985 with the exchange rate dipping as low as £1 = $1.05 (see Box 22.8).

The government attempted to arrest this fall. The Bank of England sold large quantities of dollars and other reserves. Interest rates were raised dramatically. Minimum lending rate was even reintroduced on 14 January for one day to drive up interest rates by 2 per cent. Eventually the crisis was averted at the end of February by concerted action between European central banks, which jointly sold $11 billion over a period of a few days.

Box 22.8

Sterling Under Pressure

The sterling crisis of January/February 1985

As Figure 22.21 shows, the period from 1981 to 1985 was one of a massive decline in the $/£ exchange rate. The pound fell from a high of around $2.40 at the beginning of 1981 to a low of $1.05 in February 1985.

But this fall was not steady. It was greatly influenced by speculation. Whenever speculators believed that the rate would fall there would be a new wave of selling sterling (and buying dollars), and sure enough the rate would fall – and often quite dramatically.

So what determines the expectations of speculators? The answer is that there are a number of factors: predictions of changes in inflation, interest rates, economic growth rates, etc. But one important determinant of speculation is the actions of government.

In June 1984 the pound fell from $1.40 to $1.32. To prevent a further fall the government raised interest rates by 2¾ per cent over the following couple of weeks. As a result the pound stopped falling. Speculators believed that the government 'meant business' and thus stopped selling pounds.

But in November 1984, when the exchange rate was again falling (from $1.26 to $1.22), the government *reduced* interest rates. This time the government was more concerned to stimulate demand and prevent a further rise in unemployment. This triggered off a massive selling of sterling, a problem aggravated by the growing attractiveness of the dollar. The problem is that, if markets get the impression that the government is prepared to see a small fall in the exchange rate, then speculation will cause a large fall. But it was not until January 1985, with the exchange rate down to $1.12, that the government eventually raised interest rates.

By this time speculation had reached fever pitch, and it was not just the pound that was coming under pressure. Unprecedented sales of sterling and other currencies took place as dealers rushed to buy the soaring dollar. The following is an extract from the *Financial Times* of 26 February 1985:

Banks powerless as dollar soars

Central banks stood by powerless yesterday as a remarkable surge in the dollar's value swept it to record highs against sterling and other European currencies.

Although it weakened slightly in late trading ... the dollar had earlier recorded the steepest one-day climb traders could remember. In Europe it rose nearly 1.5% against other major currencies. The central banks failed to mount even token resistance.

Sterling closed in New York at $1.0565 after finishing in London down 2.25 cents at an all time low of $1.054. The French franc, Italian lira and many other currencies were at their lowest ever against the dollar ...

Foreign exchange dealers said the wave of dollar buying orders from commercial customers and speculators led to frantic trading ...

Dealers cited as reasons for the latest surge ... the expectation of higher US interest rates and President Reagan's rejection of moves to depress the US currency.

Central bankers acknowledged that intervention against such a strong trend would have been hopeless ... The West German Bundesbank, which has so far taken the lead in trying to slow the dollar's rise, now believes intervention can only be effective if the US authorities play a major role.

But then the following day the central banks fought back. In a joint action between central banks across the world there was a huge sale of dollars from their reserves. The following extract is from the *Financial Times* of 28 February:

Dollar falls in chaotic trading after central bankers' intervention

Large-scale and concerted intervention by central banks sent the dollar plunging against other leading currencies in chaotic trading on foreign exchange markets yesterday.

The central banks, led by West Germany's Bundesbank and including most other European central banks and the Bank of Japan, sold between $1.5bn and $1.75bn, according to senior European monetary officials.

The intervention, one of the largest ever and the first joint move for more than a month, triggered off what dealers called panic selling of the US currency ...

Mr Volcker [US Federal Reserve Board chair] ... stressed the useful role which official intervention in the foreign exchange markets could play, although he reiterated that intervention must be 'complementary and subsidiary to more basic measures to have a lasting impact.'

Over the next few days the fall of the dollar continued, and the pound consequently rose against it. Within a few weeks the exchange rate was around $1.25, and a few weeks after that it was around $1.40.

? How in practice could central banks decide when to intervene?

Up until early 1985, destabilizing speculation had worked to drive the dollar up and other currencies, especially the pound, down. After February 1985, speculation went into reverse. The dollar was now falling. People therefore sold dollars and bought other currencies.

Whether the action by the central banks in February 1985 would inevitably have worked even if there was still upward pressure on the dollar, or whether it merely acted as a trigger to initiate a fall in the dollar which had already become overvalued in the eyes of many speculators is debatable.

1. Why would the pound not have gone on falling indefinitely?
2. Was there anything that the UK could have done to prevent the massive fall in the dollar/pound exchange rate from $2.40 in 1981 to only just above $1.00 in early 1985? (See Figure 22.21.)

Mixed fortunes for the pound: 1985–88

After February 1985 the dollar fell and the yen rose. Although there were still considerable currency fluctuations after that, the dollar did not return to those record high levels. So why did it fall?

- US money supply was growing more rapidly.
- US growth was more sluggish. US interest rates were thus falling, and falling relative to international rates (see Table 22.2).
- This led to a fall in the capital account surplus (see Table 22.3).
- There was still a growing current account deficit (see Table 22.3).
- Speculators generally believed that the dollar had been overvalued.

Sterling at first appreciated: not only relative to the dollar, but also relative to the trade-weighted index (see Figure 22.21). This was encouraged by high interest rates in the UK. Interest rates had been driven up in an attempt to maintain monetary targets and to encourage the recovery of sterling (see Table 22.2).

In 1986, however, oil prices fell: from $28 per barrel in 1985 to $13.50 in 1986. This was due to an increasing oil glut, as individual oil producers, both within and outside OPEC, attempted to increase their share of the oil market. Oligopolistic collusion between oil producers was breaking down. The pound, as a petrocurrency, therefore depreciated.

Also, as 1986 wore on, and as a general election drew closer, so people began to believe that the government would engineer a pre-election boom. Certainly, £M3 was being allowed to increase well above original targets. (In the 1987 Budget, targets for £M3 were dropped.) The prediction of a boom plus a relaxed monetary policy therefore led to expectations of a depreciation of the pound, which speculators then helped to bring about. The exchange rate index fell from over 96.6 in the spring of 1986 to 84.6 in October.

To what extent could the exchange rate movements in this period have been (a) predicted; (b) prevented?

But then in 1987 the pound began to rise again. Oil prices were firmer; inflation had fallen to just over 3 per cent (the lowest for twenty years) and interest rates were still very high relative to those of other countries. The Chancellor, Nigel Lawson, anxious to avoid repeating the damage to UK industry that was done by the high exchange rate of the early 1980s, was keen to prevent the pound rising. He was also keen to keep the exchange rate pegged as closely as possible to the German mark. The reason for this was his aim of the UK eventually joining the pegged exchange rate of the European Monetary System. (see Section 22.7 and Box 22.7).

But how was he to keep the exchange rate from rising? The answer was to lower interest rates. Thus between October 1986 and May 1988 interest rates fell from 11 per cent to 7½ per cent. (An added reason for reductions in interest rates occurred after the October 1987 stock market crash. The government was afraid of a recession and was thus concerned to boost aggregate demand.) For several months the policy of shadowing the D-Mark seemed to work. The exchange rate was effectively pegged at around DM2.95; the economy grew and unemployment fell.

A deteriorating balance of payments: 1988 onwards

Keeping the exchange rate down through reductions in interest rates, plus a policy of reducing income taxes, was causing the economy to expand rapidly. The current account thus moved rapidly into deficit (see Box 22.1) and inflation began to rise sharply. In June 1988 the government was forced to raise interest rates again in order to dampen demand.

The current account continued to deteriorate. Within three years an annual current account surplus of over £3000 million had been transformed into a deficit of over £20 000 million as Table 22.5 shows.

Table 22.5 UK balance of payments current account: 1985–89 (£m)

1985	1986	1987	1988	1989
+3355	+151	−2906	−14 665	−20 851

Source: *Economic Trends* (CSO).

But whereas a high rate of interest was used to slow down the growth in demand and thus also to help reduce the growth in imports, it also had the effect of keeping up the exchange rate. This only increased the difficulties for UK exporters in competing abroad, and thus prevented an improvement in the current account.

Nevertheless in mid-1989, with the current account still deteriorating, the exchange rate began to fall. The fear of the authorities was that with such a huge deficit, once the rate began to fall, speculation would cause the fall to be very severe. Thus the government was forced to maintain high interest rates in order to attract sufficient capital account inflows to finance the deficit and stave off panic selling. The Bank of England was frequently forced to intervene in the foreign exchange markets to steady the rate, especially after the announcement of a bad monthly set of trade figures.

But despite these difficulties, one development over the years has made the job of financing a current account deficit easier. This is the growth of 'hot money': the huge quantity of liquid funds in the international money markets. If the government raises interest rates, this can attract vast sums into the country – more than enough to finance even a large current account deficit. The problem with this is that these funds can just as easily be withdrawn again. As a result the government may have very little discretion over the level of interest rates.

? To what extent was there a conflict after 1988 between using interest rates to affect the rate of inflation and using them to maintain a given exchange rate? Explain under what circumstances there was and was not a conflict.

Conclusion: the volatility of exchange rates

Exchange rates in recent years have become extremely volatile. Currencies can gain or lose several percentage points in the space of a few days. These changes can then make all the difference between profit and loss for trading companies.

But why have fluctuations increased? There are a number of reasons:

- The adoption in the early 1980s of monetarist policies by most Western governments. This involved monetary targets. To keep to these targets meant allowing interest rates to fluctuate as necessary. This in turn caused exchange rate fluctuations.
- A huge growth in international financial markets. Banking throughout the world has become increasingly international rather than national. This has encouraged the international transfer of money and capital.
- The abolition of exchange controls. With a few exceptions, such as Japan, most industrialized countries have abolished exchange controls. (The UK did so in 1979.) This has further encouraged the international movement of capital.
- The growth in information technology. With the simple use of a computer and a VDU, capital can be transferred from London to Tokyo, to New York or to Paris in a matter of seconds.
- The preference for liquidity. With the danger of currency fluctuations, companies prefer to keep their financial capital as liquid as possible. They do not want to be locked into assets denominated in a declining currency.
- The growing speculative activities of trading companies. Many large companies will put together a team of dealers to help manage their liquid assets: to switch them from currency to currency in order to take advantage of market movements.
- The growing speculative activities of banks and other financial institutions.
- The growing belief that rumour or 'jumping on the bandwagon' are more important determinants of currency buying or selling than cool long-term appraisal. If people *believe* that speculation is likely to be destabilizing, their actions will ensure that it is. Many companies involved in international trade and finance have developed a 'speculative mentality'.
- The growing belief that governments are powerless to prevent currency movements. As short-term capital (or 'hot money') grows relative to official reserves, it is increasingly difficult for central bank exchange market intervention to stabilize currencies.

 Could world governments have prevented or lessened any of these causes of growing exchange rate volatility?

Although most governments and firms dislike highly volatile exchange rates, there have been few serious suggestions that the world could return to a fixed exchange rate, or a Bretton Woods type system – at least not in the foreseeable future. Nevertheless, there have been suggestions made for reducing volatility. Two of these – international harmonization of economic policies, and an adjustable peg system between a group of currencies (as in the European Monetary System) – are discussed in section 22.7.

▲ SUMMARY

1. Since the early 1970s the world has largely been on a dirty floating exchange rate system. The degree of intervention, however, varies from country to country and from time to time. The forms of intervention include central bank purchases and sales of currencies, changes in interest rates, exchange controls and, over the longer term, demand management policies.

2. With the collapse of the Bretton Woods system, dirty floating was felt to be the best compromise. It would give the necessary degree of exchange rate flexibility in a world where shifts in currency demand and supply were becoming much larger. It would also release domestic policy from being dominated by balance of payments considerations. At the same time, the intervention could (in theory) prevent violent exchange rate fluctuations and allow a more orderly adjustment to new equilibrium exchange rates.

3. Nevertheless there are problems under dirty floating of predicting long-term equilibrium exchange rates. What is more, with the massive growth in 'hot money' since the early 1970s, it has become increasingly difficult for countries on their own to counteract speculation. The main weapon of intervention has become the rate of interest. There may be a conflict, however, in using interest rates both to control exchange rates *and* as the weapon of domestic monetary policy.

4. Sterling exchange rates have shown considerable volatility over the years, with large divergences from the purchasing power parity rate.

5. After the first oil crisis and a high domestic rate of inflation the pound fell. After 1976, however, with inflation falling, a growing oil surplus, a rise in the price of oil and a tighter monetary policy, the pound soared. The rise was made steeper by the recession, which began earlier in the UK than in other countries.

6. With the rise in the value of the dollar in the early 1980s – as a result of high US interest rates – the pound fell again. There was massive speculation, leading to a crisis in early 1985.

7. Following concerted international action to arrest the rise of the dollar, together with the perception that the dollar had 'overshot', the dollar fell again and the pound rose. For a time (1987–8) the UK government targeted the German mark. With UK inflation having fallen, and interest rates still high by international standards, interest rates had to be reduced in order to prevent an appreciation of the pound. The lower interest rate, however, contributed to a massive expansion of the money supply and a correspondingly large rise in demand. The current account moved sharply into deficit.

8. The volatility of exchange rates around the world has tended to grow. There are many reasons for this, including a growth in international financial markets and a liberalization of international financial movements combined with easier computer transfer of funds, a growth in speculative activities and a growing belief in the impotence of governments acting on their own to stabilize rates.

22.7 Concerted international action to stabilize exchange rates

International harmonization of economic policies

One of the major causes of currency fluctuations is the very different economic policies followed by different countries. For example, an expansionary fiscal policy plus a tight monetary policy can lead to huge currency appreciation if other countries do not follow suit. This is what happened to the dollar in 1983 and 1984. The problem is then amplified by speculation. Divergences in *interest rates, growth rates* and *inflation rates* are the main problems.

For many years now the leaders of the seven major industrial countries – the USA, Japan, Germany, France, the UK, Italy and Canada – have met once a year at an economic summit conference. Top of the agenda in most of these has been how to generate world economic growth without major currency fluctuations – and a central requirement for achieving this has been the *harmonization* of economic policies between nations. In particular, harmonization of interest rates has been seen as the prime requirement for currency stability. High US and low Japanese interest rates have been the major cause of the huge Japanese capital account deficits and US capital account surpluses, and of the high dollar relative to the yen.

Box 22.9

'Seven Men in a Boat'
Attempts at harmonization

In recent years, governments of the major industrial nations have tried to come to terms with the ever growing interdependence of their economies. Economic disruptions in one country (e.g. a worsening US budget deficit or a unilateral decision by, say, Germany or Japan to raise interest rates) can have profound effects on the world economy.

As a result of the potentially highly unstable nature of economic relationships, financial ministers and heads of state have met on a regular basis to try to harmonize their policies. But the key problem in this has been the nations' overriding self-interest. Before a country will agree to a package of policies it must be convinced that it is in its own interests.

In 1987 the *Group of Seven (G7)* – the UK, West Germany, Japan, France, Italy, Canada and the USA – decided to try to stem the fall of the dollar caused by the huge US budget deficit. The *Louvre Accord*, as it became known, was an agreement to co-ordinate interest rate reductions and exchange rate intervention. The US, however, failed to allow its interest rates to rise relative to the other countries, or to intervene sufficiently on the foreign exchange market. The agreement collapsed.

In order for policy co-ordination to succeed, the parties to such agreements must be seen to be taking actions to benefit the *others* and not necessarily themselves. One suggested reason for the USA's reluctance to follow the Louvre Accord was the lack of policy initiatives in both Japan and Germany to limit their trade surpluses, either by domestic measures or through an appreciation of their exchange rates. In response, the USA was only too willing to allow the dollar to fall and US industry to improve its competitive position, regardless of the inflationary impact on the world economy.

Successful policy co-ordination requires that serious imbalances in world trade should be kept to a minimum. But such is the size of the US and UK current account deficits (and the Japanese and German surpluses) that huge pressures are placed on the foreign exchange market. The imbalances create massive capital flows and great uncertainty. As a result speculation is likely to be a far more powerful determinant of events than any agreement made by finance ministers.

? Why is it difficult to reach international agreement on policy co-ordination when the economies of the world are badly out of line in the first place? Why, having once reached an agreement to co-ordinate policy, is it difficult to put it into practice if the world economies are badly out of line?

But how can harmonization be achieved? As long as the US budget deficit remains high, it is going to be difficult for US interest rates to be kept low without a large increase in US money supply and possible inflation. The solution has been sought in Japanese (and German) reflation: expansionary fiscal policy, but only a mildly expansionary monetary policy so as to achieve growth but a rise in interest rates. The higher demand would cause an erosion of these countries' current account surpluses. Higher interest rates would erode their capital account deficits.

There are serious difficulties with international policy harmonization, however:

- Monetary targets involve letting interest rates fluctuate with the demand for money. Harmonizing interest rates would involve abandoning monetary targets.
- Countries have different internal structural relationships. Countries with higher endemic *cost* inflation would require higher interest rates and higher unemployment if international inflation rates were to be harmonized.
- Countries have different rates of productivity increase, product development, investment and market penetration. Thus the growth in exports (relative to imports) will differ for any given level of inflation or growth.
- Countries may be very unwilling to change their domestic policies to fall in line with other countries. They may prefer the other countries to fall in line with them! Japan, for example, on several occasions has been reluctant to reflate. .

If any one of the three – interest rates, growth rates or inflation rates – could be harmonized across countries, it is likely that the other two would then not be harmonized. One solution would be to concentrate monetary and fiscal policies entirely on targeting the exchange rate. If governments were prepared to accept large interest rate fluctuations, it might be possible to keep the exchange rate reasonably stable. But this is little more than a return to fixed exchange rates, with a resulting total constraint over domestic policies!

Total harmonization may not be possible. Nevertheless most governments favour some movement in that direction: some is better than none.

> 1. What practical problems would there be in achieving a general harmonization of economic policies?
> 2. Would harmonization be in the interests of *all* countries?

Greater exchange rate rigidity between specific currencies: the EMS

One means of achieving greater currency stability is for countries to group together into blocs, and to peg their exchange rates to each other, whilst floating against the rest of the world. This will have two main advantages:

- Trade will be encouraged between the members of the bloc. The greater the harmonization of policies within the bloc, and therefore the less frequent any adjustments of the pegged rates, the more will trade be encouraged.
- The combined reserves of all countries in the bloc can be used to prevent excessive fluctuations of the bloc's currencies with the rest of the world.

One such bloc is the *exchange rate mechanism* (ERM) of the *European Monetary System* (EMS). Although the UK was a formal member of the EMS ever since it was formed in 1979, it was reluctant to join its fellow European Community partners in the exchange rate mechanism. Until Greece and then Spain and Portugal joined the EC, the UK was alone in staying outside the exchange rate mechanism. Spain joined the mechanism in 1989. The UK eventually joined in 1990. From the outset, all members of the EMS participated in lending central bank support to each other's currencies, but only the members of the exchange rate mechanism pegged their rates to each other (jointly floating against other currencies).

How successful has the EMS been in creating stability and trade? Was the UK right to stay outside the exchange rate mechanism for so long? Should similar blocs be created in other parts of the world?

The features of the EMS exchange rate mechanism

Members' currencies are denominated in ECUs (European Currency Units). The ECU is a unit of account valued in terms of a combination (or 'basket') of EMS currencies, including sterling. Each currency has a different weight in the ECU, depending on the size of the country and the importance of its currency in foreign exchange markets. For example, the pound has a weight of nearly 14 per cent, the D-Mark a weight of just over 32 per cent and the Luxembourg franc a weight of 0.3 per cent. Currencies' fluctuations are limited to 2.25 per cent either side of any other ERM currency (6 per cent in the case of the UK and Spain until they felt ready to adopt the ± 2.25 band). Central banks must intervene once these limits are reached. Members must deposit 20 per cent of their dollar and gold reserves with the European Monetary Co-operative Fund (EMCF). In return the EMCF provides credit facilities to support the agreed exchange rate between members.

Box 22.10

Currency Realignment in the EMS
Harmony means stability

The exchange rate mechanism of the European Monetary System (EMS) by pegging the exchange rates of the member countries to the European Currency Unit (ECU), and thereby to each other, should encourage trade between the member countries.

Unless the member countries' inflation rates, growth rates and interest rates are in harmony, however, the pegged rates may become disequilibrium rates. To correct for this, realignments have been necessary from time to time. But as the table shows, these realignments have tended to become smaller and less frequent in recent years as the economies of the EMS have become more in tune with each other.

The currency stability of the members of the exchange rate mechanism is further highlighted by tracing the path of the pound and the German mark against the European Currency Unit. The stability of the D-Mark is shown by its relatively smooth trend. This is in marked contrast to the volatility of the pound, which during the period shown was outside the exchange rate mechanism.

The consequences of this for international trade are highly significant. The volatility of sterling put UK exporters at a considerable disadvantage in a highly competitive European and world market.

European currency values against the ECU:
1979–85 (1979 = 100)

Source: G. Dennis, 'The European Monetary System', *The Economic Review*, November 1986.

? If membership of the exchange rate mechanism of the EMS brings the advantages of currency stability, why did the UK resist joining for so long?

Currency realignments in the EMS

	Dates of realignments										
	4/9 1979	30/11 1979	22/3 1981	5/10 1981	22/2 1982	14/6 1982	21/3 1983	21/7 1985	7/4 1986	4/8 1986	12/1 1987
Belgian franc	0.0	0.0	0.0	0.0	−8.5	0.0	+1.5	+2.0	+1.0	0.0	+2.0
Danish kroner	−2.9	−4.8	0.0	0.0	−3.0	0.0	+2.5	+2.0	+1.0	0.0	0.0
German mark	+2.0	0.0	0.0	+5.5	0.0	+4.25	+5.5	+2.0	+3.0	0.0	+3.0
French franc	0.0	0.0	0.0	−3.0	0.0	−5.75	−2.5	+2.0	−3.0	0.0	0.0
Irish punt	0.0	0.0	0.0	0.0	0.0	0.0	−3.5	+2.0	0.0	−8.0	0.0
Italian lira	0.0	0.0	−6.0	−3.0	0.0	−2.75	−2.5	−6.0	0.0	0.0	0.0
Dutch guilder	0.0	0.0	0.0	+5.5	0.0	+4.25	+3.5	+2.0	+3.0	0.0	+3.0

Source: 'What has the European Monetary System Achieved?', *Bank of England Discussion Paper*, no. 31.

There is also an agreement whereby, if a country's exchange rate diverges by more than three-quarters of the 2.25 per cent of its central rate, all the EMS members will meet to consider whether a *realignment* is necessary and what internal policies ought to be adopted by the divergent country.

How successful has the EMS been?

In a system of pegged exchange rates, it would be ideal if countries harmonized their policies to avoid excessive currency misalignments and the need therefore for large devaluations or revaluations. For a time there was only limited success here. In the early 1980s French and Italian inflation rates were persistently higher than German rates. As a result there had to be several realignments, and these countries had to pursue tough deflationary policies.

Realignments were therefore relatively frequent at first – approximately two per year. This was frequent enough to prevent severe balance of payments disequilibria from building up, and thus helped to reduce speculation. It was also frequent enough to allow the realignments to be relatively small (often involving only one or two currencies), and yet still be sufficient to prevent countries from experiencing a significant gain or loss in competitiveness as a result of different rates of inflation.

Central bank intervention has reduced speculation and thus reduced short-run exchange rate volatility. Realignments have reflected differences in countries' underlying economic conditions, rather than speculative pressures. Certainly compared with the dollar, pound and yen, the EMS currencies have been extremely stable, not only relative to each other, but also relative to the average of all other currencies.

After 1987 realignments became unnecessary. This was due to a growing convergence of members' internal policies. Rather than setting independent monetary targets (with the resulting interest rate and exchange rate volatility), France, Italy and the other members increasingly adopted exchange rate stability as their major monetary goal. This disciplined them into adopting the lower inflation rates experienced in Germany, especially as it was the D-Mark exchange rate with their currencies that had become the effective target.

 Under what circumstances may a currency bloc like the EMS (a) help to prevent speculation; (b) aggravate the problem of speculation?

The UK and the ERM

Both politicians and academics were generally against the UK joining the ERM in 1979:

- The UK had a higher 'endemic' inflation rate than the EMS countries (except Italy). This would soon cause a misalignment under fixed rates.
- The UK is an oil exporter whereas the EMS countries are oil importers. Changes in oil prices would thus cause misalignment. There were high international oil prices at the time, and sterling was seen as a 'petrocurrency'.
- The UK's medium-term financial strategy involved setting monetary targets. This necessarily involved allowing interest rates to fluctuate as necessary to keep within these targets. Interest rate fluctuations would have caused balance of payments disequilibria under a fixed exchange rate.

By the late 1980s, however, opinion had changed:

- There was general agreement that exchange rate volatility is undesirable.
- The UK inflation rate had come down and was similar to the European average (although by the end of the 1980s it had risen above the European average again).
- Oil prices had fallen, and oil was no longer such an important element in the UK's balance of payments.
- Targeting money supply had been abandoned.

From early 1987, UK monetary policy became more geared towards keeping the exchange rate with the D-Mark within a relatively narrow band. The UK became a sort of 'shadow' member of the ERM. The Bank of England tried to keep the exchange rate at around £1 = DM3.00 (see Box 22.7). By early 1988, however, the higher interest rates in the UK than in Europe, a relatively weak D-Mark, and the still

Box 22.11

Britain's entry to the ERM
The start of a long haul

The following is an extract from an article by Martin Wolf in the *Financial Times* of Monday 8 October 1990, the day the UK entered the exchange rate mechanism of the EMS.

> The political reasons for the Chancellor of the Exchequer's decision to put sterling into the exchange rate mechanism of the European Monetary System last Friday are transparent: about two-thirds of UK housing is in owner-occupation, while just 20 per cent of the labour force is employed in manufacturing and at most 40 per cent in sectors subject to some degree of international competition. Any policy that promises both lower interest rates and inflation, combined with a squeeze on jobs and profits in less than half of the economy, looks like the answer to a hard pressed government's prayers.
>
> None the less, over the long haul the destination is the same as that of domestic monetarism. If the exchange rate is fixed, inflation must converge upon that in the anchor country. The Bundesbank's target inflation rate for Germany is about 2 per cent, which is a little below the country's average over the 1980s. It is possible that German unification will raise this average more than merely temporarily. It would be unwise to assume it.
>
> The UK must now adopt the policy described by the French as 'competitive disinflation'. Over the 1980s unit labour costs in German manufacturing rose at 1½ per cent a year. In the UK productivity growth in manufacturing
>
> seems to have been some 4½ per cent a year. If that high rate could be sustained (itself unlikely) then wage costs per hour in British manufacturing must ultimately rise by not more than 6 per cent a year, if the exchange rate target is to be combined with steady growth. 'Competitive disinflation' would demand wage inflation of 4–5 per cent a year, less than half of today's rate.
>
> When the countryman was asked how to get to Dublin, he replied that the traveller would have done better not to start from where he was. The UK, too, would have done better to start somewhere else. But it has no choice. The period (and the pain) of adjustment must now be as long (and as great) as is required to get from here to there, with 'there' defined as steady growth at the UK's underlying rate of 2.5–3 per cent a year, combined with wage inflation running at, or below, 5 per cent a year.
>
> 'There' can also be defined more broadly. One central difference between Germany and the UK is the way in which a liberalised UK financial system has generated credit growth during the 1980s. Between 1985 and July 1989 the respective increases in broad money – mainly cash and bank and building society deposits – in Germany and the UK were 37 per cent and 126 per cent, in spite of higher interest rates in the UK. Such differential growth in relative money supplies would normally preclude fixed exchange rates.

relatively low rate of inflation in the UK meant that there was considerable buying of sterling. To keep the exchange rate from shooting up, the government had to sell large amounts of sterling and hence build up the reserves. More particularly, Nigel Lawson, the Chancellor, felt obliged (against the advice of Margaret Thatcher) to reduce interest rates.

 Why could interest rates not be used as a weapon both to control inflation and to maintain a stable exchange rate?

But within a few months the problem was reversed. With low interest rates and easy credit, the UK was experiencing a large consumer boom. As imports poured into the country and the current account plummeted, so the government had to raise interest rates again, both to curb inflation and this time to prevent the pound from falling.

Critics of the UK joining the ERM argued that, if the D-Mark had never been shadowed and interest rates maintained so low, the subsequent excessive reflation could have been avoided.

The main argument against UK membership of the ERM was that it would involve a loss of independence in monetary policy: interest rates would be tied to those of the other EMS countries (see Box 22.11). In reply it was pointed out that with an absence of exchange controls, the pursuit of an independent interest rate policy even outside the ERM had become virtually impossible. Any change in German interest rates forced Britain to make similar changes if massive capital flows and resulting large swings in exchange rates were to be avoided.

By 1990 the government was committed to the UK joining the ERM. The last obstacle was the UK's high rate of inflation compared with the other ERM members. By the Autumn, however, inflation appeared to have peaked and, with intense political pressure (from both inside and outside the Conservative party), John Major, who was then the Chancellor, announced that the UK was joining the ERM at a central parity of DM2.95 and would adopt the broad ± 6% band for fluctuation against other ERM currencies.

But even though inflation was now falling, it was still substantially above the EC average. So what, under these conditions, was the effect of using interest rates to maintain the exchange rate within the fixed band?

As Box 22.11 illustrated, the fear expressed at the time of entry was that interest rates would be pushed downwards towards the level of other member countries. This would mean that the only effective control against inflation would be the exchange rate. If UK exports were to be competitive, unit labour cost and other cost increases in the export sector would have to be brought down to the EC average. Only that way could bankruptcies and unemployment in the export sector be avoided. But this would then place a heavy burden on the export sector, a discipline not shared by large parts of the service sector, which did not face international competition.

As it turned out, the economy moved sharply into recession and inflation fell rapidly. There were thus calls from industry for cuts in interest rates to arrest the decline in aggregate demand. But too rapidly falling interest rates would push the pound towards the bottom of the band. The effect was that the Chancellor, Norman Lamont, felt unable to make substantial cuts in interest rates, with the result that the economy continued to plunge into recession.

An exchange rate rule had replaced monetary discretion.

> **?** Does ERM membership strengthen the argument for a prices and incomes policy for members with higher than average inflation?

European monetary union (EMU)

> The foreign exchange markets were thrown into confusion yesterday when Nottingham's Chancellor of the Exchequer (Socialist, Mr R. Hood) announced an emergency package of measures to bolster his town's currency: a 10 per cent devaluation of the Nottingham pound; a 2 per cent rise in Nottingham interest rates, measures to reduce Nottingham's PSBR; and other measures to restrain the excessive growth of credit in the county. Commenting on the measures, Nottingham's Shadow Chancellor (the Revd F. Tuck) claimed that this demonstrated the total failure of Nottingham's medium-term financial strategy, and was a capitulation to the speculators of London and Derbyshire who had been selling Nottingham pounds and buying London dollars and Surrey crowns on a massive scale because of Nottingham's balance of payments deficit. This means that Nottingham will not now be joining the British Monetary System.[4]

Nottingham as an independent economy, with its own Chancellor, its own currency and its own central bank! It sounds ridiculous. But perhaps in the year 2000 the idea of an independent UK with *its* own economic policy, *its* own currency and *its* own central bank will seem equally ridiculous.

Chapter 21 looked at the Single European Act and the removal of trade barriers in the EC after 1992. But many of the advocates of a single market, including President

[4] D. Llewellyn, 'Monetary Union in Europe', *Banking World*, November 1988, p. 30.

Box 22.12

The Effects of Removing Capital Controls in the EMS

A problem for high-inflation members?

Back in 1979 when the exchange rate mechanism of the EMS was set up, the international movement of capital was tightly controlled in all member countries except West Germany and Holland. The effect of these capital controls was to allow member countries to pursue relatively independent economic policies. They could, for example, have lower interest rates than the other members provided they could prevent the outflow of capital.

Controls were seen as important as long as inflation rates differed across the EMS. First of all, it would be necessary for countries with high inflation rates to have higher domestic interest rates if they were to reduce the growth in their money supply and get inflation under control. If there was to be no realignment, then without controls the higher interest rates would encourage a massive inflow of capital which would make control of the money supply difficult.

Secondly, with different inflation rates it would be difficult to avoid realignments indefinitely without substantial current account problems. Without controls, the possibility of a realignment would probably cause large speculation and a large change in interest rates to counteract it.

As the 1980s progressed, however, most of these capital controls were lifted, and by 1990 they were virtually all gone. Did this mean that speculative flows increased? Did it mean that realignments would have to be more frequent?

As it turned out there was no need for realignments!

There were two reasons for this:

- With the *possibility* of speculative movements having increased, the EMS governments became even more committed to maintaining existing parities. As markets became convinced of this, the degree of speculation tended to decline, and with it the need for governments to counter it with interest rate changes.
- There was a growing convergence of the EMS economies, with a considerable narrowing of the differences in members' inflation rates.

Nevertheless convergence was not complete. Italy, for example, continued to have inflation rates above the EMS average. With controls having disappeared, this posed Italy a dilemma. Either it kept its interest rates above those in the rest of the EMS with a resulting large inflow of capital, or it kept its interest rates down with a resulting rise in aggregate demand. Either way it would be difficult to bring inflation down. If a realignment was ruled out, the competitiveness of Italian goods would gradually decline and the current account would go deeper into deficit. But at least this would put some downward pressure on wages and other costs.

? Did an absence of capital controls make UK entry to the ERM more problematic, given that the UK's inflation rate was higher than the EMS average.

---

of the European Commission, Jacques Delors, argue for much more. The EC's Delors report of 1989 advocated a complete European Monetary Union (EMU). This would involve the complete economic and financial integration of the EC countries: a United States of Europe. This European Monetary Union would be like the current 'British Monetary Union': the economic union of England, Scotland, Wales and Northern Ireland.

Under the Delors plan, EMU would be achieved in three stages. The first stage would be the completion of the single European market with free trade and free capital and labour movements. The next stage would involve the harmonization of monetary policy across the Community with moves towards a European central bank. The third stage would involve the creation of a single European currency – a European currency union.

The Delors plan has widespread support throughout the Community among both governments and opposition parties. A single European currency is seen to bring two major advantages. The first is that it would eliminate the costs of converting

Currency union

A group of countries (or regions) using a common currency.

currencies. With separate currencies in each of the EC countries, these transaction costs can be very large, especially when the various parts of a good are made in several different countries. With the encouragement of trade and factor movements that the single market will bring, these transaction costs are likely to rise as long as separate currencies remain. The second advantage of a single currency is that it removes all problems of uncertainty about exchange rates, interest rates and inflation rates. Even with the ERM, realignments may still occur from time to time if separate currencies remain.

Monetary union was bitterly opposed, however, by Margaret Thatcher and others, who see within it a surrender of UK political and economic sovereignty. This is a serious problem, they argue, if the UK economy is at all out of harmony with the rest of the Community. For example, if UK has a higher endemic rate of inflation (due, say, to greater cost-push pressures – perhaps caused by a lower growth in productivity than in Europe), then how is it to make its goods competitive with the rest of the Community? With separate currencies it can devalue or run a deflationary monetary policy. With a single currency it could become a depressed 'region' of Europe, with all the problems of depressed regions *within* a country. This may then require significant regional policies – policies which might not be in place (or, if they were, which might be seen as too interventionist by the political right).

In 1990, John Major, put forward an alternative to the Delors proposal for a single EC currency. This was for a 'hard ECU'. The idea was that the ECU would be a separate currency acceptable throughout the EC that would be used in *addition* to existing currencies. It would effectively only replace existing currencies for inter-EC and international trade. The other eleven EC countries, however, were generally unimpressed with this proposal, seeing it as little more than a blocking move to the establishment of a genuine common currency.

> **[?]** By what means would a depressed country in an economic union with a single currency be able to recover? Would the market provide a satisfactory solution to its problems or would (Union) government intervention be necessary? If so, what form could that intervention take?

▲ SUMMARY

1. Currency fluctuations can be lessened if countries harmonize their economic policies. Ideally this will involve achieving common interest rates, growth rates and inflation rates. The attempt to harmonize one of these goals, however, may bring conflicts with one of the other goals.

2. One means of achieving greater currency stability is for a group of countries to peg their internal exchange rates and yet float jointly with the rest of the world. The exchange rate mechanism of the European Monetary System is an example. Members' currencies are pegged to the European Currency Unit, but may be realigned if necessary. The need for realignments has diminished in recent years as the economies of the EMS have converged.

3. The ERM is seen as an important first stage on the road to complete European monetary union. The aim of most of the EC countries is for an eventual currency union: a single European currency with a common monetary policy operated by an independent European central bank. This would have the advantage of eliminating the costs of converting currencies and the uncertainties associated with possible changes in inter-EC exchange rates. It might make adjustment to domestic economic problems more difficult, however, with certain countries becoming depressed 'regions' of the EC.

Economic Development in the Third World

23.1 The problem of underdevelopment

In this final chapter we turn to the economic problems of the poorer countries of the world. These include all the countries of Africa and Latin America and most of the countries of Asia. More than three-quarters of the world's population lives in these countries. As Theodore Schultz said when accepting the Nobel prize in economics in 1979:

> Most of the people of the world are poor, so if we knew the economics of being poor we would know much of the economics that really matters.

This first section looks at the nature and extent of their poverty and the means by which it can be measured. Section 23.2 examines the trade relations between the poorer countries and the advanced industrialized world. In section 23.3 the focus shifts to some of the internal problems faced by developing countries: problems such as the neglect of agriculture, the use of inappropriate technology and the rise in unemployment. The final section looks at one of the most serious problems facing poorer countries: the problem of huge international debts.

The gulf between rich and poor countries

The typical family in North America, Western Europe, Japan and Australasia has many material comforts: plentiful food to eat; a house or apartment with electricity, running hot and cold water and probably central heating; an inside toilet connected to an underground sewerage system; access to free or affordable health care and education; numerous consumer durables such as a car, washing machine, vacuum cleaner, television and stereo system; holidays away from home; visits to the cinema, concerts, sports events, etc. These and many other features of life in the affluent countries are taken for granted by many of their citizens. There are some people, it is true, who are very poor. A minority cannot afford even the basics of life, such as adequate food, shelter and clothing. For most people, however, such poverty is something they never experience and perhaps only rarely witness.

In most of Africa, Asia and Latin America the picture is quite different. The majority of people live in poverty. For them life is a daily struggle for survival. Affluence does exist in these countries, but here it is the fortunate few who can afford good food, good housing and the various luxury items that typify life in the industrialized world.

A large proportion of the inhabitants live in the countryside. For many in Latin America and Asia, this means living in a family with many children and working on a small amount of land with too little income to buy adequate agricultural machinery, fertilizers or pesticides. With a rapid growth in population there is less and less land to go round. As land is passed on from generation to generation it is divided up between the offspring into smaller and smaller plots. Many who cannot make ends meet are forced to sell their land to the local landlords. Then as landless labourers they have to accept very low-paid jobs on the large farms or plantations. Others try to survive by borrowing, hoping to be able to pay off their debts with future crop sales. But often the only source of finance is again the local landlord who charges exorbitant rates of interest. As a result they end up in a state of 'debt bondage' where they can never pay off their debts but year in year out have to give part of their crops to the landlord as interest.

Others come to the rapidly growing cities. There at least there are some jobs. But far more people migrate to the cities than there are jobs available. Thus the number of unemployed in the cities grows inexorably. People are forced to do anything to earn a living: selling wares on street corners, or working as casual labourers, domestic servants or shoe shiners; some resort to prostitution and crime, others merely beg. All round the outskirts of cities throughout the Third World, shanty towns mushroom as the poor flock in from the countryside. Families crowd into one- or two-roomed shacks, often with no electricity, no water and no sanitation. There are schools in these towns, but often parents cannot afford to allow their children to attend. Instead they have to send them out to work to supplement the family's meagre income.

Statistics cannot give the complete picture, but they can give us some indication of

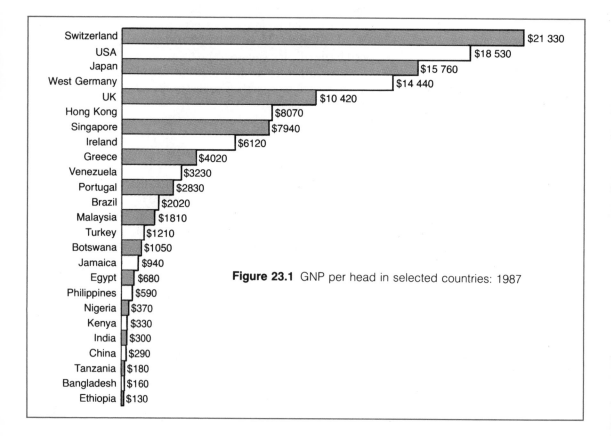

Figure 23.1 GNP per head in selected countries: 1987

Country	GNP per head
Switzerland	$21 330
USA	$18 530
Japan	$15 760
West Germany	$14 440
UK	$10 420
Hong Kong	$8070
Singapore	$7940
Ireland	$6120
Greece	$4020
Venezuela	$3230
Portugal	$2830
Brazil	$2020
Malaysia	$1810
Turkey	$1210
Botswana	$1050
Jamaica	$940
Egypt	$680
Philippines	$590
Nigeria	$370
Kenya	$330
India	$300
China	$290
Tanzania	$180
Bangladesh	$160
Ethiopia	$130

the gulf between rich and poor countries. Here are some examples:

- Over 75 per cent of the world's population lives in developing countries but earns only about 20 per cent of the world's income.
- The GNP per head of the 42 poorest countries of the world in 1987 averaged only $290. For the richest 25 it was $14 430. For the UK it was $10 420, for West Germany it was $14 400, for Japan it was $15 760, for the USA it was $18 530 and for Switzerland, at the top of the list, it was $21 330 (see Figure 23.1).
- The average annual GNP-per-capita growth rate between 1965 and 1987 was 5.1 per cent in East Asia but only 0.6 per cent in Sub-Saharan Africa. It was 2.3 per cent in the advanced industrialized countries.
- The average life expectancy at birth in the 10 poorest countries of the world is 49 years. It is 76 years in the 10 richest countries.
- Developing countries suffer higher rates of inflation than advanced industrial economies. Upper-middle-income developing countries have higher rates than lower-middle-income countries, which in turn have higher rates than low-income countries. Between 1980 and 1987 the average annual rate of inflation was 601.8 per cent in Bolivia, 298.7 per cent in Argentina, 166.3 per cent in Brazil and 101.5 per cent in Peru. In Latin America and the Caribbean as a whole it averaged 109.1 per cent. By contrast, it averaged 5.4 per cent in East Asia and 5.2 per cent in the advanced industrialized countries.

Table 23.1 gives more details.

Table 23.1 Selected world statistics

	Low-income economies[1]	(Sub-Saharan Africa)	Lower-middle-income economies[2]	Upper-middle income economies[3]	High-income economies[4]	All countries
Population (millions)	2823	442	610	432	777	4638
GNP per capita ($ per annum)	290	330	1200	2710	14430	3010
Population growth (average annual % 1980–87)	2.0	3.1	2.2 (middle income)		0.7	1.8
Growth in GNP per capita (average annual % 1965–87)	3.1	0.6	2.2	2.9	2.3	1.5
Growth in GNP per capita (average annual % 1980–85)	3.9	−3.7	−0.3 (middle income)		1.5	0.6
Inflation (average annual % 1980–87)	13.3	15.2	36.7	86.8	5.2	13.7
Life expectancy at birth (years)	61	51	64	67	76	65
Number of people per doctor (1984)	5410	23760	3330	1170	470	3930
Infant mortality per 1000 live births (1980)	76	115	61	50	10	60
Percentage of age group enrolled in secondary eductaion (1986)	35	16	51	59	92	50
Urban population as a percentage of total population (1987)	30	27	51	66	77	44

[1] Those countries with a GNP per head in 1987 of below $500.
[2] Those countries with a GNP per head in 1987 of between $500 and $2000.
[3] Those countries with a GNP per head in 1987 of between $2000 and $6000.
[4] Those countries with a GNP per head in 1987 of over $6000.

Source: *World Development Report 1989* (World Bank).

Box 23.1

Dimensions of Poverty
Differences between developing countries

There are many differences between developing countries. These differences make it difficult to isolate a simple set of causes of poverty and a simple set of policy solutions that can apply to *all* developing countries at all times. We have already seen that developing countries differ markedly from one another in terms of per-capita GNP. They also differ in the following ways.

Size
Some developing countries are very large. China, the biggest, has a population of 1100 million and an area of 9.6 million square kilometres. India has a population of 800 million and an area of 3.3 million square kilometres. With a large home market and probably a wide range of raw materials and industries, such countries are less likely to be so reliant on international trade. They may, however, be more difficult to administer. By contrast, other developing countries have tiny populations. Fifty-four have populations of less than 1 million. Many of these are also tiny in area, especially island countries such as those in the Caribbean. But some countries that are large in area also have very small populations: for example, the Saharan country of Mauritania has a population of only 1.9 million.

Resources and climate
Some countries are richly endowed with raw materials and have fertile lands and a favourable climate. Clearly these countries have an enormous advantage over those which are poorly endowed.

Infrastructure
If a country has good roads and communications, a developed financial and distributional system, an efficient administrative system and a developed and universal system of education, it will be able to take much better advantage of economic opportunities. Some of the least developed countries have a very poor infrastructure. In much of tropical Africa, for example, roads are little more than dust tracks that are full of holes and become virtually impassable in the rainy season. There is a joke in Africa that if you see a car driving in a straight line the driver must be drunk! As Julius Nyerere, the former President of Tanzania, once remarked, 'Man has now succeeded in reaching the moon, but we are still trying to reach the village.' The worse a country's infrastructure, the bigger a handicap it faces in trying to develop.

Cultural and social factors
People's outlook, adaptability and attitude towards work will affect the speed of economic development. These attitudes will depend on social, cultural and religious factors and the changes people have already experienced.

Many of these attitudes will have been affected by their historical links with developed countries. Most developing countries were at some time colonies of Western European countries, and as such have inherited some of the institutions, values and social patterns of these colonial countries. For example, the educational system in many countries is modelled on that in the colonial country.

Degree of industrialization and urbanization
The middle-income countries tend to have a higher degree of industrialization and urbanization than the low-income countries. In many African countries over 80 per cent of the labour force are engaged in agriculture, whereas in some Latin American countries the figure is less than 40 per cent.

Relations with the developed world
A very large proportion of the national income of some developing countries, particularly the smaller ones, is earned from exports, and they are heavily dependent on imports to provide essential raw materials and capital equipment as well as consumer goods. Others, such as China and India, are much more self-sufficient. This is due partly to their sheer size, but partly to deliberate policies of discouraging reliance on international trade. To the extent that trade brings advantages and disadvantages the experiences of 'outward-looking' and 'inward-looking' countries will be very different.

There are other ways in which relations with the developed world will differ from one developing country to another. Some are heavily reliant on the importation of foreign technology; others are less so. Some openly encourage multinational companies to set up plants in their countries; others try and prevent or at least limit the process. Some welcome military 'support' from the USA or USSR; others shun it. Some receive significant economic aid from developed countries; others receive virtually none.

Political structure
Some developing countries are democracies; some are dictatorships. Some are capitalist; some are socialist. Some engage in national economic planning; others rely on the market. Some have a large public sector; in some it is relatively small. Most importantly for economic development, some developing countries have governments and institutions that are adaptable and willing to adopt the changes necessary to transform their economies; others have powerful interest groups (like large landowners or the military) who see change as a threat to their privileged positions.

The meaning of 'development'

Countries want to develop. But just what do we mean by 'development'? The simplest definition of the level of development is the level of human welfare. The *rate* of development then becomes the rate of increase in welfare. But this definition does not take us very far because we then have to ask what is meant by 'welfare'.

Development is thus clearly a normative concept. Its definition will depend on the goals that the economist assumes societies want to achieve. So how do economists define and measure development?

The basic needs approach

A starting point is to identify the basic needs that people have if they are to be able to realize their potential as human beings. Different economists have identified various lists of requirements, including the following items:

- Adequate food, shelter, warmth and clothing.
- Universal access to education.
- Availability of adequate health care.
- Availability of non-demeaning jobs.
- Sufficient free time to be able to enjoy social interaction.
- Freedom to make one's own economic decisions.
- Freedom for people to participate in the decisions of government and other bodies that affect their lives.

? What other items might be included as basic needs?

There are four major problems with defining development in terms of a basic list of requirements.

The first is in deciding *what to include*. Any definition of *economic* development would clearly include people's *material* standard of living. But how wide should the concept of development be? Should it include social and political factors? Should it include items such as 'self-esteem', freedom from servitude, freedom to choose one's social relations, religion, lifestyle, place of abode and traditions?

The second problem is in *measuring each of the items*. Purely economic indicators, while only providing part of the picture of human welfare, are relatively easy to measure. It is possible to measure such things as income per head, literacy rates, mortality rates, the number of doctors and nurses per head, and calorific and protein intakes per head; and in each it is possible to measure their distribution. The main measurement problem with these economic indicators is in acquiring the statistics. It is much more difficult, however, to measure the achievement of social and political objectives such as self-esteem.

The third problem is in arriving at a *single measure* of the level of development. Even if you can measure each of the items unambiguously, you cannot simply add all the items together. You cannot add the average calorific intake to the number of doctors and nurses to the percentage of homes having various basic amenities such as running water. Each of the items is measured in different units. You can only meaningfully add things up if they are expressed in the same units, or if appropriate *weights* are attached to each of the items. To attach weights, however, requires agreement on the relative importance of each of the goals: e.g. how much extra food is equivalent to an extra nurse, or how many extra homes with running water are equivalent to a life saved. Clearly the assigning of any such weights would be highly controversial.

The fourth problem is in deciding the importance of the *distribution* of the various items. If, say, the average calorific intake increases or the average mortality rate decreases, but the poorest sections of the population have less to eat and suffer an increase in the level of poverty-related deaths, can the country really be said to have experienced an increase in the level of development?

But despite these problems, many economists have argued that the basic needs approach does provide a useful 'checklist' to see whether a country's so-called development is broadly based or merely confined to just one or two indicators. The more indicators that are improving and the more rapidly they are doing so, the more justification there is in saying that development is taking place.

Would it be possible with this basic needs approach to say (a) that one country was more developed than another; (b) that one country was developing faster than another?

Using GNP to measure development

The desire to have a single measure for development and thus to be able to make simple comparisons between countries has led to the universal use of real GNP per capita as the main indicator. It has some major advantages:

- It takes into account virtually all the goods and services produced in a country, and converts them into a single measure by the use of market prices.
- Although markets are by no means perfect, they do at least reflect the strength of demand and the opportunity costs of supply.
- The rules for the measurement of GNP are universally agreed.
- Virtually all countries compile GNP statistics for inclusion in United Nations, World Bank and IMF official statistics.
- Although not every item that affects human welfare is included in GNP, a sustained rise in GNP is generally agreed to be a *necessary* condition for a sustained rise in welfare.

What is the difference between saying that a rise in GNP is a *necessary* condition for an increase in human welfare and saying that it is a *sufficient* condition?

- There is a fairly close correlation between the level of per-capita GNP and other indicators such as mortality rates, literacy rates, and calorific and protein intake. As a result, when economists have devised alternative composite measures to GNP (hoping to come up with a superior measure), they have tended not to lead to a significant difference in the rank order of countries' levels of development.

Nevertheless the use of GNP to measure development has come in for a lot of criticism. After all, GNP measures *output*, and output is not the sole contributor to human happiness. Growth in output is not the same as development. It may not be possible to have sustained development *without* growth, but could a country really be said to be developing if GNP is rising as a result of the rich élites getting a lot richer while the poor are getting poorer?

There are four fundamental criticisms of relying on simple GNP per capita as an indicator of development.

Many items are excluded. Much of production that does not get bought and sold will escape being recorded. This is a particular problem with rural societies which are largely subsistence based. People grow their own food, build their own houses, make their own clothes and provide their own entertainment. GNP statistics are therefore likely to *understate* the level of production in these societies. On the other hand, as these societies 'develop', the size of the market sector is likely to grow. With farmers moving over to the production of cash crops for sale, and with the expansion of towns, a larger and larger proportion of people's consumption will be of items they have purchased and which therefore *do* enter into GNP statistics. Thus GNP figures will *overstate* the rate of *growth* of production and consumption.

As an economy becomes more urbanized there is likely to be a growth in *external* costs of production and consumption, such as pollution and crime. Again, the GNP statistics are likely to *overstate* the *rate* of development.

As we have seen, there are non-economic factors that affect welfare. These will be excluded from GNP. Generally these non-economic factors are likely to be negative. Economic growth involves change. Traditional ways of life will be destroyed; people may find themselves increasingly in a competitive, uncaring environment; aspirations will be raised by observing the lifestyles of the rich few, and yet the poor will not have the means of satisfying these aspirations. Again, therefore, the growth in GNP is likely to *overstate* the growth in human welfare.

Market prices may be highly distorted. GNP is based on market prices, but these prices may be distorted for a number of reasons. Markets are often highly fragmented, and there is little competition to ensure that prices reflect undistorted marginal costs. Companies often have considerable monopoly power to push up prices of manufactured goods; landlords often have power to push up rents; moneylenders often have the power to charge high interest rates to people in financial difficulty. At the same time governments may impose price controls on food; employers with monopsony power may be able to pay very low wages; foreign companies may have the power to drive down the price of local raw materials and other inputs.

? How would a redistribution of income to the powerful be likely to affect GNP?

Exchange rates may not reflect local purchasing power. GNP statistics are initially compiled in terms of the domestic currency. For purposes of international comparison they then have to be converted into a common currency – usually the US dollar – at the current exchange rate. But exchange rates reflect demand and supply of *traded* goods; they do not reflect the prices of *non-traded* goods. Generally the price of non-traded goods and services in developing countries will be lower (at current exchange rates) than the price of similar goods and services in advanced countries. The *level* of GNP is therefore likely to *understate* the level of production in poor countries compared to advanced countries. If, on the other hand, the proportion of traded goods increases over time, the *growth* of GNP will again *overstate* the growth in production.

The general conclusion from each of these three criticisms that we have examined is that GNP figures for developing countries underestimate the true level of production and welfare. The daily GNP per head in the poorest countries is only about $1. Although they live in grave poverty, people do survive on these incomes. It would be impossible, however, to survive in the USA or other advanced countries on $1 a day. On the other hand, the growth in GNP in developing countries is likely to be an overestimate of the growth in production and welfare.

Simple GNP per head ignores the distribution of income. During the 1980s, faced with a mounting burden of debt and the need to expand their exports, many developing countries achieved relatively rapid growth in per-capita GNP as they sought overseas investment, privatized their industries and cut the levels of public provision. But with a deepening of poverty, a growing inequality in the distribution of income and an increase in unemployment, few would argue that this constituted genuine 'development'.

Many who have advocated the concentration on GNP and its rate of growth have argued that the rich may be the first to benefit from prosperity, but that gradually the benefits will 'trickle down' to the poor. In practice the wealth has failed to trickle down in many countries. The rich have got richer while the poor have got poorer.

▲ SUMMARY

1. There are a number of ways of categorizing countries according to their level of development. A simple division is between richer and poorer countries. The poorer countries are given various labels such as 'developing', 'less developed', 'Third World', 'underdeveloped' or 'emerging' countries.
2. Developing countries vary enormously one from another in terms of size, resources and climate, infrastructure, cultural and social factors, degree of industrialization and urbanization, relations with the developed world and political structure.
3. The level of development of a country can be defined in terms of the extent to which it meets basic needs for human life. There is no universal agreement, however, about which items should be measured or about how to measure and weight them. Nevertheless the approach

provides a useful indicator of whether development is broadly based and how rapidly the most serious problems of poverty are being tackled.

4. The most widely used measure of development is GNP. Nevertheless there are serious problems with using GNP: many items may be excluded, especially for a more subsistence-based society; prices may be highly distorted; exchange rates may not reflect local purchasing power; and the statistics ignore the question of the distribution of income. Nevertheless there is no other single measure of development that is used in all countries, and it does provide some guide, albeit an imperfect one, to relative levels of development in different countries and over different periods of time. Clearly the statistics have to be expressed in terms of *real per-capita* income.

23.2 International trade and development

The importance of international trade to developing countries

The role of international trade is one of the most contentious in development economics. Should countries adopt an open trading policy with few if any barriers to imports? Should governments go further and actively promote trade by subsidizing their export sector? Or should governments restrict trade and pursue a policy of greater self-sufficiency? These are issues we will be looking at in this section.

Whether it is desirable that developing countries should adopt policies of more trade or less trade, trade is still of vital importance. Certain raw materials, capital equipment and intermediate products that are necessary for development can only be obtained from abroad. Others *could* be produced domestically, but only at much higher cost. In some cases it might be possible for a country to develop without trade. China under Mao, from the revolution in 1947 to his death in 1976, followed a policy of virtually no trade with the outside world. But such cases are exceptions. Certainly for smaller countries, with small domestic markets and a lack of resources, an absence of trade would greatly hinder development. Thus for most policy makers it is a question not of free trade versus no trade, but rather of more trade versus less trade.

As countries' economies grow, the proportion of trade to national income tends to rise. This is illustrated in Table 23.2, which shows exports for various countries as a proportion of GDP for the two years 1965 and 1985. Three general points emerge from these data: smaller countries have a larger proportion of exports to GDP than large ones; exports form a smaller proportion of GDP in poorer countries than in richer countries; exports formed a higher proportion of GDP in 1985 than they did in 1965.

 What exceptions are there in the table to any of these three general points? What explanation can you give?

Table 23.2 The growth in the relative size of the export sector

Country[1] or group of countries	Exports as a % of GDP	
	1965	1985
Low-income economies (1–42)	7	10
India (21)	4	6
Sub-Saharan Africa	25	21
Lower middle-income economies (43–77)	16	23
Upper middle-income economies (78–95)	18	28
Brazil (78)	8	14
South Korea (85)	9	36
Hong Kong (102)	71	106
Oil exporters	16	21
High-income oil exporters	61	47
Industrial market economies	12	18

[1] Countries numbered in ascending order of GNP per capita.

One of the most important considerations affecting a country's trade policy is the state of its balance of trade. Many countries are desperately short of foreign exchange: their demand for imports has grown rapidly and their exports have not kept up. Given this situation, should a country concentrate on expanding its exports, or should it reduce imports and replace them with home-produced goods (or go without them altogether)?

Trade strategies

As they develop, countries' policies towards trade tend to change. Typically they go through various stages.

Primary outward-looking stage

Traditionally, developing countries have exported primaries – minerals such as copper, tin and uranium, and cash crops such as coffee, tea, cocoa, sugar and tropical fruit, and non-foodstuffs such as cotton, rubber and jute – in exchange for manufactured consumer goods. In their early phase of development, countries have little in the way of an industrial base, and thus if they want to consume manufactured goods they have no option but to import them.

Secondary inward-looking stage

Most developing countries saw little prospect for rapid economic development by relying on primary exports. They therefore sought to draw lessons from the experience of the advanced countries. The main conclusion was that industrialization was the key to economic success.

But if developing countries were to industrialize, this would require foreign exchange in order to purchase the necessary capital equipment; and with only a slow growth in primary exports, where was the foreign exchange to come from? The answer was to cut back on all non-essential imports and thereby release foreign exchange. The policy became known as import-substituting industrialization (ISI). The process by which this was done was to impose tariffs and other restrictions on those imports for which a domestic substitute existed or which were regarded as unimportant.

Secondary outward-looking stage

There were limits to import substitution. Once an industry or agricultural sector had satisfied domestic demand, it would have to seek markets abroad if expansion was to

Import-substituting industrialization

A strategy of restricting imports of manufactured goods and using the foreign exchange saved to build up domestic substitute industries.

continue. What is more, as we shall see, import substitution brought a number of serious problems for developing countries. The answer seemed to be to look outwards again, only this time not to primary exports, but to the exports of manufactured goods. Many of the most economically successful developing countries (especially the 'South-East Asian tigers': Hong Kong, Singapore, South Korea and Taiwan) have owed their high growth rates to a rapid expansion of manufactured exports.

Are these three stages inevitable steps in the process of development? Do they necessarily occur in this order? What are the advantages and disadvantages of each of the stages? These are questions we will now examine.

Approach 1: Exporting primaries – exploiting comparative advantage

The importance of primary exports

Despite moves towards import substitution and secondary export promotion, many developing countries are still heavily reliant on the export of primaries. This is illustrated in Table 23.3. It shows primary exports as a percentage of total merchandise exports in the two years 1965 and 1987.

Table 23.3 The importance of primary exports

Country[1] or group of countries	Primary exports as a % of total merchandise exports	
	1965	1987
Low-income economies (1–42)	75	51
Low-income economies excluding China and India (18, 21)	90	75
Zaire (4)	92	94
Uganda (17)	100	100
India (21)	51	31
Sub-Saharan Africa	92	88
Lower-middle-income economies (43–77)	86	53
Philippines (46)	95	38
Mauritius (69)	100	59
Malaysia (73)	94	61
Upper-middle-income economies (78–95)	86	37
Brazil (78)	92	55
South Korea (85)	40	7
All developing countries (1–95)	83	45
High-income economies (96–120)	31	21
United Kingdom (104)	17	23
W. Germany (110)	12	10
Japan (116)	9	2

[1] Countries numbered in ascending order of GNP per capita.

Primary exports constituted 83 per cent of total developing country exports in 1965. Although this had fallen to 45 per cent by 1987, it was still much higher than the figure for advanced countries (21 per cent). For the low-income developing countries excluding China and India, both of which had had extensive programmes of industrialization, primaries still constituted 75 per cent of exports in 1987. For the poorest African countries the figure was even higher.

The justification for exporting primaries

There are three major arguments that have traditionally been used for pursuing a policy of exporting primaries. In each case the arguments have also been used to justify a policy of free trade or virtually free trade.

Exporting primaries exploits comparative advantage. Traditional trade theory implies that countries should specialize in producing those items in which they have a comparative advantage: i.e. those goods which can be produced at relatively low opportunity costs. For most developing countries this means that a large proportion of their exports should be primaries.

The reason for differences in costs between countries may be the *different skills* of labour and the *different technologies* available to them. This was the traditional basis for trade put forward by the classical economists such as David Ricardo and John Stuart Mill (see Box 21.2). Countries should specialize in those goods they can produce *most efficiently*. In this version of comparative advantage, developing countries should specialize in primaries because they have developed the labour skills and technologies in these products.

The reasons for differences in comparative costs were examined more closely by two Swedish economists, Eli Heckscher and Bertil Ohlin. The Heckscher–Ohlin theory is that comparative cost differences arise from differences in *factor endowments*. Some countries such as Canada, Australia and New Zealand have an abundance of land. Therefore land is cheap. As a result they have a comparative advantage in foodstuffs which are produced by extensive farming methods. The advanced countries of Western Europe have a relative abundance of capital. Capital equipment and the technologies embodied in it is therefore relatively cheap. As a result such countries have a comparative advantage in capital-intensive goods such as 'high-tech' manufactured goods. The resource that is most abundant in most developing countries is labour. Labour costs are therefore relatively low. This means that developing countries have a comparative advantage in traditional products, such as crops produced by intensive-farming methods and minerals mined labour intensively.

> **Heckscher–Ohlin version of comparative advantage**
>
> A country has a comparative advantage in those goods that are intensive in the country's relatively abundant factor.

The Heckscher–Ohlin theory states that: *a country should specialize in those goods which are intensive in the country's abundant factor.* Thus labour-abundant developing countries should specialize in labour-intensive products. By exporting these products, which will typically be primaries, they can earn the foreign exchange to import those goods which use large amounts of capital and other resources that are in short supply.

According to the Heckscher–Ohlin theory, international trade would not only lead to a higher level of consumption, it would also lead to factor price equalization. By this is meant the erosion of income inequalities between trading nations. For example, if wages are low in developing countries, then trade will increase the demand for their labour-intensive products and thereby push up wages. Thus the gap between wage rates in rich and poor countries will narrow.

> **Factor price equalization**
>
> The tendency for international trade to reduce factor price inequalities both between and within countries.

> **?** 1. What effect will trade have on the price of capital in developing and developed countries?
> 2. If land is abundant in a given developing country, in what sort of products will it have a comparative advantage? What will happen to rents and the price of land in this country when international trade starts?

In a similar way, international trade will also erode income differentials *within* countries. The demand for exports will increase the demand for the relatively cheap factors, and imports will reduce the demand for the relatively expensive ones. Thus the cheap factors will go up in price and the expensive ones will come down. Greater factor price equality results.

> **?** It is sometimes claimed that trade with the Third World is unjust because it leads to the importation of goods produced at pitifully low wages: that by importing such goods the First World is exploiting the Third World. How can the Heckscher–Ohlin theory be used to refute this claim? Does any truth at all remain in the claim?

Vent for surplus

Where international trade enables a country to exploit resources that would otherwise be unused.

Exporting primaries provides a 'vent for surplus'. Some countries may have resources that would simply not be used were it not for trade. Trade thus provides a vent for surplus: i.e. a means of putting these resources to use.

There are two ways in which these surpluses of resources can occur. The first is where the domestic market is simply not big enough to consume all the available output of a particular good. The most obvious example is with minerals. There is far too little demand within Zambia to consume its potential output of copper. The same applies to Namibian uranium or Malaysian tin.

The second is where there is a lack of some complementary input, which can prevent the use of certain resources. There is much disguised unemployment and underemployed labour in the rural sector of many developing countries. The opening of a mine or plantation can utilize this surplus of labour by producing products for the export market. Without the foreign capital and expertise that such export-orientated projects attract the project might never get under way, even if there were a sufficiently large domestic market.

Exporting primaries provides an 'engine for economic growth'. According to this argument, developing countries benefit from the growth of the economies of the developed world. As industrial expansion takes place in the rich North, so this will create additional demand for primaries from the poor South. The extra revenues this earns for the South enable its inhabitants to consume more industrial goods. Thus growth is *transmitted* from developed to developing countries.

The weakness of traditional trade theory in the context of development

Although there is some validity in each of the above arguments, there are nevertheless a number of reasons for questioning whether they do in fact justify a policy of relying on primary exports as the means to development.

Comparative costs change over time. Factors are not fixed in quantity or quality, and thus even if a country has a comparative advantage in primaries today it does not follow that it will still have in ten, twenty or fifty years' time. Over time, with the acquisition of new skills and an increase in the capital stock, a developing country may find that it now has a comparative advantage in certain *manufactured* products, especially those which are more labour intensive and use raw materials of which the country has a plentiful supply.

> **?** Would it matter if comparative advantage changed over time? Could the country's economy not simply adapt to the new situation and change its pattern of specialization?

Concentrating on primary production may hinder growth. The theory of comparative advantage is based on the assumption of fixed production functions and factor supplies, and hence of a given production possibility curve. Trade then allows countries to consume beyond this production possibility curve. This was illustrated in Chapter 21, Figures 21.1 and 21.4. As the economy grows, however, this production

Box 23.2

Sugar and Beef and All Things Tariffable
Barriers to Third World food exports

Sugar and beef are the Third World's two agricultural commodities most affected by trade barriers erected by the industrial countries. They account for approximately half of all the lost export earnings in agricultural trade resulting from such protectionism.

The costs of such protection include two elements: the loss of export revenue and welfare costs. Welfare costs can be defined as 'the amount of money that exporters would need to be paid to make them as well off with protection against them by the industrial countries as they would be without such measures'.

A survey carried out for the World Bank[4] into the magnitude of these costs covered 17 industrial countries and 58 developing countries. The tables show the results.

Sugar

(a) Estimated effects of trade barriers on sugar exporters (millions of 1980 dollars)

	1979–81 (annual average)	1983
Welfare costs		
Latin America	670.4	1111.0
Africa	76.7	130.9
Other LDCs	507.3	886.2
Total	1254.4	2128.1
Loss of export revenues		
Latin America	2224.2	3391.0
Africa	269.2	421.9
Other LDCs	2614.9	3578.1
Total	5108.3	7391.0

The loss in foreign exchange from trade barriers on sugar amounted to a huge $7.4 billion. The magnitude of this is clear when we see that the aid programme of all industrialized countries totalled only $22.5 billion in the same year.

Beef

(b) Estimated effects of trade barriers on beef and veal exporters (millions of 1980 dollars)

	1979–81 (annual average)
Welfare costs	
Latin America	506.4
Africa (Sub-Saharan)	7.6
Other LDCs	21.7
Total	535.7
Loss of export revenue	
Latin America	4692.6
Africa (Sub-Saharan)	99.0
Other LDCs	303.5
Total	5095.1

Although the costs to beef exporters were less than those to sugar exporters, they were still substantial. One important point here is that the costs are highly concentrated in Latin America, and especially in Argentina and Brazil, the world's two major beef exporters.

It is clear from both tables that Latin America has suffered most acutely from protection against developing country food exports. Ironically, it is these countries that have the biggest international debts in the Third World.

[4] J. Zietz and A. Valdez, 'The costs of protectionism to less-developed countries: an analysis for selected agricultural products', *World Development Report 1985* (World Bank).

possibility curve will *shift outwards*. The problem with concentrating on primaries is that the curve may then shift outwards more slowly than if the country had pursued a policy of industrialization. If this is true, in the long run the static benefits of free trade will be outweighed by the dynamic benefits of industrialization.

The benefits from trade may not accrue to the nationals of the country. Trade may provide increased net benefits, but who gets these benefits? If a mine or plantation is owned by a foreign company, it will be the foreign shareholders who get the profits from the sale of exports. In addition, these companies may bring in their own capital and skilled labour from abroad. The benefits actually gained by the local people will probably be confined to the additional wages they earn. But with these companies being in a position of monopsony power, these wages are often very low. In the extreme case, the export sector may be little more than a foreign enclave: a patch of the USA, the UK or France within the Philippines, Kenya or Senegal.

 Why does this argument make GNP a better indicator of development than GDP? (see Section 13.6.)

Trade may lead to less equality not more. Trade shifts income distribution in favour of those factors of production employed intensively in the export sector. If exports are labour intensive, greater equality will tend to result. If, however, the exports are land intensive, then trade will redistribute income in favour of the landowners. In countries where land is unequally distributed, trade will only make the large landowners (such as plantation owners) even richer. Similarly, with raw-material-intensive products (like minerals), trade will redistribute income in favour of the mine-owners, who may well be foreign nationals.

Exporting primary exports may involve external costs. Mining can lead to huge external costs, with the despoiling of the countryside, damage to the health of miners and the breaking-up of communities as miners have to leave their villages for long periods. Similarly, plantations can lead to the destruction of traditional communities and their values.

Balance of payments problems may result. If a country pursues a free-trade policy and imports of consumer goods are widely available, the production and sale of primary exports may not be able to keep pace with the increased demand for imports. The resulting balance of trade deficit will create various adjustment costs.

Trade may adversely influence tastes. The more freely a country trades, the more will people's aspirations for a 'better life' be fuelled. If people cannot afford to buy the goods imported from the affluent world, their frustrations are likely to increase. There will have been a decline in economic welfare.

All these arguments cast some doubt on whether a policy of relying on free trade in primary exports is the best way of achieving economic development. These doubts have been given further justification by various trends in the international economy that have worked against primary exporters.

Problems for primary exporters: long term

Long-term trends in international trade have caused problems for primary exporting countries in three ways: (a) exports have grown slowly; (b) imports have grown rapidly; (c) the terms of trade have moved against them.

Slow growth in exports
Low income elasticity of demand for primary products. As world incomes grow, so a smaller proportion of these incomes is spent on primaries. The reasons differ somewhat between food and raw materials.

Since food is a necessity of life, consumers, especially in rich countries, already consume virtually all they require. A rise in incomes, therefore, tends to be spent more on luxury goods and services. To the extent that expenditure on food products does increase, the extra expenditure tends to be more on the processing and packaging of the food rather than on its basic ingredients. Thus imports of the basic ingredients only rise slowly. The exceptions are certain 'luxury' imported foodstuffs such as exotic fruits.

In the case of raw materials, as people's incomes grow they tend to buy more and more expensive products. The extra value of these products arises not from the extra raw materials they might contain, but from their greater sophistication. Thus if a person can now afford to buy a more luxurious video recorder with all sorts of remote features, the video recorder will probably not contain any more imported raw materials than a more basic model.

Agricultural protection in advanced countries. Faced with the problem of a slowly growing demand for food produced by their own farmers, advanced countries increasingly imposed restrictions on imported food. For example, massive protection of the sugar beet industry in the European Community greatly reduced the exports of Third World sugar cane producers.

The development of synthetic substitutes. Compare typical durable consumer goods of today with those of twenty years ago and one of the obvious differences is the materials of which they are made. Instead of steel, wood and rubber, the modern products are made largely with plastic of one sort or another. It is the same with industrial equipment. Imported raw materials have in many cases been replaced by synthetic substitutes.

A similar trend was observed with clothing: polyester, nylon and acrylic fibres were replacing cotton. In recent years, however, there has been a reversion of demand to 'natural' fibres.

Miniaturization. Another major feature of industrial development has been the process of miniaturization. As microchips have replaced machines, so less and less raw materials have been required to produce any given amount of output.

Low price elasticity of demand for primaries. Given the basic nature of primaries, their overall demand tends to be relatively price inelastic. There is no substitute for food, and in the short run there is often no substitute for minerals. On the other hand, the demand for any *one* primary product, and especially the demand for any one *country's* primary exports, will be very price elastic: there are plenty of other countries producing substitutes.

 Under what circumstances would developing countries face an infinitely elastic demand curve for their exports?

The high price elasticity of demand for an individual country's primaries will encourage countries to produce as much as possible (as long as price remains above marginal cost), but as all countries do the same, the low overall price elasticity will have the effect of depressing primary product prices.

Rapid growth in imports

High income elasticity of demand for imported manufactures. Whereas the demand for most primary exports grows slowly, the demand for imports of manufactured goods into the developing countries grows rapidly with the growth of their income. This is partly due to the process of the better off in these countries being able to afford luxury goods, and partly due to the development of new tastes as people are exposed to the products of the developed world in shop windows, in adverts and through seeing others consuming them.

Low price elasticity of demand for imported manufactures. Because of a lack of domestic substitutes, the price elasticity of demand for manufactured imports is low. This gives market power to the overseas suppliers of these imports, and thus tends to raise their price relative to exports.

The terms of trade

The net effect of all these factors is a long-term decline in the terms of trade for primary exporters, where a country's terms of trade are defined as the average price of its exports divided by the average price of its imports (P_x/P_m). This effect can be seen in Table 23.4, which shows this terms of trade for Sub-Saharan Africa, the region whose exports contain the highest proportion of primaries.

Table 23.4 Change in the terms of trade for Sub-Saharan African countries (average annual %)

1965–73	1973–80	1981	1982	1983	1984	1985	1986	1987	1988
−8.5	5.0	−1.4	−4.8	−0.1	1.8	−3.3	−23.2	3.3	−5.3

Source: *World Development Report 1989* (World Bank).

The one major and dramatic exception to this rule has been the case of oil. With the worldwide growth in transport and other forms of energy consumption, the demand for oil grew rapidly. Given the lack of immediate substitutes and the determination and organization of OPEC, the oil exporters were able to push up the price of oil, first in 1973/74 and then again in 1979/80 (see Box 6.6).

Problems for primary exporters: short term

There are also problems for primary exporting countries in the *short term*.

The prices of primary products are subject to large fluctuations. This causes great uncertainty for primary exporters and makes it virtually impossible for the government to predict how many imports the country can afford. As the current account of the balance of payments fluctuates wildly, so this tends to cause large swings in exchange rates or requires massive government intervention to stabilize them.

The causes of the price fluctuations are (a) a low price elasticity of demand and supply of primaries and (b) substantial shifts in their demand and supply. We looked at the causes of low price elasticities above. But why are demand and supply curves likely to shift substantially?

The demand for *food* is relatively stable, but the demand for minerals varies with the trade cycle and tends to vary more than the demand for consumer goods. The reason is to be found in the *accelerator principle* (see section 14.4). Since the *level* of investment demand depends on the size of *changes* in consumer demand, investment will tend to fluctuate much more wildly than consumer demand. But since many minerals are inputs into *capital* equipment, this means that their demand is also likely to fluctuate more than consumer demand.

The supply of minerals is relatively stable (unless there is a strike or a mining disaster). The supply of cash crops, however, varies with the harvest. Many Third World countries are subject to drought or flood, and these can virtually wipe out their export earnings from the relevant crop.

> **?** If a disastrous harvest of rice were confined to a particular country, would (a) the world price and (b) its own domestic price of rice fluctuate significantly? What would happen to the country's export earnings and the earnings of individual farmers?

Box 23.3

When Driving and Alcohol Do Mix
A case of import substitution in Brazil

Two major changes in world trade hit Brazil in the 1970s. The first was the fourfold increase in world oil prices. Brazil has very little oil of its own. The second was the slump in the world sugar cane market as a result of northern countries' protection of their sugar beet industries. Brazil was a major cane sugar exporter.

Faced with a resulting large increase in its import bill and a slump in its sugar exports, the Brazilian government came up with an ingenious solution. It could use surplus sugar cane to make alcohol, which could then be used instead of petrol for cars. Large distilleries were set up to convert the sugar cane into alcohol. At the same time cars were produced (e.g. VW beetles) that could run on alcohol rather than petrol. Thus by one measure two problems were alleviated.

But despite the production of alcohol-powered cars, Brazil continued to import massive amounts of oil, which by 1980 absorbed almost 50 per cent of total export earnings.

With a price-inelastic world demand and supply for primaries, shifts in either curve will lead to substantial fluctuations in world prices. The problem is most serious for countries that rely on just one or two primary products, such as Ghana on cocoa, Colombia on coffee, Zambia and Zaire on copper, and Bolivia on tin. For such countries diversification into other primaries would help to reduce their exposure.

Approach 2: Import substituting industrialization (ISI)

Dissatisfaction with relying on primary exporting has led most countries to embark on a process of industrialization. After all, industrialization seemed to hold out the prospect of higher growth rates. The rate of growth of both demand and technological advance was higher in industry than in primary production. Some developing countries (the newly-industrialized countries – NICs) are already well advanced along the industrialization road. Others have not yet progressed very far, especially the poorest African countries.

But how were countries to industrialize? The most obvious way for most of them seemed to be to cut back on imports of manufactures, and to substitute them with home-produced manufactures. Of course this could not be done overnight: it would have to be done in stages. The simplest method was to start with the final stages of production: i.e. assembly. Thus if a country decided to set up in tractor production, it would start with an assembly plant: instead of importing tractors, it would import all the parts necessary for assembling into tractors. The next stage would be to start making some of the components – not all at once but again in stages. It would still be necessary to import the machinery to make these components. In the final stages of import substitution all, or virtually all, of the inputs into production would be made domestically. Most developing countries have at least started on the first stage. Several of the more advanced developing countries have component-manufacturing industries. Only a few of the larger NICs, however, such as India, Brazil and South Korea, have built extensive capital goods industries.

The method most favoured by policy makers has been to engage in a process of tariff escalation. Under this policy, tariff rates (or other restrictions) increase as one

Tariff escalation

The system whereby tariff rates increase the closer a product is to the finished stage of production.

moves from the raw material to the intermediate product to the finished product stage. Thus finished goods would have higher tariffs than intermediate products. This would encourage assembly plants to be set up. The assembly industry would be protected by high tariffs from imported finished products, and would be able to obtain its components at a lower tariff rate. In other words, the tariffs would lead to a bigger rise in prices than in costs, and hence profits would rise.

One of the problems with ISI is that countries are desperately short of resources to invest in industry. As a result, a policy of ISI has usually involved encouraging investment by multinational companies. They may be offered tax concessions, cheap sites, the cutting of red tape, government contracts, cheap finance, etc. But even without specific 'perks', multinationals will still probably be attracted by the protection afforded by the tariffs or quotas. Rather than having to scale the protective walls from outside as importers, they themselves can be protected from outside competition if they set up within the country.

Adverse effects of import substitution

Some countries, such as South Korea and Taiwan, pursued an inward-looking ISI policy for only a few years. For them it was merely a stage in development, a stage rapidly to be followed by a secondary outward-looking policy. Infant industries were initially given protection, but when they had achieved sufficient internal and external economies of scale the barriers to imports were gradually removed. The infants were weaned off the protection.

The countries that have continued to pursue protectionist ISI policies have generally had a poorer growth record (see Table 23.5). In addition, the ISI economies have tended to suffer from other problems, such as a deepening of inequality. The rich have tended to get richer, but few if any of the benefits have trickled down to the poor.

Table 23.5 The relative growth performance of secondary inward and secondary outward-looking economies

	Average annual % rate of growth in real per-capita GNP	
	Strongly outward-orientated countries	Strongly inward-orientated countries
1963–73	6.9	1.6
1973–85	5.9	−0.1

Source: *World Development Report 1987* (World Bank).

The development of the modern industrial sector has often been to the detriment of the traditional sectors and also of the export sector.

The criticisms of ISI are numerous. ISI is claimed to lead to inefficiency, distortions of the market, balance of payments problems, lower growth, higher inflation, greater inequality and generally an undesirable pattern of 'development'. Let us examine these arguments.

It has run directly counter to the principle of comparative advantage. Rather than confining ISI to genuine infant industries and then removing the protection as the 'infant' matures, ISI has been applied indiscriminately to a whole range of industries. As a result many of their products are now produced at much higher costs than those of the equivalent imports. The result is a waste of resources. Countries are producing goods in which they have a comparative *disadvantage*. If these industries are to survive foreign competition, they will need *continuing* protection.

If a country specializes in a good in which it has a comparative *disadvantage*, where will it be consuming with respect to its production possibility curve?

It has cushioned inefficient practices and encouraged the establishment of monopolies. Without the competition from imports, many of the industries are highly inefficient and wasteful of resources. What is more, in all but the largest or most developed Third World countries the domestic market for manufactures is small. If a newly established industry is to be large enough to gain the full potential economies of scale, it will necessarily be large relative to the market. This means that it will have considerable monopoly power to raise prices. Thus not only are costs higher, but profit margins may also be higher than in advanced countries.

A related problem is that of overcapacity. In many countries, plants run at well below full capacity simply because of a lack of demand.

It has involved artificially low real interest rates. In order to encourage capital investment in the import-substituting industries, governments have often intervened to keep interest rates low. This, however, has tended to encourage the use of capital-intensive technology with a consequent lack of jobs. It has also tended to starve other sectors in the economy (such as agriculture) of much-needed finance, since they have not had access to capital at these low interest rates. It has also discouraged savings.

It has led to urban wages above the market clearing level. Wages in the industrial sector, although still low compared with advanced countries, are often considerably higher than in the traditonal sectors. They are pushed up by firms seeking to retain labour in which they have invested training. Governments, seeking to appease the politically powerful urban industrial working class, have often passed minimum wage laws. Trade unions, although generally less widespread in the developing world than in advanced countries, where they do exist tend to be mainly confined to the new industries. All these factors have the effect of increasing industrial wages, which in turn further encourages firms to use capital-intensive techniques in order to economize on wage costs.

It has involved overvalued exchange rates. By restricting imports, import substitution tends to move the current account of the balance of payments into surplus. This leads to an appreciation of the exchange rate. This is often seen as desirable by developing country governments, which welcome the downward pressure this creates on the price of imported inputs and hence on the costs of the new industries. Governments often actively intervene to keep up the exchange rate as part of their fight against inflation.

But if a higher exchange rate makes imported inputs cheaper, the result will be to discourage the establishment of *domestic* industries supplying those inputs. The spread effect of the industrialization to supplying sectors will thus be reduced.

Also a higher exchange rate discourages exports. Developing countries, having little or no economic power, are usually price takers in world markets. They face a given *dollar* price for their exports. If the exchange rate appreciates, domestic currency will buy more dollars; or put another way, a dollar will exchange for less domestic currency. Thus exporters will earn less domestic currency as the exchange rate appreciates.

With an overvalued exchange rate those goods with little or no protection will be cheaper. A major example is food. Due to pressures from the growing urban population for cheap food, governments are reluctant to impose tariffs on basic foodstuffs such as grains and meat. This then makes it difficult for local farmers to obtain a reasonable price for their crops, and thus discourages agricultural investment.

 Why is an overvalued exchange rate likely to encourage the use of capital-intensive technology?

It does not remove the balance of payments constraint on development. Many of the new industries are highly dependent on the importation of raw materials, capital equipment and component parts. Sometimes it can even cost as much foreign exchange to import the inputs as it does to import the finished product! (Yet it is still profitable for the new industries to do so because the inputs have a lower tariff.) In this case no foreign exchange is saved at all.

What is more, foreign inputs, unlike foreign finished goods, are often only supplied by a single firm, which can thus charge monopoly prices. For example, assume that a developing country wants to buy cars. If it imports the finished cars, it can choose makes from Japan, France, Germany, Italy, the USA, etc. Supply is relatively competitive. If, however, as part of an ISI strategy it sets up an assembly plant to produce Fiat cars, then it will have to buy the inputs from Fiat, even if the assembly plant is not actually owned by Fiat. The country now has to buy from a monopoly.

Finally, a large proportion of the extra income generated by these industries tends to be spent on imports. The new urban élites who benefit from these industries, either as profit earners or as skilled personnel, tend to have a high propensity to consume imported consumer goods.

Protection has not been applied evenly. Many different tariff rates are often used in one country: in fact a policy of tariff escalation demands this. In addition, governments often use a whole range of other protectionist instruments – such as the licensing of importers, physical and value quotas, foreign exchange rationing, multiple exchange rates (where less essential imports come in at a less favourable exchange rate), stamp duties and port duties. These are often applied in a haphazard way. The result is that protection is highly uneven.

Effective rate of protection

The percentage increase in an industry's domestic value added resulting from protection given to that industry.

Economists have developed the concept of effective protection to measure the true degree of protection an industry gets. What effective protection measures is the extra domestic value added that protection gives an industry. By *'domestic value added'* we mean the difference between the world market price of the finished good and the cost of the imported inputs used to make the good. Thus if a developing country set up an industry assembling cars which had a world market price of £8000, and if the imported parts to make each car cost £5000, the domestic value added would be £3000 per car. Put another way, by assembling the cars itself rather than importing finished cars, the country would save £3000 of foreign exchange per car.

To show how we calculate effective protection, consider first the simple case of a 10 per cent tariff on the finished car (a 10 per cent 'nominal' rate of protection) and also a 10 per cent tariff on the imported inputs. The price of an imported finished car (and hence the price at which a domestically produced one can also be sold) rises to £8800. The imported inputs rise to £5500. Domestic value added thus rises to £3300 (i.e. £8800 − £5500). This is a 10 per cent rise in value added. The effective rate of protection is thus 10 per cent. This is the same as the nominal rate. The effective and nominal rates will be the same when there is the same rate of tariff on both the finished good and the imported inputs.

Now let us consider the case where the government, through a policy of tariff escalation, puts a 20 per cent tariff on the finished car and a 10 per cent tariff on the imported inputs. The finished car rises in price to £9600. The imported inputs, as in the previous example, cost £5500. Value added has increased to £4100 (i.e. £9600 − £5500). This is an increase of £1100 over the original value added of £3000 – an increase of 36.7 per cent. Thus although the nominal rate of protection is now 20 per cent, the *effective* rate is 36.7 per cent. In other words, the car manufacturer is able to gain a 36.7 per cent increase in value added compared with the free-trade position.

Box 23.4

When a High Value was Given to Smelling Sweet

Effective protection for the perfume industry[5]

Many countries have attempted to save foreign exchange by cutting down on luxury imports. They do this by putting very high tariffs or other restrictions on these products.

There is an ironical outcome of this, however. It gives very high levels of effective protection for *domestic* producers of these products. In Brazil in 1966 the effective rate of protection for the perfume industry was a massive 8480 per cent. There was thus a much bigger incentive for domestic producers to set up in the perfume industry than in industries that might be considered to be more important!

Other examples of massive effective protection from the same period were a 9900 per cent rate for silk and art-silk in Pakistan, a 2320 per cent rate for electric lamps in the Philippines, a 380 per cent rate for textiles in Argentina and a 212 per cent rate for motor vehicles in Mexico.

[5] This box is based on material in I. Little, T. Scitovsky and M. Scott, *Industry and Trade in Some Developing Countries* (Oxford University Press, 1970).

Formally, the effective rate of protection can be defined as:

$$\frac{V^* - V}{V} \times 100$$

where V is the free-trade domestic value added, and V^* is the value added after the imposition of tariffs. It can be seen from this that there are three variables that determine the rate of effective protection:

- The tariff rate on the finished good (the nominal rate of protection). The higher this is, the higher will be the value of V^* relative to V, and hence the higher will be the effective rate of protection.
- The tariff rate (or rates) on the inputs. The higher these are, the lower will be the value of V^* relative to V, and hence the lower will be the effective rate of protection.
- The level of value added as a proportion of the price of the finished good. The higher this is, the lower will be the effective rate of protection (assuming tariff escalation).

 To demonstrate this last point, work out the effective rate of protection in the following three cases:
(a) Free-trade finished good price = £100; free-trade cost of imported inputs = £40.
(b) Free-trade finished good price = £100; free-trade cost of imported inputs = £80.
(c) Free-trade finished good price = £100; free-trade cost of imported inputs = £100.
In each case assume that a 50 per cent tariff is imposed on the finished good and a 10 per cent tariff on the imported inputs.

Evidence shows that in many countries effective protective rates vary massively from one industry to another. For example, according to World Bank estimates, in 1980 effective rates of protection in manufacturing ranged from −85 per cent to 219 per cent in Brazil and from −62 per cent to 1119 per cent in Nigeria! Clearly such huge differences in effective protection impose massive distortions on the market and destroy any hope of a 'rational' allocation of resources.

 Under what circumstances could the effective rate of protection be negative?

Income distribution is made less equal. The modern sector often has few links with the traditional sector. Additional incomes generated by the modern sector tend to be spent on modern-sector goods and imported goods. Thus there is a multiplier effect *within* the modern sector, but virtually none between the sectors. Also, as we saw above, an overvalued exchange rate leads to a bias against agriculture, and thus further deepens the divide between rich and poor. Finally, the relatively high wages of the modern sector encourage workers to migrate to the towns where many, failing to get a job, live in dire poverty.

Social/cultural problems. A policy of ISI often involves imposing an alien set of values. Urban life can be harsh, competitive and materialistic. It has to be seriously questioned whether, even if ISI leads to a rise in consumption, it really leads to an increase in human welfare.

Environmental costs. The drive for industrialization may involve major costs to the environment. Many of the new industries belch noxious fumes into the atmosphere, pour poisonous chemicals into rivers and dump toxic waste in landfills.

Finally, import substitution is necessarily limited by the size of the domestic market. Once that is saturated, ISI can come to an abrupt halt. At that stage, further expansion can only come from exporting; but if these industries have been overprotected, they will be unable to compete in world markets.

This has been a long list of problems and not all apply with equal force to all secondary inward-looking countries. Also, different economists will put different emphases on them. Neo-classical economists stress the problems of market distortions, arguing that ISI leads to great inefficiency. Neo-Marxist economists, on the other hand, stress the problems of dependency it creates. Many of the new industries will be owned by multinational companies which import unsuitable technologies. The countries will then become dependent on imported inputs and foreign sources of capital.

Approach 3: Exporting manufactures – a possible way forward?

The countries with the highest rates of economic growth have been those that have successfully made the transition to being exporters of manufactures. Table 23.6 shows the growth rates in per-capita GDP and the share of manufactures in exports of some of these countries.

Table 23.6 Growth rates and export performance of selected secondary outward-looking countries

	Average annual per-capita growth in GNP (%) 1965–87	Share of manufactures in merchandise exports (%)		Annual average growth rate of exports (%)	
		1965	1987	1965–80	1980–87
Brazil	4.1	9	45	9.3	5.6
Malaysia	4.1	6	40	7.6	6.6
South Korea	6.4	59	92	27.2	14.3
Singapore	7.2	35	72	4.7	6.1
Hong Kong	6.2	87	92	9.5	11.4
All developing countries	2.7	19	56	3.1	5.0

Source: *World Development Report 1989* (World Bank).

The transition from inward-looking to outward-looking industrialization

First we must be clear what is meant by 'outward-looking industrialization'. It could simply mean an abandonment of biases in favour of import substitution. In other words, there would be no bias *either* way: there would be a *neutral trade regime* where production for the home market and for export would get equal treatment by the government. A country could go further, however, and actively *promote* exports. It could, for example, subsidize exports or give tax concessions to exporters. In most cases, however, when a country is referred to as 'outward looking', what is meant is simply that it is not biased *against* exports: that it is neutral.

But how is a country to move from import substituting to being outward looking? One approach is to take it industry by industry. When an industry has saturated the home market and there is thus no further scope for import substitution, it should then be encouraged to seek markets overseas. The trouble with this approach is that, if the country is still protecting other industries, there will probably still be an overvalued exchange rate. Thus specific subsidies, tax concessions or other 'perks' would have to be given to this industry to enable it to compete. The country would still be highly interventionist, with all the distortions and misallocation of resources this tends to bring.

The alternative is to wean the whole economy off protection. Three major things will need doing. There will need to be a devaluation of the currency in order to restore the potential profitability of the export sector. There will also need to be a dismantling of the various protective measures that had biased production towards the home market. Finally, there will probably need to be a removal or relaxing of price controls. But these are things that cannot be done 'at a stroke'. Many years of protectionism may have led to a highly distorted economy with a mass of restrictions. Firms may have to be introduced gradually to the greater forces of competition that an outward-looking trade policy would bring. Otherwise there may be massive bankruptcies and a corresponding massive rise in unemployment.

The benefits from a secondary outward-looking policy

The advocates of outward-looking industrialization make a number of points in its favour.

It conforms more closely to comparative advantage. Countries pursuing an open trade regime will only be able to export goods in which they have a comparative advantage. The resources used in earning a unit of foreign exchange from exports will be less than those used in saving a unit of foreign exchange by replacing imports with home-produced goods. In other words, resources will be used more efficiently.

It will lead to more employment. According to the Heckscher–Ohlin theory, the manufactured goods in which a country will have a comparative advantage are those produced by labour-intensive techniques. Export expansion will thus increase the demand for labour relative to capital, and thus create more employment.

It can lead to a more equal distribution of income. The increased demand for labour will tend to lead to a rise in wages relative to profits.

 Will the adoption of labour-intensive techniques *necessarily* lead to a more equal distribution of income?

It removes many of the costs associated with ISI. Under a policy of ISI, managers may spend a lot of their time lobbying politicians and officials, seeking licences (and sometimes paying bribes to obtain them), adhering to norms and regulations or trying to find ways round them. If an outward-looking policy involves removing all this, managers can turn their attention to producing goods more efficiently.

Economies of scale. If the home market is too small to allow a firm to gain all the potential economies of scale, these can be gained by expanding into the export market.

Increased competition. By having to compete with foreign companies, exporters will be under a greater competitive pressure than industries shielded behind protective barriers. This will encourage (a) resource saving in the short run, both through their better *allocation* and through reductions in X inefficiency (see Box 5.5), and (b) innovation and investment, as firms attempt to adopt the latest technology, often obtained from developed countries. They cannot afford a 'quiet life'. They have to compete to survive.

Increased investment. To the extent that outward-looking policies lead to a greater potential for economic growth they may attract more foreign capital. To the extent that they involve an increase in interest rates they will tend to attract more savings. To the extent that they lead to increased incomes additional savings will be generated, especially given that the *marginal* propensity to save may be quite high. The extra savings can be used to finance extra investment.

Drawbacks of an export-orientated industrialization strategy

Many of the problems associated with a *primary* exporting strategy do not apply to a *secondary* exporting one. For example, the income and price elasticities of demand for manufactures are generally much higher than those for primaries. Nevertheless some of the problems of an outward strategy still remain.

The export of manufactures is seen by many developed countries as very threatening to their own industries. Their response is often to erect trade barriers. These barriers are often highest in the very industries (such as textiles, footwear and processed food) where developing countries have the greatest comparative advantage. Even if the barriers are *currently* low, developing countries may feel that it is too risky to expand their exports of these products for fear of a future rise in barriers.

 Consider the arguments from the perspective of an *advanced country* for and against protecting its industries from Third World imports of manufactures.

The success of developing countries such as Hong Kong and South Korea in exporting manufactures does not imply that other developing countries will have similar success. As additional developing countries attempt to export their manufactures they will be facing more and more competition from each other.

Exporting manufactures may thus be a very risky strategy for developing countries. Perhaps the best hope for the future may be for a growth in manufacturing trade *between* developing countries. That way they can gain the benefits of specialization and economies of scale that trade brings, while at the same time producing for a growing market. The feasibility of this approach depends on whether developing countries can agree to an open trade policy between themselves.

▲ SUMMARY

1. Trade is of vital importance for the vast majority of developing countries, and yet most developing countries suffer from chronic balance of trade deficits.
2. Developing countries have traditionally been primary exporters. This has allowed them to exploit their comparative advantage in labour-intensive goods and has

provided a market for certain goods which would otherwise have no market at home. It has also provided a means whereby growth can be transmitted from the advanced countries.

3. There are reasons for questioning the wisdom of relying on traditional primary exports, however. With a low world

income elasticity of demand for primary products, with the development of synthetic substitutes for minerals and with the protection of agriculture in developed countries, the demand for Third World primary exports has only grown slowly. At the same time the demand for manufactured imports into developing countries has grown rapidly. The result has been a worsening balance of trade problem; and with a *price*-inelastic demand for both imports and exports, the terms of trade have worsened too. In addition to these problems, there is also the danger that comparative costs may change over time; that most of the benefits from primary exports may accrue to foreign owners of mines and plantations, or to wealthy élites in the domestic population; that mines and plantations can involve substantial environmental and other external costs; and that export earnings can fluctuate, given instabilities in supply and unstable world prices.

4. Import-substituting industrialization was seen to be the answer to these problems. This was normally achieved in stages, beginning with the finished goods stage and then working back towards the capital goods stage. ISI, it was hoped, would allow countries to benefit from the various dynamic advantages associated with manufacturing.

5. For many countries, however, ISI brought as many, if not more, problems than it solved. It often led to the establishment of inefficient industries, protected from foreign competition and facing little or no competition at home either. It led to considerable market distortions, with tariffs and other forms of protection haphazardly applied and with resulting huge variations in effective rates of protection; to overvalued exchange rates with a resulting bias against exports and the agricultural sector generally; to a deepening of inequalities and to large-scale social problems as the cities expanded, as poverty and unemployment grew and as traditional values were undermined; and to growing environmental problems. Finally, the problem that ISI was supposed to ease – the balance of payments constraint – was in many cases made worse as the new industries became increasingly dependent on imported inputs and as growing urbanization caused a growing demand for imported consumer goods.

6. The most rapidly growing of the developing countries are those that have pursued a policy of export-orientated industrialization. This has allowed them to achieve the benefits of economies of scale and foreign competition. It has allowed them to specialize in goods in which they have a comparative advantage (i.e. labour-intensive goods) and yet which have a relatively high income elasticity of demand. Whether countries which have pursued ISI can successfully turn to an open, export-orientated approach will depend to a large extent on the degree of protectionism they face from advanced countries and on the degree of competition they face from other developing countries.

23.3 Structural problems within developing countries

The neglect of agriculture

In their drive to industrialize, many developing countries have taken their agricultural sector for granted. The general view in the 1950s and 1960s was that agriculture was useful to the extent that it provided food for the expanding towns. But it was essentially seen as a resource to be tapped rather than developed. The key to growth and modernization was industry not farming. The result of these attitudes was that the rural sector was neglected.

The process of import-substituting industrialization has been highly damaging to agriculture, especially in the poorest countries such as those of Sub-Saharan Africa. With a backward and rundown agricultural sector, with little or no rural infrastructure, many countries today face a food crisis of immense proportions. Unable to produce enough food to feed their growing populations and increasingly unable to afford the imports of food to make up the shortfall, people have died in their thousands. One year's poor harvest can mean mass starvation. Harrowing scenes of famine and death from countries like Ethiopia and the Sudan have become all too familiar.

In the last twenty years opinions have gradually changed. It is now realized that the relief of poverty, unemployment and the maldistribution of income can best be achieved by improving productivity and incomes in the rural sector. No longer is agriculture seen as a sector to be 'squeezed' like an orange. Rather it is seen as a sector in its own right that must be developed in harmony with the urban sector. What is required is sectoral balance. Agricultural output must be increased for the benefit of rural and urban dwellers alike. At the same time industrial output can be given new markets in the rural sector if rural incomes expand.

To achieve rural development, the urban bias of previous policies must be reversed. More than this, there have to be positive policies to encourage a more efficient use of land and to help the vast numbers living in absolute poverty. The following are some of the possible ways forward.

Price reform. The price of food needs to be raised relative to the price of industrial goods. This will increase the profitability of agricultural production and enable farmers to afford to invest in irrigation, agricultural implements, land improvement, etc.

Devaluation. If the currency is devalued, this will increase the price of food imports and thus make it easier for domestic food producers to compete. It will also increase the profitability of food exports.

Government support for rural infrastructure projects. If food is to be marketed, there must be adequate rural infrastructure. Government road-building schemes and the setting-up of marketing boards can make a dramatic difference to the viability of commercial food production.

The provision of finance. Farmers need access to cheap finance and not to be forced to borrow at sky-high interest rates from local moneylenders. This can be achieved by setting up rural banks specializing in the provision of finance to small farmers. These could be nationalized institutions, or the government could give incentives to private banks to expand into the rural sector.

The adoption of new technologies and practices. There have been rapid advances in agricultural technology in recent years. The development of new fertilizers, pesticides, simple but effective agricultural machinery, and most of all of new high-yielding strains of grain, especially wheat and rice, have helped to transform traditional agriculture in certain Third World countries such as parts of India. There has been a *Green Revolution.*

Other countries, however, and especially those of Sub-Saharan Africa, have made little progress in adopting these technologies. This is due partly to an inability to afford the new equipment, chemicals and seeds, partly to the lack of infrastructure to make them available, and partly to their unsuitability to the generally more arid African conditions.

Governments can help by funding research into the best farming methods and inputs for local conditions. They can also help by providing finance for the adoption of the new methods.

Education and advice. Many farmers are simply unaware of new more efficient farming methods. Training schemes or rural advisers can help here.

Land reform. Many farmers operate on tiny plots of land that can never yield an adequate income. As the population grows, land holdings are divided and subdivided as they are passed from generation to generation. The average size of plots thus gets smaller and smaller. Increasingly, farmers get into debt and are forced to mortgage their land to large landowners at high interest rates, or to sell it to them at low prices. The number of landless labourers or farmers in 'debt bondage' therefore grows.

A solution to this problem is the redistribution of land. Clearly this cannot be done unless there is a government sympathetic to the rural poor and willing to take on the inevitable opposition from the large farmers. Often these large farmers are politically powerful and have the police on their side.

Two of the most successful developing countries, Taiwan and South Korea, despite having right-wing governments, underwent a radical redistribution of land from rich to poor in the late 1940s and early 1950s. In both countries the growth of the agricultural sector has been rapid and yet continues to be egalitarian, based as it is on small, but not tiny, peasant holdings. In both countries extreme rural poverty has been eliminated.

The encouragement of rural co-operatives. If small farmers get together and form co-operatives, they may be able to afford to share agricultural equipment such as tractors and harvesters; they may be able to undertake irrigation schemes; they may be able to set up input-purchasing and crop-marketing and distribution organizations; they may be able to gain easier access to credit; they may be in a better position to negotiate with government agencies and be a channel through which the government can provide technological and financial assistance. In many countries, national or local governments have actively encouraged such co-operatives by providing subsidies, tax incentives and advice, and by passing favourable legislation.

Inappropriate technology

The technology employed in a country depends on the type of development strategy it is pursuing. Some strategies lead to the adoption of relatively labour-intensive technologies (technologies with a high labour/capital ratio). Others lead to relatively capital-intensive technologies (technologies with a high capital/labour ratio).

Neo-classical theory suggests that countries should use techniques that are intensive in their abundant factor. This is simply an extension of the Heckscher–Ohlin theory, only this time it is applied to the choice of techniques rather than to the choice of goods. Given that developing countries are generally abundant in labour and have a relative scarcity of capital, the argument suggests that they should adopt labour-intensive techniques: techniques that use relatively more of the cheap factor (labour) and relatively less of the expensive factor (capital).

With the advent of policies of industrialization, however, came strong arguments for adopting capital-intensive technology. Capital-intensive technologies were seen to be more advanced. These were the technologies that were developed in rich countries, countries with sophisticated research facilities. The argument here was that, despite having a higher capital/labour ratio, these techniques nevertheless had a low capital/output ratio. The equipment might be expensive, but it would yield a very high output and would thus cost less *per unit* of output.

> **?** If a modern capital-intensive technique has a higher capital/labour ratio *and* a lower capital/output ratio than a traditional labour-intensive one, what can we say about its labour/output ratio relative to the traditional technique?

A second argument was that, if multinationals were to be encouraged to invest in developing countries, they had to be allowed to bring with them their own technology – technology that was almost invariably capital-intensive. In other words, the choice was not between more labour-intensive and more capital-intensive techniques, but rather between having *extra* capital (by allowing multinationals to invest) and not having it at all.

A final argument in favour of capital-intensive technology was that it provides a greater level of profit, and that this profit will then be reinvested, thereby causing a faster rate of economic growth. There are two assumptions here. First, if a more labour-intensive technique is used, the wage cost will be higher per unit of output,

---

Box 23.5

Inappropriate Technologies
When 'modern' is not best

Marsden cites the following examples of the inappropriate use of capital-intensive technology in various Third World countries:[6]

- The large public-sector shoe factory which operated at 20% of capacity because it had no means of reaching the small private shoe retailers who handled 90% of the shoe trade.
- The battery plant which could satisfy a month's demand in five days.
- The woollen-textile factory which had a 10% material wastage figure (costing precious foreign exchange) because its management did not know how to set and control material usage standards.
- The $2 million date-processing plant which had been out of action for two years, ever since a blow-out in the cleaning and destoning unit, because there were no service engineers who knew how to repair it.
- The radio assembly factory whose production line broke down repeatedly because of the high rate of absenteeism among key workers . . .

- One country imported two plastic injection-moulding machines costing $100,000 with moulds. Working three shifts and with a total labour force of fifty workers they produced 1.5 million pairs of plastic sandals and shoes a year. At $2 a pair these were better value (longer life) than cheap leather footwear at the same price. Thus 5,000 artisan shoe-makers lost their livelihood; this, in turn, reduced the markets for the suppliers and makers of leather, hand tools, cotton thread, tacks, glues, wax and polish, eyelets, fabric linings, laces, wooden lasts and carton boxes, none of which was required for plastic footwear. As all the machinery had to be imported, while the leather footwear was based largely on indigenous materials and industries, the net result was a decline in both employment and real income within the country.

[6] K. Marsden, *'Progressive technologies for developing countries'*, in R. Jolly *et al.* (eds.), *Third World Employment* (Penguin, 1973), pp. 320–2.

---

leaving less for profit. Secondly, a smaller proportion of wages will be saved (and thus be available for investment) than of profits.

 Do you think that these are realistic assumptions?

Given these arguments, many Third World governments actively encouraged the use of capital-intensive techniques; some still do. But also there were other features of ISI that unintentionally led to biases in favour of capital-intensive technology. These included the following:

- Low interest rates to encourage investment.
- Wages above the market clearing level, driven up by minimum wage legislation, trade union activity, or firms trying to ensure that workers they had trained were not 'poached' by other firms.

(The effect of low interest rates and relatively high wages is to encourage the substitution of capital for labour.)

- An overvalued exchange rate. This lowers the relative price of imported inputs, which under a policy of tariff escalation have low tariffs. This encourages the use of import-intensive technology, which also tends to be capital intensive.
- The ignorance of many multinational companies of alternative efficient labour-intensive technology.
- The bias of engineers. It is engineers rather than economists who are often instrumental in deciding which production techniques a firm will use. Engineers

tend to be biased in favour of *mechanically* efficient techniques, which tend to be capital intensive, rather than *economically* efficient techniques, which may well be labour-intensive.

 What is the difference between *mechanical* efficiency and *economic* efficiency?

In recent years, with the criticism of ISI has come the criticism of capital-intensive technologies. Simply in terms of economic growth, they may not be superior to labour-intensive ones. They may be quite unsuited to the conditions of developing countries:

- Capital-intensive equipment may require more maintenance.
- It may have to be imported, and may use a high proportion of imported inputs. This will put a strain on the country's balance of trade. By using less domestic inputs there will be less spread effect to other sectors of the economy: there will be a smaller multiplier effect.
- There may be problems of hold-ups, breakdowns and incorrect usage due to problems in obtaining parts and an absence of properly trained maintenance staff.
- Even if they do generate higher profits there is no guarantee that these will be reinvested. They may simply flow abroad to foreign shareholders, or be spent largely on luxury consumption if the profits initially stay within the country (and a high proportion of luxury goods are imported anyway).
- Capital-intensive techniques often involve large-scale production. There have been many examples of countries opening up plants that are simply too large relative to the market. As a result they never operate at full capacity, and thus may operate inefficiently.

In addition, capital-intensive technologies have other detrimental effects. As we shall see shortly, they worsen the unemployment problem. Also, as these are large-scale technologies, the firms using them usually locate in the cities. This tends to worsen the problem of dualism. Inequality between urban and rural incomes tends to grow; and with relatively few workers being employed in these industries at relatively high wages, the gap between their wages and those of the urban poor tends to grow also.

Dualism
The division of an economy into a modern (usually urban) sector and a poor traditional (usually rural) sector.

The concentration of large-scale plants in cities can cause severe problems of pollution, especially if the government is not very strict in enforcing pollution control.

 Why may Third World governments be less strict than developed countries in controlling pollution?

So what can be done to encourage a more appropriate technology? Part of the solution lies in correcting market distortions: there will probably need to be a devaluation of the currency and a rise in interest rates. This would remove two of the key factors favouring capital-intensive industry.

Then there will probably also need to be positive encouragement given to the invention or adoption of *efficient* labour-intensive technologies. This could involve government-sponsored research, information centres to provide details of the various techniques used around the world, education and training schemes for managers and workers, the provision of advice on production, marketing, distribution, etc., and incentives for inventions (such as subsidies or patent protection)..

The government could help to encourage small businesses (which typically use more labour-intensive techniques) by, for example, setting up development banks which provide services specifically for small businesses and which grant loans at similar rates to those charged to large firms; encouraging the formation of co-operatives through tax concessions or subsidies, or by reducing the amount of red tape such organizations are likely to encounter; and providing small workshops or other premises at low or zero rent.

Finally, the government can actively encourage the economic development of the countryside and thus help to break down the dualism between the rural and urban sectors and stop the mass migration of people to the cities. Policies could include the building of roads, the provision of government rural advisory services on new techniques and business practices, the setting-up of rural banks, higher prices for food and the products of handicraft industries, and tax incentives for rural investment.

 What difficulties is a government likely to encounter in encouraging the use of labour-intensive technology?

Unemployment

Imagine the choice of living in a large family in the countryside with too little land to be able to feed you and the other family members, or of seeking your fortune in the city where there are nowhere near enough jobs to go round. It is not much of a choice. But it is the sort of choice that millions of people throughout the Third World are forced to make. Open unemployment rates in developing countries are generally much higher than in developed countries: rates in excess of 20 per cent are not uncommon.

But even these high rates grossly understate the true extent of the problem. With the system of extended families, where the family farm or the family trade occupies all the family members, people may not be out looking for jobs and are thus not openly unemployed, but their output is nevertheless very low. There is simply not enough work to occupy them fully. This is the problem of disguised unemployment. Then there are those who manage to do a few hours' work each week as casual labourers or as petty traders. These people are underemployed. When you add the problem of disguised unemployment and underemployment to the problem of open unemployment, the problem becomes overwhelming. There seems no escape for the mass of the Third World's poor. And the problem has got worse in recent years. With the world recession of the early 1980s and with the debt crisis faced by large numbers of Third World countries, they have been faced by declining rates of growth and in many cases a decline in output. This has therefore deepened the unemployment crisis.

The causes of the unemployment problem are deep seated and complex, but four stand out as being particularly important in most developing countries.

Underemployment

Where people who want full-time work are only able to find part-time work.

Disguised unemployment

Where the same work could be done by fewer people.

Rapid population growth

With reductions in mortality rates (due to improved health care) which have not been matched by equivalent reductions in birth rates, populations in most Third World countries have grown rapidly for many years now. The labour force has thus grown rapidly too. The growth in production has simply not been fast enough to create enough jobs for these extra workers.

Capital-intensity bias

As we have seen, import-substituting industrialization has involved a bias in favour of capital-intensive technology. This has led to the production of goods and to the use of processes that provide only limited employment opportunities. As long as the relative price of capital to labour is kept low, or as long as there is a lack of modern efficient

Box 23.6

The Growth of Urban Shanty Towns
A consequence of rural–urban migration

Table (a) shows the extent of slums and squatter settlements in various Third World cities. In many large cities more than half the population live in make-shift dwellings.

(a) Slum dwelling in Third World cities

City	Population living in slums and squatter settlements (%)
Latin America	
Bogota, Colombia	60
Mexico City, Mexico	46
Caracas, Venezuela	42
Middle East and Africa	
Addis Ababa, Ethiopia	79
Casablanca, Morocco	70
Kinshasa, Zaire	60
Cairo, Egypt	60
Ankara, Turkey	60
Asia	
Calcutta, India	67
Manila, Philippines	35
Seoul, South Korea	29
Jakarta, Indonesia	26

Sources: *World Population Growth and Global Society*, report no. 13 (Population Crisis Committee, Washington, 1983), quoted in M. Todaro, *Economic Development in the Third World* (Longman, 1989).

The major factor contributing to the growth of these shanty towns has been the massive levels of rural–urban migration (see Table (b)). It has been estimated that migrants constitute between 35 and 60 per cent of urban population growth.

(b) Rural–urban migration as a source of urban population growth: 1970s

Country	Annual urban growth (%)	Share of growth due to migration (%)
Argentina	2.0	35
Brazil	4.5	36
Colombia	4.9	43
India	3.8	45
Indonesia	4.7	49
Nigeria	7.0	64
Philippines	4.8	42
Sri Lanka	4.3	61
Tanzania	7.5	64
Thailand	5.3	45

Source: K. Newland, *City limits: Emerging constraints on urban growth* (Worldwatch, paper no. 38, Washington, 1980), quoted in Todaro, *op. cit.*

labour-intensive techniques available, or as long as multinational companies choose to bring in their own (capital-intensive) technology, so there will continue to be a lack of demand for labour.

Rural–urban migration

Throughout the Third World, people flock from the countryside to the towns and thereby swell the numbers of urban unemployed. But why do they do it? If life in the shanty towns is wretched, what is the point? The point is that for most of the migrants there was no chance at all of getting another job in the countryside, whereas in the towns there is at least some chance. If one in five migrants gets a job, then you might be the lucky one.

The decision to migrate thus depends on four main factors:

● The income differential between the countryside and the town. The more that jobs in the town pay relative to what the migrant could earn by staying behind on, say, the family farm, the more the person is likely to migrate. If their decision was to be totally rational, they would also take into account the differences in the cost of living between the two areas.
● The chance of getting a job. This will depend on the rate of urban unemployment.

*Box 23.7

Third World Unemployment
Three simple models

In this box we will look at three models that have been developed to explain Third World unemployment. The first one focuses on the limited choice of techniques open to much of industry. The second focuses on the biases in favour of capital-intensive technology. The third focuses on rural-urban migration.

Limited choice of techniques
The simplest version of this model assumes that there is only one technique available to firms and that just two factors of production are involved – labour and capital. Firms will thus face a right-angled isoquant. This is illustrated in diagram (a).

(a)

Each isoquant shows a particular level of output (Q). Given that there is only one choice of technique, involving a particular combination of labour and capital, then for each amount of capital used a *particular* amount of labour will be needed – no more and no less. Any extra labour will simply be idle.

For example, if each machine required one operative and if ten machines were available, then ten operatives would be required. An eleventh would add nothing to output. Similarly, if there were ten operatives available, an eleventh machine would be idle.

If, in the diagram, the total supply of capital were $\overline{K}$, then firms would require L_1 of labour. But if the total labour force were $\overline{L}$, then $\overline{L} - L_1$ workers would be unemployed.

Thus the lack of availability of labour-intensive techniques means that there is not enough capital to employ everyone.

Capital-intensity bias
This model assumes that there *are* labour-intensive techniques available, but that firms choose not to use them. Assuming again that there are just the two factors, labour and capital, this time firms will face *curved* isoquants. In other words, the firm can choose to combine labour and capital in any proportions it chooses. This is illustrated in diagram (b).

Assume that the total supplies of capital and labour are $\overline{K}$ and $\overline{L}$ respectively. With a price ratio given by the slope of the isocost AB, the factor market will clear. All capital and all labour will be employed at point d on isoquant Q_1.

Managers, however, may have a bias in favour of capital-intensive techniques. Alternatively, the price of labour may be above the market clearing level, or the

The higher the rate of urban unemployment, the less the chance of getting a job and thus the less likely is the person to migrate.

- The 'risk attitude' of the person: in other words, how willing potential migrants are to take the gamble of whether or not they will get a job.
- The degree of misinformation. People may migrate to the towns, attracted by the 'bright lights' of the city and the belief (albeit probably misplaced) that their prospects are much better there.

 What would be the effect on the level of urban unemployment of the creation of jobs in the towns?

External influences
Most developing countries are highly dependent on international economic forces. If the world economy goes into recession, Third World exports could fall dramatically,

*Box 23.7 (cont'd)

(b)

price of capital may be below the market clearing level, so that the isocost is steeper than AB (e.g. CD). In either case, if $\bar{K}$ capital is used, *less* than $\bar{L}$ labour will be employed. With an isocost of CD, only L_1 will be employed. $\bar{L} - L_1$ will be unemployed. There will also be a lower level of output, since production is now on the lower isoquant Q_2.

 If there were three techniques available, what would the isoquant look like? Would it make any difference to the conclusions of this model?

Rural–urban migration

This model assumes that migration depends first on the difference between urban wages (W_u) and rural wages (W_r). The bigger the differential, the more will people wish to migrate. Secondly, it depends on the likelihood of getting a job. The more likely people are to find a job, the more likely they are to migrate.

These two can be combined in the concept of an *expected urban wage* (W_u^e). This is the *actual* average urban wage multiplied by the probability of getting a job. Thus

if the average wage were £40 per week, and if there were a 50 per cent chance of getting a job, the expected urban wage would be £20. If the chance were only 25 per cent, the expected wage would be only £10, and so on. This can be expressed formally as:

$$W_u^e = W_u \cdot L_m / L_u$$

where L_m is the total number of workers employed in the urban sector and L_u is the total labour supply (employed and unemployed). Thus L_m / L_u is the employment rate, which can be taken as an indication of the probability of getting a job.

So when will rural workers migrate to the towns? According to the model this will occur when:

$$W_u^e > (W_r + \alpha)$$

where α is a term representing the costs of migration. In other words, people will migrate when, after taking the cost of migrating into account, they can expect to earn more in the towns than in the countryside.

But as people migrate, W_r will tend to rise as the supply of rural labour falls, and W_u^e will tend to fall as the new arrivals in the towns increase L_u and thus reduce the likelihood of others getting a job. An equilibrium urban unemployment will be reached when:

$$W_u^e = W_r + \alpha$$

At that point migration will stop.

Thus in this model, urban unemployment will be greater (a) the higher is the level of the actual urban wage (W_u), (b) the lower is the level of the rural wage (W_r) and (c) the lower are the costs of migrating (α).

 If more jobs were created in the towns, how, in the rural–urban migration model, would this affect (a) the level of urban unemployment; (b) the rate of urban unemployment?

especially if developed countries respond to their own unemployment by using protectionist measures against Third World imports. If world interest rates go up, highly indebted developing countries may be forced to adopt deflationary policies in order to cut their import bill. As the growth of Third World industries slows down, so unemployment will tend to rise.

There is no simple cure for Third World unemployment. Nevertheless there are certain measures that governments can take which will help to reverse its growth:

- The government can encourage the use of more labour-intensive techniques by adopting the sorts of policy outlined earlier.
- It can help to reverse rural–urban migration by reducing the rural 'push'. This will involve policies of encouraging rural development and thereby providing jobs away from the big towns.
- It can provide jobs directly by embarking on labour-intensive infrastructure

construction projects. For example, it can employ gangs of workers to build roads or dig irrigation ditches.

- It can adopt policies that help to reduce the rate of population growth: policies such as educational and propaganda programmes to persuade people to have smaller families, measures to raise the economic and social status of women so that they have a freer choice over family size, and policies directed at tackling extreme poverty so that the very poor do not feel the need to have a large family as an insurance that they will be supported in their old age.

 1. Is there any potential conflict between the goals of maximizing economic growth and maximizing either (a) the level of employment or (b) the rate of growth of employment?
2. What is the relationship between unemployment and (a) poverty; (b) inequality?

Inflation

Inflation rates are generally much higher in developing countries than in the advanced industrialized countries. The average annual inflation rate for developing countries between 1980 and 1987 was 43.9 per cent, whereas for developed countries it was 5.2 per cent (see Table 23.1 above for more details). They also vary enormously from one developing country to another, with rates of well over 100 per cent not uncommon, especially in certain Latin American countries.

Theories of inflation developed in the West (such as demand-pull and cost-push) have been inadequate to provide a full explanation of the problem. Whenever there is rapid inflation in developing countries there is also a rapid expansion of the money supply. But does this provide a *full* explanation? Is the expansion of the money supply the fundamental cause of the problem, or is the money supply merely growing in response to other deeper causes?

Structuralists

Economists who focus on specific barriers to development and how to overcome them.

Structuralist economists have argued that the deeper causes of inflation are the structural rigidities inherent in Third World economies, which frustrate attempts to expand the economy. The change from a traditional primary outward-looking economy to an inward-looking industrialized one demands fundamental changes in economic structures. There needs to be a supply of food to feed the cities, a supply of appropriately educated and trained labour (and not just a plentiful supply of unskilled labour), the provision of capital equipment and raw materials, the provision of a transport and financial infrastructure, and so on. Inevitably, with all these extra demands for resources and facilities, bottlenecks will occur. There will be a shortage of tax revenues to finance all the desired government spending; there will be a shortage of foreign exchange; there will be a shortage of food; there will be a shortage of certain skills. In many parts of the economy there will simply be inadequate supplies to match the demand. The result is higher prices.

If supply bottlenecks are to explain *continuing* inflation, they must be validated by an increase in aggregate demand. Why will governments allow demand to expand? Structuralists explain this by arguing that very often governments simply cave in to price and wage demands arising from the bottlenecks. In addition, they may not have the political power to constrain the growth of credit or raise sufficient tax revenues to cover the growing levels of government expenditure. Alternatively, the government may choose to increase the size of the budget deficit quite deliberately in its desire to spend more on building the economy.

Monetarists challenge these arguments by claiming that there *has* to be an expansion of the money supply if there is to be sustained inflation, and that therefore the cure for inflation must be to slow down the rate of monetary growth. If bottlenecks *are* significant in developing countries, then it is the natural rate of unemployment they will affect, or the rate of growth of output potential. Monetarists therefore separate anti-inflationary policy (i.e. monetary policy) from supply-side policies to increase output and employment. As far as these supply-side policies are concerned, most monetarists argue that bottlenecks are best relieved not by 'throwing money' at them, but by freeing up the market and removing price distortions (such as artificially low interest rates, an overvalued exchange rate and controlled food prices).

For structuralists the cure for inflation lies ultimately in alleviating the bottlenecks. This will require more than simply freeing up the market (though for some this is an important ingredient). It will require measures such as a carefully designed system of education and training, the provision of transport infrastructure and schemes of rural development. Developing countries have too many problems of externalities and monopolistic vested interests to leave the relief of bottlenecks to the market. Nevertheless most structuralists do not dismiss monetary (and fiscal) policies as short-term devices for preventing structural rigidities causing inflation.

 What common ground is there between structuralist and monetarist explanations of inflation and lack of growth in developing countries?

▲▼ SUMMARY

1. The urban/industrial bias of many development programmes has led to the neglect of agriculture. The effect has been a deepening of rural poverty and a growing inability of the rural sector to feed the towns. Policies to reverse this trend include the raising of food prices, devaluation of the currency, government support for rural infrastructure projects, the provision of lower-interest finance to the rural sector, encouragement for the adoption of new labour-intensive techniques in farming and the use of new high-yielding seeds, land reform and the setting-up of rural co-operatives.

2. Development programmes have often encouraged the use of capital-intensive technology through policies of low interest rates, relatively high urban wages, an overvalued exchange rate or encouraging investment by multinational companies. These capital-intensive technologies were often seen as advantageous in that they yielded higher profits and thus more surplus for reinvestment. Often these technologies were more sophisticated than labour-intensive techniques, and sometimes they had a lower capital–output ratio despite having a higher capital–labour ratio. Nevertheless, labour-intensive techniques may involve less maintenance and less reliance on imported inputs and foreign skilled personnel; the profits generated from them are more likely to be retained within the country; they are likely to create more employment and a more equal spread of the benefits of economic growth; and they may be less polluting.

3. Unemployment is a major problem for most developing countries, both in the countryside – where in many cases it is in the form of disguised unemployment or underemployment – and in the ever growing shanty towns surrounding the cities. The causes are complex, but include rapid population growth, biases towards the use of capital-intensive technology, and a vulnerability to world economic fluctuations and to changes in international demand for developing country exports. Urban unemployment has grown rapidly as people have migrated from the countryside, attracted by the relatively higher wages, the 'bright lights of the city' and at least the *possibility* (however remote) of getting a job.

4. Inflation too is a major problem for many developing countries. Again the causes are complex. At a superficial level, inflation is caused by excessive monetary growth. At a more fundamental level, the problem is one of structural rigidities, with supply being unable to expand sufficiently in response to demand stimuli, whilst the government, impatient for growth, runs large budget deficits and the people demand higher living standards.

23.4 The Third World debt problem

A serious consequence of the oil shocks of the 1970s and the reactions of the developed world to these shocks has been a major debt crisis in developing countries. Attempts to service these debts – to pay interest and pay back capital (amortization) –

have caused severe strains on the economies of many developing countries. By the early 1980s the problem had become so severe that many developing countries found it virtually impossible to continue servicing their debt. There was a growing fear that countries would default on payment, thereby precipitating an international banking crisis.

The first oil shock and its aftermath: 1971–78

Between 1971 and 1973, developing countries' balance of payments had generally fared well, helped by a world commodity price boom. This position was then dramatically reversed after 1973 with the increase in oil prices and the resulting world recession. Oil imports cost much more and export demand was sluggish. The effect on oil-importing LDCs' balance of payments is illustrated in Table 23.7. Their current account deficit rose from 1.1 per cent of GNP in 1973 to 4.3 per cent in 1975.

Table 23.7 Current account balance as % of GNP for oil-importing LDCs: selected years

1971	1973	1975	1978	1981
−3.0	−1.1	−4.3	−2.5	−5.1

Source: *World Development Report 1985* (World Bank).

It was not difficult to finance these deficits, however. Flows of aid and loans from both governments and international agencies were increasing. The oil surpluses deposited in commercial banks in the industrialized world provided an important additional source of finance. The banks, flush with money and faced with slack demand in the industrialized world, were very willing to lend. The various flows are shown in Table 23.8. As can be seen, the biggest increase occurred in bank loans, which increased from $3 billion in 1970 to $12 billion in 1975. These flows enabled LDCs to continue with policies of growth.

Table 23.8 Capital flows to LDCs: selected years ($bn)

	1970	1975	1980	1981	1983
Official aid	8.1	20.1	37.5	37.3	33.6
Official loans	3.9	10.5	24.5	22.2	19.6
Private investment	3.7	11.4	10.5	17.2	7.8
Bank loans	3.0	12.0	23.0	30.0	36.0

Source: *World Development Report 1985* (World Bank).

After 1975, the balance of payments position of most LDCs improved. The reasons for this were as follows:

- The world recession of 1974–75 was short-lived. Aggregate demand quickly recovered as mild expansionary policies were pursued. The rise in world demand helped LDCs to regain their growth in exports. Exports from LDCs between 1973 and 1980 grew at an annual average of 4.6 per cent only slightly below the 5.0 per cent average from 1965 to 1973.[7]
- Relaxed monetary policies in many industrialized economies, combined with the higher oil prices, led to rapid inflation. This helped to reduce the real value of LDCs' debt.
- The relaxed monetary policies also meant that interest rates rose less quickly than

[7] *World Development Report 1986* (World Bank).

inflation. *Real* interest rates were thus low. This made the servicing of their debts relatively easy for LDCs.

The second oil shock and its aftermath: 1979 onwards

The second oil shock of 1979/80, like the first one, caused a large increase in the import bills of LDCs. But the full effects on their economies this time were very much worse, given the debts that had been accumulated in the 1970s and given the policies adopted by the industrialized world after 1979.

Table 23.9 illustrates the worsening debt position of LDCs after 1979, compared

Table 23.9   The growth of Third World debt: average of all LDCs: selected years

	1974	1980	1982	1984
Ratio of debt to GNP (%)	15.4	20.9	26.3	33.8
Ratio of debt to exports (%)	80.0	89.8	115.0	135.4
Ratio of debt service to exports (%)	11.8	16.0	20.5	19.7
Ratio of interest payments to GNP (%)	0.8	1.6	2.3	2.8

Source: *World Development Report 1985* (World Bank).

with the position in 1974. These are averages for all LDCs. Certain countries fared very much worse than this. For example, in 1984 the ratio of debt service to exports was 26.6 per cent for Brazil, 31.9 per cent for Egypt, 34.3 per cent for Mexico and 38.3 per cent for Bolivia.[8]

But why were things so much worse this time?

- The world recession was deeper and lasted longer (1980–3), and when recovery came, it came very slowly. LDCs' current account balance of payments deteriorated sharply (see Table 23.7). This was due both to a marked slowing down in the growth of LDC exports and an actual fall in exports in 1982, and to a fall in LDC export prices. Export prices of oil-importing LDCs fell by 2.1 per cent in 1981, 4.8 per cent in 1982, 1.0 per cent in 1983, 1.3 per cent in 1984 and 1.6 per cent in 1985.[9]
- The tight monetary policies pursued by the industrialized countries led to a sharp increase in interest rates, and the resulting fall in inflation meant, therefore, that there was a very sharp increase in *real* interest rates. This greatly increased LDCs' costs of servicing their debts (see Table 23.9).
- The problem was made worse by the growing proportion of debt that was at variable interest rates. This is illustrated in Table 23.10. (This was largely due to the increasing proportion of debt that was in the form of loans from commercial banks.)

Table 23.10   Percentage of LDC debt at variable interest rates: selected years

	1974	1978	1980	1981	1982	1983
All LDCs	16.2	27.3	33.2	36.7	38.7	42.7
Major borrowers	18.4	32.5	40.5	45.0	46.7	51.2

Source: *World Development Report 1985* (World Bank).

 Referring to Table 23.8, how had the *proportions* of capital inflows into LDCs from different sources changed since 1970?

[8] *Ibid.*
[9] *Ibid.*

Box 23.8

The Great Escape
Capital flight in the 1980s[10]

One of the more bizarre features of the Third World debt crisis has been the phenomenon of 'capital flight'. Countries deeply in debt have been forced to borrow more money to finance these debts. But much of this money, rather than being used to pay previous debts or to restructure the economy, has simply been put on deposit by private individuals and firms in foreign banks, or has been used to buy foreign property or stocks and shares.

Evidence suggests that up to 1982 in eight highly indebted countries (Argentina, Brazil, Chile, South Korea, Mexico, Peru, the Philippines and Venezuela) for every dollar lent to these countries an average of 30 cents flowed back as 'capital flight'. By the end of 1984 private overseas deposits of these eight countries amounted to nearly $47 billion (about 12 per cent of their total foreign debt).

Capital flight usually occurs when individuals or firms believe that they can obtain a better return for their money abroad (after taking risks into account). Capital flight can thus be caused by overvalued exchange rates (making foreign assets appear cheap), the fear of devaluation, high and fluctuating rates of inflation, political instability, poor domestic investment prospects, or the corrupt obtaining of money and the wish to 'launder' it abroad.

Although capital flight slowed down somewhat in the late 1980s, the accumulated amount of capital held abroad remains high.

 In what ways can capital flight be damaging to a developing country's economy?

[10] This box is based on a box with the same title appearing in *The Banker*, September 1987.

Coping with debt crisis: rescheduling

After 1979 many developing countries increasingly found themselves unable to service their debts. Several countries, such as Brazil, Mexico, Bolivia, Zaire, Peru, Ecuador, Sudan and Senegal, declared their inability to maintain payments without help.

Dealing with the problem is essentially a two-stage process. The first is coping with the crisis in the short run. This will usually involve some form of rescheduling of the repayments. The second stage is trying to deal with the underlying causes of the problem. Here we will focus on rescheduling.

Commercial bank loans have in many cases been renegotiated. This normally involves a small advisory committee that liaises with the country and the banks concerned. The agreement can involve a simple delay in repaying loans for a number of months. Or it can involve a more complex rescheduling of debt to cover a number of years. This essentially involves lengthening loans. In all cases, however, interest still has to be paid at current rates.

Official loans are renegotiated through the 'Paris Club'. Industrialized countries are members of the club, which arranges terms for the rescheduling of their loans to LDCs. Again, agreements normally involve delaying the date for repayment of loans currently maturing, or spreading the repayments over a number of years. Paris Club agreements are often made in consultation with the IMF, so that a programme can be worked out with the LDC for tackling its underlying economic problems.

 What are the relative advantages and disadvantages to a developing country of rescheduling its debts compared with simply defaulting on them (either temporarily or permanently)?

Box 23.9

'Ecocide'
Debt and the environment

When heavily indebted nations are put under pressure to repay their debts, they are likely to face a number of difficult questions: which part of their domestic budget can they reduce; how can they reduce the inflow of imported products; or how can they generate greater amounts of foreign currency (i.e. what more can they export)? At some point it will be difficult to make further cuts in government budgets and imports will be at a minimum. For many of the poorest countries the question thus becomes 'What can we sell abroad?'

The answer that many of these countries have come up with is the intensified extraction of minerals and ores or intensified farming. But a consequence of this may be massive environmental damage. It is only in recent years that green issues have become top of the agenda and the IMF and World Bank have been forced to consider the ecological costs of their loan and adjustment programmes.

An example of a country forced into what has been called 'ecocide' in response to its huge debt burden is Brazil, with its Grande Carajas iron ore project. Proposed in 1980, the Carajas scheme has been estimated to cost some $62 billion and has involved massive deforestation of an area larger than France and Britain together. The Brazilians' willingness to incur such environmental damage was due to the fact that Carajas was seen as a 'national

export project' – something else to sell to keep creditors happy.

Projects like Carajas and the cutting down of the rain forests to provide timber and to clear the land for farming have enormous long-term consequences. Deforestation at current rates will, it is predicted, lead to a dramatic change in the world's climate.

If we are to reverse or even slow down the destruction of the forests, then actions to reduce debt seem crucial. It is hardly surprising to find that the principal tropical rain forest countries – Brazil, Indonesia, Zaire, Peru and Colombia, which between them account for some 60 per cent of what is left of tropical rain forests – are also amongst the world's top debtor nations.

1. If reductions in Third World debt are in the environmental interests of the whole world, then why have developed countries not gone much further in reducing or cancelling the debts owed to them?
2. Would it be possible to devise a scheme of debt repayments that would both be acceptable to debtor and creditor countries and not damage the environment?

Dealing with the debt crisis: structural reform within the developing countries

Some of the problems have lessened for LDCs in recent years. Interest rates have come down; the world has slowly recovered from the recession of the early 1980s; oil prices fell after 1985 (although this was a blow for oil-exporting LDCs like Mexico, Venezuela and Nigeria, which relied on oil exports to help service their debts). Nevertheless the problems remain serious for many LDCs, and they are under continued pressure to make painful policy adjustments.

The types of policy recommended by the IMF include:

- Tight fiscal and monetary policies to reduce government deficits, reduce interest rates and reduce inflation.
- Supply-side reforms to encourage greater use of the market mechanism and greater incentives for investment.
- A more open trade policy and devaluation of the currency in order to encourage more exports and more competition.

A more interventionist solution would include:

- Greater planning to encourage investment and infrastructure development.

Box 23.10

Swapping Debt for Equity
A solution to Third World debt?

With many banks in the West facing the prospect of Third World countries unable to pay their debts, several of them have favoured an ingenious scheme to convert debt into company shares. The process of these 'debt–equity swaps' is simple. Banks agree to accept part ownership in Third World companies in return for writing off a certain amount of the debts owed to them.

This solution to the Third World debt crisis is much more market based than other solutions. It is a solution agreed by individual debtors and creditors for their mutual interests. Other solutions, by contrast, typically involve the imposition of a package of measures by some agency like the IMF or the World Bank, in exchange for a certain amount of debt rescheduling.

Debt-equity swaps help to alleviate one of the major problems for the debtor nations: insufficient liquidity. By swapping debt for equity, banks provide these countries with much-needed liquidity and at the same time avoid the possibility of them defaulting on their debts and precipitating a worldwide banking crisis. The actual amount of debt and equity swapped will depend on negotiation. In practice, the banks have often been prepared to offer a good 'price' for equity in order to persuade the debtor countries to agree to the deal.

The advantages of these swaps are thus on both sides. Not only is debt exposure reduced for the banks, but the debtor gets a new source of badly needed investment and an effective cancelling of some of its debts.

Given these obvious advantages, why has the debt–equity strategy failed to be adopted on any significant scale?

The system has serious drawbacks. Banks must first be able to take a loss on discounted debt. This is not always possible. Also the companies whose shares they acquire may not be the ones they would normally choose to invest in.

As far as the debtors are concerned, they may not welcome the increased foreign ownership and control of their companies. In the long term, the increased outflow of funds in the form of profits and dividends may make their debt problem worse.

Thus ultimately a solution based on the mutual interest of debtor and creditor must be seen to confer clear benefits on *both* parties if it is to be adopted. The problem with debt–equity swaps is that the benefits do not always outweigh the costs.

 Would the objections of developing countries be largely overcome if foreign ownership was restricted to less than 50 per cent in any company? If such restrictions were imposed, would this be likely to affect the 'price' at which debt was swapped for equity?

- Reduction in imports if necessary by the use of tariffs, quotas and other forms of trade restriction.
- Policies to encourage greater self-sufficiency of economies.

 Compare the advantages and disadvantages of these two sets of policies.

But whether the approach is market orientated or planning orientated, there are substantial short-term costs for developing countries. Their balance of payments has to improve, and this means reducing the consumption of imports and diverting resources away from domestic consumption into exports. That means a reduction in their standard of living: a harsh penalty for some of the poorest countries in the world.

 Imagine that you are an ambassador of a developing country at an international conference. What would you try to persuade the rich countries to do in order to help you and other poor countries overcome the debt problem? How would you set about persuading them that it was in their *own* interests to help you?

▲ SUMMARY

1. After the 1973 oil crisis many developing countries borrowed heavily in order to finance their balance of trade deficits and to maintain a programme of investment. Despite this increase in Third World debt, a combination of low real interest rates, a recovery in the world economy and high international rates of inflation allowed developing countries to sustain moderate rates of economic growth after 1975.

2. After the 1979 oil price rises, however, the problem of Third World debt became much more serious. The resulting world recession was deeper than that of the mid-1970s, and real interest rates were much higher. Debt increased dramatically, and much of it at variable interest rates.

3. Rescheduling can help developing countries to cope with increased debt in the short run.

4. If the problem is to be tackled, however, then either debts have to be written off – something that banks have been increasingly forced to do – or the developing countries themselves must take harsh corrective measures. The IMF favours policies of deflation and market-orientated supply-side policies. An alternative is to pursue a more interventionist policy of restricting imports and encouraging investment in import-substituting sectors of the economy.

Postscript: The Castaways or Vote For Caliban

The Pacific Ocean –
A blue demi-globe.
Islands like punctuation marks.

A cruising airliner,
Passengers unwrapping pats of butter.
A hurricane arises,
Tosses the plane into the sea.

Five of them, flung onto an island beach,
Survived.

Tom the reporter.
Susan the botanist.
Jim the high-jump champion.
Bill the carpenter.
Mary the eccentric widow.

Tom the reporter sniffed out a stream of drinkable water.
Susan the botanist identified a banana tree.
Jim the high-jump champion jumped up and down and gave them each a bunch.
Bill the carpenter knocked up a table for their banana supper.
Mary the eccentric widow buried the banana skins,
But only after they had asked her twice.

They all gathered sticks and lit a fire.
There was an incredible sunset.

Next morning they held a committee meeting.
Tom, Susan, Jim and Bill
Voted to make the best of things.
Mary, the eccentric widow, abstained.

Tom the reporter killed several dozen wild pigs.
He tanned their skins into parchment
And printed the Island News with the ink of squids.

Susan the botanist developed new strains of banana
Which tasted of chocolate, beefsteak, peanut butter,
Chicken and bootpolish.

Jim the high-jump champion organized organized games
Which he always won easily.

Bill the carpenter constructed a wooden water wheel
And converted the water's energy into electricity.
Using iron ore from the hills, he constructed lampposts.

They all worried about Mary, the eccentric widow,
Her lack of confidence and her –
But there wasn't time to coddle her.

The volcano erupted, but they dug a trench
And diverted the lava into the sea
Where it formed a spectacular pier.
They were attacked by pirates but defeated them
With bamboo bazookas firing
Sea-urchins packed with home-made nitro-glycerine.
They gave the cannibals a dose of their own medicine
And survived an earthquake thanks to their skill in jumping.

Tom had been a court reporter
So he became a magistrate and solved disputes.
Susan the botanist established
A university which also served as a museum.
Jim the high-jump champion
Was put in charge of law enforcement –
Jumped on them when they were bad.
Bill the carpenter built himself a church,
Preached there every Sunday.

But Mary the eccentric widow . . .
Each evening she wandered down the island's main street,
Past the Stock Exchange, the Houses of Parliament,
The prison and the arsenal.
Past the Prospero Souvenir Shop,
Past the Robert Louis Stevenson Movie Studios,
Past the Daniel Defoe Motel
She nervously wandered and sat on the end of the pier of lava.

Breathing heavily,
As if at a loss,
As if at a lover,
She opened her eyes wide
To the usual incredible sunset.

Adrian Mitchell[1]

1. Had the castaways reduced their problem of scarcity by the end of the poem?
2. Could the 'usual incredible sunset' be described as an economic good?

[1] In G. MacBeth (ed.), *Poetry 1900–1975* (Longman, 1979), p. 320.

Index